GIACOMO GASTALDI MAPS

THE WORLD

GIACOMO GASTALDI MAPS THE WORLD

A GENERAL STUDY AND CARTOBIBLIOGRAPHY

By Douglas W. Sims

THE BOREAS PRESS

RIVER FOREST, ILLINOIS

2025

First edition: April 2025

Printed and bound in the USA

Published by the Boreas Press <info@BoreasPress.net>

Design by Touchstone Graphic Design

Not-quite Library of Congress Cataloging-in-Publication data

Sims. Douglas William, 1945-2023

Giacomo Gastaldi maps the world : a general study and

cartobibliography / Douglas W. Sims.

xiv, 905 p. : 127 maps, ills. ; 26 cm.

Includes bibliography.

1. Gastaldi, Giacomo, ca.1500-1566. 2. Ramusio, Giovanni

Battista, 1485-1557. Navigazioni et viaggi. 3. Cartography—Italy—History—

16th century. 4. Map publishing—Italy—Venice—History. 5. Continents.

6. America—Maps—16th century. 7. Asia—Maps—16th century.

8. Africa—Maps—16th century. 9. World maps—History—16th century.

10. Bering Strait Region—History—16th century.

ISBN: 979-8-89282-126-1 (paperback)

ISBN: 979-8-89282-147-6 (digital)

For Ewa

CONTENTS

Foreword

I first met Doug Sims at an International Conference on the History of Cartography (ICHC) in the 1980s, possibly at the 1987 conference in Paris. We hit it off because of a shared interest in the bibliography of the history of cartography and in sixteenth century mapping. Over the years, our acquaintance deepened and I shared with him some of the work I was doing on my *Maps of the Sixteenth Century and Their Makers*. His enthusiasm was energizing, and we kept in touch at conferences, by email, and through my two visits to his home in Brooklyn.

Doug's enthusiasm for Giacomo Gastaldi was well-known to many in the field who would receive his hand-made Christmas cards, always featuring a Gastaldi map. In 2003 he finished the first version of this book, and I persuaded him to supply a photocopy to the Newberry Library, where I was then Curator of Maps. The introduction to that volume proclaimed it to be a work in progress, and indeed at only 250 leaves, it was very much a first draft. Doug continued to devote all his "leisure hours", when he was not teaching English to new immigrants, refining and elaborating his thesis, which was basically that Gastaldi was truly a great cartographer, certainly one of the greatest (if not *the* greatest) of the sixteenth century, and that his achievements had not received their due in the literature.

Sometime around 2010, Doug entered into an agreement with the research group EXPLOKART at the University of Utrecht to publish his book, but after several years of working with each other, it became clear that Doug's and EXPLOKART's visions for the finished product would never satisfactorily align. Consequently, their agreement was dissolved.

However, Doug's eagerness to have his work on Gastaldi published remained as strong as ever, and he redoubled his efforts to finish the manuscript. Although it was still a work in progress, the bulk of the book, and its general shape, were determined and solid. In the fall of 2022 I agreed to read the entire work and provide Doug with feedback, and our work together began in earnest. Doug sent me chapters, and I responded using "track changes".

But time was not on Doug's side. He and his wife Ewa, both of whom had suffered serious medical problems over the years, entered a new period of failing health. Chronic ills, new ills, and advancing age were a disastrous combination for them, and their care for each other, as well as themselves, began to take a terrible toll on their time and energy. As a result, I was hearing less and less from Doug about the comments and suggestions I had offered, and by August 2023 I had heard my last from him.

Around Christmastime, I realized I had not gotten the traditional Gastaldi card from Doug. Then I got a note from his sister Margot in Kansas City informing me that he had died on December 19th at Staten Island Hospital, from burns suffered in a fire at his home a month earlier.

I told Margot that I would endeavor to see his Gastaldi book into print, and she agreed to help me with editing and proofreading. Doug left a massive and complex manuscript, verbose and heavily documented. He had obviously taken to heart the old speaker's maxim to "Tell them what you will tell them. Then tell them. Then tell them what you told them." He was so aware of this trait that he felt it necessary to defend it in a prologue entitled "A Word to the Wise Regarding Repetition." We decided to spare the reader that apologia and have done some other judicious pruning, but early on declined to second guess Doug's text. Certainly, there are parts which puzzled me or made me want more discussion with Doug for clarifications. That, of course, was impossible. Thus, the great bulk of the work, surely 99.9% of it, is in Doug's own voice and wording, as his inimitable style attests.

It is our good fortune that Doug was obsessed with Giacomo Gastaldi. Thanks to that preoccupation, Gastaldi now has the first monographic work devoted to him, in any language. Doug would be the first to admit that there is much more that is unknown about the great cartographer, but this book marks a solid foundation for new research.

Robert W. Karrow
Senior Research Fellow
The Newberry Library

ACKNOWLEDGEMENTS

[Editor's note: Doug prepared these acknowledgements when he made a typescript of an early version of this book. He did not find time to revisit it before his death. In the intervening years, a number of people he recognized have passed away, retired, or left their positions. We have decided to present his acknowledgements as he wrote them, without inserting "the late" or "formerly" when it might reflect the situation today.]

This book could never have been completed without the assistance of many people, and I welcome the opportunity to express my gratitude to them here. For general assistance and advice I am indebted to Marica Milanesi of the Università di Pavia; Corradino Astengo of the Università degli Studi di Genova; George Carhart of the Osher Map Library, Portland, Maine; Ron Grim of the Norman B. Leventhal Map Center, Boston Public Library; Peter Barber of the British Library; Ed Dahl of the National Archives of Canada; Evangelos Livieratos of the Aristotle University of Thessaloniki; the late Professor David Woodward, co-founder of the History of Cartography Project of the University of Wisconsin at Madison; Ananda Abeydeera of Paris; and György Danku of the National Széchényi Library, Budapest. At my "home library", the New York Public Library, I am grateful to Alice C. Hudson, Chief of the Lionel Pincus and Princess Firyal Map Division; Geospatial Librarian Matthew A. Knutzen; senior map cataloger Nancy Kandoian; Alexandra Cabreja; and Michelle Hernandez.

Endless appreciation for reading various parts of the book and providing helpful suggestions go to Tony Campbell, George Carhart, Ed Dahl, David Cobb, John Docktor, Bob Karrow, Joel Kovarsky, Dee Longenbaugh, Barbara McCorkle, Margot Sims, and Chet Van Duzer. Bob Karrow, Curator of Special Collections and Maps at the Newberry Library, provided assistance in a number of ways, and at one point responded cheerfully to what must be considered an unreasonable request, made at short notice, to see a very large number of original sixteenth century maps; Richard Betz, proprietor of Hemispheres Antique Maps and Prints, has been a constant ready source of advice and encouragement, and has provided me with several map reproductions; Peter Meuer has also tendered much advice, as well as locating one unique map for me, and providing me with a reproduction of still another unique map.

Caleb Keefer, of Graham Arader Galleries, New York, has performed numerous favors for me, including providing high-resolution reproductions of a large number of maps; Jessica Maier, at the same establishment, provided me with a series of readable piece by piece enlargements of an extremely lengthy text on the Gastaldi-Camocio-Bertelli America map; my nieces, Katharine Sims-Drew and Rebecca Talbott, helped with various quandaries; Professor Albert Ganado, of Valletta, Malta, supplied me with a copy of an important work of his which I was unable to obtain at any library.

The number of individuals from whom I received assistance in obtaining reproductions of maps in numerous institutions is quite large, and I do not even have the names of all of them, but mention must be made of Piero Falchetta of the Biblioteca Marciana in Venice; Richard Workman of the Harry Ransom Center of the University of Texas at Austin; and Douglas Long and Rose Pusateri of Chicago. Special mention must be made of Pilar Chiás Navarro, of the Escuela Técnic Superior de Arquitectura y Geodesia, at Alcalá de Henares, and of Regine Gerhardt, Universität Hamburg, each of whom obtained for me excellent reproductions of unique maps which I had little hope of obtaining at all, though I needed them very much.

Graham Arader of New York graciously provided me with high-resolution reproductions of a large number of maps in his possession at no charge. In my endless search for a copy of the original Venice edition of Gastaldi's 1560 map of Southeast Europe which was complete and in good condition I am indebted to several persons, including Henrik Dupont of Det Kongelige Bibliotek, Copenhagen; Christos Zacharakis; personnel unknown to me by name at the Bibliothèque Natonale, Paris; and, especially, to Jan Mokre of the Österreichische Nationalbibliotek, from whom I finally obtained a copy when I had almost lost hope of doing so.

Special gratitude goes to Paul van den Brink, University of Utrecht, for assistance in locating copies of rare maps; to Andrew Cook, of the India Records Office in the British Library, who benevolently intervened for me in a unique way at a crucial moment during the gestation of this work; and also to Jude Leimer, Managing Editor of the History of Cartography Project at the University of Wisconsin at Madison, who is responsible for my initiating the present book, although I believe she is as yet unaware of it as I write. For assistance with computer graphics, and other bewildering aspects of the cyberworld, I owe thanks to Anita Flejter, Mariusz Nutkowski, and Marcin Wisniewski. For pure encouragement and moral support, I an especially grateful to Willy Dobak, of the United States National Archives; to John Beneducci of Brooklyn; and to Graham Arader,.

But my greatest debt of gratitude of all goes to my beloved wife Elzbieta, whose endurance was tried beyond all reason as time wore on and on, who did without in so many ways, as a project which was intended to last about two years became one of decades, and who nevertheless stood by me and never flagged in continuing to give me her support and encouragement. May I strive to repay her and find her forgiveness.

Addendum from the Publishers

That this physical book exists at all is due to Graham Arader who generously underwrote the costs of digitization and formatting. His timely support and continued encouragement have been essential. And we must acknowledge the much-tried but untiring work of Kevin Theis of Fort Raphael Publishing Company. Kevin wrestled with formatting this massive tome for many days and remained calm and supportive, even when our demands seemed outrageous. You are the best, Kevin!

1.1 Preliminary Remarks

The name of Giacomo Gastaldi[1] is instantly familiar to any historian of cartography and any dealer in or collector of old maps, as well as, to a lesser degree, to historians in other areas. Indeed, with the great increase in the last fifty years in popularity in the use of reproductions of old maps as wall décor, and, perhaps especially, on calendars, the name is no doubt by now peripherally familiar to a wide portion of the population in general. It is also a commonplace to see him referred to as "the great Gastaldi," or similar phrases. Yet, there has been no attempt anywhere to date to tell us what this assumed greatness consists in. Indeed, Gastaldi might be referred to as just a conspicuous blur in the minds of scholars. He published a tremendous number of maps. We have 124 in our cartobibliography (compared to previous listings, all with less than 110), all produced over a remarkably short period of only about 25 years, from the early 1540s to 1564 or 1565, and possibly 1566. And many of these maps were shortly after reprinted, often many times, by various Venetian map and print publishing houses, such as those of the Tramezzini, Camocio, the Bertellis, Forlani, Zaltieri, and others, as well as by Roman publishing houses, such as those of Lafreri, Duchetti, de'Nobili, and others, and this continued at a lesser pace well into the seventeenth century, with the houses of Valeggio and the Scolaris,[2] with the result that there were literally several hundred Gastaldi maps in print, and Gastaldi was everywhere for anyone interested in maps or in geography in general, and, as implied above, the same is true today among historians of cartography.

But Gastaldi isn't really about quantity of maps, and indeed I think these large numbers have obscured what is truly important about Gastaldi. While we will deal with all of Gastaldi's maps in this book, his real accomplishment lies in a

---

[1] There are sundry variants to the name. The last name is found as Gastaldo, Castaldo, Castaldi, Gastaudi (Almagià believes this last variant is probably the way the name actually sounded (1939, *carta*, 6)), Gastaldus and others; and the first name can be found as Jacopo, Iacopo, Jacomo, Iacomo, and others. Furthermore, it is not uncommon to find the article "di" meaninglessly inserted, as "Giacomo di Gastaldi", etc., and all or nearly all of these forms can be found used by Gastaldi himself, who had a particular indifference to orthography. The spelling we use here is perhaps not the commonest in his time, but is certainly the most common in twentieth century scholarship. Through the seventeenth to nineteenth centuries, we find almost exclusively Castaldo.

[2] We shall have occasion to examine the most important of these houses in greater depth than has been done previously near the end of this work.

rather small number of his maps, which are quite astonishing, indeed breathtaking. We shall bring this out sharply in a section toward the end of this chapter, and from that point on in this book we will deal principally with these outstanding works. But for the most part, our first chapter is of an introductory nature, and we must say some important words along general lines, principally concerned with what general biographical information is available about Gastaldi. We have brought together here all extant pieces of biographical information, some known before and some introduced here for the first time, part of the fruit of over thirty years of research, with an unprecedented fullness of detail, and we have tried to relate them to each other and to Gastaldi's work overall as well as we have been able. We have also, for the purpose of providing future scholars with lines of further investigation which might allow them to finally break through the impenetrable barrier of obscurity in which Gastaldi's life has always been cloaked, introduced some informed speculations, as well as pointing out numerous other possible lines of pursuit, often by means of pinpointing sundry persons whose lives may have touched Gastaldi's, and providing bibliographical access to these persons.[3] Immediately following this more purely biographical section, we include a discussion of several technical or official aspects of Gastaldi's maps, such as his engravers and publishers, and his privileges (copyrights), and we will find that looking into these areas can also provide very valuable insights into Gastaldi's life and character. We cannot, regardless of thirty years and more of research, provide the reader with a full and smoothly flowing biography, but we will remove some of the fog that has surrounded Gastaldi, and if a good deal of mist remains, we hope that we have found sufficient signposts for future researchers that eventually perhaps the mist too can be dissipated.

---

[3] Still other such lines of pursuit might be found in Gastaldi's dedicatees. Of Gastaldi's dedication in his 1548 Ptolemy to Fra Leone Strozzi, Fahy says: "Biographers of Gastaldi have not explored the implications of this dedication, which may throw light on the nature of his employment prior to 1539." (1993, 114, note 18). But it is precisely the problem of what these "implications" might be that presents something of a problem here. So far, no serious study that I know of has addressed the significance of these dedications, and there are only scattered isolated suggestions, which we haven't the space to present here. The most frequent suggestion is that they are connected to patronage in one sense or another, but other ideas also exist. See the transcriptions of the title cartouches of the 1559-1564 maps and a few others in our cartobibliography for Gastaldi's dedicatees. His most frequent dedicatee is Johann Jacob Fugger. We have refrained in this chapter from citing older works which do nothing other than repeat Ortelius's list of Gastaldi maps, or which include simply mentions of Gastaldi's 1548 Ptolemy, but those who may be interested in these will find the references in Manno and Promis (1881), and in Grande (1902). We have also omitted, though a couple can be found in the book elsewhere, the many encomia extant on Gastaldi, which are frequent both on the many reprints of Gastaldi's maps, and also in the writings of modern authors. The best encomium possible is the great maps published in 1559-1564, all of which are reproduced here.

1.2 Before Venice: Searchings and Speculations

Gastaldi was from the northwestern Italian province of Piedmont,[4] as he himself attests on virtually all his maps, even on the manuscript maps which he made in connection with his work as a hydrographical engineer for the Venetian Republic, and upon other documents, such as privilege requests, suggesting a pride in his birthplace.   It also perhaps suggests a strong bent of independence, considering that Gastaldi was living in a proud state which expected immigrants to openly embrace their new home and urged them to apply for citizenship. Gastaldi seems to be obstinately insisting on being acknowledged as Piedmontese, and not Venetian.[5] This bent of independence seems also to be reflected in the fact, brought out below, that he invariably did his best work in maps conceived and initiated by himself. On one map, his 1544 Spain, he is more specific, and tells us that he was from the Piedmontese town of Villa Franca,[6] and we can presume that he was born there, probably sometime between 1490 and 1510; his death date of October 19, 1566 is securely known.[7] This Villa Franca can assuredly only be that Villafranca which is about 35-40 km. south-southwest of Torino, close to the confluence of the Po and Chisone Rivers.   Manno and Promis (1881, 852) speak of a writer who wrongly implies that Gastaldi was from the maritime Villa Franca, near Monaco, but that town was then and is now in Liguria, and certainly could not be Gastaldi's Villa Franca di Piemonte.   The only other Villa Franca in Piedmont is Villafranca d'Asti, about 12 km. west of the larger town of Asti in Piedmont, dating from 1275,

---

[4] To what degree we should really consider Piedmont as part of Italy in the sixteenth century is perhaps questionable. Braudel, speaking of the Treaty of Vaucelles (1556) says: "France was allowed to keep her conquests, notably Savoy and Piedmont . . . . Piedmont, in the sixteenth century could hardly be called part of Italy." (1972-73, 2, 937-38). Piedmont in general was closely associated with House of Savoy from the eleventh century, and through that House often with the Spanish throne, although political affiliations were both complex and unstable for the area over the centuries.

[5] Note also the wording in the dedication on Gastaldi's 1559 First Part of Asia to the "Duke of Savoy, Prince of Piedmont [from] his compatriot and most demonstrable signor, Giacomo di Gastaldi, piedmontese" (see note 19 below, where this dedicatory line is given in full.).

[6] See the inscription in full in our cartobibliography (map 1). In modern sources, the town is invariably rendered Villafranca. Gastaldi separates the two parts in the only three places where he mentions it, in the title cartouche of the Spain (villa franca), on his 1555 Piedmont (Villa franca), and his posthumous 1570 Lombardy (Villa Franca). Note the inconsistency in capitalizations. Gastaldi's maps were highly inconsistent in orthography (just as he was in rendering his own name, as we have seen in note 1), probably more so than was usual in an age where this was common.

[7] Almagià (1939, carta, 9).

but this is always named in full Villafranca d'Asti, and is not a candidate for our Villa Franca, which can only be the one near Torino.[8]

Unfortunately, we know nothing certain about his life between this time and the beginning of his activities in Venice. However, while the facts brought together for the first time in the following four paragraphs are not so neatly interconnectable as we might wish, they do provide us with some tentative glimpses into a milieu which I think can only be that from which Gastaldi came, a milieu which interestingly contains connections with the nobility, participation at the highest ranks in the army of Philip II, and two persons with cartographic abilities.

Firstly, in 1522, the nobleman Pietro Marmosia ceded to the Duke of Savoy a home in Villafranca which formerly belonged to one Matteo Gastaldi. This duke would have been Charles III ("Charles the Good"), ninth Duke of Savoy (1486-1552), who reigned long (1504-1552), and who was followed by Duke Emmanuel Philibert, of whom we shall speak further below. This fact, first brought to light only in 2002 by Emanuela Mollo,[9] is important because no one had previously succeeded in placing any Gastaldi in Villafranca before 1603,[10] and because the connection with the Duke of Savoy, however tenuous it might be, is suggestive of a possible connection with our Gastaldi, in light of further information brought out in the following paragraphs.

Secondly, we learn from Roland that one Giovanni Battista Castaldo (not to be confused with our Gastaldi, although it is true that our mapmaker is often given as Castaldi/Castaldo; he can, however, no doubt be considered as from the same family, as posited by Karrow, 1993, p. 246) was serving in the capacity of some commanding officer in the 1540s in the campaigns against the Protestants,[11] and Roland does not hesitate to state that he was "from the family of the illustrious

---

[8] See also the several page section on Gastaldi in Grande (1953), which is a history of Villafranca.

[9] In Comba and Sereno (2002, 1, 27 and 30, note 5).

[10] In Comba and Sereno (2002, 1, 27 and 30, note 4), and Grande (1902, 4-5). Grande had found in the parish archives of Villafranca the record of a marriage between one "Giacomo Gastaudi" of Racconigi with a "Margherita "iraudo" in 1603, and a record of the baptism of their firstborn in 1604 (Racconigi is perhaps 10 miles (16 km.) east of Villafranca.). This was the earliest record he could find of any Gastaldi, causing Grande to sense an element of doubt about Gastaldi's birthplace (Grande, 1902, 4). However, grounds for this doubt were not very strong even then, since the extant parish records dated only from "1582 or a little later" (Grande, 1902, 4), and a period of about 20 years with no births, marriages or deaths is not long enough to cause any particular astonishment, if the familial clan were not a large one.

[11] Roland (1913, 19-20), basing his information on Louis Gollut's 1592 history of the Sequanoise Province and the county of Franche-Comté in Charles Duvenoy's edition of 1846.

Piedmontese geographer."[12]   This Giovani Battista, who, as we shall see, rose to become one of only five commanding generals in the armies of Philip II, and must have had some training in topography and mapping, very possibly was the same Giovani Battista Gastaldi who made a map of the vicinity of Nice in 1564 in connection with an earthquake which occurred there on July 20 of that year.[13] Also, the young nobleman Ferdinand de Lannoy, Count of La Roche (1520-1579),[14] who had had mathematical, topographical, and cartographical training in Italy,[15] served in the campaign under Giovanni Battista Gastaldi, and they were probably on familiar terms.[16]

        Thirdly, at a somewhat later time, in a 1559 Spanish ambassadorial relation, published by Jose García Mercadal, we find that, among the five main generals leading the armies of Philip II were "two Italians, the Duke of Savoy and Giovanni Battista Gastaldi" (in the Spanish text "Juan Bautista Castaldo"),[17] which cannot but bring to our minds the 1522 acquisition by the previous Duke of Savoy of the former home of Matteo Gastaldi, with obvious underlying implications of a

---

[12] Roland (1913, 20). Bagrow also seems confident that the two are of the same family; see note 16 below. Karrow simply states that: "Most likely, Giovanni was related in some way to Giacomo." (1993, 246).

[13] Karrow (1993, 246), citing an 1839 history of the Maritime Alps by Pietro Giofreddo, who refers to the map's maker as "Giovanni Battista Gastaldi Piemontese", which led some to speculate that the map was by our Giacomo, and that Giofreddo had scrambled the name. But the map, which was printed in copperplate, still survives in two copies, and Almagià confidently asserted that it was not in fact by our Giacomo (Almagià, 1939, carta, 9).

[14] Dates per Meurer (1991, 180). Karrow (1993, 332-33), says "about 1511 to 1579." Roland (1913, 19) says 1524-1579, and says he entered the army "hardly having left his boyhood."

[15] Karrow (1993, 332).

[16] They are registered twice as co-combattants in the campaigns, in 1546 and 1549 by Gollut, as see Roland (1913, 20, note 1). Bagrow, in regard to Lannoy's participation alongside Giovanni Battista in the campaign against the Protestants, makes the statement, "Here he fought at the side and under the command of a representative of the renowned Piedmontese Gastaldi family of geographers" (1928-30, 1, 126), but the statement must be accepted with caution since, while it is likely that our Gastaldi and Giovanni Battista were of the same family, it has not been definitely determined. Lannoy would later produce at least three maps between 1563 and 1568, at least one of which, a map of Burgundy, would be printed in all editions of Ortelius's Theatrum from 1579 to 1601 (Karrow, 1993, 332-33). He was a favorite of Cardinal Antoine Perrenot de Granvelle, who recommended him to Philip II as "a great draftsman and an excellent geometer," leading to Lannoy's appointment as governor of the city of Gray in 1564 (Karrow, cit., 332). For much more on Lannoy, see Roland (1913, 19-37), and Meurer (1991, 180), both with further references. Considering that the possibility that Gastaldi taught mathematics at Torino, brought out below, is not yet well-documented, and the relationship between Giacomo and Giovanni Battista is uncertain, but could be direct brotherhood, is it too incautious to wonder if our Gastaldi may have been among the young Lannoy's teachers?

[17] García Mercadal (1952-1962, 2, p. 1140). Note also the dedication to the 10th Duke of Savoy from our Giacomo, on a 1559 map (note 19 below).

considerable prominence of this Gastaldi family. It seems likely that they are all indeed kinsmen, especially considering that, except for this Matteo, no sign of any other Gastaldi has turned up for the early sixteenth century in Villafranca. On the next page of the same ambassadorial relation, Giovanni Battista's talents as a general are highly extolled.[18] The Duke of Savoy who was Giovanni Battista's co-general is Emmanuel Philibert, tenth Duke of Savoy (1528-1580, and a duke from 1553-1580), a cousin of Philip II, and a man of considerable prominence in history,[19] about whom several substantial books have been written, and of whom we shall speak again in a moment. We must note, however, that in still another Spanish ambassadorial relation in García Mercadal, also of 1559, a note of possible discord arises in the picture which we have been painting, unless there is some error or misprint, for Giovanni Battista Gastaldi is mentioned again, and still specifically as a general of the army, but he is said to be seventy-six years of age![20] This is 1559, so, if indeed it was he who made the Nice earthquake map of 1564, he must have been eighty-one years old when he did so. True, there is nothing impossible about this, and instances of historical figures maintaining their stamina into their seventies and even eighties certainly exist, but the fact does give us pause. Still, the officer Gastaldi in 1546 and the general of 1559 seem clearly to be the same man. And the mapmaker of 1564 *could* conceivably have been him as well, but he might also have been an offspring of the general, or other scion of the family.

Fourthly, and lastly, on October 10, 1566 (just nine days before our Gastaldi's death), Duke Emanuel Filiberto, just spoken of, evidently in need of a capable cartographer in connection with some extensive public improvements he wished to make in Savoy, wrote to his ambassador in Venice, one abbot Perpaglia, inquiring if "that piedmontese who was so excellent at making maps and descriptions of countries is still in existence . . . because we might wish to make use of him, and if he might have died . . . if he has left any student of his to whom he

---

[18] García Mercadal (1952-1962, 2, 1141). On the same page, Lannoy is also discussed, and we find that he has been promoted and has the reputation of being a man "of much valor and good counsel."

[19] He is also the man to whom Gastaldi dedicates his 1559 First Part of Asia, one of the first two maps from the magnificent set of maps produced in 1559-1564: " To the most serene signor the signor Duke of Savoy, Prince of Piedmont [from] his compatriot and most demonstrable Signor, Giacomo di Gastaldi piedmontese and cosmographer in Venice." It may be significant that this Duke Emmanuel Philibert seems to have been an avid supporter of the Accademia Venetiana (see Grande, 1902, 93-94), to the cosmography section of which Gastaldi, along with Livio Sanuto, had been appointed.

[20] García Mercadal (1952-1962, 2, p. 1131).

might have taught his profession, for we will make use of him."[21]   There is room
here to speculate that it would have been from his co-general Giovanni Battista that
he had come to know of our Gastaldi, and also room to speculate that by October of
1566 Giovanni Battista had died, since it would seem natural that he would
otherwise have turned to the latter with this question, instead of Perpaglia,
presuming he was indeed our Gastaldi's kinsman and still in touch with him, a
likely enough possibility in an epistolary age.

While there is less cohesiveness and less surety as to the relationships
implied by the above related facts than we might wish, they certainly provide a
fairly strong foundation to speculate that Matteo Gastaldi, Giovanni Battista
Gastaldi, and Giacomo Gastaldi were of the same family, and that this family was
one of some consequence, with high connections and probably some wealth.   A
home which the Duke of Savoy elected to acquire could not but have been a place
of some elegance.   While the grounds for speculation are somewhat thinner here,
one cannot suppress an inclination to wonder if in fact Matteo might not have been
Gastaldi's father, and if the house spoken of might not have been the birthplace of
our Gastaldi.   In any event, we present these tidbits of information, which, as we
have said, have never been brought together before, and in some cases have not
been noticed at all before now, in the hope that they might help conduct us to other
threads of pursuit which could lead to more information on a life which has so
stubbornly refused to reveal itself.

Continuing along speculative lines, though in a different vein, this might be
as good a place as any to insert the following observation from Johann Gregorii in
1713 which has also not been noticed before:[22]   "Johannes Castaldus, from
Piedmont, lived in Torino as a doctor and mathematician.   He made to the honor of
his fatherland sundry maps which were very pleasing at that time.   One finds from
the same *orbis universalis Typum magna forma,* and just the same in smaller form.
Also, maps of Asia, Africa, Spain, Italy, Sicily, Corsica, Hungary and Piedmont,
which are published partly in Venice, partly in Rome," but unfortunately does not
give his source.   The last part of this, the little list of maps, seems taken straight
from the Gastaldi entry in Ortelius's "Catalogus" (cf. Karrow, 1993, 23).   As to
Gastaldi's being a mathematician, we find in a work (first edition 1959) by Carlos
Quirino the following short statement: "Born in Piedmont, Italy, Gastaldi taught

---

[21] Emanuela Mollo in Comba and Sereno (2002, 1, 27 and 30, note 1).

[22] Gregorii (1713, 113-14). The fact that there is no true German equivalent to Giacomo (English James)
perhaps accounts for Gregorii's usage of "Johannes."

mathematics in Turin and later he became a cosmographer to the Venetian Republic."[23] Edward Bernard, seems to list Gastaldi ("Castaldo") among those in whose works can be found commentary on Archimedes's *Circuli Dimensio (The Measurement of a Circle)*, but the passage is obscure to me, so I am unsure. [24] I know of no such commentary, nor of any other reference to such, though it is clear that Bernard was a much respected scholar.[25] As to Gastaldi's being a doctor, it is true that many cartographers practiced or had studied medicine, including Algoet, Cuspinianus, L'Ecluse, Fine, Fries, Geminus, Honter, Lazius, Mellinger, Sambucus,[26] and Etzlaub,[27] and the text of Gastaldi's Ptolemy of 1548 was translated into Italian by the physician Pietro Andrea Mattiolo. Morison says of Toscanelli that he "was a leading Florentine physician in an era when the best astronomers and cosmographers were apt to be medicos, since they alone acquired enough mathematics to be men of science."[28] None of all this, however, provides us with more than general plausibility for the notion; it does not provide any solid reason to think that Gastaldi had been a doctor, and I know of no other source besides Gregorii who makes this claim.

---

[23] Quirino (1963, 75). Note that this is somewhat different than Gergorii's statement, and neither Gregorii nor any works of the kind are found in Quirino's bibliography, so he must have gotten it from elsewhere. Unfortunately, he too does not give us his source. I have long suspected, on the basis of such hints as this that, lost somewhere in the printed literature of the late sixteenth and seventeenth centuries, there exists a source which gives some biography on Gastaldi, but have had no luck in identifying such a source. Nor have I so far been able to find any other mention of Gastaldi's having lived in Torino, or being a mathematician, or teaching mathematics other than these two references. Though Gastaldi certainly used no precision mathematics in his cartography, other facts brought out below show us that he definitely had some mathematics under his belt.

[24] Bernard (1704, p. 8 (under Archimedis Opera. Viz., in paragraph I. Circuli dimensio . . . , second to last name in paragraph)).

[25] As we shall see below, Gastaldi worked as a master-mason at times, and he also worked as a hydrographical engineer for the State, and so he clearly had, as already noted, some mathematical abilities, though probably mathematics that was basically pedestrian and unoriginal. The mathematics of most teachers of the subject at the time would typically have been on this level.

[26] Karrow (1993, respectively, 34, 138, 159, and 160, 168, 191-92 and 204, 250, 302, 334 and 343, 371, 458).

[27] Kretschmer (1986, 1, 205).

[28] Morison (1974, 27). One might argue, I think, with this observation.

Fig. 1.1. The only known portrait of Giacomo
Gastaldi. See Appendix 2.

Fig. 1.2. Giovanni Battista Ramusio. Engraving
of a medal, reproduced in
Museum Mazzuchellianum (Venice, 1761), vol. 1.
pl. lxiv.

1.3 Venice: Beginnings

Paolo Sereno recently made the apt observation: "If Gastaldi is a protagonist in the building of modern cartography, this is not due only to his remarkable capability, but also by virtue of his having found in Venice, where he immigrated from Piedmont, an ambience of refined humanistic culture, of relative political stability and blooming economy, of precocious experience in governing of territory, a crossroads of accumulation and elaboration of geographical knowledge which urged cartography towards an effort at refoundation of contents and methods . . . ,"[29] and Emanuele Mollo, in the same collection makes the observation, equally apt and serving as it were as a compliment to Sereno's , that, while we don't know the date of Gastaldi's moving to Venice, we can reasonably assume that it occurred fairly early, for the "familiarity and connections which Gastaldi had with intellectuals and high functionaries of the Republic demonstrates a long presence in the Venetian ambience, in which the cartographer must have been molded. The work itself of Gastaldi reflects fully the characteristics of the cultural debate underway at Venice in those years."[30] And, finally, Busolini notes in the same vein: "At the beginning of the 1540s Gastaldi must have been already known in the educated circles because he began to work on a series of maps",[31] meaning the maps for the 1548 Ptolemy. To put the best and most profitable perspective on these insightful statements, we need to add one more. While Gastaldi's cartographic career was an extremely prolific one it was *not* extremely long. All his maps were produced between the early 1540s and 1566, the year of his death, a period of only about twenty-five years.[32] By comparison, for instance, Ortelius's cartographic activities spanned fifty-one years, from 1547 to 1598,[33] and Mercator's fifty-six years, from 1537 to 1598. So, the unknown period of

---

[29] Sereno, in Comba and Sereno (2002, 1, 33).

[30] Mollo, in Comba and Sereno (2002, 1, 29).

[31] Busolini (1999, 529).

[32] There are only twenty years between his first definitely dated map, the 1544 Spain, and his last printed map, the 1564 Anatolia, but as we shall see, he had very possibly, indeed probably, already been at work on some of the maps for his Ptolemy by 1542, and also quite possibly on a large Africa which was not published at the time.

[33] He was admitted to the Guild of St. Luke as an illuminator of maps in 1547 (Karrow, 1993, 1). His first actual map appeared only in 1564.

Gastaldi's life is quite long,[34] and the known active period quite short. Clearly, he must have worked with remarkable speed and intensity.

Moving on to specifics we note that the first that we know for certain about Gastaldi, other than the fact of his birth in Villafranca at an unknown date, is that in 1539 he applied in Venice for a privilege to publish a *lunario perpetuo*.[35] The importance of this fact is that it is the earliest date we have definitely putting Gastaldi in Venice. It shows too that he had some interest in astronomy, but the age was full of scholars who had a dilettantish interest in astronomy, and this datum does not tell us if his interest was higher than that or not, although information brought out below in this chapter suggests that it was not. A lunar perpetuo simply allows one to tell the phases of the moon for future (or past) dates, based on the moon's repeating nineteen-year cycle, and such devices had been around a very long time indeed, possibly since Babylonian times.

1.4 Ramusio, Pedrezzano, Mendoza

1.4.1 *Preliminary Remarks*

It is just shortly after this, in the 1540s, that Gastaldi begins to come into somewhat fuller view in Venice, and this is mainly connected with three persons who influenced Gastaldi: Giovanni Battista Ramusio, Giovanni Battista Pedrezzano, and Diego Hurtado de Mendoza. Although chronologically the first *definitely documented* association between Gastaldi and these three persons is the reverse of what we have just written, it is very likely that Ramusio was the first. One thing is certain, that Ramusio, who was Secretary to the Venetian Senate, and his activities and works, had from an early time virtually to the end of Gastaldi's career, even after Ramusio himself had died, an incomparably greater influence on Gastaldi and his maps than any other person or factor. So, we shall start with him, then proceed to the others, and finally review the interrelationships among the three of them, and between them and Gastaldi. Gastaldi's cartographical beginnings also stem from this decade, but that will begin to emerge when we begin speaking of

---

[34] For instance, if he were, say, seventy when he died, the unknown period would come out to about forty-six years, enough time, for example, for him to have lived, say, fifteen years in Torino (if that insufficiently documented residence is in fact correct), with still another fifteen years to become familiar with educated circles of Venice. If he possessed the longevity of Giovanni Battista Gastaldi, probably a relative, the unknown period could have been quite long.

[35] Almagià (1939, *carta*, 7 with note 10.)

Pedrezzano and Mendoza. At the start, we will be looking at information of a more purely biographical nature. The earliest biographical facts related to connections between Ramusio and Gastaldi come to us from a series of interesting letters from two persons to Ramusio, or to his son Paolo.[36]

1.4.2 *Letters to Ramusio*

The first solid evidence of intimacy, or indeed contact of any kind, between Ramusio and Gastaldi comes from an April 3, 1546 letter from the well-known writer, language reformer, and theologian Cardinal Pietro Bembo to Ramusio, in which we learn that Gastaldi, along with two other tutors (or three, if we include Ramusio himself, as Bembo does in his letter), is regularly giving private lessons to Ramusio's son Paolo in Ramusio's home;[37] Bembo doesn't say what subjects Gastaldi is teaching Paolo, but from a different letter to Ramusio, written May 10, 1549 from the famous doctor and astronomer Girolamo Fracastoro, we learn that the subjects are geography and astrology.[38] These are the only two original references to Gastaldi's tutoring in Ramusio's home,[39] and while it does establish intimacy and trust between Gastaldi and Ramusio, Grande[40] unjustifiably represents these tutoring lessons given *en famille* as constituting a school proper,

---

[36] Unfortunately, we do not have the corresponding letters in which Ramusio writes to these friends.

[37] Bembo (1809, 127-28); Grande (1905, "relazioni," 187-88). The lessons are being given also to the sons of several other prominent Venetian dignitaries. Daria Perocco brings out aspects of this tutoring which make it clear that Ramusio's esteem for Gastaldi was already very high indeed (Perocco, 1994).

[38] Atanagi (1582, 342). At the time, the terms astrology and astronomy were used virtually interchangeably, for reasons we haven't time to go into here. This is an opportune place to clear up an important misunderstanding. It is clear from the writings of many scholars that the title alone of the lengthy 1905 Grande work just cited, which in English would be: "The Geographical Relationships between P. Bembo, G. Fracastoro, G. B. Ramusio, and G. Gastaldi," has led many to envision some informal geographical club consisting of these four persons. Actually, the only relationship between the pair Bembo and Fracastoro, and Gastaldi, is entirely indirect, and consists only of information in epistolary communications between Ramusio, Bembo and Fracastoro. It is clear that the latter two are, via Ramusio, familiar with Gastaldi's activities, though it is not clear to what degree, and there is no indication at all that either of the two ever had any direct contact with Gastaldi himself, in person or by letter. This is not to say necessarily that there *was* no such contact, but only that Grande's work contains no indication of such, nor does any other information we have from other sources which have turned up so far. Much more important persons to Gastaldi's career at the time were Pedrezzano and Mendoza.

[39] And thus we unfortunately can't say if the lessons began before 1546 or ended past 1549.

[40] 1905, "relazioni," 186-89 and 193-94.

which is incorrect.[41]   Grande also errs, I think, when he interprets a somewhat obscure passage in a postscript to Bembo's April 3, 1546 letter as meaning that Gastaldi was actually living as a resident in Ramusio's home at the time he was giving these lessons.[42]   In the passage, Bembo thanks Ramusio for taking into his home, at Bembo's behest, the son of another dignitary (see note 37 above) so that he can receive the lessons as well, and then still more lavishly thanks, through Ramusio, one of the other tutors, Giovita Rapiccio, for taking Gastaldi into his room so that the "young dignitary" will have more spacious quarters.[43]   Now, it is clear that the young dignitary was indeed temporarily taking up residence in Ramusio's home, but, in my firm opinion, the meaning of Rapiccio's accepting of Gastaldi into his room is that formerly Gastaldi and Rapiccio had had separate rooms in which to do their tutoring, whenever they came to Ramusio's home for that purpose, but that now they would both be doing their tutoring in one room.[44]

The reasons for my interpretation of this are several, and I think they are worth pointing out. In the first place, we have no reason to believe that Gastaldi, who seems at all times a very resourceful person, would have been in such low financial circumstances that he would need to assent to the very inconvenient arrangement of living in a single room with another resident.   Two further circumstances provide further reinforcement for this view. In 1555 Gastaldi drew up a will which still exists,[45] since he was suffering from some serious ailment, whether illness or injury he does not say, and in the will he states that he has a wife, Anzola, and that he had had a previous wife Ieronima, by whom he had a daughter Isabetta, who was still living.   Thus, while it is not certain, it seems likely that Gastaldi in 1546 was a married man, very possibly with a daughter, and this family could hardly have been living in one room with still another occupant. Furthermore, Gastaldi in 1546 was, as we shall see, in the midst of preparation of sixty maps for the 1548 Pedrezzano edition of Ptolemy, and he could not well have pursued this work in the cramped quarters suggested by Grande. There is also the fact, as we shall see, that Gastaldi was the master-mason or master-builder in the

---

[41] Parks (1955, 133-34), and Skelton (1970, xii and xvi, note 36) agree with this conclusion.

[42] Grande (1905, "relazioni," 186 and 188); and (1905, carte, 71).

[43] Bembo (1809, 128).

[44] Having done a good deal of tutoring myself, I can say that it is certainly preferable to be alone in a room with one's student, but it is certainly possible for two tutors to work simultaneously at the opposite ends of a single room.

[45] The will is quoted in full in Almagià (1939, carta, 9).

construction of a chapel in 1548, with the implication that he probably had been in this business for a while, which would suggest he was a man of reasonable means, not in need of a patron to provide his living quarters. Finally, we have direct testimony of Gastaldi's possessing his own house in 1549, the last year from which we have evidence of Gastaldi's tutoring in Ramusio's house. Gastaldi was directed in 1549 by the Venetian Council of Ten to draw on a large framed canvas a gigantic map of all of Africa, apparently at least several meters in width, which was then to be painted on a wall of the Ducal Palace (cf. below in this chapter and cartobibliography entry no. 65). While it was evidently originally intended that Gastaldi make the large canvas drawing in his own residence, it seems that this had to be done elsewhere, for a May 6, 1549 document of the council states that the framed canvas was "much larger than the house of the said Maestro Jacomo" (Lorenzi, 1868, 266), meaning that there was, not surprisingly, no wall space of sufficient dimensions where the canvas could be secured.

In any event, we have a definite connection between Gastaldi and Ramusio in 1546. Now, let us back up for a moment, for, before this 1546-1549 tutoring of Paolo, which is solidly documented, there does exist an intimation of a slightly earlier (1545) connection between Gastaldi and Ramusio. In a letter to Ramusio of April 3, 1545 (exactly a year to the day before the letter mentioning Gastaldi as a tutor), Bembo gratefully says to Ramusio, "I have received the Spain, which you sent me, which by all reason must be very accurate."[46] The reference can only be to Gastaldi's unequivocally dated map, the 1544 Spain, a fact already recognized by other scholars.[47] The immediate implication is that Gastaldi in 1545 provided Ramusio the copy to send to Bembo, and one even seems to sense that Ramusio was there, so to speak, even the year before, 1544, when Gastaldi completed the map, and this I feel intuitively was actually the case, and furthermore, again on intuition, I suspect the Ramusio-Gastaldi connection went back even before that time an indeterminate way. But no documentation exists to make this intuition a genuine determination, and it certainly could be wrong. For the possibility exists that Ramusio, who we can assume with certainty followed the map market, simply

---

[46] Bembo (1809, 125). Bembo in the same letter also thanks Ramusio for a "copy-book on the parts of Africa", of which we shall speak shortly.

[47] Grande (1905, "relazioni," 193-94); Biasutti (1920, 417), who by some momentary oversight refers mistakenly in note 2 on the same page to the map as a woodcut (he was probably confusing it with Paletino's 1551 map (Karrow 1993, 60/1); Parks (1955, 145-46), who also mentions a second possibility as to what the "Spain" might be, but the suggestion is an unnecessary and gratuitous insertion. The reference is unquestionably to Gastaldi's Spain.

purchased, as anyone could, a copy of the new Spain in 1545 and sent it to Bembo, and for this reason, the 1546 tutoring letter remains the earliest unquestionably documented connection between Ramusio and Gastaldi.

We continue with the unfortunately so limited tidbits of information gleanable from correspondence to Ramusio from Bembo and Fracastoro.[48] In the May 10, 1549 letter cited in note 47, Fracastoro says that he agrees with Gastaldi that the extant planetary calculations are wrong, but not for the reasons Gastaldi says, which he calls fantasies.[49] Fracastoro was unquestionably correct, but we can't hold this against Gastaldi very strongly. No one at the time understood the revolutions, periods, and irregularities in the motion of the planets, and there were sundry ideas, most of them not deep, and all of them essentially fantasies, to use Fracastoro's appropriate term. Even the great Kepler, who, with the aid of theory obtained from Copernicus, and extensive observational data obtained from Brahe, eventually got the picture pretty much correct in a general sense, produced, in 1595 at the age of twenty-four his *Mysterium Cosmographicum,* which consists of a fascinating, but utterly fantastic, description of the solar system. So Gastaldi was at least in good company with his fantasies. Actually, the main problem at the time was simply that astronomers did not yet possess the necessary theory, the necessary accurate instruments, nor the necessary resolve, to come up with correct theories of

---

[48] Unfortunately, as noted earlier, we have only a one-sided record. The letters with information on Gastaldi are all from Bembo and Fracastoro to Ramusio. The corresponding letters from Ramusio to them have not been found to date. In all there are five of these letters which have bearing on Gastaldi: Three from Bembo to Ramusio of April 3, 1545; March 13, 1546: and April 3, 1546, all published in Bembo (1809, 124-28); one from Fracastoro to Ramusio of May 10, 1549, and one from Fracastoro to Ramusio's son Paolo of January 21, 1550, both published in Atanagi (1582, 341-43 and 347-48 respectively). There are a number of editions of Atanagi's collection of correspondence, of different formats and paginations, but all, I think, include a full table of contents in which it is easy to find the wanted letters. One of the letters, that of Bembo of April 3, 1545, contains no direct information on Gastaldi, but only on the tutoring lessons. It does not state that Gastaldi is yet among the tutors, although the sense is that the tutoring is something new, and so far the only tutor is Rapiccio, teaching literature. Note that Bembo died in January, 1547 and Fracastoro in 1553, and, as implied earlier, there is no positive evidence that they personally had much effect on Gastaldi's career.

[49] While the main current fame of Fracastoro, doctor, astronomer, and poet, lies in his coining the word syphilis in one of his poems, he was an astronomer of note. His principal astronomical work *Homocentrica* (1538) adheres to the ancient geocentric concept of the solar system, and he continued in this belief after the publication of Copernicus's *De Revolutionibus* in 1543, which introduced the correct idea of heliocentricity. But we must recall that the great majority of astronomers continued to believe in geocentricity for quite a few years, and acceptance of Copernicus's ideas came slowly. *Homocentrica* was a good and serious work, and contains a number of new and correct ideas, which we needn't go into here. But his responses to Gastaldi's astronomical ideas as transmitted by Ramusio are cogent and correct, and show that he was in the forefront of astronomers of his time.

the planets, sun, and, especially, moon.[50] It took another two hundred years of slow and anguished labor by a good number of the world's best astronomers working with the best existing instruments and extensive government financing before such observations could be of any practical used in determining longitude. The only exception was that the first Cassini had by 1668 developed a set of tables relating to the moons of Jupiter which were sufficiently accurate to be successfully used for finding longitude.

Finally, in the same letter to Ramusio, and, in more satisfactory detail in the January 21, 1550 letter to Paolo Ramusio, Fracastoro speaks against a longitude finding method supposedly discovered by Gastaldi involving conjunctions of the moon with planets or stars. First, we should note that, while perhaps Gastaldi came up with the idea on his own, it was not new, for it had been suggested by Rui Faleiro in about 1518, by Antonio Pigafetta, and others, and a variant of it had been described by Werner in 1514, followed shortly by others. Fracastoro's interesting response shows him, as noted, as being much ahead of most scholars of the time with pretensions to astronomical knowledge, such as Werner, Apian, or Gemma Frisius. He replies that eclipses of the moon have always been the only method of viability,[51] and that Gastaldi's method wouldn't work because the time of conjunction would not occur at the same time in different places due to lunar parallax.[52] Here, Ramusio's astronomer friend truly shines, for, from lengthy

---

[50] At all times in history, until about the late eighteenth century, the phrase "theory of Mars," or "theory of the moon", etc., invariably meant one thing and one thing only: a hypothetically correct day by day (later hour by hour) tabulation against time at some specific point (i.e., meridian) on earth of the positions of the sun, moon, and planets (then all called planets) on the celestial grid. In short, it is that which is found in astronomical tables, or, more specifically, ephemerides.

[51] Though he does not note the level of viability, or certainty, of that method, which was extremely low, far too low to be of value for an area as small as Europe, for the degree of surety that could be attained from it would be quite low, though theoretically some limited but real advantage could be gained from it as regards two observers located at places very remote from each other, as points in Europe and, for example, India, China, America, etc.

[52] Like some other savants of the time, notably Alonso de Santa Cruz in his *Libro de las longitudines* (printed in full in Cuesta Domingo, 1983-84), but a good many others as well, Fracastoro uses the term "aspect" ("aspetto") for parallax, although the correct technical term had long existed. The term aspect used in this sense is, however, reasonably appropriate. (The position of the moon against the background of stars can vary up to more than a degree, depending upon the *aspect* from which it is seen, that is, depending upon the part of the earth from which it is seen at any given moment.) Here the tremendous problem of parallax arises from the simple fact that the moon is so close to the earth that, seen from different points on the earth at the same moment in absolute time the moon will appear to be in a different place against the starry background, with the maximum displacement being greater than the width of two lunar diameters! This problem of parallax would hound longitude hunters for centuries.

investigations into this area, I can assert that very, very few indeed were capable of grasping the nature of this hindrance to the would-be method, and Fracastoro's objection is right on the mark. Errors of up to 30° or more could occur on the ground from this extremely troublesome factor alone. There were, however, several other quite serious problems as well, which we shall not go into here.[53] All in all, Gastaldi's astronomical ideas were unoriginal, dilettantish, pedestrian, like those of so many who dabbled in astronomy at the time, and would not stand up to the scrutiny of the true astronomer Fracastoro. But, again, we cannot judge Gastaldi very harshly on the point, for the situation was no doubt the same with virtually all cartographers of the time. There is no more to glean on Gastaldi from the Bembo and Fracastoro correspondence with Ramusio, and we turn now to Gastaldi's connections with Pedrezzano.

1.4.3 *Pedrezzano the Publisher*

In 1548 there appeared Gastaldi's edition of Ptolemy, though perhaps it would be more correct to call it Giovanni Battista Pedrezzano's edition, for the arguments of Conor Fahy, the best authority on the book,[54] that the project was conceived by Pedrezzano, who then took on Gastaldi as partner, are fairly convincing. The printer was Nicolo Bascarini. We shall speak more about this work below, and about the sixty Gastaldi maps in it. At the moment we wish to concentrate on the fact that, although it was published in 1548 according to the title page (but with a colophon dated 1547), all agree, and it could hardly be otherwise, that the book required several years to produce. Work on the maps for the book clearly goes back before 1548, because some of the maps are inferior to Gastaldi maps of the same areas which precede that date.[55] Indeed we know beyond question that work on the book goes back at least to 1545, for a modern marginal note printed aside one of the names in Ptolemy's list of names speaks of an event which occurred in "the past year 1544."[56]

---

[53] The parallax problem here is not at all the same as the simple one regularly encountered in taking altitudes of the moon, where one can simply correct the altitude by recourse to tables, although even this correction could not be dealt with adequately at the time, for lack of a good lunar parallax theory, and thus tables as well, in general. But in the present case, the level of difficulty of the parallax problem approaches the arcane, if not the eerie.

[54] Fahy, (1993, 93 and 97).

[55] Fahy (1992, 92).

[56] Fahy (1993, 98).

But there is still an earlier date in the book. The simple titles of the maps all run across the top edge of the maps, and one, but only one of them, the modern Germany, ends in the date 1542 (MDXXXXII). This is a little puzzling, for its presence imparts a small element of incongruity and inconsistency to the work, and the fact it occurs in a work clearly dated 1548 might make one doubtful of the date's validity. Fahy twice expresses reservations as to accepting 1542 as the date when the map was made.[57] However, Almagià seems to accept the date without question,[58] and Meurer, who says the map is taken from a late 1530s derivation of the Eichstädt map, itself derived from the Cusanus type, and noting that the workmanship is rougher than in any of the other maps, says that the date is quite correct, and that the map is the first one Gastaldi drew for the Ptolemy, which would make 1542 the year Gastaldi began work on the maps.[59] Perhaps Gastaldi decided to leave a record of the date he began work on the project. Whatever the case, I agree with Almagià and Meurer, and can give further reasons. As we shall see below, probably to the surprise of readers previously familiar with Gastaldi, it is likely that Gastaldi himself engraved these maps, and that they were the first, but not the only, maps he engraved. The Germany is unquestionably the most poorly made and engraved map, giving much credence to the idea that it was Gastaldi's first map. In any event, Fahy too thinks 1542 is the most likely date for the beginning of the project, although based on more general considerations.[60] This, then, is perhaps the most likely date of the project's commencement. Milanesi expresses the opinion that work on the Ptolemy "must have been begun about 1540",[61] a little earlier than our tentative date. While the only thing we can be absolutely certain of is that work began at least as early as 1545, I think 1542 is almost certainly the starting date, though preliminary planning could have gone back to 1541 if not 1540.

All of the maps in the book are double-page openings, with text by Gastaldi on the recto of the left half of all the modern maps. In the text on two of the modern maps of parts of Africa, Gastaldi proudly tells us that soon much more detail as to Africa will be available, for he is at present making a very large map of the continent, such as has never been seen before. It seems clear from his words that he

---

[57] Fahy (1993, 92 and 103).

[58] Almagià (1939, *carta*, 7).

[59] Meurer (2001, 122-23).

[60] Fahy (1993, 103).

[61] Milanesi in Lago (2002, 213).

feels the map is probably not far from publication, although no such map would in fact be produced for a long time.[62] Also, we reserved mentioning until now that, in the April 3, 1545 letter to Ramusio in which Bembo thanks Ramusio for "the Spain",[63] he also thanks him for a copy-book (*quinterna*) on the parts of Africa, and expresses amazement at the amount of detail, which he has never seen before. Biasutti considered that the reference was to a several-sheet map of Africa, the one that Gastaldi mentions,[64] and I agree with him that it refers to the large Africa Gastaldi is making, but a copy made for Bembo of textual data accumulated by Gastaldi for the making of the map, and not the map itself, for it is hard to see how the term *quinterna* could refer to a map. Parks suggested that the reference was to the text of Leo Africanus, which would appear in volume one of Ramusio's *Navigazioni,* and which would provide Gastaldi with so much information on northern Africa, but that text is very long, 206 folio pages in the printed edition of Ramusio, and a text this long does not, again, seem to well accord with the term *quinterna.*[65] If Biasutti and I are correct, this would definitely give us a close connection between Ramusio and Gastaldi in 1545, and perhaps the implication of an earlier one, but, again, the reference is too laconic for us to feel quite sure.

Before leaving Gastaldi's Ptolemy, we need to say, for reasons which shall become clear shortly, a few words about its publisher Giovanni Battista Pedrezzano. As Fahy shows, he was "a figure of some importance and originality,"[66] who produced and sold books "of solid intellectual content", including, besides Ptolemy, other works by the ancient classical writers, and commentaries on them,[67] and some on Arabic classics as well,[68] and works on geography.[69] He also published a number of serious works by Spanish authors, and for a period of several years, in the early 1530s, published almost exclusively not

---

[62] Of this project we shall speak more shortly, and at greater length in chapter 10.

[63] See above, in the section on Ramusio.

[64] See Biasutti (1920, 416-19), and in our chapter 10.

[65] Parks (1955, 146). Parks, one should note, was unaware of the existence of the pending large Gastaldi Africa.

[66] Fahy (1993, 93).

[67] Fahy (1993, 94, 95, 108).

[68] Fahy (1993, 95, 108, 109).

[69] Fahy (1993, 95, 108, 109).

only Spanish works, but in the Spanish language,[70] a period Fahy once refers to as his "Spanish period."[71] As noted, these observations will be of use to us shortly.

1.4.4 *Mendoza the Patrician*

We turn to the third of our early contacts, Mendoza. In 1544 Gastaldi published his first definitely dated map, his large four-sheet map of Spain, which we have already briefly mentioned, and about which we shall have more to say below. Gastaldi acknowledges in the map's dedication the assistance of Diego Hurtado de Mendoza (1503-1575), the then Spanish ambassador to Venice.[72] Hernando Rica wrote recently that probably simply because it was Gastaldi's first map, the map of Spain had received little attention,[73] a comment which the present writer ruefully admits applies perfectly to him. Although I have studied Gastaldi since the late 1970s, it was only much later that I finally saw the importance of this map, due to a combination of the reason given by Rica, and the fact that I had never seen the map except in a photocopy I had made long ago from a small, dark, poor reproduction in some dealer's catalog. I never even bothered to notice Karrow's notation that it was a four-sheet map, and of considerable dimensions. We shall speak more of it shortly. At the moment, we wish to speak of the man who provided Gastaldi with information on Spain, and to whom Gastaldi dedicated the map, Mendoza. His importance I missed also, and it has been missed by everyone who has written anything on the map.[74] Mendoza was not just your everyday Spanish ambassador to Venice. He was very probably the most important Spanish

---

[70] Fahy (1993, 95-96).

[71] Fahy (1993, 113, note 17).

[72] I am aware of three other circumstances which also might suggest further connections between Mendoza and Gastaldi. According to Wagner, Francisco Lopez de Gomara, the Spanish writer whose *Historia general de las Indias* (see our bibliography) was the only significant textual source Gastaldi used in his maps of America besides Ramusio, was living, evidently temporarily in Venice in 1545 in Mendoza's quarters (Wagner, 1948, 270). Also, Mendoza evidently helped Guillaume Postel compile an Arabic lexicon (Weill-Secret, 1987, 277-78, in note 114, with further references), and as we shall see in chapter five, good reason exists to think Postel may have been associated both with Ramusio and Gastaldi. And perhaps suggesting ties between Gastaldi, Pedrezzano, and Mendoza is the fact that Pedrezzano dedicates his 1550 Italian edition of Herberstein, containing Gastaldi's map of Muscovy (our no. 67), to Mendoza.

[73] Hernando Rica (1995, 125).

[74] Almagià, for example, seems quite unaware of Mendoza's great importance, when, in speaking of Gastaldi's sources of information for the map of Spain, he refers to him as "one Diego Hurtado de Mendoza" (1939, *carta*, 14).

ambassador ever sent to Venice, and, though I may go too far here, one could probably argue that he was the greatest Spanish ambassador to any place in Italy ever![75] He was an imposing and influential figure who was allowed to speak before the Venetian Senate, and did so forcefully, and was listened to. He also was a writer and poet, as well as one of the great bibliophiles of his time, a fact which will be of significance to us later. He also had an interest in geography, and in fact appears in Ortelius's list of cartographers (as Mendezius) from 1584, and apparently one of Ortelius's maps, a map of Peru, stems from him.[76] The 1913 *Catholic Encyclopedia* says he is "one of the greatest figures in the history of Spanish politics and letters." But besides this, he was brother to Antonio de Mendoza (1495-1552) who was the first and most important Viceroy to New Spain,[77] whose official chronicler was Gonzalo Fernández de Oviedo (with whom the Viceroy shared a deep interest in geography), and who was a regular correspondent both of Ramusio and Fracastoro. Clearly, these facts and connections surrounding Diego Hurtado, unnoticed before in works on Gastaldi, are rife with suggestion, and offer various threads to follow for future scholars of Gastaldi and his circle.

Thus the basic facts concerning Gastaldi's contacts in the 1540s with these three personages. Now, let us review these three connections once again to reveal some possiblities not brought out in our relation of the basic details, adding as we go a few observations, and finally ending with an interesting conjecture concerning Gastaldi and Ramusio, a conjecture which some may feel too bold.

1.4.5 *A Second Look and Some Speculation*

Starting with Gastaldi's connection with Ramusio, we find that the earliest definitely established contact between them dates only back to 1546. There are fairly strong indications of a connection in 1545, and less strong indications for a connection in 1544, but they cannot be proven. We find an earlier definite

---

[75] I base my assessment, which, if too rosy, is only slightly so, on Levin (2005, passim, per index). A good number of full-length studies on Mendoza exist, some in English as Spivakovsky (1970), and Hobson (1999).

[76] Meurer (1991, 194).

[77] On Antonio de Mendoza, see Aiton (1927), Vázquez (1987), and Avalos Guzman (1991). It was probably from his brother that Diego Hurtado obtained the material for his map of Peru, for after his fifteen years as Viceroy of New Spain he became Viceroy of Peru.

connection between him and Pedrezzano in 1545,[78] though there are rather strong indications of a connection as early as 1542 if not earlier. But these indications are not quite certain, and the earliest we can be certain of is 1545, nevertheless still a year earlier than the earliest definite connection with Ramusio of 1546. At a still earlier date of 1544, we find a definitely established connection with the Spanish ambassador to Venice, Mendoza, who provided Gastaldi with data for the 1544 map of Spain. This in fact is the earliest proven date of a connection between Gastaldi and any other person.[79] Looking at the maps themselves, we arrive at the same earliest definite date, 1544 for that of Spain. Earlier dates are likely for some of the Ptolemaic maps, and possibly for the giant Africa Gastaldi was working on, but again nothing definite.

Now, while one tends, regardless of the above, to still consider Ramusio as Gastaldi's earliest contact in his cartographic career, and perhaps his inspiration for that career, we note the following circumstances. We know that Mendoza had a certain interest in geography, and, more important for us at the moment, we know that he was a great bibliophile, indeed one of the greatest in the sixteenth century, and all works on him give much attention to this aspect of his activities. We also know that our publisher and bookseller Pedrezzano specialized in books of a scholarly and serious nature, that one of his interests was geography, and, most significantly, that he especially had a predilection for Spanish writers, and even went through what Fahy has referred to as a "Spanish period", during which he not only published and sold the works of Spanish writers, but often printed them in the original Spanish. Nothing could be more natural than that the ambassador Mendoza would have come to know of his shop, if indeed he hadn't known of it before leaving Spain, and that he would have frequented it. Clearly, if this were so, and Pedrezzano's Ptolemy, a book which would surely interest Mendoza, were under way, Mendoza might have met Gastaldi in this way, and enlisted Gastaldi to

---

[78] The earliest date, recall, when we can be absolutely certain that the Ptolemy edition was under way, due to the notice added by Gastaldi concerning a 1544 event which he says occurred in "the past year 1544."

[79] We have not mentioned a definite connection with Matteo Pagano (fl. 1538-1568) in 1546, when Pagano printed a map of the Danube regions (no. 4) for Gastaldi, since this is no earlier than the earliest date we have for the much more important Ramusio, and no hint of an earlier connection exists. No evidence at all exists of any connection with the cartographers Battista Agnese (fl. 1535-1564) or Giovanni Andrea di Vavassore (fl. 1510/15-1572), although we can be sure Agnese influenced Gastaldi, as we will see in the following chapter, and he may have been influenced by Vavassore, simply because his large and important maps, published in Venice would have been in circulation. But we know nothing of any personal contact between Gastaldi and Agnese or Vavassore. On Pagano, see Almagià (1939, *carta*, 10-12); Bagrow (1940); and esp. Destombes (1973). On Agnese, see Wagner (1931), and Milanesi (1990). On Vavassore, see Bagrow (1939).

make the map of Spain for him; and from this arises the further possibility that it was Mendoza who acquainted Gastaldi with Ramusio, and not vice versa, as is usually assumed. Certainly the dates, so far as we know them, allow for this. And even the contrary possibility, although less likely, also exists, that Mendoza, acquainted with Gastaldi and aware of his talents by virtue of facts unknown to us, introduced Gastaldi to Pedrezzano as a person who could produce the maps for an edition of Ptolemy.

But we can't know, and we bring out the above simply to leave no stones unturned. The scenarios described do not in fact seem very likely ones. For, regardless of our paucity of definite dates, the scenario which is usually suggested in the literature still seems to me the most likely, that is, that of the persons with whom we know Gastaldi had contact in this dimly lit period, Ramusio remains most likely to have been the first. For one thing, it seems quite probable that Ramusio would have known Gastaldi already for an appreciable amount of time before he would have entrusted him with the tutoring, in his own home, of his son Paolo, of which we first hear in April 1546. For another thing, while the Mendoza-Pedrezzano possibility related above is not unrealistic, it seems more likely that it would have been Ramusio, with his high post with the Venetian Senate, who first became associated with the ambassador, and then familiarized Gastaldi with him. Furthermore, we know that, not only the bibliophile Mendoza, but Ramusio too had a strong and active interest in literature, including the classics as well as writings on travel and exploration,[80] and it could well have been Ramusio, who was well-connected in the Venetian publishing community, and who would certainly have been familiar with the shop of Pedrezzano, who acquainted the latter with Gastaldi, and got the wheels rolling on the 1548 Ptolemy.

---

[80] For full documentation of Ramusio's interest in classical literature, see Parks (1955), an excellent work. But the reader must be advised to read Parks with his critical senses well alert as regards one point. Parks's work is mainly a reaction against Del Piero (1902), the main general work on Ramusio and his works. Del Piero depicts Ramusio as having a lifelong very active interest in geography and the literature of travel, especially on the new discoveries, all culminating in later years in his *Navigationi*. Del Piero's picture of Ramusio is basically correct, but he gives little notice to the fact that Ramusio had a very significant interest in classical literature as well. Parks goes quite overboard in correcting this, typical of writers in such circumstances and quite unjustifiably minimizes, at every chance, indeed almost marginalizes, often gratuitously, the geographical interests of Ramusio. The truth, not surprisingly, lies between the two, but if either of the two sometimes intersecting interests predominated, it would certainly be geography. Ramusio must have already been long interested in both in 1519, when he was 34, for in the dedication in the 1519 third decade of his edition of Livy, Franciscus Asuianas addresses Ramusio as being "a long-time student of the classics (*bonae literae*) and of geography (*cognitione orbis terrarum*)." (Parks, 1955, 134).

Ramusio's familiarity with Venetian publishers could possibly even have provided Gastaldi with the publisher of his *Lunario perpetuo* for which he took out a privilege in 1539. Here, admittedly, we are speculating rather liberally, for, even if Ramusio had a hand in the initiation of the Ptolemy, and even if that project stems back to 1542, there is still a three-year gap from 1539 to 1542. But we have seen that the available solid facts are simply too few to make much headway, and we may say that, from desperation perhaps, we intentionally and openly introduce with this little observation a greater liberality to our speculations, to act as it were as a prelude to a still far more liberal speculation, for which we may be criticized; but we feel that we are justified in presenting the possibility which we shall present now simply because we think that it might very possibly not be noticed again, and, while perhaps unlikely, it could be true, and if it be true it is obviously of great importance, and thus we feel we would be seriously remiss in omitting it. Is it just possible that Ramusio and Gastaldi first became acquainted due to a chance meeting in their youth, when Gastaldi was, say, in his upper teens and Ramusio his early twenties, that they struck up a friendship on the basis of mutual interests, perhaps cosmography, that they then continued to correspond over the years, with Gastaldi eventually moving to Venice at Ramusio's suggestion, perhaps shortly before we first encounter Gastaldi in Venice, but perhaps earlier, in the 1530s, or even 1520s, and that a combination of a mutual interest in cosmography and geography and a talent for depicting evinced by Gastaldi in the process of work as a master-builder (about which more below) eventually coaxed Ramusio into suggesting to Gastaldi to try his hand at map-making? Here no doubt the reader will say that we have, in our liberal speculations, passed beyond the limits of the reasonable into the realm of the outlandish. But note the following circumstances, which are suggestive, even if only remotely so.

Ramusio, in fact, was in Gastaldi's homeland Piedmont in 1507, when Ramusio was twenty-two, and Gastaldi perhaps a few years younger. Ramusio, who had just begun a lifelong career with the government two years earlier, was attached at the time as secretary to a year-and-a-half-long Venetian embassy to France, perhaps because of his excellent knowledge of French.[81] The eighteen-month embassy lasted from October 1505 to May 1507, and included the cities of Tours and Blois and probably Paris, though I don't know in what order, before returning to Italy through Piedmont, and on the return trip was escorting the King

---

[81] On this embassy, and the facts connected with it related here, see Parks (1955, 129-30).

of France himself, Louis XII.[82]   It was probably the fact that the King's business was taking him to Genoa that the embassy made its return through Piedmont. Though I don't know the exact route of return, a journey from Tours or Blois could certainly have taken the embassy through Gastaldi's part of Piedmont, and, in fact, Ramusio was dispatched to Genoa with the King from the Piedmontese town of Alessandria, just over 50 miles east of Villa Franca.   Now they were traveling eastward, and a previous stayover could well have been in Villa Franca, and, at the casual rate they were evidently traveling (the embassy we recall lasted eighteen months) they were probably making their stopovers for several days.   Now, an official embassy, and especially one escorting a major king, would no doubt make their layovers with prominent citizens of whatever area they were in, and we recall that in 1522 the nobleman Pietro Marmosia had ceded to the Duke of Savoy a home in Villa Franca, which had previously belonged to one Matteo Gastaldi, the only Gastaldi scholars have so far succeeded in locating in Villa Franca in what would have been the years of our Gastaldi's youth.   A home chosen by the Duke of Savoy, and before him another nobleman, could not but have been a sumptuous one, and though we know nothing of Matteo Gastaldi, he must have been a person of some wealth and prominence to have possessed this home before Marmosia, and certainly 1507 is long enough before 1522 that he could have been in possession of it in that year.   Clearly, some possibility does exist that the embassy laid over there, perhaps for more than one night, that our Gastaldi was Matteo's son or other kinsman, and that he and Ramusio at the time struck up a lasting friendship.

It is true that the threads holding all this together are thin, but the possibility is a real one,[83] and although Parks evidently bases himself only upon the *Diarii* of the famous chronicler Marino Sanudo,[84] one would think that the chances were good that some more detailed account of this embassy could well exist in the Venetian archives which might throw further light on the question.   One might object to the suggestion of an interest in cosmography being held at the time by

---

[82] Louis XII ("Father of the People") lived 1462-1515 and reigned 1498-1515. No other journeys are known to have been made by Ramusio in his life, except a probable trip to Rome (Parks, 1955, 129).

[83] We can put an alternative slant on this. If the embassy did indeed lay over at this house, Ramusio would probably have met all members of the household in a passing way; but perhaps a friendship proper was not struck up with Giacomo himself, who, for all we know, with our very fluid and unstable knowledge of time frames here, may still have been a child, but with the head of the household, and it was this latter who began a correspondence with Ramusio, and he who at some point later interceded on behalf of his son to obtain an invitation to Venice from Ramusio.

[84] Parks (1955, 129).

Gastaldi, on the basis of the fact that his first map of Piedmont, in the 1548 Ptolemy, is a very poor map, not reflecting a good knowledge of the country at all. But we know that Gasaldi's interests in cosmography and geography were of a very broad nature, and not at all of a local one, and a poor knowledge of one's local geography is not incommensurate with a cosmographical interest of this nature. Nor, if indeed there is any substance to the statements of Gregorii and Quirino about Gastaldi living in Torino before moving to Venice, does that in any way contradict our conjecture, for, as noted, we have no basis to impose any but the very loosest of time frames to any of these events.

While we can add nothing of a truly solid nature to what we have conjectured, I would note that, although I may be reading too much into the facts, several things do indicate that Ramusio felt a particular admiration for and intimacy with Gastaldi which might suggest long familiarity, for instance in his choice of Gastaldi not only to tutor his son Paolo but to make the maps for his master-work, the *Navigazioni*. Note, too, the implications of the following. Fracastoro the astronomer, as we have seen earlier, declares in a letter to Ramusio that Gastaldi's astronomical ideas are wrong. Fracastoro is absolutely correct in his criticism, and I'm sure that he knew he was correct. But he concludes by asserting that perhaps Gastaldi's ideas are just too deep for him to grasp, and that he is sure that Gastaldi must be a great genius. He clearly was simply being delicate, and wished to avoid offending his friend Ramusio, who clearly was much taken with Gastaldi and his ideas.

It is worth noting that, in these hypothetical circumstances, if Gastaldi arrived in Venice already knowing Ramusio, and conceivably at his invitation, then, even if this were to have occurred at a late time, as in the late 1530s or later, the observations of Sereno, Mollo, and Busolini, that, in order for Gastaldi to be found in contact by the 1540s with the Venetian elite, he must have been there for a good number of years, would be nullified, for if Gastaldi came to Venice already a friend of Ramusio, that association would put him immediately in contact with the social and intellectual elite.

While these hypotheses are not impossible, we do not really feel them to be very likely; as stated, we felt that it would be a mistake to omit such speculations, as they might direct future scholars to possibly fruitful areas of research. It is no doubt more likely that the first meeting of Gastaldi and Ramusio was of a much more mundane nature, and more likely to have been in Venice than elsewhere. But that Ramusio was in some way connected with the initiation of the Ptolemy project, and also with the giant Africa map project, projects which most probably stem from the early 1540s, and that his association with Gastaldi goes back at least somewhat further even than this, seems likely to me, if only on the basis of their very close mutual interests.

Having completed our survey of Gastaldi's connections and possible connections with these three figures through the 1540s, hoping that we have thrown some light on this crucial period, crucial mainly because the 1540s contain the seeds of Gastaldi's cartographic beginnings, we proceed to a presentation of the known biographical facts from the end of this period on.

1.5 Venice: Later Biographical Glimpses

While Gastaldi may make little formal usage of mathematics in his cartographical work, we know that he must have had some mathematical training, for in 1548 he built, or rather directed, and probably planned, the building of a chapel for the Venetian church Santa Maria Nuova, which we know from an inscription carved in one of the stones of the chapel.[85] Gastaldi's signature in the stone inscription runs thus: "M. IAC. MVRATOR PIAMÕTESE GASTALDO ET CÕPAGNI." Whether the phrase "and company" carried the same connotation then as now I don't know, but if so perhaps this implies that he was and had been in this business regularly, as a master-builder or master-mason, although he had also been making maps for several years, and no doubt receiving financial compensation for it. Biasutti says good reason exists to think Gastaldi may indeed have first come to Venice from Piedmont as a builder, noting that many other cartographers had begun in that way, including "Pirro Ligorio and Bellarmato, and many others,"[86] and Barber notes, speaking generally of the time around 1530-1540 in England, that often "the native master-mason . . . was being transformed under the pressure of circumstances from medieval architect-builder into military engineer and surveyor-cartographer."[87]

---

[85] Cicogna (1824-53, 3, 307); Bagrow (1928-30, 1, 80); and Biasutti (1908, 60), all of whom give the inscription in full. The inscription was one of thousands recorded over a good number of years by Cicogna for his classic multi-volume work *Delle Inscrizioni Veneziane*, published from 1824 to 1853. It is interesting to note that the church, and therefore the inscription, are no longer extant. By 1808 the church had become structurally unstable and was turned into a warehouse, and in 1852 it was demolished (Franzoi and Di Stefano, 1976, 161). If Cicogna had not made his timely recording of this inscription not long before the church was demolished, this valuable bit of history would have been lost forever.

[86] Biasutti (1908, 60).

[87] Barber in Buisseret (1992, 33). On p. 35 he gives some examples of such by name.

Gastaldi also worked for the government of the Venetian Republic, and in several capacities. We shall first mention his work as what in modern terms we would refer to as a hydrographical engineer, work which he performed for a period which has so far remained indeterminate. This work often involved the making of drawings, plans or maps of hydrographical features or larger drainage areas within the bounds of the Republic. It also often involved surveying, which would have required some mathematical background, although of a fairly rudimentary nature, for the surveys conducted by these bodies would not involve actual triangulation until a later time, and were of a less precise nature.[88] The discovery of this fact, that Gastaldi was at least at times employed by the government in engineering work, was made in 1914 by Mario Baratta, who uncovered in the Venetian archives, in the documents for the administrative department called the *Savi ed Esecutori alle Acque,* which we may refer to as simply the Ministry for Waters, six such plans and maps by Gastaldi dating from 1551 to 1565.[89] Later, in 1947, Almagià discovered fourteen more such engineering maps by Gastaldi, but this time in the documents of the department called the *Magistratura per i Beni Inculti* (The Ministry for Uncultivated Lands),[90] varying in date from 1557 to 1563, and said that there could be still others in that department's archives, and he also found evidence of Gastaldi working for still another department, the *Camera dei Confini* (The Chamber of Boundaries?).[91] John Plumb has spoken of the Venetian archives as "the greatest collection of archives ever accumulated by a single city,"[92] and when I looked into

---

[88] See the special note at the end of our cartobibliography.

[89] Baratta (1914).

[90] These bodies consisted of a *magistratura,* made up of patrician *provveditori* selected by the Senate. Below these were the *proti,* senate-elected intermediaries and advisors between the patrician overseers and the *periti,* which latter were the actual engineers, who were sometimes assisted in their work by the *proti.* In about 1560, the *Provveditori dei Beni Inculti* began a series of projects on unprecedented scale which would last for forty years (Cosgrove, 1988, 256-57; Tafuri, 1989, 120 and 184-87; Michieli, 1919, 32). Shortly after this time, Gastaldi, a *perito,* was twice nominated, in 1561 and then 1563, for the office of *proto,* but failed by a small margin to be elected. (Almagià, 1947, 189; and Baratta, 1914, 126-28). Perhaps his persistent habit of referring to himself as Piedmontese, instead of Venetian, played a role in the negative votes of some of the proud Venetian patricians of the Senate. It is perhaps worth adding here that it is possible that the stepped up activities of the *magistratura* about 1560 meant an increased work load for Gastaldi, slowing down his work on the great maps of 1559-1564, and perhaps one could posit this as a possible reason for his not producing maps of western Europe, instead of the reasons I posit at the end of chapter ten, for, as my discussion there shows, this question cannot be resolved with certainty.

[91] Almagià (1947), who stated (at 188) that the maps found possessed "little geographical interest."

[92] Plumb (1964, 230).

Andrea da Mosto's classic work on the *Archivio di Stato di Venezia*,[93] which categorizes all of the myriad government departments, I found that the number of departments extant in the sixteenth century which could possibly have need for engineering plans or maps was overwhelming. Furthermore, to make matters worse, Braudel speaks of "the impossibly dispersed Archives of Venice,"[94] and indeed much which belongs there is not.[95] Clearly, consolidating all the possible Gastaldi engineering plans and maps would be, at the best, a very daunting proposition, and, at the worst, unfeasible if not impossible.[96] Unfortunately, then, we obviously cannot say by how much time, if any, Gastaldi's affiliation with the government in this regard precedes the year 1551.[97]

Fortunately, except for being uncertain whether a possible official connection some years before 1551 might have had an effect on the beginning of Gastaldi's cartographic career, especially as regards possibly providing the channel through which he met Ramusio and others, the extreme incompleteness of information available to us in this area has little or no effect at all on the present work. It might at first be thought that, since at least some of these drawings and maps were based on survey, they might tell us something of Gastaldi's working methods in producing some of his printed maps, that is, those maps which made Gastaldi famous and which alone make up the subject of the present work, but this is a mistaken notion, and it is important to dispense with it.

In the first place, as we have already seen, the surveys performed at the time by these engineers were of a primitive nature with little of a precise mathematical nature, and furthermore, as we gather from Almagià in a bold but unquestionably

---

[93] Da Mosto (1937-40).

[94] Braudel (1972-73, 2, 1245).

[95] Brogan (1952) has much information on where many of the misplaced archives are to be found, in sundry European repositories, and Brown (1864) reveals what accounts for their dispersal.

[96] Nevertheless, some decades ago, an enormous project was set afoot and pursued to unearth all map materials in the current archives, and catalog the materials by author and subjects, and there is some suggestion that an indeterminate amount of further Gastaldi material was unearthed, but the outcome or status of this project today is rather mysteriously unclear, as see the special note we have appended to the end of our cartobibliography.

[97] Woodward (1997, 7) states of Gastaldi: "His official position afforded him the opportunity to be well connected with the academic and political elite of Venice," but until other materials might emerge, we cannot say this as regards his early cartographic career.

correct observation, Gastaldi never made personal surveys for his printed maps.[98] Almagià doesn't give direct documentation for this statement, which is actually made in reference to Gastaldi's cartography of Italy, and indeed it would hardly be possible to do so. But, on the basis of simple logic, it is clear from the ceaseless intensity of Gastaldi's many activities in Venice that he could not have been traipsing about Italy, not to mention further afield, making surveys or taking astronomical observations for his 124 maps, virtually all of places far from Venice. As Almagià, Biasutti, Banfi and others have observed, his maps are works of synthesis and compilation from data obtained from secondary sources, such as marine charts and other maps, descriptive works, such as, mainly, Ramusio's *Navigazioni e viaggi,* itineraries, lists of localities, and the like.[99] Indeed, it is the most astonishing thing about Gastaldi that he managed on the basis of such materials to arrive for the first time at generally correct images of all the far continents,[100] and for that matter it is generally revealing that such tremendous advances could be made with virtually no personal recourse at all to formal mathematics.[101]

We return to Gastaldi's employment by the government, in connection with a quite different sort of work than that dealt with above, both more interesting, and more easily expounded. In May 1549 the Venetian Council of Ten commissioned Gastaldi to make a map of Africa on the wall of the Sala dello Scudo in the Ducal Palace.[102] Gastaldi drew the map in charcoal, the actual painting was done by the painter Vitruvio Buonconsiglio, and work was finished by summer 1550. No trace of the map remains. In August 1553 Gastaldi was again commissioned to make another wall map for the Ducal Palace, which, according to the surviving instructions,[103] would have covered an enormous geographical area including

---

[98] Almagià (1929, 26b). For some limited discussion of Gastaldi's actual working methods, see chapter four, and, esp., chapter seven.

[99] On this in general, see for example Almagià (1929, 26 and 27); Almagià (1939, *carta*, 14; Almagià (1948, 21-22 and 40); Biasutti (1930, 553-54); Banfi (1947, 28), and many other places.

[100] See for a quick but quite convincing documentation of this astonishing fact our chapter three, and our chapter four, or indeed our entire work from that point on, which is mostly concerned precisely with this impressive achievement.

[101] On this point, see the end of our chapter four .

[102] Actually, he was first commissioned in 1548, but the map he drew then for some reason was found unsatisfactory (Karrow, 1993, 224), and he was recommissioned in 1549.

[103] Lorenzi (1868, 277-78). This second commission clearly shows the Council's satisfaction with the first wall map.

Central and Eastern Asia, and all of America as far as the parts discovered by Cartier (i.e., New France) -- in other words, all of North America. A map of similar but not the same coverage is still there, but several scholars believe it is not the map that Gastaldi made, and that that map no longer exists, or that the extant map is much changed from Gastaldi's original. I too have serious doubts that the current map reflects Gastaldi's original, but for different reasons.[104]

In the same month of August 1553 Gastaldi was commissioned by the Senate to make an enormous world map which the Republic would present to the son of Sultan Suleiman, a work for which Gastaldi was paid very generously. This map too is presumably no longer extant, although it is hard to be certain, for only in recent years have the Islamic countries begun to show interest in looking into a large number of repositories in their world untouched for centuries.[105] It is clear that the Venetian government had much faith and trust in Gastaldi in such matters. He seems to be the only person who was entrusted with such projects, though I am not certain of this, and they speak of him endearingly enough in the surviving documents.[106] But there is no evidence that he was endowed with an official title, and this will be a good place to dispense with a myth that this was so.

It is often said that Gastaldi bore the official title of Cosmographer of the Venetian Republic, based on the fact that Vincenzo Coronelli refers to him in 1695 as "Giacomo Castaldo Piedmontese, cosmographer of the Republic of Venice."[107] But no contemporary documentation of this exists, and Gastaldi never refers to

---

[104] For a fuller treatment of these two maps, including references to all the documents on them printed in Lorenzi (1868), see the comments in the entries for them in our cartobibliography, nos. 65 and 72.

[105] On this map see a fuller story in our chapter two. It is worth pointing out that the scholar who uncovered the only information on this map, in the regular Venetian archives, does not, as is unfortunately normal in such cases, tell us what it was that led him to this part of the archives, and there seems an underlying assumption that it may have been found there by chance, which obviously implies that in both the archives of the Council and the Senate, there certainly remains the possibility of further information on Gastaldi, and that no systematic search for such information has been made, and, indeed, may be very difficult or impossible to make.

[106] In the preserved documents printed by Lorenzi (cf. note 105 above), there are ten references to him as "Master Jacomo of Piedmont, our cosmographer". Note that they do not hesitate to refer to him as he himself did, as "Piedmontese", even though these were members of the Council of Ten, the heart and soul of the pride of Venice. There may be something more than national pride in the regular addition by Gastaldi of this element to his signatures, which has so far escaped us. Note, too, in a different vein, that the significance of this occasional work, but on very important projects, impresses this writer as perhaps of greater significance in assessing Gastaldi than his work as engineer for various bodies. In this last arena, Gastaldi was outshone in his time by at least two persons, Christoforo Sabbatino and Christopher Sorte.

[107] In Coronelli's "Catalogo degli avtori antichi, e moderni, che hanno scritto, e trattato di Geografia," in his *Atlante veneto* (Venice, 1695). I quote after Armao (1957, 23). On Coronelli in general see Milanesi (2016).

himself thus, nor does anyone else at the time to the best of my knowledge. The closest are the mentioned references to him in documents of the Council of Ten as, "Master Jacomo of Piedmont, our cosmographer."[108] Gastaldi usually refers to himself as "Cosmographo in Venetia," or something similar. The earliest usage of the title form that I know of is by the French geographer Mallet in 1683, who refers to "Jacques Castaldo, Cosmographe de la Republique de Venise,"[109] but it very possibly occurs earlier. Grande in 1902 noted that Coronelli had held the same title, and thus would have been in a position to know,[110] and other writers have followed him in that vein. But Coronelli's actual title was Cosmografo della Serenissima Repubblica. Furthermore, it was invented by the flamboyant Coronelli himself in 1685, when he managed to convince the Council of Ten to allow him to officially apply that title to himself and even to receive a regular emolument for it. The council later thought better, for in 1705 it stripped him of both title and emolument. In explaining their reasons for the 1705 measure, they mention, "The title of Cosmographer and the professorship enjoyed by Coronelli, being totally new and created by him."[111] Coronelli had perhaps read that his illustrious forebear had had a similar title, as in Mallet, and decided to apply it to himself. In any event, it must be considered as questionable at best that the title existed in Gastaldi's time, and that he bore it.

Only one further official affiliation in Gastaldi's life is known. Private literary and scientific academies for the social and intellectual elite were a popular thing at the time in Italy. One such, envisioned at its start as to be one of the greatest, was opened in 1557 by the patrician Federico Badoer (or Badoero, or Badoaro), who gave it the name Accademia Venetiana, though it was also often called the Accademia della Fama. This was not an academy in the sense of a school (nor were other similar bodies), but a forum for the intelligentsia from various fields, who could meet and discuss new ideas, perhaps then putting these ideas into print, or possibly implementing them, although the academy was so

---

[108] See note 107 above.

[109] Mallet (1683, 1, 193).

[110] Grande (1902, 38-39).

[111] Gatti (1976, 29 and 1143). The original documents granting the title and remuneration are printed in Luisetto (1988, 1025-26).

short-lived there was unlikely to have been time for the latter.[112] The academy had four departments (*consigli*), which were broken into sections (*stanza*), which were in turn broken into various faculties.   There were approximately one hundred members in all. Gastaldi and the patrician Livio Sanuto were selected to represent the faculty of geography (or cosmography -- the two terms are used interchangeably in the several contemporary documents referring to the faculty), which came under the section mathematics, part of the *Consigio delle scientie*[113]

Here a word on the documentation of Gastaldi's membership in the academy is due, for it has never been made clear before.   Grande first mentions the fact (1902, 93, 95 and 100), but does not give us the source for his information, other than the uninformative remark at page 100 that "we find him named at that time [1560] in the Instrument of Deputation of the Academy of Fame, as a member of it", without telling us what this "Instrumento" is.   The document is the last of three constitutions written for the academy in 1557, 1559 and 1560, each more comprehensive than the preceding (Rose, 1969, 192).   It was written by the academy's founder, Badoer, and was printed by the prestigious Aldine Press by Paolo Manucio, as were all the academy's printed works. (see in our bibliography at Badoer, 1560 for the complicated details connected with this very rare item. It is known only in two copies, neither of which I have seen.   Fortunately, it was reprinted by Maria Domenico Pellegrini in 1808 (Pellegrini, 1808, at pp. 49-68 in

---

[112] On the academy, see Rose (1969), the best general treatment, and Tafuri (1989, 114-22 and 242-48), both with extensive further references. Regarding its geographical activities in particular, see Woodward (1996, *Maps*, 18-19). All works which the short-lived academy produced were published by the Aldine Press, the most prestigious in Venice, and an excellent full descriptive catalog of the fifty-seven works published, individually numbered, is in Renouard (1834, 267-81). See also Pellegrini (1808), which includes reprints of four important works of the academy which deal with the academy itself, including a prospectus of proposed projects. Editorially, Pellegrini is a nightmare, for he constantly fails to follow the orthography of the original, sometimes illogically and confusingly inserts material of unclear relationship to the materials around it, and in general is very poorly organized,

[113] Livio Sanuto (1520-1576), from a noble Venetian family, is best known for his *Geografia*, published posthumously in Venice, 1588. The book is the first full geography and atlas of Africa, although death prevented Sanuto from realizing his full intention, which was a similar volume for each continent. Obviously, the title of this volume does not correspond well to its contents. But, fortunately, the first volume of the set was to contain a rather lengthy preface outlining geographical knowledge of the whole globe at the time, and by good fortune this preface to the whole work was printed in the only volume published (see also our chapter ten). Sanuto is also known for a large set of globe gores attributed to him (Woodward, 1987; see also Skelton [1965, v-x]; Bury [1990], and Lefevre [1942]). His brother Giulio Sanuto worked together with him on these projects. On Giulio, see Bury (1990), with other references. Although we know of no mutual activity of Gastaldi and Livio, their interests were similar, and he should be counted among those whose study might lead to information on Gastaldi, and, though less so, the same is true of his brother Giulio, who some say engraved the maps for the 1561 Ruscelli Ptolemy, which were mostly copied directly from Gastaldi's of ca. 1542(?)-1547 for the 1548 Pederezzano-Gastaldi Ptolemy.

the part of the work printed in volume 23). As noted above, Pellegrini is an editorial nightmare. The valuable reprint begins near the bottom of page forty-nine, with no introductory comments at all, and directly after a small list of works completely unconnected with the document. It begins with the words "Instrumento di deputazione," etc., and continues through page sixty-eight. At pp. 61-64 of this document there is inserted rather abruptly a list of the names of the ninety-nine members of the academy. The obscure and florid language which directly precedes this list might make one feel unsure of the list's nature, but for affirmation that it is definitely a list of the academy's members, see Rose (1969, 199. esp. note 41 there). The list is broken into a number of little sections, each representing one of the academy's faculties or sections. Gastaldi and Sanuto are under the heading "cosmografi", at p. 63 in the Pellegrini reprint.

The academy was short-lived. It was closed by government intervention in 1561, ostensibly due to enormous foreign debts incurred by its founder Badoer, and it is perhaps due to this fact that many modern writers on Gastaldi have tended to shy away from the subject of the academy, fearing that it might detract from his name. But a glance at the many Venetian luminaries appointed or elected to the academy, including Francesco Sansovino, Bernardo Tasso, Francesco Patrizio, Agostino Valier, Alvise Mocenego, Paolo Ramusio, Alessandro Contarini, and many others, is sufficient to put any doubts to rest as to the honor of being selected for membership.[114]

Tafuri says that "the real motives behind the elimination of the Accademia and the *damnatio memoriae* to which it would be relegated are probably more complex than one might think",[115] and argues very convincingly that the new institution actually posed something of a threat to the government: "Let there be no doubt about it: the Accademia's ambition was to be recognized as the depository of 'public knowledge'; and it came close to expropriating prerogatives that the entire patriciate had been guaranteed by the Venetian constitution."[116] The sense of the present writer is that Tafuri's incisive comments are almost certainly correct.

As we see in our cartobibliography entries (97.-100 and 107.-117), it is virtually certain that Gastaldi produced some rather interesting, though not

---

[114] See Rose (1969, 199 and 214-15), Tafuri (1989, 114 and 246-47, in note 96), and Pellegrini (1808, 61-64).

[115] Tafuri (1989, 114).

[116] Tafuri (1989, 116). For more on the genuineness of the prestige of the academy, including the addressing of a number of laudatory letters to it by several cardinals, and pope Pius IV's admiration for it, see Grande (1902, 93), Rose (1969, 207-08), and Tafuri (1989, 114-15).

spectacular, works in connection with his membership in the academy. We shall not speak of them now, but only in the cartobibliography, because of some points of uncertainty concerning this work, although we do say a few preliminary words about them at the end of the present chapter. As to the spectacular cartographical project of 1559-1564, dealt with in chapter ten and elsewhere, that was certainly an independent enterprise of Gastaldi, very possibly contemplated for many years, and, as we shall see below, it had nothing to do directly or officially with the academy.[117] Nor is there any known cooperative undertaking involving Gastaldi and his fellow academician Livio Sanuto. However, in keeping with our expressed policy in the present chapter of drawing attention to every possible person who might have been connected with Gastaldi, we note the following. One of three regents heading the mathematics stanza is one Francesco Tiepolo, while one Antonio Tiepolo is among the regents of a law stanza (Pellegrini, 1808, 63 for both). One of these must be the person academy member Bernardo Tasso speaks of when, in praising the Accademia in his famous 1560 *Amadigi*, he mentions "the exquisite Tiepolo the Geographer, who knows every shape and place in the world" (Tafuri, 1989, 120-21). Although he would have been only about thirty-two years old at the time, Antonio is probably that same Tiepolo, member of a very prominent Venetian family, who later became ambassador to Spain, then Poland, then Constantinople, and had an active interest in far places, including the American Indies. On him see Donazzolo (1929, 9, 128, and 141-43), Monga (2000) and Monga(1999, 48). On both Tiepolo's, see Cicogna (1824-1853, at indexes). There exist indications that Gastaldi may have been working together with other persons in his very latest years, or that other persons may have revised some of his work not long after his death, and this ;"exquisite Tiepolo the Geographer" would clearly be a candidate, especially since he was affiliated with the academy.

We have dwelt on the topic of the academy principally for the purpose of removing any sense that some sort of stigma attaches in any way to Gastaldi as a result of his membership in it. The honor of being chosen as one of its principals is an unblemished one.

---

[117] See, however, chapter ten, note 31, and in the cartobibliographical entries mentioned above, where we shall have occasion to speak of projected Gastaldi projects mentioned in a 1558 prospectus of the academy.

1.6 Technicalities and Officialdom

We have found it convenient and useful to include here some information on the technical and official aspects of Gastaldi's maps (engraving, publishing, privileges [copyright]), for various reasons, but most importantly because a scrutiny of these areas throws some further light, in unexpected ways, on aspects of Gastaldi's activities which may be called biographical in general.

We shall start with the engravers. Here we are in for some surprises. Gastaldi's maps were among the most reprinted in history, especially in Italy, but also abroad, and the reprints much outnumber the originals. Thus, when we scan a list of sixteenth century Italian maps, as, for example, in a cataloging of a Veneto-Roman atlas (Lafrerian atlases), most of the Gastaldi maps will be reprints.[118] These reprints almost invariably name the engraver, and very often at least one other person as well, besides the cartographer. Since these reprints or re-editions almost invariably predominate in such collections to a high degree over examples which are original editions, the very important fact brought out in the following paragraph has gone unnoticed.

Of 124 Gastaldi maps by our count, one is manuscript, and two are painted wall maps. Another twenty-four are either woodcuts, or, we should say, since some of these never reached the press, were intended to be woodcuts.[119] So there are ninety-eight copperplate maps. On only nineteen of these maps, always speaking of course of the original editions, is an engraver named. Five of these nineteen maps are posthumous, so out of ninety-three copperplate maps produced in Gastaldi's lifetime, only fourteen of them carry the name of an engraver, eleven of them that of Fabio Licinio. Of course, other copperplate maps exist without an engraver named, but it is very common for the engraver to be named, at least in Italian maps. So seventy-nine out of ninety-three, about 85%, is a very large number. Who engraved the other seventy-nine maps?

The bulk of the seventy-nine maps are the sixty maps included in the Pedrezzano-Gastaldi Ptolemy of 1548, and fifteen more are made up by a group of unique maps recently brought to light by Peter Meurer,[120] consisting of four Ptolemaic maps (two ancient and two modern), and eleven "Strabonian" maps, both evidently

---

[118]For Veneto-Roman atlases (often referred to in the literature as "IATO atlases" for "Italian-assembled-to-order-atlases") see our first Appendix.

[119]We speak of some of those maps intended for Ramusio's *Navigationi* which never made it into print. In all but the first editions of Ramusio's volumes, incidentally, the maps are replaced by copperplate editions.

[120] Meurer (2004) and see our cartobibliography, nos. 97-100 and 107-117.

intended for aborted editions of Ptolemy and Strabo.   The other four maps are Gastaldi's 1544 Spain, 1545 Sicily, 1546 world, and 1550 Moscovia.[121] The first copperplate Gastaldi map which indicates an engraver, Enea Vico, is Gastaldi's 1552 Germany. Of the Spain, Woodward wrote: "Giacomo Gastaldi . . . who had a fine chancery hand, may have also engraved his first published map, La Spagna (1544) himself,[122] and Karrow notes of the same map: "Gastaldi's map has the look of a beginner still unsure of his rhythm and spacing (he is said to have engraved it himself.)"[123]   Nordenskiöld does not hesitate to say of the sixty maps in the Pedrezzano-Gastaldi Ptolemy that they "had been handsomely engraved in copper by the famous cartographer Gastaldi",[124] nor do Laor or Tooley.[125]   Jo Margaret Mano expounds this all a little further. Having noted that Gastaldi refers to himself as a ;"cosmographer", she continues: "This term is confusing, and does not tell us whether he was responsible for drafting the maps or engraving and publishing them as well," then shortly after she comes to the conclusion: "It is reasonable to believe Gastaldi began by engraving his own maps . . . His early maps of Spain (1544) and the world (1546) are exquisitely and minutely detailed, use a distinctive undulating wavy pattern to depict the ocean and contain only his name."[126]   Mano doesn't mention the Ptolemy maps, or the 1545 Sicily, but the engraving style is the same, especially the "distinctive undulating wavy pattern to depict the ocean," at least in maps which touch upon the ocean or sea.

This idea is not at all implausible. A good number of sixteenth century cartographers also had engraving talents, including Oronce Fine,[127] Sebastian Münster,[128] Thomas Geminus, Augustin Hirschvogel, Jodocus Hondius, and Christoph Zell,[129] and no doubt others, and, of course, the engraving talents of

---

[121] Our nos. 1, 2, 3, and 67.

[122] Woodward (1987, 186).

[123] Karrow (1993, 110).

[124] Nordenskiöld (1889, 26, and again on p. 29), and still again shortly after (1897, 129).

[125] Laor (1986, 90), and Tooley, Bricker and Crone, 1989, 58.

[126] Mano (1987, 5). Mano errs when she states, as many have done, that his major engraver and the most prolific was Fabio Licinio" (Mano, op. cit., 6). Licinio engraved only eleven Gastaldi maps, but they include the most important (and most often reproduced), which has led to this idea. If she had said he was the best and most important, that would be correct.

[127] Hamon, in Balteau, 1933- , Vol. 13, col. 1371.

[128] Lach (1965-93, Vol. 2, bk. 2/3, 340).

[129] Karrow (1993, respectively, pp. 250, 295, 405 and 591).

Mercator are well-known, and he engraved all of his own works up to the famous 1569 world map,[130] and perhaps some of his later maps, though he also hired engravers, and, after his eyesight became poor, had to depend entirely on others. He also taught his sons and grandsons how to engrave, and occasionally taught others as well, such as Johannes Corputius.[131]   Furthermore, as Bury says, "engraving was practiced by Gentlemen amateurs, along with painting in the sixteenth century," and he gives examples of this from Vasari.[132] Hamon states the same;[133] and, of course, there were a good number of engravers in Venice in the early 1540s, mostly producing subject prints, from whom Gastaldi could have learned engraving.[134]   I think it very likely that the opinions of Nordenskiöld, Woodward, Laor, and Mano are correct, and that Gastaldi probably engraved all of his own copperplate maps up to 1552, and possibly also the later maps found by Meurer.[135]

There is little more to say of particular note regarding Gastaldi's engravers. His engraver for the great 1559-1564 maps of course is Fabio Licinio. It is true that the block cutter for the woodcut maps in Ramusio's *Navigazioni* is also unknown, but while no other likely candidate comes to mind besides Gastaldi himself for the early copperplate maps, a good possible candidate for the Ramusio woodcuts does exist, Matteo Pagano, who engraved four separate woodcut maps for Gastaldi, the first in 1546 (our no. 4), four years before the first Ramusio map of 1550 (no. 67), but I would not venture further than to call this a quite reasonable possibility.[136]

As to publishers, we also run into a surprise, or we at least seem to, at first. Out of the 119 maps published in Gastaldi's lifetime,[137] other than those published

---

[130] Karrow (1993, 382; see also 376-77 on the milieu in which he learned his engraving).

[131] Karrow (1993, 388). See much on Mercator's engraving activity in Crane (2002, 69, 73-74,75, 80, 113, 117, 156, 171, 172, 178, 218, 225, 235, 255, 259 and 270).

[132] Bury (1990, 19, and 24, note 74).

[133] Hamon (op. cit., in note 128, col. 1371).

[134] Bury (2001, throughout the book, passim).

[135] See our cartobibliography, nos. 97-100 and 107-117. Perhaps a further note of support for the idea that Gastaldi himself engraved these maps, instead of entrusting it to someone else, is provided by the distinct streak of independence which we have detected in his character.

[136] Since we really don't know, it is not altogether impossible that Gastaldi cut these woodblocks, but it seems very unlikely. Note, however, that Mercator was capable of cutting woodblocks (Crane, 2002, 113).

[137] For information on the publishers and engravers of the five posthumous Gastaldi maps, see cartobibliography entries 120-124.

in books,[138] there seems to be only one for which we can find a publisher's name, that is, no. 70, the 1552 Germany, whose publisher is given as Gabriel Giolito. But this apparent absence of publishers is an illusion, for Gastaldi himself, along with Licinio, is, besides the cartographer, the publisher of the great maps of 1559-1564, and I suppose he is also the publisher, or the entrepreneur (if there is really a difference here), for his first three maps, the 1544 Spain, the 1545 Sicily, and the 1546 world map.[139] The four separately printed woodcut maps cut for Gastaldi by Pagano were presumably printed and sold by him at his establishment and shop "in Frezaria al insegna della Fede" ("in Frezaria [Street] at the Sign of Faith").

What of the privileges (*privilegi*, singular *privilegio*)? Basically, as the need for it grew with the rise of printing and selling books, the institution of privileges (which, as we shall see, is different from the permission, or license, to print, although they are sometimes confused with each other), evolved imperceptibly over time out of the much older institution of patents, which goes back several centuries before the privilege.[140] It is simplest to explain the essence of both of them using a typical example of a patent rather than a privilege, and so we shall do that here. Let's say a man has found, perhaps after many years of work and effort, a way to build better and stronger bridge supports, a thing obviously of benefit to all in a society. But he hesitates to implement his new idea even once, because he knows that others, some of them having talents in business and in forming what we would call companies, talents which he himself lacks, will begin using his new idea at will, and he will receive no compensation for his years of work. So he turns to the king for a patent, which states that, under penalty of law, no one can use this new method except the inventor, other than with the inventor's permission, for which he may charge a reasonable fee. The king grants the patent, for a fee, and both the inventor and the king benefit. The inventor can now

---

[138] In these cases, of course, the publishers of the maps were the publishers of the books, Pedrezzano for the Ptolemy, the Giunti for the *Navigationi*, and Pedrezzano again for the *Comentari della Moscovia, etc.*, of 1550, with Gastaldi's Moscovia. We can't say, however, that the maps were actually printed in the shops of these people, and on this point we are in the dark.

[139] An interesting little question is what arrangements he made for the selling of these first maps. It is hard to venture a guess, but perhaps the most likely is that he sold them through the shop of the Giunti, whom Ramusio knew well, or through Pedrezzano's establishment.

[140] Witcombe (2004, 21-28). I have also looked into this development quite deeply myself, but shall not add my findings here, which do not contradict those of Witcombe (2004) and Brown (1891), and the findings reported in the following paragraphs are based in general on those two works, and upon my own experience with reading these documents themselves, mostly those for Gastaldi, but also some others. Mainly, scholarship in this area has arisen only in recent years, Brown being the only significant exception.

implement and release his idea, for he will receive compensation for his work. The king benefits because he knows the new idea, freed by his patent to come into effect, will benefit his whole realm directly, and indirectly as well, since it stimulates activity good for the economy in general, besides adding to his own revenue due to the patent fee paid. The writer's and printmaker's privilege evolved out of this, and in a way was just a special sort of patent, which works upon obviously analogous lines.

While both the writer and the printmaker, and also the government, benefit from the *privilegio*, we usually think in terms of the writer. The word privilege does not imply permission granted by the government to the creator of a work to publish it. That would be a permission or license to print, and, in Venice it was applied for and (perhaps) granted by the *Riformatori dello Studio di Padova*, and was required if the book were on a particularly delicate subject, as politics, religion, or important living persons. The privilege was applied for and granted by the Venetian Senate, and was *not* required, if the book publisher were willing to take the risk, which he might be if his work was, say, of a specialist nature interesting to few, which would be unlikely to be printed by others in any event. The word privilege is to be understood as meaning only the privilege holder had the right to print the work, and others did *not* have this right, unless he willingly passed it on to them, presumably for a fee. So the privilege implies a sort of ascendancy over other potential printers, who do not have the permission to print it without the privilege holder's consent. The holder and dispenser of permission here is the privilege holder, not the government. The role of the government is simply to provide the power to enforce the privilege holder's privilege, that is, his right to give or refuse permission to others to print his work. The factor of revenue for the State seems to have been of some importance to the government, for it appears that the number of years for which the privilege was to be in effect, most commonly five, ten, fifteen or twenty years, though other spans can be found, simply depended on how high a fee was paid.

There were always two documents involved (occasionally more for special circumstances) as regards privileges, and also licenses to print: a hand-written request (*supplicatio*) by the seeker of the privilege or the license, and a hand-written grant (if granted, as they usually were, at least as regards privileges) written by a member of the Senate or some functionary working under the Senate, or of the *Riformatori dello Studio di Padova*, as the case may have been. The requests are usually much longer than the grants, and are usually written in a neat, legible hand to show respect to those being applied to, which is fortunate, for they can often provide valuable details to us about the work and its preparation, while the latter are usually short, laconic, and often scrawled and barely legible. The dates on both documents are always exact, that is, to the day, and it is interesting to note that, as to privileges (I can't speak on this as to licences, but probably the case was often different with them), usually the date of the request and the date of the granting are the same, implying that very possibly the whole procedure was usually treated perfunctorily, perhaps with the applicant simply presenting his request and paying his fee, and the privilege dispenser simply quickly reading or looking over the request, and quickly scribbling out his grant to the request, and the applicant was on his way. All in all, as regards privileges, the most important factor for the State seems to have been simply the revenue obtained, although it is true that it also helped keep the publishing business stimulated, with resultant benefits to the public.

While they were usually applied for by publishers, anyone involved in the process of producing a map (or other print) could apply, including the original cartographer, the engraver, the printer, etc., and, while I am not yet quite certain on this point, it appears that once a privilege had been obtained for a work by one of these involved persons, none of the others could apply on his own for a privilege for the same work, or perhaps they could theoretically, but it was simply never done. There is the implication here that the holder of the privilege was by virtue of that the main entrepreneur in the project involved, although it is perhaps not possible to be quite sure, for any number of unwritten arrangements between the persons involved could have been made, I suppose.

A notice of the privilege granted was of course engraved on the work, including the number of years it was granted for. Though scholars have sometimes used privilege requesting or granting documents as evidence of the date of a work, this is not a good idea. There was no government stipulation as to when a privilege for a particular work was to be applied for. One could apply before work had begun, while work was in progress, or after a work was finished, and a work could take several years to finish, or perhaps not even be begun for some time after a privilege was granted. Several of Gastaldi's preserved requests for privileges are for works which in fact he made only several years later. Examples of works for which privileges were taken out, while the work never appeared at all, are also known, though none for Gastaldi.[141] On the other hand, while the colophon in the Pedrezzano-Gastaldi 1548 Ptolemy is dated October, 1547, the application for privilege is dated after this, on November 5, 1547 (Fahy, 1993, 93).

Typically, the applications, or supplications, are formulaic. They begin with obsequious expressions made to the Senate, then, with some variation in order of presentation, an observation on the efforts expended and expenses incurred by the applicant, and a statement that the applicant should rightfully receive recompense for his efforts, which should not be taken away from him by others; a comment on the usefulness for all of his product, and, always lastly, a drawn-out and imploring plea that if anyone should violate his privilege, the government will take quick and severe steps to deal with the offender, ending then with more obsequious remarks.

Most, but not all, of Gastaldi's maps are covered by privileges, either for single maps, or for a small group of maps named in a single request, or they are covered by a privilege taken out for a whole book in which they appear, as the maps in the Pedrezzano Ptolemy, or the maps in the three volumes of Ramusio's *Navigazioni*. I don't know the significance of the fact that a few are not covered. As regards the impressive individual maps from the boom period of 1559-64, most of the original privilege documents have come to light over the years, though in some cases only the granting, and they have been published in various places, either in full or in part or in resumé. In chapter ten, we give the places where they have been published,[142] and, in the following note, a quotation in full, in English, of

---

[141] Examples also exist of a single privilege covering several maps named in the application, and even of what we could call blanket privileges, providing government protection for *anything* published by an applicant during the course of a specified number of years. Two examples are found in Gallo (1950, 93-94, incl. note 9 on p. 94), obviously of greater value than privileges for individual works, and I am not sure how to interpret this fact. My guess is that it was simply a matter of money, government revenue, and probably very high fees were asked for such privileges. Licenses to print and privileges, as said, are different things, with the former a graver matter from the standpoint of the government, and, in fact, in many years of looking at these things, I have never had the sense that the matter of privileges was one of great concern for the Senate, and probably after having obtained their fee, since they had more important things to think about, they concerned themselves no further, unless perhaps asked for intercession by someone whose privilege had been violated. Certainly the publication of a non-controversial new work was not as important to society at large as a means to built better and safer bridge supports.

[142] See chapter ten, note 8.

the most important of the few not published elsewhere, by way of example.[143] See also the comments to entry no. 69 in our cartobibliography, on the Gastaldi map of southwest Asia of 1550 or later, concerning the privilege for that map.

1.7 Gastaldi's Crown Jewels

We have still one more avenue to follow which can reveal yet a little more of a biographical nature, in the sense of throwing some tentative light on certain points of character and certain aspirations of Gastaldi, and at the same time defining the principal direction of the remainder of our book. We have, as we have said, 124 maps in our cartobibliography. Discounting five posthumous maps leaves 119.[144] Out of these 119 maps, only twenty-one are separate maps *made upon Gastaldi's own initiative*. All the rest were initiated by others. The majority of these were parts of large sets of maps occurring in books, or sets of books, e.g. the Ptolemy maps just mentioned, the Ramusio *Navigazioni* maps, and the Strabonian maps and new Ptolemy maps, undoubtedly commissioned by someone for aborted editions of Strabo and Ptolemy. These twenty-one maps initiated by Gastaldi himself can tell us a lot about Gastaldi.

---

[143] The item quoted here is the request of July 29, 1559 for item no. 4 in the note in chapter ten just referred to. It is a multiple request for a privilege for Gastaldi's three Parts of Asia, and his Greece, Italy, and Lombardy. The request begins with a headline reading "Most Serene Prince and Most Illustrious Council", under which follows the main text: "Just and honest has ever been the institution of this most serene and most felicitous dominion to wish that those who virtuously toil in any profession to the highest usefulness and convenience to many, as I Giacomo Gastaldi, Piedmontese cosmographer, have done in my profession, should receive for their toils what emolument they might be able, and that that which is so much due to them might not be taken away by others: I, Jacomo the aforesaid, wanting sole right to have printed, with much expense and toil to me, and to universal convenience and usefulness, three Parts of Asia, that is to say the country of the Turkish sovereign Sophi, and the country of Arabia desert, and felice now called Aiaman, and the country of Cathay, with India, and similarly Greece, and Italy, and of Italy Lombardy in particular, and all these countries will be with the names modern and ancient: I reverently petition that the True Serenity might be content to render to me privilege for XV years that others may not, in this city or in any other city or place of its jurisdiction, print or sell the said maps of mine under penalty of losing the works, and the monies given to me as is customary in similar cases, or as may seem best to the True Serenity, so that with this favor and example, in the future I may be able so much the more readily, without regard to expense, to attend to the bringing forth of many other works of mine, to universal benefit to all; and in good grace I worshipfully entreat the True Serenity." (From Archivio di Stato di Venezia, Senato Terra, filza 29). I am very grateful to the late David Woodward for providing me with a copy of the original document. Though no documents have been found for them, we know that, besides the privileges for the maps noted in our note 8 in chapter ten, privileges were taken out for the 1545 Sicily and the 1562 Polonia (northeast Europe), for privilege statements are engraved in their cartouches.

[144] We omit these because of the impossibility of knowing if they were changed or added to by later hands after Gastaldi's death. They are dealt with adequately in our cartobibliography (nos. 120-124).

They show us, first off, that, unlike almost all other cartographers of the time, who, as a perusal of Karrow shows immediately,[145] were principally interested in producing maps of their homelands or parts of their homelands, Gastaldi was from the start drawn to the mapping of far places. Gastaldi's first four maps, all of them part of our central corpus of twenty-one maps, are his 1544 Spain, 1545 Sicily, his 1546 woodcut Danube lands map, and the 1546 world map.[146] In fact, other than the little map of Italy, and some Italian provinces in the 1548 Ptolemy, maps which he could hardly do otherwise than include in their context, and not representing a conscious choice, Gastaldi shows no interest in an area which could be called Italian until his 1555 map of Piedmont, over ten years into his career, but even here we may have our reservations, for, as we have seen from Braudel (see note 4 above), "Piedmont, in the sixteenth century could hardly be called part of Italy." Not until 1561 does Gastaldi produce a separate large map of Italy (no. 101), and even that map may well have been inspired as a sort of offshoot of the map of southeast Europe of 1560 (no. 96), and in fact I believe that this may have been the case.[147] Make no mistake: Gastaldi's main interests from the start lay with faraway lands, and it was mostly maps of faraway lands that made and make him famous.

They show us also that Gastaldi invariably did his best work when making maps conceived on his own. Only then did he work with full brilliance and a fully-

---

[145] Karrow (1993). The same emerges from a perusal of Meurer (1991), or, for that matter, even Ortelius's list of cartographers.

[146] Gastaldi received information from Mendoza for the Spain, and evidently information from Maurolico for the Sicily, but there is no indication that he was commissioned by these men to make these maps. This Sicily cannot be taken as indication of an interest in places Italian, as opposed to far places. While Italian speaking, Sicily was under the Spanish crown from 1503 until the early 18th century, at times under or affiliated with the House of Savoy.

[147] Both Almagià and Biasutti express the opinion that, regardless of their dates of publication, the Italy was finished in manuscript before the southeast Europe, but their only evidence for this seems to be the fact that the Italy is mentioned in a privilege application of 1559, precisely the one we have quoted above, in note 144. But one cannot, as we have seen, depend on privilege application dates in dating maps, and especially when the maps contain clear dates which obviously show that the 1561 Italy was published after the 1560 southeast Europe. It is true that Gastaldi does mention, as said, a map of Italy in the application of 1559, but my suspicion is that at the time Gastaldi published his 1559 Danube basin map, which is really just the upper half of the 1560 Europe, he had already visualized and probably at least sketched the entirety of the 1560 southeast Europe, and it was the fact that a little over half of Italy straggles rather awkwardly into that map from the northwest which prompted him to produce a separate Italy. From a series of maps, which we shall not recount in detail, beginning from the 1560s to the 1580s, which show Venice at the upper left corner, the whole of the Adriatic, and then a large section of the eastern Mediterranean and the Near East, one gets the impression that, for a Venetian, this was really the "home territory" and area of influence, and not the peninsula of Italy proper.

fired inspiration. For, without exception, all of those eighteen Gastaldi maps which I consider his best and most impressive come precisely from this small group.[148] Not one falls in the group of ninety-eight other maps. Note that this is not just a matter of size, for of course most of the separate maps are larger than the maps in books, but of overall quality. Of course, not all of these ninety-eight maps are worthless. It was the sixteenth century, and there were more bad maps around than good ones. And some of these ninety-eight maps, for example the three 1554 maps from the second edition of volume one of Ramusio's *Navigazioni*, were sharp improvements over previous works, and, though less so, so were the extra-European 1548 Ptolemy maps. Nevertheless, it is abundantly clear that Gastaldi did his finest work when he was the man in charge, when he was working for himself, again indicative of a strong streak of independence.

Still another circumstance worth pointing out is that, although they are not maps of continents or parts of continents, Gastaldi's first two separately printed maps, the 1544 Spain and the 1545 Sicily, are quite accomplished productions, and their overall look and style remind one of the superb maps produced in 1559-1564 by Gastaldi and Licinio, even if they are not *quite* as elegant as the later maps. No other maps between this time and 1559 have this look about them. The 1546 Pagano-engraved woodcut of the Danube lands to be sure is an impressive production indeed, but elegance it lacks. And, again, there was the giant Africa being worked on in the background, obviously reminiscent of the later set merely by virtue of its subject. There may be here the implication that Gastaldi from the start was, in a perhaps not quite fully formulated sense, contemplating a program of production similar to that which occurred in 1559-64, but simply was prevented from pursuing it by economic considerations, the mundane necessity to make a living, and the demands on his time resulting from that.[149]

But, while there may have been earlier glimmerings of the spectacular explosion of cartographic activity and talent of 1559-1564, it is precisely the maps produced in those years, all conceived and executed by Gastaldi, and engraved by Licinio (the sole exception being the great 1561 *Cosmographia vniversalis* world

---

[148] Of course, subjectivity plays a role here. But I have been looking at these maps for many years, and I feel certain that the same list of maps, or one very close to it, would be generated by any careful observer. The eighteen maps are our nos. 1-4, 69, 80, 92-96, 101-104, 106, and 118-119. Gastaldi's Lombardy would certainly qualify for this group, and just possibly his Padua, but these are posthumous maps.

[149] The whole question of Gastaldi's motivations and goals is a troubled and problematic area, which we explore in considerable depth in the final section of chapter ten. It is not impossible that Gastaldi himself had some difficulty in clearly defining his goals.

map, engraved in wood by Matteo Pagano), which make up Gastaldi's masterworks. These are Gastaldi's jewels. We can say, without fear of error, that, if all of Gastaldi's maps had been lost, except these nine Gastaldi-Licinio maps,[150] and the 1561 *Cosmographia vniversalis* world map, ten maps in all, the loss would be a relatively minor one, and Gastaldi would still be among the greatest cartographers in history. In fact, we may go still farther with this. For the same would be basically true even if we reduced this number to only *four* (or six, depending on how one counts) of these maps, the First, Second, and Third Parts of Asia, which, although the three parts are not designed so that they fit together to make a single map, one might consider as a single map,[151] the ca. 1560 America (no. 94), the 1564 Africa (no. 118), and the great 1561 world map (no. 104). These are Gastaldi's crown jewels. We can see that, consistent with his beginnings, it was in reaching for far places that Gastaldi shone the brightest, and the farther from home, from Venice, from Italy, from Europe, as you will, the brighter he shone. It is principally these large multi-sheet maps of the far continents, or large parts of continents, which stand out with such an incomparable brilliance by comparison with all of his other maps. They are truly breathtaking. For in these maps of Africa, Asia, and America Gastaldi does an amazing thing. He depicts for the first time ever in human history all three of these far continents in general correctly as to their overall form, as well as filling their interiors, also for the first time, and this also often in general correctly. This single astonishing fact, which we shall document fully in chapters three and four, is unquestionably the single most important fact about Gastaldi, and we shall pointedly repeat it more than once, in hopes of bringing it home once and for all. If I have any fear that I might have failed to make some point clear enough in this book, it is this one. For these maps *are* Gastaldi. And it is they, how they were made, and their final metamorphosis into continental wall map series, which make up the principal subject of our study.

---

[150] There are actually two other Gastaldi-Licinio maps in Gastaldi's repertoire, an undated Malta (no. 87) and an undated Corsica (no. 88), which, though of some interest, we consider as distinctly incidental works, and treat mainly in the cartobibliography. One must also include no. 94, the ca. 1560 America, in the Gastaldi-Licinio period maps, even though it was not engraved and published until after Gastaldi's death. Finally, although all other Gastaldi-Licinio works are Gastaldi first editions, there is one exception. Licinio in 1556 engraved in copper a second edition of Gastaldi's 1555 woodcut Piedmont. This 1556 edition would be just before work began on the 1559-64 maps, which we estimate at 1557, and in the author's opinion, Gastaldi here may have been trying Licinio out as his engraver, and the same could well be true of the two undated island maps, which is the reason that we have dated those also as tentatively ca. 1556(?).

[151] Giovanni Francesco Camocio in the 1570s, after Gastaldi's death, would do an excellent job of combining the three together into a single map (map no. III in our cartobibliography), as see in our chapter eleven.

The maps, of course, are not perfect, and here and there, inevitably for the time, a fair amount of false information sneaks in, including even a certain amount of legendary information.[152] But this does little to diminish the astounding precedent which they set.

Thus, inevitable shortcomings aside, it was without a doubt Gastaldi who first brought these continents to life in the European consciousness, and without a doubt also it is these maps and no others, amounting as they do to a virtual cartographic revolution, which establish the fact that Gastaldi was in truth a great cartographer, an observation which, as I noted earlier, has often been made, but never expanded upon and given foundation. Note that these three continents make up over three-fourths of the land surface of the planet; before Gastaldi, the areas they cover were not at all yet in focus, and large, grossly misshapen features still remained. Then, suddenly, they *were* in focus. So Gastaldi's advance here could well be argued as making up the greatest single cartographic advance in history.[153] A heady claim? Indeed, but we shall substantiate it beyond argument in chapter three. No claim even approaching the sweeping nature of this one can be made concerning any other of Gastaldi's many maps, in which, to be sure, improvements over previous maps can be found, and even rather significant ones, but all of them, relatively speaking, are incremental by comparison, and it is one of my principal goals in the present book to bring this fact home, which has not been done before. Why it has escaped scholars is something of a mystery, but no doubt among the reasons is the fact that the sheer number of Gastaldi's maps has obscured it, smothered it. Clearly, although these amazing maps are there to stare us in the face, the fact of their astonishing progress over previous depictions of the continents has for some reason remained elusive.

We shall not ignore the other Gastaldi-Licinio maps from 1559-1564, for they are notable productions, especially the southeast Europe and perhaps the Polonia (northeast Europe, our no. 106), which make an important contribution to the whole of eastern Europe, and possibly a more important contribution than has been yet recognized, for they still remain under studied. So we give them, and also the 1561 Italy, due notice in chapter ten and also in our cartobibliography, where in fact their entries are much longer than most. We also investigate Gastaldi's world

---

[152] See for more on this chapter four, note 80.

[153] Ptolemy's tremendous advance appears unprecedented to us, but we have no means to put it in perspective. How great an advance his maps were over previous maps, we don't know, for the maps are quite lost to us. The maps, of course, covered only one-fourth of the earth's surface.

maps, but especially the 1561 *Cosmographia vniversalis* to which we devote a lengthy section in chapter two. Indeed, we treat all of Gastaldi's production in the book, although we often do not treat individually in our main text the maps in the map sets, the Ptolemy maps, the Ramusio maps, and the maps for the uncompleted editions of Strabo and Ptolemy, though we do so in our cartobibliography. But the principal subject of this book is the brilliant continental maps, and we investigate in depth how they were made, what it was that made them possible at all, certain great problems that had to be resolved to make them, and also their aftermath, for they inspired and made possible the durable cartographic form of sets of wall maps of the four continents which lasted into the eighteenth century.

1.8 Closing Comments

Having avowed our main purpose, let us quickly outline what lies ahead. We have outlined what is in this book in the introduction. Indeed, we have done so twice, in different ways, because we believe the main conclusions arrived at in the book, brought out nowhere before, to be of first importance to the history of cartography, and the presentation of things in the book can sometimes necessarily be intricate, and perhaps at times can even difficult for the reader to follow. Thus, we shall present an outline once again, in still a different way, a repetition which we feel will not be superfluous. First, we shall close this first chapter by a short examination, in a different sense from what we have done previously in this chapter, of the Ptolemy maps of 1548 and then the Ramusio maps in the *Navigazioni*, showing that the maps of the far continents in these two sets distinctly prefigure the great maps of 1559-1564, and also make very significant progress over all maps of these areas before them, as well as underlining still further the fact that Gastaldi all along had an impulse to reach for these far realms. In our second chapter, we treat Gastaldi's world maps as a subject apart. In chapter three we document beyond question the tremendous extent of Gastaldi's advance over all previous maps of the extra-European continents. Chapter four begins with an overview of Ramusio, and then shows that it was Ramusio's vast accumulation of geographical information on the far continents that provided Gastaldi with the main sources of his maps, and no doubt to a high degree the inspiration for them as well. Chapter five is a necessary interjection to counter an old and incorrect notion, stemming from Ortelius, that Gastaldi copied his Asia from the Arab geographer Abulfeda.

The remaining chapters address several related subjects, and have broadly the purpose of placing Gastaldi's work within the context of his time. Chapter six reviews the development of the four-continent idea, which will be useful to us in all of the chapters which follow it. In chapter seven we discuss one especially thorny geographical problem of the age, which plagued all cartographers of the time, and especially any cartographer who wished to make separate continental maps of Asia and America, that is, the question of the geographical relationship of these two continents in higher latitudes. In chapter eight, we expound Gastaldi's eventual resolution of, or mode of dealing with, the problem. In chapter nine, we discuss an unsigned Venetian wall map of America, a map which has been subject to much confusion in the literature, due principally to a faulty assessment made by Almagià in 1923. The map had been pronounced by most, but not all, scholars as a work of Gastaldi, and we finally establish that this is correct beyond doubt, though the map remained in manuscript until it was published by other hands in the 1570s and 1590s. In chapter ten, we attempt to pinpoint exactly Gastaldi's purpose in making these great continental maps, in particular exploring the question of whether he consciously intended to make a set of modern maps covering the whole world, including western Europe, for which he made no maps in 1559-1564, although we are unable to reach a definite conclusion on this point.

The eleventh chapter relates the attempt of Camocio in the 1570s to make a four-continent set of wall maps, consisting wholly of Gastaldi's cartography for the far continents, and partly for Europe, an attempt which failed when it was near completion, evidently due to Camocio's death from the plague. Chapter twelve relates the realization of Camocio's idea of a set of four-continent wall maps, still using principally Gastaldi's cartography, in the mid-1590s, in the famous San Marco shop of the Bertellis, at the hands of Donato Bertelli, and finally that set's further fate in the hands of the Scolari family.

We then go on to make a short survey of the maps in the 1548 Ptolemy and of those made for Ramusio's *Navigazioni*, with an eye to revealing to what a notable degree they prefigure the main maps of 1559-1564, in the sense of their surpassing their predecessors as regards coverage of the extra-European world.
There are typically twenty-seven truly Ptolemaic maps in editions of the *Geography*, a world map, ten maps for Europe, four for Africa, and twelve for Asia.[154] Beginning with the 1482 Florence edition, the third printed edition, there

---

[154] Gastaldi's 1548 Ptolemy has only twenty-six of the ancient maps, for he does not include the world map.

began to appear some modern maps, four in this 1482 Florence edition, and the number of such modern maps increased after that in various editions of Ptolemy. There were five in the 1482 Ulm Ptolemy (published after the Florence edition), six in the 1507 Rome edition, twenty in Waldseemüller's 1513 Strassburg edition, twenty-three in Fries 1522 Strassburg edition, and twenty-one in Münster's 1540 Basle edition. Then came the Gastaldi-Pedrezzano edition of 1548, which was the first edition with more modern than ancient maps. Those modern maps were thirty-four in number, thirteen more than in Münster's. In general, the European modern maps were mediocre to poor. But it is in the number and quality of modern maps of non-European areas that the work excelled most sharply, with seventeen modern maps, compared to but five in the 1513 Waldseemüller Ptolemy, the next highest. We will look at them quickly continent by continent. There were five maps for Africa, which covered the entire continent. The greatest previous number had been two, and these were Waldseemüller's of 1513 which, apart from not covering a good portion of the northeast part of the continent, were by the 1540s obsolete, and contained none of the interior detail of the 1548 maps, which was mostly based on information obtained since 1513. There were five maps also for America, giving fairly representative coverage of the continent. No previous Ptolemy had had more than one primitive map devoted to America. Waldseemüller's single map of the continent was, of course, in 1513, hopelessly primitive, and the few later ones occurring in other Ptolemy editions were not much better. The Gastaldi-Pedrezzano edition of Ptolemy was a completely unprecedented little assortment of maps, with the modern, non-Ptolemaic depictions in the main quite correct. Nordenskiöld referred to them as the first atlas of the New World.[155] There were seven maps for Asia, with fairly representative coverage for the continent. Again, the best and fullest previous coverage, slightly better than for Africa and America, was three maps in Waldseemüller's 1513 Ptolemy. Only one of them, his "Indiae", goes beyond the Near East,[156] and like the Africa maps, it is badly out of date, with a coastline that remains very primitive, not showing any of the extensive further modern knowledge gained after Albuquerque's opening of Malacca, much of which we do find in Gastaldi, no doubt partly from Portuguese charts, and probably partly

---

[155] Nordenskiöld (1897, 182).

[156] It is true that in Fries's 1522 Ptolemy, the maps of which are badly made copies of those in the 1513 Ptolemy, two more maps for far eastern Asia are added, but they can hardly be considered as true modern maps, simply reproducing the depiction of these parts as shown on the Behaim globe made in 1492 (Nordenskiöld, 1889, 21), well before any of the modern discoveries in the Far East had even occurred.

from Ramusian texts, though it is hard to say how much of Ramusio's material was yet in hand at this date. Waldseemüller's outdated maps also include no interior detail, of which there is an abundance in the 1548 maps.

Thus, we see there was nothing approaching Gastaldi's sets of modern maps of non-European areas in any other Ptolemy. (Nor, for that matter, was there anything rivaling this set of maps in any other, non-Ptolemaic context, as we shall see in chapter three.) Gastaldi in fact does hedge in two great areas. He shows nothing of north central or northwest North America; and in Asia he shows, beyond Persia, only the southern part of the continent, omitting north central and northeast Asia, and there is a gap of 16° in southern Asia, between the eastern border of his Calecut (123° E) and the western border of the India Tercera Nova (140° E). My guess is that Gastaldi, like Mercator and others, continued to feel uncertainty as to how many south Asian peninsulas to depict, and by hedging in this way, he could leave room where one more might occur. This lacuna would be rectified in Gastaldi's following set of extra-European maps, to be discussed next, the Ramusio maps. It is abundantly clear, that in 1548, and in the several years preceding, when the maps were being made, Gastaldi's sights were already set on regional maps of the far continents, on which there is a much greater stress than had been the case with any previous cartographer.[157]

Then, shortly after, in ca. 1553-1556/57, we see the same stress repeated in the regional maps made for Ramusio's *Navigazioni*, but this time to the complete exclusion of European areas, for Ramusio's three-volume work is devoted exclusively to Africa, Asia, and America, although the break-up is not exactly, as one might expect it to be, one volume for each continent. For, although volume three is virtually completely devoted to America, volume one covers both Africa and coastal Asia, while volume two covers interior Asia. The maps were in three sets, one set per volume, covering of course the areas dealt with respectively in these three volumes.

Very unfortunately, only one of these three sets survived and is thus known to us, that of 1554 in volume one,[158] , which included maps of Africa, southwest

---

[157] We cannot say precisely how and by whom the decisions were made as to which areas were to be covered by the modern Ptolemy maps. Not being a geographer, Pedrezzano perhaps left this up to Gastaldi. But we cannot but wonder, considering the notable stress on foreign coverage, if Ramusio did not have a hand as a sort of volunteer consultant. For much more information on the Gastaldi Ptolemy, see the compound cartobibliography entry (5.-64.), and the individual entries 5 to 64 for the separate maps.

[158] This set, three woodcuts, first appeared only in the 1554 second edition of volume one. They were not in the 1550 first edition of the volume.

Asia and southeast Asia, but we know for certain that all three sets existed. As to volume two, on central Asia, we know from the two-page address to the reader by Tommaso Giunti, Ramusio's publisher and good friend, that the latter had given over to Giunti, a few months before his death in July, 1557,[159] the text of volume two, "together with several maps of lands of which mention is made in this book", that is, the maps of central Asia. But in the same place, he tells us that a fire had occurred in his printing house in November, 1557, and the maps and an indeterminate amount of the text were destroyed in the fire (which of course explains the printing only in 1559). As to volume three (1556), we learn from Ramusio in a lengthy, nebulous, and very difficult passage at the end of his dedicatory epistle, dated June 20, 1553, to Fracastoro at the beginning of the volume, that he has had Gastaldi make a set of four maps, embracing, we can assume, larger or smaller regions of the Western Hemisphere, and covering the hemisphere as far as it was known.[160] However, for some reason, although discussed in the dedication to Fracastoro, the maps were not published in the volume. We devote considerable attention in our cartobibliography at entry no. (73.-76.) to the question of why these four maps were not published.

However, the volume one maps are full double page foldouts in a folio volume, and the others must have been the same, and their general style and amount of area coverage must have been basically the same. Volume one has three maps, volume three was to have four, and volume two was to have "several", probably meaning three or four, the former I think more likely. Though there are fewer maps per continent than there were in the Ptolemy, the maps are almost five times larger than the Ptolemy maps, and the scale is thus much larger. Most importantly, they are geographically better than the Ptolemy maps, representing thus a distinct step forward, especially as to the two maps of southwest and southeast Asia. The gap of 16° in the south Asian coast and near inland has been filled in, the Malay peninsula, very odd in the Ptolemy, is much improved, all due mainly to new information from João de Barros's *Asia*, the first decade of which was published in Lisbon in 1552, and translated by Ramusio into Italian for inclusion in the 1554 second edition of volume one, which, as we have said, is the edition in which the maps first appear. All in all, there is very notable improvement

---

[159] The volume was first published in 1559, the only volume to be published posthumously.

[160] We forbear here to give our own lengthy interpretation of this very difficult passage, a correct rendering of which requires taking recourse to sources outside the letter itself and considerable explanatory asides. But we present our free translation, which we believe correct in all details, in our cartobibliography, at entry no. (73-76).

over 1548, although Gastaldi's 1548 extra-European maps remained their best predecessors, for no one anywhere had in the meantime stepped in to improve over the 1548 maps, just as no one would improve on the Ramusio maps between the time they came out and Gastaldi's project of 1559-1564. Thus, although those 1559-1564 maps represent almost a quantum leap over the Ramusio maps, it is a fact that it was Gastaldi alone who first correctly mapped the non-European world, in three steps, in 1548, then 1553-1556/57, and then with finality in 1559-1564. Though we don't have them, the maps for volumes two and three can no doubt be assumed to be of comparable quality to the volume one maps.[161]

It is true that Gastaldi was here working under commission from Ramusio, on a project in the conception of which he had no direct hand. But Gastaldi's strong personal interest in far places before this time is already well-documented, both in his earliest self-initiated maps, especially the giant Africa he was creating in the 1540s, followed by the Ptolemy, in which the decision to greatly increase the coverage in special maps of the non-European world over previous editions of Ptolemy, surely represents partially, and perhaps wholly, Gastaldi's personal involvement. So it can be assumed that Gastaldi felt considerable vested interest also in the new Ramusio maps, quite above and beyond any remuneration, in the sense of self-satisfaction and fulfillment in the area of his greatest love, when he achieved improvement once again in the depiction of these far regions. After all, they were, as had been the 1548 maps in their time, the best maps of these areas that had ever existed. And they were the second step taken towards the revelatory maps of 1559-1564.

---

[161] One shortcoming in the Ramusio maps is that the quantity of interior locales shown is inexplicably much smaller than it could have been in light of the vast data available in the Ramusian accounts in the same volume, for there is much available space for more, a feature unquestionably dictated by Ramusio, and much reminiscent of the so-called Ramusio map of the Western Hemisphere of 1534, on which see Holzheimer and Buisseret (1992), including a reproduction of the map. For more on the Ramusio maps, see our cartobibliography entries 68, (73.-76.), 73-76, (77.-79.), 77-79, (81.-86.), 81-86, (89.-91.), and 89-91.

2.1 Preliminary Remarks

Gastaldi's world maps are a thing apart from the rest of his cartography, just as they are with any cartographer, so I have decided to give them a chapter of their own. The greater part of the chapter is devoted to the great world map "Cosmographia Vniversalis." That is a very important map in its own right, but it will also prove vital to us, in its depiction of America, in connection with Gastaldi's map of America, which became part of an important set of four-continent wall maps, which we will discuss in a later chapter. But we begin for now with Gastaldi's 1546 "Vniversale."

2.2 The 1546 "Vniversale" and Its Derivatives

This is Gastaldi's first world map,[1] and only his third dated map, after his 1544 Spain and his 1545 Sicily. What prompted him to turn to a world map at this point is unknown. However, as we have seen, it was precisely in 1546 that Gastaldi is recorded as teaching cosmography to Ramusio's son Paolo and a select group of other students, and we can assume that the notions of cosmography he was teaching them were as depicted on this map, and it is certainly possible that Ramusio and the students had a role in influencing him to publish those ideas in the form of this map. We shall speak more of what some of these ideas were later in this section. The map gave rise to many later editions, all essentially the same in their main details. They are also all on the same elegant oval projection, so that the projection became a hallmark for Gastaldi, and he is often credited by scholars with devising the projection,[2] and this was true in Gastaldi's time as well. Giuseppe Moleto wrote in 1573 that, "fra tutte le forme, mi piace quella, ch'è di un sol pezzo, ch'è uenuta fuori in stãpa di legno, & di rame insieme sotto nome di Iacomo Gastaldo Piemõtese. In q[ue]lla forma adunque si ueggono

---

[1] Our no. 3. On this map, Gastaldi identifies himself only as "Giacomo Cosmographo in Venetia."

[2] The projection is not strictly oval; it is closer to elliptical, though it is not exactly that, either. I shall retain the former term to avoid confusion.

i Meridiani essere linee curue, & i Paralleli linee rette, & si descriue cosi," (among all the forms of world maps, I like that which is of one piece, which has come out in print in wood, and in copper as well under the name of Jacomo Gastaldo Piedmontese, in which form then the meridians are seen to be curved lines, and the parallels straight lines, and it is drawn thus), after which there follows a diagram of the projection.[3] Jacques Severt in his 1590 book on projections devotes a small chapter to Gastaldi and his oval projection, and also gives a diagram of the projection.[4] A number of more discriminating modern commentators have been quick to acknowledge that a number of previous maps had oval projections,[5] but that used on Gastaldi's maps represents a noteworthy innovation,[6] and indeed it does compare very favorably with predecessors. Its simplicity and clarity are apparent by comparison with others, and the net seems not to interfere at all with the main image behind it. However, although Gastaldi was the first to use it in a printed map, it was not devised by him, but by Battista Agnese.[7] Agnese had been using the projection at least as early as 1536, the date of his earliest known atlas. A comparison shows that the projections are identical.[8] Furthermore, while on Agnese's earlier world maps, the meridians are spaced at 10° intervals, as they are on Gastaldi's 1546 world, he later began to achieve an even higher degree of clarity to the picture by spacing the meridians at 15° instead of 10°,[9] and Gastaldi later does the same in his "Cosmographia Vniversalis." Finally, we find that the only other projection used by Gastaldi which employs curved meridians, the hemispheric

---

[3] In Malombra's 1574 edition of Ptolemy (Malombra, 1574, pp. 60-61 of the section by Moleto, which carries its own title page dated 1573).

[4] Severt (1590, 103-04). He also speaks of Gastaldi at pp. 5 and 91.

[5] See Shirley, 1987, nos. 28 (1508 Roselli), 59 (1528 Bordone), 67 (Münster-Holbein, 1532), 76 (Münster, 1540), 81 (Cabot, 1544). For a general history of oval projections see Fiorini (1881, chapter four), and Fiorini (1895, 180-201). For Ancient and Medieval antecedents, see Harley and Woodward (1987, 137, 171-72, and 312-13 with ill. at p. 352), and Brown's comment at (Brown, 1949, 140).

[6] See for example Grande (1905, carte, 93-95), and Minella (1993, 33).

[7] On Agnese, see Wagner (1931; and 1937, 18, 21-23 and 26-29), and Almagià (1944, 62-71 and pls. 32-36).

[8] For the 1536 projection, see the reproduction of Agnese's 1536 world in Almagià (1944, pl. XXXIII). Another cartographer who was using the projection, Francesco Ghisolfi, was apparently copying from Gastaldi. On him see Astengo (1993), and Wagner (1937, 1, 29).

[9] See the 1542 world map in Almagià (1944, pl. XXXV).

projection used in his 1556 map of the Western Hemisphere, was also used before by Agnese.[10]   Agnese's maps are less well known for their geographical accuracy than for their exceptional beauty,[11] and from an esthetic standpoint, the choice to use the projection was a good one. Nor was anything lost in accuracy.   Still another geographer with an eye for the appealing considered it the best choice, for it is precisely this projection that Ortelius adopts for the world map in his 1570 *Theatrum Orbis Terrarum*.

In general, Gastaldi did not attempt to be innovative in projections, and he seems to have eschewed complexity in this regard. Except for the world maps and the map of the Western Hemisphere just mentioned, all his maps are drawn on one or the other of two simple projections, the trapezoidal, which had been devised by Donnus Nicolaus Germanus and had often been used in the modern renditions of the Ptolemaic maps, and the still simpler plain rectangular projection, that virtually prescribed by Ptolemy for regional maps, for he gives no other, while for world maps, he offers a choice of three projections. In both, all meridians and parallels are straight lines. There are no curved meridians on Gastaldi's maps except the worlds and the Western Hemisphere map, and there are no curved parallels at all. Furthermore, the projections and the grid are indicated on the regional maps only via the degree markings on the borders.   There are no latitude or longitude lines drawn in except, again, on the worlds and the hemisphere,

---

[10] See the reproduction of a 1543 Agnese hemispheric map in Portinaro and Knirsh (1987, p. 72). It's clear that manuscript atlas makers of the time were experimenting a lot with various projections (see Astengo, 1993). That Gastaldi was impressed with Agnese's overall ground plan for his world maps can perhaps also be detected in the lack of a border for the 1546 map, and the similar general style and cherubic character of the windheads around the maps, especially apparent in the smaller copy of Gastaldi's world in his 1548 Ptolemy.

[11] As we shall see shortly, however, they may also have been sometimes notable for geographic innovation as well, and Gastaldi may well have used them at times. Wagner wrote that, "all that we have to show the progress of Spanish discovery as delineated on the general map in Seville between 1529 and 1544 must be looked for in his maps." (Wagner, 1937, 1, 18) Wagner refers of course, to the *Padron Real*, the map which was kept updated by the Spanish as new discoveries were made. Agnese's atlases were clearly valued, for over seventy examples survive.

almost without exception.[12]   But we know that, while Gastaldi could not be called a truly accomplished mathematician (very few cartographers were), he had a reasonably good base in mathematics, and we should not take these facts as indicators of a lack of competence on Gastaldi's part.   In my opinion they probably represent a healthy and perhaps commendable disdain for complexity where there was no need for it.   These simple projections are very utilitarian, both to the draftsman, the engraver, and the map reader. Anyone who has attempted to follow coastlines or interior features on maps using, for instance, cordiform or double cordiform projections, which serve no real use other than to advertise the virtuoso talents of the map-maker, since from the practical side they simply distort things far more than is necessary, will appreciate the clarity which comes from simplicity in projections such as those used by Gastaldi. It was no doubt the clarity and simplicity of the Agnese projection that led Gastaldi to adopt it.

To return to the 1546 "Vniversale."   The original edition is quite elegant overall, although it does exhibit some faults.   For instance, the engraving of the wavy lines in the sea is too heavy in many places, and the coastlines are sometimes not well enough defined, as Shirley notes.[13]   It may well have been engraved by Gastaldi himself, as brought out in the previous chapter.   However, the map is basically a very attractive one, as are all of the more attractively engraved later editions. Most of these belong to the prominent series of copperplate editions produced in Venice from 1560 on by Camocio, Forlani and Bertelli.   We shall start with a short description of the two exceptions to this.   Matteo Pagano engraved the only woodcut edition, the undated "Dell'Vniversale."[14]   It is in two sheets, and is the largest format of Gastaldi's world ever produced, being a quarter again as large as the better

---

[12] The only exception is the 1559-60 map of southeast Europe (no.96), which perhaps amounts to two exceptions, since the north half came out before the south, and was sold as a separate map. One might object to the statement that the parallels are always straight in the Gastaldi maps taken as having a trapezoidal projection. Often the convergence of meridians is very slight in these, and one could argue that a slight arc was to be understood in the parallels. Indeed, it is impossible to say, since the lines are not drawn in, for whether straight or slightly arced, they will come out the same as to the latitude markings on the sides of the maps. But I feel it is safe to presume that the projection on Gastaldi maps showing a convergence of meridians is in fact trapezoidal, as it definitely is on the 1560 Southeast Europe, with parallels drawn in.

[13] Shirley (1987, 96).

[14] Our no. 66.

known 1565 Forlani edition.[15] It is the least easily dated of all Gastaldi's maps. Several estimates have been given, but they are guesses and none are convincing.[16] The only thing that might point to a date is that the texts in two large legends atop the map are taken almost verbatim from the texts on the back of two maps in Gastaldi's 1548 Ptolemy, the oval world and the map of South America, so probably it came shortly after that, which is why we tentatively assign to it the date ca. 1550(?). In 1555 Gerard de Jode published an edition in Antwerp, also larger than any of the Venetian copperplate editions.[17] The long Venetian series begins with a Forlani-Camocio edition on one sheet in 1560, the smallest in size.[18] There followed a 1562 Forlani edition dedicated to Count Geronimo Canossa, also in one sheet, but larger than the 1560 variant, and we shall speak more of it in a moment.[19] Then followed a Forlani-F. Bertelli edition of 1565, considerably larger in size and on two sheets.[20] Gastaldi's name is nowhere on this 1565 edition, nor on the following two, a fact I mention since it may well have some significance I haven't grasped. A D. Bertelli edition followed in 1568,[21]and finally, a Forlani-Duchetti edition in 1570.[22] I have given this rather monotonous enumeration to stress the extraordinary fortune and

---

[15] It is 4158 sq. cm., compared to 3311 for the 1565 variant.

[16] Caraci's estimate of between 1548 and 1552-53 (1936, 131-33) is the only exception, but his arguments are vitiated by invalid assumptions involving the development of Gastaldi's thinking concerning the relationship of Asia to America.

[17] It is 3800 sq. cm. Of this map, a 1590 edition appeared in which the Strait of Anian separates Asia from America (Shirley 1987, no. 174).

[18] Shirley (1987, no. 106) and Woodward (1990, nos. 1.01-1.02). Of this, there were printings of 1562 and 1594, and, oddly, two very late printings of 1651 and 1751, on which the Strait of Anian has been altered on the plate.

[19] Our no. 105. It is sufficiently different from the other late editions of the 1546 map to be considered a separate Gastaldi map, for reasons explained below, in chapter eight. It was reissued in 1564 and 1576.

[20] Though still not so large as the Pagano woodcut (Shirley, 1987, no. 115; Woodward, 1990, nos. 35.01-35.07). There were at least seven later issues, two more of 1565, two undated, one of 1571, one after 1571, and one in 1599. Bagrow and Wagner cite a 1562 edition of this, but it is evidently a ghost, as cf. Shirley (135), and Woodward (22). Minella (1993, 87-88) devotes two pages to a 1563 edition, but this too is probably a ghost for the 1565, since the final 5 in that is very similar to a 3, as cf. Shirley (135).

[21] Shirley (1987, no. 118).

[22] Shirley (1987, no. 121), and Woodward (1990, no. 82).

popularity which the map enjoyed, especially from 1560. It must have contributed considerably to Gastaldi's renown. Wroth referred to this series of derivatives as "a succession of informative and spectacularly beautiful, separately printed maps,"[23] and indeed there are sundry additions in names and interior detail to these various derivatives, much no doubt taken from the 1561 "Cosmographia Vniversalis." But they are for the most part incremental and incidental in nature,[24] and there is little substantial difference between these and the 1546 original except that, as noted, these later engravings are all more attractive. The one partial exception is the 1562 Forlani world dedicated to Canossa, which perhaps differs significantly enough from predecessors to justify the claim made by Forlani in a legend that it is a new map made for him by Gastaldi.[25]

Besides the late editions of 1590, 1651 and 1751 which included the Strait of Anian, mentioned in the notes to the above enumerated editions, there were two earlier world maps which derived from this line and which contained the Strait of Anian. One was larger than any of the above maps and was in four sheets, put out by Camocio in 1567, bearing the same title in full as the great 1561 "Cosmographia Vniversalis."[26] We shall speak more of this map later in the present chapter. Finally, there was an anonymous, undated world in two sheets titled "Totius Orbis Descriptio."[27] Although not a world map, we must also mention here the well-known 1566 Forlani-Zaltieri "Nova Franza," the first separate map of North America ever made.[28] Its similarity to the northwest quadrants of the last two maps, especially the latter, suggests that it was taken from them. The map has neither grid nor border graduations; to disguise the fact it was copied directly from such a

[23] Wroth (1970, 203).

[24] In general, the differences are less significant than those occurring on the Canossa map (see note 19 above).

[25] We quote from this legend from the map in chapter eight, where the points of departure from previous editions are also detailed. All the same, the map, like the others, is basically an edition of the 1546 world, and not really a new map as Forlani rosily implies.

[26] Shirley (1987, no. 117); Woodward (1990, nos. 66.01-66.03); and Beans (1933). There were later issues in 1569, 1581 and perhaps 1593.

[27] Shirley (1987, no. 120).

[28] Woodward (1994), Woodward (1990, nos. 37.01-37.02. It also is undated.

map.[29] These maps are something of hybrids. They derive in general form and style from the series beginning in 1546, but incorporate some features wholesale from the 1561 world map, especially the Strait of Anian. What hand Gastaldi might have had in producing these last three maps is unclear, but I suspect he had no direct part in any of them, and they were worked up by someone such as Camocio or someone in his employ, even though he seems to tell us in the dedication to the 1567 world, which we quote below, that it is by Gastaldi.

No attempt to identify the 1546 map's sources has been made, except as regards the American coastlines, and to a lesser degree that continent's interior. Unquestionably, the principal source for the coast was the cartography of Ribero, a point agreed on by all.[30] For the North American east coast this Ribero cartography was constructed largely on information from the Gomez voyage, and Wroth wrote that the 1546 world and its derivatives were "particularly significant because it was their influence which ensured that the Ribero-Gomez cartography should prevail in the more important maps of the northeastern coasts until well after the opening of the seventeenth century."[31] However, not just the northeast, but all the American coasts are primarily from Ribero.[32] A secondary source of importance was Maggiolo's 1527 world map,[33] and there may well also be information from Santa Cruz's maps.[34] To what degree Agnese may have been also a source

---

[29] See Marinelli (1917), who determined the map was derived from the northwest quadrant of the long line of Gastaldi worlds, though he did not suggest it was from a variant with the strait added in a later revision of the plate, for none of those was yet known at the time he wrote.

[30] Wroth (1970, 202), Minella (1993, 61), Grande (1905, *carte*, 100 and 106). On Diego Ribero see Cortesão (1960, 1, 87-100), and Vigneras (1962). There were presumably numerous copies of Ribero's famous manuscript planisphere made, and additions were made to them as time passed. We have no idea which copy Gastaldi had at hand, nor its date. All the surviving examples are reproduced in Cortesão (1960, 1, pls. 37-41, and 5, pl. 523).

[31] Wroth (1970, 202). For the Gomez voyage, see Morison (1971, 326-31 and 336-37), and Sauer (1971, 62-69).

[32] Grande (1905, 106 and 134). Grande has a useful comparative list of toponyms found on the American coasts of the 1546 world, and on Maggiolo, Ribero, and Agnese (132-63).

[33] Grande (1905, 106). On Vesconte Maggiolo and his cartography see Caraci (1937 and 1958).

[34] Minella (1993, 59 and 61). For Alonso de Santa Cruz, see Wagner (1942), Dahlgren (1892), and Martín Merás (1986).

for Gastaldi is not yet perfectly clear. Wagner said that Gastaldi either used Agnese, or some Spanish maps that Agnese used.[35] Grande maintained that names occurring in common between Agnese and Gastaldi maps represent borrowings by Agnese from Gastaldi, not vice versa.[36] Minella just notes there are a few Gastaldi names found in Agnese, but not in Ribero.[37] We cannot solve this here, but offhand, considering that Ramusio was regularly receiving new manuscript maps from sources in the Spanish New World, and making them available to Gastaldi, as we see in cartobibliography entry no. (73.-76.), the borrower would seem more likely to have been Agnese, but of course it is quite possible that both cartographers borrowed from each other at different times. We must note as well, that, of 193 American coastal names on the 1546 world, fifty-six (about 29%) are not accounted for at all in the sources examined. Very likely some of these would be found in Ramusio's texts or on some of the maps Ramusio obtained from New Spain, but we have no idea what those maps might have been. Inland America is based in part on the explorations of Fray Nizza, Coronado, and Orellano, accounts of which are all to be found in Ramusio.[38] No determinations for the rest of the world have been made, but Milanesi asserts that a major source in general for the world map would be Ramusio,[39] and this we can reasonably assume to be true.

There are on the 1546 "Vniversale" two features of great interest which prefigure to some degree those later ideas of Gastaldi which gave rise to the concept of a very narrow strait between Asia and America, that is, the Strait of Anian. The first has not been noticed before. The map, as is often observed, is among those on which Asia and America are connected by a land bridge, but Gastaldi differs from predecessors as to the north-to-south width of the land bridge connecting Asia to America. All former maps showing such a connection, as for example those of Fine,[40] depict the south

---

[35] Wagner (1937,I, 26).

[36] Grande (1905, 134).

[37] Minella (1993, 61).

[38] Grande (1905, 101-02).

[39] Milanesi (1993, 41).

[40] Shirley (1987, nos. 66 and 69).

coast of this land bridge as reaching a northern maximum of only about 18° N latitude. But in the 1546 Gastaldi world map, this south coast attains a height of ca. 38°,[41] slightly over twenty degrees higher! We might say that in the former type, as in Fine and others, America is a *part* of Asia, while in the Gastaldi type, it is only *connected* to Asia.[42] The fact suggests that Gastaldi may already have been thinking along the lines which eventually led him to entertain the idea of sundering the two continents.[43]

The second feature is the presence in capital letters of the name "TERRA ARSAROT" high in the land bridge between Asia and America. This is "the 'Land of Arsarot' which joins North America with northeast Asia."[44] The name is that of a conjectural land to which some believed the lost tribes of Israel had wandered after their dispersal from the Holy Land. For several centuries, at least until the end of the eighteenth, some would speculate that the lost tribes had found their way into America, and that they were progenitors of the American Indians. Some speculated further that their presence in the New World indicated that there must be a connection in unknown northern regions between the Old and New Worlds, or that at least they must come very close together somewhere.[45] These ideas first began to germinate at about this time, or possibly slightly earlier. The presence of this name on the land bridge implies that it played a role in Gastaldi's adoption of the notion that the two continents were connected. Unfortunately, Gastaldi left us no written record of his thoughts on the important question of the relationship of the two worlds, but the indications are pretty clear that by some time in the 1550s he had come to the conclusion that the Old and New Worlds must either be connected or separated only by a very short distance in order to account for the presence of similar human and animal life in both worlds, since all had to have sprung ultimately from Noah's Ark on Mount Ararat after the Deluge. He would depict both concepts on different maps,

---

[41] It is a little difficult to catch the exact northmost point in Gastaldi's strongly undulating coastline.

[42] See chapter eight, note 91, for later maps which adopted this depiction.

[43] This is all discussed in greater depth in chapter eight, where likely sources for Gastaldi's new idea are discussed.

[44] See Milanesi (1992, 36-38).

[45] See chapter eight, where all of this is gone into in depth.

but it was impossible to determine which was correct. We shall look at the record of Gastaldi's thinking in these regards in depth later in this work.

2.3 The World Maps in Gastaldi's 1548 Ptolemy

Gastaldi made two small modern world maps for his 1548 Ptolemy, but they are not remarkable. One, titled "Universale Novo", is just a reduced version of the 1546 world map,[46] and should perhaps be considered as part of that series. The other is a fanciful little map criss-crossed (in imitation of portolan charts), with a web of rhumb lines, which produce a rather attractive geometrical design, but which serve no practical purpose, entitled "Carta Marina Nova Tabula." It is remarkable for one feature, the depiction of a land connection between northeast North America and Europe, at northern Norway, the significance of which we will speak of later, in chapter eight.[47]

2.4 The Giant World Map for an Ottoman Prince (1553)

Venice had long-standing and valuable trading relations with the Ottoman world, and it was common for the Republic to provide high-ranking Ottoman figures with valuable gifts of various kinds. It was evidently some time in 1552 that one of Sultan Suleiman's sons, Bayezid, sent a messenger to Venice's *bailo*, the Republic's permanent representative in Constantinople, Domenico Trevisan, asking that he acquire for him in Venice a map of the world. Trevisan relayed this to Venice, and on December 15, 1552 the Senate wrote to him that they had given orders to acquire this map of the world, "of the very best and special kind that can be found," which would be sent as soon as possible, "because of our interest in pleasing his lordship."[48]

---

[46] Our no. 63.

[47] Another odd feature is a long arm of the sea running deep into northwestern North America from the northern part of the great gulf between eastern Asia and western North America, which I think may be a tentative interpretation of a very unclear passage which occurs in Ramusio's edition of Marco Polo, about which we shall also speak more later. We speak of these two maps in greater depth in our cartobibliography, nos. 63 and 64.

[48] Fabris (1989, 8), and Arbel (2002, 21-22).

But on March 22 (or April 22),[49] 1553 they wrote that they were unable to find a map which would be of sufficient quality to satisfy the prince, and they had therefore issued an order to have such a map made, apologizing for the delay and saying they would send the map when they received it.[50] This commission went to Gastaldi, and, since the order to acquire a map was given in late 1552, and evidently some time had been fruitlessly spent seeking one, the second order, to have one made, was probably given not long before the spring 1553 letter. The map was ready by August 25, 1553, as we learn from a communication from the Senate to Trevisan in which they say that such diligence was used that they trust the recipient will be satisfied.[51] The map was sent and was presented to Bayazid by the baillo's dragoman, although the sultan apparently did not actually receive it until late 1554 or early 1555.[52]

On August 28, 1553, just three days after we learn the map was ready, the Senate took the following decision:

> It has been recently written to our *bailo* in Constantinople, that in order to gratify the Lord Sultan Selim, son of the most Serene Lord Turk, instructions have been issued to make the map of the world requested by him so insistently, as this council has learned from the letters of our said *bailo*. Since this work had been assigned to Master Giacomo Piamontese, a man of great knowledge in this art, who was promised for his work and expenses the sum of 140 ducats, for [a map] measuring five *brazza* in width and two and a half *brazza* in height, it is proper to provide that the said Master Giacomo would be paid his reward, having fulfilled the promise. It is therefore decided

---

[49] There is some confusion with the date, which need not concern us here (Fabris, 1989, 9-10).

[50] Fabris (1989, 9), and Arbel (2002, 22).

[51] Fabris (1989, 10).

[52] Fabris (1989, 11). It is unclear whether a short Council of Ten reference of November 18, 1553, to a world map for a sultan is in reference to this or perhaps some other map. Fabris (11 and note 27 there), and Arbel (2002, 22) do not agree. Partly because of this unclear reference, Arbel hypothesizes the existence of other maps made at the time for other sons of Suleiman, but there seems little basis for this. There is also not enough evidence to assume, as he seems to do (Arbel, 25), that Gastaldi made the Hadji Ahmed world map (Shirley, 1987, no. 103), although that is possible, and it is certainly possible, perhaps likely, that Gastaldi was connected with that in some way.

that 140 ducats should be paid out from our Signory's treasury to the said Master Giacomo Piamontese as a recompense for the said map of the world.[53]

It is only from this record, discovered by Arbel, that we learn of the map's author, and of its size, and of the fee paid to Gastaldi for it. The map was truly enormous. Its width and height of 5 *brazza* and 22 *brazza* come out to 3.19 x 1.59 meters, for a total surface area of ca. 5.07 sq. meters, more than three times as large as his *Cosmographia vniversalis* (1.64 sq. meters), and even half again as large as Waldseemüller's gigantic 1516 "Carta Marina" (3.31 sq. meters).[54] These astonishing dimensions are apparently correct. Arbel gives a conversion factor of .638 meters for one *brazza*, and Woodward notes that the "Venetian *braccia* varied from 63 to 68 centimeters depending on its function,"[55] so these are evidently the same measuring unit. The price paid for it, 140 ducats, was also large, equal to an entire year's salary of a senior official (*masser*) in Venice's shipyard,[56] and Gastaldi apparently completed this work in only five months' time. What material was this map, presumably manuscript, made from? We can only guess, but it must have been in a number of pieces, perhaps sewn together if on cloth or glued together if on paper or vellum. We also have no idea what picture of the world it presented, but at this date it almost certainly showed the Old and New Worlds as connected, for Gastaldi made no maps showing a separation until several years later. We can also assume that much on the map would have been influenced by the materials which his friend Ramusio had been accumulating for years, about which we will say much more below. The map's text must have been in Turkish to be read by an Ottoman prince, so we can assume that Gastaldi had help in this, probably from Michel Membré, an interpretor in Turkish and Arabic for the Venetian Republic, with whom

---

[53] Arbel's translation (2002, 22). He gives also the original Italian at p. 28.

[54] Arbel (2002, 27-28, note 28).

[55] Woodward (1987, 3-4).

[56] Arbel (2002, 24).

Gastaldi had worked before in 1550.[57]   Though we do not know how it looked, the map was of great importance, and it provides us with another indicator of how highly Gastaldi's talents were already regarded by the Venetian government at the time.   We see from the letter of August 25 that the map was much esteemed, and it seems likely that the Senate's satisfaction with Gastaldi's work on this had some influence in their decision of August 9, 1553, to commission him to make his map of Asia for the walls of the Doge's Palace.[58]

2.5 The Great "Cosmographia vniversalis"

Gastaldi's fine large woodcut map of the world in nine sheets,[59] the *Cosmographia vniversalis* (our no. 104), the original edition of which was 1561, is one of his greatest productions, and one of the great maps of the sixteenth century.   The only surviving copy, which is undated and bears no indication of publisher or engraver, was first discussed adequately by Almagià in 1939."[60] It disappears from view after this, until turning up in the possession of an unnamed German antiquarian from whom it was acquired by the well-known Amsterdam dealer Nico Israel, in whose catalogue twenty

---

[57] We speak more of Membré, who was also closely associated with Ramusio, in cartobibliography entry no. 69.

[58] Lorenzi (1868, 277-78). See also cartobibliography entry no. 72.

[59] The map when fully laid out as intended consists of two rows of four sheets each, with the half sheets at the left, for eight full sheets and two half sheets. The two half-sheets are printed on one full sheet and must be cut apart for mounting. Thus, the number of sheets as printed was nine.

[60] Almagià (1939, "Intorno," 260). On this page, Almagià mistakenly notes that one full sheet of the map had been reproduced full size in the first of three parts of Francesco Pullè's *La cartografia antica dell'India*, 3 vols. (*Studi italiani di filologia indo-iranica*, vols. 4, 5, and 10) (Firenze, 1901, 1905 and 1932), but actually it appears in the third volume published in 1932. The reproduction, of the top right sheet, showing most of eastern Asia, is excellent. In general, Almagià's observations here on the provenance of the map are confused, and we shall only note that he says that in 1899 it "was located in the Library of the Marquis and Marquise Panciatichi in Florence," and then that it "had passed to a different Italian city" (1939, "Intorno," 260). Francesco Pullè (1850-1934) says that it "had reposed . . . in the Panciatichi Collection in the Palazzo di Borgi Pinti in Florence," and then continues that it was "placed generously at my disposition by the Marquise Paolucci in the year 1898. Now the map has passed to Padua to the honorable Count Arrigoni degli Oddi," who, he says, preserves it with great care, having had each of its nine sheets individually framed (Pullè, 1901-32, in Part III of 1932, at p. 165).

it appeared for sale in 1978;[61] it was shortly after purchased by the British Library, where it now resides. Israel, well known internationally, was the nestor of Dutch antiquarian dealers, especially in the area of maps and atlases, and handled a large amount of extremely valuable cartographic materials over some fifty years. In an interview conducted by Lida Ruitinga and Jan Werner for the Dutch periodical *Caert-Thresoor*, he stressed its importance: "What do you consider the most important document that has gone through your hands?" "I think the Gastaldi world map."[62] The map was intended to be accompanied by a 1561 booklet by Gastaldi, titled *La Vniversale descrittione del mondo*, published, like the original map, by Matteo Pagano, of which we shall have more to say shortly.

The importance of the map is easy to state. It capsulizes all of that great Gastaldian advance in extra-European cartography which we briefly surveyed in chapter one and shall look at in greater detail in chapters three and four. It was the first map to show a North America which was both separate from Asia and had a width and general form approaching to reality, a feature quickly adopted by others. It was also the first to show a generally correct relationship of Asia to America, with its Strait of Anian, and also the first to incorporate the generally correct southern coastline of Asia and improved African interior of Gastaldi's continental maps, and all of these features were adopted by Mercator, Ortelius and later cartographers. A glance backwards in Shirley shows quickly that it is in fact the first world map in which the entire world takes on a generally correct overall outline. All the tremendous deformities which characterize all previous world maps without exception in one respect or another here for the first time disappear. It is, in a word, the first world map ever made which shows the whole world in generally correct form in all its major features. In a famous old work of 1879 by Charles P. Daly, then president of the American Geographical Society, in which he makes a very early attempt at a general history of cartography, Daly takes the history only up to the appearance of Mercator's well known 1569 world map, of which he gives one of the first

---

[61] Elte and Israel (1978, 43-44, with reproductions of parts at pp. 38 and 42).

[62] Ruitinga and Werner (1994, 99).

reproductions.[63]   His rationale for stopping at this time was that with this map, the world's overall outline had been achieved, and that all after that was just technical improvement.   But there is no question that it was Gastaldi who first achieved this correct depiction, eight years earlier in this "Cosmographia Vniversalis." All in all, it is a spectacular piece of work, one of the most impressive maps of the sixteenth century. Its only shortcoming is in Europe, where we find a discomfiting crowding of names, and, because of the limitations of the woodcut technique, some are unreadable.

This point begs the question as to why indeed Gastaldi chose the wooodcut technique to produce this magnificent work. Even before the map had been found, and was known only through mentions of the Gastaldi-Pagano booklet, Bagrow had suggested that the map may never have been published, since Pagano was a xylographer, and Gastaldi would not have wished to make a map in the antiquated woodcut method.[64] Caraci said he saw no reason for Bagrow's doubt,[65] but indeed the fact that it would be a woodcut did stand out as an odd choice.   Gastaldi used the much more precise copperplate technique on all of the maps of his peak period of 1559 on, and indeed had produced no woodcut map since his 1555 Piedmont.[66] Why, for this magnificent world map, which one could argue was his most impressive work, would he choose this more challenging medium?   The answer may lie in simple economics. As we shall see in chapters eight and nine, Gastaldi at this time would have been in a serious quandary as to whether to depict Asia and America as separated or connected, for no one knew, and he might also have expected that at any time the correct answer might be revealed by continued Spanish explorations. It would be natural, in such a situation, to seek the least expensive means of production, since, if new explorations suddenly rendered the map outdated, the loss would be minimized. Woodward says: "Since the blocks were faster to produce and

[63] Charles P. Daly, "On the Early History of Cartography; or, What We Know of Maps and Map-Making, before the Time of Mercator," *Journal of the American Geographical Society*, 11(1879), 1-40. This was the annual address before the society.

[64] Bagrow (1928-30, 1, 91-92). On the tremendous superiority of *intaglio* over relief woodcuts as to precision work, see esp. Ivins (1969, 47-50).

[65] Caraci (1936, 137, note 1).

[66] Our Cartobibliography no 80.

cheaper than copper plates, and the paper less expensive and rarely watermarked, woodcut prints were cheaper for the consumer. Size for size, they cost about a tenth or a twelfth of the price of their copperplate equivalents. Woodcuts were consequently less collectible and more ephemeral . . ."[67] So Gastaldi was perhaps just observing prudence and hedging his bets. Or perhaps he was unable to find a copper plate engraver who was willing to take on the risk, considering the inherent unpredictability involved. Whatever the explanation, the decision was to carve the map in wood.

The map, as said, was originally sold together with a small booklet by Gastaldi, with the title *La Vniversale descrittione del mondo*.[68] The booklet amounts to a short cosmographical description of the world, beginning with the four elements, the sphericity of the earth, the concepts of longitude and latitude and of the five climatic zones, and a standard description of the difference between cosmography, geography, chorography, and topography

---

[67] Woodward (1996, *Maps*, 33). Conor Fahy refers to "these cheap and easily produced maps" (*Imago Mundi*, 49(1997), 175, in a review of Woodward). See also Verner (1975, 65) on the high cost of copper.

[68] *La Vniversale descrittione del mondo, descritta da Giacomo de' Castaldi Piamontese*. IN VENETIA, per Matthio Pagano, in Frezzaria, al segno della Fede. M.D.LXI. (24 unnumbered pages in 8-mo). Copies are in the Biblioteca Marciana (call no. 6. D. 201), the Biblioteca Trivulziana, and the Biblioteca comunale Passerini Landi. Repr. facs. In Minella (1993, [95]-[105]). Also reprinted, not in facsimile, by Giuseppe Caraci in Caraci (1936, 226-37). There is a single typographical error in Caraci's reprint, which is important enough to be pointed out. On p. 13 occurs the phrase "il stretto detto Anian" ("the strait of Anian"), the first known mention in print of this name. This unfortunately came out printed with an m in the reprint (A*m*ian), and it's important to know that this does not represent some early variant spelling, but only a typographical error made in 1936. There is also a 1562 edition, a copy of which is in the John Carter Brown Library (call. No. H562. G255a), which was reprinted in facsimile by George Harry Beans as no. 21 in his *Tall Tree Library Publication* series (Jenkintown, Pa., 1940) and there is a 1565 edition, whose publisher was Francesco de Tomaso de Salo, a copy of which is in the British Library (call no. Maps. 197.a.10); and also a 1571 edition, also published by Salo in the Biblioteca Universitaria in Pavia, Italy (call number MISC. 8. - t. 171a 5). Although statements to the contrary can be found, all three editions are quite identical in their text except for a very few unimportant punctuation changes. There is also a Latin edition, *Universali mundi descriptio*, published by Pagano, of which there is a 1562 copy in the Bibliotheque Nationale, Paris (cf. *Catalogue Général des Livres Imprimés de la Bibliothèque Nationale*, vol. 57, col. 906), and a 1568 copy in the Bayerische Staatsbibliothek (call no. Res/ Geo.u. 143m), also cited by Sandler (1894, 404, note 3), I know of no other editions than these six, four in Italian, and two in Latin. Perocco (1994, 218) gives library locations for ten copies, but does not give their dates. While the 1561, 1562, 1565 and 1571 Italian editions are the same, as noted, there are differences in page signature numbers, with the 1561 edition having both an A and B series, while the 1562 edition has only an A series. To simplify, and to avoid confusion, I use here the page numbers assigned by Caraci in his 1936 edition, which are as follows: p. 1 is the title page, its blank verso is unnumbered; p. 2 is the first page of text, containing at top a repeat of the title, followed by text beginning "L'Vniversale machina della Terra," etc., its verso is p. 3, and so on to the last page with text, p. 22, the verso of which is blank.

(pp. 2-4).[69] Next comes a rather long discussion of old vs. new ideas as to habitability of the earth's climatic zones (pp. 5-10), followed by a description, one after another, of the confines of the four continents (*parti*) (pp. 10-14), then a listing of the provinces in each of the four parts (pp. 14-18); and ending with a separate section on the gain or loss of a day resulting from circumnavigation of the earth (pp. 20-22). In describing the confines of Asia, he twice mentions the Strait of Anian, separating Asia from America in the north, the earliest known use of that name in any printed text. But interspersed here and there are passages describing features of a particular world map (*Mapamondo*), and it's clear that the booklet was written specifically to accompany our world map. We shall look at the passages describing features of the world map below.

Both the map and the booklet are also known from three archival references. First there is a July 30, 1561 license to print to Gastaldi from the Reformers of the Studio of Padua stating that, since "nel libretto, il qual và insieme col mapamondo di Jac(om)o piamõtese di Gastaldi, nõ vi è cosa alcuna contraria alle leggi, concedono licenza, et possa essere stampato in questa città" (in the booklet which goes together with the mappamondo of Jacomo piamontese di Gastaldi, there is not anything contrary to the laws, they concede license, and it may be printed in this city),[70] and that clearly refers to our booklet and map. Shortly after, on August 18, 1561 there is a request for privilege written by Pagano, in which he states, that, "Io Matteo Pagano . . . Ho cõ lungi mie fattiche, tempo, et spese dissignato et intagliato un Mapamondo di fogli xii grandi reali" (I Matteo Pagano . . . have with my long labor, time, and expense drawn and engraved a world map of twelve *grande reale* sheets); followed immediately on the same day by a fifteen-year concession to Pagano of the requested privilege for this "mappamondo

---

[69] For an English translation of the section giving the difference between geography, chorography, and topography, see Woodward (1996, *Maps*, 6).

[70] Venice. Archivio di Stato. Senato Terra. Filza 34. Gastaldi. 30 July 1561; I am very grateful to the late Professor David Woodward for providing me with the text of this document.

di fogli dodici grandi reali" (world map of twelve *grande reale* sheets).[71] Thus the map would be a large woodcut Gastaldi world map in twelve sheets.[72] These notices assure us that Pagano, who did much other work for Gastaldi as xylographer (or for whom Gastaldi did much work as inventor of materials, for these interrelationships are often unclear), cut and published the map, and give us the year 1561, and since we do possess copies of a 1561 original edition of the booklet, and copies of later printings (but none earlier than 1561), the implication is that the map was published on schedule in that year.

In 1939 Almagià raised a series of four objections to the present map's being an authentic exemplar of the original 1561 map. He believed it to be an unauthorized reworking of the original in which changes had been made, most notably the addition of an extended Southern Continent at the bottom of the map. Indeed, later findings have shown that the extant copy is not from the original issue, for it is on seventeenth century paper, so obviously was printed in that century.[73] Nevertheless, there is a very sizeable body of evidence which indicates that the present map is a fully faithful reflection of the original 1561 map in all its major details, and perhaps literally in all details, although whether it represents a reengraving or was pulled from the original blocks, which is possible, would seem to be indeterminable. In the rest of this section, we will present this evidence. It will be convenient to start with Almagià's series of four objections. First, he said, the present

---

[71] Archivio di Stato di Venezia. Senato Terra. Filza 34, Matteo Pagano, 18 agosto, 1561; and Venice. Archivio di Stato. Senato Terra Reg. 43, carta 97 V. I don't think the fact that Pagano says in his request that he has "drawn (*dissignato*)" the map causes any problem. In many languages it is usual not to distinguish between "doing" something and "having something done," just as in English it is common to say that we have painted our house, when we mean someone else painted it. In all Slavic languages, although it is possible to make the distinction, it is practically never done. A Slavic speaker will invariably say, "I fixed my watch yesterday," whether he actually fixed it or had it fixed, and this is true of all such activities. This is just an instance of such usage by Pagano, I believe.

[72] I have not succeeded in determining exactly what size the *grande reale* sheets would have been, and so leave that detail out of consideration. There does not seem to be certainty on the subject. For some discussion, see Woodward (1996, *Maps*, 25 and 108, note 71), and Conor Fahy, in a review of Woodward in *Imago Mundi*, 49(1997), 175. Fahy gives four paper size designations with corresponding sizes, one being *reale*, 61.5 x 44.5 cm. The individual sheets of the surviving Gastaldi 1561 world map are 44.5 x 40 cm.

[73] Karrow (1993, 241, based on information provided by David Woodward). Almagià used the word "contraffazione", implying perhaps a pirated edition. However, the original fifteen-year privilege had long expired before the present printing.

map's lengthy title (which we quote below) said that others were involved, while Gastaldi worked alone; second, as already noted, that the map included a large extended Southern Continent, while Gastaldi's other world maps did not, and Gastaldi made no mention of such a continent in his booklet (Almagià was mistaken, as we shall see, for he mentions it twice clearly); third, that Pagano had asked for a privilege for a twelve-sheet map, while this was a nine-sheet one; and fourth, that this map does not contain Pagano's printer's device, although he habitually included it.[74]   In 1990, Corradino Astengo reexamined the evidence, observing in reply to Almagià's objections that the map was a sufficiently large and complex production that it would not be surprising if other hands had been involved; that the Southern Continent is indeed mentioned by Gastaldi in his booklet, contrary to Almagià's assertion;[75] that it was customary to request a privilege before the work had actually been done, and that Pagano might have reduced the format from twelve to nine sheets after obtaining his privilege; and finally, that the engraving of the blocks might have been completed by a different xylographer, accounting for the absence of Pagano's device.[76] As to this last point, the fact that our copy was printed in the seventeenth century provides a much simpler answer.   Pagano's device was simply removed, standard practice, by some later owner of the blocks, perhaps whoever owned them when this example was printed in the seventeenth century, or perhaps earlier. All of Astengo's responses have validity, though they cannot be called conclusive, but we can offer much more, and more specific, replies to the objections of Almagià. Let's look first at the claim of involvement by other hands.

At the top of the large ca. 1561 Gastaldi world map in the British Library[77] is written "COSMOGRAPHIA VNIVERSALIS ET EXACTISSIMA IUXTA POSTREMUM NEOTERICORVM TRADITIONEM" ("Universal And Exact Cosmography After The Most Recent Scholarship"), and at the bottom, in

---

[74] Almagià (1939, "Intorno," 263-66).

[75] Actually, as noted, he mentions it twice (Gastaldi, 1561, 13 and 14).

[76] Astengo (1990, 15-17).

[77] Our Cartobibliography no. 104.

continuation as it were, "IACOBO CASTALDIO NONNVLLISQUE ALIIS HVIVS DISCIPLINAE PERITISSIMIS NVNC P(RI)MVM REVISA AC INFINITIS FERE IN LOCIS CORRECTA ET LOCVPLETATA" (By Iacobus Gastaldus And Now For The First Time Reviewed And In Numerous Places Corrected And Augmented By Some Others Most Expert In This Discipline). Now, it is impossible, due to the sprawling Latin syntax here, so typical of the time, to be certain which of two possible referents for the ablative forms "nonnulisque aliis . . . peritissimis" the writer has in mind, and thus impossible to say which of the following three interpretations is the intended one: (1) cosmography, by Gastaldi and by others, now corrected [by unnamed hands]; or (2) cosmography, now corrected by Gastaldi and by others; or (3) cosmography by Gastaldi, now corrected by others. I think the last is correct, with the full intention being: "Cosmography . . . by Iacobo Gastaldo and now for the first time reviewed and in numerous places corrected and enriched by some others most expert in this discipline." A 1571 passage by the philosopher and minor cosmographer Giasone de Nores, which seems most likely is in reference to this map, tends to confirm this. Nores, who has given the confines of the parts of the world, says he has referred for these confines partly to Strabo and Ptolemy, and "parte alla figura del disegno fatto da Messer Iacomo Guastaldo Piemontese, ricoretto, & reuisto poi con grandissima diligentia da huomini intelligentisimi di questa professione, nel quale si potrà comprender il tutto particolarmente." (partly to the image of the map made by Messer Iacomo Guastaldo Piedmontese, corrected and reviewed then with the greatest diligence by men most skilled of this profession, in which all can be understood in detail.)[78]

The implications of involvement by other hands in the Gastaldi 1561 world map seem odd to me. Everything else we know of connected with it implies that it was a work of Gastaldi's alone. The 1561 booklet is clearly stated to be by Gastaldi, and the July 30, 1561 license to print granted to

---

[78] Nores (1571, fol. 47v). Nores repeats the statement in another work in 1589, with slight changes in wording and a more familiar spelling for Gastaldi ("fatto in piano da Messer Iacomo Gastaldo," etc.) (1589, fol. 6v). Regardless of his references to Strabo and Ptolemy, his confines and provinces are mostly directly from Gastaldi's booklet, and he mentions Gastaldi's "Stretto di Anian" twice (1571, 43v and 45r; 1589, 5r and 7v). Nores, a Cypriot, moved to Padua about 1570, when the Turks took Cyprus, and remained there to his death in 1590, teaching philosophy (*Archivio Biografico Italiano*, fiche I 705, 60-61). On him see also Riccardi (1952, 2, cols. 202-03 with references).

Gastaldi speaks of, "the booklet which goes together with the mapamondo of Jacomo piamontese di Gastaldi." (cf. Note 9 above.) There is also nothing in the booklet itself which implies anything but that the map is entirely Gastaldi's. There are a few occurrences of the rhetorical first person plural (pp. 4, 7, 22), common then as now, but they have nothing to do with the authorship of anything, and the important passages are all securely in the first person singular ("I reserve to describe them . . . ," "I will give into the light . . . ," etc.). Everything about the map points to Gastaldi alone, and this is especially true of the cartography for the depictions accord well in general with those on Gastaldi's regional maps of continents and parts of continents. Also, as regards claims of extensive corrections, it was not just common, but usual practice, that sixteenth century map printers and sellers wished to make their products appear as up to date as possible, and we must always take with a grain of salt statements made in the titles, dedications, etc. on such maps.[79] I find these unnamed experts and unspecified corrections very questionable, and suspect that the map as we have it may represent a slight reworking made sometime after Gastaldi's death in 1566, and probably before Nores's comments of 1571,[80] but that in all its important features, it presents the same picture of the world as the original 1561 map. The only major feature for which there is much likelihood of there having been any change would be the gigantic Southern Continent, about which more below, but while a prominent addition, it has no effect on the image of the "real world" above it

---

[79] A couple of examples will suffice. A legend on a 1599 reedition of Gastaldi's Italy (original 1561) declares: "Ecco la Geografia di tutta l'Italia di Iac(om)o Gastaldi di nuouo in questa ult(im)a impressione reuista emendata coreta et ampliata," (Here is the Geography of all of Italy by Gastaldi newly reviewed, emended, corrected and enlarged in this last impression,) but Almagià states, "Regardless of the declaration of the legend, it carries no alteration worthy of remark," and notes that indeed it continues to show the same orthographical errors of the original. (Almagià, 1948, 32). Compare also the claim, in the text on the map of America in the later Scolari variants of the set of four-continent wall maps inspected later in chapter twelve, that the four maps have been "newly reviewed, emended, and augmented," although there is clearly very little difference between the maps in these later sets and those in the much earlier set in the James Ford Bell Library. Drake Passage has been cut through on the America, but other than that, there seems to be little if any difference. Indeed, the fact that the publishers of these maps regularly speak in hyperboles and superlatives which are often unjustified will be familiar without documentation to readers familiar with practices of the time.

[80] And this invites the conjecture that the 1568 edition of Gastaldi's booklet, which, like the big map, is in Latin, may have accompanied this issuance of the map (see note 68 above). Unfortunately, no one has yet had the opportunity to check this 1568 edition for possible changes.

and it is almost certain that this was on the original edition of the map anyway, as we'll see later in this chapter.

What of the disparity in the number of sheets of the map compared to the number expressed in the privilege request and concession? Astengo suggests that plans could have changed after the privilege was obtained, and Woodward has suggested the same.[81] At first glance, it would seem, from Pagano's request itself, partly quoted above, that the twelve blocks had already been prepared before the request was made. But the context is hardly a disinterested one for Pagano. Certainly, any publisher might naturally hesitate to embark on the engraving for any project of this magnitude before he had assured himself that he would have permission to print and publish. Misrepresentations in such a context do not amount to a desire to deceive with bad intentions in mind, but just prudence. I suspect that he had not yet embarked on the actual xylography, but knew he had a very large map in mind and thought first of using smaller sheets.

On the other hand, this can't be proved, and the map could be a re-engraving.[82] We recall Giasone de Nores's 1571 reference, quoted above, to a "map made by Messer Iacomo Guastaldo Piedmontese, corrected and reviewed then with the greatest diligence by men most skilled in this profession," which much resembles the statement at the bottom of the British Library map that it is "by Iacobus Gastaldus and now for the first time reviewed and in numerous places corrected and augmented by some others most expert in this discipline,"[83] implying that Nores is very possibly referring precisely to our map, and that there may have been a revised edition somctime before 1571, which could be this nine-sheet variant. Whether this would also have been by Pagano, whose device was subsequently removed by a later owner of the blocks, or someone else we can't say. The information we have on Pagano and the party who apparently succeeded him in business "in Frezzaria, al segno della Fede," Francesco di Tommaso da

---

[81] Astengo (1990, 16), and Woodward (1979, item no. 53).

[82] Making changes in the woodcut form is much more difficult than in copper (Woodward, 1975, 48), so if revisions were desired, perhaps cutting new blocks would be more economical than revising the old blocks.

[83] See several paragraphs back for the Latin, and discussion of possible translations of it.

Salò e compagni, is fragmentary and contradictory. Most terminate Pagano's activity in 1565 or earlier, and it is also stated that in that year Tommaso da Salò assumed his business,[84] and indeed we do have a 1565 Italian edition of Gastaldi's booklet which was published "IN VENETIA, per Francesco de Tomaso di Salò, e compagni, in Frezzaria al segno della Fede." But Sandler had in his possession a 1568 Latin edition of Gastaldi's booklet which was published in "Venetiis, per Matthaeum Paganum in frezzaria ad insigne Fidei."[85] The fact the booklet exists in Italian and Latin editions suggests the map may have, also. And the three facts, that Nores's statement implies a possible revised edition before 1571, that the 1568 booklet was in Latin, and that the known artifact is in Latin, are suggestive.[86] However, without more solid facts, we cannot come to any definite conclusions here. One can only speculate.

While there may be uncertainty as to whether the preserved map is printed from the original blocks, perhaps revised, or from newly cut blocks, there is an abundance of indications that the original map did indeed come out pretty much on schedule, and that it looked very much like the current map in all its major details, including the Southern Continent. This latter is Almagià's last and greatest objection, and we shall answer it shortly. First,

---

[84] Destombes (1973, 124 and 125), Bagrow (1940), Almagià (1939, *carta*, 12).

[85] Sandler (1894, 404, note 3). The whereabouts of the copy Sandler had in hand is now uncertain, but I suspect for reasons it is not necessary to go into here that it is that which is now in the Bavarian State Library (cf. note 68 above), and even if not, they are unlikely to differ in any way. Perhaps Pagano and Tommaso di Salò ran the business together, or Pagano reacquired it from Tommaso by 1568.

[86] On the other hand, it is not impossible that Tommaso da Salò might have done a re-engraving. Very little is known of him. His having reprinted ca. 1565-67 a two-sheet 1559 view of Venice engraved by Pagano doesn't tell us much, but if an unconfirmed report of a twelve-sheet new edition of the same by Tommaso is correct (Destombes, 1973, 128), he would make an obvious candidate for the world map. Both Pagano and Tommaso also published books. The latest edition I know of by Tommaso is an anonymous *La representatione di santa Margherita vergine et martire, Nuouamente ristampata*, with colophon, "In Venetia; appresso Francesco de Tomaso di Salò, e compagni, in Frezzaria, al segno della Fede, 1576," in Harvard's library. The online SBN (Servizio Bibliotecario Nazionale) has twelve editions, all 1565-1574, mostly quarto and octavo editions, with ca. thirty to sixty leaves. Great Britain's online union catalog COPAC shows two editions, one dated 1550? which is probably an error. Several editions later than 1565 evidently lack the "in Frezzaria, al segno della Fede." One of the SBN's editions is, incidentally, an anonymous *Calendario perpetuo. Con il lunario et feste mobili*. In Venetia: in Frezzaria, al segno della Fede, 1566, a single leaf. As noted in chapter one, our earliest notice of Gastaldi is of a 1539 privilege for a "lunario perpetuo," which Almagià said he had been unable to find (1939, *carta*, 6-7).

however, it will be convenient to present several other pieces of important evidence indicating that the present map is the same as the original 1561 map.

We mentioned that Gastaldi's 1561 booklet *La Vniversale descrittione del mondo* was published by Pagano as accompaniment to the map, and that it includes passages describing several features of the map.[87] According to these passages, the map would have twenty-four parallels and twenty-four meridians, all 15° appart,[88] a very unusual spacing arrangement.[89] It was also to have eighteen northern and eighteen southern climatic zones indicated on its perimeters.[90] It would furthermore contain certain geographic features mentioned in the booklet, notably the Strait of Anian. All this accords exactly with the map we have in hand. The map also contains a copy of a diagram explaining time variation as one encircles the globe which is identical to a diagram which occurs in the booklet (p. 21).

We saw above that Giasone de Nores refers in 1571 to a Gastaldi map in terms that much suggest he is speaking of our map. There also exist manuscript maps from the 1560s which reproduce quite exactly the delineations in the known map, and since it is obvious that these are completely derivative products, copies of the map had to have existed before them. First, there is a Turkish world map, from an atlas known as the Ali Macar Reis atlas, which is dated 1567, and which reproduces the outlines of the British Library world map quite exactly.[91] Finally, there exist some Joan Martines atlases of the 1560s-1580s which contain maps of the American northwest coast which copy to the smallest detail the depiction on the British

---

[87] The passages describing the map are at pp. 4-5, 9-10, 14, 15, 18, 19.

[88] Gastaldi (1561, 9-10).

[89] No other map in Shirley up to the time has this arrangement, and the next in time which does, Porcacchi's 1572 world, is clearly copied from Gastaldi's map.

[90] Gastaldi (1561, 18).

[91] See reproductions in Harley and Woodward (1992, 282), in *Imago Mundi*, 23(1969), p. 91, and in Sezgin (2000, atlas volume, p. 96). The same outline is also repeated in another Turkish atlas, as seen in *Mercator's World*, 2(1997), no. 3, p. 26. Both maps include the extended Southern Continent.

Library map (ignoring completely the projection they are taken from),[92] and a number of the Martines atlases also contain a little two-hemisphere world map (diameters, ca. 16.60 cm), which also follow the British Library map exactly, being slightly enlarged copies of the double-hemisphere inset world map on the British Library map (diameters ca. 13.25 cm.). The earliest example of this world map is in a Martines atlas dated 1562, in the library of the Hispanic Society of America, New York (reproduced in Sider, 1992, 26), although that doesn't contain the larger maps of the northwest American coast. Caraci examined this map via a reproduction published in 1911 by Stevenson,[93] and commented that, "a glance at the reproduction of it given by Stevenson is sufficient to perceive that the planisphere is nothing but a pure and simple copy, naturally simplified and schematized, of a printed model."[94] He made a detailed comparison of the 107 names on the Hispanic Society world map with the names on the Camocio 1567 world map, and came to the conclusion that the Martines world map was a much reduced direct copy of the Gastaldi world map described in Gastaldi's 1561 booklet.[95] This rather remarkable indirect deduction, made before the *Cosmographia vniversalis* had turned up, was essentially correct, except that the Martines is not of course a reduction from the big oval map, but a slight enlargement of the double hemisphere inset map in its lower corners.[96] Note that both of the

---

[92] For example, see Caraci (1926-32, 2, pls. 21, 28, 29), from an atlas in the Biblioteca Angelica, Rome (Fondo antico 1311). The attribution to Martines is made at p. 31. See also Kretschmer (1892, pls. 27 and 30), from an atlas in the Correr Museum, Venice (Portolan no. 2). This atlas too is attributed by Caraci to Martines (pl. 29). Though it would take too much space to explain why, I highly suspect that quite a few other of Martines's earlier atlases will contain the same. See also Biagiotti (1990), with a catalog of Martines atlases; and Astengo (1996, 42-43), locating forty-two Martines atlases.

[93] Stevenson (1911), and Caraci (1936, 203-20).

[94] Caraci (1936, 204).

[95] Caraci (1936, 220).

[96] The two-hemisphere inset has just slightly more names than the Martines, but all Martines's names and their placement are as on the inset.

Turkish copies mentioned above, and this 1562 map, all contain the extended Southern Continent.[97]

The delineations on these maps are quite exactly in agreement with those on the "Cosmographia Vniversalis." But besides these, there are a good number of other maps from the 1560s and 1570s which were also clearly derivative productions which stem from this model. They are, in short: (1) a 1574 Forlani map of America, probably engraved ca. 1570;[98] (2) a large set of globe gores attributed to the Sanuto brothers and known as the Holzheimer gores;[99] (3) the maps of northeast Asia and northwest North America in a set of painted wall maps by Egnazio Danti (ca. 1560s-1570s) in the Medici Guardaroba of the Palazzo Vecchio in Florence;[100] (4) the world map and maps of America and Asia in a set of painted wall maps in the Palazzo Farnese at Caprarola (reproduced in Portoghesi, 1996); and (5) the

---

[97] Besides the Stevenson reproduction, the 1562 Martines is reproduced in Sider (1992, p. 26). There is a mild discoloration over the last figure "2" in the date of the Martines world, clearly visible in the reproduction in Sider (1992, 26). Edward Luther Stevenson believed that this represented an erasure, and that the "2" had been changed from some other digit (Stevenson, 1911, 53). Caraci, who had Stevenson's work in hand, made no note of Stevenson's observation, evidently not agreeing with it, and simply gives the date as 1562 with no reservation. In fact, I have inspected this atlas very closely in person and can state categorically that this discoloration is not an erasure, and the date is as originally engraved. The discoloration is probably from some spillage (perhaps candle wax?). There are many instances of course of dates being changed on maps, especially printed, but sometimes manuscript; but the reason is always clear. Without going into a wordy discussion, I invite the reader to speculate what possible reason one could have had to change the final figure on such a map, made not for practical use, but elegant display. Even if the atlas were one intended for use by seamen, the only possible change which could have made sense would have been from 1560 or 1561 to 1562. Other sources besides Caraci have also dated the atlas just as 1562 (Codazzi, 1922, 906; Almagià, 1944, 79, note 1; Astengo, 1996, 37; and notices in *Rivista geografica italiana*, 1910, 195-96, and in the *Bollettino* of the Società Geografica Italiana, 45(1908), 594-95). Note also the opinion Caraci expressed slightly earlier, also evidently founded on toponymic comparisons made before the British Library map had come to light, that all of Martines's world maps and regional maps of the New World from the period 1562-1572 are copies from Gastaldi (Caraci, 1935, 661 and 662.).

[98] Woodward (1990, no. 83, with reproduction).

[99] Woodward (1987), and Shirley (1987 no. 129).

[100] Levi-Donati (1995, pp. 23 and 77), and Kish (1951, 52-54).

two-hemisphere world map in the Terza Loggia of the Vatican,[101] an odd example, but definitely appertaining to this type.[102]

Still further evidence that the map was printed and released in the 1560s, and known to geographers, is provided by Camocio in his 1567 world map.[103] It is certainly this map that Camocio refers to as being too large to handle easily:

> Cum multi hactenus varias, . . . Cosmographiae ediderint chartas, eas tamen aut maiori forma, quam ut commode a studiosis tractari minibus possent, aut forma tam exigua. Vt multa in iis praetermittere, etiam cognitu vel maxime necessario, necesse fuerit, Visum est mihi in studiosorum gratiam exactissimam hanc Iacobi Gastaldi, Cosmographi excellentissimi, pest omnium neotericorum traditions, summa diligentia, meisque non exiguis expensis, delineateonem, in aes, idque hac mediocri forma incisam, in lucem dare: . . . (Although hitherto many cosmographers may have published various maps, [these] however either of form larger than suitable for handling by the studious, or else of form so small that many of the things most indispensable for understanding are omitted in them. It has seemed necessary to me, with an eye to gratifying the studious, that I should engrave in copper for giving into the light in this medium-sized form with the greatest accuracy and with no small expense of mine, this most exact delineation according to all the new information, of the most excellent Cosmographer Iacobi Gastaldi: . .).[104]

---

[101] Almagià (1955, 28-29, with plate between).

[102] I exclude one other such map, Gastaldi's map of America (no. 94), not because it was not properly published until the 1590s, but because its drawing actually precedes the "Cosmographia Vniversalis" by a short time, and it actually is the latter map's prototype as to the depiction of America, as will be made clear in chapter nine.

[103] Shirley (1987, no. 117). See also Karrow (1993, no. 30/93.2), and also earlier in the present chapter.

[104] The ellipsis in the Latin omits only the words "Praesul. Rme," which I was unable to decipher. It is probably some form of address to the dedicatee, Agostino Valerio. The Camocio map apparently appeared in response to difficulties encountered in handling the gigantic 1561 "Cosmographia Vniversalis." The depiction of the area around the Strait of Anian on this map, while inspired by the type as seen on the 1561 world, is of a rather different sort, being about five degrees lower, and with the strait itself much less narrow.

Camocio's allusion to maps "of form larger than suitable for handling by the studious," and the fact he's putting this out "in this medium-sized form" are certainly to the large ca. 1561 Gastaldi world map, the "Cosmographia Vniversalis." This Camocio map itself, although it clearly repeats in many places delineations from the long series of Gastaldi world maps beginning in 1546 and continuing through the 1560s and beyond, is obviously based on the 1561 world in part, especially in the areas around the Strait of Anian,[105] and this is also supported by the fact that it bears, as noted, the exact same title. Furthermore, a still earlier map, the Ortelius 1564 world map,[106] was also clearly influenced by the ca. 1561 world, even if Ortelius hadn't yet fully accepted Gastaldi's very narrow Strait of Anian, and its title also was partly inspired by the title of the ca. 1561 world map. All the evidence adduced so far shows beyond doubt that the 1561 world was published, available to geographers, and well known in the 1560s, and that its delineations were as on the preserved map. Note, too, that on all the maps cited which copied the delineations of the Gastaldi world, the extended Southern Continent is present. This fact alone is perhaps enough to counter Almagià's last objection. However, there is much more evidence indicating that Gastaldi would indeed have had good reason to add this feature, and, since the point was Almagià's strongest one, it will be worthwhile to present this evidence.

Although Almagià felt particularly certain that the extended Southern Continent on the "Cosmographia Universalis" would not have been put there by Gastaldi, his bases were not very sound. One was that "there is not the slightest mention made in the booklet"[107] of the continent. Astengo pointed out that there is such a mention. In fact, there are two. In describing the limits of Asia, Gastaldi establishes a parallel at 15° S latitude which he says,

---

[105] Although the 1561 world was still unknown when he wrote, Caraci had on the basis of involved but valid comparisons already predicted that the Camocio world was based on the, at that time, lost world map in its nomenclature (Caraci, 1936, 133-37 and 204-22).

[106] Shirley (1987, no. 114).

[107] Almagià (1939, "Intorno," 263).

"divides Asia from the unknown new World towards the south."[108] And in describing the limits of Africa, he establishes a parallel below Africa at 44° S latitude which "divides Africa towards the south, from the new parts."[109] The notices are short, but we recall this is a twenty-two-page octavo booklet which covers the world. No place named in the booklet gets more than a short mention. The other basis was that no known Gastaldi world maps contain the extended Southern Continent, but only a very limited one, and he cited in evidence all the maps in the long series from 1546 to and past the 1560s.[110] But we note that all of those maps also lack the Strait of Anian, which *is* on the big world map. Clearly, we cannot take the absence of a feature on all the long series of maps as evidence that that feature on a different map cannot be Gastaldi's, for we know the strait is indeed Gastaldi's. Furthermore, all of those world maps which clearly derive from the original 1561 world, and which all contain the Strait of Anian, also contain the extended Southern Continent,[111] certainly implying that their prototype did as well.[112] As we demonstrate at length in chapter seven, as regards areas of the globe for which there was no reliable information, cartographers sometimes gave variant views, none of which could have represented conviction, or even really opinion, and, as we show in the same place, Gastaldi was not just among those who presented, and simultaneously entertained, such variant views, or possibilities, the policy of doing so is indeed one of the defining characteristics of his cartography throughout his career. No one could have really known the geography of the southern polar regions, and we can be sure Gastaldi's original depiction of the area was not

[108] Gastaldi (1561, 14).

[109] Gastaldi (cit., 13).

[110] Almagià (1939, "Intorno," 265). Almagià, incidentally, included the 1555 Gastaldi world published in Antwerp by de Jode, although he hadn't seen that. But there the depiction of the continent doesn't fit either recipe. It is much more extended than Gastaldi's original depiction, but nevertheless much less extended than on the 1561 world map, "Cosmographia Vniversalis". See repr. in Shirley (1987, no. 100). In any event, this is De Jode's recension, not Gastaldi's.

[111] That is, the mentioned Turkish maps, the Martines maps, the Porcacchi 1572 world (Shirley, 1987, no. 127), and the Holzheimer gores (Shirley no. 129); and also, though coming from a different line of derivation, the "Totius Orbis Descriptio," (Shirley no. 120), and the Camocio world just mentioned.

[112] See also a few pages below on the 1559/60 Hadji Ahmed world map in which Gastaldi very possibly had a hand.

based on sure knowledge, or that it was an idea he was in any way bound to. It was conjecture, a possibility, and there was more than enough present in the sources Gastaldi most used, in the way of unconfirmed reports and conjecture, to justify his entertaining another idea, and depicting it as a possibility on his maps, as the following examples will confirm.

In his discourse on the ancient voyage of Hanno to Carthage in volume one (1550) of the *Navigazioni*, Ramusio, repeating the words of a Portuguese pilot, has noted that the king of Portugal prohibits inland exploration in Africa, from which he continues:

> & sopra tutto e vietato il poter nauigare oltra il capo di Buona speranza a dritta linea verso il polo Antartico, doue è opinione appresso tutti li pilotti Portoghesi che vi sia vn grandissimo continente di terra ferma, laqual corra leuante & ponente sotto il polo Antartico & dicono che altre volte vno eccelente huomo Fiorentino detto Amerigo Vespuccio con certe naui de i detti Re la trouò & scores per grande spatio, ma che dapoi è stato prohibito che alcun vi possa andare (and above all it is prohibited to sail beyond the cape of Good hope to the starboard towards the Antarctic pole, where it is the opinion of all the Portuguese pilots that there be a very large continent of firm land which runs east and west under the Antarctic pole, and they say that formerly an excellent Florentine man called Americo Vespucci with certain ships of the said king found and coasted it for a great distance, but that since it has been prohibited that anyone can go there).[113]

Ramusio mentions the continent shortly once again in volume three (1556), in the dedication to Fracastoro which opens the volume. He has said that perhaps the discovery of the passage to Cathay is being reserved by God for some great explorer, and continues, "come fa anco il discoprir l'altra parte della terra verso l'Antartico: il che fin al presente nõ vi è alcuno che habbia voluto, ò tentato di fare" (as also the discovery of the other part of the earth

---

[113] Ramusio (1967-70, 1, 114r; Milanesi ed., 1978-88, 1, 561.)

towards the Antarctic: which up to now there is no one who has wished or tried to make).[114]

As we saw earlier (chapter one, note 72), among the few non-Ramusian sources used by Gastaldi was Gómara's great account of the Spanish exploration and settlement of America, which was published in December of 1552, and probably was available to Gastaldi sometime in 1553. After his rapid description of the periplus of the North American coast, he notes rather meaninglessly that there are many other islands and lands in the world, and continues:

One of these is the land of the Strait of Magellan, which runs toward the east and according to appearance is very large and extends close to the Antarctic Pole. They think that on one side it reaches almost to the Cape of Good Hope, and on the other to the Moluccas, because the ships of the viceroy Don Antonio de Mendoza encountered a land of Negroes which extended for 500 leagues, and they believed this was a continuation of that of the strait just referred to.[115]

Tommaso Giunti, Ramusio's publisher, in the revised version of his "Alli lettori" which appears first in the 1563 third edition of volume one, having noted that Ramusio's death was a great loss to learned men, for he intended to continue producing material on his subject, and always strove to steal some time from his great public obligations as secretary to the Venetian Council of Ten to work towards that end, then continues:

Cosi Iddio n'hauesse concesso gratia, che viuendo lui fosse stata scoperta, & pienamente conosciuta quella parte ch'è verso mezzo dì, sotto il Polo Antartico, che egli haueria fatto ogni opera di hauerne le relationi, & li Viaggi, per potere vn giorno dar fuori ancho il Quarto Volume, talche non hauesse fatto piu di bisogno leggere, ne Tolomeo, ne Strabone, ne Plinio, ne alcun' altro de gli antichi scrittori intorno alle cose di Geografia (Thus had God granted the favor, that while he lived that part which is towards the south, under the Antarctic Pole,

[114] Ramusio (1967-70, 3, 6th page of dedication to Fracastoro; Milanesi ed., 1978-88, 5, 12.)

[115] Quoted after Wagner (1929, 431).

might have been discovered and made fully known, he will have made every effort to obtain the relations, and the voyage accounts, to be able one day to give out also the Fourth Volume, so that there might no longer have been need to read either Ptolemy, or Strabo, or Pliny, or any other of the ancient writers regarding geography).[116]

The passage is somewhat puzzling. With a few exceptions, Ramusio's three completed volumes cover almost all of the important explorations which had occurred, and it is hard to imagine what material he had in mind that could be sufficient to warrant a whole fourth volume.[117] But to judge from his words, it seems that Giunti envisioned that this Southern Continent would be its main bulk, and his observation that *if* this volume had come out, *then* Ramusio would truly have replaced the classical writers, both implies that Ramusio had not quite done so with his three volumes, and that the Southern Continent was not considered by him as something peripheral in nature, but a bona fide important part of the earth.   Indeed, there is no question that the conjectured Southern (and for that matter Northern) Continent would not have been envisioned as some frozen and forbidding

---

[116] Ramusio (1967-70, 1, 2nd page of Giunti's "To the reader" ; Milanesi ed., 1978-88, 1, 8.) On discussion of the Southern Continent in general in Ramusio's circle see Grande (1905, "relazioni," 115-19). Gastaldi could also have been influenced by other cartographers in this. Mercator, in his 1541 world map, shows the continent, and has two legends of interest, one saying that its existence is certain, though its limits are not yet known (Nordenskiöld, 1889, 107; and Almagià, 1939, "Intorno," 263), and the other that some Portuguese were driven there by wind in 1500 on a voyage to India (McClymont, 1921, 13 and 41). See also just below on the continent as shown on maps of Fine, Monachus, and Hadji Ahmed. Another believer in a Southern Continent, which he called Chasdia, was Guiallume Postel, who may well have been personally acquainted with both Ramusio and Gastaldi (Milanesi, 1989).

[117] Ramusio himself refers once to such a fourth volume, in his discourse on the several relations concerned with Pizarro's conquest of Peru in volume three; Giunti also mentions it near the end of his note to the reader at the head of volume one. Having spoken of various matters connected with South America, especially but not entirely dealing with the conquest, the conquistadors involved, and their later fates, Ramusio ends the discourse with the sentence, "Et questa narratione con breuità habbiamo voluto discorrer per satisfatione de' lettori, laqual piu distintamente leggerãno nel 4. vol." ("And this narration we have wished to briefly present for the satisfaction of readers, who will read [it] more distinctly in vol. 4"). Ramusio makes no allusion to the Southern Continent in the discourse, although if he really intended a fourth volume, he must have had something more in mind than the material discussed in the discourse, which could never make up a whole other volume. These are the only two allusions in the *Navigationi* (or anywhere) to a fourth volume. Milanesi implies the fourth volume idea may have been more Giunti's idea than Ramusio's (1984, 55). She once refers to it as "the mythical fourth volume" (cit., 60; see also 41, 46, 59 on the elusive volume), and see our chapter four, note 10.

wasteland similar to the real Southern Continent, but a viable, livable, and populated quarter of the earth, so there is all the more likelihood that Gastaldi might have considered it worthy of inclusion on his maps.

The ancients, we know, had considered that, of the earth's five zones, only the two temperate ones could be lived in. The torrid zone and the two polar ones were uninhabitable. This question of the habitability of the earth was one of great interest at the time.[118] Ramusio discusses it at some length in his discourse (dated 1553) to Fracastoro at the head of volume three (1556), revealing that the moderns had demonstrated that the ancients were incorrect as to the uninhabitability of the extreme zones, and concludes with the observation:

> Hora per le cose dette di sopra, penso che non ci sia piu dubbio alcuno, che sotto l'Equinottiale, & sotto ambidue i poli, non si troui la medesima moltitudine de gli habitanti, che sono in tutte l'altre parti del mondo (Now considering the things said above, I think that there is no more doubt at all, that under the Equinoctial, and under both the poles there might be found the same multitude of inhabitants which there are in all the other parts of the world).[119]

Giunti too, in the "alli lettori" just quoted from, notes that modern explorers have uncovered things unknown to the ancients: "onde si puo chiaramente comprendere, che d'ogni intorno questo globo della terra è maravigliosamente habitato, ne vi è parte alcuna vacua: ne per caldo o gielo priua d'habitatori" (by which it can clearly be understood, that on every side this globe of the earth is wonderfully inhabited, nor is there any part empty: neither from heat nor cold wanting in inhabitants).[120]

Gastaldi himself devotes near five full pages to the subject of habitability in his 1561 booklet, much more than to any other subject.[121] He

---

[118] On discussion of this in Ramusio's circle, see Grande (1905, "relazioni," 114-15).

[119] Ramusio (1967-70, 3, 2nd to 4th pages of discourse to Fracastoro. Quoted line on 4th page; respectively in Milanesi ed., 1978-88, 5, 5-9, and 9.)

[120] Ramusio (1967-70, 1, 2nd page of "Alli lettori" of Giunti; Milanesi ed., 1978-88, 1, 8).

[121] Gastaldi (1561, 5-9).

discusses at length first the polar zones, then the torrid one, noting in both cases that the ancients had come to their conclusions without having gone to these places, and he speaks of the trade in these zones, the fertility of the land, the astronomical factors effecting their habitability, etc. He concludes the section on the polar zones by noting that the moderns

> hanno praticato, & negociato in diuersi paesi, principiando sotto al circolo Artico, e distendendosi uerso il Polo Artico infino a gradi 80. di latitudine, o uoglia dire di larghezza, li quali hanno ritrouato diuerse Regioni habitatissime, ne mi estendero a scriuerle, ma per uerificar il detto loro, dirò della Region di Finmarchia, nella quale ui è la Città Vardans habitatissima, che ha il Polo eleuato sopra il suo Orizonte gradi 75" (have frequented, and traded in, various lands, beginning under the Arctic circle, and extending themselves towards the Arctic Pole as far as 80 degrees of latitude, or rather of height, the which have found various most populous Regions; I'll not go on to describe them, but to verify their word, I will speak of the Region of Finmark, where there is the very populous city of Vardans,[122] which has the Pole elevated above its Horizon 75 degrees).[123]

He continues that while it's true that it's intemperate, and the people do not get about and trade in winter, but in summer every sort of fruit grows except grapes, concluding: "dunque diremo, che è habitata, ma luoco intemperate, & in simile sono i Meridionali" (Therefore we will say that it is inhabited, but an intemperate place, and it is the same with the Southerners).[124]

I have made these rather lengthy observations to show that good reasons exist to show that Gastaldi could have entertained the possibility of there being an extended Southern Continent, a real part of the earth, and not

---

[122] This is Vardo, still in Finmark County, far northeast Norway, formerly a center of trade with Russia and Finland. Vardohus fortress was built there in 1307. Its actual latitude is 70° 22' N.

[123] Gastaldi (1561, 6-7).

[124] Gastaldi (1561, 7).

a wasteland.[125]   This, the fact that it was normal for Gastaldi and others to entertain variant ideas about unknown regions, and the fact that all of the various maps which obviously stem, directly or indirectly, from the 1561 map, convince me that the original map most likely did contain this extended Southern Continent.   Furthermore, I would add (and this is especially important, since it involves a map predating the 1561 world map) that Gastaldi was evidently involved in the making of the 1559/60 Hadji Ahmed map, on which the extended continent is taken from Fine's 1531 world.[126] All in all, there is every reason to believe that the British Library's *Cosmographia vniversalis* is a fully accurate reflection of the original map. We have but one question left to ask.   We have seen earlier in this chapter that one cannot take very seriously claims on these sixteenth- century Venetian maps that a map has been improved, updated, augmented, etc, as we see in the title of the copy which we possess of this map.   Such claims appear in a context which is anything but neutral, where the prime interest is convincing customers to buy.   Is it just possible that the map we have is literally unchanged from the original, not just in all major but all minor details as well?   Frankly, I consider it quite likely. Certainly, it is hard to imagine that much could have been done in the way of additions and improvements. As we have seen, Gastaldi's depictions of the extra-European world had advanced to such a degree that few significant changes would be seen for some time.   In his 1567 Asia, which follows Gastaldi, Ortelius did make some improvements as to the southeast Asian islands, probably based

---

[125] On the *Cosmographia vniversalis* there are two pictures of native inhabitants, both hunters, one dispatching his prey, the other lugging his prey home on his back.   There are also numerous animals, real and fictitious.

[126] The Fine map has the legend: "The Southern Land, recently discovered, but not yet explored" (quoted after Karrow, 1993, 408). According to Wilford (1981, 139), Fine's was the first map to give real definition to the continent. Monachus's ca. 1527-30 world had it, but with a somewhat blocky appearance. It contains the legend: "This part of the world not yet discovered by our navigators." (after Karrow, 1993, cit.). There are two legends on the "Cosmographia Vniversalis" itself. One is on the continent below Africa: "TERRA DE VISTA. Fu discoperta questa terra da Portogalesi per fortuna ma non si fermorno" (Land of Sighting [?]. This land was discovered by chance by the Portuguese but they did not tarry). The other is south of Gilolo and the eastern Moluccas, at the west edge of the map: "TERRA INCOGNITA MERI(DI)ONALE DISCOPERTO (sic) NOVAMENTE" (Unknown Southern Land Newly Discovered). See also Arbel (2002). Interestingly, apparently some Arab geographers had also believed there to be such a Southern Continent (see the *Bulletin* of the Société de géographie, Paris, for July, 1848, 15).

on some recent Portuguese chart. But Ortelius's changes are not reflected in the copy of the *Cosmographia vniversalis* we have. If there really were changes, they were probably restricted to small additions or changes in toponyms, or incidental and mostly meaningless adjustments made in such features as coastlines, interior hydrography or orography, since much of this was guesswork anyway.

In any event, we can affirm that in the main, in the map which we have, we see the only surviving picture of Gastaldi's 1561 world map, and, in my opinion, this is probably true also of the Southern Continent there depicted. Certainly, we know it is true in the area of the Strait of Anian, which is essentially identical on the maps upon which that feature was obviously derived directly from this map, or directly related to the depiction on this map, that is, the Holzheimer gores; the 1567 Turkish world map; the painted wall maps at Florence, Caprarola, and the Vatican; and the Martines maps, especially his maps of the northwest coast mentioned above, which are of sufficiently large scale that they include the exact detail of the area as on the Gastaldi world map. In fact, our principal reason for investigating this map in some depth has been to establish that Gastaldi's original Strait of Anian did indeed have precisely the appearance that it has on this map, a point of major importance to us since it lies at the heart of our chapter eight.

CHAPTER 3 - GASTALDI'S GREAT ADVANCE IN CARTOGRAPHY

3.1 Preliminary Remarks

Although there is, of course, a general awareness that Gastaldi made some large maps of the continents, in whole or in part, and though these maps are generally pronounced as being great works, these pronouncements have all been of a general and banal nature. No direct and outspoken declaration of the stunning superiority of these maps over all earlier maps of the extra-European continents has ever been made, other than the statement made in the first chapter of the present book. Due to reasons for which one can find explanations, but not with certainty, it simply has not been divined. In fact, I had not noticed it myself in some twenty years of looking at Gastaldi and his works until intuition, or insight, or something else, compelled me to begin making the kind of simple comparisons as those that follow here, which will document beyond question that which we have so far only stated. We start with Africa.

3.2 Africa

With this continent, our task is much facilitated by the publication at 't Goy Houton in 2007 of Richard Betz's *The Mapping of Africa*, a comprehensive illustrated chronological cartobibliography of all full maps of Africa up to 1700.[1] Just turning the pages of this book until we have reached Gastaldi's 1564 Africa (Betz no. 9) gives us a demonstration of the astonishing superiority of Gastaldi's Africa over all previous maps of the continent as graphic and revealing as we could wish for. As with the other continents, the improvement in Gastaldi's 1564 Africa (our Cartobibliogaphy no. 118) over previous maps was by no means incremental; it was a leap, a gigantic bound forward. The map was in the first place enormous by comparison with any previous maps, but it was also covered with

---

[1] Betz's book is a production of the Explokart Program at the University of Utrecht.

information, both on the coasts and the interior. In fact, if we look at the best full map of Africa which preceded it (excluding for the moment Gastaldi's own pre-1564 Africa maps), Münster's 1540 woodcut "Africae Tabvla," (Betz no. 3), the difference is so startling that we might at first think we have made a mistake, and that surely some other cartographer produced something better between 1540 and 1564, but such is not the case, unless we take into account Gastaldi's own earlier work, upon which note it will be appropriate to make an aside which will be relevant to all three far continents, and will give a better and clearer perspective to our discussion.

We intentionally left out of the comparison made above between Gastaldi's 1564 Africa and preceding maps of that continent Gastaldi's own maps of Africa before 1564, but it must be noted that, in Gastaldi's own earlier work, and in his alone, we do indeed find worthy transitional work; there was the very large 1549-50 map of Africa painted on a wall of the Venetian Ducal Palace (no. 65), and in 1554 there appears in the second edition of the first volume of Ramusio's *Navigazioni* a rather good Africa much superior to the Münster map (Betz, no. 4; our no. 77), both mentioned in chapter one. There is also an even better 1562 Forlani Africa (Betz no. 6), but we know Forlani made no major original maps, if any at all, and it is generally agreed, by Karrow (1993, no. 30/98.1) and Betz, and the present author, that this map was copied by Forlani from Gastaldi's wall map of Africa in the Ducal Palace (our no. 65), so it too is Gastaldi, a copy from part of his ever-improving image of Africa culminating in the 1564 map. Gastaldi's two maps covering southern Asia in the same volume also played such a transitional role for that continent, as did his 1553 painted wall map in the Ducal Palace (our no. 72, and see chapter one), as well as his ca. 1550 or later map of western inland Asia (our no. 69). Likewise for America there was his map of the Western Hemisphere, which appeared in volume three of the *Navigazioni* in 1556 (our no. 86), as well as the presumably rather large ca. 1553 map of America compiled from Spanish sea charts, as well as the four regional maps of America derived from that which were intended for volume three of Ramusio's *Navigazioni* (nos. 73-76, discussed in chapter one), and finally the large inset of most of America on the 1549-50 Africa wall map in the Ducal Palace (cf. no. 65 in our Cartobibliography), unfortunately none of these still extant except the 1556 Western Hemisphere. It is important to remember, as we go along, that these "interim" maps were better than anything which had been previously produced by any other cartographers. Furthermore, as we also saw briefly in chapter one, Gastaldi had still earlier, in his 1548 Ptolemy, given incomparably better and wider representation of modern maps for all three of the extra-European continents than had any previous edition of Ptolemy. Thus, there is a clear three-stage progression in three series of maps through Gastaldi's career leading from 1548 to ca. 1553-1556/57 to 1559/64 as regards mapping of the extra-European world, with several individual "interim" maps of these areas appearing from time to time, all showing steady progress, while there was very little or no progress from other quarters. In the remainder of our survey, we shall omit mention of specific previous Gastaldian maps. We return to our comparison of Gastaldi's Africa with what preceded it.

While there was clearly no map of the whole continent before Gastaldi's which could provide any comparison at all, somewhat more viable contenders than Münster's can be found in a 1513 two-part map of most of Africa by Waldseemüller, reproduced by Nordenskiöld (1889, 115 and 119), and in the image of Africa on a few world maps. Waldseemüller does in fact capture the African coastline fairly well for his time in these maps, though omitting a good-sized portion of northeast Africa, and also in his world maps, but while they are quite large for the time, they are nevertheless, taken together, three to four times smaller than the huge Gastaldi Africa (ca. 4,200 sq. cm. for the 1513 maps together compared to ca. 15,000 sq. cm. for the 1564 Africa). Although it is true that Waldseemüller does very liberally provide coastal names which he has taken from sea charts, the maps are basically quite primitive, with the few data found in the near empty interior being quite medieval. Most of the modern accounts which provided the information filling Gastaldi's Africa did not exist at the time. The same is true of course of the images of Africa on Waldseemüller's enormous world maps of 1507 and 1516,[2] as well as on the 1525 Fries world[3], taken from

_____

[2] Shirley, 1987, nos. 26 and 42.

[3] Shirley, 1987, no. 56.

them, all which images are also about three times smaller than the image of Africa on the 1564 map. In pure terms of size, nothing else in the sixteenth century before Gastaldi approaches these early Waldseemüller giants, with the largest Africa image on a world map for the period probably being that on a 1558 Vopel-Vavassore world,[4] where the image is about 2,420 sq. cm., between six and seven times smaller than the Gastaldi Africa, and others get progressively smaller. The Africa on the great 1541 Mercator globe[5] covers about 740 sq. cm., about twenty times smaller. Furthermore, none of these contain, of course, any but a small fraction of the data on the Gastaldi map, and none include anything at all from the lengthy new accounts of Leo Africanus, Francesco Alvarez, Odoardo Barbosa, João de Barros, and others, which appeared in Ramusio's *Navigazioni* in 1550 and 1554, and of which Gastaldi made extensive use as we shall see shortly. Other than the basic coastline as given by Waldseemüller in 1513 and 1516, Gastaldi's 1564 Africa presented the large-scale modern picture of Africa to mapreaders' eyes as if from out of nowhere. There was literally nothing worthy of note before it that could be compared to it, except Gastaldi's own progressively improving maps.

3.3 Asia

The departure from previous depictions by Gastaldi's Asia of 1559-61 (nos. 92, 102 and 103) is even more spectacular and complete than for Africa. Again, as with Africa, the picture of Asia is huge and crammed with information, a grand sweeping panorama with no predecessor. As with Africa, the only viable map of all Asia before Gastaldi's was Münster's of 1540, and the comparison is just as startling (cf. for Münster, Skelton (Münster), 1966, pl. XIX, and our Cartobibliography no. 111, the composite picture of all of Gastaldi's Asia as it occurs in the Bell atlas.). Again, we can

---

[4] Shirley, 1987, no. 102.

[5] Shirley, 1987, no. 78.

do a little better by resorting to previous images of Asia on world maps,[6] but there is less to offer than for Africa. Asia on the gigantic Waldseemüller world maps is so thoroughly a mixture of the medieval and the Ptolemaic that we don't need even to consider them, and the same is true of all maps through the period. Nordenskiöld's observation on Gastaldi's Asias, that, "as regards the outlines of the coasts they are superior to all previous maps of Asia known, either drawn by hand or printed,"[7] does not really capture the magnitude of the difference. Perhaps the best overall image of Asia before Gastaldi's is that on Mercator's 1538 world,[8] but there aren't a twentieth, if a thirtieth, part of the toponyms, and the map retains the two great Ptolemaic peninsulas beyond India. There are many more toponyms on the 1541 Mercator globe gores, though still only a fraction, less than a fourth, of what are on the Gastaldi Asia, and here the Asian south coast is still worse than on the 1538 map, with not two, but three peninsulas east of India. There are no other real contenders. The Asias on the 1544 Cabot world,[9] and on the 1554 Tramezzini world[10] are about one tenth and one twelfth the size of Gastaldi's, with proportionate quantities of data, and there are still troubles with the south coast.[11] Finally, as with the Africa, there is extensive Asian material from Ramusio in Gastaldi's Asia which was not available to these mapmakers, and is not represented in their maps. For Asia, we see, there was not even a fairly correct continental coastline before Gastaldi, as there had been for Africa from Waldseemüller. Again, Gastaldi presented Asia to the

---

[6] Again, as noted, there are the two Gastaldi maps which cover southern Asia in Ramusio in 1554, and good coverage in the 1548 Ptolemy, which we do not take into account here.

[7] Nordenskiöld (1897, 160). At p. 161 he adds, "real reform in the cartography of southern and eastern Asia was first realized by the works of Gastaldi."

[8] Shirley, 1987, no. 74.

[9] Shirley, 1987, no. 81.

[10] Shirley, 1987, no. 97.

[11] The Cabot map does not carry the Asian south coast to the end at all and has no Asian east coast. The Vopel-Vavassore 1558 world mentioned in the comparisons made as to Africa cannot be used here for comparison at all, for on it Asia and America are one, but its Asia is no more spectacular in general than its Africa. There is no need to bring into consideration several small, sketchy and very primitive maps of parts of Asia, as Fries's two thoroughly medieval sections of eastern Asia in his 1522 Ptolemy (repr. Nordenskiöld, 1889, 99 and 101), the little sketchy maps of Johannes Honter, or the manuscript maps of Pietro Coppo.

world with no notable predecessors, creating the modern map of Asia practically single-handed.

3.4 America

For America, we have Gastaldi's beautiful map, probably from 1559 or 1560 (no. 94), which remained in manuscript, for reasons explained in chapter nine, until the 1570s. It was published in ca. 1575/1577 by Camocio. However, the publication aborted due to Camocio's sudden death from the plague in the mid-1570s, while in the process of revising some points of the map, leaving the map such that three parts were missing. Also, in the process of revising it, parts of the original map were probably destroyed. No one knew what Camocio had had in mind in his revisions, and the map was left in limbo. In the 1590s Donato Bertelli divined what Gastaldi's original manuscript had looked like, and he printed the map complete for the first time (nos. VIII and XII). In 1561 Gastaldi made his giant woodcut world map (no. 104), in which the America is copied directly from the original ca. 1559/1560 America. It was no doubt using this map that Bertelli was able to reconstruct the original Gastaldi America image. It has been suggested that the Camocio-Bertelli map (ca. 1575/77 and ca. 1596) stems directly from the 1561 printed world map (no. 104), but this is unlikely for several reasons, as shown in chapter nine. Here, as with Africa, much of the basic coastline had already been caught before Gastaldi, including the entire South American and Central American coastlines, and fairly good representations of the North American east coast. Nevertheless, Gastaldi again does not leave us disappointed, for he gives North America for the first time a broad east to west extent, having added a reasonably adequate northerly and especially westerly extension to the continent, with a more or less proper relationship in the west to Asia, at his Strait of Anian, which we shall discuss below. A glance backwards in Shirley, from Gastaldi's ca. 1561 world map, shows immediately that it was precisely at this time that we first see a North America which looks like the real continent. All former maps which showed a full North America at all depicted the continent as far too narrow, and with far too much sea between it and Asia in the north. The broadest North America's before Gastaldi's were those of Tramezzini in 1554, and the characteristic Mercator type of 1538, repeated in several maps afterwards. For comparison of the America on the Scolari-Gastaldi America, or Gastaldi's 1561 world with these two maps see Shirley (nos. 97 and 99 respectively).[12] In addition to this great stride in the right direction, Gastaldi fills South America, Central America and Mexico with toponyms and hydrographical and orographical detail, not all of it accurate. All former maps, though they had coastal toponyms, were completely or nearly completely lacking in interior names, except perhaps the Vopel-Vavassore world of 1558, which has a few, but only a small fraction by comparison with Gastaldi.[13]

3.5 Some Closing Comments

Taken together, the three depictions, Gastaldi's Africa, his Asia, and his America not only give for the first time a generally correct picture of the world beyond Europe, but they also give this picture on a scale several times larger than ever offered before, as well as filling the picture throughout with an unprecedented array of toponyms and other geographical details. If there is question about the cartography of Europe in the Venetian four-continent sets of wall maps, of which we speak in our last chapters, there is certainly no question about what cartography, and what cartographer, made such four-continent wall map series possible in general, that is, as regards the other three continents. How could Gastaldi, certainly a drawing room cartographer, have done this? How could anyone have all but single-handedly brought the modern cartographic picture of all the non-European world from the state it was in before Gastaldi, as shown by our comparisons, to this very large and generally correct picture of 1559-64? Part of the answer to this question, treated only rather cursorily in our chapter one, is that he did not really do so single-handedly, for most of the information gathering was not done by Gastaldi, but by his friend Giovanni Battista

---

[12] One should consult the ca. 1555 Florianus rendition of the Mercator type (Shirley, 1987, no. 99), since in the original of 1538 (Shirley no. 74), the image of America is badly broken up by the cordiform projection.

[13] As to hydrography, a good many earlier maps did contain the two large South American rivers so familiar to historians of cartography, the Amazon and the Plata. Much of Vopel's South America is filled with pictures of animals and natives, and we see the same on many others, as the 1544 Cabot world.

Ramusio, Secretary of the Venetian Senate, and later of the Council of Ten, who for thirty years and more tirelessly gathered information on the new discoveries as a labor of love, and who put this information at Gastaldi's disposal, and then at the disposal of the world when he published his great three-volume *Navigazioni e viaggi* of 1550-1559. But we get ahead of ourselves, for this we shall show in detail in the next chapter. For the moment, a few more comments will provide us with some further perspective on the extent of Gastaldi's advance as to mapping of the world beyond Europe.

Of the eighty-seven cartographers in the list of mapmakers which Ortelius includes in his 1570 *Theatrum Orbis Terrarum*, only ten besides Gastaldi made any contribution to modern mapping of non-European areas before 1566, the year of Gastaldi's death, other than, in a few cases, maps of the world, or of the Holy Land. They are as follows, giving last name only,[14] with a general indication of what they made in the way of maps of extra-European lands: Boileau de Buillon (three small 1555 maps, Africa, Asia, America), Bordone (about fifteen small maps of non-European areas, mostly islands, 1528), Chaves (a small 1548 map of America), Coppo (1520 and 1528, about ten to twelve manuscript maps of parts of Africa, Asia, America, folio size), Fries (1522, copies of the Waldseemüller maps listed below, and two primitive maps of parts of eastern Asia, taken from the 1492 Behaim globe), Gutiérrez (1550 Atlantic Ocean, and 1562 wall map of America, one of the few significant extra-European contributions of the period, but coming after most of Gastaldi's work was already done, and omitting all of northwestern North America), Honter (several small maps of parts of Asia and Africa, 1542 and reprints), Münster (three primitive and simple maps of Africa, Asia, America), Nicolay (1554 Atlantic Ocean with parts of America and the Old World), Waldseemüller (1513 America, a two-part map of most of Africa, Asia Minor, Asia). All other seventy-six cartographers made only maps of European areas, except, as noted, some of the world or the Holy Land. While there were no doubt a few produced by people not in Ortelius's original list, the added contribution would probably not be very significant.

---

[14] This little survey is based upon Karrow, and I use his forms for the cartographers' surnames in all cases.

None come to my mind as I write. Note especially that there were no maps of non-European areas by Ortelius before 1567 or Mercator before 1585, again excluding world and Holy Land maps. Donald Lach wrote that, "The history of Renaissance geography divides into two interrelated parts: the topographical descriptions of Europe and the depiction of the overseas world as it was gradually revealed."[15] Clearly, it was Gastaldi (and Ramusio) who brought about the greatest single advance as to the latter.

We give here, to conclude this short chapter, comments of various scholars on the later influence of Gastaldi's maps, from which it is clear that his depictions had taken the picture of the world to such a point that it was difficult for later mapmakers to find means to improve on it. Stevenson wrote, "To Gastaldi's Africa are traceable practically all important features of that continent, as they appear in the maps of the following century and a half."[16] Skelton was even more bullish: "Gastaldi's map of Africa . . . served European cartographers as a prototype for nearly 200 years."[17] Most recently, Phipps and Sdiri, speaking of the 1564 Africa, state, "From this period on, every African map would largely draw on Gastaldi's, including those of Abraham Ortelius (1570), Gerhard Mercator the Younger (1595), and Henricus Hondius (1631). Two centuries were to pass before new geographical information appeared on maps."[18] The same comes out as to the Asia. Biasutti wrote, "the Gastaldian influences in the cartography of Asia are also easy to follow . . . Here it is sufficient to bring out that all the maps of the seventeenth century, and even some after, keep numerous and significant traces of it,"[19] and he goes farther as to some parts of the map: "It is obvious that, especially for the portions of the continent contained between the Red Sea, the Mediterranean, the Caspian and the Indus, nothing is found to replace the drawing and the data of Gastaldi until the 18th century."[20]

---

[15] Lach (1965-1993, 2, 2/3, p. 447).

[16] Edward Luther Stevenson's review of Biasutti *Geographical Review* 11, no. 4 (1921): 641).

[17] Skelton (1962, 82).

[18] Phipps and Sdiri (1994, 6). Wulf Bodenstein has given an excellent demonstration of just how very closely Ortelius followed Gastaldi in his Africa (Bodenstein, 1998, 185-207).

[19] Biasutti (1923, 310).

[20] Biasutti (1923, 310).

Most recently, Sezgin, whose wide survey covers not just Ortelius and Mercator, but almost all the cartographers of Asia, says there was no substantial progress over Gastaldi to the mid-seventeenth century.[21] As to America, one need only glance through the works of Shirley and Burden to see that practically all world maps and maps of America from the 1560s to the mid-seventeenth century adopt Gastaldi's broadened North America and its close approach to Asia at the Strait of Anian, and a diminishing number continue to show this to the end of the seventeenth century.

Of course, all this doesn't mean that Gastaldi was accurate in everything on his maps by any means, for he certainly wasn't. Some of what Gastaldi showed was wrong, but much of this as well continued to be shown for a long time by others, and in such cases, it was just the tyranny of an established image, hard to break away from if there were no real information to the contrary. Skelton notes mistakes in Gastaldi's Africa which continued for 200 years.[22] But a great deal was correct and, *most importantly*, as we have stated before and shall intentionally state still again later for much deserved emphasis, in the main, the overall world picture as shown on these large maps, all compiled in the short space of five years, 1559-1564, was correct for the first time in history. While it may be difficult for the reader to believe, this unprecedented achievement has, for reasons which escape me, never been acknowledged, and indeed has gone quite unnoticed in our literature, even though, in doing what he did, Gastaldi essentially laid the physical foundations for all modern cartography of the extra-European world which would follow. Let us at this point insert a rapid overview of the period following Gastaldi's. For general perspective purposes, this will be useful and appropriate in any event. But, as we shall see, it will also allow us to adequately accentuate how jarring has been the absence of a recognition of this major link in tracing the development of cartography.

Gastaldi and his work, concluding with the four-continent sets of the 1570s and 1590s based upon his cartography, ended an era, the era of Italian predominance in cartography. The principal successor was the Netherlands.

---

[21] Sezgin (2000, 2, 157).

[22] Skelton (1961, 566).

Low Country cartography began to decisively eclipse Italian in 1570 with Ortelius's *Theatrum Orbis Terrarum*,[23] which continued to be published after his 1598 death into the earlier seventeenth century, and then also by the works of the De Jode family which continued until the end of that century. These were followed by Waghenaer's first printed sea atlas in the 1580s, and in the great Mercator atlas of 1595, and the first works of Hondius, Blaeu, and Linschoten, all from about the time when Donato Bertelli finally first completed the Gastaldian four-continent set of ca. 1596, of which we shall speak in chapter twelve, in a sense the swan song of the Italian school. This was followed by further consolidation into Dutch hands of cartography in the seventeenth century in the works of Janssonius, the Danckaerts family, the Vissschers, Allard, De Wit, the Van Keulen family and others. But, besides this, from about the time of the founding of the Dutch East India Company, i.e., the VOC (Vereenigde Oost-Indische Compagnie) in 1602, to later in the century, the Dutch also contributed to exploration proper, mapping the Asian archipelago properly, uncovering large parts of Australia and New Zealand, as well as much of Japan, and the Asian east coast up to Sakhalin, considerably extending the basic world outline which Gastaldi had first established correctly. Also relevant to cartography, as we shall see, the Dutch invented the telescope in 1608,[24] and in the 1650s Christiaan Huygens invented the pendulum clock. Although Dutch navigators sometimes used magnetic declination to roughly judge the eastward longitudinal progress of the VOC's ships to the East Indies, they made little real progress in the old bugaboo of longitude determination. This was accomplished only by Cassini I in the 1670s to 1690s by observation of Jupiter's moons, but to do this successfully required both Lipposhay's telescopes and Huygens's pendulum clocks.

This very rapid survey of Gastaldi's successors is, as noted, useful for perspective purposes, but we have a second motive in presenting it. For

---

[23] Besides this, there were significant earlier signs of Low Country activity, as in Mercator's 1554 wall map of Europe, and his 1569 world, as well as the still earlier globes of Gemma from the 1530s, the great maps of Deventer, beginning also in the 1530s, and some others.

[24] The best candidate for the discovery would be Hans Lipposhay, but Zacharias Jansson, Jacob Metius, and others are also candidates.

there is an underlying great difference between the nature of the facts just related, and the fact of Gastaldi's accomplishment related above. That is, while the facts just presented make up a crucial phase in the history of cartography, and they have long been so recognized in the literature,[25] the achievement of Gastaldi is also a crucial historical fact in the history of cartography, but has, as we have pointed out, gone altogether unrecognized. Furthermore, the contribution of the Dutch period has been rather fully described and defined, as has been that of Ptolemy, and the French school which generally succeeded the Dutch school, and the English school which succeeded the French school. But the contribution of Gastaldi, the main representative of the Italian school, has remained in shadow, not fully described, unrecognized, and undefined. This, most likely, is mainly due to the simple fact that there have existed doubts about his authorship as concerns the depictions of Asia and the America, doubts which we remove with finality in chapters six (Asia) and seven to nine (America)

How Gastaldi could have accomplished what he did we have briefly hinted at earlier in this chapter. In our next chapter, we shall explore this in depth, giving full sources, and we shall bring out aspects of the question not yet touched upon, and end up with a picture which we believe is virtually full and complete.

---

[25] In recent years these facts have been brought into much clearer and more detailed view by the EXPLOKART project, for instance as to the production of atlases (Peter van der Krogt), and the production of separately published maps and sets of wall maps of the four continents (Günter Schilder), and in many other areas, but in a general way, the contribution of the Low Countries to the history of cartography has been recognized and defined in a general way for quite some time.

CHAPTER 4 - RAMUSIO AND GASTALDI: THE BACKGROUND AND SOURCES OF GASTALDI'S HALLMARK LATER MAPS

4.1 Preliminary Remarks

We saw in the first and third chapters that the set of large maps of continents and parts of continents which Gastaldi produced in his later years were preceded by two other projects which also aspired to some degree to provide modern cartographic coverage for all the world. It is valid to consider them as precursors to the later works. But the maps of these projects were quite small by comparison to the later maps, and very little of the vast panorama of place names and geographical features which we see on the later maps could have been mined from them. How indeed could Gastaldi have produced his Asia, his Africa, and his America, which suddenly produced a generally correct picture of the world beyond Europe where there had been nothing approaching it in general correctness before, in the short period of five years, from 1559 to 1564? A good part of the answer lies in the fact that Gastaldi was spared one of the most time consuming phases of map production that a cartographer must normally deal with, that is, the phase of information gathering. For, as we have suggested already, and shall now show in detail, Gastaldi to a great extent compiled these maps from the vast store of information which was made readily available to him by his friend Ramusio, information which the latter had been assiduously gathering over a period of many years, and which would ultimately be published as his famous collection, the *Navigazioni e viaggi*. We will first look at this great compilation and how it was put together, and then at Gastaldi's usage of it.

4.2 Ramusio and his "Navigazioni e viaggi"

Giovanni Battista Ramusio's *Navigazioni e viaggi* was published in Venice in three thick folio volumes by Tommaso Giunti, in 1550, 1556, and 1559.[1] This important compilation is, Skelton notes, "generally recognized as the first great collection of travel literature," and he continues: "His expressed purpose was the reform of modern geography and cartography; his plan, the publication of primary documents illustrating the most recent travels and discoveries in all parts of the earth; and his method, the critical selection of the best texts available, accompanied by commentaries. These editorial principles were already known and practiced in other fields, such as canon law and classical literature. By his application of them in the geographical field, Ramusio introduced, in the words of one of his more perceptive biographers, 'the concept of a documented history of travel and geography'."[2] Ramusio's work was just as striking an advance over its predecessors as Gastaldi's maps were over theirs. Skelton states plainly: "Ramusio had no precursors."[3] To be sure, there were two previous compilations of voyages and travels, Fracanzano da Montalboddo's *Paesi*

---

[1] Dates and volumes are not in sequence: vol. 1(1550), vol. 3(1556), vol. 2(1559). This was the first edition. There were five later editions of vol. 1, three of vol. 2, and two of vol. 3 (see Parks, 1970, 1 for details). For full titles, bibliographical details, and contents of all editions of all volumes, see Sabin (1868-1936, vol. 16, pp. 303-16). There have been two recent reprintings. The first is a three-volume facsimile edition containing an introduction by Raleigh Ashlin Skelton, and an analysis of contents by George B. Parks, published by the Theatrum Orbis Terrarum Ltd. Press in Amsterdam, 1967-70, which reprints the third (1563) edition of vol. 1, the third (1583) edition of vol. 2, and the third (1606) edition of vol. 3. The other modern edition is with reset modern type, in six volumes, two each for the original three volumes. It was published by Einaudi of Torino, 1978-1988, and is edited by Marica Milanesi. This last is unquestionably the best and most useable edition, containing extensive new indexes, with information on name variants and more at many of the entries, with a series of maps showing the routes covered in the various accounts, with solid and detailed introductory material at the head of each account, and with extensive notes throughout. This Milanesi edition is indispensable for anyone wishing to do serious work on the *Navigationi*. The full text of this edition has been now made available in digital form online, and is thus now a searchable text. On Ramusio himself, see Parks (1955), Skelton (1970), and esp. Milanesi (1984, 25-168), all with many further references.

[2] Skelton (1970, v). The "perceptive biographer" is Parks.

[3] Skelton (cit., xiv). In fact, one Alessandro Zorzi did make such a collection between 1507 and 1538, but he never reached publication (Donattini, 1992, 119-20). There is no evidence that Ramusio drew upon Zorzi's materials. (This is not the Alessandro Zorzi who is possibly author of charts ascribed to Bartolomeo Columbus).

novamente retrovati, published in 1507 in Vicenza,[4] and the 1532 Basel collection, *Novus Orbis*, put together by Simon Grynaeus and Johann Huttich, both of which were popular enough to be reprinted several times, and Skelton notices them. But, besides the fact that they were much more limited, single volume compilations, he observes that "the selection was . . . haphazard and confined to readily accessible materials,"[5] and that neither "provided a comprehensive and methodical synthesis of the new geographical knowledge won by the exploratory voyages."[6] He adds that, "Ramusio's technique as a collector and as an editor is in refreshing contrast" to them.[7]

Although there were three extra-European continents, and three huge volumes of the *Navigazioni*, there is not a clean correspondence between the two. Volume one, sometimes called the Africa volume, contains all of Ramusio's material on Africa, but it also contains all his material on southern Asia, from the Arabian Peninsula to the Moluccas.[8] Volume two is about travels and ventures in interior, more northern Asia. As Milanesi has pointed out, his divisions here are based upon trade routes rather than geographical

---

[4] On this collection see Schiavo Musi (1952). The collection treats Cadamosto, Cabral (with Sintra), Columbus, Vespucci, and Pasqualigo on the Corte Reals.

[5] Skelton (cit., xiv). The same observation is made by Nordenskiöld (1889, 105).

[6] Skelton (cit., vi).

[7] Skelton (cit., xiv). And he adds here on Ramusio that the "book has the formal completeness and unity which characterizes a work of art and enables it to satisfy the mind and ego." Parks noted that "the *Viaggi* is the first large published collection of historical documents other than collections of laws and decretals" (Parks, 1955, 127). Also John Locke, if the generally made attribution is correct, eulogizes "Ramusio's collection of voyages and travels, the most perfect work of that nature extant in any language whatsoever, containing all the discoveries to the east, west, north, and south; with full descriptions of all the countries discovered; judiciously compiled and free from that great mass of useless matter, which swells our English Hakluyt and Purchas; much more complete and full than the Latin de Brye, and in fine, the noblest work of this nature." From "An Explanatory Catalogue of Voyages and Geographical Works, by Mr. Locke," a separately paged appendix to Clarke (1803), at p. 173.

[8] It also oddly contains the accounts of one New World explorer, Vespucci.

entities.[9]   Volume three is consistent, being devoted to the New World.[10] Besides the accounts of voyages and explorations which are the main bulk of the work, there is considerable auxiliary material, most of it interesting commentaries by Ramusio.[11]   The first edition of volume two was much smaller than the other two volumes, due to the loss, in a printing house fire, of much worked up manuscript material, as we are informed by Giunti in his preface to that volume.   In the second edition of 1574, volume two had become comparable in size to the other volumes due to the addition of considerable material, and it seems likely that some or all of the added items were among the material which had been intended for the original edition.

It will be useful to us to cite some further facts concerning Ramusio to underline how extensive and far-reaching his collecting activities were. Ramusio's activity as a collector and editor of accounts of exploration and travel extend over at least thirty years, from about 1525 to the mid-1550s. Throughout this time, and indeed before and after it, Ramusio occupied important positions in the service of the Venetian state, from 1515 to 1553 as secretary of the Senate, and from 1553 until his death in 1557 as secretary to the powerful Council of Ten,[12] and this brought him into regular contact with various highly placed persons and much assisted him in the gathering of accounts which would otherwise have probably been impossible to obtain. Important personages from whom Ramusio obtained or probably obtained materials included Andrea Navagero, Venetian ambassador to Spain and

[9] See Milanesi (1984, 40-44, 50-51 and 54-56).

[10] There is also mention of a proposed fourth volume, which did not materialize, although it's not quite clear exactly what it was to contain. It was evidently to deal with parts of South America, but perhaps also the Pacific and the unknown Southern Continent. See Ramusio (1967-70, 1, second page of Giunti's "alli lettori;" and 3, 309v-310r; respectively in Milanesi ed., 1978-88, 1, 8; and VI, 667-71.) See also on this Milanesi (1984, 41, 55, 59, 60; and our chapter two, note 117).

[11] There are about 110 pages of this material, exclusive of indexes, on which see below. Cicogna gives a very convenient and complete list, with comments, of all of Ramusio's commentaries in the *Navigationi* (Cicogna, 1824-53, 2, 322-24).

[12] It is widely but erroneously stated that Ramusio was secretary to the Council of Ten from 1533. But it was precisely on July 7, 1553 that Ramusio became secretary to the council. Fabris (1989, 10 and 14) quotes the original document. The mistaken idea arose from a typographical error of "1533" for "1553" in the following passage from Cicogna: "Del 1533 a' 7 di luglio fu ascritto fra' Secretarii del Consiglio de' Dieci" (Cicogna, 1824-53, vol. 2, 316). The date is the same to the day of Ramusio's dedication to Fracastoro at the head of his edition of Marco Polo in vol. two of the *Navigationi*, and that dedication has the feel of having been brought to an end abruptly and perhaps prematurely.

close friend of Ramusio;[13] Diego Hurtado de Mendoza, Spanish ambassador to Venice and brother of Antonio Mendoza, first and most famous viceroy of New Spain in America;[14] Francesco Contarini, Venetian ambassador to Flanders;[15] Damião de Góis, Portuguese humanist and chronicler;[16] Gonzalo Fernandez de Oviedo, official Spanish chronicler of the Indies (America) and not only a friend and frequent correspondent of Ramusio,[17] but also a long-time business partner;[18] and Pietro Bembo, Cardinal and lifelong friend of Ramusio, himself in contact with New World figures.[19]

Nevertheless, even with such connections, Ramusio had sometimes to go to much trouble obtaining items. He tells us he obtained his Barbosa account "con grandissima fatica, & difficoltà" (with the greatest efforts and difficulty),[20] and he finally obtained a copy of Conti's voyages "dopo molte fatiche spese in vano" (after many efforts spent in vain),[21] only to find it was defective, forcing him to use a different text.[22] Tommaso Giunti, publisher of the *Navigazioni*, in his notice to the reader in volume two says Ramusio collected his materials "cõ incredibile diligenza & giudicio" (with incredible diligence and judgment). Clearly Ramusio went to great pains to collect his materials. In a letter to Ramusio of February 14, 1539, his long-time friend, the physician and poet Girolamo Fracastoro, jests with him about his "correspondence" from the New World, Greenland, the Equator, and the

---

[13] Skelton (cit., vii-viii); Parks (1955, 134-38).

[14] Parks (1955, 130-31, 142 and 145; and 1970, 32). Diego supplied Gastaldi with the materials for his 1544 map of Spain, as we have seen above.

[15] Parks (1955, 130, 144, 145; and 1970, 32).

[16] Parks (1955, 146), and Skelton (1970, viii-ix).

[17] Parks (1955, 139, 141-42, 143).

[18] Gerbi (1985, 165-73 and, reproducing the original contract, 411-16), and Milanesi (1984, 65-66).

[19] Parks (1955, 145, 147).

[20] Ramusio (1967-70, 1, 287v; Milanesi ed., 1978-88, 2, 541.)

[21] Ramusio (1967-70, 1, 338r; Milanesi ed., 1978-88, 2, 785.)

[22] Parks (1970, 13).

North and South Poles.[23]   In quite a few cases it is not known from whence Ramusio got his sources.

Many of the accounts in the *Navigazioni* were original with Ramusio. They had never been published anywhere before, and some remain to this day the only source for certain explorations.   They include such important items as Leo Africanus's lengthy description of the central and western parts of the whole of the north half of Africa, based on personal travels and observations in the 1520s.   The also lengthy account of Francisco Alvarez, covering the eastern part of northern Africa, based on observations made in the 1520s, is partly original, collating a manuscript account which the Portuguese Damão de Gois provided Ramusio with a published text of 1540.[24]   Completely original are Thome Lopez's valuable account of India, Barbosa's account of southeast Africa, India and places between, Tomé Pires's famous "Suma oriental," covering south and southeast Asia and China, some original Jesuit communications from Japan, and Giovanmaria Angiolello's historical and geographical account of Persia.   Ramusio's famous version of Marco Polo, of which he was especially proud,[25] even though it was among the four items not from the sixteenth century, contains much which is original. Although Polo, of course, had been available before, Ramusio compiled his version from several manuscripts unknown before, and a huge portion of it is entirely new in Ramusio.   Perhaps most impressive of all was the number of previously unknown accounts dealing with the New World in volume three, including a valuable anonymous relation on Cortes, and original accounts of the explorations of Nuño de Guzman, Francisco Ulloa, Vasquez de Coronado, Marco da Nizza, Hernando Alarcón, Fernando Pizarro, Francisco de Orellano, Giovanni Verrazzano, and Jacques Cartier's first voyage. Although several of these are not among the lengthiest items, many were the only accounts of their respective discoveries available.   While just under a third of the total bulk of the *Navigazioni* is

---

[23] Parks (1955, 140), and Skelton (1970, ix). Fracastoro also helped Ramusio obtain materials, as see our Cartobibliography entry no. (81.-86.).

[24] Skelton (1970, viii-ix).

[25] He devotes twenty-seven pages of introductory material to it, several times longer than the introductory material to any other account.

original materials, it still amounts to some 656 folio pages of new information.

But the bringing together and rendering into a single vernacular of the other, non-original accounts, those which had already been printed, was of no mean significance in itself for cartography. It is worth reminding ourselves that the considerable advances made by Waldseemüller in the 1516 *Carta marina* were, as he tells us himself, principally based on accounts which had been brought together by Montalboddo and published as his *Paesi*, and, although all the accounts had been published separately before, it was from this compilation that Waldseemüller took his information. Gathering information to make maps of far countries was clearly not an easy thing to do at the time, even if the accounts were in print. E. G. R. Taylor, in cataloging some early English geographical libraries, noted that: "Much critical work on early maps and documents is vitiated by the assumption that the early author had access to all the material in existence when he wrote. Such was not the case: libraries even so complete as the two cataloged were very rare indeed, and many books . . . were practically unprocurable."[26] Thus, printed materials were also sometimes hard to come by. Ramusio tells us, for instance, that he had great trouble getting a copy of the printed account of Conti's voyage,[27] and he succeeded only with difficulty in obtaining a mutilated copy of Alvarez's book.[28] Obtaining a representative assortment of accounts covering the many rapidly occurring advances in geographical knowledge was clearly not an easy thing. We recall that, as astonishing as it seems, there had been no real advances in the cartographic picture from the time of Waldseemüller's 1516 *Carta marina*. There had been nothing but sketchy and inferior maps such as those of Münster and Honter. Yet it was precisely in this period between Waldseemüller and Gastaldi that the far-reaching explorations of Coronado, Pizarro, Verrazzano, Cartier, and many

[26] Taylor (1930, 162). The two libraries were those of Dee and Lumley. Compare what Taylor says with the findings of Lavis-Trafford, who makes it clear that the picture on sixteenth century maps is by no means an accurate reflection of the total of topographical information available at the time (1950, 15-16, 25-31, 47-50, 57, 85, 107-08, 123), though here he is speaking of European areas, especially Piedmont.

[27] Ramusio (1967-70, 1, 338r; Milanesi ed., 1978-88, 2, 785.)

[28] Parks (1970, 9).

others for America, and of Magellan, Gaetano, and Villalobos for the Pacific and the Asian archipelago, had occurred. All of these and more were gathered by Ramusio and included in his *Navigazioni*, and all were used by Gastaldi, as we will see.

To really get a full measure of the quantity and variety of materials gathered by Ramusio one needs to peruse Parks's extensive catalog of the contents,[29] or to peruse the collections themselves. Still another revealing measure of the great bulk of information brought together is provided by a perusal of Ramusio's extensive, though nevertheless inadequate, indexes to the *Navigazioni*.[30] Each volume contains a lengthy index of places, persons, and subjects, for a total of 158 pages of index. My own rapid examinations show there to be just short of 5,000 place names in the index, and since my investigations also show there to be a good number of places missed in the indexes,[31] the number is surely closer to 6,000 and very possibly more. Here was a harvest indeed for replacing the Ptolemaic corpus, and we recall that it all refers to lands beyond Europe. The Italian historian Giovanni Nicolo Doglioni said that "Ramusio has replaced in authority the writings of Ptolemy, Strabo, and Pliny."[32] Nothing close to Ramusio's mass of information had ever been gathered together before, and wouldn't be again until later in the century in England, with Hakluyt. We should add, too, that Ramusio generally omitted materials connected with the exploits at arms of the explorers and similar material, concentrating in particular on geographical information.[33]

We have noted that Ramusio's stated purpose, in gathering all these accounts, was to provide the materials from which better, modern maps could be made. Let us now look at this in Ramusio's own words. In the dedication to Fracastoro at the head of volume one, on Africa and Asia,

---

[29] Parks (1970).

[30] Only the first edition of volume one had no index.

[31] The thorough indexes in Milanesi's edition pick up all places in the work.

[32] Doglioni (1594). I quote from the 1605 edition, p. 485, after Lach (1965-1993, 2, 1, 333, note 214).

[33] See, for instance, what he says in this regard in his notice to the reader at the head of his extracts from Barros in 1554. (Ramusio (1967-70, 1, 384r; Milanesi ed., 1978-88, 2, 1043.)

having expressed the desire that his work might be a thing of wonder for men of letters and science, he then becomes more specific:

Ma la cagione che mi fece affaticar volentieri in questa opera, fu, che vedendo, & considerando le tauole della Geografia di Tolomeo, doue si descriue l'Africa, & la India esser molto imperfette, rispetto alla gran cognitione che si ha hoggi di quelle regioni, ho stimato douer esser caro, & forse non poco vtile al mondo il mettere insieme le narrationi de gli scrittori de' nostri tempi, che sono stati nelle sopradette parti del mondo, & di quelle han parlato minutamente, alle quali aggiugnendo la descrittion delle carte marine Portoghesi, si potrian fare altre tante tauole, che sarebbero di grandissima satisfattione à quelli che si dilettano di tal cognitione, perche sarian certi de i gradi delle larghezze, & lunghezze almanco delle marine di tutte queste parti, & de' nomi de luoghi, città, & signori, che vi habitano al presente, & potrian conferirle con quell tanto, che ne hanno scritto gli auttori antichi. (But the reason which made me toil gladly in this work was that seeing and considering that the maps of Ptolemy's *Geographia* describing Africa and India were very imperfect in respect to the great knowledge that we have of these regions, I thought it proper and perhaps not a little useful to bring together the narrations of writers of our day who have been in the aforesaid parts of the world and spoken of them in detail, so that, supplementing them from the description in the Portuguese nautical charts, other maps could be made to give the greatest satisfaction to those who take pleasure in such knowledge, for they will be certain of the degrees of latitude and longitude at least of the coasts and all those parts, and of the names of places, cities, and kingdoms, which there are at present, and will be able to make comparison with that which the ancient authors have written about them).[34]

[34] Ramusio (1967-70, 1, second page of dedication to Fracastoro; Milanesi ed., 1978-88, 1, 4-5) Translation adapted from that of Skelton (1970, vii). In Ramusio's various commentaries to many of his accounts, there are endless references to things now known which were unknown to the ancients. Ramusio's remark here that via his materials scholars would now be certain of the longitudes of places must be taken with a grain of salt, as we shall see towards the end of this chapter.

While, as we have seen, a small start had been made towards achieving this with the maps produced for the volumes themselves, these were pitifully inadequate for displaying the vast amount of data accumulated by Ramusio.

4.3 Ramusio and Gastaldi

To anyone even partially familiar with the nature and content of Ramusio's *Navigazioni*, the nature and content of Gastaldi's large maps of continents or parts of continents, and the clear connections between the two men, the suggestion that Gastaldi obtained the information for his maps from Ramusio's collection of exploratory accounts comes naturally. At least four scholars have made categorical (indeed, too categorical, as we shall see), statements to that effect. First Nordenskiöld in 1897, even before anyone had really touched upon the question of Gastaldi's sources, had written of Ramusio, "It is a natural supposition that the learned geographer and collector of such an influential position in Venice, who had for forty years been the Secretary of the Council of Ten,[35] had provided Gastaldi with the new material for the large maps of Africa and Asia."[36] Next, Grande, in 1905, who has been speaking of the Gastaldi maps in the *Navigazioni*, states, "the Ramusian collection is without doubt the principal source of Gastaldi, not only for these, but for all the other geographical maps. In fact, one can affirm, without fear of error, that all the copious Gastaldian cartographic production has its scientific basis in the work of Ramusio."[37] Grande, in this blanket statement, carelessly fails to specify that he has in mind Gastaldi maps of extra-European areas, for the *Navigazioni* deal, of course, only with Africa, Asia, and America, and obviously could have had no influence on Gastaldi's many maps of European areas.[38] More recently, in 1970, Skelton

---

[35] This of course is an error, as we have seen.

[36] Nordenskiöld (1897, 161). Note that Nordenskiöld appends: "As far as is at present known, Gastaldi has not issued any equally important map of the New World." No copy of Gastaldi's America had yet turned up when Nordenskiöld wrote (see chapter nine).

[37] Grande (1905, "relazioni," 186).

[38] Nor, of course, could Ramusio have influenced Gastaldi's manuscript maps made for the Venetian Republic.

stated, more carefully, that "Gastaldi's largest maps are associated directly with the texts printed in the . . . volumes of the *Navigazioni*, from which are derived their new geographical concepts and much of their nomenclature."[39] Finally, in 1993, Milanesi says, "in the maps of [Gastaldi] are rendered graphically, in all likelihood, the cosmographical opinions of Ramusio, and, with certainty, the information collected by him on the various parts of the world, and published in the *Navigazioni e viaggi*. This is evident both in the content of his continental and regional maps, as well as in his very successful world maps (*universali*), the prototype of which was engraved in copper and printed at Venice in 1546."[40]

We must make one significant qualification to all this right from the start, besides the obvious one concerning maps of European areas. None of these writers thought to make mention of the role of navigational charts in Gastaldi's maps. We recall that the proposed program outlined by Ramusio himself for making modern maps of the world outside Europe specified that the coasts ("le marine") would be taken from navigational charts, while the inland ("fra terra") would be taken from the accounts in the *Navigazioni*, and as we shall see, both in our text and countless times in our cartobibliography entries, Gastaldi did take most of his coastlines from such charts. But for the interiors of the continents, the general observations of these scholars have been quite borne out by the work of other scholars. The author has been gathering information on Gastaldi's sources for many years, some of it hidden in obscure places. The following paragraphs, which do not represent original scholarship on the part of the writer, but a consolidation of the work of many scholars published during the course of a century or more, should establish with finality the general validity of the observations of the above scholars. We will start with Africa.

Renato Biasutti made an in-depth study of Gastaldi's 1564 Africa in 1920,[41] including a full investigation of its sources. The coastlines and some coastal hydrography are from nautical charts, especially those by Portuguese

---

[39] Skelton (1970, xii.)

[40] Milanesi (1993, 45).

[41] Biasutti (1920).

cartographers, but also some from the Dieppe school.[42]   But the
overwhelming majority, probably at least 90%, of interior features, including
toponymy, hydrography, orography and information given in short legends,
is from Ramusio, principally from the accounts of Leo Africanus and
Francisco Alvarez for all of the north half of the continent, and João de
Barros for southern Africa, though there are also elements from the accounts
of Alvise Cadamosto, Andrea Corsali, Duarte Barbosa, et al.[43]   Biasutti
believed that the map had been drawn some years before it was first
published, in two stages, one in 1544-45, and the second around 1554, after
the first parts of Barros had been obtained.[44] The first draft was "conducted
almost exclusively on the geographical material which Ramusio was
gathering," and it was brought up to date about 1554, "utilizing the
information of de Barros."[45]   Ramusio, he says, "must have furnished to
Gastaldi the new geographical materials which he was collecting for the
Navigazioni, perhaps discussed with him the value and interpretation of
given data, and arrived with him at the intention of renewing the map of the
immense continent on the bases of modern geography alone," and concludes:
"The map of Africa is in reality a new proof of the intellectual affinity, the
genuine friendship and of the profound esteem which bound the two men,
and simultaneously attests to the skill and the erudition of both."[46] The map,
however, does contain, out of about 1,200 place names, some eighty-five
names which are not from Ramusio or the sea charts.[47]   There are also a few
isolated gleanings from other sources, such as four names in Egypt taken
from Ziegler,[48] and there are still traces from Ptolemy, as there would be on
all maps for over 200 years, especially as regards the concept of the south
central African lakes system from which the Nile and other rivers were taken

---

[42] Biasutti (1920, 330, 332, 333-35, 340, 345, 393-94, 403); he identifies some of the charts.

[43] Biasutti (1920, 333, 337-43, 346, 394-97, 416, 419, 433).

[44] Barros first appeared in the *Navigationi* in the 1554 second edition of volume one. Its first appearance in
Portuguese was in 1552.

[45] Biasutti (1920, 433).

[46] Biasutti (1920, 419).

[47] Biasutti lists them at pp. 398-404, and gives hypothetical sources for some of them, but many are
completely unidentified.

[48] Biasutti (1920, 337).

as arising. This lake region, however, is only partly after Ptolemy, for much of this too is after Barros.

Other scholars who have dealt with the question of the map's sources have come to the same conclusion as Biasutti, including Skelton: "The interior of equatorial and northern Africa, in Gastaldi's map, is drawn almost wholly from materials published in 1550 in the first volume of Ramusio's *Viaggi*, namely the "Description of Africa" by Leo Africanus and the "Relation" of Alvares.[49] As regards southeast Africa, the Congo, and the south central African hydrographical system, other scholars' studies are also in line with Biasutti. Randles determines that these areas are mostly from Barros,[50] as do other scholars.[51]

We are not fortunate enough to have, for the other two extra-European continents, such clear and unequivocal assessments as those given by Biasutti and Skelton for Africa. Nevertheless, what we do have also points squarely enough to Ramusio as Gastaldi's main source. Stefano Grande in 1905 made a book-length study of all of Gastaldi's maps of America which were known at that time (the maps of parts of America in Gastaldi's 1548 Ptolemy, and in the *Navigazioni* itself) and states that the *Navigazioni* is "the principal source of Gastaldi."[52] Other than for coastal areas, in every instance where Grande identifies a source for data on the map, the source is Ramusio, and in most instances the source was used before it had been published.[53] It was in this same year that Grande expressed his opinion, quoted above, that all of Gastaldi's cartography is from Ramusio. Again, we must not forget that the coasts are taken from nautical charts, which Grande

---

[49] Skelton (1961, 562). So closely does the map follows its sources, he says, that Alvarez's "Itineraries can readily be followed on the map" (1961, 567), and "the map serves as a graphic index to Alvarez's text." (Skelton, 1962, 83).

[50] Randles (1958, 132-36, 143, 145-49). He says that it sticks to Ptolemy in some details, however (140-41).

[51] Simar (1919, 39), and Schilling (1892, 488 and 495-96).

[52] Grande (1905, *carte*, 70).

[53] Grande (cit., 38, 39, 45, 55, 56, 57, 59-60, 60, 61, 80, 82, 83, 88). For conclusive evidence that Gastaldi's late America from the 1559-1564 Gastaldi-Licinio period (Cartobibliography no. 94), which was unknown to Grande, was compiled principally from sources compiled by Ramusio, with lesser information from Gomara, see chapter nine.

identifies mostly as being those of Ribero, Agnese, and Maggiolo.[54] Also, as was the case with the Africa, a few data are from sources other than Ramusio. For instance, the name *Sierras Nevadas* appears on the map of the Western Hemisphere on the northwest coast in about 41°.[55] The name is from the Cabrillo voyage, not in Ramusio, and can only have been taken from Francisco López de Gómara's *Historia general de las Indias*, published in Saragossa in 1552-53, where the toponym occurs in a small list of names assigned during the voyage. More Cabrillo names also appear on the northwest coast on the ca. 1561 Gastaldi world map in the British Library, *Cosmographia vniversalis*, but the great majority are clearly from Ramusio.

For Asia, we do have several studies which touch upon the question of Gastaldi's sources, most of them in regard to the large 1559-61 three-part Asia which is of greatest interest to us, and again, the findings are that the main source is Ramusio, although we must always presume that for the coastlines, the source was Portuguese nautical charts. Unfortunately, the studies deal only with certain parts of Asia. The daunting task of sifting through all the voluminous material on Asia in Ramusio, and comparing it with the discouragingly extensive toponymy on the three parts of Asia has never yet been undertaken.[56] The first to identify Ramusio as a Gastaldi source for Asia was Nordenskiöld, in an 1899 study.[57] Nordenskiöld was not making a general comparison of Asian materials from Ramusio and Gastaldi's Asia. He was interested only in the version of Marco Polo's travels which was in the *Navigazioni*. He found that, "in the interior of Asia, from Mesopotamia to the Pacific, we find almost all those names which are used in the description of Marco Polo's travels, and with an orthography which, barring some few systematic alterations, is identical with that used in Ramusio's celebrated *Delle Navigazioni e Viaggi*.[58] The same comparison

---

[54] Grande (cit., 44, 51, etc.).

[55] Wagner (1937, 46).

[56] Almagià apparently intended to publish such a study. Speaking of the Asia in 1948, he said: "For a detailed study on the sources of this Gastaldi map I refer to a work of mine of proximate publication," (1948, 37), but no such study appeared.

[57] Nordenskiöld (1899).

[58] Nordenskiöld (cit., 400).

was made in 1955 by Rodolfo Gallo, who arrived at the same conclusion,[59] and also showed there could be no doubt that Gastaldi took his names *directly* from Ramusio's Polo, while Nordenskiöld had entertained also the alternate possibility that both were from some earlier common source. There are of course many names and features on Gastaldi's Asia which are not in Ramusio's Polo, including not only all in those areas not covered by Polo, but also some in the areas covered by him, as Nordenskiöld notes. He observes, as would be expected, that coastal or island names are taken from navigational charts.[60] Nordenskiöld loosely mentions the possibility that information from Venetian or Fugger archives may have been used, a random suggestion which has been picked up by some later writers. Why Nordenskiöld did not mention the obvious and much more likely possibility that the many names not found in Polo were taken from the extensive materials in the accounts of Duarte Barbosa, Giosofat Barbaro, Ambrogio Contarini, Hayton Armenio, Giovanmaria Angiolello, Nicolo Conti, Lodovico Varthema, Andrea Corsali, Tomé Pires, João de Barros, and a good many others, all in the same volume with Polo, I don't know. Perhaps he felt that he would be opening himself to reproach for not having checked those himself, but so far no one has.

Both Gezelius and Dahlgren in 1910 and 1911 identify the letters from Jesuit missionaries published in the second edition of Ramusio's first volume in 1554 as the source for Japan (*Giapan*) on Gastaldi's map.[61] Speaking of the great Lake Chiamay of Further India and the river systems connected with it, which occur in literature for the first time in those parts of Barros which were published in Ramusio, Hedin, discussing Gastaldi's Asia, says: "The hydrography is in perfect accordance with the text of

---

[59] Gallo (1955, 212-13 and 224-31).

[60] Nordenskiöld (cit., 400).

[61] Gezelius (1910, 134), and Dahlgren (1911, 20).

Ramusio."[62]   Almagià recognizes the influence of Hayton Armenio, in Ramusio's volume two, in Gastaldi's depiction of the area of the Altai Mountains in Central Asia on Gastaldi's map of the continent (1948, 64). In discussing the letters of Andrea Corsali, which deal with his voyage to Abyssinia, Arabia, and India, Luzio writes that: "They were certainly used, in the Ramusio edition, by Giacomo Gastaldi, who draws from them a number of data for his well-known map of Asia, as is revealed by the identity of form of spelling of various names of places and from several short legends which appear in this and which have complete correspondence with the information given by Corsali."[63]   Luzio does not make an in-depth survey, giving only a sampling of names and legends dealing with Abyssinia, Arabia and the Persian Gulf.   Most recently, Suarez identifies Antonio Pigafetta's account of Magellan's voyage, and, to a lesser degree, Maximilian Transilvanus's account of the same, both in Ramusio, as the principal source for archipelagic Asia on Gastaldi's maps of Asia, both those on the 1554 map of southeast Asia in volume one of the *Navigazioni*, and the great 1559-61 Asia in three parts.[64] Without giving specifics, Suarez cites as lesser sources Oviedo and an account of a voyage of Ruy Lopez de Villalobos and Juan Gaetano, both in Ramusio, and a voyage of Loaysa and Salazar, not in Ramusio. Since the areas dealt with by Suarez are largely island areas, we can safely assume that much is from Portuguese sea charts.[65]

.

---

[62] Hedin (1917, 232). See also Hedin (1919, 317-18), on the same. This was also the source for this lake and its rivers on the Gastaldi map of eastern Asia in Ramusio's 1554 edition of volume two, although here the correspondence is less perfect, for here Gastaldi has only four rivers leaving the lake instead of six as in the Barros text (Hedin, 1917, 231). Perhaps the much smaller scale made it impracticable to include all the rivers in the Ramusio map.

[63] Luzio (1947, 26-27).

[64] Suarez (1999, 130-57). Suarez nowhere specifically identifies the Pigafetta and Maximilian texts used as those printed in Ramusio, but we can assume these were the ones used. The Ramusio text of Pigafetta, an abridged account, which had been published before (Parks, 1970, 14), was the only version available at the time. The full text did not become available until 1800 (Parks, cit., 14; and Skelton (Pigafetta), 1969, 15-18). Ramusio knew of the full account, but he was unsuccessful in obtaining it, and concluded that it had been lost in the sack of Rome (Gerbi, 1985, 100).

[65] Suarez does not specifically state this, just mentioning loosely "Portuguese sources," or similar phrases (cit., 131, 142, 147), but from what we have seen already, and according to Ramusio's own words, it is undoubtedly the case.

There is no more, I think.[66]   In any event, no more has come to my attention in many years of investigating Gastaldi.   Large parts of Gastaldi's Asia are not touched in these studies, and no areas have been exhaustively researched.   No general study for the continent has been done, as was done for Africa by Biasutti, and America by Grande.   In a very general way, we do have some assurance that Gastaldi's three parts of Asia would be mainly from Ramusio, for Biasutti's observation that the 1554 maps of Asia in Ramusio "are a schematic reduction of" the 1559-61 maps is clearly in the main correct,[67] and Ramusio himself says that the 1554 maps are taken, for the coasts, from Portuguese nautical charts, and for the inland, from the accounts in the *Navigazioni*.   However, apart from the fact that the chronology of the comparison is obviously backwards, and the fact that the later maps reach 15°-20° higher than the 1554 maps, the late Asia contains many times more names.   What makes it likely that Ramusio is the main source across the three parts of Asia is just that all studies which have touched on the question of Gastaldi's sources for Asia, have identified the *Navigazioni* as the main or only source, while no study has demonstrated otherwise, and we know Ramusio is the main source for Africa and America. These things, together with the facts that Ramusio's stated purpose in gathering his accounts was to provide the material to make better modern maps, that Gastaldi made just such a set of maps, and that Ramusio and Gastaldi were closely connected, certainly make valid the conjecture that Ramusio was just as much Gastaldi's main source for Asia as he was for Africa and America.   Indeed, it is hard to imagine that Gastaldi did not make use of those extensive modern Asian materials in the *Navigazioni* which have not been investigated yet.

As with Africa and America, there are minor exceptions.   We have already mentioned that Suarez mentions data from the Loaysa voyage, of

---

[66] Two other scholars who deal with Gastaldi's Asian cartography treat the question of his sources only as regards the maps in the *Navigationi* itself. They too mention no other source than Ramusio. Unno says "almost all of the place-names found in Ramusio's [Gastaldi's] map of the East Indies correspond to those in Barros's description," meaning Barros as in Ramusio (Unno, 1985, 291). Abendanon identifies Celebes as coming from Barbosa in Ramusio (Abendanon, 1915-18, 4, p. 1899).

[67] Biasutti (1923, 308).

which there is no account in Ramusio, and the northmost parts of the First Part of Asia no doubt contains information from Herberstein, which we can assume Gastaldi knew, since he made the map which appears in the 1550 Italian edition of Herberstein's work.[68]   Also, as with Africa, there remain some traces of Ptolemy, as there would in all maps of those continents at least to the seventeenth century.   His dependence on him however, was not great. Hedin, surveying the old cartography of India stated:

> A great stride in the right direction is marked by Jacopo Gastaldi's epoch-making map of India from the year 1561.   It is only in the hydrography of the Ganges and the Indus that Ptolemy can be traced, but for the rest, he has completely disappeared.   Gastaldi is not satisfied with the classical names of the Himalayas; he speaks instead of Monte Dalangver, M. Naugracot and M. Ussonte. Of Tibet he has nothing to tell, but of the regions surrounding it he gives so ingenious a representation, that one almost has a foreboding that the unknown land will soon appear of its own accord.[69]

Most likely these great advances in India are due to accounts from Ramusio, the most likely accounts being those of Barbosa, Varthema, Corsali, Lopez, Conti, and Pires.

All in all, although a definitive statement can be made only after a one-to-one check of Ramusian vs. Gastaldian place names has been undertaken,[70] everything indicates that our hypothesis that Gastaldi's Asia is

---

[68] The *Navigationi* contains Herberstein, but only beginning with the 1574 second edition of volume two. It's possible it was intended for the first edition of 1559, for we know much material for that volume was destroyed in the printing house fire of 1557 (Parks, 1970, 17).

[69] Hedin (1917, vol. 1, xxv). Hedin says that Gastaldi's interior of Asia is better than Witsen's of 1687 (xxvi-xxvii).

[70] For the scholar who would undertake this task, there exist several aids. Ramusio's original indexes, as faulty as they are, could be useful, as also the lists of ancient and modern names accompanying Gastaldi's Parts of Asia, which include full coordinates for the places listed for the first two Parts of Asia. Most important, indeed indispensable, are Milanesi's new indexes to her edition, which include variants, modern equivalents, and comments. She also has route and itinerary maps. Her text, as mentioned, is also available in digital form, although the indexes and maps are available only in the printed edition. The great problem is orthographical inconsistency. The age is notorious for this, and Gastaldi is among the worst offenders.

principally based on Ramusio seems quite justified. There is, however, one other source I am aware of which Gastaldi might have made some use of, and it should be mentioned here.

The great official Portuguese chronicler João de Barros, parts of whose *Decades* are published in volume one of the *Navigazioni*, was also compiling a Latin *Geographia universalis* with maps,[71] and omitted much geographical description from his *Decades*, reserving it for the *Geography*. Barros, renowned as a geographer, used Arabic, Persian and, especially, Chinese geographical works, for the translation of which he had educated slaves,[72] and of course he had access to all the Portuguese accounts, and the Portuguese nautical charts. Cortesão wrote that, "Judging from the accuracy and richness of the numerous geographical descriptions he wrote in the *Decades*, those "tables" must have been of the greatest interest and undoubtedly presented the most advanced knowledge of the time."[73] The first draft of the *Geography* was virtually complete when Barros died in 1570, but it is not known what became of it. Barros refers to it several times in his *Decades*,[74] including three times in his book nine, chapter one, which is one of the Barros chapters which Ramusio prints.[75] In the second of these three references, he also mentions maps of his cosmography which are taken from a printed Chinese cosmography. Again, Ramusio, in his preface to Polo in his volume two, makes reference to some facts concerning Cathay and India, "come nella tauole della Geographia delle Illustre Sig. Gio. De Barros Portughese si potrà copiosamente uedere" (as one will be able to see copiously in the maps of the *Geography* of the illustrious Mr. João de

---

[71] Baião (1932 and 1945-46), Lach (1965-1993, 1, 192, note 207, 413, 504, 756), and Boxer (1981, 115 and 130).

[72] Boxer (1981, 119), Harrison (1961, 158). On Chinese maps used and seen by him, including a printed Chinese cosmography, see Boxer, 106. The Chinese cosmography was probably something like the *Guang yutu* of Luo Hongxian of ca. 1555, on which see Yee (1994, "Reinterpreting," 50-51 and 59-60) Yee (1994, "Taking," 125), and Ledyard (1994, 241).

[73] Cortesão (1960, 5, 180).

[74] Baião (1945-46, 1, lvi) gives all the places in the *Decades* where it is referred to.

[75] Ramusio (1967-70, 1, 388r, 388v, 390v; respectively, in Milanesi ed., 1978-88, 2, 1060, 1061 and 1071). Each time he refers specifically to the *maps* of the *Geography*.

Barros).[76] Kazutaka Unno feels Ramusio may have seen and used Barros's *Geography*,[77] and Sven Hedin felt quite certain that he had,[78] and if Ramusio saw and used it, we can safely assume Gastaldi did as well. Personally, I do not think this likely. We know of no direct contact between Ramusio and Barros, as there was with Oviedo, and it's hard to imagine that a copy of a work just in stages of completion could have been provided to Ramusio, although it's not impossible that some parts were. I also suspect that certain features of the south and southeast Asian coast which would surely have been on Barros's maps, since they are on several Portuguese nautical charts of the time,[79] such as the bulge of Further India, would have been on Gastaldi's Asias if he had seen Barros's maps, but they are not there. This is

---

[76] Ramusio (1967-70, 2, fol. 5r [1st pagination]; Milanesi ed., 1978-88, 3, 28). Ramusio also refers to the Chinese cosmography mentioned by Barros, and also perhaps refers again to the *Geography* (although the passages are not clear), in three other places (cit., 1, in the short text preceding the maps near the head of the volume, and at fols. 377v and 384r; respectively in Milanesi ed., 1978-88, 1, [911]; 2, 109; and 2, 1043).

[77] Unno (1985, 291).

[78] Hedin (1919, 315-16).

[79] See Cortesão (1960, all vol. 1).

not conclusive, however, and the possibility does exist that Gastaldi might have seen and used Barros's maps.[80]

4.4 By Way of Closing

We have come to the end of our chapter. It is not a very long one. But, by virtue of the invaluable light it throws on Gastaldi's most important cartographic work, it is one of the most important chapters of our book, important enough that, to deepen our perspective of it, it will be well worth recounting it from a different vantage point, followed by making a few relevant observations which we have not yet made.

---

[80] We should note, finally, that there is a certain amount of fictional information on Gastaldi's maps, as there is on all cartographers' maps of the far continents, but we cannot say that they represent invention on the part of Gastaldi personally, even though it is true that Gastaldi has twice been accused of including fictitious places on his maps, once by an ancient and once by a modern writer. Antoine Baudrand in 1683 speaks of "fictitious, that is, nonexistent and never having existed, cities and places indicated on maps, and above all on the Venetian ones of Giacomo Gastaldi." (quoted after Milanesi [1994, 453]), although Vitale Terrarossa rises up in defense three years later in a different work (Milanesi, cit., 453-54). Albert Kammerer claims that part of Gastaldi's Arabic nomenclature in Arabia is fantasy (Kammerer, 1952, 27), and we may add to Kammerer's observation that certainly part of Gastaldi's geography of Arabia is necessarily fantastic. For Gastaldi fills the Arabian peninsula with a number of kingdoms, and their cities, and he does this for southeast Arabia as well as the rest, although we know that, then as now, there is nothing in inland southeast Arabia except the great Rub-al-Kali desert. However, in neither case can we be sure that the fantasies are of Gastaldi's invention. We have seen in the present chapter that the principal source and inspiration for Gastaldi were Ramusio's numerous accounts, but we have also seen that he did have other sources, sometimes fairly significant, as Gomara for America, and there are likely some sources still unidentified for other continents. In Near Asia, for instance, either Michel Membré (see Cartobibliography entry no. 69) or Guillaume Postel (see chapter five), who had been to and returned from the Near East, could have brought back so far unidentified texts, and it is certainly possible that Gastaldi unwittingly copied some false data from such unknown sources. And as to Arabic names, their transcription into the Latin alphabet can be a thing of great difficulty and uncertainty, as see our chapter five. Incidentally, much use of fictitious names on old maps is presented by Durand (1952, 205-06), and Claudius Clavus was especially prone to this, as see Björnbo and Petersen (1909, 81-100), and there were assuredly others. Indeed, the old maps are covered with them if we include such things as Mercator's four polar islands, or the Great Southern Continent. And in modern times, we find that no less a geographer than August Petermann included on his Arctic maps imaginary geography, mountains, etc., including even nonexistent islands to which he gave the names of his friends! (Paul van den Brink, in comments made in response to a talk given by Bruno Schelhaas on July 22, 2007 at the 23rd ICHC in Bern). In any event, it was the sixteenth century, and Gastaldi's maps were the first modern maps to fill the interiors of the far continents, and it is quite natural that, perhaps in response to the traditional cartographer's *horror vacui*, in the maps there should be misplaced, mistranscribed, and sometimes nonexistent places, whatever the source for them might have been. In any event, in face of the general unprecedented overall accuracy of these maps, these things do little or nothing to detract from their groundbreaking and revelatory nature.

Let us start by stepping back briefly into the fifteenth century. In the 1480s and 1490s, the slow southward progress of the Portuguese along the west African coast suddenly turned into an exploration in great sweeping leaps and bounds, beginning with Diogo Cão's push far southwards to about 28° South on the west African coast in 1482 and 1485, followed by Bartolomeu Dias's bold rounding of the cape in 1487, and then the finding by Vasco Da Gama of a faster way to make towards the south by sweeping far out into the Atlantic before heading southeast and his pushing on far past the cape to Calcutta and Goa in 1496-99, and finally the opening up of the whole of the Far East by Albuquerque and others, all the way to the Moluccas and even up the east Chinese coast to about 30° N latitude, all by the 1520s. Corresponding to this juggernaut to the East was another to the West, accomplished by the Spanish. Starting with Columbus, they began their astonishing series of discoveries to the West. These explorations, supplemented somewhat by French and English ventures to far northeastern North America, once begun, proceeded at a tremendous pace, a pace which continued unabated until precisely 1542/43, when Juan Rodriguez Cabrillo and Bartolomé Ferrelo made their push up the North American west coast from New Spain (Mexico) to ca. 40° N. latitude.

By this time, in the East, the entirety of the African coast, east and west, had been revealed, as well as the entirety of the Asian south coast, and its east coast up to 30° N; and in the West, the entirety of the east coast of America, both North and South, all the long way from Labrador down to Tierra del Fuego had been brought into view, as well as the entirety of the South and Central American west coasts, and with the explorations of Cortes, followed by those of Cabrillo and Ferrelo, the North American west coast up to about 40° N. And a great deal of inland exploration had also occurred, especially in America, but much less in Africa and Asia.[81] All this at a feverish pace in the course of only about sixty years! And there and then, with Cabrillo and Ferrelo, the great surge stopped. By comparison with the fevered activity of 1482-1543, the entire period following, up to the present day, was mostly one of incremental advances. Yes, there were some brilliant forays, such as the discovery of Australia by the Dutch in the seventeenth

---

[81] We shall have more to say below on this dearth of information provided on African and Asian interiors.

century, or the opening up of the northernmost Pacific by the English in the eighteenth century, but the greater part of the extra-European world in its main outlines had been found out by 1543. I believe I have not seen before in my reading a recognition of these facts, i.e., that from the 1480s to the early 1540s European exploration continued unabated at an almost unbelievably whirlwind rate, that the result was the uncovering of close to all of the major parts of the world by 1543, that the maelstrom of activity suddenly lost its steam at that date, and that exploration, however occasionally impressive, would never again reach the fever pitch of these first sixty years. This fact explains the extraordinary longevity of Gastaldi's influence on other cartographers into the eighteenth century, as brought out in chapter three. The influx of new material was simply much decreased after his time, and he had captured almost all of the flood of new information up to his own time. And it is worth noting that, since Gastaldi had for the first time established the forms of all the major bodies of land generally correctly, in that sense his influence does not extend only to the eighteenth century, but right up to our own times as well.

This tremendous burst of discovery, revealing most of the world for the first time in history to Europeans, went on at such a rapid rate that it was difficult, indeed impossible, for the residents of Europe to keep up with it, for the information spread slowly or not at all. Some champion was needed to make the necessary exertions to bring all the new information together, and that champion of course was Ramusio. It was his information gathering activities which documented the whirlwind of discovery which we have just briefly described. The documentation, as we know, was of two sorts, a collection of sea charts which provided the world's coastlines, and the vast collection of textual accounts described earlier in this chapter, which documented the interiors, although in fact there is also in Ramusio's accounts a good amount of coastal information as well.

But, while his documentation of the great discoveries is perhaps his most prominent contribution, there is a very substantial body of information of another kind in Ramusio's collection, generally given less notice, but vital to his purpose. Ramusio wanted to provide the information necessary to fully revamp, extend and generally replace the ancient geography, including the inlands of both the large sections of the far continents which Ptolemy had mapped so poorly, and of the lands which Ptolemy had not known at all. And documenting the great discoveries was not enough, except in the case of America, where the relatively copious information available on the interior was part and parcel of the great discoveries. But as to Africa and Asia, the exploratory accounts did not offer very much in the way of information on the interiors.

Accordingly, Ramusio had to seek out much material of a different kind. Thus the majority of information on African interiors does not come from exploratory accounts proper, but from accounts of other kinds, as Francisco Alvarez's account of Ethiopia, compiled during a Portuguese diplomatic mission in the 1520s, or the lengthy account of virtually all the vast Maghreb (Islamic northern Africa), quite unknown to Europeans before, in the 1520s by the Muslim scholar Leo Africanus, who knew the area well. For interior Asia, covered by volume two of the *Navigazioni*, the information is mostly not from explorer's accounts either, but the accounts of travelers and merchants, and while there is considerable sixteenth century material, Ramusio had to settle, as regards many areas, for accounts dating from the fourteenth and fifteenth centuries, still "modern" of course, by comparison to Ptolemy. And by 1553, Ramusio had the invaluable geographical information of Barros, which provided extensive concise information on the coasts *and* interiors of both southeast Africa, and all southern Asia.

Ramusio, in short, had all the information necessary to compile maps which would nearly completely exile the old geography of the world, and replace it with modern geography, and this was his dream. He stated, as we have seen, that the coasts would come from the sea charts, and the interiors from the texts he had gathered. Ramusio's friend Gastaldi had access to Ramusio's mass of geographical material some years, and in many cases, I suspect, many years before it was printed, giving him time to study and assimilate well the vast body of information, some time before it became generally available. And Gastaldi fulfilled Ramusio's dream spectacularly, as we know, between 1559 and 1564, creating three great continental depictions which showed for the first time the general form of the world's continents as they actually were, and also filled up their interior as had never been done

126

before, usually with correct information. For the first time, most of the world as it actually was could be surveyed on paper.[82]

Unfortunately, there is a note of the tragic to this story, basically a story of resounding victory. For, at the end of his preface to volume three, Ramusio takes on a saddened tone, as if he felt that he had largely failed in his enterprise, and no doubt this is the way he still felt when he died in 1557. If only he had lived a few years longer, and seen Gastaldi's great continental maps! He would have seen that his endeavor had been one of the most spectacularly successful in the history of geography. Still, even without having seen Gastaldi's maps, Ramusio's disappointment in the outcome of his efforts seems hard to account for. Milanesi has intimated that perhaps Ramusio felt that the distinct shortage of geographical coordinate data in his collection was seen by him as a shortcoming, and this may be the explanation. Ramusio lived in an age when no geographer could astronomically find coordinate data to a high degree of surety, especially as to longitudes, although every geographer tacitly pretended that he could. The great difficulties involved, insurmountable at the time, at least as to longitude, created a great air of mystery about this problem. Everyone felt that very possibly there were, somehow, somewhere, wise and mystical savants, holders of secret information, who actually could find longitude with requisite surety. No one was willing to admit that he couldn't, from fear of being shown as inept in his profession if one of these nonexistent holders of secret information was then to step forth out of the shadows and show that it *could* be done. Throughout the literature of the time which touches on the subject, we find everywhere between the lines this reticence to be forthcoming in the matter.

Whatever the reason for Ramusio's dissatisfaction, it certainly was not justified, for, as we have seen, it was almost entirely through Ramusio's vast accumulation of data that Gastaldi was able to surpass by leaps and bounds any previous printed maps of Africa, Asia, and America, in the process imparting to the picture of the world the greatest single advancement ever made or to be made. But, we recall from chapter three that there have been

---

[82] Gastaldi also, in 1561, we must not forget, created his great "Cosmographia Vniversalis" world map, treated here at length in chapter two, which basically shows the same picture, though on a smaller scale.

doubts as to Gastaldi's authorship of maps of Asia and America. If, in fact, these two maps, or even one of them, were not the work of Gastaldi, or not wholly the work of Gastaldi, then the claim that Gastaldi made the single greatest advance in the history of cartography disappears. So we must dispel these doubts if our claim is to stand. We shall do so in the next chapter as regards Asia, concerning which there has floated about a rather unclear notion since the time of Ortelius, that Gastaldi constructed his Asia based on material from the fourteenth- and fifteenth-century Arabian geographer, Abulfeda, though Ortelius's hazy wording does not make it clear whether he means that Gastaldi copied from a map by Abulfeda, or obtained his data from Abulfeda's famous *Geography*. The doubts as to his authorship of the America we will remove in the ninth chapter.

4.5 A Note on Coordinates

It is quite interesting, revealing, and instructive to note how little in the way of mathematics went into the compilation of Gastaldi's great continental maps. Neither Gastaldi, who worked always in Venice, nor anyone else of course had troops of people surveying or taking astronomical observations in these far continents. Rather, in the interiors, it was entirely a matter of approximate determinations based on very vague indications of distances expressed in terms of days of travel and sometimes not even that, and directions expressed in major compass points only, or more often in such terms as "towards sunset" or "left of sunrise", etc. The coasts were from sea charts, and here some rudimentarily formal mathematics would have been involved, in the taking of some latitudes, and compass-determined azimuthal directions of coasts, plus plain dead reckoning, but besides the fact that none of this was very accurate, all of this would have been done by the Portuguese and Spanish mariners and chartmakers themselves, not by Gastaldi. From the beginning of his career to the end, as we bring out especially in chapter seven, Gastaldi treated terrestrial coordinates, especially longitude, and fairly often not only coordinates, but the depiction of large land features and formations as well, with a certain nonchalance which in fact was in perfect accord with the realities of his time, that is, with the levels of surety attainable at the time in these regards, which levels were quite low. And yet his maps, with their generally correct forms for the continents, are there for us to see. How truly astonishing was his achievement will be brought out by the considerations in the following two paragraphs.

While there were a number of problems which made the attainment of accuracy impossible in the sixteenth century, focusing on the greatest problem of all, longitude, will serve us best in the short demonstration which we wish to make here. Longitude could only be very roughly estimated, resulting in unknown distortions of all forms across the maps. This is attested by the serious differences in longitude of the same places across world maps and other maps of the time, and by the fact that when Jean Dominique Cassini (Cassini I) began finding nearly accurate longitudes across the globe in the late seventeeth century, it was found that even the best maps had been very badly in error. The presence of longitude graduation on a map tends to subconsciously lull us, when we notice it at all, into thinking that it is in some sense necessarily "real", that is, based in some sense on actuality.[83] The illusion unquestionably arises from the fact that on modern maps, this is indeed the case. But this was not so, and could not be so for sixteenth-century maps. There existed a very, very few desultory attempts to find the longitude of individual places in the sixteenth century, and there were in the first half of the seventeeth century a couple, I think no more, equally desultory, and nonproductive ventures to organize broader attempts to find the approximate longitudes of a number of places scattered over larger areas of the earth. The most ambitious of these was an attempt guided by Fabri de Peiresc (1580-1637) to find key longitudes of selected places over an area including much of Europe, North Africa, and the Near East, by simultaneous observations of the lunar eclipse of August 28, 1635 by persons

---

[83] The author has spent several years on this question, going into it in great depth, including an analysis of literally all methods of attempting to find one's longitude, from the earliest times to the twenty-first century, but focused on the sixteenth century. This cannot be gone into here, but will be dealt with in a separate study. [The publishers hope to locate this essay among Doug's effects.]

Peiresc had stationed at the key positions, but the attempt failed to elicit any meaningful results.[84]

From the 1670s to the 1690s, Cassini, with the tremendous funding provided by Colbert under Louis XIV, and with the active cooperation of Jesuit priests stationed in key spots world-wide, trained by himself, and equipped with telescopes and the pendulum clocks of Huygens, began for the first time ever making meaningful longitude attempts aplenty by timing simultaneous occultations and eclipses of Jupiter's moons by the mother planet, and comparing these times with the times of the same occultations at the meridian of Paris as indicated in Cassini's famous 1668 tables (and in some cases with Cassini's personally observed timings in Paris). Only then, *and not before*, did longitudes begin to be found with some surety -- to be precise, a rather astonishing level of surety not lower than three arc minutes of accuracy, and it was found that, for places in the Far East, in Siam, China, the Philippines, etc., the longitudes which had been shown on the maps of the time differed between 20 and 30 full degrees from those found by Cassini, and similar errors were found for other parts of the world.[85] So we see here that, regardless of the thoroughly misleading presence of marked and numbered parallels and meridians, and the just as misleading lists of purportedly correct and meaningful coordinates of places, the age of mathematical cartography had not yet arrived in the sixteenth century, and it was in fact quite unreachable at the time. *And yet, despite this fact, Gastaldi's spectacular continental maps are undeniable evidence that outstanding cartographical progress could nonetheless be made without recourse to formal mathematics, but only to extant sea charts, and extensive studied usage of textual materials.* Gastaldi got the general forms, and Cassini finally wrenched them into mathematical accuracy.

---

[84] See Chapin (1957). The inherent elements producing uncertainty in the method, the slow motion and fuzziness of the edge of the earth's shadow on the moon, the inability to find local solar time to a sufficient degree of accuracy (Huygens's clocks, and the tables and techniques needed for setting them to the local time of whatever place the longitude for which was being sought, were yet to come), and a non-professional, insufficiently prepared, and indeed insufficiently interested squadron of stationed personnel, were the main reasons for the failure.

[85] While the story of Cassini's achievement has been told, and well, by several, as by Brown (1941), authors have remained mute on the virtual nothingness which came before him, seemingly unaware of it, so that the tremendous novelty and setting of precedence of his work has not yet received proper recognition.

CHAPTER 5 - GASTALDI AND THE ARAB GEOGRAPHERS

5.1 Gastaldi and Abulfeda: Introduction

There have been several assertions that Gastaldi used, or may have used, Arabic sources in compiling some of his maps, especially those of Asia, sources, that is, over and above the narrative of Leo Africanus in Ramusio, which we know he used extensively in his great map of Africa. We shall look first at the most long-standing such claim, that he used the *Geography* compiled in the Arabic language by the Syrian prince, geographer and scholar Abulfeda (1273-1331), who completed the work in 1321.[1] We will look in a moment at the claim that Gastaldi used Abulfeda, who made the claim, and upon what basis. Answering this claim is a rather complex matter, and it will be useful to us first to say a few words about Abulfeda's work, and about how it was first brought to Europe by the French Orientalist, visionary, linguist, and occasional cartographer, Guillaume Postel (1510-1581).[2] The actual name of Abulfeda's work, transliterated, is Taqwīm

---

[1] I use the title *Geography* after the title used by Joseph Reinaud and Stanislas Guyard in their French translation, the only really full translation ever made into a western Language (Reinaud and Guyard, 1848-1883). The appearance of the first volume in 1848 spawned two ostensible article-length reviews, one an anonymous work in the *Bulletin de la Société de Géographie* [Paris], July 1848, 5-19; the other by Joseph Hammer-Purgstall in the *Sitzungsberichte der Kaiserlichen Akademie der Wissenschaften, Philologisch-Historische Classe*, 2(1849), 59-75 and 85-109, but their authors use the occasion for general discussion of Arab geography, and really tell us nothing of Reinaud's work proper, probably abstaining from critiques of the translation until the anticipated last volume appeared. That did not occur for thirty-five more years, and, as far as I have been able to determine, no real review of the work was ever published. Russian Arabicist Krachkovskii said the translation is one of the best in its field, and will last (1957, 394). On Abulfeda and his book, see Jourdain (1811), Lelewel (1852-57, 1, 147-53 and 5[Epilogue], 45-47), Sarton (1947, 793-99), Krachkovskii (1957, 595-99), Vernet (1970), Holt (1983; an English translation of his autobiography), Reinaud (1840, vii-xxviii), Reinaud and Guyard (1848-1883, 1, ii-xxxviii). Lelewel gives a true analysis of the work, and, though 150 years old, it is the only such ever written to date. A wealth of information, especially on early references and on manuscripts of the work, is hidden in Sale (1734/35, 114-16 and 1737, 525-28), which I have not seen cited before. Because the present chapter is not directed toward Arabicists, and the subject of Arab sources is a peripheral one to this book as a whole, I have decided to use the traditional westernized forms of Arabic names as opposed to the more correct modern forms, that is, Abulfeda, instead of Abu al-Fida, Idrisi, instead of al-Sharif al-Idrisi, etc. A good modern translation into Spanish of Abulfeda's section on that country, not surprisingly the only European area well covered, with an introduction by F. Molla, is in the *Boletín* of the Sociedad geográfica de Madrid, 48 (1906), 81-104, which seems to have been overlooked by everyone.

[2] On Postel, see Bouwsma (1957), Weill-Secret (1987), and works cited below. For his work as a cartographer, see Destombes (1985), and Meurer (1991, 218-20).

al-buldān, for which a myriad of renderings have been offered by scholars, perhaps the best being *A Description of the Countries*.[3] The work is a compilation of the works of over fifty Arab geographers who preceded Abulfeda, principally Biruni (*Canon*), Ibn Said, Khwarizmi (*Kitab Rasm*), an anonymous Persian (*Kitab al-Atwal' Book of Longitudes and Latitudes*), Ibn Hawqal, Yakut, Ibn Alatir or Aladir (*Lobab*), Idrisi and Ptolemy. The first four named were his main sources for geographical coordinates of places. The work consists of a lengthy general prologue, followed by a description of the whole world, as perceived by and known to, Abulfeda, broken into twenty-eight numbered regions. It naturally stresses the Near and Middle East. Because at each major place named Abulfeda usually provides several differing pairs of coordinates taken from different geographers, the work has often been referred to as "Abulfeda's comparative tables," or some similar phrase, but the work is much more than a set of tables, giving extensive description, mainly geographical, but also historical, of the places named.

Reinaud hailed the richness of the geographical material in the work, and called it "a capital work in its field, like the treatise of Idrisi; Europe in the Middle Ages produced no work which could be compared with it,"[4] while Lelewel calls it "an invaluable manual for the geographical knowledge of the Arabs, a storehouse filled with variety."[5] It was very warmly received in the East, enjoying great popularity in its time and later, and it had a number of imitators.[6] But there are many problems with the work, informational, technical, and stylistic, and since these problems will be of pertinence in what we say below, we shall say a few words about them. Anyone who reads through a couple of Abulfeda's longer chapters will understand the repeated use by his critics of such terms as repetitiveness, indecision, contradictions, incoherencies, etc.[7] For example, Lelewel speaks, in reference to Abulfeda's treatment of the River Jordan, of his "reechoing

---

[3] Writers have occasionally confused the phrase al-buldan with the name of the author, Abulfeda.

[4] Reinaud and Guyard (1848-83, 1, cdliii).

[5] Lelewel (1852-57, 1, 149).

[6] Reinaud and Guyard (1848-83, 1, cdxlvi and cdliii-cdliv), and Krachkovskii (1957, 392).

[7] See for instance Lelewel (1852-57, 1, 148 and 150-51 and atlas, p. ix), Hettner (1927, 39), Oehme (1978, 367-69).

the constant confusion on the point in the data taken from other geographers. This entanglement in the description of Abulfeda is tiresome,"[8] and as to his description of the Euphrates, he speaks of the "labyrinth of his indigestible erudition."[9] He is astonished how Abulfeda could have come up with a "toothless Nile," and misshapen Persian Gulf.[10] Technical problems are as bad. Vernet says: "The longitudes recorded in the *Taqwim al-buldan* often contain obvious errors that are a result of their having been taken from sources that did not adopt the same prime meridian (some used the western coast of Africa, others the Canary Islands); poor conversion of the distance

GUILIELM, POSTELLUS, Philologiæ Prof. Lutetiæ Paris,

Courtesy National Galleries of Scotland

---

[8] Lelewel (1852-57, 1, 150-51).

[9] Lelewel (1852-57, 1, 151).

[10] Lelewel (1852-57, 1, 151).

between extreme points on an itinerary into degrees and minutes of latitude and longitude; and faulty use of the canvas maps in use in the Near East,"[11] and Reinaud notes that when he does give longitudes based on different prime meridians, he doesn't inform us of this.[12] Such errors also regularly occur in areas which were closest to Abulfeda, and which he should have known best.[13] Oehme noted that the coordinates that Abulfeda gives in his "Prologue" for some places differ for the coordinates given for the same places in the general descriptions of countries.[14] Lelewel describes the great difficulties encountered if one attempts to make a map based on the

---

[11] Vernet (1970, 29); Sarton, too, notes that his "coordinates are often erroneous, sometimes grossly so" (Sarton, 1947, 797). We have mentioned the subject of prime meridians, and shall mention them again several times in this chapter. We intentionally avoid here a detailed discussion of this subject since it would be lengthy, technical, and inappropriate in the present work. We only note the following. With a few unimportant exceptions, those maps which show a prime meridian are world maps or maps of Africa, and we can now easily make a preliminary survey of sixteenth century prime meridians thanks to the works of Shirley (1987) and Betz (2007). Restricting ourselves of course to the maps in these works which are reproduced well enough to obtain meaningful results, we made such a survey, and anyone who wishes may readily do the same should he wish to confirm our results. We found that, in the sixteenth century, there were well over twenty Western Ocean prime meridians in use, all running through one or another of the islands in the Cape Verde group, the Canary group, the Azores group, or Madeira. The group whose islands are used most often on the maps is the Cape Verdes, and *not the Canaries*. When an island in the Canaries (which run east and west through over four degrees of longitude, and *not* straight north and south, as do Ptolemy's equivalent, the Fortunate Islands) is used, which is fairly frequently, the island most often chosen was the *eastmost* Canary, and *not* the *westmost*, as often tacitly assumed. On only a small number of maps is the westmost island chosen, and on only two is this westmost island Ferro, another common tacit assumption; for while the group runs basically east and west, the interpositions of the three westmost, Gomera, La Palma, and Ferro, close together, were clearly not well known at the time, for, albeit barely, the westmost is usually La Palma, or even Comara. Adding chaos to confusion, *whatever island* we choose on the old maps, whether in the Cape Verdes, the Canaries, the Azores, or Madeira, that island's angular (longitudinal) distance from the west end of the European mainland (chosen for various reasons as the southwest tip of Portugal, technically incorrect, but the discrepancy being of no relevance in our comparative survey), varies back and forth through the century like a shuttlecock with its distance from the mainland varying up to five degrees! The implication of a wellspring of profound confusion here for historians of cartography, unrecognized before as far as I know, is undeniable. For example, if we have a graduated sixteenth century map of Germany, and Frankfurt is at, say, $32°15'$ E, what meridian is this figure purportedly being counted from? The cartographer never tells us, nor could he really have said himself with any surety, considering that clearly no one knew within about five degrees how far west of European points *any* of the Western Ocean islands lay. As said, we shall not pursue this further now. We only point it out, for it seems inescapable that the seeds of much confusion are here, and any tacit assumption that there somehow existed in the sixteenth century (as there has in *reality* existed in our times for a century and a quarter) a single prime meridian from which all makers of graduated maps were counting is clearly wrong. All of this cries out for an open investigation, but it cannot be done here.

[12] Reinaud and Guyard (1848-83, 1, cdli; see also ccxxxiii-ccxxxiv for more on the confusion in meridians).

[13] Lelewel (1852-57, 1, 152), and Renaudot (1733, xiv-xv).

[14] Oehme (1978, 369).

information given by Abulfeda, and concludes that, "Abulfeda was deprived of the geographical instinct, that he is found quite bad in the great questions, and that he did not at all meet with the truth," and that "Abulfeda is certainly not comparable to his predecessors."[15] There are also serious organizational problems with the work, as well as tremendous orthographical difficulties, often making translation near impossible, which we'll return to below.

Abulfeda's *Geography* was one of a number of rare Oriental manuscripts which were first brought to Europe in 1550 or 1551 from the Middle East, probably Damascus, where they had been stolen, "part from private persons, part from churches," by Postel, whom we have mentioned. We learn this astonishing fact from a confession included by Postel in a testament written in early 1551, shortly after he had undergone an experience in which he said that the spirit of a deceased holy woman, known as the Venetian Virgin, whom Postel had known earlier in Venice, had entered into and become a part of his corporeal being.[16] Postel had found the manuscripts during the second of his two trips to the Near East, in 1549-1550/51, and, although he made several attempts to obtain the funds to purchase them, he clearly failed.[17] Of all the manuscripts he brought back, it is abundantly

---

[15] Lelewel (1852-57, 1, 151 and 153).

[16] Postel tells us of the theft in a testimony written evidently December 1551 or January 1552. See Secret (1959, 458-59), and Secret (1962, 34, note 2); and fuller later, in Secret (1972, 39-40) and Weill-Secret (1987, 89-91 and 282, note 173). The most pertinent lines from the relevant part of the document read: "Finally the wretched conscience of the proud and arrogant Postel led by the judgement of God was constrained to confess his hidden wickedness, to such an extent that not only to the priest and in confession but before all the world . . . to from his own hand declare himself a thief, sacrilegious person, and violator of faith and of affection between God and men. For, having always tried through languages and learning and principally the Arabic language to be rendered famous and renowned, he is constrained to make known to all the world through letters for executing his testament written to Thomas Giunta or to his brother at Venice that the books which he brought to the West to amplify his glory were for the most part stolen, part from private persons, part from churches, and for as much directs by testament that 32 *écus* might be repaid to the said Giunta for the money lent on the said books, to that end that having received his sum he might return to the Orient the said books to be restored to those whose they are." Postel at the time was a relatively young man of forty-one, and would live another forty years, but he apparently thought he was in danger of death due to his extraordinary experience, which occurred to him in December, 1551.

[17] On the various attempts to obtain funds, see Bouwsma (1957, 16), Weill-Secret (1987, 82-83 and 277, note 14), Vogel (1853, 55). One of those to whom Postel turned for financial assistance was Gabrielle de Luels d'Aramon, French ambassador to Constantinople, to whose embassy Postel attached himself when he coincidentally encountered the embassy in the East. Among the members of Aramon's entourage was the cartographer Nicolas de Nicolay, whom we shall speak of again. On Nicolay and this embassy, see Karrow (1993, 436-37).

clear that it was the Abulfeda that he most treasured.[18] Postel was the first to bring a copy of Abulfeda to Europe, and the work appears to have been completely unknown in Europe before.[19] Indeed, Abulfeda was the first of any of the classical Arab geographers to become known in Europe.[20] Postel was compelled to give up his Abulfeda, and a number of other manuscripts, in pawn, to the Palatine Elector Otto Henry, Duke of Bavaria, in March, 1555,[21] and they became a part of the Duke's library at Heidelberg. All these manuscripts were transferred in 1622-23 to the library of the Vatican, where they still reside.[22] Postel made several attempts to retrieve his manuscripts, but with no success.[23] Let us now return to the claim that Gastaldi used Abulfeda in his map of Asia.

5.2 *Gastaldi and Abulfeda: Ortelius's Claim*

It was Ortelius who first claimed, in an address to the reader in a large cartouche at the lower right of his 1567 Asia taken from Gastaldi's 1559-61 Asia, that Gastaldi's map was taken from Abulfeda, although, as we shall see, Ortelius could not at the time have seen Abulfeda's work, in translation or otherwise. Ortelius says:

> Abraham Ortelius of Antwerp to his honest observers. Since, honest observers, Giacomo Gastaldi, a man worthy for geography, has rather recently published a map of Asia, following the version of Ismael

---

[18] Levi della Vida (1939, 326, and other places). See also Fueck (1955, 57).

[19] Bayle (1697, 50, note B), Vogel (1853, 57, note 2), Jourdain (1811, 225). See note 161 on other manuscripts of Abulfeda's *Geography*.

[20] Peschel (1877, 160), Sezgin (2000, 1, 3). Europeans apparently began to learn of Idrisi, the second to become known, only late in the sixteenth century.

[21] On this pawn see Levi della Vida (1939, 308-09, 312-17 and 319), Weill-Secret (1987, 111-12, 120 and 121), Vogel (1853, 57-58).

[22] The Abulfeda *Geography* and an Arab medical text are bound together in one codex of 168 folio leaves which carries the Latin title, "Geographia Abilfedeasi adglutinati [sic] su(n)t in fine computationes Medicae," with call mark Arabo 266. The *Geography* is the first 125 leaves of the codex (Levi della Vida, 1939, 293-94), and Levi della Vida (1935, 15).

[23] On this, see the special note, "Postel's 1567 Letter to Ortelius," at the end of the chapter.

Abulfeda,[24] the Arabian cosmographer (which author was brought to Europe from the Middle-East by Guillaume Postel, the famous mathematician and a man very skilled in many languages, even Arabic; and we look forward with great anticipation to a complete translation by him sometime, for the common good of cosmography), in many sheets, but quite unequal in size so that they could not possibly be joined together, a few years ago in Venice, without the name of the author; it has been decided to issue this single map for the convenient use by scholars. . . . Antwerp 1567.[25]

The claim was repeated after Ortelius on the undated Asia by Bonato Bertelli (see Almagià 1948 in the legend on the Bertelli map, at pl. XVIII),

---

[24] The phrase is "secundum traditionem Abilfedee Ismaelis." Although it has been suggested that this could refer to a map by Abulfeda, as we shall see, there exists no possibility that Abulfeda made a map of Asia, and if he had, it could only have been a quite poor one, considering the gross inaccuracies in some of his data.

[25] I have used Schilder's translation (1987, 63-64). The legend continues, mentioning improvements Ortelius has made in the map. Schilder gives the whole legend. The map Ortelius refers to, of course, is Gastaldi's three-part Asia of 1559-61. The allusion to issuing "this single map for the convenient use by scholars," is in reference to the fact that Ortelius combined Gastaldi's three maps into one large one. Compare the words of Camocio in the dedicatory legend on the Asia map in the Bell Library, quoted below in chapter eleven. Ortelius's assertion was repeated afterwards by other writers, and over time took on some changes. John Greaves, in his notice to the reader at the head of his 1650 translation of two chapters from Abulfeda, tones down Ortelius's statement, saying just that Gastaldi used Abulfeda to correct the coordinates of many places in Asia (Greaves, 1650, 1st page of "Lectori"). This was repeated by others, as Bayle (1697, 50). Greaves also makes the odd statement, on the same page, that Ortelius often cites Abulfeda in his *Thesaurus Geographicum* (1596; see Karrow, 1993, p. 25), "not as having seen them himself, but on the authority of Gastaldi." This gross misunderstanding arose from the fact that Ortelius repeats, though less fully, his claim of 1567 at the entry for "Babylon" in the *Thesaurus* (Levi della Vida, 1939, 326, note 2, who quotes the passage). Though Ortelius cites Gastaldi as an authority at many other places in the *Thesaurus*, he is doing so on Gastaldi' s own authority, not as a second-hand authority after Abulfeda, whom Ortelius does not mention anywhere else other than at Babylon. Greaves apparently presumed all the citations were after Abulfeda based on Ortelius's comments at the Babylon entry, probably together with a knowledge of the original 1567 statement. Greaves's supposition was repeated by others, as Bayle (1697, 50), and it was no doubt this statement, probably with a knowledge of the Abulfeda extracts printed in Ramusio (about which see below), that led to the strangest twist in this thread, when Johann Gottfried Gregorii stated that "Jacobus Castaldus, of Piedmont, translated the Opus Geographicum of the learned Arabian Prince Abulfeda into Italian and had the same published at Venice" (1713, 162), and I have seen this repeated later by others. We see how distorted things can become over time. It is not necessary to refute this absurd statement, although Christian Sandler seemed to tentatively accept it (1894, 405). The story takes still another turn in 1695 when Coronelli stated that Gastaldi made not just his Asia, but also his maps of Africa and Europe (!) after Abulfeda (quoted in Armao, 1957, 23), and this too came to be repeated by others, as Christian Hübner (1710, 23-24) and Gregorii (1713, 162).

and by others; as we see in the following paragraph it has continued to be given attention by some scholars in our times.

Apparently the first to notice this legend on the 1567 Ortelius Asia in modern times was Almagià in 1923,[26] who at the time simply noted that: "It is for now impossible to test the validity of this reproach." Giorgio Levi della Vida, researching in the Vatican Library various Oriental manuscripts which had once belonged to Postel,[27] noticed in Josias Simler's 1555 additions to Conrad Gesner's bibliography a passage stating that Postel had made a compendium of Abulfeda's *Geography* and left it with Ramusio at Venice.[28] Ramusio, Levi adds, must have passed this compendium on to Gastaldi, who would have then used it in making his map of Asia, as Ortelius states. But really testing the hypothesis would take him too far outside his area.[29] Almagià, taking up the subject again in 1948,[30] notes that Ramusio much praises Abulfeda's work in his *Navigazioni*,[31] and says that "the hypothesis would be very likely that Ramusio might have passed the copy of the work of Abulfeda to his friend Gastaldi and that the latter might have used it in some way."[32] Almagià also makes known a relevant letter of April 9, 1567 which Postel wrote to Ortelius after the latter had sent a copy of the 1567 map to him as a gift. Although Gastaldi is not mentioned in the letter, and although, as Almagià so correctly states, "Postel's Latin is not always clear," one can deduce that Postel is grateful for his name having been placed in the address to the reader on the map, and he states that his contribution could have been more fully documented had it been possible for him to get hold of the Abulfeda manuscript, which was by then in the possession of Otto Henry of Bavaria.[33] The question is also discussed more recently by Günter Schilder,

---

[26] Almagià (1923, 298).

[27] Levi della Vida (1939, 290-337).

[28] Levi della Vida (1939, 326-27). The passage, quoted below in full, is in Simler (1555, p. 1).

[29] Levi della Vida (1939, 327). As we shall see, it is unlikely any such compendium ever existed.

[30] Almagià (1948, 63-64 and 65-66).

[31] Ramusio is quoted in this below.

[32] Almagià (1948, 65).

[33] Almagià (1948, 65-66). I don't think Postel's very vague comments in this letter can be taken as indicative of much of anything. The question of what Postel may be saying here, and his motivations for saying it, are explored here in a special note at the end of the chapter.

who pretty much follows Almagià.[34] Both Almagià and Schilder tentatively accept the possibility that Gastaldi may have used Abulfeda, seemingly even including the possibility he actually copied his Asia from an Abulfeda map no longer extant, and that he did this without giving Abulfeda credit.

Not all have been disposed to entertain Ortelius's claim so seriously. Rodolfo Gallo categorically denied that Gastaldi would have used Abulfeda in any way.[35] More recently, Thomas Suarez is unable to take Ortelius' words seriously at all, calling it all "an interesting myth," and concluding with the following on Abulfeda's *Geography*: "This work, itself an undistinguished compilation of earlier material, would have been quite worthless to Gastaldi. Gastaldi's map is derived directly from Spanish and Portuguese exploration and is vastly superior to Arab knowledge of the region, prior to the advent of a European presence in Southeast Asia."[36] Suarez is speaking in particular of Southeast Asia, and, as we shall see, regarding not only that area but some others, his judgment is quite correct. The most recent, and strongest, denial of Ortelius's claim has come from Fuat Sezgin, of the Johann Wolfgang Goethe University, Frankfurt, in a lengthy study of the influence of Arab cartography on the West.[37] Sezgin repeatedly draws attention, as we have done several times, to the extraordinary suddenness of the change wrought by Gastaldi's new maps of Asia, their strong influence on Mercator and Ortelius,[38] and to Ortelius's legend about Gastaldi and Abulfeda, and concludes that it "is highly telling that Ortelius believed, that the origin of Gastaldi's 1561 map of Asia could be accounted for only through the tradition of Abulfeda. We know today that the comparative tables of Abulfeda would not have sufficed and were unsuitable, to serve as the basis of the Gastaldi map,"[39] and: "When

---

[34] Schilder (1987, 63-68).

[35] Gallo (1955, 215-16).

[36] Suarez (1999, 131). Suarez is correct, but, besides Portuguese sources, Gastaldi also made much use of sources of another kind from Ramusio, as we have seen in chapter four.

[37] Sezgin (2000). We will speak at length of this work in a following section. He has also published a short work reviewing the main points of the larger work (Sezgin, 2001).

[38] Sezgin (2000, 2, 97 and 102-03), and Sezgin (2001, 25).

[39] Sezgin (2000, 1, xx-xxi).

Abraham Ortelius . . . felt himself induced to remark on his edition of this map, that his predecessor had been able to bring about his version owing only to the Arab geographer Abulfeda, then this means that the new depiction was a startling thing for the contemporaries."[40] Finally, still in reference to the Ortelius legend, he says:

> We should so interpret this reaction, that Ortelius was simply dumbfounded by the abundance of place names on Gastaldi's map of Asia, furnished with longitude and latitude scales, and found no other explanation for this other than Abulfeda's comparative tables of geographical coordinates. Whether the places occurring in Gastaldi's map were actually found in Abulfeda's book, and whether the coordinates ascertained through the scales were in congruence with the longitudes and latitudes of the corresponding places, Ortelius could not judge.[41]

Considering what we have brought out in previous chapters on the sudden, and quite unprecedented, appearance of Gastaldi's continental depictions, I feel Sezgin has very much hit the nail on the head here. [42] Ortelius felt there had to be some extraordinary explanation for Gastaldi's new cartography, and knowing from two sources with which we know he was familiar, Ramusio himself and Simler (in his revision of Gesner),[43] that Postel had brought Abulfeda back from the East and deposited certain materials from it with Ramusio, this was the explanation he latched onto.[44] As we shall see, it is quite clear that Ortelius himself had not yet seen Abulfeda's *Geography*, so his judgment had to have been an indirect one of this nature. Nevertheless, the question is not an easy one, for, even if Ortelius arrived at his conclusion without having actually seen Abulfeda, the notion that it would have been natural that Gastaldi, or any other

---

[40] Sezgin (2000, 2, 455).

[41] Sezgin (2000, 2, 103-04).

[42] "Ortelius believed he had gotten to the bottom of the secret," inserts Sezgin (2001, 25).

[43] We quote the relevant passages from both below.

[44] I do not, however, agree with Sezgin's own explanation for Gastaldi's map, which is discussed later in this chapter.

cartographer of his time would have made use of such a source if it became available certainly does come naturally. While it was over 200 years old, so was Marco Polo, and we know Gastaldi made extensive use of that, and he made use of the work of Hayton Armenio, also over 200 years old. Furthermore, while neither Polo nor Hayton was really a geographer, and neither gave coordinate positions for places, Abulfeda was a geographer, and did give such positions, and he was a native of the Near East, while Polo was just a traveler. Why would one *not* use him? Indeed, Gastaldi's contemporary, the cartographer Nicolas de Nicolay, speaks in 1567 of the fact that Postel had brought back "the cosmography of Abil Fedeas, Mesopotamian prince who has described all the Oriental parts of Asia by its longitudes thus as Ptolemy which is an inestimable boon to our Latin homeland."[45] Furthermore, as we shall see, Ramusio much praised Abulfeda, as did some other sixteenth century personages. In the next paragraphs we shall show easily that Gastaldi certainly used no map of Abulfeda, and that he just as certainly did not use his text and tables for any areas beyond the Middle East. But the question of whether Gastaldi would have made partial use of Abulfeda for the Middle East (and if not, why) is more complex, and we shall broach it later.

Let us dispense first with the notion that there could have been an Abulfeda map of Asia which Gastaldi copied. Lelewel, having noted that there was in general very little mention of maps at all in Abulfeda's *Geography*, observes: "Abulfeda has touched on the question of the construction of maps, when he speaks of the reduction in distances in longitudes and latitudes: but one has no positive proof that he himself ever made a map. One could even doubt that he had ever seen any map whatever, if he had not found out the maritime position of the town of Antalia on a painted map, [and] if he had not expressly cited the map of Haraïr."[46]

Lelewel himself constructed, as he did in the case of several Arab geographers who left no maps, a map based on Abulfeda's coordinates and other data, at least as well as he was able to. But the resultant picture shows extraordinary distortions, which Lelewel describes, adding that, "It is rather

---

[45] Nicolay (1567), page reference unknown to me. I quote Nicolay after Chesneau (1887, lv-lvi). Nicolay also speaks of Postel's having pawned the book to Otto Henry, confusing the date of the pawn, 1555, with the date when Postel first obtained the manuscript, 1549.

[46] Lelewel (1852-57, 1, 150).

difficult to explain their origin."[47] When we consider further that Abulfeda himself says nothing of maps in his own explanations of why he wrote his book, and what he includes in it,[48] and when we remember that, although Ramusio had the greatest interest in maps and refers to them repeatedly in the *Navigazioni*, and although he much lauds Abulfeda's work, and speaks of it at some length, as we'll see below, he makes no mention of any map in the manuscript which Postel brought from the East, and we can safely assume there was no Abulfeda map.

Nor is this surprising. It takes but a moment to realize that it could not have been otherwise. We recall Abulfeda's geography is a compilation from many previous works from the ninth to thirteenth centuries. His figures for latitudes and longitudes of places, perhaps the most important part of the work from a cartographic standpoint, were taken from tables of geographical coordinates, of which a good number appeared through the centuries, regularly borrowing from their predecessors. One point universally noted and stressed in modern discussions of these tables is that they were never used to make maps, and indeed were never developed for such a purpose. In volume two, book one of *The History of Cartography* we read that, "The ultimate outcome of all these tables of longitude and latitude was virtually nothing cartographic,"[49] and, "while great sophistication was reached in developing the mathematical and astronomical bases of celestial and geographical cartography, little or no attempt was made to translate the existing theoretical knowledge into cartographic practice."[50] They were developed for astronomical, astrological, and perhaps religious reasons, as well as for "general scientific curiosity."[51] Durand says:

---

[47] Lelewel (1852-57, 1, 151), and see the odd map, which is map 59 on pl. 23 in the atlas of 1850. In the 1845 edition of the atlas, the edition reprinted for the facsimile edition of Lelewel, the map is on the nineteenth plate. The plates unfortunately are unnumbered, and one must count from plate 1.

[48] Reinaud and Guyard (1848-83, 2, pt. 1, 1-3).

[49] Tibbets, in Harley and Woodward (1992, 106; see also 107).

[50] Karamustafa, in Harley and Woodward (1992, 7). On the same, see Trimingham (1957, 137), Durand (1952, 101), Wright (1923, 96 and 97-98), Krachkovskii (1957, 390), Sezgin (2000, 1, 215), and Jourdain (1811, 221). We must add here that, on the basis of extensive research, the notion that "great sophistication was reached in . . . the astronomical bases of . . . geographical cartography" should in our opinion be taken with a hefty grain of salt.

[51] Wright (1923, 76 and 98).

The fact seems to be that the excellent measurements of latitude and longitude carried out by the Arabs were undertaken primarily in the interests of astronomy and astrology. Tables of solar and planetary motions are valid for only one position on the earth's surface. In order to transpose them for use at another point, it is necessary to know the exact longitudinal and latitudinal distance from the original station. In the Middle Ages, as now, the co-ordinate lists appended to astronomical tables were intended to facilitate transpositions of this sort.[52]

These tables were perhaps originally fairly good, although, of course, they were imperfect.[53] They were especially deficient as to longitudes: "Longitudes are just so much guesswork. In no case do we know how the Arabs arrived at their values, except by playing with the figures of their predecessors."[54] Over time the copying, recopying and sometimes altering of the tables resulted in degeneration of their integrity:

> Tables of this sort often gave variations of the same placenames or even assign different names to the same place as well as different coordinate values. Later authors tend to pick and choose. They combine or duplicate material in a completely arbitrary manner, so that as time goes on the tables become impossible to use in any scientific way."[55]

Also, at times, determination of a longitude figure from some newly designated central meridian resulted in changing "in a haphazard manner values they had received from other sources, causing ultimate confusion in

---

[52] Durand (1952, 102). See also Tibbets and Mercier, in Harley and Woodward (1992, 101 and 175), and Jourdain (1811, 221). Again, we must note that the statement about "excellent measurement of latitude and longitude carried out by the Arabs" must be looked at quite askance as to the longitudes.

[53] Reinaud and Guyard (1848-1883, 1, cclix).

[54] Tibbets, in Harley and Woodward (1992, 94, note 20), who continues, "Nor do we know how Ptolemy arrived at his figures." See also Minow (2001, 49), with the same. Durand says many positions were worked out from itineraries (1952, 105). Here he is probably correct.

[55] Tibbets, in Harley and Woodward (1992, 98).

some of the later tables."[56] This problem of a lack of a standardized usage as to a prime meridian was a major factor in corruption of the tables. Some used, or claimed to be using, Ptolemy's meridian through the Canary Islands, while others used the west coast of Africa, and, for that matter, no clear idea existed as to where those places themselves were located exactly.[57] Furthermore, as noted earlier, the geography of Ptolemy's Canaries (Fortunate Islands) was not at all the same as ours (or the sixteenth century's), a point of fundamental significance which, in our literature, has not yet sunk in.

Wright makes note of the humorous result which would ensue, "if one should try to draw a map of the world from the coordinates given in these lists,"[58] and we have already mentioned the absurdly distorted picture of the Middle East which resulted from Lelewel's attempt to make a map based on Abulfeda's coordinates, and Lelewel's vexation is apparent when he speaks of "the two meridians which too often confuse the compilation of Abulfeda and maybe all the Arab geography."[59] Had there been all along a cartographic tradition, where the interpositional relationships of the various places was shown graphically, that is, on maps, that no doubt would have acted as a kind of control, and many or most of these displacements would probably have been caught. But there was none, and the mistakes increased in number and seriousness over time. When we remember that Abulfeda came at the tail end of all this and was accumulating data from tables many or all of which had become corrupted, and was also evidently making his selections rather carelessly,[60] we understand the gross errors in his compilation already mentioned, and we understand the impossibility of making from it a truly viable map, as Lelewel attempted to do. But we also

---

[56] Tibbets, in Harley and Woodward (1992, 104).

[57] Reinaud and Guyard (1848 and 1883, 1, ccxxxiii-ccxxxiv and ccxxxv). See also Regier (1987, 359-61), who mentions another central meridian through Basra, and note the odd meridian 28°30' west of Toledo, which we'll speak of below. On prime meridians located in mythical places, see Tibbets, in Harley and Woodward (1992, 104). See especially our comments above in note 11 of the present chapter.

[58] Wright (1923, 97).

[59] Lelewel (1852-57, 1, 113).

[60] Lelewel (1852-57, 1, 150) and Oehme (1978, 367 and 369).

understand why Abulfeda, following the tradition of his numerous predecessors, probably never even had any intention of making a map from his data. And finally, we note that this is in accord with what we know of Arab cartography of the period. As many writers have noted, there simply were no Arab maps of the period drawn to scale, or at least none have come down to us.[61] Indeed, we don't need their authority, for a glance through volume two, book one of *The History of Cartography*, or Sezgin's atlas, or Konrad Miller's work,[62] reveals this immediately. Not only are there none drawn to scale, there are none which contain anything like the extensive interior toponymical and topographical detail of Gastaldi's Asias.

We can thus discount altogether any notion that Gastaldi might have copied his Asias from an Abulfeda map. If he used Abulfeda, he used some form of his text. But here, too, we can categorically state that, for large portions of his map, it is quite impossible that he could have used the Arab geographer, for Abulfeda himself tells us at the beginning of his work that there are several major areas of the continent which he does not cover at all or covers only very scantily. Abulfeda says, after having enumerated the types of geographical works written before his time:

> After mature consideration, we have brought together in this resumé that which was scattered in the books mentioned above. We have not however pretended to treat here of all the regions of the earth, nor even the greatest part among them; that is a thing which it cannot be hoped to accomplish; for the totality of the books which are devoted to this science contain only a very small portion of it. Indeed, although the empire of China may be vast and its cities may be numerous, only scanty and incomplete notices of it have reached us; and these notes are far from being trustworthy. It is the same with India; that which has reached us about that country is confused and uncertain. One can say as much of the countries of the Bulgars, of the countries of the Circassions [northern Caucasus], of the countries of

---

[61] Beckingham (1983, 9), Needham (1959, 561-65), Reinaud and Guyard (1848-1883, 1, cclxii). See also the comments in Harley and Woodward (1992, 6 and 512-13).

[62] Miller (1926-31).

the Russians . . . these regions are numerous, these kingdoms are considerable and extremely vast; and yet, in view of the few notices which we have of them, we do not know the names of their cities and that which makes up the general appearance . . . Most of the works of geography have described in an exact manner only the Muslim lands; they are far even from having described all of these.[63]

There are three important areas of Asia which are entirely untouched upon in Abulfeda: all of Further India, all of archipelagic Asia, and Japan. Gastaldi, we know, had plenty of material in Ramusio on all three of these areas, as well as all the areas Abulfeda mentions as being poorly covered. For Further India, there was much in Ramusio's editions of (to name the most important) Pires, Barbosa, Barros, Santo Stefano, Varthema, Polo and Corsali.[64] For archipelagic Asia, there was Gaetano (Villalobos), Pigafetta's and Maximilian's accounts of Magellan's voyage, Conti, Santo Stefano, Varthema, Polo, Corsali, and the anonymous Dieppe captain's account. For China and Japan, besides Ramusio's Polo, there is much information in Pires, Hayton Armenio, Conti, the Jesuit letters, Corsali, Barbaro and Barros, as well as smaller amounts in Barbosa, Giovio, and Pigafetta. For India, which became a central base for Portuguese activities, there was a tremendous amount, including extensive data in Pires, Barbosa, Barros, Corsali, Conti, Varthema, Cabral, Empoli, Gama, Lopez, and smaller notices in Alvarez, Barbaro, Santo Stefano, and the Comito Veneziano report. For Russia, the Caucasus, and more northern areas, there were Hayton, Campense, Giovio, Barbaro, Contarini, Interiano, and small amounts in Angiolello, the merchants to Persia report, and Polo. All of these were areas either barely touched on by Abulfeda, or completely untouched. And while Abulfeda does provide extensive information, as he says, on the Near and Middle East, Gastaldi had much from Ramusio for these areas as well, and quite a bit of it

---

[63] Abulfeda (Reinaud and Guyard) (1848-1883, 2, part 1, 2-3).

[64] For bibliographical details about the locations of these individual accounts in Ramusio, see Parks's excellent catalog of contents, which carries its own index (Parks, 1970), and his incisive discussion of the individual accounts. See also Milanesi's comments at the head of each of the accounts in her 1978-88 edition of Ramusio.

much more recent, including information from Pires, Barbosa, Corsali, Conti, Varthema, Barros, Angiolello, Barbaro, Contarini, the Comito Veneziano report, the merchants to Persia report, plus smaller amounts in Santo Stefano, Cabral, Alvarez, and Polo.

It is worth pointing out also that it is questionable if Gastaldi's not naming a source could make a valid point of reproach in any event. Gastaldi does not name any sources in any of his great continental maps, and he does so only in a few of his other maps. Nor is it that common to find sources named on the maps of other cartographers of the period. There by no means existed some sort of understood practice in this regard which Gastaldi was somehow violating. Ortelius regularly names his sources, but he was an exception, and the obvious rationale was that he had collected maps from many cartographers and published them as they were given to him, a completely different thing. Even he fails occasionally to give credit, as, for instance, for his Asia Minor, which is after Gastaldi, though Gastaldi is not named (Almagià, 1948, 35). Note that Gastaldi never names his friend Ramusio as a source, although he was certainly the main source for most non-European areas. The fact is, when most cartographers of the time compiled a work from various sources, it was very unusual that those sources would be named, and indeed it would seem a little pointless, if not gratuitous. Mercator names no sources for his great 1554 Europe, nor do most others. Stating that Gastaldi used Abulfeda "without giving credit" implies that we are holding Gastaldi up to some standard which didn't exist and would have been rather superfluous if it did. In any event, as we now see, if Gastaldi did make use of Abulfeda, it was quite limited.

If Gastaldi made any extensive use of Abulfeda's *Geography*, it would have been only for the Near and Middle East. But even for this area, we can make a blanket limitation from the outset that Abulfeda could certainly not have been the only source, for, though I have made no attempt at a detailed count, there are clearly not nearly enough names total in Abulfeda to account for all on Gastaldi's Asias. For example, in Abulfeda's first section, on Arabia, one of his best covered areas, there are only 163 names, and this includes a good number of places mentioned in passing, with no real locational data at all, while there are close to 300 names in Arabia on

Gastaldi's Second Part of Asia. Probably not more than half of Gastaldi's *could* have come from Abulfeda, and a cursory inspection shows the same is probably true of other areas. Still, half is a lot, and the possibility of extensive usage in the Near and Middle East remains a strong possibility.

5.3 *Gastaldi and Abulfeda: Further Considerations*

It is clear that, if Gastaldi used Abulfeda, he could only have used what had been made available to him by translation from Arabic. As we shall see below, what was available had been translated by Postel, who had brought the manuscript from the East. Though there is nothing vaguely resembling a compendium or epitome of Abulfeda in Ramusio, as is often mistakenly stated, there are a few small passages quoted or paraphrased by Ramusio after Postel in the prefatory material to his edition of Marco Polo in the *Navigazioni*,[65] with the purpose of helping to clarify some places in Polo. The problem of correct proper name transliterations from Arabic is a thorny one indeed,[66] as we shall see, and there often is enormous variation between one source and another. In the passages from Abulfeda which are in Ramusio, there are thirty-seven place names, and we know that in them we have Postel's renderings. I have found definite correspondences for twenty-two of these on Gastaldi's Asia, and there is little agreement between Postel's Abulfeda forms and those Gastaldi uses on his map. The forms, Postel's first, followed by Gastaldi's, are as follows: Alessandretta/Alixandreta,[67] Ardiul/Ardouil, Armenia/ARMENIA, Bochara/Buccara, Caffa/caffa, Calat/ Aclat, Caraman/CARAMANIA, Comager/cumania, Constantinopoli/ Constantinopoli, Coruch/curco, Elatach[river]/Volga altri ledil f.,

---

[65] The notion, apparently first given currency in modern times by E. G. R. Taylor (1930, 132 and 193; and 1935, 19), on the basis of faulty information from Josiah Simler, that Ramusio included in his work a compendium of Abulfeda's *Geography* is quite incorrect. (For more on this, see note 130 below, and the places referred to there.) All the passages and information from Abulfeda can be found, passim, on the following pages in Ramusio (1967-70, 2, second to fourth pages of "Prefatione" to Polo, and fols. 13v-14v and 16v-17r; and a one-page list of some coordinates from Abulfeda on fol. 18r; respectively, in Milanesi ed., 1978-88, 3, 24-27, 56-60, 68 and [list of coordinates] 72.). We shall cite these passages more fully below, along with their correspondences in Reinaud and Guyard's Abulfeda.

[66] See the special note at the end of this chapter, "Postel's Translating of Abulfeda."

[67] Not the Egyptian city, but in the northeast corner of the Mediterranean.

Elcur[river]/cor. F., Elgil/GILAN, Giorgian/Girgian, mar el Azach/MARE
DELLE ZABACHE, Natolia/NATOLIA, Seleucia/seleschia, Tarso/tarso,
Terbestan/TAPERISTAN, Turquestan/TVRCHESTAN, Van-van, Vastan/
Vacstan.[68] Whatever source Gastaldi took these names from, it does not
seem to have been from passages translated from Abulfeda by Postel, and
Postel's translations would have been the only available.

Besides the short passages from Abulfeda, Ramusio also includes a
short (one-page) list of some place names from Abulfeda, followed by
Abulfeda's coordinates for them, longitude then latitude. The facts that the
list is so selective and that there seems to be no particular criterion for having
chosen the places recorded, suggests that Postel was having trouble
rendering some place names from the Arabic, and as we shall see, there are
regularly tremendous problems involved in this, due to peculiarities in the
way Arabic letters are written, a problem concerning which we shall later
quote Postel himself. Oddly, though there are thirty-two pairs of coordinates,
there are corresponding place names to the left for only twenty of them. For
the other twelve, there is no referent, no place name given, so they are
coordinates for unknown places, and are quite meaningless. The likely
explanation is that there was still hope these place names could be
deciphered from Abulfeda, but they were not, and the sheet got to the printer
as we see it. In any event, the significance of the list for our purposes now is
that there is strong disagreement between these coordinates of Abulfeda, and
the positions in which the named places are found on Gastaldi's map, and so
we know that Gastaldi did not follow Abulfeda for these locations. This
great discrepancy between the coordinates given in the little list of Abulfeda
names and the positions of the same places on Gastaldi's map had been
noticed before, by Nordenskiöld,[69] and by Grande.[70]

Almagià suggested the possibility that perhaps the differences were
accounted for by the use of a different prime meridian by Abulfeda, implying
that Gastaldi could have made the adjustment himself.[71] Ramusio was

---

[68] But Vastan in Gastaldi's list of "nomi" for his First Part of Asia.

[69] Nordenskiöld (1899, 404).

[70] Grande (1905, "relazioni," 149-50).

[71] Almagià (1948, 66).

indeed aware that Abulfeda usually used a different prime meridian than that through the Canaries, and even states that one must make a ten degree adjustment in using Abulfeda's figures,[72] and it may well have been this statement that suggested to Almagià his idea. But the explanation is not valid, and in fact is typical of the facile and thoughtless statements thrown out whenever such areas are touched upon in our literature (as if the general misunderstanding of such areas somehow justifies making untested and overtly incorrect statements, with which the literature has swarmed from the start). If the suggestion were valid, there would have to be general consistency in the degree of difference between the Abulfeda's coordinates and those of Gastaldi, while in fact, there is much variation in the degree of difference between the two for the various cities named. I made the same comparison, for ten well-known places not in Ramusio's list, between Gastaldi's map and Abulfeda's figures as in the Reinaud-Guyard translation and got the same results. The ten places, using Gastaldi's spellings, and with the *difference* in longitude between the two sources indicated in parentheses, are: Antiochia (1°10′), Sinopi (6°40′), Aleppo (8°33′), Baruti (9°05′), Alessandra (9°06′), Damasco (9°30′), Ierusalem (12°30′), Bagdat (9°10′), Buccara (20°55′), Cabul (22°20′). Note that there are also considerable differences in latitude figures between the two sources, although of course not as great, the differences varying from an insignificant quarter of a degree to over six degrees, the average difference being around two degrees.[73] It would seem that, if Gastaldi took into account Abulfeda's positions at all, he

---

[72] Ramusio says that, "this author does not commence in longitude from the Fortunate Isles, as does Ptolemy, but from the furthest littoral of the coast of Africa, and this is said to differ ten degrees from that which Ptolemy does. And therefore I advise the reader wanting to compare them to those of Ptolemy, to strike off ten degrees in the longitudes which here below will be quoted from the said." (Ramusio, 1967-70, 2, 5th page of "Prefatione"; Milanesi ed., 1978-88, 3, 25). Ramusio could have gotten this only from Abulfeda himself (Abulfeda, in Reinaud and Guyard, 1848-83, 2, pt. 1, 96), so this part must have been among those translated by Postel.

[73] Here, of course, there is no possible question of beginning from different bases.

would have done so only in a most general (and unverifiable) way, perhaps doing a little pushing and shoving to and fro, here and there.[74]

We could close here, but as we have seen, real reasons exist which imply that Abulfeda should have been a valuable source for Gastaldi in the Middle East. It was, after all, a work by a geographer who was himself from the Middle East, and he gave coordinate figures. The question of why Gastaldi would not have used it hangs heavily over all this, and is a sufficiently nagging one that we might wonder if something in our analyses so far has been wrong. I think we can come to a conclusion on this pretty easily. We saw that Nicolay was aware of its potential and stated so. Ramusio also much praises it, in the July 7, 1553 "Prefatione" to edition of

---

[74] A direct check of names in Abulfeda, as we have him in Reinaud's and Guyard's translation, against the names on Gastaldi's map, the traditional method in such cases, cannot provide conclusive results in our case, at least not working within the parameters imposed upon the present researcher, due to the following. Without having made an actual name by name comparison, a preliminary investigation assures me that not more than about ten percent of the names in Abulfeda's section on Arabia have definitely recognizable correspondents on the Arabia in Gastaldi's Second Part of Asia. However, as we show in a special note at the end of this chapter, due to tremendous difficulties involved in the transliteration of proper names from Arabic to Roman alphabet languages, it is quite possible for one interpreter to come up with a rendering of a name which is largely or entirely unrecognizable next to the rendering of the same name by a different interpreter. When the proper name is a generally known place, as Beirut, Samarkand, Aleppo, etc., there is usually no problem, but if it is not, the problems can be insurmountable. To make more meaningful comparisons here, one would need to have access to the original Postel manuscript, and also have knowledge of the Arabic language, and the present writer has neither. Nevertheless, my very preliminary findings do show little correspondence between Gastaldi and Abulfeda, just as have all other avenues of approach we have used so far. It is worth noting that it has been shown that, on the well-known Hadji Ahmed world map made in Venice in ca. 1559 (Shirley, 1987, no. 103), although its author mentions Abulfeda as inspiration for his map, there is also no agreement at all between locations of places on the map and Abulfeda's figures (Ménage, 1958, 309, note 1). The principal source seems to have been Fine's world map, from which it is largely copied. The only other source of note mentioned by Ménage is Ramusio (Ménage, 1958, 295, note 2, 305 and 306). Arbel seems to suggest Gastaldi as the author of this map (Arbel, 2002, 25), and this writer tends to agree.

Marco Polo in volume 2 (1559) of the *Navigazioni*.[75] It was only with the help of this book, he says, that he was able to elucidate and understand several passages from Polo, and in this "Prefatione" and in a "Dichiaratione d'alcuni luoghi ne libri di M. Marco Polo" (Explanation of several places in the books of M. Marco Polo) which follows shortly after, he draws on information from Abulfeda's work several times to this end.[76] He also tells us in the "Prefatione" that Abulfeda had been knowledgeable in philosophy and astrology, that he "reduced, as into a compendium, all that which many Arab authors had already written about degrees of longitude and latitude of the said parts," and generally praises him in other ways, concluding with: "Now this book of geography is not fully translated, but there lacks the greater part of the commentaries concerning each province, which if it were

---

[75] Ramusio (1967-70, 2, 2nd to 3rd page of "Prefatione"; Milanesi ed., 1978-88, 24-25).

[76] Ramusio draws on Abulfeda eight times in the prefatory material. In two instances, he directly quotes from Abulfeda, once an eighteen-line quote, and once a five-line one, and these twenty-three lines are the sum total of what we have anywhere translated from the Arab geographer by Postel. The rest are paraphrases or, in two cases, simple mentions of a place name. The passages are of some interest, for they are unquestionably the first extracts and information ever published in a western language taken from the work of one of the classic Arab geographers. For the student who might wish to follow this up, the passages (cited from the 1967-70 edition, all from the first pagination preceding the Polo account, and with corresponding locations from the Milanesi 1978-88 edition), together with the corresponding passages in Abulfeda (cited from the 1848-1883 Reinaud-Guyard edition), are as follows: (1, paraphrase) Ramusio, 2, 3rd to 4th pages "Prefatione" (Abulfeda, 2, pt. 1, 40, 282-84, and cf. also 319-21); (2, place name citation) Ramusio, 2, 4th page, "Prefatione" (Abulfeda, 2, pt. 2, 216); (3, paraphrase) Ramusio, 2, fol. 13v (Abulfeda, 2, pt. 1, 14, and cf. also note 4 same page, and p. 26); (4, paraphrase) Ramusio, 2, fols. 13v-14r (Abulfeda, 2, pt. 1, 35-36, and cf. also 2, pt. 2, 32 and 133); (5, place name citation) Ramusio, 2, fol. 14r (Abulfeda, 2, pt. 2, 208ff on Turkestan); (6, quotation) Ramusio, 2, fol.14r (Abulfeda, 2, pt. 1, 42-44); (7, paraphrase) Ramusio, 2, fol. 14v (Abulfeda, 2, pt. 1, 52 and 2, pt. 2, 143 and 148-49); (8, paraphrase and quote) Ramusio, 2, 16v-17r (Abulfeda, 2, pt. 2, 122, and (the quote) 2, pt. 1, 24). The corresponding places to the above eight citations from the 1967-70 edition of Ramusio are found, respectively, in Milanesi's 1978-88 edition, as follows: (1) 3, 25-26; (2) 3, 27; (3) 3, 56; (4) 3, 57-58; (5) 3, 58; (6) 3, 58-59; (7) 3, 59-60; and (8) 3, 68. The last quote is given in our chapter eight. Other than the one-page list of place names with coordinates looked at earlier here, there is no more Abulfeda material in Ramusio. There is no "compendium" of Abulfeda in Ramusio as is sometimes stated.

all Latin, we would have a detailed geography of the parts of Asia and Africa of which notice was had at his time, and we would know the names of the provinces, cities, mountains, rivers, and seas, as [they] at present are called, with the degrees of longitude and latitude . . . which would be one of the beautiful and rare things that could be seen in these times." It's clear that Ramusio feels sanguine about Abulfeda, but it is also clear that much is not translated, including evidently many names and coordinates. Outside Italy, it also came to be highly regarded, and much sought after, especially among northern geographers and scholars. Josias Simler, in his additions to Gesner's bibliography, carries the entry: "Abulfeda, eminent cosmographer, equal or superior to Ptolemy in the description of the world subject to the Islamites, with the names adapted to our times, was brought from the Orient by Guillaume Postel: of which book Postel has left a compendium from his translation at Venice to Ramusio, in order that he might publish it in the second volume of the new world."[77]

Throughout the latter part of the century, we find Abulfeda's *Geography* praised and sought after by Dee, Mercator, Hakluyt and Ortelius, although it is clear from the nature of the statements that none of them had ever seen it.[78] In 1631-32 Wilhelm Schickard declares that European-made

[77] Simler (1555, 1). The phrase "the second volume of the new world" is obviously a garbled reference to the *Navigationi*. It is no doubt this reference principally that gave rise to the notion of a compendium given to Ramusio or printed in Ramusio. As we know, nothing was published in Ramusio except a few short extracts and paraphrases, and there is nothing in Ramusio's comments on Abulfeda in his "Prefatione" to volume two which suggests he had come into possession of anything that could be called a compendium. To make a true and proper compendium, one really needs to start from a full text, and we can be sure that was not available.

[78] For paraphrases of Dee's comments, from an unpublished 1577 work, see Taylor (1930, 132); for Mercator's comment in a 1580 letter to Hakluyt, see Hakluyt (1903-05, 3, 281); for John Newberie seeking a copy of Abulfeda in 1583 for Hakluyt, see Hakluyt (1903-05, V, 452). Hakluyt adoringly publishes a passage from Ramusio's extracts from Abulfeda in 1589 (Hakluyt, 1903-05, 3, 412-13) and there is a mention by Ortelius to Camden of supposed preparations by Hakluyt in 1588 to publish Abulfeda, which Ortelius heard of from his friend Emanuel (Demetrius) van Meteren, which assuredly grew out of reports of his preparing the last mentioned quote from Abulfeda's passage in Ramusio (Camden, 1691, 33).

maps are highly defective, and begins to translate Abulfeda, thinking that therein lies the best hope for reforming cartography,[79] and later in the same century, Melchisédech Thevenot speaks of, "Abulfeda, the most exact of all the geographers, and the only from which we are to hope for the positions of the cities of the Orient."[80] There were no doubt many others infected with this Abulfeda euphoria, even much later.[81] But those who looked deeper invariably came out with a different impression. Schickard in the end could not translate Abulfeda, much less use him for a reform of cartography, and in the end speaks of the corruptions and inconsistencies in the text.[82] Eusebe Renaudot wrote in 1733: "All the learned, and, upon what they have said, all that were strangers to the Oriental tongues, have fed up the public with the excessive commendations they have bestowed on Abulfeda's work, though often without knowing why or wherefore."[83] That this was still going on even in the early nineteenth century is clear from Jourdain's reaction against it: "History may draw some fruit from [Abulfeda], but the geographer, properly speaking, will find here only information very imperfect, and which will never be able to serve to rectify the geographical maps of the Orient."[84] Ullmann, in fact, observes that Abulfeda was overvalued from the start.[85] We recall Abulfeda was the first ancient Arab geographer's work to reach Europe, and it was no doubt its novelty that gave rise to its exaggerated reputation. In any event, I think we have enough here to show that Abulfeda was much lauded and had great appeal, indeed was a sensation, as long as it remained distant, inaccessible, untranslated, and thus an unknown quantity, but once one delved into it, it was found seriously wanting. Renowned Polo scholar Andrew Muller, and indeed "many learned Orientalists," thought that

---

[79] Oehme (1978, 311 and 366).
[80] Thevenot (1663-96?, 1, in a two-page *avis* preceding his account of Anthony Jenkinson's travels. The account occurs in varying places in Thevenot, depending on the copy one is consulting).
[81] Oehme (1978, 364-66).
[82] Oehme (1978, 368).
[83] Renaudot (1733, x).
[84] Jourdain (1811, 220).
[85] Ullmann (1978, 121-22).

it would certainly elucidate Polo "and afford us a fair prospect of China,"[86] but in fact Abulfeda's section on China, never translated until Guyard finished his edition in 1883, has but four pages, and definitely identifies only nine places, this, note, concerning a place as vast and populated as China![87] We recall Lelewel's and Sezgin's observations that one could not make a good map from Abulfeda. And we've seen it has the fatal flaw that it sometimes gives longitudes from a source using a different prime meridian than most, without informing the reader of this, although the significance of this is a hard thing to assess.

We don't know how much of Abulfeda Postel managed to translate.[88] We have only one statement in this regard that might be taken as reliable. Postel himself told his friend Andreas Masius in a letter of Mar. 20, 1555, that he had undertaken a translation of Abulfeda, then observed:

> Sed nonsum ausus sequi reliquum Versionis, propter carentiam punctorum et non distinctas literas *be, te, the, nun, je,* quae corpore literae non different, donec alterum etiam exemplar nanciscerer. Verti tamen generalem descriptionem totius Operis . . ." (But I have not risked to pursue the remainder of the translation, until I might chance upon a different copy, because of missing points and the letters *be, te, the, nun, je* not having been differentiated, which letters are [thus] not

---

[86] Renaudot (1733, x-xi).
[87] Reinaud and Guyard (1848-1883, 2, pt. 2, 122-25).
[88] See our special note on this question at the end of the chapter.

distinguished in substance. All the same I have translated a general description of the whole work . . .")[89]

The five Arabic letters Postel mentions are notoriously difficult in Arabic.[90] But where he stopped, how much he did, and what order he was translating things in, we have no way to know for sure. But if he translated any sizeable portion at all, it couldn't have been long before a few of the renegade longitude figures, originating from sources which used a different prime meridian than that of most, appeared in the corpus. In fact, it is likely that three of the places occurring in the two small samples we looked at earlier are such. In the first set, consisting of the names taken from the Abulfeda coordinates list in Ramusio, the longitudinal difference between the locations as on Gastaldi's Asia and in the Abulfeda list is, for all places but one, Tiphlis, within two or three degrees at the most from the average of about

---

[89] From letter quoted by Levi della Vida (1939, 314). Levi della Vida, who in this same work is the first to note the reference to a compendium given to Ramusio by Simler in 1555, interprets Postel in this passage as referring to a started but unfinished compendium. However, Postel is clearly speaking here of an attempted and abandoned full translation. The only reference to a compendium is that of Simler, and since his source for the citation was probably Postel himself (since Simler also includes reference to other of the manuscripts Postel brought back), which would mean Simler himself never saw the item, it is possible Postel exaggerated, or perhaps used the word compendium for lack of a better term for what may have just been a series of extracts, which certainly better accords with what Ramusio appears to have been in possession of. In any event, there is no other mention of a compendium at the time. Dee mentions one briefly in 1577, in an unpublished work (Taylor, 1930, 132), and Mercator makes a passing mention of one in a 1580 letter (Taylor, 1935, 1, 161), but Dee was clearly depending on Simler, and no doubt Mercator's comment ultimately goes back to the same. Levi also speaks of Postel giving the supposed compendium to Ramusio in 1554, but this is a supposition, and certainly a wrong one, for we know Ramusio already possessed what he had of Abulfeda in July, 1553, when he wrote the preface to his Polo, and it seems unlikely he received Postel's manuscript and papers from Postel himself.

[90] When diacritical marks, or points, are omitted in conjunction with these five letters, which often enough happens, they become indistinguishable. See Kennedy (1983, 101), and Beckingham (1983), and the special note at the end of this chapter, "Postel's Translating of Abulfeda."

16°45′, but for Tiphlis, the difference is only 5°32′, a little over ten degrees from the average difference, and this probably stems back to a usage of a prime meridian ten degrees different from that used by most sources in Abulfeda. For the second group, consisting of random major cities chosen by the present author, the longitude difference between Gastaldi's Asia and Abulfeda for two cities, Buccara and Cabul, is close to ten degrees higher than the highest for any of the other cities, and there is much less variance in range across all of the other places. Probably, the longitude figures for these three places are based on a prime meridian ten degrees different from the norm.

Gastaldi, like all cartographers of the time, was determining locations for places on his maps of Asia by the old method of itineraries, that is, by pushing and shoving things to and fro, a method primitive, but workable to a degree. One couldn't hope for latitudinal or, especially, longitudinal accuracy, but by consulting and comparing various sources, texts, one could push and shove places about until at least *relative* interpositional relationships between places were close to correct, certainly more than sufficiently close to correct, that when one of these renegade longitude figures popped into the picture, causing a sudden approximate ten degree leap in inaccuracy, it would be immediately apparent. This is what I believe basically happened, and what accounts for the fact that in the samples we used, there was no sign at all of any use of Abulfeda by Gastaldi. The tables, after all, were corrupt, and in particular contained the fatal flaw of occasional places which were assigned longitudes based on different prime meridians. Gastaldi, I believe, simply became aware of this fatal flaw, after which he would naturally enough have declined to use the source anymore. As we have abundantly shown, Abulfeda's *Geography* was a sensation until tried out. Probably Gastaldi was as interested at first as were Ramusio or Nicolay, but once he had started working on it, he was bound to have run into these occasional figures which were wildly off. In any event, whatever the reason, we have certainly found no definite use by Gastaldi of Abulfeda's *Geography* in his maps.

5.4 *Gastaldi and Sezgin's Theory*

157

Professor Fuat Sezgin (1924-2018) of the Institute for the History of Arabic and Islamic Sciences at the Johann Wolfgang Goethe University in Frankfurt, Germany, began in the 1960s actively pursuing a program of publishing classic works of Arabic-Islamic science and scholarship, and works about them, certainly a very welcome initiative, considering the West's always low level of understanding of the Arabic-Islamic world. In 2000 he published a volume titled *Mathematische Geographie und Kartographie im Islam und ihr Fortleben im Abendland* (*Mathematical Geography and Cartography in Islam and Their Adoption in the West*).[91] It is an enormous work in three large volumes, and has a sixty-nine-page bibliography, and 187 pages of indexes, an atlas volume, and a good, detailed table of contents. It covers an enormous amount of material and will be useful as a reference work for many years to come, both for text and reproductions. It is filled with factual information on a large number of persons and subjects, all readily accessible via indexes, and, as far as I can judge with my limited experience in the area, reliable and accurate in the main. But I must disagree strongly with what he has to say about Gastaldi and his cartography of Asia.

As we have seen earlier, there was virtually nothing in the way of modern cartography of Asia before Gastaldi except the ugly schematic map of Münster, and a few small and sketchy maps of some parts of the continent. Gastaldi's large and detailed Asia in three Parts had no precedents whatsoever, and its sudden appearance was impressive, even overwhelming, as we have seen in the case of Ortelius. Sezgin notices this and points it out repeatedly in the course of his discussions.[92] For instance: "The importance of the innovation introduced by Gastaldi in European cartography of the old Oecumene cannot be praised highly enough."[93] Where does this unprecedented improvement come from, he asks naturally enough, and concludes that it must have come from Arab-Islamic models which came into

91 Sezgin (2000). Sezgin also published an article (2001), which gives the key points of his ideas. A short review of the book by Helmut Minow appeared in *Cartographica Helvetica*, 24 (July, 2001), 48-49, which gives a short resume of Sezgin's ideas.
92 Sezgin (2000, 1, 397, 627-28,; 2, 97, 99, 102-03, 108, 111, 112, 116-17, 455).
93 Sezgin (2000, 2, 111).

Gastaldi's hands. This conclusion is repeated often,[94] and these Arab-Islamic models would stem apparently from about the second quarter of the sixteenth century.[95] These presumed models would have underlain not just Gastaldi's 1559-61 Asia, but also the Asia maps which appeared first in the 1554 second edition of volume one of the *Navigazioni*,[96] and we are told that these models would have been based on a prime meridian passing 28°30′ west of Toledo.[97] What it is about Gastaldi's maps of Asia that leads Sezgin to the conclusion that they go back to models based on this old prime meridian we are not told, nor are we told what significance, if any, we should attribute to the assumption that they do.

The main problem with Professor Sezgin's conclusion is that he never gives any concrete reason for having come to it. There are no artifacts to support it. There are no Arab-Islamic maps of the period, or of any period before Gastaldi's time, which bear the slightest resemblance to Gastaldi's maps of Asia, or which could have served as models for them (nor are there any western ones, except for the Portuguese charts as regards the coastlines alone). Nor are there any references to such maps, nor, as far as I can make out, is there any reason or necessity to posit that such ever existed, other than as an explanation for the sudden appearance of Gastaldi's Asias. Nor does there seem to be much evidence of any other kind. When Professor Sezgin states his conclusion, and he does so several times, it is usually statement alone, emphatic, but undocumented (an example: "without going into further reflections, might I still once more give voice to my interpretation, that Gastaldi must have had as models maps from the Arab-Islamic world, where

[94] Sezgin (2000, 1, 353, 397, 629; 2, 100, 106, 107, 114, 116). Sezgin seems unaware of the vast resources in Ramusio.

[95] Sezgin (2000, 2, 102, 110-11, 115).

[96] Sezgin does not accept that the Ramusio Asia maps are by Gastaldi, although he treats of them considerably in his section devoted to Gastaldi (2000, 2, 99-116).

[97] Sezgin (2000, 1, 397, 628,; 2, 92, 100, 101-02, 106, 107, 110, 114, 115). This 28°30′ meridian is an old one which resulted from a shortening of the width of the Mediterranean Sea by Arab cartographers. There is no need to go here into the interesting history of this meridian, the best and clearest discussion of which is still that in Wright (1923, 90-97); shorter, but also clear, is Durand (1952, 100-01 and 103).

longitude degrees were coordinated with the prime meridian passing 28°30′ west of Toledo and 17°30′ west of the island of Ferro"[98]). When he does lend documentation to the statement, it is in such broad terms that it does not demonstrate anything.[99] For instance, at one point, he says in regard to Gastaldi's 1559 First Part of Asia: "Not only the grid underlying the map, but the whole topographical content shows, that we have to do with a model of Arab-Islamic origin. It obviously came into Gastaldi's hands in the more mature years of his employment with cartography."[100] But there is nothing preceding or following here to tell us what it is about "the grid underlying the map" or the "whole topographical content" that should lead us to the conclusion that it goes back to an Arab-Islamic model. In another place,[101] he states that the coordinates of many places on Gastaldi's First Part of Asia are in accord with the coordinates in Arab-Islamic geographical tables of

---

[98] Sezgin (2000, 2, 106).

[99] An exception perhaps is his observation that the Asia maps in Ramusio are south-oriented (Sezgin, 2000, 2, 100 and 102-03), and we recall this is true as well of the Gastaldi map of Asia in the Ducal Palace in Venice. This does make one think of Arab sources, but it does not do so strongly. By no means were all Arab-Islamic maps south-oriented (Harley and Woodward, 1992, 518), and south-oriented maps are not as rare among European cartographers as we usually think. For instance, in Heijden's survey of European-made maps of the continent of Europe, six out of the first sixteen maps are oriented with south at the top (Heijden, 1992). (Very possibly our notion that almost all European maps are north-oriented is partly just due to little preference having been given to reproducing south-oriented maps.) Also, as regards these maps in Ramusio, we recall that he himself describes their sources thus: "In the present three maps the coasts are described following the navigational charts of the Portuguese, and the inland, following the writers, which are contained in this first volume" (Ramusio, 1967-70, 1, [fol. 35r], preceding the three maps after the index; Milanesi ed., 1978-88, 1, [911]), and he makes the same observation on the title page of the volume. In fact, we show in our compound Cartobibliography entry no. (77.-79.) that the source for the southern orientation is probably simply Ramusio, basing himself not on Arab sources, but upon Aristotle's ideas in his work *De Caelo*.

[100] Sezgin (2000, 1, 397).

[101] Sezgin (2000, 2, 109).

coordinates, as far as these are preserved, but gives no examples, and the statement is far too broad to have any significance.[102]

True, as we read there are many, if not overmany, presentations (sometimes with tables, often without) and discussions of variations in longitude between two or more places, variations in the widths of seas or land masses, and variations in total relative longitudinal difference between two points far distant from each other, in the maps of Gastaldi, Mercator, Ortelius, Arab-Islamic sources, etc., and one senses that Sezgin felt that these were in some way key factors, key distances, key demonstrations, but in fact it is often not clear why these comparisons are being presented to us and what they are supposed to be taken as demonstrating. We seem to drift from one to another of these expositions without any sense of knowing where we are going or why. The feeling this writer gets is that Professor Sezgin took considerations of longitudinal positions and longitudinal differences between remote points somewhat too seriously in these early works, whether western, or Arab-Islamic.

---

[102] Many such tables exist, and there is much variation among them, so there is no way to know what tables Sezgin had in mind here. In any event, the observation is inconsistent with his main theory. Did Gastaldi copy Arab-Islamic maps, or did he take figures from Arab-Islamic tables? True, a combination of the two would not be impossible, but as we remarked earlier, these old tables were not generally used to make maps. The same sort of vagueness which we see in Sezgin's statement here is seen more explicitly in a table which is presented in volume two at pp. 113-14. The table compares the coordinates of thirty-nine places as given in four sources, Gastaldi, Mercator, Arab-Islamic, and modern. But how are we to take the figures under the column "Arab-Islamic"? Whose Arab-Islamic coordinates are they? Where are they from? We know there was much disagreement among Arab geographers and astronomers on coordinate values, and, we recall, one of the most characteristic features in Abulfeda is his giving of coordinates from varying sources. Regarding the great disagreement among different Arab geographers in this regard see also the telling table given by Tibbets in Harley and Woodward (1992, 99). So, are the figures in the column under "Arab-Islamic" in Sezgin's table developed selectively from several geographical tables? If so, on the basis of what criteria? Or are they some kind of averages? Without knowing these things, the column of figures becomes meaningless, as does the table itself and any conclusions based on it. At some other places too we are left in the dark as to the bases of Sezgin's expositions.

Several times, Sezgin expresses amazement at Gastaldi's coordinates.[103] ("Where did these coordinates come from?"[104]). But in fact there is nothing astonishing about Gastaldi's coordinates at all. They are very far from the truth in all cases, just as they would be for all cartographers for centuries to come.[105] It might be useful to say a few words here relative to the question of the degree of seriousness with which we should delve into questions of mathematical accuracy when studying these sixteenth century maps, especially of far parts of the world. Fifty-some years ago, Marcel Destombes, in speaking of a large ca. 1587 set of twelve globe gores made in Antwerp, and based mostly on works of Ortelius and the Postel 1581 world map,[106] said of the treatment of the land masses on that map: "The treatment is systematic to allow for the copious nomenclature, sacrificing accuracy to clarity. We are therefore dealing with a map which is exclusively geographical, containing no nautical information, with a great philological index rather than a mathematical work. It is therefore unrealistic to calculate coordinates . . . ."[107] This, I think, perfectly applies to Gastaldi's Asia as well, as to all of his maps of non-European areas, as well as the maps by others of those areas in those times. What, really, could a cartographer of the day do as to these more remote areas? Having accepted, perhaps more or less subconsciously, one or another estimate of the earth's circumference, and thus too, for the length of a degree, he had then to make the best estimate he could as to what extent of the total circumference to ascribe to Eurasia as a whole, as far as he knew it, and then within the parameters of that estimation,

---

[103] Sezgin (2000, 1, 627-28; 2, 97) and Sezgin (2001, 25).

[104] Sezgin (2001, 25).

[105] It is worth pointing out that, although Sezgin does not think Gastaldi used Abulfeda, and specifically states that Abulfeda was out of date by comparison with the more recent models Gastaldi presumably used (Sezgin, 2000, 1, 107), the fact is that Abulfeda's figures are better than Gastaldi's for most places, always excepting for the renegade figures that pop up in Abulfeda. Both geographers were way off, but Abulfeda usually rather less so for Middle Eastern places. The fact was also noticed by Ménage as regards positions on the Hadji Ahmed map (Ménage, 1958).

[106] Shirley, 1987, no. 144.

[107] Destombes (1970, 86); the map is Shirley no. 156.

to approximate as well as possible the interrelative positions of the various places of which he had information. There was no other way.

In all cases, the greatest problems came from the impossibility of accurately establishing one's vital bases, that is, the circumference of the globe, the length of a degree, and beyond that, the great difficulty of obtaining reliable data as to comparative positions of places known by name. In all cases, that of Ptolemy, the Arab scientists' geographical tables, and western sixteenth century maps, there is a certain degree of relative correctness in the interpositional locations of places across Asia, but at the same time there is in all cases and for all locales enormous and consistent errors as regards absolute longitudinal positions for the simple reason that the whole picture is tremendously askew as a result of the bases being totally incorrect. Thus, we know for certain that in all these cases, no longitudinal positions indicate astronomically determined locations, and the ultimate derivation for all positions had to have been by comparisons of information in itineraries and similar textual sources, and I suspect Gastaldi was well aware of all this himself. There is no more reason to be astonished at the locations of Gastaldi's places, than there is to be astonished at the locations of places on Mercator's or Ortelius's maps of the area, or those of anyone else. All were badly off. What is impressive in Gastaldi's Asia, however, is the sheer size of the map, the quantity of information, the number of place names. *We should not, that is, confuse what is to be sure an impressive display in quantity for an impressive display in mathematical accuracy. The former there is, but the latter there is not.* What we are saying, with Professor Sezgin's observations on Gastaldi in mind, is that there is not yet, in Gastaldi's maps of far countries, anything to be amazed at in the way of geodetic accuracy, and consequently nothing of that nature crying out for explanation. What does cry out for explanation is the pure bulk of place names, but the obvious first place to turn here is to the tremendous quantity of information accumulated in Ramusio. While this remains to be checked for many areas of Asia, it is certainly the most likely source for the majority of the data on the map.

It is impossible (and also unnecessary) to deny altogether Sezgin's theory, and it is worth pointing out that, of all places in the West, Venice is certainly the most likely place to have been reached by documents of the sort Sezgin suggests, and not just because of its high level of activity in cartography. The amount of interaction of various types between Italy in general, and Venice in particular, and the East, at the time was enormous. Just a glance at certain places in Braudel's modern classic *The Mediterranean and the Mediterranean World in the Age of Philip II* shows what massive trade and activity were going on between Italy and the Levant in the sixteenth century,[108] and he speaks in one place of "the 4,000 Venetian families living in the Levant, in Damascus, Aleppo, Alexandria, Cairo, even in Baghdad," this in the 1580s, but we can be sure this was not a new situation at the time.[109] We also remember Gastaldi's evidently close connections with Michele Membré, interpreter for the Republic in the Levant,[110] and he probably was personally acquainted with Postel, who had great interest in the East, and had traveled there twice. We also know that Gastaldi was acquainted with the illustrious Spanish sometime ambassador to Venice, Diego Hurtado de Mendoza, who provided him with the information for his first map, the 1544 Spain; and Mendoza, who learned Arabic in Granada before going to the University of Salamanca, collected many Greek and Arabic manuscripts, which he would later give to the Escorial.[111] But these facts only establish that the time and place were right. They in no way give direct support to Sezgin's theory. There is still no necessity that I can see for the theory, and there is no positive evidence at all to support it, regardless of a flood of irrelevant verbiage and circumlocution

---

[108] Braudel (1972-73, 1255-56).

[109] Braudel (1972-73, 560). Fabris too, speaks of a circle of erudites in sixteenth century Venice interested in the East, as reflected in Venetian publishing (Fabris, 1989, 13).

[110] See Perocco (1994, 215-16), and Almagià (1962). See also, on the intense and complicated connections between Membré, Tramezzino, Ramusio, and the eastern world the work of Bragantini (1987).

[111] Dannenfeldt (1955, 107).

in Sezgin which alleges that there is.[112] I have read and re-read Sezgin's section on Gastaldi, and his remarks on so-called "Arab-Islamic" coordinates. There is simply no evidence whatsoever to give the slightest basis to the statements on Gastaldi's use of Arab-Islamic sources. Sezgin simply repeats and repeats but gives no evidence to support his claims. Indeed, no reason exists even to have made these claims. This is simply pseudo-scholarship, based on nothing but repetition, argument by brainwashing one might say. Gastaldi's Asia is based on Portuguese charts, and to a degree, the *Navigazioni*, for the coast, and for the interior, on Ramusio, as shown in our chapter four, although it is possible that a few names from that which Postel managed to translate from Abulfeda might have slipped in.

Besides Abulfeda and Sezgin's theory, there has been one other suggestion that Gastaldi used Arab sources in his maps. It has been suggested that the information on Gastaldi's map of Africa in Ramusio is partly from Idrisi.[113] As we have seen, Biasutti has established that the map is based on information from the texts in Ramusio. S. Maqbul Ahmad discusses the influence of Idrisi in Europe, and concludes: "If there was any influence of al-Idrisi in western Europe, it was only indirect."[114] If indeed there are any elements from Idrisi in the Gastaldi Africa, they would be of such an indirect nature as Ahmad suggests. While Leo Africanus mainly uses his own experiences in his account of North Africa, he also made some use of information from medieval Arab geographers, including Idrisi.[115]

Summing up, I see little to no evidence that Gastaldi used Arab sources in compiling his Asia. It is true that there remain large portions of his

---

[112] The most convincing evidence of this is in the atlas volume to Sezgin's work itself, which contains all known Arab-Islamic cartographical works. There are also no known Arab-Islamic texts which could account for Gastaldi's tremendous array of detail and names. But the massive topological and other data in the first two volumes of Ramusio's *Navigationi* provide more than enough to account easily for the amazing manifestation of information on Gastaldi's map..

[113] Norwich (1997, 9).

[114] Ahmad, in Harley and Woodward (1992, 172).

[115] Bartold (1947, 130).

map for which no one has yet attempted to isolate the sources, and as already noted, no one has yet undertaken the grueling task of comparing all the names on the map with the vast number of place names in the Ramusio Asia accounts. However, for all areas of Asia for which research has been done, the source has been exclusively Ramusio. No work has yet shown any other source for any parts of Asia. Ramusio has also been shown to be the source for the overwhelming majority, perhaps over 90%, of the data on Gastaldi's 1564 Africa, and Ramusio is unquestionably the main source for Gastaldi's America. Finally, we know that Ramusio's stated main purpose in making his compilation was to provide information for the creation of better modern maps of the world beyond Europe. Certainly, then, at the present stage of research, it is reasonable to postulate that the most likely principal source for the unchecked parts of Gastaldi's Asia was Ramusio.

SPECIAL ENDNOTES TO CHAPTER 5

1 Postel's 1567 Letter to Ortelius

Ortelius sent to Postel a gift copy of his 1567 Asia, made after Gastaldi, the map upon which we find, in the note to the reader, Ortelius's claim that Gastaldi took his Asia from Abulfeda, quoted near the beginning of this chapter. Postel wrote to thank him April 9, 1567 in a letter which is preserved, and this letter has been taken as indirect confirmation of Gastaldi's use of Abulfeda.[116] Indirect, because Postel does not actually state in this very vague latter that Gastaldi used Abulfeda. Indeed, as Almagià notes, Postel's Latin is not always clear, and it is hard to be sure what he does state. The letter is known through the collection of Ortelius correspondence published by Jan Hendrick Hessels in 1887.[117] Hessels, a recognized authority in Latin, gives running summary paraphrases in the third person for the letters he publishes, with numbers inserted in the paraphrases corresponding to numbers he has inserted in the main text, for orientation. It

---

[116] Almagià (1948, 65-66).
[117] Hessels (1887, letter 19, pp. 42-43).

is the first four sentences which are relevant here. For the first three of them, Hessels has:

> 1. The writer, thanking Ortelius for his maps of Asia, points out that it has appeared in the same form, in which he had long been thinking of sending forth some day, by his own exertions, or through others, the inhabited portion of our Northern region on a universal chart. 2. The map is somewhat larger than a quadrant, but he feels sure that when it is enlarged with its three other quadrants, it may take the place of the best map and astrolabe ever published. 3. He thinks a publication of their common studies may some day be advantageous to the Church of Christ, in the name of which he thanks Ortelius for claiming for him the praise of which the Italians had deprived him.

Nothing is very clear here, presuming Hessels's rendering of the bad Latin is correct. We can intuit that the last clause should be taken as implying his belief that Gastaldi should have given some credit to Postel on the map,[118] and from the fourth sentence we can perhaps intuit that this credit deserved would consist in his having provided to Gastaldi information from Abulfeda, but, if that is his intent, we might wish he had been a little less abstruse in saying so.

The fourth sentence is: "Si quando ex Bibliotheca illa Ducis Bauariae D. Otthonis Henrici vbi ducentis aureis numis Abilfedeam nostrum cum alijs voluminibus oppignerare sum coactus, licebit recuperare, erit vnde et meorum laborum et tue diligentiae assertionisque nostrae sedulitatis testimonium possis abunde confirmare." While the prudence of Hessels and Almagià in avoiding a direct translation of this is undeniable, and while the present writer can certainly not claim any great expertise in Latin (even when good Latin), I think the following comes pretty close to a correct understanding: "If at any time one will be able to recover our Abilfeda with fourteen other volumes from that library of the Duke of Bavaria D. Otto Henry where I have been compelled to pawn [them] for the sum of two

---

[118] Gastaldi, as we have pointed out, never names any of his sources, not even Ramusio, on his extra-European maps, and rarely on his others.

hundred gold florins, [it] will be wherewith *you* can abundantly corroborate testimony both of my labors and of your conscientious advocacy, as well as of our earnestness."[119] There seems to be a subtle suggestion or hope here that the affluent Ortelius might recover the manuscripts and that it would be advantageous for him to do so. Hessels, in fact, who may well have been aware of nuances of meaning in the passage which are not evident to me, summarizes the sentence as follows: "4. He requests Ortelius to recover, if possible, from the library of Duke Otho Henry of Bavaria, the Abulfeda and fourteen other volumes which he had to give in pawn there for two hundred gold-florins." Upon this, we can attempt to reveal what is perhaps the real *raison d'étre* for Postel's response to Ortelius.

Postel was greatly stricken at being compelled to give up his beloved manuscripts in pawn in early 1555, especially at what he considered to be a paltry price for them. Levi della Vida notes that, in his March 20, 1555 letter to his friend Andreas Masius, he laments the loss "in terms so bitter and moving, that they merit being reproduced in their entirety."[120] Shortly after pawning the manuscripts, he came up with a plan by which he hoped to ransom them, as he informed Masius in a letter of June 7, 1555. The letter, poorly preserved, is missing much of the relevant parts, but the plan apparently involved negotiations connected with his plans to publish an Arabic New Testament.[121] But the plan failed, very possibly because of Postel's being imprisoned for suspicion of heresy while the negotiations were going on.[122] In 1563 he devised a more promising means for retrieving the manuscripts, by which a wealthy Augsburg patrician, Johann Georg Paumgartner, agreed to redeem the manuscripts in return for some other manuscripts which Postel had in keeping in Paris. Postel had assembled these manuscripts at Lyon to make the trade, but they were unfortunately lost

---

[119] Stress added.

[120] Levi della Vida (1939, 313-14) gives the letter in full, as does Chaufepié (1750-59, 3, 221-22). A resumé in German is in Lossen (1886, 196).

[121] Levi della Vida (1939, 314-15), who also quotes those parts of the relevant passages which are still extant.

[122] Levi della Vida (1939, 315, note 1).

when Calvinists plundered that town.[123] About a year later, Postel transferred his rights to the pawned manuscripts to the Jesuits, with whom he had ties even though he had been ousted from the order, apparently in the hope that they would be able to succeed where he had failed, but when they tried to redeem the manuscripts from the successors to Otto (who had died in 1559), they were told that no manuscripts with Postel's name and hand were in the library.[124]

Was Postel's motivation in writing Ortelius the fact that he could use the communication as a pretext for suggesting that Ortelius retrieve the manuscripts? This is what I suspect was the case. The observation that Ortelius could find in the manuscripts confirmation of Postel's labors, and justification for Ortelius's praise of him looks concocted and gratuitous, and the references to "our Abilfada" and "our earnestness" also look odd, too coaxing. Postel was aware that Ortelius himself had said in the 1567 legend "we look forward with great anticipation to a complete translation by him sometime, for the common good of cosmography." How could he provide such if he didn't have the manuscript? As to Postel's intimation that he had had some hand in the making of the map himself, it is extremely unlikely that he could have done so. The parts of Asia treated most fully by Abulfeda are those parts where he himself had been, that is, Syria, northern Arabia, and the lands north of Syria from eastern Asia Minor to upper Mesopotamia.[125] So it would have been in this geographical area that Postel's translations for Abulfeda could have been most useful to Gastaldi. But all of these areas fall in the area of Gastaldi's First Part of Asia, which was published in 1559, and we know that Postel was in a Roman prison for heresy from November 1555 to August 1559.[126] Finally, I would add that, in regard to Ortelius's original 1567 notice on the map, his own words to the effect that a full translation is hoped for show that he could not have seen all of Abulfeda, and, in all that I have come across on the subject, there is

---

[123] Levi della Vida (1939, 315-17), Wiell-Secret (1987, 120-22), and Vogel (1853, 57).
[124] Vogel (1853, 57).
[125] Reinaud and Guyard (1848-1883, 1, cdxlvii).
[126] Bouwsma (1957, 24).

nothing that would indicate that any copy of Abulfeda could have come his way at all. This would seem to find some confirmation in Mercator's words in a 1580 letter to Hakluyt, where he interjects parenthetically toward the end, "I am glad the Epitomie of Abilfada is translated, I would we might have it shortly."[127] Surely if Ortelius had had access to Abulfeda by 1567, Mercator would not still be waiting to see it in 1580.[128] Sezgin's idea that Ortelius simply felt there had to be some explanation for the sudden appearance on the scene of Gastaldi's unprecedented Asia, and that he latched onto Abulfeda as the explanation is undoubtedly correct. It was just an early instance of that illusion of the inaccessible Abulfeda as the be-all and end-all for geography which would last right into the early nineteenth century.

2 Postel's Translation of Abulfeda

Postel's was the first attempt ever to translate Abulfeda into a western language. How much did he translate? The question is of some relevance here, for all that survives which was translated by him consists of twenty-three lines quoted in Ramusio, plus a few short paraphrases, and no positive evidence has ever been offered that he did more. References to a supposed compendium seem apocryphal. If all that existed was the handful of material in Ramusio, the whole question of whether Gastaldi used Abulfeda would not really exist, so we would like some idea of how much was translated, and therefore available to Gastaldi. We get mixed signals on the question. Postel himself tells us in March 1555 that he was obliged to stop what was evidently a full translation attempt because of the impossibility of distinguishing some of the letters, but that he has all the same "translated a general description of the work."[129] Simler in the same year just says that

---

[127] This notion, almost certainly rumor, probably was gotten from John Dee (see note 79); in any event it surely goes back to the statements in Simler and Ramusio.
[128] One draws the same intimations from a 1588 letter from Ortelius to Camden (Camden, 1691, 33), and a 1594 one from Hakluyt to Ortelius's friend Van Meteren (Taylor, 1935, 420).
[129] Quoted after Levi della Vida (1939, 314). This passage is quoted above in the present chapter.

"Postel has left a compendium from his translation at Venice to Ramusio."[130] Ramusio gives a little more in his comments on Abulfeda in his July 1553 "Prefatione" to Polo, some of which we did not quote earlier, but will do now.[131] At the start of the passage, Ramusio says that he would not have been able to understand certain passages in Polo "if good fortune had not in the last months caused to come into my hands a part, recently translated into Latin by a man of this age well versed in many languages,[132] of an Arab book compiled over 200 years ago by a great prince of Syria called "Abilfada

---

[130] Simler (1555, 1). This is the only actual reference to a compendium made by Postel, and my own feeling is that this compendium is apocryphal, due to some confusion. On this, see above, notes 66, 78, and 90. Note that Ramusio speaks, correctly, of Abulfeda's whole work itself as being a "compendium" in the passage in which he speaks of Abulfeda in the "Prefatione" to Polo in volume 2, and this may have contributed to confusion, although it is true Ramusio's words from 1553 were not published until 1559, so Simler could not have seen them when he made his 1555 entry.

[131] Ramusio (1967-70, 2, 2nd and 3rd pages of "Prefatione"; Milanesi ed., 1978-88, 3, 24-25).

[132] It is generally accepted, and without doubt correctly, that the "man of this age well versed in many languages" is Postel. The failure to mention him by name is no doubt due to the fact Postel was in trouble with the Inquisition at the time due to suspicion of heresy (Almagià, 1948, 65, note 4). That the extracts are indeed rendered by Postel is put beyond all doubt by the fact that, in the passage describing an annual miracle of fish in Lake Geluchalat in Armenia Postel, who was an avid student of biblical geography, has added two biblical place names, Assiria and Media, which are not in Abulfeda's original, nor would they be, since they had not existed as political entities in the region since biblical times. Compare Ramusio (1967-70, 2, 14v; Milanesi ed., 1978-88, 3, 59) and Reinaud and Guyard (1848-1883, 2, pt. 2, 143 and 148-49).

Ismael."[133] Further on, in a passage which we quoted in part earlier, he observes that, "this book of geography is not fully translated, but there lacks the greater part of the commentaries concerning each province, which if it were all Latin, we would have a detailed geography of the parts of Asia and Africa of which notice was had at his time, and we would know the names of the provinces, cities, mountains, rivers, and seas, as [they] at present are called, with the degrees of longitude and latitude, according as they are written by these Arab authors, that is, Attual, Canon, Bensidio, Resum, Cusiro . . . ,"[134] and, finally, at the end, having noted what a good thing we would have were it all translated, he concludes: "But to perform this so great benefit for the world the munificence of some great prince, who might wish to make its coming to light provided for, would be necessary; which perhaps will bring him glory no lesser, and more durable and fixed in the hearts of men and of all posterity, than that which can proceed from grand empires and triumphs obtained with arms." Finally, we know for certain that Postel did translate a little, for we have the two direct quotes from Abulfeda, making twenty-three lines total in Ramusio, and a comparison with the 1848-1883 translation of Reinaud and Guyard shows that his translation was in fact

---

[133] The original here runs "una parte d'un libro Arabo ultimamente tradotta in Latino per un'huomo di questa età ben intendente di molte lingue, composto gia due cento, & piu anni d'un gran principe di Soria detto ABILFADA ISMAEL." At first glance the translation "a part of an Arab book recently translated into Latin by a man of this age well versed in many languages, composed over 200 years ago by a great prince of Syria called Abilfada Ismael" might seem to be more likely Ramusio's intention here, but this would permit the interpretation that the whole book had been translated into Latin and Ramusio himself tells us clearly later in the same passage that it is far from complete, and both Postel himself, in 1555, and Ortelius in 1567 also tell us it's incomplete ("We look forward to a complete translation by him sometime."). No one familiar with Ramusio's rambling sentences and sprawling syntax will question the validity of my reading, I think.

[134] Attual refers to the Kitab al-Atwal (Book of Latitudes and Longitudes) by an anonymous Persian geographer. On it, with some speculation as to the author's identity, see Reinaud and Guyard (1848-1883, 1, lxxxix-xc), Harley and Woodward (1992, 97), Lelewel (1852-57, 1, 112-13 and V[Epilogue], 46). Canon refers to al-Biruni's Masudic Canon. Bensidio refers to the work of Ibn Said. Resum is evidently a reference to the Kitab Resm al-mamur of al-Kindi. I do not know to what Ramusio's Cusiro refers (perhaps Qiyas?).

fairly good.[135] He also had provided enough that Ramusio was able to accurately paraphrase at some length in several other places in the text, as we have seen.

All of this doesn't tell us a great deal, but it is clear that, although he attempted a full translation into Latin, he succeeded in completing only part of it. Ramusio says that much of the "commentaries" are missing, though it is not too obvious what he means here, and, most importantly, many place names and coordinates are missing ("we *would* have a detailed geography," and "we *would* know the names of the provinces, cities, mountains, rivers, and seas . . . with the degrees of longitude and latitude"). Whether the "general description of the work," which Postel says he completed, the supposed "compendium" mentioned by Simler, and Ramusio's "part . . . of an Arab book" all refer to the same thing is also not clear. Finally, and this is important I think, we know that the translating must have been quite extraordinarily difficult, for Ramusio tells us at the end that rendering it all into Latin would be possible only with the patronage and "munificence of some great prince." It will be worthwhile, in this regard, to show in some detail just how extraordinary were the difficulties Postel was up against in his task.

One of the most valuable things in Abulfeda would be the place names, and their positions on the earth as given by the coordinates. In translating from a geographical work written in any language which uses the Roman alphabet, this would be the easiest part of the job, not really requiring much true translating at all. This itself would make a sort of compendium, and, for a cartographer at least, it would be the most vital information. But

---

[135] See note 76 above, where the corresponding references are given. There are some indications Postel may have erred a little, and perhaps omitted small bits which were too puzzling, but there are always differences between the manuscripts of Abulfeda, and Reinaud and Guyard were using different, and better, manuscripts than Postel. (On the very considerable differences among manuscripts, partly due to the fact Abulfeda himself made various changes from time to time, see Lelewel (1852-57, 1, 148), and Reinaud (1840, xli).) To make a definitive judgement, one would need the Arabic passages as they occur in the Vatican manuscript Postel used. But all in all, Postel's renderings are rather good considering the enormous disadvantages he was working with, about which more below.

in translating from Arabic, this can be the hardest part of all, and it is easy to understand why. The Arabic alphabet, which consists, like other Semitic alphabets, entirely of consonant symbols,[136] is written with eighteen basic characters, or cursive shapes. For eight of these shapes, placing combinations of dots, or points, above or below the shapes gives variants, different letters, and thus we get the full complement of twenty-eight consonant symbols. For two of these eight variable forms, three consonants exist, and for the other six, two each exist. All in all, only ten of the twenty-eight consonants have a unique form, while eighteen do not, and so, if dots are missing or misplaced, there are eighteen letters subject to confusion. Using the simplified transliterations given in the alphabets table in my Merriam-Webster dictionary, the confusable groups of letters are as follows: b,t,th; j,h,k; d,dh; r,z; s,sh; s,d; t,z; >gh[137] As regards the first set, still further confusion is possible if a scribe is not very careful, for the basic shape is very similar to that for two of the unique letters, n and y.[138] (These are the five letters (ba, ta, tha, nun, and ya) which Postel refers to in a passage quoted earlier by the names be, te, the, nun, je.) So, this is the most troublesome group.

But the other groups also cause much trouble, especially j,h,k; r,z; s,d; and t,z. For any word even two or three letters in length, there is likely to occur one or another of these letters, and usually more for longer words. Scribes often miscopied dots, or combined sets of dots for different letters. Often, they left dots out altogether, no doubt mainly because, in making their copies, they had in mind readers who were both native users of Arabic, and, in the case of texts such as Abulfeda's, persons with an interest in and knowledge of Middle Eastern geography. They had no reason to suspect that a European with little knowledge of Arabic, and almost no knowledge of Middle Eastern place names was going to be their reader. Often a tiny mark on the paper could be mistaken for a dot which should not be there. C. F.

---

[136] The long vowels and the diphthongs are ambiguously represented, while short vowels are most commonly left out altogether, although there does exist a way to indicate them.
[137] The symbol > represents here a deep guttural or glottal sound.
[138] And a sixth, p, is also similar, though it occurs only in the Persian variant of the Arabic alphabet.

Beckingham, in an interesting piece, "Arabic Texts and the Hakluyt Society,"[139] from which much of what is said here is taken, notes that, "the opportunities for textual corruption are prodigious," and adds, "I will say only that dots alone distinguish between N, T, TH, B, Y and P. What happens when, as is sometimes the practice of scribes, dots are omitted altogether, I leave to your imagination." Another authority in the area, Edward S. Kennedy, simply states that "the reading of unknown placenames written in a bad or careless hand is subjective guesswork at best."[140] The situation is made worse by the fact that, although vowel sounds can be shown, they are usually omitted. For regular dictionary words, an experienced reader can usually make his way, and for geographical names of well-known places, there would also be relatively little problem. But for completely unknown place names, it would often be impossible to know what the scribe had intended. As to the numbers, there was a distinctive set of digits, the same set that developed into the present Arabic numerals. But a few adhered to an older system, where, as in other Semitic languages, the numbers were indicated by letters of the alphabet,[141] and, unfortunately, Abulfeda used this system in indicating longitude and latitude figures, so the same problems applied.[142] To make matters worse, Abulfeda used a particularly odd form to represent zero,[143] and this apparently accounts for the consistent misreadings noted by Ménage in the list of Abulfeda coordinates Postel prepared for

---

[139] Beckingham (1983).

[140] Kennedy (1983, 101).

[141] Nine of the letters were for digits 1-9, nine for 10-90, nine for 100-900, and the 28th for 1,000, although not in alphabetical order. For more on Abulfeda's system of representing numbers and the difficulties caused by it, see Jourdain (1811, 220), and Reinaud (1840, xlv).

[142] Abulfeda's use of these number forms was evidently quite unusual. Sarton says, "It is very remarkable that in his indications of geographical coordinates (degrees and minutes, etc.) he always uses the literal (abujad) numerals (e.g., lam for 30, sin for 60), not "Arabic numerals" (Sarton, 1947, 797). Thus, it is all the less likely that Postel, with his limited Arabic, would have been prepared to cope with this usage.

[143] Reinaud (1840, xlv) and Reinaud and Guyard (1848-1883, 1, cdxlix, note 1).

Ramusio.[144] Nor was this all, either. Reinaud describes still other orthographical difficulties,[145] and, more significant, points up serious and confusing syntactical and organizational problems in Abulfeda's text.[146]

Some notion of the great difficulty of translating Abulfeda can be demonstrated by the number of scholars who projected or began translations, but failed, even though all of them had access to cleaner manuscripts than did Postel, including T. Erpenius in 1612,[147] W. Schickard in 1631-32,[148] Samuel Clerk and William Guise of Oxford, late seventeenth century,[149] J. Golius in mid-sixteenth century,[150] L. d'Arvieux and M. Thevenot in the mid to late seventeenth century,[151] T. Hyde of Oxford in the late seventeenth century,[152] J. Gagnier in the early eighteenth century,[153] and L. Langlés, evidently in the early nineteenth century.[154] There is, it is true, another list of scholars who did manage to publish something, but the fact that they all restricted their translations to only one, or, in a couple of cases, two of Abulfeda's twenty-eight regions is also a testimony to the difficulty of the task: J. Greaves (Khwarizm and Transoxiana, 1650),[155] M. Thevenot (Sind

---

[144] Ménage (1958, 310, note 2). Wilhelm Schickard, working, as had been Postel, from a corrupt Abulfeda manuscript in 1631-32, noted in a letter to John Greaves that the manuscript was "generally very doubtful in the numbers, so that no tables, or at least only incorrect ones, could be formed by it." Quoted in Sale (1737, 525).

[145] Reinaud and Guyard (1848-1883, 1, cdlvii-cdlix).

[146] Reinaud (1840, xxxviii-xl), and Reinaud and Guyard (1848-1883, 1, cdxlix-cdl).

[147] Levi della Vida (1939, 339 and 368), Greaves (1650, 1st and 2nd page of ALectori"), Juynboll (1931, 109), Bayle (1697, 50), Sale (1734, 115),

[148] Oehme (1978, 311, 353, 356, 362-73), Seck (1978, 35-36), Ullmann (1978, 110, 114-15, 117, 120-23), Sezgin (2000, 2, 81-84), Reinaud and Guyard (1848-1883, 1, cdlv).

[149] Jourdain (1811, 226), Sale (1734, 115, note B), Smith (1707, in article on Greaves, p. 31).

[150] Juynboll (1931, 142).

[151] Jourdain (1811, 226), Sale (1734, 115, note B), Renaudot (1733, x).

[152] Jourdain (1811, 226).

[153] Reinaud and Guyard (1848-1883, 1, cdlv), Sale (1734, 115, note 18), Jourdain (1811, 226 and 228).

[154] Jourdain (1811, 226, note 2).

[155] It is often mistakenly said that Greaves's 1650 work was a full translation of Abulfeda.

and Hind, 1672 or earlier), J. Gagnier (Arabia, 1712), J. de la Roque (Arabia, 1718), L. A. Muratori (the prologue, 1740), J. B. Koehler (Syria, 1766), J. D. Michaelis (Egypt, 1776), F. T. Rinck (Africa, below the Maghreb, 1790, and Arabia, 1791), J. G. Eichhorn (Maghreb, 1791), E. F. C. Rosenmüller (Mesopotamia, 1791), C. Rommel (Arabia, 1802), A. Herbin (parts of Egypt, 1803), P. J. Wustenfeld (Arabia, 1835), J. Goldemeister (India, 1838), and C. Solvet (Maghreb, 1839), most in Latin.[156] Reinaud made general reference to the fact that such works had been printed, though he did not name most of them, noting that they were not produced with a desirable degree of critical attention.[157] In fact, no one scholar has ever published a full translation of Abulfeda's *Geography*. The celebrated J. J. Reiske did publish in 1770-71 a Latin translation of all but four regions,[158] and Reinaud, we know, did publish all through the seventh region in 1848, but the work was finished only in 1883 by Guyard. Note that, unlike Postel, all of these later scholars also had the benefit of the works of previous Arabicists to work with,[159] and some even had access to editions of the original works from which Abulfeda

---

[156] I believe there were no more besides these before the twentieth century. For a 1906 Spanish translation of the part on Spain, see note 1 in this chapter. The reader who might wish full details on all these editions, which are not in our bibliography, is referred to Lelewel (1852-57, 148-49), Reinaud (1840, xlvi), Levi della Vida (1939, 336), Jourdain (1811, 227-28), the Library of Congress's *National Union Catalogue, pre-1956 imprints*, vol. 2, 262-64, the British Museum's *General catalogue of printed books*, etc., vol. 113, cols. 46-49, and the Bibliothèque Nationale's *Catalogue general des livres imprimés*, etc., vol. 1, 81-82.

[157] Reinaud (1840, xlvi). He makes an exception as to Gildemeister.

[158] The translation was published in the 1770 and 1771 volumes of the *Magazin für die neue Historie und Geographie angelegt von D. Anton Friedrich Büsching*. For the four regions not included, Arabia, Syria, Khwarizm, and Transoxiana, the translations of Greaves, Gagnier, and Koehler already existed, thus the omission.

[159] See the several published aids and grammars Schickard was using in the 1630s (Ullmann, 1978, 110). Greaves in 1650 had all this and then some, and he himself notes what great progress had been made in the field in the decades before him (Levi della Vida, 1939, 325, note 1).

had compiled his own work.[160] Just as importantly, the later scholars all had access to much better manuscript copies, at least from Greaves's time on.[161]

Postel was largely without such advantages,[162] and he was stuck with a single manuscript, which we learn from himself was corrupt.[163] And while it is also true that he would have been one of the most knowledgeable persons in Europe at his time in the Arabic language, and in fact it was he who produced the first ever published grammar of the language, it is also true that he was a pioneer in working with Arabic, for the formal study of the language begins only at his time, and we must wonder how much such a pioneer could have translated from an extremely difficult work such as Abulfeda's, especially working with a single bad manuscript. Johann Fueck, one of the twentieth century's deans of Arabic studies, wrote a history of

---

[160] By Reinaud's time, many of these were available (Reinaud, 1840, xlv-xlvi), although he says he still found himself uncertain at times (Reinaud and Guyard, 1848-1883, 1, cdl). By Guyard's time, practically all were available, and he gives a good review of them (2, iii-vii).

[161] Greaves had five manuscripts, including one he had himself purchased at Constantinople, and two he obtained from his friend Edward Pocock, who had presumably bought them in Constantinople, where he purchased many manuscript works in the late 1630s (see Sale (1737, 525), and Sale (1741, 560)), and he also had access to Postel's original manuscript, as well as a copy of it which had been made by Erpenius. I have made no in-depth attempt to isolate all manuscripts. The best is a manuscript in the University of Leiden library including additions in Abulfeda's own hand. There are at least two in the Bibliothèque Nationale, Paris besides the Schickard copy mentioned just below. A manuscript once in the Imperial library, Vienna, is now presumably in the Austrian National Library, and a later copy of it made by Wilhelm Schickard in the early seventeenth century is also in the French library. The manuscript in the Vatican Library is that originally brought to Europe by Postel, and evidently a copy of it made by Erpenius exists. There is a manuscript in the British Library, and evidently a very good manuscript in the Bodleian Library at Oxford. (For all of these, see Reinaud (1840, viii, note 1 and xli-xlii, including note 2 on xlii), Reinaud and Guyard (1848-83, 1, cdlil), Levi della Vida (1939, 334-35), Brockelmann (1938, 49), Lelewel (1852-57, V[Epilogue], 47), Jourdain (1811, 224-26), and Bayle (1697).

[162] Not quite completely, however, for he had a good manuscript Arabic-Latin glossary (Levi della Vida, 1939, 320), and also a manuscript Arabic grammar composed by Leo Africanus (Levi della Vida, cit., 311, 313 and 321).

[163] A clear idea of the extreme difficulties of working with such a corrupt manuscript comes out in the sad story of Schickard's attempt, as brought out by Oehme (1978, 362-73).

Arabic studies in Europe, in which he speaks of Postel's "grammar, which at every page . . . demonstrates that he has not become master of his subject."[164] It does not, he says, show the alphabet correctly, and does not show the diacritical points. Derived verbal stems are almost entirely missing, and there are other defects.[165] Postel's Arabic translation of the Lord's Prayer at the end of the work "shows that Postel's Arabic knowledge lacked a solid foundation,"[166] and he judges the work in the end as "quite defective."[167] A much more positive opinion of Postel's grammar is given by Secret.[168] The Arabic scholar Joseph Scaliger in the early seventeenth century declared the grammar bad, said it could not be useful, and gives assurance that Postel "was not as learned in Arabic as he wished to seem."[169] Elsewhere Scaliger, who had been a student of Postel's, said that Postel wasn't as at home with Arabic as he would have people believe, and said he really didn't have a good fundamental knowledge of any language at all.[170]

Considering the great difficulties concerned with translating Arabic geographical texts in general, the fact that Abulfeda's is much harder than most, the fact of his evident inability to transcribe many of the all-important place names (as evidenced by the absence of 40% of the names in Ramusio's list of thirty-two Abulfeda coordinates), that he was working with a corrupt manuscript, and that he gets poor marks as an Arabicist from his critics, it would not seem at first glance likely that Postel could have translated much of Abulfeda, although it is true too that he did at least a passing job in the small extracts we have by him. Let us explore as well as we can one more avenue, before coming to our final conclusion, the question of how much time Postel could have found to devote to his efforts to translate his manuscript.

---

164 Fueck (1955, 40).
165 Fueck (1955, 60-61).
166 Fueck (1955, 61).
167 Fueck (1955, 61).
168 Secret (1962).
169 Quoted in Weill-Secret (1987, 213).
170 Fueck (1955, 47).

From the time Postel arrived in Venice with the manuscript in 1550 or early 1551 until the time he was forced to give it up in pawn in March 1555, after which he obviously could have worked no more on the manuscript, he was extraordinarily occupied. He felt that he had an evangelic mission before mankind, and had to get his message out quickly,[171] and it is hard to imagine where he would have found time to work much on the manuscript in that period. But Postel was in possession of the *Geography* for up to a year and a half before he arrived in Venice with it, and he could have worked on it in that period. Indeed, the circumstances indicate this is very likely. Postel arrived in the Middle East from Venice in the summer of 1549, and in November the same year, having obtained his manuscripts, he left Jerusalem for Constantinople, where he arrived in January 1550. There is much disagreement as to how long he remained in Constantinople before returning to Venice. Statements vary, from saying he left about mid-1550 to saying he remained until early 1551, if not slightly later. He may have been there as little as six months, or as much as close to a year and a half. In any event, nothing is known of what he did there, so there is a good space of time unaccounted for. We recall that the Abulfeda was far and away his most treasured find,[172] and the indications are that it was the only one of Postel's manuscripts obtained on his trip that he actually worked on.[173] Postel had obtained on his first trip to the East in 1534-37 both a very good Latin-Arabic lexicon, and a copy of the Arab grammar by Leo Africanus mentioned in note 163 above.[174] It seems likely he would have taken these

---

[171] Bouwsma says: "Between 1551 and 1555 he published at least twenty-three books, prepared a series of broadsides to spread his message, wrote long letters to influential personages all over Europe, petitioned the Parliament of Paris to back him against the Sorbonne, traveled through France, Switzerland, Italy, and Austria, and taught and preached at every opportunity. He was impelled by a sense of extreme urgency. His calculations pointed to 1556 as the fateful year for the human race; time was evidently running out" (Bouwsma, 1957, 17-18; see also 16 and 21-22). For more on Postel's extreme activeness at this time, see Levi della Vida (1939, 312 and 325), and Weill-Secret (1987, 83, 106-07 and 278, note 118).

[172] Levi della Vida (1939, 326). This is also obvious from the fact that, whenever we find him lamenting the pawn to Otto Henry, it is invariably the Abulfeda he mentions in particular and refers to its great monetary value as well (see Vogel, 1853, 57) and Levi della Vida (cit., 313 and 315).

[173] Levi della Vida says of the fifteen Postel manuscripts that the Vatican received from the Heidelberg library that "they carry almost no trace at all of having passed through [Postel's] hands," except the Abulfeda (Levi della Vida, 1939, 325-26).

[174] Levi della Vida (1939, 320-21).

two items with him on this second trip, and if so, he could have worked on the Abulfeda during his stay in Constantinople, a city where he also could perhaps have gotten some assistance with the translation if he ran into difficulties.[175] What facts we can muster indicate that this must have been the time when Postel would have rendered what he could from the manuscript, and, if the amount of time be uncertain, here is a considerable space of time in which Postel would have been able to work on the manuscript.

Now, with what we have up to this point, I think we can arrive at a very likely notion of how much Postel was able to render into Latin from his manuscript, and thus how much Gastaldi might have been able to use, since he clearly could gain nothing from the original Arabic, and we can also provide a near certain solution to the question of what in fact was the ever fleetingly referred to "compendium". Ramusio tells us in the preface to his volume two, dated July 7, 1553, that he had received part of Abulfeda translated into Latin "in the last months," so probably sometime in spring of that year. He could not have received the Abulfeda material directly from Postel, for Postel was in Venice in 1553 only from August, when he arrived after a two year period in France, until the end of the year, when he was off for Vienna.[176] As we saw earlier,[177] Postel's manuscripts were in hock in January, 1552 with the Giunti brothers, Ramusio's publishers, with whom Postel was close.[178] Thus it would seem most likely that it was from the Giunti, with whom of course Ramusio was also close, and who would also have an interest of their own in any improvements that Ramusio could make to a book they were going to publish, that Ramusio borrowed Postel's

---

[175] For various and sometimes conflicting reports on Postel's two trips to the East and the works brought back, see Vogel (1853), Levi della Vida (1939, 309-12 and 320-25), Bouwsma (1957, 5-7 and 16), Chesneau (1887, lv [here quoting Nicolay from 1567] and 138-39), Weill-Secret (1987, 31-42, 78 and 81-84), Fueck (1955, 50-57), Codazzi (1952, 174-75 and 177), Chaufepié (1750-59, 3, 216 and 221-22).

[176] Bouwsma (1957, 16-18 and 21-22), and Weill-Secret (1987, 106).

[177] See note 16. See also Secret (1962, 34, note 2) on the pawn to the Giunti.

[178] Postel sometimes lodged with the Giunti brothers when he was in Venice, and he also sometimes gave their printing house as a mailing address through which he could be reached (Weill-Secret, 1987, 154 and 295, note 284) and Codazzi (1952, 178).

materials.[179] What might have been in the Postel materials obtained, on loan to be sure, from his close friends, the Giunti?

Ramusio, as we have seen, states in his comments that "the good reader might taste in a few places" of Abulfeda's work, and tells us elsewhere: "Now this book of geography is not fully translated [nor would it be until 1883], but there lacks the greater part of the commentaries concerning each province." Now, we know that Ramusio in his commentaries uses Abulfeda material at eight places (see note 76), for a total of 118 lines. But only slightly less than a fourth of the time Ramusio actually quotes from Abulfeda (twenty-three lines), while in ninety-five lines he is paraphrasing. It is reasonable, then, to assume that it was only in quite limited places that Postel was able to produce actual translations (though, to his credit, considering the daunting difficulties involved, rather good ones, as comparison with Reinard and Guyard show), but for the great majority he was able to provide only synopses, providing only the general gist, and no doubt in some places only skeletal clues, and the places where Ramusio paraphrases would be taken from such. This surely was the "compendium", so often vaguely referred to,[180] and, since none such accompanies Postel's manuscript, as we now have it in the Vatican, we may assume, as of course we would expect, that when Postel retrieved these materials from the Giunti in order to pawn the manuscript to Otto Henry for a higher price, he retained this partial translation. What became of it, we don't know. Note that, since the coordinates are complete, but some of the corresponding place names are missing in Ramusio's list of thirty-two Abulfeda coordinates, and Ramusio

---

[179] At the head of the table of Abulfeda coordinates in Ramusio (Ramusio, 1967-70, 2, 18; Milanesi ed., 1978-88, 3, 72), of which we have already spoken, Ramusio has a short "to the reader," which states: "These longitudes and latitudes which we will describe below here have been taken from the book of Mr. Abilfada Ismael, a copy of which came into my hands, and [which] I hold very dear, and they will be of use regarding several lands and places named in the present volume, published by us to this end, so that the good reader might taste in a few places of the beauty of the book of the aforesaid Mr. Ismael, having come divinely to light in our times." He seems here to be speaking of the whole original manuscript, and since the manuscript and the parts Postel had translated would presumably have at all times been together, he probably got both from the Giunti brothers. I do not know what accounts for the fact that in the 1559 first edition, the line "a copy of which came into my hands, and [which] I hold very dear," is omitted, occurring only in later editions.

[180] Which, we recall, was slightly inaccurately described by Simler as having been left with Ramusio. Probably the state of the translation was similar to that of Schickard when that scholar had done all he could do. That still exists, and Ullmann (1978), and Oehme (1978) give good descriptions of it.

gives Abulfeda coordinates in some of the Abulfeda passages in the *Navigazioni*, there is the implication that Postel had succeeded in deciphering Abulfeda's method of designating numerals. But, while this would have been the most important data for a map-maker, Gastaldi would no doubt have been able to catch the scattered ten degree discrepancies in Abulfeda, and it would most likely have been this consideration which determined him to reject Abulfeda's figures as unreliable. In any event, we know for certain from direct comparison that Gastaldi did not use Abulfeda's figures, which differ so much from his own.

CHAPTER 6 - BACKGROUND AND DEVELOPMENT OF THE FOUR-CONTINENT IDEA

6.1 Preliminary Remarks

In the remainder of our study, we wish to throw as much light as possible on the crucial period of Gastaldi's work, 1559-1564, in which he virtually single-handedly created history's first generally correct maps of the extra-European continents, and in the process provide answers to some outstanding questions. Almagià has observed that at his death Gastaldi must have left maps in various stages of completion.[1] Was it Gastaldi's intention in his activity of 1559 on to provide universal modern separate coverage of all four continents? We know that he produced maps in this period covering only the eastern half of one continent, Europe. Did he perhaps complete such a set of maps in manuscript? And, finally, is there any possibility that he not only did so, but then proceeded to work up from them individual full continent maps corresponding to that for Africa, to produce the first set of four-continent wall maps? As we shall see, five instances are preserved of a Venetian set of wall maps of the four continents which clearly mostly derive from Gastaldi's work, and as we shall also see, a number of commentators have counted Gastaldi among those who have made sets of four-continent wall maps. Our basic conclusions will be: (1) that Gastaldi's apparent project of ca.1559 on was probably not that well thought out and that he most likely had never fully visualized what his final goal was to be; (2) that it is unclear whether he intended to arrive at a universal modern coverage for the whole globe and that possibly this was not clear even to him at the time; (3) that he probably did not finish such a set of maps in manuscript, at least not in any complete and viable form, and lastly; (4) that it may be considered certain that he did not himself work up a set of four-continent wall maps proper, and that the existing sets were worked up by other hands from Gastaldian or principally Gastaldian material. We shall furthermore see that Gastaldi's apparent inability to clearly envision a final goal and formulate a sound overall plan to reach it arose from specific and identifiable problems,

---

[1] Almagià (1939, *carta*, 9).

and that the most serious of these problems was the impossibility of determining whether Asia and America were connected or not, whether they were one or two continents. We will also see that Gastaldi was able to arrive at a partial solution to this problem, i.e., that the continents had to be either connected or, if not, come very close together (the latter choice depicted as his Strait of Anian), but that this partial solution was still not sufficient to allow him to proceed with full surety in depicting the continents. Before proceeding directly to the subject of Gastaldi's activities from 1559, it will be useful and instructive to gain some overall background orientation by reviewing the development of ideas concerning the number of continents up to and in Gastaldi's time. It will be useful to us in several ways to have this in mind as we proceed through the remainder of the book.

6.2 The Conceptions of Geographers in General

For over a millennium and a half before the time of Christopher Columbus, most of the western world traditionally held the world's land surface to be broken up into three large continents, Europe, Asia and Africa (or Libya, as it was then more often called). The change from this tripartite scheme to a quadripartite scheme which included America did not, as we shall see, occur immediately after Columbus's discoveries, and it was not at all such a smooth and automatic transition as one might think. But by the latter part of the sixteenth century, most had come to accept that the world consisted of four continents, Europe, Africa, Asia and America,[2] and, not surprisingly, the cartographic genre of sets of wall maps of the four continents came into being. While there were antecedents, or attempted antecedents, which we will examine in detail, the genre had definitely become a successful one by about the mid-1590s, with the appearance in Venice of the Donato Bertelli Gastaldian set, and in Antwerp the set of Cornelis de Jode, put together from the work of his father Gerard, followed by Jodocus Hondius's set of 1598, which was itself then followed by Willem Blaeu's famous 1608 set and its derivations by Henricus Hondius and Claes

---

[2] For an excellent review on the number of continents from ancient to modern times, see Lewis and Wigen (1997, 21-33).

Visscher.[3] This quadripartite continental scheme remained in effect throughout the eighteenth century and even into the nineteenth, and throughout the period such cartographic publishers as the Danckaerts family, Wit, Jaillot, Delisle, Covens & Mortier, and others continued to produce such sets. The latest set I know of is one by Clouet of 1788-93,[4] but the form probably continued into the early nineteenth century.[5] Certainly the concept itself was still current in the early part of that century. Martin W. Lewis and Kären Wigen state that, "All things considered . . . the fourfold scheme prevailed well into the 1800s,"[6] and they quote the English geographer Maunder as observing in 1854, "It was usual until the present century to speak of the great divisions of the earth as the Four Quarters of the World, VIZ; Europe, Asia, Africa, and America."[7] It was by far the longest-lived scheme of early modern and modern times. But "The transition from a three-fold continental scheme did not occur immediately after Columbus. First, America had to be intellectually 'invented' as a distinct parcel of land -- one that could be viewed geographically, if not culturally, as equivalent to the other continents."[8]

If we look only at the very earliest post-Columbian literature which touches upon the question, we might pause at accepting this. Duarte Pacheco

---

[3] Schilder gives a very full and readable history of the famous Blaeu maps of the four continents (Schilder, 1996), as well as an excellent survey of the four-continent wall map series by Gerard and Cornelis Jode and others which preceded the Blaeu maps ("Sets of Wall Maps of the Continents, Published in the Netherlands before 1608," in Schilder 1996, pp. 35-75.) Other volumes in his series *Monumenta Cartographica Neerlandica* fully document later Dutch sets of four-continent wall maps. The popularity of the form in the late sixteenth and seventeenth centuries is documented by surviving household inventories (Woodward, 1996, *Maps*, 80-81; Ambrosini, 1981, 69-71).

[4] See notice in *Imago Mundi*, 38(1986), 104.

[5] An 1840-42 Brué and Picquet set of continental wall maps may be such a set (*Imago Mundi*, 37(1985), 94). Note also two nineteenth century book titles: J. MacCarthy, *Choix de voyages dans les quatre parties du monde . . . entrepris depuis l'année 1806 jusqu'a ce jour* (Paris, 1823); and F.-C. Vibert, *Traité pratique de la reduction des monnaies, changes étrangers, poids, measures: et des usages des principales villes de commerce des quatre parties du monde* (Paris, 1844).

[6] Lewis and Wigen (1997, 30).

[7] Lewis and Wigen (1997, 31).

[8] Lewis and Wigen (1997, 25). The authors give an excellent review of the various schemes for the number of continents from antiquity to the present day in the section, "The Development of the Continental Scheme," pp. 21-33 (with 214-21).

Pereira writes in 1505 that the world has a fourth part,[9] the anonymous *Globus mundi* of 1509 tells us in its title of a "fourth part of the terrestrial orb recently discovered by Americo [Vespucci],"[10] Johannes Stobnicza says in 1512 that while there used to be three parts of the world, America is now a fourth,[11] and Johannes Werner in his commentaries to his 1514 translation of parts of Ptolemy also recognizes America as a fourth part.[12] But it was a false start. I have made a check of the opinions and thoughts of over sixty sixteenth century cosmographers, about forty of them before the 1560s, and another dozen or so for the later part of the century, and the results confirm the assessment of Lewis and Wigen.[13] Almost all of these opinions are gleaned from books, cosmographies and geographies proper, but a few are taken from textual material on maps, as indicated in the notes. The results are summarized in the following paragraphs.[14]

Seven cosmographers do state unequivocally that there are four parts of the world, and that America is the fourth part, or at least is one of the four parts: Gemma (1530), Franck (1534), Girava (1556), Hadji Ahmed

---

[9] Pereira (1937, 14-15). The work was finished in 1508, but this part was written by 1505, according to Zerubavel (1992, 79).

[10] *Globus mundi; declaratio sive descriptio mundi . . . alijsq[ae] permultis de Quarta orbis terraru parte nuper ab Americo reparta* (Argentinae, 1509).

[11] Stobnicza (1512, fol. vii).

[12] Werner (1514, 1, 43-48).

[13] The works of another nine cosmographers I checked had nothing on the question: Maurolico (1543), Medina (1545), Dodoens (1548), Cortes (1551), Fine (1551), Boileau de Bouillon (1555), Borrhaus (1555), Barozzi (1588), and Gallucci (1588). For Fine, there are earlier editions, but they were not available to me, and I believe they are the same in the later edition. In some of these, the question was not touched on because the work was purely theoretical in nature, consisting entirely of mathematical and astronomical presentations, with no geographical details proper. Others seem simply to avoid the question.

[14] Interestingly, the concepts of there being four parts of the world and of a fourth continent occasionally also occur in classical and Medieval documents, although of course not with reference to America. See Uzielli (1893) and Bertolini (1929). See also Hieronymo de Girava's comments on Herodotus in this respect (1556, 61).

(1559/60), Postel (1561), Porcacchi (1572), and Anania (1576).[15] Egenolff (1535), Gutiérrez (1562), and Wytfliet (1598[1597]) do not specifically state that there are four parts of the world, but they do so imply by calling America a fourth part.[16] Apian (1524[1544]) and Arrivabene (1554), with just a hint of equivocation, speak of the four *principal* parts of the world, one of them America.[17] Ruscelli, in 1562, speaks of the "three principal parts, known and described by the ancients," and then of "this other, fourth and so large part, newly . . . discovered by the Spanish and Portuguese."[18]

But there is much less agreement among the majority. Some cosmographers vacillate, giving status to America as a part of the world at one time, but denying it at another. Many more refrain altogether from giving it continental status, while some say that there are *more* than four parts to the world. Waldseemüller states clearly enough in 1507, after having given the three parts known to the ancients (Europe, Africa, and Asia) that "another fourth part has been discovered by Americus Vesputius,"[19] but in 1513 speaks of "the three parts of the world."[20] In a more famous case of opinion switching, Schöner states in 1515 that there are four parts of the world, and the fourth is America,[21] but in 1533 implies that Vespucci, who had thought America an island, was wrong in considering it a fourth part of the globe, for Magellan's voyage had now proved America "to be continuous

[15] Gemma (1530, pt. 3, ch. 1), Franck (1534, 3v, 23v and 210v), Girava (1556, 61-62), Hadji Ahmed, in the text on his 1559/60 world map, as paraphrased in Ménage (1958, 294-95), Postel (1561, 1), Porcacchi (1572, 110-11), and Anania (1576, 7th page of "Prohemio al lettore"). The name Hadji Ahmed is probably a pseudonym. Anania actually says there are just two great continents (*continenti*), the Old World, with Europe, Africa, and Asia, "and the other, which is called the New World because it was hidden from the ancients." Anania's usage of the word continent in a sense similar to current usage was exceptional at the time, as see below.

[16] For Egenolff, see Lach (1965-1993, 2, 2/3, 339); Gutiérrez, in title to his 1562 map, and in cartouche below it; and Wytfliet (1598, 97; 1st ed. 1597). For a reproduction of the Gutiérrez map, see Burden (1996, no. 32). For the cartouche text, see Hébert and Pflederer (2000, 47).

[17] Apian (1544, 2v and 32r) and Arrivabene, quoted by Kretschmer from a 1556 manuscript (1892, 426). Apian says the same in his 1524 first edition, but I only have page numbers available for the 1544 edition.

[18] Ruscelli (1564, [2]; 1st ed. 1562).

[19] Waldseemüller (1507, fol. 15v). The erroneous notion that Vespucci had discovered America was common in the sixteenth century.

[20] Waldseemüller (1513, verso of title page).

[21] Schöner (1515, fols. 17v and 61v.).

with upper India, which is part of Asia."[22] Note that Schöner's criterion for assigning or not assigning fourth part status to America here seems to depend on whether or not the New World was separate from Asia or not, which might seem logical enough. As we shall see, however, many who considered America an other part of the world did so regardless of whether it was considered as connected to the Old World or not. In any event, no one really knew or could have known whether there was a connection or not.

Johann Eichmann (called Dryander), in his 1544 edition of Apian's cosmography, states twice that there are but three parts of the world,[23] but elsewhere in the same work says there are no longer just three parts, for now there is a fourth, found by Vespucci.[24] Bellinato in 1573 states there are three parts ("In how many parts is it divided? In three, Europe, Africa and Asia."),[25] but later in the same work adds, "The new World can *perhaps* (*forse*) be called the fourth part of the world;"[26] and in the same year, Bordini speaks of "three *principal* parts of the world,"[27] but elsewhere says America "is *called* a fourth part of the world."[28] But many of the cosmographers state without reservation that there are but three parts of the world, and never give any status to America at all, including: Glareanus (1527), Vadianus (1534), Stöffler (1537), Rithaymer (1538), Signot (1539), Münster (1540, and 1550), Honter (1542), Passi (1558?[1564]), Citolini (1561), and Gwagnin

---

[22] Schöner (1533, sig. E5r). For discussions of this astonishing instance of misinterpretation of facts, see Deane (1885), Kretschmer (1892, 411-15), and Wieder (1925-32, 1, 3). We unfortunately cannot explore here the failure of the majority to appreciate the implications of Magellan's voyage, and the persistence of the idea of a small Pacific, especially North Pacific, but the notion of a close proximity of the China coast and North American west coast persisted strongly not only in maps (and whether the continents were considered as separated or not), but even more clearly in written Spanish documents even into the seventeenth century.

[23] Dryander (1544, pt. 1 ch. 14, 2nd page; and on 1st page of the ten-page "summario" at end of book.).

[24] Dryander (1544, pt. 1, ch. 14, 2nd page).

[25] Bellinato (1573, 7).

[26] Bellinato (1573, 48).

[27] Bordini (1573, 472).

[28] Bordini (1573, 452).

(Guagnini) (1578).[29] Many of these do mention America under one name or another, but give it no status as a continent, while a few make no mention of the New World at all, as if it didn't exist (Stöffler, Signot, Passi, Gwagnin).[30] The Italian poet Bernardino Baldi, in 1576 in his most famous work, *La nautica*, seems to leave it to the reader whether America should be considered a continent. He tells us that the world is embraced by a "great wet arm,"

> E che in tre larghe parti ella è divisa:
> Europa, Africa ed Asia; a cui conviensi
> America anco aggiunger, che dal nostro
> Mondo fu pria da vasto mar disgiunta.

> (And that in three large parts it is divided:
> Europe, Africa and Asia; he whom it befits
> America also [might] add, which from our
> World was before by vast sea separated.)[31]

Part of the problem with recognizing the New World as a part of the world was in all likelihood not geographical, but perceptional, with many Europeans not accepting the Indians as fully human, and some perceiving them outright as animals, with accompanying doubts as to the validity of considering America as a true part of the world.[32] In fact, self-centered Europe had long considered that remote and uncultivated regions were hardly real parts of the world. The fifteenth century Venetian historian Bernardo Giustiniani wrote that, "The great wildernesses and deserts or the peoples rather savage than human are not to be adjudged parts of the world.

---

[29] Glareanus (1527, 23r and 24r), Vadianus (1534, 29-31), Stöffler (1537, [10v] and [11r]), Rithaymer (1538, 5, 8 and 64), Signot (1539), cited here after Lach (1965-93, 2, 2/3, 273), Münster (1540, 160r; and 1550, in ch. 16 of section, "Das erst büch der Cosmography"), Honter (1542, 1st page of 2nd book), Passi, *Tavola* (1558?, in "lettori" at end of work; also under entry. "Asia"), Citolini (1561, 126, 163 and 346), Gwagnin, on p. 1 of his account as added to 1583 edition of vol. two of Ramusio, as see in Ramusio (1967-70, 2, folio 1r of 3rd pagination; Milanesi ed., 1978-88, 4, 319) (First published 1578, as see Parks, 1970, 26).

[30] Oddly, Rithaymer notes that Egypt is sometimes identified as a fourth part of the world (1538, 64).

[31] Quoted after Cirillo Sirri (1994, 283).

[32] Hanke (1937, 68-70, 72-73, 96-98); see also Gerbi (1973, 64-66, 68, 69 and 71).

Those are proper parts of the world which under more agreeable regions of the heavens are inhabited by men not leading life so much after the manner of wild beasts as filled with humanity and natural reason."[33]

No doubt another factor contributing to the confusion was the lack of a good term, or conception even, for what we now call continents (a problem not at all fully clear even today). The term usually used was "parts," but the word was just as broad and vague in meaning then as now. Gastaldi regularly used the term to refer not only to the continents, but also to sections of Asia, Europe, etc., that is, as parts of parts. The word continent(s) was beginning to be used by a few cosmographers to refer to the major parts of the earth,[34] but the great majority used the term "parts" instead, a term too broad in meaning to give a sense of sureness as to what was being spoken of. A number of the cosmographers include a section in their works where they define geographical terms,[35] and most do contain the term "continent." But there is no consensus as to its meaning, and it is defined in very vague terms, as in Apian in 1524, who says: "Continent (*continens*) is termed all firm and fixed land, which is neither island, nor peninsula, nor isthmus, but is totally constant and coherent unto itself,"[36] and who includes among continents France, Bohemia, Saxony, etc., and this sort of confusion existed for long afterwards.[37] Lewis and Wigen treat the problem of the definition of the word continent and note that, "in early modern English, any reasonably large body of land or even island group might be deemed a continent."[38] This continued at least to the end of the sixteenth century, and no doubt into the seventeenth. In Gerrit de Veer's narrative of Willem Barents's voyages to Novaya Zemlya, first published in 1598 and included in the 1606 third

---

[33] Giustiniani (1608, book 2, p. 43), which I quote after Tenenti (1973, 42, note 81). Giustiniani lived 1408-1489.

[34] Gemma (1530, pt. 1, ch. 90), Glareanus (1527, 23r), Rosaccio (1598, 7v-8r), Citolini (1561, 163 and 346).

[35] For example: Apian (1524, pt. 1, ch. 17), Gemma (1530, pt. 1, ch. 9), Glareanus (1527, ch. 20), Rithaymer (1538, 4-5), Porcacchi (1572, 2nd to 6th pages of "Prohemio"), Myritius (1590, pt. 1, ch. 14).

[36] Apian (1524, 57).

[37] Myritius includes among continents Saxony, Bavaria, Austria, Pannonia, etc. (1590, pt. 1, ch. 14).

[38] Lewis and Wigen (1997, 29).

edition of Ramusio's volume three,[39] the word is used dozens of times and clearly usually just means "mainland." He also speaks six times of the "continent of Novaya Zemlya," three times of the "continent of Waygats," twice of the "continent of Russia," and once of the "continent of Tartary." We continue with our survey of the cosmographers.

Some cosmographers used schemes different altogether from the three- or four-part schemes, and, as we shall see, there was a touch of this is Gastaldi's thinking as well, in more ways than one. Enciso in 1519 has a six-part scheme, first dividing the world into two great "parts," one including everything east of the Ferro meridian,[40] and the other all west of it, after which he divides the part east of Ferro into four "parts," Europe, Asia, Africa, and the East Indies (*indie oriental*), and then the part west of Ferro confusedly in two parts, one north of Ferro (here evidently using Ferro as establishing a latitude line as well as a longitude line), and the other "south and west" of Ferro, which he calls West Indies (*indies occidentals*), while giving no name to the part north of the Ferro line.[41] Some add in a supposed southern or northern continent, affecting the number total. Tyard in 1557 adds the southern, for a total of "five Parts."[42] Even in Ortelius in 1570 there is uncertainty, regardless of the unequivocal four maps for four continents which begin his *Theatrum*.[43] On the second page of the address to the reader he says there are "four quarters or principal parts," Europe, Asia, Africa and America, but on the front overleaf of the world map, he says the ancients had three parts, Europe, Asia and Africa, but now America is a "fourth part," and

---

[39] Ramusio (1967-70, 3, 398v-430r; Milanesi ed., 1978-88, 1083-1242). The account should have been included in volume two. Gilbert speaks of how, in old times, the sea "cut off Sicilia from the Continent of Calabria" (Hakluyt, 1903-05, 7, 161).

[40] The meridian of Ferro (Hierro) runs through the Canaries. Ferro is in 27°45' latitude, so his dividing line for the north and south parts of the New World is about in the middle of the Florida peninsula. Enciso is the only writer I have encountered so far who specifically chooses Ferro for his prime meridian.

[41] Enciso (1519, sigs. GVIv-GVIIr). Barlow does the same in 1540-41 in his cosmography, which is mostly just a translation of Enciso (Barlow, 1931, 148). See Enciso's further comments on this at his sigs. AIIr (not in Barlow), and BIXv-BXr (Barlow, 32-33).

[42] Tyard (1950, 107-10). Tyard's classification is unique. He says that the world's five parts consist of two Asias, one Europe, and two Africas, where one of the Asias is the New World, and one of the Africas is the Southern Continent.

[43] Ortelius (1570).

that under the south pole is "a fifth." Also in the dedicatory poem at the head of the volume there are said to be five parts (*QVINQVE ORBIS PARTES*), and the fifth, the Southern Continent, is called "MAGELLANICA." He also informs us, on the overleaf, of Mercator's scheme of three "continentes," the Old World, America, and "the south main, which some call Magellanica."[44] Garzoni (1585) recognizes "six most principal (*principalissime*) parts" of the world, adding a northland, "Grutlandia," and a southland, which he says "is unnamed for the present,"[45] and Rosaccio does the same, asserting that there are four principal parts, but that because of the possible northland and southland, which he leaves unnamed, one can "with reason say that there might be six."[46]

6.3 The Conceptions of Gastaldi

Gastaldi, in his 1561 *La Vniversale descrittione*, expresses equivocation in this regard in several ways. First of all, while he does speak of, "tutte Quattro le parte d'essa Terra, & Mare, che fin hora se n'ha cognittione, cioe l'Europa l'Africa, l'Asia, & le parti nuouamente discoperte, nominate dal Volgo Mondo nuouo," (all the four parts of this Earth, & Sea, of which knowledge has been had up to now, that is, Europe, Africa, Asia, and the parts newly discovered, commonly called new World,)[47] we find he gives tentative recognition to two others. In describing the "confines" of Asia, he establishes a parallel at 15° S latitude which he says "diuide l'Asia dal Mondo nuouo incognito uerso l'Austro" (divides Asia from the unknown new World towards the south.)[48] Again, describing the confines of Africa, he establishes a parallel below Africa at 44° S latitude which "diuide l'Africa uerso Austro, dale parti nuoue" (divides Africa towards the south, from the

---

[44] On Mercator's scheme, see also Nordenskiöld (1889, 107).

[45] Garzoni (1996, 394-95).

[46] Rosaccio (1598, 5v-6r). Petrus Plancius gave a different six-part scheme, with Europe, Asia, Africa, Mexicana, Peruana and Magalanica, according to Wieder (1914-15, 172), and in this was possibly the first to recognize North and South America as separate continents. There is perhaps a hint of such a division in Gastaldi's *Vniversale descrittione*, as we shall see below.

[47] Gastaldi (1561, 4).

[48] Gastaldi (1561, 14).

new parts.)[49] And in describing the confines of Europe, he establishes a parallel through the Drobasof Sea (part of the Arctic Ocean), which "diuide la Europa dalla Grutlandia parte nuoua uerso Tramontana" (divides Europe from the new part of Grutlandia towards the north.)[50] And, as we saw in chapter two and will see again, per the ideas of Gastaldi, Ramusio, Giunti and others, these would not have been ice-bound wastelands, but well populated parts of the earth. There is also perhaps just a note of equivocation in his description of the New World. Having said that the New World is divided into two main parts, Peru (South America) and New Spain (North America), and that New Spain consists of twelve provinces, he lists them, ending with "la duodecima e Quiuira, la quale confina con la parte dell'Asia uerso Ponente" (the twelfth is Quivira, which borders with the part of Asia towards the west.)[51] The wording here seems, at least to me, to hedge a little, possibly implying a land border between Quivira and Asia, although elsewhere he describes a meridian through the Strait of Anian as separating Asia from the New World.[52] This may not be such a quibbling point as it seems, for, as we shall see, there can be no doubt that Gastaldi, at this time and at all times from some indeterminate point in the 1550s, perhaps most likely 1557, remained undecided as to the question of whether Asia and America were connected or separated, and that, although it was impossible to show it in any single map, his Strait of Anian was just one of two alternate concepts, the other being that the Old and New Worlds were just as solidly joined as on his original 1546 world map.

The most telling indication of equivocation on the point in the booklet comes in the paragraph where Gastaldi enumerates the provinces of the New World. He has just done the same for Europe, Africa, and Asia, and, in each case, he heads the paragraph with a statement of the number of provinces in that part. For instance, for Africa: "La seconda parte nominata Africa si diuide in sette Prouincie. La prima delle quali è la Barbaria, l'Egitto. La seconda Numidia. La terza Lybia," etc. (The second part named Africa is

---

[49] Gastaldi (1561, 13).

[50] Gastaldi (1561, 12).

[51] Gastaldi (1561, 18).

[52] Gastaldi (1561, 13).

divided into six provinces. The first of which is Barbary, Egypt. The second Numidia. The third Lybia, etc.)[53] But, at the New World, he first divides the *part* into two other *parts*: "La Quarta parte detta il Mõdo nuouo, o uuol dire l'Indie Occidentali, la si diuide in due parti, cioe il Perù, & la nuoua Spagna; la parte del Perù si diuide in sette Prouincie, la prima delle quail, è la Castiglia de l'oro; la secõda è Paria," (The fourth part called the new World, or rather the West Indies, is divided into two parts, namely Peru, and new Spain; the part Peru is divided in six provinces, the first of which is Castilla del Oro; the second is Paria,) etc., naming all six provinces, after which he continues, "E la parte seconda detta la nuoua Spagna si diuide in dodeci prouincie, La prima e Nicaragua: la seconda e Santo Dominico, ouero l'Isola Spagnola," etc. (And the second part called new Spain is divided into twelve provinces, The first is Nicaragua: the second is Santo Domingo, or the island Hispaniola, etc.)[54] It is only at the part America that Gastaldi does not move directly into enumerating the provinces, but instead feels compelled first to break the part into two sub-parts, and only then to enumerate the provinces, first of the one, and then of the other, separately. This is perhaps an instance of an early sensing that each of the two enormous halves of the megacontinent America were individually worthy of continental status, but I much suspect that it is more a reflection of something else, as follows.

As we shall see below, in chapters seven and eight, neither Gastaldi nor anyone else knew or could have known whether Asia and America were separated or not, and it would be a long time after before the problem was solved. His famous depiction of the two continents approaching close together in the north, at his Strait of Anian, represented neither conviction nor even opinion, but simply a suggestion, a possibility, and he all along would have simultaneously entertained the possibility that the two continents were solidly joined, though it was of course not possible to depict both possibilities in one map. My own suspicion, though it can't be proved, is that Gastaldi's dividing of the New World into two parts reflects a wish to keep the two halves to some degree disassociated from each other since it would be valid to assign continental status to South America, connected (like

---

[53] Gastaldi (1561, 15).

[54] Gastaldi (1561, 18).

Africa) to other land only by a very narrow isthmus, regardless of whether this continental status could be assigned to the northern half. That this is the case gains some more support from the fact that there is a very interesting further indication of Gastaldi's feeling uncertainty as to the continental status of North America, while at the same time feeling certainty on the same point as regards its southern counterpart South America.

This further indication we see in a legend on his undated world map, "Dell'Universale,"[55] which shows the New World firmly connected with the Old, as on his 1546 world map. While, in the 1561 booklet, he gives half-status, so to speak, to each of the two parts of the New World, in the legend on the "Dell'Universale" he seems to tacitly deny that North America has any status at all beyond being a part of Asia, while South America is a new part of the world. The legend sits prominently above the left half of the map, that is, the part devoted to the New World, although it unavoidably also shows part of easternmost Asia, blending into the New World. However, although the legend is clearly addressed to all of that part of the map directly below it, its text recognizes only South America: "Qvesta parte di terra nuoua ritrouata da Christoforo Colombo Genouese, & da molt' altri huomeni illustri, e diuisa in diuerse Regioni, cioe il Peru, la Castiglia de l'oro il Brasil, e il Quito & molt' altre," etc. (This continent of terra nuova[56] discovered by Christopher Columbus of Genoa, and by many other illustrious men, is divided into diverse regions, that is Peru, Castilla del Oro, Brazil, and Quito & many others, etc.) The legend continues, giving various descriptive and historical facts about these areas of South America, and ends with a statement that all this "terra noua" extends from 50° S, at the Strait of Magellan, to 10° N,

---

[55] Our map no. 66. This legend is taken nearly verbatim from the back of the map of South America in Gastaldi's 1548 Ptolemy.

[56] Cf. the name Gastaldi uses for South America on the map of that continent in his 1548 Ptolemy: "Tierra nova" (our map no. 58). The map is the first ever separate map of South America. I have used the word "continent" here to render "parte" to avoid the confusion of the phrase "this part of Terra nuova," which might be taken as meaning a section as opposed to the whole. That "part of Terra nuova" definitely means "continent of Terra nuova" and not "section of Terra nuova" is confirmed by the fact that the usage of the partitive "of" in this sense is widespread in maps of the time. Compare Gastaldi's title in his 1564 Africa: "Il disegno della geografia moderna de tutta la parte dell'Africa," means "of the modern geography of all the continent of Africa," not all of some *part* of Africa. In the present passage, the rendering "this part of Terra nuova" would be too easily misunderstood. The problem points up again the difficulties which could arise as a result of the sixteenth century usage of the word "part" to refer to a continent.

followed by the names of the South American rivers. It simply ignores North America completely, implying an unwillingness to make a commitment as to whether North America here should be taken as part of the Old World or the New. We shall see still other strong suggestions of uncertainty in Gastaldi as to the relation of the Old World and the New in the next two chapters.

6.4 Visual Conceptions

Note that all of the expressed opinions that there were four continents given in our survey of cosmographers above were textual statements, not graphic representations or accompanied by graphic representations. They were simply opinions buried in books on cosmography. We have no certain knowledge of the notion's having emerged into the light from a passive textual context to a bold visual one until 1570 when Ortelius opens his *Theatrum Orbis Terrarum* with four consecutive maps of the principal parts of the world, America, Asia, Africa and Europe, in that order. After Ortelius came Giovanni Lorenzo d'Anania's unattractive little set of four-continent maps in his 1573 cosmography,[57] the four-continent set in Thevet's 1575 *Cosmographie universelle*,[58] the set in Gerard de Jode's 1578 *Speculum*, and others later, and also, of course, the 1574 painted wall maps at Caprarola.[59] Nor were there any other kinds of graphic representations of the four-continent notion until (also in the 1570s) when allegorical representations of the four continents first began to appear in art. There is such a set, in fresco by Taddeo Zuccaro, in the same hall at Caprarola where we find the painted four-continent wall map set of which we shall speak shortly, and Partridge says that this "is the earliest extant painted ensemble at the beginning of a

---

[57] See Hellwig (1994, with maps reproduced at 112-15).

[58] Karrow (1993, 532-33, nos. 77/5, 77/8, 77/24, 77/33).

[59] I have not tried to trace down a reference by Raemdonck in the *Bulletin* of the Societé de Géographie d'Anvers, vol. 4(1879), pp. 261 and 361 to an April 30, 1571 Plantijn reference to a "4 parties du monde de Belleforest." The only Belleforest work I know of off-hand is his 1575 edition of Münster. We shall speak more of the Caprarola maps below.

long tradition."[60] Indeed, the four-continent theme did quickly become one of the most popular ensemble themes, and remained thus for several centuries, in all art genres.[61] Art historian Suzanne Boorsch has written: "I suspect that the single most important contribution directly to art history of the discovery of America -- until very recent times -- was the addition of the Four Continents to the roster of secular iconographical subjects. They joined the four elements, four seasons, four temperaments, and four times of day as convenient series for allegory or decorative schemes."[62] But there was nothing graphic before the 1570s.

The scheme was also very popular in one other area of visual representation, the more ephemeral medium of processions, royal entries, pageants, ballets, etc.,[63] and only in this area have I found any reference to visual representations of the four continents before 1570. The first occurred in the *tableau vivant* of the four continents in 1564 and 1566 for the annual *Ommegang* pageant in Antwerp,[64] and the second in a procession in 1571 in

---

[60] Partridge (1995, 440). Partridge suggests they may have been inspired by the allegorical figures on the title page of Ortelius's *Theatrum*, which should then itself perhaps be considered the earliest such example, but we recall that the Ortelius title page continent allegories also contain one for the fifth continent, Magellanica. Köllmann, in a work which Partridge calls "the fundamental article on the personification of the continents," also gives the Caprarola set, which he dates as ca. 1572-74, as the earliest in a long list (Köllmann, 1967, cols. 1107-1202, at col. 1164.) In his monumental catalog of European art arranged by themes, which, regardless of its title, gives exhaustive lists going back to late Medieval times, at least to the late fourteenth century, and covering all genres (frescos, engravings, plaques, etc.), Andor Pigler also gives the Caprarola frescos as the earliest dated example (Pigler, 1974, 2, 521-23). He precedes it in his listing by two undated frescos by Paolo Farinati, one in the Casa Castellani at S. Pietro in Monastero, Verona, and the other in the Villa Stegagno (formerly Villa Della Torre), also Verona. His placement of these two at the head of the list is clearly not to be taken as an indication of chronological precedence, but just uncertainty as to where they belong in the basically chronological listing, and Lionello Puppi tells us that Farinati was working in the two named places in the late 1580s and 1590s (Puppi, 1968, pp. xxxvi, note 100; 62, in note from previous page, and 130).

[61] Le Corbeiller (1961), and Hyde (1924).

[62] Boorsch (1976, 506). We see, not surprisingly, from Pigler, that fourfold series themes were much more prevalent than series in three, or five, or other numbers. We can probably assume that this universal attraction to fourfold schemes itself played a subconscious role in the appearance of the four-continent scheme among the map producing community as well.

[63] Boorsch (1976), and Hyde (1926).

[64] Williams (1960, 352-53). The continents were depicted on the skirts of participants.

the Piazza S. Marco in Venice, in celebration of the anti-Turkish league between Venice, the Papacy, and Spain.[65]

It is widely known that in sixteenth century Italy a good number of painted mural wall maps were executed in public buildings or the residences of the wealthy. These mural maps provide some further confirmation that in the early 1560s, when Gastaldi was making his most important maps, the old Ptolemaic convention of showing the continents in parts, which we briefly described in chapter 1, still held the field strongly for those who would present the whole world in a series of special maps, while the four-continent idea would arise only a few years later.

There are only four which make up true series or cycles of such maps,[66] and of these, one, a cycle in the Galleria delle Carte Geografiche in the Vatican Belvedere is of no interest to us, being a series of maps of parts of Italy.[67] But the other three, noted in chapter two, all represent the entire world in painted maps, and they can be revealing for us. We shall describe each of them briefly, and then point out their significance for the present study. The first in order of time is a series of maps painted on the walls of the West and North Wings of the Terza Loggia of the Vatican.[68] There are thirty maps in all, one world, ten parts of Europe, ten parts of Asia, three parts of Africa, and five parts of America. The cycle followed a plan of unknown authorship, but it's clear there was a syncretistic concept behind it.[69] The main authors, or painters, were Giovanni Antonio Vanosino and, later, Egnazio Danti.[70] Work began from 1560,[71] under Pius IV and at the end of his reign in 1565 the West Wing was complete, and the North Wing had been started.[72] Work was halted under Pius V, (1566-1572), but was

---

[65] Ambrosini (1980, 66-67). Note that in a 1549 royal entry of Prince Philip into Antwerp, a *tableau vivant* included figures only for the three parts of the world Europe, Asia, America (Le Corbeiller, 1961, 209).

[66] An excellent concise description of the four is given by Schulz (1987).

[67] On this cycle, see Almagià (1952), and Gambi and Pinelli (1994), with reproductions of all the maps.

[68] Almagià (1955), which reproduces all the maps; Schulz (1987, 101-07).

[69] Schulz (1987, 104 and 107).

[70] Almagià (1955, 3 and 27).

[71] Almagià (1955, 3). Elsewhere, Almagià says work on the maps began in 1559 or 1560 (1952, 12).

[72] Almagià (1955, 1 and 2).

taken up again and completed under Gregory XIII (1572-1585), and it presumably followed the original plan."[73] None of the source maps used was later than 1562,[74] and fewer of the source maps are Gastaldi's than for the other two sets. The Africas are from Gastaldi, and four of the Asias, but only three of the Europes are from Gastaldi.[75] It is especially for north Europe that Gastaldi sources are lacking, and Gastaldi seems to have been weak as to northern Europe, especially northwestern Europe.

The second set is painted on cabinet doors in the Sala delle Carte Geografiche (also called the Sala della Guardaroba Nuova) of the Palazzo Vecchio, in Florence.[76] It contains fifty-three maps, thirteen of Europe, fifteen of Asia, twelve of Africa, nine of America, and four of Polar regions. The original impetus came from Duke Cosimo I de' Medici, the palace's owner, and the original intent was to follow the order of Ptolemy as much as possible, but with modern maps, although that wasn't followed.[77] Gambi says, after Almagià, that "it was the first attempt to realize a coherent and comprehensive, if somewhat unusual, sequence of maps of all the known regions of the planet."[78] The main authors were Egnazio Danti and Stefano Buonsignori.[79] Work began in 1563 and was not completed until 1586.[80] The cartography is "mostly derived from that of Gastaldi."[81]

---

[73] Schulz (1987, 105) says the "original program was continued with only slight alteration."

[74] Almagià (1955, 25).

[75] Almagià (1955, 25, 30, 31).

[76] Levi-Donati (1995), who reproduces all the maps; Schulz (1987, 98-99); Almagià (1952, 14-16).

[77] Almagià (1952, 13). In Vasari's description of this project, he says: "Over the doors of these cabinets, within their ornaments, Fra Ignazio [Egnazio Danti] has distributed fifty-seven pictures about two braccia high and wide in proportion, in which are painted in oils on the wood with the greatest diligence, after the manner of miniatures, the Maps of Ptolemy, all measured with perfect accuracy and corrected after the most recent authorities, and with the exact charts of navigation . . . ."(Vasari, 1906, VII, 633-34) The maps of course are not the maps of Ptolemy corrected, but they do reflect the Ptolemaic practice of making a number of regional maps for each continent, as see just below. Probably Vasari, who does not seem to know much of cosmography proper, simply heard that Danti was following Ptolemy in this way, and interpreted that as meaning the Ptolemy maps themselves were being followed.

[78] Gambi, in Gambi and Pinelli (1994, 89).

[79] Schulz (1987, 98).

[80] Schulz (1987, 98).

[81] Milanesi, in Gambi and Pinelli (1994, 110).

The last set, already briefly mentioned, is painted on the walls of the Sala del Mappamondo (also called the Sala della Cosmografia) in the Palazzo Farnese of Caprarola, near Viterbo.[82] Here there are only a world map, and four large painted wall maps of the continents, plus two smaller maps, one of Italy and one of the Holy Land. The plan was conceived in 1573 by Fulvio Orsini,[83] and executed quickly by Vanosino in 1573-74.[84] The source for the Asia and the Africa are Gastaldi's maps of those continents,[85] and the main sources given for Europe by Kish are also Gastaldi maps, though I think he may be partly in error here.[86] For America, the source was virtually certainly Gastaldi's image of America from the 1561 *Cosmographia vniversalis* world map.[87]

All three sets contain a good representation of Gastaldian cartography, but especially the second, begun after Gastaldi's project of 1559-1564 was well under way, and the third. The first, conceived about 1560 (possibly 1559), consists of maps of parts of the continents, as does the second, conceived about 1563. The last, conceived in 1573, at approximately the time when Camocio was working on the first of his continental wall maps of which we shall speak at length in chapter eleven, but probably earlier than the time when he decided to extend this into a full set of the four continents, probably ca. 1575, but certainly not before 1574, consists of whole wall maps of the four continents. While this is not absolute proof of anything, it certainly is in accord with our suggestion that in the early 1560s, when Gastaldi was working on his project, the notion of a set of large maps, one

---

[82] Schulz (1987, 99-101), Kish (1953), Partridge (1995). Fairly good reproductions of all the maps are in Portoghesi (1996, pp. xciv-xcv, xcvi-xcvii and xciii), and also in Faldi (1981, 250-59), where there is also a good photograph of the entire room, at p. 130.

[83] Partridge (cit., 413-14).

[84] Schulz (1987, 100).

[85] Kish (1953, 53-54).

[86] Kish (1953, 53).

[87] It would not have been from the Gastaldi America itself, which, though drawn ca. 1560, was not properly published until the 1590s. Kish (1953, 54) suggested as sources for the Caprarola America, the 1574 Forlani America (cf. Woodward, 1990, no. 83, with a reproduction), and the undated Forlani South America (cf. Woodward, 1990, no. 11, and a reproduction in Nordenskiöld, 1889, fig. 80), and, while possible, I think it unlikely. The "Cosmographia Vniversalis" world was still little known, and had not been reproduced anywhere when Kish wrote, and my feeling is that Vanosino was probably unaware of it.

each for each continent, had hardly arisen yet, and representations of the world in modern maps were still following the format of continents shown in parts, while four maps for four continents would still have to wait a few years. This Caprarola set of maps of 1573-74 is, incidentally, the first large complete set of four-continent wall maps, although painted and not printed.

It is clear from all this that in the 1560s acceptance of the notion of there being four continents was only barely beginning to reach a level sufficiently high for it to begin appearing in visual representations, and that this did not really start to take good hold until the early 1570s. This finding can give us some grounds for doubt that it would have been such a natural thing for Gastaldi to have embarked in the early 1560s on a project for representing the world in four large maps of individual continents, a question we will investigate further below.

As noted at the head of this chapter, our review here of the development of sixteenth century ideas concerning the number of continents will be useful to us in the following chapter, and the rest of our book. In the following chapter, we shall present still some more ideas of various geographers, including Gastaldi, ideas relatable to the question we have explored here, but this time focusing more narrowly on but two continents, Asia and America, and the problem of whether they were connected or separated.

CHAPTER 7 - AN UNSOLVABLE CARTOGRAPHIC RIDDLE: THE GEOGRAPHICAL RELATIONSHIP OF ASIA AND AMERICA

7.1 Opinions, Hedgings, and Confusion

One of the greatest problems, perhaps the greatest, with mapping the world's continents was how to depict the relation of Asia and America, a problem that was unsolvable at the time. What was Asia? What was America? What was the New World? Where did Asia end? Where did America begin (in the west)? Were they one entity, or were they distinct? Let us take a look at what our cosmographers thought on this score. We will see that there was tremendous uncertainty on the question, that there was a reluctance to commit oneself on the question, to the point of resorting to sundry ruses and artifices to avoid direct answers to the question, and that Gastaldi was just as uncertain, and just as inclined to avoidance, as the rest. This, I believe, was among the principal problems hindering Gastaldi from formulating a good plan for depicting the whole world during the years from 1559 on. This question, of course, is related to how many continents there were, as examined in the last chapter, for if they were separated, America would definitely be a separate, and a fourth, continent. Nevertheless, it is an interesting fact that, for many cosmographers, the notions of four principal continents, and of America being the fourth continent, did not necessarily imply that the New World was separated from the Old at all. Gemma in 1530 does not hesitate to state that there are four parts, and the fourth is America, but he also states that it is unknown whether the New World is joined to Asia or not.[1] Schöner, too, although in 1533 he rejects Vespucci's claim that America is a fourth part of the globe since it's connected to Asia, contradicts himself in saying earlier that a fourth part has been seen and partly explored, called Brasil.[2] More to the point, Girava states in 1556 unequivocally that there are four parts, the last the "Indias, ó Nuouo Mundo," but his world map accompanying the book shows a clear broad

---

[1] Gemma (1530, pt. 3, ch. 30, 2nd page).

[2] Schöner (1533, C4r).

connection of the type initiated earlier by Monachus ca. 1527 and Fine in 1534.[3] Again, while it is stated clearly in the lengthy text on the 1559/60 Hadji Ahmed world map that there are four parts and that the New World is the fourth part,[4] the map itself shows a clear connection.[5] Postel, too, as we have seen, has no reservations in saying there are four parts, and the fourth is America, although in both his manuscript ca. 1560 cosmography and his 1561 printed one, he states it is not yet known whether the two continents are connected or separated;[6] and, while Gutierrez, on his 1562 map of America twice calls the continent a fourth part of the world, he clearly hedges as to the question of a connection with Asia, cutting his depiction in the west very short to avoid showing anything beyond the lower California peninsula.[7]

Similar double-think is evinced by both Arrivabene in 1554, and Garzoni in 1585, who consider America as one of four parts of the earth, but they both present lists of toponomy in which there is wholesale mixing together of Old and New World place names. Arrivabene includes among New World place names Gogh, Magogh, Bangella, Cataio, Moluche (all clearly Asian place names), as well as Nuoua hispagna, Il bacalos, Terra florida, Peru, Brasil, etc.,[8] and Garzoni does the same.[9] A similar sort of confusion is seen in the fact that many scholars took the term New World as denoting not just America, but all the areas which had been explored by the Portuguese and Spanish.[10] Donald Lach says of Münster: "His conception of the 'New World,' all those newly discovered places unknown to the ancients, became as broadly influential as his writings. Like others of his

---

[3] See Girava (1556, 61-62). For the map, see reproduction at Shirley no. 101.

[4] See Ménage (1958, 294-95); and again in a very interesting section of the text not noticed by Ménage, but given in French translation by Avezac (1865, 719).

[5] Though the map is clearly in general inspired by the 1534 Fine world, the connection type adopted is much different from that shown by Fine, as see chapter eight.

[6] Postel (1561, 4); and Milanesi (1992, 35, note 19, and 35), citing Postel from a ca. 1560 manuscript work.

[7] See Karrow (1993, 285-87) for Gutierrez; and also our chapter six, note 16.

[8] Quoted in Kretschmer (1892, 428).

[9] Garzoni (1996, 432-33). The same occurs in the cosmography of Francesco Filopono, about which more below, and in Myritius (1590, 120).

[10] Besides the comments here, see on this Lewis and Wigen (1997, 217, note 59), and Morison (1974, *Southern Voyages*, 155).

time he included within this conception the newly discovered places of Asia as well as America,"[11] and, again, of the very rare *L'histoire du noveau monde descouvert par les Portugalois, escrite par le Seigneur Pierre Bembo* (Paris, 1556), the same writer says, "the author treats the Portuguese conquests in Asia and Magellan's voyage to the Moluccas as integral parts of the opening of the 'New World.'"[12] Franck has a twenty-eight-page section on the "newly found world," but almost half of it is on areas of Asia,[13] and Garzoni in 1585 speaks of Marco Polo and Lodovico Varthema as being among those "who treat of the New World."[14] The famous collection edited by Simon Grynaeus, *Novus Orbis Regionum* (Basle, 1532; German edition title: *Die New Welt*, etc.), sometimes cited as being on America, contains at least as many texts on Africa and, especially, Asia, as for America.[15]

What comes through most clearly from the above examples is that nothing was clear regarding the relation of Asia and America. It is perhaps not surprising then, that none of the cosmographers surveyed ever actually offered any discussion on the question of whether Asia and America are physically separated or connected. Indeed, very few even offer a clearly stated opinion. None, in fact, make a straightforward statement that the continents are separated, although a few do tell us indirectly, or by implication, that they are separated, by stating that America is an island or islands, as do Apian (1524) and Münster (1540),[16] A few state they are connected, but give no real reasons, as do Verrazzano (1524), Monachus (ca.

---

[11] Lach (1965-93, 2, 2/3, 339).

[12] Lach (cit., 302). Lach doubts Bembo's authorship, though the work does include much from another Bembo work. The question is unsettled.

[13] Franck (1534, 210-37), of which 220-34 only are on America.

[14] Garzoni (1996, 432-33). Varthema voyaged through south Asia as far as the Moluccas.

[15] For more examples of the same confusion, see (Lach, 1965-93, 1,2, 235, note 229 and 2, 2/3, 516-17). The multiplicity of names applied to America also implies much uncertainty. Besides America, the New World, and the West Indies (which meant all the American New World at the time, not just the islands), we find it called "the New Asia" by Tyard in 1557 (Tyard, 1950, 109), while Postel (1561, 2) includes as variants Atlantis and Atlas. Porcacchi offers three unusual variants, Santa Croce (1572, 101), and the American Indies and France Antarctic (1572, 102), the last taken from Thevet (1558), while Monachus offers "India Culuacano" (Monachus, ca. 1529, fol. 4v), which evidently derives from Culiacan in northwest Mexico, discovered and explored by Nuño de Guzman.

[16] For example, Apian (1524, p. 69; 1544 edition, fol. 32R), and Münster, in the text overleaf of his map of the "New Islands (1540, at pl. XVII), and others.

1529), Vopel, (1545), and Schöner (1533).[17] Monachus to be sure promises to show us that Asia and America are one, but he never shows, he just tells, and tells, and tells. Vopel informs us, in a legend on his map, that in an audience with Emperor Charles V he spoke with some of Cortes's men, who convinced him that the two continents were connected, but he doesn't say what it was that convinced him. Nor does Schöner in 1533 make it clear why the results of Magellan's voyage should have had the extraordinary effect of leading him to believe that the continents were joined when he had previously considered them as separated.

Several of our cosmographers state more reasonably and honestly that it is unknown whether the two continents are connected or not, including Gemma (1530),[18] Ramusio (1536),[19] Rithaymer (1538),[20] Arrivabene (1554),[21] and Filopono (1557),[22] and we see the same in a very few maps, such as Cabot's 1544 world[23], Gastaldi's 1556 map of the Western Hemisphere,[24] and Ruscelli's 1561 world map.[25] But the great majority of the cosmographers do not even offer this. They simply avoid making a statement as to whether the Old and New Worlds are separated by water or not.

Just how confounded cosmographers of the day were by this question is shown by the following. It was common for cosmographers, in their works, to provide descriptions of the boundaries of continents. It was customary, wherever possible, to describe these boundaries by recourse to bodies of water or watercourses, seas, gulfs, rivers, etc., and sometimes, when none such were available, using parallels and meridians, established at

[17] Verrazzano, in his 1524 letter to the king (quoted in Kretschmer, 1892, 423, and in many other places), Monachus (ca. 1529, sig. F4v, and in Kretschmer, 1892, 415-16), Vopel, in long text at lower left on his world map (Shirley no. 102), and Schöner (1533, sig. E5r).

[18] Gemma (1530, pt. 3, ch. 30, 2nd page).

[19] After Milanesi (1992, 30, note 11).

[20] Rithaymer (1538, 111).

[21] After Kretschmer (1892, 427).

[22] After Kretschmer (1892, 430).

[23] Shirley no. 81.

[24] See our map no. 86.

[25] Shirley no. 110.

some latitude or longitude as necessary. But when it became necessary to describe the east boundary of Asia, or the west boundary of the New World, a number of cosmographers, Gastaldi included, resorted to a device which allowed them to avoid coming into direct confrontation with the question of where Asia ended and the New World began. Enciso, in 1519, is the first I know of to apply the technique. He simply says that the New World, which he divides into the West Indies and some unnamed northern part, runs from the meridian through Ferro on to the west.[26] He does not say how far west, and gives no eastern end of Asia. Essentially, he's just saying that the New World constitutes everything west of this prime meridian.

Very interesting are the similar methods used by two Italian cosmographers, contemporaries of Gastaldi, both of Mantua,[27] and from their words it is very clear that they are adopting their methods specifically to avoid committing themselves on the question of whether Asia and America were connected or not. The cosmographers are Ippolito Arrivabene (1554) and Francesco Filopono (Philopono) (1557).[28] Both state that it is not known whether the Old and New Worlds are connected or separated, but that they will accept for the purposes of their descriptions that they are connected. But in his section, "Confini de il Mondo nuouo," for the eastern boundary of Asia (and the western boundary of America) Arrivabene just gives the 180° meridian from pole to equator, then proceeds to work his way around the whole New World by arbitrarily establishing one after another a series of parallels and meridians.[29] He stops at one point to stress that the New World is not to be taken as passing anywhere to the east of the prime meridian

[26] Enciso (1519, GVIv-GVIIr).

[27] It is not clear if they were originally of Mantua or were there in connection with service to the Gonzaga family.

[28] The manuscript cosmographies of these two persons were discovered by Konrad Kretschmer, Arrivabene's in the Vatican, Filopono's in the Naples National Library. Kretschmer printed extracts from them related to the New World (1892, 424-35), where the original Italian for the sections quoted here can be found, but they seem to have gone unnoticed. Both seem to have been connected with the house of Gonzaga, under which Mantua achieved great splendor. On the Gonzaga family's interest in cosmography, see Bourne (1999), Fiorani (1996, 145, note 47), and Almagià (1929, 36 and 37). Francesco Gonzaga was patron of Magini (Almagià, 1922), and Prince Curzio Gonzaga was involved in the construction of a gigantic globe (Woodward, 1987, 2 and 18). Arrivabene was very possibly connected with the prominent publishing family Arrivabene of Mantua, who also published some things in Venice (Grendler, 1977, 105-12).

[29] Kretschmer (1892, 427-28).

(*prima linea ò meridiano*), where Europe lies.[30] Filopono describes the boundaries of Asia, but has to hedge on the eastern end, saying that the ancients stopped at 180°, and that "the authors of our time" are also uncertain.[31] Then he opens his description of the New World, which follows, with the rather confused words: "First is it to be known that all which remains to be said about the rest of Asia will be included under this name of new World; therefore that we will include this part of Asia unknown to the ancients, up to 225° longitude where some would have it that there is a gulf (*Golpho*), which extends up to the north pole, and divides this part from the new world. Others would have it that it be joined with it and all the earth without any division by water. Now whether this be or not, we do not inquire into. We will leave it thus undiscussed describing it joined, and we start from [the] 180° meridian,"[32] after which he proceeds more or less as Arrivabene, concluding with, "Thus is this part of the sphere unknown to the ancients almost half the sphere."[33] This is in Filopono's fifth book, on the New World. In his fourth book, on Asia, from which Kretschmer extracts a short passage, he also noted the two opposing conceptions of the relationship of the continents, ending with the laconic observation that he leaves "the belief to each as he pleases."[34]

We find Gastaldi resorting to essentially the same expedient. In 1548, in the overleaf text to the world map "Vniversale Novo," in his Ptolemy, Gastaldi says:

> L'Universale Orbe della Terra fu diuiso secondo gli antiqui in tre parti, cioè Europa, Aphrica, & Asia. Le quali parti hanno di longitudine gradi. 180. principiando alle isole canarie, il primo grado. . . . Tutto il resto che si vede di longitudine, che sono altri gradi. 180. e stato discoperto da moderni, cioe, le Indie occidentali che il uulgo chiama mondo nuouo, . . . il quale e verso occidente, alle

---

[30] Kretschmer (1892, 428).

[31] Kretschmer (1892, 429-30).

[32] Kretschmer (1892, 430).

[33] Kretschmer (1892, 430).

[34] Kretschmer (1892, 430).

sopradette Isole Canarie, pero somando questi gradi. 180. verso oriente discoperti dagli antiqui, con li gradi. 180. uerso ponente discoperti da moderni fanno gradi. 360. che e tutto il circolo delle Equinoctiale nella Sphera." (The Universal Orb of the Earth was divided according to the ancients in three parts, that is Europe, Africa, and Asia. Which parts have 180 degrees of longitude, beginning from the canary islands, the first degree. . .All the rest which is met with of longitude, which are another 180 degrees has been discovered by the moderns, that is, the west Indies which is popularly called the new world, . . . which is towards the west of the aforesaid Canary Islands, [and] by summing these 180 degrees towards the east discovered by the ancients, with the 180 degrees towards the west discovered by the moderns makes 360 degrees which is the whole circle of the Equinoctial in the Sphere.)[35]

Here he has defined the limits of the New World without recourse to descriptions of land or water. The New World is simply all that was not included in the 180° known to the ancients. Note that Gastaldi avoids specifically stating that the New World is a "part" of the earth, which he hasn't hesitated to do for the three old parts.[36]

In 1561 in his *Vniversale descrittione*, Gastaldi, in giving the bounds of the New World, follows the same sort of avoidance policy to a lesser degree, though it is not as obvious at first that he is doing so. He has just before given very detailed and rather lengthy descriptions of the boundaries (*confini*) between the three parts of the Old World,[37] sticking to the

---

[35] The entire legend of this 1548 world map overleaf is repeated verbatim, with a few orthographical changes, in the right of two long legends at the top of Gastaldi's undated woodcut world map "Dell'Vniversale" engraved by Pagano (Our map no. 66), which suggests its date may be close to that of the 1548 Ptolemy; but this is not conclusive, and the Pagano world remains the most undatable of Gastaldi maps. None of the estimates made to date are more than guesses. Note that on Gastaldi's 1548 map of South America in his Ptolemy (our no. 58) there is a great deal, thirty degrees or more, of what appears to be a gratuitously included Atlantic Ocean east of the continent, and a small corner of the Old World is shown. The same is seen in Gastaldi's ca. 1560 map of America (no. 94).

[36] Bellinato perhaps is following Gastaldi when he says the original three parts included all from the Fortunate Isles (Ptolemy's name for the Canaries) to 180° East, and this fourth part contains all from the Fortunate Isles to the west including all else for a full circuit of the earth (1573, 49).

[37] Gastaldi (1561, 10-14).

traditionally used watercourses as much as possible (Don River, Pontes Euxinus, Hellespont, Strait of Hercules, Red Sea, etc.), and he does give a more definite east bound to Asia, using the Strait of Anian to establish a north-south dividing line between Asia and America.[38] But for the New World he avoids altogether such a direct description of bounds. Rather, having given the bounds of Europe, Africa, then Asia, he concludes with, "questi confini dãno la separatione a tutte le quattro parti come chiaramante si ha detto, & similmente il Mondo nuouo resta in mezzo de sopradetti confini delle altre parti" (these boundaries give the separation of all the four parts as has clearly [?] been said, and similarly the New World is located in the midst of the aforesaid boundaries of the other parts).[39] But this is not at all clear, and again reflects an avoidance policy, as above in 1548. It also tends, as do the procedures followed by Enciso, Arrivabene, and Filopono, to include the world's water surface, as well as land surface, in the division of the globe into continents. He has described Europe's west boundary thus:

> La diuisione dell'Europa uerso Ponente, e il Mare Oceano, distendendo però una linea che uadi sempre uerso Settentrione, et includa la Isola d'Irlanda, infino al paralello, che passa per il mare Drobasaf. E quella linea diuidera l'Europa uerso Ponente dal Mondo nuouo (The division of Europe towards the West, is the Ocean Sea, extending thereupon a line which goes always towards the North, and includes the Island of Ireland, as far as the parallel, which passes through the Drobasaf [i.e. the White] sea. And this line will divide Europe towards the West from the new World).[40]

This implies that all the water between the two continents belongs to one or another of them, as in fact does also the line Gastaldi establishes to separate Asia in the east from the New World, for the line runs straight south from the Strait of Anian to the island Gilollo in the Moluccas. Gastaldi seems to tacitly be attempting to justify this earlier in the booklet when he refers to

---

[38] Gastaldi (1561, 13).

[39] Gastaldi (1561, 14).

[40] Gastaldi (1561, 11-12).

"tutte Quattro le parte d'essa Terra, & *Mare*, che fin hora se n'ha cognittione, cioè l'Europa l'Africa, l'Asia, & le parti nuouamente discoperte, nominate dal Volgo Mondo nuouo" (all the Four parts of the Earth and *Sea*, which are known so far, that is Europe, Africa, Asia, and the parts newly discovered, popularly called the new World).[41]

Gastaldi's uncertainty as to the relationship of Asia to America, and reluctance to commit himself, is apparent in another place, his great three-part map of Asia. In both the First and Second Parts of Asia, he gives us in the dedicatory legend detailed descriptions of the boundaries of the areas covered by the maps, and also proudly states that for all places the latitude and longitude are shown, and indeed both are marked degree by degree in the margins. But on the Third Part of Asia, the little dedicatory legend gives us only the title of the map, the dedicatee's name, and Gastaldi's signature. No description of bounds is offered, and no mention is made of latitudinal or longitudinal limits of the map; in fact, latitudes are shown only in five degree increments, and longitudes are shown only on the equator at the bottom of the original 1561 edition of the map, also only in five degree increments (cf. our Cartobibliography entry no. 103). But since we don't know the projection, we can't divine what the easternmost limit of longitude is for Asia at the north end of the map. As to how close we may be to America Gastaldi does not wish to venture a statement, nor does he wish to venture an opinion as to the longitudinal eastward extent of Asia. There are various signs that not only was Gastaldi dismayed as to the relation of the continents, but also could not come to a decision as to what total part of the earth's 360° should be assigned to Eurasia, America, and the Atlantic Ocean, which three expanses account, at the latitude of the Strait of Anian, for the entire earth's circumference on the maps where we find the strait, and that the uncertainty apparently was experienced by others who adopted his views. There are considerable differences in the widths assigned to the three on the 1561 *Cosmographia vniversalis* (159° width, from 160° W to 11° W), the Holzheimer Gores (138° width, from 173° W to 35° W),[42] Gastaldi's America

---

[41] Gastaldi (1561, 4).

[42] Shirley (1987, no. 129).

(also 138° width, but from 144° W to 6° W),[43] and the maps which derive less directly from the 1561 world, as the undated "Totius Orbis Descriptio" (131° width, from 153° W to 22° W),[44] and the 1567 Camocio world map (135° width, from 153° W to 18° W),[45] etc. There was no way anyone at the time could have estimated longitude figures for farthest Asia or America with anything less than a 20°-30° allowance for error at the least, and Gastaldi was well aware of the fact. Gastaldi also exhibits, as already noted, uncertainty as to the Asian north, for his map stops at 50° N. My own opinion is that this is at least as much due to uncertainty as to whether Asia should meet with America or not, as it is to lack of knowledge of extreme northern Asia, although both probably play a part.

Some of the clearest evidence of uncertainty on the part of Gastaldi as to whether the two continents were continuous or not is provided by several maps which were not directly made by Gastaldi, but which are obviously directly influenced by his ideas. They also make it clear that the confusion continued quite unabated after 1561, when the *Cosmographia vniversalis* world map appeared, showing the continents separated, and suggests that there probably existed preliminary Gastaldi manuscript models that either showed variant possible depictions, or left certain areas blank, and that these models were known to others, or at least the ideas shown in them were known to these others, and that these others were also mulling over and no doubt discussing the same problem. First, the modern world map in Girolamo Ruscelli's 1561 Ptolemy[46] shows a tentative connection between the two continents, resembling the tentative connection in Gastaldi's 1556 map of the Western Hemisphere. As in that map, the tentative connection is shown by a dotted line. But while the highest latitude reached by the south coast of the land bridge is about 38° N (as in the 1546 world), Ruscelli's reaches about 48° N latitude, a full ten degrees higher. In another instance, we find that in the northeast sheet of Camocio's composite Gastaldi Asia which occurs in the Bell Library's Venetian set of four-continent wall maps

---

[43] See nos. VIII and XII in the last section of the Cartobibliography

[44] Shirley (1987, no. 120).

[45] Shirley (1987, no. 117).

[46] Shirley (1987, no. 110).

(our no. III), the east coast of Asia in about 51° N latitude takes a sudden turn to the east and continues thus off the edge of the map, implying a possible connection to the east with the New World in this higher latitude.[47] In both the original Third Part of Asia of 1561, and the ca. 1570 Olgiato variant, the Asian east coast continues steadily to the north, running off the map at the top, even though the Olgiato variant does reach up to ca. 55° N latitude, like the Bell Library Asia (The 1561 original edition reaches only 50° N.). Knowing the uncertainty and problems connected with this area, we can be sure this little variation in the Bell Asia is not some thoughtless flourish by a draftsman or engraver. Its presence is clear testimony that either some trial sketches by Gastaldi for the area existed, or else that others besides Gastaldi were familiar with his ideas, and were experimenting on their own, or, perhaps most likely, both situations obtained.

Another interesting example in maps not created by Gastaldi, but no doubt much influenced by his late cartography, is the depiction on two of the regional maps, that of northwest North America, and that of northeast Asia,[48] in the set of fifty-three painted wall maps decorating the doors of the cabinets in the Sala delle Carte Geografiche (Sala della Guardaroba) of the Palazzo Vecchio at Florence, spoken of earlier. This project, we recall, was conceived in 1563 by Duke Cosimo I de' Medici, and begun in the same year by Egnazio Danti, when Gastaldi was well along with his series of large maps of parts of the world, and the cartography is "mostly derived from that of Gastaldi."[49] Almagià wrote of this set of maps that, "it represents in essence the first attempt . . . to realize a complete and organically conceived, if formally unusual, collection of cartographic representations of all the regions of the world, in other words, a modern atlas: indeed if the general design and the distribution of the maps goes back to 1563, the ordered collection precedes not only the *Theatrum* of Ortelius (1570), but also the *Tavole moderne di Geografia* put in circulation at Rome by Lafreri and analogous collections by Venetian engravers and printers."[50] As with many

---

[47] See fig. 7.1.

[48] See notes 52 and 53 below for locations of reproductions.

[49] Milanesi (1994, 110).

[50] Almagià (1952, 16).

of the maps, the derivation from Gastaldian prototypes with these two maps is obvious at a glance, both in the contours of coasts, and in the nomenclature (ANIAN PRO, GOLFO DI CHEINAN, MANGI, STRETTO DI ANNIAN in Asia, and TOLM. P in America, and others).[51] But unlike the known late maps of Gastaldi which show the area, including the "Cosmographia Vniversalis," in these two maps the coasts, and indeed the inland areas as well, are cut short about ten degrees south of the top border of the map.

The frame of the map of northwest North America, "L'ultime parti note nel Indie Occidentali" (The furthest parts known in the West Indies), made in 1564,[52] goes up to 51° N latitude, but all above ca. 41° is painted a hazy white. The untitled map of northeast Asia, made in ca. 1575,[53] runs up to 62° N latitude, but all over ca. 52° is in the same noncommittal haze as on the other map. As noted, the map contains the name "STRETTO DI ANNIAN," written vertically below the hazy section, but whether there is actually a strait above or not cannot be said. On both of the maps, in the undepicted area, is written, "Terra o mare incognito" (Land or sea unknown), and each contains a large cartouche filled with text, partly taking up the empty space.[54] There must have either been some Gastaldi models which showed variant depictions, or which left some areas blank, as in these examples, or else there was a general awareness of the uncertainty connected with these areas. In any event, the uncertainty reflected in these wall maps, and in the two printed maps noted above, must surely have reflected the uncertainty of Gastaldi himself, and it was assuredly this uncertainty, or

---

[51] It is not impossible that the Giunti, who published the great collection which contained the greater part of the information that Gastaldi used to make these later maps, had a hand in suggesting the original idea to the duke. Their publishing house was at least as prominent in Florence as in Venice, and there were works by Danti printed in Florence by the Giunti under the patronage of Duke Cosimo, with frontispieces carrying the motto "Cosimo, order of the cosmos" and surmounted by a map of the world (Milanesi, 1994, 113).

[52] Levi-Donati (1995, pl. 2, p. 23).

[53] Levi-Donati (1995, pl. 29, p. 77). The map is undated but is so clearly a partner to the map of China (pl. 28, p. 74), which makes its continuation to the west, that it must have been made at about the same time. The whole project continued until about the late 1580s. Danti made thirty-two of the maps in two periods, 1563-1565 and 1573-1575, and all or most of the rest were painted by Stefano Buonsignori from 1576 to an uncertain time, probably in the late 1580s. None of these paintings has ever been altered (Milanesi, 1994, 110).

[54] The substantial texts, clearly well-preserved, are unfortunately unreadable from the available reproductions in Levi-Donati (1995), and in Kish (1951, pl. op. p. 52).

indecision, that prevented Gastaldi from immediately publishing his ca. 1560 America (no. 94) corresponding to the maps of other continents, as we show below in chapter nine.

7.2 An Option by Bilateral Thinking

Was there perhaps a way to solve this problem without really solving it? Could a cartographer simply say: It was either this way or the other way, without committing himself one way or the other? He couldn't well do this on one map. But we suggest that he *could* do it simply enough on two or more maps including the same area, by showing one depiction on one map, and the other on another map. Much has been written of the power of maps in the sense that, for some reason, our minds have a strong tendency to take it for granted that what is depicted on a map is really there in actuality, even if it isn't. And concomitant with this notion is an also strong tendency to believe that when a cartographer depicts something on a map, his depiction necessarily reflects his opinion, if perhaps not his conviction. But in this section, we will show that it was not at all uncommon for the old cartographers to simultaneously depict one and the same area differently on different maps, and in the section following this one, we will show that, of all cartographers, it is probable that it was precisely our Gastaldi who most frequently availed himself of this option, and indeed not just frequently, but, at least in a sense, constantly and ceaselessly. In fact, it quite pervades his cartographic thinking and production from the beginning of his career to the end, to the point that we may refer to it as his *philosophy of cartography*. Finally, in the following chapter we shall see that, while Gastaldi's final resolution to the question of the relationship of the two continents was partly due to a truly brilliant bit of deductive reasoning, he was nevertheless in the end compelled, in order to finalize that resolution, to resort to the tactic of dual portrayals.

As we have seen, the great majority of sixteenth century cosmographers simply avoided altogether the question of whether Asia and America were separated or not. Even those few who offer an opinion do not say why they held that opinion. There was in fact little basis for discussion. No one knew whether the continents were connected or not, and no one could have known. Hesitance to commit was understandable. Mapmakers, too, could follow an avoidance policy if they wished. As we have seen above, a few did this, leaving those parts of their maps blank which were still undiscovered. Later, in the seventeenth century, this would become the usual policy. Wright's great world chart of 1599 held itself strictly to showing only those coasts actually discovered.[55] This wasn't immediately adopted by others, but by the 1620s a few were following his lead, and more and more did so in the ensuing decades, until the 1660s, when it had become the standard, and would remain the standard until the eighteenth century, when real information would at last begin to be available.

But, with the few mentioned exceptions, the sixteenth century cartographers seemed to have had an aversion to leaving empty spaces on their maps. They wanted a full picture, and we know that almost all world maps in the period before and during Gastaldi's time do take a stance one way or the other. Hartmann (1535?), Mercator (1538 and 1541), Demongenet (1552), Tramezzino (1554),[56] and others, all show a clear separation, while Monachus (ca. 1529), Fine (1531 and 1534), Vopel (1536 and 1545), Gastaldi (1546, etc.), Hadji Ahmed (1559/60),[57] and others, all show a clear connection. But they are silent witnesses. Just as we are not told, by those few cosmographers who express an opinion as to the relation of Asia and America, why they hold that opinion, we are not told here, either. One thing is certain. Once a cartographer had decided to draw a map of the world, he had to show one concept or the other, presuming he was not willing to leave empty spaces. That is, there was no way, working in his graphic medium, that he could just leave "the belief to each as he pleases," as Filopono could do in his textual medium. He was inexorably bound to commit himself one way or the other; there was no "or" available to him.

In light of this inexorable necessity to depict, either this way or that way, but *depict*, in light of the complete lack of stated reasons for views expressed by the cosmographers, and in light of the utter lack of real information available on the question, can we really speak of conviction

---

55 Shirley (1987, no. 221).

56 Shirley (1987), nos. 72, 74, 78, 93 and 97 respectively.

57 Shirley (1987), nos. 57, 66 and 69, 73 and 102, 85, and 103, respectively.

when we refer to a cartographer's depicting of the relation of the continents in one way or the other? We often speak, in reference to a cartographer's depiction of some unknown part of the globe, of his "thinking" this, or "believing" that, or "having the opinion" that such or other depiction was correct, and we speak of a cartographer's "changing his mind" or "changing his opinion," etc., when he adopts a depiction different from that given by him formerly. But how justified, how correct, are such statements? I think the question is an important one in attempting to assess sixteenth century cartography of unknown areas in general, and a crucial one in attempting to understand Gastaldi's thinking as regards the relation of Asia to America, as regards his famous innovation, the Strait of Anian, discussed in the following chapter, and finally as regards his project to provide an orderly large-scale set of maps of all the world's non-European continents (and perhaps of Europe as well, though this is unclear). In the following paragraphs, we will show, using other areas of the globe for which there existed uncertainty, and conflicting possibilities or opinions, that a common expedient in such instances was simply to show one possibility on one map, and another possibility on a different map. We shall also see that Gastaldi was perhaps more inclined to resort to this expedient than any other cartographer of the time.

All students of the history of cartography are well aware of that overarching dichotomy which so characterizes European cartography of the late fifteenth century, and the early to mid-sixteenth century, in which cartographers regularly produced books with whole series of maps of the same areas which differed from each other, sometimes quite radically. These were, of course, the Ptolemaic maps and their modern counterparts, and it's clear that no one felt that it was strange that there should be differing depictions of the same areas all together under one cover. But the same phenomenon is also common in the sixteenth century as regards two different modern conceptions of one area. A few examples will suffice: Waldseemüller's 1507 world map, which shows North and South America separated by water, while in the inset on the same map, they are connected;[58] Waldseemüller's 1513 set of two maps of Africa, one of North Africa, the

[58] Shirley (1987, no. 26).

other of South Africa, in which the hydrography of the north half does not meet up with the hydrography of the south half;[59] the very different depiction of northeastern North America on the 1558 Vopel-Vavassore world and the same area in the inset of the same map;[60] the radically different depictions of the whole Asian east coast and also the Asian archipelago on two maps which occur together in Ortelius's 1570 *Theatrum Orbis Terrarum*, the "Asiae nova descriptio" and the "Indiae Orientalis";[61] the very different location of Japan on two of the maps in the Cosimo di Medici Guardaroba wall map series discussed earlier;[62] the very different North Atlantic depictions on the world map in the 1561 Ruscelli Ptolemy, and on the so-called Zeno map in the same book. A truly extraordinary example, though of a very different sort, is provided by the Veneto-Roman (Lafrerian) atlases, which were presumably compiled by customers' preferences, in very many of which we find world maps showing Asia and America connected side by side with maps showing the opposite. Clearly the clients were not perturbed by these variant depictions, though they knew both could not be correct. Obviously, we cannot say that one of the two depictions in the Waldseemüller, Vopel, Ortelius, and Ruscelli double depictions represented the cartographer's opinion, let alone conviction, while the other did not. Clearly, in all cases, we are dealing with just two suggestions, two possibilities, although looking at any of the depictions apart from its partner depiction, it would be natural to think of it as representing the mapmaker's solid opinion. As noted, much has been written on the great power of images, and not in vain, for it is very hard to look at any map standing alone and not consider that we are looking at the cartographer's *belief*.

In the above examples, we have one cartographer offering different depictions of one place at the same time, that is, in one map, and its inset, or in one map book. Can we doubt that in at least some cases we should apprehend in the same spirit different depictions of the same area by one

---

[59] See Nordenskiöld (1889, figs. 8 and 9).

[60] Shirley (1987, no. 102). Probably the same is true of the 1545 original of which we have no copy.

[61] Karrow (1993), nos. 1/8 and 1/68. Excellent though small reproductions are given side by side in *Journal of the International Map Collectors' Society*, 77 (summer 1999), 56-57.

[62] Pointed out by Lach (1965-93, II:3, 464).

cartographer in maps published at different times, such as the very different pictures of eastern Asia and the New World given by Münster in 1532 and 1540,[63] or in Mercator's 1538 depiction of three south Asian peninsulas versus his 1541 depiction of four such peninsulas?[64] In both cases, both depictions are quite wrong, so in neither case does the second depiction represent a correction on the basis of newly obtained correct information. Indeed, in the case of Mercator, the correct number of south Asian peninsulas is two, so the later depiction is more incorrect than the first. These depictions are just different suggestions, different possibilities. We can't be at all certain that the cartographer really had any basis for preferring the second depiction over the first, and we cannot speak for certain of his having "changed his mind," or "changed his opinion," even if in certain cases this was true. We have said above that we see this policy of variant depictions in Gastaldi's maps more than in the maps of any other cartographer, and we shall demonstrate this now. The discussion will allow us to elucidate a crucial aspect of Gastaldi's attitude toward cartography in his time, and at the same time throw more light on his working methods in general than we have done so far.

7.3 A Cartographer's Philosophy

In 1939, Almagià, speaking of the maps in the 1548 Gastaldi Ptolemy wrote:

But the net which encloses the 'Tavole Nuove', even limited to those of Europe, is not unique; in fact often each map stands alone as a product independent of the others. Thus it occurs, for example, that in the two modern maps of France and of Germany, the coordinates of the localities common to both do not coincide (see, for instance, Magonza), as also the coordinates of Messina do not, for example, coincide in the modern map of Italy and in that of Sicily, nor the coordinates of Otranto in the map of Italy and in that of Greece, etc.

---

[63] Shirley (1987), nos. 67 and 77.

[64] Shirley (1987), nos. 74 and 78).

Hence we do not yet find in the Ptolemy, which appeared in 1548, but was put together in the preceding years, a completed work of coordination of the various maps into a single grid. It is indeed probable that precisely in working on the modern maps of the Ptolemy, Gastaldi noticed the necessity of this coordination or fitting of the modern maps into a single net, and perhaps he thus must have gotten the stimulus to seek out, at least for the better known countries of Europe, better cartographic materials than those which he had been able to find for the aforesaid modern maps." (Almagià, 1939, *carta*, 15; repeated more briefly in 1948, 21).

Almagià here clearly expects that Gastaldi will in the future seek out "better" sources from which he will be able to obtain consistency in his coordinate nets. But it never happens! It never even comes close to happening. Not only do coordinate inconsistencies on different maps for the same places, often much larger than these, especially for places far from Europe, continue to occur throughout Gastaldi's career, but also much larger inconsistencies occur, including differences in large and major landforms. A few examples will suffice. In his 1548 Ptolemy, inconsistency comes out very strongly as to the depiction of very large areas or features in the two very different modern world maps he includes, his "Vniversale Novo,"[65] and his "Carta Marina nova."[66] The differences are numerous and large, as anyone can quickly verify by comparing the reproductions of the two maps in Nordenskiöld (1889, pls. 45 (2) and 45 (3)). In a much later and more prominent example, Gastaldi's 1561 Second Part of Asia (no. 102) extends far to the west, catching a very sizeable portion of northeastern Africa. Due to this extension, we obtain a prominent image of the whole area of the Horn of Africa, the Gulf of Aden, and the Red Sea. Now, if we compare this area on this Second Part of Asia with the same area on Gastaldi's 1564 Africa (no. 118), we soon notice that the ratio between the length of the northern side of the Horn of Africa and the length of the Red Sea, that is, the distance between Cape Guardafui and the Strait of Bab el Mandeb versus the distance

---

[65] Our no. 63.

[66] Our no. 64.

from Bab el Mandeb and Suez, differs strongly between the two maps. Taking the former as our base, in 1561 the ratio is about 1 to 2.50, but in 1564 it is about 1 to 1.66, a sizeable discrepancy. Again, taking the axis of the Red Sea, in 1561 we obtain an azimuth of about 29 degrees west of north, while in 1564 we obtain about 40 degrees west of north. Although the different projections, trapezoidal in 1561 and rectangular in 1564, can account for some of the difference, it would account for a very small amount. And, in light of this of course, latitudes, and, especially longitudes, of places cannot but vary considerably between the two maps, as indeed they do. Perhaps the most salient example of this inconsistency is in the many differences, in both coordinates and in large features and forms, between the continental depictions on the 1559-1564 maps and the same on the contemporaneous *Cosmographia vniversalis* world map of 1561, where one can quickly find many differences, both in the coordinates and in larger differences, as in the form of the eastern coast of Asia, or the area of northeastern Africa, or in the shape of California or India, and many other instances. But these are only a few cases by way of example. If we include all of the differences, including disagreements of only a few minutes in coordinates, as the examples Almagià noted, the number of such inconsistencies in Gastaldi's maps is virtually endless. Of course, there were a good many times when Gastaldi actually did obtain newer more correct information on some area, usually through Ramusio, and changed that area accordingly. Nevertheless, a high degree of flux and inconsistency always remained, even in these areas, just as in all others.

Was Gastaldi indifferent, unconcerned as to consistency here? We may answer without trepidation: Indifferent and unconcerned he was indeed, to the end of his career! But the record indicates to us that there was unquestionably rationale behind this indifference, and this rationale was, without doubt, as shall be clear momentarily, a major factor in his resounding success in making three series of maps from the 1540s to the 1560s which successively show the greater part of the world better than it had been shown before, culminating in the great continental maps of 1559-1564. Gastaldi's intention was to get the picture right in a *general* sense, and he did it. He was indeed, beyond question, quite consciously indifferent to trying to get it right in a *precise* sense, for the simple reason that he knew that this was quite impossible in his time.

He knew that the Portuguese and the Spanish in their voyages took azimuthal bearings which were taken with only a most primitive understanding of magnetic declination; that they also took distance measurements based purely on dead reckoning; and that they took some latitudes which, while reasonably good, were far from truly accurate. He knew too that the Portuguese did not bother themselves with longitude, and that the Spanish could only provide the very roughest of estimates. And he knew that, combining these basically faulty sources of information they did what they could to produce depictions of the African, Asian and American coasts. The overall result was rather good for the time in a general way, but of course there was a broad element of error, and regular disagreement between charts, and neither they nor anyone else could possibly have gotten very close to true accuracy. The same was true of information from the Ramusian texts, except that here what little numerical data which was given was of a still much more approximate nature than that of the Portuguese, as reflected in their charts. We have concentrated on extra-European areas, since those are the most important to us, but, while the level of surety obtainable for European areas was of course much higher, a quite impenetrable veil of inaccuracy and uncertainty still reigned there as well in the sixteenth century.

In short, *Gastaldi fully recognized, and openly and unstintingly acknowledged to himself the realities and limitations of his times, kept his heud out of the clouds, and did not waste time and effort trying to reach the unreachable.* This, we submit, was his philosophy of cartography, a philosophy of healthy indifference, not indifference to exactitude as an abstract notion, but indifference to an exactitude unachievable in his particular endeavor. This philosophy of indifference was well founded, and in perfect accord with the ineluctable truth that *all* the world's geography was in great flux and uncertainty in the sixteenth century, and precise facts were usually just not available.[67] Because of this, he was able to work with speed

---

[67] I may add, incidentally, that anyone who inspects Ortelius's *Theatrum* will see that he too must have shared Gastaldi's openmindedness in this regard to a considerable degree, for there are a good number of coordinate and land form differences in the same areas on different maps in that work as well.

and fluency, and it was this that afforded him the possibility of reaching his goal. And reach it he did, precisely by virtue of this liberating and thoroughly logical philosophy. He probably gave a little more thought to his latitudes than his longitudes, which latter he probably estimated quickly, in short order and in an offhand way,[68] there being little reason to fret over them beyond that, and where there was uncertainty (and uncertainty was everywhere in the sixteenth century), his depictions varied accordingly from map to map.[69] How else indeed, than by a conscious disregard for impossible-to-attain precision and consistency could Gastaldi have accelerated his efforts and production to the point that he could make at least 124 maps of all parts of the globe, including much of Europe, and including

---

[68] Sometimes borrowing a few Ptolemaic coordinate values as a skeletal frame for European, and other areas within the old Ptolemaic *ecumene*, although Gastaldi shone his brightest precisely in areas beyond that old *ecumene*. This borrowing of selected Ptolemaic coordinates has been noted in a number of places by Almagià (for example: 1929, 23, 27, 28; 1939, 17; 1948, 22, 34, 36; and other places). It had been noted earlier in a rather inexplicit way by Biasutti (1908, 16-18), who, however, failed to grasp what Gastaldi was doing, and implied to the point of gross exaggeration the extent of Gastaldi's borrowings from Ptolemy in a peculiar table, though exactly what this table is supposed to demonstrate Biasutti never really tells the reader (1908, 17-18). An in-depth analysis of the table reveals it to be essentially meaningless in many of its entries, but a *superficial* perusal of it serves only to distort things, creating a very wrong impression, and tending, if I may coin a term, to "over-Ptolemaicize" Gastaldi. It was no doubt an awareness of this negative implication of his table that prompted Biasutti's memory to fail him at one point, where he makes the strange asseveration, without giving references (which, after all, do not exist), that Lelewel, Nordenskiöld and Gallois somewhere refer to Gastaldi's work as "Ptolemaic" (1908, 54). I have years since read every word Lelewel and Nordenskiöld ever wrote about Gastaldi, and can state with perfect assurance that neither says anything of the kind anywhere, and indeed Nordenskiöld devotes considerable space to stressing that Gastaldi is among the main harbingers of modern, i.e., non-Ptolemaic cartography (for example, in 1889, at 116-32, esp. 116 and 122, but in other places as well.) I have not read all of Gallois, but have read much, and have encountered no such comments, so I suspect the same is true of him. Finally, clearly in support of his Gastaldi-Ptolemy "thesis" (I use quotation marks, for he never really states a thesis), Biasutti makes a peculiarly circuitous claim which we haven't room to state or expound on here (though the reader can look it up at Biasutti's p. 116, note 3), other than to say that we have checked the claim out thoroughly against the original sources named by Biasutti, finding that it is quite incorrect.

[69] It would take me too far off course to present a more detailed exposition of Gastaldi's probable working method in these maps, especially as regards his coordinate grids. I will note only that, in my considered opinion, this whole understudied area is probably complicated a great deal more than has been realized due to longstanding unspoken but implied incorrect assumptions concerning prime meridians in the sixteenth century (see chapter five, note 11), and I feel that, presuming that my tentative conclusions are correct, Gastaldi's selective, *and quite limited*, use of Ptolemaic coordinates, was a perfectly valid and logical procedure, not in any way regressive; and I further feel that some intuitive or empirical application of today's simple cosine rule (the longitude varies as the cosine of the latitude), although not yet formulated in our straightforward terms at that time, was perhaps sometimes being used by Gastaldi. Unfortunately, going into these things here would take us much too far afield.

some of the greatest maps ever made, in the short space of just over twenty years? Nevertheless, a good general picture of the world he did indeed capture, and it is there for us to see. But we must not look for or expect consistency in detail from map to map, and often enough we must not look for consistency in larger, broader features either.

The greatest differences in depictions are found in areas completely unknown, in Gastaldi as in other cartographers, and there still remained quite a few of these unknown areas, where one could resort only to guesses, imagination, or myth. The unknown area which makes up the principal topic of the present chapter, the far northern Pacific, where was hidden the secret of the relation of Asia to America, holds much greater interest for us than the others. We have looked at many ideas of other geographers on this topic, all of them ideas guided essentially by guess, just as was always the case with depictions of any other unknown areas. But for Gastaldi this particular case was very special, for two reasons. In the first place, it was especially important to Gastaldi, because his aspirations included separate maps of the two continents of Asia and America, so that some suitable solution *had* to be arrived at. In the second place, no doubt because of a driving impetus arising from the fact that a satisfactory answer was vital, Gastaldi managed to coax from his intellect a partial (and partially adequate) solution not by guess, but by a valid process of inference, even though no soul alive had any information on the area, by recourse to a train of logic which we consider as among Gastaldi's crowning achievements, and perhaps the most astonishing and impressive *tour de force* in pure ratiocination ever made in the history of geography. Nevertheless, even though Gastaldi performed this brilliant intellectual feat, and even though he managed thereby to greatly narrow down the possibilities as to the correct depiction of the relationship of the two continents, and in fact even succeeded in approaching to the truth, final and absolute resolution of the problem continued to elude him for the rest of his life. And yet, regardless of this, he *did* depict the correct relationship in some maps (though not in others, resorting thus to our procedure of variant depictions), and this basically correct depiction *did* come to take hold in cartography, by virtue of considerations of an essentially non-geographical nature. How these things came about makes up the business of the following chapter.

CHAPTER 8 - A WORKABLE SOLUTION: GASTALDI'S STRAIT OF ANIAN

8.1 Preliminary Remarks

The strait of Anian, as the reader will no doubt know, is the name given to a strait depicted as running north and south in high northern latitudes between Asia and North America, much resembling the present Bering Strait, although it first appeared on old maps in the early 1560s, almost 170 years before Vitus Bering discovered the actual strait in 1728. It is an old puzzle in the history of geography, and no one has ever offered a

Gastaldi 1555

Gastaldi 1561

satisfactory explanation for it.[1] We first see it on Gastaldi's "Cosmographia Vniversalis," and on a number of other Italian maps shortly after. Once it had been adopted by Ortelius in 1570 in his *Theatrum Orbis Terrarum*, it appeared on almost all world maps until the 1640s, when it began to be replaced on better world maps by a depiction which opted not to show the American northwest coast above an insular California, and which left an empty void between California and an east Asian coast some 50°-60° away, or else showed in that space an indistinct and disconnected south coast of a conjectured land, often referred to as Jesso or Company Land, names derived

---

[1] There is a voluminous literature on this subject, which will be reviewed fully in a work in progress, *The Straits of Anian in History, Cartography and Myth*, from which the present chapter is for the most part condensed. [The publishers have not yet discovered this work among Doug's papers] For the present, I will just cite the principal works that have appeared which touch in any way on the question of the origin of the strait on maps. Chronologically, they are: Kohl (1911, but written 1850s), Ruge (1873, and edition 1888), Kretschmer (1892), Sandler (1894), Ruge (1896), Sykes (1915), Marinelli (1917), Berg (1919), Vignaud (1921), Wagner (1926), Gould (1929), Nunn (1929), Berg (1935), Hennig (1935), Berg (1936), Rickard (1941), Parker (1956), Astengo (1990), Milanesi (1992). The last two named are much more valuable than any before, especially that of Milanesi. As can be seen, after the 1930s, there was little, and after 1956, nothing until recently. Milanesi is really the first to have made any meaningful contribution since the 1890s. The most valuable early work was all done by the German scholars Ruge, Kretschmer, and Sandler, who established the source of the name, and the fact that the strait was created by Giacomo Gastaldi. Before that, writing on the subject had been largely undirected and chaotic, and was much vitiated by the fact that the earliest maps with the feature were not known (cf. note 34 below). None of the works mentioned make any real headway as to the origin of the concept before Astengo and Milanesi. Marinelli did briefly introduce one not-too-helpful suggestion, but it was invalid since based upon a misapprehended chronology, as shown by Caraci (1936, 123). Hennig, still occasionally cited, is daydreams, reverting to the old idea that perhaps there had been a real discovery, for which it must bring in the tales of Mendes Pinto, closer to Münchausen than true history. Nunn, the most often cited of all the works, rambles, and is hard to follow, facts pointed out by its reviewers in the *Geographical Review* (1930, 353-54), and the *Geographical Journal* (1932, 342-43). Besides the fact that it in no way fulfils the promise of its title, simply reestablishing the facts already brought out by German scholars, it roundly throws readers off the right track by a gross misinterpretation of Oviedo, as see note 87 below. There are endless other works on various subjects which contain material on this, but they cannot be gone into in this short note. Most notable are various works of Bancroft, Winsor, Wagner, Almagià and Caraci. However in none of the works mentioned so far is any real attempt made to explain how the idea of the strait first arose, and thus the present chapter is the first such attempt. There are also endless works on Anian which do not touch on the subject of the original strait, but a different strait with the same name which arose slightly later, which also can't be gone into here. Finally, there is Anian as dealt with in sundry ways in a tremendous number of books from the early seventeenth to the nineteenth centuries. Two interesting examples are Goldson (1793), and Amoretti (1811), and a number from the seventeenth and eighteenth centuries are cited below. Many of these forgotten works are of extraordinary interest in tracing the development of various old ideas connected with sundry aspects of the Strait of Anian. For more on this, and on "The Second Strait of Anian" see the special note at the end of the chapter.

from the 1643 discoveries of the Dutch explorer Vries.[2] But it certainly did hold sway on most world maps for a fairly long period after its adoption by Ortelius.

How indeed did this strait come into being on the maps so long before its actual discovery? For one hundred years, since the studies of Sandler (1894) and Ruge (1896), on the basis of different grounds than the *Cosmographia vniversalis*, which was actually publicized only in 1939, it has been generally accepted that it was Gastaldi who first came up with it. But how? We believe we have the correct answer, an answer which directly ties in with Gastaldi's strivings to depict the non-European continents. But before presenting it, it will be useful to dispense conclusively with a notion which has floated through the literature for over 250 years, the notion that perhaps the strait was based on real information somehow obtained in connection with some actual voyage.

8.2 There Was No Discovery Voyage

When, in the early 1750s, world maps began to belatedly show the actual strait revealed by Bering's expeditions of the1720s and early 1740s, the idea first arose, among those few who remembered the old maps, that perhaps someone had already discovered the strait some 200 years earlier, and knowledge of it had somehow become lost over time. The earliest I am aware of to propose this was Philippe Buache, himself something of a historian of cartography, as well as cartographer, geographer, and

---

[2] The depiction of the strait did not by any means, as sometimes stated, continue up to the time the real Bering Strait began to appear on maps. Though it did continue to appear on maps after the mid-1600s, it appeared on fewer and fewer until, by the end of the century, it had disappeared. Maps showing the Bering Strait first began to appear in the early 1750s. In the fifty years before that the old Strait of Anian running north and south between the two continents was quite forgotten, although a different one, running northeast from the California coast towards, but usually not reaching, the area of Hudson's Bay, replaced it. (See the special note, "The Second Strait of Anian," at the end of this chapter.) In fact, even before the 1640s, when the empty void, or Jesso type of depictions began to oust the old strait, the precursors of these new types are traceable in maps as far back as the 1620s and 30s, so the old original Strait of Anian actually enjoyed an undisputed heyday only for about fifty years, from 1570 to about the 1620s. Indeed, Wright had exiled it already on his world chart of 1599 (Shirley no. 221), and there is little sign it was ever taken too seriously by anyone at all in English and Spanish circles even from the beginning. All of this will be fully covered in the work in progress.

mythologist.[3] Buache, in discussing the recent Russian discoveries in 1753, wrote:

> Il y a plus de 180. ans que les meilleurs Géographes de ce temps ont commence à mettre un Détroit entre l'Asie & l'Amérique, auquel ils donnoient le nom d'*Anian*, don't l'entrée Méridionale étoit à 180. ou 190. degree de Longitude, & qui s'étendoit depuis le 56. de Latitude jusqu'au de-là du 62.[. . .]Divers Ecrivains célébres chercherent ensuite les fondemens du Détroit d'Anian; & leurs efforts n'ayant pû rien produire, ce Détroit devint fort incertain, & peu à peu il disparut des meilleures Cartes[. . .]Aujord'hui que nous connoissons un Détroit vers le Nord, près des Côtes de la Tartarie, qui sont bien plus avancées au Nord-est qu'on n'avoit lieu de croire ci-devant, ne pouvons-nous pas dire que c'est celui auquel nos Anciens ont donné le nom d'Anian? Les resemblances me paroissent à remarquer. L'un & l'autre a son entrée au Sud vers le 180. Degré: ils se trouvent entre les Côtes Orientales d'Asie ou de Tartarie, & celles du Nord-Ouest de l'Amérique; ils s'étendent jusqu'au Cercle Polaire, après quoi les Terres tournent du côté de l'Amérique Septentrionale au Nord-Est, & du côté de la Tartarie ou de l'Asie au Nord-Ouest. . . . Tout cela ne peut-il pas faire conjecturer qu'ils ont eû réellement la connaissance du Détroit en question, & l'idée d'une suite de Côté que leurs successeurs ont trop rabaissé, & qu'ils ont rempli de diverses choses Presque à l'aventure[?]. (It is more than 180 years since the better geographers of the time started to place a strait between Asia and America, to which was given the name *Anian*, the southern entrance to which was at 180 or 190 degrees of longitude, and which extended

---

[3] On Buache, see Kish (1976), and Lagarde, in Kretschmer (1986, 119-21). On him as a historian of cartography, see Harley, in Harley and Woodward (1987, 10), and Lagarde (1989, 35).

from 56° latitude to as far as 62° [4][. . .]Various celebrated writers sought thereafter the foundation for the Strait of Anian; and their efforts not having succeeded in producing anything, the strait became very doubtful, and little by little it vanished from the better maps. [. . .]Today when we know of a strait in the north, hard by the coasts of Tartary, which are much more advanced to the northeast than one formerly had good reason to think, can we not say that this is that to which our forebears gave the name Anian? The resemblances seem remarkable to me. Both have their entrance in the south at about 180 degrees: they are between the east coasts of Asia or Tartary, and the northwest coasts of America; they extend to the Polar Circle,[5] after which the North American coast turns to the northeast and the coast of Tartary or Asia to the northwest. . . . Does not all this permit the conjecture that they actually had knowledge of the strait in question, and an idea of the lay of the coast which their successors too much undervalued, and which they filled up with various things virtually at random[?].)[6]

Buache also correctly conjectured that the concept of the strait would have first arisen in the mind of some Italian thinker:

---

[4] In fact, in the first maps to show the strait, as the "Cosmographia Vniversalis" and Gastaldi's America, and all others in that group, the strait is at about 51° N latitude, while in those which were directly taken from those, as the Forlani-Zaltieri North America and the "Totius Orbis Descriptio," it is even lower, in about 45° N latitude. Buache had probably not seen any of the maps of the first group, but as we see just below he did know the Forlani North America. The figures he gives reflect the strait's placement on maps of the Low Country cartographers, Mercator, Ortelius, etc., who placed the strait higher than it had been on the original Italian maps to show it.

[5] Again, we point out that on the original maps, the strait is a good fifteen degrees below the Arctic Circle. The original latitudinal location of the strait no doubt grew out of an interpretation of a rather questionable passage in Barros, which stated that, according to Chinese sources, the Asian east coast was known to extend to 50° N latitude, beyond which it was unknown, as we shall see below.

[6] Buache (1753, 16-17, 18 and 18-19). Buache's observations are repeated twelve years later by Engel (1765, 86-87). Buache says still more on the strait later in his work, where he suggests that it would have been Spanish or Portuguese navigators who had seen the strait (cit., 66), and there is also an interesting passage reflecting an opinion that the Spanish had all along been holding secret information about the strait, and a wish that they would come forward with what they knew (cit., 68). This notion, that the Spanish knew things they were keeping from others, had long been current, and was especially strong among the English; it continued for long afterwards as well, and indeed shades of it can still be detected in the literature. As we will see, there was never the slightest foundation for it.

Les cartes les plus anciennes que j'ai vû, & qui sont toutes Latines, marquent cependant ce Détroit en Italien, *Stretto di Anian*: ce qui me fait soupçonner que le premier qui en a fait mention, est quelque Mathématicien d'Italie . . . . (The oldest maps which I have seen, and which are all [in] Latin, nevertheless denote the strait in Italian, *Stretto di Anian*: which causes me to suspect that the first to make mention of it, is some Italian mathematician . . .)[7]

It is also clear, from the following, which is very probably the first mention in the literature of the Forlani-Zaltieri "Nuova Franza," that Buache had seen that map, in the 1566 dated variant:

La plus ancienne Carte que j'aye trouvé jusqu'à present, qui marque cette continuation de Terres jusqu'àu Détroit d'Anian, est une Carte Italienne de l'Amérique Septentrionale faite en 1566. (The oldest map which I have found to the present, which shows the continuation of land as far as the Strait of Anian, is an Italian map of North America made in 1566.)[8]

This suggestion that the strait may have actually been discovered continued to be repeated by some scholars over a good many years. It is suggested by as serious a scholar as Nordenskiöld as late as 1897.[9] Since it is the only thing in the way of a real attempt at an explanation that has ever

---

[7] Buache (cit., 19); repeated in Engel (cit., 87). For the origin of the name Strait of Anian, see the special note at the end of this chapter, "The Name Anian."

[8] Buache (cit., 66); repeated in Engel (cit., 89). For the 1566 map, see Woodward (1990, no. 37.02); reproduced in Nordenskiöld (1889, fig. 81), Wagner (1929, pl. XVI), and Wagner (1937, pl. XII).

[9] Nordenskiöld (1897, 100). It has been unearthed at least once in the 20th century, by Hennig in 1935.

been offered,[10] and since it occurs fairly frequently in the older literature, it will be worth spending a little time here to conclusively put the notion to rest. Few serious and well-informed scholars of sixteenth century American exploration have continued to entertain this possibility since the appearance in 1929 of Henry Raup Wagner's *Spanish Voyages to the Northwest Coast of America in the Sixteenth Century*.[11] Wagner's work pretty much brought down the curtain on the old notion, which had held sway through the nineteenth century and into the twentieth, that there had been extensive attempts by the Spanish along the North American west coast to find a strait to the Atlantic. Although so much bad and sensationalist history had been written by Wagner's time, the notion is still commonly repeated in histories of New Spain, Mexico, California, etc. Very little interest was shown by Spain in finding such a strait, even after the appearance of Gastaldi's Strait of Anian in 1561, and still less before that. There were two series of voyages up the west coast, five expeditions from 1532-1539 under Cortes, and three from 1540-1542 under Viceroy Antonio Mendoza,[12] together with his partner, Pedro de Alvarado, master of a good fleet of vessels. The five Cortes voyages explored all the present coast of Mexico from Tehuantepec up to the northern end of the Gulf of California, and the last, under Ulloa in 1539, also explored the west coast of Baja to an unknown point above Cedros Island. None got as far as the southern limits of the present United States. The first two of the Mendoza voyages also got no higher on the coast, although the first, under Alarcon, which explored up the Gulf of California, sailed a ways up the Colorado River in smaller boats. The

---

[10] There were nothing but vague suggestions, such as one that, since a narrow strait had been found in the south by Magellan, perhaps the cartographers decided by analogy that there should be one in the north as well. These old ideas are all reviewed in the mentioned work in progress, but none carried any weight, and it is hardly worth taking the time to present them here. Oddly, there were many more theories as to the origin of the name than the geographical feature proper. Perhaps the feeling was that if its name were understood, the rationale for the strait itself would follow. Some of these old theories were interesting in themselves, and lasted long enough that revealing their origins is worthwhile. They are also brought out in the work in progress, but for present purposes, the correct origin, given in the special note, "The Name Anian," at the end of the chapter, will serve our purposes well enough.

[11] Wagner (1929). The information in the following paragraphs is taken from this milestone work unless otherwise indicated.

[12] This viceroy was, as we have seen, brother to Diego Hurtado de Mendoza, the Spanish ambassador to Venice who provided Gastaldi with information for his first map, the 1544 Spain.

second, which was to sail under the command of Diego Lopez de Zúñiga, to whom the extant instructions are addressed, but which in the event sailed under Francisco de Bolaños, became stranded on the Baja coast, and had to be rescued. Only the last, the famous Cabrillo voyage of 1542-43, got above Mexican waters, and managed with great difficulty to reach perhaps somewhere between 40° and 42° on the present upper California coast.

Both Cortes and Mendoza also sent out several other voyages from the west side of Mexico. These, however, were not coastal voyages, but voyages for the Moluccas, and they departed straight across the Pacific. Note that, while the voyages up the coast ceased after the Cabrillo voyage's end in 1543, not to be taken up again until very late in the century, the trans-Pacific exploratory voyages continued until 1565, when Andrés de Urdaneta finally succeeded in finding a return route from Asia to America east across the Pacific for Spain, after which annual regular trade voyages began and continued until the early nineteenth century.

The purposes of the voyages of Cortes and Mendoza up the coast were general exploration, investigation of trade possibilities with the Indians and of the feasibility of establishing settlements. The 1540-42 expeditions also had another goal, one which seems to make no sense to us now. That is, they were conceived of as making up part of a joint effort together with the voyages for investigation and reconnaissance of trans-Pacific routes. At first, this seems incomprehensible to us today, but so it was. Concerning the relationship between the 1542 voyage from Mexico to the Moluccas under Ruy López de Villalobos, and the voyage of Cabrillo, I quote from Harry Kelsey's excellent work on the latter:

> Alvarado and Mendoza planned that the two fleets would approach the Spice Islands and China in a sort of pincer movement. Villalobos was to sail directly across the Pacific, while Cabrillo would seek the same goal on a northwesterly route along the coast. If this seems to show a monumental disdain for geography, it did not seem so implausible at the time. No one then had any clear concept of the shape of the Pacific basin or of the great distances involved. It was generally assumed that North America was either an extension of the Asian mainland or very close to it and that the Especieria and the

Moluccas were islands near this shared coastline. Thus when Cabrillo's men returned, they reported that the fleet had come very close to the coast of China, an opinion backed by prominent navigators who had themselves been to the Moluccas.[13]

In general, it is clear from these and other sources that at the time the Spanish concept of the northwest coast above Mexico was that it continued generally northwest or west-northwest for a way, then began to curve westward, then southwestward, until it ran into the China coast, south of which lay the Moluccas, and that China and the Moluccas were not all that far from the northwest Mexican coast, which is very like what we see in Gastaldi's 1546 world.[14]

It is clear from the existing record that outfitting these voyages involved a great deal of time and expense, that only persons commanding wide authority and with great power, such as Cortes or Mendoza, could have hoped to carry out such projects, and our record of their activities is pretty complete. But more important, more telling for our purposes, was the fact that Spain simply had no interest in exploring far up the west coast. "This was a money-oriented venture," says Kelsey of the Cabrillo voyage,[15] and

---

[13] Kelsey (1986, *Cabrillo*, 103). For more on the purposes of these voyages, see pp. 95-110 in Kelsey, and also Wagner, the latter especially as to the Cortes voyages. Making the unlikely still more unlikely, the instructions for the voyages up the coast also included a directive to keep an eye out for Coronado's overland expedition, which had begun in 1540 and returned in September 1542, with the purpose of making contact with it, and providing it with supplies from the ships. Kelsey says: "Not only did the planners underestimate the distance across the Pacific Ocean, they all clearly had little concept of the size of the North American continent, and they seemingly thought Coronado was heading northwest, rather than northeast" (cit., 110). Also in reference to the Coronado expedition, Reinhartz and Jones note that, "In 1540, even with the reports of Cabeza de Vaca and others, the Spanish really knew very little about the North American interior. They still underestimated the width of the continent by almost ninefold and thought it to be much smaller north to south and much closer to Asia than it actually was" (in Allen, 1997, 1, 273).

[14] The whole subject of the extreme foreshortenings of distances in the concepts of the time as regards the shape and size of the North Pacific basin, and of the northwest American coast above Mexico, with its resultant mental picture of northwestern North America above Mexico as being located very close to the Asian east coast or else merging right over into it, and of a North Pacific which was quite narrow or amounted to no more than a large gulf between the continents, is gone into in depth in the mentioned work in preparation. There is a great deal which is of interest on this subject, but for the present, the comments of Kelsey, Reinhartz and Jones correctly give the overall impression that was had.

[15] Kelsey (cit., 110).

this was very true of all the Cortes and Mendoza enterprises. I quote Mathes:

> By the end of 1542 the first great phase of exploration northward from New Spain had terminated, with generally negative results. No detailed diaries, logs, rutters, or navigational charts of the region had been prepared, and those that survived the tragic Rodriguez Cabrillo expedition were unclear. None of the areas visited had shown evidence of civilization approaching that of the Mexicans, nor had any similar sources of precious metals been located. Rather, increasingly hostile inhabitants, climate, and terrain appeared to be the rule as expeditions went farther northward. The isolation of California, the contrary winds and currents along its Pacific coast, and the evident poverty of its natives made it a particularly difficult area to explore and settle, and thus, within a decade of its discovery, it was relegated to a position of geographical, political, and economic unimportance in the scheme of Spanish imperial design.[16]

Only in trans-Pacific voyages did Spain show any continued interest, this, as noted, in hopes of finding a return route to New Spain across the Pacific from the Orient. In 1565 this was finally found, and from that time, very profitable annual trade galleons made the crossing over and back right up to the early 1800s. These regular voyages all returned east or east by southeast by catching trade winds in high latitudes, ca. 40° N or higher in the west Pacific in the late spring or early summer, generally about June, which carried them across. The combination of latitude and time of year was the secret to the return, which had been sought since the early 1520s. This return voyage, however, was still trying, and always took at least twice as long as the almost always very easy crossing to the west. They would normally catch sight of the California coast at various latitudes varying from about 42° N down to Baja, after which they would sail easily on down the coast to the west Mexican ports. Unlike sailing up the coast, which was tortuously difficult, sailing down was always a cinch. The next phase of interest in the

---

[16] Mathes, in Allen (1997, 1, 410).

northwest coast after Cabrillo began only in the 1580s, when the crown began to designate that certain of the regularly returning cargo ships be directed to make surveillance of the coast as they came in and down from the west. This was done three times, in 1584 (Gali), 1587 (Unamuno), and 1594-95 (Cermeño), and only when this method proved fruitless did the crown send out one more expedition, outfitted specifically to explore the northwest coast, under Sebastian Vizcaino in 1602-03. This may (or may not) have gotten a degree or so higher than Cabrillo in 1542-43, but produced nothing of sufficient promise for the crown to continue. [17] There were no more voyages from 1603 to 1769, when the third and last phase began, which lasted into the 1790s and involved both Spanish and English vessels, and during which the whole northwest coast up through Bering's Strait was finally actually explored.

The sum total of indications of interest in locating a strait on the northwest coast in the period before 1561, when Gastaldi's strait first appeared on maps, is two, the first amounting really to just an idea, abandoned and never acted upon, and the other probably apocryphal. The first involves Cortes, in the 1520s; the second involves some very questionable 1574 testimony given concerning the Bolaños voyage of 1541. Cortes, in his fourth letter of relation of October 15, 1524 to the Spanish king Charles V, eight years before the first of his west coast voyages actually began, speaks of plans to send ships up both the east and west coasts in search of a strait said to run from the area of Baccalaos, in the vicinity of Newfoundland, southwest to exit somewhere near the Spice Islands (again the bizarre geography). Cortes, who has just said he intends to explore up the east coast to Florida, continues:

---

[17] There is, of course, a strong note of anti-climax in all this. Sailing up the coast was a great fight, but sailing down was all but a relaxed cruise. Although the return voyage across the Pacific by the Manila Galleons (the name by which the ships which began to regularly ply the route from 1565 came to be called), was difficult since long, it was a regular passage, and many a wealthy young Spanish nobleman made a small fortune by making the crossing, and they must at times have had a leisurely view of the same coasts which Cabrillo and Vizcaino fought so hard to climb.

And from there to continue up this same Florida coast[18] northwards to Los Bacallaos,[19] for it is believed that there is on that coast a strait leading to the Southern Sea.[20] If it is found, it will, according to a chart I have, come out very close to the archipelago which Magellan discovered by your Highness's command.[21] And if Our Lord God be pleased that we find this strait, it will prove a very good and very short route from the Spice Islands to Your Majesty's realms, for it will be two-thirds shorter than the one now sailed, and will be without hazard or peril for the ships, for they will always come and go through the realms and dominions of Your Majesty, so that whenever they are in need they may repair without fear or danger to one of Your Highness's ports[. . .]though I assure Your Majesty that I have had to borrow all the money for it, I have determined to send three caravels and two brigantines in this quest (although I believe it will cost me more than ten thousand *pesos de oro*) and add this service to the others I have performed. For I hold this to be the most important of them if, as I say, the strait is found, and, even if it is not, many great and rich lands must surely be discovered, where Your Caesarean Majesty may be served and the realms and dominions of Your Royal

---

[18] There was little consensus at the time as to what was intended by many of the geographical names in use. The name Florida often, as here, included virtually all of the North American east coast from present day Florida up as far as Maine, if not further.

[19] This name Baccalaos, variously spelled, is a key one in the sixteenth and seventeenth centuries in connection with notions of a hoped-for Northwest Passage. The name originates from words for codfish in Iberian languages, and was generally applied to Newfoundland, but sometimes had a broader connotation. It became very common, when speaking of a possible strait leading from the area of Newfoundland southwestwards and into the South Sea (Pacific) in lower latitudes, to speak simply of going "by way of Baccalaos." An old story that the name was given by Sebastian Cabot after an Indian word for codfish is nonsense. On this term, see Sauer (1971, 24 and 232), Morison (1971, *Northern Voyages*, 203 and 221), Quinn (1979, 1, 463). Wagner's idea that the name is first used in 1540 by Münster is clearly off, for here is Cortes using it in 1524. This notion of a strait running diagonally southwest from the Newfoundland-Labrador area to the Pacific evidently first arises in the 1520s, about the time Cortes is writing here. In the 1570s, beginning in England, the name Anian becomes transposed in the minds of some to this strait.

[20] The Pacific.

[21] Cortes's reference to a chart showing this strait is the earliest reference to any map showing such a strait that I know of. The archipelago means the southeast Asian archipelago. This notion of a strait leading from northeast North America southwest to enter the Pacific in the area of the Spice Islands was very common, and is found often in the seventeenth century. Such amazing foreshortenings of distances as regards the Pacific and North America were the rule at the time.

238

Crown much increased. Should there, however, prove to be no such strait, then it will be most useful for Your Highness that it be known, for some other means may be found for Your Caesarean Majesty to benefit from the Spice Islands and all the others which are adjacent to them. In this I offer myself to Your Highness's service and will be greatly pleased if Your Majesty choose to command me, in default of that strait, to find some such means whereby Your Majesty would be well served and at less cost. May Our Lord grant, however, that the fleet succeed in its purpose, which is to discover the strait, because that would be best; and I am sure it will, because nothing can eclipse Your Majesty's Royal good fortune, and diligence, careful preparation and determination will not be found wanting on my part to carry it out.

Likewise I intend to send the vessels which I have built on the Southern Sea. If Our Lord so wishes these will sail at the end of July of this year, 1524, down the same coast in search of that strait, for, if it exists, it cannot escape those who go by the Southern Sea and those who go by the Northern,[22] because those who go in the south will follow the coast until they find it or reach the land discovered by Magellan,[23] and the others on the north until, as I have said, they reach Los Bacallaos. Thus on the one coast or the other they cannot fail to discover it. I assure Your Majesty that according to the information I have received of lands up the coast of the Southern Sea, I would have profited considerably, and served Your Majesty too, by sending these ships there, but as I have been told of the great desire which Your Majesty has to discover this strait and the great service which its discovery would render to Your Royal Crown, I lay aside all

---

[22] The Atlantic Ocean.

[23] In this sentence Cortes capsulizes the two beliefs which were held at the time, and continued long after to be held, that the west coast of New Spain (Mexico), which, at the time of this letter, was known only up a very short distance, probably not as high even as present day Acapulco, either led to the southwest end of a strait or free passage northeast into the Atlantic, or else continued northwest a ways, and then dropped back down again southwest, melding into the China coast. "The land discovered by Magellan" means the Philippines, not the area of Tierra del Fuego, as one might gather.

those other interests and advantages, of which I have heard many tales, in order to follow this course.[24]

But just two years later, in his fifth letter of relation of September 3, 1526, Cortes has become much less sanguine about the strait, and barely mentions it. He has been speaking of a fleet of vessels he has prepared for exploration up the west coast of Mexico:

> And I pray to Our Lord that by this journey I shall render a great service to your Majesty's good fortune, for even if no passage is found I hope to discover a route to the Spice Islands so that Your Majesty may be informed every year of what is done there. If Your Majesty chooses to grant me the favors which I asked for concerning that discovery, I will undertake to discover a route to the Spice Islands and many others, if there be any between Maluco, Malaca and China, and so arrange matters that the spices shall no longer be obtained by trade, as the king of Portugal has them now, but as Your Majesty's rightful property . . .[25]

In fact, this is the last mention of the idea of a Cortes search for a strait, either by Cortes, or by anyone else, that I am aware of, and he clearly abandoned the idea, very likely as a result of hearing of the results of Gomez's voyage up the east coast for Spain in 1524-25, and perhaps also that of Verrazzano of 1524, which voyages had run the entire North American eastern seaboard without finding any evidence of a strait.[26]

The second possible indication of interest in finding a strait somewhere up the west coast seems quite apocryphal to me. In 1574, some thirty-three years after the abortive Bolaños voyage of 1541, which stranded

---

[24] Cortes (1986, 326-28).

[25] Cortes (1986, 444-45). For a somewhat different rendering of this last passage, see Jeremy Moyle's translation in Gerbi (1985, 372-73).

[26] Various problems continued to prevent Cortes from sending his fleet up the west coast, though, as we have seen, he did finally send up five voyages in 1532-39 for different purposes. There is not a word of interest in seeking any strait in the surviving documentation and accounts of those voyages, whose principal objects were general exploration and possible finding of a route to the Moluccas by following the coast westward.

on Baja, an elderly seaman in his 60s, one Juan Fernandez de Ladrillero, said in a deposition before an inquest that he was on the Bolaños voyage, and that their instructions included a directive to look for a strait, called the Strait of Bacalaos, which supposedly led from the area of Bacalaos into the South Sea.[27] The full original instructions to Zùñiga are extant,[28] and certainly contain no mention of a search for a strait. But Ladrillero's statement implies that this directive would have been received only at the last moment, when the party who delivered their ships to them for the voyage also delivered an extract out of a letter from the king to the viceroy, in which it was stated that the king had had word of an unidentified Portuguese gentleman who had supposedly passed through such a strait.[29] This testimony seems quite apocryphal to me, and has all the earmarks of other tales of the kind that would pop up from time to time in the late sixteenth century and seventeenth century. I know of no other reference around the time of the Bolaños voyage of 1541 to reports of any Portuguese gentleman having passed through a strait.[30] The inquest at which Ladrillero testified in 1574 had been called to investigate a report that Richard Grenville of England was preparing an expedition into Spanish American territory, and the chief object of the inquest was to try to determine if Grenville could enter the South Sea by some strait at the north.[31] Did Ladrillero concoct his story to achieve recognition for himself, as a holder and provider of valuable and secret information? This is certainly what I suspect. In any event, even if true, this late testimony is the only reference to any actual voyage before 1561 which might have had as part of its instructions a search for a strait, and that was for a strait running northeast to the Newfoundland area along the backside of a North American continent not yet conceived by anyone as

---

[27] His full statement, which deals with various things, is printed full, in English translation, in Wagner (1929, 66-71).

[28] Also printed in Wagner (1929, 418-25). Zùñiga, we recall, was replaced by Bolaños as commander of the expedition.

[29] Wagner (1929, 69).

[30] Wagner asserts that the story of such a strait seems to have first become current in Mexico only about 1555, about fourteen years after the Bolaños voyage (cit., 318, note 22). He unfortunately does not document this.

[31] Wagner (1929, 63).

having any great width above Mexico. The voyage, as we know, foundered at Baja California, and no voyage got higher than Cabrillo's of 1542-43, which perhaps reached 40° to 42° N.[32] No Spanish voyager sailed up into Arctic America, and certainly none would have wanted to.[33]

It is, after all, abundantly clear to any mind freed of illusions in the matter, upon objectively looking at the first maps with the Strait of Anian,[34] that this could in no way be the result of information obtained from actual voyages. There is no sign on these maps of the huge peninsular westward

[32] This all is in sharp contrast to the statement still commonly made that the Spanish were persistently banging away along the North American west coast in the sixteenth century in an all-out attempt to find a strait through to the North Sea (Atlantic), a strait often referred to in our modern literature as the Strait of Anian, even in reference to times before 1561, although the name certainly did not exist before about that time. It is not possible to go into it in depth here and now, but in the mentioned work in progress, it will be shown that this idea of a determined Spanish search for a strait up the Northwest Coast arose mainly as a result of presumptions made by English writers, writing in ignorance of what was actually going on in western New Spain, that such must be the case, and also as a result of a tendency on the part of some nineteenth-century Spanish historians to add fuel to the notion by putting an extremely wide interpretation to Spanish exploratory voyages to the Americas almost all the way back to Columbus, implying that these were all in some broad way interpretable as being part of a Spanish search for a Northwest Passage from the west coast corresponding to an English search from the other side, as is done by the historian Navarrete. The impression one gets is that this was done in response to English histories of their search for the Northwest Passage from the east and, perhaps especially, as a continuation of the great rivalry (although at this late date sometimes a fairly friendly rivalry) which arose in the 1770s-1790s when the English and Spanish were simultaneously making genuine and intensive voyages far up the west coast to finally settle its real geography.

[33] Nor would anyone else have wanted to. There is no record of any English, French or Dutch vessels entering the Pacific until some years after this time, and the record is pretty clear. We don't think it necessary to consider the possibility of some miracle sailor from one of these lands, or any other, sailing, unbeknownst to the world, around and into the Pacific, and then up on a goose chase to the American Arctic for no imaginable reason. Nor was there any reason for the Portuguese, already comfortably ensconced in southeast Asian waters, to attempt to sail up into the Asian Arctic. We also feel it unnecessary to fiddle with any such notion as information about the area for some reason filtering down through sundry native tribes, only partly because no indigenous peoples of the area could possibly have had any notion there was any special significance to their remote water world.

[34] The three principal maps to show Gastaldi's original concept of a very narrow Strait of Anian, along with the year when they originally became known to modern scholars, are: (1) Gastaldi's America, made ca. 1560 (our no. 94), though not properly published until the 1590s, as we shall see in chapter twelve; the 1561 world map, "Cosmographia Vniversalis," brought to light in 1939 (Almagià, 1939, "Intorno"); and the Holzheimer globe gores, unearthed in 1969 (Skelton, 1969, *globe*). Before this, the only maps known which depicted the original idea were a few Martines world maps which had been copied after Gastaldi, but they are of such small scale the extreme narrowness of the strait is not obvious on them. A few Martines atlases also contain some much larger regional maps, and at least one of them shows the North American Northwest Coast, copied directly from the "Cosmographia Vniversalis," and here the very narrow strait is shown clearly (cf. in chapter two). It was reproduced by Kretschmer (1892, pls. 27 and 30), but was not widely known. No Anian researcher ever mentions it, and no other map with the important feature was known until 1921, when Chadenat and Vignaud brought to light the first known, but defective, copy of Gastaldi's America, as we shall see in the next chapter.

extension of North America we call Alaska, occupying 28° of longitude, and forming the roof of the eastern half of the North Pacific basin, nor is there any sign of the still larger corresponding eastward peninsular extension of Asia running above the Sea of Okhotsk and eastward to Bering Strait through a full 48° of longitude, forming the roof of the western half of the Pacific basin, Consequently, there is no North Pacific Ocean at all. Above the approximate furthest north known point at the time, that is, ca. 42° N latitude, we see no great ocean, 70°-80° wide, but just the little Gulf of Cheinan, approximately 6°-8° east to west at its widest. The strait proper on these maps is not in 66° N latitude, but in 51° N latitude, and we know that navigators of the time could come up with rather good latitude figures, often less than a degree off, and only rarely as much as 2°-3° off. And, most importantly, the strait is far too narrow. The actual strait is approximately 2° in width, or about 55 miles wide at the narrowest, but the strait as shown on the maps showing the earliest, the original Gastaldian, depiction, the ca. 1561 "Cosmographia Vniversalis," Gastaldi's map of America, and the Holzheimer gores, is so narrow that the coastlines at the narrowest point all but touch. The strait is less than 2° wide, but, in fact, it is probably unrealistic to speak here of longitudinal width at all, for the fact that a separation at the narrowest point is detectable at all is no doubt simply a concession to the fact that, at this scale, one could not show a still closer approach without leaving it unclear to the map viewer whether he were looking at a tiny separation or a tiny connection, a tiny strait, or a tiny isthmus. Indeed, on one map, the Gastaldi America, the coastal shadings on the two sides of the strait so fully blend together that one must look twice to feel sure of a separation at all. As we shall see, probably what the cartographer, Gastaldi, had in mind here, was something like the strait between the Sea of Marmora and the Black Sea, the Bosphorus, which, while seventeen miles long, is at the most two miles wide at its narrowest point, and perhaps had in mind something even narrower than that. It is clear from Gastaldi's America, the 1561 *Cosmographia vniversalis* world map, and the Holzheimer gores,[35] that the delineating of the passage in such a way that at one point the two sides of the strait almost touch is deliberate, and this

---

[35] The first two are our nos. 94 and 104 respectively. The gores are reproduced in Woodward, 1997.

deliberateness is also clear in the fact that the name of the strait is written in the waters above the strait, instead of through the strait as would be more normal, for the point of extreme close approach would necessarily have been eradicated if the latter had been done.[36] Any explanation for this strait must account for this intentional extreme narrowness.

Nor do we have to depend on the discrepancy between the maps and reality to show us there had been no actual discovery. Indeed, we are fortunate enough to have testimony, from the horse's mouth as it were, that between Cabrillo's voyage of 1542-43 and the appearance of the strait in 1561 there had been no further discoveries on the northwest coast. From the late 1550s until 1564 there were extensive preparations in western New Spain for a trans-Pacific expedition under Miguel López de Legazpi to find a return route from the Orient back to New Spain. The Augustinian friar Andrés de Urdaneta was selected to accompany the voyage as a navigational consultant, and it was he who discovered the return route (the Manila galleon route) in 1565. Urdaneta seems to have been one of those rare souls in history who was genuinely of a sterling character in all regards, and he had had extensive experience in trans-Pacific navigation. According to Wagner, Viceroy Luis de Velasco informed the king that he was "the best and most careful cosmographer in the country."[37] Fairly early during the preparations for the Legazpi expedition, in 1561, Urdaneta wrote a long memorandum to Philip II describing three possible outgoing routes, depending on the time of the year when the fleet might depart.[38] The memorandum was written

---

[36] On one of the three maps, Gastaldi's America, there is no name given to the strait. The explanation for this is found in chapter nine.

[37] Wagner (1929, 104). On Urdaneta see Mitchell (1964), Morison (1974, *Southern Voyages*, 492-95). There is no foundation for a tale about Urdaneta's claiming to have come through a strait from the South Sea to Germany [!], as asserted by Humphrey Gilbert in his discourse on the Northwest Passage (Hakluyt, 1903-05, VII, 179-80), and see below in chapter nine, note 89, for another spurious claim by Gilbert of a supposed sailing by Urdaneta through a Northwest Passage. Gilbert's 1576 discourse, while an invaluable record of ideas of the time as to the possibility of a Northwest Passage, is the purest propaganda, and so freely mixes up names, events, and ideas that it would take a tract three times as long as the discourse itself just to unravel them. The eighteenth-century German historian George Forster seems also to have contributed to spreading the tale, as see Mitchell (cit., 147-48).

[38] The memorandum is printed in full in *Colección* (vol. 2, 1886, 119-38). For a partial synopsis and translation, see Mitchell (cit., 106-10 and 146-47).

sometime between March and September, 1561.[39] Urdaneta thinks it would be best to leave New Spain between the start of October and November 10, and recommends an outgoing course. In the event the departure should be after November 10, but before about January 20, he recommends a different course. Finally, he recommends still a third course should the fleet depart still later:

> If it should turn out that we cannot leave the coast of New Spain some time in January to sail toward the south as just stated, we should wait until the month of March or later, until we have good winds with which to sail on the side of the Arctic Pole or north, following the coast of New Spain, which trends toward the west-northwest. Given propitious winds for this purpose we should sail, although perhaps somewhat distant from the coast, up to the latitude of 34° or more, where we should endeavor to examine the country on the coast which Juan Rodriguez Cabrillo discovered. Taking what was necessary of what might be found on that coast and having communicated with the Indians, although only by signs, about a big water beyond toward the land side, of which they had given information to Juan Rodriguez Cabrillo, we should follow the coast in search of it, in order to see if that water might be sea and if the end of this land be there. We should soon know if it is salt or fresh water and if God should be pleased that we discover what it is, we should take the direction from there towards the west on a southwest course down to 37° or 35° of latitude, sailing directly west from this point and discovering what there is between this land and China, to a point close to the islands of Japan, if

---

[39] It was written after a March, 1561 communication from the king to Urdaneta (Mitchell, cit., 105), and from information in the memorandum itself, it is clear that it was written before October, 1561.

we should not discover something sooner of such importance that we would be contented with it.[40]

Here is evidence made to order, written in New Spain in 1561, and from an informed authority as possible to his king, and it is quite clear that no one had yet followed up Cabrillo's discoveries. The cartographic historian Erik W. Dahlgren made use of a different part of Urdaneta's memorandum, and for different reasons than ours here, but his words in reference to it are as appropriate for our purposes as they were for his: "It is absolutely impossible, of course, that in these papers Urdaneta should have deliberately concealed any part of his knowledge concerning previous voyages and discoveriesCon such an occasion as this the love of secrecy of which the Spaniards have so often been accused would have been as unnecessary as imporoper; and with about the same degree of certainty we can characterize it as improbable that any earlier voyage or discovery should have escaped Urdaneta's notice."[41]

Nor were there any illusions in Venice on the score. Philosopher and encyclopedist Alessandro Citolini tells us in his 1561 *Tipocosmia* that nothing is yet known of the lay of the sea around northwest America and northeast Asia.[42] Guillaume Postel, too, in his 1561 cosmography, says that he refuses to take a stance on the question of whether Asia and America are separated or connected, since nothing is yet known about it,[43] as he did also

---

[40] *Colección* (1886, 132-34). I have used Wagner's translation (1929, 106). Mitchell's translation is very similar (cit., 109-10). Mitchell says: "One thing is clear: Urdaneta's interests are more expansive than those of men directed to a single objective such as the Philippines" (cit., 110), and observes that the lines "suggest Urdaneta's interest in the discovery of a North-West Passage" (109). Wagner says: "His object as expressed here was no doubt to interview the Indians on the Santa Barbara Channel to see if he could find out something more than Cabrillo had," and: though not so stated, Urdaneta evidently expected to go up above 41° to see what was beyond the farthest point of Cabrillo's discoveries" (1929, 349, notes 55 and 56).

[41] Dahlgren (1916, 34; in reprint, 60). Spanish ignorance of the coast above Cabrillo's limits is also reflected at another point, although a little later in the memorandum, where Urdaneta lets himself fall prey to one of the apocryphal stories of straits through the continent which were current, in this case a piece of nonsense about the French having sailed through from the Atlantic to the South Sea (*Colección*, cit., 136-38; translated in Mitchell, cit., 146-47; and partially, by Mathes, in Allen, 1997, 1, 412). We shall speak again of Urdaneta and his ideas concerning the American northwest coast in our next chapter.

[42] Citolini (1561, 81-82). On Citolini and his *Tipocosmia*, see Renieri (1997), and Della Giustina (1999).

[43] Postel (1561, 4).

in his ca. 1560 unpublished cosmography.[44] He also apparently chides Gastaldi in this latter work for his audacity in offering the new depiction.[45] And Ruscelli, in the modern world map in his 1561 Venetian Ptolemy, leaves the question open by showing an indefinite dotted line between Asia and America at 48° N latitude, similar to the depiction of Gastaldi five years earlier in his 1556 map of the Western Hemisphere, but with a higher point of possible connection.[46] Perhaps the most interesting and conclusive evidence that Gastaldi's new depiction was not the result of some revelatory and new information comes indirectly to us from the residents of Venice themselves, along with other clients of the Venetian map publishers, for the new innovation clearly did not find the reception it should have if it were known to represent real information which rendered older concepts obsolete. Ronald Vere Tooley in 1939 brought together the results of his collation of the contents of some thirty-five of the Veneto-Roman composite atlases, sometimes called Lafrerian or "IATO" (Italian-assembled-to-order) atlases, which began to appear in Venice ca. 1565, and whose contents, which vary from atlas to atlas, presumably reflect the preferences of individual clients.[47] Although Tooley's survey could have been more accurate in some regards, it is certainly sufficiently dependable for our purposes here, and it is very revealing as to preferences regarding the question of the relationship of Asia to America.

Close to seven times as many customers preferred the Gastaldi world maps showing a connection over maps showing the Strait of Anian, and another indicator of a strong preference for this depiction, and of the continued currency of it, is shown in the fact that at least sixteen of the twenty or so variants of the original 1546 world map came out after 1561, including new and larger engravings of it in 1562 and 1565. (Of forty-six Gastaldi world maps occurring in the atlases in Tooley's listings, forty show

---

[44] Per Milanesi (1992, 37). Postel was in Venice, the city he loved most, from ca. late 1560 to spring, 1561, evidently for the last time in his life (Bouwsma, 1957, 24-25; and Destombes, 1985, 361).

[45] Milanesi (1992, 38). I have not yet seen this passage, so do not know its precise gist. The date 1560 for the work is an estimate, although it is possible that Postel could have been criticizing Gastaldi's concept before 1561, for, as we shall see, it certainly must have existed before that date.

[46] Shirley no. 111.

[47] Tooley (1939).

a connection as opposed to only six which show a separation.) In general, compared to the massive and steady output of these world maps showing a connection, there were only a few copies put out or purchased of the world maps showing the strait, and the known copies of two of these, the large 1561 world map, and the undated "Totius Orbis Descriptio," exist in what appear to be only proof copies, and do not seem to occur at all in the atlases, where world maps with the strait are present only in a few copies of the 1567 Camocio world map and its later printings.[48] The new concept, to be sure, is much better represented in the atlases by the Forlani-Zaltieri map of North America alone,[49] with just under half of the atlases containing either the 1566 dated map or its undated variant. Still, while some atlases contain only maps showing a connection, there is not one, at least among those represented in Tooley, which contains only maps showing a separation. There are copies of three other types of world maps showing a separation in the atlases besides those with the Strait of Anian, one by Mercator, one by Florianus after Mercator, and one anonymous one, put out by Tramezzini, all three showing an older wide type of separation, and there are eight to nine times as many copies of these as of the new Gastaldi type with the Strait of Anian. Many of the atlases contain more than one world map, with one, the Triestino atlas, containing as many as eight. Most interestingly, a large number of atlas clients chose to include in their atlases both maps showing a connection as well as maps showing a separation, and this is in accord with what we have seen earlier as regards a tendency to simultaneously entertain different ideas as to unknown areas. The total of both preferences, when taking into consideration all types of separations, seems to come out very close to even. By my count, of ninety-nine world maps in the atlases collated by Tooley, fifty-one show a separation, of one kind or another, while forty-eight show a connection, so indecision seems pretty complete.

Clearly, the Strait of Anian did not take Venice or the world by storm, and clearly there was nothing like a consensus as to the question of the relationship of the two continents. There were other Italian cartographers, too, who did not accept the innovation, as Giorgio Sideri (Callapoda), whose

---

[48] Shirley no. 117.

[49] Woodward (1990, no. 37.01-02).

1563 world map shows a connection of the type in the 1546 Gastaldi world,[50] and Francisco Basso, whose 1570 globe shows the old connection type.[51] Interestingly, this latter work, which shows the Golfo de Tonza between Asia and America as on the 1546 world, also shows a second gulf, a large but very enclosed one cutting northwest a ways into China from a latitude in the 30s, and this gulf bears the name, "Golfo de Anian," showing that not quite all who adopted this name felt it should be applied to a strait. Only after the new concept was adopted by Ortelius in 1570 in his widely influential *Theatrum Orbis Terrarum* did the new concept begin to be widely adopted, although, as we have pointed out elsewhere, that hegemony did not last as long as is often implied,[52] and was not at all as universal as we usually think. In this regard, we can again cite the Veneto-Roman, atlases, for many of these were compiled far past 1570, and nevertheless continued to show indecision, a tendency to show variant views, and a low preference for maps with the new Strait of Anian. All in all, then, we find after 1561 the same uncertainty regarding the question of Asia and America that we found in our cosmographies before that date. The simple fact is, they did not know, they could not know. There was still no consensus, but general disagreement and uncertainty, and the new concept seems to have been looked on doubtfully by many, as it evidently was by Postel. And the first occurrence of the concept on maps in ca. 1561 was clearly not an earth-shaking event.[53]

So indecision and uncertainty still ruled among geographers, and, furthermore, it also still ruled in the mind of Gastaldi himself. In 1562, one year after the appearance of Gastaldi's 1561 *Cosmographia vniversalis* with the Strait of Anian, Forlani put out a new, considerably enlarged edition of Gastaldi's original world map (our no. 3), showing the continental

---

[50] See reproduction in Kretschmer (1892, pl. 22).

[51] Repr. Kretschmer (cit., pl. 29).

[52] See our special note, "The Second Strait of Anian," at the end of this chapter.

[53] Compare this with the observation so frequently made in twentieth-century literature that some great "change" occurred in Gastaldi's cartography in 1562, and that his new idea immediately took over the cartographic world. The idea arose principally because the first appearance in print of the name "Strait of Anian" is in Gastaldi's *La Vniversale descrittione del mondo*, and for many years the only edition known was 1562, the actual first edition of 1561 being brought to light only in the 1930s, by Caraci (1936).

connection, and in his dedication to Count Geronimo Canossa on it, Forlani says:

> Molto tempo è ille sig(n)or mio ch' ho un interno desiderio di dare al mondo una Vniuersale descrittione di tutta la terra conosciuta fin qui, al qual desiderio ha dato compimento l' ecc(ellen)te m(esser) Giacomo gastaldo cosmographo raro; percioche egli questi mesi addietro me ha dato un disegno, ó descrittione uniuersale di tutta la terra, per la piu piena et copiosa di quanti fin qui sene sono uedute . . . . (It is a long time sir that I have an inner desire to give to the world a Universal description of all the earth known up to now, to which desire the excellent Mr. Giacomo Gastaldo, exceptional cosmographer, has given fulfillment; for he has these months past given me a drawing, or universal description of all the earth, fuller and more copious than those which have been seen hitherto . . .)[54]

The tendency of the time, stronger if anything in Forlani than in most, to hyperbole, is here, for the map does not contain a great deal which is different from previous editions. Still, it is considerably larger, and it may be considered as a new production, for, besides simple differences in décor and in some place names, the east coast North American river system is much different and more expanded than in previous maps in the series, the orography of South America is considerably changed, being notably more spread about, and there appears for the first time a prominent western tributary to Gastaldi's north-south running Amazon, coming across the continent from what would be the area of the northern Andes. Of Forlani's words in the dedication, Woodward has noted that, "We assume that, since Gastaldi was still alive and well-known in Venice at the time, he was telling the truth,"[55] and the present writer too feels there is no reason to doubt Forlani here. This might at first seem to present an irresolvable problem, if we were to assume that a cartographer's depictions must always represent conviction at the moment he made his map, but as we have seen in chapter

---

[54] Forlani's dedication is transcribed and translated in full in our Cartobibliography entry no. 105.

[55] Woodward (1992, 57).

seven, this is definitely not always the case, and, not rarely, one cartographer's different depictions of the same area do not represent changes in conviction at all, but just variant possibilities concerning an area on which he could not be sure, a thing which the visual medium of cartography makes it impossible to show in a single map. In fact, in the present case, far from presenting an irresolvable conundrum, the reappearance of Gastaldi's original concept in the 1562 map one year after the appearance of a very different concept in his 1561 world map probably provides us with the key we need to understand his thinking. For, while there is, I think, no way Gastaldi or anyone else could have picked out one depiction and said that it was correct, there is, as we shall see, a clear way he could have arrived at the conviction or opinion that the two continents must *either* be fully connected, *or* approach extremely close together at some point.

We trust that the detailed foregoing exposition has put to rest any notion that Gastaldi's strait was based on any real information. Now we may proceed to present the evidence for what we believe to be the actual rationale behind the strait, as stated near the beginning of this chapter. The evidence can be divided into two types, which we shall call zoological evidence and geographical evidence. We will present these in two sections, followed by our final conclusions.

8.3 The Zoological Evidence

Corradino Astengo makes note of the fact that among the rationales for sixteenth century cartographers' depiction of the continents of Asia and America as joined would be that this depiction would provide a satisfactory explanation for the mystery of the origin of the inhabitants of America, and then speaks of the extremely narrow strait on the 1561 Gastaldi world map, "which, although cleanly separating America from Asia, could have been easily crossed in remote times by the descendants of Adam."[56] Marica Milanesi touches on the same idea in speaking of Gastaldi's strait: "We don't know how the cartographer might have come to this change of opinion, which permitted him to reconcile the two theories on the interrelationship

---

[56] Astengo (1990, 2 and 3).

between Asia and America. A very narrow strait separated the two continents, which the experts of the New World like Oviedo declared to be quite distinct; but these remained close enough to appease those who demanded how the descendants of Noah, and the animals of the ark might have come to reach and populate, after the flood, an America separated from Asia by oceans too wide."[57] These authors' statements contain the germ of our own thesis on Gastaldi's thinking, which it will be easiest for us to here capsulize by resorting at first to a sort of presentation by reverse chronology, that is, by presenting some recent ideas on the subject, then moving step by step backwards in time to earlier centuries.

The most widely accepted current theories concerning the origin of the first inhabitants of the American continent involve their having first arrived from the Old World across the area of the present Bering Strait, and many theories concerning the origin of much of American wildlife follow a similar vein. But these ideas are far from new. Although often upon the basis of different premises or suppositions than at present, they have been tossed around among scholars for centuries.[58] From the sixteenth to the eighteenth centuries, and in some cases into the nineteenth and even twentieth centuries, the most common main underpinning of the idea was essentially religious, involving the one great assumption that all current human and animal life on the planet had to originally stem from those humans and animals which survived the great Flood, or Deluge, that is, from those who were on Noah's ark when it came to rest on Mount Ararat. There were also, however, from the time of the earliest literary ruminations on the subject, discussions containing discernible threads of thinking we would now term anthropological or ethnographical, although much (but not quite all) of the thinking and conclusions arrived at were fallacious. These discussions

---

[57] Milanesi (1993, 43). Cf. also her observations in another work: "We are able to recognize in the Strait of Anian the sustainers of the isolationist thesis: the Portuguese and Spanish pilots, the authorities on the New World like Oviedo and Gómara, the already authoritative Flemish cartographer [Mercator]. But neither is the classic idea of a unique *ecumene* trammeled: the strait is narrow, the form as a whole of the terrestrial mass does not change, America is equally an appendage of Asia, after the fashion of Africa in which the isthmus between the Mediterranean and Red Seas has been cut through, as the ancients had done so many times." (Milanesi, 1992, 49). This 1992 contribution is an especially valuable and interesting work.

[58] Most in the following paragraphs, unless noted otherwise, is from Huddleston (1967), Garcia (1981), Glaser (1973), and Schmidt (1988); also Arias Montanus (1572). Many more (and more specific) references are given on this in the mentioned work in progress.

252

became frequent toward the end of the sixteenth century, but their antecedents went back to the early sixteenth century, at least. By the early seventeenth century they became widespread and in the forefront, and there developed an enormous literature on the subject, almost all of which is now completely forgotten. Besides the great biblical premise, discussions regarding the origin of the human inhabitants of the New World, the Indians, centered on various considerations of physical appearance, customs, usages and habits, perceived linguistic similarities, etc. Endless signs were detected in these areas, most often incorrectly, of similarities between the Indians and various Old World cultures, with Jewish and Tartar races being the most frequently cited as the Indians' predecessors. There was a great deal of talk of the lost tribes of Israel, of their postulated wandering into the New World, and of their presumed new homeland of Arsarot, which figures prominently in the land bridge between Asia and America on Gastaldi's 1546 world map.[59] There was also much on possible migrations of Tartars, Scythians, Phoenicians, Cambrians, Chinese, Trojans, Greeks, Romans, and many others, and lists of supposedly interrelated words and grammatical structures were produced. Some tried to break away from the paradigm of a necessity of a physical connection between the two worlds, exploring what possibility there might have been of the primitive first populations having had enough knowledge of navigation and vessel-building to have sailed to the New World over something greater than a very short distance. But most presumed the Indians had come over some land connection, or near connection, existing somewhere in the still unexplored north.

An important corollary in many of these discussions involved the question of how the common animals had gotten to America, and, again, this usually went back in the main to Noah and the ark.[60] The presence in the New World of all sorts of species was considered, including those useful for domestic purposes, or even as pets, and the possibility of certain animals' having been brought along intentionally on boats by more advanced primitive peoples was considered. But the presence in both worlds of those wild beasts which could be of no possible use to man, even as pets, beasts

---

[59] For more on this, see just below.

[60] Besides the references given in note 58, see on this Browne (1983), Bancroft (1886), Allen (1949).

which were often indeed dangerous to man, as bears, lions, tigers, wolves, took a special place in the discussions, and the near universal consensus declared it inescapable that the two worlds must somewhere be connected or nearly connected. This remained a central point through the years, and the centuries of frustration and perplexity on the point seem to be summed up in the title of a work published in 1763 by Francisco Xavier Alexo de Orrio, *Solution to the Great Problem of the Population of the Americas, in which . . . there is Discovered an Easy Path for the Transmigration of Men from One Continent to the Other: and How There Could Pass to the New World, not only Beasts of Service, but Also the wild and Harmful Animals . . .*[61] Even here there had occasionally been other explanations offered, such as that perhaps the wild beasts had for some divine reason been transported by angels, or by giant birds, such as the mythical roc. But the great majority considered that the point could only mean that the New and Old Worlds were connected or came very close.

Note that there are, of course, a good number of New World animals which do not occur in the Old World. It is natural that the novel and different should at first make a greater impression than the familiar, perhaps to the point of one's not noticing the latter, and it may have been this that caused one early observer, Humphrey Gilbert, to go quite overboard in 1576 and make the absurd asseveration that *all* New World fauna differed from that of the Old World. This, he maintained, could only mean that the two continents must be unconnected. It is hard to believe that Gilbert would not have known by his time of the many reports of almost all the commonest and most familiar Old World animals occurring in the New World, including bears,[62] wolves, foxes, lions, deer, boars, leopards, lynxes, dogs, sheep, goats,[63]

---

[61] Alexo de Orrio (1763), in Spanish.

[62] Both bears of the regular variety, as well as polar bears, as see below. Polar bears were known to Europeans, and, in fact, they are mentioned as occurring in Sweden by Piero Quirini in the *Navigationi* (Ramusio, 1967-70, 2, 210r; Milanesi ed., 1978-88, IV, 95).

[63] While there were differences between Old and New World sheep and goats, this fact is not generally mentioned in the accounts, so it would not be known to readers. In general, in this time over 200 years before Darwin's ideas, it was not usual to dwell much on small distinctions. Bears were bears, lions were lions, deer were deer, etc.

martens, rabbits, hares, squirrels, rats, lizards, etc.[64] He nevertheless seems not to have been aware of this, or if he was, he pretended not to be.[65] Within a relatively short time, the fact that New World fauna was predominantly the same or similar to that of the Old World had become common information, and accordingly, Gilbert's notion is not found past the sixteenth century.[66] There was one other idea which for a while was given as speaking against a connection between the continents, slightly better founded than Gilbert's, but it too was soon rejected as untenable. It was said, particularly in reference to the theory that the Indians had descended from Tartars or Scythians, two cultures which made extensive use of horses, that the lack of that animal in the New World would indicate that the continents were unconnected.[67] But the notion had little strength, for there were too many possible variant explanations. America may have first been settled by people who had lost their way, straggled over, without their domestic animals. Tribes could have crossed over too far north to bring them. The crossing could have been made by Tartars before they became a horse culture. Or indeed the Indians'

[64] There were also a certain number of reports of Old World animals in the New World which were erroneous, but there was no way a reader could have known that, and they too must have influenced thinking along these lines. Although he does not mention it in his account as published in Ramusio, evidently Marcos da Nizza spoke of having heard that there were camels and elephants beyond the area of Civola that he had traveled to in the lands above Mexico. One Geronimo Jiménez de San Esteban, writing in an October 9, 1539 letter of Nizza's journey, says, "it is said that in the country beyond there are camels and elephants" (Quoted in Wagner, 1967, 94-95). Again, also in October, 1539, in another letter concerned with Nizza, Rodrigo de Albernez, treasurer of New Spain, wrote that, "there are camels and elephants and cattle of our kind as well as wild ones" (Quoted in Sauer, 1971, 128). The notion there were camels in the New World seems to have been fairly widespread, and Gastaldi must have heard it. Fracastoro suggests that the Spanish could make use of camels in transporting goods across the Panama mountains (Grande, 1905, "relazioni," 141-42), and the Spanish writer Gaspar de Carvajal refers to llamas as camels (Pastor Bodmer, 1992, 167). A Franciscan friar speaking in 1541 of the "cattle" of Civola, says: "These cattle are like those of Castile, and some larger[. . .]Marco Polo, in chapter XV of his treatise, says he has seen these same cows, with the same kind of hump" (Quinn, 1979, 1, 411-12). The friar clearly believes in his account that the area beyond Civola runs on into eastern Tartary in Asla.

[65] Gilbert's purpose was to promote his Northwest Passage project. Since the natural implication of the presence of many like and similar animals in the two worlds would be that the worlds were connected, which would preclude any possibility of a Northwest Passage, it would have been anathema to Gilbert's project to acknowledge the great predominance of similar species.

[66] Astonishingly, an unwary George Nunn, probably on the basis of the cited passage from Gilbert's well-known work, took Gilbert's fatuous reasoning seriously enough that he allowed it to obscure for him the clear statements of Oviedo to the effect that there was an overwhelming similarity between New and Old World fauna. See note 87 below.

[67] The earliest I know of to suggest this was Sanuto (1588, fol. 17r).

ancestors may not have been Tartars, or any other horse using culture.[68] So this argument, too, had little strength, and it is no longer found past about the mid-seventeenth century. In general, it was pointed out, the absence of certain species could not be taken as indicative of much of anything. As Ptolemy himself had said, there were many places in the Old World which contained animals which were not found in other parts of the same, and this was obviously true. While there were elephants, camels, tigers, etc., in Asia, there were none in Europe, and certainly no one claimed that Europe and Asia were not connected, and the same was true of Africa. It was the predominance of similar fauna, and its implication of a connection or near connection which mainly held the field all along, and after mid-seventeenth century, acceptance of this argument became pretty much universal. It was repeated with great consistency and seems to have been one that had great force for the minds of the times. The only point which remained undecided was whether there was a connection or just a near approach. This no one was able to decide upon, until Bering's time. The information just wasn't there.

The earliest clear statement that the similarity of human and animal life in the two worlds must indicate that they were connected or nearly so comes from the Spanish Jesuit missionary José de Acosta in 1581.[69] Acosta was sent in 1571 from Spain to America, where he remained for sixteen years. In 1573-74 he traveled widely, gaining the knowledge he used in his writings. In 1581 he wrote his first great work, the *De Natura Novi Orbis*.[70] Here he discusses at great length the question of the origin of the human and animal life of the New World,[71] touching on many of the areas just reviewed. The two starting points for his argument were the facts: (1), that there existed

[68] Also, there could have been confusion on this point, too, among European readers, for reports of horses in the New World did exist, from Columbus's time on (Nunn, 1992, 74 and 76). See also Giglio (1560, 213), although his horses have horns.

[69] On Acosta, see Burgaleta (1999), and O'Gorman (1972).

[70] He did not obtain a license for the work until 1586, and it was published only in 1588 (O'Gorman, cit., 230 and 240). Acosta shortly after translated this work into Spanish, and it made up the first two of seven books of his more famous *Historia Natural y Moral de las Indias* (Seville, 1590). An English edition appeared in London in 1604, *The Naturall and Morall Historie of the East and West Indies*, of which a two-volume edition was published by the Hakluyt Society in 1880 as nos. 60-61 in the first series.

[71] Acosta (1604, 41-81, and in other places).

in the New World both human and abundant animal forms which were common to the Old World, and (2), that after the Deluge, there had been no living things left on earth, except those on the top of Mount Ararat in Asia. From here he explores in depth all possible explanations for these life forms' having found their way to the New World. His full argument is far too long to repeat here in its entirety but the conclusion he arrives at is that, "the confines of the Indies, Europe, Asia and Affricke have some communication with one another, or at least, approach very neere together."[72] He restates this, but in much fuller and more definitive terms, later in his work:

> That . . . confirms me in my opinion, (whereof I have amply discoursed in the first book,) that the first inhabitants of the West *Indies* came by land, and so by consequence, . . . that the first continent of the *Indies*, joynes with that of Asia, Europe, and Affrike, and the new world with the old, although they have not yet discovered any country that toucheth and ioynes with the other world; *or if there be any sea betwixt the two, it is so narrow, that wilde beasts may easily swim over, and men in small boats.*[73]

Acosta in fact states at least six times in his *Naturall and Morall Historie*, that the Old and New Worlds are connected, but in every instance recognizes the alternative possibility that they are separate but "very neere."[74] He ascribes more significance to the presence of animal life than human life, for the purpose of his argument, since it is conceivable, if unlikely, that men could have come to the New World by boat, even if a great deal of water lay between the New World and the Old. Most significant of all, he says, is the

---

[72] Acosta (cit., 69).

[73] Acosta (cit., 503). Emphasis added. Though there is no clear earlier expression of this notion that I have found, the germs of this kind of thought can be detected in the following 1578 words of George Best, although he is apparently speaking with only the Old World in mind: "For it is to be thought that only such countries in times paste have been known as either did bounde and hang together, or else were separated by very narrow seas as are Europa, Affrica, and Asia out of which from either to other a man may travaile by lande, or else shall finde in some places very narrow seas separating them, and so mighte saile from the one to the other onelye by lande-markes wythoute the arte of navigation, by cause the one was within a ken of the other" (Best, 1867, 31).

[74] Besides the references given, pp. 67, 68, 71 and 78.

presence of ferocious and vicious animals which could be of no use to men, such as tigers or bears, since the tamer, domesticated animals might have been brought by men in boats. However, he shows, through arguments that are convincing, but too long to repeat here, that, although not impossible, it is most unlikely that men could have come here by any long voyage, in times long before the age of discovery.[75]

The problem with Gastaldi is that we can't directly know the rationale behind his thought, since he left almost no writings, at least which have come down to us.[76] Of course, he might have discussed such things in letters, but we have none. But the components of Acosta's thought have antecedents which go back to Gastaldi's time, and earlier, and as we shall see, Gastaldi would have been well aware of them, especially as regards the most vital part of Acosta's argument, the presence of Old World wild animals in America. And the extreme narrowness of Gastaldi's strait, together with the fact he was evidently undecided between this depiction and the one with a full connection, certainly implies that this must have been his reasoning. As we shall now see, strong bases exists indicating that Gastaldi would have been thinking along these lines, that he would have been cogitating about the presence in, and the thus implied passage to, the New World from the Old both as regards human populations, and as regards animal populations.[77]

---

[75] This was the reasoning evinced by almost all thinkers on the subject in later times. Huddleston says: "Between 1589 and 1638 the published members of the "costan school [Acosta (1589-1590), Herrera (1601-1613), Torquemada (1631[sic]), Solórzano (1629-1646), and Calancha (1638)] had gradually eliminated trans-Atlantic origins and routes via the South Pacific. Geography of faunal distribution had convinced them that the first settlers must have come into the New World by way of the still undiscovered Straits of Anian" (Huddleston, 1967, 109). In fact, the same arguments are found in many authors all along, well into the mid-eighteenth century, as Lipsius (1604), Bochart (1646 and 1663), Horn (1652 and 1666), Pythius (1656), Alexo de Orrio (1763), Engel (1767), to name just a few. Indeed, it is really the same theory held today, and seems in all likelihood the correct one.

[76] There is a tantalizing legend on the De Jode edition of Gastaldi's world map, which appeared in 1555 in Antwerp, just below the equator below the eastern Chinese coast, which reads: "Qoud in describendo America ab alijs Cosmographis discrepauimus tamque contiuentem [sis] cum Asia fecerimus non sine ratione id a nobis factum est" (Although we shall be so much in disagreement with other cosmographers in portraying America and have depicted [it] continuous with Asia, this has not been done by us without reason.). But we are not told what the reason is! It is possible De Jode was not really aware of Gastaldi's rationale, and simply included this legend to forestall criticism. Interestingly, this legend remains on a ca. 1590 variant of the map, even though there the Strait of Anian has been cut through (Shirley no. 174).

[77] We recall that, at the time, the world took the saga of Noah and the Ark quite literally.

The record is not as extensive as concerns human populations as regards animal ones, but it is clear and sufficient. As Milanesi has recently brought out, we know that the most important element, the possible location of the lost tribes' new homeland, Arsarot, in America, was part of Gastaldi's thought from the beginning, for this mythical land occurs prominently in the land bridge between the continents on his 1546 world (our no. 3), and in later copies of that map. Whence Gastaldi obtained this idea, we don't know. It was not Ramusio. But we do know that the idea had been afloat at least since the 1530s, and that it is expounded upon by a Spanish physician identified only as Dr. Roldan in ca. 1540.[78]

As regards the fact that Old World animals were common in the New World, the record is clearer. We can be sure Gastaldi was aware of this, for Ramusio's *Navigazioni* is filled with it. We select some of the more significant such passages. Verrazzano, describing the eastern coastal regions of North America, relates that, "there are animals in the greatest number, as stags, deer, lynxes, and other kinds . . . ."[79] Cortes, describing Montezuma's palace, says: "In this house there were several large low rooms filled with big cages . . . In all, or in most of them, were large numbers of lions, tigers, wolves, foxes and cats of various kinds . . . ."[80] Vespucci says, of the lands he coasted, "here are seen all sorts of lions, bears, and other animals."[81]

---

[78] For Milanesi, see her 1992 work. On the earliest development of the idea of Arsarot in America, from the 1530s, including Roldan's ideas, see Hanke, 1935, 72-73; and, more fully, Gliozzi, 1977, 49-60 and Schmidt, 1988, 174-80. It would not be surprising if this idea arose still earlier, for it originates from the apocryphal Book of Esdras, and Quinn quotes the following from Columbus: "Note that the blessed Ambrose and Augustine and many others have held Esdras to be a prophet and that they have approved his book as it appears below by the extracts which are made from his books. And they do not appear to be apocryphal." (Quinn, 1979, 1, 134). A possible source for Gastaldi's ideas on Arsarot would have been Guillaume Postel, who was much interested in that, as in all biblical geography (Secret, 1998). Postel certainly must have been in contact with Ramusio (Almagià, 1948, 63-64, 65 and 66). Meurer thinks Gastaldi himself had contact with him (Meurer, 1991, 218), and the present writer agrees. Postel spent considerable time in Venice, the city he loved more than any other, and, though there is no space to go into it here, there were between the two men a large number of common interests, and common acquaintances, including, besides Ramusio, Diego Hurtado de Mendoza, the Spanish ambassador who provided Gastaldi with the information for his 1544 map of Spain, Matteo Pagano, who published several Gastaldi maps, and Giovanni Battista Pedrezzano, who published Gastaldi's Ptolemy, the Giunti brothers, as well as others.

[79] Ramusio (1967-70, 3, 351v; Milanesi ed., 1978-88, VI, 901).

[80] Ramusio (cit., 201v; Milanesi ed., 1978-88, VI, 84). Pagden's translation from Cortes (1986, 111).

[81] Ramusio (1967-70, 1, 131v). Vespucci also mentions wild boars (131r), and, elsewhere, large rats, lizards, and serpents (129v)(respectively in Milanesi ed., 1978-88, 1, 676; 1, 675; and 1, 668).

Martire, describing, after Cabot, a sort of game which the bears of eastern North America make of catching fish, says, "the said Sebastian Gabotto said to have seen . . . that many bears which are found in this country came to make a sporting hunt of these fish Baccalai in this manner."[82] Ramusio relates of Cortereal that he saw "people who cover themselves with sewn-together furs of marten and of various other animals [and] . . . he saw many birds and other animals, [and] gigantic bears, all white . . . ."[83] Pizzaro speaks of the "Casali" of the Indians, "which are pastures with sheep of various kinds, that is, some small, *like ours*, and others so large that they are used in carrying things . . . ."[84] Marcos da Nizza tells us that during his trek, he was "always well supplied with victuals, of deer meat, hares and partridges," and "I was brought much deer meat, as [also] rabbits, quails."[85] But the most important source in Ramusio in this regard is undoubtedly Oviedo, who systematically presents what is probably the first catalogue of New World animals. Some of these, he says, are just like their Old World counterparts, and the differences that are found in some animals between the two parts of the world occur, "according to the locality or the constellation under which these animals have been bred."[86] The following are just a few of the animals he describes:

> In Tierra Firme there are royal lions *exactly like those in Africa*[. . .]There are also leopards in Tierra Firme, *similar in shape and appearance to those to be seen here and those of Africa*[. . .]There are foxes *of the same appearance of those of Spain*, but not the same color[. . .]There are many deer *exactly like those in Spain, in color, size, and other features*[. . .]There are likewise very many fallow deer, especially in the province of Santa Marta. *They are of the same shape and size as those in Spain*[. . .]In Tierra Firma the

[82] Ramusio (1967-70, 3, 30r; Milanesi ed., 1978-88, V, 173).

[83] Ramusio (cit., 346v; Milanesi ed., 1978-88, VI, 878). Cf. note 62 above.

[84] Ramusio (cit., 314v; Milanesi ed., 1978-88, VI, 698). Emphasis added.

[85] Ramusio (cit., 299v and 298v; respectively, in Milanesi ed., 1978-88, Vi, 597 and 602).

[86] Ramusio (cit., 45v; Milanesi ed., 1978-88, V, 255).

Carib arrow-shooting Indians have small cur dogs . . . *and they are of all the colors of dogs in Spain.*[87]

Once again we find consolidated in Ramusio for Gastaldi what was almost certainly a greater concentration of pertinent information than was available in any other source,[88] this time indicating an overwhelming preponderance of similar, instead of dissimilar, fauna, between the two worlds. While to be sure, there are references to New World animals which do not occur in the Old World, they are far fewer in number, and as we have seen, the fact cannot be taken as indicative of anything as regards a separation or connection of continents. Even a half century earlier, in 1500, it was on the basis of this criterion of a commonly shared fauna that Vespucci had come to the conclusion that the New World was "bounded by the eastern

---

[87] Ramusio (cit., 46v-48r; Milanesi ed., 1978-88, V, 254-67). Emphases added. Oviedo also notes that there are "many lizards *similar to those in Spain* . . . ." (51v; Milanesi ed., V, 288). Emphasis added. Translations are those of S. A. Stoudemire, in his 1959 English edition of Oviedo. I have intentionally selected here those passages from Oviedo where he specifically states that the animals named are the same as their counterparts in the Old World. Many other American animals in Oviedo, indeed the majority, also have same or similar corresponding species in Europe or Asia. It is hard to explain Nunn's thorough failure to grasp that the clear implication of Oviedo's catalogue of American animals is that New World beasts are predominantly the same as or very similar to Old World ones, other than by assuming a far too hasty reading of Oviedo (Nunn, 1929, 18-21, esp. 18-19). Making no mention at all of the many Old World animals which Oviedo so explicitly describes as being the same as their counterparts in the Old World, he proceeds to name seven Old World animals which do not occur in the New World, and then wonders why it never occurred to Oviedo that he could have supported his opinion that the continents were separate by pointing out that none of the Old World's animal forms were found in the New World! It would be hard to find a statement which could more thoroughly throw a reader off the right track than this. Four from Nunn's list of seven animals do, incidentally, occur in the New World (sheep, goats, cattle, dogs), and, if there are differences at the species level, we know that most writers of the time failed to note those minor distinctions which would have made this clear to readers, such that readers back home could only assume that identical beasts were being spoken of. Even in the case of those three animals in Nunn's list which truly do not occur in the New World (elephants, camels, horses), reports of them nevertheless occurred in the literature (see notes 64 and 68), and, again, readers would have had no reason to doubt these. There is no escaping the fact that reports of New World fauna told of a quite overwhelming preponderance of life forms which were the same or similar to those in the Old World, sometimes even more so than was actually the case, although for the most part the reports were in fact quite correct.

[88] There were, of course, other sources with such information, and had been from early on. Nunn quotes Cantino in 1501 on "wolves, foxes, tigers, and sables" (1992, 131). An anonymous 1515 publication speaks of lions, leopards, lynxes, and genets (Parker, 1957, 31). Geronimo Giglio, in a section added to the 1558 Italian edition of Boemus, mentions a large number of animals common to both worlds, including, besides many of the animals named already, crocodiles and cows. (In 1560 Venice edition, 189r-236r). He also, in his first chapter, touches on the origin of man, the Deluge, and the animals of the ark, though not with particular reference to the New World.

parts of Asia . . . because . . . we saw divers animals, such as lions, stags, goats . . . which are not found on islands, but only on the mainland,"[89] and he had been aware of far fewer common species than was Gastaldi. As we have seen elsewhere, there is a wealth of indications that Gastaldi was perplexed and confounded on the question of the relationship of the continents, and that considered, I think we can assume that the great significance of this criterion to the question would have occurred to him. Its immediate implication is clearly that the continents were connected, or, if separated, the separation was sufficiently small that wild animals and primitive men could have swum across, or floated across on driftwood or in rudimentary boats.

8.4 The Geographical Evidence

The evidence presented so far all implies a connection between the continents. What would have prompted Gastaldi to entertain the opposite possibility, that the continents were separated? There would have been, I think, not one factor, but a series of them. Probably the most persuasive would have been certain information received about 1553 from Barros and Gómara, but we shall look at these last, after presenting some more general factors for background. Firstly, it should be remembered that Gastaldi probably would have been, by the 1550s anyway, favorably predisposed to the possibility of a separation from the start just because of the great simplification of things it would offer as to making a series of maps of the various parts of the world. Secondly, Gastaldi would have known of course that many other mapmakers had all along depicted the continents as separated, and this too might have made considering the different possibility easier.[90] Finally, it is worth bearing in mind that, in a way, Gastaldi can be

---

[89] Vespucci (1951, 277). Translation of Huddleston (1967, 5). These words of Vespucci do not occur in the Ramusio Vespucci letters.

[90] I do not personally feel that a wish or hope that there be a northwest or northeast passage, often cited as a possible factor influencing those who adopted the idea of a separation of the continents, would have played much, if any, role, in Gastaldi's thinking, although it is true that Ramusio devotes a lengthy discourse to the subject of routes to the Spice Islands, and seems interested in the possibility of a northwest passage, so there may have been some influence of an indirect nature from him or others. All in all, one would think that Venetians would prefer that such a passage *not* be found, for it could only increase the damage to the Venetian economy already done by the opening of the cape route by the Portuguese.

detected as heading towards a separation even in his first world map in 1546, for he sharply differs from predecessors as to the north-south width of the land bridge connecting Asia to America, a fact we have already mentioned briefly in chapter two. In all previous maps showing a connection, such as Monachus ca. 1527, Fine 1531, 1534, Vopel, 1536 (Shirley nos. 57, 66, 69 and 73), the south coast of the land bridge rises only to about 18° N latitude at its highest, while in Gastaldi's 1546 world it rises to about 38°-39°, creating Gastaldi's great "GOLFO DI TONZA" between the continents, the first true sign of a North Pacific Ocean.[91] Thus the land bridge is already much narrowed, by a full twenty degrees or more, and there is clearly much more individuality imparted to the two continents, although there is still a quite solid connection. The designation "Tonza" is the name of one of the greatest of the Chinese coastal provinces, and is taken from Marco Polo, although this form of the name does not occur in the Ramusian edition of Polo which Gastaldi would later use,[92] and so Gastaldi must have correctly perceived that Polo's description strongly implies the existence of a substantial east oceanic coast to China, a thing obvious enough to modern readers of Polo, but evidently not so obvious to Fine or Vopel or some others, who used Polo extensively, but have nothing like an east coast to China. But Gastaldi's sharp raising of the coast was also certainly influenced by one of the very rare instances where actual latitude figures were available for these remotest parts of the world, when Marcos da Nizza relates in 1539 sighting

---

[91] Besides the long series of Gastaldi worlds, this sort of connection was also adopted on the Hadji Ahmed map (Shirley no. 101), where one must give close attention, due to the distorting projection, to determine that it is precisely this type, and not the Fine type; the 1561 Honter world (Shirley no. 108); the 1590 Myritius world (Shirley no. 175), and on several manuscript maps, including some by Giorgio Sideri detto Callapoda (cf. 1563 world reproduced in Kretschmer, 1892, pl. XXII); a 1570 globe by Francisco Basso (Mediolenso) (reproduced in Kretschmer, 1892, pl. XXIX); and some maps by Francesco Ghisolfi (see Astengo, 1993, figs. 2, 4, 5, 6). On Sideri in general, see Raynaud-Nguyen (1985, with an inventory of works in note 4), Wroth (1970, 194-96), and Astengo (1996); on Basso, see Astengo (1991), and Stevenson (1921, 163-64); on Ghisolfi, see Astengo (1993), and Wagner (1937, 1, 29).

[92] The name is found in this form only in the very rare abridgement of Polo sometimes referred to as the Venetian or Italian epitome of Marco Polo, which occurred in many editions from the late fifteenth century far into the seventeenth century. I have seen only two editions of this exceedingly rare item, that of 1533 (Polo, 1533), where the name is rendered Tonza, and a 1555 edition published by Matteo Pagano, where it is rendered with the tilde Tõza. It is found in chapter 116 of the unpaginated books. In the Ramusio edition, it is given as Concha (Ramusio, 1967-70, 2, 48v; Milanesi ed., 3, 245), while other common spellings are Choncha, Chonka, Conca, Koncha, Tonzo. It is apparently equivalent to the modern province of Fukien on the coast.

the American west coast in 35° N during his northern trek in search of Civola and the Seven Cities, the only latitude figure in Ramusio for the North American west coast above the limits of the expeditions sponsored by Cortes, which did not get past Baja California.[93] One can perhaps sense a slight prefiguring of his later idea in this raised connection.

Now we can move on to the more explicit factors which would have influenced Gastaldi to consider separating the continents. There are several places in Ramusio where opinions or ideas are expressed which state or imply that the continents should be separated. While many of these passages have a semi-apocryphal or uncertain air about them, which I feel Gastaldi would have been aware of, it is no doubt significant that there are, against them, no statements at all in Ramusio which state or imply the opposite, and they could certainly have influenced Gastaldi.[94] Some of the statements are made by Ramusio himself in his discourses. In one place, Ramusio speaks of an ambassador from Muscovy who states twice that one could "easily" sail by the north coast of Asia from Muscovy to China, and Ramusio does not gainsay him.[95] Then, on the same page, Ramusio asks rhetorically why the princes who govern New France and Baccalaos do not institute a search for a strait to Cathay and the Moluccas since, although he seems uncertain, he believes there is likely to be such a strait.[96] In a different discourse, Ramusio speaks of Cortereal's intention of finding a strait through America to the Spice Islands, although he does not volunteer here any opinion as to the validity of this notion.[97] In still another discourse, Ramusio relates that Sebastian Cabot had informed him that there was a clear strait through from

---

[93] Ramusio (1967-70, 3, 299r; Milanesi ed., 1978-88, VI, 599). Gastaldi could have had access to this report as early as ca. 1540-42, the time when Ramusio probably obtained it (Parks, 1970, 32; and 1955,"Ramusio's Literary History," 130 and 144-45).

[94] There is also, in the fact that there is nowhere expressed in the *Navigationi* the opinion that the continents are connected, the implication that Ramusio's own opinion was that they were separated, especially since a number of the statements are made by Ramusio himself in his discourses. Thus Ramusio himself may have had some influence in causing Gastaldi to reconsider or qualify his original view.

[95] Ramusio (1967-70, 1, 374r; Milanesi ed., 1978-88, 982-83).

[96] Ramusio (1967-70, 1, 374r; Milanesi ed., 1978-88, 2, 984-85).

[97] Ramusio (1967-70, 3, 346v; Milanesi ed., 1978-88, VI, 877). The notion that Cortereal was seeking a strait, which apparently first arises in the 1530s, was quite unfounded, as see the special note,"Cortereal and the Strait of Anian," at the end of the present chapter.

the area of New France to the China coast.[98] All other statements to the effect that the continents should be separated in the *Navigazioni* are in the words of the authors of the accounts proper. Paolo Giovio expresses his opinion that one should probably be able to sail the Asian north coast east from Russia and to Cathay.[99] Cortes, in his fourth letter of relation to the king of Spain, says that it is considered certain that there is a strait through North America from the Atlantic to the South Sea (Pacific), in a passage which we have already quoted in full earlier in this chapter from a different source.[100] An authority of a different nature would have been the Arab geographer Abulfeda, from whose fourteenth-century work Ramusio gives several short quotations and paraphrases in the prefatory material to his edition of Marco Polo in volume two.[101] At one point, we find the following:

> And Abylfada Ismael himself, describing the confines of the region of Cine, says that . . . "the Ocean of the East turns towards the region of Cine, and goes towards the north, and having finally passed the said region reaches thence to Gogi and Magogi, that is to the confines of furthest Tartari, and thence to some lands which are unknown: and running ever to the west, passes over the northern confines of Rossia, and goes toward the northwest'[102]

How reliable an authority Gastaldi may have considered Abulfeda to be is very hard to say. My own suspicion, as regards the present passage in particular, is that he would have taken it with a grain of salt. However, it is clear from Ramusio's words of praise in his Polo preface,[103] that he held Abulfeda in high regard, and Gastaldi must have given some notice to the

---

[98] Ramusio (1967-70, 3, fol. [*4v]; Milanesi ed., 1978-88, V, 12). Here Ramusio does preface Cabot's opinion with the remark that, "it is still not clear to us . . . whether through this part it is possible to go to the province of Cataio."

[99] Ramusio (1967-70, 2, 134r; Milanesi ed., 1978-88, 3, 682).

[100] Ramusio (1967-70, 3, 245r-v; Milanesi ed., 1978-88, 293).

[101] He gives no more than this. For the mistaken notion that he included a compendium of Abulfeda in the *Navigationi*, see chapter five, at note 130, and the places referred to there.

[102] Ramusio (1967-70, 2, 16v-17r; Milanesi ed., 1978-88, 3, 68).

[103] Ramusio (1967-70, 2, 3rd page of "Prefatione"; Milanesi ed., 1978-88, 3, 24).

passage, perhaps especially when considered together with the words of Barros given below.

Still another authority worth quoting in full is Gonzalo Fernandez de Oviedo. Oviedo is speaking in general terms of the New World, concerning which:

> by virtue of its not yet being fully discovered, it is not known if it ends in land or sea, or if all of that part is surrounded by the Ocean Sea. That which I am most inclined to believe, and the opinion is not only mine, but has been coming to be believed by many others in recent times, is that this land is neither part of Asia, nor does it join with that which the ancients called Asia.[104]

Oviedo, with whom both Ramusio and Fracastoro regularly corresponded, was official Spanish historiographer of the Indies, and his opinion would undoubtedly have been held in high regard by Gastaldi. While all of these could have influenced Gastaldi to consider the possibility that the continents might be unconnected, the most influential and persuasive statements, I think, would have been those of Gómara and Barros, both of which Gastaldi would have first become aware of about the same time, ca. 1553, and my suspicion is that it would have been shortly after this time that he began to seriously entertain the possibility that the continents could be separated, as long as there was a very close approach at some point.

Francisco López de Gómara's great *Historia general de las Indias* was first published in 1552-53. Ramusio makes use of him in his discourses to his 1556 volume three,[105] and we can probably assume he had obtained a copy by 1553, which Gastaldi would undoubtedly have seen. At one point in his history, Gómara lists, from south to north, many (but not all) of the place names on the west coast of America which were derived from the Cabrillo expedition, along with the distances between them, and his lines effectively exclude the possibility of America being connected with Asia:

---

[104] Ramusio (cit.,III, 140v; Milanesi ed., 1978-88, V, 737).

[105] Parks (1970, 31, 33 and 34).

From the Sardinas to Sierras Nevadas, it is 150 leagues, passing by Puerto de Todos Santos, Cabo de Galera, Cabo Nevada, and Baia de Los Primeros. Sierras Nevadas are in 40°, and the last country marked out and graduated in that direction, although the coast still continues to the north to where it closes the country as an island at Labrador or at Gruntlandia. In this last stretch of country there are 510 leagues . . . . The account which I give of the number of leagues and degrees is according to the maps of the royal cosmographers. These do not receive or put down the account of any pilot except under oath or without witnesses.[106]

Gómara's report of the west coast being known up to 40° N latitude was correct, and was based on information from Cabrillo's voyage of 1542-43, although Gómara does not make specific reference to the voyage or to Cabrillo.[107] It was five degrees higher than any previously available latitude figure for the west coast of North America, and Gómara, like Oviedo, was an authority of some stature. The datum would probably have gained reinforcement for Gastaldi by virtue of still another passage in Gómara, even though the passage amounts to a misinterpretation by Gómara of an already spurious report which appeared, ironically, in Ramusio's first volume in 1550.[108] His misinterpretation gives the impression that Coronado had reached the west coast in about 40° where he saw ships, whose occupants gave out that they were 30 days in reaching there, leading Coronado to assume they were from China.[109]

---

[106] López de Gómara (1552-53 [1852], 164). I use Wagner's translation (1929, 431).

[107] Elte and Israel, in their 1978 catalog entry for the "Cosmographia Vniversalis," say that map seems to be the first with Cabrillo names on the Northwest Coast (Elte and Israel, 1978, 40-42). This is correct, but it appears to me the names are from this Gómara account of Cabrillo's voyage, which would mean Gastaldi knew that voyage only through this very imperfect account, which is really just a partial list of names, source unidentified. See Wagner's full list of Cabrillo names (1937, 42). For further references on the voyage see note 115 below.

[108] Ramusio (1967-70, 1, 374r-v; Milanesi ed., 1978-88, 2, 985).

[109] On Gómara's rather involved misconstruction, which we need not go into here, see Wagner (1929, 59-60), and Wagner (1937, 44-45 and 50-52), where there is also a reproduction of an anonymous Italian manuscript map probably of ca. 1558-60, which contains on the west coast in 40° the legend, "Ship of Cathay or China," and at 45° the legend, "Francisco Vasquez de Coronado discovered to here."

The first Decade of João de Barros's *Asia* was published in 1552. Ramusio published six chapters from it, those specifically on geography, in the second edition of his volume one in 1554, and we can be sure that he had the Decade by 1553 from a reference to Barros in his preface to his Polo (dated 1553) in the same volume,[110] and that Gastaldi had seen it by that time as well. Included in the chapters extracted by Ramusio is a periplus, or description, of the Asian coast all the way from the Red Sea to the east end of Asia, then north along the China coast. Barros divides the coastline into nine parts to facilitate description. The first eight parts cover all from the Red Sea to the South China Sea, and then up to 30° N latitude on the Chinese coast, which he says is the furthest point yet navigated by the Portuguese. Thus his last, ninth, part is not known yet by experience to Europeans, but he adds:

> However, according to the cosmography of China (which we have spoken of above), the maritime provinces of this kingdom run approximately toward the northwest; there are three of them, Nanquij, Xanton, Quinsii, where the king makes his residence the greater part of the time, which is in forty six degrees, and the coast runs still from this province, as far as fifty degrees, in which there are contained four hundred leagues, where ends the most eastern and northern terra firma that we know.[111]

As with Oviedo and Gómara, Barros was an official historiographer of great repute, and again we can assume Gastaldi would have held him in high regard. This 50° point was far and away the highest actual latitude figure yet available for either shore of the Pacific Ocean. As we will see in the next chapter, there exists reason to suspect Gastaldi looked upon this figure with a hint of skepticism, and certainly the fact that he takes great liberties in his interpretation as to some other parts of the same passage demonstrates a certain disregard for Barros's statements here. Nevertheless, it is also very

---

[110] Ramusio (1967-70, 2, 2nd page of "Prefatione"; Milanesi ed., 1978-88, 3, 22).

[111] Ramusio (1967-70, 1, 391v; Milanesi ed., 1978-88, 2, 1074). The passage this is from is dealt with further in our chapter eight.

clear that the northeast China coast on the third part of his great 1559-61 map of Asia[112] is taken directly from Barros, including the location of Quinsay at precisely 46° N, and including the fact that the map stops right at 50° N latitude, with the coast disappearing to the north off the map at that point.[113] Gastaldi was clearly much impressed with this passage, and, although it was probably a tentative acceptance to a degree, he did accept the 50° figure for this map of east Asia.[114]

This statement of Barros concludes what would have been available to Gastaldi from Ramusio.[115] Indeed, after some twenty and more years of researching this area, I think I can say with something very close to complete assurance, that, with Barros, and what we have said in the last note, we have fully exhausted here all possible information which could have been

---

[112] Our no. 103.

[113] The Strait of Anian is located at a little over 50° on the great 1561 world map (no. 104), and the maps enumerated in chapter two which are directly copied from it.

[114] There is but one other place in Ramusio where we find information, indirect in nature, which could be useful in attempting to determine how far north Pacific shores might reach. In a Jesuit letter from Japan which is first included in the 1554 second edition of volume one, there is the very inexact statement that Japan is at the latitude of Italy, which, if taken literally, would put Japan somewhere in the range of 38° to 47° N latitude. It is questionable, I think, whether this rather vague datum would have played any role in Gastaldi's thinking.

[115] There were two more sources which could have provided relevant information, but, as far as I have been able to determine, Gastaldi would either have known of them only indirectly and imperfectly, or, in the case of one, not at all. In 1542-43 the voyage of Juan Rodríguez Cabrillo up the west coast of North America reached ca. 40° to 42°. Evidently Gastaldi had no report of this other than that of Gómara, already mentioned, who, in his 1552 *Historia general de las Indias*, includes a partial list of Cabrillo's names without actually mentioning the voyage or Cabrillo, and says that the highest point known on the coast is Sierras Nevadas in 40° N latitude. See on this voyage Wagner (1929, 72-93, 426-31, 450-63), Wagner (1937, 40-53), Wagner (1941), and Kelsey (1986, *Cabrillo*, esp. 160.) In 1522, Gonzalo Gómez de Espinosa reached 42° or 43° N latitude in the western Pacific in a failed attempt to sail east from the Moluccas to Mexico, incidentally establishing that the coasts of the Pacific must reach above that point, even though he was far from either one. See Wright (1945, 61-62), Brand (1967, 116-17 and 119), Landín Carrasco (1992, 1, 161-86), and Lévesque (1992, 305-06). There is no account of this which contains the important latitude figure that could have reached Gastaldi as far as I have been able to discover after much searching, except that, on some of Ribero's famous planispheres, a small picture of Espinosa's ship, the "Trinidad," is found in about 42° latitude with a legend reading, "This is the ship 'Trinidad' trying to sail across the South Sea. It went up to 42 degrees, but, meeting contrary winds there, returned again to Maluco, because it had been six months at sea, was leaking badly, and lacked supplies." (Quoted after Kelsey, 1986, "Finding," 150). We know from Grande that Gastaldi had seen at least one Ribero map, but whether or not it was one with this legend, we can't know, and, in any event, with no corroboration from other sources, Gastaldi might well have looked askance at this information. Two other attempts to cross the Pacific from west to east just might have barely reached above 30°, that of Saavedra in 1529, and Torre in 1543-44. On them see the works cited for Espinosa.

available to Gastaldi, or to any European at the time, from Ramusio or otherwise, regarding North Pacific shores or the question of the relationship of Asia to America. We have, in this, together with what we have said earlier regarding the fauna and humanora of the New World, and regarding the ideas of other thinkers, all the ingredients we need to provide us with the answers we seek. It will be useful to begin by pointing out that we have here some pretty clear indication of the nature of Gastaldi's mentality, that is, of the general stance he would have taken towards all this material. We get this from his known reaction to the statements of Abulfeda and Gómara. These two authorities alone, among all cited, make *unqualified* statements to the effect that the two continents stand quite alone, unconnected to anything, as we have seen above. Abulfeda states unequivocally that Asia is completely surrounded by the ocean to the east, and to the north as well, and Gómara does the same for America. Gastaldi had seen both of these sources before 1556, probably by 1553, and if he were a credulous fellow, they should have settled the issue. Indeed, either one alone should have. Yet we have his 1556 map of the Western Hemisphere, which leaves the area between Asia and America blank. So we have Gastaldi's skepticism documented.[116] This will be useful to bear in mind as we proceed.

8.5 Our Conclusions

The two sorts of evidence we have given above, which we have called zoological evidence and geographical evidence, are basically contradictory. The logical conclusion of the first is that the continents are connected. The logical conclusion of the second is that they are separated, and there is nothing in the latter case which implies anything as to the width of the separation. This separation could just as well be wide as narrow. It is only when we try to reconcile the two that it occurs to us that we can affect this reconciliation only via the stipulation that, if they are connected, they must approach very closely if we are to account for the movement of people and animals between the two continents. We can assume that Gastaldi, who

---

[116] Ramusio, on the other hand, seems to have been a little less critical, although, as we have seen, he too could have reservations about the information he received.

surely pondered the question over many years, was aware of this stipulative solution, and the extremely narrow strait on his 1561 *Cosmographia vniversalis* world map and his ca. 1560 America surely implies that he was there making use of it.

But this solution is not at all completely satisfying in and of itself. In the first place, we believe Gastaldi to have been a perspicacious fellow, and we believe that at all times, he was well aware that, while there was considerable basis for conviction where the zoological evidence was concerned, this was not so for the geographical evidence, for all of it is of a rather questionable and speculative nature, and thus by no means convincingly closes the possibility of a solid connection. And in the second place, we have already seen, in chapter two, and again, earlier in this chapter, that Gastaldi, as well as some others in Venice did indeed, at least for several years, continue to abundantly produce maps which did in fact show such a solid connection after the narrow strait had first appeared, and customers everywhere continued to buy, often simultaneously in one and the same composite atlas, maps which showed both the one conception and the other. There was no conviction, and both possibilities continued to be entertained at the same time, as we have in fact seen earlier.

Yet, while both depictions continued to be shown in Venice, side by side, to the end of the century (precisely 1599; see Shirley, in his no. 115), we can intuitively detect that there was a preference for the depiction with a close separation. Gastaldi chose it for his most important world map, the 1561 *Cosmographia vniversalis* (no. 104). It was chosen by other Venetian cartographers, who were familiar with Gastaldi's ideas for their most important world maps, including Camocio's large four-sheet world map of 1567 (reissued 1569, 1581, and 1593), dealt with briefly in our chapter two, section 2 (and see Shirley, no. 117). Although it was not a world map, Forlani's famous ca. 1566 "Noua Franza", also discussed briefly in our chapter two, sec. 2 (and see Woodward, 1990, nos. 37.01 and 37.02), the first map of North America alone, also has this depiction. And, of course, for the first time outside of Italy, Gastaldi's Strait of Anian appears on Mercator's 1569 world map, and in the next year in the first edition of Ortelius's *Theatrum Orbis Terrarum* in 1570, after which it continued to appear on all but a very few world maps (except for the straggling reissues in Italy, until

1599, of the several editions of Gastaldi's original depiction with connected continents); it continued until well after the middle of the 1700s, and the alternative depiction of a solid connection was rather quickly booted out of the picture and forgotten.

What accounted for this victory, when no reliable evidence existed to prove there was not a connection? The prominent coexistence of the two opposing ideas in Italy, through the 1560s, and, even if less often, until the end of the century is accounted for quite fully in our previous chapter: When the geography of an area was simply unknown, it was common procedure that cartographers would give quite different depictions of the same area in different maps. But how did the depiction showing a close separation come to be the preferred one in Italy, and the one which became universal, in and out of Italy? No facts existed to justify this.

There is an answer at hand, but it has nothing to do with facts, evidence, or proofs, geographical, biological, or otherwise. It has to do with more subtle things. Look well and broadly at Gastaldi's famous world map of 1561 (no. 104), not seeking details, but an impression of the whole, and take note of the following three things: (1) The depictions of the two great parts of the world, the Old World and the New World, are in strong harmony with each other, in the sense that all of the Old World is to the right of the prime meridian (itself neatly cutting the map in two), and all of the New World to the left of the prime meridian, the division is simple and clear (and keep in mind the passion for symmetry of the Renaissance mind);[117] (2) note that, in this visualization of things, if a cartographer wished to make, not a world map, but separate continental maps of Asia and America (as Gastaldi did), again, the divisions are obvious, with each continent fitting into a simple quadratic frame, with no parts of the other continent lopping over into the same rectangle; there is resolution and conciseness, not the conflict, the ambiguity, and the indecision inherent in the depiction with the two continents connected; (3) complementing these two ideas, and giving it more impetus as the choice to make, would be the fact that, in the sixteenth century, many Europeans considered that the inhabitants of the New World

---

[117] On many world maps, including those of Mercator and Ortelius, this symmetric distribution is taken to an idealized extent, with the land nestling close to the border on both sides, while at the map's edges we see a thin presence of water all around.

were barbarous, or worse, not really people at all, but animals; consequently, the depiction with a separation neatly divided the civilized world and its peoples, from the uncivilized world and its peoples. It can only have been such considerations which would have influenced Gastaldi, and other cartographers to accept, perhaps in part subconsciously, the depiction with a separation. And the considerations of Mercator, Ortelius, etc. would have been the same. But the decision, we must remember, was based upon considerations of convenience, utility, esthetics, and perhaps ethnology; and not on facts. It was to provide greater strength for our theory, which we consider unquestionably true, that the second part of this chapter (and, indeed, the chapter as a whole), is so lengthy. With all other ideas thoroughly discredited, our theory obviously grows in credence. With this in mind, contemplate the following: If facts and evidence tell us that there must be a connection or else a close separation, but we have no clue to help us decide which, the sensible and obvious course would be simply to select the depiction which provided the greatest convenience and satisfaction.

It remains to say a few words concerning the question of when the kernel of Gastaldi's conception of a very narrow strait first occurred to him, for I think this can be narrowed down considerably. In the first half of the sixteenth century, there was held by some a notion that there might be a land connection between the two worlds which ran approximately from the region of Labrador to the area of northern Norway. Ramusio makes mention of the idea in his famous discourse on Spice Islands routes in volume one of the *Navigazioni*, although he then in the same sentence says he thinks it unlikely and that more likely there is open sea up there.[118] And in fact, Gastaldi himself does show a narrow isthmus connecting the two areas on the Carta Marina map (our no. 64) in his 1548 Ptolemy. Ziegler in his 1532 Scandinavia map also shows such a narrow connection between Europe and the New World (repr. in Nordenskiöld, 1889, p. 57) as does Monachus in his 1527 world map (Shirley no. 57). I haven't discovered whence this idea first arose, but as long as it existed, the notion that New World human and animal populations could have come to America *only* via an America-Asia connection could hardly be a very compelling one. This possibility of an

---

[118] Ramusio (1967-70, 1, 374r; Milanesi ed., 1978-88, 2, 984-85)

America-Europe connection was conclusively put to rest by Richard Chancellor's voyages of 1553-55 around Scandinavia to Russsia's northern shores in the area of present-day Archangel. Word of this voyage, though without Chancellor's name, the voyage being described simply as one undertaken by England under the auspices of King Edward VI, first appears in Ramusio in the "Dichiaratione", written by Ramusio himself, which precedes Polo's account in the *Navigazioni*'s second volume.[119] While this volume was first published in 1559, it had been ready for the press in 1557 when a printing-house fire destroyed the set type; furthermore, Ramusio died in 1557, so he clearly had word of the voyage by that time or perhaps slightly earlier. Gastaldi would surely have known of it as well from him, leaving his mind free to develop the lines of reasoning brought out in this chapter, and it must have been sometime around 1557 or slightly later that his idea first came to him. But it must always be remembered that this strait was never a matter of real knowledge or conviction. It was a matter of one or other of two possibilities, and a preference for one of them as being amenable to the needs of a cartographer. The illusion of real knowledge or conviction arises completely from the resemblance to reality, although, as we have seen earlier in this chapter, that resemblance is actually more superficial than at first seems the case.

The available facts and evidence suggest that the idea we have presented here is probably correct, in the main, although the fact remains that we have arrived at it by deduction, and no unequivocal statement from Gastaldi or others exists. In the event, it is unlikely we will ever be able to arrive at absolute certainty on all details of the matter. Nevertheless, if we are correct, it is worth observing that Gastaldi's thought processes were essentially identical to those of Acosta and the many who followed him. Pablo Martinez del Rio, in a work which includes a review of ideas concerning the origins of the Amerindians, quotes Acosta's lines in which he states, after lengthy discussion, that the two continents must be either connected or come very close together, the latter being a statement of the actual fact, and then observes: "I believe that when the reader arrives at the

---

[119] Ramusio (1967-70, 2, 17v [first pagination, i.e., the last page of the "Dichiaratione]"; Milanesi ed., 1978-88, III, 70)

274

end of this book he will agree that these lines are proof of one of the most extraordinary instances of scientific perspicacity known in all the history of human thought."[120] We must agree with Martinez's accolade to Acosta, for we do not have absolute proof that Gastaldi arrived at the same conclusion, and in the same way, before him, and in any event, Acosta was the first to write it down clearly. Nevertheless, if indeed Gastaldi's thought process was as we have outlined, then that process is reflected in the Strait of Anian as seen on the "Cosmographia Vniversalis," and it is carried over after that into the maps of Mercator, Ortelius, De Jode, and many others; and, in light of this, we may validly wonder to what degree that depiction on maps of the time may have played a role in providing Acosta with the inspiration for that part of his own theory which recognizes the quite correct possibility of a close approach of the continents.

And this ends our examination of the origin of Gastaldi's famous Strait of Anian, which we believe to be the most complete explanation ever offered.. We trust that our findings have removed the enigmatic air which has always surrounded the subject. There is nothing mysterious about the Strait of Anian.

Settling the question of Gastaldi's Strait of Anian has been an important reason for writing this chapter. After all, we wish our book to be a general one about Gastaldi. But it is not the main reason! The main reason for revealing what we believe completely explains the appearance on maps of the strait is something which we have mentioned in the course of our discussion above, but not in a sufficiently pointed way. It must be, here at the end of this chapter, be stated in a way that underlines and accentuates it as forcefully as possible: Gastaldi, no fool, knew well that his narrow strait was not a thing that had been proven. He knew that both the possibility of a solid connection or a close approach still existed, and the thought that his depiction was a revelatory truth, as has so long been thought, would never have entered his head. (It would not be shown to be certain by anyone until the eighteenth century.) We repeat, for emphasis: *Gastaldi was unsure which of the two possibilities was correct when he showed the strait first in 1561, and he would remain uncertain until his death in 1566.* Establishing

---

[120] Martinez del Rio (1952, 24).

this awareness of his *uncertainty* is the main purpose of the entire present chapter. Without a solid knowledge of it, it would be impossible to follow our next chapter, chapter nine.

SPECIAL ENDNOTES TO CHAPTER 8

1 The Name Anian

The name Anian was taken from the name of the province Ania, which Gastaldi places near the east Chinese coast in ca. 51° N latitude. This province of Ania derives from a passage found in chapter five of book three of Ramusio's Marco Polo, published in volume two of the *Navigazioni* (1559). The passage, which occurs at a point when Polo is departing the northeast coast of China by ship, is as follows:

> Partendosi dal porto di Zaitum si nauiga per Ponente alquanto verso Garbin, mille, & cinquecento miglia, passando un colfo nominato Cheinan, ilqual colfo dura di longhezza per il spatio di due mesi, nauigando uerso la parte di Tramõtana, ilqual per tutto cõfina verso Scirocco cõ la prouincia di Mãgi, & dall'altra parte con Ania, & Toloman, & molte altre prouincie cõ quelle di sopra nominate (Departing from the port of Zaitum one sails by the West somewhat towards the southwest, fifteen hundred miles, passing along a gulf named Cheinan, which gulf extends in length for the space of two months, sailing towards the north part, which [gulf] borders towards the southeast entirely with the province of Mangi, and on the other side with Ania, Toloman, & many other provinces named above with those.) (Ramusio, 1967-70, II, 51r; Milanesi ed., 1978-88, III, 256).

It is hard to make sense of the passage, as it often is in Polo, but this is not of great importance to us here, since, as we have seen, the concept of the strait did not derive from this passage, only the name. All of the names of this passage are found in the area around the Strait of Anian on Gastaldi's maps, and on those maps derived from them. On his Third Part of Asia, we find MANGI PRO, ANIA PRO, GOLFO DE CHEINAM, porto de zaiton, the latter just below 39°. On the 1561 *Cosmographia vniversalis* we find MANGI PRO, ANIA | N (with the final N written below the ANIA), GOLFO DI CHEINAN, Zaiton, at ca. 36° N, TOLMAN, which Gastaldi has placed on the other side of the strait in the New World. On the large Gastaldi America map in the four-continents sets, we also find Tolman pro on the New World side of the strait, and the COLFO DI CHEINAN. And so forth with other maps of the series, including the painted wall maps mentioned earlier. On these maps the Gulf of Cheinan is the part of the ocean just below the strait, Ania(n) is west of the strait, and Tol(o)man east of it. We discuss below, in the second note, how the change from Ania to Anian probably occurred. Polo's Ania is clearly the source of the strait's name, but since there have been scholars, unaware of the facts just given and influenced by a host of old and incorrect theories as to the name's origin, who have expressed doubts on this, it is worth mentioning that the identification is made more certain by two facts. Firstly, both Nordenskiöld (1899), and Gallo (1955) have shown that *all* of the names in Ramusio's Polo are found on Gastaldi's Asia. Secondly, and most importantly, the chapter in which the passage occurs is one of many which are not found in any other early edition of Polo besides Ramusio's, and two of the passage's names, the Gulf of Cheinan, and the province of Ania, do not occur at all in any other edition of the account. The fact that the name derives from Ramusio's Marco Polo has led a good many to think that the rationale itself for the strait might be sought there, but there is, of course, no basis for this idea, although it is no doubt true that part of the rationale for Gastaldi's original 1546 Gulf of Tonza does come from Polo, as we have pointed out in the present chapter. We shall not discuss here Gastaldi's decision to locate Ania in the north, when it probably actually belongs in the south, but will do so in our work in progress, *The Straits of Anian in History, Cartography and Myth*, from which most of the present chapter is condensed. A final comment: The reader will have noticed that the Polo passage quoted above is so garbled and chaotic that it is open to as many interpretations as a passage from Nostradamus. A good number of scholars, recognizing that the name was from the passage, have quoted the passage in their works, thinking or imagining that the strait itself was somehow to be found there as well. But twist and turn as one might, one will find no inkling of anything that could be construed as a strait in this passage. Gastaldi simply chose the name from a coastal province, in the same way that mapmakers have borrowed coastal names to designate water features, and vice versa, since time immemorial.

The place name Ania, which occurs in the often quoted passage from Ramusio's Marco Polo, provided the name for the strait, but that was all, and even that was indirect. Ania in Polo is not of course the name of a water feature, but a land one, a province on the more northerly stretches of the China east coast, which is where Gastaldi placed it according to his reading of the text. (His placement of the province Ania there is not at all as illogical as some have thought, if one takes into account the overall context in which it occurs, for Polo has just departed by ship from somewhere pretty high on the ocean coast, although it is true that in actuality Marco Polo's Ania probably originally stems from his placename "Amu", which occurs in inland southern Asia.) In any event, when Gastaldi decided to represent on some maps the Old and New Worlds as sundered, but just barely so, the result was a tiny hypothetical passage which had never existed there before, a new feature which sprang into being as it were as a by-product of his rationale. It was of course nameless, so, adopting the natural practice of naming water features after already named land features, Gastaldi gave it a name after an adjacent coastal province, although I think he probably did not immediately apply any name to it at all, as elaborated in chapter nine below. He did the same, we recall, with the name Tonza given to the great gulf between Asia and America on his 1546 world map, a name taken from the coastal province Tonza, as shown in the present chapter. Note that this name Ania is ideally suited as a proper place name in Italian, a fact which may well have subconsciously influenced Gastaldi in seeking a coastal name for the strait. That is to say, it ends in -ia after a consonant, which is common in Italian rendering of geographical names, as Italia, Venezia, Sicilia, India, Bolivia, etc. Note too that the corresponding adjectival form for such names is often in -no: italiano, veneziano, siciliano, etc. The corresponding form for Ania would be Aniano. Finally, note that it is just as common to use adjectival and prepositional phrase structures interchangeably in Italian as it is in English (car door/door of the car//Magellan Strait/Strait of Magellan), and it was no doubt as a result of a mixture of these factors, and the age's notoriously cavalier approach to matters of orthography and usage that gave rise to the form Anian. We see the form Stretto di Aniano in a few early sources, as in the text added to the Gastaldi America in the Venetian set of maps of the four continents, and in the maps of Urbano Monte (Monte, 1994, chap. 1, in pl. 3; and chap. 8, in pl. 22, in legend). Such a change would have been made all the more natural by the fact that it is common for a final -o to elide in Italian (sono " son/fanno " fan/etc. "Son io", says Rigoletto, instead of "Sono io", for example, or take the name of Mozart's famous opera "Cosi fan tutti", instead of "Cosi fanno tutti", etc, etc.). Gastaldi was probably a great deal more lax in his usage as regards orthography and norms for proper names as was his age in general, and we regularly see him using variant forms even of his own name (Giacomo Gastaldi/Giacomo di Gastaldi/Jacopo Castaldi/Jacopo di Castaldi/etc.) If there had been any special fascination attached to the name Anian at the time, as there would be later, perhaps that would have brought about an early standardization of one form, but there was none. For that matter, the orthography of the names even of famous places seems at the time to have been just as subject to orthographical corruption as the names of lesser known places. Still another common phenomenon of the time which could have affected changes was the very common usage of a tilde over a vowel to indicate a following -n, and indeed we find Toscanelli in 1567 using the form "stretto Aniã" in giving the confines of Asia (1567, sig. f5v), even though a few lines earlier he has used the form "stretto di Anian" (The form Aniã in the first phrase, lacking the preposition di, should perhaps be technically looked on as a truncated adjectival Anian(o), but it is clear that it was just such niceties that no one was worried about.) Clearly the difference meant little to Toscanelli. The original form Ania does also occur as the name of the strait, as in Anania's book, where we find "Stretto d'Ania" (1576, 225). The variants Ania, Aniã, Anian, Aniano were all used, though it was the form Stretto di Anian that caught and stuck for most mapmakers.

3 The Second Strait of Anian

Once it had been adopted outside Italy, the Strait of Anian held sway on printed world maps for quite some time. Its depiction was, however, fairly general among cartographers in the Low Countries, whose maps long dominated the market, and the Strait of Anian as shown by Ortelius was by no means taken as gospel by many in Spain and England, who from early on began to apply the name to a different concept, that of a strait running northeast-southwest from the area of Baccalaos (modern Newfoundland) to an indeterminate point rather lower on the west coast. It was in England in the 1570s that this application of the name Anian to a northeast-southwest strait (also known as the Northwest Passage) first arose. This fact was first noted by Wagner in 1926 (p. 18; see also San Pío, 1992, 81.) and it can first be detected in the writings of Richard Grenville, George Best, Richard Willes, and John Dee. The confusion was perhaps occasioned by maps such as that by Gilbert (repr. Hakluyt, 1903-05, VII, op. 176), even though the name does not appear there, and, especially, Jean Cossin (repr. Stokes, 1915-28, II, pls. 15 and 16), on which the name occurs in the strait. On both of these maps, due to a distorting projection, the strait between Asia and America can be apprehended either as a north-south strait or a northeast-southwest one. After this, we first find this new usage in Spanish documents of the 1580s. From this time on, both this idea and the original one existed side by side for many years, the one on maps, the other in literature, until the mid-seventeenth century, when the northeast-southwest Anian began to appear on maps as well, though only the western entrance to it was usually shown. By the end of the seventeenth century it had ousted the original notion completely, and in the first half of the 18th century and considerably later the name was used exclusively to refer to the later idea. Over the years, apocryphal tales of passages through such a strait would arise from time to time, adding fuel to the interest in the strait, and to the belief that it actually existed. The most famous of these tales were the oft-mentioned accounts of Fuca, Fonte and Maldonado, but there were others. Tremendous confusion arises in the second half of the eighteenth century when the old half-remembered Anian came to collide with the newly discovered real Bering Strait, with the result that, from that time on it becomes increasingly difficult to tell what the writers are referring to when they use the name, and this state of affairs continued right through the nineteenth century and into the twentieth. It is still quite evident today. Writers on Spanish America, and writers on the history and lore of British Columbia, where the last of Anian finally came to rest at the turn of the nineteenth century, and indeed the majority of writers on the history of discovery and exploration in general, when using the name, usually have in mind the northeast-southwest Anian, while historians of cartography usually have in mind the original north-south Anian, and it is clear that scholars of one area consulting works of writers in the other are still a little confused. It will probably come as a surprise to cartohistorians that the total amount that has been written on the strait understood as a northeast-southwest passage vastly surpasses the amount written on it as a north-south passage, and the literature is so filled with the notion that the name usage for the northeast-southwest strait goes back to the time when such a passage was first conceived, in the ca. 1520s (indeed earlier, for it is sometimes even used in reference to the Spanish search ca. 1500-1520 for a strait across Central America), that one can find many references in all but the most meticulously careful writers (as Kelsey) to not just Cabrillo, but also Cortes, Coronado, etc., and even Piñeda in 1519, looking for this "Strait of Anian." Nevertheless, it is quite certain that this usage of the name does not go back in contemporary literature to before the 1570s, and that the name itself did not exist until ca. 1561. Spanish speaking users of the name early on assimilated the acute accent for Anián, and that is the way it usually now appears in literature on Spanish America. Finally, it should be noted here, that throughout the period of this second strait, but especially ca. 1600-1770, there was an extremely active interest in Anian, and it was much discussed in the literature. This active interest was by no means limited to geographers, but also occurred among zoologists, philosophers, theologians, and occasionally others, including legal scholars and poets. The feeling one gets now in poring over this now utterly forgotten literature is that intellectuals of the time in any field would have been familiar at least with the term. This interest was for many quite absorbing, amounting to a fascination in the minds of some. Strangely, the notion of Anian seems to have often been unclearly defined in the minds even of those who wrote on it, sometimes indeed to the point that it would be unclear to the writer himself whether the name were to be taken as applying to a strait or something else, as in the case of the philosopher and scholar Hugo Grotius in 1642 (Grotius, 1884, 8). One gets the impression that this very unclarity accounted for much of the fascination that attached to the second Strait of Anian, and that one of the principal factors contributing to its long life and high interest was the fact that no one seemed quite sure of what the strait was or where it was supposed to be. While its usual guise was as a passageway running northeast from the California coast toward the area of Hudson Bay, we find writers seeking it all over, from the Gulf of Lower California to above Vancouver, and sometimes far in the west, in regions above Japan. One guise in which it never seemed to appear after the end of the seventeenth century was its original one as a short north-south strait in high latitudes between Asia and America.

4 Cortereal and the Strait of Anian

We saw earlier in this chapter that Ramusio in 1556 spoke of Gaspar Cortereal seeking a strait through North America to the Spice Islands. This notion had arisen only shortly before, perhaps as a result of Gemma Frisius's including on his globe a Strait of the Three Brothers, suggesting the three Cortereal brothers. Or it may have arisen slightly before the globe, and given rise to Frisius's depiction. In any event, it does not occur in the earliest references to the Cortereal voyages, and it is quite certain that Cortereal (like John Cabot) was not looking for a strait through or around North America, for no one yet had the slightest idea that there was a North America. The northern lands discovered by Cabot and the Cortereals were considered as parts of Asia. In the last three decades of the eighteenth century, when there occurred the first (and only) series of voyages up the North American west coast in search of the Strait of Anian, there also arose an accompanying flurry of writing on the topic. In this atmosphere of excitement, there arose a great interest in where the *name* Anian had come from. The name Strait of Anian had by that time come, as we saw in the previous special note, to designate a strait running northeast-southwest through America from somewhere along the present United States western coastline northeast to Hudson Bay or the Atlantic, similar, of course, to the old idea as on the Frisius globe and other maps, and similar to the idea suggested by Cortes in 1524. Lo, eighteenth-century historians, especially the German scholar George Forster, latched onto the old reports of a Cortereal strait hunt and the Gemma Frisius Three Brothers Strait, and proposed out of all this that the name Strait of Anian had been bestowed by one of the three Cortereal brothers. This notion, borne out of enormous confusion, was much repeated in the nineteenth century and later, and it so permeated the literature that it can still occasionally be found expressed today.

CHAPTER 9 - GASTALDI'S AMERICA

9.1 Stating the Problem

Where is the Gastaldi America in the set of continental and other maps made by Gastaldi and Licinio in 1559-1564? The question positively glares us in the face. Neither Bagrow nor Karrow list such a map. But certainly, there *should* be a large Gastaldi map or set of maps corresponding to those for Africa and Asia, and the notion that Gastaldi would not have made an America to accompany them can hardly be realistically entertained at all considering what we know of his previous history. The known facts of Gastaldi's career up to the time of the 1559-1564 maps shout out to us that we should expect a Gastaldi America here. In the first place, while Gastaldi's interest in all three of the extra-European continents is clearly evinced before the Gastaldi-Licinio period of 1559-1564, there are not just as many, but rather more maps or sets of maps of America in the period than there are for Africa or Asia.

There was the set of modern maps of parts of America in Gastaldi's 1548 Ptolemy, the first set of maps giving representative coverage of the continent, which Nordenskiöld called the first atlas of America (1897, 182);[1] there was the large inset map of most of America, perhaps one meter square, on the 1549-50 Africa painted on a wall in the Doge's Palace;[2] there was the 1553 or earlier map of America compiled from an assortment of Spanish sea charts made for the purpose of using it as the basis for a set of maps intended for Ramusio's volume three;[3] there was the 1553 set of maps, made from the previously mentioned map, consisting of four regional maps presumably giving representative coverage for the continent, made for Ramusio's volume three, although they were not in the end published in the volume;[4] there was the western half of North America, or perhaps all of North America (it is unclear which), making up the eastern part of the giant map of parts of Asia

---

[1] See Cartobibliography nos. 58-63.

[2] See Cartobibliography no. 65.

[3] See Cartobibliography no. (73.-76.).

[4] See Cartobibliography no. (73.-76.).

and America painted on a wall in the Doge's Palace;[5] there was the map of America (the Western Hemisphere) which actually appeared in Ramusio's 1556 volume three in place of the four maps made in 1553 mentioned above, together with the map of Hispaniola which also appeared in that volume, and which in the circumstances we may consider as accompaniment to the other map;[6] and there were two maps, of northeastern North America and of Brazil, taken from a set of anonymous French maps obtained by Ramusio, and included also in Ramusio's 1556 volume three,[7] making a total of seven maps or sets of maps, as opposed to six each for Africa,[8] and for Asia.[9] Thus, if anything, the cartographic record documents a perhaps slightly greater interest in America on the part of Gastaldi than in the other two non-European continents. Note especially here the strong sense of regular continuum and improvement beginning with the modern Africa, Asia and America maps in the 1548 Ptolemy, followed by the improved Africa, Asia and America maps made for Ramusio's *Navigazioni* from ca. 1553-1556/57, followed in turn by the great 1559-1564 maps, where we naturally expect to find culmination in a still better map of America, just as we find for Africa and Asia.

---

[5] See Cartobibliography no. 72.

[6] See Cartobibliography nos. 86 and 81.

[7] See Cartobibliography nos. 82 and 83.

[8] For Africa there was the large Africa unknown to us which Gastaldi began work on in the 1540s (see chapter ten in the section, "The Maps Made on Gastaldi's Initiative in the 1540s"), the regional African modern maps for the 1548 Ptolemy (Cartobibliography nos.31, 33, 35, 36, and 38), the 1549-50 Africa painted on a wall of the Doge's Palace (Cartobibliography no. 65), the map of the Nile Basin in the 1550 first edition of Ramusio's volume one (Cartobibliography no. 68), the map of Africa in the 1554 second edition of Ramusio's volume one (Cartobibliography no. 77), and the map of Guinea (West Africa below the Tropic of Cancer) taken from one of the anonymous French maps obtained by Ramusio, and included in his 1556 volume three (Cartobibliography no. 84). There were no more.

[9] For Asia, there was the set of regional Asian modern maps for the 1548 Ptolemy (Cartobibliography nos. 40, 42, 45, 47, 49, 54 and 56), the map of part of western Asia made sometime between 1550 and 1555 (Cartobibliography no. 69), the eastern part of Asia making up the western part of the giant map of parts of Asia and America painted on a wall of the Doge's Palace in 1553 (Cartobibliography no. 72), the two maps of southwest and southeast Asia in the 1554 second edition of Ramusio's volume one (Cartobibliography nos. 78 and 79), the map of Sumatra taken from one of the anonymous French maps obtained by Ramusio and included in his 1556 volume three (Cartobibliography no. 85), and the ca. 1556/57 regional maps of Central Asia made for Ramusio's volume two, though lost to fire in 1557 (Cartobibliography entries nos. 89-91). There were no more.

Correspondingly, what we know of Gastaldi's sources suggests that he probably had somewhat more information available to him on America than on the other continents. For one thing, we know from Ramusio that Gastaldi had access to a good number of regional sea charts of American areas [see Cartobibliography no. (73.-76.)], as well as access to world charts of the types of Ribero and Maggiolo [see Cartobibliography entry no. (58-62)], while for Africa and Asia we can say for certain only that he had charts of the latter type. Furthermore, we have much more in the way of documented connections by Ramusio with Spanish informants (America) than with Portuguese informants (Africa and Asia).[10] Again, while Ramusio is the main source for all three continents, it is only for America that there has been isolated a major secondary source used by Gastaldi, Gómara's 1552-53 *Historia general de las Indias*, heftily supplementing Ramusio with another 261 leaves in folio on the Americas. But, besides this, Ramusio himself offers somewhat more on America than on the other two continents. In his 1556 volume three on America, there are 496 leaves, while his 1550 volume one contains 409 leaves and his 1559 volume two contains only 185 leaves.[11] And modern scholars assure us that the quality of the material in this America volume is in no way lacking.

In the introduction to his monumental five-volume *New American World*, David Quinn, who has been surveying the printed sources of information on America, and lamenting how little there was, continues:

> The real turning point came with the publication of the first volume of Giovanni Battista Ramusio's collection *Navigazioni e viaggi* at Venice in 1550. Ramusio took the whole of the recently discovered extra-European lands as his field and by 1559, when this publication was complete in its three volumes, much of value on North America had

---

[10] Parks, 1955 and 1970. And, in Diego Hurtado de Mendoza, brother, we recall, of Antonio de Mendoza, Viceroy of New Spain, we find a possible informant on America to Gastaldi himself, but no Portuguese counterpart.

[11] As to volume two, we recall that much was lost in a 1557 printing house fire. The 1574 second edition, which probably includes some narratives that were lost in the first edition, has 276 leaves, still much smaller than volume three on America.

been included. The most important texts were those by Giovanni da Verrazzano in his voyage of 1524 up the North American coast, and full accounts of both the first and second Cartier voyages of 1534 and 1536, while there was also important light shed on Coronado's expedition of 1540-1542. Thereafter English, French, and German writers were to go to Ramusio as to a treasure chest, plundering it for references and for texts to translate into their own languages; this process had been completed only by the end of the sixteenth century.[12]

Earlier, Henry Harrisse, in his *Bibliotheca Americana*, had stated

> The publication of Ramusio's *Raccolta* may be said to open an era in the literary history of Voyages and Navigation. Instead of accounts carelessly copied and translated from previous collections, perpetuating errors and anachronisms, we find in this valuable work original narrations judiciously selected, carefully printed, and enriched with notices which betray the hand of a scholar of great critical acumen. Nor should we forget that we are indebted to Ramusio for the preservation of accounts of voyages of the utmost importance to the student of American history; and did his work contain only the *Relatione d'un gentilhuomo del Sig. Fernando Cortese*, and the first voyage of Jacques Cartier to Canada, these two capital relations would entitle the *Raccolta* to a prominent place in any American library.[13]

So once again, we cannot but ask: Where is the Gastaldi map of America? It is simply inconceivable considering the things brought out above that there would not be an America to accompany the Africa and the Asia.

While one could hypothesize that such a map had indeed existed, but no copies survived, noting that no copies are extant for a good number of maps which are known to have existed, and that this is especially frequent as regards large multi-sheet works, the fact that the map is conspicuously absent

---

[12] Quinn (1979, 1, lxv).

[13] Harrisse (1866, 457).

in several registers in which it should have occurred suggests that is not the case here, and that in fact it is certain that no such map existed, at least in printed form. In the maps section of a 1573 catalog of the dealer Georg Willer, we find both the Africa in eight sheets, and the Olgiato edition of Gastaldi's Asia in ten sheets, but no America.[14] Again, Ortelius, in his list of works by Gastaldi, includes Asia and Africa, but no America.[15] Also, in a 1604 letter Jan Raedemacker, describing a unique little atlas of thirty-eight maps, mostly Italian, compiled for personal use by Ortelius sometime in the 1560s, informs us that it contained Asia, Africa, Tartary, Egypt and various European lands, but no map of America.[16] Also, as we have seen, a number of applications for, and concessions of, privilege, for Gastaldi maps survive in archives, and while it is true that we can't know what may or may not be missing from these archives, almost all of Gastaldi's later works are represented in the surviving documents, including the Asia and the Africa, but there is no mention of an America. Again, while Gastaldi's Asia and Africa both occur in the Veneto-Roman (Lafrerian) atlases, there is never any sign of an America. From all of these things, we can assume that no Gastaldi America existed in print.

Yet, five copies are known of a large unsigned and undated multi-sheet America which looks precisely like the work of Gastaldi and no one else. Furthermore, in all five cases, this America makes up part of a Venetian published four-continent wall map set originally compiled in the first half of the 1570s in which the Africa and Asia are taken from Gastaldi's maps of those continents, and the Europe is partly so. Again, no one in Italy was making original large multi-sheet continental maps in the 1560s except Gastaldi, and no one at all was making them in the 1570s.[17] Also, while in two of the five sets, the America is incomplete, in those three sets where it is

---

[14] Bagrow (1948, 55).

[15] See Karrow (1993, 29). A similar later list, obviously inspired by Ortelius's, but with additions, also includes Asia and Africa, but no America (Barcía Carballido y Zúñiga, 1737-38, 3, col. 1342).

[16] Hessels reproduces the letter (1887, 772-79).

[17] Nor was anyone anywhere else making them, with the single exception of Gerard de Jode in the Netherlands, who produced a wall map of Africa (after Gastaldi) in 1569, followed in 1576-1587 by maps of the other continents (Schilder, 1996, 38), though it is unclear whether he intended, when he had all four continents, to sell them as a set. But the present Italian set clearly has nothing to do with De Jode.

complete there is a lengthy type-set descriptive text which is meant to apply to the four-continent set as a whole, and this text is headed by a conspicuous large-print title stating that the text gives a "description of the four parts of the world by Giacomo Gastaldi."[18] Is this America the Gastaldi America which all reason tells us should have, nay, must have, existed? This is the question to which we seek an answer in the present chapter. Before proceeding directly with this investigation, let's pause and give a concise description of each of the five just-mentioned four-continent wall map sets, which will be useful to us in this chapter as well as in the following three.

9.2 The Four-Continent Sets Containing America

The five descriptions, in which provenance details are presented first, are given here chronologically according to the time when each of the sets first came to light in modern times. The first description is much more detailed than the others, since it contains that copy of the America which figures most prominently in the present chapter, and it will thus be of much use to us to bring out several facets of the map at the present time.

9.2.1. *The James Ford Bell Library Set*

This set first showed up in the possession of the Paris antiquarian Charles Chadenat ca. 1920, and the well-known historian of discovery and cartography Henri Vignaud wrote an article on it.[19] The sheets of the maps in this set are not pasted together to make whole individual wall maps. Rather, the sheets are as pulled from the copper plates and they have been bound together in a limp vellum binding to make up an atlas (though they were not originally intended for this purpose, and, especially in terms of the break up of the geography into distinct geographical entities, the "atlas" is hopelessly ineffectual). The sheets of the atlas make up thirty-three atlas plates, plus one map sheet being a single-sheet 1562 world map, brought into

---

[18] This title is given in full in transcription of the original Italian and English translation at the beginning of chapter twelve.

[19] Vignaud, 1921. On Chadenat, see Barbat, 1937.

service from old stock. This unique and bizarre atlas bears the contemporary manuscript title "Quatro parte del Mondo." In the 1920s the atlas became part of the collection of Sir Leicester Harmsworth (Woodward, 1997, 3), and in 1939 it was put up for auction for Harmsworth by Sotheby's (Heijden, 1992, 96), though I have been unable to ascertain who purchased it. Its whereabouts are unknown from this time to 1956, when it turned up in the hands of one Michael Sinelnikoff of Orion Books, London (Parker, 1991, 121-23), from whom it was purchased in the same year by John Parker for the James Ford Bell Library (Parker, 1956, 4), where it now resides under the call number B1560 fCa. This set was originally compiled, as we shall see in chapter eleven, principally from Gastaldi's works, by Giovanni Francesco Camocio between the early to mid-1570s,[20] The Africa is a direct copy from Gastaldi's 1564 Africa, with changes in decor, etc.; the Asia is taken completely from Gastaldi's three-part Asia of 1559-61, but Camocio has very successfully combined the three parts into a single map; and the Europe is a direct copy from the 1564 map of Europe and western Asia (of which we shall speak more later), signed by Giovanni Pietro Contarini, but Camocio has eliminated the western fourth of Asia. This Contarini map has not been studied in any depth, but appears to contain much from some of Gastaldi's maps of parts of Europe, as his 1544 Spain (no. 1), his southeast Europe (no. 96), perhaps his Poland (no. 106), and possibly more; the America is directly from a Gastaldi manuscript America (about which much more below), although the suggestion has been made that it is taken from the America on Gastaldi's giant 1561 world map (no. 104). The plates of this map of America were not quite completed according to Camocio's aspirations, due to his untimely death (the completed sheets are shown in figure 9.1). All of the four maps were intended to be of the same size and shape and were all to have the sheeting arrangement shown in figure 9.2.

However, in the uncompleted America, the map which interests us most at the moment, two parts of the continent are missing, a large section of middle North America, and a much smaller section comprising a small expanse of northwestern Mexico including also the tip of the Baja peninsula;

---

[20] The current set, however, is a slightly later printing, for two of the maps, the Europe and the Asia, are dated 1579, in both cases changed from an earlier date.

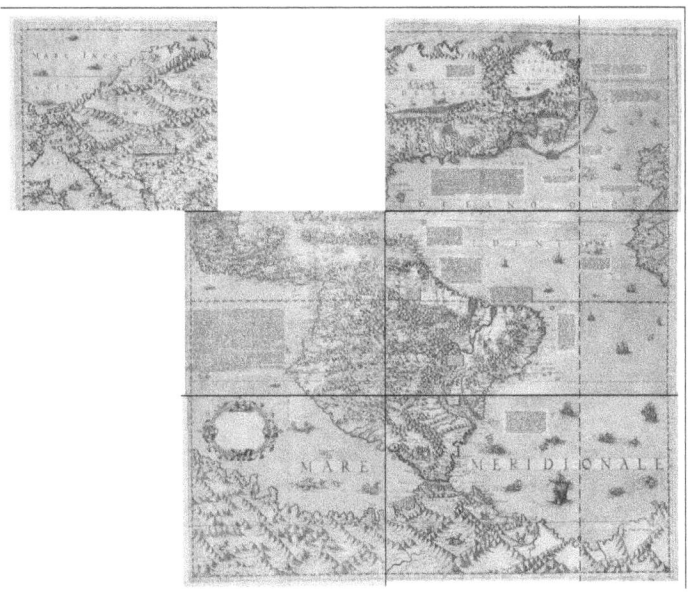

Fig. 9.1. The uncompleted America Map in the Bell Library

a sizeable tract including part of the Pacific Ocean and the imaginary Southern Continent in the southwest periphery of the map is also absent. Clearly, the map was intended to have the coverage implied in figure 9.2. Figure 9.3 gives the letter designations for each sheet of the uncompleted map to facilitate discussion. Ordinarily, when we speak of parts of a map as missing, we mean that a *sheet* or *sheets* are missing, but in the present case, an extraordinary one, using this terminology is not quite correct and would

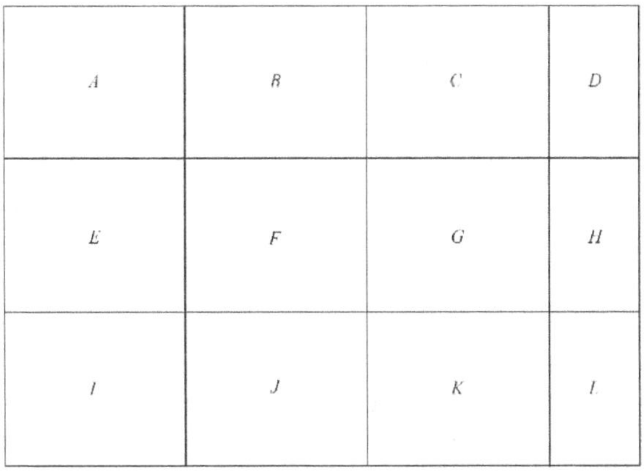

A	B	C	D
E	F	G	H
I	J	K	L

Fig. 9.2. Sheet layout of the Camocio Continental Maps

be misleading, for reasons which shall become clear as we go along.

Apropos of this, note, in figures 9.2 and 9.3, the peculiar proportions of the absent rectangular sections by comparison with the usual sheet shapes of the maps in the set (as in figure 9.1), and note also the peculiar sheeting segmentation of the complete copies of the map (as in figure 9.4). We discuss how the map came to be in this condition later in this chapter.

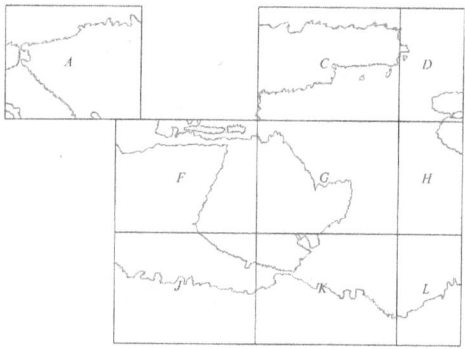

Fig. 9.3. Sheet designations for the
uncompleted America Map

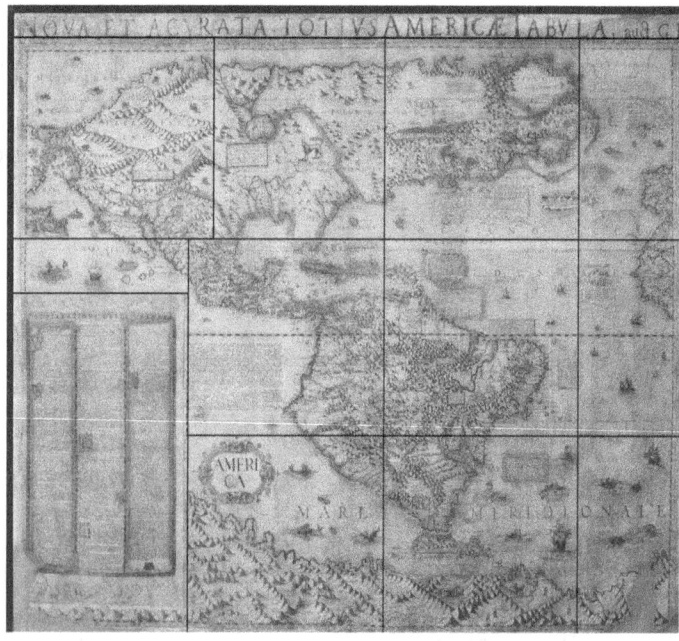

Fig. 9.4. Actual sheet lines of the Complete America Map
(Arader copy, Cartobibliography XII.)

Note that the map's large cartouche (fig. 9.2, sheet J), which would have contained the author's name, the date, and perhaps a dedication, is empty. But it is vital to pause here a moment in order to stress that, other than the missing contents of the cartouche, the cartography in all of the sheets present is complete down to the last- and most-minute detail. Nothing, however small, is missing or incomplete. Furthermore, both the drawing of the map and its subsequent engraving were done with the greatest care, and it is immediately evident that both the cartography and the engraving reflect a very high degree of meticulousness, attention to detail, expertise, and experience. Accentuation of these facts will be useful to us below.

Fig. 9.5. Ghost coastline on sheet C

Nevertheless, although at first glance we notice nothing unusual except the lack of two parts of the continent and of the cartouche's contents, a closer inspection reveals several peculiar features which clearly do not reflect the original intentions of either the draftsman or the engraver. Firstly, we see (figure 9.5) what appears to be a sort of ghost coastline skirting the west edge of sheet C and meandering southward from about 58° W longitude on the North American east coast from 36°30′ N latitude to the bottom of the sheet at 26°25′ N latitude. The engraving work seems tentative, for the original sea stippling which ran all the way to the western edge of the sheet

Fig. 9.6. Ghost coastline on lower
right corner of sheet A

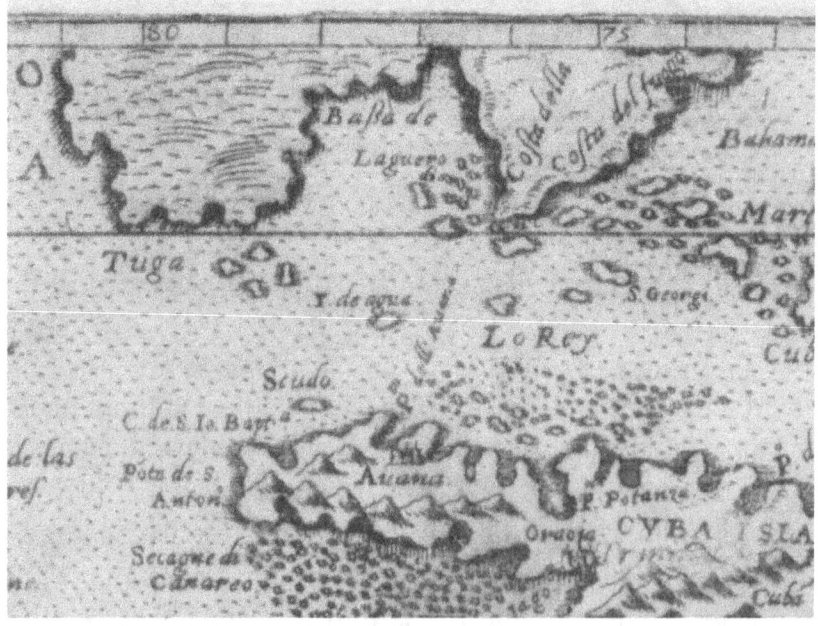

Fig. 9.7. Double Florida on sheet F

everywhere here has not been removed and runs right across the land, and there is also no coastal hachuring as seen everywhere else on the continent's coasts. This coastline is not quite complete, for it runs westward off the sheet between 27°35' to 30°20' N latitude, and, inexplicably, we find what is clearly to be taken as its continuation at the right side of sheet A (!), running from 27°35' to 30°20' and, again, having a tentative look, lacking coastal hachuring (figure 9.6).

Next we notice (figure 9.7) at the top edge of sheet F, just above Cuba, the tip of the Florida peninsula, and to the left of it, a *second* ending of that peninsula. Again, it seems rather tentatively engraved, lacking the coastal hachuring of the original peninsula to its right. Also, unlike the original peninsula, it contains no names or inland features, although the points of the sea stippling originally occupying the area have been disguised by extending them into a series of short slightly curved lines which are evidently intended to impart the impression of some kind of relief or texturing across the land, though the attempt is not very convincing. Moving back to sheet A, we see (figure 9.8) an odd snaky line running meaninglessly from the southeast corner of Japan southwards, then curving markedly to the east and then south again, running thence off the sheet. It seems somewhat more resolutely engraved than the preceding two features.

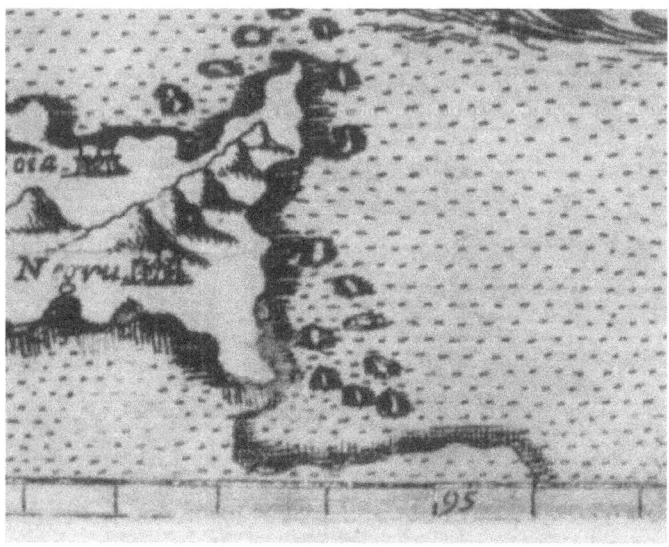

Fig. 9.8. Snaky line south of Japan on sheet A

296

Besides these odd lines, there is one more indication of meaningless, indeed, in this case, nonsensical tinkering with the map. It is clear, as we have seen, that the only proper place for the top left sheet (sheet A) is as in figure 9.2, and that a sizeable chunk of America is missing between that sheet and the next sheet to the right. Consequently, of course, there should be a quite considerable gap in the numbering of the longitude graduation marks at the right end of this top left sheet, and the left end of the sheet to the right (sheet C) in figure 9.2, a gap of ca. 39° or 40°. But no such gap in numbering is present! Impossibly, the numbering sequence of the longitude marks continues uninterrupted from the left end of the sheet at the right onto the right end of the sheet at the left! That is, beginning from the third such marking to the right of the left end of the right sheet, we have 56°, 57°, and 58° W longitude, and beginning from the right end of the left sheet, whose proper position is ca. 40° to the left, or west, of the other sheet, the sequence mysteriously and nonsensically continues westward in the same progression, 59°, 60°, 61°, and so on, to 106° W., This is an absurdity which puts the east end of Asia even further east than Columbus had in mind. In the copy of this map corrected by Donato Bertelli ca. 1596 (of which we shall have much to say), the numbering of this spread of longitude is adjusted correctly to meet Gastaldi's intentions, that is, 100° W to 148° W). What sort of black magic is this?[21] The longitude numbering on the northwest sheet is clearly bogus, and has been applied as part of a hopeless, half-hearted attempt to obscure the fact that parts of the map have simply become lost due to an extraordinary glitch, as we shall see. Finally, latitude graduation has been applied to the left sides of sheets F and J. In this case, the graduation is correct, but it is clear from figures 9.2 and 9.1 that the line formed by the left edges of sheets F and J could not have originally been intended to be the west end of the map, and thus no graduation markings were originally intended here. While this is evident enough in itself, we shall give conclusive proof of it shortly.

---

[21] To emphasize the absurdity of this, we recall that Columbus thought that the east end of Asia was 225° E, leaving only 135° of water between the east end of Asia and the Canaries. But on our bastardized copy of the America, due to the hefty omission of 40° of longitude, the east end of Asia comes out only 101° west of the Canaries (or 259° E, a number which would have sent Columbus into paroxysms of delight! It is even farther east than the east end of Asia on the Behaim globe, where Asia attains to 253° E longitude.

Because sheet A is the same size as sheets C, F, G, J and K (all of them the size of the standard main sheets in Camocio's set of maps, as see figure 9.1), and because the left sides of F and J have latitude graduations, and, following the bogus latitude numbering applied to the top of sheet A, it would seem that we should shunt sheet A as in figure 9.2 to the right and obtain a fair rectangle with uninterrupted graduation all around. But the picture which would be obtained by doing so (see figure 9.9) is so thoroughly ridiculous, with Japan meeting up with northern Mexico, the Baja peninsula meeting up with the tip of Florida, and other gross absurdities, that we know of course that no one in their right mind would ever have pasted it together in this way and attempted to sell it.

And in fact this Bell set of maps does not (and could not) occur in the form Camocio originally intended, a set of wall maps of the four continents. Rather it occurs in the unlikely form of an atlas, the sheets of the four maps

Fig. 9.9. Absurdly closed-up America, showing sheetlines

298

making up its pages.[22] In this form, it was evidently thought or hoped that the tinkerings and doctorings described above would perhaps be sufficient to delude one who perused the book's pages into not noticing the gross discontinuities in the geography of the defective America map. How the map came to be in this condition will be brought out below.[23]

9.2.2. *The Correr Museum Library Set*[24]

There are two types of these five sets. The first and original type is represented by type one, of which we have just spoken, compiled by Giovanni Francesco Camocio in ca. 1570-75 (?), and of which only one copy (that in the Bell Library) is known. The second type, represented by all remaining items in this account, nos. two to five, is basically the continuation and culmination, of the failed Camocio set, and it was compiled by Donato Bertelli at some time between 1592 and 1604, which date span is certain. We shall arrive at a more precise estimate for Bertelli's compilation (ca. 1596) in chapter twelve. Two of the four maps are from Camocio's plates, with the name changed, that is, the Europe (this copy dated 1585 ("158V"), altered from an earlier date by hand) and the undated America. The Africa and the Asia are compiled by Donato Bertelli himself,[25] but they simply copy Gastaldi. The Africa, as with Camocio's Africa, is once again taken exactly from Gastaldi's 1564 Africa. The Asia is copied directly from Ortelius's 1567 wall map of Asia. But Ortelius's map is also straight from Gastaldi, with these differences: Ortelius has given the map a different (and better) projection (although the place coordinates have not changed from Gastaldi),

---

[22] We shall shortly speak again of this atlas, and at greater length in chapter eleven, including a full bibliographical description of its makeup.

[23] Though we have virtually combined the atlas-bound sheets together in the way described, as in our figure 9.9, as have at least two other scholars (Burden, 1996, p. 45; and Woodward, 1997, figure 4), it goes without saying that the actual sheets were never combined in this way in the sixteenth century, and so these "reproductions" do not reflect anything that ever actually existed in reality.

[24] No printed notice of the set appeared until 1923 (Almagià, 1923), which is the date when it first became known to scholars, two years after Vignaud's 1921 first printed notice of the set now in the Bell library.

[25] All four maps in the present Correr set have been reproduced, the Europe in Heijden, 1992, pp. 94-95; the America in Caraci, 1927, pls. 32-40; the Asia in Gasparrini Leporace (1954, pl. 19), and the Africa in Betz (2007, p. 126).

a north coast has been added to Asia, and some improvements have been made in archipelagic Asia. No copy of either of the Bertelli maps, whether making up part of a four-continent set, or as an individual map, carries a date, though they both carry dedications to Paolo Nani as Procurator of St. Mark's, and since he became procurator in November 1573 (and retained that position until his death in 1608), they were made after that date. Sets three, four, and five have all served as seventeenth century wall maps for someone. But the second set, in the Correr Museum, is different. Its America is still in the incomplete condition as in the Bell Library set, and the Europe is missing seven of twelve sheets. Only the four sheets in the top row and the first sheet in the second row are present (that is, sheets A, B, C, D, and F as in fig. 9.1). The Bertelli Africa and Asia are complete. It appears to have come into Bertelli's hands ca. between 1585 and 1596. All in all, the set gives a rather desultory impression. But in fact, it is quite interesting and valuable, due to one detail which provides us with valuable information unavailable elsewhere. At the bottom of the cartouche of the Europe in the Bell set, we find engraved "Alla libreria della Piramide" (At the shop of the Pyramid), where "Piramide" is Camocio's shop insignia. At the bottom of the Correr set's Europe cartouche, though both maps are from the same plates, we find in this place only "Alla libreria della," but no insignia, and the signs of an erasure are clearly evident (see figure 9.10).

Fig. 9.10. Erasure on the Europe map in the Correr set

Then, in the Europe of set four, in this place, and still from the same plate, we find "Alla libraria della S. Marcho" (At the shop of St. Mark's), where "S. Marc[h]o" is the insignia of Bertelli's shop. We don't find this in set three for reasons we needn't enter into here (see Cartobibliography entries [V.-XII.] and [V.-VIII.]), and in set five, the Europe map is missing. But the insignia "S. Marcho" would usually have been in the sets sold. Clearly, Bertelli was, when he had these maps in hand, changing the set from a Camocio set to a Bertelli set, and we see him at work in this Correr set.

We should note that, when Bertelli obtained the Europe and the America, he did not receive them together with the Africa and Asia, which came from his own shop, and were in fact worked up by his own hands (see the beginning of chapter twelve). Therefore, the question of whether the parts of the present group of maps should really be considered as an integrated historical artifact is rather problematic. Tending to give strength to doubts in this regard, is the fact that the maps are now four of seventy-one loose sixteenth century maps in a folder in the Library of the Museo Correr,[26] and they are not located together in this folder. Their numbers are: Europe (4), Asia (67), Africa (68), America (70) (Gallo, 1954, pp. 6, 34, and 51-52). But they are treated in the literature as a set (Almagià, Caraci, etc.), and we believe there is good reason to do so. For sets three, four, and five, as we shall see, all come from the shop of the Scolaris, who had obtained them from the Bertellis, as detailed in chapter twelve. No copy of the set which was sold to a customer out of the Bertelli shop has come down to us. Though the Scolari copies are of course the same, one would like to have a copy of the Bertelli original. The present set, while it was not intended for sale, was in the shop of S[an] Marco, and was in Donato's hands when he was working up the set, which gives it some historical significance, and it can be taken as representing the Bertelli original. So, albeit still unfinished, we can justifiably consider it as a set, the only one we have which dates from the time when the set was in the Bertelli shop, and, indeed, it has special significance in that it reflects the time when the set was being worked up.

---

[26] The folder is identified as "Venezia Correr, Carte geografiche a stampa del >500 (folder no. 32.)", sometimes alternatively referred to as "Cartografia cartella 32". Of the seventy-one maps, fifty-five were given to the Marciana Library in the first years of the nineteenth century by Girolamo Ascania Molin, but later they were moved to the Correr Library. (Gallo, 1954, 6). Our four maps were all among those donated to the Marciana Library by Molin, as see the notation "Prov. Molin" on maps nos. 4, 67, 68, and 70 in Gallo. On Molin, see Civici musei veneziani (1988, 91-94).

9.2.3. *The University of Texas Set*

This set first appeared in an H. P. Kraus catalog in 1949 (Kraus, 1949, 10-12 and pls. XI-XIV). It next appeared some twenty years later in another Kraus catalog (Kraus, 1969?, 22-27), when it was purchased by the Harry Ransom Humanities Research Center at the University of Texas at Austin, where it now resides with the provisional call number of Cartography Collection Kraus 12, I, II, III and IV. Whether it remained with Kraus from 1949 to 1969, or was sold and then later re-obtained by him, I have not been able to discover. This set is complete, including the America, and is a 1655 printing by the Scolaris from plates made by Donato Bertelli ca. 1596, as we show in chapter twelve. The Africa and Asia are the same Bertelli variants as occur in the Correr set, as well as in the following two sets. The Texas set has remained virtually unknown to the scholarly world, except for passing mentions by Burden (1996, 47) and Woodward (1997, 24). For much more detail on this set, see our Cartobibliography at no. (V.-VIII.).

9.2.4. *The First Graham Arader Set*

This set first appeared in the hands of the Chicago map dealer George Ritzlin in the 1980s, after which it was for several years in the possession of Philip Burden, and was finally acquired by the New York antiquarian Graham Arader, who still possesses it. It is complete, *including* the America, and is a ca. 1662 Scolari printing from the Bertelli plates represented in the Texas set discussed above. It has also remained practically unknown to scholars except for passing remarks by Burden (1996, 47 and 49) and Woodward (1997, 24). For much more detail on this set, see our Cartobibliography at no. (IX.-XII.).

9.2.5. *The Second Graham Arader Set*

This set came up for sale at Sotheby's, London, in May 2002, and was purchased by Mr. Arader, in whose possession it remains. It is another example of set number four. The set lacks the Europe, but the other maps are complete, including the America. It has remained unknown to scholars.

9.2.6 *The Majority Opinion as to the Authorship of the America*

We return to the America. This map, though not officially signed, looks, as we have said, in all respects exactly like Gastaldi. It shouts Gastaldi. It is drawn in exactly the same general style as Gastaldi's maps, and the method of delineation of principal features, such as the coastlines and rivers and their contours, the hydrography, the orography and the forestry, as well as the style of drawing of the mountains and hills, the nature of their clustering and shading, as well as the clustering of the forests, is the same in every respect as typical Gastaldi work of the period 1559-1564. The same is true as to the method of designation of centers of population, the occasional vignettes showing human or animal activities, the level of density of cities and towns, and indeed the level of density of features in general, and the sparse but appealing decorative features, and, in short, every type of feature. But there is also something more, of great importance, and less immediately obvious than these things; the following will show that the map shouts Gastaldi not only in these more salient, external attributes, but also in its internal attributes, if I may put it that way, by which I mean its underlying mathematical scheme, that is, its distinctive projection, and furthermore, the very distinctive way that projection is used.

I admit that my own first reaction, some time ago, to this map was subdued, and I felt that it was probably copied by someone from Gastaldi's 1561 *Cosmographia vniversalis*, and it even seemed that it had been copied slavishly, that is, without the proper adjustments being made such that it would conform to its rectangular projection.[27] But a comparison of full reproductions revealed that the America was definitely not slavishly copied from the world map, and that the two depictions, while essentially the same, were quite different in absolute shape, precisely due to their both being quite properly and professionally accommodated to their respective projections,

[27] The impression was probably obtained by looking only at partial reproductions of the two maps, as in Wagner (1926), Parker (1956, 6)(for the America), and Elte and Israel, (1978, 38 and 42) (for the world map), by the fact that I was not yet aware of the full copies of the America, and perhaps also by being influenced by uncritical readings of Almagià (1923) and Caraci (1927), which works we shall look at below.

which will be clear from comparing the giant 1561 world map and the Arader America (figure 9.11).[28]

Clearly it had not been copied blindly from the world map, and its rectangular projection had been validly used, which suggests that it had not been copied from another map and was an original Gastaldi production. For while the use of the rectangular projection is not common for continents, it is precisely the projection which Gastaldi uses on his Africa.[29] And still more telling, it is used in the same *way* as in his Africa, that is, with the length of a degree of longitude proportionately longer than a degree of latitude, which as far as I know is unique to Gastaldi, and in fact is not a very good choice of projection here.[30] Exactly the same defect is seen in the America, but more pronounced, since the proportion of a degree of longitude to a degree of latitude is still greater than in the Africa.[31] Thus, not just the outward appearance, but even the basic mathematical scheme itself of the map unmistakably bears the mark of Gastaldi.

[28] It is most immediately clear in the form of South America, but it is clear in all places.

[29] Gastaldi also uses the projection in his great 1546 map of the Danube countries (our no. 4), as well as on most of the modern maps in his Ptolemy.

[30] The usage in fact has a notable drawback to it, especially the further one is from the equator, since it exaggerates east-west distances by comparison with north-south ones. Biasutti, speaking of the use of this unusual projection on Gastaldi's Africa, observed that it has "the shortcoming of flattening out latitudinally the geographical shapes distant from the equator. The projection therefore exaggerates the defect which first catches the eye in the appearance of the continent, and which Gastaldi has in common with the Portuguese sea charts and all the cartography of the sixteenth century, of the excessive extent given to northern Africa from west to east." (Biasutti, 1920, 330). In general, the rectangular projection was quite good enough at the time for maps of smaller areas, as typically found for parts of Europe. But it is not well suited to maps of continents or large parts of them.

[31] This was evidently necessitated here by the fact that the map covers a broad range of longitude, especially since the depiction is carried in the east all the way to the far west end of Europe, and the vast area could not be accommodated in the normal landscape format without introducing this latitude versus longitude proportion, exaggerating east-west distances still more than in the Africa. (We remember, too, regarding this area coverage, that Gastaldi defined the New World as everything west of a north-south line at the west end of Europe, giving us still another point of consistency between the ideas of Gastaldi and the map, which runs to the west end of Europe.) The full America on the 1561 world map is about 23° lesser in width than on the America, but this is quite consistent with Gastaldi (or for that matter any cartographer in the sixteenth century), for we recall his disregard for consistency in longitudes (see in chapter seven, in the section "A Cartographer's Philosophy"), especially in the farthest reaches of the world, where it is common to find on sixteenth century maps longitude variations of 20° to 30°, and in this case obviously, lessening the longitudinal breadth of America would certainly be of the greatest of assistance in helping to reconcile the geographical breadth with the landscape form of the whole map.

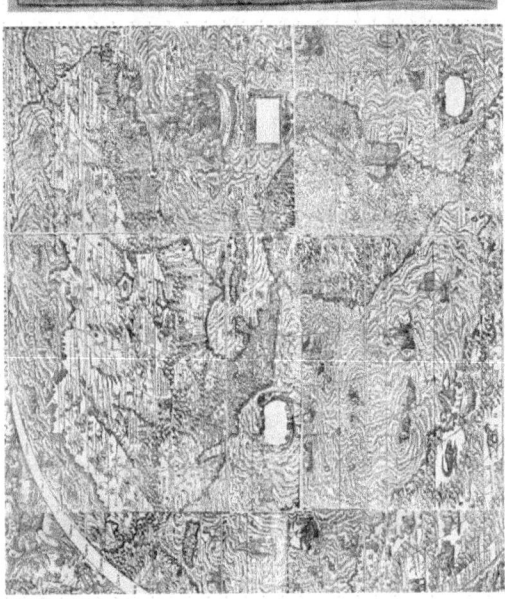

Fig. 9.11 America on the 1561 world map and on the Arader copy of the America map

In fact, the majority of scholars who have commented on it have unequivocally declared it to be by Gastaldi, including Charles Chadenat in 1921,[32] Henri Vignaud in 1921,[33] Isaac Newton Phelps Stokes in 1922,[34] Henry Raup Wagner in 1929 and again in 1937,[35] H. P. Kraus in 1949 and again in 1969,[36] John Parker in 1956,[37] Theodore Layng in 1956 and 1964,[38] Graham Arader in 2002,[39] and an anonymous writer for Sotheby's in 2002.[40] In 1939, Ronald Vere Tooley, following Caraci, called the map "anonymous,"[41] but in 1968, after having learned of the Kraus copy, of which we shall speak below, he lists it without reservation among Gastaldi's works.[42] The entire set is also referred to in 1604 as a Gastaldi set in the account books of the Officina Plantiniana, as see chapter twelve, in the section 12.2, "A terminus a quo and a terminus ad quem." Two other authorities, Burden and Woodward, suggest Gastaldi for the map, but in an indirect way, as we shall see below. Only one scholar, Almagià, has declined to touch the subject of attribution at all, and one other, Caraci, rather surprisingly following on the heels of Almagià's badly mistaken reasoning, which we shall now examine, attempted to disassociate Gastaldi from the map. We proceed to Almagià's thesis.

[32] This according to Stokes, who saw the map in the summer of 1921 in Chadenat's shop in Paris (Stokes, 1915-28, 4, [941]).

[33] Vignaud (1921, 2). Accepted by his reviewer in the Geographical Journal, 58 (1921), 396.

[34] Stokes (1915-28, 4, [941]).

[35] Wagner (1929, 358-59; and 1937, 1, 57 and 2, 283[no. 83]).

[36] Kraus (1949, 11 and 1969?, 22).

[37] Parker (1956, 5-8).

[38] Layng (1956, 136; and 1964, 486).

[39] Graham Arader, private communication, May 6, 2002.

[40] Sotheby's, London, Auction May 8, 2002, 10:30 A.M., lot 277.

[41] Tooley, (1939, no. 83).

[42] Tooley, in Map Collectors Circle. Map collectors Series, vol. 5, no. 50 (1968), 180.

9.3 Almagià's Impossible Thesis

After Vignaud in 1921, Almagià was the next to inspect the map, although, like all, much too cursorily.[43] Having given a short but adequate description of the basic characteristics of the map, Almagià continues: "Reserving to another occasion a more detailed study of this map and of its sources, I shall point out here that the sheets of the first series, which embrace all of North America, cannot be made to coincide with those of the second,"[44] after which follows a description of various chaotic meetings of geography between sheets, as described above, when one closes the sheets to make a perfect rectangle. In other words, Almagià has adhered to the longitude numbering as given and closed the picture accordingly so there are no gaps in the depiction, although the depiction presents a geographical absurdity.

It is important to understand Almagià's perception of the artifact here. He makes no mention of the incongruity of the continuation in the longitude numbering, nor does he mention the hopeless gestures at rectification by engraving imaginary continuations. While it may be hard for us to believe now, since we know what the full map looked like from the other copies, Almagià had seen no such copies, and it is clear that he did not perceive that by shunting the northwest sheet left ca. 36°, one obtained a sensible picture albeit with missing parts, and that some tremendous shop glitch could only be responsible. The map, to him, *was* in its original form, as absurd as that original form was. In other words, he treated the "map" as if it were a finished product! Caraci, as we shall see shortly, made his own misjudgments about the map, but at least he was aware, and stated clearly that it was "unfinished" (1927, 48b). Almagià himself, speaking of Gastaldi a quarter of a century later, and enumerating some of his works, says, "perhaps he was also preparing a map of the entire New World, which he did not succeed in completing" (1948, 22a). He can only be speaking of this America, although in 1923, he does not venture to name an author.

---

[43] Almagià (1923, 300-02), writing on Molin's copy in the Correr Museum Library.

[44] Almagià (1923, 301).

Having made it clear that he took the map as a completed work, Almagià then proceeded to give his opinion as to how this absurd form had been arrived at: "I cannot explain this singular fact otherwise than by supposing that the engraver of the map would have had under his eye two different sources, one for North America, the other for South America, and that he has made the engraving directly from these, without having first executed a drawing; having started with South America and continued with the eastern sheets of North America, and having almost finished the work, it would have been noticed that it was not possible to obtain a coincidence; therefore he would have neglected the finishing touches of the map (title, dedication, scale, etc.)."[45]

While Almagià is a trifle obscure here, the words "without having first executed a drawing" make it clear what he has in mind. He visualizes a shop-technician who, perhaps pressed for time, is seeking a short-cut which combines two stages in the map production process into one, that is, the stage of drafting a working drawing and the stage of engraving, a thing no engraver would ever attempt to do, for, as the following paragraphs show, combining these two stages into one is something which literally cannot be done in reality. In short, the problem with Almagià's explanation is that it is literally impossible, and completely ignores the realities of engraving, and the always essential preparations for engraving.[46]

Very close to nothing has been written in our history of cartography about the absolutely indispensable step of preparing the plate for engraving by lightly waxing the plate, then using a *modello,* or paper drawing, exactly the same size as the desired print, and containing upon it all the details of

---

[45] Almagià (1923, 302).

[46] Before demonstrating the impossibility of Almagià's thesis, however, it is worth pointing out that, apart from that, and even allowing for the sake of discussion, the existence of a draftsman-engraver who could not only engrave directly to the plate by eye, but could even do so and mellifluously combine the depictions from two maps into one, how can we accept, considering the utterly chaotic picture obtained in the closed map, that this shortcut-seeking engraver could fail to see long before finishing his engraving, that his work was headed for utter failure, and that he would continue to be unable to perceive this right up to the point that he had engraved every detail except the contents of the cartouche? And again, note the impossible incongruity in the suggestion that the same person who produced in the sheets present the superb drawing and engraving described earlier, a person who was obviously a very talented, experienced and professional individual, could possibly make a blunder the grossness of which is hard to imagine. As we'll see now, the whole procedure is an impossible one in any event, but that is not the point here. The point is that he who produced the exquisite work in the sheets could not possibly be the same person who committed the type of blunder Almagià implies.

that print, to transfer the lines of the desired print onto the plate. While there is still no adequate treatment of the subject which is devoted to the history of cartography in particular, in 2001 print historian Michael Bury finally did justice to this process, breaking much ground, in his book *The Print in Italy, 1550-1620*.[47] Bury here deals with prints in general, but the material is applicable to cartography, that is, geographical prints as well, and in other sections of the book he does devote some special sections to cartography (including some on the work of Gastaldi). We shall not attempt to repeat all he says but shall extract from his presentation sufficient information to demonstrate the complete impossibility of Almagià's thesis.

Engraving is not drawing. A pencil or a pen moves very lightly and agilely across the paper, and a talented artist can copy by eye, from another artist's work. It was done regularly. But a burin on copper offers incomparably greater resistance to motion, and the engraver must have visual guidance in the form of visible delicate lines incised into a wax coating carefully and evenly applied to the surface of the plate. Of course, one can scratch and scrape all he wishes directly onto a plate, and whatever he scratches in will indeed print out. One handy with a burin could in fact no doubt produce crude pictures in this way. But any serious and delicate work, intended to produce anything of quality, demands the sort of drawing called a *modello*.

How is this done? Bury describes several processes and brings in considerable detail as well as a fair number of examples. As said, we shall describe only what we need to make our point. In all cases, one must start with the waxed plate, and a paper *modello* or fair copy containing all details, and exactly in the size of the wanted print.[48] The procedure easiest to describe is as follows: One first waxes the plate evenly. Then he takes the completed drawing and rubs the back of it with charcoal or chalk until it is completely covered. Then he turns the drawing back around, and lays it face

---

[47] Bury's first chapter is wholly devoted to the subject, pp. 13-28.

[48] However, a few types of detail need not be shown on the drawing, as coastal hachuring, or sea stippling.

up on the plate, taking care that it meets the plate squarely.[49] Then one takes a tracing instrument and goes over the whole drawing line by line. The best tracing instrument would be fine-pointed, but not so fine as to pierce the paper, probably something similar to the end of a modern fine ballpoint pen. Care was taken, but not always successfully, to not actually pierce the paper.[50] When the tracing was finished, the paper was lifted from the plate, and in all places where tracing had been done, a clear, but perhaps light, line of charcoal or chalk was visible on the wax, for the engraver to follow, and the actual engraving could begin, through the wax, and into the copper of the plate. When the engraving was all done, the plate was heated to remove the wax, and printing could begin. Bury describes several other procedures, but all involve the waxing of the plate, and the use of the paper *modello,* and we shall not describe them all here.

We see that Almagià's idea of a simultaneous draftsman-engraver is a chimera, a fantasy with reality only in his mind.[51] But there is more still of relevance brought out by Bury here. When one follows the procedure we have described, the image comes out the right way around on the plate. What is to the left in the drawing will come out to the left on the plate, and what is to the right will be to the right, etc. But the print pulled from the plate will, of course, come out the wrong way around. For many subjects, says Bury, the artists and engravers of the time were simply not concerned by this fact, and went right ahead with their work. Indeed, a backwards image in such cases as a picture of a horse, or a wolf, a fish, a flower, and many other subjects, such as gardeners planting, or builders constructing something, or soldiers in battle, caused no concern. But sometimes this would not do, and it was imperative to reverse the image. The example Bury gives is Christ giving his blessing, in which the right hand must not come out to be the left hand. In the case of maps, of course, reversal is *always*

---

[49] It is obvious that the paper would have to be secured once laid in place, a point Bury doesn't go into. If there was considerable empty border on the paper, one could place it so that the edges of the paper extended beyond the ends of the plate, which would be lying flat upon a table, and secure the paper with small nails or pins; there were probably other ways to make the paper secure.

[50] Sometimes a second paper copy (or modello or fair copy) of the original was made by the artist (or cartographer, etc.) to assure a paper image would be preserved, if this was considered important.

[51] In justice to Almagià, he did not of course know the things which Bury's extensive documentation shows that he dug out only after long and painstaking research, much of it in archives.

necessary. No one will buy a backwards France, or an Italy trending to the southwest, etc., etc. We shall not describe how this was done in detail, but the simplest, if not the best, way was to burnish and oil the original paper, so that the paper became transparent, and the image visible from the back, then apply the charcoal or chalk medium to the right-reading surface of the *modello,* lay the paper on the plate face down, and continue as above. Another method, evidently cleaner and better, was a double process. One completely chalked a blank sheet with colored chalk, then secured the fair drawing face up on that sheet and traced as above. The tracing in this case would leave a reversed image on the back of the original drawing, which was then laid on the plate face down (i.e., the original drawing against the waxed copper plate), and the image traced onto the wax, following the chalk lines on the back of the original. There were still other ways, but we shall not describe them here.[52] Thus, Almagià's draftsman-engraver would not only have had to engrave by eye (an impossibility in itself) he would have to do it backwards! And if we wish to add more impossibility to already doubled impossibility, since in this case we are dealing with multi-sheet maps, he would have had to do all this such that the lines crossing from sheet to sheet all met exactly as necessary.

Now, consider for a moment the implications of all this in our case. The sheets which are present are, as we pointed out earlier, exquisitely engraved. So, clearly, the complex double procedure described by Bury lies behind these sheets. For each sheet, a reversed *modello* was carefully made up, this *modello* was then laid on a waxed plate and carefully traced in order to transfer the entire image to the wax surface, and finally the colored lines in the wax were carefully followed with a burin to engrave them into the copper plate. All of this was long, difficult and tedious work for the engraver, and perhaps for others as well, if the *modello* and its tracing were

---

[52] Oddly, one such process, pouncing, is mentioned by Bury, but not described by him. It involves laying the drawing on the waxed plate, poking thousands of holes through along the lines with a pin, then applying a very fine powder to the drawing's surface, which powder penetrates the holes, and adhering to the wax, leaves a sufficient outline for the engraver to follow. By the purest of chance, I encountered two descriptions of this process in two very standard works on the history of cartography, although, as said, I have never seen the more usual processes described in our literature anywhere. See Delano Smith in Harley and Woodward (1987, 391), and Nordenskiöld (1897, 18), who describes the process, though he refers to it as pouncing only at p. 24.

done by other hands, and furthermore it was also very expensive work for which the publisher had to pay. Now, let us look again at the absurd image in figure 9.9, and ask ourselves the question: Would anyone in their right senses go to the trouble and expense we have described to reproduce this image, as ridiculous as it is repugnant? Very obviously not. Clearly, there are missing pieces here of more than one kind; there are missing pieces of the map, and there are missing pieces to the story. Since this trouble and expense would never have been expended unless the publisher felt certain beforehand that it was going to lead to a complete and sensible image, work would never have even begun if he didn't have this complete and sensible image before him in the first place. So, regardless of whatever glitch intervened to prevent this complete and sensible image from being fully engraved in copper, it is certain that such an image, a full America, did already exist on paper when work was begun, and it is equally certain that Almagià's hypothesis must be rejected as completely impossible. And it is also certain that the original intention of the publisher, Camocio, was as in figures 9.2 and 9.3, and not as in figure 9.9.

9.4 Caraci, Burden, and Woodward

Almagià's hypothesis is illogical, a chimera. But if taken seriously, it imparts a strong undeserved stigma both to the map and its maker. The map becomes relegated to a sort of limbo, a misfit artifact created by an unknown misfit craftsman, hardly more than a curiosity.[53] Unfortunately, the hypothesis was taken seriously by three other scholars, and it much influenced and vitiated their opinions and discussions. First was Caraci (1926-32, 2, 37-48).[54] Caraci examined all the many legends on the map, transcribing and translating them in full, and discussing them in some depth, as well as, to a lesser extent, investigating some of the toponyms. He found

---

[53] None of this, of course, as mentioned earlier (see note 53), would be commensurate with the exquisite nature of the drafting and engraving of the extant sheets, as described earlier, but Almagià was for some reason disinclined to notice this, or perhaps just too much in a hurry to devote to the map the time it deserved, which is what I suspect was actually the case.

[54] Caraci's article is mostly taken up by transcription and translation of the many and sometimes lengthy legends on the map and cannot really be considered a general study of the map. The present chapter is, in fact, the first true study the map has received.

that the great majority were from Ramusio, and the rest from Gómara, precisely the sources we know Gastaldi used most, and if anything further were needed to clinch Gastaldi's authorship, this was it. But under the influence of the stigma imparted to the map by Almagià, whom Caraci quotes and unwarily accepts, Caraci, driven by a misguided determination to distance Gastaldi from the map, twists and turns at six points in his article to avoid the correct attribution of the map to Gastaldi by Vignaud, whom he also quotes.[55]

The alerted reader will have no trouble in discerning the thoroughly strained and unconvincing nature of Caraci's mostly gratuitously inserted objections, and there is no need to go into them in detail here. But we should mention that at one point Caraci goes so far as to attempt to disassociate Gastaldi from Ramusio. At page 46, in note 81, Caraci, aware that the close affiliation between Gastaldi and Ramusio was well known, volunteers that recent studies have shown that "Gastaldi used a certain number of data, over and above what we know from Ramusio," but he gives no references, though he is usually a stickler for references. Now, since his article is specifically about the America map, this broad statement is both irrelevant and misleading. It is true, of course, that, besides Ramusio, Gastaldi made use of nautical charts for the coastlines in all of his maps, and it hardly need be stated that Gastaldi did not use Ramusio in making his maps of European areas. But since Caraci's statement does not specify that he has these things in mind, and could therefore be interpreted as implying something quite different, I think it important that the following statement be made: The *present writer has been studying Gastaldi for over thirty years, and believes he may state with assurance that he has long since exhausted the secondary literature on him. And it is quite certain that no study or discussion of sources for any Gastaldi map of any non-European area has ever come to any other conclusion than that the principal or, in most cases, exclusive source was Ramusio, excepting the coastlines. There is no exception.* Thus,

---

[55] Caraci, cit., at pp. 39, 46 note 81, 47 (three places), and 47 note 85. It was clear enough that the set, and the glitch which resulted in the misbegotten America, dated from a time considerably after Gastaldi's death. Obviously, then, Gastaldi could have had nothing to do with this glitch, and no reason existed to shield him from anything. The confusion and lack of clear critical thinking which permeates the writings of Almagià and Caraci on the map is astounding.

the strength of the implication of Gastaldi's authorship of the America map, inherent in the fact that the legends are mainly from Ramusio, stands undiminished. In general, the association between Ramusio's work and Gastaldi's maps of extra-European areas is very clear, thorough and strong, and a key element in understanding both men. Any statement implying otherwise is misleading and detrimental, and cannot help us, but only hinder us. Attempting to disassociate Gastaldi from Ramusio is like trying to distance Wagner from German mythology, or Gauguin from Polynesia.[56]

Actually, Caraci's greatest sin where the Gastaldi-Ramusio connection is concerned is one of omission. He makes no mention anywhere, though to do so would be germane to his findings, of the numerous scholars, such as Biasutti, Nordenskiöld, Hedin, Gezelius and many others, as brought out in our chapter four which show overwhelmingly and unequivocally that Gastaldi used principally Ramusio for non-European areas in general. One begins to gather from this and the last paragraph a hint of the degree to which the headlong campaign to deny Gastaldi authorship of the America can contribute to distorting the entire picture of Gastaldi and his work, far beyond simply considerations connected with the America itself.

Caraci, however, to his credit, having finished his review of the map legends, does begrudgingly admit, if rather confusedly, that, "What we have said here will suffice to show how nevertheless *a priori* the agreements noted between the legends of our map and Ramusio must compel us to think of Gastaldi."[57] Indeed! But this single statement in the right direction does little to lessen the damage done for an uncritical reader by Caraci's generally relentless campaign throughout his work to distance Gastaldi from the undeservedly disgraced America, and the principal effect of the work is simply to further calumniate this map supposedly produced by some anonymous inept in a Venetian shop.

---

[56] There is much more in Caraci of a similar ilk, but we shall not go further into it. The reader who might wish to do so can follow the references above.

[57] Caraci (1926-32, 2, 46, note 81).

After Almagià's and Caraci's phobic battering of the America,[58] its repute (and that of its presumably anonymous author) was so stained that its status as simply a curiosity, if not a pariah, seems to leave the last two writers to express reservations as to Gastaldi's authorship, Burden in 1996, and Woodward in 1997, unable to take the map seriously at all.[59] The observations on our map made by them are rambling, haphazard, and uncritical, although I believe we may excuse these usually very worthy scholars, since they were clearly working under the influence of the egregiously misdirected writings of Almagià and Caraci. Overall, the air of their comments would be befitting an artifact of doubtful integrity, a curiosity, as Almagià and Caraci had essentially made it out to be, which undoubtedly accounts for the offhand and random nature of their comments. The student finishes reading through these comments with a feeling of having flailed about aimlessly, and a sense of having gained, instead of solid information, only solid confusion. For instance, Burden in one paragraph (cit., 46) loosely discusses the possibility that Gastaldi made the map, concluding the paragraph with the observation that he "does not believe that Gastaldi had any direct part in this work," although it is clear that he is speaking specifically of the spoiled variant, which indeed, of course, Gastaldi truly had no part in. He then opens the following paragraph with: "This leads us to the next possibility, which is that they are most likely the work of Giovanni Francesco Camocio." The statements befuddle the mind. For there can be no question of the map's being by *either* Gastaldi (a cartographer) *or* Camocio (a publisher). As we shall see, it is by *both* Gastaldi *and* Camocio. Gastaldi was the cartographer, the draftsman, and Camocio, some years later, dealt with the engraving and the publishing. It is imperative, as with any printed map, but especially one which is problematic, to sharply distinguish the two stages, the two operations, from each other, if we hope to make any sense of anything. The thinking here hails back to Almagià's chimerical conflation of cartographer and engraver. This impossible notion underlies, and runs like a poisonous vein through, the comments of Caraci, Burden, and Woodward, hopelessly vitiating them, and

---

[58] Always remembering that they had in mind the two bastardized copies, the only ones known to them.

[59] Burden (1996, 45-47); Woodward (1997, 9 and 22-23).

this is the main reason it is hard to make much sense of their observations. We feel no need to sift through their comments in any detail.

Nevertheless, to Burden must go the credit of first suggesting in print that the America might have been copied from the 1561 *Cosmographia vniversalis* world map (our no. 104), certainly a more realistic and enlightened observation than had previously been made regarding the map's origin, and a solid step forward in relating the map, if only indirectly, to Gastaldi,[60] even if this idea, as we shall see, does not in the end stand up to inspection. Woodward also accepts the thesis of the America being copied from the world map, even stating it as a fact.[61]

9.5 The Suggestion of Burden and Woodward

The suggestion of Burden and Woodward, that the America was copied from the America on the 1561 world map, is one which has a genuine air of possibility about it, and it puts them in the camp of those many who have opined that the America is by Gastaldi, even if only indirectly, for the *Cosmographia vniversalis* itself is of course by Gastaldi. If the America is not Gastaldi, it is Gastaldian, and the cartography is Gastaldi's. But, as said, the suggestion does not stand up to scrutiny. For one thing, it is not consistent with the known genesis of the other three maps of the set, all of which derive directly from models from 1559-1564 which were separate continental maps themselves, and not taken from a world map, and we can assume that Camocio would have preferred that the same be true of the

---

[60] Burden (1996, 46). The "Cosmographia Vniversalis" had been unknown to Almagià and Caraci, prompting them both to suggest several unlikely cartographical sources for the map which in fact it could have had nothing to do with, and there is no need to repeat their conjectures here, other than to mention that they undoubtedly contributed to the general confusion around the map.

[61] Woodward (1997, 22). He also offers a short explanation of the condition of the bastardized variant which is not altogether clear, but is reminiscent of Almagià's old explanation, and just as impossible for the same reasons (1997, 9). Burden does the same (1996, 46). Woodward also errs, as did the present writer formerly (see above in the present chapter), in stating that the shape of the continent on the America is just like that on the "Cosmographia Vniversalis", and not accommodated properly to its projection (Woodward, cit, 22), which is quite incorrect. Neither Burden nor Woodward takes any notice of the opinions of the many authorities cited earlier who unequivocally attribute the map to Gastaldi. Perhaps they were unaware of them, or possibly they were so inexplicably mesmerized by Almagià's impossible idea and the resulting unjustified devaluation of the map, that they simply did not wish to acknowledge them.

fourth and last continent, America. More significantly, we note the obvious fact that the America contains a large number of sometimes quite lengthy legends which are not to be found on the world map, and it also contains a larger number of toponyms than America on the world map, especially in South and Central America. If we posit, then, that the America was copied by a publisher from the world map, then we must *ipso facto* assume that he took the trouble to dig deep and long in the texts of Ramusio and, to a lesser degree, Gómara[62] in order to find appropriate material for this bevy of legends, located at numerous places all across the map. While I don't doubt that Camocio could have handled without trouble the conversion of the image of America from an oval projection to a rectangular one,[63] the type of time-consuming book work needed to come up with the extensive texts of the legends does not seem to me the sort of labor that Camocio would have been likely to enter upon.

But besides these more general considerations, there are two very precise and definite considerations which conclusively close the book on this possibility, and which simultaneously help us date the time of composition of Gastaldi's original manuscript America. Firstly, on the America, unlike on all other of the large maps which depict the Strait of Anian, no name has been given to the strait. We remember that, if our ideas are correct, Gastaldi's thinking was that the continents were either solidly joined, or, if not, came very close together, close enough to allow for occasional movement between the continents, accidental or otherwise, by both people and animals. By the nature of this idea, one's consciousness is focused solely on passage from landmass to landmass. The union of waters resulting has no significance. It has no connection to the mental process which produced the cartographic datum, and in fact comes about as an incidental by-product. It would be altogether natural that it would not occur to one at first that there were any necessity to name this coincidentally produced feature, and indeed, the fact that it were quite conjectural might cause one to consider naming it as a

---

[62] As we have seen, Caraci (1926-32, 2, pp. 40-46) has shown that these texts are the sources for all the legends, and they are probably also the principal source for the increased nomenclature.

[63] We should remember that this rectangular projection, of an extremely unusual type, is the same as that used by Gastaldi in another of the four-continent maps, Gastaldi's authorship of which has never been doubted by anyone, that is, the Africa.

rather presumptuous act. This, I think, is very possibly the explanation for the lack of a name here, and we can even suggest what circumstances might have caused Gastaldi to nevertheless apply a name not long afterwards.

We recall that in his 1561 booklet *La Vniversale descrittione del mondo*, Gastaldi describes one after the other the confines of the continents,[64] and in all cases uses named geographical features to do so, preferring names of water features when possible, after the recommendation of Ptolemy. Gastaldi never uses these features themselves to describe the confines, rather he uses them as points through which, from which, and to which he establishes lines which then are described as extending (*estendendo, distendendo*, etc.), or continuing (*continuando*), to such or other place, or which are drawn (*si tira*), or which we follow (*seguitando*), to such or other place, and which make the boundaries. Sometimes the lines are meridians or parallels, but sometimes not. The words line (*linea*), meridian (*meridiano*), and parallel (*paralello*) occur thirty-one times in the process, most often line (*linea*), which occurs twenty times. The whole system depends on the names of the geographical features for its points of reference, most of them generally known names. Twice, in describing the limits of Asia, he must use the strait to establish such a point of reference:

> La terza parte nominata Asia, ha i suoi confini uerso Leuante, benchè nel detto Mapamondo pare che sia uerso Ponente; il stretto detto Anian, et si distende con una linea per il golfo Cheinan, e passa nel mare Oceano de Mangi fino al Meridiano che è al fin dell'Isola di Giapam uerso Leuante, etc. (The third part called Asia has its confine[65] toward the east, although on the said world map it appears that it is toward the west, the strait named Anian, and it extends with a line through the gulf Cheinan, and passes in the Ocean sea of Mangi up to the meridian which is at the end of the Island of Giapam toward the west, etc.);

---

[64] Gastaldi (1561, 11-14).

[65] Gastaldi has the plural "confini," but should have used the singular, since this is clearly the referent for the verb form "si distende" which comes shortly after. Such points of grammatical disagreement are frequent in Gastaldi's writing, as they were for many at the time.

Fig. 9.12. Detail of the Strait on
Bell Library sheet A

and again, having made his circuit of Asia, he concludes,

> e il suo confino uerso Settentrione, è una linea la quale principia alla
> linea della fonte del fiume Don, nel mare Sitico, fin'al stretto Anian,
> etc. (and its confine toward the north, is a line which begins at the line
> from the source of the river Don, in the Scythian sea, as far as the
> strait Anian, etc.).

The implication is strong that it was only upon describing these bounds,
using predominantly water courses, which, of course, must have names if the
description is to be intelligible, that he was first compelled to borrow the
name of a land province to give to his strait, and since not just the booklet of
1561, but the accompanying world map of the same date include the name,
but the America does not (and we recall that this America is notable for its
precise attention to every last detail), the America could not have been
copied from the world map, and must somewhat precede it in time.

The second circumstance relates to the physical appearance of the
strait on the map. Even though the America presents the largest-scale
representation of the strait out of those inter-related first maps which show it,
on this map the continents are made to approach so close at two points in the

319

wriggling strait that the coastal shadings overlap, and they do so deeply at the northern of the two points, to the point that one must look closely to be sure that there is indeed a separation instead of a connection (see figure 9.12).

The map is drawn with great care, and this can only have been intentional. Of course, for the two landmasses to approach so close that animals could actually have occasionally swum the distance, or effected a crossing on a floating log, etc., a gap so small is necessary that it could not possibly be shown really clearly except on maps of much larger scale than these, and in drawing the feature here it appears that in an attempt to approximate this tiny gap the coasts have been pulled together so closely that there is a disconcerting hint of uncertainty that there is truly a separation. It is the sort of feature that might have provoked criticism, or self-criticism, and in fact on all the other maps, the appearance is that care has been taken to provide as close an approach as possible at the scale being used while still making it sufficiently clear that there is indeed a separation, with two separately distinguishable coasts on either side of the strait. The America, as we have pointed out, was engraved with exquisite care and attention to detail. It is, I think, not conceivable that, if someone had copied the Bell America from the world map, he could have omitted this important and conspicuous name, and that he would not have left a perceivable gap between the two continents, as we see on the "Cosmographia Vniversalis," and these considerations definitely disallow the possibility that the America was copied from the world map.

Now let's see what this finding does for us. We have known all along that the compilation of the set of wall maps by Camocio occurred in the 1570s. And we also know that the maps of the set are almost entirely from Gastaldi's cartography. Gastaldi died in 1566, so obviously the Gastaldi models for the maps used were not specifically created as models for the four wall maps just before they were made. They are taken from Gastaldi models made considerably earlier. The Asia was made from the Three Parts of Asia *printed and published* in 1559-1561, and the Africa and the Europe were *printed and published* in 1564, and, we add, that the period covered is the span 1559-1564 when all the great Gastaldi-Licinio maps were produced.

Now, from what we have just seen, the implication is inescapable that the original model for the America map was not the *Cosmographia vniversalis* of 1561, but had to have preceded it. The intimation is clear that the original had to have been made the first years of the Gastaldi-Licinio period, that is, sometime in the period from 1559 to earlier 1561, before the *Cosmographia vniversalis* was made. But as we have seen, the evidence speaks very strongly against there having existed a *printed and published* America in this period. The only possible answer that fits all the facts is that Gastaldi produced his America in manuscript, just as the other maps were originally produced in manuscript, but while those maps went on to be published, the America was not. In our scenario, we must assume that, for some reason, unlike the other maps, Gastaldi decided to temporarily hold back the America in manuscript, that it remained in manuscript until his death, and that Camocio at some later date came into possession of that manuscript. The information in the following paragraphs gives decisive support to such a supposition.

First, we note that there is abundant precedence, as we have mentioned elsewhere, for Gastaldi's holding maps back in manuscript form, for whatever reasons, perhaps seeking further information, perhaps uncertain yet about certain areas on the maps, or perhaps for other reasons. There is the 1567 Puglia, the 1568 Padua, and the 1570 Lombardy.[66] Also, Gastaldi's map of Anatolia is implied as being forthcoming in 1559, since it is mentioned in a privilege application for that year,[67] though it didn't appear until 1564. Most significantly, there was his giant Africa which we know he had been working on in the 1540s,[68] and to judge from the way Gastaldi speaks of it at that time, it seems likely it was in completed form not long after. But he did not publish it at that time, very probably because he was waiting for more information, which indeed he would get from Barros in 1554, or perhaps slightly earlier, and even when it was complete in the form

---

[66] We do not at all agree with Almagià's hypothesis of a lost ca. 1559 woodcut edition of the Lombardy, as see our Cartobibliography entry no. 124.

[67] Almagià (1939, *carta*, 8); and Almagià (1962, 2, note 3).

[68] See note 8 above.

we know it, which we see from Karrow may have been no later than 1562,[69] it was not published until 1564. Probably he was waiting for still more information, which, as we shall see, was certainly the case with the America. No doubt there were other such held-back maps. As Almagià said,[70] there were probably various maps in sundry stages of preparation when Gastaldi died, and my instinctive feeling is the same. And, as to the America, we can adduce very strong and specific reasons why that map in particular would have been among those for which Gastaldi had good reasons to temporarily hold it back from the press.

9.6 Why Would Gastaldi Have Held his America in Manuscript?

As we saw in the previous chapter, Gastaldi did not and could not know whether Asia and America were connected or separated. Strong reasons existed to *prefer* a separation over a connection, reasons rooted in esthetics and convenience of presentation; similarly strong reasons existed to prefer a connecton or near-connection, reasons rooted in the evidence of human and animal life in America. Actual geographical proof (an eyewitness account) did not exist. Gastaldi and others felt quite at liberty making world maps which showed either one concept or the other. But Gastaldi could not have in good conscience felt so free to take this liberty with one of the great showpiece continental maps he and Licinio were producing at the time, far superior products to any that Gastaldi had produced before, and products upon which his reputation would depend.[71] Willy-nilly, one might say, since no one knew the real relationship of the two continents, if one were going to make a map of America at all, he would have no choice but to take the risk,

---

[69] Karrow (1993, 243-44).

[70] Almagià (1939, *carta*, 9).

[71] There is, besides, a subtle distinction between the showing of conjectural geography on a map of a particular area, and the showing of that same conjectural geography on a world map. On a world map, one must show *all*, simply because it is inherently demanded by the nature of the map's subject, which is the whole earth. But a map of a particular area reflects a conscious choice of that area by the mapmaker, with the attendant implication that he has good information on that area, and thus his sense of responsibility for showing things correctly in that area is higher than in the case of a world map.

and commit himself one way or the other.[72] But what if one had good cause to believe that the true relation of the continents might shortly be revealed? In such a case, he would certainly not rush forward but bide his time. The logical procedure in such a case would have been to draw the whole map, to not waste time if the expected information came, but hold it back from the press until that information came, at which point he could go straight into print. The northwest sheet, the only sheet which would vary sharply depending upon the information received could be left blank, pending the awaited new information, or two variants could be drawn, allowing him to go to press immediately. Gastaldi was obviously energetic, and probably worked fast, and this is no doubt the alternative he would have chosen.[73] As we shall now show, Gastaldi would indeed have had good reason to believe that the question might soon be resolved by new information from Spanish sources, and therefore hold his America temporarily in manuscript.

As early as 1536, Ramusio had felt confident that the mystery of the relationship of America in the west to Asia would soon be resolved. It was in the introductory material to a little work on the Magellan navigation which Ramusio edited in this year, when Ramusio had already been gathering information on the discoveries for over ten years,[74] that he expressed his original optimism. He wrote, "si può tener per certo, che alli tempi nostri si verrà a cognitione, se la parte della nostra terra ferma della Asia si congiungne in Oriente con la terra ferma delle Indie occidentali di sopra il tropico del cancro" (it can be held for certain that in our times there will come cognition whether the part of our terra firma of Asia joins in the East

---

[72] Nor could he well have resorted in the case of the America to the compromise he used to bring out his Asia, where he simply stops the depiction at 50° N, leaving the possibility of a connection or a separation, since the east coast of America was known up to 60° N, and indeed considerably higher figures existed, including a claim by Cabot to have reached 67° N, a reading cited by Ramusio himself in the discourse to Fracastoro at the head of volume three of the *Navigationi* (Ramusio, 1967-70, 3, 6th page of the discourse to Fracastoro; Milanesi ed., 1978-88, 5, 12). With other cartographers (and Gastaldi himself) showing the American east coast up to latitudes such as these, it could hardly have seemed a viable procedure to cut that coast at 50°, which would be inevitable if he were to do so at the west coast.

[73] There would be no risk in these advance drawings, for the information received would not be very detailed in nature, but principally would simply provide the answer to the long-sought question of whether the two continents were connected or separated.

[74] Parks (1955,"Ramusio's Literary History," 134-40).

with the terra firma of the west Indies above the tropic of Cancer).[75]
Ramusio had good reason for his optimism. During only 40 or 50 years, the
entire east coast of the continent had become known up to at least 60° N, and
in the south all the way to Tierra del Fuego, and the entire west coast of
South America and Central America had become known as well, while
Cortes and Guzman were busily revealing the northwest coast of Mexico.
Within a few years after this, Ramusio and with him, Gastaldi, would receive
word of Ulloa reaching at least 30° in 1539-40, and Marcos de Nizza
sighting the west coast in 35° N latitude, followed again still later by
information received about 1553 from Gómara of the coast then being
known up to 40°, due to the explorations of Cabrillo, although Gómara fails
to name that explorer. Gómara also contradictorily states, in the same work,
that the coast was then known up to 45° N, a fact which may have led
Gastaldi to mistrust him (for the documentation of these explorations, see the
previous chapter). Nevertheless, it was clear that progress up the west coast
continued, although the solution to the problem of the relationship of the two
continents had still not been found. While it was probably the continued lack
of a solution to the great problem that made up the strongest element of the
vexation and impatience Ramusio expresses in the 1553 dated preface to
volume three of the *Navigazioni* at the insufficiency of geographical
information available on the New World, it is also obvious that he and
Gastaldi would have had in general strong foundation for expecting that the
wanted information might become available at any time.

But besides these general bases for expectation of new Spanish
knowledge, there is excellent reason to believe that Gastaldi had a more
specific basis for this. The Spanish were at the time preparing for a new
expedition from the west coast of New Spain, of which we have spoken
some in chapter eight. The principal purpose was to sail across to the East
Indies, and then try to find a route back, a problem which Spain had been
trying unsuccessfully to resolve for forty years, since the time of Magellan's
voyage. But, as we shall see shortly, due to the aspirations of the
expedition's Pilot Major, chosen in 1553 by the king, and current ideas

---

[75] Ramusio (1536, fol. 4). I have quoted after Milanesi (1992, 30, note 11). The ascription of the work to
Ramusio, once considered equivocal, has been definitely established (Donattini, 1992, 122, 124-29, 131 and
150, no. 54).

concerning the proximity of the East, and the misunderstood nature of the northwest coast, there was reason to believe that the expedition might well follow that northwest coast far to the north. Preparations for the expedition went back to 1557.[76] The most knowledgeable person regarding trans-Pacific sailing was the friar and cosmographer Andrés de Urdaneta, a resident of New Spain of whom we have spoken before as a person with much interest in the question of the Northwest Passage,[77] and of the relation of the New World to China, etc. Though, because of his religious occupation, he could not be chosen as commander-general of the expedition, he was asked by King Philip to serve as chief pilot, and to him was given the choice to select the commander. He chose Miguel López de Legazpi, a personal friend, and the great expedition is usually referred to as the Legazpi Expedition.[78] In a long memorial to the king of ca. spring 1561, Urdaneta discusses aspects of the voyage, including several possible routes for the departing expedition to follow. Urdaneta speaks of word having been received in New Spain of a French voyage which succeeded in sailing through a passage from the Atlantic to the Pacific, existing there between 40° and 50° N latitude, and among the routes he recommends for the new voyage is one following the west coast of New Spain north to the areas discovered by Cabrillo and Ferrelo in 1542-43.[79] He wishes to explore for a "big water" of which the Indians had spoken in signs to Cabrillo, to find out if the land ends in that direction, and try to find out what lay between New Spain and

---

[76] Levesque (1992, vol. 2, 25), says Viceroy Luis de Velasco ordered preparation of ships to begin December 13, 1557. He was acting on an order of the king (Levesque, cit., 29) which had to have been issued several months earlier, and no doubt there had been discussions of the idea in Spain some time before that order was sent. Morison (*Southern Voyages*, 493), says mistakenly that the king's order to Velasco was of September 24, 1559, but that is the date of the king's request to Urdaneta to serve as chief pilot to the expedition.

[77] See our previous chapter for more on Urdaneta, and on his interest in the Northwest Passage, including general references on Urdaneta.

[78] Morison (*Southern Voyages*, 493) refers to it as the Legazpi-Urdaneta voyage.

[79] We remember it was believed that this coast had a much more westerly trend than it has in reality, that China and the Orient were not far distant, and that the west coast might run right into China or come close to it. Cabrillo's men believed that they had almost reached China in their 1542-43 voyage up the west coast, and the idea that that coast was close to China remained current at the time of Vizcaino's expedition up the coast in the early seventeenth century.

China.[80] Though Urdaneta thought the expedition might leave as early as autumn, 1561,[81] preparations dragged on and it did not depart until November 21, 1564, and Urdaneta was back in Acapulco only in October of 1565. Word of it would not have reached Europe until sometime in 1566, too late to be of any use to Gastaldi, who died in that year. While the voyage succeeded in finding a return route, it did not solve the question of the relationship of America to Asia, and no further attempts to solve that were made until many years later.

Now, not only is it clear that Urdaneta had much interest in the Northwest Passage and related questions, there is reason to believe that he spoke of this to others, evidently to the point that tales seem to have arisen to the effect that he actually discovered it.[82] But, apart from Urdaneta, no doubt other highly placed persons knew of and discussed the impending voyage, at various times from its inception ca. 1557. We recall that Ramusio had important contacts with prominent Spaniards, and this is principally how he came by his vast information on the Americas. In the case of one of the most important of these persons, Diego Hurtada de Mendoza, who was the Spanish ambassador to Venice (and whose brother, Antonio Mendoza, was the first Viceroy of New Spain), we know that Gastaldi himself was well acquainted, for he had provided Gastaldi with the information for his large 1544 map of Spain.[83] It is reasonable to assume that Gastaldi may well have had other such contacts through Ramusio, as well as possibly through his own associations with the Venetian Senate, for the Senate entrusted Gastaldi with important cartographic projects on at least three occasions, and referred

---

[80] See our previous chapter, at note 38 and in the quote from Urdaneta on the same page for reference to modern printings of the full memorandum, and for a quotation of the part spoken of here from Mitchell (1961, 109-10), who, as mentioned earlier, says Urdaneta's interests are clearly wider than just a voyage to the Philippines, and believes Urdaneta was interested in discovery of the Northwest Passage.

[81] Quoted in Mitchell, (1964, 107).

[82] In a letter to the king of January 30, 1565, Pedro Menéndez de Avilés, Admiral to the Indies fleet (and mentioned by Urdaneta in regard to the Northwest Passage in his 1561 memorial), says that Urdaneta had had information of such a possible strait for many years, and "that he discussed the way of promoting its discovery" (quoted in Mitchell, 1964, 147); and the English nobleman Humphrey Gilbert said that in 1568 a Spanish nobleman by the name of Salvatierra told him that Urdaneta had found a Northwest Passage in about 1556 or 1557 (Mitchell, cit., 147) a little past our time, but implying that talk no doubt stemming from the great expedition had probably been spreading about for a long time. See also chapter eight, note 37.

[83] Gastaldi may have maintained a contact with Mendoza, who died in 1575.

to him as "our cosmographer." It would also be reasonable for Gastaldi to have maintained these contacts after Ramusio's death in 1557, and, of course, also reasonable to presume that he, just as Ramusio, would have been particularly interested in any geographical information he could obtain. Also significant here is the fact that, though Spain had its own mapmakers, these were principally makers of coastal charts of the new Spanish colonial lands, and Spanish officials seem to have turned to the Venetian cartographic community, the most active in the world at the time, for printed maps, implying intercourse between highly placed Spaniards and the Venetian mapping community. In 1568 Luis Hurtado de Toledo, then Spain's ambassador to Venice, had an atlas compiled to his order in Venice for King Philip,[84] and several Veneto-Roman atlases of the period still exist in the Spanish National Library in Madrid which came directly from the old King's Library. In short, substantial reason does exist to believe that Gastaldi would have had knowledge of Spain's projected expedition, of the fact that it was thought possible that the expedition might resolve the question of the relation of America to Asia, and of the fact that it was thought (as by Urdaneta himself, as we have seen) that the expedition might depart as soon as 1561. Gastaldi knew that previous Spanish expeditions had succeeded in pushing knowledge ever farther, and certainly, with the eminent possibility of receipt of conclusive information on the old question, he would not have been inclined to rush ahead and commit himself in print on a map of America when his depiction might then be proved quite wrong within a year or so of publication.

These were good reasons indeed to hold back temporarily on the publication of the map of America, by a man who we know was in the habit of holding in manuscript maps for which he believed he could receive new information, and I think we need have no doubt that this is precisely what Gastaldi was doing. Here then is the reason there was no *printed* Gastaldi America corresponding to the Gastaldi maps of Africa and Asia which Camocio used in his four-continent attempt. And here, right in front of our eyes all along, in the sets of wall maps of the continents, is the Gastaldi

---

[84] Beans (1943, 1-2 and 5). The atlas was compiled by the well-known Venetian printer and publisher Bolognino Zaltieri.

America which logic has told us all along had to have existed as accompaniment to the Gastaldi Africa and Asia.

We may consider our case closed at this point. The America is definitely Gastaldi, in the direct sense, and was copied from a ca. 1560 (or possibly very slightly earlier) Gastaldi manuscript America, which was made as a complement to the Africa and Asia but was left for the time in manuscript. However, we still have one more loose end to tackle before closing our chapter, the question of how the defective incomplete form of the map which we see in the Bell and Correr copies arrived at its condition.

9.7 How Did the Bell and Correr Copies Become Spoiled?

Here we cannot hope to come up with a complete and exact answer. But some of the added engraved markings described earlier, together with certain shortcomings in Gastaldi's original cartography, provide us with two clues which will be sufficient to arrive at a general idea of a scenario which cannot be far from the correct one. We start with the shortcomings in Gastaldi's cartography. In the very earliest years of the cartography of the North American east coast, that is, up to the time some real knowledge of the principal section of that coast, that part between the far northern lands in the area of Labrador, and the far southern parts, from about Florida on southwards, began to be brought into view in the 1520s by Verrazzano and Gomez, maps showed the eastern most extent of North America, in the far north, as extending far beyond the easternmost extent of the sister continent to the south, South America. But thereafter, the opposite becomes the case, and South America's maximum eastward extent begins, properly,[85] to exceed that of North America, and, though by no means with perfect consistency, this difference in the right direction continues to grow over the years from ca. 1530 to the 1560s on maps.[86]

But some mapmakers shortly began again to give North America a greater eastward extension than was being shown by most. My instinctive

---

[85] Actually, the easternmost reach of North America is ca. 22 degrees west of the east end of South America.

[86] This short survey is based upon the chronological presentation of world maps and maps of North America in the works of Shirley and Burden.

feeling is that this new and incorrect eastward thrust of North America is not a revival of that of the earliest years, but due to some different misunderstanding, but I admit that I have not been able to put my finger on what its source might be.[87] Whatever its cause, it reaches its maximum in the maps of Gastaldi.[88] It is conspicuous on Gastaldi's 1561 *Cosmographia*

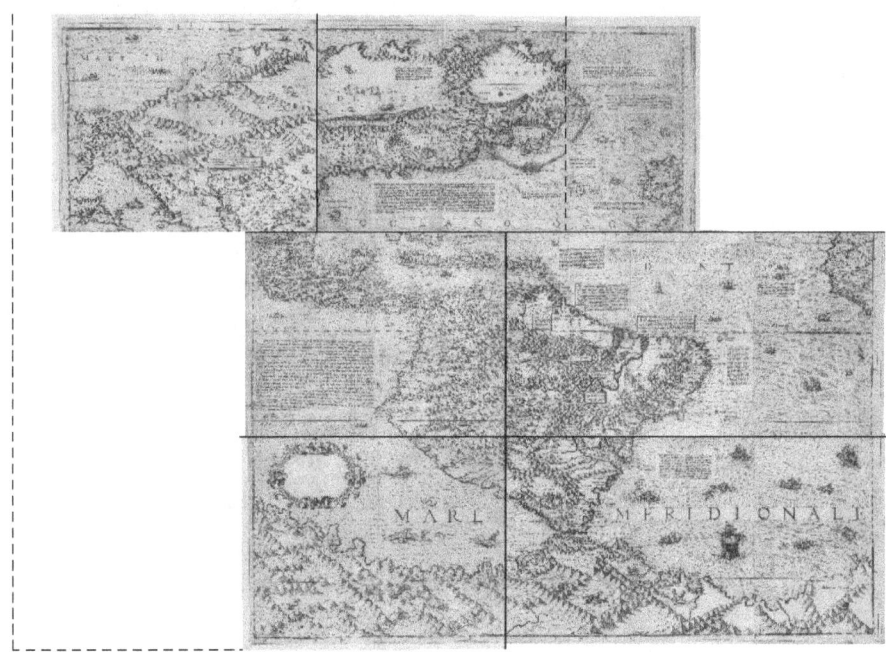

Fig. 9.13. Apparently intended arrangement of incomplete Bell Library America

vniversalis world map, where the east end of North America is about 11° east of the east end of South America. In the Gastaldi America, it is approximately the same, ca. 12°, but, due to Gastaldi's rectangular projection, the distorting effect of which becomes proportionately greater the further we are from the equator, the visual effect is of a truly enormous eastward extension, resulting in an unappealing picture, unique and inconsistent with any other map. A glance at the America (see figure 9.4) reveals immediately the unnatural impression made. I have included here

---

[87] Again, we can conveniently trace these opposed tendencies in Shirley and Burden.

[88] It is far less pronounced in Gastaldi's 1546 world map (and in later editions of that as well), where he seems to take a middle of the road approach to the point, so whatever swung him in the new direction occurred after 1546.

(figure 9.14) a reproduction of a map showing the correct tendency, one in fact close to reality in this regard, and have intentionally chosen for the purpose a map published by Camocio, copied directly from a 1553 map by Nicolay. Thus, our first clue.

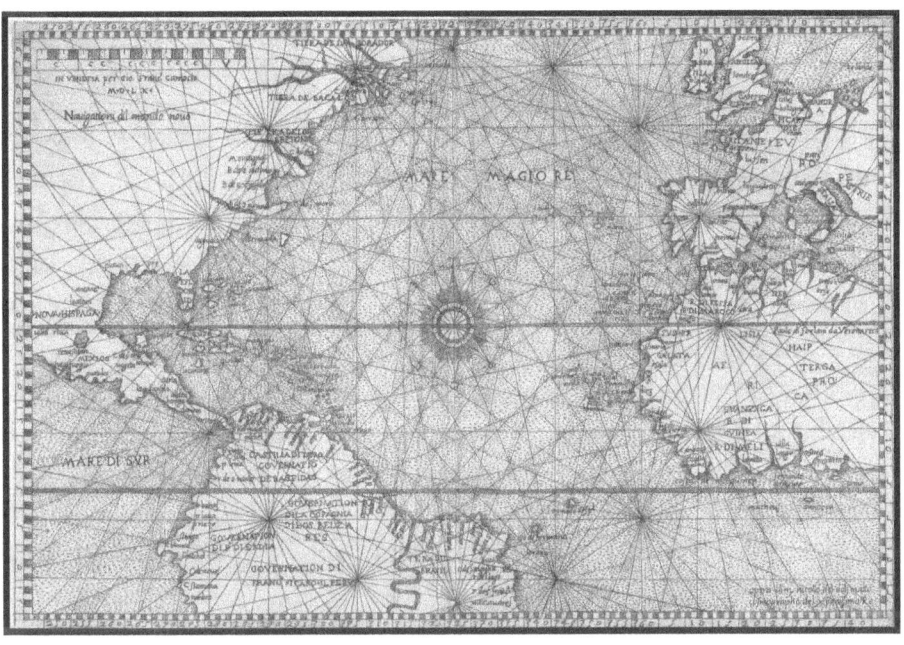

Fig. 9.14. Camocio's 1560 "Navigazioni dil mondo novo."

Now, note the tentatively engraved coastline, described earlier, at the left edge of sheet C (figure 9.5) and the fact, very fortunate for us, that a small part of this coastline appears in sheet A, as also noticed earlier (figure 9.6), so that to obtain the full coastline one must place these two sheets together side by side. This was clearly the intention, as it was also clearly the intention to excise the whole area covered by sheet B in the original manuscript.[89] Now note further that this added coastline is obviously a replacement for that part of the Mexican eastern coastline which had appeared above sheet F, and which had originally been in the discarded sheet B area, so that the intention was that the added coastline in sheet C should meet with the more southerly part of the Mexican east coastline rising out of sheet F. The only possible arrangement of the sheets of the incomplete

---

[89] Also clear in the complete, and correctly arranged incomplete, copies of the map. See figures 9.2, 9.3 and 9.12.

copies which will meet all these requirements and produce such a juncture is that shown in figure 9.13.

At first glance this seems to make no sense, producing an eight-sided map. It also seems to make the whole of the image broader than the original map. But actually, the map is slightly narrower in this arrangement. For the area covered by sheet B has been removed, and sheet A has been shunted slightly to the right, necessary to assure both that the north and south parts of the Mexican coast meet, and that the added coastline in sheets C and A is complete; and we recall that the original manuscript would have included the area shown with dashed lines in figure 9.10, an area filled almost entirely with part of the Pacific Ocean, and part of the imaginary Southern Continent. Although that never came to be engraved,[90] it would, if engraved, take care of justification of the left side of the map.[91] Finally, to bring the map into square, a sheet, approximately square, would have to be added in the upper right, which sheet could consist, for example, of simply a large wind rose in the North Atlantic, just as Camocio adds in the Indian Ocean on his map of Asia (map III).[92]

Some other adjustments would have to be made, which we will not go into. But notice that the eastward extent of North America comes out in the completed picture, in relation to South America, to be much improved, indeed not far from reality, and incidentally also very similar to its extent on the 1560 Camocio Atlantic Ocean map (after Nicolay) mentioned just above. So what we are suggesting here is that, at some point after work was already well along on engraving the map's sheets, Camocio began experimenting with the idea of improving the depiction by much shortening Gastaldi's overextended eastern North America. Judging from what remains, he probably would have had the map's engraving begun with the sheets to the right, and sheets C, D, F, G, H, J, K and L would have already been engraved

---

[90] The area, in the complete map as reconstituted by Donato Bertelli in the 1590s (see chapter twelve) came to be occupied by the large text spoken of earlier.

[91] The small sliver of this unimportant area which extends west of the left end of the top row as a result of slightly shunting sheet A to the right would have to be sliced off, that is, not included, in the printed version, which would present no problem. The implication would seem to be that the original manuscript must have extended slightly farther to the left all along the western border of the map (cf. fig. 9.10).

[92] The part of Spain and a small part of Africa at the far right of sheet D would have to be burnished out as well.

when he would have begun contemplating and weighing the feasibility of his idea, while sheet A would probably have been the last engraved,[93] after he had begun tinkering with his plan for improving the map. If he had decided that it was not feasible, that too many changes in engraving already done would have to be made, he could always revert to the original picture, although, having committed himself to at least an assessment of the idea by having sheet A engraved, it would be necessary to return the excised area of sheet B using a sheet for that area which was incommensurate in size with the other sheets, but this would not be a problem, and, as we shall see, it is precisely what Donato Bertelli did in the 1590s to finally complete the map, returning it to its original form.

Now, it is generally accepted that Camocio, who disappears from the record in the mid 1570s, fell victim to the great Venetian plague of 1575-1577,[94] and this gives us the denouement of our hypothesis. Having had sheet A engraved, and no doubt being still in the midst of contemplating his new idea, Camocio died, leaving behind him an uncompleted America. Those around him were probably incapable of following what Camocio had been doing, and incapable of completing the America, presuming they had any chance to do so at all, for the shop may well have closed after Camocio's death. So the America remained unfinished and no four-continent set yet existed.

---

[93] It is clear, since Camocio had assuredly segmented in pencil or light charcoal a full assembled manuscript of the map, possibly Gastaldi's original, according to the sheet segmentation which he gave all the maps (see fig. 9.1, and chapter eleven, note 24), that, when he had sheet A engraved, its coverage would not have been the coverage of the originally envisioned northwest sheet, although its dimensions remained those of all the larger sheets of the map. Its right several centimeters would have been originally intended as the left several centimeters of the sheet originally intended as being left of sheet C, while the left several centimeters of the sheet, omitted, would have extended the map somewhat further into Asian territory, so that the longitudinal width of the area beyond the left end of America in the west would have been much closer to the longitudinal width of the area shown beyond the right end of America in the east.

[94] Gallo (1950, 96), and regularly repeated by other scholars since. Only in one small point would I revise this long-standing idea. It is invariably stated that Camocio would have died from the plague precisely in 1575, the beginning year of the plague. But there is an uncertainty of 2-3 years at either end of the span in which Camocio began his first continental map and partly completed his last one, and no facts exist which will allow us to more definitely define the period. Now, we know from Jonathan Swift's *Journal of the Plague Year*, that life went right on, though no doubt under a pall of fear and gloom, in London when the plague roiled there in 1665, and we can be sure it did so in Venice as well. So it is quite possible that Camocio died in 1576, and not outside possibility that it was even in 1577.

What happened after this is unclear, but at some point in time someone, perhaps the surviving personnel of his shop, or perhaps someone else who had come into possession of the plates of the uncompleted America, decided to attempt to sell the whole four-continent set in the form of an atlas, of which we have one exemplar in the Bell set, in which form it might not be noticed that the America was not complete. It would have been they who engraved, this time not in tentative fashion, the odd line running from southeast Japan to provide a continuation (ludicrous, but perhaps not noticeably so to one turning the pages of an atlas) of the east coast of Mexico, and also they who engraved the bogus longitude numbering in sheet A so that there would be no gap in numbering from page to page,[95] as well as the graduation at the left of sheets F and J. Thus of the five peculiar additions to the two incomplete copies of the map noted earlier, two, the tentatively engraved ones, i.e., the ghost coastline and the second Florida, would have been made by Camocio in connection with his revision idea, while the other three, resolutely engraved, would have been made by later hands when the four-continent set was converted to an atlas.

There is no reason to attempt to follow Camocio here in any more detail than in the general presentation above, for we are dealing with hypothesis, and a general notion is the best we can hope for. But judging from the fact that the markings on the map pretty definitely indicate that the sheets were intended to be brought together as in figure 9.13, it seems very likely that what Camocio had in mind was a melioration of Gastaldi's overextension of North America eastward, and that the above scenario, or one close to it, is generally correct. In any event, our scenario shows that a reasonable rationale for the map's incomplete condition can be found, without resorting to the unreasonable (and impossible) scenario suggested by Almagià. As a last word, while we can say little about the fate of the plates in the years shortly after Camocio's death, we can say for certain that they had come into the hands of Donato Bertelli, who returned the map to its

---

[95] It would not have been necessary to burnish out previous correct numbering, for, by our thesis, none would have yet been applied. Camocio, by our thesis, would have been weighing the feasibility of proceeding with his idea as against reverting to the original Gastaldi depiction, and the longitude numbering in the sheet would have varied depending on the course taken, so Camocio would presumably not have added graduation to this sheet yet.

original condition as in Gastaldi's manuscript, no later than the early to mid-1590s, as we shall see in our final chapter.

With the affirmation that the map discussed here can only have been by Gastaldi, all doubt is removed of his authorship of all three of the continental maps discussed in chapter three. And in removing this doubt, we establish beyond discussion that in the three continental depictions Africa, Asia, and America, all made in the years 1559-1564, Gastaldi established cartographically, the general correct forms for the greater part of the globe. While the term cartography can be extended to include cosmic spaces, and even mental and emotional "spaces," its most basic business is the mapping of our world's land spaces, and, by that definition, one could argue that Gastaldi was not just one of the world's greatest cartographers, but the greatest! I will not take that stance here, because the multiplicity of aspects concerned with the question of what makes a cartographer great or not are legion, and the statement sounds exceedingly brash. But again, *if* we stick to the simplest and most basic of terms, the assertion is more than plausible. A final point. As to the suggestion of Burden and Woodward that the image of this continent could have been taken from the America on the 1561 world map (no. 104), if it is impossible to utterly disprove it, we feel that the arguments we have presented make it very unlikely. But even if it were to be taken as true, the image was directly copied from Gastaldi, nevertheless.

CHAPTER 10 - THE MAPS OF 1559-1564: THE HEART OF GASTALDI'S LEGACY

10.1 Preliminary Remarks

As we have noted earlier, Gastaldi's most impressive production occurred in the years 1559-1564. In these years he produced, together with the talented Fabio Licinio as engraver,[1] nine large multi-sheet copperplate maps, among them the maps for which he is most famous, and all of them superb and spectacularly attractive productions. In chronological order these maps are a 1559 map of west central Asia (Cartobibliography no. 92), the first of three maps which together make up a general map of Asia, a 1559 map of the Danube Basin (no. 93), a 1560 southeast Europe (no. 96), a 1560 map of Greece (no. 95), a 1561 map of Italy (no. 101), a 1561 southwest Asia (no. 102) and a 1561 eastern Asia (no. 103),[2] these last two maps complementing no. 92 above, followed by a 1562 map of northeastern Europe (no. 106) and, finally, in 1564, a giant map of Africa (no. 118). To this period also belongs Gastaldi's ca. 1560 map of America, discussed in the previous chapter, although, as we have seen, it was not engraved by Licinio, or anyone else, within Gastaldi's lifetime.[3] An important point to note here is that in the maps of Africa, Asia, and America there are virtually no derivative elements at all taken from any previous printed modern maps (although there is much, of course, taken from various sea charts); they are in no respect the result of accumulated cartographic data taken from predecessors. They are

---

[1] Licinio (1521 to Nov. 8, 1565), from a family of artists, was one of the most skillful map engravers of the sixteenth century. According to Borroni Salvadori, some of his plates passed to Camocio. As is usually the case with engravers, little is known of him. See Ludwig (1903, 51-52; 44-57 on the Licinio family as a whole), Borroni Salvadori (1980, lii-liv and index), Almagià (1949, 116 and index), and the *Archivio Biografico Italiano*, 1, fiche 567, 14 (Nagler), and II S, fiche 46, 408 (Pellicioni).

[2] The two narrow south sheets of this map, showing southern archipelago Asia, though presumably drawn in 1561, were not published until several years later. They were engraved by Paolo Forlani (we shall speak more of this just below.) Examples of the map consisting of only the two upper sheets are rarer than full examples

[3] It is unclear whether we should consider two other much smaller single-sheet Gastaldi-Licinio maps, one of Malta (no. 87), and the other of Corsica (no. 88), as part of this set. They are undated, and not at all of the order of significance as the main maps. For the most part, we leave them out of consideration in the following discussion. They are adequately treated in our Cartobibliography.

in fact primary models.[4] Note also that these three continental maps, taken together with the maps of southeast Europe and northeast Europe, provide coverage for three out of the four then recognized continents, and a major question we will be seeking the answer to in this chapter is whether Gastaldi was attempting, though if so he fell just short, to provide full modern cartographic coverage for the world, a thing unprecedented at the time. Finally, in this same period, he produced his great 1561 *Cosmographia vniversalis* world map. This map is not actually part of this set, for it is not a copperplate map engraved by Licinio, but a woodcut engraved by Matteo Pagano. But Gastaldi speaks of some of the above maps, in passages which we shall quote below, in his booklet *La Vniversale descrittione del mondo* which accompanies the world map, in such a way that he seems to have considered the world map as, to some degree, an adjunct to the continental maps. While we have already spoken of most of these maps separately at considerable length, in the present chapter we wish to discuss the set of maps as a whole, with the intention of attempting to determine to what extent they make up a cohesive project, and of what this cohesiveness consists.

10.2 Gastaldi and Licinio

The earliest documented contact between Gastaldi and Licinio is 1556, when Licinio engraved a copperplate edition of Gastaldi's 1555 Piedmont (no. 80), and it is my guess that it was at this time, or shortly after, that Gastaldi, impressed with Licinio's fine engraving work, chose him as his engraver. It seems very likely, considering the fact that the maps are quite elaborate productions, and the fact that we see no maps from the ever-active Gastaldi, or from Licinio, between ca. 1556 and the release of the first of the great maps in 1559, that there would have been a couple or so years of planning and preliminary drawing, and perhaps the making of business arrangements for the vending of the maps, perhaps most likely through familial connections of Licinio, about which more below, before actual production began.

---

[4] See in this regard chapter three.

This coalition between Gastaldi and Licinio lasted until 1564, when it ceased with the Africa (no. 118), and it will be worth our while to pause a moment to make the circumstances of this cessation as clear as possible. Another Gastaldi map, his Anatolia (no. 119), was published in this same year 1564 and shortly after appeared the last printed cartographic production of Gastaldi's lifetime, which we can assume went on sale as soon as it was engraved in ca. 1565/66. This last production was not truly a separate map, but the narrow lower two sheets of the 1561 east Asia (no. 103), mentioned above in note 2.[5] Both the 1564 Anatolia and the ca. 1565/66 addition to the east Asia were engraved by Paolo Forlani,[6] and not Licinio. Now, Licinio died in 1565 at the relatively young age of about forty-four years of an unknown cause. Since his last map was the 1564 Africa, it is reasonable to assume that his affliction, whatever it was, had begun to debilitate him about the time he finished the Africa, at which time Gastaldi turned to Forlani for an engraver. This is given further support by the fact that, while the image of Africa itself is superb, the finishing touches seem to have been done poorly and hurriedly, as we see both in the very erratic way the graduation was applied,[7] and in the careless and hasty line work in the large box in the northeast corner of the map containing both the title text and the list of ancient and modern names. The box is not sufficiently set off from the map, being defined by single lines (themselves being incomplete in three places) instead of the usual two lines with hachuring between them, giving the sense of a tablet, and the title box within is not set squarely in its place. Furthermore, the list of ancient versus modern names contains no explanatory title as we see for the other maps ("I Nomi Antichi et Moderni di, etc."). Thus the chronology of the two 1564 maps is clear, with the Africa preceding the Anatolia, and it is clear that the maps from the 1559 First Part

[5] See also on this entry 103 in our Cartobibliography. We do not enter this ca. 1565/66 addition as a separate production in the Cartobibliography, since it was simply a later extension of the 1561 map and became a part of that map in copies of the map sold after its completion. The cartography is clearly Gastaldi's.

[6] The Anatolia carries Forlani's name as engraver ("Paulo Forlani Veronese intagliatore"). The other does not, but Woodward, who studied Forlani's changing engraving style at length, attributes the engraving work to Forlani, and arrives at the date 1565 or 1566 (Woodward, 1990, no. 36, esp. under "Remarks"; and 1992, p. 52 and figs. 6 and 7). Woodward's figure 7 shows the two narrow sheets as engraved on a single plate. When printed out, the top sheet, which is upside down on the plate by comparison with the lower one, is intended, when cut out, to be turned around and pasted to the left end of the lower sheet.

[7] This peculiar graduation is described fully in our Cartobibliography entry no. 118.

of Asia to the 1564 Africa are an unbroken set all engraved by Licinio, while both of the two maps engraved by Forlani came out after the Gastaldi-Licinio venture had come to an end due to Licinio's having become incapacitated. This fact will be of use to us in a moment.

Up until 1559 almost all of Gastaldi's maps had been made at the behest of other persons, on contract as it were, with them (Pedrezzano, Ramusio, the Venetian Republic, et al), with the one notable exception of the first four dated maps of 1544-1546, which make up a very worthy small set in their own right, as shown in chapter one, and at the end of the present chapter. But beginning in 1559, and continuing through 1564, we will show that Gastaldi was his own proprietor, together with his chosen partner, Fabio Licinio, who served as engraver, but also, as we shall see, fulfilled other functions in the business as well. All the copyrights (*privilegi*) were applied for and granted to Gastaldi himself.[8] This and the two following considerations tell us that the business was entirely in their hands, that the directing of the operation was completely independent of any others, that Gastaldi and Licinio themselves handled in one way or another all aspects of the enterprise, and that they may be considered as partners, co-entrepreneurs[9]: For one thing, no names except Gastaldi and Licinio ever

---

[8] The only Gastaldi maps from the period 1559-1564 for which privileges are not known are the southern half of the map of southeast Europe and the map of northeast Europe. There are seven such privileges which are definitely known for Gastaldi works. For some, only the concession of privilege is known, for some both request and concession. The requests are generally more informative. I list here the known privileges, their dates, what they were for, and literature references, where in most cases the texts of the privileges are given in part or full: (1) 1539 for a "lunar perpetuo", concession (Almagià, 1939, *carta*, 6-7); (2) July 15, 1550 for Asia, together with Michele Membré, request (Fabris, 1989, 9), concession (Almagià, 1962, 3); (3) April 29, 1559 for Natolia, and the north part of Gastaldi's map of southeast Europe, concession (Almagià, 1962, 2, note 3); (4) July 29, 1559 for the three Parts of Asia, Greece, Italy, and Lombardy, concession (Almagià, 1962, 2, note 3); (5) July 30, 1561 for 1561 world map and accompanying booklet, privilege to print (mentioned by Woodward in *Mapline*, special no. 4(1979), item 53); (6) August 18, 1561 to Matteo Pagano for publishing Gastaldi's 1561 12-sheet world map, concession (Almagià, 1939, "Intorno," 260); (7) September 11, 1564 for Africa, Natolia and Lombardy, request (Almagià, 1939, *carta*, 8). There also exist, not previously recorded in the literature, the requests for nos. 4 and 6, and the concession for no. 7. The request for no. 4 is printed in full in our chapter 1, note 143. Parts of no. 5 and the request for no. 6 are quoted in the present work, where the 1561 world map is discussed in chapter two. I am very grateful to the late David Woodward for providing me with the texts of most of these documents. Other than one for the 1539 "lunar perpetuo", there are no privileges known for Gastaldi before 1555. For more on Renaissance *privilegi* for prints in general in Venice, see chapter 1.
[9] The relationship would be similar to that described by Fahy (1993, 96-98) between Pedrezzano, the main proprietor or entrepreneur in the production of the 1548 Ptolemy, and Gastaldi (here as partner).

appear on any of the maps,[10] and, furthermore, there is never indicated the name of a publishing house or shop,[11] which invites us to assume that Gastaldi and Licinio handled not only the drawing and engraving of the maps, but also handled the other aspects of the business. There exist two less obvious facts which confirm beyond doubt that this is true, and that Licinio especially acted in other capacities besides engraver in the business.

The first fact comes to us from the little words or abbreviations which are placed before or after the names of persons who took part in the creation of a map, and these leave us, in the present case, in no doubt that Licinio served not only as engraver, but also as printer and vendor. On many of Licinio's maps, we find "fecit" or just "f." next to Licinio's name on a map, which can only mean engraver. But on four maps, his function is indicated by the abbreviation "ex"/"Ex": map 87, ca. 1556 Malta ("ex"); map 88, ca. 1556 Corsica ("Ex"); map 101, 1561 Italy ("ex"); and map 118, 1564 Africa ("ex"). This abbreviation is ambiguous, for it can stand for either "excidit/ excidebat", indicating the engraver (Woodward, 1992, 46), or for "excudet/ excudebat", indicating the printer (Woodward, 1992, 46) or the publisher (Manasek, 1998, 275; Tooley, 1985, 62). But in one instance, our map 103, the 1561 third part of Asia, Licinio does not abbreviate, but gives his function designation in full: "Fabius licinius Excudebat", which can only mean "printer" or "publisher".[12] The second fact confirms beyond doubt that Licinio handled the sales. All of the maps in the great bloom period beginning in 1559, contain Licinio's name and Gastaldi's, except two, which do not contain Licinio's name at all, that is, no. 119, 1564 Anatolia, and the bottom half of no. 103, the third part of Asia, which bottom half was not published until ca. 1565/1566. Licinio died November 18, 1564, and probably was somewhat debilitated by some time earlier in that year, for there are slight irregularities, mentioned earlier, in the engraving of no. 118,

---

[10] There do occur the names of dedicatees, but this obviously is irrelevant to the present discussion.
[11] This too reminds us of Gastaldi's earliest maps.
[12] In fact I know of five sources which refer to Licinio fulfilling these roles: Gustav Ludwig twice refers to Licinio as a "stampadore" (printer) (1903, 51 and 52); Biasutti states that, besides being an engraver, Licinio was also sometimes a vendor of maps (1908,7, including note 1) Borroni-Salvadori refers to him as a printer (1980, liii); the online author information sources of the Bibliothèque Nationale, Paris, include bookseller and publisher among his functions; and the OCLC's online "WorldCat Identities", also include bookseller and publisher as among his activities. Unfortunately, none of these give us the sources for their information.

the 1564 Africa, involving the border lines around the title text, and also in how the latiutude and longitude graduation are handled. It is clear that Licinio had nothing to do with the 1564 Anatolia, whose engraver is signed as Paolo Forlani, nor had he anything to do with the two lower sheets in the third part of Asia, which Woodward has shown were also engraved by Forlani ca. 1565/1566.[13] But in these two maps, and in these two alone, we find a vendor's name, the San Marco shop of the Bertellis. In the lower left corner of the left of the sheets added to the third part of Asia, we find "Si uenda alla libraria d'l San Marco in Venetia" (Sold at the San Marco bookshop in Venice), and at the end of the dedication on the 1564 Anatolia (which, like the bottom two sheets of the third part of Asia, was engraved by Forlani) we find "Alla libraria d' la insegna di S[an] Marco" (At the bookstore of St. Marks). Clearly, in losing Licinio, Gastaldi lost not only his engraver, but also his vendor.

An interesting question: Why did Licinio incise in full on the third part of Asia, as he did nowhere else, the word Excudebat, showing him as vendor or publisher? Off-hand one would expect Licinio to take more pride in his role as engraver than in his role as vendor/publisher, but it may be that the role of publisher seemed to his mind at the moment a more prestigious one. I suspect that in the several maps mentioned above where Licinio left the abbreviated form of "ex" or "Ex" on the map, he was quite consciously aware that he was leaving a mark which could be interpreted either as engraver or vendor/publisher, or which could be interpreted as both at the same time.

As to Gastaldi, it seems worthwhile to make the following observation. Gastaldi here would have been responsible for the choice of subjects and how they were drawn. The only other place we see this in his work is in Gastaldi's first four maps to be published (nos. 1-4), which are the only other maps comparable in quality to the maps of 1559-1564. Gastaldi did his best work when he was the man in charge, working essentially on his own

Finally, we note that there are several notable points of uniformity among the maps in this Gastaldi-Licinio set. All have the same clean, sharp,

---

[13] Woodward, 1992, 52..

uncluttered look; there are no large and prominent cartouches, and little abstract décor, but with animals and sundry other figures depicted inland. Each contains a simple box of dedicatory text, with the first line engraved in large characters, which could be taken as a title, but there is no large, separate title anywhere. Typically, though not in every case, the text describes the bounds of the area covered, states that longitudes and latitudes of places are indicated, and that there is provided a scale in Italian miles, and ends with a notice of *privilegio*, sometimes two, one of fifteen years from the Venetian Republic, and one of ten years from the papacy.[14] Typically, also, there is a list of ancient vs. modern place names for places on the maps, often printed as a separate sheet, but sometimes printed in a framed panel on the map itself, in instances where the number of ancient correspondents to modern place names is small, and in one instance (his 1560 map of southeastern Europe) where the number of names is large, printed as a separate small booklet.[15] There is, however, no such list for the map of northeast Europe. In addition, all the maps exhibit great beauty, and are informed with a powerful visual appeal which is hard to explain, but which draws the viewer's eye towards and into the map. Clearly, Gastaldi had much of the artist in him, and it is regrettable that I do not possess the necessary art historian's knowledge to go into this aspect of Gastaldi's work more deeply, for it is certainly one of the central elements of his work. However, as we shall see, there are also many exceptions to this uniformity, especially as regards the maps of parts of Europe.

10.3 An Attempt at Universal Modern Coverage?

Let us now turn to the question posed earlier about whether or not Gastaldi's intention in this set of maps was to provide, for the first time in the history of mapping, modern cartographical coverage for the entire world. As we have seen, the maps cover three out of four continents, all except western

---

[14] Though no application for, or grant of, privilege has been found for one of the maps, that of northeastern Europe, we know there was one, for there is a privilege notice printed on the map.

[15] This idea was not new with Gastaldi. Münster before him did it, and others before him. Gastaldi, however, probably did it more extensively than any other. But, as Banfi has shown, the ancient and modern equivalents given by Gastaldi are often incorrect (Banfi, 1947, 40-41), although my guess is that they are also with others.

Europe. We also know that Licinio became incapacitated in 1564, the year of the last of the maps, that he died the next year, 1565, and that Gastaldi himself died in the following year, 1566. Obviously, this immediately suggests a very neat and simple interpretation of things: Gastaldi intended to provide modern world coverage, but, because of his partner's death and then his own, he did not have time to finish the job. *A priori*, the facts seem to justify this explanation, and indeed the scenario is not impossible; but, as we shall see, much speaks against it and, as we shall also see, the suggestion that Gastaldi would not have had time before his death to make these maps is not very convincing upon inspection. And, in general, as we go along, we shall find that things are by no means so simple here, and that in fact, it would be a sad mistake to accept this hypothesis without looking into it more deeply.

So we enter the fray, even though at first sight it may seem that no fray exists. We start by stating a couple of caveats. Firstly, we must stress that we can in no way consider the fact brought out just above, that there are a fair number of points of formal uniformity in the maps as an indication of an intention of full world coverage, as tempting as that might seem, for the one idea does not at all automatically follow from the other. Really, all we can say, at least so far, is that the similarity in overall characteristics is simply the striking look that Gastaldi and Licinio decided to give to their maps, and while it does provide a sense of unity to the maps, it is a unity of design and not of purpose.

That said, we should bring out a consideration which perhaps can validly be taken as indicative that Gastaldi might have been inclined to consider a project aimed at modern world coverage, although the circumstance is assuredly not a very concrete one. There exist in several Italian works of the period passages showing that the need for a new cosmography of the world was current in the minds of Italian geographers in general at that time. Ruscelli several times makes extensive reference to a project which he proposes to undertake, which would consist of a large number of modern maps covering all the world.[16] There is no sign that this ambitious project was ever actually begun. In the anonymous one-page "Alli

---

[16] Ruscelli (1561, fol. 2r of the book's dedication, and at pp. 57-59 of his commentaries on Ptolemy); and more extensively in Ruscelli (1562, in the dedication to Cardinal Borromeo at the head of the book).

lettori" at the head of Livio Sanuto's famous book on Africa, which contains a series of modern maps covering all Africa, the writer says of Sanuto that, "He died at the age of 56 years when he was about to begin describing the other parts of the world separately."[17] Another such passage, including reference to Gastaldi himself, is something of a puzzle. In the "Alli lettori" at the end of an anonymous little work generally attributed to Carlo Passi, which work serves mostly as a sort of gazetteer to places mentioned in Paolo Giovio's famous *Historie* of his times (first ed.. Florence, 1550-52), Passi, having stressed how many modern and ancient names he has gathered, and that it is not alone Giovio's book that has occasioned him to take up this work, continues, "rather I had and still have the intention to make a universal Geography, conferring [in] it with M. GIACOMO CASTALDO, who has no match in this."[18] My guess is that Passi's (or whoever's) envisioned project involving a coalition with Gastaldi was more of a pipedream than reality, and nothing came of it, as in the case with Ruscelli. But the passages do indicate an awareness of the need for a new world description of some kind.[19]

We move ahead to an area more directly concerned with our question, that is, the part of Europe for which we have Gastaldi-Licinio maps, eastern Europe, to see what light these maps might be able to throw upon our discussion. We start with the 1560 four-sheet map of southeast Europe (no. 96). The area coverage of this map seems arbitrary. There is no natural or logical center of unity. The top half consists of inland countries with little or

---

[17] In Sanuto (1588, in the "alli lettori"). Though Sanuto's book was published only in 1588, it was written much earlier, perhaps in the 1560s, and possibly even earlier. No one knows when he was born, nor how long after he finished his book on Africa he died (see Skelton's introduction to the 1965 modern facsimile edition of Sanuto's work.)

[18] Passi (1564, in the mentioned "alli lettori"). Though I quote from the 1564 edition, the earliest I have seen myself, there are many editions, sometimes with small variations in the title. Although it sometimes occurs as a separate publication, it most often accompanies the various editions of Giovio, and its first appearance seems to be in the 1555 edition of Giovio, as implied by a notice in the printed library catalog of the British Museum, vol. 86, col. 469. Whether the passage itself occurs in the earliest edition, I cannot say, but it certainly appears in a 1558 edition seen by Grande, as see Grande (1902, 40) and Grande (1905, "carte", 96.) (Grande gives the date only in 1902).

[19] We shall quote, later in this chapter, several passages by Gastaldi himself regarding his activities of 1559-1564, though unfortunately, they are not very enlightening as to the question of whether he considered these activities as an attempt at a new general world description. See also below in note 31 the quotation from a prospectus published by the Accademia Venetiana, of which Gastaldi was a member, which is perhaps relevant here, though I feel this passage should be taken with a grain of salt.

no political, cultural, or historical unity among them. Then, in the southeast part of the map, we have Greece, also with little or no political, cultural, or historical unity with the countries above, and lacking geographical unity as well, for it is not at all an inland country, but a peninsula with island-studded seas all around it. And finally, in the lower left sheet, the southern half of Italy meanders out of nowhere onto the map, also remote in the senses mentioned from the areas depicted in the other sheets, and remote from its own invisible northern half, off the map.[20] One might, then, advance the suggestion that the explanation for the map's area coverage could be simply that it covered the southeast part of Europe, as part of some predetermined scheme for breaking up the continent into several parts, as had been done for Asia. But this suggestion is not very convincing, because in 1546 Gastaldi had made another large four-sheet map (no. 4), comparable in size and scale, whose area coverage, most of north central and south central eastern Europe, was also arbitrary,[21] and we know for certain that this 1546 map was not part of any plan to cover all of Europe in a set of maps. Rather we suspect that the explanation for the coverage is simply that Gastaldi had managed to come by enough new and original information, information not on any previous printed maps, to justify making a map of it, a suggestion the rationale for which will become clearer below.

There are also several facets of this map in which it is quite inconsistent with the conventions followed in any of the Gastaldi-Licinio far continent maps, which fact seems to disqualify the notion that it was part of a coordinated plan to provide a set of maps which would cover all of Europe and correspond to the maps made for the far continents. Firstly, the form of the map itself (not just its projection) is trapezoidal, like no other map in the Gastaldi-Licinio set, or any other Gastaldi map for that matter. This obviously sets it off from the other maps, and the presence of slanted sides

---

[20] Actually, the whole east coast is present, but the west coast is chopped off quite low. We see now, incidentally, the reason for the usual scattering of these sheets in the Veneto-Roman atlases.

[21] For reasons of convenience and economy of space, we refer, in our Cartobibliography, to this production as Gastaldi's map of the "Danubian Lands", which nominally provides a rationale for its coverage, but in fact the coverage extends far beyond the area which could be called Danubian Lands, reaching in the north as far as Saxony, Thuringia, north central Poland, and the Smolensk region of Russia, and in the south including much of Italy, and parts of Greece and Turkey. The south half of the 1546 map, incidentally, coincides with the north half of the 1560 map, and there is much improvement in this large area on the 1560 map by comparison with the 1546 map.

hardly accords well with the notion that another part-map to the left was envisioned as its complement. Secondly, for some reason, Gastaldi here has drawn in all the parallels and meridians, which we see on no other of the Gastaldi-Licinio maps, and again sharply in contrast with those maps. Again, while on the well planned three-section Asia, each section bears a part name (A . . . PRIMA PARTE DEL ASIA . . .", A . . . SECONDA PARTE DELL'ASIA . . .", etc.), there is no part number assigned in the title of this map, nor in the title of the map of northeast Europe to the north of it. Clearly, there is much evidence arguing against any supposition that the map is part of a planned intention to cover Europe and complement the continental maps as part of a whole-world modern coverage attempt. Still other factors impart doubt to this, though in an indirect way which is hard to assess, and we shall only mention them and not try to analyze their meaning further. The genesis of the map is disconcerting. The top half, in two sheets, was issued alone the year before, 1559, as a separate map (no. 93), and the lower two sheets were added only in 1560.[22] This resulted in the full southeast Europe map, but there is room to wonder whether this was the original intention or an afterthought, for the two lower sheets are a full 130 mm. greater in width north to south than the two upper sheets. Furthermore, Gastaldi mined out of this map a separate map of Greece in 1560 (map no. 95), consisting of the lower right sheet plus part of the sheet to its left,[23] and one can posit that Gastaldi's 1561 Italy (no. 101) was inspired by and partly mined out of this map.[24] As noted, we shall not discuss these machinations further, but there seems to us to lurk here an intimation that Gastaldi was much focused on this map as a thing unto itself, instead of part of a set of maps covering Europe, and that there is lacking a sense of a singleness of purpose.

Turning to the map of northeast Europe (no. 106), we first note one fact which at first would seem to suggest the possibility that the two maps were part of a plan to cover Europe, that is, the northeast Europe overlaps at the bottom with the southeast Europe, and we can presumably take it that this was intentional, giving a continuum to the maps such that they provided

---

[22] See Cartobibliography entries no. 93, 95 and 96 for full detail on this.

[23] See Cartobibliography entries 95 and 96 for detail on this.

[24] See our comments in Cartobibliography entry no. 101.

coverage for almost all of eastern Europe.[25] Nevertheless, this overlap is problematical in more ways than one. It is only twenty-four arc-minutes in width,[26] barely enough to follow from one map to the next, compared to the very ample planned overlap of about ten whole degrees between the parts of Gastaldi's Asia. This small overlap, while to be sure present, is not at all commensurate with the notion of a well-planned set of maps covering the continent, and in fact, as we shall see in a moment, it is likely that the map was an afterthought, first conceived of only in 1561 or perhaps 1562. Another disconcerting feature is that the northeast Europe and southeast Europe do not meet squarely at their, respectively, south and north edges. The north border of the southeast Europe runs from 33°09' to 56°50' E longitude, while the south border of the northeast Europe runs from 40°50' to 65°15' E longitude, so that the northeast Europe covers 8°25' more at the east, and the southeast Europe covers 7°41' more at the west, while in the well-planned Asia, the parts meet squarely. Disconcerting too in the northeast Europe is the fact that the north part of the western border awkwardly chops Scandinavia squarely in half, with the east half on the map, but the west half off it. Both of the last two factors make the question of how one would proceed with continuation to the west a problematical one, just as does the slanted left border of the southeast Europe, and all three of these factors imply the lack of any pre-formulated plan for full coverage of Europe, with the suggestion that very possibly no such intention ever existed at all. And one other consideration, if correct, tells us that the northeast Europe was not yet even envisioned when the southeast Europe was made. For there is good reason to posit that the original instigation for making the northeast Europe came only in 1561, a year after the southeast Europe had

---

[25] In neither of the two maps is coverage literally complete. A goodly portion of northern Sweden, Finland, and European Russia fall off of the north end of the northeast Europe map, and the south part of Crete falls off of the south end of the southeast Europe map, and all of the Crimea and a very sizeable part of the lands just to the north are not on either map, although these areas definitely fall within Europe according to the definition of the bounds of the continent given by Gastaldi in his *La Vniversale descrittione del mondo*. We recall that Asia over 50° N latitude was not shown on Gastaldi's Asia. But this area was unknown, while southern Crete was quite well known, the Crimea and the lands just north of it were reasonably well known even in ancient times, and the northmost delimitations of Europe had been more or less set by the 1553-55 explorations of Richard Chancellor, of which Gastaldi was aware, if only imperfectly, as see chapter eight, in the section, "Our Conclusions."

[26] Amounting to about 3 cm. on the southeast Europe, and only about 12 cm. on the northeast Europe, which is on much smaller scale than the southeast Europe.

346

been completed, when original textual information on the area would have become available to Gastaldi.[27]

While the results of our inquiry so far cannot be said to be overly conclusive, clearly the implication that Gastaldi had no intention of mapping western Europe is stronger than the implication that he did. But a sense of uncertainty about this is unavoidable, for the simple reason that the suggestion that Gastaldi had no intention of making maps of western Europe does not seem a natural one. It runs blatantly counter to what we would expect, since he had made maps of eastern Europe and all the rest of the continents. Why he would have had no intention to provide maps for the last eighth of the world is a question which needs an answer. For the moment, we will leave this conundrum unanswered and continue to present all the basic evidence we have been able to compile which is relevant to our inquiry. We can learn no more, I think, from the maps of eastern Europe. Let us see what we can learn from Gastaldi himself.

Gastaldi, of course, left no written description of his intentions. But he does give us a few hints in two short passages in his booklet *La Vniversale descrittione del mondo*,[28] and in the text box on the 1559 first edition of his First Part of Asia, which passages we shall quote here, but principally with the purpose of showing that here, too, there is little of solid value to latch onto, for these passages too are mostly of an inconclusive and noncommittal nature.

At the end of the main part of the 1561 booklet, which was as we have seen, published as accompaniment to his 1561 *Cosmographia vniversalis* world map, having named the provinces of the four main parts of the world, Gastaldi continues:

---

[27] This is brought out in entry 106 in our Cartobibliography. There is, we should note, one other point in which the northeast Europe is inconsistent with the other Gastaldi-Licinio maps. It has no list of ancient and modern place name equivalents. However, the map was clearly made more hurriedly than the exquisite southeast Europe, and perhaps Gastaldi lacked the opportunity, or perhaps the initiative, to work up such a list, for isolating the ancient equivalents for modern places in an area relatively remote from Greece and Rome would no doubt have been more difficult than for most places, although Gastaldi managed to compile a moderate such list for eastern Asia. It goes without saying, of course, that no such list was made for America, where there obviously could be no ancient equivalents.

[28] For the pagination which we use for this work, see chapter two, note 68.

Similmente tutte le Prouincie del mondo si diuideno in Regni, Regioni, Territori, con le lor Città, Castalli, & Monti, Laghi, Fiumi, Mari, Golfi, Porti, & Isole: la diuision delle quali non la descriuero qui altramente. Ma le risaluo a scriuerle con le parti, che daro in luce alla giornata, piu particolarmente che non sono descritte nel Mapamondo: nel detto Mapamondo ui e descritto qualche cosa in generale per esser fatto a piccolo cõpasso, ma nelle parti che si danno fuori ui sara ogni particolare. (Similarly, all the Provinces are divided into Kingdoms, Regions, Territories, with their Cities, Castles, Mountains,& Lakes, Rivers, Seas, Gulfs, Ports, & Islands: the division of which are not described here otherwise. But I reserve to describe them with the parts, which I will give into the light from time to time, in more detail than they are described on the Mappamondo: in the said Mappamondo some things are described in a general way by virtue of being made on small scale, but in the parts which are being given out there will be every detail [p. 19]).[29]

[29] I have been closely studying this significant passage for many years and can assure the reader that the rendering given here is in general correct. In particular, the translation of the Italian word "parti", used twice here by Gastaldi, is important. Gastaldi speaks of "the parts which are being given out." In 1561, when this was written, this can refer only to the *parts* of continents which were indeed being given out by Gastaldi at the time, that is, the 1560 "Geographia particolare d'una gran *parte* dell'Europa, etc." (Detailed geography of a large *part* of Europe, etc." [map no. 96]), covering all of the southeast part of Europe, and the three parts of Asia, i.e., the 1559 "IL DISEGNO DELLA PRIMA *PARTE* DELASIA [sic], etc." ("MAP OF THE FIRST *PART* OF ASIA, etc." [map no. 92]), the 1561 "IL DISEGNO DELLA SECONDA *PARTE* DELL'ASIA, etc." ("MAP OF THE SECOND *PART* OF ASIA, etc." [map no. 102]) and "IL DISEGNO DELLA TERZA *PARTE* DELL'ASIA, etc." ("MAP OF THE THIRD *PART* OF ASIA, etc." [map no. 103]). While the word "parti" was often used at the time to refer to parts of the world in the sense of continents, that is definitely not Gastaldi's intention here. Gastaldi was not publishing any maps of full continents at the time, and in fact he would publish only one map of a full continent in this Gastaldi-Licinio period, that is, his large map of Africa, and even that map was published only in 1564, three years after the passage quoted here. Besides, when the word "parts" was used in this sense of continents, it was virtually always used together with the phrase "of the world" ("parts of the world" or "part of the world"), and not standing alone, as here. (see also our comments on the equivocal nature at the time of the words "part" and "continent" in chapter six. Woodward gave an English translation of part of the passage quoted here, but without the corresponding original Italian, and rendered the word "parti" as "continents" (2007, 786), implying that the sense could be that Gastaldi was working on a set of maps of the four continents at the time. But this translation is not correct, and, as we shall see later in this chapter, Gastaldi made no set of maps of the four continents, and it is extremely unlikely that the idea would even have crossed his mind. Incidentally, I also disagree with Woodward's translation of the problematical idiom "alla giornata" here, for which numerous renderings exist. He renders it as "any day", but I am virtually certain that the intended sense here is as we have rendered it above, that is, "from time to time."

Loosely, one might construe this as meaning he will provide large sectional maps for all parts of the world, but the statement as made is far too broad, noncommittal, and generally not sufficiently forthcoming, if indeed not hedging, to justify drawing such a conclusion, and he certainly nowhere states here unequivocally that he means *all* parts of the world.

There is one more passage of relevance, slightly earlier in the book. It is even less helpful than the first one, but we shall quote it for the sake of completeness. Perhaps some other scholar will divine from it something which has escaped us. In the section on European provinces, which number twelve by Gastaldi's reckoning, he states after giving the names of the first four that, "la Quinta non è nominata con nome particolare, ma con diuersi nomi di Regioni; & benche non sieno descritte nel detto Mapamondo: ne dirò alquante" (the fifth is not designated by a particular name, but with diverse names of regions; & although they might not be described in the said Mapamondo, I will give several of them [p. 14]), and he names Switzerland, Bavaria, Austria, part of Hungary, Sclavonia, Croatia, Bosnia, and Dalmatia, all of which refer to the map of southeast Europe, completed the year before. Then at the end of the same Europe section he notes that: "A queste Prouincie non gli scriuono i confini: mi riserbo a scriuerli nelli dissegni particolari." (The confines of these provinces are not marked: I reserve to myself to mark them in the detailed maps [p. 15]).[30]

---

[30] Note that in this and the previous quote Gastaldi seems to connect the "Cosmographia Vniversalis" vaguely with the maps of the Gastaldi-Licinio effort, almost as if the world map were the general presentation, while the special maps are to be taken as accompaniment to it, although the world map did not appear until two years after the special maps began to appear, and the world map is a woodcut by Matteo Pagano. But note also, that these three little phrases, all beginning with a definite article, i.e., "*the* detailed maps", "*the* parts which I will give into the light from time to time", and "*the* parts which are being given out", appear in the text quite abruptly and unexpectedly. There is no antecedent whatsoever to them in the text to orient the reader as to what he means by "*the* parts", etc., so one does not feel too secure as to what he is talking about.

As mentioned, the only other information he gives us on his activities at the time is in the textbox of the first edition of the First Part of Asia, where, in the dedication to the "Duke of Savoy; Prince of Piedmont", he says:

> Presto mandero alla stampa l'altre due parti del Asia, che seguitano la prima uerso oriente, et uerso Austro con la Grecia che la sequita uerso Ponente le qual' parte sarão descritte con i nomi moderni et antiqui come e questa prima parte, et similmente faro all'italia, et a molte altre prouincie che saria lungo scriuerle, ma presto le mandaro all' vostra Altezza. (Soon I shall put into print the other two parts of Asia, which extend the first toward the east, and toward South with Greece which extends it toward the west, which parts will be described with modern and ancient names as is this first part and I will do similarly for Italy, and for many other provinces which it will be [too] long to write out, but soon I shall transmit them to your highness.)

Notice that none of these unfortunately very few notices from Gastaldi ever make any specific reference to western Europe, but they do make very specific allusion to maps of parts of eastern Europe, as well as parts of Asia, which we know he made.[31] Thus, while there is certainly no expression of

---

[31] One other statement could possibly be taken as referring to the Gastaldi-Licinio project which for completeness we should include. We recall the Accademia Venetiana, established in 1557 (see chapter 1), to the Cosmographical/Geographical faculty of which Gastaldi and Livio Sanuto were assigned as heads. In 1558, the academy published a prospectus, of which we speak again in the Cartobibliography, in entries (97.-100.) and (107.-117.), which included a list of projected works for each faculty. There are fifteen such works for the Cosmographical faculty, the first and principal of which is given as: "Recens geographia, in qua descripta est universa terra, et mare, dehinc singulae provinciae, tum quae ad orientem, quaeque ad occidentem, tum quae ad septentrionem et meridiem vergunt, una cum regionibus, urbibus, montibus, et fluviis, quibus addita sunt nomina, tum vetera, tum recentia cum parallelis, et gradibus, opus multo amplius, et aptiore digestum ordine, quam ea quae et ab antiques, et a recentioribus conscripta sunt" (Modern geography, in which is described the whole earth, and sea, then individual provinces, both which to the east, and which to the west, and which to the north and south are situated, together with regions, cities, mountains, and rivers, to which are added the names, both old and modern, with parallels, and degrees, a work much more ample, and arranged in more suitable order, than those which by the ancients and the more modern have been composed [Accademia Venetiana, 1558, under the heading "Geographia"]). Whether this rather vague description, possibly written by Gastaldi and/or Sanuto, but also very possibly by another hand, should be taken as referring to the Gastaldi-Licinio activities, which probably began about 1557, a couple of years before the appearance of the first map in 1559, is hard to say, but I think probably not. Concerning, however, two other projects mentioned in this list (and not impossibly some others), we know Gastaldi did have a connection, as see Cartobibliography nos. (97.-100.) and (107.-117.).

any intention to provide maps for all of Europe, or all of the world, there is again perhaps a slight intimation that Gastaldi had no clear intention of the kind, though, of course, we are still faced with our unbroached question of "Why not?"

There is another consideration which suggests that Gastaldi had no intention of providing coverage for western Europe. As implied earlier, we can demonstrate that the premise that Gastaldi did not have the time to make maps of western Europe before death took him does not stand up at all well to inspection. In 1560, Gastaldi completed the southeast Europe (our no. 96), and, as we established with finality in our previous chapter, must have completed the America in manuscript at about the same time. In 1561, he completed not only two large parts of Asia, and the Italy, but also the giant world map *Cosmographia vniversalis* , and then in 1562 the map of northeast Europe. But from 1562 to 1564, there seems to be nothing. As we see in Cartobibliography entry no. 118, the Africa may have been ready by 1562, though it was engraved only in 1564 by Licinio. Now, at the rate Gastaldi had been working, surely there would have been time from 1562 to 1564 to make the maps covering the remaining half of Europe. In fact, he would have had until 1565 (and even possibly until sometime in 1566), for in 1564 appears the map of Anatolia engraved by Forlani, presumably selected by Gastaldi to replace an ailing Licinio, and we know that Gastaldi was still healthy and active at least until July 1565,[32] so Forlani could have engraved the western parts of Europe as well. So, there were at least three years in which the remaining parts of Europe could have been drawn and engraved. But there are no signs of them, no maps, no manuscripts finished or unfinished, no copyright notices, and no mention of them anywhere. Thus, presuming that our analysis is sound, there would seem to be no explanation for the absence of the maps except that Gastaldi had no intention of making them. But, once again, "Why not?"

Why not? Could the answer be simply that he did not have the necessary sources available to him? At first the suggestion seems ludicrous, considering what we know of the cartography of the times. There is no

---

[32] Karrow (1993, 247). We have no clue as to Gastaldi's condition from this time until his death in October, 1566, but it is as reasonable as not to assume that he could have remained healthy and active some time into 1566, not impossibly up to the day of his death, since we do not know how he died.

doubt that Gastaldi would have had the sources at hand to compile two or three large maps covering the missing blocks of Europe, for a glance at Tooley's catalog of Veneto-Roman atlas maps,[33] shows that the Venetian and Roman map publishers had copied and printed very good maps, by northern and other cartographers, of all the regions of western Europe before the start of the Gastaldi-Licinio partnership of 1559-1564, maps which would have been immediately accessible to Gastaldi.[34] So Gastaldi certainly had the sources at hand to make large sectional maps covering western Europe, and thus complete coverage of all four continents, and he apparently had plenty of time to do so.

10.4 A Probable Resolution to Our Question

We seem to be at an impasse. Things don't seem to make sense. But if we broaden our horizons a bit, looking in other directions, we will find that the answer to our problem is a simple one, if a little subtle. The answer is in two parts. The first part will show us that, regardless of indications which seem to speak to the contrary, Gastaldi would not in fact have had the necessary means to provide maps for western Europe *which would have satisfied his own dictates*. The second will show us that he would furthermore have had no reason to be vexed or preoccupied by this situation, indeed probably would not have been much concerned at all. Together, they will show us what Gastaldi was all about when working independently of others.

For the first part, we need only to briefly survey the nature of Gastaldi's sources, *all the time bearing in mind in particular those maps which Gastaldi made on his own volition, and thus working according to his own standards*. For his most important maps, the continental maps of Africa,

---

[33] Tooley (1939). Tooley breaks his presentation into countries and provinces.

[34] In Tooley, we find maps for these countries from the following years: France, 1554 and 1558/Germany, 1548, 1552, 1553,1559/British Isles, 1546, 1549, 1555, 1556, 1559/Belgium, 1558/Holland, 1556, 1558 plus numerous Dutch provincial maps from the 1550s. For Spain, besides his own Spain of 1544, Tooley has maps from 1552, 1559 and 1560, but Gastaldi would also have known Vincenzo Palatino's great woodcut Spain of 1551 and its 1558 edition by Pagano (Schilder, 1987, 91-94 and 98-101; Karrow, 1993, nos. 60/1 and 60/1.3). Palatino's map outmoded Gastaldi's only seven years after the latter was made. But it is worth noting that the improvement of Gastaldi's Spain over preceding maps was much greater than the improvement of Palatino over Gastaldi.

Asia, and America, this is very simple. They are, as we already know and has been pointed out once earlier in this chapter, completely original products. No one has ever isolated a single source for any of these maps which was a previously printed and published map. They were compiled entirely from manuscript maps, that is, the portolan charts, and textual sources, mainly, though not entirely, the accounts in Ramusio. And here we have our keynote. Gastaldi had no interest in producing a map which was simply copied from a previously published map or maps. The same is true as regards those maps of parts of Europe which were made on Gastaldi's own volition, although in some cases not entirely so, since Gastaldi did not have for Europe a vast trove of original information such as that provided by Ramusio for the far continents. There are six of them, the 1544 Spain (no. 1), the 1545 Sicily (no. 2), the 1546 map of a huge tract of central eastern Europe (no. 4), the 1560 southeast Europe (no. 96), the 1561 Italy (no. 101), and the 1562 northeast Europe (no. 106).[35] The coasts in all cases are from manuscript sea charts. The interior of the Spain and the Sicily are from information obtained from, respectively, Mendoza and Maurolico.[36] For the 1560 southeast Europe, only one previously printed source has been identified, covering a relatively small part of the map, Lazius's 1556 Hungary, and the same is true of Italy proper on the 1561 Italy, where only Tuscany is covered by Bellarmato's 1536 map of that region, or one of its later editions. The sources for all the rest on these two maps are unknown.[37] For the 1546 map of a large tract of eastern Europe, several printed sources have been tentatively identified,[38] but the sources for half or more of the map are unknown. For the northeast Europe, Wapowski's 1526 Poland (or Grodecki's 1557 Poland based on Wapowski), apparently accounts for the area covered by that country on the map, though no true study has been made yet, and much remains of unknown origin, but it also no doubt contains original contributions from Maciej z Miechowa's 1561 text on the two

[35] We do not list separately the 1559 Danube Basin (no. 93) and the 1560 Greece (no. 95), since those maps simply make up part of the southeast Europe.
[36] See Cartobibliography entries nos. 1 and 2.
[37] See Cartobibliography entries nos. 96 and 101.
[38] See Cartobibliography entry no. 4. Except for Secretarius's Hungary, the sources are only offhand suggestions made by Almagià, at least one of which has been shown to be wrong.

Sarmatias, as well as elements which are original in the sense that they are taken from Gastaldi's own 1546 map of much of eastern Europe.[39]

While most of the sources for the Italy and the southeast Europe, at least half of the sources for the 1546 map of much of eastern Europe, and probably part of the sources for the northeast Europe are unknown, they are not in any event from previously printed maps. Since the many areas unaccounted for are reasonably correct and have been found by Almagià and Kret to be much better than any previous maps, we know *ipso facto* that sources existed, and we can only assume that these consisted mainly of now unknown or lost manuscript materials, maps or texts, but probably both, and perhaps some oral information. The main point we wish to make here is that, for these parts of Europe in particular, but not for others, it almost certainly would not have been very difficult to obtain such new information, especially if one actively attempted to do so. The vast amount of valuable goods which Venice's merchant fleets brought into the city, and which made the Republic the wealthy and prominent place that it was, had to be distributed, partly to Italian places,[40] though a much greater bulk would have been distributed overland northwards, to major east European centers, such as Vienna, Prague, Buda and Pest, Belgrade, Cracow, etc., from which in turn more local distributions would have been made. The immeasurable importance of these vital economic lifelines, which we could think of as arteries to the heart of the Republic, the city of Venice itself, meant of course that these places were not only of great economic significance to Venice, but

---

[39] See Cartobibliography entry no. 106. The map has received only superficial attention so far, and there are very likely elements from unidentifiable sources.

[40] The Italian part of this distribution would mostly have been effected by stops made at Italian ports of call, such as Brindisi, Bari, Pescara, Ancona, Pesaro, Rimini, etc., as the homecoming ships came up the Gulf of Venice.

political as well.[41] We also know that the Republic, apparently more than any other nation, actively pursued a course of obtaining information, no doubt including such things as manuscript maps and written reports, on areas which were of political and/or economic significance to it.[42]

So there would have been a ripe harvest of data on these areas available through these lines of communication for the person who took the trouble to obtain it, and Ramusio and very possibly Gastaldi himself would not only have been much inclined to take this trouble, but had solid government contacts which would have facilitated it. So, we have every reason to posit that Gastaldi could have obtained much original information on these European areas, and, concomitantly, that he would have chosen to make maps specifically of these regions. Gastaldi in Venice would have had every opportunity to tap lines of communication in western Europe for new information, if it existed, with the result that he would have been unable to make any significant further contributions to the cartography in the maps of western Europe already extant. He would have been reduced to slavish copying exactly from these maps, an idea which would not have appealed to him after the strikingly original maps he had produced of other areas. This would not necessarily mean that Gastaldi looked upon this as a point of pride, but simply as a mundane fact. If others had already mapped these areas as well as they could, what purpose could be served by simply copying them if he had no further information than they had, a likely enough state of

---

[41] We have a record of Ramusio asking for and receiving information, some of it geographical, from a Venetian legation secretary in Buda, who reported being in Transylvania within two days' journey of Tartary, and who spoke some of natural phenomena in Hungary, and also of the famous geographer Ziegler being in Buda (Parks, 1955, 134). This was very early for us, in 1520, but Parks adds that Ramusio's interest in eastern Europe continued, and certainly, considering his position with the Venetian government, Ramusio could at will have continued soliciting information from members of Venetian legations to Hungary or other eastern European places. No record of his doing so is known, but such activity would certainly have been characteristic enough of Ramusio, especially if he were urged by Gastaldi. It is not surprising that the sparse record in general of the activities of Ramusio concentrates on his efforts to gather the information on the far continents which resulted ultimately in his famous *Navigationi*, and that information on any exertions he might have made as to obtaining data on more local, European, areas would have been passed over as of relatively peripheral interest.

[42] For more on this, see Cartobibliography entry no. 96.

affairs for those areas?[43] Thus the first part of our answer to why Gastaldi would have had no intention of providing maps of western Europe corresponding to those for eastern Europe. The second part will show us that Gastaldi would not in any event have been predisposed to make such maps. It will also give us a better understanding in general of the nature of his motivations and intentions and reveal that we have been all along imposing upon Gastaldi's story a historical development which had not yet occurred at his time. We will find that Gastaldi's attention was almost certainly never directed toward attempting to attain full modern world coverage. He was doing something else. We need to step away from Gastaldi for a moment, and step ahead in time to Ortelius.

Ortelius's 1570 publication of the *Theatrum Orbis Terrarum* was a bold venture, and a pace-setter in the best sense. The book itself contains a four-continent set, although of course not wall-maps, and this was the first truly viable such set, even if on quite small scale, quickly followed by Anania in 1573, and many others, and shortly after followed by the four-continent wall-map sets proper, printed, and in a few cases painted as mural sets. But mainly the *Theatrum* was an atlas of the world. Ortelius knew, as we have seen elsewhere, and will see again in a moment, that there remained sizeable portions of the globe unexplored, and he knew that there had been reports of sightings of land which *could* be parts of large unknown continents. So, the world was not fully known. But he forged ahead anyway and published his *Theatrum.* For this he can only be congratulated, for, in doing so, he broke through a formidable barrier indeed. Thousands of other atlases followed over the centuries, and even in the late nineteenth century, and perhaps even in the early twentieth, there still remained a number of empty spaces on the map, progressively of less and less importance, but *there* nonetheless, and if we had waited until absolutely *everything* was discovered, we would have had no atlases at all until about the 20th century. Thus, Ortelius's initiative was in no sense premature, and we may credit him with a very important, nay, revolutionary realization, that when *most* of the

---

[43] It is true that Gastaldi had, due to special circumstances, obtained original information for his Spain in 1544 from Mendoza. But in 1551 his Spain had been superseded by that of Palatino, and he probably would not have been able to obtain further new data by which he could in turn have superseded Palatino's map by the time of the Gastaldi-Licinio partnership of 1559-1564.

world's most important lands had been discovered, there was need for an atlas to systematically document it all, and partly precisely so that mankind could properly pace itself, and head in the right directions to get the job literally and finally done. While it has been pointed out often that the *Theatrum* was a watershed in several ways in the history of mapping, I feel that this subtle but far-reaching aspect of his atlas, which allowed cosmography to move forward more freely, has perhaps not received the recognition it deserves. To repeat, the unknown and uncertain areas of the globe were still there, and still considered, but quite suddenly they had taken on a quite distinctly peripheral air compared to the principal known bodies of land. Concomitantly, since at Ortelius's time, and for quite some time to come, these principal known bodies of land amounted in general to four large continents, the four-continent idea arose quite naturally, and the two forms quickly came to be considered, and properly enough, as depictions of the whole world. But now let's move back in time again, only a few years, to Gastaldi.

This had not yet happened in Gastaldi's time. Although the acceptance of the idea of there being four continents was taking form, ambivalence due to the very possible presence of still other large land masses, perhaps of continental proportions, was still quite strong, and Gastaldi himself was among those who specifically pointed this out. As we have seen in chapter six, while Gastaldi in his *La vniversale descrittione del mondo* gives the four parts which were becoming generally recognized (Africa, Asia, America, Europe), he also gives distinct tentative recognition to two others, twice as to a possible Southern Continent, and once to a Northern Continent or landmass which he calls "Grutlandia," and as we have shown at length in chapter two, these would have been visualized by Gastaldi as livable and populated regions.[44] Furthermore, among Gastaldi's

---

[44] And in actual fact, this was correct, for the north coast of the Southern Continent on Gastaldi's "Cosmographia Vniversalis", and on some other cartographers' maps, rises very high in the unexplored far southwest Pacific, and thus includes virtually all of unknown Australia, which contained, and had contained for thousands of years, literally hundreds of cultures, and it was true of the Arctic areas as well, even if the cultures present were very sparse. Even Ortelius recognizes the existence of a fifth continent, and not just as a hypothesis, and he even gives it the name "Magellanica", as do some other cosmographers, as Garzoni in 1585 and Rosaccio in 1598. See chapter six for all of this).

own circle, Giunti, Ramusio's publisher, takes the Southern Continent quite seriously indeed, and evidently so did Ramusio, for Giunti speaks of Ramusio's intention to include it in a fourth volume of the *Navigazioni,* and in fact, Ramusio himself does speak of such a fourth volume (see Giunti's quote in chapter two).

Thus, for Gastaldi, the conception of full modern coverage of the world, would have been an idea that did not come so easily and naturally at all, for such coverage still remained literally out of reach. The basic guiding principle as to what areas he decided to map seems to have been simply to map those areas for which he had original information. This statement may seem like a tautology, for it was certainly true of any *bona fide* mapmaker, but there was one tremendous difference between Gastaldi in this respect, and most other cartographers of the time, and here we are perhaps close to the heart and soul of what Gastaldi was all about. For, while the great majority, indeed nearly all, of the many mapmakers which fill Karrow's 1993 classic work did indeed choose to map areas about which they had information, those areas are almost inevitably the areas in which they lived and worked. That was the heart of their interest. But Gastaldi mapped areas for which he had information *no matter where those areas were located,* and, if anything, seemed to actually prefer the farther regions. The heart of his interest was not his homeland, but the whole world, in a word all that portion of the world for which he had new information, and, because of the tremendous European expansion of just over fifty years' time, and because of Ramusio's indefatigable documentation of this expansion, that portion of the world for which he had new information was huge indeed.

Thus, if we seek a concise description of Gastaldi's basic motivation, it would be that he mapped those parts of the known world for which he had substantial new information to add beyond that shown in previous cartography.[45] But Gastaldi certainly had no, or very little, information on the Southern Continent or on Grutlandia. This lack of knowledge about several large sections of the globe, making it impossible to make genuine special maps of these areas, introduces an important nuance to Gastaldi's not providing maps of western Europe. For, taken in this context, the omission of western Europe no longer amounts to the omission of the last remaining area, that is, it was not the last remaining block in an otherwise complete picture. It was simply one of several areas for which he did not have any new information over and above what the cartographers of those lands themselves possessed. And thus, there would have been no sense of urgency for attaining coverage for western Europe.

Our conclusions in this section are just a shade more conjectural and inconclusive than we might have hoped for, but our information is simply too limited to arrive at anything more definite, that we have in fact exhausted our resources, and any attempt to go further would simply result in empty pondering.

10.5 The Maps Made on Gastaldi's Initiative in the 1540s

It will be appropriate to conclude this chapter with a few words on the only other Gastaldi maps made on his own volition, besides the Gastaldi-Licinio maps of 1559-1564, that is, the small but significant group of separate maps made in the 1540s. In a broad sense, these maps could be taken as heralding the efforts of 1559-1564, and it is possible that Gastaldi had harbored from the start of his career a desire to map parts of the world far from his homeland, and that only the everyday exigencies of life and providing a living for himself and his family impeded him from following this with regularity, a suggestion we have made elsewhere. There is the large

---

[45] We recall that in general we have in mind here maps made on Gastaldi's own volition. However, while the picture is not yet fully clear, the indications are that Gastaldi's policy was for the most part the same as regards the maps made for others. The only Gastaldi map known to have been basically simply copied from a previous map is the pre-1552 Germany (no. 70), made, we can no doubt assume, on contract for Gabriel Giolito. Even in this case, Gastaldi made some slight additions, although not very successfully according to Meurer (2001, 244). Generally, we may say that the generalization stated repeatedly by Lavis-Trafford (1950), that sixteenth century cartographers mainly constructed their maps by following previously existing maps is quite incorrect in the case of Gastaldi.

and impressive four-sheet Spain of 1544 (no. 1), which is strikingly similar in all points of style and convention to the later maps, then the 1545 Sicily (no. 2), also similar to the later maps, except that the engraving in these maps is not as fine.[46] Next, there is the influential 1546 world map (no. 3), followed by the very large four-sheet map of central eastern Europe (no. 4). These are all worthy products of the first order. But most importantly, as regards analogy with the Gastaldi-Licinio maps, there is the giant Africa (no. 118) which we know Gastaldi was working on in the 1540s, as first noticed by Biasutti, and of which we have made mention several times previously. We shall now give Gastaldi's own description of it, as far as it goes.

On the verso of the map "Africa nova tabvla" in Gastaldi's 1548 Ptolemy,[47] after having given some general description of Ethiopia, Gastaldi continues: "Nella nostra Aphrica la quale (come io spero) verrà tosto in luce, sarà ogni cosa particolarmente distinta di questa parte della Ethiopia, la quale è sotto lo Egitto, cosa maravegliosa e non più veduta" (In our Africa, a wonderful thing not seen before, which [as I hope] will soon come into the light every thing about this part Ethiopia, which is below Egypt, will be distinguished in detail). Again, on the verso of the map "Marmarica nova tabvla" there,[48] we find written:

> Anchora questa Marmaricha hoggi si domanda tutto Barberia, sotto alla quale sono diversi regni, cioè il Regno di Nubia, quello di Gaoga, Borno, et molti altri li quali meglio si vederanno più particolari quando daremo fora tutta la nostra Aphrica, e tutti questi Regni e molte regioni e provincie che sono al presente nell'Aphrica, che saria cosa molto lunga a narrarla in questa poca scrittura pero mi riservo al grande disegno di tutta l'Aphrica per mare e per terra, a dimostrarla come si ritrova hoggi (This whole Marmarica is still today called Barberia, in which there are various kingdoms, namely the Kingdom

---

[46] As brought out in chapter 1, it is quite possible that Gastaldi himself engraved his own earliest maps. The engraving, in fact, is reasonably good, though of course not up to Licinio's.

[47] Our map no. 38. Regardless of its title, the map does not show all of Africa, but all the great south projection of Africa plus part of central and east Africa up to northern Ethiopia. The title may simply mean the part that was unknown to Ptolemy.

[48] Map no. 35. The map covers eastern Libya and western Egypt.

of Nubia, that of Gaoga, Borno, and many others which will be seen better [and] in more detail when we give out our entire Africa, and all these kingdoms and many regions and provinces which are at present in Africa, which will be a thing too lengthy to recount in this short writing, but I propose to show how it is found today by the large map of all coastal and inland Africa).[49]

Biasutti believed that the map Gastaldi refers to here was an already worked up large Africa in several sheets which would already have resembled the large 1564 Gastaldi Africa which would appear sixteen years later, except for some significant additions which would have been made about 1554, after the appearance of the first *Decade* of Barros's *Asia*, of which we have spoken in chapter four. Skelton generally expressed reservations about Biasutti's idea.[50] Whatever the map was, clearly Gastaldi had some large and impressive Africa map project in hand, and that he had reason to hope that this would "soon come into the light." The phrase "I propose to show," etc. immediately reminds us of his words about his forthcoming *parti* in his 1561 *La Vniuersale descrittione del mondo*. But we know that no map corresponding to that described in 1548 as coming out soon appeared for sixteen years, until 1564. The Gastaldi Africa in the 1554 second edition of Ramusio's *Navigazioni*, though impressive by comparison to all before it, could not have been this detailed map, and even if it were, there was still a six-year gap between it and the 1548 promise of a map soon to appear.

The existence of these works in the 1540s suggests that perhaps the activities of 1559-1564 were the culmination of a sort of intention to cover the world as known up to Gastaldi's time which Gastaldi had perhaps cherished all along, as long as he had something new to offer, an intention which he was not able to consistently pursue earlier in his career due to sundry obligations, but which, for unknown reasons he found himself in a position to pursue in the years just before the 1559-1564 maps began to appear. Perhaps in these years 1556-1558 something happened in Gastaldi's

---

[49] Both passages are also quoted full in Biasutti, 1920, 416.
[50] Biasutti (1920, 416-19 and 433); Skelton (1961, 563, note 1). Skelton does not give his reasons for questioning Biasutti's reasoning, which seems quite sound to me.

financial situation which permitted him then, having found the great engraver Licinio, to embark in earnest on a project which had been in his heart from the 1540s.[51] It must not be forgotten, though, that twice earlier in his career, he succeeded, not at all so spectacularly as in 1559-1564, and in maps on a much smaller scale, in achieving essentially the same end, in the 1548 modern maps, and in those of 1553-1556/57, even if those projects were not under his own proprietorship, and those efforts, as we have stated several times, can certainly be considered as the precursors of the 1559-1564 maps.

If we cannot be entirely certain about Gastaldi's intentions, no uncertainty exists as to his influence. It was beyond doubt the cartographic explosion of 1559-1564, especially as regards the far continents, that both inspired and made possible the appearance shortly afterwards of modern world atlases and the great four-continent sets, essentially completing the transition from ancient Ptolemaic to modern cartography. In our next two chapters, we shall bring into focus the genesis of these great four-continent sets from the work of Gastaldi.

---

[51] This exhausts the maps which we believe may have had in Gastaldi's mind some perhaps loose cohesion of purpose which became realizable only in the late 1550s. We omit consideration of the Italian province maps, most of them of unknown dates of composition, since published, except for the 1555 Piedmont, after Gastaldi's death, and which seem more like incidental works unrelated to a broader plan, and we also omit Gastaldi's two island maps, of quite secondary importance in any event, mostly for the same reasons. As regards Gastaldi's last printed map, the 1564 Anatolia (no. 119), it is unclear whether it should be considered as a product of Gastaldi's own volition, for it is not impossible, though it seems unlikely to us, that it was contracted for by the Bertellis, whose shop address appears on the map; and it is also unclear what the rationale for the map was, and how it would have fit in with the Gastaldi-Licinio maps. See also our comments at Cartobibliography entry no. 119.

CHAPTER 11 - CAMOCIO'S GASTALDIAN FOUR-CONTINENT WALL MAP ATTEMPT OF THE 1570s

11.1 Preliminary Remarks

From what we've seen in chapter ten, there certainly would seem to be no reason to expect a four-continent set of wall maps per se from Gastaldi. Yet, in his repertoire there are maps of continents or large parts of continents, and, as we saw in chapter nine, there do exist five examples, not all quite identical, of a set of four-continent wall maps which all clearly contain principally Gastaldi's cartography, two of them sixteenth century printings from an unknown publisher, and three seventeenth century printings by Stefano Scolari.[1] No doubt these facts have given rise to fairly frequent statements or intimations that Gastaldi himself created such a set. Burden notes, "The full set of continental maps have often been labeled as Gastaldi maps."[2] In a notable instance of this, Heijden writes that "Gastaldi has been the first to make a series of large maps of the four continents, setting an example that was widely followed by others,"[3] and Werner Stams says, in his article on printed wall maps, that these "were at times worked up as continent series, by J. Gastaldi among others."[4] Most recently, Woodward has suggested that Gastaldi may have been working on such a set of maps (2007, 786), but the suggestion is based on an incorrect translation of part of a passage in Gastaldi's 1561 booklet *La Vniversale descrittione del mondo*, as we have shown in the previous chapter. There are a number of other such

---

[1] See reproductions corresponding to Cartobibliography entries I to XII for reproductions of all the maps from the three extant complete examples of these sets, derived, as said, mainly from Gastaldi, but not created by him in this form of continental wall maps in a coordinated set.

[2] Burden (1996, 65).

[3] Heijden (1992, 65 and 140).

[4] Stams (1986, 873).

references,[5] and in fact I myself for a considerable time entertained the possibility some years ago.

None of those who have stated or implied that Gastaldi made a four-continent set has attempted to develop an argument to support the idea with the single exception of Heijden, whose argument, as we shall see, rests upon grounds quite thin and it seems to me that he goes a bit too far on the basis of altogether insubstantial information. Heijden's book is basically a cartobibliography of maps of Europe, so he concentrates first on that map. He says he mailed to John Chalmers at the Ransom Research Center at the University of Texas at Austin, where one of the three later sets of the four-continent maps is located,[6] a photo reproduction of the Europe in the James Ford Bell Library set,[7] and asked Chalmers if the Europe in the Texas set was printed from the same plate as the Bell Europe, to which Chalmers replied, "In my opinion, the answer is no."[8] On the basis of this, and an invalid point based on a misunderstanding, which we shall elucidate in a moment, and a couple of circumstantial factors,[9] Heijden comes to the conclusion that the Texas Europe must have been printed from an original mid-sixteenth century plate engraved from some presumed original map of Europe by Gastaldi

----

[5] For example, in Parker (1991, 122), Kraus (1949, 12; and 1969(?), p. 23), a recent notice in *Imago Mundi*, 52 (2000), 182, in the notices of recent items of interest; and no doubt many others. In fact, in their own time, the completed sets of these maps seem to have been referred to as Gastaldi sets. As mentioned in chapter nine, the America map in one of the of the later, completed examples of these sets contains the slightly misleading phrase: "Description of the Four Parts of the World by Giacomo Gastaldi . . . " (see chapter twelve, at section 12.2, "A terminus a quo and a terminus ad quem" for the full title of this text, in Italian and English, and more on the text itself). These sets evidently sold well at least until the late 1660s, and the giant world map "Cosmographia Vniversalis" was being sold into the seventeenth century (The only copy known was printed in the seventeenth century as we have seen in chapter two), so Gastaldi's name retained some prominence in cartography at least until those times.

[6] The Asia is dated 1655, the only map in the set carrying a date.

[7] Itself dated 1579, though the date has clearly been altered from an earlier one (see figs. 11.1 and 11.2, which reproduce this date figure greatly enlarged.)

[8] Heijden, 1992, 65. Basically, the two maps look the same, except that in the Texas copy the title cartouche in the upper left sheet has been changed, as has the background marine décor (ships, sea monsters, etc.). Nevertheless, I have confirmed that it is in fact a different engraving.

[9] The map, as we shall see, and as Heijden acknowledges, is a direct copy from the 1564 Contarini map of Europe. This map is reproduced in Heijden (1992, pp. 66-67, no. 18). Heijden, apparently implying an attribution of the Contarini map to Gastaldi, notes correctly that no other map by Contarini is known, and that Gastaldi was producing more than anyone else at the time (Heijden 1992, 97). But, while these facts are true, they provide no conclusive evidence of anything, though we shall discuss such factors below.

himself! He numbers this unattested first printing of the map as no. 17 in his cartobibliography, and dates it as "before 1564."

Now, apart from the fact that the determination made by Chalmers could hardly be considered as conclusive at the time, the conclusion reached by Heijden on the basis of it can only be regarded as a heroic leap of faith. There are six copies of the Europe known, one in Rotterdam, as a separate map, dated 1573, that in the Bell set dated 1579 (changed from an earlier date by hand), that in the Correr set dated 1585, two undated copies in later, seventeenth century, complete sets of the maps, one possessed by Graham Arader of New York and the other in the set at the University of Texas, and an undated seventeenth century single copy at Yale University. Only that in Texas contains décor different from the others, and in fact, it is, as we have said, indeed from a different engraving of the Europe.[10] But since it is from a mid-seventeenth century set, the obvious conclusion is that it is a late reengraving made in the seventeenth century, a logical enough eventuality since the map evidently sold well over many years, and its original plate could well have become worn out. Certainly, no reason exists to assume that the plate behind this mid-seventeenth century printing was older than the plate which produced the copies dated 1573, 1579, and 1585.[11]

Heijden's only evidence for the other three maps is the fact that the maps in the Texas set have large title strips pasted to the top which end with the abbreviation "Auct. G.I."[12] But even at a first glance, interpretation of this abbreviation as meaning G[astaldi] I[acomo] seems a little odd. There is

---

[10] See more on this in entries (V.-VIII.) and V in our Cartobibliography.

[11] Next to the new title cartouche in the Texas map is a figure of some monarch riding the waves in a water chariot. The monarch is not identified. Heijden asserts that the king is Charles V, who died in 1558, and resigned the throne in 1556, so this would suggest that the presumed Gastaldi plate went back at least to 1556, quite impossible. Still another cartobibliographer of Europe uncritically, accepts Heijden's determination, and dates the map as "1550-1560 circa" (Borri, 2001, 98). However, he identifies the monarch as Phillip II, who reigned 1556-1598, as do also Lentz (1994, at no. 28), and Kraus (1949, 12 and 1969(?), 27). The entries for this map in Heijden and Borri both refer to a map which most assuredly never existed.

[12] Heijden, 1992, 65. The title strips also occur in the complete set of the maps owned by Graham Arader (Mr. Arader owns two of the five known sets, one of them lacking the Europe). By way of example, the full title strip on the Europe reads "NOVA ET ACVRATA TOTIVS EVROPAE TABVLA. Auct: G.I:" (see our maps VI to XII, all of which contain the title strips). The title strips do not occur in the two sixteenth century copies of the sets.

no Italian tradition or practice of inverting surnames and Christian names as far as I know.[13]

In fact, these initials do not mean Gastaldi, and it is worthwhile clarifying things here, for others, including H. P. Kraus, have made the same incorrect assumption. The initials actually mean "Guglielmus Iansonnius" or perhaps "Guglielmo Iansonnio", respectively the Latinized or Italianized forms of Willem Janszoon [Blaeu]. Willem Janszoon never used the last name form "Blaeu" until he was about fifty years old, first evidently in ca. 1621,[14] but always used the first two names only. So, what are Blaeu title strips doing on these Italian maps? The answer lies in the sometimes-makeshift practices in the Italian map trade of the seventeenth century. In 1608 Blaeu made a very successful set of four-continent maps, and some years afterwards (it is not known exactly when) the Venetian publisher Stefano Scolari published an Italian rendition of the 1612 edition of the set, and pasted to the top of the maps large full-length title strips, ending in the initialized forms just described. It was, as we have mentioned, Scolari who also published the later editions of the Gastaldian four-continent sets, and he simply brought these Blaeu title strips into service on these maps, knowing that there was sufficient similarity between the two cartographers' initials that the form "G.I." would be taken as Gastaldi.[15]

Thus, the "G.I." definitely cannot be taken as a genuine or definite indication that the map it is located on is by Gastaldi, and, especially, cannot be taken as an indication that these four maps were created by Gastaldi in the four-continent form in which we see them, a thing which must not be confused with the fact that most of the cartography was in fact borrowed

---

[13] There is such a practice, and, in formal situations, it is quite universal and rigidly followed, in Slavic societies. If Anton Chekhov were asked, in formal circumstances, his name, he would unquestionably answer "Chekhov Anton", with no pause between the words, and with no comma if it were written. But even in these societies, there does not exist a practice of inverting name forms given as initials.

[14] Van der Krogt (1995, 84).

[15] Gastaldi is recognized as source for the maps in the dedicatory epistles on the Africa and Asia of the later sets, and on the America his name occurs in the title of the lengthy box of text making up the large southwest sheet of the map, already mentioned above. But, perhaps significantly, since, unlike the Africa, Asia and America, it is unclear how much of the cartography in the Europe is from Gastaldi, his name does not occur on that map.

from Gastaldi's maps.[16] Heijden presents no further support for his idea, except for simply stating twice that Gastaldi made the first four-continent set.[17] So we see there exists no evidence at all for this idea of Gastaldi himself producing a four-continent set, as opposed to someone else, Camocio, producing a four-continent set after Gastaldi's death on the basis of Gastaldi material, a quite different thing. Nevertheless, we shall obstinately broach the idea once more below to remove any lingering notion that Gastaldi made a four-continent set or had any intention to so.

Now we may move on to the real genesis of the Gastaldian, or (almost entirely) Gastaldi-based four-continent sets, and demonstrate that they unquestionably came originally from the mind and shop of Giovanni Francesco Camocio,[18] who is thus the father of this famous form, which would flourish for over two centuries, although, as we have seen, he did not quite succeed in finishing the last map, the America, and thus the set. We can assume that, since he was less than one map away from completing his impressive four-continent set, his drive would have been very strong to conclude the job, and that he would have done so if he had been able. This consideration lends certainty to the surmise, discussed briefly in chapter nine, that Camocio succumbed to the plague of 1575-77 (probably in 1575, after which we find no mention of him), though no one has doubted this since it was first posited by Gallo in 1950.

Camocio was probably intellectually a cut above the typical publishers and printers of his time. Menato (1997, 237) says some historians maintain that he was the brother of the celebrated Hellenist Giovanni Battista Camocio, while Palagiano (1974, 288), just says he is considered a relative "if not direct brother" of Giovanni Battista, and Gallo (1950, 93) simply calls him Giovanni Battista's "namesake". But while the relationship seems indefinitely attested, Camocio was, for the seven years before we first see his interest in maps, that is, 1552-1559, a book publisher, and his repertoire included several commentaries on prominent Greek thinkers, including

---

[16] For more on these title strips which were with questionable legitimacy used on the later Gastaldian map sets, see Di Palma (1991, 525-26), and Schilder (1996, 77 and 190-93; note esp. the reproduction on p. 192.)

[17] Heijden (1992, 65 and 140).

[18] On Camocio in general see Gallo (1950); Palagiano (1974); Menato (1997, 237-38); Ganado (1994-95, 1, 267-71); Bury (2001, 223); Almagià (1948, 116-17); and Borroni-Salvadori (1980, lxiv-lxv).

Aristotle (one of them by Piccolomini, and another by Giovanni Battista Camocio), as well as others on Hippocrates, Galen, and Diocles of Carystus, and a number of medical texts.[19] He also made a good number of prints after paintings of the great masters, including Titian and Michaelangelo (Gallo, 1950, 93), probably on contract with these artists themselves, as was commonly done. But most telling of all, he himself translated at least two works from Greek into Latin (Meurer, 1991, 125). And, as we shall see, he certainly played a much more active part than was usual in his capacity as a map publisher (from 1559), fulfilling the role of a designer or planner, and a quite imaginative and venturesome one.

11.2 The First Bid for a Four-Continent Set of Wall Maps

Camocio's original four-continent set, incomplete in one continent, provides us with a wonderful example of something which all historians of cartography have known intuitively all along: that is, that there unquestionably existed a certain number of maps, some of them of much import, of which neither examples nor written records have come down to us at all, and so we don't even know of their one-time existence. For, while, as we said, five sets have come down to us, none of the latest four contains the slightest indication that Camocio initiated the set, or that this occurred in the 1570s. It is due only to the very fortunate finding of a single example of the original set, the Bell Library set, that we know of it at all.[20] Its preservation is due to a peculiar quirk of fate. The sheets of the maps were of course intended to be pasted together, and the full maps framed and proudly displayed as wall maps, which is precisely the form in which all three of the seventeenth century printings were originally found preserved. But because, as we have seen, one of the four maps of the Camocio set, the America, was not completed, it could not be sold as a wall map, and without it the set itself could not be sold as a four-continent set. Stuck, as it were, after Camocio's untimely death, with one map in incomplete condition, it was decided, rather unethically, to attempt to sell the set as an atlas, in which form the absence of

---

[19] My source is the Servizio Biblioteca Nazionale (SBN), the online union catalog of Italian libraries.

[20] For the provenance of the set, see chapter nine.

some parts of one continent would be much less obvious to the prospective purchaser. And thus, the wall maps, intended for ostentatious display, were relegated to serve in a guise inappropriate both to their form, and to the proper make-up of a world atlas. But it is due only to this sad circumstance that the maps' sheets, bound between covers as the leaves of an atlas, came to be preserved in superb condition. We will now describe this atlas.[21]

The atlas is in a typical sixteenth century limp vellum binding ca. 29 x 41 cm., and on its cover is a manuscript title "Quatro parte del Mondo" ([The] Four parts of the World). It contains seventy-one leaves, arranged as follows: First is a single-sheet world map signed by Camocio.[22] A flyleaf follows which is blank except for the manuscript word "Europa," after which are nine double foldout plates (thus eighteen leaves total) making up the Europe.[23] The same pattern of flyleaf with manuscript title (Africa, then Asia) followed by nine double-spread plates occurs then for the Africa, then the Asia, and finally, a flyleaf with "America" followed by the six double-spread plates of the incomplete America.

This copy of the atlas (there were probably others, as we shall see) was not produced in Camocio's lifetime.[24] Two of the continental maps are dated, the Europe 1579 (M.D.LXXIX), and the Asia also 1579 (M D LXXV4).[25] Nevertheless, this copy of the atlas clearly provides, along with some other facts, very certain proof that the set was originally compiled by

---

[21] See reproductions corresponding to Cartobibliography entries I to IV for reproductions of the maps, with the individual sheets assembled together to make images of full wall maps.

[22] It is Tooley's no. 8 in his 1939 work. It is, strangely, dated 1562. As Woodward says (1997, 5), it must have been salvaged from old stock. It is basically a reengraving of Gastaldi's 1546 world map, with minor changes.

[23] The sheeting arrangement is actually twelve sheets (as in figure 9.1), nine whole sheets and three half-sheets at the right, but in the atlas, the half sheets have been pasted to the sheets to their left, and then folded inward to not exceed the bounds of the atlas. The maps have therefore sometimes been described as nine-sheet instead of twelve-sheet maps, causing some confusion. In the Correr set, these half sheets are loose and not pasted to the sheets to their left.

[24] Actually, no copy of the so-called atlas was produced in his lifetime. When he died, not having completed the America, his intent was still a set of wall maps.

[25] Both of the dates have clearly been changed (see figs. 11.1, 11.2, 11.3 and 11.4 for enlarged reproductions of the dates), and in the author's opinion, it is quite impossible to determine what the original dates were from these changed dates, though attempts, mostly serendipitous in my opinion, have been made (see Caraci, 1927, 37-38; Caraci, 1962, 51-52 and 55-56; and Woodward, 1997, 6, 9, and 25-26.). See more on these dates below.

Camocio in the 1570s; and, in my opinion, probably in the period ca. 1570 to ca. 1575 (?).[26] As to Camocio's authorship, for one thing, both the Europe and the Asia contain long dedicatory epistles signed by Camocio, along with his characteristic address "Alla libraria della Piramide" (see figs. 11.1, 11.3, 11.5 & 11.6 at the end of this chapter) and in these legends he not only specifically tells us that he produced the maps, but also mentions others in the set that he has made before, and in the Asia also tells us that, having made maps of Africa, Asia, and Europe, he intends to move on to an America, so that the whole world might be enjoyed.[27] While, on the Africa, the dedicatory cartouche has been left blank in the Bell copy, and there is thus no Camocio signature on it, Camocio tells us on the Asia that he made an Africa, and, Caraci notes, the map is definitely done in Camocio's later style,[28] and the same can be said of the America, also unsigned. Also, there is the fact that all the maps were given the same peculiar and distinct sheeting arrangement.

This is a good place to say a few words on this sheeting arrangement decided on by Camocio, consistent throughout the set, which shows the unusual level of versatility and talent exhibited by Camocio as publisher. He was without question the basic guiding hand, planner and designer in this, as well as in some other of his works, and not just a publisher in the sense of a businessman alone.[29] We have already mentioned the segmentation of sheets which Camocio gave to each of these maps (see figure 9.1 at the end of this

---

[26] It is not possible to establish with certainty the beginning and end dates. My reasons for the estimate given are made clear further below. The earliest previous estimates for the start date have been 1570, and for the end date 1575, but none of the estimates, including my own, can be given full credence. But Camocio's authorship is certain.

[27] We quote the relevant parts of this Asia dedication below in the section, "ASIA". For the full dedications as they appear on the maps, see the enlarged figs. 11.5 and 11.6. A full English translation of the Italian text on the Europe, only moderately good, is in Gallo (1950, 101).

[28] Caraci, 1962, 53, who describes this style.

[29] Another good example is his successful fusing of major elements of Gastaldi's 1561 "Cosmographia Vniversalis" world map with the same cartographer's depiction of the world in his 1546 world map and its derivatives to produce his large four-sheet 1567 world map (Karrow, 1993, p. 241, no. 30/93.2; and Shirley, no. 117.).

chapter).[30] But we did not mention that the sheet segmentation of the maps he was copying from was quite different, which would have presented a task that was not simple. The Africa and, we can assume, the America had an arrangement of eight equal-sized sheets, four above and four below, as in figure 11.7. In figure 11.8 we superimpose one sheet arrangement over the other, and we can see at a glance the difficulties involved. The original Europe (the 1564 Contarini map, minus an eastern sliver, as we shall see) with twelve equal-sized sheets, in three rows of four sheets each, was probably still more difficult. And more difficult by far than these, was the Asia, of which difficulties we shall speak separately below. Finally, as we shall see, Camocio was capable of making actual major geographical changes, justifying the fact that some historians have referred to him as not just a publisher, but also a cartographer.[31]

What impelled or inspired Camocio to venture on the first four-continent set? We can identify certain currents and events which surely contributed to it. In the first place, although not in sets, using maps as wall décor goes back to the first half of the sixteenth century.[32] More to the point, there were the single-sheet four-continent sets of Ortelius in 1570 and Anania

---

[30] The most likely explanation I can find for this sheeting arrangement is that the size of the large sheets was dictated by the materials available. That is, at the time Camocio began these maps, the sheet size of the larger sheets was limited to the size of the largest plates he, or his unknown engraver, had on hand, or were able to acquire. Alternatively, perhaps no paper was available which would exceed the size of his larger sheets, and even the length of the bed of the rolling press on which the maps were printed could have played a limiting role. The maps, incidentally, as we see from their dimensions given in the Cartobibliography, are in fact not at all exactly equal in width or height, but in all cases, Camocio partitioned each image north-south into three equal spans, and east-west into three equal spans plus one span which was half the width of the equal spans. So, likewise, the individual sheets themselves are not exactly the same size from map to map. The overall difference in size is not perceivable to the eye when perusing the maps on walls, especially if placed, as would be usual, on four different walls.

[31] For example, Bagrow-Skelton (1985, 236) and Tooley (1979, 10).

[32] Ambrosini (1981, 67-69).

in 1573 (in Anania, 1576(1573)).[33] Also, a limited number of wall maps of individual continents already existed.[34] Very possibly another influence was the first painted four-continent wall map series at Caprarola, in Camocio's own Italy, done in 1573-74.[35] While Camocio had already begun his maps before this, it only becomes certain in the dedication in the Asia we possess, which I date speculatively at ca. 1573-1574 (?), that he intended to map all four continents, so the Anania and Caprarola maps could have affected his decision. Finally, there is the fact that Camocio himself had produced at least four previous single-sheet maps of Europe,[36] three one-sheet continental maps of Africa,[37] and a map which shows most of America and the Atlantic (figure 9.14)[38] Though there seems to be no map of all Asia, the 1563 Africa already mentioned actually extends considerably further east, showing southern Asia as far as Western India, and there is a 1565 Anatolia, after Gastaldi.[39] And, in general, a perusal of those pages in Tooley which catalogue maps of the extra-European continents (Tooley, 1939, 19-21) shows that Camocio had a much greater interest in those regions than anyone other than Gastaldi himself. Clearly, whatever the reasons were, Camocio was more inclined towards an interest in making maps of non-European continental areas than other map producers.

---

[33] It should be mentioned that there was one, but only one, precedent to this, thirty years before the *Theatrum*. Münster's 1540 *Geographia* includes a modern set of the four continents. The set is a little awkward in several ways. Europe is split up from the maps of the far continents by other maps; the integrity of the Asia is a little questionable, for at the east it wanders over a good distance into the New World map, and its title, "India Extrema", is a little disconcerting; and the maps are generally quite primitive in appearance. Nevertheless, it basically qualifies as a set of maps of the four continents, if with some slight reservations, and it was repeated in at least twenty-seven editions of Münster's *Geographia* and *Cosmographia* to 1628, so it probably had some influence on the growth of the idea, and perhaps influenced Ortelius to a degree. See Karrow (1993, 421, 423-26, 428, 430 and 433-34).

[34] For example, Mercator's 1554 Europe, Guttierez's 1562 America, Gastaldi's 1564 Africa, and Ortelius's 1567 Asia.

[35] On the Caprarola maps, see Partridge (1975). The wall maps are reproduced in fine color in Portoghesi (1996, pls. XCIV-XCV.) The cartography is mostly Gastaldi's (Kish, 1951).

[36] Two in 1568 (Tooley, 1939, nos. 32 and 33), one in 1570 (Almagià, 1948, 84-85), and one in 1571(?) (Gallo, 1950, 96).

[37] One in 1562 (Woodward, 1992, 49-50), one in 1563 (Tooley, 1939, no. 70), and one of Africa after the Ancients in 1566 (Tooley no. 41).

[38] Tooley (1939, no. 77).

[39] Karrow (1993, p. 246, no. 30/103.1); and Tooley (1939, no. 65).

We said that, of the five extant sets of the Gastaldian four-continent maps, it is only from that in the Bell Library that we can learn that it was Camocio who created the set in the beginning. It is interesting, and will be useful to us in our presentation, to reveal what accounts for this fact. As we have said, the America was finally completed in the 1590s, and along with it, the Venetian four-continent set became a reality. However, Camocio's original Africa and Asia were replaced by different maps, two wall maps published by Donato Bertelli, of which we shall also speak more in their place. They are similar to the original maps, and they are very much still basically Gastaldi, but they are different productions, and there is no sign of Camocio's name or style in them. Furthermore, the dedication on the Europe has been burnished out, and replaced with only the name of the continent in large letters, while the America, is unsigned in all sets. Thus it is that the four-continent set in the Bell Library is the only set extant which consists entirely of Camocio's original maps, the only maps which reveal to us that Camocio was the original father of the set.

11.3 Comments on Each of the Four Individual Maps, and Tentative Observations on Their Sequence of Appearance

Let us now turn to a discussion one by one of the original Camocian maps,[40] stressing especially their origins cartographically, and seeking, one last time, any indication that all of these maps could possibly have been made by Gastaldi himself in the form in which we know them, that is, as a set of wall maps of the four continents, in order to put that notion to rest with finality. We shall first discuss the Africa and the America, which require little attention, and then the Asia and the Europe, which present more complexities.

---

[40] As regards two of the maps, of course, the Europe and the America, the discussion also applies to the copies of those maps in the other sets as well. As said, we shall speak more later of the Bertellian Africa and Asia.

11.3.1 *Africa*

Of the Africa, little need be said. It is clear that Camocio copied it directly from Gastaldi's eight-sheet map of Africa (Cartobibliography no. 118). This is true also of the Bertelli variant which appears in all the other sets, although it is true there are small orographic and hydrographic differences between them. We might note that, while the Africas of the sets are just editions of the original Gastaldi map, that map itself gives no indication that it should be thought of as being part of a four-continent set.

11.3.2 *America*

As with the Africa, we need say little about the America. We know that Camocio took the map directly from Gastaldi's manuscript ca. 1560 America, and that Camocio at the time of his death was attempting, or contemplating an attempt, to make one major change in Gastaldi's cartography, the shortening of Gastaldi's eastward overextension of North America. We know no more of how Camocio obtained this manuscript map than we know how Ferrando Bertelli obtained the manuscripts for the 1567 Apulia and the 1568 Padua, or how Lafreri obtained the manuscript for the 1570 Lombardy. But the natural supposition is that the America and the others were purchased from Gastaldi's estate, which would presumably have reverted to Gastaldi's family after his death. So, the most likely seller would have been Anzola Gastaldi, his second wife,[41] who was probably considerably younger than he, and most likely survived him by a number of years. As with the Africa, we have no reason to think that the original manuscript America was conceived by Gastaldi as part of any four-continent set. While it is clear that the Africa and the America were conceived as continental wall maps, this is not the case, as we shall now see, with the Asia and the Europe.

---

[41] This we learn from Gastaldi's testament of 1555, as see chapter 1, in the section,"Letters to Ramusio.".

11.3.3 *Asia*

The derivation of the Bell Asia is clear also, for in it Camocio reproduces practically exactly Gastaldi's three-part Asia of 1559-61, bringing those three parts together to make a single map. This is an artifact of great value, since it is the only extant copy of the only map to bring all three Gastaldi Asias together in a single image. We give Camocio's dedication to Gottardo Murari, followed by an English translation, the accuracy of which we can vouch for only to the extent that Camocio's sprawling and tortured syntax allows us:

> Secondo li scrittori antichi, et moderni Mag(nifi)co Sig(no)r mio l'habittation di l'uniuerso si distingue in 4 parti, cioè Asia, Africa, Europa, et Nouomondo: Et essendo poste a luce due di esse parti, cio è Africa, et Europa, fu ancho dall'Ecc(elentissi)mo Gastaldo data fuori in uarij pezzi la p(rese)nte Asia, li quali per essere difficil alli studiosi, et per accompagnare le due predette parendomi cosa necessaria, mi son mosso senza riguardo di fatica et spessa a dar fuori ancho questa bella parte de l'Asia nel simil modo non piu fatta con speranza anche de la Quarta, acciò intieramente si goda detto uniuerso. (According to the ancient and modern writers my Magnificent Lord the inhabited part of the universe consists of four parts, that is Asia, Africa, Europe, and the New World. And two of these parts, Africa and Europe, being brought out, I am moved without regard to labor and expense to give out also this beautiful part of Asia not made before[42] in such fashion, this seeming to me a necessary thing in order to accompany the two aforesaid and because the present Asia was given out by the most excellent Gastaldo in variable parts, presenting difficulty to scholars;

---

[42] I do not find in modern Italian this odd little usage or idiom of "non più" carrying the meaning "not before" or "never before" or "before now", but it seems to have been common enough at the time, for Gastaldi uses it on the back of his Africa nova tabvla (see our map no. 38.) in his 1548 Ptolemy in a line we have quoted at the end of the previous chapter, in which he refers to a large Africa map he is evidently making as a "cosa maravegliosa e non più veduta." Note also the title of a 1544 Venice published work by Alvise Cà da Mosto in the New York Public Library: *Nuouo Portolano non piu stampato molto particolare de'l Levante e de'l Ponente*, etc. (*New very detailed portolan of the East and the West not/never published before*). The idiom may have been Venetian dialect.

with hope of the fourth so that the whole said world might be enjoyed.)

At this point, we must interrupt our comments and insert something about the dedication to Count Antonio Valmarana on the Europe. This will allow us to go into some important details on the Asia and Europe, and will also allow us to draw some tentative conclusions concerning the dates of the maps, and for the set as a whole, and offer a very likely sequence of appearance for the maps. The Europe dedication reads:

> Havendo nelli passati miesi in luce posto, mag[nifi]co et Ill[ustrissim]o Sig[n]or mio, la descrittione dell'Asia in bella et cómoda forma, la quale esse[n]do piaciuta alli studiosi di tal scientia son stato diuerse fiate da loro stimolato a douerla accompagnare con una simile Europa . . . (Having published in the past months, my magnificent and most Illustrious Sir, a depiction of Asia in a beautiful and convenient form, which, having pleased all students of this science, there have been repeated suggestions to have it accompanied by a similar [map of] Europe . . .)

We are left with a direct contradiction, unsolvable, for we do not know the original dates of the maps. On the Europe, he says that he has already made an Asia. On the Asia, he says that he has already made a Europe (and an Africa). Caraci and Woodward have noted this discrepancy, but they do not offer any real conclusion. We have a solution which cannot be proved, but is certainly possible, and it answers all questions and removes all contradictions perfectly. We think the most likely explanation is simply momentary oversight, inattention on the part of Camocio or his engraver. That is, when, in the map of Europe, he says he has already made a map of Asia, he simply slipped, made an oversight, as anyone can do and occasionally does, and, due to inattention, perhaps from fatigue, he simply wrote Asia where he was supposed to write Africa. Note that these two relatively short names, both beginning with capital A, are the names of the two extra-European continent names in the Old World, and note, too, as see below, that the upcoming Asia map would probably already have been discussed in the shop, and very possibly was already underway. It would be natural enough for a fatigued or distracted mind to make such a slip. Note also what we get if we assume he meant Africa. The Africa would be first, the Europe would be second, and the notice on the Asia which says that Africa and Europe (in that order) had already come out would be in perfect order, and his stated hope for a fourth, meaning America, would make perfect sense also, for we know that the failed America had to have come last. Note something else. The order Africa-Europe-Asia-America follows the order of simplicity of production, which would no doubt be a consideration. The Africa was copied straight from Gastaldi. The Europe required the excision of the west fourth of Asia from the right of the Contarini map, from which the Europe was then directly copied. The Asia required considerably more, that is, the need to combine into a single map Gastaldi's three parts of Asia, requiring some ingenuity on the part of Camocio. The America would have been most difficult of all, both because it was being worked up from a manuscript copy, and, perhaps still more significantly, because Camocio had clearly decided to improve on Gastaldi's geography.

Note also that we have a tentative, but fairly strong, *terminus ad quem* for the whole operation. No historical record of Camocio past 1575 exists, and he presumably died from the plague that year (Gallo, 1950, 96). Since it was almost surely this that stopped work on the America, which was clearly the last map, we can, considering the lengthy manipulations that Camocio was making on the map, posit that work on the America began in 1574 and halted in 1575, our tentative *terminus ad quem*. We also have a weak *terminus a quo* in the fact that 1571 is the earliest possible date for one of the maps by those who have made attempts to decipher the crudely changed dates on the maps which have come down to us. Noting that the first true four-continent set printed, though not in the form of wall-maps, was the set in Ortelius's 1570 *Theatrum*, which most likely played a role in Camocio's inspiration, we feel it safe to surmise that the set developed approximately in the years 1570 to 1575, which agrees exactly with Woodward's statement that, "The plates for the four wall maps in the Camocio atlas were most likely engraved between 1570 and 1575" (1997, 26), an estimate which he may have arrived at by a different train of thought, which he does not state.

Furthermore, while we recognize that it will never be possible to arrive at precise dates, we feel it safe, on the basis of the above discussion, to make, for dating purposes, the following tentative estimates: History's first attempt at a four-continent set of wall maps, from inspiration to its incomplete denouement, took place in ca. 1570-1575 (?). The individual maps were most likely produced within the following two-year spans: Africa, ca. 1571-72 (?); Europe, ca. 1572-73 (?); Asia, ca. 1573-74 (?), and America, ca. 1574-75 (?), and these are the dates we will use for them. The "circa" and the question mark provide a curtain of leeway, for certainty is unattainable.

Precision, in fact, is of no real importance to us, and the above arguments serve our true purpose quite adequately: We know that it was Camocio who first expressed an intention to make a four-continent wall-map set (see the passage from the dedication on the map of Asia: "with hopes of the fourth [continent] so that the whole said world may be enjoyed"); and it was Camocio who attempted to do so at the same time, falling just short due to his death from the plague. We also know, from earlier chapters, that certainly over 80%, and perhaps 90%, if not more, of the material for the set was taken from the work of Giacomo Gastaldi, without whose material, it could not have been accomplished at all.

We return to Camocio's text on the Asia in the four-continent set, from which we digressed to elucidate, as far as possible, the dates of the maps which comprise it. It is from this Camocian Asia text that we learn that it was he who combined the separate three parts of Gastaldi's Asia into one. This was an impressive piece of compilation on the part of Camocio, and another testimony to his remarkable talents in manipulating cartographical material. It could not have been simple to fuse Gastaldi's three parts into this single map. The only problem which Camocio's compilation presents is the small bit of the Asian continent which runs eastward off the map, as if to meet up with America, near the northeast corner of the top right sheet. There is nothing like this on the original Gastaldi Asia three, or on the later Olgiato edition of that map. We know from other Gastaldi maps of the area that, at this point, Asia and America are extremely close in Gastaldi's concept, so the likelihood that this little extension is to be taken as an indication of a connection with America in a high latitude is strong. As we have stated in chapter nine, it is probable that Gastaldi had in hand variant sketches for northwest America; he probably had corresponding variant sketches for northeast Asia as well, and this depiction most likely reflects such a variant. Almagià has pointed out that the Venetian publishers no doubt made use of surviving uncompleted Gastaldi material after his death.[43] In any event, it is clear that it was Camocio who compiled Gastaldi's three parts of Asia into a single map. To argue that there existed already a combined Asia made by Gastaldi himself, we would have to assume that Camocio is lying outright in his statements quoted above, and we have no basis for such an assumption.

11.3.4 *Europe*

What of the Camocio map of Europe? Camocio copied the map, in every detail, from the 1564 map of Europe together with the western end of Asia signed by Giovanni Pietro Contarini,[44] except that the Camocio copy omits the Asian part of the map. In the present section, we focus on the 1564 original which Camocio copied, or copied most of (although, as shown below, our reproduction is of the printing which we estimate tentatively as ca. 1572-73 (?) (but changed by hand to 1579), which is identical except for the date).[45]

Camocio's copying is exact, so the relatively sparse information that has been offered by scholars as to the sources of one or the other apply equally to either. The fact that the map carries a signature by another party should in theory settle outright that the map is not by Gastaldi. But the world of sixteenth century Venetian map publishing is never a fully open book, and since at first glance there is enough reason to suspect Gastaldi's hand in this, we shall take a second look. No other map by Contarini is known, and this

---

[43] Almagià (1939, *carta*, 9).

[44] Reproduced in Heijden (1992, pp. 66-67, no. 18).

[45] The map carries the following legend in a decorative cartouche upper left: "Joannis Petri Contareni Elegantissima totius Europae ac parties Asiae, nec non littorum Africae descriptio jn lucem nunc edita qui non sine maximis uigilijs eam ab egre gijs Geographis passim collagens et in aere post modum incisam studiosis spectandam praebuit CUM PRIVILEGIO PER ANNOS XV" ("Giovanni Petro Contarini has compiled this very beautiful map of all of Europe with parts of Asia, and besides the coast of Africa, with great care from the data of diverse leading geographers and after that engraved it in copper, [and] placed it at the disposal of the interested"). Camocio did not copy this text onto his map.

looks like the production of an accomplished hand. It has in many places much the look of Gastaldi's work, and the map appeared at a time when Gastaldi was producing large-scale maps of most parts of the world.[46] There is considerable overlap between the southeast part of the map and parts of Gastaldi's first part of Asia, and the similarity is striking, but the most logical conclusion to draw from this is not that we are looking at a Gastaldi production, but simply that for this part of the map Contarini copied from Gastaldi's First Part of Asia, for Contarini clearly copied from many maps in making his own. The map is also on a slight trapezoidal projection, the projection most used by Gastaldi. But these circumstances cannot solidly demonstrate anything, and certainly some parts of the map do not look like Gastaldi. For instance, the axis of Italy is not at all like Gastaldi's and seems almost Ptolemaic.

What little has been determined as to the sources of the map is only a little enlightening. The most important fact is a negative one, that the map definitely does not use as a source the famous 1554 Mercator Europe.[47] Nor is it based, in the north, on the well-known works of Olaus Magnus or Cornelius Anthonisz.[48] Gallo believed that the map was compiled from maps of individual countries,[49] and a glance backwards through Van der Heijden's illustrated cartobibliography of maps of Europe as a whole tends to confirm this,[50] since no whole Europe resembles our map, as do the findings of Lynam and Koeman as far as they go. Lynam believed the map's Britain to be from Lily's 1546 map, and Iberia to be from Gastaldi's 1544 Spain,[51] and Koeman said that the map has an "unmistakable affinity" with a number of Gastaldi maps of parts of Europe, which he does not specifically name.[52] No more has been offered to date, and these findings are not from studies in depth. Furthermore, the fact that a certain amount of Gastaldian cartography

---

[46] Similar observations, as we have seen, were also made by Heijden.

[47] Almagià (1923, 299), Gallo (1950, 103), Koeman (1978, 10).

[48] Gallo (1950, 103).

[49] Gallo (1950, 102).

[50] Van der Heiden (1992).

[51] Lynam (1937-38, 23).

[52] Koeman (1978, 9 and 10).

has been used, though perhaps not in an in-depth way, simply would indicate that Contarini used some Gastaldi sources, hardly a surprising thing.

Little is known of Contarini other than that he was the illegitimate son of a nobleman from the old and powerful Contarini family, and that he was a minor historian.[53] Is there any reason at all why a map made by Gastaldi might appear under Contarini's name? Interestingly, there was an instance slightly earlier in Venetian map history that suggests that something like this actually occurred. In 1555 Antonio Florianus, an artist and sculptor, who was not a nobleman, but whose mother and wife were both of noble families, and who was himself among the popular members of the Council of the Commune in Venice, published a world map in gores, although no other map is known by him.[54] Florianus's map was copied from Antonio Salamanca's version of Mercator's 1538 world map (although it is true that its projection in gores was new), but neither Salamanca nor Mercator is given credit on the map. But again, this interesting case cannot be taken as evidence of Gastaldi authorship in our case.

If we are to speculate that the map is by Gastaldi although it bears Contarini's name, we must assume that this was for some reason agreed upon between the two, and that they were friends. That Gastaldi rubbed shoulders with noblemen we know. His co-chair in geography in the Accademia Venetiana, Livio Sanuto, was of a noble family, as was also Tiepolo, who headed the department of the academy which included geography, and there were other noblemen in the academy whom he would have known. Among the academy's prominent members was Alessandro Contarini. There are also signs of interest in geography by the Contarini family, and there were various connections between persons in Gastaldi's circle and members of this great family. Lynam suggests that geography may have been Contarini's hobby,[55] and the fact that Forlani dedicated to Contarini his map of South America (Peru), a map which could be by Gastaldi, and which has clear connections

---

[53] All that is known of Contarini is in Lynam (1937-38), Gallo (1950, 102, esp. in notes), Caraci (1926-32, 1, 7, note 15), Caraci (1927, "Avanzi," 189, note 1), and Van der Heijden (1992, 66 and 68). Lynam notes that "it is hard to understand why a man like him would have compiled it at all" (cit., 23).

[54] Gallo (1949, 35-38).

[55] Lynam (1937-38, 23). The fact that the family traded heavily in the Levant, and had a business house at Jaffa, accords with this (Lynam, cit., 22).

to the depiction of South America on the Gastaldi America map, accords with this. A lengthy eight-page dedication to Giacomo Contarini, with much information on the Contarini family name, heads the 1574 Ruscelli-Malombra edition of Ptolemy.[56] Ramusio and Fracastoro were themselves in a circle of literati which included Gasparo Contarini, a much more prominent member of the family,[57] and Ramusio at least once obtained material for his *Navigazioni* from Francesco Contarini, a Venetian envoy to the Spanish emperor, and very possibly obtained from the same Contarini his very valuable geographical materials on Fra Marco da Nizza and Coronado.[58] Fracastoro was also in communication with the diplomat Marc' Antonio Contarini,[59] and it is likely that other connections between the illustrious family and Gastaldi's circle could be found if one tried to find them.

But indirectly relating the Contarini family to Gastaldi does nothing for us, and we can pull nothing solid out of it. I can think of no convincing reason why Gastaldi would have made the Contarini map from which Camocio's Europe is taken, and then asked Contarini to accept authorship of it. With no proof to the contrary, we must accept Contarini's authorship, as indicated in the signature. And, finally, there is another point, subtle, but quite convincing, against the original Contarini map being part of a Gastaldi four-continent plan: The Contarini map is not a map of Europe! It is, as we have seen, a map of Europe *and* of western Asia. It clearly could not fit into any plan, by Gastaldi or by anyone else, for a four-continent set.

*   *   *

We trust that the reader will agree that our discussion of the Asia and the Europe, taken together with the facts presented at the start of this chapter,

---

[56] Also, many years before this time, the Giovanni Matteo Contarini who designed the famous 1506 world map (Shirley no. 24), was also a member of this family (Lynam, 1938, 23).

[57] Grande (1905, "relazioni," 95, 106, 133-34), and Parks (1955, 132). Gasparo was involved in failed negotiations with Sebastian Cabot on a project to find a new route to the Spice Islands, and Milanesi, (1984, 67) mentioning Fracastoro, Bembo, and Navagero as being among those interested in geography at the time, also mentions Gasparo with them.

[58] Parks (1955, 143-45).

[59] Grande (1905, "relazioni," 106).

as well as the assessments made in our previous chapter and in chapter six, are sufficient to remove any lingering notion that Gastaldi might have made, or intended to make, a set of wall maps of the four continents in his own time, and that we may now safely close the door on this notion and banish it from the literature. It was never more than a mirage arising from inadequately critical inspection of the materials and facts available. It was Giovanni Francesco Camocio who first conceived of the four-continent wall map form, and, although he principally used Gastaldi's cartography to do so, it was he who all but completed the first such set of maps.[60]

11.4 The Interim: From Camocio's Death to the Realization of the Four-Continent Set

What befell the plates for these maps in the period between Camocio's death and the time when the set was finally completed in the 1590s by Donato Bertelli, as we shall see in our next chapter? Here we can say very little. We have no definite information on what party or parties might have been in possession of the plates in this interim. We know one thing: Whoever owned them, the maps were not sold as a four-continent set, for with the America incomplete, no such set yet existed. But one would expect that individual examples of the three completed continental maps were sometimes sold, probably more of the Europe than of the others, most of which will have simply disappeared, unfortunately the fate of almost all very large maps from this time.[61]

---

[60] Thus, although Camocio's set of maps derives in the main from Gastaldi's work, it was definitely not simply copied from a four-continent set proper which had been made by Gastaldi, as has been hypothesized (Woodward, 2007, 787).

[61] One individual example of the Africa, missing seven of its twelve sheets, probably from this interim period, is known (Betz, 2007, 117). Several individual copies of those sheets of the America which represent sufficiently distinct geographical subjects by themselves are known, one of sheet A, and one of sheet F in the British Library (Woodward, 1997, 22); sheet C is in the Leiden University Library, and was reproduced long ago in Part 1 of *Remarkable Maps*, and sheet G was in the George Harry Beans collection (*Imago Mundi*, 5 (1948), 72), and is most likely now in the John Carter Brown Library at Brown University. According to Woodward (1997, 22), another copy of sheet G is in the Leiden Library also, but I suspect confusion with the Leiden sheet C. No separate copies of the Asia are known, and no separate copies of the Europe are known from the period under consideration, although there is the superb 1573 copy of the Europe in Rotterdam, and there is evidently a later seventeenth century copy of the Europe in Yale University Library, according to Heijden (1992, 93), although I was unable to locate it there.

Also, of course, we know that at least once, the maps, including the incomplete America, were bound as an atlas. Was the single example known to us a one-time experiment which due to good fortune did not perish over the centuries? One consideration suggests that this was not the case, and that, while it may be doubtful how well they might have sold,[62] the intention was to attempt to sell them regularly. For, while the engraving work needed in order to help make the subterfuge effective, that is, the latitude scale added to the left sides of sheets F and J, the bogus longitude numbering applied to sheet A, and the curved line hooking up southeast Japan with Mexico, would not be overly arduous, it nevertheless would amount to enough labor that it seems unlikely that it would have been undertaken unless it were believed that some profit might be obtained from it. So, the implication is that other copies of the defective atlas were made.

As to where, when, and by whom the surviving example of the atlas was made (which was some time after the original copies of the maps were made), we are also faced with much uncertainty. Based on watermark evidence, Woodward (1997, 4 and 25-26) posited that the atlas would have been made in Rome around 1590 or shortly afterwards, by Pietro de' Nobili. But, besides the fact that this watermark evidence is not convincing to me, this hypothesis does not add up considering other evidence. Only two of the maps in the atlas are dated, the Europe and the Asia, which both carry the date 1579. But in both cases the dates have been changed, and very carelessly,[63] and Woodward found that the date change in the Europe had been done in manuscript (Woodward, 1997, 6). But since Woodward's hypothesis is based upon watermark evidence, this necessarily means that the assumption is that the maps were actually printed in Rome ca. 1590.[64] But, obviously, neither De' Nobili, nor anyone else, would print a map in 1590 or thereabouts, and then change the map's date, whatever it had been originally,

---

[62] Besides the fact that it is questionable how many prospective clients could have been successfully deceived into thinking that the America was whole by the cosmetic tinkering in three sheets of that map, the individual sheets of wall maps are hardly well suited to the purpose of making up a world atlas. There are of course no overlaps, and the area coverage of each of the pages of the would-be atlas is quite arbitrary, reflecting no plan at all, and with a few sheets showing virtually nothing but empty stretches of ocean.

[63] See figures 11.2 and 11.4, enlargements of these two dates.

[64] As opposed to the atlas being put together from stock printed earlier, in either Rome or Venice.

to 1579, a time eleven years earlier. So, this hypothesis does not stand up well, and in lack of good reason to posit otherwise, we feel that the most likely date for its manufacture would be 1579 as written on two of the maps.

Let us turn to a different and more important question. We know that part of the surviving fragments of the Europe and the America in the Correr set were acquired by the Bertelli shop at some point (the Africa and the Asia came from Bertelli's own hands, for it was he who made, or soon would make, them). When were the Europe and the America obtained? It is possible in fact to establish a solid *terminus a quo* for this, due to peculiar circumstances. We know that in both the Bell Library set and in the Correr Library set, there occurs one map which contains a changed date which very oddly contains an Arabic number: In the Bell Asia the date 1579 is expressed as MDLXXV4, and in the Correr Europe we have 1585 expressed as MD8V, though in both cases there was adequate space to express the dates correctly in all Roman numerals (see figs. 11.4 and 11.9). I have never before seen this sloppy procedure, which implies that the writer of these dates (both dates are entered in manuscript probably after some burnishing out of former characters), was unfamiliar with usual practice, and probably was unfamiliar with how to correctly form Roman numerals. We have assumed earlier that after Camocio's sudden death, the denizens of his shop went on running the business as well as possible, if for no other reason than to have a living. (Lending further credence to this is the fact that the Camocio shop was equipped also for book publishing and bookbinding, and the 1579 four-continents atlas is a book in a soft vellum binding.) It can only be one and the same person, or perhaps group of persons, from these shop denizens who created both of these date forms, one in 1579 and the other in 1585. The latter number tells us something. Since it could only have been done by a person or persons among the Camocio shop personnel, the map and its plate had not yet been acquired in 1585 by the Bertelli house, where making such a mistake would be impossible. This gives us our solid *terminus a quo* for Donato's having received the material, and for the time he began his restitution of the set. That is, it could not possibly have happened *before* 1585. Unfortunately, we cannot be certain that a sheet already dated 1585 could not have been supplied to Donato at some time *after* 1585. But it could not have been before that, and any piece of chronological information is always potentially useful.[65]

---

[65] Adding to the difficulties and uncertainties there is the peculiar fact that none of the copies of the Camocio maps in the two incomplete sets bear any other publisher's name besides Camocio's, although the maps in the two incomplete sets which we know must certainly have been made after his death. Perhaps there was concern over the possibility that his maps were protected by a *privilegio* and that Camocio's heirs might take action if another publisher applied his name to the maps. It is known that Camocio obtained a blanket privilege of fifteen years in 1568 for all works published by him, which would have run until 1583 (Gallo, 1950, 93-94).

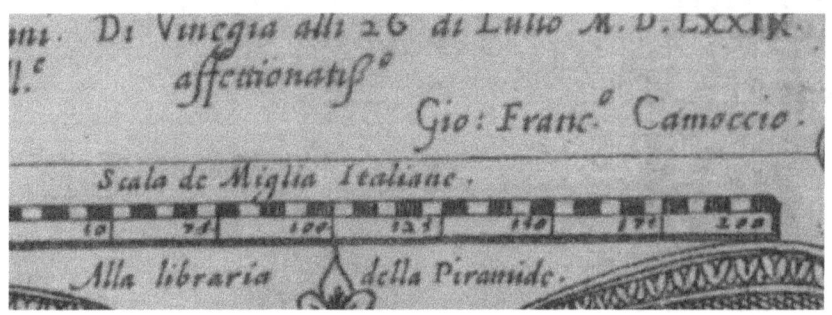

Fig. 11.1 Signture and address, cartouche of Camocio Europe

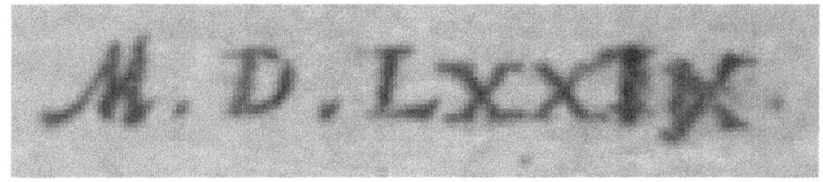

Fig. 11.2 Date on Camocio Europe

Fig. 11.3 Signature, address and date on Camocio's Asia (map. III)

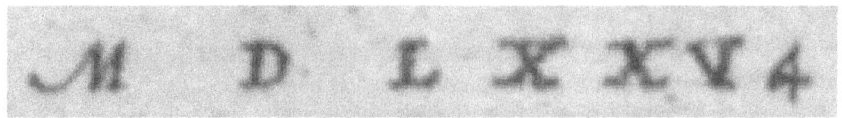

Fig. 11.4 Year from Comocio's Asia (map III)

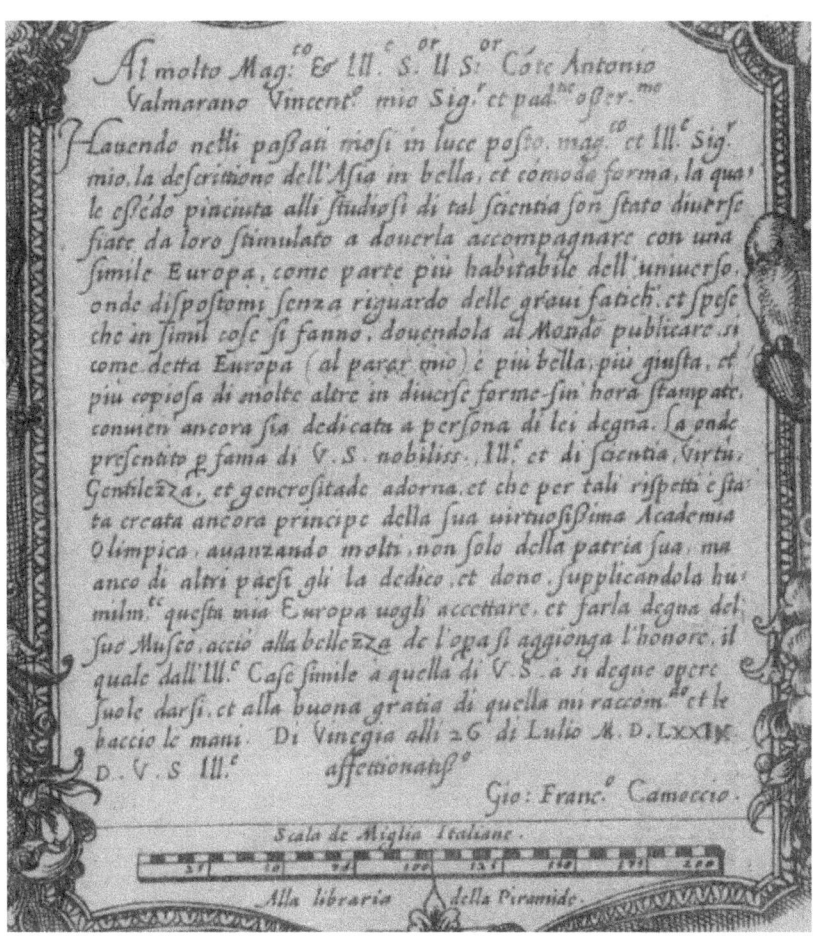

Fig. 11.5 Dedication from Camocio's Europe (map I)

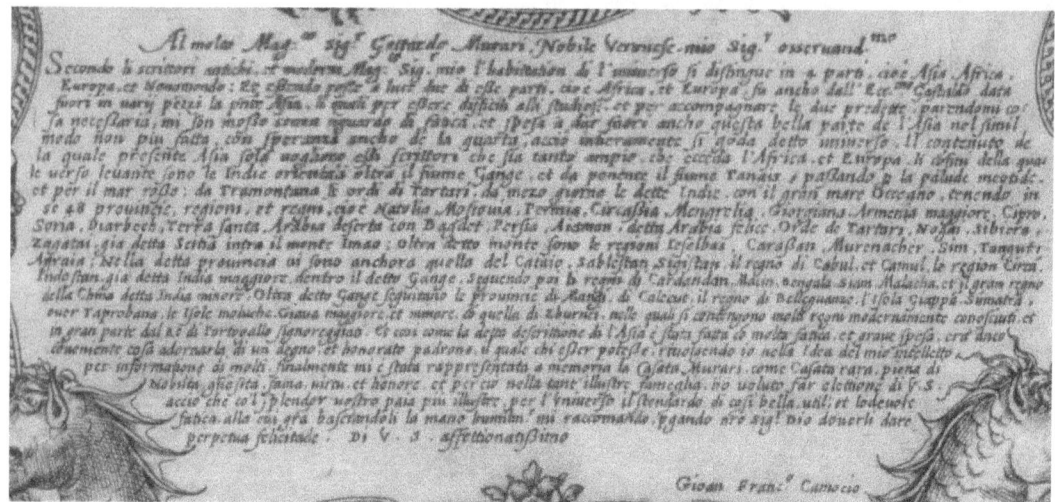

Fig. 11.6 Dedication from Camocio's Asia (map III)

A	*B*	*C*	*D*
E	*F*	*G*	*H*

Fig. 11.7 Standard 4 up and 4 down sheet arrangement

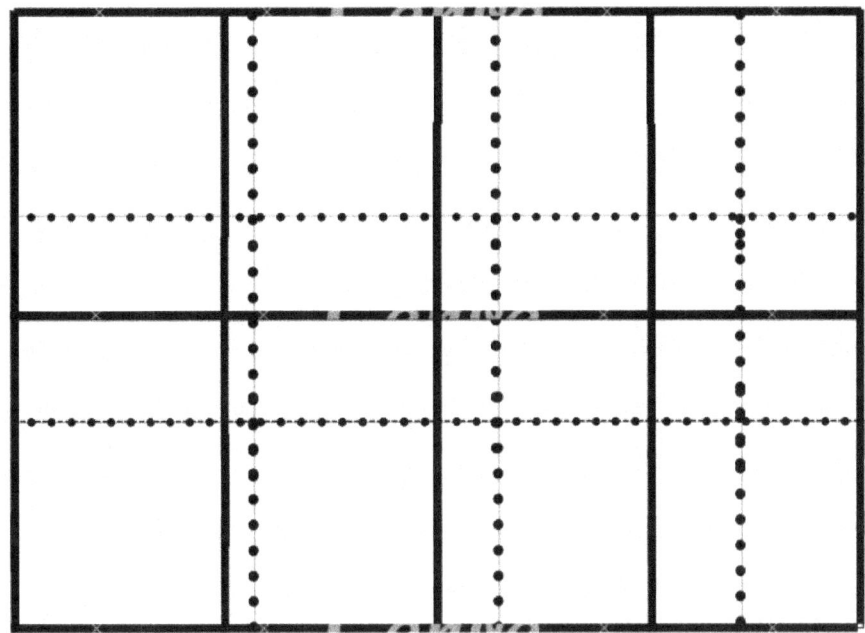

Fig. 11.8 Standard and Camotian (dotted) sheet arrangements combined

Fig. 11.9 Year date from Correr Europe cartouche

12.1 Preliminary Remarks

The fine Camocian set's period of rather debased service as a pseudo-atlas came to an end with the reconstitution of the American map. The parts of the continent which had been excised (or perhaps it is more accurate to say omitted, for these parts were, of course, in the original Gastaldi manuscript map), were filled in (see sheets B and E in figs. 9.12 and 9.3) by recourse, we can assume, to Gastaldi's *Cosmographia vniversalis* ,[1] and the empty large area in the lower left (as in fig. 9.2, which originally had contained a large portion of the Pacific Ocean, and below it, the greatly extended part of the fictional Southern Continent, as on the *Cosmographia vniversalis* , was given over to a large sheet consisting entirely of letterpress text, about which it will be useful to say a few words. The text sheet bears the title, "Dichiaratione Delle Qvattro Parti Del Mondo Di Giacobo Gastaldo Raccolta Da Piv Famosi Cosmografi Et Historici" (Description of the four parts of the world by Giacobo Gastaldo gathered from the most famous cosmographers and historians). It was certainly not written by Gastaldi, as we shall see.[2]

In the first paragraph the writer tells us that the ancients had divided the world into three parts (*parti*), Asia, Africa and Europe. They were ignorant of the rest because of the impassable ocean. But the moderns have found a new land which, because of its size, its fertility, and its other boons,

---

[1] When the cartography was completed, by Donato Bertelli as we shall see, the small sheet E was, by some computational oversight, made only about half as wide north to south as it should have been. The little sheet completes all necessary geography, but should have been carried further south, depicting only ocean waters, in order for it to properly fill the space above large sheet 1, containing text. Since this was not done, the text sheet is not large enough to neatly fill the space below sheet E, and it was pasted onto a blank sheet of the correct size such that part of the unfilled space falls above the text and part below it, minimizing the noticeability of the unfilled space. This is indicated by the two red lines in sheet I in figure 9.12.

[2] This would be evident in any event from several points. Although he used several variants for his given name, the name form Giacobo is one he never employed. The phrase "by Giacobo Gastaldo" would not have been included in the text of the title in this way were he the writer. And neither Gastaldi, nor any in his circle ever referred to the New World under the name "America," which occurs several times in this text. They invariably said "New World." On this point see Grande (1905, "Carte," 128-32).

deserves to be called a new world, which more particularly is called America. Thus the moderns have enlarged the ancients' division of the earth from three into four parts, Asia, Africa, Europe, and America, "qualli chiaramente si vedono con molta diligenza delineate nelle presenti quatro Tauole di nouo reuiste, emendate, & accresciute, con vn facile, & chiara ma breue dichiaratione delle qualità delli Paesi" (which clearly are seen delineated with much diligence in the present four maps newly reviewed, emended, and augmented,[3] with a simple and clear but brief description of the attributes of the Lands), which will include their confines, main provinces, customs, inhabitants, and most important things. The rest of the text consists of four long sections, one each for each of the continents (*parti*), first Europe, then Asia, then Africa, then America. The America section opens: "L'America ò Mondo nouo, oltre alle molte Isole delle quali diremo più a basso si diuide in doi grandissime Peninsule congionte fra di loro con vn istimo, vna delle quali si chiama America Settentrionale, l'altra l'Australe: . . . ." (America or new World, other than the many islands of which we will speak below, is divided into two very large peninsulas joined to each other by an isthmus, one of which is called North America, the other South: . . .).[4] We return to our description of the revitalized four-continent set.[5]

Unlike the America, the Africa and the Asia were replaced by different versions of those continents which had been made and published by Donato Bertelli.[6] These maps have a sheeting arrangement of eight equally-sized sheets, four up and four down, and are undated. Both maps are

---

[3] This is mostly propaganda, although a few changes have been made, such as the addition of the name "VIRGINIA", invented in the 1580s by Sir Walter Raleigh, and on the Arader sets, Drake Passage has been cut through, and there are probably other smaller additions. Some have mentioned the addition of the name "Florida", but this was not new, and in fact occurs in Gastaldi's list of New World place names in his 1561 booklet.

[4] The concept of America as broken up into a great northern part and southern part was just coming into existence. Here it is taken from Giovanni Botero's *Relationi Vniuersali,* which, as we shall soon see, the unknown writer made much use of in his text.

[5] We shall shortly have more to say about this text, however, which will prove vital in helping us find the date when the set was completed.

[6] See plates VI and VII, and X and XI. The Bertelli shop insignia was San Marco. We shall speak much more below about this shop. It had a high repute, although many of its maps were simply later reprints of maps originally published elsewhere.

dedicated to Paolo Nani in the capacity of Procurator of Saint Mark's, a post Nani held from November 22, 1573 until his death in 1608,[7] so they had to have been made between the former date and the time when the four-continent set was brought to fruition. Other than this, although I have borne the question in mind for over twenty years, I have never been able to find grounds to fix this date more precisely. Perhaps they were begun in competition with Camocio when the latter's four-continent set was approaching completion and possibly Bertelli intended a four-continent set of his own but dropped his plan when the plague began decimating Venice, possibly moving temporarily to Padua, where much of his family was located. We can only speculate, but this scenario seems the most likely to me.

The Bertelli Africa, like Camocio's, is a direct copy from Gastaldi's 1564 Africa, and is thus an edition of that. The Asia is a direct copy of Ortelius's 1567 wall-map of Asia,[8] which is itself taken directly from Gastaldi's Three Parts of Asia, except that Asia has been given a north coast, there are some small improvements in insular eastern Asia, and the map's projection has been changed. However, the coordinate grid is exactly the same as on Gastaldi's original map.[9] Like the Ortelius map from which it is copied, all text is in Latin, and the same is true of the map of Africa.[10] The two maps, we see, are still, either in the direct sense (the Africa), or in the essential sense (the Asia) by Gastaldi. The map of Europe remained basically the same, except that the dedicatory text was removed by

---

[7] Caraci (1926-32, 2, 37, note 3).

[8] Donato's copy is identical in dimensions and scale to the Ortelian original. But the engraving on the Ortelius map is much finer than on the Bertelli copy. On this map, see Schilder (1987, 59-84, with a full-size reproduction on plates 3(1)-3(8)). On the Bertelli Africa, see Betz (2007, 126-28).

[9] Schilder (1998, 110).

[10] Other than the copies of these two maps which occur in the four-continent sets, one separate copy of each is known. The Asia is in the Vatican Library, to which it was bequeathed in 1933 from the former collection of prints and drawings of the British archeologist Thomas Ashby. It is discussed by Almagià (1948, 63-66, and reproduced there at plates 17-18). The Africa, formerly in the Ashburner collection, was purchased by the Biblioteca Medicea Laurenziana in Florence, but Betz (2007, 127) was unable to locate it there.

burnishing it out, although the burnishing was too hurriedly done, and replaced by simply the name of the continent in large letters.[11]

12.2 A Terminus a quo and a Terminus ad quem

So, when, where, and by whom was the America completed, and along with it the four-continent set, albeit with the original Camocian Africa and Asia replaced by Bertellian ones, though still very much basically Gastaldi? We shall start with the question of when. If we had a shortage of evidence as regards when and by whom the ersatz atlas was made, this is fortunately not true of the much more important question just posed. Here, fortune has smiled upon us and left us with clues which easily allow us to come up with a nearly exact answer.

To begin with, we have a ready-made and certain *terminus a quo,* and also a ready-made and certain *terminus ad quem* which allow us to immediately narrow the time down to within twelve years. The *terminus a quo* is given to us by the unknown writer of the lengthy type-set text at the lower left of the America map of which we have just spoken, in his description of America. He notes that in America there are many rivers, woods, plants, and animals, "come rifferrise Gioan Bottero nella sua Relationi" (as Giovanni Botero reports in his Relations), a reference to Giovanni Botero's immensely popular and widely read *Relationi Vniuersali,* the first two parts of which were first published in 1591-92 in Rome, with at least seventeen editions published in Italian by 1600. Many editions appeared in the seventeenth century as well, at least into the 1670s, and there were also translations into Latin, English, German, Spanish, and Polish. In all, there were four parts to Botero's work, the first on world geography, the second on politics, economics and social conditions in the most important nations. The last two parts are on religion, and were published only in 1595-96. But the writer of our text was certainly drawing on part one, first

---

[11] There are, as brought out in chapter nine, three of these revitalized sets extant, all late printings by the Scolaris in the 1650s and 1660s, though as we shall see the set was first completed in the 1590s. One of the sets is in the Ransom Research Center of the University of Texas at Austin, and the other two are in the possession of Graham Arader of New York. For provenance details, see chapter nine, subsections three, four and five of the section "The Four-Continent Sets containing the America", and for cartobibliographical details, see nos. V-XII of our Cartobibliography.

published with part two in 1591-92, as two volumes. Actually, the title page of volume one of this first edition says 1591, while the colophon of part two, the second volume, says 1592. The impression I receive is that volume one, though printed in 1591, was not released until it and volume two were put on sale together in 1592, but I cannot be certain. In any event we have a certain *terminus a quo* of 1592 for the map text, and thus also for the map and for the date of its final completion, and possibly 1591. It was not earlier than this.

Our ready-made *terminus ad quem* is of a quite different nature. In the account books of the Officina Plantiniana, the firm of the deceased great Antwerp publisher Christoffel Plantijn there is an entry for a December 14, 1604 sale through Plantijn's establishment to Joan Baptista Vrients of ten uncolored sets of Gastaldi four-continent maps: "10 Partes quatuor Gastaldi bl. 6 flY..fl. 60" (10 four parts by Gastaldi, uncolored 6 florins Y..60 florins).[12] Vrients was an important dealer and cartographer himself,[13] and we can be sure that the reputable Officina Plantiniana would not have attempted to sell him, or anyone else, ten four-continent sets which included a deformed incomplete America, so here we have certain evidence that the Gastaldian set had been completed by 1604. Thus, while the only completed sets which have surfaced so far are very late printings from the mid-seventeenth century, we know, thanks to the Botero reference and the Plantijn business's account books, that the set was first completed and put on sale sometime between 1592 and 1604.

We cannot say more with absolute surety, but fortune still smiles on us, even if less brightly, for strong grounds exist from which we can by postulation narrow this down to a two-year span within which it was in all probability completed. This has been assumed, by some dealers and auction houses, to have been done by Donato Bertelli, no doubt since the signed Asia and Africa of the set are his. As we shall see, this assumption is correct, but intuitive, and we will be able to establish it with much greater certainty. Finally, we will broach the question of how and when the plates got eventually from the Bertellis to the Scolaris, a very important question in

---

[12] Schilder (1987, 128); and Schilder (1996, 36, note 32).

[13] On Vrients see Schilder (1987, 122-45).

concluding our story, for the only three surviving sets known to date come, as we have said, from the Scolaris, in the 1650s and 1660s. However, establishing what we can on these questions will not be quite so simple as it was for us to arrive at our very solid span of 1592 to 1604. We will have to first establish a good number of background facts about publishers of, and the publishing of, maps in late sixteenth century and seventeenth century Italy, facts which have not been at all solidly established before. In the process, our span of 1592-1604 will give us a very convenient frame of reference upon which to build our further investigations.

To start with, we need to say a few general words about the state of the Italian, principally Venetian, map industry in the period named, and then move on to more specific indagations. So far in the literature, this period has been, if we may so put it, something of a wasteland in the history of cartography, with only a very vague picture emerging as to what was going on. We will bring a little more definitude and perspective to the period, and, having done so, will return much better equipped to the question of the birth, vicissitudes, and fate of our four-continent set.

12.3 An Overview of the Venetian Map Publishing Industry, ca. 1570s to 1660s

The author has made what we may call a *relatively* in-depth study of the period and its players. He has not exhausted all possible sources,[14] but he has carefully and analytically exhausted far more sources than has ever been done before. Basically the method was to bring together all information I could find on the principal players of the period, with an eye to establishing for each of them more reliable dates for their periods of activity, and any other relative data, such as principal places of operation (Venice, Padua, or elsewhere) and what role or roles were played by them (publisher, engraver, dealer, etc.), and, of course, with the main focus of all being the determination of who could have, or couldn't have, had anything to do with the production of the completed four-continent set, and its history after its

------

[14] A thing which indeed would be quite impossible at the present time. See our special note at the end of the chapter on available information sources on the Venetian map publishing community and the extent to which they have so far been exhausted.

completion, by a sort of process of elimination. After a preliminary assessment of all those who could have been involved past 1592 in either the original completion of the set, or involved in later reprintings of it, all based on a rapid preliminary survey of the secondary sources enumerated just below, the persons focused on were: the Bertellis (Andrea, Donato, Ferrando, Francesco [not son of Pietro], Francesco [son of Pietro], Lorenzo, Luca, Nicolò, Orazio and Pietro;[15] Pietro de' Nobili (the only Roman investigated); Donato Rasciscotti; the Scolaris (whom, for reasons which will become clear, we will not name separately here), and the Valeggios (Francesco, Giacomo, and Nicolò). Having established this list, my procedure was to meticulously check, map by map, through the same sources used to establish the preliminary list, that is, the listings in six substantial catalogs of sixteenth and seventeenth century Italian maps, beginning of

---

[15] There is occasional reference to one Domenico Bertelli, a very shadowy figure whom I suspect may not have existed at all (Almagià, 1948, 117, note 5 seems to imply the same), purportedly active according to Borroni in the business only in 1590[!], as a printer and engraver. For the few modern references to him, besides Almagià, see Borroni (1967, "Donato," 490a); Borroni-Salvadori (1980, lxvii with note 6), and Ganado (1994-95, 1, 131 with note 2, and 138). At 131, Ganado slips badly, due to some oversight or inattention, stating, after having spoken of the earlier Bertellis, that the Bertelli business "seems to have been later inherited by Domenico Bertelli, who was active in the 1590s", accompanied by a note in which he gives reference to three pages (lv, lxi, lxix) in Borroni-Salvadori, 1980. But there is no reference to any Domenico Bertelli on any of these pages, though there are references to other Bertellis, including Donato, and at p. 138, he states: "Occasionally, Donato has been confused with Domenico Bertelli, a printer and engraver, who worked in Venice in 1590 and, according to Le Blanc, even in Rome. Domenico's imprint was like Donato's *ad signum Bibliothecae D. Marci,* and his editorial address was likewise: *"Venetia alla libraria del segno di S. Marco in merzaria."* This is all complete nonsense. I suspect Domenico may be a ghost who came into existence in the older and often unreliable literature of such as Le Blanc, Nagler, Gori Gandellini, etc., either through some confusion with Donato, or possibly confusion with the engraver Domenico Zenoi, who did much engraving work for the Bertellis, and sometimes signed his works simply "Domenico", without the "Zenoi", although it is true Zenoi disappears in the mid-1570s, very possibly a victim of the plague. In any event, if Domenico existed, he certainly never inherited the San Marco business. Most often it is said that the shop passed from Donato to Andrea in 1594, which would accord well enough with the floruits of these two. But actually, even these statements are simply borrowed from the person's floruits. There do not exist, in actuality, any statements whatsoever from the time telling us who was at the head of the famous shop at any time. Donato and Andrea could well have been equal partners. We do know, however, that Donato alone ran the business from ca. 1572, when Ferrando leaves the scene, and Andrea appears first in 1593 or 1594, for no maps come from the San Marco address during this time except Donato's. Finally, Tooley (1979, ad nomen) mentions a single map, an "Isola de Palmera" by one Nicolò Bertelli, but this is from 1713, and the latest date we have for any Bertelli work which definitely comes from the original clan is a 1656 book reprinting by Pietro Bertelli's son Francesco, so this Nicolò is unlikely to be from the same family. Thus, so far, it would seem that the Bertelli clan consisted of ten persons, or perhaps eleven, if Domenico is real. However, as we shall see, we have turned up an eleventh (or twelfth), one more Pietro, previously unrecognized, but very important indeed. We shall speak more of him below.

course with Tooley's well-known list of 1939.[16] This was followed by index, or alphabetical entry checks for each of the names given above in nine major works containing many scattered pertinent entries.[17] Then I carefully studied six promising texts, which were especially useful in obtaining a clear picture of the activities of the Bertellis,[18] and consulted Bury's catalog of publishers, engravers, etc. in Italy, 1550-1620.[19] In the case of the Scolaris, I checked still three other sources, of a different nature, and with resounding success, as will be seen. Most of those in the original list were quickly eliminated, as we shall soon see.

Besides serving our general purposes well, this little experiment also revealed a good number of errors commonly encountered in the literature, concerning some of these personages, but unfortunately we will not be able to go through all of this here, though we have done so when it seemed pertinent to our ends. The rest will have to wait for another time. Two results of the survey turned out to be vital to us: first, the general light thrown on the period, and, second, the illumination brought to the questions of the genesis, the following vicissitudes, and the ultimate fate of our four-continent set, and we shall present our results in this order, for an understanding of the first contributes in an important way to the understanding of the second.

The peak of the Venetian map industry was in the mid-1560s. After this, it began to decline, but at first only slowly, and in general it retains its luster into the early to mid-1570s, the period when Camocio made his four-continental wall maps attempt. But then it begins to steadily and more sharply decline, continuing inexorably to do so well into the seventeenth century. There is no question that one great blow, the first one, was the

---

[16] The six works checked through are Tooley, 1939 (614 maps); Borroni-Salvadori, 1980 (484 maps); Meurer, 2004 (191 maps); Gallo, 1954 (150 maps); Bella, 1986 (148 maps); and Woodward, 1990 (basically on Forlani, but mentions many later editions of maps in its entries.)

[17] The nine works are Almagià (1929); Almagià (1948); Kret (1978); Ganado (1994-95); Karrow (1993); Bagrow-Skelton (1985[1951]); Menato (1997); Sicco (1985); and Shirley.

[18] The texts are Gallo (1950); Borroni (1967,"Donato"); Borroni (1967, "Ferdinando"); Borroni (1967, "Luca"); Borroni (1967, "Pietro"); and Palagiano (1974).

[19] In Bury (2001, pp. 221-36).

appearance of Ortelius's *Theatrum Orbis Terrarum* in 1570,[20] followed shortly by Gerard de Jode's *Speculum Orbis Terrarum,* in 1578,[21] which had a tremendous effect by shifting the locus of map production to the Low Countries. But, though I can't document it, my instinctive feeling is that it was the 1575-77 plague which dealt the most serious blow, and it seems to have reverberated to Rome as well, probably because the two centers had always worked hand-in-hand to a considerable degree. Three of the best-known and skillful engravers, Zenoi, Olgiati, and Forlani, probably fell to the plague, for their activities all stop in 1574, while still another, Nelli, disappears in 1579, two years after the plague. And several notable publishers and printers also evidently fell to the plague, Camocio, last heard of in 1575, Zaltieri, who is last heard from in 1576, and Pinargenti, unheard of after 1577. The drop in quality and quantity of engraving is quite noticeable after this period. The general loss of vitality is evinced very clearly in the ever-increasing re-use of old maps and old plates, first made and published in the 1540s to early 1570s, most often simply reprints from the old plates, only occasionally new engravings, but still copied from the older maps. Fewer and fewer truly new maps appear.[22] These facts in themselves have no direct bearing on the question of our four-continent set, but it was surely these general aspects of decline which led to the onset of the type of disorder and heedless practices brought out in the next paragraphs, and this will have important bearing on tracing the history of the set.

The general desultoriness, loss of vigor, and decline comes through most strongly, and in my opinion most interestingly, and certainly most importantly for us, in the following. During the time when the industry was

---

[20] By the time of the Venetian plague of 1575-77, there had been no less than thirteen different issues of the atlas, in four languages, Latin, Dutch, German, and French (Karrow, 1993, 22, and, esp., Betz, 2007, 124.).

[21] The Italian composite atlases, i.e., IATO or Veneto-Roman (VR) atlases, with their varying and irregular contents, and, worst of all, their complete lack of any critical attempt to include only the *best* available depictions of the countries and regions shown, but rather an arbitrary inclusion of *all* depictions of areas, could in no way compete well with the atlases of Ortelius and De Jode, with their well thought out selection of contents.

[22] We know that, even at the industry's height, many of the maps produced in Venice were taken from maps obtained (at fairs, markets, by direct order) from northern cartographers. Was there perhaps a drop in the number of such maps for some reason? I haven't tried to look into this.

flourishing, besides the constant influx of new maps, mostly from other lands, there were also reprints and re-engravings of somewhat older maps, just as there would be in the later period. But in these cases, it was customary to burnish out the old date and the old publisher, and engrave in new ones in their places. In general, this was regularly and painstakingly done, and usually no sign of the previous date or publisher remains. But, in the latter quarter of the century, publishers grew lax and lazy, and it became common to find reprinted maps where the old publisher's name and/or the old date were not sufficiently burnished out, and can often still be read. This then is taken still further by some, as in the case of de' Nobili (this being in Rome), whose work begins in the 1580s, who almost never bothers to burnish out previous printers or dates at all, although he invariably adds his name to the plates as well.[23] Then, towards the end of the sixteenth century, Francesco Valeggio enters the scene in Venice as a map publisher, and also takes up this practice, at least in part, for on many, but not all, of the maps he reprints, he simply leaves the original date as it is.[24] But the practice peaks

---

[23] And sometimes, if the map is in more than one sheet, he adds his name to each sheet. One feels that to him, the name addition is more like a brand, simply indicating that he owned the plate, and indeed, that really was his only involvement. Examples of de' Nobili's practice are a map of Genoa, originally published by Lafreri in 1573, where the old date and Lafreri's signature remain, but de' Nobili's name is added, too (Bella, 1986, no. 55, with a reproduction), a Greece, originally 1558 Vincenzo Luchini, where again the old date and signature remain, though de' Nobili's is added as well (Bella, 1986, no. 62, with a reproduction). For an example of this with a subject print, see Borroni-Salvadori (1980, xlvii, note 2). The practice, we would add, was not followed in Rome only by de' Nobili. Orlandi also often did this. For a particularly odd example, see Bella (1986, no. 131, with a reproduction), where an Orlandi map of Toledo dated 1602 also carries, conversely to the above examples, de' Nobili's signature, and the date 1585. (According to Ganado (1994-95, 1, 225), the year 1585 was the only one in which de' Nobili changed the original dates on acquired plates to the current date, 1585, which I personally suspect is the year when he began.)

[24] Valeggio's floruit is ca. middle to late 1590s to ca. 1630 or a little later. The other significant reprinter of earlier plates at this time was Donato Rasciscotti (fl. ca. 1580-start of seventeenth century), who obtained and reprinted earlier plates of Tramezzini, Rota, and the Bertellis, though he cuts a much smaller figure than Valeggio, and his total production of reprints was only about one-fifth that of Valeggio. More important for us, since among the questions we will attempt to answer is how the four-continent set eventually made its way to the Scolaris, is the fact that, while former publishers' names often occur on works which are reprints by the Scolaris of earlier works, scholars give as being among these former names Camocio, the Bertellis, Van Aelst, and F. Valeggio, but make no mention of Rasciscotti (Almagià, 1948, 118; Borroni-Salvadori, 1980, xlviii, note 1, and lxix, note 1). This accords with the findings of my own survey, and thus Rasciscotti falls from the ranks of those who hold interest for us, and the same is true of Nicolò Valeggio (fl. 1560s-1570s, with a very few ghost-dated works from the 1590s and even the very early seventeenth century) and his son Giacomo (fl. 1570s-1580s); but many of the plates of Francesco Valeggio passed eventually to the Scolaris. Some of Rasciscotti's plates were very old, and perhaps they ended up in the melting pot, as did some of those of de' Nobili (Borroni-Salvadori 1980, xlvii).

in Venice, with the Scolaris in the seventeenth century, who very commonly follow the practice of de'Nobili, leaving the former publishers' signatures, and sometimes the dates, unchanged, while adding their own signature. For example, Forlani produced a map of the Territory of Verona by Bernardino Brognolo dated exactly October 25, 1574. The plate found its way to Valeggio, who published an issue of it, and then to Stefano Scolari,[25] who published it again, still with the date October 25, 1574 and the name Forlani, as well as the name of Valeggio, and with Scolari's signature added as well.[26] The map was published again, by a different Scolari, with the date changed to October 25, 1700 (MDCC), but Valeggio's signature still remains, along with Scolari's.[27] This example will suffice, but it is very common to find Scolari-published maps still bearing the name of a previous publisher (Valeggio or otherwise) still intact. For convenience, we will give these leftover signatures the name "ghost signatures", for, as we shall see, the concept will be an important one in our determinations regarding the four-continent set.

12.4 The Bertelli Family and Their San Marco Establishment

In this rather bleak period from the second lustrum of the 1570s on in Venice, one figure stands out as remaining pretty much normally active, and generally not changing his editorial practices, and that is Donato Bertelli. Ganado says, "Donato retained his pre-eminence long after both his associates and competitors had disappeared from the scene," and on the same page states: "Throughout the second half of the sixteenth century Donato Bertelli was one of the central figures in the printing, publishing and trading of maps"[28]; and Almagià's assessment, after speaking of him, would make

[25] Probably some time after 1620, for there is no clear evidence of map publishing by the Scolaris before then. The map, incidentally, was also published by Andrea Bertelli in 1612, as we shall see below, evidently his last publication. So it came into the hands of Valeggio after that (for the progression of passage of plates as to the Bertellis and Valeggio is always from the Bertellis to Vallegio, and never vice-versa), who erased Andrea's name, and then from Valeggio to Scolari.

[26] Woodward (1990, p. 54, no. 97).

[27] Ganado (1994-95, 1, 389, no. (b)).

[28] Ganado (1994-95, 1, 138).

him *the* central figure: "Donato Bertelli then would have been, in the sale of maps at Venice, the principal inheritor and continuer of the most active producers of the second half of the sixteenth century."[29] And certainly, in the survey I have made, his name is the only one that occurs with uninterrupted regularity and frequency through the period.

And furthermore, a vital fact in regard to the four-continent set, as we shall soon see, my survey revealed that that he was the only member of the broad Bertelli family whose name appears through the period in any connection at all with the famous address "*Venetia, libraria de l'insegna del S[an] Marco in merzaria,*"[30] from the time Ferrando Bertelli leaves the scene in 1571 or 1572, until the time Andrea Bertelli first shows up in 1593. This address (by which we mean its physical presence as printed on maps), as we have just implied, will be vital in more ways than one in connection with the final much more precise determinations than those we have made so far in connection with the four-continent set, and it behooves us to look at it for a moment. It most often occurs in Italian, but it also occurs, not infrequently, in a Latin form, as: *Venetiis, apud Donatum Bertellium ad signum Bibliothecae divi Marci.*" There are endless variations, from map to map, as to the order of words, or abbreviations, or omissions of parts, etc., in these inscriptions, and there are probably very few instances of two maps where the address is identical. The two longer forms just given above in italics are ideal full forms written up by myself from inspection of many instances.[31] Any one or more of the following elements may be missing: Venice (Venetia, usually), or a particular publisher's name, or the word "appresso", or Alibraria" or "de l'insegna" or the street name "in merzaria", but "S. Marco" (occasionally "S. Marcho"), or in Latin "divi Marci" will regularly be found, along with at least one other element of the full address.

---

[29] Almagià (1948, 117b).

[30] The address will be immediately familiar to those with an interest in sixteenth century Italian cartography. Without question, more maps issued from this address than from any other in the history of Venetian cartography from the time Donato's first map was published here in 1558 until an indeterminate time past the turn of the seventeenth century. Most often, the address includes the name of a particular Bertelli (always, as far as I have been able to discover, either Donato, Ferrando, or Andrea), as for example: "*Venetia, appresso Donato Bertelli, alla libraria de l'insegna del S. Marco in merzaria.*" There were numerous variants in how these words were written, about which more below.

[31] Ganado (1994-95, 1, 137-38) gives a good number of variants, but there are many more.

Sometimes Donato signs with only his initials "D.B.",[32] but in such cases the expression "San Marco" in one form or other will always be present. Indeed, from the time Ferrando leaves the scene in 1571/72, the shop name always occurs, and it is only the period from the mid to late 1570s onwards which is vital to our questions concerning the genesis of the Bertelli variant of the four-continent set. Ferrando does not always include the shop name.

A short history of the establishment will not be out of place here. The first time a map, or any work published in this shop, appears is in 1558 on a map of Italy published by Donato Bertelli and titled "Italia Nuova", a re-engraving of an earlier map.[33] This is followed by Donato's 1559 edition of Gastaldi's Germany,[34] and by his 1559 map of Austria and Hungary.[35] In 1560, he publishes a map of Transylvania and neighboring regions,[36] and he continues to publish maps uninterruptedly on into the 1590s. Only in 1561 do we find Ferrando entering the scene with a 1561 Lombardy, no copy of which is known.[37] I found no Ferrando work before this date, and in fact the

---

[32] In fact, occasionally no publisher name at all is given, but if so, the shop name will invariably occur. An example is in Borroni-Salvadori (1980, no. 32).

[33] Almagià (1929 16a (no. B)). The engraver, identified as only "Domenego" is Domenico Zenoi, as see Almagià (1948, 99). Of mistaken claims of an earlier map by Donato, we shall speak in a moment.

[34] Almagià (1948, 26-27); Gallo (1954, p. 41, no. 28*).

[35] Tooley (1939, no. 120); Gallo (1954, 48, no. 55*); and in the online Vatican catalog. These three sources cite the map correctly, as also its date: MDLVIIII. Due no doubt to some momentary distraction or failure of attention, Almagià in 1948 gave the date of the Vatican example which he was inspecting mistakenly as MDLIII (1553), and then confounded things still further by following this with the statement: "The last two I's could be a later addition," implying that the map's original date could even be 1551! (1948, 99); the sense is that he is speaking of an altogether different map, and perhaps the peculiar error was due to some small organizational error made later in coordinating his notes, as anyone can do. Later, Borroni-Salvadori (1980, no. 254) cites the map correctly as 1559, but presumes it is a later issue of the nonexistent 1553 map, for whom she of course cites Almagià (1948, 99) (she repeats the error at her no. 96), and the same error is made in Bella (1986, p. 22, no. 14), who also cites Almagià, 1948, 99; and also in Ganado (1994-95, 1, 110), and possibly others. No 1553 edition of this map exists. As noted, the same copy of the map as that Almagià was inspecting, and still with the same call number, is found in the online Vatican library catalog correctly dated 1559 (MDLVIIII). And, finally, Ganado, in his survey of Malta siege maps, seems, although the passage is a bit obscure, to suggest that an undated Donato Bertelli map of the siege "was published perhaps in or after 1552" (1994-95, 1, 138), but he gives no good reason for it. The first map from the San Marco shop was most certainly the 1558 Donato Bertelli Italy, followed then in unceasing succession for many years by many other maps.

[36] Almagià (1948, 27-28).

[37] Almagià (1929, 28a (no. B)). There is also very possibly a 1561 Ferrando Britain, of which also no copy is known (Meurer, 2004, 20, no. 6).

most authoritative scholars give his floruit period as 1561-1572 or 1561-1571.[38] Yet, while no one states it overtly, intimations in the literature are common that the *libraria del S. Marco* was Ferrando's business, and that Donato joined up later.[39] But since works from the S. Marco shop are documented clearly for Donato from 1558, and only from 1561 for Ferrando, Donato was obviously operating in the San Marco shop three years before Ferrando.[40] Still, the notion pervades the literature that Ferrando came first, and with it the unstated implication that it would have been he who started the business. For us, it is important, for, as we shall demonstrate, it was Donato who completed the four-continent set, and so we wish to have a correct picture of him in general.

In fact, I have discovered that neither of the two seems to have founded the famous shop. On his first map, the "Italia Nuova" mentioned above, Donato signs himself very strangely in the signature and address line: "A*lla libraria del. S. Marco|Donato de Piero 1558|Domenego V. F.*"[41] But on his 1559 Austra and Hungary, his name comes out as we are accustomed: "A*lla libraria de l'insegna del S. Marco| Donato Bertelli|domenego*

---

[38] Almagià (1948, 117a) and Borroni (1967, "Ferdinando," 491) both say 1561-1572; Bury (2001, 222) says 1561-71. A few others give an end date of 1574 or 1575. This is, I am fairly certain, due to confusion concerning a town book with which Ferrando had no connection, as see Gallo (1950), but no one gives a start date earlier than 1561.

[39] An ideal example is Borroni, 1967, "Donato," 490a; but there are many; indeed, the literature swarms with them, but we'll not list them here.

[40] Bury (2001, 222) speaks of them as equal partners, which was probably the case, but clearly Donato was there first. Probably the notion of Ferrando being the principal, and Donato subordinate, comes from the fact that during his relatively short floruit period Ferrando's production was much more spectacular than Donato's, with about 200 prints produced, including, besides maps, subject prints of all kinds (religious, mythological, historical, popular, etc) (Borroni, 1967, "Ferdinando," 490b; and Menato, 1997, 122). Indeed, for Ferrando, the quantity of such prints apparently much exceeded that of geographical prints, i.e., maps. Donato produced subject prints as well, but far fewer than Ferrando, and since the old writers, as Le Blanc, Nagler, etc. were interested mainly in subject prints, Ferrando would have been their major interest, and Donato would have been much less important. Probably this is where Donato's supposed subordinate status comes from, and out of it grew the idea, or I should say intimation (for writers are never clear and specific on the point), that Donato entered the business after Ferrando. In the present investigation, of course, Ferrando plays no direct role at all, but, since, as we shall see, the San Marco shop plays such a significant role in the question of the four-continent set, it seemed to me best to obtain a clear picture of the establishment's history, which, in any event, has not been done before.

[41] Almagià (1929, 16a). Domenego is the engraver Domenico Zenoi, who often signed without the last name (Almagià, 1948, 99), and "V. F." stands for "Venetiano Fecit" (Ganado, 1994-95, 1, 3), so the line translates "Engraved by the Venetian Domenico [Zenoi]".

venetiano F. MDLVIII,. "[42] And similarly on his 1559 Germany,[43] and indeed on all later works. What does this "Donato de Piero" mean in 1558? Bury[44] has recently discovered a February 12, 1587, testament for Donato Bertelli where he refers himself as "Donato Bertelli fu di m[aestro(?)] Pietro libraro all insegna di S. Marco." Now, one does not need a comprehensive Italian-English dictionary to find that the preposition "di" is regularly used to mean "offspring of" in Italian. In the well-known little pocket-book dictionary I have in my hands at the moment, *The Bantam New College Italian and English Dictionary* of Robert C. Melzi (New York, 1978 and numerous later editions), we find among the definitions of "di": "son of", e.g., *Carlo Giovannini di filippo* Carlo Giovannini son of Philip; daughter of, e.g., *Anna Ponti di Antonio* Anna Ponti daughter of Anthony." And the word "fu", besides meaning simply "was", has its own independent meaning Alate, deceased" (and can mean, standing alone, "son of the late" or "daughter of the late" as we learn from the same small dictionary), so that Donato's phrase, while the structure seems slightly awkward, certainly means "Donato Bertelli son of the late master[?] Pietro bookseller at the sign of St. Marks."[45] And, finally, since the use of "de" for "di" was common in the still not fully standardized Italian of the sixteenth century, "Donato de Piero" on the 1558 map means simply "Donato son of Pietro" and the implication is that the "Libraria del S. Marco" probably belonged to Donato's father Pietro and it was simply a bookshop in the basic sense only, though he also no doubt sold prints and maps as well; and only with the appearance of Donato's 1558 Italy did publishing become part of the business. Probably the shop would have been founded not long before by Pietro, who presumably moved from nearby Padua to do so, for Donato sometimes referred to himself as from Padua.[46]

---

[42] Gallo (1954, p. 48, no. 55*).

[43] Borroni-Salvadori (1980, p. 26, no. 70): *"In Venetia appresso Donato Bertelli | libraro al segno del San Marco | Domenico Zenoi Venetiano Fecit."*

[44] Bury (2001, 121-22).

[45] I am not sure how to render the "m." in the phrase, and, have translated it as "m[aestro]", although, since Pietro, who had evidently died only shortly before 1587, seems never to have engraved or printed, it is hard to see why the word "maestro" would be used, but perhaps it was simply out of endearment by Donato, or possibly Pietro acted sometimes as a planner or designer, constantly necessary, but a function not usually recognized on a work. The "m." may simply mean "messer", evidently close to simply "mister."

[46] Ganado, 1994-95, 1, 137.

Being only a dealer, a seller, there is no reason we would now encounter this Pietro's name. I think the San Marco shop may well have ended, as will be made clear below, as it began, that is, as a sales shop only, sometime in the first third or so of the seventeenth century.

We continue with our account of the shop's history. In its later years, in about 1593, after the long period in which evidently only Donato Bertelli kept the San Marco business running, Andrea Bertelli enters the business.[47] Andrea is the last recorded Bertelli in the San Marco shop, a fact which will be of some significance for us below, so it behooves us to say a few words about him and the length of his activity in the shop. His known floruit period is rather short. Borroni gives 1594-1601,[48] and Menato gives the same.[49] Almagià alone gives 1591 to 1601, but the 1591 is clearly just some confusion between the original production of a map of Trevigiano of that date by Bonifacio, and Andrea's 1601 issue of that.[50] I found a total of eight maps (other than two possibly ghost-dated ones, cited below) ranging from 1593 to 1612, and I think this is probably his correct floruit period, or very close to it.[51] Note that there is one great time gap in Andrea's floruit period, 1601 to 1612, and we shall speak more of this, and of Andrea's floruit in

---

[47] The notion that the business passed into his hands (and, by implication, out of Donato's), as stated or implied by some (Borroni-Salvadori, 1980, 490b; Menato, 1997, 122) seems to me to be something which has been repeated uncritically from writer to writer, coming I suspect from some very early sources, as Nagler, Le Blanc, etc. There certainly is no documentation for it. Andrea simply joined his older relatives' business, just as Ferrando (and not vice versa) joined the business of (the older) Pietro and his son Donato in 1561. We know absolutely nothing of the status of their relationships in the company. All may have been treated as full partners. If any one head was looked up to as the guiding hand, it would, of course, be the older, experienced one, and not that of an incoming novice.

[48] Borroni (1967,"Donato," 490b).

[49] Menato (1997, 122). But he contradicts himself later on the same page when he says Andrea's activities can be followed from 1595 to 1606 in the record book (*mariegola*) of the guild. For *mariegole* see the special note at the end of this chapter.

[50] Cf. Almagià (1948, 117b and p. 5 of the same work). There is no 1591 Andrea work cited anywhere that I found.

[51] The eight maps are a 1593 world after Camocio (Karrow, 1993, in no. 30/93.2); a 1594 Padua after Gastaldi (Borroni-Salvadori, 1980, lxix, in note 1) (apparently first issued by Andrea without changing the original 1568 date); a 1594 view of Venice (Menato, 1997, 122); a 1595 Switzerland after Lazio (Almagià, 1948, 44); a 1595 Asia evidently taken from Ortelius (Karrow, 1993, no. 1/4.2); a 1595 Brescia Territory (Almagià, 1948, 87); a 1601 Trevigiano Territory after Bonifacio, already mentioned (Almagià, 1948, p. 5); and a 1612 Verona Territory after Brognolo (Almagià, 1929, 38a) (also apparently first issued by Andrea without changing the original date, 1574).

general below. One should perhaps beware of ghost dates in Andrea's work. Mention is made of a 1568 Andrea issue of Gastaldi's Padua, which is the original date of Gastaldi's Padua, published by Ferrando, and is far too early for Andrea,[52] but he shortly afterwards re-issued it dated 1594 (see note 51 above). Also, Gallo gives a 1574 Forlani Verona issued by Andrea,[53] also impossible, and again Andrea then re-issues it dated 1612.[54]

Donato's floruit is even more important to us. It has been given differently by different scholars (usually, but not always, expanded over previous estimates), much more in about the last century and a half than is typical. Nagler had said 1560-1570,[55] but this was changed some time after that into 1563-1574.[56] Almagià in 1929 gives 1558 as his earliest map, as we have seen, and in 1948, says he found maps with Donato's name up to 1589 (1948, 117b), for a floruit of 1558-1589. It was probably Bagrow who expanded this to 1558-1592, and this has been pretty much universally accepted since then.[57] We have succeeded in expanding this to 1558-1594, with a 1593 Africa,[58] and a 1594 world map reprint,[59] and considering our admittedly still defective but nevertheless much improved base of data, and the only incrementally different nature of our new floruit over the one which has stood for some years, our new floruit is probably correct or very close to it.

As to the rest of the Bertelli clan, they were either book publishers and booksellers, or print publishers, but these latter published subject prints (by which I mean religious, mythological, historical prints, or engravings

---

[52] Tooley (1939, no. 430).

[53] Gallo (1954, 54, no. 41*).

[54] See note 51 above. In general, the confusion (most of it stemming, I suspect, from ghost-datings and ghost-addresses) surrounding the sundry issues of this map in the literature is truly chaotic, but we cannot go into this here.

[55] According to Ganado (1994-95, 1, 137).

[56] Per Borroni (1967,"Donato," 490).

[57] Bagrow-Skelton (1985, 136); then: Borroni (1967,"Donato," 490); Borroni-Salvadori (1980, lxviii); Coccio (1991, 291); Menato (1997, 122). There are in fact three maps for 1592, a Greece, a Marche and a Lombardy (Almagià, 1929, 19b (B) and 28a (D)), and Almagià (1948, 29-30).

[58] Betz (2007, 107).

[59] In the Vatican Library's online catalog, under author Bertelli, Donato.

after the paintings of the great masters). Several operated in Padua,[60] and could have no direct connection to the San Marco shop, including the later Pietro (dates ca. 1571-1621), and both Francesco's. Luca, too, the most important of the clan besides Ferrando and Donato, started a bookshop in Padua in 1564 (the first thing we hear of any Bertelli after Ferrando and Donato, and their father), which lasted 30 years to 1594,[61] but he regularly operated in Venice as well producing subject prints (though his bookshop must have often tied him to Padua), but there is no sign of the San Marco address. Sometimes on his prints we just see "apud Luca Bertellium et socios" or "L.B. et socius", which phrase "et socius" is generally hypothesized as referring to Orazio Bertelli, probably his assistant. At least one print has the address "Venetiis in aede Salvatoris,"[62] which, according to Menato was a Venetian bottega, though he doesn't say whose,[63] while Bury (2001, 222) implies he had a "shop at St. Bartolomio," and says he's described in a 1578 Marciana document as "Luca Bertelli fu de Ms Piero libraro a S. Bartolomio", so possibly he was brother to Donato. Perhaps he associated himself from time to time with different bottegas, while keeping his residence in Padua near his bookshop. In any event, there's no sign of any connection with the San Marco shop.[64] Lorenzo and Nicolò functioned in Venice, but exclusively as book or subject print publishers. A smattering of map production did exist outside the San Marco shop, but it was a peripheral and quite insignificant thing. Ganado (1994-95, 1, 131) says that Luca "also dabbled in distribution of maps," and in fact I found two maps

---

[60] Donato himself, and thus his father Pietro, very possibly originally came from Padua, for Ganado (1994-95, 1, 137), and Borroni (1967,"Donato," 490) say that he described himself as "Donatus Bertellius patavinus", although neither says where it is that he does this, and I certainly haven't encountered it.

[61] Borroni (1967,"Luca," 492b).

[62] Borroni (1967,"Luca," 492).

[63] Menato (1997, 123).

[64] Borroni-Salvadori (1980, lxix, in note 1) makes the egregious error of stating in passing that the S. Marco business passed to Andrea from Luca[!]. Luca had no connection with the San Marco business, and, if it really "passed" into the hands of Andrea (instead of Andrea simply becoming a part of the business), it is clear that it did so from the hands of Donato, not Luca. A surfeit of wearisomely recited minutiae (always some of it of questionable validity) is unavoidable in these modern works on the sixteenth and seventeenth century Italian publishing industry, and no doubt the common errors and mental slips occur because of the swirl of these endless minutiae in the heads of the writers.

and two city views by him, a 1571 world map (Woodward, 1990, no. 35.06), an undated Malta (Ganado, cit., 1, 131-32 with a good reproduction at 2, pl. 29), a 1565 view of Algiers (Woodward, cit., no. 38), and a 1589 view of Rome (Tooley, 1939, no. 496), but none of them came from the S. Marco shop, although some might have been produced in Venice (place of publication is not given on them), and I found three maps from his apparent assistant Orazio, a 1570 Italy, 1570 Western Hemisphere, and undated Peloponnesus, all without a San Marco address (Meurer, 2004, nos. 64, 65, 168). I found no other maps from the non-San Marco Bertellis, although one of the works published by the book publisher Pietro was a *Theatricum Urbium Italicarum* of 1599, a book of Italian city views, but it too, not surprisingly, lacks any connection with the house of San Marco. Clearly, none of these people had any connection to the San Marco business, and none of them could have had any connection with the completion of the four-continent maps, since, as we shall see, the set was certainly completed at that famous address.[65]

12.5 A Late Dynasty: The Scolari Family of Venice

Now we need say only a few words about the Scolaris, mentioned briefly above who published the only complete sets we know to date, and we will finally be in a position to give much better definition to the fate of the four-continent set, both as to when and by whom it was brought to culmination, and as to its later fate after that.

The Scolaris,[66] who come very late in the day in the Venetian map industry, have always had only a very shadowy existence in the literature. Invariably, we encounter only one Christian name, Stefano, giving Stefano Scolari, though occasionally we hear of one Stefano Mozzi Scolari, of whom more below. But Bury, in his "Biographies of Printmakers, Dealers and Publishers" (in his 2001 work, pp. 221-36), has an entry for one Giuseppe Scolari (fl. 1592-1607), a painter, designer and woodblock cutter active in

---

[65] We might add that, besides what we have said here, the floruit periods of most of these other Bertellis would alone disqualify them from any connection to the four-continent set's restoration.

[66] The reader may be surprised at my referring to the family in the plural, for usually only one Stefano Scolari is named. The explanation will be clear shortly.

Venice, who produced a number of woodcut prints, and presumably the first Scolari in the print business, and he must be father to the clan. Bury mentions no Stefano, but his book covers 1550-1620, and I have found no sign of a Stefano Scolari print before 1617. For the Scolaris, in my survey, I used, besides all the sources enumerated above, three other sources as well, i.e., the OCLC online union catalog (WorldCat); the SBN (Servizio Bibliotecario Nazionale), Italy's online union catalog for all Italian libraries, and, finally, ordinary Internet searches, and the very successful results certainly confirm the usefulness of our ever-growing electronic resources.

I found a total of forty-nine works (fifty-five if we individually count the eight maps of two different four-continent sets), all under the name Stefano Scolari, including five books (1594 to 1687), twenty-one maps (ten from 1620 to 1720, and eleven more undated), six views (five from 1629 to 1677, and one more undated), eleven subject prints (seven from 1617 to 1699, and four more undated), one set of globe gores (1666), and two sets of four-continent maps (1640s to 1660s, but date of first publication unknown).[67] Except for a map of Verona Territory, first published in 1620 followed by three known reprintings (1700, 1720, and an undated issue), two reprintings of a 1620 Italy (1657, 1662), and one undated reprinting of a 1678(?) world map, none of the works, of any genre, are re-issues,[68] so there are at least forty-three distinct works. The full date span is 1594-1720. Now, this is a span of 126 years, and, clearly, there has to be more than one Stefano Scolari here. Apparently, there were three or four generations of Scolaris, all named after their fathers, most likely, that is, father, son, grandson, etc. Some confirmation is perhaps given to this by the fact that on five works (1657, 1677, 1687 and two undated works), we find the name as "Stefano Mozzi Scolari,"[69] seeming to imply that maybe one of the breed tired of the confusion, and decided to use his middle name as well. The shop, from all I have been able to determine from often incomplete information on these works, remained the same the whole time, and the full signature and address

---

[67] Besides the Gastaldian set, the Scolaris produced an Italian edition of the 1612 variant of the famous 1608 Blaeu four-continent set, of which at least six exemplars exist, one dated 1646 (see Schilder, 1996, 189-95).

[68] Nor, it must be added, am I certain that these Verona, Italy, and world maps are simply re-issuings of each other.

[69] In one case "Mozo" instead of "Mozzi."

would be: *"à Stefano Scolari all'insegna delle Tre Virtù à S. Zulian in Venetia,"* although, as with the Bertellis, there were many variations, and shortenings, and in fact works seem most commonly signed simply "Stefano Scolari", or, more often, "Stefano Scolari formis" (or "forma", or abbreviated "for", or just "f" or "F").[70]

While we can't draw hard and fast conclusions, due to the presence of sixteen undated works and the problem of ghost-datings, there is no solid evidence of any kind of subject print publishing until 1617, and no sign of map publishing until 1620. Also important is the fact already mentioned that it is common on the prints to find previous plate owners' names left intact on the maps, besides the Scolari signature being added. This seems especially true of the many Scolari plates which were obtained from Francesco Valeggio, but it is possible that it was regularly if not always done; I cannot be certain because in many instances the sources available to me did not provide sufficiently detailed information. But I do know for certain that there is no Valeggio signature or address to be found on any of the Scolari Gastaldian four-continent maps, nor any other ghost signatures, except those of the Bertellis and the San Marco business. This fact will come to our aid twice just below.

12.6 Culmination of the Four-Continent Wall Map Set, and Its Aftermath

Now, finally, with what we have clarified concerning those times (and the practices of those times), and concerning those who could in any way be connected with the Gastaldian four-continent set, the majority of whom we have already eliminated along the way, we may return to that set, establish firmly who brought it to culmination, narrow down to near exactitude when it was completed, and also obtain at least a good general idea of its history from the time it was brought to culmination, and the time when the Scolaris produced the three sets which have been preserved.

---

[70] The word formis/forma indicates here plate owner, for most, possibly all, of the Scolaris' productions seem to have been reprintings, although they probably had a certain amount of engraving done for them, as see the comments in our cartobibliography, at no. (V.-VIII.) and no. V. Also, on the 1720 Verona we see "Stephanus Scolari sculpsit", which would indicate that this Stefano was the engraver.

As to the first, the Scolaris have left us just enough in the way of ghost signatures to settle the issue. As we know, dealers, such as Kraus, and Sotheby's, and others[71] have in a general way connected the Bertellis as well as the Scolaris to the set, even though these two families cannot really be considered as contemporaries, and, to be sure, the names and addresses of both establishments occur on the maps.[72] Dealers have associated the maps with the Bertellis on the basis of the simple fact that the Africa and the Asia are known to have been originally made by Donato Bertelli, and contain his signature, and indeed the facts suggest rather strongly that it would have been precisely Donato Bertelli who revived the failed four-continent set. That is, the facts at first *seem* to provide a logical enough basis to show that the set was originally from him and his shop. But in fact, the thinking here is fuzzy, and not so very logical at all. *Suggestion,* to be sure, that the connection is correct, is strong, and even very much so, in light of the fact that no maps are known by the Scolaris before 1620, and in light of the fact that we already know for certain that the maps had to have been completed between 1592 and 1604, and also the fact that there are no ghost signatures of Valeggio, or anyone else, except the Bertellis on the maps. It would seem that the set could only have originated with the Bertellis, and any thought of either Valeggio or the Scolaris having had anything to do with the genesis of the set seems excluded. Nevertheless, the proof is not as solid as we would wish so far, even though we know also that in general Valeggio and the Scolaris did not produce original work, but reprinted earlier works of others.

But just because our knowledge remains rather hazy on the period and its players, we lack absolute certainty here. We are not absolutely *certain* that Valeggio couldn't have obtained both the remains of the Camocio set as well as the Donato Bertelli Africa and Asia, replaced the Camocio Asia and Africa with the Bertellian variants, and repaired the debilitated America, as

---

[71] Extraordinarily, considering the tremendous significance of these map sets, no other authorities of any kind have broached the question at all, and the maps have remained very close to altogether unknown in the scholarly community. What lesson there might be in this fact, I don't know.

[72] In the Texas set, the name Scolari appears on all the maps except the America (twice on the Africa); in the sets belonging to Graham Arader, the Scolari name appears on the Africa (once), and on the Asia. The San Marco address, and the name of Donato Bertelli appear on the Africa and the Asia of both the Texas and Arader sets, and, most importantly, as we shall see, on the Arader Europe. For the exact location on the maps, and quotations of these various signatures and addresses, see our Cartobibliography entries nos. V to XII.

unlikely as it seems. His floruit period does not contradict this, in any event. And we are not absolutely *certain* that the Scolaris *never* removed his imprint from plates obtained by him. And likewise, although we are pushing unlikelihood still further, we cannot be absolutely *certain* that the Scolaris weren't producing cartographic material by 1604, and that they themselves might not have obtained the Camocian and Bertellian continents, and done the same as we have just suggested was remotely possible for Valeggio. And still one other unlikely but possible scenario remains, that is, that it was indeed the Bertellis who revitalized the set, but Andrea instead of Donato, although here too unlikelihood is strong simply because of Andrea's small and unspectacular production in cartography.

But, very fortunately for us, there is one ghost address line which neatly closes the door on Valeggio or the Scolaris, and unquestionably establishes that it was indeed in the Bertellis' San Marco shop that the completion of the four-continent set occurred. This telltale address occurs on only one map, the Europe of the first Arader set,[73] at the bottom of the title cartouche, between the indication of scale, and an ornamental scroll close below it, and it simply says "A*lla libraria della S. Marcho.*" See this inscription in fig. 12.1, and compare it with the address line in the same place in the original Camocio issue of this Europe, as in fig. 11.1, which reads "A*lla libraria della Piramide*", Camocio's address, as we have seen. While it is perhaps subtle, further reflection shows that we have in this little phrase rock-solid proof that it was a Bertelli who completed the set, as we shall now demonstrate. We will first eliminate Valeggio and the Scolaris (and anyone else outside the San Marco shop). Finally, we will eliminate Andrea, generally on the basis of other considerations, but also partly on the basis of a certain peculiarity in this same ghost address line.

Consider: If Valeggio, or the Scolaris, or anyone else, had come into possession of the uncompleted Camocio four-continent set, and decided to rejuvenate it, the conjecture that they might have decided to replace the original Africa and Asia with the Donato Bertelli ones is, as we have noted, a perfectly possible one, presuming they had come by the Bertelli plates, and

---

[73] It would certainly occur on the other Arader set as well, except that the Europe, we recall, is missing in that set.

of course the presence of Bertelli's name on them would be quite natural, for the simple reason that he made them. But the Europe could not possibly contain the Bertelli address according to such a supposition. It would, of course, contain Camocio's, "A*lla libraria della Piramide*." In other words, the presence of a Bertelli address on the Asia and Africa could prove nothing to us, for they were made in the first place by a Bertelli, and in an era where leaving ghost signatures was common, the presence of the address would be natural no matter by whom and/or when the two maps were used in completing the four-continent set. But the Europe was not made by a Bertelli. It was made by Camocio, and the presence on it of the Bertelli address certainly proves that it made a stop in the house of San Marco, and along with it the defective, uncompleted America, and presumably the original Africa and Asia as well, which Bertelli naturally enough preferred to replace with his own maps of those continents. Note too that the long text on the America required typesetting, and the Bertellis were equipped for this, while the Scolaris and Valeggio produced only engravings, and could not have done this, at least not in-house.

     Eliminating Andrea is rather less vital for us, for the most important thing is that the set originated in the Bertellis' San Marco shop, and not at the hands of a Valeggio or a Scolari. However, it will help us to narrow down the date the set was completed if we can pinpoint Donato as its originator. And in fact, based on some general considerations, as well as some more specific ones, we may safely, I think, draw the conclusion that it can only have been Donato who envisioned and carried into effect the restoration of the four-continent set. In the first place, considering the relative ambitiousness and novelty of the project, it is natural to think first of Donato since he was clearly the most experienced by far of the two, with a prolific, lengthy and impressive career behind him. Then there is the obvious fact, already mentioned, that two of the set's maps, the Africa and the Asia, are signed productions of Donato, and the very close resemblance in style between these two maps suggests that, whenever he made them, he was quite possibly considering a four-continent set of his own, which would certainly predispose him to conceiving the idea of carrying Camocio's initiative through to completion, while we know that Andrea had no experience at all with wall maps. The way in which the address line is couched on the Europe also points to Donato. It ends in "S. Marcho" instead of the more usual "S. Marco", and the only previous usage of the form "S. Marcho" attested is by Donato, in an undated map of Malta.[74] There is also the possibility, brought out below, that the San Marco shop came into possession of Camocio's remnants altogether before Andrea's floruit begins, in the 1580s, although this is only speculative.

We might note in addition the fact that the completion of the set required some engraving, and, while no evidence exists of Andrea ever having done any engraving, there is evidence of Donato having done limited engraving (Borroni, 1967), although it is true that the engraving could have been contracted for. Still, this consideration aside, we feel that the circumstances and facts presented above provide us sufficient indication that the project must have been Donato's, although, of course, it is possible that Andrea might have provided some assistance. The instincts of Kraus and Sotheby's were correct, and, indeed, from the facts already gone over, viz., that the four-continent set had to have been restored between 1592 and 1604, that no maps are known before 1620 by the Scolaris, the complete absence of any ghost signature by Valeggio on any of the maps, the substitution of two of Donato's maps for two of the original Camocio maps, and finally the unmistakable presence of the Bertellis' San Marco address, we may consider our case as demonstrated. The four-continent set of wall maps was completed in the San Marco shop by Donato Bertelli.

Can we go any farther? Can we narrow this down more? We saw, in the section "*A Terminus a quo and a Terminus ad quem*", at the beginning of this chapter, absolute certainty beyond 1592-1604 could not be achieved. But we stated that we could strongly postulate a date span of two years, namely ca. 1595-1596 if we first presented a body of data concerning the Venetian map industry from ca. 1570s to the 1660s (plus a bit for the 1550s

---

[74] Ganado (1994-95, 1, 138). Ganado's estimated date for this map, already spoken of, is at least six years too early. Note that Donato, in this altered address line, lazily ignores proper grammar. He has preserved Camocio's "della", correct before the feminine noun "Piramide", but incorrect before the abbreviated masculine "santo". It should read "del S. Marcho."

and 1560s), which would give us the needed footing to establish this probability.[75] We begin.

We have a flourit period for Donato of 1558-1594, a period of thirty-seven years. He was long-lived. He died June 22, 1623.[76] We don't know his birthdate, but he probably began working in his father's shop as a young man. We shall venture that he began work at age eighteen, which would put his birth at about 1540. Exactitude is not important here. We simply want to estimate the length of his life, and to show that it was quite long. So, if he was born in 1540, or close to it, then, in 1623, which date is certain, he would have been eighty-three when he died. Now, with a flourit ending in 1594, when Donato would have been fifty-four or thereabout, if we accept our reasonably estimated birthdate of 1540, and a death date of 1623, we have twenty-nine years from end of flourit until death. Now, a man who is ca. fifty-four years old and in bad health is not likely to live another twenty-nine years, to be eighty-three. Donato had always been active, so when he was fifty-four years of age and presumably in good health, why should he stop working? Here, the date 1594 (and the date 1595) take on much relevance. There are many possible explanations, but we have one ready-made: the preparation of the four-continent set. The fact that from 1595 on we have nothing suggests that he then started work on rejuvenating the set in 1594 or 1595. He could have first received the material at about that time, or perhaps received it earlier, but sat on it for a while, unsure what to do with it. For he had not tackled a project of these proportions before. What did he need to do with the materials at hand to come out with a four-continent set? He needed to rub out Camocio's lengthy dedication on the Europe, and replace Camocio's insignia with his own, a detail.[77] His own Africa and Asia were presumably already prepared, or soon would be.[78] Presenting the most

---

[75] It will also give us the opportunity of making a concerted effort to examine the history of several Venetian map publishing houses in greater depth than has been done before.

[76] See note 85 below.

[77] On this, see the section "The Correr Museum Library set" in chapter nine.

[78] See the start of Chapter twelve on Donato's wall-maps of Africa and Asia, both deriving directly or indirectly from Gastaldi maps. The dates of these maps are unknown, other than that we know they were made after November 1573. Did Donato make these up in particular for the four-continent set? Since both maps are direct copies from already existing maps, they would not make for complicated work. Only new border designs and other decor would have been new.

difficulty would be the restoration of the America to its original condition, probably by reference to Gastaldi's image of America on the giant 1561 world map, which could involve engraving as many as three new plates. In this scenario, the job would have been Donato's last active piece of production, and the most impressive one of his life, and having started it, and divining its potential, he probably would not have diverted his attention from it until it was finished. By this scenario, having begun work on it in late 1594, he probably would have finished it by late 1595 or 1596.

There happens to be a particular circumstance that tends to lend some credibility to this scenario. In 1594 no one had ever made a true four-continent set. Gerard de Jode had, it is true, made wall maps of the individual continents over many years beginning in 1569,[79] but whether he ever intended for them to be taken as a coordinated set is unknown. The erratic time pattern of production argues against the idea. But in the first lustrum of the 1590s, his son Cornelis decided to make such a set, based upon his father's. In 1595, he published a work apparently intended to accompany his upcoming four-continent set of 1596, in which, no doubt, he speaks of the impending set.[80] By our postulations above, Donato would have been working on compiling the spoiled Camocio set. The Italian cartographers generally kept up with what the northern cartographers were doing, and Donato may well have seen Cornelis's 1585 advertisement, and been inspired to increase his postulated efforts to get his set out by 1596. (Alternatively, he may have not yet begun his set, but saw Cornelis's work, and felt goaded to start work on his own, in which case it probably would have appeared ca. 1596/97.) No copy of the first edition of the Bertelli four-continent set is known, nor is there any record of when it first appeared. But we know for certain it was out by 1604, and we know the plates eventually went to the Scolari's, who published them regularly, as we shall see just below; and three exemplars of these sets exist today. And we know that more than half of the maps still bear, besides the Scolari name, that of Donato Bertelli, or the "S[an] Marc[h]o" insignia of his shop, consistent with

[79] They were not printed at the same time. The dates were: Africa (1569); America (1576); Asia (1577); Europe (1587). (Schilder, 1996, 38).

[80] Unfortunately, no copy of this work survives (Schilder, 1996, 38).

the practice of the Scolari's (and many other very late sixteenth century and seventeenth century Italian map publishers) of leaving on plates the names and/or insignia of previous plate owners, along with their own, though at different places on a given map.

To be sure, we could wish for more solid evidence to work from here, but we have pretty much squeezed dry what fragmentary information we have, and it seems likely that the above scenario is correct, or close to it. We tentatively assign the approximate date for the time of Donato's completion of the set as ca. 1596 (?), together with a "circa" and a question mark (?), with the understanding that the date of 1596 is a very rough estimate, although we feel that it is likely to be correct within a year or two. We doubt that any better result can be conjured up, without new information. It is, in fact, not of such great significance. What is most important for us here is to show how the basically Gastaldian set in the James Ford Bell Library, the unique example of the original abortive set was finally brought to fruition by Donato Bertelli.[81]

Following the maps from this point to the time some Stefano Scolari published the sets we know of from 1655 and 1662 is an even shakier proposition, for the record is still more threadbare, but we are by no means without resources for reasonably solid deliberations, and we can come up with some reasonably likely answers.[82] It will be helpful by way of preliminary groundwork to point out that there are three factors, none of them solidly conclusive, but nevertheless suggestive, which intimate that the new four-continent set sold well. Firstly, there is the fact, as we have seen, that Baptiste Vrients ordered no less than ten of the sets from the Officina Plantiniana in 1604, which number shows that Vrients was expecting good sales, and there is also here perhaps an implication that the Officina had still more in stock, unless he was ordering them, by virtue of some Italian contact which Vrients did not have, from Italy. It also shows that the set was selling well outside Italy, and at that even in the Low Countries, which had by this

---

[81] Note that it is not possible for us to establish priority as to whether De Jode's set or Bertelli's set came out first, since we know that De Jode's definitely came out in 1596, which is the same year that we have deduced as the best conjecture as to when, in the span 1592-1604, Bertelli's set was first published.

[82] It is only on the Asias that the Scolari sets are dated. See our cartobibliographical descriptions of these maps, nos. VII and XI for the precise location on the maps of these dates.

time plenty of its own maps for sale. Secondly, there is the fact that at least three sets survived, which is a fairly high survival rate for very large wall map sets, suggesting there had been many. And thirdly, the sets were still selling in the 1660s, ca. seventy years after their creation, and for all we know, they probably sold longer.[83] One more observation on these lines is worth making. In the Low Countries, once the four-continent form was established by the De Jodes, it was regularly followed, every few years, by the four-continent sets of other cartographers. But Donato's Gastaldian set was the only set existing in Italy for a long time, until Scolari began at an indeterminate time to make Italian copies of the 1612 variant of Bleau's famous 1608 set, the earliest dated example of which we know being 1646.[84] This absence of any local competition also no doubt much contributed to its success. Thus, the suggestion that the set was a moneymaker gives us some cause to posit that the Bertellis would have wished to hold on to them for a long time, and the following considerations imply that they indeed did so.

Our survey showed that Valeggio was a major operator, and most, though not all, of his business consisted of reprintings from plates formerly owned by other publishers, and more such plates were obtained from the Bertellis than from any other house. It also showed that many of Valeggio's plates then went to the Scolaris, and that the Scolaris did not generally bother to remove the signatures and/or addresses of previous publishers, though they also added their own. The maps in the three Scolari sets are still

---

[83] Perhaps part of the apparent popularity of the set, even in the north, is due to insufficient alacrity in attempts to market the two sets by the De Jode family, that of Gerard de Jode, which set was complete by 1584, although it is not known to what degree they were marketed as a four-continent set, and that of Cornelis de Jode of 1596. There are few records of sales of the set (Schilder, 1996, 38), and after Cornelis died, the plates were bought by Vrients, and it is not clear whether he published from the plates or not (Schilder, cit., 39). In any event, the survival rate is very low. Of Gerard's set only one individual copy each of two of the maps, Asia (found in 1983 by Schilder) and Europe (surfaced in 1979), and possibly one sheet of his America (Schilder, 1996, 47-49 with ill's 2.32, 2.33, and 2.34) are known. Of Cornelis's set, only a single copy of one map, the Africa, is known, also found by Schilder, in 1975 (Schilder, 1996, 41 and ill. 2.32). The survival rate is about as bad for Jodocus Hondius's set of about 1598, for which one copy each of the Europe and Africa survive, and two sheets of the America (Schilder., 1996, 55-59), and it is nil for his set of 1602, the existence of which is uncertain. No doubt things picked up with the appearance in 1604, the same year as the Officina Plantijniana sold ten of Bertelli's set to Vrients, of Claesz.'s set, and certainly it picked up beginning in 1608, with the first publication of Blaeu's famous and very successful set. As to the question of priority between Cornelis de Jode and Bertelli, one can only guess, for De Jode's set appeared in 1596, and we have set the date of Bertelli's as ca. 1596 as well.

[84] Schilder (1996, 189-95); and Betz (2007, 274-76).

conspicuously covered with Bertelli ghost signatures and addresses, and there are no signs of any attempts to remove them, but, as we have noted earlier, none contain any sign of a Valeggio signature, or address. From these facts, the implication seems pretty conclusive that the plates were indeed lucrative, that the Bertellis held these lucrative plates long, that the plates never made a stop with Valeggio, but rather they passed directly from the Bertellis to the Scolaris at some point.

Here, at first, we seem to encounter a little problem, though it is, I think, very easily resolved. The problem is an apparent missing link. For what evidence we have tells us that the Scolaris did not enter upon map production until around 1620. But the ends of the floruit periods of the two last known denizens of the San Marco shop, Donato and Andrea, are, respectively, ca. 1594, or possibly somewhat later, and 1612, which seems at first sight to leave a gap of at least eight years. But I think if we do a bit of poking around, all can be brought into pretty clear focus, nevertheless. Let's start with Donato. He restored the set, and while not an enormous job, it would not have been easy, and we can fully assume that he would not have entered upon it at all if he were not going to receive some benefit from doing so. Now, Donato, as mentioned earlier, lived to an old age. He died June 22, 1623.[85] Nevertheless, since his first map is from 1558, he was no longer young when he completed the four-continent set. Whether sales from the set were so good that we could call it a golden goose we can't say, but there is room to speculate that Donato at this time decided, perhaps via some agreement with Andrea, to rest upon his laurels, and retire into inactivity. On the other hand, and this seems more likely to me, perhaps he did something like this, but nevertheless remained active, or semi-active in the San Marco shop for an indeterminate amount of time, but only as a dealer, although possibly also directing shop hands in making pulls of the four-continent set, or of other ghost-dated maps.[86]

---

[85] Bury, 2001, 222. Bury discovered this in the Archivio di Stato di Venezia, in connection with the testament mentioned earlier, and though Bury seems to feel not quite certain of this, saying "it was probably the date of his death," the nature of the evidence he gives seems quite certain to me; cf. Almagià (1939, *carta*, p. 9 with note 21), on the documents recording Gastaldi's death. The nature of these records seems to be the same.

[86] The earliest pulls of the four-continent maps were probably dated, but we have no copies from the period and cannot say.

The same is true of Andrea. He could well have continued the shop past 1612, but as a dealer alone, or sometimes printing ghost-dated maps, but producing no newly dated issues. We must remember too that quite possibly compilation of composite atlases in the shop was continuing apace, and in these there is always a broad range of dates and changing them to fit the time of sale of such an atlas was clearly not, and had never been, done. So, a floruit period only tells us the limits of newly produced products, whether truly original compilations, or re-engravings, or just reprints with only a date change. It does not necessarily mean that the person had left his business at all. We point out Menato's finding that Andrea's activities could be followed in the guild record book from 1595 to 1605,[87] yet there is a gap in Andrea's production from 1601 to 1612. Clearly, he was doing something in 1601-1605, and was still in business, but not producing new works. We remember too, that, before Donato made his 1558 Italy, the older Pietro was apparently running the San Marco business purely as a dealer's shop. Andrea's gap in personal production from 1601-1612 suggests to me that at that time, the shop was reverting in this direction, and after 1612, did so once and for all, selling books, prints, maps, very possibly compiling composite atlases, and, especially, printing copies of the four-continent set.[88] The ultimate demise of the San Marco shop is lost in the mist, but my feeling is that it probably continued in this status for an indeterminate time.[89]

So, we cannot say with any precision when the plates passed from the Bertelli shop to the Scolaris. The approximate record says the Scolaris did not begin producing maps until the 1620s, and the earliest dated Scolari-Blaeu set is 1646, and the earliest dated Gastaldi-Scolari set is from 1655,

---

[87] Menato (1997, 122). See also our special note at the end of the chapter on the registers, or *mariegole,* of the printers and booksellers guild.

[88] An alternative scenario, as regards the four-continent set, might be that the shop reverted to a sales shop alone, and the actual printing was done by arrangement with the later Pietro (life dates ca. 1571-1621) and his son Francesco, the last recorded Bertelii, whose floruit of ca. 1621-1656 runs past the mid-seventeenth century, who were both copperplate publishers as well as typographers. It is true that Pietro and Francesco operated in Padua, but Padua is very close to Venice, and some sort of arrangement could have been made; and, even if they were not part of the San Marco establishment, the four-continent set would still remain in the family. But there is no need to fall back on this here, and I don't think it too likely. More likely the San Marco business continued on its own as we have been describing.

[89] It is interesting to note that, presuming that the shop did so continue for a good number of years, there might have been a Bertelli or two who joined the shop in this period about whom we know nothing at all!

neither of which later dates can tell us anything very specific regarding our question. We can however observe that in our survey we found no sign of the Scolaris venturing into the production of multi-sheet maps before 1646. The few maps I found up to that time are all smaller single sheet maps, and so, on the basis of this, and the fact that the general odds would seem to be against the 1655 edition's being the first Scolari publishing of the set, perhaps the best estimate, highly approximate, would be ca. the 1640s as the time when the four-continent set passed from the Bertelli family to the Scolari family. We can, alas, do no better.

After the Scolaris obtained the plates, we know that they continued to publish them at least until 1662, and possibly later. Ironically interesting is the fact that we cannot speculate on which Stefano Scolari was publishing them at what times, but the Scolari signatures on the 1655 and 1662 sets seem different to me. We do have Stefano Mozzi Scolari (who on one piece signs himself as "bresciano"), with a hazy floruit of 1657-1687, so perhaps he did the Arader sets, and some earlier Stefano the Ransom Center set.[90] As a final observation, it is not impossible that there was more than one Scolari shop. Maps from the San Marco shop *always* showed the shop insignia, at least from the early 1570s onwards, but occasionally did not give a particular Bertelli's name. On the contrary, Scolari maps *always* show the publisher's name, but rarely the insignia or address. So, we can't be sure there was just one shop.

12.7 Summary and Conclusion

Giacomo Gastaldi: Gifted visionary and imaginative maker of maps far ahead of his time. There's never been another cartographer remotely like him. Unlike most sixteenth-century cartographers, Gastaldi had little interest in mapping areas anywhere close to his home, which was first in Piedmont and then in Venice, but always hungered to map the unknown, to reach out to extra-European continents and present them to the world on exquisitely executed maps. For all his talent, vision and imagination, Gastaldi kept his

---

[90] We should mention that the Europe in the ca. 1655 set is a different engraving from the Europe in the 1662 set, although the 1662 Europe is clearly from Camocio's original plates. See our Cartobibliography entries no. (V.-VIII.) and no. V for an explanation of this peculiar fact.

head out of the clouds and worked steadily and confidently within the scientific limits that his own time imposed on his work. The most persistent and perplexing unknowable for cartographers—not to mention navigators—in the sixteenth century was the inability to determine longitude. The solution to that riddle was two hundred years away in Gastaldi's lifetime. He was not discouraged. He gave a metaphorical shrug and worked within the limits of his time's knowledge. He would do the best he could with the knowledge within his reach. And the best he could do was astounding.

Besides the longitude problem, there was an ongoing debate about whether Asia and America were separate land masses or connected. There were fervent believers in both possibilities, and there were those who simply could not decide. Gastaldi did not let this debate, which absolutely could not be resolved with the knowledge of the time, interfere with his work. It was one or the other, and it didn't matter tremendously to him which would eventually be proved to be correct. He gave another metaphorical shrug, and sometimes made maps showing a connection and sometimes made maps with a strait between the land masses. What he wanted was the big picture. Gastaldi's indifference to the problems he knew could not be solved allowed him to work with great speed and fluency. Fortune had also smiled on him in bringing him together with invaluable colleagues, particularly Giovanni Batista Ramusio, who gathered enormous amounts of information from voyages and explorations, which he enthusiastically shared with Gastaldi to use in his maps; and Fabio Licinio, an extremely talented engraver who was able to bring Gastaldi's glorious maps to fruition.

Gastaldi's greatest maps were created between 1559 and 1564. These great continental masterpieces brought the continents of Asia, Africa, and America into European consciousness. They represent, arguably, the single greatest cartographic advance in history, and laid the foundations for all the extra-European mapmaking that followed. The depictions of those continents turned out to be largely, almost eerily, correct. Eventually, they were wrenched into mathematical accuracy, but it was the vision of Giacomo Gastaldi that brought their essence to the world. My hope is that this book will enlarge the recognition Gastaldi so richly deserves and acquaint a wider audience with his remarkable achievements.

The most important single source of information on the Venetian publishers, dealers, printers, etc. of this period, as any, has always been the sundry little notices on the maps themselves. This source has far from been exhausted. There are at present known probably slightly over 100 Veneto-Roman or IATO atlases, or significant collections of sixteenth century Italian maps most of which no doubt originally came from these atlases for the most part. Probably less than half of these have been catalogued, and far less than this have been catalogued with the requisite thoroughness to be dependable in such a survey as that we attempted for the present chapter. In fact, over half of these catalogings consist of very abbreviated entries, of considerable use, but far from sufficient for deep cartobibliographical work. Thus, a great mine of information still waits to be brought out. Unfortunately, doing so will be no easy or fast task.

Still another source of possibly great value has hardly been touched and remains very little known, although a handful of informed Italian scholars have made limited use of it. This source is what I shall call for the moment the record book of the Guild of Printers and Booksellers of Venice, which guild was established on January 18, 1548 (Brown, 1891, 81, 83, and 87). All guilds everywhere in Europe had such books, and they are all similar in content, generally containing three things: the statutes of the guild, a register of members, and a sort of minute-book, recording proceedings of meetings, but also often carrying much other information on the affairs of the guild, as recorded by the guild's scribe. Sometimes the members register makes up a separate volume or even series of volumes. In Venice and Venetian owned territories, these record books were called *mariegole* (singular *mariegola*). Indeed, the word, the source of which is unknown, was used exclusively in Venetian territories. More expectable, or typical, names were used for such record books elsewhere. Few survive, but that for the Venetian Guild of Printers and Booksellers does. It is in the Library of the Correr Museum (under the number Classe IV, no. 119), which museum received it from the estate of the great nineteenth century Venetian scholar

Emmanuele Cicogna, who appended some other relevant documents to it, among them some materials by himself, including among other things a running catalogue of Venetian printers and booksellers from 1469 to 1796, and gave to the whole of the compilation the following manuscript title: "Matricola dell'arte dei stampatori e librai ec. ec. In Venetia dal 1469 al 1856, non che diversi decreti a stampa relativi" (Matricula of the Guild of Printers and Booksellers etc. etc. in Venice from 1469 to 1856, as well as diverse decrees relative to printing.) Note that because the time span given by Cicogna in his compilation of related materials runs from 1469 to 1856, it is impossible to determine from this title the time span covered by the *mariegola* proper, since its beginning date, 1469, far precedes the foundation of the guild in 1548, and the end date far exceeds its demise, which would have been in 1797, when Napoleon closed all the guilds by decree after taking the Republic, but I suspect this *mariegola* is preserved right up to 1797.

Brown prints parts of the mariegola, but confusedly, and omitting an unknown amount of the minutes and records, without telling the reader he has done so, to wit: His Document III (1891, 241-48) he calls "Mariegole of the Guild of Printers and Booksellers." But besides the fact that he misspells the term which designates the record book (the word is invariably feminine "*mariegola*" with plural "*mariegole*"; a masculine variant "mariegole" definitely never existed), his document III prints only that part of the *mariegola* which contains the guild's basic statutes, and no more. His document IV is called "Minute-book of the Guild of Printers and Booksellers" (1891, 249-336). This is itself part of the mariegola, not a separate document, and Brown, as said, without telling us, has omitted unknown amounts and portions, and his document IV is really just extracts. This I know from a personal communication from Piero Lucchi, Librarian of Manuscripts at the Correr Museum (actually a lengthy April 14, 1998 MAPHIST response by Lucchi to a request sent to MAPHIST on the same day by the present author.) Lucchi's response was written with the manuscript literally under his eyes, and among the things he mentions are the minutes of the meeting of the guild for April 1, 1571, in which it is recorded that among those present that day was Donato Bertelli, and this little datum was misrecorded by someone, perhaps Cicogna, and gave rise long ago to a myth that 1571 is the date that Donato joined the guild, an error which has been repeated since by countless authors. As Lucchi accentuates, the datum is nothing of the kind, and just records his presence that day at the meeting, his date of joining being some time earlier. This meeting record is *not* among the materials published by Brown in his Document IV, and the facts just recited are sufficient to show that it is vital that the entirety of the *mariegola* be printed, along with any other material in Classe IV, no. 119 (Brown does publish Cicogna's 1469-1796 list of printers, as his Document VI, at pp. 395-420).

Donato printed several books, though his main publishing interest was maps, and one might wonder if the guild was only for book printers. But we know from Menato (1997, 22) that the activities of Andrea Bertelli, a much later (fl. ca. 1593-1612) and less prominent name in the San Marco business, are recorded in the *mariegola,* and Andrea printed only maps. No books are recorded as being published by him. So, at least by his time, but very probably from the start, the guild included among its "stampatori" those who published maps, and no doubt other prints as well. An interesting nuance here is that the guild is said to be for "printers and booksellers," without specific mention of publishers. And, in fact, there can be little doubt that all of our map publishers published from shops which also sold books. Thus, by virtue of their bookseller status, they should be in the guild records even if their actual personal printing was restricted to maps, and even if map printers were not understood as included among the "printers" in the guild's name. I think it is worth pointing this out, although I think in fact printers of copper engravings probably were understood as being included under the heading 'printers". I should note that it is vital, for anyone who wishes to investigate these old *mariegole* to first consult the recent works of Alessia Giachery, which can be found easily by consulting the free online union catalog of Italian libraries, the SBN (Servizio Bibliotecario Nazionale), though one article of hers cannot be found there (Giachery, 1998).

Finally, we should note, in Venice, all guilds had an agreement with one or other of the Catholic churches or monasteries of the city, by which the church provided a meeting place for the guild, while the guild was responsible for the upkeep of the church. The *mariegole* were kept in the church's sacristy, and other guild documents were kept in these sacristies as well. Very many of these old churches still stand, but, as I understand things, obtaining permission to explore the contents of these sacristies is extremely difficult. Finally, legal records concerned with some guild map publishers probably still exist, though I know nothing of them, except that to find them, one needs to know the name of the map publisher's lawyer (personal communication from David Woodward). Standard records of dates of birth and dates of death, as well as dates of marriages, likely still exist in clergy records for some of these people. And it is not impossible that still other sources of information exist of which I am unaware. Clearly, the bottom of the barrel has not yet been scraped on possible data sources on the map publishers and printers of Venice.

APPENDIX 2 : ON THE PRESERVATION OF GASTALDI'S CARTOGRAPHIC LEGACY

In terms of pure numbers, the majority of Gastaldi's maps were published in books, mainly in the 1548 Ptolemy, and in volumes one and three of Ramusio's *Navigationi*, and this fact assured that these maps would not perish. But it was in his large separately printed maps that Gastaldi made his main mark. Let us speak for a moment of the fact of the survival of these separate maps to our time, a point of much importance in our story. Without these maps, we would have no story, nor would Gastaldi, whose legacy would be lost, for in fact these maps are the story's foundation. Both he and we are indebted to their survival. How did it come about, in an age from which so many maps of other countries are lost to us?

Probably, the great majority of the copies of Gastaldi's maps, as well as those of others, which were printed in Venice, and then often in Rome, were sold individually, and no doubt almost all maps so sold have long since disappeared, victims of the ravages of time, like so many of the maps of northern cartographers, many of which survive only as fragments or not at all. But, fortunately, somewhere around 1565, someone in Venice, most likely someone in the Bertelli's famous San Marco shop in Merzaria Street, but perhaps Camocio or Forlani or someone else, came up with the idea of binding together in book form assortments of these maps, varying in number from about twenty to as many as perhaps two or three hundred, and marketing them thusly. From all appearances, the number of maps and their selection were things left to the discretion of the customer, who decided what he wished to have, which was then bound up and sold to him.[1] [2] These individualistic compilations were, then, in this form, atlases in a sense, and the order in which the maps were entered in the binding generally followed the order, as far as that was possible, which had been followed by the outdated but revered Ptolemy.

---

[1] The Bertellis, Camocio, and others dealt in and published books, and binding was probably done in the shop itself.

It must not be thought that these compilations were the first true modern atlases. That honor goes without reservation to Abraham Ortelius, with his *Theatrum Orbis Terrarum* of 1570. The Venetian atlases do not qualify because there was of course no consistency in the contents from atlas to atlas, and, most importantly, no expert editorial hand was involved in their compilation. There were usually several maps available in stock of any particular country or region, for the Venetian publishers indiscriminately copied and published all maps they could come by from other lands, and we often find that the selection made for a country was a poor one, sometimes the worst, while Ortelius spent much effort in always trying to obtain the best map for each region. Also, the Venetian atlases had no title page, and no preliminary material, but were just a bare collection of maps bound between covers. However, it is valid to consider them as precursors to the true atlas, and they form up part of its pre-history. The practice of compiling these atlases was then shortly after taken up in Rome by Antoine Lafreri, with the difference that Lafreri added a title page: *Geografia. Tavole moderne di geografia de la maggior parte del mondo di diversi autori, raccolte et messe secondo l'ordine di Tolomeo, con I disegni di molte città et fortezze di diverse provintie. Stampate in rame con stvdio et diligenza in Roma.*[3]

These were expensive books, and many of them found safe havens in the carefully shelved book collections of noble or wealthy persons, and thus many of them survived the centuries.[4] It is only due to the preservation of these atlases that most of the legacy of sixteenth century Italian map production was not lost, although there are quite a few cases where only one example of a map has made it through to us, and this is true of several Gastaldi maps, so there may be a few which have not turned up yet, or even a few which are lost forever. In any event, it is due principally to this fortunate historical accident that the whole, or nearly the whole, of Gastaldi's

---

[3] It is not impossible that some atlases without the title page could be Roman, for we don't know whether Lafreri began adding these title pages as soon as he began making these atlases.

[4] The author has been keeping a sort of record of these atlases, and other significant collections of Italian sixteenth century maps, which themselves no doubt descend from such atlases which were at some time or other disbound, and the total number of such atlases and collections is now slightly over 100. Only about half have been cataloged.

production has reached us, and we are able to piece together a reasonably good and complete history of his work.

Ironically, as important as these compilations have been in the preservation of sixteenth century Italian cartographic heritage, there has never existed a suitable term for referring to them. Certainly, as the following comments will make clear, they are in need of such a suitable term, and we will conclude the ensuing observations with a suggestion which we think will be satisfactory. Up to about the time of Nordenskiöld, they were very little known, and in the rare instances in which they were referred to, they were usually called "the Roman atlas", due of course to the Lafreri title page in some copies, a name quite wrong, since it is now long recognized that they originated in Venice. Nordenskiöld referred to them as "Lafreri's atlas", a name still fairly commonly used, though some have revised this to "Lafrerian atlas" or "Lafreri-type" atlas, but again, the name is misleading, still implying a Roman origin. The well-known one-time collector of sixteenth century Italian maps, George Harry Beans, to circumvent this, coined the phrase "Italian Assembled to Order Atlas" (or, abbreviated, "IATO atlas").[5] But both Beans's denomination *and* its abbreviation are clumsy in the extreme. They do not roll but stumble off the tongue, and are denizens not of the land of euphony, but the land of cacophony, and the abbreviation IATO sounds like the initials of some organization. The phrase also, obviously, lacks conciseness. No doubt due to these esthetic unpleasantries, this phrase too has found only limited acceptance, and the most recent attempt at a name has been to simply refer to them as "Italian composite atlases", or even "sixteenth century Italian composite atlases". But, besides the fact that this is more of a description than a denomination, it is also unsatisfactory because there are any number of possible understandings of the phrase "composite atlas", Italian or otherwise, so the phrase is too broad to serve as a designation of this

---

[5] I note that a number of foreign writers acquainted with Beans's denomination have taken Beans's phrase "Assembled to Order" to refer to the fact that the atlases were assembled according to the *order* of Ptolemy, but this is quite wrong. The phrase "Assembled to Order" in Beans's appellation means assembled to the *order* of individual customers, that is, assembled according to his (the customer's) specifications as to the choice of maps to be included, just as a suit, or a home, or even an automobile, or whatever, "made to order" always means in English made according to the customer's order, that is, according to his specifications or directives.

particular form; furthermore, as with Beans's denomination, it is anything but concise.

I have been studying these atlases for many years, and for the last fifteen years or so I have invariably referred to them in my own personal notes as Veneto-Roman atlases, or, abbreviated, simply VR atlases. Both the term and its abbreviation are concise, and they are articulated smoothly and easily, and, most importantly, the term has an unmistakable uniqueness and it expresses its object much better than any previous term, even preserving the historical precedence of Venice over Rome by putting "Veneto" first. It is my hope that this term, which we use often in the present work, will be adopted, putting an end to the difficulty in which we have always found ourselves when wishing to refer to these very important compilations, which have preserved so well the heritage of sixteenth century Italian cartography.

APPENDIX 3: THE PORTRAIT OF GASTALDI

The portrait of Gastaldi reproduced as figure 1.1 is the only one known, and was first brought to light by Roberto Almagià.[6] It was drawn by the Milanese historian and sometime cartographer Urbano Monte (1544-1613), and is found in a 318-folio manuscript work by him titled "Trattato Vniversale Descrittione, et Sito de Tvtta la Terra Sin Qvi Conoscivta, etc."[7], in the Biblioteca Ambrosiana in Milan, with call number MS A.260.Inf.[8] Monte, note, uses for Gastaldi the given name form Iacomo, which at the time was perhaps as common as the form Giacomo, the form usually used in our time. The Gastaldi portrait is at folio 269 recto, which may also be designated as plate (*tavola*) no. 59. To understand this dual designation, and in general to gain a complete and correct bibliographical perspective concerning this portrait, which perspective was extremely difficult for me to piece together, some background is necessary.[9]

In 1587 Monte completed a gigantic sixty-four-sheet circular world map on a north polar projection. He then composed the tract named above, basically a lengthy accompaniment to and commentary on the world map, which tract he finished in 1590.[10] Monte made at least two other copies of the map, one now in private hands,[11] and another which was completed by 1604. Monte introduced several changes to this latter copy, only one of

---

[6] Almagià (1939, *carta*, [19]). Almagià gives a reproduction of the portrait at p. 6, but it is a very small and poor reproduction. No truly adequate reproduction of the portrait has been made before that in the present book.

[7] The very lengthy full title is given in Almagià (1941, 157).

[8] A microfilm of the manuscript, under the same call number, is also available at the library of the Medieval Institute at Notre Dame University, which possesses a complete microfilm collection of the manuscripts of the Ambrosiana Library, and a copy of the film may be ordered therefrom for a fee.

[9] The documentation for the basic explanatory facts in the following two paragraphs is all from Almagià (1941), and from Maurizio Ampollini's introduction to Monte (1994), unless specifically indicated otherwise.

[10] This first copy of the map, and its accompanying text survive, in the library of the Venegono Seminary near Milan, and this copy of the map has been reproduced, sheet by sheet, with introduction and commentary by Maurizio Ampollini (Monte, 1994).

[11] On this copy, see Goss (1981). It was unknown until it came up for sale by Sotheby's in 1981. According to Goss, Sotheby's stated that the copy was dated 1587, which is the same date as the original at the Venegono Seminary, but I suspect there is some kind of equivocation here.

which interests us, the addition of the portraits of thirty-three geographers,[12] which make up part of a broad band, or garland, of sundry décor surrounding the map.[13] Monte then decided to have both the map and the *Trattato* published together as a set. The sixty-four sheets of the map were duly engraved, and proof prints were pulled.[14]

But for some reason, the project went no farther, and the *Trattato* was not printed, presumably due to some objection on the part of the publisher. No doubt disappointed and disgruntled, Monte had his manuscript tract and the printed proof sheets all bound together, the printed map sheets sewn in with the manuscript pages of the tract, with the map sheets dispersed through the book in appropriate places according to the text, and this is the quite unusual artifact we now possess in the Ambrosiana Library, consisting of a book which is part manuscript and part printed. Monte paginated his work strangely. He paginated everything in one continuing sequence, including in the pagination not only the tract's manuscript pages, but also the map sheets,[15] and even the empty backs of the map sheets! The pagination is peculiar in still another way. If we open the book at random, and we see in the upper left corner of the left page, say, the folio number 117, and then we look at the page to the right, we see 117 again, in the upper right corner! And when we turn the page, we see 118 on the left page and 118 on the right page, and so on through the book. Monte numbered by page spreads instead of by leaves. So, 117 verso is not on the other side of 117 recto, but on a different sheet of paper, to the left of 117 recto. Although the actual geographical sheets of the map are distributed evenly through the text, Monte

---

[12] The geographers' names are given at the bottom of each portrait. Gastaldi is given as IACOMO GASTALDI".

[13] The sixty-four sheets of the enormous map (radius'1.37 meters) are not rectangular, but curved on either one or two sides, depending upon where they fall in the sheeting arrangement, which consists of five concentric circular series of sheets, four in the center, eight in the band around them, twelve in the next band, and, finally, twenty sheets each in the outer two bands. Almagià gives a diagram showing schematically the entire arrangement of the sheets (1941, 160); he also names all the geographers, one of which of course is Gastaldi (1941, 168). The size of the individual portraits varies slightly, but they are roughly 5 x 6 cm, except one, a self-portrait of Monte himself, which is much larger than the others. These portraits, as implied, do not occur in the other copies of the map.

[14] A copy of the Urbano map, with various interactive versions, is reproduced at Davidrumsey.com/luna/servlet/detail/Rumsey~8~1~303668~90074325

[15] Each map sheet makes up one double-page spread.

had all of the sheets containing the portraits and other décor sewn in together, making up folios 244-279. The Gastaldi portrait is at folio 269 recto.[16] But sometime in the recent past, the Ambrosiana has assigned plate numbers as well to those of Montes folios which are actually printed sheets, with Gastaldi's portrait coming out as plate (*tavola*) no. 59 (269 recto).[17] What can we say as to the authenticity of the portrait? Is it true to life? Almagià simply said that it probably came from a print which was circulating at the time, though no copy of such is known.[18] But even if Almagià's hypothesis be correct, that would still not guarantee that the surmised print itself was to life. Could Monte himself, who assuredly drew the portrait, have done so from life? Monte, in fact, was something of a portraitist himself. During the first embassy from Japan to Italy in 1585, Monte drew portraits of the members of the embassy, as well as a portrait of one P. Mezquita, a Portuguese Jesuit who accompanied the embassy.[19] Furthermore, Monte left us self-portraits on most of his works, including the one on the title page of the Trattato cited earlier, and on the three known copies of the world map. Also, of all the geographers whom Monte depicts, it is abundantly clear from numerous passages in Almagià's 1941 study that the geographer whose works Monte made most use of is Gastaldi, and this fact and the fact that both were Italian would seem to lend a little support to the idea that Monte might have drawn Gastaldi's portrait from life. But, while not impossible, other facts speak rather strongly against this. Monte was born in 1544, and Gastaldi died in 1566, so, if Monte drew Gastaldi's

---

[16] This copy of the portrait is, I believe, unique. Shirley (1987, in no. 246) states that the original manuscript drawings from which the surviving proof sheets were made are also in the Ambrosiana, and implies the same elsewhere (1987, in no. 239), but I am virtually certain, for reasons too long to go into here, that this is not the case, and the idea perhaps arises from confusion connected with the facts that the proof sheets are located in an artifact whose lengthy text is itself indeed in manuscript, and that the copy of the map in the Venegono Seminary is in fact manuscript, as is the copy sold by Sotheby's in 1981.

[17] As far as I am aware, no attempt has ever been made to actually assemble the sixty-four proof sheets into a whole map. [Publisher's note: The David Rumsey page referenced in note 14 above, does, in fact, reproduce the entire map as a single sheet on a polar projection, and also shows the map transformed to a rotating globe.]

[18] Almagià (1939, [19]).

[19] Almagià (1941, 158, note 6).

portrait, he could not have done so when he was older than 22 years of age. Furthermore, the earliest indication of which we have knowledge of any interest in geography on the part of Monte is 1587, the date he finished his original world map, so we have no particular basis to posit that Monte would have had any reason to seek Gastaldi out in the mid-1560s.[20] In the end, unfortunately, with what information we have, no foundation exists upon which we can make any sound judgment as to the authenticity of the Gastaldi portrait.

---

[20] It is not impossible that there might be evidence of an early interest in geography in Monte's four-volume manuscript historical chronicle of Milan, preserved in the Ambrosiana, and mentioned by Almagià (1941, 158).

Il Sommario italiano è una sinossi dell'Introduzione del libro, dei capitoli e della cartobibliografia.

Sommario dell'Introduzione del libro

Il lettore troverà nei sommari dei singoli capitoli le stesse informazioni presenti nell'Introduzione del libro. È una notevole eccezione. Ciò che segue è trattato nell'Introduzione del libro, ma non nei sommari dei capitoli. Numerosi studiosi hanno chiesto in merito alla considerevole lunghezza del libro, approssimativamente 800 pagine. Ci sono tre ragioni:

1. Nei capitoli 3 e 4 mostriamo che, considerate congiuntamente, le tre grandi rappresentazioni di Gastaldi dei tre continenti extraeuropei, Africa, Asia e America, sono tutte realizzate tra il 1559 e il 1564 e costituiscono il più grande miglioramento della cartografia del mondo nella storia. Ma una piccola minoranza di studiosi aveva espresso riserve riguardo alla paternità del Gastaldi rispetto all'Asia e all'America. L'eliminazione di ogni dubbio ha richiedesto 4 capitoli: il capitolo 5 per l'Asia e i capitoli 7, 8, e 9 per l'America.

2. Il libro prende in considerazione tutti gli aspetti della vita di Gastaldi per i quali abbiamo informazioni, includendo sia soggetti cartografici sia non cartografici e tratta di tutte e 124 le carte del Gastaldi nella cartobibliografia di 185 pagine, includendo in ogni caso commenti di parecchie pagine.

3. Abbiamo dovuto dedicare molto spazio alla correzione delle numerose inesattezze e confusioni sulla letteratura intorno a

Gastaldi e al suo lavoro. Queste inesattezze cominciarono seriamente intorno al periodo 1900-1920, ma la situazione diviene peggiore tra il 1920 e il 1930. Nella maggior parte questi problemi era causati del fatto che numerose carte importanti di Gastaldi erano completamente sconosciute agli studiosi fino a quando alcuni esemplari vennero alla luce in tempi piuttosto recenti (1921, 1939, 1949, ecc.). Entro la metà del XX secolo questi errori avevano talmente preso piede da rendere poco comprensibile il lavoro di Gastaldi. Questa mancanza di chiarezza contribuì ad una sottovalutazione dell'opera gastaldina con una conseguente riduzione di contributi accademici. Ho trascorso molto tempo per rintracciare le fonti di questi errori, rimuovendo gran parte delle inesattezze e restituendo chiarezza e correttezza all'opera di Gastaldi.

Capitolo 1

Il capitolo primo tratta dei soggetti vari, biografici, generali, ecc.: le prime citazioni riguardo a Gastaldi; i rapporti con esponenti di governo e patrizi (ad esempio Giovanni Battista Ramusio e Diego Hurtado de Mendoza) e con editori e stampatori (Giovanni Battista Pedrezano e Nicolò Bascarini); la sua edizione di Tolomeo del 1548 (trattiamo di questo libro maggiormente nella cartobibliografia); il suo lavoro come idrografo governativo; la sua associazione con l'Accademia Veneziana. Ci occupiamo anche dell'incisione delle sue carte e in merito ai suoi *privilegi*. Il capitolo sottolinea la scarsità delle informazioni biografiche intorno al Gastaldi.

Capitolo 2

Nel capitolo secondo parliamo delle carte del mondo di Gastaldi: la sua famosa carta del 1546 e le sue numerose edizioni; la grande carta fatta per un principe ottomano, ma in modo particolare ci occupiamo della carta del mondo del 1561, alla quale sono dedicate numerose pagine.

Capitolo 3

Queso capitolo è breve, ma molto importante. Paragona le migliori carte gastaldine di Africa, Asia e America alle migliori carte realizzate in precedenza. In tutti e tre i casi il miglioramento apportato da Gastaldi è notevole, ed infatti le sue carte ebbero una forte influenza per oltre un secolo. Se consideriamo tutti e tre i continenti insieme, il miglioramento dell'immagine cartografica del mondo nella sua interezza è davvero sorprendente, si tratta del più grande perfezionamento nella storia della cartografia. Alcuni eruditi (ma non la maggioranza) hanno avuto dubbi per quanto concerne la paternità del Gastaldi relativamente alle carte di Asia e America. Tra i principali obiettivi del volume vi è la rimozione definitiva di questi dubbi.

Capitolo 4

In questo capitolo ci si chiede come sia stato possibile per un cartografo migliorare l'immagine di questi tre continenti. La risposta risiede nella collaborazione di Gastaldi con il segretario del Senato della Repubblica di Venezia Giovanni Battista Ramusio, intorno al 1540. Il Ramusio nutriva un profondo interesse verso le scoperte geografiche d'oltremare. In circa 30 anni Ramusio accumulò un'enorme quantità di relazioni di viaggio di esploratori e viaggiatori di mare e di terra, molti delle quali manoscritte. Il Ramusio spesso riuscì ad ottenerle in virtù dei suoi rapporti con il governo veneziano e con gli studiosi di paesi stranieri. La raccolta iniziò intorno al 1520, ma la loro pubblicazione avvenne molto più tardi in tre tomi (nel 1550 il primo: Africa e Asia costiera; nel 1559 il secondo: Asia interna; nel 1556 il terzo, l'America), col titolo *Navigationi et Viaggi, ecc.* Ma Gastaldi, in alcuni casi, ebbe modo di consultare le relazioni anche un ventennio prima della loro pubblicazione. Finalmente, e in aggiunta a questa straordinaria collezione di narrazioni, sappiamo che Ramusio ebbe una quantità sconosciuta di carte nautiche portoghesi e spagnole a disposizione di Gastaldi e non pubblicate nell'opera ramusiana. Ecco le vaste fonti, le relazioni e le carte manoscritte utilizzate dal Gastaldi per elaborare le sue sorprendenti carte.

Capitolo 5

In questo capitolo dimostriamo senza ombra di dubbio che Gastaldi fu l'unico autore della grande carta dell'Asia del 1559-61 (si vedano i numeri 92, 102, 103). L'erudito francese Guillaume Postel viaggiò da Venezia a Damasco negli anni 1549-1550/51 e tornò con parecchi libri arabi, inclusa la *Geografia* di Abulfeda, libro sconosciuto in Europa. Ramusio, che conosceva Postel, scrisse di questo nella prefazione della sua edizione del *Milione* di Marco Polo all'interno del secondo volume delle *Navigationi*. Abramo Ortelio di Anversa lesse questa prefazione e, senza altre fonti, dichiarò che Gastaldi migliorò notevolmente l'Asia in base al lavoro di Abulfeda, tuttavia non precisando se si riferisse ad una fonte cartografica o scritta. Nessuno ha mai menzionato di una carta geografica realizzata da Abulfeda e vi sono fondati motivi per credere che Abulfeda non abbia mai fatto costruito una carta; per quanto concerne il libro di Abulfeda, ne esiste dal 1883 una traduzione completa (2 tomi) in francese di Reinaud e Guyard. In generale, il libro di Abulfeda contiene solo una piccolissima percentuale dei toponimi di Gastaldi. Ad esempio, Abulfeda ammette che i geografi arabi avessero scarse conoscenze della Cina, infatti il suo libro riporta soltanto mezza dozzina di toponimi cinesi in confronto alle centinaia della carta gastaldina (e nell'opera di Ramusio). Un altro esempio: Abulfeda non dice una parola intorno all'enorme arcipelago asiatico sud orientale, a differenza di Gastaldi che tratta abbondantemente questa regione. Inoltre, varie circostanze ci dicono che Ortelio non ebbe mai modo di consultare la *Geografia* di Abulfeda e, anche se la vide, non avrebbe potuto leggerla. Eccetto Postel che ne aveva tradotti alcuni frammenti sparsi, nessuno aveva tentato di tradurla. Gastaldi non prese nulla da Abulfeda. Ortelius semplicemente non riusciva a immaginare in quale altro modo Gastaldi fosse riuscito a realizzare la sua straordinaria mappa. Le fonti certe di Gastaldi erano le relazioni del lavoro di Ramusio nei tomi I e II, e le carte nautiche da lui ricevute. In questo modo noi giustifichiamo una di queste due carte di cui parliamo nel capitolo 3 restituendo la paternità a Gastaldi. Per scagionare anche la seconda carta, l'America, riguardo alla quale si nutrivano dubbi sulla paternità di Gastaldi, dovremo attendere il capitolo 9 quando avremo più informazioni.

Capitolo 6

I capitoli 6 e 7 sono necessari per la comprensione del capitolo 8, il quale è necessario per la comprensione del cruciale capitolo 9. Il capitolo 9 conferma la ingiustamente dubitata paternità del Gastaldi di una stranamente poco conosciuta grande carta dell'America di cui due esemplari difettosi vennero alla luce negli anni '20 del ventesimo secolo, e più tardi tre esemplari completi di un'edizione successiva vennero alla luce nella seconda metà del ventesimo secolo. Il nostro capitolo è il primo passo per provare che Gastaldi è certamente l'autore della questa carta. Nel capitolo si discute lo sviluppo storico dell'idea dell'esistenza di quattro continenti (il medesimo soggetto è trattato anche nei capitoli 11 e 12). Osserviamo che nel Cinquecento non vi era una chiara riflessione riguardo a questa idea a causa del fatto che non esistevano informazioni attendibili sulla relazione fra il Mondo Nuovo e il Mondo Vecchio. Erano separati o uniti? Ecco il soggetto del nostro capitolo seguente.

Capitolo 7

Nello capitolo 7 scriviamo riguardo alle idee correnti nella prima metà del XVI secolo rispetto alle relazioni geografiche fra Asia e America. Vengono discusse molte idee intorno a questo enigma. Alla fine la maggioranza accettò l'esistenza di uno stretto a nord tra i due continenti.

Nel capitolo si riflette sul fatto che uno stesso cartografo possa mostrare diversamente la medesima area geografica in due carte e che questo non necessariamente significhi un cambio

d'opinione nella carta con la data più tarda. Al contrario, questo
può significare che semplicemente il cartografo non ha certezze
riguardo a quella regione, oppure non ne sa niente. Probabilmente
né l'una né l'altra rappresentazione si prestano ad indicare la verità
o la convinzione del cartografo. Sono semplicemente due
possibilità. Questa idea sarà molto importante nel capitolo 8.

Lo stretto geografico menzionato più sopra è naturalmente il
famoso Stretto di Anian, il quale somiglia molto allo Stretto di
Bering, scoperto quasi anni 200 dopo che quello di Anian
comparve sulle carte, e questo rimase un enigma per quasi anni
300. È risaputo che questo stretto apparve per la prima volta nelle
carte di Gastaldi, ma le sue ragioni sono state conosciute soltante
in parte e nel nostro seguente capitolo 8 ne daremo una esauriente
spiegazione.

Capitolo 8

Questo è un lungo capitolo che tratta dello Stretto di Anian,
di grande importanza nella storia. Nel corso di oltre due secoli gli
studiosi lo investigarono senza successo, ma intorno alla fine del
XIX secolo gli storici compresero che l'idea veniva da Gastaldi,
senza capire come. Noi proponiamo la nostra interpretazione
pensando sia corretta.

Nelle *Navigationi et viaggi* di Ramusio, fonte principale di
Gastaldi, si parla di innumerevoli animali e in quasi tutti i casi
quelli del Mondo Nuovo sono gli stessi del Mondo Vecchio o
molto simili. Lo stesso dicasi per gli esseri umani. L'implicazione
è chiara: o i due continenti sono connessi, oppure sono molto

vicini in qualche punto a nord. Ma quale delle due ipotesi è vera? All'epoca non esistevano certezze per decidere.

In merito a questo la nostra argomentazione diviene sottile, ma crediamo che il lettore sarà d'accordo con noi. Né l'una, né l'altra furono accolte da Gastaldi o da altri, benchè alla fine una divenne prevalente. Note bene: nel 1561 Gastaldi fece una carta del mondo colla separazione dei continenti (la nostra numero 104), ma nel 1562 ne fece un'altra con la connessione (numero 105). La stessa credenza era osservata da altri cartografi italiani per oltre un decennio dopo il 1560. C'erano carte del mondo con la connessione e carte con la separazione (ad esempio la *Totius Orbis Descriptio* e altre). Ma sembra che Gastaldi propendesse per la separazione nella sua grande e importante carta del mondo del 1561 (numero 104). Perché? Non è difficile rispondere. Vi sono parecchie risposte. Guardate ad esempio la famosa carta del mondo appena menzionata e prendete nota dei seguenti fatti:

1. Le rappresentazioni delle parti del mondo, Vecchio e Nuovo, sono perfettamente in armonia con tutto il mondo vecchio alla destra del primo meridiano e tutto il mondo nuovo alla sinistra del meridiano, semplicemente e chiaramente (e tenete presente la passione per la simmetria del Rinascimento);

2. Se il cartografo avesse voluto fare carte separate di Asia e America e non una carta del mondo è tutto semplice e chiaro; non c'è né conflitto, né ambiguità o indecisione nella rappresentazione con la connessione tra i due continenti;

3. Nel Cinquecento molti popoli europei consideravano gli abitanti del Mondo Nuovo barbari oppure animali; di conseguenza

la rappresentazione con la netta separazione divideva il mondo civilizzato da quello non civilizzato. Potrebbero essere state queste considerazioni ad influire su Gastaldi e altri cartografi per accettare, forse in parte inconsciamente, la rappresentazione con la separazione. E le considerazioni di Mercatore, Ortelio e tutti coloro che accettarono l'idea della piccola separazione di Gastaldi sarebbero state senza dubbio le stesse. Nessuno poteva saperlo. La decisione era fondata su questioni di convenienza, estetica e forse etnologiche, ma l'incertezza persisteva. Nella mente di Gastaldi non c'era convincimento. Questo è vitale per affrontare il capitolo 9.

Capitolo 9

Forse è il nostro capitolo più importante. Il lettore ricorderà che nel capitolo 3 ho parlato delle grandi rappresentazioni dei tre continenti extraeuropei: Africa, Asia e America. In esso abbiamo affermato che prese le carte tutte e tre insieme, si tratta del più grande miglioramento geografico nell'intera storia della cartografia. Vi sono stati dubbi in merito alla paternità del Gastaldi per quanto riguarda l'Asia e l'America. Abbiamo tolto i dubbi sull'Asia nel capitolo 5. Qui togliamo i dubbi sull'America.

Dobbiamo ricordare che la carta dell'America è piuttosto rara e stranamente poco nota e non menzionata nei lavori su Gastaldi. Sospetto che questo sia il risultato di giudizi erronei che iniziarono quasi 100 anni fa: li correggeremo. La prima carta divenne nota agli studiosi nel 1921, ma ne mancavano tre parti. Eccetto le mancanze è molto bella e ben fatta, sia rispetto alla geografia sia per quanto riguarda l'incisione. Un secondo esemplare, sempre in mancanza delle stesse tre parti, apparve in

1923. Finalmente negli anni 1949, circa 1980(?) e 2002, apparvero tre esemplari completi di edizioni più tarde che contengono il nome di Gastaldi, benchè siano quasi completamente sconosciute nel mondo degli studiosi. Non esistono altri esemplari.

A seguito della comparsa del primo esemplare incompiuto nel 1921, la maggioranza degli studiosi lo attribuirono senza esitazione al Gastaldi. Ma in due diedero un'interpretazione veramente bizzarra riguardo alla condizione incompiuta della carta. Questa interpretazione infondata e ingiustificata fece ombra alla carta, insinuando dubbi rispetto alla competenza dell'autore. Questa interpretazione bizzarra era attribuita all'adulterazione della numerazione della longitudine sull'orlo superiore del foglio di nord-ovest della carta, riguardo alla quale diremo più avanti.

Come si spiega la condizione della carta? Innanzitutto è necessario sapere che questa era la quarta in una serie di carte di quattro continenti del mondo, la prima serie nella storia. Questa serie fu preparata da Giovanni Francesco Camocio tra il 1570 e il 1575 (?). Prima carta Europa, in seguito Africa (ricavata dall'Africa del 1564 di Gastaldi), quindi Asia (da Gastaldi del 1559-61). Mancava solo l'America.

Sembra che Camocio tentasse dei miglioramenti nella carta del Gastaldi, in particolare nella rappresentazione della parte di nord-est dell'America del nord, dove davvero la rappresentazione del Gastaldi era piuttosto cattiva ed enigmatica. Camocio apparentemente manipolava i *modelli* della carta, e/o forse i fogli manoscritti originali della carta e faceva modifiche della grandezza e/o del contenuto di due o tre dei *modelli*, e probabilmente sostituì uno o due di questi *modelli* con esemplari nuovi. È impossibile essere certi del suo operato, perché certamente i materiali manoscritti con i quali lui lavorava sparirono molto tempo fa (probabilmente subito dopo il suo lavoro con essi). In ogni caso, qualunque cosa avesse fatto, fu colpito dalla peste e le sue intenzioni morirono con lui. Quali erano le sue intenzioni? Questo non era chiaro a quel tempo e non lo è nemmeno adesso. Comunque, il risultato è una carta dell'America incompleta e priva di tre parti. In merito alla presenza di numerosi dettagli enigmatici incisi sulla carta, sappiamo che dopo la morte di Camocio mani sconosciute fecero parecchi inutili tentativi per recuperare la carta e inclusero falsi numeri di longitudine sull'orlo superiore del foglio di nord-ovest, dove Asia e America del nord quasi si incontrano. Nei due esemplari incompleti la numerazione della longitudine va di 58° W a 106° W, un'assurdità che situa il termine orientale dell'Asia anche oltre le fantasticherie di Colombo. Nelle edizioni più tarde e corrette (ne parliamo nel capitolo 12), completate da Donato Bertelli, i numeri vanno di 100° W a 148° W, in conformità con le presunte intenzioni del Gastaldi.

Quale era la carta manoscritta con la quale lavorava Camocio? All'apparenza era quella dell'America realizzata da Gastaldi nel 1560 circa, che tuttavia lasciò temporaneamente non pubblicata, così come aveva fatto in precedenza con parecchie altre carte (numeri 120-124 nella cartobibliografia) perché sperava di migliorarla con materiali nuovi. Sappiamo che Gastaldi fosse incerto riguardo alla questione della separazione o connessione tra Asia e America. Evidentemente sperava che la grande spedizione spagnola di Legazpi nell'ovest e nord-ovest del Messico fino all'Asia, già in preparazione nel 1560, potesse portare alla

447

soluzione. Questo il motivo per cui Gastaldi sospese la stampa della carta dell'America in attesa di informazioni attendibili. Ma la spedizione del Legazpi partì più tardi del previsto e tornò in Messico soltanto nell'anno 1565. Le informazioni dei risultati della spedizione probabilmentre non raggiunsero Venezia fino all'anno 1566, anno della morte di Gastaldi. In ogni caso la spedizione non risolse il mistero.

Per questo la carta è rimasta manoscritta fino all'utilizzo da parte di Camocio per la sua serie dei quattro continenti. Egli cominciò a prepararla per la stampa, ma l'improvvisa morte ne arrestò il progetto. Come vedremo nel capitolo 12 Donato Bertelli alla fine riuscì a completarla intorno al 1596.

In ogni caso è chiaro che le condizioni della carta trovata nel 1921 sono il risultato di una problema enorme causato della morte di Camocio nel 1575/76, quando la carta era ancora nella bottega e certo non può essere di Gastaldi che era morto nel 1566. È chiaro che la carta dell'America realizzata da Gastaldi circa nel 1560 era il giusto accompagnamento alle sue rappresentazioni dell'Africa e dell'Asia, ed è altrettanto vero che le fonti principali per l'America erano le relazioni e le carte nautiche che gli procurò Ramusio, come con l'Africa e l'Asia. Alla fine possiamo affermare (come detto nel capitolo 3) che con le sue grandi carte continentali degli anni 1560-1564, Gastaldi apportò il più vasto miglioramento mai compiuto nella rappresentazione del mondo. Un'affermazione che può sembrare stravagante, ma le mappe possono essere messe davanti ai nostri occhi!

Capitolo 10

In un anno imprecisato, ma forse intorno al 1566, Gastaldi e il noto incisore Fabio Licinio divennero soci. Questa partnership continuò fino all'anno 1564, quando Licinio si ammalò. Negli anni 1559-1564 i due produssero la maggior parte delle migliori carte di Gastaldi; tutte sono realizzate nel medesimo stile e sono sorprendentemente belle.

In tutte le carte appaiono soltanto i nomi di Gastaldi e Licinio, e da questo possiamo dedurre che l'impresa appartenne solo a loro. Le carte includono le tre grandi continentali gastaldine di Africa, Asia e America, l'ultima fu incisa e pubblicata molto più tardi, ma la sua immagine era già nella carta del mondo del Gastaldi del 1561 (numero 104 nella cartobibliografia). La stretta somiglianza nello stile e il fatto che le carte includano le tre carte continentali e anche carte che mostrano la totalità dell'Italia e praticamente la totalità dell'Europa orientale, suggeriscono la possibilità dell'intenzione di Gastaldi di mostrare il mondo intero nella cartografia moderna, o la serie dei quattro continenti.

Nella seconda parte del capitolo approfondiamo la possibilità che una presentazione così unitaria dei continenti fosse l'obiettivo principale di Gastaldi. Tuttavia, per ragioni piuttosto complesse, che non possiamo affrontare in questa sintesi, concludiamo che la sua motivazione principale fosse semplicemente quella di essere un cartografo appassionato che preferiva realizzare mappe di aree per le quali aveva accesso a nuovi materiali e poteva quindi apportare miglioramenti. Ed è questo che in realtà facevano la maggior parte dei cartografi, anche se Gastaldi ebbe un grande vantaggio derivato dall'enorme quantità di informazioni prese da Ramusio relativamente al mondo extraeuropeo e a quello europeo.

L'ambasciatore Mendoza gli diede delle informazioni per la sua carta della Spagna del 1544 e per la sua notevole carta della Sicilia ricevette informazioni forse dal Maurolico e/o dai contatti spagnoli del Mendoza. Probabilmente ebbe anche fonti per la sua carta dell'Italia, dell'Europa centrale e dell'Europa di sud-est, ma semplicemente non le conosciamo. Da notare che almeno due considerazioni producono l'illusione di un grande piano alla base dei lavori: la somiglianza dello stile di tutte le carte di Gastaldi-Licinio e il fatto che Gastaldi avesse realizzato le carte complete di tre continenti. Ma l'idea dell'esistenza di un grande piano è solo un'illusione.

Abbiamo eliminato l'idea che Gastaldi realizzasse la serie di carte dei quattro continenti, che sarebbe stata la prima nella storia. Una quantità considerevole di studiosi ha affermato o implicato che lui l'avesse realizzata o almeno tentata, e fu questa idea che in principio mi spinse a studiare questo autore. Negli ultimi due capitoli mostreremo che, per quanto Gastaldi non realizzò mai la serie dei quattro continenti, furono quasi interamente le sue carte che fornirono il materiale per fare la prima di tale serie. Nel capitolo 11, parliamo del primo fallito tentativo degli anni circa 1570-1575, a causa della morte del compilatore Giovanni Francesco Camocio, prima del completamento della quarta carta dell'America e mostriamo nel capitolo 12 che la serie alla fine fu completata circa nel 1596 da Donato Bertelli.

Capitolo 11

I miglioramenti apportati alle mappe di Gastaldi influenzarono per oltre un secolo le mappe pubblicate separatamente, le mappe contenute negli atlanti e le serie di mappe dei quattro continenti. Ma in quest'ultimo genere la loro influenza fu notevole per due motivi: in primo luogo, le mappe continentali di Asia, Africa e America di Gastaldi costituirono un precedente per le mappe continentali, e in secondo luogo, vediamo che le serie realizzate da altri si basavano sulle mappe di Gastaldi, almeno fino alla metà del XVII secolo, come vedremo nel capitolo 12.

Secondo la mia interpretazione il primo tentativo fu fatto da Giovanni Francesco Camocio intorno al 1570/1572, quando realizzò la carta murale dell'Africa, copiata esattamente dall'Africa del 1564 di Gastaldi. Tra il 1572/73 Camocio fece una carta dell'Europa anch'essa copiata da quella del 1564 di Giovanni Pietro Contarini, che include molto materiale gastaldino, anche se non è attribuibile a lui. Circa nel 1573/74 fece l'Asia, per la quale combinò le tre parti dell'Asia di Gastaldi del 1559-61. Fino a questo punto, non possiamo affermare che Camocio intendesse una serie di quattro carte murali, benchè fosse molto probabile. Ma nel testo di questa carta dell'Asia dice che, avendo fatto le carte dell'Africa, dell'Europa e dell'Asia, ha "speranza anche de la Quarta [America], acciò intieramente si goda detto uniuerso". Camocio iniziò probabilmente la carta dell'America nel 1574 terminandola per la maggior parte, tentando qualche cambiamento nella parte parte nordorientale della carta, ma morì di peste nel 1575. Nessuno potè capire le manipolazioni effettuate da Camocio con i fogli, i *modelli* e con l'incisione, e il progetto fu abbandonato. Donato Bertelli lo ravvivò intorno all'ultima decade del secolo, come mostriamo nel capitolo 12.

Capitolo 12

Cosa avvenne con le lastre della sfortunata serie dopo la morte di Camocio nel 1575? Questo non è chiaro, ma sappiamo che la bottega dei Bertelli ottenne la maggior parte delle lastre di Camocio in un momento imprecisato, ma probabilmente fra il 1580 e il 1590. Nella carta dell'Europa venne cancellata l'insegna del Camocio e rimpiazzata con quella dei Bertelli e fu cancellatta anche la dedica del Camocio. Fu ripresa anche l'immagine dell'America, ripristinata alla sua condizione originale, probabilmente usando l'immagine dell'America derivata dalla grande carta del mondo del 1561 di Gastaldi. Per quanto concerne l'Africa e l'Asia, Donato Bertelli le sostituì con due sue carte murali, entrambe di derivazione gastaldina. L'Africa di Donato Bertelli è una altra copia dell'Africa del 1564 di Gastaldi. Per l'Asia copiò quella del 1567 di Ortelio, che a sua volta è copiata dall'Asia del 1559-61 di Gastaldi, con tre cambiamenti: sostituì la proiezione di Gastaldi con un'altra differente (e migliore), benchè le coordinate geografiche siano esattamente le stesse di Gastaldi; Ortelio aggiunse anche la costa settentrionale dell'Asia e apportò parecchi miglioramenti nella rappresentazione dell'arcipelago dell'Asia sud-orientale. Donato terminò la sua serie fra il 1592 e il 1604, ma stimo che la serie fu completata intorno al 1596 (?). Sembra che questa serie si vendesse bene e che i Bertelli la conservassero per molto tempo.

L'ultima vendita di un Bertelli avvenne probabilmente tra il 1620 e il 1630, tuttavia alcune considerazioni contenute nel nostro libro suggeriscono che il negozio di San Marco continuò a svolgere solo la funzione di punto vendita (come aveva iniziato) e che probabilmente vendeva regolarmente questo set dei quattro continenti. Le nostre scarse informazioni suggeriscono che questa serie passò nelle mani della famiglia Scolari non molto tempo dopo di 1640. Sappiamo che si vendevano bene perchè abbiamo tre esemplari di questa serie con l'insegna e la firma degli Scolari, benchè loro avessero mantenuto in più della metà delle carte, le dediche, le firme e l'insegna del Bertelli. Scolari e molto altri venditori di carte del XVII secolo vendevano regolarmente carte stampate da lastre ottenute dai precedenti proprietari, queste carte contenevano informazioni non cancellate relative ai precedenti proprietari.

Le tre serie degli Scolari sono datate una 1655 e due 1662. Queste informazioni appaiono solo sulle carte dell'Asia in tutte e tre le serie. Così abbiamo due carte di Gastaldi, Africa e America, che sono copie dirette dagli originale di Gastaldi, ancora in vendita fra il 1660 e il 1670, e probabilmente anche più tardi.

Cartobibliografia

La cartobibliografia comprende 185 pagine e praticamente è di per sé un libro. Contiene schedature relative a 124 carte di Gastaldi, 15 in più rispetto ad elenchi realizzati in precedenza. Le informazioni nelle schede non sono limitate ai dettagli delle descrizioni tecniche, ma includono molti commenti storici rispetto alle fonti e ai metodi usati da Gastaldi e da altri soggetti. Molte schedature sono veri e propri articoli di 5 o 6 pagine; alcuni includono informazioni nuove e inedite; tutte le mappe esistenti sono riprodotte. La cartobibliografia può essere considerata un complemento al testo principale del libro.

CARTOBIBLIOGRAPHY AND DISCUSSION OF THE SOURCES AND CONSTRUCTION OF INDIVIDUAL MAPS

Introduction to the Cartobibliography

The following Cartobibliography of Gastaldi's maps is chronological, beginning from his first known dated map of 1544. It comprises the first editions of all 121 printed Gastaldi maps which the author has come to be aware of in over thirty years of researching Gastaldi, plus three very large non-printed maps (a manuscript world map and two continental maps painted on the walls of the Venetian Ducal Palace, nos. 65, 71 and 72), for a total of 124 map entries, fifteen more than any previous listing. It also includes, at its ending, twelve more maps, numbered I-XII, consisting of the maps in three four-continent sets of wall maps which were produced after Gastaldi's death by other hands, but were taken almost entirely from Gastaldi's maps. The first such set, of the 1570s (nos. I-IV) was not completed due to the sudden death of the publisher before the last map, of America, was completed. Nevertheless, it was the first-ever attempt at a four-continent set of wall maps. This set was completed ca. 1596 by Donato Bertelli and re-issued regularly until the end of the seventeenth century. No full copies of the ca. 1596 set are known, but one ca. 1655 and a ca. 1662 set (nos. VI-VIII, and IX-XII), printed by the Scolaris, survive. These sets are very much part of the Gastaldi story, even if the first fully printed set appeared successfully only in the 1590s, thirty years after Gastaldi's death. Indeed, they amount to the culmination of his most important work, although the finally completed set (represented by nos. V-XII, in two variants) has strangely remained almost completely unknown to the scholarly world.

A fair number of Gastaldi maps were contracted as a group, by another party. For example, maps 81 to 86 were made for Ramusio for volume three (1556) of his *Navigazioni*. Therefore, much of the story of these maps is involved with the contracting. Consequently, as in all such cases in this Cartobibliography, I have included an entry for the group as a whole ("nos. 81-86"), followed by entries for the individual maps. In the case cited, the inclusive entry is given as: "(81.-86.) Six Maps Which Appeared in volume three of Ramusio's *Navigazioni,*" which multiple entry is then followed by six individual entries (81, 82, 83, 84, 85, 86), which contain information relative only to those individual maps.

A primary goal in the present Cartobibliography has been to focus strongly on the work which Gastaldi himself produced and avoid as much as possible the peripheral activities by sundry other parties who copied and recopied his maps into the seventeenth century. We have in mind such persons as Forlani, the Bertellis, Camocio, Zaltieri, Zenoi and many others, who reprinted, recopied, reengraved and republished an enormous number of Gastaldi maps. In a few cases, Gastaldi had very short or one-time significant relationships with these people, almost entirely within the last years of his life. Such cases are brought out in our book. But there was such a mountain of simple derivatives of Gastaldi's maps made by people over the sixteenth and into the seventeenth century to a degree that, if they were all brought in, they would smother Gastaldi, as, in fact, they have tended to do in past scholarship. We wish to bring out Gastaldi himself, as sharply and clearly as we can. Considering this goal, the fact that the Cartobibliography is limited to the first editions of his maps, has proved to afford a considerable advantage to the writer, for the Cartobibliography amounts to a sequential presentation of his cartographical career, without the intrusively distracting elements inevitably introduced by listings of derivatives. We do not ignore derivatives entirely, for, as regards all those maps for which derivatives exist, we have included references to the various works which include notation of such derivatives, although for some maps, there are derivatives which have never yet been mentioned in any source.

We do not include the manuscript maps which Gastaldi made during a yet undetermined number of years in the employ of the Venetian Republic as what we would now call a hydrographical engineer. The means by which these maps were compiled have nothing to do with how Gastaldi's printed works were derived. They have no connection whatever with his printed cartography, and thus this activity is extraneous to the spirit of the present work. Furthermore, so far no one has any idea how many of these maps may still exist in the papers and folios of various departments of the government in the Venetian Archives. At the present time, some basic details of eight are available in print, the existence of twelve more is known, but no details are available, and the implications are that there are probably others, the number of which could be small or could be enormous. Certainly, if anything, they are evidence of the prodigious energy and activity of Gastaldi. For extant bibliographical and other details about these maps, see the lengthy notice at the end of this Cartobibliography, and also some lesser comments in chapter one.

Having made these preliminary observations, we move on to a description of the format of our Cartobibliography entries, which is consistently used for every entry in the Cartobibliography. The following elements, always in the order given here, are found in each entry:

Map number, together with the modern name, or a modern description, of the place or area covered by the map (Spain/Southwest Asia/Germany and part of Poland/etc.).

Place and date of publication.

Statement of whether the map is woodcut or copperplate, followed by dimensions of the map, and the number of sheets. The dimensions are given in metric units, to a half centimeter, always with the shorter side (usually the height) first, followed by the longer side.

Scale of the map, as given in the scale bar on the map, when such is present. The scale is given using the unit of measure employed in the scale bar and its equivalent in centimeters, to a tenth of a centimeter. (For example: 100 Italian miles=3.8 cm.)

A presentation of all textual material which provides any basic information on the map as a whole and its creation, including any title or titles, names of persons connected in any way with the map, as cartographer, engraver, publisher, etc., as well as dedicatees, and any dates. There often will be more than one such text on a map, varying in length from a word or two to several paragraphs, and these texts are given one after the other in the order which seemed to us most logical. The location of the text on the map is given first, followed by an exact transcription of the original text, using the symbol "|" to indicate the beginning of a new line. This transcription is then followed by an English translation in parentheses. Some of these texts can be quite lengthy, sometimes amounting simultaneously to a title, which turns into a descriptive or historical text, which in turn becomes a sometimes long-winded and usually adulatory dedication to some dignitary. For the benefit of scholars, to whom anything in such a text could possibly be of value, in the current Cartobibliography all such texts have been, without exception, transcribed and translated into English in their entirety, with no omissions, to the best of our ability. Simple informational inscriptions which occur here and there within the body of the map, providing sundry local information, such as local customs, or the presence of certain types of wildlife in an area, etc., are not transcribed and translated.

Reproduction of the map.
For all extant Gastaldi maps we include a small reproduction.

Comments, in general, on the map. This section, often the longest one, always begins with a statement of the latitude and longitude limits covered by the map, the map's projection, if determinable, and any other technical data which might be relevant, but the section is mainly concerned with the geographical area shown, its history and significance, and an attempt to put the map in perspective in relation to Gastaldi's work. Often, with more significant maps, a strong stress is laid on the question of Gastaldi's sources for the map. These comments vary much in length, depending on the overall importance of a map. For some of the most important maps, besides the regular comments, the reader is referred to places in the main text of the book for further discussion. At the end of the section references are given to sources which provide information on later editions and derivatives of the map, if such exist, although the reader should bear in mind, as mentioned above, that for a number of Gastaldi maps, the record of derivatives remains incomplete, in some cases extremely so.

Locations of copies of the map including the call number in almost all cases. The library names are given in abbreviated form, and a list of keys to the abbreviations will be found at the end of the Cartobibliography.

References to literature on the map. The references are given in chronological order. Here, our policy has been to stress the inclusion of sources which provide scholarly information and discussion relevant to the map's history proper, as opposed to simple technical cartobibliographical information on the map, since such information is given with unprecedented fullness in our own Cartobibliography. We have followed our guiding criterion here even in cases where the amount of historical or other valuable information is very small, if that small amount of information was judged by us to be important and was not to be found elsewhere.

Locations of reproductions of the maps. In the considerable number of cases in which we are aware of more than one reproduction, we have intentionally restricted our listings only to reproductions of high quality and preferably of larger size. There exist a good number of reproductions which are so poor or so small, they could be of little scholarly use. In many cases, we have provided URLs to online reproductions, but as the web changes so rapidly, users would do well to search for other reproductions.

1. Spain
-Venice, 1544
-Copper engraving, 66.5 x 91.0 cm., on four sheets
-No scale bar

In text box at lower left of southwest sheet:
Giacomo Castaldo Piemontese de Villa franca, Cosmografo. | Alli Spettatori. Salute. | Questa è la uera descrittione di tutta la Spagna da me composta per | commune utilita de gli huomini & meritamente dedicata in Segno di | gratitudine al Molto I[lustri]ss[imo] Signor Don Diego Hurtado de Mendoza | dignissimo Orator Cesareo nella Inclita Citta di Venetia impero che oltra la | mia deuotione a, sua signoria Ill[ustrissi]ma debbiamo tutti da quella | riconoscere la miglior parte della presente fatica, per hauermi data | chiara notitia de' nomi moderni di tutte le citta et luoghi compresi | in questa figura. Voi vedetela, leggetela, et uiuete felicj. In Venetia. 1544. (Giacomo Castaldo Piedmontese of Villa franca, Cosmographer. To onlookers. Salutations. This is the true map of all of Spain compiled by me for the common usage of men and meritably dedicated in Sign of gratitude to the Very Illustrious Gentleman Don Diego Hurtado de Mendoza most dignified Imperial Ambassador to the famous city of Venice to whom other than having my devotion we all owe his most Illustrious lordship the major part of the interpreting of the present work, for having given to me clear information of the modern names of all the cities and places included in this figure. May you observe it, read it, and live in happiness. In Venice. 1544.)

Comments:
The map is graduated in twelve-minute increments in latitude and longitude, from 35°00' to 45°00' N, and from 2°00' to 21°00' E, and is on a rectangular projection. It is Gastaldi's first dated map, although we may consider it as virtually certain that he had been making the maps for his 1548 Ptolemy in manuscript at least from 1542, as shown in chapter one. However, unlike those maps, the present map is a large and very ambitious work, in four sheets. Almagià says that it "opened a new period in the modern cartography of the Iberian peninsula." (1948, "First," 31). It reminds one much of the great multi-sheet maps Gastaldi would create from 1559-1564 in partnership

with Fabio Licinio, and in fact it is considerably larger than some of the most important of those maps, including the 1561 Italy, and the First, Second and Third Parts of Asia. The engraving work is not as fine as that of the expert Licinio, but it is fairly good, and, as we have shown in chapter one, the most likely candidate for the engraving is Gastaldi himself. It is certainly an impressive production for a debut, and it presents a notable improvement over any previous map of Spain, even if its hegemony was short-lived, being outmoded in only seven years by the still larger 1551 map of Spain by Vincenzo Palatino, followed by several other worthy maps and culminating in the great 1571 map by Carolus Clusius (Schilder, 1987, 90-99). No doubt it has received relatively little attention simply because it was Gastaldi's first dated production.

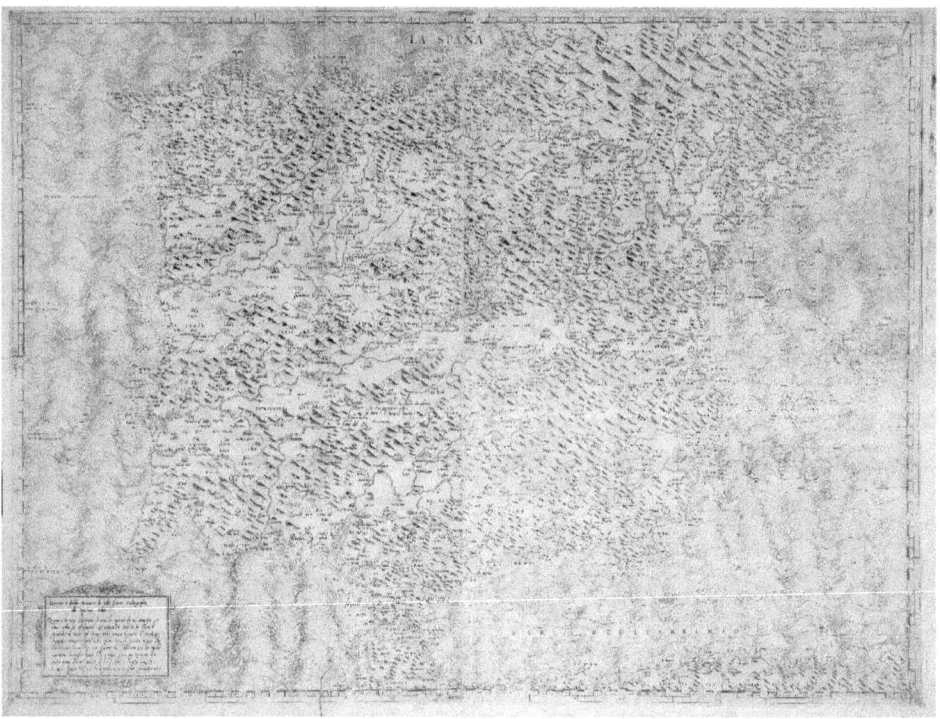

1 Spain 1545 Chicago Newb

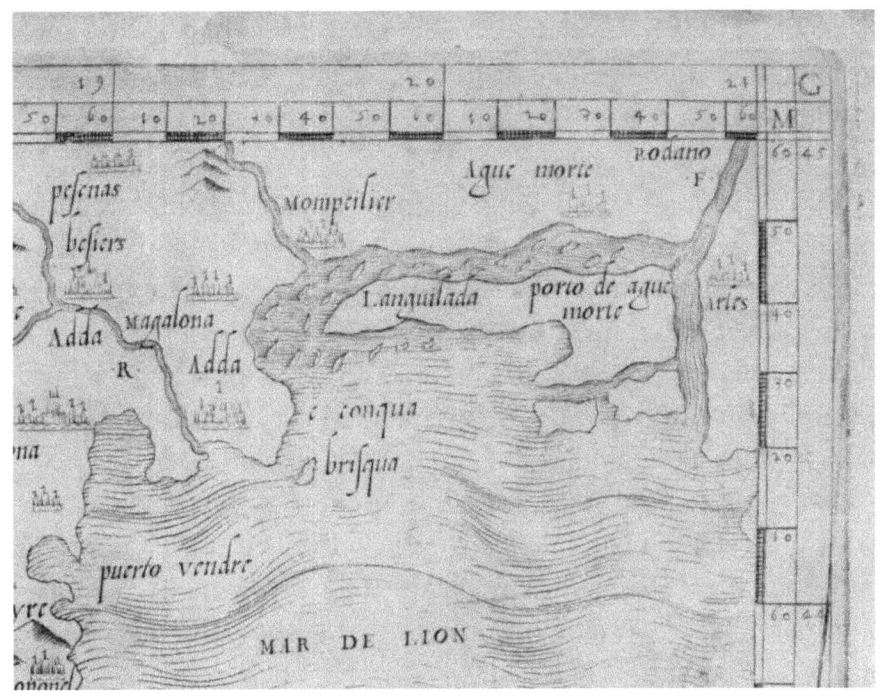

1 Spain 1545 (detail) Chicago Newb

How was Gastaldi, who lived in Venice and certainly had no opportunity to roam through a country hundreds of miles away, able to make such a map? As we see in his dedicatory message above, Gastaldi says that the ambassador Mendoza, of whom we have also spoken much in chapter one, provided him with the modern names of the places on the map, whether directly or through Ramusio is unknown, though Destombes refers to Mendoza as Gastaldi's "patron" (1973, 122). We must assume that he means the modern names as opposed to the Ptolemaic names. All well and good, but this can't possibly explain the tremendous improvement over Ptolemy in the overall shape of the peninsula, in the relative placement of the towns, in the general hydrography and orography and other features. Gastaldi assuredly must have obtained much more information than simply the modern names, either from Mendoza or elsewhere.

As to the general form of the peninsula, the source was virtually certainly portolan charts, which Gastaldi is known to have made use of regularly. As to the interior, the question is more difficult, but we recall that Spain was one of the first countries for which modern maps began to appear in the printed editions of Ptolemy, alongside the Ptolemaic maps, beginning with the 1482 Berlinghieri Ptolemy, and in fact no less than six further editions with modern maps of Spain appeared between that time and the appearance of the 1544 map (1482, 1507, 1511, 1513, 1522, and 1540), as well as a few separate modern maps of Spain, including one by Martellus from the end of the fifteenth century, and an anonymous map of ca. 1520-1530 (reproduced in Schilder, 1987, p. 90), so part of the detail may have come from some of these maps. However, that the level of improvement attained by Gastaldi could be fully explained by recourse to these generally primitive models does not seem very convincing, and we would like to offer a different, though tentative, explanation.

There were several large-scale initiatives taken up in the sixteenth century for the mapping of Spain (see Parker, 1992, 126-35 and Marcel, 1899, 173-86 and 189-93), but only one of these occurred before the time of Gastaldi's map, that of Fernando Colón, son of Christopher Colón (Columbus), and a team of associates, working under the authorization of Charles V. Colón's enterprise, the first ever of its kind, lasted from 1517 to 1523, but, oddly, and for unknown reasons, it was peremptorily brought to a halt by the Royal Council at the latter date, although Colón had clearly not lost favor, for in 1524 he was among those appointed to the Council of Badajoz, formed to attempt to determine the limits between Portuguese and Spanish territory in the area of the Spice Islands (Núñez de las Cuevas, 1991, 181). But the project must have been near completion, for Colón had by this time accumulated data on the positions of no less than 7,000 towns (Parker, 1992, 28), as well as much other data, and Kagan says he had done this "throughout the peninsula" (1989, 47). His extensive manuscript data survived, and was eventually published in 1908-1915, and reprinted in 1988 (Colón, 1988). Could Mendoza, or perhaps some other Spanish dignitary known to Ramusio, have possessed a copy of the manuscript, which was then provided to Gastaldi? I can think of no other informational source extensive enough to account for Gastaldi's many improvements. Since Colón's "Descripción y cosmografía de España", or "Itinerario", as it is often called, is in print, this can be checked out by some industrious scholar, though it will be long, tedious work. Skelton's suggestion that one of Ramusio's Spanish correspondents supplied a map of Spain from which Gastaldi made his map (1970, xii) seems very unlikely to me, and there is nothing to support it.

Location of copies:
Chicago Newb(Novacco 6F 24)/ Cambridge Harv(51-2501)/ Washington LC(G6540 1544.G3 Vault Oversize) /Paris BN(GE C- 10494)/ Paris BN(GE B- 1530)/ Wien ÖNB(K III 109630 Kar)/ Madrid BN(Mv/3.España.Mapas generales.1544)/ London BL(K.71.3)[1987]/ Rotterdam MMPH(WAE 815) [1987]/ Firenze BMar(in atlas Stampe 423)[2005]/ London BL(M.T.11.gg.1. (1).)[2003].

References:
Marcel, 1899, 186-87; Bonacci, 1905, 824; Grande, 1905, "relazioni", 194; Almagià, 1948, "First", 31; Skelton, 1970, xii; Destombes, 1973, 122; Schilder, 1987, 91; Meurer, 1991, 152; Parker, 1992, 128; Karrow, 1993, 216-17; Bifolco and Ronca, 2018, 2: 1100.

Reproductions:
Schilder, 1987, 91; Bifolco and Ronca, 2018, 2: 1100-01.
https://collections.Newberry.org/asset-management/2KXJ8ZSA2Q51O? &WS; https://gallica.bnf.fr/ark:/12148/btv1b53223510q?rk'1974258;4

2. Sicily
-Venice, 1545
-Copper engraving, 37.0 x 54.0 cm., on two sheets.
-100 Italian miles = 17.0 cm.

In text box at northwest corner of map:
Descrittione della sicilia con le sue Isole, della | qual li nomi Antichi et Moderni et altre | cose notabili per un Libretto sono bre- | uemente decchiarati, con gratia et priuilegio. | per Giacomo Gastaldo Piemon- | tese, Cosmographo. In Venetia. | .1545. (Map of Sicily with its Islands, of which the Ancient and Modern names, and other notable things are briefly described via a Booklet; with grace and privilege. By Giacomo Gastaldo Piedmontese, Cosmographer in Venice. 1545.)

2 Sicily 1545 Chicago Newb

Comments:

The map is graduated in ten-minute increments in latitude and longitude, from 36°37' to 39°14' N, and from 35°52' to 40°27' E, and is on a rectangular projection. This is Gastaldi's second dated map, though, as pointed out in our previous entry, we can assume that Gastaldi had been making maps in manuscript for his 1548 Ptolemy since at least 1542. The engraving is quite good, and, as with Gastaldi's other earlier copperplate maps, the most likely engraver would be Gastaldi himself, though this is not proven. A peculiarity of the map is that just below the southwest most corner of the title cartouche, itself in the northwest corner of the map, we can make out what remains of a poorly burnished out inscription, many of the characters of which are visible, but just barely so, and it is often hard to be certain as to their reading. It was first noticed by Ruge (1904-1916, Part 4, p. 987), who believed that it may contain the engraver's name. Karrow suggested that it may be part of an earlier cartouche's script, perhaps from a completely different print (Karrow,

465

1993, 217a). But Valerio (2013, Vol. 1, 126c) has shown convincingly that the inscription indicates one of the climata seen at the edge of Ptolemy's maps (see Harley and Woodward, eds., 1987, 182-83), and often seen on the maps of Renaissance cartographers, including, very often, Gastaldi's. Another example of such a clima, clearly visible, is seen on the same map just above the southwest corner.

This rather unassuming little map presents a quandary to us. There is a tremendous amount of important background information connected with this map which is filled with complexities, uncertainties, and no small amount of controversy. It is not possible to go into all of this at the present time, for it would require many pages. For now, we must limit ourselves to the information which is most basic, and which is well established, although we will make passing mention of some of the less certain aspects of the map's story

At the end of the title, as see above, Gastaldi implies rather clumsily that the map is intended to be accompanied by a booklet ("Map . . . of which the Ancient and Modern names, and other notable things are briefly described via a booklet"). The booklet, anonymous, is named *La descrittione dell'isola di Sicilia. In Venetia per Nicolo de Bascarini,* !546. It is in twenty unnumbered leaves (forty pages). De Stefano (1920) has shown that it was virtually certainly written by Francesco Maurolico, the well-known Sicilian mathematician and scientist. This has been repeated by all later writers as a fact, but, though I generally agree, I hesitate to state this as a fully established fact. I shall give a few comments on this booklet which will be of use to us below. About half the booklet, approximately twenty pages, deals with geography in one way or another, including an eight-page list of ancient and modern place names at the end. The list does not give geographical coordinates, as we find on the similar lists accompanying five of Gastaldi's maps from his peak period of 1559-1564, and it gives no locational information at all, except a very few insignificant comments in a few cases. (There is no mathematical information of any kind in the booklet.) So, the list of names is only peripherally geographical, and it is more historical in nature, leaving only twelve pages on geography. The rest of the book, about twenty more pages, is of a historical and social nature, and includes a fourteen-page history of the island (called a history of the kings, but containing much more than that), several pages giving a long list of current aristocrats (mostly barons, with some counts, etc.), with their governed areas named (but *not* geographically located), shorter lists of prominent past ecclesiastics and scientists, and several pages on the fertility of the soil, with much attention to Sicily's famous grain. As we see, the book is by no means exclusively a geographical one, but deals with much more, albeit rather desultorily. One might even question whether the map was an adjunct to the book, instead of vice versa. But there are other, more serious, problems, with the relationship between the booklet and the map, which we shall bring out below. Library locations for copies of this booklet are given at the end of this entry.

A word on the odd date discrepancy between the map (1545) and the booklet (1546). There are several possible explanations. Perhaps the map was printed very near the end of 1545, and the booklet very near the beginning of 1546. Another possibility involves the Venetian dating system (*more veneto),* in which the new year began on March 1. But this was not observed with great consistency, especially as regards non-native Venetians and foreigners dealing with Venice, and others. If both the map and the book were published in 1546, per the Julian calendar between January first and March first, then, if the map's publisher used the Venetian system, the date would be 1545, and if the book's publisher used the Julian calendar, the date would be 1546. We shall speak more about this booklet soon.

It should be noted here that at least two writers have stated that a letterpress broadside with the title *"Siciliae locorum nomina antiquis recentioribusq[ue]vsurpata"* is to accompany this map (Biasutti, 1908, 34, note 1, and Karrow 1993, p. 217a, no. 30/B), and it is not impossible that there are copies of the map accompanied by this list. However, the list was not intended to accompany this map, but a ca. 1560 derivative of it: "Siciliae insvlarvm (ut antiquit Diodorus) optima et mediterranei maris maxima . . . nomina tam antiquis quam recentioribus saeculis usurpata, in altera Tabella adijci curauimus . . ." (the full title is eighteen lines long) (n.p., Roma?) n.d. (ca. 1560?), as see Almagià (1929, p. 23a, no. C(B), and esp. Borroni-Salvadori (1980, pp. 24-25, nos. 64 and 65). The names in this list are taken from those in the placenames list at the end of the 1546 book described above. (Copies of this later list can be found in: Firenze BN (12.-44.), v. 1, no. 66; idem, v. 3, no. 45; Chicago Newb(Novacco 2F 177; Wolfenbüttel, HAB (2.3 Geogr.20, no. 31). We return to the map proper.

Like all Gastaldi's first four maps, it is among his more important ones, again, like the Spain, worthy of the maps of 1559-1564, though smaller than any of those. The level of improvement over previous maps, always the only valid basis for judgement, is astonishing, especially as regards the orientation and physical shape of the island, that is, the level of accuracy of the azimuthal bearings of the three coasts of the triangle, though to be sure, they are still not perfect, especially as to the north coast. But there are a large number of improvements throughout the island, both on the coast and in the interior, not only as to placement of features, but also as to their number. On the coast Gastaldi has over twice as many names as Ptolemy (47 vs. 23), while for the interior there are over three times as many (113 vs. 35). There was no notable improvement afterwards for about two centuries (Di Vita, 1905, 761; Enrile, 1908, 56), a record unequalled by any other Gastaldi map except the continental maps of 1559-1564. In a word, all previous maps of Sicily published are quite simply primitive by comparison, as a glance at Vladimiro Valerio's recent two-volume cartobibliography of Sicily reveals immediately (see Valerio, 2013, vol. 1, pp. 95-126). Gastaldi's advance here is altogether startling. There were a very large number of later editions and derivatives.

As we learn from Almagià (1929, 23; and 1948, 22-23), the perimeter was obtained from portolan charts. Then, Almagià gives the foundation for the coordinate net. His description is basically correct, but too elliptical to be fully clear. Almagià says that the foundation for the coordinate net was established by assigning three Ptolemaic half-coordinate values, as we may call them, to the three corners of the island, that is, the Ptolemaic longitude to the southeast cape (Cape Passaro) and to the western cape (Cape Boeo), and the Ptolemaic latitude to the northeast cape (Cape Faro), after which Gastaldi adjusted the positions of all the towns and features in relation to these points on the basis of modern information, taken from the sea charts for the coasts, and from information from the Sicilian mathematician Francesco Maurolico for the interior, by which he means information from the booklet described above.

Almagià's words, the best we have for now as to a description of Gastaldi's basic procedure is good, as far as it goes, but only up to this last statement, that the information from the interior was taken from the booklet *Descrittione*, etc., presumed as having been written by Maurolico. For at this point, a careful investigation of things brings out a very big problem. A careful place by place inspection of all places in the interior of the main island on the map (places on small peripheral islands or on the Calabrian mainland not being taken into account), and all interior places named in the booklet (indeed all places named in the booklet) shows that twenty-nine places (twenty towns, five castles, one cape, one lake, one bridge, and one storage warehouse [fondaco] on a river) which are in the interior of the map are not named in any way in the booklet. Three of the twenty-nine do occur in the list of ancient and modern place names at the end of the book, but no locational information is given. (As a side note, it is worth mentioning that in general, agreement between the modern place names in the book's list of names and the names given in the main body of the work is poor.) The places missing altogether in the book, but present on the map are: Acis, atalanli, fondoco bolo, calatanixetta, calatavirtui, camaranta, carao, cattamo, centorbi, k. cifala, galiano, lo inazarino, Mirto, Molta, musulumani, Lo muxaro, La nonciata, s peri, Pettineo, pollana, Raptus Pserpine, k. Re Ioãni, Roccella, roma, s libricci, ponte di s paulo, s philipo de agirone, spir linga k., k. taui. Where did they come from? Furthermore, the booklet includes in its geographical information a periplus of the island counterclockwise from Messina, giving the places where the rivers disembogue, and there are a few disagreements between book and map. And there are other disagreements. Clearly, the booklet is not the source for much of the inland information on the map.

There is reason to believe that Gastaldi came into further geographical information from Sicilian sources. Sicily, we recall, was solidly part of the Spanish Empire from the late fourteenth until the early eighteenth centuries. Under Ferrate Gonzaga, Viceroy of Sicily from 1535-1546, there began a major fortification of Sicily which had nominally begun the year before but got into full gear only in 1535. The project was in response to the growth in frequency of depredations from Muslim forces and pirate attacks (Tadini, 1977) and this ongoing project continued for many years (Mazzarella, 1985, esp. at chapter three and at pp. 131-33), eventually resulting in about 200 defensive towers being built all around the Sicilian coast, as well as major fortifications being built around the principal cities. The work was begun by the military engineer Ferramolino da Bergamo (see Tadini, cit.), and subsequently continued by other engineers. Such work could hardly go forth without surveying and no doubt manuscript mapping. Gonzaga was Viceroy from 1535 to 1546, and all of that part of this ongoing activity which occurred in that time took place under his reign. Now, we recall that, from 1539-1546, the Spanish ambassador to Venice was Diego Hurtado de Mendoza, and we recall that in 1544 he provided Gastaldi with information on Spain which helped the cartographer make his map of Spain. It would have been simple for Mendoza to obtain from his fellow Spanish official in Sicily information on the great work ongoing and transmit it to Gastaldi. He might even have had his own reasons for wishing for a map of Sicily. Since it was part of the Spanish Empire, Charles I would no doubt wish to have a good map of the island. No serious map of the place had ever been published, as we saw above, and Venice, where the king was sending Mendoza, had become a major map producing center. Making it still easier for Mendoza to obtain information from Gonzaga was the fact that the two had known each other at least since 1527, when they were together at the Sack of Rome; they were present together at the Emperor's coronation in 1530, and they were also together at the great 1535 taking of Tunis (as was also, by the way, Ferramolino da Bergamo), and the two would become close friends (for all this, see Spivakovsky [1970, 160]). Gastaldi obtained the substantial information which was not in the *Descrittione* somewhere, and information coming in from Sicilian authorities is surely the most likely place.

And still another possibility has been suggested concerning the map. It has been posited that Gastaldi was not the map's author at all, but rather it was made, presumably at Gastaldi's behest, by Maurolico! This is supported by a single source, but it cannot be dismissed offhand, considering that it comes from Maurolico's nephew, Francesco Maruli, Baron della Foresta, who wrote and published a biography of his illustrious uncle in 1613 (Maruli, 1613). The biography is confusedly, and overly tersely, written in many places, the place of interest to us among them. At page 7, Maruli, having spoken rapid fire of several other works written by his uncle, mentions Maurolico's treatise on Sicilian fishes, written 1543 (though unpublished until 1808), written for some party in Rome identified only as one "Gillo", and he then continues: "come altresi à Giacomo Castaldo Piamontese cosmografo, il disegno di tutta l'isola di Sicilia, che stampessi poscia in Roma più d'una volta" (as also for Giacomo Castaldo Piedmontese Cosmographer, the drawing [map] of all the island of Sicily, which was afterwards printed in Rome more than once). He says no more, and he seems to know little about the map, for, while indeed the map was very successful in Rome, the baron makes no mention of the fact that it was published most often in Venice, including the original printing. He also makes no mention of the booklet *Descrittione dell'isola di Sicilia*, which De Stefano and many others claim was certainly written by Maurolico.

A few writers have accepted Maruli's claim. Others have rejected it. Others have mentioned it but have given no opinion as to its validity. Some have not mentioned it at all, no doubt some because they thought it not worth mention, and others because they had not heard of it. In fact, so far, no one knows the truth. We shall quickly note several factors which seem to give circumstantial evidence supporting the idea. But we shall end with a simple observation which throws a formidable monkey wrench into the works as regards this notion.

Maurolico's book was dedicated to Giovanni III Ventimiglia, Marquis of Gerace, whose grandfather was Giovanni II Ventimiglia, 6th marquis of Gerace. This Giovanni II was among the most illustrious of the old and prominent Ventimiglia family and served twice in the prestigious office of Stratigoto of Messina (1532-1534 and 1540-1541). There was no one of higher authority in Messina than the Stratigoto, except the Viceroy himself, whom of course the stratigoto knew well, and during Giovanni II's second term, who would have been Viceroy Gonzaga. Giovanni was also close to Maurolico, whom he adored, for Giovanni was a lover of the sciences, and Maurolico, who was Sicily's greatest mathematician, astronomer, and scientist in general, often spent extended periods of time in Giovanni's castle in Gerace, at Giovanni's behest. And, of course, Giovanni II and Viceroy Gonzaga were well acquainted.

It is clear from the last paragraph that paths via which one could learn of the important defense work going on the island of Sicily, and paths connected to documents related to that, were just as open to Maurolico via his connections, as they were to Gastaldi, with his connections. But there is a serious problem with the idea that Maurolico could have made the map. All scholars since De Stefano in 1920 have accepted that the book is by Maurolico, and I accept it as well, with only the slightest reservation. But: If Maurolico both wrote the booklet, and made the map, then why are there such significant geographical discrepancies between the two?

Here we must stop, though there is more which we haven't had time to go into. As said above there remains pertinent information which we could bring in, and endless possibilities for discussion. There is also obviously a myriad of paths here which any interested scholar might follow, with hopes that they might take him not only to further information on the Sicily map, but just possibly to further information on Gastaldi himself. But, as said, this shall all have to await another time.

There were many derivatives of this map, for which see Enrile, 1908, 43-57; Almagià, 1929, 23; Almagià, 1948, 22-23; Karrow, 1993, 217-18; and especially the comprehensive two-volume cartobibliography of maps of Sicily by Valerio, 2013.

Location of copies:
Wien ÖNB(K I 109551 Kar)/ Paris BN(GE DD- 655(54 RES)/ Paris BN(GE D- 7656)/ Paris BN(GE D- 7770 (RES))/ Paris BN(GE D- 7784)/ Paris BN(GE DD- 2987(5679))/ Paris BN(GE D- 17088)/ London BL(Maps K.Top.84.1)/ Chicago Newb(Novacco 4F 347)/ Madrid PR(MAP/454, no. 48)/ Firenze BMar(in atlas Stampe 423)[2005]/ Sint-Niklaas KOKW(Atlas 408 IATO (no. 43))[1994]/ Firenze BN(12.-.44,v. 1, no. 67)[1980]/ Greenwich NMM(C3995, no. 54)[1971]/ London RGS(Map Room, 264.G.2, no. 48)[1915]/ Madrid PR(MAP/464, no. 72)[1915][Wieder errs dating this copy 1544]/ Dillingen SB(X,122, no. 56)[1911]/ Roma BN((711.6.G.3, no. 63)[1876]

Location of Copies of the Booklet Descrittione dell'isola di Sicilia:
Bayerische Staatsbibliothek (Epist. 885); Universitäbibliothek Bern (VI R

321); Biblioteca Nazionale Centrale, Firenze (PALAT.5.7.1.3); Biblioteca di archeologia e storia dell'arte, Roma (RARI99A); Biblioteca Nazionale Centrale, Roma (RB. 1155.3); Biblioteca Angelica, Roma (F.ANT BB.8 14/3: and (F.ANT BB.* 16); Biblioteca Nazionale Marciana, Venezia (call number unknown to me); University of Glasgow Library (call number unknown to me).

References:
Maruli, 1613, 7; Porena, 1895/96; Macrì, 1896, 114-15 (220-21 in the 1901 edition); Ruge, 1904-1916, Pt. 4 (1911), p. 98, no. 85(47); Di Vita, 1905, 759-61; Enrile, 1905, 767-72; Biasutti, 1908, 12 nt. 1, and 33-36; Enrile, 1908, 40-43 and 56; De Stefano, 1920; Almagià, 1929, 23; Almagià, 1948, 22-23; Bella, 1986, 132 (no. 124); Meurer, 1991, 154; Lago, 1992, II, 283; Karrow, 1993, 217; Perini, 1996, 122; Lago, 2002, 498 and 502-05; Milanesi, in Dentoni Litta, et al, 2003, 163-64; Meurer, 2004, 92(no. 78); Valerio, 2013, passim (see index at Gastaldi); Bifolco and Ronca, 2018, 3:2084.

Reproductions:
Almagià, 1929, pl. 29; Meurer, 2004, no. 78; Valerio, 2013, vol. 1, p. 127 (fig. 17a); Bifolco and Ronca, 2018, 3: 2084-85. https://collections.Newberry.org/asset-management/2KXJ8ZSKAVFE0? &WS

3. World
-Venice, 1546
-Copper engraving, 37.0 (29.0) x 53.0 cm., on one sheet
-No scale bar

At top center of map:
VNIVERSALE (WORLD MAP)

At bottom center of map:
GIACOMO COSMOGRAPHO | IN VENETIA MDXXXXVI (GIACOMO COSMOGRAPHER IN VENICE 1546)

Comments:

The map is graduated in whole degrees of longitude on the equator, and whole degrees of latitude on the sides, with meridians and parallels drawn in at ten-degree intervals. The prime meridian runs through modern day Senegal, and on the two sides Gastaldi includes Ptolemy's old system of climata. It is on the oval projection, as are all its many derivatives, and for long this projection was taken to be an innovation of Gastaldi, even in the sixteenth century (Karrow, 1993, 218). Gastaldi took the projection from Agnese, as shown in chapter two, and it was constructed empirically. It is a simple unpretentious projection, and I believe Gastaldi had simplicity consciously in mind when he selected it. It is eminently suited for doing what it is meant to do, showing the spherical world in plane, and in fact it resembles almost to an illusion of identity, many modern day projections, although those are constructed mathematically. There are in fact, in all of Gastaldi's work, only four projections, none of them elegant or pretentious, and none of them created by Gastaldi, i.e., the oval projection, for his world maps, a hemispheric projection for one map, that of the Western Hemisphere in Ramusio's 1556 volume three, and the rectangular and trapezoidal projections, used in all of his regional maps. The present projection was also adopted by Ortelius for the world map in his *Theatrum Orbis Terrarum*. The map exhibits a remarkable artistic sense in its lack of a traditional border and especially in the striking, and, I believe, unique, cloud banks protruding from the edge of the main depiction. No engraver or publisher is named, but as shown in chapter one, Gastaldi is most likely himself responsible for the engraving. The engraving shows the characteristic undulating wavy pattern to represent the sea, instead of the more usual stippling, just as in the first two maps, and in the 1548 Ptolemy, and the engraving work has been lauded as of high quality (Brown, 1952, no. 121; Schwartz and Ehrenberg, 1980, 61). The peculiarity of the map is its signature. It is the only map in which, although Gastaldi gives his Christian name, he indicates neither his surname nor his Piedmontese nationality. Its most salient feature geographically is the broad land bridge connecting Asia with America, although the south coast of the bridge is much higher, about 38°, than in any previous maps showing such a connection, lessening the sense that Asia and America should be considered as one continent. It was no doubt partly due to the map's many later editions that this depiction became one of the most important and influential of the century.

Minella has made the interesting observation that, based on toponymic evidence, there is reason to think that this map is later than the similar small "Vniversale Novo" world map (our no. 63) in the 1548 Ptolemy (Minella, 1993, 58), and, since the making of the maps for the Ptolemy probably began about 1542, this is a reasonable enough conjecture. Another interesting observation, which, if correct, also seems at first to contradict chronology, is made by Grande, who detects on the North American west coast the influence of the Cabrillo-Ferello expedition of 1542-43 (Grande, 1905, *carte*, 102), although Ramusio includes nothing on this, and the earliest known printed mention, which gives some of the coastal names from that expedition (although without mentioning Cabrillo or Ferello) is by Gomara in 1552-53.

Shirley observes that, except in America, mountains take up most of the interior (1987, no. 85). It is perhaps because of this that, other than two discussions of the Polar regions of the map by Bjørnbo (1912, 314-19), and by Grande (1905, *carte*, 98-99), and short comments on Scandinavia by Richter (1967, 71), discussions of the map's sources seem to be limited to America. Two scholars, Grande and Minella, have made systematic comparisons between the coastal names of America (Grande for both North and South America, and Minella only for South America) and the names for the same areas on several portolan charts. Both found the most frequent source by far to be the charts of Ribero for all coasts (Grande, cit., 100 and 104-06; Minella, 1993, 58-61), but a significant number of names come from Agnese, and Wagner considered Agnese the main or only source for the California coast (Wagner, 1937, 1, 26). A few names seem to come from a 1542 Santa Cruz chart and the 1544 Cabot world map. Less attention was given to the interior, but for western North America, Grande found the names to come from the explorations of Marcos de Nizza, Coronado, and Alarcon (Grande, cit., 101), the accounts of which are all in Ramusio, who was undoubtedly the general source, and for South America, Minella finds too that most of the names are from Ramusio (Minella, cit., 61).

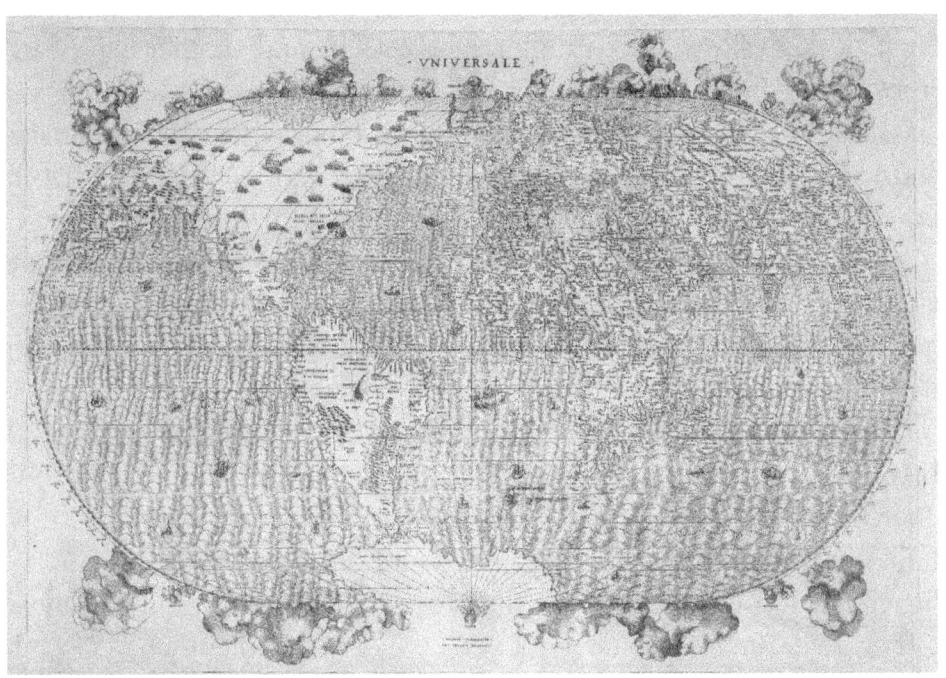

3 World (1546) Chicago Newb

As to the general contour of the American coasts, there is actually no great difference between the sea charts, but an exception is the North American east coast, especially the more northerly parts, and here sixteenth century cartographers had something of a problem, due to significant differences in the contours as well, of course, as in the different toponymies applied, between the reports from the voyages of Gomez as opposed to Verrazzano. Their reports differ enough that they often cannot be reconciled, with the result that two different schools of thought existed through the century and further as to which depiction to give to this area. Gastaldi depicts the Gomez concept in the present map, but on his 1548 map of eastern North America (no. 60), he depicts the Verrazzano concept. Both Wroth and Schwartz and Ehrenberg take Gastaldi to task for this inconsistency in his work (Wroth, 1970, 202-03; Schwartz and Ehrenberg, 1980, 40). But their criticism is quite unjustified. The fact is, no one in Europe could possibly have said which depiction was correct. There was absolutely no way to know.

Knowledge of the area was, willy-nilly, in flux and, as our chapters seven and eight tell us clearly, it was altogether characteristic of Gastaldi, in such circumstances, to show one depiction on one map, and another depiction on a different map. The present instance is simply another example of the way in which Gastaldi's mind worked in such circumstances, the way he felt such a conundrum should be approached, and a little reflection will show that the attitude was an eminently logical one, indeed the *only* logical one. For insisting on one of a choice of depictions when there was no way to know if it was the correct one or not is certainly not showing conviction, but plain bullheadedness, hardly a laudable trait. Gastaldi was simply keeping his mind open.

We need to make two closing comments. Firstly, we should mention, as noted by some writers (as Ruge, 1892, 69; and Grande, 1905, cit., 99-100) that there is no sign on the world map of the explorations of Cartier, of which Gastaldi must not have yet obtained any word; thus, though Ramusio published the accounts of the first and second voyages in 1556 in volume three (Parks, 1970, 36), he must not yet have obtained them when Gastaldi made this map in 1546. Secondly, at the John Carter Brown Library there exists a proof state of this map, with call number Cabinet. A546 1, which was purchased, evidently in 1912, from a 1911 Frederik Muller catalog. It lacks the clouds around the map, the forests and figures in North America, the word "Amazon" in South America, and the inscription at the bottom center of the map, although considerably above where that would be, we find written in manuscript in the Southern Continent the words "1546 | Giacomo Cosmographo | in Venetia". For the later editions and derivatives of this map, see our chapter two.

Location of copies:
Chicago Newb(Novacco 4F 4)/ Cambridge Harv(51-2492)/ London BL(26.b.30.)/ Leiden UB(COLLBN 002-01-003)/ London BL(Maps K.Top.IV.6)/ Firenze BMar(in atlas Stampe 423)[2005]/ Sint-Niklaas KOKW(Atlas 408 IATO (no. 2))[1994]/ Firenze BN(12.-.44, v. 4, no. 4(not 6))[1980]/ Firenze BN(12.-.44, v. 1, no. 6)[1980]/ Roma BN((711.6.G.3, no. 3)[1876]

References:
Ruge, 1912, 69; Grande, 1905, *carte*, 97-106; Bjørnbo, 1912, 314-19;
Wagner, 1937, 26-28; Almagià, 1939, *carta*, 7, in note 13; Almagià, 1948,
38; Brown, 1952, no. 121; Wheat, 1964, 30; Richter, 1967, 71; Wroth, 1970,
201-04; Schwartz and Ehrenberg, 1980, 40 and 61; Shirley, 1987, no. 85;
Karrow, 1993, 218 (no. 30/3); Minella, 1993, 57-61; Bifolco and Ronca,
2018, 1: 226-27.

Reproductions:
Remarkable Maps, 1894, in part 4, 3rd world map; Shirley, 1987, no. 85;
Bifolco and Ronca, 2018, 1: 226-27.
https://collections.Newberry.org/asset-management/2KXJ8ZSARSWZU?
&WS

4. Danubian Lands (all of central eastern Europe)
-Venice, 1546
-Woodcut, 73.0 x 106.0 cm., on four sheets
-No scale bar

In text box just left of bottom center of the map:
*La vera descrittione di Tutta la Vnghe | ria: Trãsiluania: Valachia: Parte di
Polo | nía: Podollia: e Rossia: con Tutta la Boe | mia: Slesia: Moravia:
Austria: Parte di | Franconía: et la Bauiera: dalla parte | Australe, del
Dannubio, la Bulgaria: la Bo | ssina: Seruia: et Romanía: Parte de Italia:
Cõ | Tutta la Schiauonia: | Per Iacomo de Castaldi Geographo in
Venetia .D.M.XLVI. | Stampata in Venetía per Mattio Pagan | in Frezaría
alinsegna della Fede (The true map of All Hungary: Transylvania: Valachia:
Parts of Poland: Podolia: and Russia: with all Bohemia: Silesia: Moravia:
Austria: Parts of Franconia: and Bavaria: of the Southern parts, of the
Danube, Bulgaria: Bosnia: Serbia: and Romania: Parts of Italy: with All
Sclavonia. By Iacomo de Castaldi Geographer in Venice 1546. Printed in
Venice by Mattio Pagan in Frezaria at the sign of Faith)*

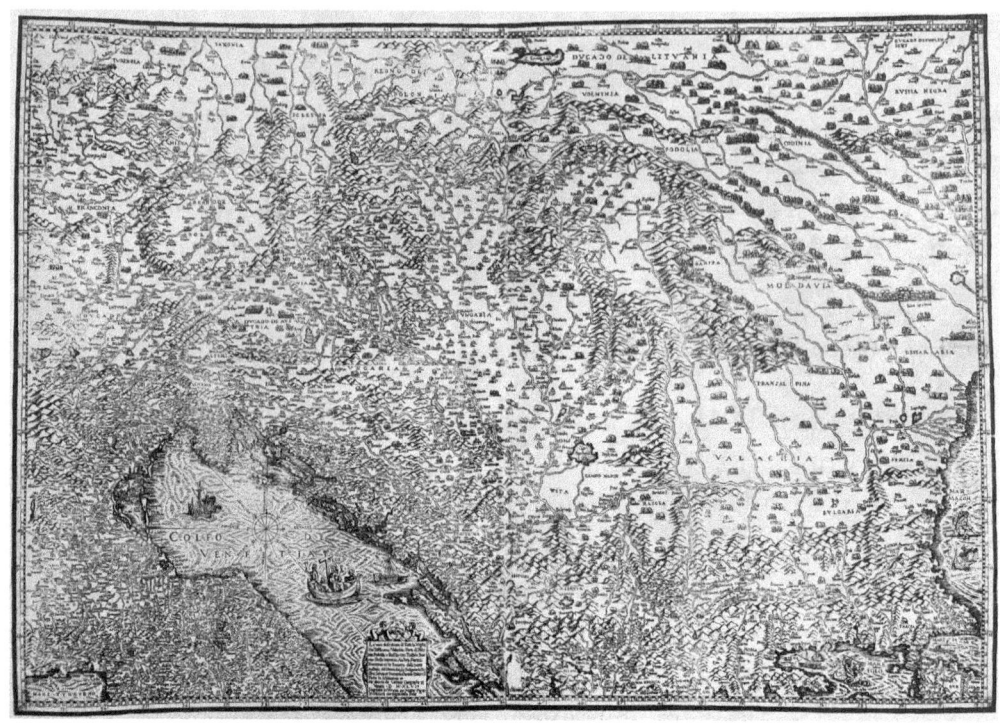

4 Danubian Lands (all of central eastern Europe) 1546 Almagià 1939

Comments:

The map is graduated in two-minute increments in latitude from 42°00' to 52°00' N, and in longitude in ten-minute increments from 32°00' to 56°00' E, and is on a rectangular projection. This woodcut was engraved and printed by Matteo Pagano, and it is the first collaboration between Pagano and Gastaldi; unfortunately, we know nothing of how this collaboration came about, and which of the two approached the other for this very large map, Gastaldi's largest to date. It covers a very large area, embracing all of the former Yugoslavia and former Czechoslovakia, as well as all but a tiny tip of Austria, all but a northern sliver of Poland, virtually all of eastern Germany, sizeable parts of northern Italy, Belarus and Ukraine, a small part of Anatolia in the southeast corner, as well as smaller parts of a few other countries. Its northern, and especially northeast portions are less dense in detail, intimating that Gastaldi had fewer sources for these areas. Its southern half generally coincides with the northern half of his later gigantic 1560 map of southeast Europe (our no. 96), which is only slightly larger than the present map. Besides these two maps, there is only one other European map by Gastaldi

479

which covers a great sprawling area of the continent, his 1562 map of northeastern Europe (no. 106). These two later maps together cover all eastern Europe, which seems to be intentional, and they *may* represent the first half of an irresolute and vague attempt to cover the continent with a series of such maps, although this is unclear and doubtful as we have shown in chapter ten.

But one is rather taken aback by the question of what in 1546 would have prompted Gastaldi to make a map of such large and irregular coverage. Almagià proposes that the rationale was a wish to portray the whole Danube Basin, the theater of important political events at the time (1939, *carta*, 12), and indeed Gastaldi depicts two opposing armies just below Vienna, undoubtedly representing the great but unsuccessful Ottoman Siege of Vienna of 1529 (Almagià, 1939, writes 1532 by error at p. 14). Alternatively, or in conjunction with this, Gastaldi may have felt drawn to depict the area because of its great commercial significance to the Republic. The tons of spices and many other goods brought from the Levant by Venetian ships found their way to all parts of Europe, but especially eastern Europe, for the Genoese (and by Gastaldi's time, the Portuguese) mainly supplied western Europe. There was major and constant merchant traffic overland between Venice and such centers as Vienna, Prague, Buda and Pest, Zagreb, Belgrade, Cracow, Munich, etc., from which the goods went to lesser centers of distribution and so on, and, along with such commercial importance there were surely standing political connections as well. Whatever was the impulse for making it, it is an impressive map, which Almagià stated was "a product far superior, in every respect, to all circulating up to that time" (1939, *carta*, 14). And it is precisely these first four maps, especially nos. 1, 2, and 4, all created in the time he was working on the Ptolemy, which make up the most important individual maps produced by Gastaldi before the brilliant period of 1559-1564. This short period 1544-1546 was a glowing debut, presaging things to come. The sense is almost that, having been chosen, or prodded, to begin the Ptolemy in about 1542, Gastaldi had found his direction in life.

As with the Sicily, Gastaldi here in constructing the map, basically used the same procedure or formula of operation as regularly outlined by Almagià in discussing Gastaldi's maps falling within the Ptolemaic *ecumene*,

virtually all of which maps contain a coordinate grid (for the present map see principally Almagià, 1939, *carta*, 12-18), i.e., portolan charts for the coasts, adoption of a number of anchor points, i.e., coordinates from Ptolemy, sometimes adopting just the longitude value or the
latitude value, in order to lay a tentative base for a grid (almost all Gastaldi maps contain one), some values of which might have been adjusted later, as he built up the map, and filling in the interior on the basis of a textual source or sources, or, most likely here I think, a combination of the two. As to the portolan charts the usage was in this case limited to the upper Adriatic coasts, the western Black Sea coast, and the northern tip of the Aegean Sea, the only seacoasts on the map, all in the southwest sheet. As to the anchor points, one must sniff them out partly intuitively, for Gastaldi doesn't usually place them quite precisely as given in Ptolemy, perhaps to disguise the borrowing, or very possibly they became, in the process of compilation, slightly adjusted for some reason. For this map, Almagià mentions only Nuremberg and Vienna, both for latitude only (Almagià, 1939, *carta*, 17), but, interestingly, Vienna's latitude is *not* taken as an anchor point from Ptolemy, but from some unidentified modern source. By some oversight, Almagià says that Constantinople is not one, for Ptolemy, he erroneously states, puts it at 41°00' N, while Gastaldi puts it at 43°00' N. But, actually, this is a Ptolemaic anchor point both in longitude and latitude (Ptolemy and Gastaldi are in exact agreement on 55°00' E and 43°00' N). Buda is also definitely from Ptolemy, and so, not surprisingly, is Venice, without question. Although, since it didn't exist yet in Ptolemy's time, and it is of course thus not in Ptolemy's list, its exact corresponding place on the Ptolemaic maps is clear. (Many fifteenth and sixteenth century printed editions of Ptolemy, incidentally, add Venice to the Ptolemaic maps.) And there are very possibly others (see also chapter seven, note 68).

As to the question of the sources used to fill in the body of the map, these are much more difficult to isolate than for the maps of single regions. Almagià says the map "is without doubt the result of a vast and complex work of elaboration and coordination of different elements . . . implying a selection, a critical and sagacious revision of material . . . Our map displays . . . a personal work of composition of very disparate materials" (1939, *carta*, 14-15), and shortly after adds that "it is evident that Gastaldi has used . . . materials diverse and of very disparate value" (1939, cit., 17), and notes, finally, that often we cannot isolate the sources with certainty (1939, 15; and 1948, 24). For Hungary, the area of the map most studied, the source is definitely Lazarus Secretarius's 1528 map of Hungray (Almagià, 1939, cit., 16; Banfi, 1947, 26 and 28; Banfi, 1956, 89). This is confirmed beyond doubt in Hrenko (1975, 112), which gives a *verzerrungsgitter* (distortion grid), the only one I have seen for any Gastaldi map, which covers a large area of our map. Lazarus's ungraduated map is oriented to the northeast, but Gastaldi took it as being oriented to the north, and incorporated it into his map accordingly, with the result that the whole area is oriented about 45° incorrectly by comparison to the rest of the map, and this is graphically apparent in Hrenko's *verzerrungsgitter*. Plihál (1998) expresses doubt, based on linguistic and orthographical considerations, that Lazarus's map was the source for the area, but there is no denying Hrenko's evidence. Banfi (1947, 24-25) detects traces also of an older map by Francesco Roselli of 1525, a lost map, and Almagià later accedes that an older map by Roselli may have been used as well (1948, 24, nt. 1). But Plihál (1998) doubts this, and even gives cause to question if the supposed Roselli map ever even existed, and, in my opinion, she is probably right. However, Hrenko says that Gastaldi has 180 new names in Hungary not on any previous known map (1975, 121), so there must have been some other source or sources.

For several other areas, the sources have been isolated with relative certainty. Bohemia is taken from the 1518 map of that country by Claudianus (Hrenko, 1975, 121; and Plihál, 1998, 2-3 and 8, with a reproduction of the Claudianus map at 3). Poland comes from Wapowski's 1528 map of that country (Almagià, 1939, *carta*, 16; Buczek, 1966, 34; Hrenko, 1975, 121). Umek, in a detailed investigation, has shown that the considerable part of Italy in the map is virtually certainly from the original of an anonymous, undated manuscript atlas of Italy consisting of twenty square maps, extant in a seventeenth century copy of an original which evidently would date from late in the first half of the sixteenth century, located in the Seminario Vescovile in Padua, and generally referred to as "the Vescovile atlas" (Umek, 2002). Almagià in 1939 had suggested that the Italian regions of Marche Trevisano and Marche d'Ancona were from Gastaldi's own modern maps of those areas in his 1548 Ptolemy, but these areas are almost certainly from the Vescovile atlas. For Istria, Almagià had given Coppo's 1525 map of the area as the source, but Lago (1981, 45-47) and Lago and Rossit (1992, 344-46), say that even a summary examination shows numerous and clear differences, and the source must be an unknown one. These findings perhaps cast some doubt upon how carefully Almagià made his original determinations in his 1939 work, the first to be published on the map, which had been unknown before. Finally, for part of Germany, Almagià suggested an anonymous 1540 woodcut map (1939, cit., 16). No determinations or suggestions have been made for the remaining areas of the map, which together amount to perhaps half or more of the entire map, except that Almagià suggests that perhaps some full map or maps of Europe were used, and suggests two, a 1536 Zell Europe, and a 1545 Methonius (Zorzi) Europe. The latter would be the more likely, for it was published in Venice one year before the present map and by the same woodcutter, Matteo Pagano. Destombes has devoted a study to this map (1973), which includes a full reproduction. While the map is primitive in its western half, preserving even Ptolemy's eastward projecting Scotland, its eastern half, that which would be useful in the present case, is rather good. Other than this, Almagià simply notes that Gastaldi used some maps now unknown, including possibly some manuscript maps circulating in Venice (Almagià, 1939, *carta*, 16; and 1948, 24), a reasonable enough possibility, and notes three sorts of maps that were *not* used, the modern maps in previous editions of Ptolemy, the maps in Münster's Cosmography, and the Cusa map.

I would like to briefly make two other suggestions not made before. Firstly, we know from Gastaldi's extra-European continental maps that Gastaldi made very extensive use of textual sources in his maps, and Münster's enormous 1544 *Cosmographia* includes over a thousand pages of *textual* geographical description of the whole world, but as much as 90% of the text is entirely on Germany and German-related places, which make up much of the western half of this map. Secondly, we have seen above that Venice had important ties to the areas to the north of it, that is, the areas on this map, and, while the masses of geographical information which Ramusio so avidly gathered over many years was principally concerned with the far continents, we know that in 1520 he requested and received from a Venetian legation secretary in Buda geographical information on "those parts" (Parks, 1955, 134). Ziegler, it is worth mentioning, was in Hungary at the time, and he assisted Lazarus in the years before 1520 with his survey for the map of Hungary he would eventually publish in 1528, and in 1520 he departed for Italy, where he remained eight years (Karrow, 1993, 604). Certainly, it is not impossible that Ramusio, the details of whose correspondence are very little known, might have made further such requests at later times for information from government representatives in those regions.

Location of copy:
Roma BVat (Stampe Geogr.I.150)(only copy known)

References:
Almagià, 1939, *carta*; Banfi, 1947, 23-28, 30 and 49; Almagià, 1948, 24 and 28; Banfi, 1956, 89; Buczek, 1966, 34; Hrenko, 1975; Lago and Rossit, 1981, 45-47 and 272-74; Lago, 1992, 311 and 344 B46; Meurer, 1991, 152; Karrow, 1993, 219-20; Plihál, 1998; Umek, 2002; Bifolco and Ronca, 2018, 1: 686.

Reproductions:
Almagià, 1939, *carta*; Bifolco and Ronca, 2018, 1: 686-87.
https://digi.vatlib.it/gds/detail/10380622

(5.-64.) The Gastaldi-Pedrezzano Ptolemy of 1548 (Venice)

The book's full title is: *PTOLEMEO | LA GEOGRAFIA | DI CLAVDIO PTOLEMEO | ALESSANDRINO, | con alcuni comenti & aggiunte fat | teui da Sebastiano munstero Ala | mano, Con le tauole non solamente | antiche & moderne solite di stãpar- | si, ma altre nuoue aggiunteui di M[eser] Iacopo Gastaldo Piamõtese cos- | mographo, ridotta in uolgare Italia | no da M[eser] Pietro Andrea Mat- | tiolo Senese medico Eccell ttissimo | CON L'AGGIVNTA D'INFINITI | nomi moderni, di Città, Prouincie, Castella, et | altri luoghi, fatta co grandissima diligenza | da esso Meser Iacopo Gastaldo, il che in | nissun altro Ptolemeo si ritroua. | Opera ueramente non meno utile | che necessaria. | In Venetia, per Gio[v]ãn[i] Baptista Pedrezano. | Co'l*

*priuilegio dell'Illustriss[imo] Senato Veneto per | Anni.X. M.D.XLVIII
(PTOLEMY. THE GEOGRAPHY OF CLAUDIUS PTOLEMY OF
ALEXANDRIA, with several comments and additions made here by Sebastian
Münster of Germany, With tables not only ancient and modern customarily to
be printed, but other new additions here by Master Iacopo Gastaldo
Piedmontese Cosmographer, translated into vernacular Italian by Master
Pietro Andrea Mattiolo of Siena most excellent physician WITH THE
ADDITION OF INFINITE modern names, of towns, provinces, castles, and
other places, made with the greatest diligence by him, Master Iacopo
Gastaldo, which in no other Ptolemy is found. A work truly no less useful
than necessary. In Venice, by Giovanni Battista Pedrezzano. With the
privilege of the Most Illustrious Venetian Senate for 10 years. 1548.)* The
colophon reads: *In Venetia, ad instantia di messer Giovãbattista Pedrezano |
libraro al segno della Torre a pie del ponte di Rialto. | Stampato per Nicolo
Bascarini nel Anno | del Signore. 1547. del mese di Ottobre. (In Venice, at
the bidding of Master Giovanni Battista Pedrezzano book dealer at the sign
of the Tower at the foot of the Rialto bridge. Printed by Nicolo Bascarini in
the Year of our Lord. 1547. in the month of October.)*

We have already spoken of this work as a whole in our first chapter,
but principally only to point out that it contains more modern maps, thirty-
four, than any previous edition of Ptolemy, and especially to note that it is the
first Ptolemy in which there is systematic coverage of the far continents, with
five maps for Africa, five for America, and seven for Asia, and it thus
evidences Gastaldi's great interest in the cartography of the non-European
world, and presages his great set of continental depictions of 1559-1564; we
also determined that the most probable span in which these maps were made
would be 1542-1547. We shall here speak briefly of its publishing details,
and give some bibliographical description, though for an exhaustive
description we refer the reader to Fahy (1993). As to the sixty maps, they are
dealt with individually in the following sixty entries.

The book is an elegant one, produced with great care. As we see from
the title, it was printed by Niccolò Bascarini, and the translation was done by
the famous botanist Andrea Mattiolo. It begins with eight unnumbered pages
of text, which include the dedication by Gastaldi to Fra Leone Strozzi, Prior
of Capua, dated January 2, 1548; an anonymous notice to the reader, and the

commentaries from Münster, followed by the main text in 214 folios, after which come the sixty double-page maps. All the modern maps are on the rectangular projection, except one, Scandinavia (no. 25), for which the rectangular projection is less appropriate, since it covers many more degrees of latitude than the others (eighteen degrees); it is on a trapezoidal projection. Finally, there is a sixty-four-leaf list of geographical names, containing 9,000 names (3,000 more than Ptolemy) and greatly surpassing anything then on the market (Fahy, 1993, 99). On the backs of the modern maps is accompanying text by Gastaldi, and, on most maps, there is a capital letter "G" in each corner, for Gastaldi. There are twenty-six instead of the usual twenty-seven ancient maps, for Gastaldi includes no Ptolemaic world map. It is the first edition of Ptolemy in Italian, and is the first octavo edition, so it is much smaller than previous editions. In the notice to the reader, an advantage of the book is said to be the fact that it is "convenient to carry in the sleeve," (actually, it is large, thick, and heavy enough that this would have to be quite some sleeve!), but, of course, if its small size is an advantage, it also brings disadvantage where the maps are concerned, and, as Shirley observes, "they are small simplified maps of not very great distinction." Indeed, taken individually, most of the maps are not especially impressive. They become rather impressive only when considered as a group, or groups, which offer, as already noted, the first reasonably good coverage of the far continents, "and some of them are of no slight interest to the history of geography," says Nordenskiöld (1889, 26), who then later states that, "it is obvious that the author has tried to obtain the best information possible concerning the countries lately discovered" (1897, 159). In fact, though their main value emerges mainly when considered as groups corresponding to the continents, and though their small size and resultant simplification of things may make the maps rather unimpressive at first, there are a fair number of the individual maps which do show innovation. This will come out when we speak of the individual maps below

Though Gastaldi has included some commentary from Münster's 1540 edition of Ptolemy, it is important to mention, as has been noted before (Almagià, 1939, *Carta*, 15) that, in his modern maps, Gastaldi does not follow Münster in any way. The only possible exception would be that in Gastaldi's depiction in his "SCHONLADIA NOVA" (entry no. 25), taken from the map of Ziegler, the more stylized depiction than that of Ziegler may have been influenced by Münster's style of drawing, but this is quite uncertain and the geography in the two maps differs in many ways. In the only two other cases where it has been implied that Gastaldi followed Münster, Gastaldi's "PRVSSIA E LIVONIA NOVA" (our no. 24) and his "POLONIA ET HVNGARIA NOVA TABVLA" (our no. 27), we show that these determinations are quite wrong in the mentioned entries. However, in the much less important Ptolemaic maps proper, Gastaldi has apparently followed Münster's area coverage in thirteen maps (our nos. 7, 9, 12, 14, 21, 34, 37, 43, 48, 50, 51, 52, 53), and he evidently follows Münster as regards geographical and other details in ten maps (our nos. 12, 21, 23, 41, 43, 44, 48, 50, 51, 57), as see the noted entries. Münster differs notably in these maps by comparison to the same maps in the two fifteenth century redactions of the Ptolemaic maps which I have had immediately available to me, those of the 1490 Rome Ptolemy, reproduced in Nordenskiòld (1889, pls. 2-27), and those of the Ebner manuscript, reproduced at the end of Stevenson's Ptolemy (1932). What the bases were for Münster's adjustments I have made no attempt to discover. It is perhaps most likely that the "additions made here by Sebastian Münster" to which Gastaldi alludes in the title of the volume are in reference to these changes

We should note in closing that no scholar has yet made a general study of the maps in the work, nor have we. Nevertheless, a good portion of the individual maps have received varying amounts of attention in the literature, in some cases considerable, and we have done our best to gather together that considerable amount of material which exists. Particularly as regards the more recent literature, some examples of which, due in general to the publication explosion, do not always find their way into the usual bibliographies, there will be works which have not caught our attention. But, while in a few cases we have had no choice but to limit our entry to the basic description and technical details, in many cases, we have been able to offer more. In the case of the twenty-six Ptolemaic maps proper (the Ptolemaic world map, as noted earlier, was not included), I have regularly made comparisons between Gastaldi's copies, and those of the 1490 Rome Ptolemy, and those of the Ebner manuscript, both mentioned just above. I have made no attempt to compare them with all available printed editions of Ptolemy.

Locations of copies (of the book)
Amsterdam UB (1804 E 16)/ Chicago Newb(Ayer 6 .P9 1548) and (Map3C G3201 AT 1548)/ Washington LC (G1005 1548 Vault) and (G113 .P8 1548) and (Thacher A844 Thacher Coll)/ New York PL(*KB 1548) and (8-*KB 1548)/ Oxford Bodl(8° P 74 Art.)/ London BL(C.20.a.1.) and (303.c.27) and (Maps C.1.a.3.)/ Copenhagen KB(169:1, 341.S-1977)/ Paris Med(G 87.A6 P97 réserve)(copy consists of the maps only, colored)/ Princeton UL(Ptolemy 1548)/ New Haven Yale(1976 1748 [2 copies]) and (Gfp94 gi548)/ Wien UB(I-182119)/ Venezia BNM(D 070D 128)/ Salamanca BU(BG/32857)/ Washington GU(02A240)/ Stuttgart WLB(40/5020-F4567/ F4569)/ Minneapolis Bell(P573)/ Milwaukee UW(G87 P848x 1548)/ Syracuse SU(G87 .P97 1548) and (912 P97)/ Rochester UR(G 87 .P87qI 1548)/ Middletown WU(SPECIAL COLLECTIONS Davison K#)/ Athens UGL(QB41 .P975g 1548) /Louisville UL(G 87 .P852 1548)Wolfenbüttel HAB(M: Lg 1890)s (All entries in the present list have been verified as for the date of this book.)

References:
Winsor, 1883-84, [pt. 4], 227-31; Eames, 1886, 35-38; Nordenskiöld, 1889, 25-26; Nordenskiöld, 1897, 119; Grande, 1905, *carte*, 28-29; Almagià, 1939, *carta*, 15-16; Almagià, 1948, 21; Brown, 1952, no. 122; Shirley, 1987, no. 87; Fahy, 1993; Karrow, 1993, 220-23; Minella, 1993, 11-14; Meurer, 2001, 123; Lago, 2002, 213 and 515, Bifolco and Ronca, 2018, 1: 104-105.

Reproductions of the maps: Bifolco and Ronca, 2018, 1: 106-15.
http://www.davidrumsey.com/luna/servlet/s/bo9636

5. British Isles (Ptolemaic)
-Venice, 1548
-Copper engraving, 12.5 x 17.0 (12.0) cm., on one sheet
-No scale bar

Along the top border of the map:
TABULA EVROPAE I (FIRST MAP OF EUROPE)

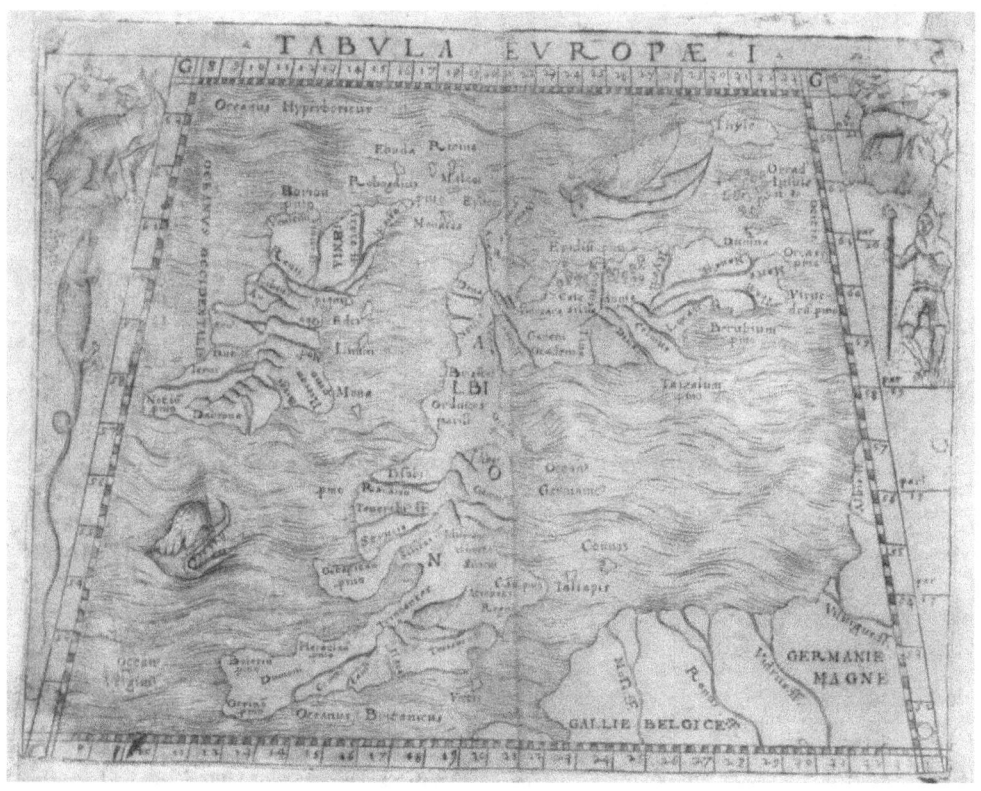

5 British Isles (Ptolemaic) 1548 Rumsey

Comments:

The map is graduated in twelve-minute increments in latitude and longitude, with each whole degree numbered, from ca. 51°12' to 63°36' N, and from 7°00' to 33°00' E. It is on a trapezoidal projection, with the convergence of meridians somewhat increased over that of Donus Nicolaus Germanus (on the confused identity of whom see Karrow, 1993, 255-56), a liberty perhaps justifiable inasmuch as Donus's application of this projection was itself a liberty, for Ptolemy's original regional maps are all on the rectangular projection, necessary in order to follow Ptolemy's procedure for establishing the grid for the regional maps (in book 8, chapters 1-2, and in the so-called captions to the regional maps; see Berggren and Jones, 2000, pp. 119-21). Though not at all comparable to Sylvanus's reworking of the maps in his earlier edition of Ptolemy, Gastaldi has made some small changes in the Ptolemaic geography, such as extending the lower part of the Welsh peninsula, adding a couple of rivers in that part of the mainland continent visible in the southeast corner of the map, etc. He has also added some unrealistic orography, a characteristic common in Gastaldi's maps throughout his career, to help fill in empty tracts. In the two empty triangular spaces at the sides of the map, larger than on the map in the earlier Ptolemy editions which I checked, he has included some interesting décor.in the form of various animals and a peasant.

Reference:
Shirley, 1980, 83.

Reproductions:
Bifolco and Ronca, 2018, 1: 106.
https://www.davidrumsey.com/luna/servlet/detail/
RUMSEY~8~1~291261~90062989

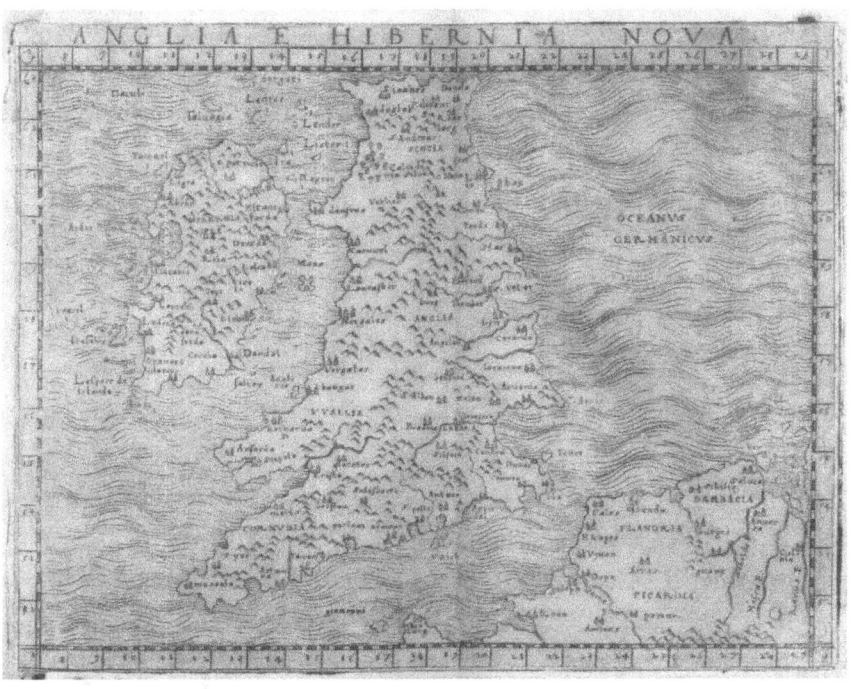

6 British Isles (modern) 1548 Rumsey

6. British Isles (modern)
-Venice, 1548
-Copper engraving, 12,5 x 17.0 cm., on one sheet
-No scale bar

At the top center of the map:
ANGLIA E HIBERNIA NOVA (MODERN ENGLAND AND IRELAND)

Comments:
Graduated in twelve-minute increments in latitude and longitude, with each whole degree numbered, from 51°00' to 63°00' N, and from 7°00' to 29°00' E, and on a rectangular projection, that prescribed by Ptolemy for regional maps. The depiction is quite primitive for its time and lacks proper form, commensurate with the fact that northwest Europe
seems to have been Gastaldi's nemesis in his career, although to be sure we do not see the Ptolemaic eastward extension of Scotland carried over. Westropp (1913, 368), speaking of Ireland on the map, says that "Irishmen will scarcely endorse his contemporaries' estimate, "Eccelentissimo cosmografo Piamontese."" Shirley says Gastaldi has reverted here to Waldseemüller's 1513 map, although "more up to date sources were certainly available both north of the Alps (e.g. Münster's map of England and Wales) and in Italy through the recent publication of Lily's map of the British Isles in Rome." Indeed, why Gastaldi did not use these sources, especially Lily, is something of a mystery, and suggests that at this early date Gastaldi was little familiar yet with the Venetian map industry, beginning to surge at this time. If this is the case, then, since it is in general the maps of the northwest part of Europe which are by far the poorest in the Ptolemy, these were perhaps the first to be made, for his depictions of the other three quarters of Europe are much better. The present map is, I believe, the poorest modern map in the book, except perhaps the modern Germany (no. 13), and possibly Gastaldi's poorest map in general. In this regard, it is worth pointing out that Ruscelli, in his 1561 Ptolemy, generally copies all the Gastaldi 1548 regional maps, somewhat simplified though on a rather larger scale, with the single exception of this map, which is replaced with another.

Reference:
Shirley, 1980, 33-34.

Reproductions:
Bifolco and Ronca, 2018, 1: 106
https://www.davidrumsey.com/luna/servlet/detail/
RUMSEY~8~1~291263~90062991

7. Iberian peninsula (Ptolemaic)

-Venice, 1548
-Copper engraving, 12.5 x 17.5 (13.5) cm., on one sheet
-No scale bar

At the top of the map:
TABULA EVROPAE II (SECOND MAP OF EUROPE)

7 Iberian peninsula (Ptolemaic) 1548 Rumsey

Comments:
Graduated in twelve-minute increments in latitude and longitude, with each whole degree numbered, from 34°00' to 47°00' N, and from 0°00' (!) to 21°00' E. Gastaldi changes the area coverage somewhat, extending the picture one degree south, following Münster, and he does this in many of the Ptolemaic maps, sometimes changing it up to a good number of degrees. It is on a trapezoidal projection as on the first printed Ptolemaic maps, but with a greater convergence of the meridians, thus creating considerable space at the sides of the map, which Gastaldi fills with animal vignettes on the left, and Ptolemy's system of climata on the right, and we see the same in all the Ptolemaic maps in the book. The map is generally faithful to the Ptolemaic original, but, as always with these maps, is quite simplified, omitting many names, due to the reduced size.

Reference:
Hernando Rica, 1995, 106.

Reproductions:
Bifolco and Ronca, 2018, 1:106.
https://www.davidrumsey.com/luna/servlet/detail/
RUMSEY~8~1~291265~90062993

8. Iberian peninsula (modern)
-Venice, 1548
-Copper engraving, 12.5 x 17.5 cm., on one sheet
-No scale bar

At top center of the map:
HISPANIA NOVA TABVLA (MODERN MAP OF SPAIN)
Comments:
Graduated in twelve-minute increments, with each whole degree numbered, in latitude and longitude, from 35°00' to 45°00' N and from 3°00' to 21°00' E, and on the rectangular projection prescribed by Ptolemy for regional maps (cf. entry no. 5). It generally follows Ptolemy in longitude graduation, although at first glance it seems not to in the west, since Ptolemy starts from

zero degrees and Gastaldi from three degrees, but the difference is an illusion and arises from the fact that Gastaldi has removed Ptolemy's tremendously overextended Great Promontory. According to Hernando Rica, it is a reduction of Gastaldi's great 1544 Spain (1995, 107).

8 Iberian Peninsula (modern) 1548 Rumsey

References:
Gallois, 1890, 215 with nt. 1; Hernando Rica, 1995, 107.

Reproductions:
Bifolco and Ronca, 2018, 1: 106.
https://www.davidrumsey.com/luna/servlet/detail/
RUMSEY~8~1~291267~90062995

9. France (Ptolemaic)

-Venice, 1548

-Copper engraving, 13.0 x 17.0 cm., on one sheet.

-No scale bar

At top center of the map:

TABVLA EVROPAE III (THIRD MAP OF EUROPE)

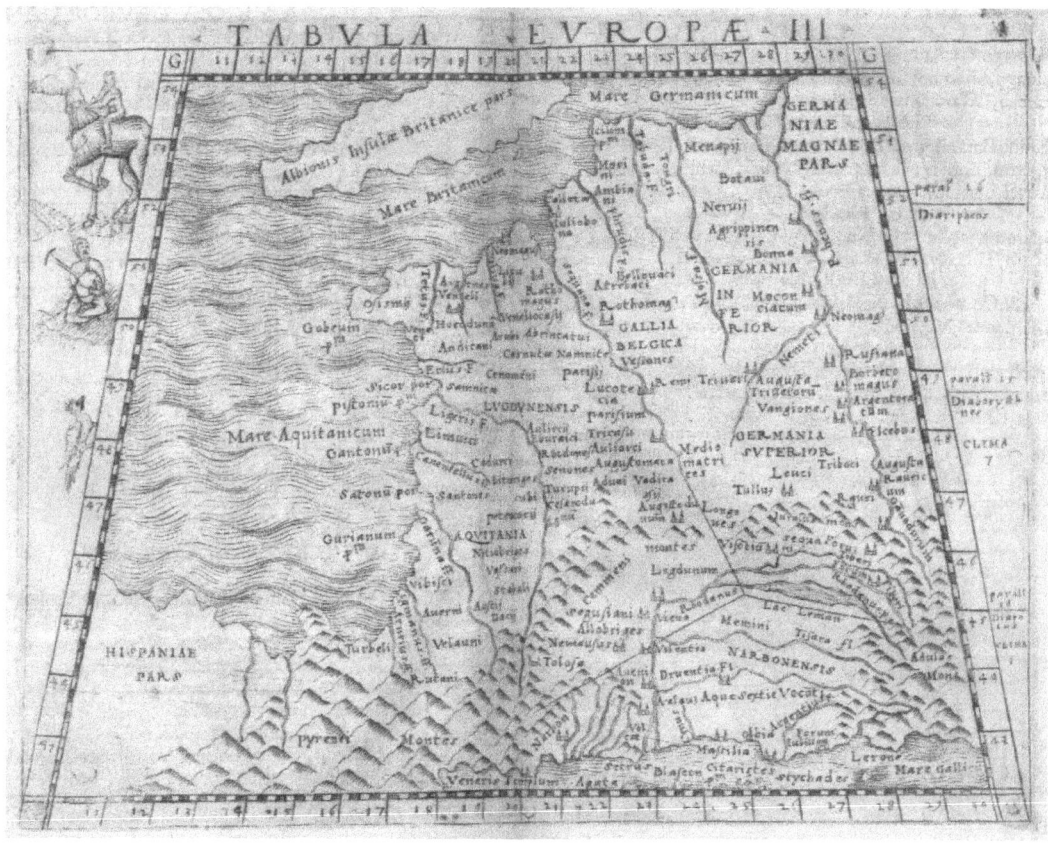

9 France (Ptolemaic) 1548 Rumsey

Comments:

Graduated in twelve-minute increments in latitude and longitude, with each whole degree numbered, from 40°00' N, and from 10°00' to 30°11' E, on the same trapezoidal projection described in no. 5, and with the usual vignettes in the leftover triangular space. Here again Gastaldi generally follows

Ptolemy faithfully, except that he extends the coverage five whole degrees to the west, after Münster.

Reproductions:
Bifolco and Ronca, 2018, 1: 106.
https://www.davidrumsey.com/luna/servlet/detail/
RUMSEY~8~1~291269~90062997

10. France (modern)
-Venice, 1548
-Copper engraving, 12.5 x 17.5 cm., on one sheet.
-No scale bar

At the top center of the map:
GALLIA NOVA TABVLA (MODERN MAP OF FRANCE)

10 France (modern) 1548 Rumsey

Comments:

Graduated in twelve-minute increments in latitude and longitude, with each whole degree numbered, from 42°00' to 54°00' N, and from 13°00' to 30°00' E, on the rectangular projection prescribed by Ptolemy for regional maps. The northern part of the map includes, on a much smaller scale, all that is included in the following map, no. 11. In general, the map is regressive by comparison with earlier works, says Rohr (1939, 186); it is significantly too wide latitudinally and longitudinally by ca. 2 degrees (Rohr, cit., 186, 189, 216), and has many smaller details wrong, some of which Rohr points out, although overly detailed comparisons and criticisms at this early time can often approach being unjustified and meaningless, in my opinion. It was the sixteenth century! Mistakes swarmed in all maps, although there were a few exceptions, as Philipp Apian's great map of Bavaria. Rohr detects the use of portolan charts (cit., 186) but contradicts himself at p. 189 where he says it is generally behind the portolan depictions. In places, he detects signs of the modern France in the 1482 Florence and 1513 Strassburg Ptolemy additions (cit., 187 and 189). He does note that Gastaldi's modern coast from Marseilles is the best of its time (cit., 187) and improves some over previous orography in two places (cit., 188). Still, the map is generally a step backwards. Now, we note, this poor map can be considered as among those of northwestern Europe and we have seen in entry no. 6 that this is by far the weakest area in Gastaldi's modern Ptolemy maps.

Reference:
Rohr, 1939, 186-90 and 216.

Reproductions:
Bifolco and Ronca 2018, 1: 106.
https://www.davidrumsey.com/luna/servlet/detail/
RUMSEY~8~1~291271~90062999

11. The Netherlands (Flanders, Brabant, and Holland) (modern)
-Venice, 1548
-Copper engraving, 12.5 x 17.0 cm., on one sheet
-No scale bar

At the top of the map:
FLANDRIA BARBANTIA E HOLANDA NOV. (MODERN FLANDERS, BRABANT AND HOLLAND)

11 Netherlands (modern) 1548 Rumsey

Comments:
Graduated in twelve-minute increments, with each whole degree numbered, in latitude and longitude, from 51°00' to 55°13' N, and from 22°04' to 29°00' E, on the rectangular projection. A considerable portion of southeast England is shown in the northwest part of the map, and it differs from that

portion as shown on no. 6, the modern map of Britain, being much better depicted and drawn. Speaking of the 1548 Ptolemy, Shirley (1987, in no. 87) states: "Although there were no later re-issues of the Gastaldi-Ptolemy atlas, Mr. Graham Franks has shown me four slightly different states of Gastaldi's small map of Flanders and Brabant from the same work." Were small revisions made in some of the maps as the printing of the edition proceeded, or did the work sell so well, that several sets of printings took place, at which times small revisions were made? In any event, the fact of these variants lends some further strength to the idea that Gastaldi himself engraved the Ptolemy's maps. Gastaldi, involved in the production, would always have had immediate access to the plates, which an outside engraver would not have had, and also to the printed copies, of which he indeed must have owned at least one for each map. That Gastaldi would have often perused the printed maps as work progressed, and caught little details which he wished to change, is certainly a natural enough supposition, and he would have been in a position to access the plates and make such adjustments with no trouble. But an outside engraver, already having been paid for his work, and gone on to other jobs, would have had no reason to repeatedly pore over the maps searching for small changes to make, and he would not have had the easy access to the plates that Gastaldi had in order to make changes

Again, we have a map of part of northwest Europe, and again, it is found wanting. For one thing, it has many misspellings, but Gastaldi was always notoriously careless about orthography. More importantly, the general outline of the region is rather poor, as noted by several writers (Heijden, 1987, 106; De Ghein, 1994, 290; Koeman, 2007, 1249), although Heijden also notes elsewhere that: "It does show more or less the real shape of the Netherlands" (1987, 19). He notes that the region is shown much better on Gastaldi's pre-1552 map of Germany (no. 70), saying the difference is "astonishing" (1987, 19 and 106). The map is the oldest copperplate map of the Netherlands alone and as a whole (Heijden, 1987, 19), though other images exist or existed, as we shall see. Sources seem to be uncertain. Heijden says it was "obviously not based on survey but copied from another map" (cit., 106), but as to more specific information, he simply says it is evidently a copy "of a map of the Cusanus-type" (cit., 19). De Ghein believes it was taken from a woodcut by Arnold Nicolaii of ca. 1547, of which no copy is known (1994, 255 and 287-88). By another theory, it may partly stem from a 1526 map by Jan van Hoirne which is not only of the Netherlands, but a larger area. Only fragments of this map are known (Heijden, 1987, 20-22; Karrow, 1993, 316), although Meurer has found a manuscript map of the Netherlands of ca. 1539 perhaps by the London printer and publisher Reynor Wolfe which was probably based on Hoirne's map (Meurer, 2002; Koeman, 2007, 1249).

References:
Heijden, 1987, 18-20, 25-26 and 106-07; Shirley, 1987, in no. 87; Karrow, 1993, 30/11; de Ghein, 1994, 255 and 287-91; Meurer, 2002; Koeman, 2007, 1249.

Reproductions:
Bifolco and Ronca, 2018, 1: 107.
https://www.davidrumsey.com/luna/servlet/detail/
RUMSEY~8~1~291273~90063001

12. Germany and surrounding areas (Ptolemaic)
-Venice, 1548
-Copper engraving, 12.5 x 17.5 (13.0) cm., on one sheet
-No scale bar

At the top of the map:
TABVLA EVROPAE IIII (FOURTH MAP OF EUROPE)

Comments:
Graduated in twelve-minute increments, with each full degree numbered, in latitude and longitude, from 46°36' to 60°00' N, and from 27°00' to 51°00' E, on a rectangular projection. Gastaldi adds one degree to Ptolemy's coverage in the south, a half degree to the north, and a full five degrees to the east, following Münster. He has also made a few changes to Ptolemy's geography. In the northeast, and running off the map, Gastaldi has added an island, or part of some mainland, to which he gives the name "DACIA", and, since the original map is fairly sparsely covered with names, he has been

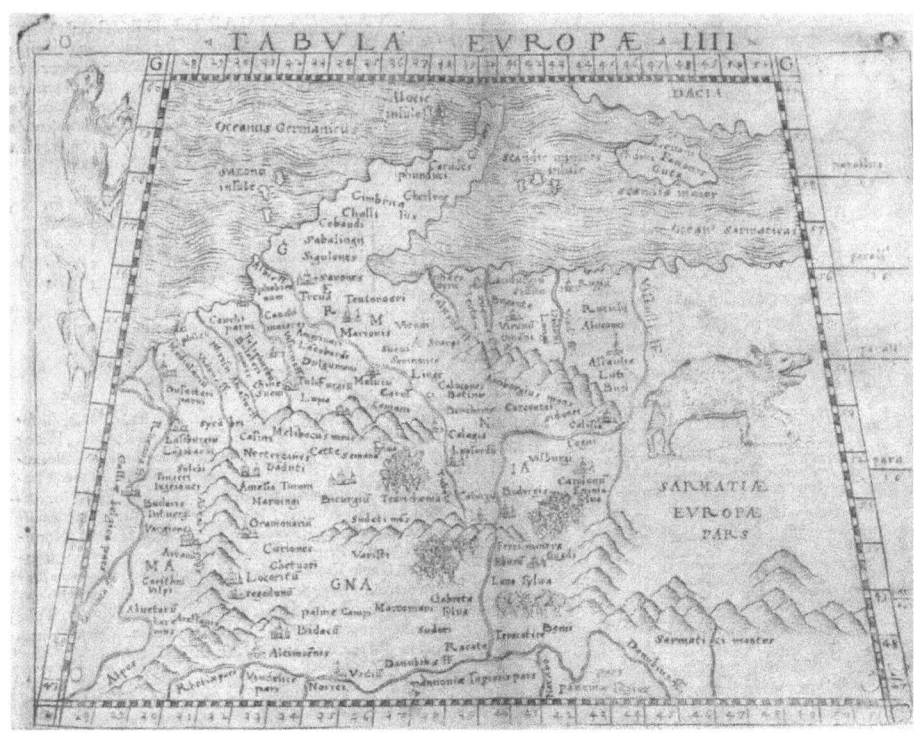

12 Germany and surrounding areas (Ptolemaic) 1548 Rumsey

able to insert a few extra names in some places, as "Cobandi" and "Tus" in the northern peninsula evidently corresponding to Denmark. I am indebted to Romanian scholar Sorin Fortiu for bringing to my attention that the same changes occur on this Ptolemaic map in Münster's 1540 Ptolemy, and we may assume that this was Gastaldi's source here, although Fortiu has also found the DACIA land in the 1482 Ulm Ptolemy and the 1513 Strasbourg Ptolemy. While the name form Dacia is the ancient designation for Romania, Fortiu points out that there is no connection between that and the present usage, and there was a period of time when at least some savants rendered Dania (roughly Denmark) as Dacia. For more of relevance to this question, see Dilke (1985, 45-46) and Linderski (1964).

Reproductions:
Bifolco and Ronca, 2018, 1: 107.
https://www.davidrumsey.com/luna/servlet/detail/
RUMSEY~8~1~291275~90063003

13. Germany (modern)

-Venice, 1548

-Copper engraving, 12.5 x 17.5 cm., on one sheet

-No scale bar

At the top center of the map:

GERMANIA NOVA TABVLA MDXXXXII (NEW MAP OF GERMANY 1542)

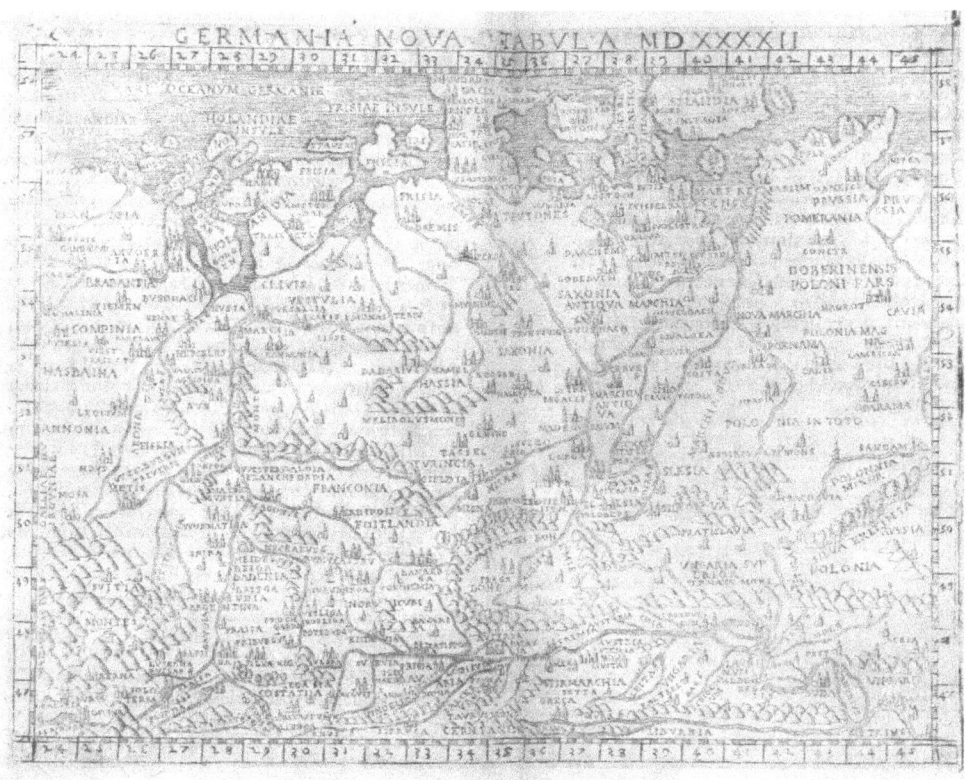

13 Germany and surrounding areas (modern) 1548 Rumsey

Comments:

Graduated in twelve-minute increments, with each whole degree numbered, in latitude and longitude, from 46°00' to 58°00' N, and from 23°00' to 45°00' E, on a rectangular projection. It is the only map in the 1548 Ptolemy which carries a date (1542), which is accepted as being its actual date (Meurer,

2001, 123; Almagià, 1939, *carta*, 7), and the fact that its execution, about which more below, is the poorest of the maps in the Ptolemy suggests it was in fact the first map made and engraved for the edition, as we have suggested in chapter one. A peculiarity of the map is that all placenames are written in capital letters. The only other map in the Ptolemy in which we find this is the second Ptolemaic map of Asia (our no. 41), suggesting that that map might have been the second map made and engraved for the edition, after which it was decided that only regional names should be so written, and names of towns in minuscules, except for a capital letter at the start, as we see in all the other maps. Another peculiarity is the extreme difficulty of finding a copy of the Ptolemy in which this map has printed well, most copies having the dim appearance of having been pulled from a plate which was worn out, although no other maps in a copy of the book have this look. They seem especially to have printed poorly in about the lower third of the map, most especially on the left side, and in the far northeast corner. Presuming for the sake of argument that our thesis that Gastaldi engraved his own early maps is correct, it is just possible that this was in fact the very first map he engraved, and that he had not yet acquired the necessary boldness to engrave as deeply as was needed, and the engraved surface indeed became worn out quite early in its career. The map is the last which we might include among those of parts of northwest Europe, and, as with all of these, it is of lower quality than the maps of other areas, indeed vying with the modern Britain (no. 6) as the most inferior in the book, both cartographically, and as to workmanship, as noticed by Meurer (2001, 123). As to source, it is taken from the so-called "Eichstädt" map, presumably in its last known edition, of 1530, or, more accurately, from the central portion of that map (Meurer, 2001, 122). The original of the Eichstätt map is the only definitely known rendition of a map of Germany presumably made in about the 1450s by Cardinal Nicolas of Cusa, the confused and uncertain history of which is probably best dealt with in English by Karrow (1993, 130-37).

References:
Feuerstein, 1912, 345; Caraci, 1927, "Giacomo," 390 nt. 48; Almagià, 1939, *carta*, 7; Banfi, 1955, 99, in note 8 continued from p. 98; Meurer, 2001, 122-23.

Reproductions:
Bifolco and Ronca, 2018, 1: 107.
https://www.davidrumsey.com/luna/servlet/detail/
RUMSEY~8~1~291277~90063005

14. Lands bordering the south side of the Danube (Ptolemaic)
-Venice, 1548
-Copper engraving, 12.5 x 17.5 (13.0) cm., on one sheet
-No scale bar

At the top of the map:
TABVLA EVROPAE V (FIFTH MAP OF EUROPE)

14 Lands bordering the south side of the Danube (modern) 1548 Rumsey

504

Comments:
Graduated in twelve minute increments, with each full degree numbered, in latitude and longitude, from 38°00' to 48°12' N, and from 29°00' to 48°00' E, on the trapezoidal projection prescribed by Ptolemy. Gastaldi enlarges Ptolemy's coverage three degrees to the south, and a half degree to the north, following Münster. The map includes most of the former Yugoslavian countries, most of Bulgaria, most of Austria, and parts of Albania, Hungary, and Germany, and does not notably deviate from Ptolemy anywhere.

Reference:
Marinelli, 1881, 102-03 (no. 515).

Reproductions:
Bifolco and Ronca, 2018,. 1: 107
https://www.davidrumsey.com/luna/servlet/detail/
RUMSEY~8~1~291279~90063007

15. Dalmatia (modern)
-Venice, 1548
-Copper engraving, 12.5 x 17.0 cm., on one sheet
-No scale bar

Along the top border of the map:
DALMACIA NOVA TABVLA (NEW MAP OF DALMATIA)

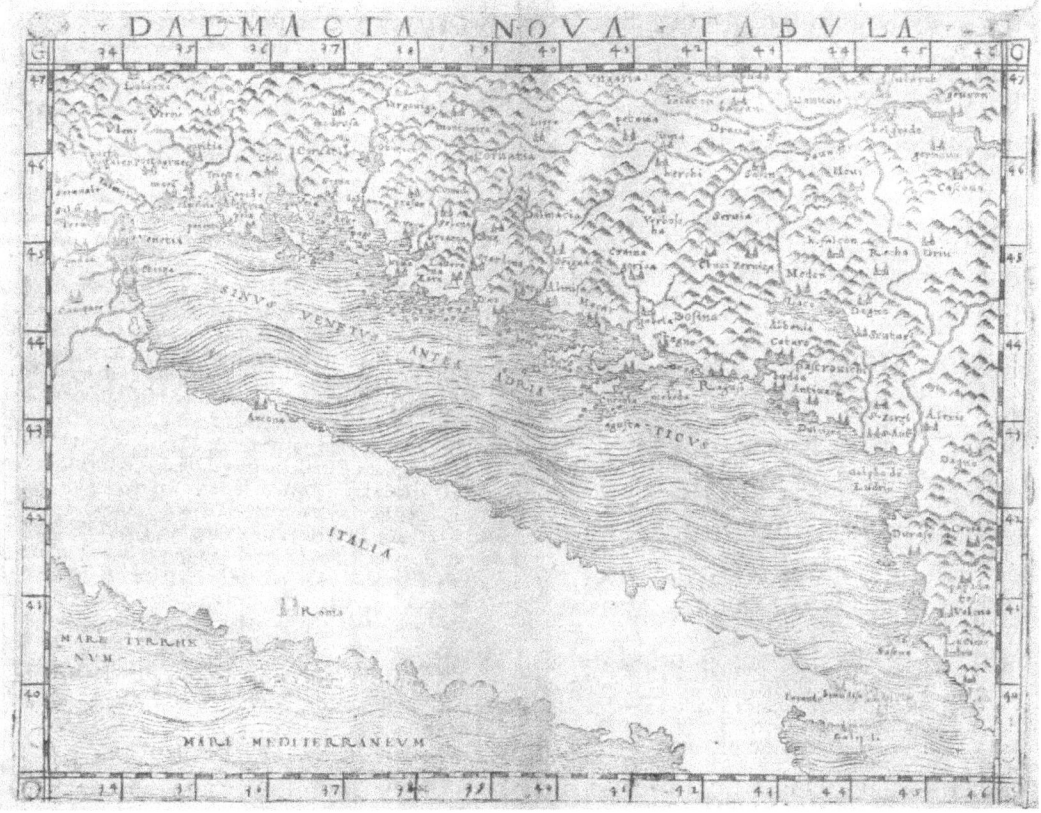

15 Dalmatia (modern) 1548 Rumsey

Comments:
Graduated in twelve-minute increments, with each full degree numbered, in
latitude and longitude, from 39°00' to 47°00' N, and from 33°00' to 46°00' E,
on the rectangular projection prescribed by Ptolemy, as in all the modern
maps of the Ptolemy (cf. entry no. 5). It is an attractive, well-made, and
well-engraved map, though an odd feature is inclusion of almost all the

506

Italian peninsula, but with the interior quite blank except for a few major points, and the area around Venice, which is filled in. Marine charts no doubt played a large role for the coasts, and we remember that this coast was closely tied commercially and otherwise to the Republic, containing stations, stopping points and commercial colonies, and some information could have come to Venice this way, and, of course, there is always the possibility of recently-made smaller regional maps, printed, or more likely manuscript, unknown to us. The only definite attempt I know of to find sources for this map is by Umek, who finds strict analogy between the Dalmatian and Albanian coasts with the Vescovile atlas, mentioned in entry no. 4 (Umek, 2002, 535), although he notes some differences in the interior. I will go out on a limb, and mention five possible sources that I have been able to come up with, in what I consider to be declining order of likelihood, though I admit that I have not yet had the opportunity to check them myself, but this could be of use to some future scholars. The most likely further source, thinking mainly of the interior, but also the coast, would be certain maps in the 1542 Kronstadt (Brasov) published *Rudimenta Cosmographica* of the Romanian cartographer Johannes Honter (Karrow, 1993, 309, nos. 41/13 and 41/14), or more likely, the same maps from the Zürich edition (Karrow, 1993, nos. 41/13.1 and 41/14.1). Second most likely would be Pietro Coppo, Venetian born, though he lived most of his life in Izola in Istria, from 1499 to 1556. A map in his 1520 manuscript "De toto orbe" is a possibility (Karrow, 1993, 120, no. 21/11). Thirdly, Waldsemüller included as the second of twenty modern maps appended to his 1513 Ptolemy one of Bosnia, Serbia, Greece, and Sclavonio (Karrow, 1993, 580, no. 80/42; and Nordenskiöld, 1889, 2a). Nordenskiöld adds that "here we have the first printed maps of Greece and the Balkan countries" but notes elsewhere that "for want of detail in the interior of the countries, we may conclude that they are copies of portolanos of the 15th century" (Nordensiöld, 1889, 70a), though Nordenskiöld of course didn't know of Umek's Vescovile atlas at the time. The fourth possibility involves no maps, but simply a possible information provider, Vincenzo Palatino (Corsulensis), who was born in Dalmatia, but then evidently lived most of his life in Italy, following a ten-year sojourn to the New World as a Dominican (Karrow, 1993, 444-46). The fifth vague possibility is Turkish sources in general, since they often plied these waters as well, although I can say nothing more specific in this regard.

References:
Marinelli, 1881, 103 (no. 516); Umek, 2002, 535-36.

Reproductions:
Bifolco and Ronca, 2018, 1: 107.
https://www.davidrumsey.com/luna/servlet/detail/
RUMSEY~8~1~291281~90063009

16. Italy (Ptolemaic)
-Venice, 1548
-Copper engraving, 12.5 x 17.0 (12.5) cm., on one sheet
-No scale bar

At the top of the map:
TABVLA EVROPAE VI (SIXTH MAP OF EUROPE)

16 Italy (Ptolemaic) 1548 Rumsey

Comments:
Graduated in five-minute increments, with every whole degree numbered, in latitude and longitude, from 37°00' to 45°30' N, and from 28°00' to 43°00' E, on a trapezoidal projection, with Gastaldi's usual somewhat increased meridional convergence by comparison with Donnus's original projection. Gastaldi as usual changes Ptolemy's coverage, but not significantly in this map. The map is somewhat more simplified than usual as to names, with a greater reduction in the Ptolemaic names, although, oddly, Gastaldi includes about a dozen names not in Ptolemy, listed by Marinelli (1881, 103, no. 517). It should be noted, regarding this statement, that Gastaldi, in all his ancient Ptolemaic maps in the 1548 Ptolemy, always draws the maps in more fluid style than in the originals, regularly introducing more curvature to features than in most earlier Ptolemy editions, sometimes including series of light undulations in coasts which are generally straighter on the Ptolemaic maps. Bad or good, this is simply his style. Borri, who in my opinion is focused a little too strongly on minutae in his cartobibliography of maps of Italy, details a number of these stylistic changes, and, evidently on the basis of this, begins his comments with the observation: "The peninsula, on the whole, shows a completely different conformation with respect to preceding Ptolemaic maps [of Italy]," an interpretation which seems to me quite incorrect and misleading. Incidentally, Gastaldi sometimes introduces such unwonted undulations of coastlines in various modern maps as well, throughout his career, which could be perhaps considered as a general stylistic defect.

References:
Marinelli, 1881, 103 (no. 517); Borri, 1999, 42-43 (no. 31).

Reproductions:
Bifolco and Ronca, 2018, 1: 107.
https://www.davidrumsey.com/luna/servlet/detail/
RUMSEY~8~1~291283~90063011

17. Italy (modern)
-Venice, 1548
-Copper engraving, 12.5 x 17.0 cm., on one sheet
-No scale bar

At the top of the map:
ITALIA NOVA TAVOLA (MODERN MAP OF ITALY)

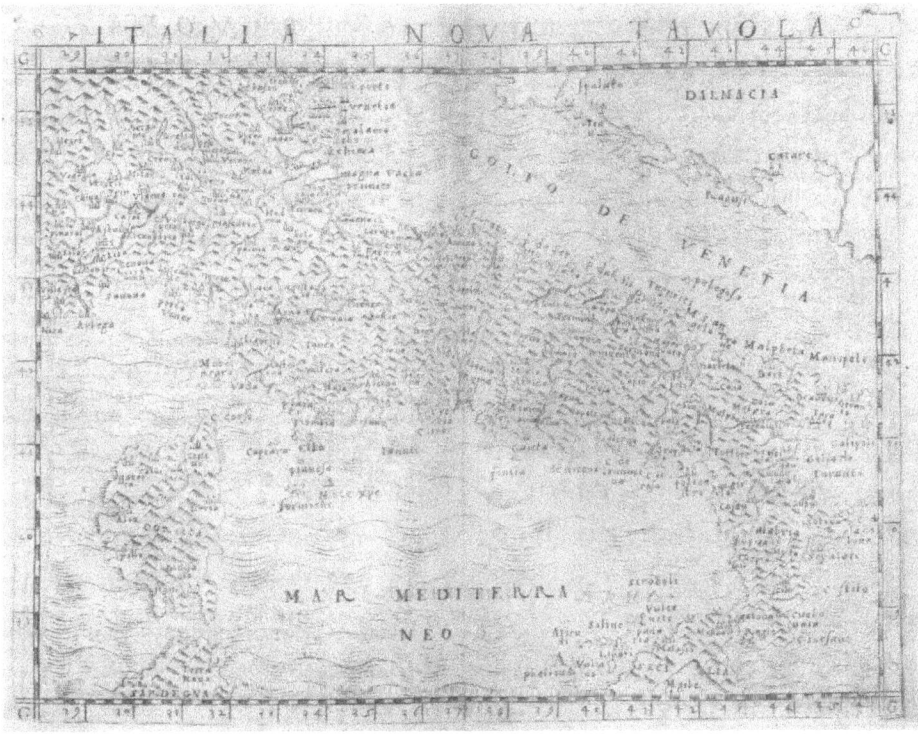

17 Italy (modern) 1548 Rumsey

Comments:
Graduated in twelve-minute increments, with each whole degree numbered, in latitude and longitude, from 38°00' to 45°24' N, and from 28°00' to 46°00' E, on the rectangular projection prescribed by Ptolemy for regional maps (cf. entry no. 5). Gastaldi's map of Italy is a poor one. Indeed it is one of the poorest maps in the Ptolemy, and overall one of the poorest maps of Italy produced to date, although it is not poor in all respects. The relative

placement of locales in the interior, and the hydrography, are reasonably good, though no better than that. But in two important broad points, Gastaldi here errs widely. Firstly, the longitudinal length of the peninsula (measured from Nice to Otranto, as seems to be customary among Italian historians of cartography), is approximately eighteen degrees. Ptolemy's length of ca. fifteen degrees was also too long, but it was much closer to the correct figure of twelve degrees. Secondly, while the axis of the peninsula, which can only be measured approximately, improves over Ptolemy, it is still much too far from reality (Ptolemy: ca. seventeen degrees south of east; Gastaldi 1548: ca. twenty-four degrees south of east; actual: ca. forty-eight degrees south of east), and several earlier cartographers do better. What accounts for this bad showing I do not know, nor has anyone else raised the question, other than to note that Gastaldi evidently made no use of portolan charts here (Biasutti, 1908, 29; Almagià, 1929, 16a, and 1961, 248), and this must surely be true, considering the poor picture presented. But why did he not? We know well that Gastaldi used portolan charts extensively in his work at least as early as 1545 with his Sicily, and probably in 1544 with his Spain. Could the Italy be one of the first maps he made, sometime between ca. 1542 and 1544, and could Gastaldi not yet have grasped the great value of these charts in mapping? All is a bit inscrutable here. In any event, as we have noted, Gastaldi is not about Italy, but about the far continents. There his brilliance comes through, even if it fades sharply close to home, as we shall see it do once again in our next entry below, the map of Piedmont. Thirteen years later, In his 1561 map, Gastaldi greatly improves his picture of Italy (no. 101)

Beginning in 1908, a notion began to take hold in the literature which could offer some exoneration for Gastaldi as regards this 1548 Italy, but it is not overly convincing in the eyes of this writer. In that year, it came to the attention of Biasutti that an anonymous 1554 map of Italy titled "Italia Nuova", much larger than Gastaldi's 1548 map was a virtually perfect cognate of the 1548 map, except for its much larger size (1908, 30; actually, Biasutti's map was of 1558; but Almagià found an edition of 1554, still the earliest known, as well as six later editions, one of which is Biasutti's edition, as see Almagià, 1929, 16a and Perini, 1996, 30). Giving no explanation whatsoever for the idea, Biasutti stated as fact that the larger, later map was a copy of some presumed earlier map, by an unknown cartographer, made originally before 1548, and that Gastaldi's 1548 map was a copy of that map as well. Now, while it is true, as any cartographer knows, that reducing a larger map to smaller size (generalization), losing some detail, is a much more common procedure than the opposite one, where a larger map is made from a smaller one, with more detail then added in, this certainly does not amount to some kind of law, and we can be sure that instances of the latter must exist. Given the simple facts that we have at hand, that is assuredly not an illogical assumption here. In our opinion, it is quite possible that the anonymous maker of the 1554 map, titled "Italia nuova", simply enlarged Gastaldi's 1548 Italy, making changes and additions gleaned from other maps. Nevertheless, Biasutti's idea has been repeated to the present day as if it were an established fact, as in Lago (1992, II, 165, at fig. 4), Borri (1999, 43, no. 32), Lago (2002, 276-77), and others. Indeed, it may well of course be true. But it has not been definitely established, as one author has acknowledged (Perini, 1996, 30), and Caraci too simply implies, more cautiously, that there is uncertainty as to whether the depiction is Gastaldi's (Ascari and Caraci, 1942-43, 210 [Caraci]). Incidentally, even if taken as true, Biasutti's idea does not fully exonerate Gastaldi in any event, since, in choosing the model, he would be endorsing it as acceptable. No discussion exists of the sources or mode of construction of either the 1548 or 1554 map, but one last observation is to the point and should be made. On Gastaldi's 1546 map of the Danube lands (no. 4), there is more than enough of the Italian peninsula on the map to show immediately that the peninsula's axis there is almost exactly correct! To be sure, there are mysteries here.

References:
Marinelli, 1881, 103 (no. 518); Biasutti, 1908, 29-33; Almagià, 1929, 16 and 24; Ascari and Caraci, 1942-43, in 1942 part, 25-26; Almagià, 1961, 248-49, 264 and 265-66; Lago, 1992, II, 165; Borri, 1999, 43-44 (nos. 32 and 33); Lago, 2002, 250 and 276-77.

Reproductions:
Bifolco and Ronca, 2018, 1: 108.

https://www.davidrumsey.com/luna/servlet/detail/
RUMSEY~8~1~291285~90063013

18. Piedmont (modern)
-Venice, 1548
-Copper engraving, 12.5 x 17.0 cm., on one sheet
-No scale bar

Along the top of the map:
PIAMONTE NOVA TAV (MODERN MAP OF PIEDMONT)

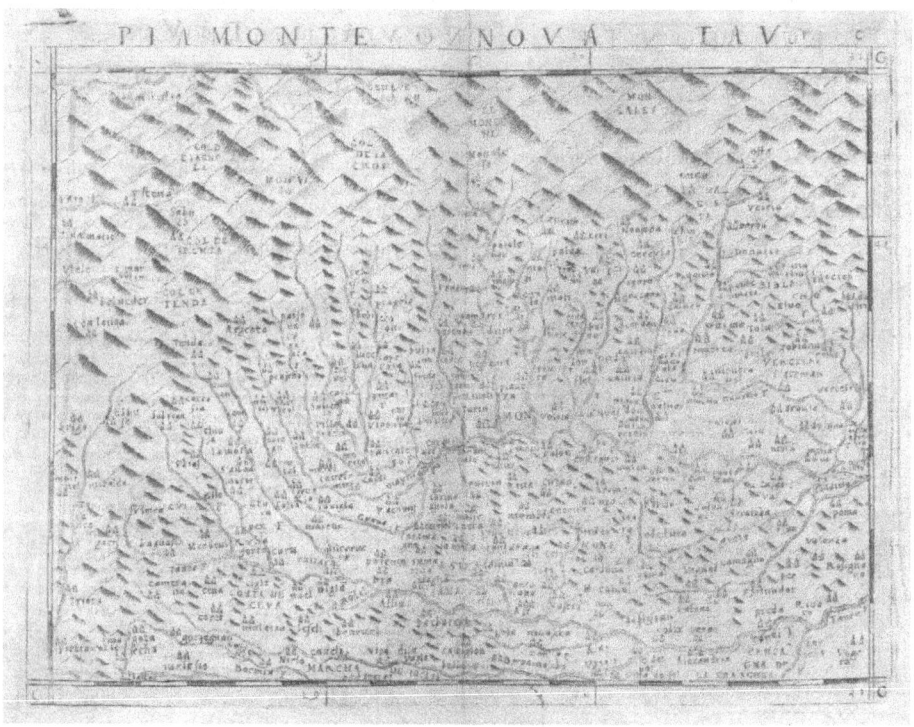

18 Piedmont (modern) 1548 Rumsey

Comments:
Graduated in ten-minute increments (as opposed to 12, as on most of the
Ptolemy maps), with each whole degree numbered, in latitude and longitude,
from 43°00' to 44°22' N, and from 28°00' to 31°00' E, on the rectangular
projection. Until 1925, when Almagià found an older Piedmont, a ca.

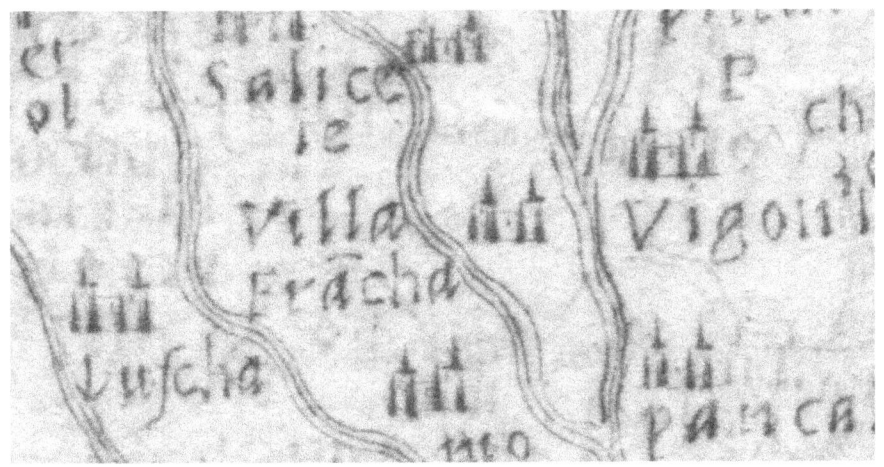

18 Piedmont (modern) 1548, detail showing Villafranca, Gastaldi's birthplace.

1538/39 undated woodcut by Pagano (Almagià, 1925), this map was thought to be the oldest map of Piedmont. Of Gastaldi's map, Milanesi doesn't hesitate to state bluntly that it is one of the worst representations of Piedmont of all time, due mainly to an extreme orientational error in which the many confluents of the Po are shown generally running north and south instead of close to east and west as they should, with the effect that this large part of the map gives the impression of having been simply turned counter-clockwise through ninety degrees, and a similar effect is seen in the orography of the area (Almagià, 1914-15, 3-4; Sereno, 2002, 319; Pressenda, 2002, 322; Milanesi, 2002, II, 17). The source of this great error is unknown. Most writers declare that the map has no connection with Gastaldi's 1555 Piedmont (Almagià, 1929, 16; and 1948, 25; Lavis-Trafford, 1950, 38; Perini, 1996, 41), but Pressenda says it has more in common with the 1555 map than Almagià says (Pressenda, 2002, 32b). Nevertheless, in the 1555 map, the orientation of the Po confluents is very much improved, and in the 1561 Italy and the 1570 Lombardy, they are shown generally correctly. The coordinates on the map are *not* like those of the 1555 map, and come from an unknown source (Milanesi, 2002, II, 17; Sereno, 2002, 319), though Gastaldi returns to Ptolemaic key-coordinates in the later 1555 Piedmont (Biasutti, 1908, 25 nt. 1).

514

As to sources, Biasutti (1908, 33) and Almagià (1914-15, 4; and 1929, 24) simply say that it is from an unknown larger earlier map. But Pressenda (2002, 322) says rather quizzically that one cannot support this idea of the map's being from a source unknown to us without more evidence (cit., 322), evidently implying that perhaps it's compiled from sources we know. Sereno in fact says its hydrography and orography (though evidently not as to their orientation) are reminiscent of that in Agnese (Sereno, 2002, 319). Almagià says that it is *not* from the ca. 1538/39 Pagano map, and Umek (2002, 536) says it is definitely not from the Vescovile atlas in Padua, mentioned in entry no. 4. I would note that, while off-hand, these facts would seem to suggest that Gastaldi in his early years in Piedmont must have had no interest in mapping, since he seems not to know the geography of his homeland, it doesn't necessarily mean that he had no interest yet in cosmography, for we know that his main interest in this area as evinced in later years had to do with far places, and such an interest would not necessarily exclude ignorance of one's local area. Nevertheless, we see in many ways in these modern maps in the 1548 Ptolemy that Gastaldi was still something of a novice to mapping proper. But this is not true as regards many of the modern maps in the Ptolemy, and we know that Gastaldi produced four excellent maps, our nos. 1-4, at the time he was working on the modern maps for the Ptolemy. There is a degree of contradiction here, but probably the answer lies in two things. Firstly, the worst of the modern maps for the book were made early, ca. 1542-1544, after which things improved; and, secondly, Gastaldi probably simply had access to better sources for some areas than for others.

References:

Biasutti, 1908, 25 nt 1, and 33; Almagià, 1914-15, 3-5, 7-8, and 14; Almagià, 1929, 16 and 24; Almagià, 1948, 25; Lavis-Trafford, 1950, 38; Capello, 1952, 119; Perini, 1996, 40-41; Pressenda, 2002; Sereno, 2002, 219; Milanesi, 2002, 1, 13 and II, 16-17.

Reproductions:

Bifolco and Ronca, 2018, 1: 108.
https://www.davidrumsey.com/luna/servlet/detail/
RUMSEY~8~1~291287~90063015

19. Treviso province (modern)
-Venice, 1548
-Copper engraving, 12.5 x 17.0 cm., on one sheet
-No scale bar

Along the top edge of the map:
MARCHA TREVISANA NOVA TAVOLA (MODERN MAP OF THE
MARCH OF TREVISO)

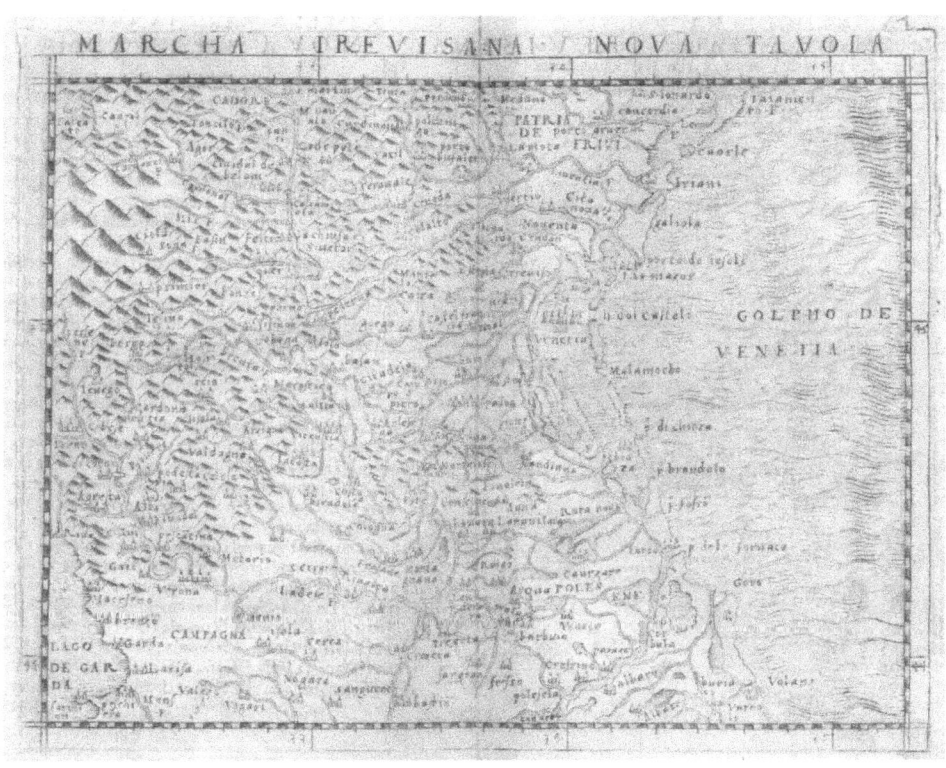

19 Treviso province (modern) 1548 Rumsey

Comments:
Graduated in two-minute increments, with each whole degree numbered, in
latitude and longitude, from 43°48' to 45°42' N, and from 32°00' to 35°18' E,
on a rectangular projection. A much larger scale map than most in the
modern map series of the 1548 Ptolemy, it covers part of the Veneto ca. forty

kilometers north and south of Venice and perhaps sixty-five kilometers west of it. There are some divergences, a few notable, in the complex cluster of hydrography and islands immediately surrounding Venice between this map and the 1561 Italy (no. 101); indeed, Almagià says that there is little similarity in general between the area as depicted here and on the Italy, and even less as to the 1570 Lombardy (1929, 30a). All in all, a mediocre map, the worst of the Italian regional maps in the Ptolemy, according to Almagià (1929, 18b). As to its source, Biasutti simply stated that it was unknown to him (1908, 33). Almagià opined that it did not seem to derive from a larger original map of the area, but seemed to have been extracted from a map, probably manuscript, covering a larger area, perhaps a map of Italy (1929, 18b and 24a). This certainly accords with the later finding by Umek that it was obviously very similar to the same area on the Vescovile atlas (see entry no. 4), and probably derived from it or both derived from a common source (Umek, 2002, 520, 521, 522 and 533). In conclusion, we should mention that there is an article by Assunto Mori (1919) on a ca. mid sixteenth century manuscript map of the area, though not covering the southern parts of the Gastaldi map, found on a flyleaf of a copy of the 1511 Venice Ptolemy by Sylvanus in the library of the Italian Geographical Society. The map has a touch of elegance and was clearly drawn by someone with cartographic skills. Mori reproduces it at p. 222.

References:
Marinelli, 1881, 103 (no. 519); Biasutti, 1908, 33; Almagià, 1929, 18b, 24a and 30a; Umek, 2002, 520, 521, 522, 533 and 536.

Reproductions:
Bifolco and Ronca, 2018, 1: 108.
https://www.davidrumsey.com/luna/servlet/detail/
RUMSEY~8~1~291289~90063017

20. The Marches (modern)
-Venice, 1548
-Copper engraving, 12.5 x 17.0 cm., on one sheet
-No scale bar

Along the top border of the map:
MARCHA DE ANCONA NOVA (MODERN MAP OF THE MARCHES)

20 The Marches (modern) 1548 Rumsey

Comments:
Graduated in twelve-minute increments, with each full degree numbered, in
latitude and longitude, from 43°00' to 44°12' N, and from 35°00' to 39°00' E,
on the usual rectangular projection prescribed by Ptolemy (cf. entry 5). This
is an attractive and well-executed little map, perhaps the best of the Italian
regional maps in the book. As to its sources, Olinto Marinelli noted over a
century ago that it appeared virtually identical to a much larger 1565 F.

Bertelli map, *NOVO ET VERO DISSEGNO DELLA MARCA DI ANCONA CON LI SVI CONFINI* (39.0 x 26.5 cm.), which is reproduced in Bella, 1986, 91 (no. 83) and in Meurer, 2004, 67 (no. 53), and he came to the conclusion that both maps stemmed from a presumed map earlier than the 1548 Ptolemy, and of larger dimensions, like the Bertelli (Marinelli, 1902, 132-34). This hypothesis was accepted as conclusive by Almagià (1929, 19a, 24a, and 31a; 1948, 91; and 1960, 11-12), and later by Bella (1986, 91, no. 83). But Mangani simply states that the 1548 Gastaldi map was the first map of The Marches, though it is clear from his bibliography that he is familiar with Marinelli's work and the three cited Almagià works (Mangani, 1992, 14). Likewise Meurer (2004, 67, no. 53), speaking of the 1565 Bertelli, simply states that it "can be traced back to a map which was designed by Giacomo Gastaldi for the 1548 edition of Ptolemy." Finally, Umek (2002, 533) notes that the 1548 map is very close in depiction to the Vescovile atlas, which we have spoken of in entry no. 4, and is also very close to the depiction on the latter map as well. He also notes that the area covered by the 1548 map corresponds to one of the twenty sheets of the Vescovile atlas (2002, 536), a fact which is untrue of the 1565 Bertelli. The Gastaldi map, though smaller, also contains some features not on the Bertelli, and applies different names to rivers (Almagià, 1929, 31a). Thus, Marinelli's idea, identical to that of Biasutti in regard to our no. 17 (Gastaldi's 1548 Italy), loses considerable credibility. (Biasutti was perhaps inspired in his notion by that of Marinelli, whom he cites (1908, 33).) The 1565 Bertelli was in my opinion developed from the rendition of Gastaldi's map in Ruscelli's 1561 edition of Ptolemy, or the 1562 or 1564 edition, all with the same maps. The 1565 Bertelli map and a 1592 reprinting are the only later editions of this map that I know of, for which see Marinelli (1902). In general, very few of the 1548 Ptolemy maps were reprinted, except, of course, in the later editions of Ptolemy which use them, beginning with Ruscelli's mentioned edition of 1561.

References:
Marinelli, 1902, 130-33; Almagià, 1929, 19a, 24a and 31a; Almagià, 1948, 90-91; Almagià, 1960, 111-12; Bella, 1986, 91 (no. 83); Mangani, 1992, 14 and 29; Umek, 2002, 533 and 536; Meurer, 2004, 67, no. 53.

Reproductions:
Bifolco and Ronca, 2018, 1: 108.
https://www.davidrumsey.com/luna/servlet/detail/
RUMSEY~8~1~291291~90063019

21. Sardinia and Sicily (Ptolemaic)
-Venice, 1548
-Copper engraving, 12.5 x 17.0 (14.0) cm., on one sheet
-No scale bar

Along the top border of the map:
TABVLA EVROPAE VII (SEVENTH MAP OF EUROPE)

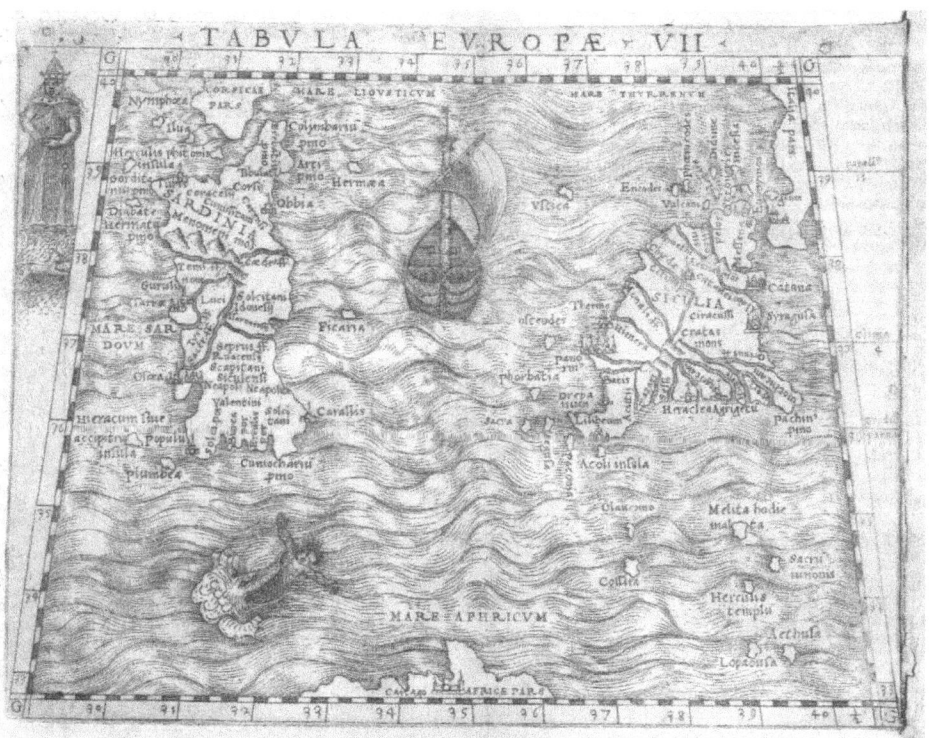

21 Sardinia and Sicily (Ptolemaic) 1548 Rumsey

Comments:
Graduated in twelve-minute increments, with each whole degree numbered, in latitude and longitude, from 32°48' to 40°00' N, and from 29°00' to 40°30' E, on a trapezoidal projection. As always in the Ptolemaic maps, there are fewer details and fewer names than in the Ptolemaic originals due to the reduced size, and thus scale. But Gastaldi, following Münster, has made some additions not found in the fifteenth century redactions of Ptolemy with which I am familiar. He has extended Ptolemy's coverage to the south by two degrees, and included the northern tip of Tunisia, and also Malta and seven neighboring islands: Glauconis (the Cittadella on the island of Gozo), Cossyra and Larunesiae (both have been identified as today's Pantellaria), Lopadusa (Lampedusa), and Aethusa (Linosa).

Reference:
Tooley, Bricker and Crone, 1989, 58.

Reproductions:
Bifolco and Ronca, 2018, 1: 108.
https://www.davidrumsey.com/luna/servlet/detail/
RUMSEY~8~1~291293~90063021

22. Sardinia and Sicily (modern)
-Venice, 1548
-Copper engraving, 12.5 x 17.5 cm., on one sheet
-No scale bar

Along the top border of the map:
SICILIA SARDINIA NOVA TABVLA (MODERN MAP OF SICILY [AND] SARDINIA)

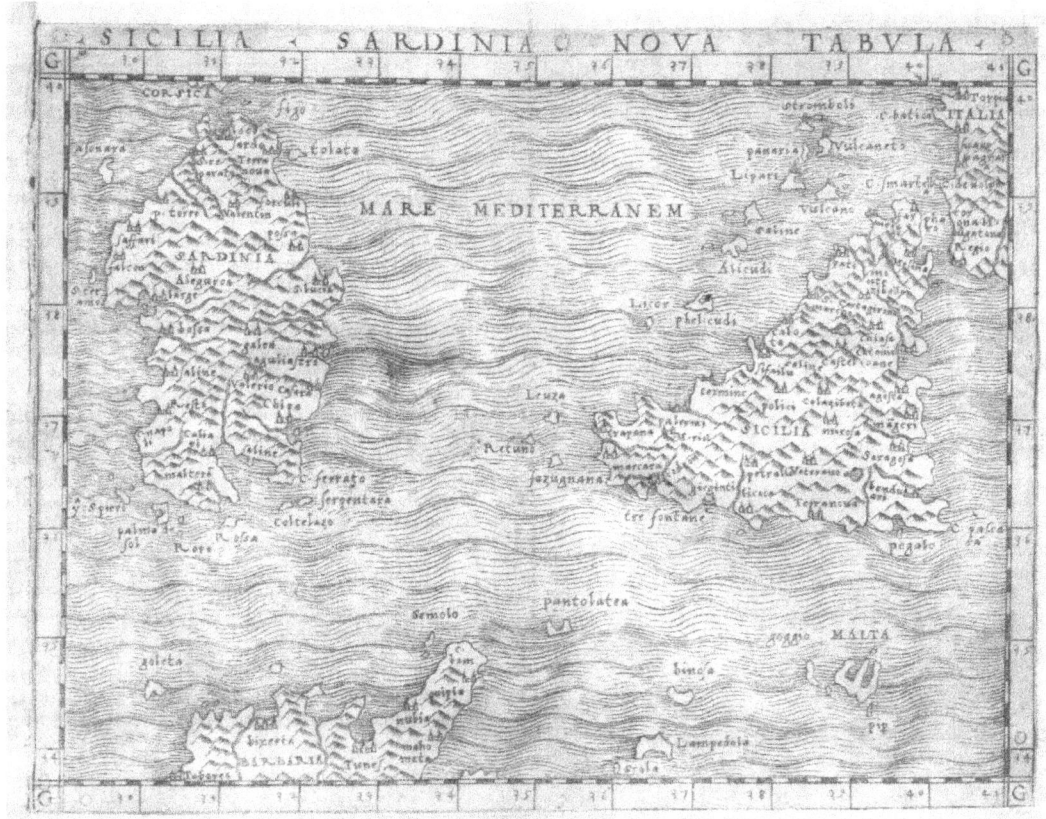

22 Sardinia and Sicily (modern) 1548 Rumsey

Comments:

Graduated in twelve-minute increments, with each whole degree numbered, in latitude and longitude, from 33°48' to 44°00' N, and from 29°00' to 41°00' E, on the usual rectangular projection of Ptolemy. Islands were always a special problem, as regards coordinates, until a much later time. Latitudes in fact could be arrived at with greater accuracy than usually thought, but, if I am not mistaken, these were rarely if ever attempted by cartographers, but by astronomers for astronomical or astrological purposes, and the expertise needed to do this well seems not yet to have filtered from the community of astronomers to that of cartographers. There exist hints that perhaps these methods were beginning to be used among a few mapmakers of northern Europe, but I have found no sign that such may have been the case by this time in southern Europe. No more eloquent evidence of this could be found than in a modern map such as this one, where we find Sardinia and Sicily almost exactly east and west of each other in a single grid, while in fact they do not coincide in latitude at any point, and even the southernmost tip of Sardinia is well over a half degree north of the northernmost tip of Sicily. The picture presented, in this regard, is one of stark unreality. Gastaldi, as he did on the Ptolemaic map of Sardinia and Sicily (no. 21), takes the depiction considerably south of the two islands, showing the northern point of Tunisia, and also showing Malta, but here the number of islands is closer to actuality than in no. 21; however, he shows the main island quite differently than in his depiction on the Ptolemaic map or from actuality, giving it an odd three-pronged shape.

As to the individual islands, Di Vita says that Sicily is sort of a hybrid, with modern elements, but more of Ptolemy (1905, 760). Biasutti simply says that it is from non-Gastaldian sources (1908, 33), which is a little unclear, and that there must have been in the sixteenth century some maps of Sicily very close to what he calls "the Ptolemaic layout of the Gastaldi type", for we find it in other maps, before and after Gastaldi, of which he gives a few examples (1908, 35, with note 3), while he later just states that it represents a type which is "archaic and incorrect" (1920, 418). Almagià says that it has no relation to previous products, and is very interesting, because it "is a first timid attempt to improve Ptolemy's coordinates on the basis of portolan charts" (1929, 23a and 24a). But Gastaldi preserves Ptolemy's coordinate data for Messina and is close to Ptolemy for the island's three corners, though not in both coordinates, but only for one. Then, within this skeletal "grid", he has tried to follow the nautical charts (1929, 23a). Inland, there is little, and there are some enormous errors (cit., 23a). It is hard to get a clear picture of things from these rather disconnected and sometimes contradictory observations, but it would seem that Gastaldi has adopted, partially, some Ptolemaic coordinate data, and then proceeded following the sea charts; and as to the interior, nothing seems definitely known, except that it contains the mentioned large errors. The map must have been made before the 1545 individual map of Sicily (no. 2), for that map is incomparably better.

For Sardinia, Almagià says that it follows, both as to the coast and coastal nomenclature, older manuscript sea charts of the fifteenth and early sixteenth century, and notes that all depictions of Sardinia from the first three quarters of the sixteenth century are poor (1929, 22b and 24b). He notes that there are only four inland names, and the orography is arbitrary (22b). Piloni (1974, no. 21) simply repeats Almagià. I have found no further information than this on Gastaldi's picture of Sardinia.

References:
Di Vita, 1905, 760; Biasutti, 1908, 33 and 36; Biasutti, 1920, 418; Almagià, 1929, 22b, 23a, 24a, 32a; Piloni, 1974, no. 21.

Reproductions:
Bifolco and Ronca, 2018, 1: 108.
https://www.davidrumsey.com/luna/servlet/detail/
RUMSEY~8~1~291295~90063023

23. Poland and eastern Europe from the Baltic coast south to the Black Sea (Ptolemaic)
-Venice, 1548
-Copper engraving, 12.5 x 17.0 (13.0) cm., on one sheet
-No scale bar

23 Poland and eastern Europe from the Baltic coast south to the Black Sea (Ptolemaic) 1548 Rumsey

Along the top border of the map:
TABVLA EVROPAE VIII (EIGHTH MAP OF EUROPE)

Comments:
Graduated in twelve-minute increments, with each whole degree numbered, in latitude and longitude, from 46°36' to 63°00' N, and from 42°00' to 73°00' E, on a trapezoidal projection. Here again Gastaldi has made additions which do not occur in the fifteenth century redactions of the Ptolemaic maps which I have inspected, although they do occur in Münster's 1540 Ptolemy, and that is no doubt Gastaldi's source here. The additions consist of a large tract of land in the Baltic Sea titled "DACIAE ET NORBEGIAE PARS", and being a continuation of the land "DACIA" in map no. 12, although its outline does not quite meet up correctly with the landform in map 12, and, to the east of this substantial land mass a large island, "GOTHI INSVLA". I do not know what the original source for these lands might be, but one can safely assume that it was not Münster, and that the comments made here in our no. 12 concerning the land DACIA on that map will apply here as well. Other than this, the map seems essentially the same as Ptolemy's, except, of course, for the usual reduced number of place names due to the Gastaldi map's smaller scale.

Reference:
Spekke, 1948, 50.

Reproductions:
Bifolco and Ronca, 2018, 1: 109.
https://www.davidrumsey.com/luna/servlet/detail/
RUMSEY~8~1~291297~90063025

24. Prussia and Livonia (modern)
-Venice, 1548
-Copper engraving, 12.5 x 17.0 cm., on one sheet
-No scale bar

Along the top border of the map:
PRVSSIA E LIVONIA NOVA (MODERN PRUSSIA AND LIVONIA)

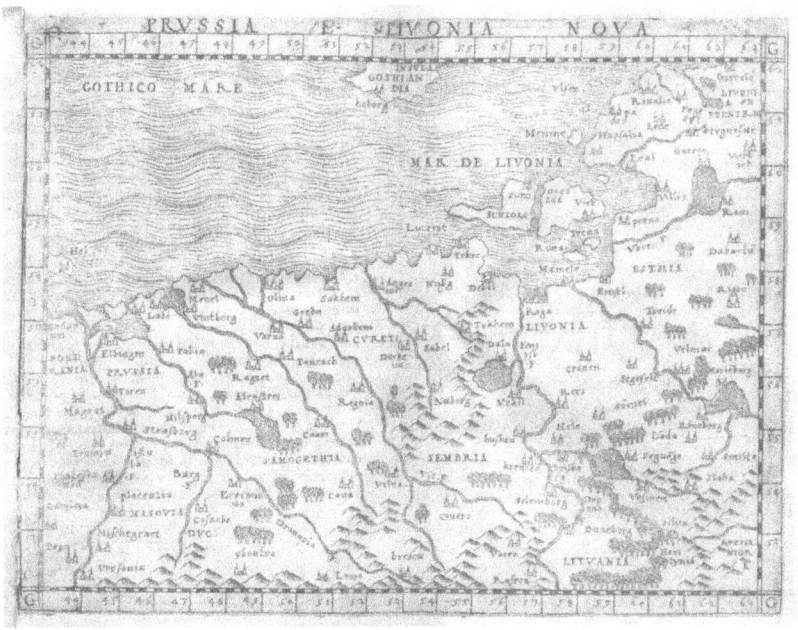

24 Prussia and Livonia (modern) 1548 Rumsey

Comments:

Graduated in twelve-minute increments, with each whole degree numbered, in latitude and longitude, from 52°00' to 62°00' N, and from 43°00' to 63°00' E, on the usual trapezoidal projection. On the Gastaldi map, as on other maps of the time, no clear distinction is made between Prussia and Livonia. Almagià, first to mention this "noteworthy" map, as he referred to it, said that he did not know its sources (1934, 145). Only in 1982 did Jäger make any investigation. According to him, the coastal features are based on the Cusanus-Eichstädt (1491) map as in the modern Livonia and Germany, etc., map in the 1507 Rome edition of Ptolemy, and Livonia is from the 1539 Olaus Magnus map (Jäger, 1982, 66), and the earlier quite limited observations of Spekke (1948, 50) and Bagrow (1975, 88a), do not contradict this, as far as they go. Kret's implication that it was based on Münster is quite wrong (Kret, 1978, 94-95). Although Gastaldi in his Ptolemy has taken some verbal commentary from Münster, and has made some adjustments after Münster in a number of the original Ptolemaic maps, none of the

Gastaldi Ptolemy's modern maps, much more important than the Ptolemaic maps, draw on Münster's modern maps, a fact we mention here often. See also our general comments to the Gastaldi-Ptolemaic maps at entry no. (5.-64.).

References:
Almagià, 1934, 145; Spekke, 1948, 50; Bagrow, 1975, 88a; Kret, 1978, 94-95; Jäger, 1982, 66, 251, 299.

Reproductions:
Bifolco and Ronca, 2018, 1: 109.
https://www.davidrumsey.com/luna/servlet/detail/
RUMSEY~8~1~291299~90063027

25. Scandinavia (modern)
-Venice, 1548
-Copper engraving, 12.5 x 17.0 (12.5) cm., on one sheet
-No scale bar

Along the top border of the map:
SCHONLADIA NOVA (MODERN SCANDINAVIA)

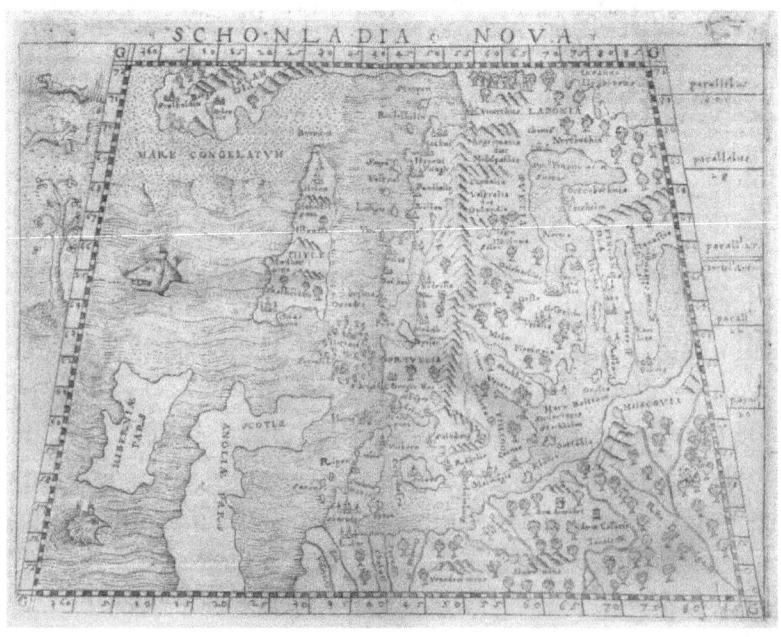

25 Scandinavia (modern) 1548 Rumsey

Comments:

Graduated in five-minute increments, with each whole degree numbered, in latitude, from 54°00' to 73°00' N, and in whole degree increments in longitude, from 5°00' W to 85°00' E. The projection is not rectangular as in all the other modern maps of the Ptolemy, but trapezoidal, for, with a latitude spread of nineteen degrees, it is not possible to arrive at the very reasonable approaches to correctness as to changes in the proportion between lengths of degrees of latitude and longitude which can be attained when the total latitudinal span covered is relatively small. Gastaldi should have used this projection in his continental depictions, Africa and America, but for some reason used the rectangular projection, probably because both of those maps cross the equator, and Gastaldi was disconcerted by the harsh break in geometrical form which occurs at the equator when using the trapezoidal form.

As to the sources of the Scandinavia map, all have unanimously stated that it was taken from Jacob Ziegler's 1532 map of Scandinavia and the North (Nordenskiöld, 1883, 31; Michow, 1907, 13; Bjørnbo, 1912, 243; Bagrow, 1928-30, 1, 117; Spekke, 1948, 47 and 50; Lister, 1970, 88; Harald Sigurðsson, 1971, 263; and Bagrow, 1975, 1, 88). The Ziegler map is reproduced in Nordenskiöld (1889, 57). However, Michow says it was insignificantly changed, and Bagrow (1975) says there were changes in the southeast corner. In fact, while it is very clear at a glance that, although the style of drawing is different, and Gastaldi has rather increased the convergence of meridians over that in Ziegler's map, which is also on a trapezoidal projection, Ziegler's map is certainly the source for Gastaldi's as regards its principal area, Scandinavia proper. It is nevertheless also clear that in the peripheral areas Gastaldi has indeed made considerable changes and additions, especially in the land mass in the northwest corner, and in the form of the British Isles. Harald Sigurðsson's observation that Münster, in his 1540 map after Ziegler, inadvertently transposed the names of Iceland (Islandia) and Thule (Thyle), and that Gastaldi repeats this error after Münster, is incorrect. Münster's Scandinavia map does not even show Iceland under any name. The transpositional error seems to be Gastaldi's own. As a final notice, no one has checked for any signs of influence from the account in Ramusio's volume three (1967-1970 edition, 150v-155v;

Milanesi edition, 1978-1988, 4, 47-98) of the voyage of Piero Quirino to northern Norway in 1431. There is a lengthy article on this voyage and account by Giuseppe Pennesi in the *Bollettino della Società Geografica Italiana*, 22 (1885), 812-35.

References:
Nordenskiöld, 1883, 31; Michow, 1907, 13; Bjørnbo, 1912, 243; Bagrow, 1928-30, II, 117; Spekke, 1948, 47 and 50; Lister, 1970, 88; Harald Sigurðsson, 1971, 263; Bagrow, 1975, 1, 88.

Reproductions:
Bifolco and Ronca, 2018, 1: 109.
https://www.davidrumsey.com/luna/servlet/detail/
RUMSEY~8~1~291301~90063029

26. Most of Southeast Europe (Ptolemaic)
-Venice, 1548
-Copper engraving, 13.0 x 17.0 (12.5) cm., on one sheet
-No scale bar

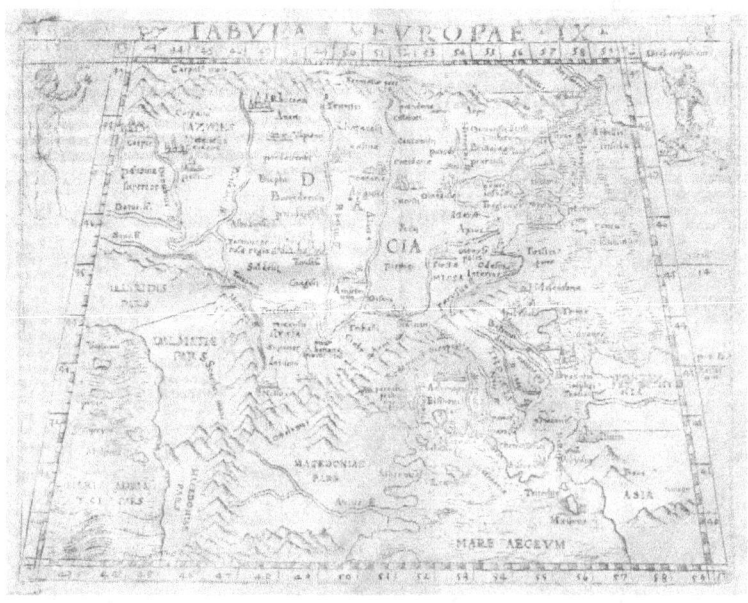

26 Most of southeast Europe (Ptolemaic) 1548 Rumsey

Along the top border of the map:
TABVLA EVROPAE IX (NINTH MAP OF EUROPE)

Comments:
Graduated in twelve-minute increments, each whole degree numbered, in latitude and longitude, from 39°00' to 49°00' N, and from 42°00' to 59°00' E, on a trapezoidal projection. Here Gastaldi follows Ptolemy faithfully, except of course for the usual loss of some detail and place names due to the reduction in scale.

Reference:
Gordeev, 2006, 123 (no. 109).

Reproductions:
Bifolco and Ronca, 2018, 1: 109.
https://www.davidrumsey.com/luna/servlet/detail/
RUMSEY~8~1~291303~90063031

27. Poland and Hungary (modern)
-Venice, 1548
-Copper engraving, 12.5 x 17.0 cm., on one sheet
-No scale bar

Along the upper border of the map:
POLONIA ET HUNGARIA NOVA TABVLA (MODERN MAP OF POLAND AND HUNGARY)

Comments:
Graduated in twelve-minute increments, with each whole degree numbered, in latitude and longitude, from 43°00' to 54°00' N, and from 42°00' to 59°00' E, on the usual rectangular projection prescribed by Ptolemy for regional maps. Originally, Almagià had said (1934, 145) that it was taken from Münster's 1540 map of Poland and Hungary, itself based on a 1526 woodcut by Berenard Wapowski. Almagià later repeating the claim, while adding that it could have been copied from the original Wapowski instead (1939, *carta,*

27 Poland and Hungary (modern) 1548 Rumsey

16 nt. 39). But Banfi noticed that the Gastaldi map is much richer in detail than the Münster rendition, and said it was thus probable that it was from the original Wapowski (1947, 30), and finally Bagrow stated without reservation that it is from the original Wapowski (Bagrow, 1975, 1, 88). But the Wapowski map itself is known only through fragments discovered in 1932 (Schnayder, 1972, 76).

References:
Almagià, 1934, 15-16; Almagià, 1939, *carta*, 15-16; Banfi, 1947, 29-30; Bagrow, 1975, 88; Gordeev, 2006, 124 (no. 110).

Reproductions:
Bifolco and Ronca, 2018, 1: 109.
https://www.lithuanianmaps.com/images/
1548_Gastaldi_polonia_et_hungaria_raremaps.jpg

28. Greece (Ptolemaic)
-Venice, 1548
-Copper engraving, 12.5 x 17.1 (14.0) cm., on one sheet
-No scale bar

Along the top border of the map:
TABVLA EVROPAE X (TENTH MAP OF EUROPE)

28 Greece (Ptolemaic) 1548 Rumsey

Comments:
Graduated in ten-minute increments, with each whole degree numbered, in latitude and longitude, from 33°36' to 42°06' N, and from 43°00' to 56°00' E, on a trapezoidal projection. Though simplified, as usual, occasionally almost to the point of schematization, the map is generally faithful to Ptolemy's original.

Reproductions:
Bifolco and Ronca, 2018, 1: 109.

https://www.davidrumsey.com/luna/servlet/detail/
RUMSEY~8~1~291307~90063035

29. Greece (modern)
-Venice, 1548
-Copper engraving, 12.5 x 17.0 cm., on one sheet
-No scale bar

Along the top border of the map:
GRAETIA NOVA TABVLA (MODERN MAP OF GREECE)

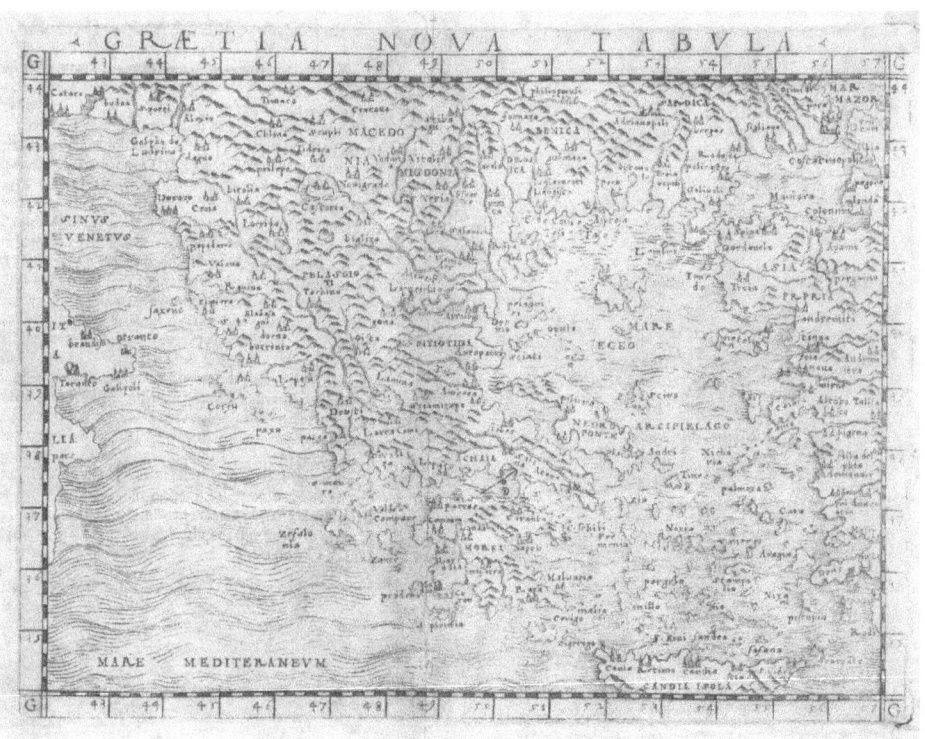

29 Greece (modern) 1548 Rumsey

Comments:
Graduated in twelve-minute increments, with every whole degree numbered,
in latitude and longitude, from 34°00' to 44°00' N, and from 42°00' to 57°00'
E, on the usual rectangular projection prescribed by Ptolemy for regional

maps (cf. entry 5). While this map is not remotely as good as Gastaldi's 1560 Greece (no. 95) and has no relation to it, it is nevertheless better than the Nicolò Sophianus map of pre-1543 which doesn't survive, although various later reprints of it occur often in the Veneto-Roman atlases. Bonacci (1905, 825) said there must have been an earlier map of larger format of which Gastaldi's map is a reduction, and Almagià later said the same (1914, 611), although he then continued to speak of the map in terms implying that it is a Gastaldi production proper. He says that the coast follows sea charts, and that Gastaldi has introduced some features of notable interest, though he doesn't specify them. The orography is arbitrary, but the hydrography better, and Gastaldi, he says, has evidently introduced some places based on contemporary information (1914, 611). At one point, Almagià states that Gastaldi has accepted some Ptolemaic coordinates for cities, "from which he has attempted or believed himself to have been attempting to thus find the correspondence with modern localities" (611). The reservation expressed in the words "or believed himself to have been attempting" is well founded, perhaps more well founded than Almagià realized. For if Almagià is correct about Gastaldi's intentions here, Gastaldi could perhaps have tried such a procedure on the basis of latitudes alone, but certainly not longitudes, for the level of uncertainty as regards longitudes, especially absolute longitudes, was very high at the time. Thus, there could be little hope for success in any procedure as that which Almagià suggests Gastaldi was perhaps following. As to the earlier map Bonacci and Almagià suggest Gastaldi began from, the most likely possible candidates would probably be Waldseemüller's modern map of Greece in the supplement to his 1513 Ptolemy (Karrow, 1993, 580, no. 80/42), or Coppo's maps of Greece of 1520 and 1524-26 (Karrow, 1993, 120, no. 21/12; and 121, no. 21/30), but the maps in Waldseemüller's supplement are in want of interior details, and were no doubt taken from portolan charts (Nordenskiöld, 1889, 70a). Furthermore, Coppo's maps are known only in manuscript, which certainly lowers the likelihood that Gastaldi would have known them. In general, the question of the sources of Gastaldi's 1548 modern Greece must be considered as unresolved and problematical.

References:
Bonacci, 1905, 825-26; Almagià, 1914, 610-11 and 619 nt. 1.

Reproductions:
Bifolco and Ronca, 2018, 1: 110.
https://www.davidrumsey.com/luna/servlet/detail/
RUMSEY~8~1~291309~90063037

(30.-38.) The Africa Maps in the Gastaldi 1548 Ptolemy

There are nine Africa maps in the Ptolemy, the original four Ptolemaic maps
and five modern maps. The greatest number of modern maps in any previous
Ptolemy had been two, in Waldseemüller's 1513 edition, and, while these
were much larger maps, they omitted much of the northeast part of the
continent, while Gastaldi's modern Africa maps cover the whole continent.
The Waldseemüller maps also lacked almost all interior detail, and of course,
they were very outdated by Gastaldi's time, when much new information was
available. Just as Almagià first noticed for the European maps in the
Ptolemy, Biasutti first noticed that the five modern Africa maps also do not
all fall within a single coordinate net (Biasutti, 1920, 406), and we have
discussed in chapter seven this attribute of indifference to consistency in this
and other regards in Gastaldi's work, which characterized all his cartography
until the end of his life. Was Gastaldi already using Ramusian materials,
which loom so large in his great continental maps of 1559-64 when he made
the extra-European maps for his Ptolemy? My assumption is that he would
have been, except of course materials which Ramusio had not obtained yet.
Biasutti, however, considered that he made no use of Ramusio's materials in
the Africa maps (1920, 406-07), and specifically states that he did not use the
account of Leo Africanus, the most important of all Ramusio's Africa
narratives (1920, 408 and 416). But Milanesi says that he *did* make use of
Leo Africanus in the Africa maps (Milanesi, 1984, 83). Nordenskiöld stated
that in the interior Gastaldi's Africa maps are still "chiefly based on Ptolemy"
(1897, 132b), but I suspect he had in mind here principally the Nile and its
tributaries. Much more work needs to be done in this area to reach a
definitive conclusion. Not surprisingly, as will be seen in the individual

entries, the Africa maps have received much less attention from scholars than the Europe maps. Some discussion of the 1548 Africa maps in general, though not individually, can be found in Biasutti (1920, 406-07, 408, 416-17 and 433).

30. Upper northwestern Africa (Ptolemaic)
-Venice, 1548
-Copper engraving, 12.5 x 17.0 (13.0) cm., on one sheet.
-No scale bar

Along the top border of the map:
TABVLA APHRICAE I (FIRST MAP OF AFRICA)

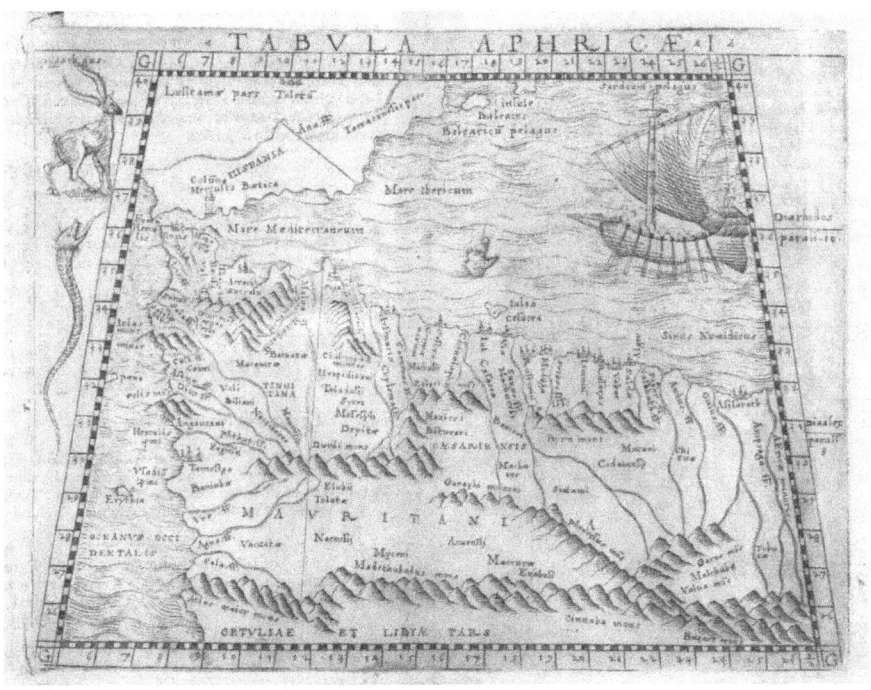

30 Upper northwestern Africa (Ptolemaic) 1548 Rumsey

Comments:
Graduated in twelve-minute increments, with each whole degree numbered, in latitude and longitude, from 25°00' to 40°00' N, and from 5°00' to 26°30' E, on a trapezoidal projection. Gastaldi follows Ptolemy faithfully in this map,

and there is less simplification and loss of detail and names than usual, simply because the original Ptolemaic map is much less dense in detail in the first place than is the case with the Ptolemaic maps of Europe.

Reproductions:
Bifolco and Ronca, 2018, 1: 110.
https://www.davidrumsey.com/luna/servlet/detail/
RUMSEY~8~1~291311~90063039

31. Northwest Africa (modern)
-Venice, 1548
-Copper engraving, 12.5 x 17.0 cm., on one sheet
-No scale bar

Along the top border of the map:
MAVRITANIA NOVA TABVLA (MODERN MAP OF MAURITANIA)

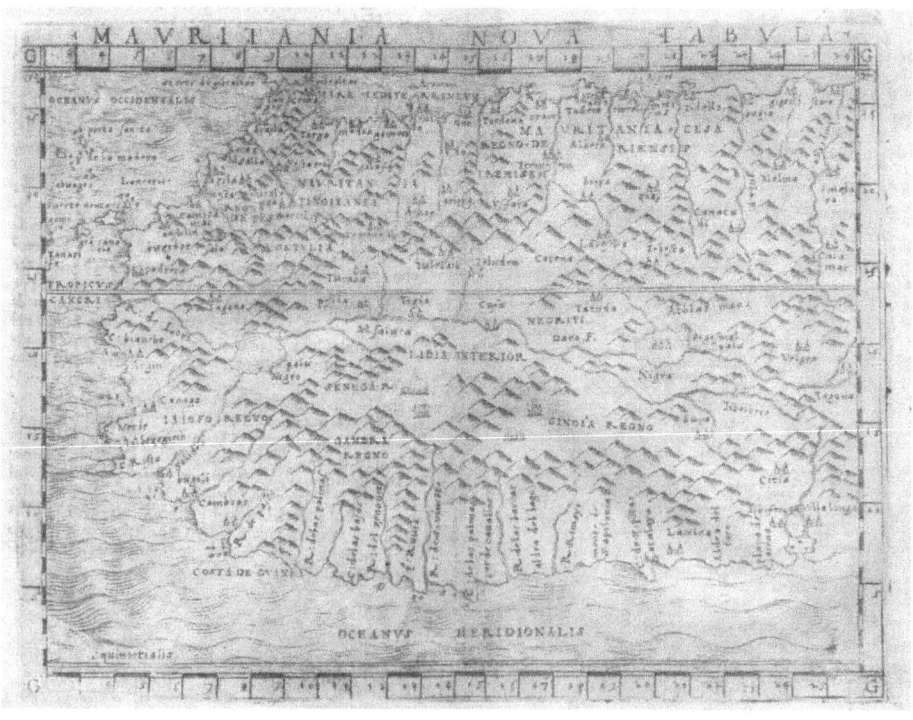

31 Northwest Africa (modern) 1548 Rumsey

Comments:
Graduated in full degrees in latitude and longitude, with every fifth latitude degree numbered, and each longitude degree numbered; from 0°00' to 37°30' N, and from 2°00' to 26°00' E, on a rectangular projection. Though all the Canary Islands appear to be shown, the prime meridian is clearly to be taken as running two degrees west of the map, as is evident from the longitude markings. It is placed about six degrees further west on the great 1564 map of Africa (no. 118). Gastaldi has probably used portolan charts for the coast, but for the coastal names may have also made use of Waldseemüller 1513. Some Ramusian information was probably used for the interior. Without doubt, Gastaldi's giant map of Africa (see the end of chapter ten), never published at the time, presuming it had been begun by the time work on this map was started, was a major source. But, as to the interior, we must make no mistake, other than a tiny handful of scattered inland features gleanable from Waldseemüller or perhaps from some portolan chart, *no information that the scholarly world knows of to date existed at the time other than that in Ramusio's accounts.* As to textual sources that we do not know of, they are extremely unlikely, for if Gastaldi knew of such sources, Ramusio would have as well, and they would be in Ramusio's volume one.

Reference:
Tooley, 1967?, p. 70, no. W7.

Reproductions:
Bifolco and Ronca, 2018, 1: 110.
https://www.davidrumsey.com/luna/servlet/detail/
RUMSEY~8~1~291313~90063041

32. North Central Africa (Ptolemaic)
-Venice, 1548
-Copper engraving, 12.5 x 17.0 (13.0) cm., on one sheet.
-No scale bar

Along the top border of the map:
TABVLA APHRICAE II (SECOND MAP OF AFRICA)

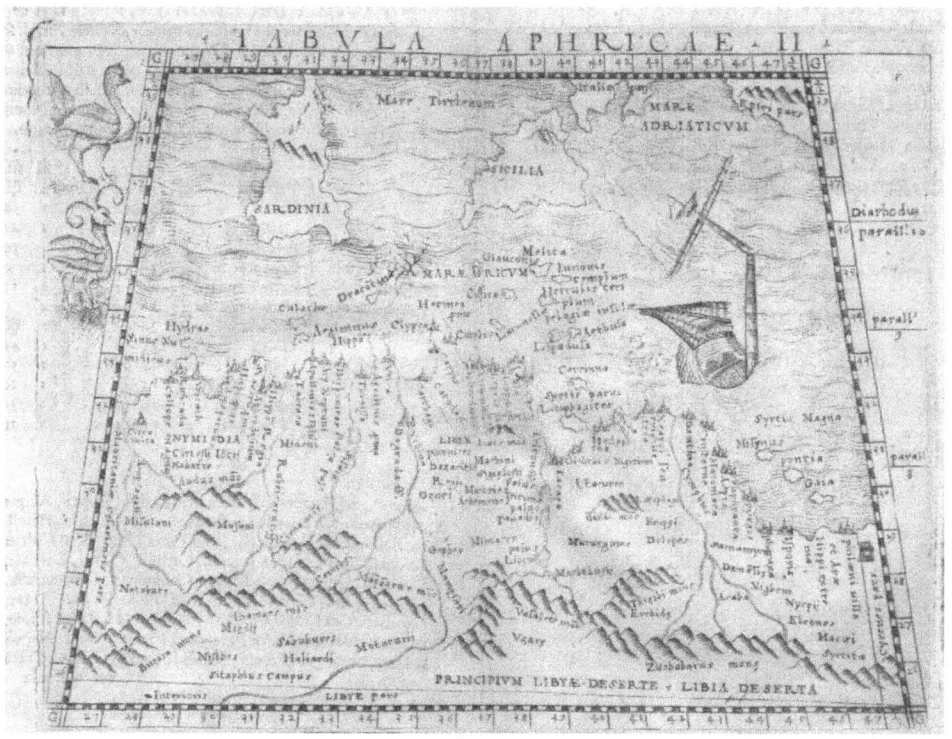

32 North Central Africa (Ptolemaic) 1548 Rumsey

Comments:
Graduated in twelve-minute increments, with each whole degree numbered, in latitude and longitude, from 25°00' to 39°30' N, and from 26°00' to 47°30' E, on a trapezoidal projection. Gastaldi follows Ptolemy faithfully in this map, and, as in the previous Ptolemaic map, there is little loss due to reduction in map size, since the Ptolemaic original is relatively sparsely detailed.

Reproductions:
Bifolco and Ronca, 2018, 1: 110.
https://www.davidrumsey.com/luna/servlet/detail/
RUMSEY~8~1~291315~90063043

33. North Central Africa (modern)
-Venice, 1548
-Copper engraving, 12.5 x 17.0 cm., on one sheet
-No scale bar

Along the top border of the map:
AFRICA MINOR NOVA TABVLA (MODERN MAP OF AFRICA MINOR
[NORTH CENTRAL AFRICA])

33 North Central Africa (modern) 1548 Rumsey

Comments:
Graduated in full degrees in latitude and longitude, numbered every fifth
degree for latitude, and at every degree for longitude, from 5°00' to 35°00' N,
and from 26°00' W to 47°00' E, on the usual rectangular projection. It
basically covers most of Algeria, most of Libya, and all of Tunisia. Part of
Ethiopia is shown, which is far too north and west and should not be on this
map at all. Gastaldi has taken liberties here with the ratio of the length of a
degree of latitude to longitude (as he did also in no. 31). His degrees of

latitude are shorter by comparison to his degrees of longitude, resulting in the ratio, or proportion, being just about the inverse of what it should be, and we find this on all the modern Africa maps in the 1548 Ptolemy, although we do *not* find it in the modern maps of Asia or America in the Ptolemy. It results in a regular distortion across the depiction, in which east-west distances are larger than they should be in relation to north-south distances. Now, Gastaldi does this also in his great 1564 Africa (no. 118), as we have pointed out in the text, and it would seem that the only rationale for this in the 1564 map was that it was the only way that he could fit all of Africa into a standard landscape type of frame. But on the regional maps this consideration does not apply. However, it *would* apply as regards the giant map of Africa of which we have spoken elsewhere (see map no. 31 above) which Gastaldi was making at the time. These facts would seem to provide pretty certain evidence that this African regional map was copied directly from the giant map, without changing the projection, and that that map was in a fairly advanced state of preparation, probably being held by Gastaldi in hopes of further information, which in fact would come, principally in the account of João de Barros in ca. 1553. Otherwise, it is hard to find a rationale for the appearance of the distorting latitude-longitude ratio on this regional map. The coasts of the giant Africa were presumably taken from portolan charts, while the interior could only have been from Ramusian information, for, as noted in the previous entry, there was no other modern information of note available on this interior. It is interesting to note that in the Mediterranean Gastaldi again shows the odd three-pronged Malta of map no. 22.

Reproductions:
Bifolco and Ronca, 2018, 1: 110.
https://www.davidrumsey.com/luna/servlet/detail/
RUMSEY~8~1~291317~90063045

34. Egypt, with eastern Libya (Ptolemaic)
-Venice, 1548
-Coppper engraving, 12.5 x 17.0 (14.0) cm., on one sheet
-No scale bar

Along the top border of the map:
TABVLA AFRICAE III (THIRD MAP OF AFRICA)

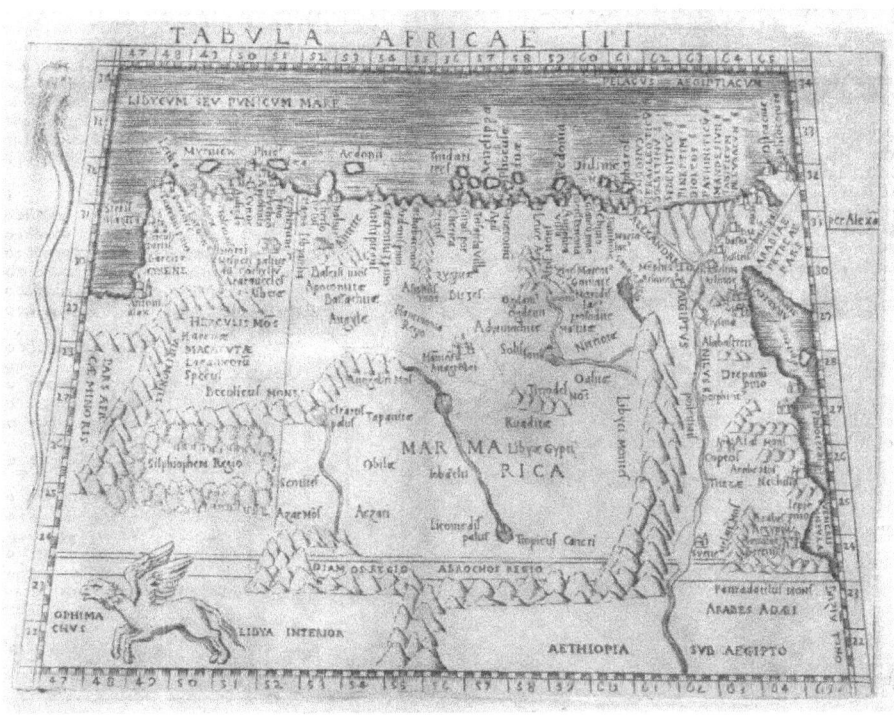

34 Egypt, with eastern Libya (Ptolemaic) 1548 Rumsey

Comments:
Graduated in twelve-minute increments, with each full degree numbered, in latitude and longitude, from 21°00' to 34°00' N, and from 46°00' to 65°00' E, on a trapezoidal projection. Gastaldi extends Ptolemy's coverage in latitude one and a half degrees both north and south, following Münster. Otherwise, Gastaldi here follows Ptolemy faithfully, except that he has removed one limb of Ptolemy's forestry in the southwest part of the map. Again, while Gastaldi has simplified somewhat due to smaller size, in the majority of

areas, he retains most detail, for, except on the coast, detail is sparse in the original Ptolemaic map.

Reproductions:
Bifolco and Ronca, 2018, 1: 110.
https://www.davidrumsey.com/luna/servlet/detail/
RUMSEY~8~1~291319~90063047

35. Marmarica (Egypt and eastern Libya) (modern)
-Venice, 1548
-Copper engraving, 12.5 x 17.5 cm., on one sheet
-No scale bar

Along the top border of the map:
MARMARICA NOVA TABVLA (MODERN MAP OF MARMARICA)

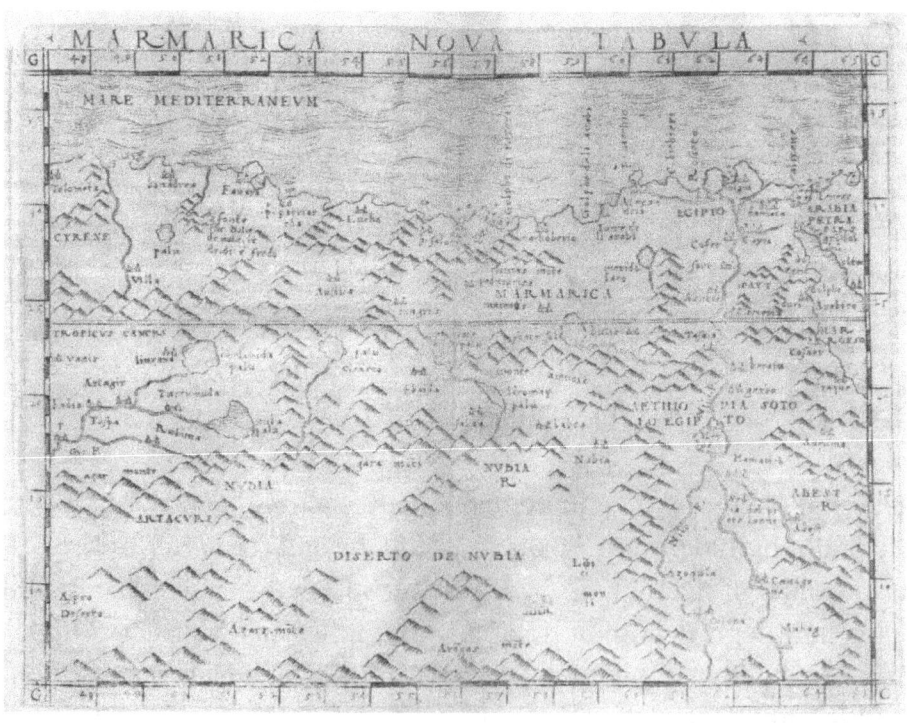

35 Marmarica (Egypt and eastern Libya) (modern) 1548 Rumsey

Comments:
Graduated in whole degrees, in latitude and longitude, each fifth degree of latitude being numbered, and each degree of longitude numbered, from 5°00' to 37°00' N, and from 47°00' to 65°00' E, on a rectangular projection. The map exhibits the same peculiar ratio of the length of a degree of latitude to a degree of longitude as in no. 33, and in all of the 1548 Ptolemy modern Africa maps, and the explanation for this will be the same as in no. 33. The name Marmarica is a very vaguely used name with variant interpretations, though often it seems to be used to refer to the middle to western littoral of Egypt. Usage was possibly different in Gastaldi's time. The map basically covers Egypt and eastern Libya. It was no doubt taken from Gastaldi's own developing giant map of Africa, itself probably from sea charts for the coasts, and Ramusian accounts for the interior. An interesting feature is that in the text on the recto of the left half of the map, Gastaldi speaks about this upcoming giant map of Africa (Biasutti, 1920, 416; the passage is quoted and translated in full in chapter ten, though it was still in manuscript at the time and would not be printed until near the end of his life, some sixteen years later (no. 118 below). Gastaldi speaks of this pending large Africa once more, in the text to map. no. 38 below, q.v.

Reference:
Biasutti, 1920, 416.

Reproductions:
Bifolco and Ronca, 2018, 1: 111.
https://www.davidrumsey.com/luna/servlet/detail/
RUMSEY~8~1~291321~90063049

36. Nile Delta area (modern)

-Venice, 1548
-Copper engraving, 13.0 x 17.5 cm., on one sheet
-No scale bar

Along the top border of the map:
AEGYPTUS NOVA TABVLA (NEW MAP OF EGYPT)

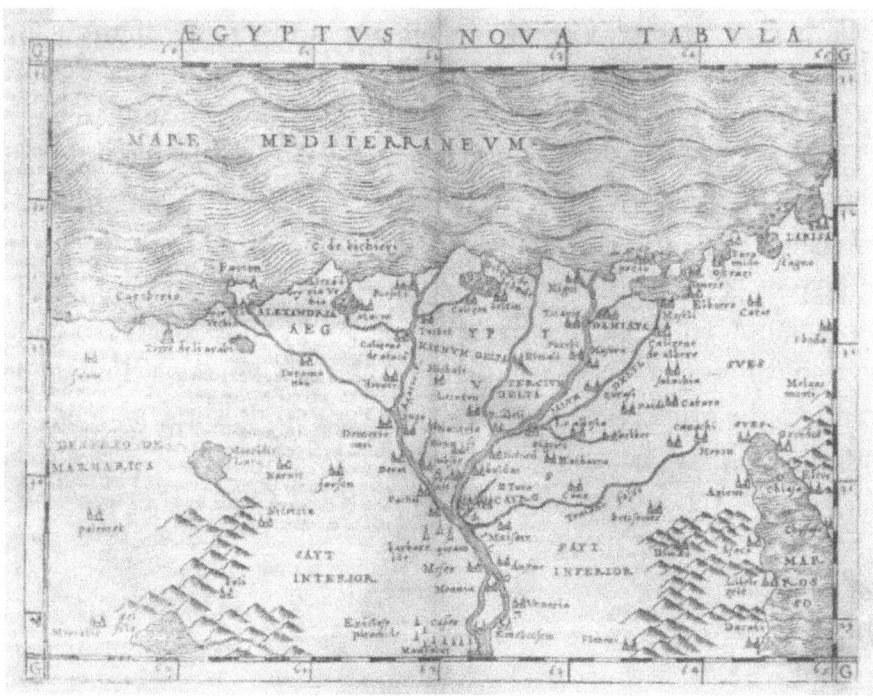

36 Nile Delta area (modern) 1548 Rumsey

Comments:

Graduated in twelve-minute increments, with each whole degree numbered, in latitude and longitude, from 28°42' to 33°00' N, and from 59°00' to 65°00' E, on a rectangular projection. The area coverage is much smaller than in the other Africa maps, and reflects a special importance given to the area for a Venetian, for much trade was carried on between the Republic and the delta area, especially Alexandria. The same area is included in its entirety, though on much smaller scale, in the previous map, no. 35. Jacob Ziegler had made a rough woodcut of the area in 1532, which occurred in a work, *Qua Intus*

Continentus Syria, etc. (Strassburg, 1532) along with seven other maps, among them the map of Scandinavia which Gastaldi used for his 1548 "Schonlandia nova" (no. 25) (Biasutti, 1920, 337; Karrow, 1993, 608, no. 86/16). Nordenskiöld referred to the Ziegler map, along with the others, as a clumsy woodcut of no special interest, but Biasutti considers that Gastaldi used this map as a basis for the present map.

Reference:
Biasutti, 1920, 337-38.

Reproductions:
Bifolco and Ronca, 2018, 1: 111.
https://www.davidrumsey.com/luna/servlet/detail/
RUMSEY~8~1~291323~90063051

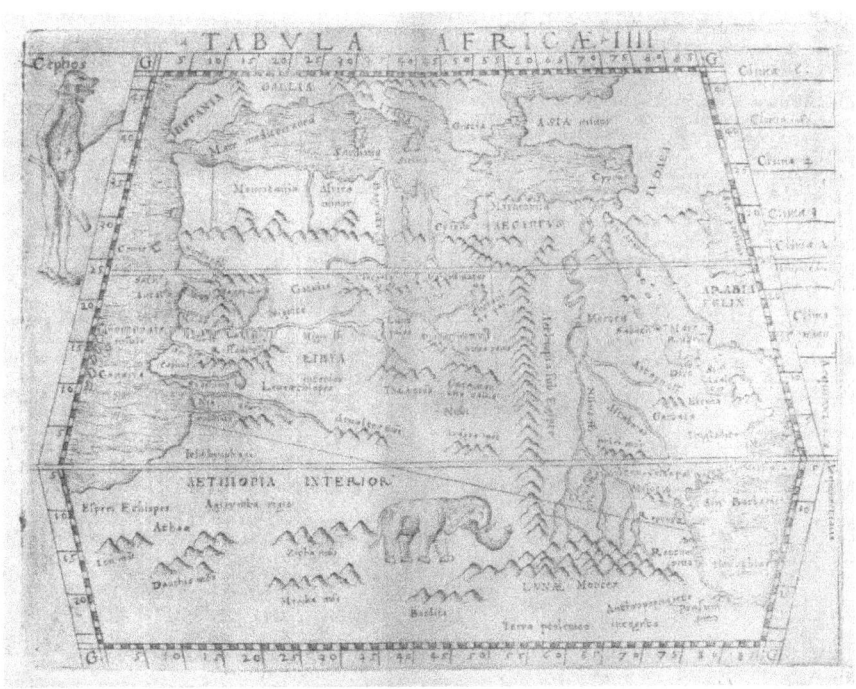

37 Northern half of Africa (Ptolemaic) 1548 Rumsey

37. Northern half of Africa (Ptolemaic)
-Venice, 1548
-Copper engraving, 12.5 x 16.5 (12.0) cm., on one sheet
-No scale bar

Along the top border of the map:
TABVLA AFRICAE IIII (FOURTH MAP OF AFRICA)

Comments:
Graduated in whole degrees, numbered at every fifth degree, in latitude and longitude, from 26°30' S to 47°00' N, and from 0°00' to 85°00' E, on a trapezoidal projection. Gastaldi increases Ptolemy's latitudinal coverage a full ten degrees to the north, and approximately ten degrees to the south, following Münster. Since the map crosses the equator, the picture results in two trapezoids, visually producing a mildly disconcerting effect, and evidently an effect which did not appeal to Gastaldi, for the projection would have been better than the rectangular projection used in his later great maps which cross the equator, his ca. 1560 America (no. 94) and 1564 Africa (no. 118). Gastaldi does use the trapezoidal projection on his 1554 Africa in Ramusio (our no. 77/Betz, 2007, no. 4), and it is used occasionally by cartographers for Africa at least until 1697 and probably later (Betz, 2007, nos. 5, 7, 10, 12, 15, 16, 20, 23, 37, 40, 42, 43, 44, 95, 121, 125, 134, 143, 146, 149, 155, and 167), although most used more suitable curvilinear projections. In fact, on any regional map covering a very large area, as Gastaldi's Africa or America, a curvilinear projection is best, but Gastaldi was apparently not adept at using curvilinear projections on maps other than world maps, and, in fact, such usage seems to have been in its infancy in Gastaldi's time. The only example I am aware of offhand being Mercator's 1554 Europe, though there may well be others. The present map shows all the areas on the other three Ptolemaic Africa maps, on much smaller scale, plus a large area to about fifty degrees further south. Except for the mentioned extension in coverage, Gastaldi generally follows Ptolemy faithfully, including his depiction of the Fortunate Islands as running directly north and south, a depiction which deserves a brief comment. This is the only map on which Ptolemy shows these Fortunate Isles, or Isles of the

Blessed, generally taken as corresponding to our Canary Islands, and Ptolemy nominally ran his prime meridian through this supposedly north-south island group. Of course, in reality, these islands do not run north and south, but generally east and west through over four degrees of longitude. Thus, although many modern historians of cartography, including the present one, have often spoken as a matter of course of a supposed Ptolemaic-based prime meridian "running through the Canary Islands" in a fifteenth or sixteenth century context, the statement makes no sense. A prime meridian must be a line only. Where in this four-degree span is this ethereal prime meridian supposed to be? While some are more specific, and single out the western-most Canary as the prime meridian island, there exists no justification for this off-hand assumption in the literature, since the notion stems in a vague and indefinite way from Ptolemy, and, since Ptolemy's Fortunate Isles run straight north and south, he of course nowhere says anything of his prime meridian running through the western-most island. There was no western-most island.

Reproductions:
Bifolco and Ronca, 2018, 1: 111.
https://www.davidrumsey.com/luna/servlet/detail/
RUMSEY~8~1~291325~90063053

38. Southern Africa (modern)
-Venice, 1548
-Copper engraving, 12.5 x 17.5 cm., on one sheet
-No scale bar

Along the top border of the map:
AFRICA NOVA TABVLA (MODERN MAP OF AFRICA)

Comments:
Graduated in whole degrees, numbered at every fifth degree, in latitude and longitude, from 40°00' S to 10°00' N, and from 30°00' to 85°00' E, on a rectangular projection. The map is of tremendous interest, for here we have the first Gastaldi map in which he is working almost entirely outside of the

38 Southern Africa (modern) 1548 Rumsey

area of Ptolemy's Ancient *ecumene*. Everything south of ten degrees south latitude falls outside of Ptolemy's limits, and thus of course the cartography is *ipso facto* modern. Gastaldi here first enters his element, the non-Ptolemaic world. It is true that we don't know the order in which Gastaldi made the maps for the Ptolemy, so it is quite possible that some other map or maps in the book which fall outside the *ecumene* actually preceded it, and there is the giant Africa upon which Gastaldi was working, but this is long lost to us, although it is safe to consider it as the first stage in a series of work-ups which eventually resulted in the 1564 Africa that we know (no. 118 below). In any event, the present map is the first non-Ptolemaic area map in the Ptolemy edition itself. It has not been studied. As to sources, we can in general presume the usual, sea charts for the coasts, and Ramusian data for the inland, though most likely taken at second hand so to speak from the giant Africa that Gastaldi was working on, and of which he speaks a second time (see no. 35 for the first time) in the text on the recto of the left side of this map (Biasutti, 1920, 416; the passage is quoted and translated here in full in the section at the end of chapter ten (pp. 360-61)).

549

References:
Biasutti, 1920, 416; Tooley, 1967, 62, no. 57.

Reproductions:
Bifolco and Ronca, 2018, 1: 111.
https://www.davidrumsey.com/luna/servlet/detail/
RUMSEY~8~1~291327~90063055

(39.-57.) The Asia Maps in the 1548 Ptolemy

There are nineteen Asia maps in the Ptolemy, twelve Ptolemaic maps, and seven modern maps, while the greatest number of modern Asia maps in any previous Ptolemy had been three, in the 1513 Waldseemüller Strassburg Ptolemy, and the only one to go beyond the Near East in Waldseemüller was his "Indiae", stopping very much short of Gastaldi's farthest east. The Waldseemüller maps were also much out of date by Gastaldi's time, for the Portuguese had made many new discoveries; they also showed virtually no interior detail, of which there is much in Gastaldi's 1548 Asia maps. As mentioned in chapter three, there are two more non-Ptolemaic maps in Fries's 1522 Ptolemy, but they are copied directly from the 1492 Behaim globe, made before the great Portuguese discoveries in the Far East had taken place. In the Asia modern maps, Gastaldi is once again attempting to arrive at a net of coordinates in which the ratio between the length of degrees of longitude and degrees of latitude are kept approximately correct, unlike his peculiar procedure in the Africa maps. As with the Africa maps, the question of how much Ramusian material Gastaldi was using remains uncertain, and will so remain until true studies of the individual maps have been made. As we shall see, as with the Africa maps, much less has been done by comparison with the modern maps of parts of Europe. The maps are the forerunners of the great Gastaldi depictions of Asia in 1559-1561, even if they are small and rather primitive by comparison.

39. Anatolia (Ptolemaic)
-Venice, 1548
-Copper engraving, 12.5 x 17.0 (12.0) cm., on one sheet.
-No scale bar

Along the top border of the map:
TABVLA ASIAE I (FIRST MAP OF ASIA)

39 Anatolia (Ptolemaic) 1548 Rumsey

Comments:
Graduated in twelve-minute increments, with each whole degree numbered, in latitude and longitude, from 35°00' to 46°30' N, and from 54°00' to 73°00' E, on a trapezoidal projection. Gastaldi generally follows Ptolemy faithfully in this map, although the simplification, and loss of detail and toponymy is more severe than usual, for Ptolemy includes a great many names for this area.

Reference:
Gordeev, 2006, 120 (no. 106).

Reporductions:
Bifolco and Ronca, 2018, 1:111.
https://www.davidrumsey.com/luna/servlet/detail/
RUMSEY~8~1~291329~90063057

40. Anatolia (modern)
-Venice, 1548
-Copper engraving, 12.5 x 17.0, on one sheet
-No scale bar

Along the top border of the map:
NATOLIA NOVA TABVLA (MODERN MAP OF ANATOLIA)

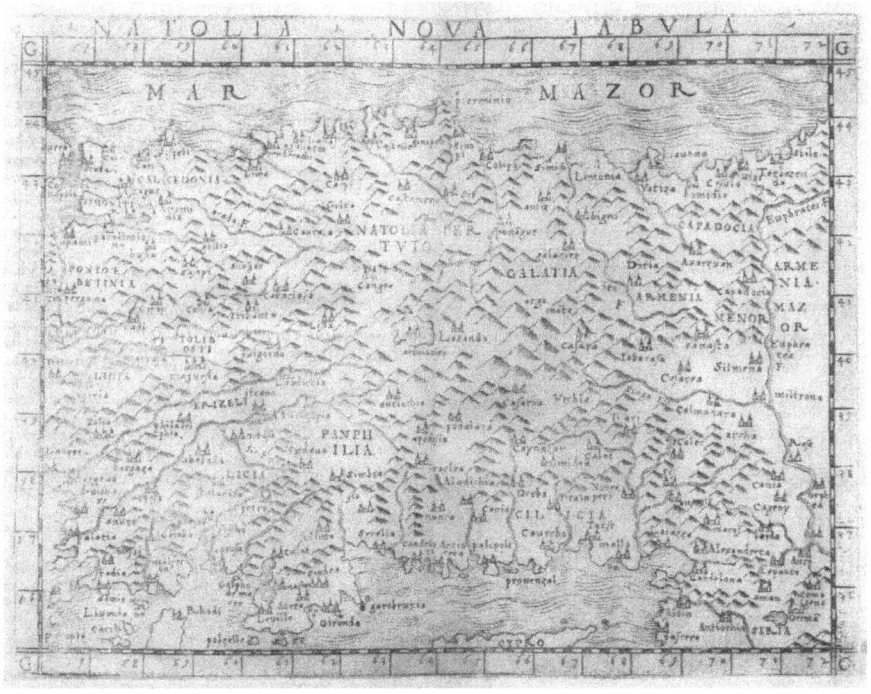

40 Anatolia (modern) 1548 Rumsey

Comments:

Graduated in twelve-minute increments, with each whole degree numbered, in latitude and longitude, from 35°00' to 45°00' N, and from 56°00' to 72°00' E, on the rectangular projection prescribed by Ptolemy for regional maps (cf. no. 5). The map basically makes a good impression, except that a small sliver of Anatolia runs off the edge of the map in the west. But as to its accuracy or sources, nothing has been written, although the usual formula, sea charts and possibly some Ramusian material, very probably played a role. However, for this large corner of Asia, Ramusio does not have a great deal to offer, and there must have been some other sources as well. As to possible maps which Gastaldi may have used, the most likely known candidates would be a large map of the country by Waldseemüller in the supplement to his 1513 Ptolemy (Karrow, 1993, 580, no. 80/45), though that is short on interior details, and Honter's 1542 map of Anatolia, almost exactly the same size as Gastaldi's map (Karrow, 1993, 309, no. 41/17.1), but I have attempted no comparisons. In general, while in Ptolemy's time, the area seems to have been well-known, in the sixteenth century, only the Mediterranean, Aegean, and Black Sea ports, that is, the littoral, would have been important to Venice as trading points. As to the rather vast interior, it mostly seems to have been off the beaten path, and, as close as it is to Europe, Ramusio, as said, does not seem to have been able to gather much information, even though he has substantial material on all lands surrounding the country. Perhaps it was the frequent tensions between the Ottoman Empire and Europe which made ingress into this area by westerners difficult or undesirable. The area would be an ideal one for Gastaldi to have attempted the approach Almagià describes for Greece (see our no. 29 above), although, as we posited there, it seems to us that this approach would have offered little positive results. The map of Anatolia in general falls among those for which we must so far consider ourselves rather stumped as to what modern sources could have been available to a European in the sixteenth century.

Reference:
Gordeev, 2006, 126, no. 112.

Reproductions:
Bifolco and Ronca, 2018, 1: 111.
https://www.davidrumsey.com/luna/servlet/detail/
RUMSEY~8~1~291331~90063059

41. The Caucasus and southern European Russia (Ptolemaic)
-Venice, 1548
-Copper engraving, 12.5 x 17.5 (10.5) cm., on one sheet
-No scale bar

Along the top border of the map:
TABVLA ASIAE II (SECOND MAP OF ASIA)

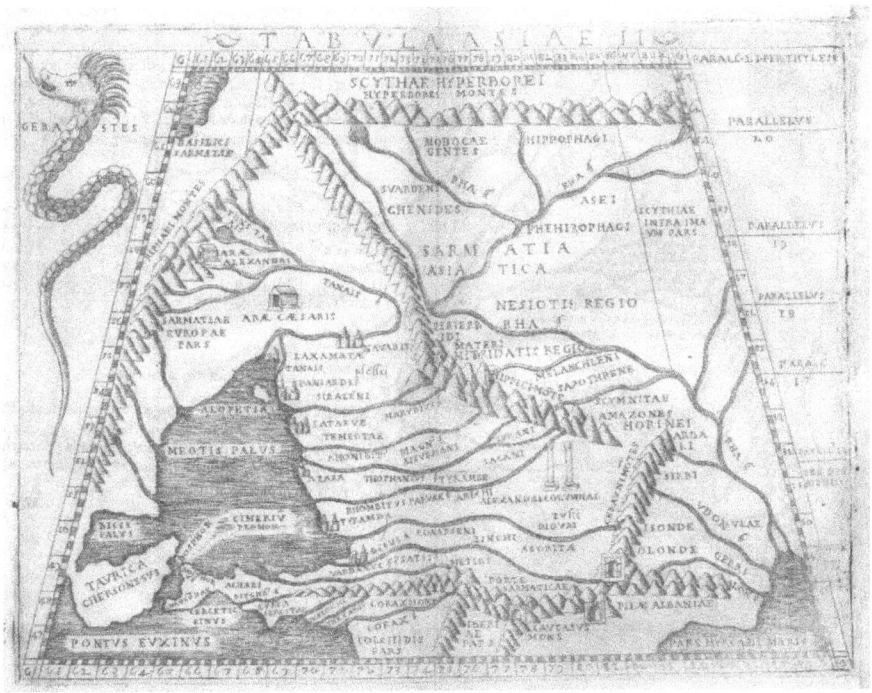

41 The Caucasus and southern European Russia (Ptolemaic) 1548 Rumsey

Comments:
Graduated in twelve-minute increments, with each whole degree numbered, in latitude and longitude, from 46°00' to 63°00' N, and from 60°00' to 88°30' E, on a trapezoidal projection. The map has the peculiar distinction of being

one of only two maps in the entire series in which all names are given entirely in capital letters. The only other map exhibiting this is no. 13, the modern map of Germany, which is dated 1542 and is accepted by most as being the first modern map in the Ptolemy. The implication would seem to be that the original intention had been to follow this policy in all maps, that it was then decided that the more usual policy was preferable, that is, only regional names in all capitals, and names of towns, rivers, etc., using a capital only for the first letter, and minuscule for the rest, and that the present map was the second one to be made for the Ptolemy. In the map, Gastaldi generally follows Ptolemy, except that he has added a lengthy mountain range running from about the center of the map northwestwards nearly to the map's end, in this following Münster. This is one of the Ptolemaic maps where the features and names are quite sparse on the original, so little is lost on Gastaldi's smaller map.

Reference:
Gordeev, 2006, 121, no. 107.

Reproductions:
Bifolco and Ronca, 2018, 1: 112.
https://www.davidrumsey.com/luna/servlet/detail/
RUMSEY~8~1~291333~90063061

42. Muscovy (European Russia) (modern)

-Venice, 1548
-Copper engraving, 12.5 x 17.0 cm., on one sheet
-No scale bar

Along the top border of the map:
MOSCHOVIA NOVA TABVLA (MODERN MAP OF MUSCOVY)

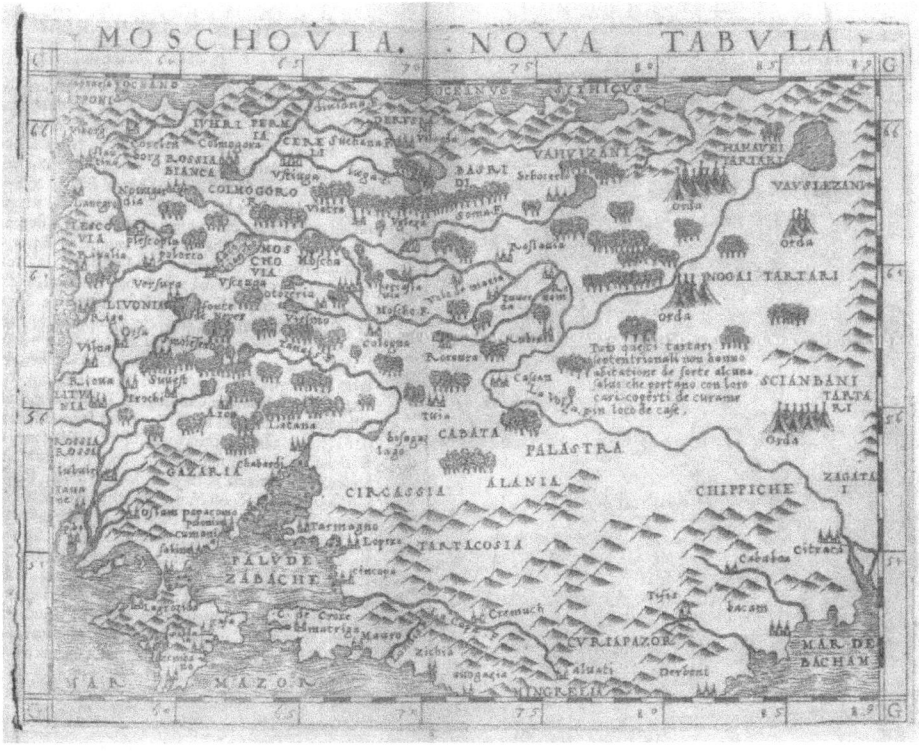

42 Muscovy (European Russia) (modern) 1548 Rumsey

Comments:
Graduated in whole degrees, with every fifth degree numbered, in latitude and longitude, from 46°00' to 67°30' N, and from 55°00' to 89°00' E, on a rectangular projection. The points chosen for numbering in the latitude graduation are peculiar: 51°, 56°, 61°, and 66°, the explanation for which I do not know. It is also a little peculiar that Gastaldi includes the map in the section devoted to Asia, although it is true that in part it does correspond to the coverage of Ptolemy's second map of Asia, which precedes it. However, not only by our definition of Europe, but also by that which Gastaldi provides in his *La universale descrittione del mondo*, the map actually covers a part of Europe, and not Asia. The ultimate source of the map is a map by Paolo Giovio, who received the information for it in 1525 from a Muscovite ambassador to Rome, Dmitry Gerasimov. No copy of the original Giovio map is known. The Giovio map was also used by Agnese in his atlases, and originally scholars believed that Gastaldi had taken his depiction from Agnese, who had taken it from Giovio (Michow, 1906, 2; and 1907, 16). But Bagrow (1962, 42-43) and Licini (1988, 74-80) are convincing in their idea that the Gastaldi map and the Agnese depictions were taken independently from a common source, presumably Giovio's map, and Licini shows that the Gastaldi map is actually the better of the two and was more influential. Indeed, judging from her assessment, it is probably one of only a very few maps in the little 1548 Ptolemy which had much real influence at all.

References:
Michow, 1906, 21; Michow, 1907, 16; Enckell, 1951, 63; Bagrow, 1962, 42-43; Bagrow, 1975, 63-64; Bagrow and Skelton, 1985, 171-72 and 246; Licini, 1988, 74-80, 93 and 103; Karrow, 1993, 267-68.

Reproductions:
Bifolco and Ronca, 2018, 1: 112.
https://www.davidrumsey.com/luna/servlet/detail/
RUMSEY~8~1~291335~90063063

43. The Caucasus and northern Iran (Ptolemaic)
-Venice, 1548
-Copper engraving, 12.5 x 17.0 (11.5) cm., on one sheet
-No scale bar

Along the top border of the map:
TABVLA ASIAE III (THIRD MAP OF ASIA)

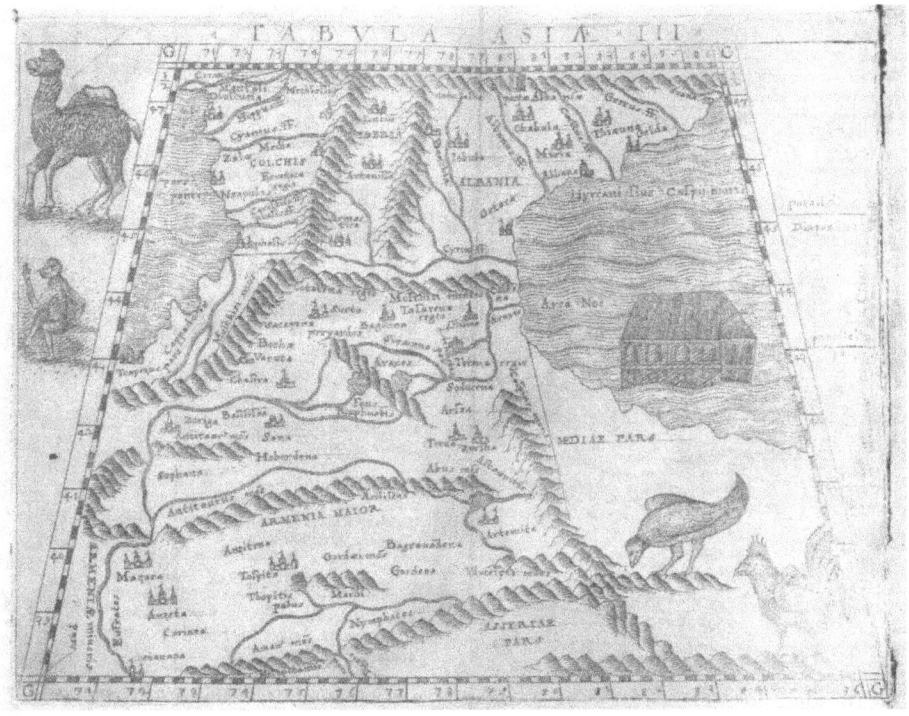

43 The Caucasus and Northern Iran (Ptolemaic) 1548 Rumsey

Comments:
Graduated in twelve-minute increments, with each whole degree numbered, in latitude and longitude, from 38°00' to 47°30' N, and from 70°00' to 86°00' E, on a trapezoidal projection. Gastaldi stops one and a half degree short in longitude coverage in the east (Ptolemy stops at 87°30' E), following Münster, the opposite of the usual case, where Gastaldi (after Münster) often extends the coverage over Ptolemy. Other than this, he follows Ptolemy faithfully, except of course for the usual diminution in details and names due to the smaller size. But note that Gastaldi has added to the map, which

includes Armenia, a prominent depiction of Noah's Ark, which reminds us of the Gastaldi's notion that there must be a land connection between the two worlds or they must come extremely close at some point, as discussed in our chapter eight. The ark, however, is also found in Münster's Ptolemy on this map. Münster may have entertained the same possibility, or perhaps the presence of the ark on Münster's map acted as part of the inspiration which led to Gastaldi's thinking on this subject. Whether any other printed Ptolemy's before Münster include the ark, I have not verified.

Reference:
Gordeev, 2006, 122, no. 108.

Reproductions:
Bifolco and Ronca, 2018, 1: 112.
https://www.davidrumsey.com/luna/servlet/detail/
RUMSEY~8~1~291337~90063065

44. Near East (Ptolemaic)
-Venice, 1548
-Copper engraving, 12.5 x 17.5 (14.5) cm., on one sheet
-No scale bar

Along the upper border of the map:
TABVLA ASIAE IIII (FOURTH MAP OF ASIA)

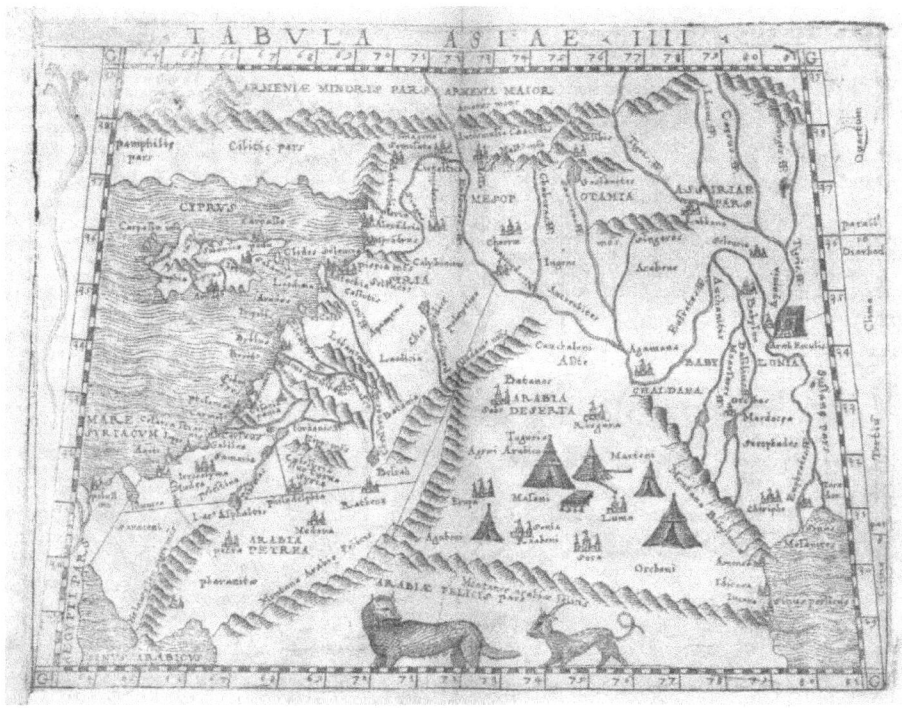

44 Near East (Ptolemaic) 1548 Rumsey

Comments:
Graduated in twelve-minute increments, with each whole degree numbered, in latitude and longitude, from 28°00' to 39°00' N, and from 63°00' to 81°00' E, on a trapezoidal projection. Gastaldi generally follows Ptolemy faithfully in this map, except that he has much straightened Ptolemy's Tigris and Euphrates river courses, and has added some rivers running north from the "Montana Babyloni" to the Euphrates, in both following Münster.

560

References:
Tibbets, 1978, 44, no. 24; Laor, 1986, 89-90.

Reproductions:
Bifolco and Ronca, 2018, 1: 112.
https://www.davidrumsey.com/luna/servlet/detail/
RUMSEY~8~1~291339~90063067

45. Syria and the Holy Land (modern)
-Venice, 1548
-Copper engraving, 12.5 x 17.0 cm., on one sheet
-No scale bar

Along the top border of the map:
*SORIA E TERRA SANCTA NOVA TABVLA (MODERN MAP OF SYRIA AND
THE HOLY LAND)*

45 Syria and the Holy Land (modern) 1548 Rumsey

Comments:
Graduated in twelve-minute increments, with each whole degree numbered, in latitude and longitude, from 31°00' to 37°00' N, and from 65°00' to 75°00' E, on the rectangular projection prescribed by Ptolemy for regional maps (see entry 5). Tibbets (1978, 43, no. 22) observes that the coastline is truer than in Ptolemy, and is doubtless derived from one of the very many earlier Holy Land maps preceding Gastaldi's, as see in the index of Karrow (1993, 783-84); perhaps still more could be found in Delano-Smith (1991). There are some differences in coordinates between this map and the same area on Gastaldi's First and Second Parts of Asia (1559 and 1561)) (Milanesi, in Dentoni Litta, 2003, 59), which of course is quite consistent with what we expect from Gastaldi as gone into in chapter seven above, and there are some significant distortions which don't occur in the First Part of Asia (Milanesi., cit., 59). The sources for the map have not been studied.

References:
Tibbets, 1978, 43, no. 22; Laor, 1986, 90; Milanesi, in Dentoni Litta, 2003, 59 (comments concerning a larger 1566 Forlani edition).

Reproductions:
Bifolco and Ronca, 2018, 1: 112.
https://www.davidrumsey.com/luna/servlet/detail/
RUMSEY~8~1~291341~90063069:

46. Iran (Ptolemaic)
-Venice, 1548
-Copper engraving, 12.5 x 17.0 (14.0) cm., on one sheet
-No scale bar

Along the top border of the map:
TABVLA ASIAE V (FIFTH MAP OF ASIA)

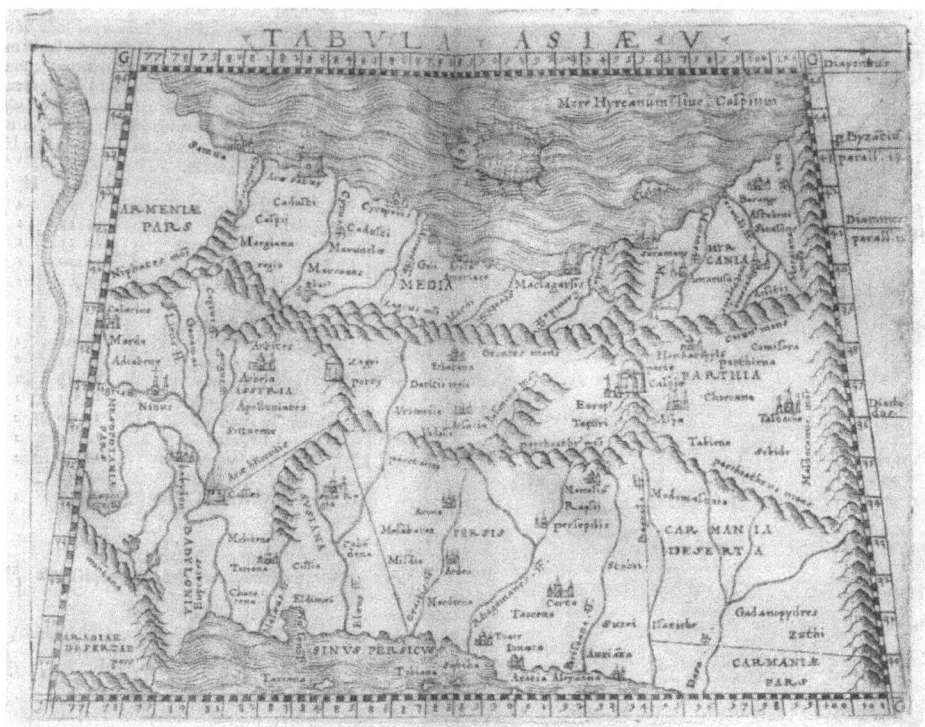

46 Iran (Ptolemaic) 1548 Rumsey

Comments:
Graduated in twelve-minute increments, with each whole degree numbered, in latitude and longitude, from 29°00' to 45°00' N, and from 76°00' to 101°00' E, on a trapezoidal projection. Gastaldi generally follows Ptolemy faithfully in this map, except for some insignificant orographical changes, and because data are relatively sparse on the Ptolemaic original, little is lost on Gastaldi's smaller copy.

Reference:
Alai, 2005, 37.

Reproductions:
Bifolco and Ronca, 2018, 1: 112.
https://www.davidrumsey.com/luna/servlet/detail/
RUMSEY~8~1~291343~90063071

47. Iran (modern)
-Venice, 1548
-Copper engraving, 12.5 x 17.5 cm., on one sheet
-No scale bar

Along the top border of the map:
PERSIA NOVA TABVLA (NEW MAP OF PERSIA)

47 Iran (modern) 1548 Rumsey

Comments:
Graduated in whole degrees, numbered at every fifth degree, in latitude and longitude (although, oddly, not in parts divisible by five; latitude numbering progresses as 32°, 37°, 42°, etc., and longitude numbering progresses as 76°, 81°, 86°, etc.); from 27°00' to 52°00' N, and from 71°00' to 111°00' E, on the rectangular projection prescribed by Ptolemy for regional maps (cf. entry no. 5). The map is an attractive one, but I can make no pronouncements as to its

accuracy or its sources, and I believe no study of it has been made. Certainly it is worthy of one, for, as far as I am aware, no modern map of the area precedes it, and Alai (2005, 1) says it is probably the first European map of Persia. Assuredly, it is not Ptolemaic, though Gastaldi retains Ptolemy's east-west axis for the Caspian Sea, and his longitudes for the east and west ends of that sea are close enough to Ptolemy's that he probably borrowed them from him. Sea charts could have played almost no role, except for the eastmost edge of the Black Sea and the northmost tip of the Persian Gulf. Other than possible wholly unknown sources, there remains only Ramusian material, and, in fact, it is almost certainly a number of accounts, many unpublished, obtained by Ramusio from Venetian diplomats and merchants who had been in Persia which served as Gastaldi's sources. As we have seen, while much of Ramusio's material was published by him for the first time, he also brought together works which had been previously published, and sometimes this material was practically as hard for Ramusio to find as the manuscript accounts. In the present case there are no less than five accounts dealing with Persia, all of which appeared in volume two of the *Navigazioni*. This volume was not published until 1559, and indeed one of our five accounts first appears only in the 1574 second edition of volume two, but since most had been published separately earlier, they were available, and Ramusio had procured his copies of most or all of these accounts by the time Gastaldi made his Persia.

The accounts are as follow: (1) That of Giosofat Barbaro, from an eminent Venetian family, who accompanied Caterino Zeno's embassy to Persia, evidently from 1471-79, the first Venetian embassy to Persia. The account, occupying twenty-one folio pages in Ramusio, was first published in Venice in 1543; (2) Zeno's own account of the embassy, which first appeared in Ramusio only in the 1574 second edition of volume two in twenty-three folio pages, and the first known published edition of which was Venice 1558, but Ramusio, who died in 1557, tells us he had owned a printed version of unknown date, though no copy of such an edition is now known; (3) The account of Ambrogio Contarini, another prominent Venetian, and also an ambassador to Persia from 1474-77. His account, which amounts to forty-two pages in Ramusio, was first published in 1486 in Venice, and again in Venice in 1523; (4) the account, thirty pages long in Ramusio, of Giovanni

Maria Angiolello, from a prominent family of Vicenza, who joined in 1486 with the Venetians, then more or less allied with Uzun Hasan, the ruler of Persia, in their fight against the Turks; Angiolello was early captured by the Turks and held for a long time, but he kept abreast of events in Persia; his work was first published in 1490 in Vicenza, though Ramusio must have had a larger manuscript version, for his published account continues to the date 1524; (5) an account of the travels in Persia from 1507-1520 of an anonymous merchant, twenty-five pages in Ramusio, though in this case no earlier printed edition is known, and it is not known when Ramusio first obtained the account. (For more detailed bibliographical and historical details on these five accounts, see Parks, 1970, 20-21 and 23-24.) So here are 131 folio pages of information indirectly or, usually, directly on Persia, most of it available in editions published before Ramusio's, which could have been supplemented by still further Ramusian material of the type which is neither ancient, in the classical sense, nor modern, in the sense of truly contemporary or near contemporary knowledge, such as Ramusio's accounts of Marco Polo and, perhaps especially, Hayton Armenio, and possibly others.

All in all, in the face of a complete lack of previous cartographic sources, the most likely assumption is that Gastaldi compiled his map from these sources, so here we would have an early instance of Gastaldi's compiling a map from various sources, mostly written accounts, essentially what he does in his great continental maps of 1559-1564. I personally suspect that more of map no. 4, his 1546 map of the Danube lands, came from written sources than has been realized. One would need to make a careful comparison of the various Ramusian accounts connected with Persia and this map in order to be certain, but, if we are correct in our suggestion, here is a map which was not, as a good number of the modern Ptolemy maps seem to be, copied from an earlier map of an area, but an original work of compilation by Gastaldi. More research will no doubt give us the answer.

Reference:
Alai, 2005, 1 and 37.

Reproductions:
Bifolco and Ronca, 2018, 1: 113.

https://www.davidrumsey.com/luna/servlet/detail/
RUMSEY~8~1~291345~90063073

48. Arabian peninsula (Ptolemaic)
-Venice, 1548
-Copper engraving, 12.5 x 16.5 (13.5) cm., on one sheet
-No scale bar

Along the top border of the map:
TABVLA ASIAE VI (SIXTH MAP OF ASIA)

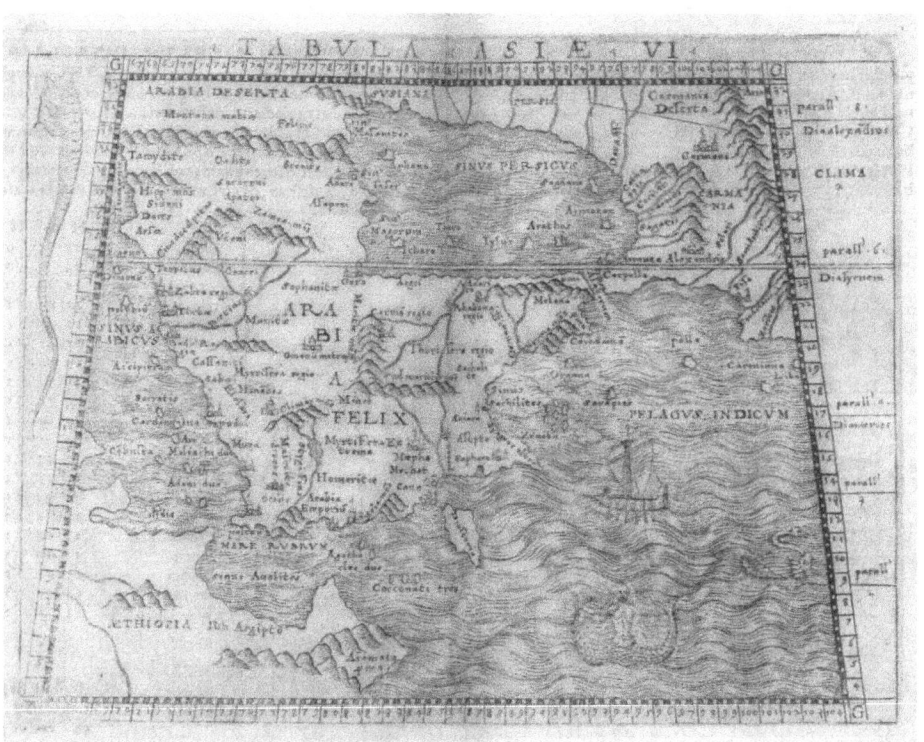

48 Arbian peninsula (Ptolemaic) 1548 Rumsey

Comments:
Graduated in fifteen-minute increments, with each whole degree numbered,
in latitude and longitude, from 3°00' to 32°00' N, and from 66°00' to 104°00'
E, on a trapezoidal projection. Gastaldi generally follows Ptolemy pretty

closely in this map, except that he omits several fair-sized islands off the northeast shore of the Persian Gulf, following Münster; furthermore, he extends the coverage six degrees further south, bringing in a moderately sized chunk of Africa in the area of the horn, and also one degree further north, and five degrees further east in latitude, also after Münster.

Reference:
Tibbets, 1998, 44, no. 25.

Reproductions:
Bifolco and Ronca, 2018, 1: 113.
https://www.davidrumsey.com/luna/servlet/detail/
RUMSEY~8~1~291347~90063075

49. Arabian peninsula (modern)
-Venice, 1548
-Copper engraving, 12.5 x 17.5 cm., on one sheet
-No scale bar

Along the top border of the map:
ARABIA FELIX NOVA TABVLA (MODERN MAP OF ARABIA)

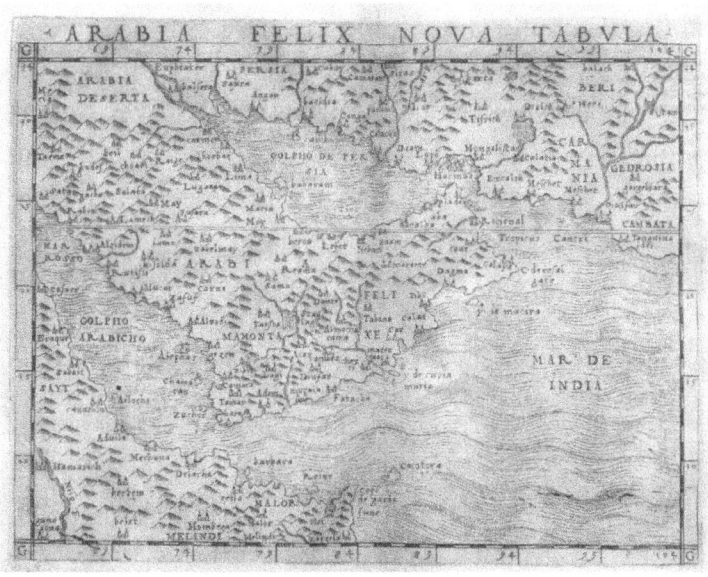

49 Arabian peninsula (modern) 1548 Rumsey

Comments:

Graduated in full degrees, in latitude and longitude, numbered at every fifth degree (for longitude, irregularly: 69°, 74°, 79°, etc.), from 5°00' to 33°00' N (but misnumbered at each side of the map as 34°00' N), and from 64°00' to 104°00' E, on a rectangular projection. "It is the first printed map to deal specifically with Arabia," says Tibbets (1978, 44), so here we have first time precedence again, as with the Persia. However, although there is some improvement over Ptolemy, the map largely retains his hydrography and orography (though Gastaldi increases the amount of the latter), the Oman Peninsula remains too long, and the Strait of Bab el Mandeb leading into the Red Sea is still much too wide, and Tibbets implies that it is only nominally a modern map of Arabia. Arabia on Gastaldi's 1561 Second Part of Asia (no. 102) would be much better, although it has shortcomings of a different nature, as we have brought out elsewhere (see chapter four, note 80). There does not seem to have been usage of portolan charts, although this is uncertain. Per Tibbets, the map does not correspond in details to the account of Lodovico Varthema, so Ramusio had perhaps not yet obtained this account, although a number of editions had been printed by the time Gastaldi was making this map (Parks, 1970, 8). There are three other voyage accounts in Ramusio which contain substantial information on Arabia of which Tibbets makes no mention, the voyage of Nicolo Conti sometime before 1444, that of Andrea Corsali in 1517, and a voyage by an unidentified group ("Comitato Venetiano") of Venetians, and, although he may not yet have obtained copies of these at the time Gastaldi made his Arabia, again, as with the Persian accounts mentioned in entry no. 47, they had all been published separately elsewhere before work began on the Ptolemy, and could have influenced the depiction in some way. For more details on the three accounts mentioned, see Parks (1970, 8, 9, 11, 13).

References:
Tibbets, 1978, 20-21 and 43-44, no. 23; McMinn, 1986, 37; Parry, 2004.

Reproductions:
Bifolco and Ronca, 2018, 1: 113.

50. South Asian Russia with part of Afghanistan (Ptolemaic)
-Venice, 1548
-Copper engraving, 12.5 x 17.5 (7.5) cm., on one sheet
-No scale bar

Along the top border of the map:
TABVLA ASIAE VII (SEVENTH MAP OF ASIA)

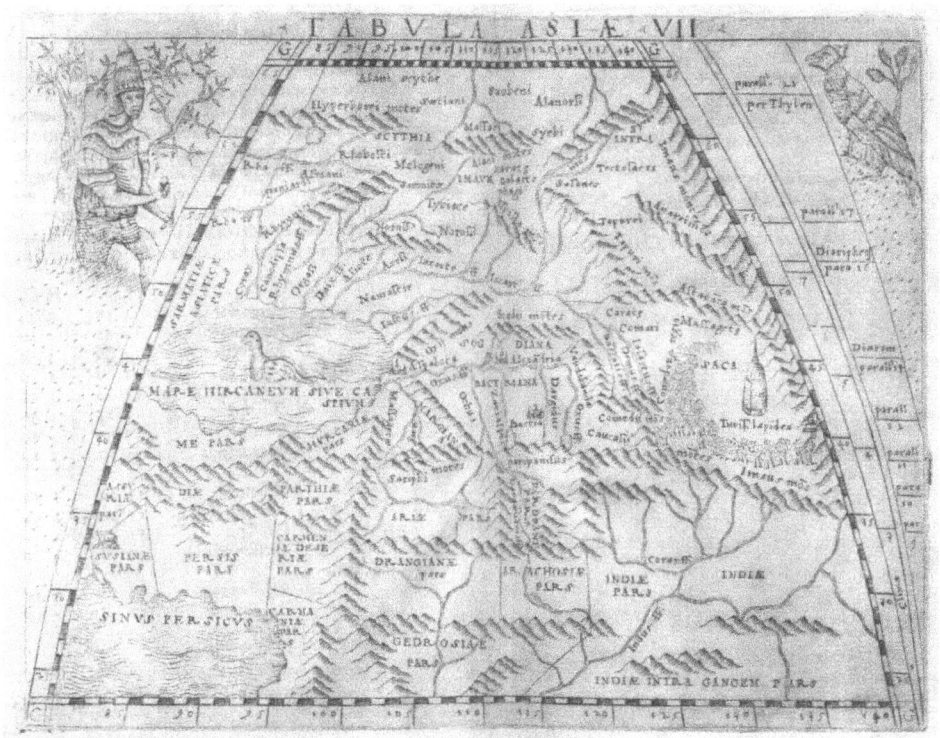

50 South Asian Russia with part of Afghanistan (Ptolemaic) 1548 (Rumsey

Comments:
Graduated in whole degrees, numbered at every fifth degree, in latitude and
longitude, from 27°00' to 65°00' N, and from 80°00' to 140°00' E. In general,
Gastaldi has followed Ptolemy in the basic geography, and there is little less

in the way of names because of the relative sparsity of detail in the original. However, Gastaldi has taken a few liberties with the depiction of mountain ranges, and at about 135° E, 43° N, he has introduced the legendary "Stone Tower" ("Turis lapidae"), which of course occurs in Ptolemy's text, although I do not find it on the fifteenth century editions of this map with which I compared Gastaldi's map. Gastaldi has also changed Ptolemy's area coverage, taking it two degrees further north, and a full twelve degrees further south, but shortening it by five degrees in the east, following Münster. But the most peculiar change which occurs, by comparison with the fifteenth century Ptolemy redactions which I have inspected, is in the right and left borders of the map, which, instead of straight lines, as in all of Ptolemy's maps, consist of convex curves. This occurs on the present map and the following one (no. 51), but nowhere else in the Ptolemy, and nowhere else in Gastaldi's cartography. Like the changes in area coverage just mentioned, Gastaldi has added this peculiar touch after Münster, and so it would surely be incorrect to speculate that we in some way might have here an embryonic attempt by Gastaldi to introduce a curvilinear projection to a regional map, a thing which he never does. The projection here must be considered as indeterminate.

Reproductions:
Bifolco and Ronca, 2018, 1: 113.
https://www.davidrumsey.com/luna/servlet/detail/
RUMSEY~8~1~291351~90063079

51. Further Asian Russia and part of China (Ptolemaic)

-Venice, 1548
-Copper engraving, 12.5 x 17.0 (7.0) cm., on one sheet
-No scale bar

Along the top border of the map:
TABVLA ASIAE VIII (EIGHTH MAP OF ASIA)

Comments:
Graduated in whole degrees, with each fifth degree numbered, in latitude and longitude, from 23°00' to 65°00' N, and from 130°00' to 180°00' E, with the same curvilinear right and left borders as in the previous map, again after Münster, making the projection indeterminate. Gastaldi has again changed the area coverage considerably, adding thirteen degrees in the south, and two degrees in the north, following Münster, but leaving the latitudes as in Ptolemy. Because of the paucity of names in the Ptolemaic original, Gastaldi seems to have lost nothing on his smaller map, and in the east center part of the map, he has added a few. He has also made rather significant changes in both the hydrography and orography, still again after Münster. Thus, in this purportedly Ptolemaic map, the master has been followed much more approximately than on the other Ptolemaic maps. As to the question of what interpretation to give to this fact, I can offer no answers.

Reproductions:
Bifolco and Ronca, 2018, 1: 113.

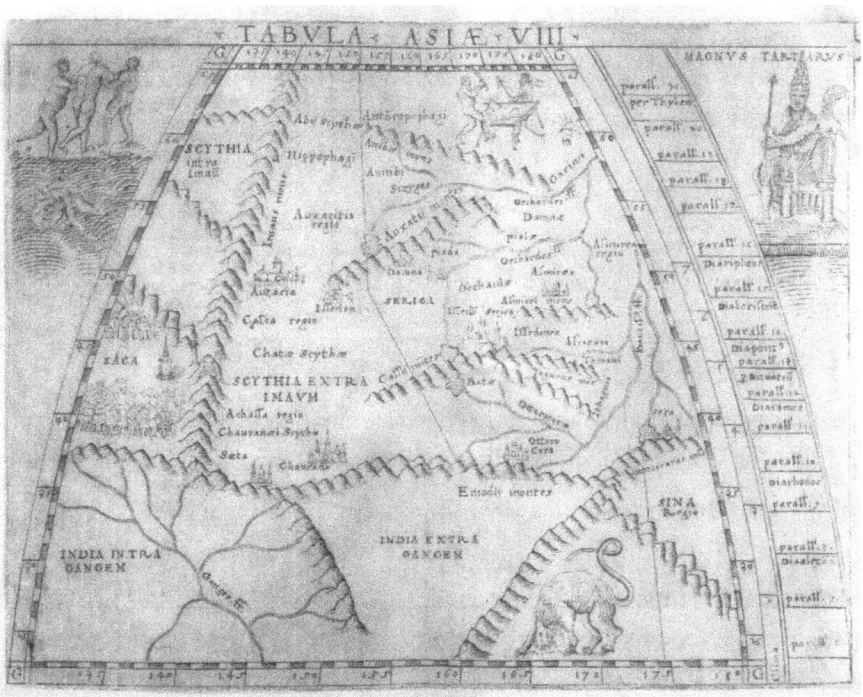

51 Further Asian Russia and part of China (Ptolemaic) 1548 Rumsey

https://www.davidrumsey.com/luna/servlet/detail/
RUMSEY~8~1~291353~90063161

52. Pakistan and part of Afghanistan (Ptolemaic)
-Venice, 1548
-Copper engraving, 12.5 x 16.0 (12.0) cm., on one sheet
-No scale bar

Along the top border of the map:
TABVLA ASIAE IX (NINTH MAP OF ASIA)

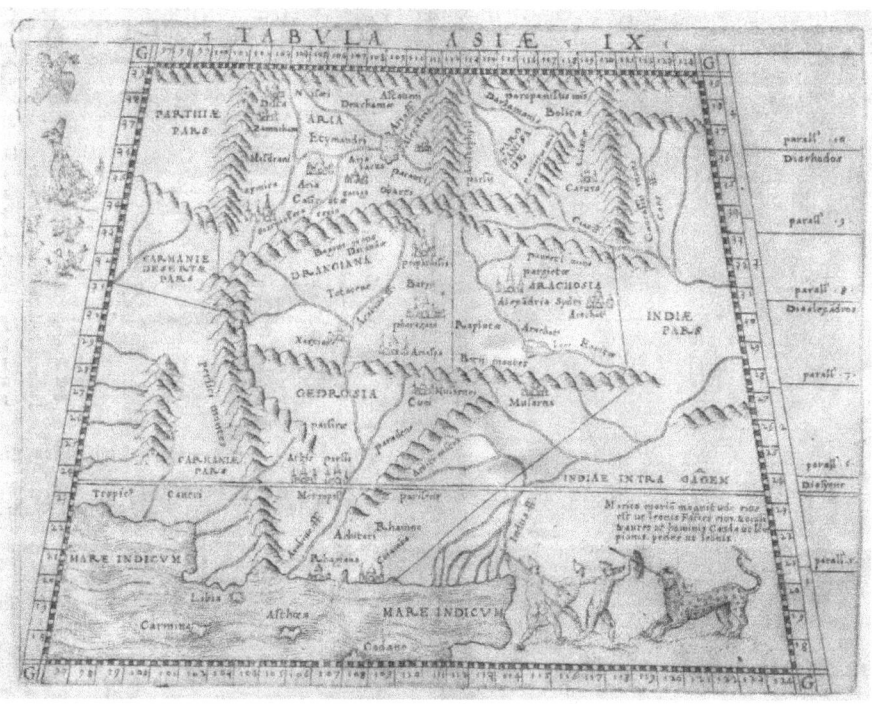

52 Pakistan and part of Afghanistan (Ptolemaic) 1548 Rumsey

Comments:
Graduated in twelve-minute increments, with each whole degree numbered,
in latitude and longitude, from 17°00' to 39°00' N, and from 96°00' to 124°00'
E, on a trapezoidal projection. Here again, though Gastaldi follows Ptolemy
as to latitudinal coverage, in longitude he has added five degrees in the west,
and four and a half degrees in the east, following Münster. Other than this,

he has followed Ptolemy rather closely, only adding a couple of short unnamed tributaries to rivers.

Reproductions:
Bifolco and Ronca, 2018, 1: 113.
https://www.davidrumsey.com/luna/servlet/detail/
RUMSEY~8~1~291355~90063083

53. India and its surrounds (Ptolemaic)
-Venice, 1548
-Copper engraving, 12.5 x 16.5 (13.0) cm., on one sheet
-No scale bar

Along the top border of the map:
TABVLA ASIAE X (TENTH MAP OF ASIA)

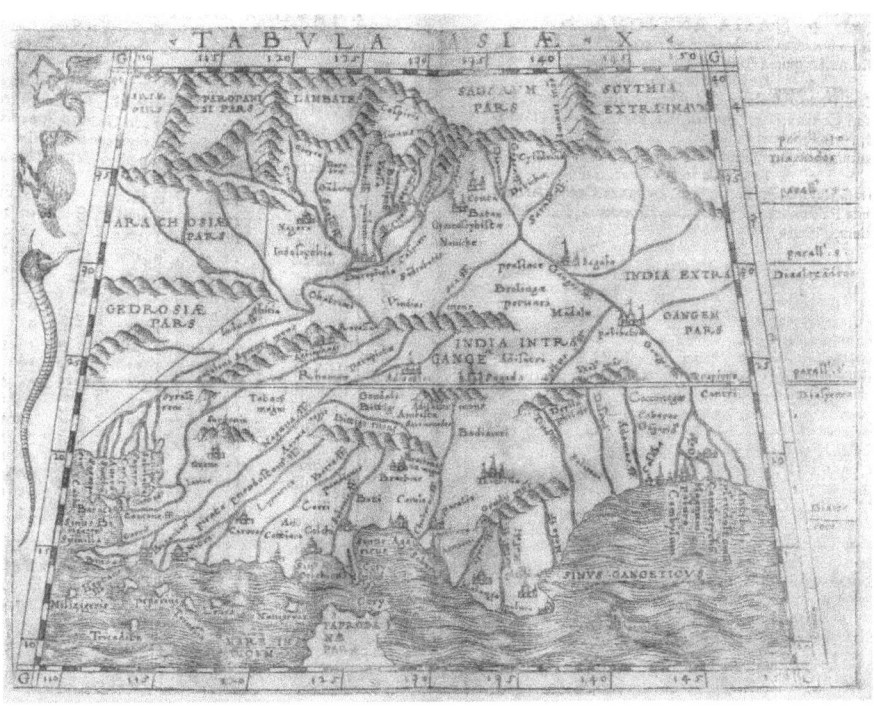

53 India and its surrounds (Ptolemaic) 1548 Rumsey

Comments:
Graduated in whole degrees, with each fifth degree numbered, in latitude and longitude, from 8°30' to 40°00' N, and from 108°30' to 150°00' E, on a trapezoidal projection. Here, though his coverage is one or two degrees greater than Ptolemy's on all sides, following Münster, Gastaldi has followed Ptolemy in general faithfully. Ptolemy's toponymy is rather dense on the map, so Gastaldi's version loses a considerable amount due to size reduction.

Reproductions:
Bifolco and Ronca, 2018, 1: 114.
https://www.davidrumsey.com/luna/servlet/detail/
RUMSEY~8~1~291357~90063085

54. India (modern)
-Venice, 1548
-Copper engraving, 12.5 x 17.0 cm., on one sheet
-No scale bar

Along the top border of the map:
CALECVT NOVA TABVLA (MODERN MAP OF INDIA)

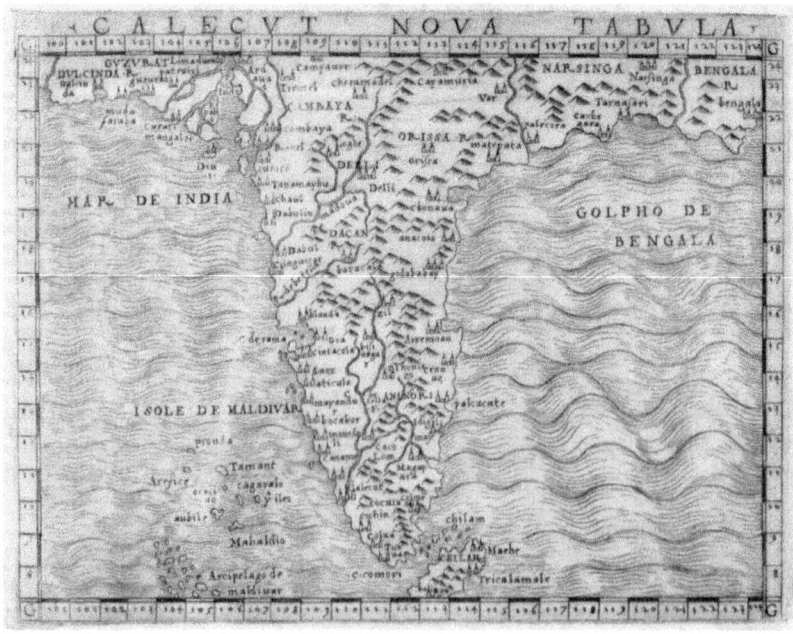

54 India (modern) 1548 Rumsey

Comments:

Graduated in whole degrees, with each degree numbered, in latitude and longitude, from 7°00' to 24°00' N, and from 99°00' to 124°00' E, on the rectangular projection. Calecut (Calcutta) was the wealthiest city in India, controlled by merchants in the hands of which most of the country's trade was concentrated, and in the earliest western accounts, we hear reference to the "kings of Calecut", and perhaps it was such considerations that prompted Gastaldi to give the name Calecut to the whole country. It is clear from Girolamo Sernigi's account of Vasco da Gama's voyage in the first volume of Ramusio that Calecut is a city, not a country, but, as so often, we don't know if Gastaldi had seen that account yet when he made this map, although it had first been published in 1507 (Parks, 1970, 5). The most striking thing about India on this map, of course, is the great narrowness of the country. It is drawn thus on some of the early universal "portolan charts", as that known as the Salviati map of 1526 (reproduced in Portinaro and Knirsch, 1987, pp. 50-51), or on Ribero's maps (1529 exemplar reproduced in Shirley, 1987, pp. xxiv-xxv), and since, as can be seen in our entries below on the Gastaldi American maps in the Ptolemy that the principal source for those, at least as to the coasts, was Ribero, that is certainly the most likely source from which Gastaldi obtained this form. Nevertheless, a glance at the pre-1548 sea charts containing India in Cortesão (1960) shows that an earlier type, beginning ca. 1510, actually shows India very considerably broader and closer to reality, while the narrow variant only shows up later, ca. the 1520s, and, after this, depending on the cartographer, both depictions can regularly be found. Apparently Gastaldi did not know the more correct form, or, not being in a position to judge which was better, elected for the Ribero type (but see also our comments at no. 78). The form is already much improved, indeed virtually normal, on Gastaldi's 1554 map of southeast Asia (no. 78), and on his 1561 Third Part of Asia (no. 103), probably from information obtained from Barros as in the second edition of Ramusio's volume one. Other than this, no study has been made of its sources. The most likely accounts in Ramusio from which Gastaldi might have obtained information on India are those of Francisco Alvarez, Thome Lopez, Giovanni de Empoli, Andrea Corsali, and Lodovico Varthema (for further bibliographical and historical details on these accounts, see Parks, 1970, 5, 7, 8, and 9). Of course, for the 1548 maps, we don't usually know which if any of these accounts Ramusio had in hand when Gastaldi was making the various maps. Although three of the named accounts had been published earlier (Alvarez, Corsali, and Varthema), it was often not at all easy to obtain copies of these published accounts. There also existed, in the present case, one previous modern map of India of sufficient size that it might have been of use, Waldseemüller's 1513 map of India in the supplement to his Strassburg Ptolemy (Karrow, 1993, 580, no. 80/47).

Reference:
Gole, 1976, 38.

Reprodutions:
Bifolco and Ronca, 2018, 1: 114.
https://www.davidrumsey.com/luna/servlet/detail/
RUMSEY~8~1~291359~90063087

55. Further India and part of China (Ptolemaic)
-Venice, 1548
-Copper engraving, 12.5 x 15.0 (11.0) cm., on one sheet
-No scale bar

Along the top border of the map:
TABVLA ASIAE XI (ELEVENTH MAP OF ASIA)

Comments:
Graduated in whole degrees, with each fifth degree numbered, in latitude and longitude, from 9°00' to 37°00' N, and from 135°00' to 180°00' E, on a trapezoidal projection. Gastaldi generally follows Ptolemy faithfully in this map, and there is relatively little loss in names and detail, since the nomenclature in Ptolemaic original is sparse.

Reproductions:
Bifolco and Ronca, 2018, 1: 114.

55 Further India and part of China (Ptolemaic) 1548 Rumsey

https://www.davidrumsey.com/luna/servlet/detail/
RUMSEY~8~1~291361~90063089

56. Further India and Archipelago Asia (modern)
-Venice, 1548
-Copper engraving, 12.5 x 17.0 cm., on one sheet
-No scale bar

Along the top border of the map:
INDIA TERCERA NOVA TABVLA (MODERN MAP OF FURTHER
INDIA)

Comments:
Graduated in whole degrees, with each fifth degree numbered, in latitude and
longitude, from 10°00' to 22°00' N, and from 140°00' to 185°00' E, on a
rectangular projection. Gastaldi's title, directly translated, "Modern Map of

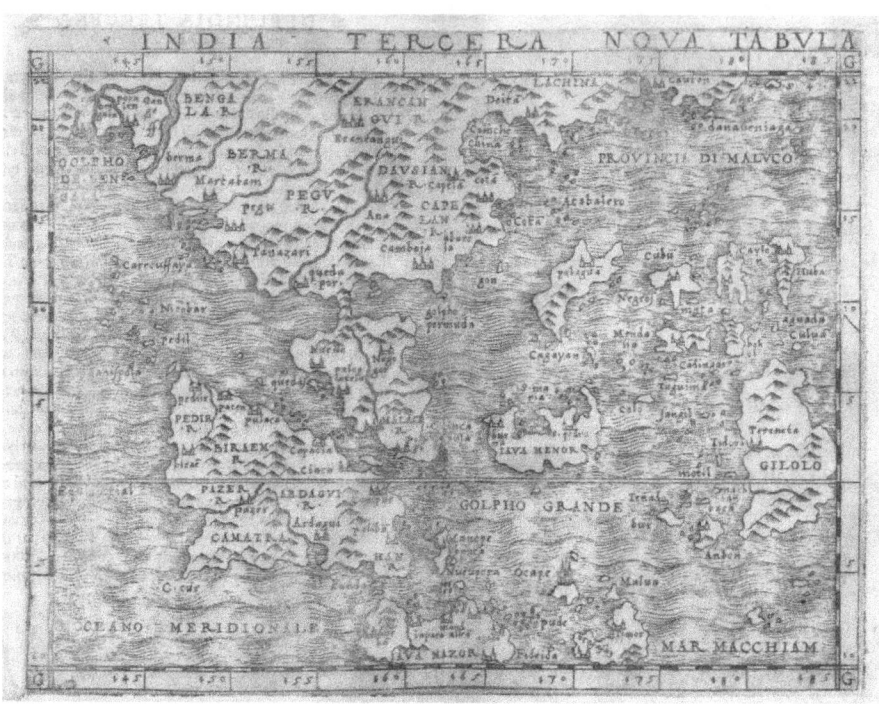

56 Further India and archipelago Asia (modern) 1548 Rumsey

the Third India", is a little puzzling, in more ways than one. For one thing,"
tercera" for "third" is neither Latin ("tertia") nor Italian ("terza"), but
Spanish, implying that this "Third India" is a Spanish interpretation of
things; probably the understanding here is that our India is the first one, the
West Indies the second, and the East Indies the third. Gastaldi's depiction
seems to have set something of a precedent in the depiction of this area
(Porena, 1888, 435), but it cannot be called a very good precedent. The map
has many misshapen land forms, both on the mainland, and, especially, in the
islands. We name but a few. The Malay peninsula is oddly shaped and much
too large east and west, and next to it Sumatra is also globular and much too
wide in form. Java is vaguely in the right place. There is no recognizable
Borneo or Celebes, although an island "IAVA MENOR" may be the latter.
Gilolo (Halmahara), the largest and most important of the Moluccas, is
enormously enlarged, probably in relation to its importance. There seems no
sign of the Philippines, either, unless they are the several islands in a group
north of Gilolo. In short, the East Indies are greatly confused. The area
would be considerably improved in 1561/1565 in Gastaldi's Third Part of

Asia, but significant confusion would still remain. The most likely Ramusian sources on the area would have been the accounts of the Magellan voyage by Antonio Pigafetta and Maximilianus Transylvanus, and the accounts of Nicolo Conti and Lodovico Varthema, and Suarez detects Ramusian sources in many places on the map (Suarez, 1999, 130-56, passim). As usual, we can't be sure which of these Gastaldi might have seen before he drew this map, and only an in-depth comparative study might resolve the question. For bibliographical and historical details on the named Ramusian sources, see Parks (1970, 7, 13, and 14).

References:
Porena, 1888, 435-36; Abendanon, 1918, 1785; Suarez, 1999, 130-56, passim.

Reproductions:
Bifolco and Ronca, 2018, 1: 114.
https://www.davidrumsey.com/luna/servlet/detail/
RUMSEY~8~1~291363~90063091

57. Sri Lanka (Taprobana) (Ptolemaic)

-Venice, 1548
-Copper engraving, 12.5 x 13.0 cm., on one sheet
-No scale bar

Along the top border of the map:
TABVLA ASIAE XII (TWELFTH MAP OF ASIA)

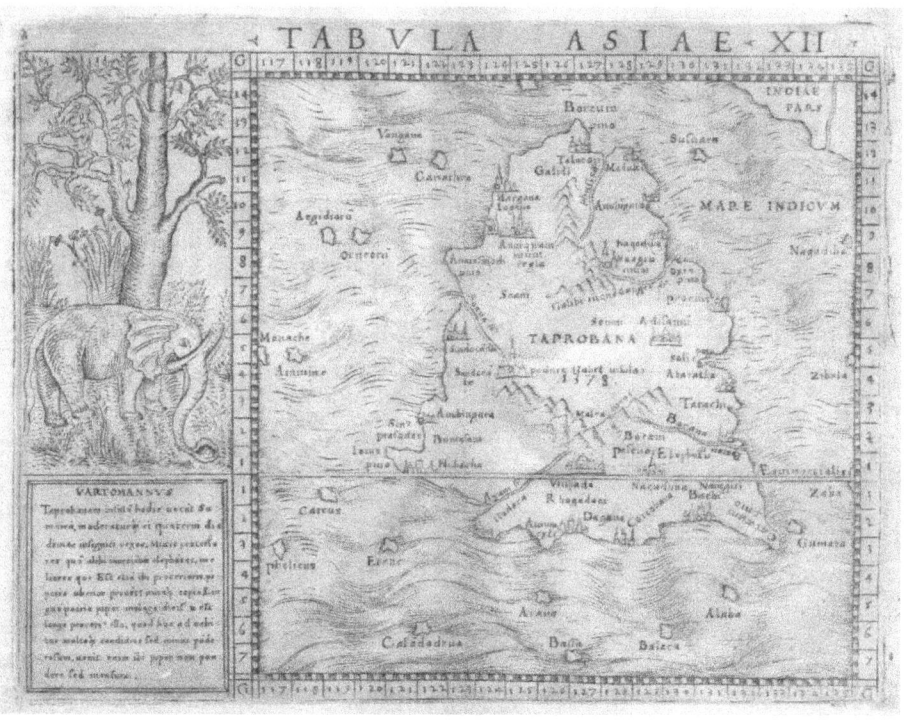

57 Sri Lanka (Taprobana) (Ptolemaic) 1548 Rumsey

Comments:

Graduated in twelve-minute increments, with each fifth degree numbered, in latitude and longitude, from 7°00' to 14°00' N, and from 116°00' to 135°00' E, on a rectangular projection. This is the only Ptolemaic map in the 1548 book which is on the rectangular projection, that originally prescribed by Ptolemy for regional maps. It is generally faithful to the fifteenth century redactions of the Ptolemaic maps except that Gastaldi shows a small corner of India in the northeast corner, following Münster. There is little or no loss of names on the little Gastaldi map, because detail is very sparse on the Ptolemaic original.

Reproductions:
Bifolco and Ronca, 2018, 1: 114.
https://www.davidrumsey.com/luna/servlet/detail/
RUMSEY~8~1~291365~90063093

(58.-62.) The America Maps in Gastaldi's 1548 Ptolemy

There are five modern America maps in the Ptolemy (there are of course no Ptolemaic ones in this case.) The greatest previous number had been but one, in Waldseemüller's 1513 Ptolemy, and that was very primitive and out of date by Gastaldi's time. This group of maps was completely unprecedented, and on the whole they are correct in their overall form, although the coordinates were still quite far from accurate, for good information in this regard simply could not yet be ascertained by anyone, especially as to longitudes. Nordenskiöld stated that: "These small maps . . . form the very first atlas of the New World" (1897, 182). Gastaldi covers the continent pretty well, both as to North and to South America, except that he shows nothing of north central and northwest North America. These maps have received considerably more attention than the modern 1548 maps of Africa and Asia. In fact, two authors have devoted full book-length works to Gastaldi's maps of America (Grande, 1905, *carte*; and Minella, 1993), including these 1548 maps and the 1556 maps in volume three of Ramusio (neither deals with Gastaldi's great ca. 1560 manuscript America, unpublished until later in the century, for they knew nothing of it), and also discuss the American parts of Gastaldi's world maps; Minella concentrates principally on South America. On the basis of toponymic comparisons, both of these authors find that the principal source for the coasts on the maps, except for two maps of small islands, Cuba and Hispaniola, was Ribero, in one of his portolan-world maps of the late 1520s (see Shirley, 1987, xxiv-xxv for a reproduction of the 1529 example), although, as Wagner (1931, 9-10) cautions, it is impossible to state that Ribero was specifically the source, because there are other such charts which show a very similar picture, perhaps derived from Ribero's earlier charts, such as the so-called Salviati map (reproduced in Portinaro and Knirsch, 1987, pp. 50-51), not to mention others which have no doubt long ago disappeared. Therefore when we say the main source was Ribero, we should understand that really we mean the Ribero-type. Both Grande and Minella also find considerably lesser, but significant, indications of the use of the works of some other cartographers, as Agnese and Maggiolo, and a couple of others. As regards one map, no. 60, of eastern North America, the situation is different and more complex, as see that entry. As regards the interiors, the main source would most likely be the American accounts accumulated by Ramusio, obtained by Gastaldi from him before he had published them, although as always the question of which of his accounts Ramusio already had in hand when Gastaldi was making the maps is problematical, and will remain so until detailed comparative studies have been made. It is an odd but true fact that, while there had been almost no modern maps of the two far continents in the Old World (Asia and Africa) by Gastaldi's time, significantly more had been done for the New World, as we see in Burden (1996), and so there is a real possibility that some names and other features of America were taken from other maps.

58. South America (modern)
-Venice, 1548
-Copper engraving, 12.5 x 17.0 cm., on one sheet
-No scale bar

Along the top border of the map:
TIERRA NOVA (NEW LAND)

Comments:
Graduated in full degrees, with each fifth degree numbered, in latitude and longitude, from 55°00' S to 15°00' N, and from 275°00' E (at the west end of the map) to 10°00' E (at the east side of the map). Gastaldi, on his America maps does not split his longitudes into two sets, from 0° to 180° east and west of some prime meridian, but counts all eastward from 0° to 360° E. The projection is rectangular. The map's foremost claim to distinction lies in the fact that it is the first map ever made of South America alone. According to

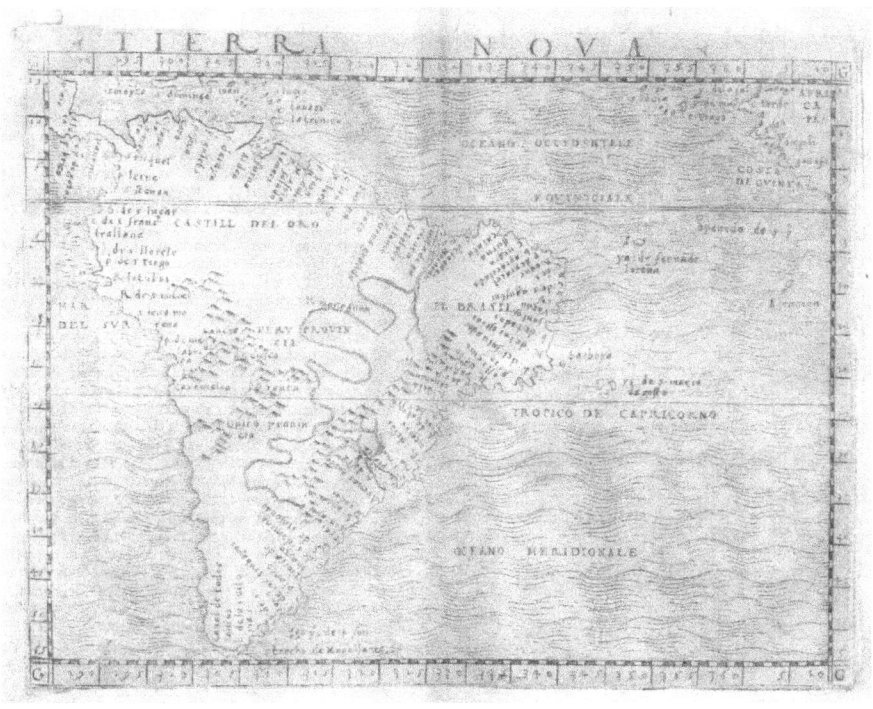

58 South America (modern) 1548 Rumsey

Grande, Tierra Nova is the name Gastaldi always applies to South America (1905, *carte*, 32). Its overall form is quite good and close to reality. Minella says that the continent remains pretty much the same on all Gastaldi maps which show it (1993, 108), but this is incorrect. On the *Cosmographia vniversalis* world map of 1561 the interior is considerably changed, and the west coast is a full twelve degrees further east. The coastline is from marine charts, and both Grande and Minella find by toponymical comparisons that Ribero was overwhelmingly the main source, with lesser contributions taken from Agnese and Maggiolo (Grande, cit., 41-42; Minella, cit., 28-30). Inland both the hydrography and the orography are poor, deviating much from reality, as for example in the northward flowing and meandering Amazon (maragnon), which I believe was common to all world maps at the time as well. Other than the defective hydrography and orography, there is very little detail inland, and only a handful of names. An interesting and odd fact is that there are no less than three nonexistent islands or island groups in the Atlantic: "openedo de s. p[iero]", "y[sl]a de fernãde lor'na", and "y[sl]e de s.

maria da gusto". If Gastaldi had Ramusian material at hand, the accounts which would have consisted of or included information on South America would be those by, or on, Gonzalo Fernández de Oviedo, Peter Martire, Hernando Pizzaro, and Francisco de Orellano. For further bibliographical and historical details on these accounts, and their locations in Ramusio's *Navigazioni*, see Parks (1970, 28, 32-33 and 34).

References:
Grande, 1905, *carte*, 30-42; Minella, 1993, 23-30, 53 and 107-08.

Reproductions:
Bifolco and Ronca, 2018, 1: 114.
https://www.davidrumsey.com/luna/servlet/detail/
RUMSEY~8~1~291367~90063095

59. Central America and southern North America (modern)
-Venice, 1548
-Copper engraving, 12.5 x 17.0 cm., on one sheet
-No scale bar

Along the top border of the map:
NUEVA HISPANIA TABVLA NOVA (MODERN MAP OF NEW SPAIN)

Comments:
Graduated in whole degrees, with every fifth degree numbered, in latitude and longitude, from 5°00' to 33°00' (33°30'?) N, and from 245°00' to 290°00' E, on a rectangular projection. "It is a beautiful and significant little map," observed Wheat (1957, 20), and in fact it is the first printed map of New Spain, if I am not mistaken. It includes all of North America to 33°00' N, the approximate northern latitudinal limit of knowledge at the time, says Grande, reached by Ulloa in 1540 (1905, *carte*, 43-44); this, however, is incorrect, for Coronado's expedition reached much higher latitudes, perhaps ca. 40°00', but Gastaldi evidently did not yet have information on that, although Ramusio obtained it, though evidently later, for information from that expedition appears on Gastaldi's 1556 map of the Western Hemisphere (no. 86). Grande

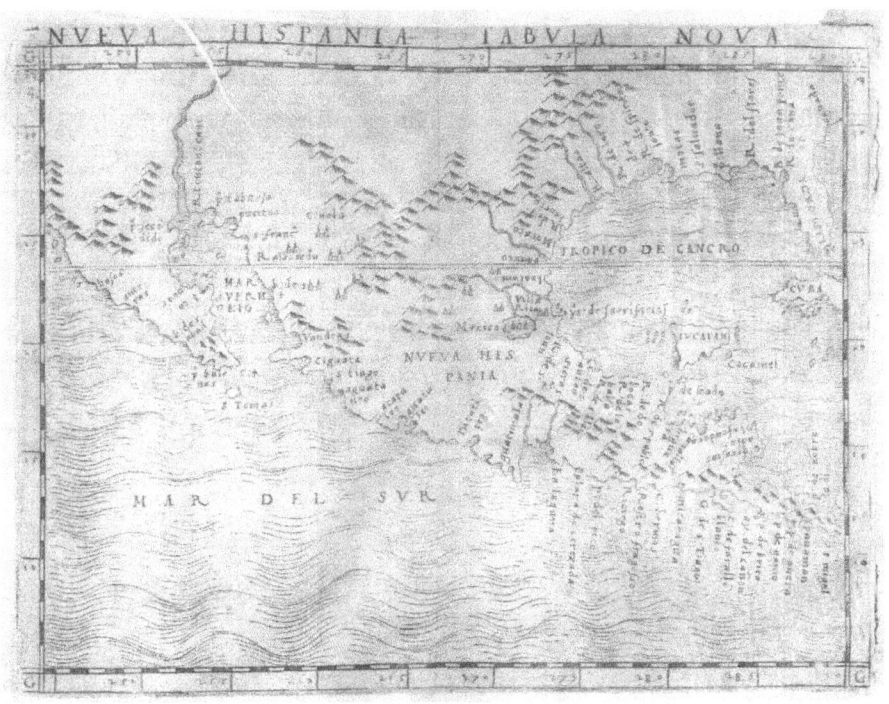

59 Central America and southern North America (modern) 1548 Rumsey

finds signs that Gastaldi used information from several expeditions, including those of Nuño de Guzman (1531), Antonio de Mendoza (1532), Fernando de Grijalva (1533), Hernando Cortes (1535), Francisco de Ulloa (1539-40), and Marco de Nizza (1539). Accounts by or on all of these except Grijalva and Mendoza are in Ramusio (see Parks, 1970, 29, 31, 32, for bibliographical and historical details and locations of the accounts in the *Navigazioni*), and Ramusio, we can assume, was Gastaldi's source. Accounts of the expeditions of Grijalva and Mendoza (the brother, we recall, of Diego Hurtado de Mendoza, the Spanish ambassador who provided Gastaldi with information for his 1544 Spain) do not occur in Ramusio, so, if indeed Gastaldi's map contains information from these expeditions, he must have obtained it elsewhere, perhaps from the parts of Oviedo's *Historia* which were not published until the nineteenth century, although his friend Ramusio could have seen them in manuscript. There is no sign on the map of De Soto's expedition, nor of the Mississippi River discovered by him. Grande, on the basis of toponymic comparisons, finds that for the coasts Ribero names predominate overwhelmingly, with a much smaller number from

Agnese (1905, *carte*, 50), except for the northernmost twenty-two names on the west coast, the source for which he doesn't identify. But judging from Wagner (1937, 1, 28), these would be from Agnese. Two peculiarities of the map are Gastaldi's placement of the lower tip of Baja California in 19°, while the real latitude is 23°, and Gastaldi's depiction of Yucatan as an island. The last is especially interesting, for on other maps in the same Ptolemy edition, as well as on Gastaldi's 1546 world map (no. 3) it is shown as a peninsula, another instance of Gastaldi's depicting a feature differently on different maps to express indecision when he had conflicting information. See Grande (1905, *carte*, 47-48) for some interesting history on the two variant depictions of Yucatan.

References:
Grande, 1905, *carte*, 43-51; Wagner, 1937, 1, 28; Wheat, 1954, 30-31; Wheat, 1957, 20; Cline, 1962, 99-100.

Reproductions:
Bifolco and Ronca, 2018, 1: 115.
https://www.davidrumsey.com/luna/servlet/detail/
RUMSEY~8~1~291369~90063097

60. Eastern North America (modern)
-Venice, 1548
-Copperplate engraving, 12.5 x 17.0, on one sheet
-No scale bar

Along the top border of the map:
TIERRA NVEVA (NEW LAND)

Comments:
Graduated in whole degrees, with every fifth degree numbered, in latitude and longitude, from 30°00' to 61°00' N, and 290°00' to 350°00' E, on a rectangular projection. This peculiar little map contains, other than four regional names in capital letters, "TIERRA DEL LABORADOR", "TIERRA DEL BACALAOS", "TIERRA DE NVREMBERG" and "LA FLORIDA",

no interior detail whatsoever, neither hydrography, orography, settlements, nor anything else, simply a great mass of emptiness, evidently to be taken entirely as land, although there is no way to be certain even of this. But there are a fair number of coastal names, and many named islands in the northeast, evidently corresponding vaguely to Newfoundland, fragmented into islands. We cannot go here into the plethora of confusing opinions which have been expressed as to the exact sources of the map, which one will find in the references given below, but all are in agreement that the map stems from the Verrazzano type of depiction of the east coast, as opposed to the very different Gomez type, seen in Ribero's maps, while in other maps in the same Ptolemy, as well as in his 1546 world, Gastaldi shows the Gomez geography. Several have expressed wonder that Gastaldi should show such contrary views in different maps of the same area (for example, Wroth, 1970, 203 and 205), but, as we have seen, nothing could be more characteristic of Gastaldi. Giovanni da Verrazzano, sailing for France, and Estêvão Gomez, sailing for Spain, were the only two explorers who had sailed the east coast of North America. Verrazzano's voyage lasted from January 1524 to July 1524, and Gomez's from September 1524 to August 1525. Their geographical reports differed very much, resulting in the institution of two schools of geography, both of which lasted into the seventeenth century. No Europeans other than them and their crews had been there. Who could say which concept was correct? Gastaldi, faced by these irresolvable contradictions, simply did as he regularly did in such circumstances. On one map, he depicted one view, and on another map the other view. A final note: The coastal and island geography of the Newfoundland area on this map is virtually identical to the geography of the area on our map no. 82, which appears in the 1556 volume three of the *Navigazioni*. This map is one of four maps which accompany an account in the volume purportedly written by an anonymous French sea captain (Ramusio, 1967-70, 3, 350v-358r; Milanesi ed., 1978-88, 6, 911-26), and the four maps are certainly those four of which Ramusio speaks, in the dedicatory epistle to Fracastoro at the head of Volume three, as having been sent him by the latter, who had received them from some unidentified Frenchmen. See more concerning these facts in our compound entry (81.-86.), and, especially, in our individual entry no. 82.

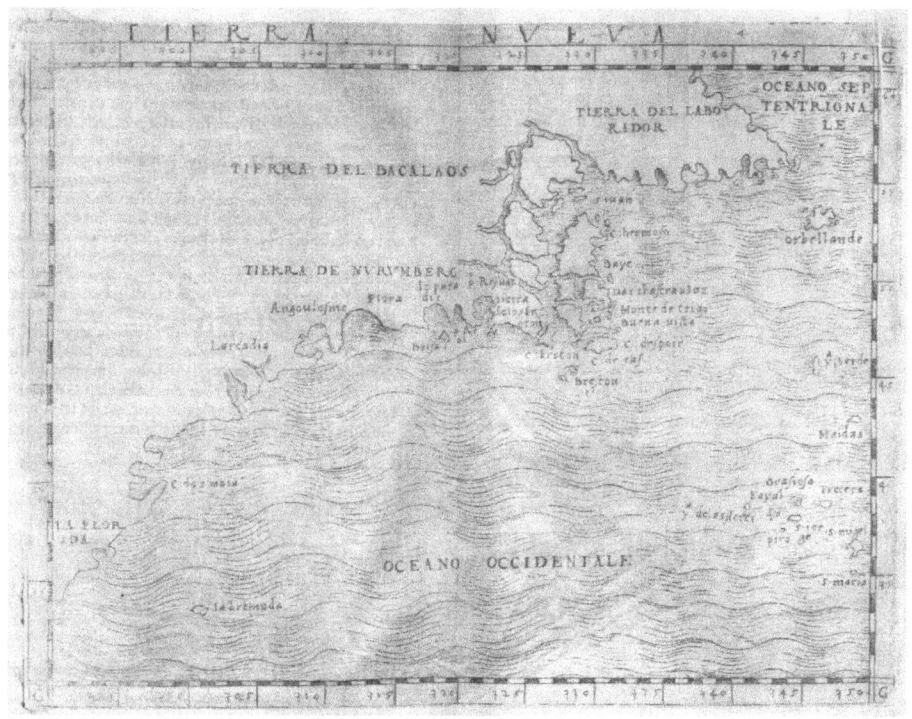

60 Eastern North America (modern) 1548 Rumsey

References:
Harrisse, 1900, 251-54; Grande, 1905, *carte*, 52 and 74-83; Wilkins, 1957, 9-11; Ganong, 1964, 124-28 and 349; Wroth, 1970, 203 and 205-09; Schwartz and Ehrenberg, 1980, 40 and 47.

Reproductions:
Bifolco and Ronca, 2018, 1: 115.
https://www.davidrumsey.com/luna/servlet/detail/
RUMSEY~8~1~291371~90063099

61. Cuba (modern)
-Venice, 1548
-Copper engraving, 12.5 x 17.0, on one sheet
-No scale bar

Along the top border of the map:
ISOLA CVBA NOVA (MODERN ISLAND OF CUBA)

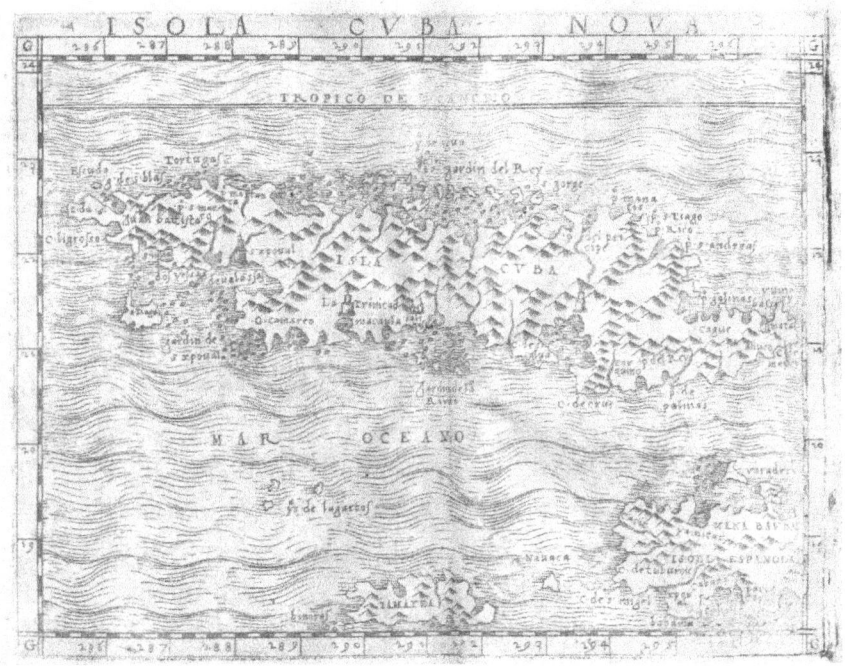

61 Cuba (modern) 1548 Rumsey

Comments:

Graduated in twelve-minute increments, with each whole degree numbered, in latitude and longitude, from 18°00' to 25°00' N, and from 285°00' to 297°00' E, on a rectangular projection. The map includes, near its southern edge, a full though small scale depiction of Jamaica, and also a nearly full depiction of Hispaniola, considerably different in form from no. 62, Gastaldi's individual map of that island. Grande notes that much earlier depictions of Cuba existed, not as separate maps, but as an island in maps covering much larger areas, and that there were serious errors in all of them (1905, *carte*, 53), and says that the first improvements of these errors came from the texts of Martire and Oviedo (Grande, cit., 54); note that these are textual and not cartographic sources. Gastaldi follows Oviedo as in Ramusio (Grande, cit., 54 and again on 55), so, though on a small scale, again we have Gastaldi working from texts instead of other maps, a procedure which he followed so often. The island in Gastaldi is eight degrees in width compared with ca. eleven degrees in reality (cit., 54).

Grande notes that the latitudinal breadth of the island north to south, approximately two and a half degrees compared to ca. three degrees in reality, is pretty good, which he says is "clear proof of the precision of the calculations of Oviedo and Gastaldi" (cit., 55). Again, we must bring Grande down to earth here. Oviedo may well have made observations of latitude, accompanied by the simple calculations needed, for it is generally known that Oviedo was capable of utilizing limited astronomical techniques, but Gastaldi uses neither astronomy or survey in his maps, even those of areas close to home, not to mention Cuba! Furthermore, even as to Oviedo, a relative error of a half degree of latitude over a small span certainly indicates no great expertise, for European astronomers could do far better at the time, though, as noted elsewhere, there exists little evidence that astronomers' skills had yet been assimilated into the geographical community in more than a very rudimentary way. Some scholars seem to wish otherwise, but I believe their reasoning belongs more to the history of psychology than that of cartography. However all this may be, we return to the map at hand. There are no internal names on the map of Cuba, but thirty-eight on the littoral, only half of which are accounted for by recourse to cartographic sources (ten from Ribero and nine from Agnese), while the other half come from Oviedo's text, which, I suspect, also includes some of the nineteen found on the above-named cartographic sources. Unlike all the other maps in the Ptolemy, this map and the following map enjoyed several separate later reissues, for which see Karrow (1993, 222).

Reference:
Grande, 1905, *carte*, 53-57.

Reproductions:
Bifolco and Ronca, 2018, 1: 115.

https://www.davidrumsey.com/luna/servlet/detail/
RUMSEY~8~1~291373~90063101

62. Hispaniola (modern)
-Venice, 1548
-Copper engraving, 12.5 x 17.0 cm., on one sheet
-No scale bar

Along the top border of the map:
ISOLA SPAGNOLA NOVA (MODERN ISLAND OF HISPANIOLA)

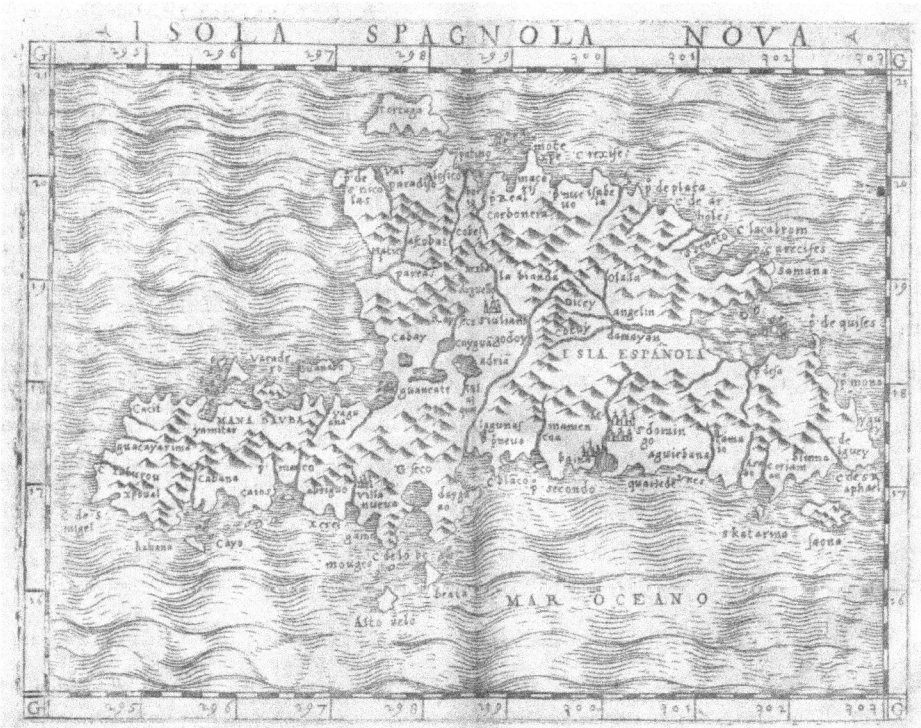

62 Hispaniola (modern) 1548 Rumsey

Comments:
Graduated in twelve-minute increments, with each whole degree numbered,
in latitude and longitude, from 15°00' to 25°00' N, and from 294°00' to
303°00' E, on a rectangular projection as prescribed by Ptolemy. The
latitudinal breadth of the island on the map is from 16°25' to 20°14' N (total

3°49'), while actual is 17°33' to 19°58' N (total 2°25'). Thus, while the southern latitude figure is off 1°08', the northern tip is off only by 16', but one must not allow oneself to be impressed by this latter figure, for there are many thousands of latitudes of places on the earth shown on old maps, which means of course that a few will by the simple theory of probability be very close, and such must be considered flukes, if we wish to keep our feet on the ground. In the present case, it is both wiser and more realistic to look upon the 1°08' error as typical of the skills behind the map's figures than the 16' error. *Only if we had a substantial group of determinations over some small area, say five instances, but better ten or more, and these were the total group, and not some selection from a larger group, and found the average error to be 16', which would eliminate the woefully ever-present and insidious element of fluke, would we have a basis to be impressed.* There is, we must note, also a Gastaldi map of Hispaniola in the 1556 volume three of Ramusio (no. 81) in which the island appears considerably narrower north to south than in this map, although we can't make precise comparisons, because that map is not graduated. Grande says that the latitudinal breadth of the island on the present map is precisely as in reality (Grande, 1905, *carte*, 58), but this is quite wrong as we have seen above. The *relative* longitudinal width of the island is 8° compared to 6°09' in reality. The orography is fairly good, and the hydrography better (Grande, cit., 59). It contains a good number of river names from Oviedo as in Ramusio, and Gastaldi gives the administrative divisions of the island, which are from Martire, again as in Ramusio. In a general way, the island conforms to the description in Martire, and Grande says that Martire is without doubt the main source for the map (cit., 60). Finally, of eighty-five names on the island, only twelve are from the maps of Ribero and Agnese, so clearly almost all are from the texts of Martire and Oviedo, and so once again we have a Gastaldi map which is fully original and compiled mainly from textual sources. Like the previous map, this map was reissued several times, for which see Karrow (1993, 222).

Reference:
Grande, 1905, *carte*, 58-62.

Reproductions:
Bifolco and Ronca, 2018, 1: 115.
https://www.davidrumsey.com/luna/servlet/detail/
RUMSEY~8~1~291375~90063103

63. World (modern)
-Venice, 1548
-Copper engraving, 13.0 x 17.0 cm., on one sheet
-No scale bar

Along the top border of the map:
VNIVERSALE NOVO (MODERN WORLD MAP)

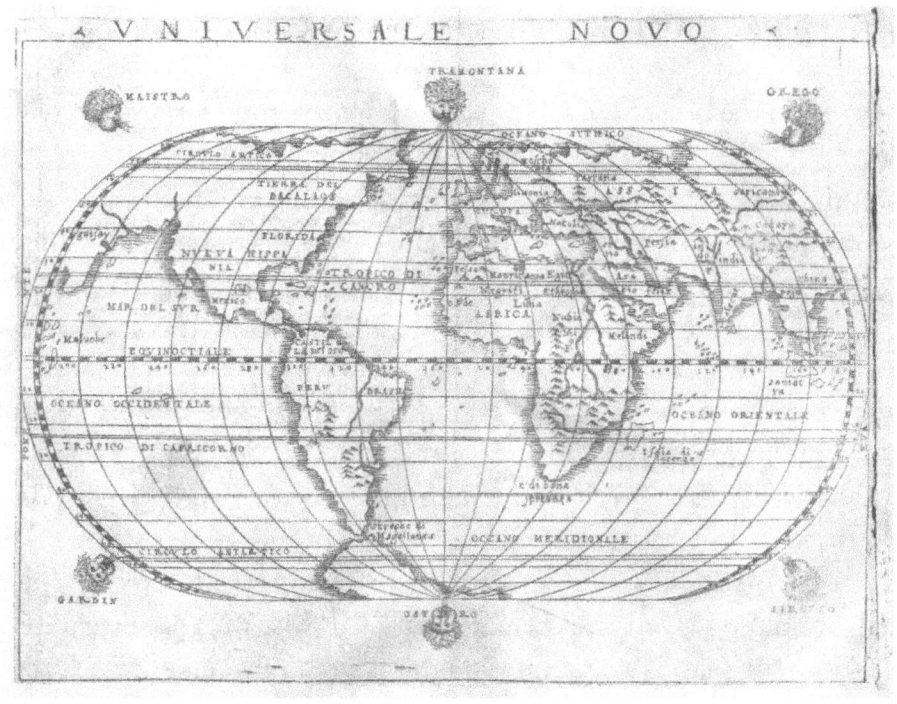

63 World (modern) 1548 Rumsey

Comments:
Graduated in two-degree increments in latitude, and four-degree increments
in longitude, on an oval projection, with parallels and meridians drawn in,
the parallels at ten-degree intervals, and the meridians at twenty-degree

594

intervals. The prime meridian passes through the eastmost of the Canary Islands. Six windheads adorn the map outside the oval. The map lacks the capital "G" found in the corners of most of the Ptolemy maps. At first glance, the map seems simply a reduction of the 1546 world map (no. 3), and several authors have stated this to be the case (Wagner, 1937, 1, 28; Shirley, 1987, no. 87). The similarity, to be sure, is striking, and the assessment cannot be considered as completely wrong. But upon inspection, we find a few significant differences. On this map, the Southern Continent rises only to the left, while on the 1546 map, it rises both to the left and right. Also, here there is nothing in the area around the North Pole, while on the 1546 there is a land mass or a frozen sea. Again, the great Totonteach River which exits at the head of the Gulf of California in 1546 here exits ca. twenty degrees further north, and not into the Gulf of California, but directly into the Pacific. Still again, while here the Amazon (Maragnon) has little curvature to it, in 1546 its course is quite snaky. And more important than all these differences, on the present map the eastern tip of South America is twenty-five degrees east of the eastern tip of North America, while in 1546, the difference is a mere two degrees. Furthermore, the undulating wavy pattern for the sea on the 1546 map (and on all the previous maps in the Ptolemy which show water) is missing here, and there is no texturing given to the sea at all (as is the case with the next map, no. 64, the last in the book). And no doubt other differences could be found. Nevertheless, we feel that the map should be considered as basically belonging to the large group of reprints and reeditions of the 1546 map which continue into the 1590s, or perhaps it is better to say that it is cognate with that group, for we cannot be certain that the present map was not actually drawn before the 1546 map. The text on the recto of the left half of the map is exactly as in the title-box text on the undated world map "Dell'Vniversale" (no. 66), which we date (tentatively) as ca. 1550. The map is not at all remarkable, but one can expect little of a world map of such small size. The question of sources has not been gone into, but Minella (1993, 33-34) notes similarities as to South America with two Agnese world maps of 1536 and 1542, and still greater similarity for that continent in the maps of Ribero (cit., 34).

References:
Nordenskiöld, 1897, 188b; Grande, 1905, *carte*, 63-65 and 107; Bjørnbo, 1912, 314-15, 317 and 320; Caraci, 1936, 121 nt. 2; Wagner, 1937, 1, 28 and II, no. 19; Shirley, 1987, no. 87; Minella, 1993, 31-34.

Reproductions:
Bifolco and Ronca, 2018, 1: 115.
https://www.davidrumsey.com/luna/servlet/detail/
RUMSEY~8~1~291377~90063105

64. World (modern)
-Venice, 1548
-Copper engraving, 12.5 x 17.0 cm., on one sheet
-No scale bar

Along the top border of the map:
CARTA MARINA NOVA TABVLA (MODERN MARINE CHART MAP)

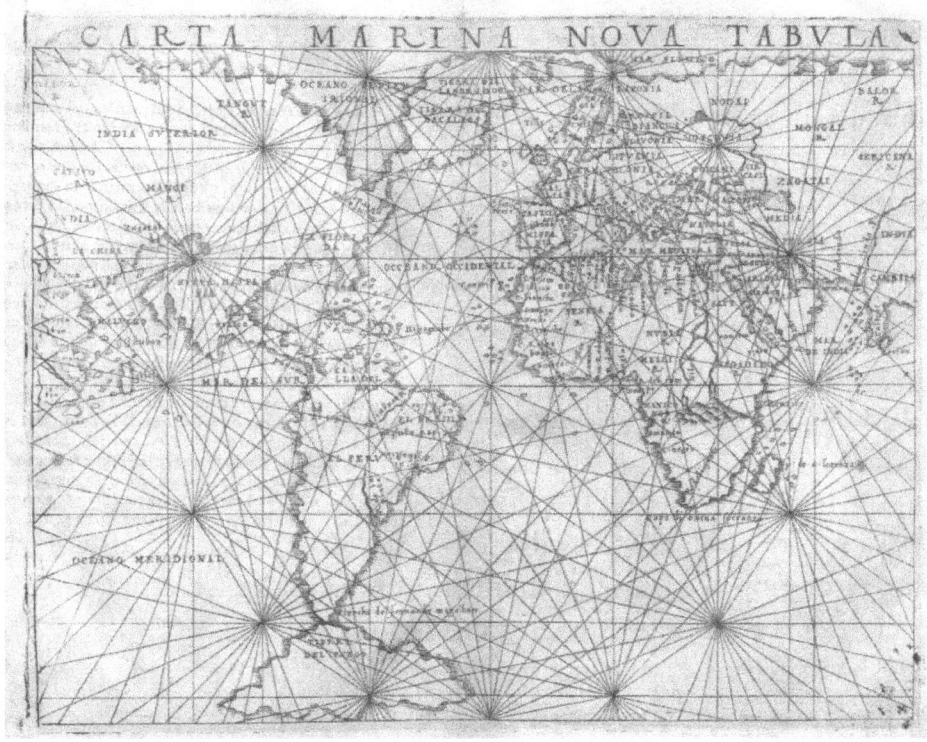

64 World marine chart (modern) 1548 Rumsey

Comments:

The map carries no graduation and is the only map in the Ptolemy not to do so. It is made in imitation of the type of manuscript maps which developed out of the old normal portolan tradition (in which the charts showed only the Mediterranean and Black seas), after Europeans began to sail the high seas, maps which were a sort of combination of world-map and portolan chart, such as the ca. 1526 Salviati map, or Ribero's maps, and which are crisscrossed by a net of rhumb-lines (perhaps it is best to say pseudo-rhumb lines), as on Gastaldi's map. Gastaldi's map, however, would have been of no use to practical navigators and was probably just intended as a theoretical example (Grande, 1905, *carte*, 67; Minella, 1993, 35). Gastaldi's text, on the recto of the left half of the map, partly quoted by Grande, tends to substantiate this idea. But what makes the map truly interesting is the extreme difference in the geography shown by comparison with the preceding world map, no. 63. Nothing could bring out more eloquently Gastaldi's philosophy of cartography as regards parts of the world's geography about which there remained uncertainty as to what was correct than the presence of these two maps together in one atlas, and, in fact, one writer has, in this case, caught the essence of things here. Lawrence C. Wroth, who has been speaking of this map, and Gastaldi's 1546 and 1548 world maps (nos. 3 and 63) writes: "The presence of these diversities of statement in three Gastaldi maps of the years 1546-48, two of them in the same book of 1548, is evidence of uncertainty in the cartographer's mind" (Wroth, 1970, 193). The number of places for which we see different depictions of the same area on this map by comparison with the preceding one is considerable, and the differences are often not small, but involve very large features. We haven't time to discuss most of them, but among the most striking such features, we mention the land bridge (incorporating within itself the lands of "Laborador" and "Bacalaos") connecting northeastern North America to northern Europe, of which we have spoken in our main text (see chapter eight, at the section, "Our Conclusions"), and also the very peculiar large gulf-like indentation into the area of northwestern North America. Some have suggested that this represents a sort of Sea of Verrazzano which was for some reason curtailed in its eastward course across the continent long before it began to get close to the Atlantic, as the

Sea of Verrazzano is supposed to do (Wagner, 1937, 2, 28; Stokes, 1915-28, 2, 16), but this is quite unconvincing. A Sea of Verrazzano which does not all but break through the eastern seaboard of North America is not a Sea of Verrazzano. I suspect that it might be an early interpretation by Gastaldi of the passage from Ramusio's edition of Marco Polo in which Polo mentions Ania and the Gulf of Cheinan, which passage we have quoted elsewhere (see "Special Endnote to Chapter Eight: The Name Anian"), presuming of course that Ramusio had the Polo manuscript with the passage in hand by the time Gastaldi made this map, which I think is likely. A reading of this confusing passage with this area on Gastaldi's map under the eye of the reader will reveal the basis for my conjecture. Only Minella has touched upon the question of sources for this map. He suggests, in a broad way, possible influence of Verrazzano, Agnese, Marco Polo, Olaus Magnus, and, finally, the undated printed map sometimes referred to as the "Florentine Goldsmith's map", made after a manuscript by Giorgio Callapoda, which Minella dates as 1544, though he doesn't say why. The map is reproduced by Shirley (1987, no. 98). But, judging from Shirley's comments, that map would probably be of 1552, too late to influence the Gastaldi map, and also, while there is on that map a great sea cutting into northwestern North America from the west, that sea is a true Verrazzano Sea type, all but protruding right through to the Atlantic, so the resemblance between the two maps is superficial and illusory.

References:
Winsor, 1883-84, in No. 27, p. 228a; Grande, 1905, *carte*, 66-68; Bjørnbo, 1912, 248-49 and 313; Stokes, 1915-28, 2, 16; Caraci, 1936, 132 nt. 2; Wagner, 1937, 1, 28 and 2, no. 16; Wroth, 1970, 192-94 and 299; Shirley, 1987, no. 88 and in no. 98; Milanesi, 1992, 30-31; Minella, 1993, 35-37.

Reproductions:
Bifolco and Ronca, 2018, 1: 115.
https://www.davidrumsey.com/luna/servlet/detail/
RUMSEY~8~1~291379~90063107

65. Africa (with an inset of most of America)
-Venice, 1549-1550
-Painted wall map of unknown size, but probably of comparable dimensions as no. 72
-Unknown if it had a scale bar

Comment
While the present Cartobibliography is in general devoted to printed maps, we have in three cases (nos. 65, 71 and 72) included non-printed maps, because of their clear general importance to Gastaldi's cartographic career. The present map is the first of those three. This map, which does not survive, was made under commission from the Venetian Council of Ten, and was drawn in charcoal by Gastaldi, and then painted by an artist Vitruvio Buonconsiglio in 1549-50 on a wall of a room called the Sala dello Scudo (Hall of the Shield) in the Venetian Ducal Palace. The map was very likely of the same or similar dimensions as map no. 72 (perhaps 2.6 x 8 meters), a truly enormous map, and was probably south oriented, like that map. According to the original instructions given to Gastaldi by the council, the map was to include all of Africa, the Mediterranean Sea, and Arabia, at least as far east as Mecca, as well as the land of Brazil (for the full text of the document giving the original instructions, see Lorenzi, 1868, 265-66, doc. No. 571). The inclusion in the instructions of Brazil reflects very unclear notions of geography on the part of the council, perhaps due to confusion in connection with Cabral's voyage. Gastaldi, having found that it was not possible to accommodate Brazil due to the shape of the space allotted for the task, offered to include, by way of compensation as it were, in an inset in the Atlantic, presumably in the space including the Bight of Benin and the part of the South Atlantic west of the South African coast, an inset which would itself have been a map of quite large size, occupying perhaps as much as a fourth of the whole enormous panel, and which would include New Spain, the Caribbean, and northern South America, including a small part of Brazil, and this compromise was accepted by the council (see doc. 573 at pp. 267-68 in Lorenzi, cit.). One might wonder, considering the original instructions, why Gastaldi did not simply include the whole of Brazil in the inset, but the fact that Gastaldi ventured to talk the austere council into allowing him to

include this map of the greater part of all of America instead of only Brazil certainly provides further attestation to Gastaldi's great interest in the new continent. Nothing remains today of the map, and it seems not to be known when and why it met its demise. None of the writers with which I am familiar broach the subject. As to the source Gastaldi used for the map, we can I think be certain that it was the large Africa upon which he had been working for a number of years, and of which we have spoken elsewhere (see chapter nine, note 8 and no. 118 below). Work on the map, we should note, is presumed to have been supervised by Ramusio (Almagià, 1929, 34), and the project may even have been initiated by him (Gallo, 1943, 59). In a later work, Gallo feels less certain of the nature of Ramusio's association with the project (1955, 212), and Karrow is noncommittal on the point (1993, 226). But considerations brought out by us toward the end of our compound entry (77.-79.) strongly suggest that Ramusio probably did play a role in directing the work. It is worth pointing out that, since, as mentioned, the inset map of the greater part of America would have been a rather large map in itself, it would have been on much larger scale than anything that Gastaldi had produced for that continent previously.

References:
Lorenzi, 1868, 265-68 (docs. 571-573); Almagià, 1929, 34 and 75; Almagià, 1939, *carta*, 8; Gallo, 1943, 59-62; Knauer, 1981, 58 and 119-22; Karrow, 1993, 223-24; Rizzo, 2006, 84a.

66. World
-Venice, ca. 1550(?)
-Woodcut, 57.0 x 77.0 cm., on two sheets
-No scale bar

In the title text box at right of top center:
DELL'VNIVERSALE. | L'Vniuersale Orbe della Terra, fu diuisa secondo gli antiqui in tre parti, cioe Europa, Aphrica, & | Asia. I equali parti hanno di longitudine gradi.clxxx.principiãdo all'Isole canarie, il primo grado. | Et e di latitudine verso Tramontana gradi seisantatre, cominciando il primo grado dall'Equinoctiale, | & verso mezzo giorno gradi diece. Tutto il resto che si

vede di longitudine, che sono altri gradi cento | ottanta, e stato discoperto da moderni,cioe l'Indie occidentali, che hoggi di il vulgo chiamano il Mon | do nuouo,perche non si ha mai inteso da niuno antiquo,che ne faceite mentione.Pero lo chiamano nuo- | uo,ilquale e verso occidente,alle sopradette Isole Canarie, Pero sumando questi gradi cent'ottanta, ver | so Oriente discoperti da gli antiqui,con gli gradi cent'ottanta verso pon'te, discoperti da moderni fan | no gradi trecento sessanta,che e tutto il circulo dello Equinoctiale nella Sphera.Et la parte di sopra gli | gradi seisantatre di latitudine settentrionale e stata discoperta da Moderni,cioe la Noruegia, e Grutlan | dia,cõ molte altre prouincie.Et la parte piu meridionale di gradi diece di latitudine, e stata anchora di- | scoperta da moderni.Benche Ariano, & Plinio dicono che fu discoperta da gli antiqui, ma non si troua | particular descriptione,come hauemo hoggi di da Moderni. | Iacomo Gastaldo Cosmographo.In Venetia. (OF THE WORLD MAP. The Universal orb of the Earth.was divided according to the ancients into three parts, that is, Europe, Africa & Asia. which parts have 180. degrees. of longitude, beginning at the Canary Islands, the first degree. And there are in latitude towards the North sixty three degrees, beginning the first degree at the Equinoctial, and towards the south ten degrees. All the rest which is seen of longitude, which are another one hundred [and] eighty, have been discovered by the moderns, that is the west Indies, which today is popularly called the new World, because there is had no knowledge of any ancient, who makes mention of it. But that which is towards the west of the aforesaid Canary Islands is called new. However, summing these one hundred and eighty degrees towards the East discovered by the ancients, with the one hundred and eighty degrees towards the west, discovered by the moderns makes three hundred and sixty degrees, which is the full circle of the Equinoctial in the Sphere. And the part above sixty-three degrees of northern latitude has been discovered by the moderns, that is, Norway, and Greenland, with many other provinces. And the part further south than ten degrees of latitude has been also discovered by the moderns. Although Arrian & Pliny say that it was discovered by the ancients, there is found no detailed description, as we have today from the Moderns. Giacomo Gastaldo Cosmographo. In Venetia.)

At lower left, outside the edge of the oval, and right of Marco Polo's portrait:

InVenetia per Matio pagan | in Frezaria al Segno della | Fede (In Venice by
Matteo Pagano in Frezaria [Street] at the Sign of Faith)

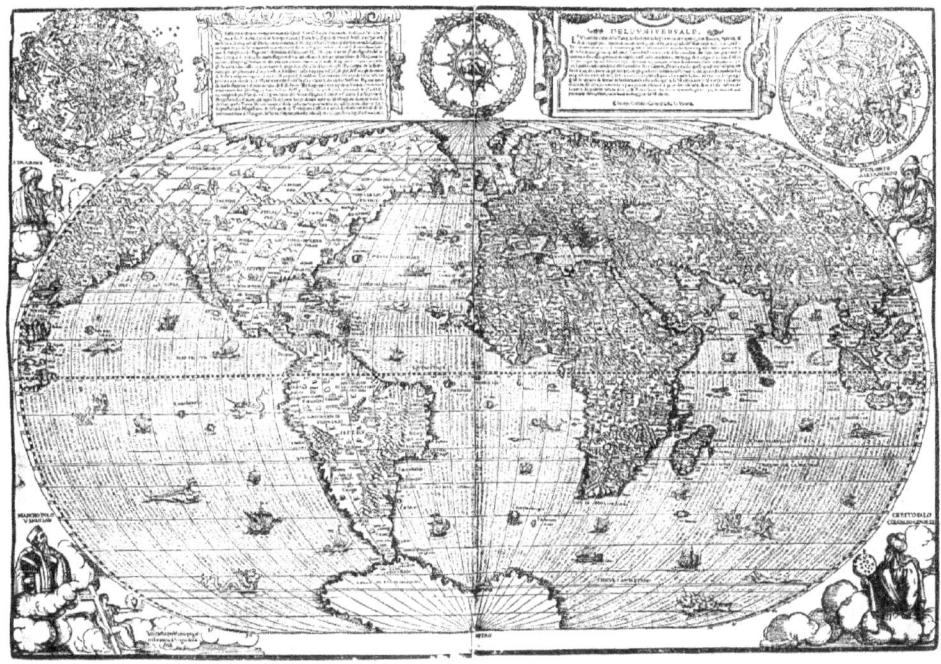

66 World 1550? London BL

Comments:

Graduated in whole degrees in latitude (on the borders) and longitude (on the
equator), with meridians and parallels drawn in at ten-degree intervals, on an
oval projection. The prime meridian passes through the eastmost Canary
Island, as on the 1546 world map (no. 3). Longitude graduation runs
eastward from here around the world 360 degrees. The map exists in only
one copy, found in the British Library in 1915 by Godfrey Sykes (Sykes,
1915, 161-62). Basically, the map is simply a copy of the 1546 world map
and is thus part of the large series of cognates of the 1546 map, most of
which would appear only from 1560 on. But it is on much larger scale than
the 1546 map, and indeed on larger scale than any of the others in the series
of cognates, including the rather large 1565 rendition by Bertelli, and is thus
by far the largest of all in that series. It has a few relatively minor
differences in its geography by comparison with the 1546 map, partly just

602

cosmetic in nature: The northeast tip of North America is truncated and does not extend to the top of the map as in 1546; and there is no Polar landmass, or frozen sea ("Mare Congellato"). In eastmost Asia, and in all of America, which have a rather blank appearance in 1546, there has been added much orography, forestry, and vignettes of animals and armed tribes, as well as some further toponyms, especially in South America; around the edges of the oval décor has been added, including the northern and southern celestial spheres in the two top corners, and portraits of four famous geographers, Strabo, Ptolemy, Marco Polo, and Columbus. The map is undated, and there has been much disagreement as to what approximate date to assign to it. But the text in the title box quoted above is found verbatim on the recto of the left side of the "Vniversale Novo" (no. 63) in the 1548 Ptolemy, which suggests to me that it probably was issued not long after that, and thus my tentative date of ca. 1550(?). Wagner (1937, 1, 28) and Bagrow-Skelton (1985, 135) give an estimated date of 1548, which is also possible.

Location of copy:
London BL(Maps C.7.c.17.) (only copy known)

References:
Sykes, 1915, 161-62; Caraci, 1936, 121, 123, 131, and 132; Wagner, 1937, 1, 28 and II, no. 17; Bagrow-Skelton, 1985, 135; Shirley, 1987, no. 89; Meurer, 1991, 149; Karrow, 1993, 30/65; Minella, 1993, 71-73; Bifolco and Ronca, 2018, 1: 228-31.

Reproductions:
Sykes, 1915, pl. 6; Bagrow, 1940; Shirley, 1987, no. 89; Meurer, 1991, pl. 30; Bifolco and Ronca, 2018, 1: 230-31.

67. Muscovy (European Russia)
-Venice, 1550
-Woodcut, 26.5 x 38.5 (26.5) cm., on one sheet
-No scale bar

In title box at middle low right part of the map:

Descriptione de la Mo | scovia. Per Giacomo | gastaldo piamõtese |
Cosmographo in Ve | netia M D L. (Map of Muscovy by Giacomo gastaldo
piedmontese Cosmographer in Venice 1550.)

67 Muscovy (European Russia) 1550 Helsinki AEN

Comments:
Graduated in whole degrees, each numbered, in latitude and longitude, from
46°00' to 60°00' N, and from 31°00' to 90°00' E, on a trapezoidal projection.
The map was basically derived from Agustin Hirschvogel's 1549 map of
Muscovy (reproduced in Nordenskiöld, 1889, p. 121; the original edition of
Hirschvogel's map was 1546), and it was made to accompany the 1550 book
Comentari Della Moscovia Et Parimente della Russia, etc, the Italian
edition, published in Venice by Pedrezzano (the publisher, we recall, of
Gastaldi's 1548 Ptolemy) of Sigmund von Herberstein's 1549 book on
Russia. The map is pasted to a flyleaf at the end of the book and is folded.
Hirschvogel's original map carries no graduation, and Gastaldi has imposed a
coordinate grid on the map, a major point which is lauded by Almagià: "The

merit of our cartographer is to have fitted Herberstein's depiction, which lacked graduation, into a net of coordinates" (1934, 145), and he notes this again later (1948, 25), as does Bagrow (1975, 88b). As to the general geographical contents of the map, opinions have oddly varied as to how much the Gastaldi map represents an improvement over the original Hirschvogel-Herberstein map. Michow repeatedly expressed the opinion that Gastaldi's map was simply an expanded copy of the original map, and had no originality about it (1884, 105; 1906, 18; 1907, 16). But Nordenskiöld stated: "There are . . . so many additions and essential improvements made in Gastaldi's map that it may be considered as an almost independent work" (1889, 114), and others followed in the same vein (Almagià, 1948, 25; Bagrow, 1962, 47 and 1975, 88). A fair assessment seems to be that in the most central part of the map, it is basically just a copy from Hirschvogel-Herberstein, but in the periphery, considered rather broadly, there is a great deal which is quite innovative. Sundry sources have been given for the improvements, including the text of Herberstein's book (Bagrow, 1975, 88; Licini, 1908, 103); sea-charts (for the Black and Azov Sea areas)(Almagià, 1934, 145); Olaus Magnus (Bagrow, 1975, 88); two of Gastaldi's own maps from his 1548 Ptolemy, the "Prvssia et Livonia Nova" (no. 24) (Almagià, 1934, 145), and the "Moschovia Nova" (no. 42) (Licini, 1988, 103), and information obtained from Venetian merchants who frequented the Black Sea area (Licini, 1988, 106). A truly definitive analysis, if possible, remains to be done, as is the case with at least significant parts of many Gastaldi maps, but the best and fullest treatment of the present map so far is that of Licini. There were several reprintings or reeditions of the map, for which see Licini, 1988, 106 and Karrow, 1993, 224-25.

Location of copies (of the book):
New York PL(*KB 1550)/ Edinburgh UL(D.S.g.4.21)/ New Haven Yale(Edb 517Hi) and (2004 745)/ Chicago Newb(Wing ZP 535 .P34)/ Cambridge Harv(Houghton Typ 525.50.450)/ Oxford Bodl(55 d.112)/ Edinburgh NLS(A.82.b)/Helsinki AEN/ London BL(150.d.12) and (G.7321)/ Paris BN(RES- M- 508) and (SMITH LESOUEF R- 9522)/ Wien ÖNB(19.T.42)/ Northridge CS(DK21 .H57 1550)/ Hartford TC(DK21 .H5317 1550)/ Urbana

UIL(X 914.7 H41 Rl 1550)/ Williamstown WC(German)/ Boston
BA($XB .H41 1550)/ Ann Arbor UML(DK21 .H536)/ Minneapolis
Bell(H133)/ Provo BY(914.7 H41 1550)/ London WellcInst(3110)/
Trondheim UB(HS, Ult. Thule, Lapon 39)

References:
Michow, 1884, 105; Nordenskiöld, 1889, 113b-114a; Grande, 1902, 71-72;
Michow, 1906, 18-19; Michow, 1907, 16; Bagrow, 1928-30, 1, 83 and 108;
Almagià, 1934, 145; Almagià, carta, 1939, 8a and 19a; Almagià, 1948, 25;
Bagrow, 1962, 47; Bagrow, 1975, 88b; Licini, 1988, 101-11; Karrow, 1993,
224-25.

Reproductions:
Bagrow, 1975, 89.
https://www.doria.fi/bitstream/handle/10024/91779/N_1958_k1.jpg?
sequence'1&isAllowed'y [the Helsinki copy]

68. The Nile Basin
-Venice, 1550
-Woodcut, 15,0 x 22.5, on one sheet
-No scale bar

The map has no title or significant texts

Comments:
Graduated in whole degrees in latitude and longitude, numbered every fifth
degree, but only on the left side for latitude, and only on the equator for
longitude, from 25°00' S to 33°00' N, and from 42°00' to 80°00' E. Because
of the limited nature of the graduations, the projection is indeterminate. The
map is oriented to the south. This was the only map in the 1550 first edition
of volume one of Ramusio's *Navigazioni*. It is one of the least important and
least striking maps in Gastaldi's repertoire. It is very schematic, and contains
few names, and this and its specialized coverage no doubt account for the
very little interest that has ever been shown in it. Its rationale for inclusion
in the volume is as follows. The great question of the Nile had occupied

heads since antiquity and resolved itself into two queries: What explained the annual floods, and what could be the source of this tremendous volume of water, questions with obvious spiritual or mystical overtones. Was it a manifestation of some God? Ramusio and Fracastoro discussed it at some length, and the essence of Ramusio's ideas is included in a five-page discourse in this volume, followed by a ten-page response by Fracastoro (for a lengthy discussion of this dialogue between the two, see Grande, 1905, "relazioni," 119-32; see also Parks, 1970, 11). Thus, the map is an occasional one, relevant only to this interchange between the two scholars, and is in no way a map intended to serve generally as illustrative material for the book, such as are the maps in the 1554 second edition of the same volume, and thus no doubt, as said, its low interest level for scholars. Biasutti, however, makes the interesting observation that, since there are significant hydrographical differences between this 1550 map and the general Africa map in the 1554 second edition of the volume, this is a definite indication of receipt by Gastaldi in the interim of new and better information (1920, 411), and this would probably be the information found in Barros's First Decade, the geographical chapter of which Ramusio includes in the 1554 second edition of volume one. The map was reproduced in all later editions of volume one (1554, 1563, 1588, 1606, and 1613).

Location of copies (of the book):
London BL(C.46.i.3)/ London WellcInst(5327/D)/ New York PL(*KB+ 1550)/ Oxford Bodl(Mason GG 180)/ Paris BN(G- 1416) and (G- 1451)/ New Haven Yale(1977 + 253)/ Austin UTL(-Q- G 159 R2 1550)/ Madrid UB(BH FLL 20682)/ Los Angeles UCLA(*Z233.G44 R149p 1550)/ Washington LC(G159 .R2 vol. 1 folio)/ Providence JCB((1-SIZE H550 .R184n, v. 1)/ Minneapolis Bell(R34)/ Roma BN(69.3.E.15)/ Venezia QS(PIANO I A 0915)/ Williamstown WC(Am1550 .R3 vol. 1 folio)/ Claremont CC(910.4 R15 v. 1)/ San Diego UCSD(G50.B7 1547 B/W Vlt)

References:
Biasutti, 1920, 411-12; Rainero, 1982, 11; Eversole, 1983, p. [2].

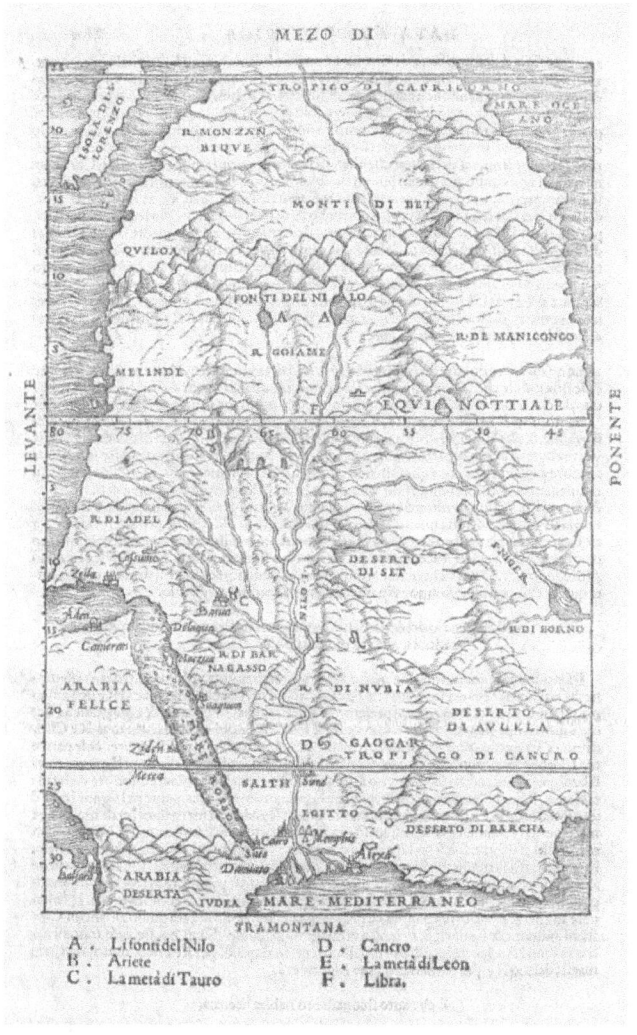

68 The Nile Basin 1550 New York PL

608

69. Western inland Asia
[Note: The following describes the only known copy, unfortunately in bad condition, of a 1555 Antwerp edition by Hieronymus Cock of a Gastaldi map, no copy of the original of which is known, although it may be considered as certain that its first edition was published in Venice at some time between 1550 and 1555, most likely at some time closer to the earlier date.]

-Antwerp, 1555 (original edition Venice, between 1550 and 1555)
-Copper engraving, 35.5 x 52.0 cm., on two sheets
-100 Italian miles = 1.5 cm.

Along the top border of the map:
TOTIVS ILLIVS REGIONIS QVAM HODIE TVRCICAM | VOCANT , NEC NON PERS IAE REGNI EXACTISSIMA DESCRIPTIO, Per Iacobum Castaldum | cosmograph apud Venetos (A MOST EXACT MAP OF ALL THAT REGION WHICH TODAY IS CALLED TURKEY AND ALSO THE KINGDOM OF PERSIA By Iacobus Castaldus cosmographer in Venice)

A text box occurs in the upper right corner beginning with the words: *TIPOGRAPHVS SPECTATORI (PRINTER TO THE OBSERVER)*, followed by seven lines of text, ending with: *ANTVERPIAE APVD HIERONYMVM COCK CVM | CAESAREAE MA[iesta]tis PRIVILEGIO AD SEXENNIVM | 1555 (ANTWERP BY HIERONYMUS COCK WITH THE PRIVILEGE OF THE SOVEREIGN EMPEROR FOR SIX YEARS 1555)*. There are too many letters and parts of words which have flaked off or worn away with time in the main body of the seven-line inscription between the words just given for the author to feel confidant of a full transcription of the original text. However, as to a translation, the following perhaps adequately or near adequately grasps the gist: *PRINTER TO THE OBSERVER Behold with the studious the chorography of all this region (which today is commonly called Turkey) and also Persia with the intermediate realms in your pleasing map, by which at almost a single glance, it is possible for you to understand the itineraries [expeditions/expedition routes/incursion routes??] against[of??] that vast enemy of the Christian race in[into??] Persia, since that advance is*

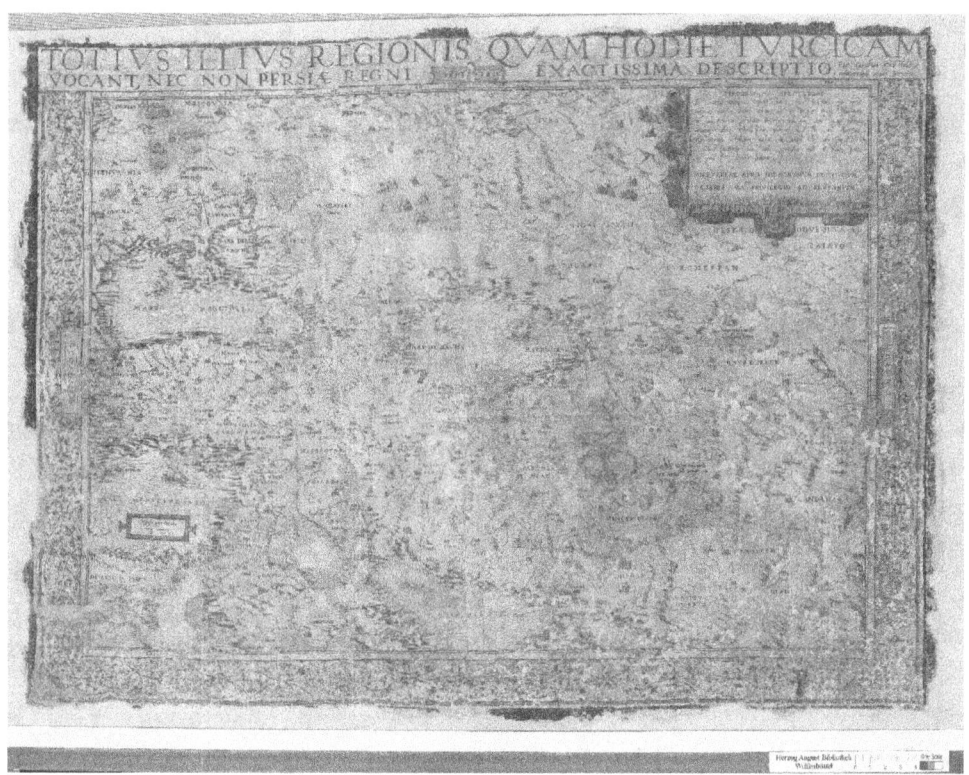

69 Western Inland Asia 1555 Wolfenbüttel HAB

indicated by dotted lines from Constantinople. Farewell, buy and enjoy our labor. Admittedly, not all is quite clear in our tentative translation attempt, but, to be sure, several (I have found four) series of red dotted lines are faintly, but quite clearly visible on the map, two of them starting at Constantinople, one of which meanders east-southeast in a slightly undulating path clear across Anatolia to the edges of Persia, and the other of which, shorter, runs southeast from Constantinople to south middle Anatolia, where it stops. There are two others, still shorter (assuming they are visible in their entirety), one of which runs inland southeast a little from near the northeast corner of the Mediterranean Sea and stops, while the fourth runs a short ways east and west perhaps in northern Iraq. None of this adds up to anything very clear, and while the syntactic and grammatical problems of the text make full clarity impossible there, these dotted lines seem to be incursion routes or itineraries by which incursions are made against the Turks by the Persians, a fact which could have been of interest to Venetian map readers, since Venice, while not really allied with, was aligned with Persia against the Turks at the time. From what I understand, there were no real actions at the time between the two nations, but only tensions, so these dotted routes may not be routes that were actually used, but considered as potential, and their presence here may be more propagandistic or sensational instead of real. In any event, it seems clear enough that these dotted lines are to be taken as itineraries or routes envisioned as being useful in some military sense, and certainly have nothing to do with routes followed by noted travelers in their peregrinations, such as Marco Polo, or Ibn Battuta, etc. The significance of these observations appended here will become clear below. We proceed to a general discussion of the map proper.

Comments:

The map, on a trapezoidal projection, is graduated in whole degrees, numbered at each fifth degree, in latitude and longitude, from 24°00' to 59°45' N, and from 43°30' to 130°00' E along the top border, and 60°00' to 116°10' along the lower border. The area coverage of the map is very similar to that in Gastaldi's 1559 First Part of Asia (no. 92), except that the present map extends slightly farther in all directions. On the other hand, the First Part of Asia is considerably larger (42.5 x 72.0 cm.), and so there is less detail on the present map, although there is clearly enough space that many more towns and details could have been included, at least in the Cock edition. The map contains only approximately a third of the nomenclature of the 1559 map. But in general it appears that all the names on the present map are found on the 1559 map, and in my opinion our map may possibly be considered as a direct forerunner to that 1559 map, and conceivably even represents a false and perhaps premature start towards the three Parts of Asia of 1559-1561. We shall further discuss this possibility, and also correct a certain misconception concerning the map which Almagià arrived at in 1962, but before we can properly proceed, we must make a short digression in order to bring out an important circumstance.

There exists an application for, and concession of, a Venetian privilege for a map of Asia, dated July 15, 1550, and made out to Gastaldi in partnership with Michel Membré. Parts of both the application and the concession have been printed. The former describes the map as being "of all the cities and kingdoms which are in the part [continent] of Asia, commencing from the Mediterranean sea and going towards the East, where is all of Turkey, Syria and Persia with the land of the Sophi [The sovereign of Persia was at the time referred to in Europe as the "Sophi", according to Almagià, 1963, 3] and from there toward the north northeast, where is the land of Cathay, [and] toward the south where India and the spice islands lie" (Fabris, 1989, in the original Italian, who gives the location of the document as Archivio di Stato di Venezia, Senato Terra, reg. 37, cc. 35v-36r; Brown gives the same passage [1891, 102] minus a little at the beginning, in English, with the location given only as "Senato Terra, filza 11"). No more of the application than we have given here is available in print. Almagià quotes from the concession of the privilege, which, as usual, is of the same date: "On the Day July 15 (1550): that with all the authority of this Council is conceded to Master Giacomo Piedmontese cosmographer and to Michel Membré Partner ["Compani"] in this that anyone else except them without their permission for the next ten years may not print or have printed or sell in this City or in any place of our Dominion even if it were printed elsewhere, the detailed map made by them of all the Cities and realms which are in Asia under penalty and with all the terms contained in their supplication." (Almagià, 1962, 3, who in note 5 gives the location of the document as: "SV, Senato Terra I, R[egistr]o 37 1550-51, fol. 35v"). Gallo (1955, 211) says only that the privilege was conceded, without quoting any of it, but gives the location as "SV, Senato Terra, filza 11, Decreto 1550, 15 luglio." Fabris (1989, 9) quotes a small part of the above, and rather over-tersely gives the location, evidently, as "filza 11, 15 luglio, 1550." It should be noted, to avert more confusion than already exists concerning this map, that both Karrow and Witcombe, having spoken of the July 15, 1550 *application* for privilege (copyright), state that nothing seems to have come of this request. This is quite wrong. The request was granted, and the map unquestionably published in Venice, for it is certainly the original of the 1555 Antwerp derivative. No Gastaldi first edition was published other than in Venice during his lifetime. Karrow seems to confuse the July 15, 1550 request for privilege, and the July 15, 1550 granting of privilege as being for different maps, but, both from the wording in the two documents and the simultaneity of their dates, it is obvious that both are for the Gastaldi-Membré Asia.

Note that we are at a disadvantage in our discussion, because we do not have in print the whole of these vital privilege documents. Clearly only a fragment of the first is in print, and the last is apparently not taken to its ending. These are certainly available in full in manuscript, for Horatio Brown in the nineteenth century recorded verbatim all Venetian printing privileges from 1527-1597 in full, and his work is preserved in the Marciana as a codex titled "Privilegi veneziani per la stampa (1527-1597)" under the call number "cod. Ital. VII, 2501 (12078)." The fullest description of Brown's very detailed work is in Mazzatinti, 1979 (109-10). Besides this, the original documents probably still exist, and could no doubt be retrieved easily enough, regardless of some inconsistencies in how they are cited by different authors, as given above. In the case of the present map, one would like to have these two documents in full, for, as we shall see, there is uncertainty as to how this map fits into Gastaldi's activities, and it is possible that something in these documents might help. We return to the main line of our text.

There is no question that a Venetian original of our map of ca. 1550 existed, and that that original was the map to which the July 15, 1550, application and concession of privilege applied. All writers who broached the subject have agreed on this (Bagrow, 1928-30, 1, 85; Almagià twice in 1948, 34 and 36; and Karrow, 1993, 229), with one exception: Almagià in a later work (1962, 9), but the basis for his objection is groundless. As we have seen, Gastaldi had a partner in this venture, Michel Membré. Membré worked for the Republic as a translator and interpreter of eastern languages, and in 1538 he was sent on a secret mission to the Sophi (sovereign of Persia), evidently to attempt to negotiate an alliance with Persia against the Turks. Now, as we have seen, there are red dotted lines on our map evidently representing general incursion or expedition routes or itineraries. But, said Almagià, there is no dotted route line for Membré's route, which is known, to and from Persia, which Almagià evidently felt would definitely be there if this were a copy of the map in the making of which Membré had had a hand. But in fact there is not the slightest reason to expect that Membré's route would have been on the map. The dotted lines on the map represent incursionary routes or itineraries, and not the private travels of any individual. And even if these lines *did* represent such travels, Membré's case would still not apply. For him, all that was important was the conference with the Persian leader. The trip there and back was incidental, and even if it had not been, it certainly would not have the same sort of significance as the incursion routes. It is true that Membré did write an account of his trip, which has recently become available in print, but it is by no means an explorer's account. There is not much of geographical value in it, and Membré's main interest was in describing human customs and living habits. It was a private one-man venture, and a secret one besides (Almagià, 1962, 3), and I can see no reason why Membré would have felt that his track should be on the map along with the other ones, of a very different nature.

Incidentally, Membré's partnership in the map venture also does not necessarily indicate a direct interest in geography but may simply have represented a business opportunity to him. Renzo Bragantini has written a very interesting article on the intense and complicated relations between Ramusio, Membré, Michel Tramezzini, and the East (Bragantini, 1987). Michel's brother, Francesco, and nephew Giuseppe, also figure in the article. And in an older work by Emile Spagni, we find Membré and one Giovanni Tramezzini working together as interpreters for the Venetian Republic (Spagni, 1900, 264-73), and Giovanni must surely be of the same Tramezzini family. Clearly, then, Membré was close to the Tramezzini clan, and of course the Tramezzini, especially Michel and Francesco, were big names in the publishing of maps and prints, as well as books. Now, Membré's account, as Almagià noted (1962, 8) shows a singular lack of interest in geography, and nothing else that I know of indicates that he had such an interest. So, what I am suggesting is that Gastaldi and Membré jointly applied for and obtained the privilege of 1550, Gastaldi as cartographer, but Membré as an entrepreneur, or publisher, intending to arrange for the printing and publishing to be done by his friends, the Tramezzini. There are overtones in such a scenario which remind one of the eventual partnership between Gastaldi and Fabio Licinio. The greatest importance of Licinio of course, was as an engraver, but, as we have seen, the vending of the maps was probably done by Licinio through his family, who had their own channels for the selling of artwork and prints.

How does the map fit into Gastaldi's work and career? Why did he make it, and why does it not correspond completely to the description, as far as we have it, in the supplication for privilege, which is for a map of *all* of Asia, which would be the case in 1559-61? We cannot go into this deeply here, but we shall make some tentative speculation. Considering the description in the privilege request, is it possible that Gastaldi intended a multi-part map covering all of Asia, but that the plan stopped short? We can think of two reasons why this could have happened. In the first place, Barros published the First Decade of his *Asia* in 1552, and Ramusio, we can be sure, obtained it the same year, or at the latest, the next. Its geographical section contains an enormous amount of new information on the continent. Perhaps Gastaldi already had another part of the map prepared but realized that it was already seriously outdated after the appearance of Barros's work and dropped it. There is another possibility. As we have shown in chapter one, no copperplate Gastaldi map until the 1552 Germany, itself not a first edition as we shall see in our next entry (no. 70), gives the name of an engraver (and no first edition copperplate Gastaldi map has the name of an engraver until his 1559 First Part of Asia and the map of the Danube Basin of the same year (nos. 92 and 93)), and quite reasonable grounds exist to hypothesize that Gastaldi himself engraved his plates up to this point. Perhaps, having completed the ca. 1550 map, Gastaldi felt that it was inadequate, which, as a reflection of the vast information available from Ramusio's many accounts, it certainly was. And perhaps, seeing that it should be done in a considerably larger size and in considerably greater detail, as well as being accompanied by two others just as large or larger if he were to cover all of Asia, Gastaldi decided to drop the task until he could find a professional engraver who could handle such a task, and handle it better than Gastaldi himself. That, in any event, is what eventually came to pass. But, whether Gastaldi was dissatisfied with the map or not, it was beyond comparison the best map of the area which had yet been produced and was a fair prelude to the 1559 map.

Location of copy:
No copy of the original Venice edition is extant, but one copy of the 1555 Antwerp edition exists at Wolfenbüttel HAB (kartens-g1)

References:

Ruge, 1904-16, Pt. 1, p. 24, no. 40; Bagrow, 1928-30, 1, 85; Almagià, 1939, *carta*, 8b; Almagià, 1948, 34 and 35-36; Gallo, 1955, 211 with 221; Almagià, 1962; Fabris, 1989, 9; Meurer, 1991, 151a; Karrow, 1993, 173, 225 and 229; Witcombe, 2004, 246-47; Bifolco and Ronca, 2018, 1;374.

Reproduction:
Reproduced above.

70. Germany
[**Note**: The following describes the earliest known edition, a 1552 copperplate, of a Gastaldi woodcut Germany of unknown date, and of which no copy is known]
-Venice, 1552 (original edition, before 1552, date unknown)
-Copperplate, 24.0 x 28.0 (34.5) cm., on one sheet (original edition, not extant, was woodcut)
-No scale bar

In right margin near top:
Il uero ritratto di | tutta l'Alama- | gna (The true picture of all of Germany). [There is an earlier state that lacks this inscription; Bifolco and Ronca, 2018, 2: 890)].

In cartouche at lower left, in the geography:
Opera di Iacopo di | Gastaldi Cosmo- | grafo In Venetia, | 1552 Cã priuileg. (A Work of Iacopo di Gastaldi Cosmographer In Venice, 1552 With privilege.)

In left margin near top:
In Venetia après- | so Gabriel Giolito | al segno della Fe- | nice (In Venice by Gabriel Giolito, at the sign of the Phoenix)

In left margin near the bottom:
Enea Vico | Parm[agiano] f[ecit] (engraved by Enea Vico of Parma)

Comments:

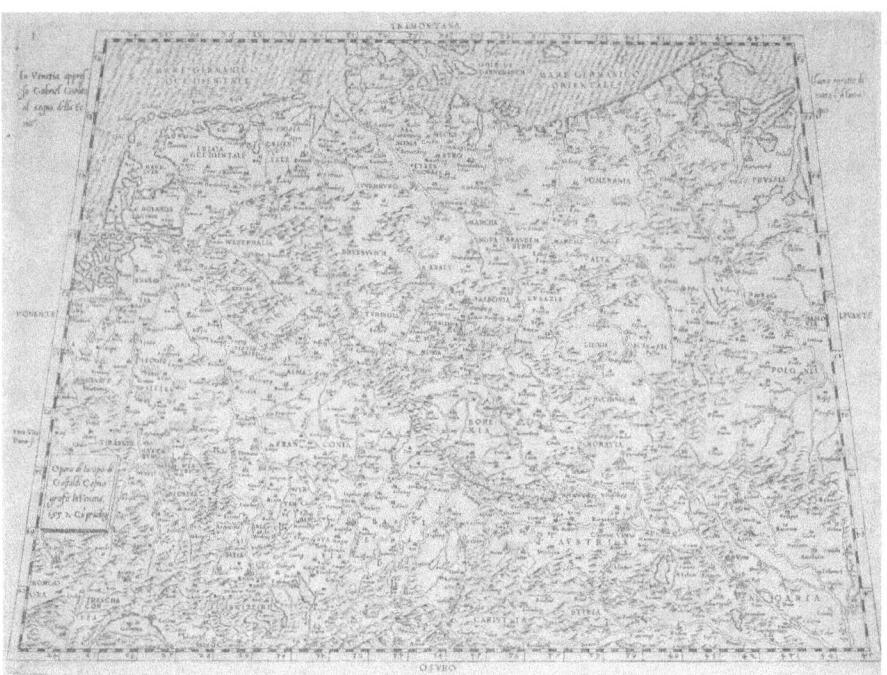

70 Germany 1552 Chicago Newb

Graduated in twelve-minute increments, with each whole degree numbered, in latitude and longitude, from 46°00' to 56°00' N, and from 23°00' to 45°00' E, on a trapezoidal projection; there is no difference between the longitude graduation at the top and bottom of the map, as would normally be the case, because the image itself is in a trapezoidal form which conforms to the graticule. This is an attractive map, but, as Almagià has pointed out, the part of Germany shown on the earlier 1546 map of the Danube lands (no. 4) was portrayed better there, and, he says, it probably did not deserve the considerable fortune that it found (1939, *carta*, 16 and 19). To be sure, it must be numbered among Gastaldi's less impressive productions, and, as we shall see, it is not in any event an original compilation, as most of Gastaldi's separately printed maps are, but is mainly copied, or derived, from an earlier work by the German cartographer Heinrich Zell, to which it corresponds closely. Probably much of its success was due to the splendid engraving job by Enea Vico, one of the greatest engravers of the time (see Bury, 2001, passim), who usually engraved subject prints of various kinds, and is little known as a map engraver, although a few other examples exist (for example, Tooley, 1939, nos. 150 and 445).

There was, for some time, considerable controversy concerning this map, begun by Caraci (1927), as to whether Gastaldi copied his map from Zell, or vice versa. The problem was that, while the earliest known edition of the Gastaldi map was 1552, the earliest known edition of the Zell map was 1560; but there was much reason to believe that there had existed an edition, or printing, of the Zell map which preceded the Gastaldi map. For one thing, on the face of it, it is much more logical to assume that an original map of Germany would have been compiled by a German, who was on the spot so to speak, than by an Italian who we know worked all the time in Venice. For another thing, the 1560 Zell map is much larger (56.0 x 73.0 cm., in four sheets) than the little Gastaldi map, and usually, though not always, the more natural assumption would be that the smaller map had been generalized from the larger one. Furthermore, there exist two small 1550 maps, one in German and the other in Latin (Bagrow, 1927, 65b; and 1928-30, 2, 112-13; Almagià, 1948, 26b; Schilder, 1996, 217), which are clearly reductions of the image in the 1560 Zell, which certainly would seem to establish that the original of the 1560 Zell could not have been later than 1550, and thus definitely preceded the 1552 map (see also Karrow, 1993, 597-98 and Meurer, 248, no. 3.3.1 on these maps; the Latin exemplar is reproduced in Meurer, 2001, fig. 3-8). We should note, too, that the 1560 Zell map, of which only one copy is known, is printed from woodblocks, and the attrition rate for woodcut maps is notoriously high; indeed it is not uncommon for no copy to exist of woodcut maps which documentation tells us definitely existed, and this is even more true of multi-sheet woodcuts, such as the Zell map.

In fact, most scholars have not inclined to Caraci's stance, and have continued to suppose that there had been at least one earlier printing from the 1560 map's blocks, dating from before 1552, and that the Italian map was derived from the German one (Bagrow, 1927, 65; and 1928-30, 2, 112-14; Banfi, 1955, 98: Karrow, 1993, 225 and 597-98; Schilder, 1996, 217-18). Meurer has subjected the question to a thoroughgoing investigation, and has put Caraci's hypothesis to rest conclusively (Meurer, 2001, 234 and 239-45), showing that the original edition of the Zell map hails back to ca. 1544 (cit.,

235-36, 239 and 241), and he has even isolated as well the misinterpretation of an old eighteenth century reference upon which one of the main foundations of Caraci's theory rested (cit., 234, with notes 35 and, esp., 36).

Finally, Meurer determined that the 1552 copperplate was not the original edition of the Gastaldi derivation from the Zell map. It was preceded by a larger woodcut edition of unknown date by Matteo Pagano, which itself was issued in at least two variants, the last one, undated, not bearing Gastaldi's name for some reason. A single copy of this latter variant exists in the library of the Sorbonne and is reproduced by Schilder (1996, 218, fig. 3.4) and by Bifolco and Ronca (2018, 2: 888-89). There is, to be sure, some strangeness in the fact that this copy does not contain Gastaldi's name. Destombes wrote of it: "It seems to us that if this map were by Gastaldi, Pagano his publisher would not have been able to avoid the obligation to put his name on it" (1973, 127). But the map and the 1552 map are truly identical images, and we know that Pagano produced some other woodcuts by Gastaldi which were then republished as copperplates, and all in all, intuitively, Meurer's determination certainly seems the correct one. In any event, this small puzzle aside, Meurer has at last resolved with finality the principal question, that of priority, and we may now rest fully assured that the prototype of the map came from Zell. There were several later printings and editions of the 1552 map, for which see Meurer (2001, 237, 239, 242, 245-48).

Location of copies:
No copy is known of the original edition, but copies of the earliest extant printing of 1552 are known: Chicago Newb(Novacco 4F 165/ Washington LC (G1015 .L25 1575b Vault Fol., no. 27)/ Paris BN(GE B- 1610)/ Paris BN(GE CC- 1380 (21 RES)/ Paris BN(GE DD- 655 (33 RES)

References:
Bagrow, 1927, 65; Caraci, 1927; Bagrow, 1928-30, II, 112-14; Almagià, 1939, *carta*, 16 nt 5, and 19a; Banfi, 1947, 31-32 and 34-35; Almagià, 1948, 26-27; Almagià, 1955, 18a-b; Banfi, 1955, 98-99 and 100; Destombes, 1973, 126 and 127; Kret, 1978, 99-100; Meurer, 1991, 271-72; Karrow, 1993,

225-26 and 597-98; Schilder, 1996, 217-18; Meurer, 2001, 234 and 239-45; Bifolco and Ronca, 2018, 2: 890-91.

Reproductions:
Meurer, 1984, 30; Meurer, 2001, atlas volume, pl. 3-3; Bifolco and Ronca, 2018, 2: 891.
https://collections.Newberry.org/asset-management/2KXJ8ZSAPQQ_Q?&WS

71. World
-Venice, 1553
-manuscript map, ca. 3.2 x 1.6 meters
-unknown if had a scale bar

Comments:
While the present Cartobibliography is in general devoted to printed maps, we have in three cases (nos. 65, 71 and 72) included non-printed maps, because of their clear general importance to Gastaldi's cartographic career. The present gigantic world map, no longer extant, was more than three times as large as Gastaldi's enormous *Cosmographia vniversalis* world map, and was made by Gastaldi at the behest of the Venetian Senate for presentation to one of the sons of Sultan Suleiman. Its interesting history is fully covered in our chapter on Gastaldi's world maps, at the section "The Giant World Map for an Ottoman Prince (1555)," where also will be found further references.

72. Asia, with parts of North America
-Venice, 1553
-Painted wall map of unknown size (very possibly ca. 2.6 x 8 meters)
-Not known if it had scale bar

Comments:
Gastaldi made, under commission of the Venetian Council of Ten, two large maps which were painted on the walls of the Sala dello Scudo in the Venetian Ducal Palace. The first was of Africa, made in 1549-50, which has been treated in entry no. 65 above. That map clearly appealed to the council,

for in 1553 he was commissioned to make a second map, evidently covering all or nearly all of Asia and all of North America, to judge from the surviving instructions printed in Lorenzi (1868, 277-78 and 279-80, documents nos. 594, 597 and 598), for doc. 594 instructs him that the map is to include the areas covered by the accounts of all the Spanish captains ("Capitani Castigliani"), the explorations of Jacques Cartier in New France, and the geography of the books of João de Barros and Marco Polo. There does exist in the palace a large painted wall map (ca. 2.6 x 8 meters) which in fact covers a little more than the eastern half of Asia, a narrow North Pacific Ocean, and about the western half of North America, but, as vast as that area is, it certainly does not include all of the area covered by Barros or Polo, not to mention the area covered by Cartier's explorations in the northeast corner of North America, to which region the map does not extend at all. This map is south-oriented. In our opinion, this surviving map is either not that which was drawn by Gastaldi, and then presumably painted on the palace wall by a professional painter, as was done with the Africa, or, if it is, it has been greatly changed by subsequent repainting, and thus does not give us a picture of Gastaldi's original map. In fact, in the middle of the eighteenth century, it was found that all the ancient maps (there were others besides that of Gastaldi) had deteriorated to the point that it was decided that a major renovation was needed for all of them, and this was performed in 1762 by the painters Francesco Grisellini and Giustino Menescardi (Karrow, 1993, 227). Opinions differ as to whether the intention was a restoration of the maps as they were, or a general replacement of the old maps with a set of new maps, but most scholars lean towards the latter possibility (Almagià, 1929, 34; and 1939, *carta*, 8, nt. 17; Wawrik, in Dörflinger, 1977, 56; Knauer, 1981, 58; Minella, 1993, 8, and others.). Karrow states: "This restoration . . . apparently amounted to a complete reworking of the maps" (1993, 227). We basically agree with this conclusion, as already stated, but for different reasons, as will be clear in a moment.

Not all have agreed with the above-cited writers, notably Gallo (1955), who, on the basis of toponymical comparisons makes a case suggesting that the present map could be a faithful restoration of Gastaldi's original map, but we are still inclined to entertain considerable doubt that the present map reflects Gastaldi's original, even if it be accepted that Grisellini

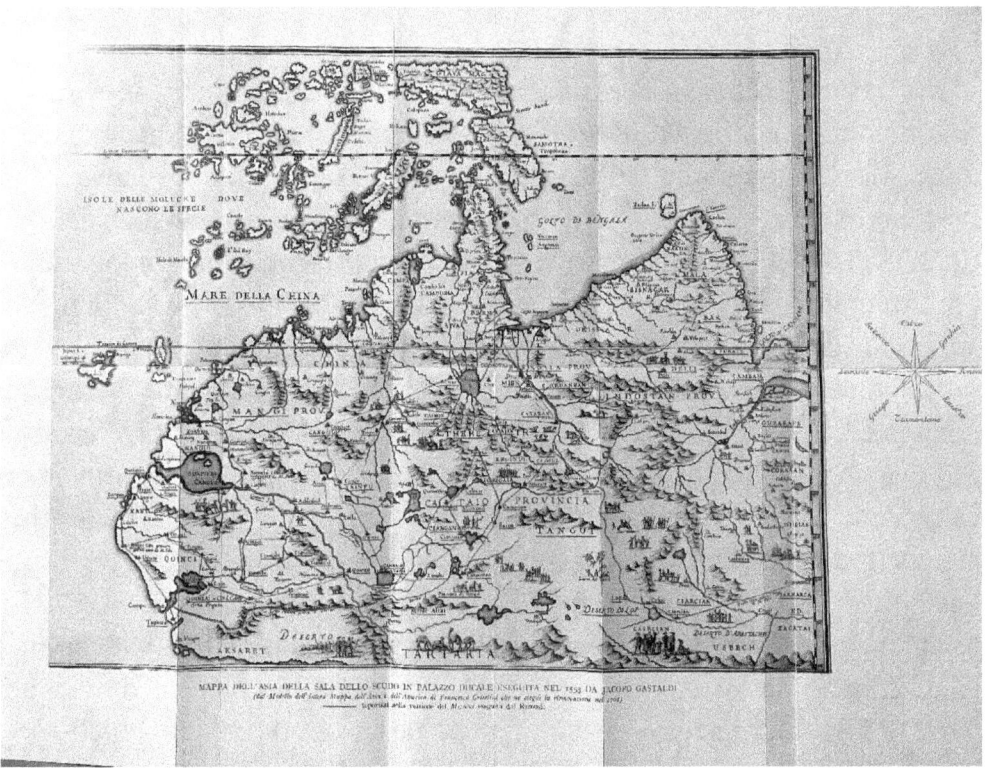

72a Mappa dell'Asia della sala dello scudo in Palazzo Ducale eseguita nel 1553 da Jacopo Gastaldi (dal Modello dell' intero Mappa dell' Asia e dell' America di Francesco Griselini che ne esegui la Rinnovazione nel 1761) (From Gallo 1955) Names underlined in red are found in the version of Marco Polo given in Ramusio.

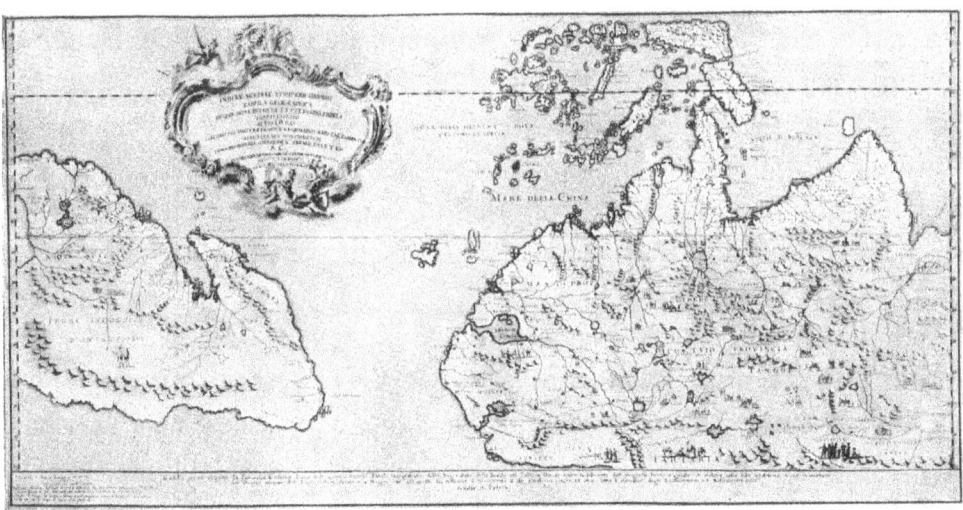

72b Modello del Griselini della Mappa dell' Asia e dell' America della Sala dello Scudo in Palazzo Ducale (From Gallo 1955)

in fact restored the map faithfully, as he found it, for in fact Gallo's case for this is pretty convincing. Rather we think that the map may have undergone a partial repainting long before 1762, perhaps early in the seventeenth century, though we have found no documents recording any such action. We think this possible for the following reasons: (1) The depiction on the present map does not accord with Gastaldi's concept of the relation of America and Asia at the time (1553), for the indications are that at the time he still entertained exclusively the idea that the two continents were connected, and he probably would have drawn that concept; (2) Shortly afterwards, Gastaldi himself established the concept that the continents were separated. The concept caught on virtually universally by the end of the sixteenth century; thus the picture of a connected America and Asia would have quickly become an outmoded one, and it might well have been wished to update the map by repainting part of it so as to sunder the two continents; (3) Girolamo Zanetti, a historian of art and antiquities inspected the maps in 1762 before their restoration and wrote a description of them which remained in manuscript until 1925, when it was published by Gian Lodovico Pertolini (Bertolini, 1925, and Zanetti, 1925[1762]). He found that the America section of the current map had been painted in oil, while the rest was in tempera (Zanetti, 1925[1762], 330-31; see also Galllo, 1955, 210), indicating that the America part had already been repainted at some time, suggesting that perhaps indeed the original map had exhibited the continents as connected, and it was decided to repaint that part such that the continents were separated, although admittedly the separation is wider than on most maps at the time (however, note Shirley, nos. 235 and 256 and some others). It was just in the sixteenth century that oil began to replace tempera in Italy as a painting medium for many artists, but some stayed with tempera, and it has never been completely replaced by oil. Many painters use tempera to the present day, and it is universally available in art supply shops. How about the narrow part of the Pacific on the map? Was it tempera or oil? The question is significant, though unfortunately we don't know the answer because Zanetti did not tell us. But it is obvious that, if a once connected Asia and America were repainted such that they were separated, the water between would have been in the new medium of oil to the Asian coast, at which point it would become tempera.

This idea still does not explain the discrepancy between the Council of Ten's original instructions and the area coverage of the map, but we recall that Gastaldi found it impossible to include all the areas that the council wanted in the 1549-50 Africa wall map (no. 65), and that Gastaldi succeeded in offering the council a compromise (see entry no. 65); it is certainly possible that he may have done that here without the fact's being recorded (in general, the documents printed by Lorenzi on the Asia are far less detailed and extensive than those on the Africa). Indeed, this seems rather likely to me, and it seems likely that the present map, although regrettably much altered from the way Gastaldi drew it, is in fact basically the same map as that commissioned to Gastaldi, for the following reason. As we have said, the map is south-oriented, which is unusual. We find this in Gastaldi only in one other place, the three maps in volume one of Ramusio's *Navigazioni*. As we bring out in our compound entry (77.-79.) below, the south-orientation of these maps for the *Navigazioni* surely reflects a directive from Ramusio. The only other Gastaldi map with south orientation is the present one (the 1549-50 Africa [no. 65] probably was also south-oriented), and it is, along with the Africa, also the only other map in which Ramusio was involved, and only one year before the 1554 volume one maps, and it is a natural enough conclusion that Ramusio prescribed the south orientation in this map as well. Gastaldi never shows south orientation except in those maps in which Ramusio had a hand. Thus, the fact of this south orientation here strongly suggests that the present map, however much it might have been altered, is the original map. If the old map had been replaced altogether, especially as late as 1762, there certainly would have been no south orientation applied to them.

We present this scenario only as a hypothesis. Much more work would be needed to arrive at a definite resolution of the question, if indeed it is possible to reach such a resolution at all. Those who might wish to attempt to explore this question further are recommended to begin with the works of Gallo (1943 and 1955), in the latter of which two works a very good hand-drawn reproduction of the current map will be found. A not overly clear photographic reproduction is in Hedin, 1917, pl. XVIII. Gallo's 1955 work, the most important, seems to have become lost in the shuffle. It is never cited.

References:
Zurla, 1818, 74-96; Lorenzi, 1868, 277-78 and 279-80 (docs. nos. 594, 597, 598); Bertolini, 1925; Zanetti, 1925 (1762); Almagià, 1929, 34 and 75; Almagià, 1939, *carta*, 8 nt. 17; Gallo, 1943, 62-64; Gallo, 1955; Knauer, 1981, 58; Karrow, 1993, 226-27; Minella, 1993, 8.

Reproductions:
Hedin, 1917, pl. XVIII (photograph, most small names and details unintelligible); Gallo, 1955, a large fold-out map at end of work, hand drawn, but very well-done, and the only really useful reproduction (reproduced here as72a); it is followed by a photographic reproduction of a manuscript map made by Grisellini in 1762, before he restored the original map (reproduced here as 72b).

(73.-76.) Four maps of parts of America intended for Volume Three of Ramusio, ca. 1553 (?)

Ramusio, we know from chapter four, gathered materials, often manuscript, but also often printed (but also often very difficult to obtain), on the far continents for perhaps as much as thirty years, and, under the encouragement of his old friend Fracastoro, finally decided, in or shortly before 1550, to publish them in three volumes, one for Africa and coastal Asia, one for inland Asia, and one for America. In the preface to Volume one he tells us, as we saw in chapter four, that his main reason for accumulating this vast bulk of material was to provide the information necessary for making better modern maps of the world's regions, breaking completely with the Ptolemaic model. He evidently did not intend to provide these maps himself, in his volumes, but just the materials for making them, for, in the 1550 first edition of his volume one, there is no set of new maps covering the area to which the volume is devoted, Africa and coastal Asia. There is, in fact, one map, but it is occasional in nature. It is our map no. 68, of the Nile Basin, and, as we see in that entry, its purpose is simply to illustrate a dialogue between himself and Fracastoro on the mysteries of the Nile, and clearly has nothing to do with providing new, modern cartographic depictions for the area covered by the volume. But Ramusio must have been criticized for this omission, for shortly after this first edition of volume one had been published, not later than 1553, but probably earlier, he decided to include in each volume a set of modern maps for the areas covered by the respective volumes. He acted on this, and maps for each volume were indeed made. But fate was unkind to Ramusio, and only one of these three sets actually made it into print, those for the first volume. Those for the second volume were lost in a printing house fire, though we are told specifically that they had been made, about which more below (see our compound entry 89-91), and those for volume three, perhaps the first to be made, succumbed to an unclear fate, of which we shall speak below.

At the end of his prefatory discourse to volume three, addressed to Fracastoro, which discourse is dated June 20, 1553, although the book was published in 1556, Ramusio includes a paragraph which tells us much about these maps, although they do not in fact appear in the book. This, we should note, was just seventeen days before Ramusio received a promotion from Secretary to the Senate to Secretary to the all-powerful Council of Ten, on July 7, 1553. Ramusio, we submit, probably already knew that this promotion was coming, and probably was preparing for the new and perhaps greater responsibilities it would entail, for there are signs that he was hurriedly trying to close out his work on the *Navigazioni* in order to concentrate fully on his new obligations. Ramusio is often diffuse and obscure in his writing, but the writing in this discourse, as also in the prefatory material to volume two, which is dated precisely on the same day as his promotion, July 7, is sometimes turgid and obscure near to unintelligibility, and they appear to have been written in great haste. The paragraph of which we have just spoken, and which we shall now quote, amounts to one long rambling sentence, and is perhaps the most nebulous and disjointed paragraph in the *Navigazioni*. But we have worked on it long, and feel that our rendering, which will require a little commentary after we have presented it, is the correct one. Words in brackets are ours.

After speaking at length on the exploits of Columbus and similar topics, ending with a quotation of a passage from classical poetry, Ramusio abruptly interjects the following paragraph: "Now, because your excellency [Fracastoro] has several times exhorted me in his letters that I might endeavor to have four or five maps made after the fashion of Ptolemy of as much as is known up to now of the part of this world newly discovered [The word "world" here is not, we think, intended to be taken as referring to the world as a whole, but to the New *World*, and the usage of the word in this sense was common at the time; neither Ramusio nor his friends, including Gastaldi, ever using the word "America", but always "the New World"], namely the coasts shown on the Marine charts, made by the Spanish pilots and captains, and [has] then determined to send to me as many of them as you had already received from the aforesaid Mr. Gonzalo Oviedo, Imperial historian [Ramusio had spoken of Oviedo, with whom both Ramusio and Fracastoro had been in friendly communication since the 1530s (Parks, 1955, 138-39), several times earlier in the discourse], both of the coasts of New Spain, and the Islands of the North Sea [Caribbean Islands; the "North Sea" at the time *always* and in all languages meant the Atlantic as a whole, all the way to Tierra del Fuego, and not the Arctic, which was always referred to in some other way, due to the facts that when Balboa discovered the Pacific (South Sea), the two oceans were at that point opposed north and south to each other across the isthmus, and the names became extended to cover the whole of the two oceans, and this practice continued long, so that, for example, when the Bering Strait was discovered in the eighteenth century, one said, if he were exiting the strait from the north, that he was entering "the South Sea"], I have not wanted to fail in complying with your wishes, and have arranged such that M. Giacomo de' Gastaldi, excellent Piedmontese cosmographer has adapted ["ridotto", but the meaning here is not "reduce" in the sense of make smaller, but "adapt, arrange" (Robert C. Melzi's *Italian and English Dictionary*), a meaning the word can also have in English] from them a universale [we shall speak more on the usage of this word in this context below] on small scale, and then divided that into four maps, with the greatest care and diligence that he has been able, so that the studious readers might see how very much notice of it has been received by means of your Excellency: for, knowing in Spain, & in France, the great pleasure which you receive from this new part of the world, and how you yourself have been accustomed to make maps of it by your own hand many times, all the lettered men continually inform you of some discovery, which has been brought to them by a captain or pilot, who might come from such parts [that is, of course, the "lettered men" received the information from captains or pilots, and then passed them on to Fracastoro; of course the captains and pilots did not come to Fracastoro in Verona]: and among others the aforesaid Mr. Gonzalo of the island Hispaniola, whom [such captain or pilot] visits one or two times every year, with some newly made chart."

The above is all one long sprawling sentence, and contains all of direct interest to us here, but Ramusio ends the paragraph still more abruptly and confusedly than he began it with a single short sentence which should have been parenthesized: "Similarly have several excellent Frenchmen done, who have sent [you] from Paris the relations of New France, together with four maps, which shall be placed in this volume in their places." This sudden insertion has nothing to do with what precedes it, except that it expands further on the notion of Fracastoro (and thus from him Ramusio) obtaining maps from foreign sources. These French maps are four in number, just as the maps made by Gastaldi for Ramusio, but the two sets of maps have nothing to do with each other. Nevertheless, due to the agreement in number, and the fact the Gastaldi maps do not actually appear in the volume, some nineteenth and early twentieth century scholars conflated the two. The four French maps, Gastaldi's only connection to which would have been to work them up into better condition for inclusion in the *Navigazioni*, have nothing to do with America, and are incidental maps which are of poor quality which have relevance only to a short relation near the end of the volume, which is where they are placed. We shall treat them in their place (see nos. 82-85).

So, returning to our main concern, what does this scramble really mean? A few comments besides those which we have enclosed in brackets in the passage itself, will make all clear. Firstly, when Ramusio uses the word "universale" he does not mean a world map. This is the most common usage of the term; but it occasionally meant a map of all of some place as opposed to part of it, and here it applies to the New World, just as it does in the New World map included in this same volume: "Vniversale della parte del mondo nvovamente ritrovata" ("Universal [map] of the part of the world newly discovered"), and just as it does in the name of a map of the New World in a small book produced by Ramusio in 1534, *Summario de la Generale Historia de l'Indie Occidentali* (the ascription of this anonymous book, once considered equivocal, has been definitely established by Donattini (1992, 122, 124-29, 131, and 150, no. 54)), the name of which map is "La carta *universale* della terra ferma & Isole delle Indie occidentali, etc." ("Universal map of the mainland and Islands of the West Indies, etc."; on this map see Holzheimer and Buisseret, 1992). Secondly, Fracastoro's words, cited by Ramusio, that he would like to see Ramusio produce "four or five maps after the fashion of Ptolemy", which at first seems meaningless and out of place in a discussion in particular on modern maps, and furthermore maps of a part of the world which Ptolemy never knew, is not in reference to Ptolemaic construction of individual maps, but to the Ptolemaic policy of presenting the continents not as maps of whole continents, but as a series of maps together making up the entire continent, and thus the "four or five maps."

Finally, Ramusio's confusingly elliptic description of the procedure by which Gastaldi produced his four maps will be made clear by the following. We know that Ramusio and Fracastoro had been in regular contact with Oviedo since the 1530s, that he had regularly sent them maps, and, from the passage we know that Oviedo had regularly been brought maps of new areas by some captain or pilot once or twice every year. We cannot tell from the compressed syntax of the preface if Oviedo, the official chronicler, is visited once or twice a year by one captain, or by a larger number of them, but the former doesn't really make much sense, while the latter does, for the Spanish main was constantly alive with maritime activity. Now, if Oviedo sent all these maps, or copies of them, to Fracastoro and Ramusio over a period of at least fifteen years, averaging "one or two" per year would give us twenty-two or twenty-three charts of parts of the New World sent over the years, but a much larger number if Oviedo was yearly brought charts not by one but by a number of pilots, which seems more likely. In any event, there would be a lot of charts for Gastaldi to work with. Of course, we do not, unfortunately, know the names of any of these chartmakers, and most likely, very few, if any, of these charts, or their original sources, still exist. Compilation of larger maps from a variety of sources is the very essence of Gastaldi's specialty in mapmaking, and so Gastaldi combined these maps of varying scale and quality into a whole map ("universal") of the West Indies, and then divided that into four maps, not in the sense of evenly slicing up a pie, but critically considering what area coverage and scale to give to each, the difference depending no doubt on considerations of population and importance, with smaller scale maps of larger areas for the less important, and the opposite for the more important (precisely per the dictates of Ptolemy, again). Probably the break-up would be similar to that found in the series of five American maps in the 1548 Ptolemy, perhaps, since the maps would be much larger than those in the Ptolemy, combining the maps of Cuba and Hispaniola into one map, along with Jamaica.

And this would seem to be the correct interpretation as regards the four New World maps of which Ramusio speaks, and speaks of as a job which is finished, which his words make very clear: "I . . . have arranged such that . . . Gastaldi . . . has adapted from them [the Oviedo maps] a universale on small scale [many of the maps brought by the pilots would be of small areas on very large scale], and then divided that into four maps, with the greatest care and diligence that he has been able," etc. These words leave no doubt that the maps were made. So where are they? They are not in the book. Caraci was the first to finally put to rest the old erroneous notion that the four French maps could correspond to the maps Ramusio speaks of, and he concludes: "It is clear that the words of Ramusio in the letter to Fracastoro refer to different maps from those contained in the third volume of the *Navigazioni*" (Caraci, 1936, 126).

What happened to those maps, and why are they not in the book? The preface is dated 1553, and the book was published in 1556. Caraci suggested that perhaps including these maps would somehow have exceeded the means of the publishers, the Giunti (1936, 129, in note, and 131, in note), but this is not very convincing, for the Giunti included the maps of the second edition of volume one a year later in 1554, and (as see entries 89-91), they were preparing in 1557 to include maps in volume two, when they and the whole text were consumed by fire. We know that in 1555 Gastaldi was suffering from some affliction serious enough that he drew up a will. Perhaps, while the maps were basically finished in manuscript, much refining of the images was still needed before they could go to the woodblock cutter, but the ever-busy Gastaldi postponed this work for the time because the volume itself was not yet ready to go to the printer, but then, in 1555, shortly before the book was to be published, he found himself unable to perform this work due to his affliction. Not knowing how long Gastaldi's affliction would last, if indeed he might not succumb to it, the Giunti decided to proceed per schedule without the maps, and without revising the preface. Readers of sixteenth century books will be familiar with the fact that it is fairly common to find in them something mentioned in a preface as being in the book, when actually it is not. Editing was lax. Or did Ramusio's friend Oviedo, official chronicler of the Spanish West Indies, answerable to the Viceroy, receive from the latter a directive that these maps should not be published, with which Ramusio could not fail to comply without putting his friend at serious risk? Probably we will never know. All that we can be sure of is that the four maps were made, but what became of them is a mystery.

Location of copies (of the book):
See at our compound entry no. (81.-86.).

73. Part of America
Map, in manuscript form in 1553, not extant, and no details known other than those in the discussion in compound entry (73-76) above.

74. Part of America
Map, in manuscript form in 1553, not extant, and no details known other than those in the discussion in compound entry (73-76) above.

75. Part of America
Map, in manuscript form in 1553, not extant, and no details known other than those in the discussion in compound entry (73-76) above.

76. Part of America

Map, in manuscript form in 1553, not extant, and no details known other than those in the discussion in compound entry (73-76) above.

(77.-79.) Three maps of Africa, and of South Asia, in volume one of Ramusio beginning from the second edition of 1554.

While the maps prepared by 1553 for inclusion in Ramusio's volume three, published only in 1556, were for some reason not actually published in that volume, the maps for volume one were published, although for the first time only in the second edition of that volume, in 1554, where they appear near the head of the volume, following the index. Probably the volume two and volume three maps, never published, were also intended to appear at the head of their volumes. The volume one maps take in the areas covered by their volume, Africa and coastal Asia, and are clearly intended as general illustrative material for the volume. They are almost exactly five times as large as the 1548 Ptolemy maps (ca. 210 sq. cm. vs. ca. 1050 sq. cm.) They are, however, fewer in number than the six 1548 maps covering about the same area, so their scale is actually about two times that of the earlier maps (instead of ca. five times). In any event, they are not only significantly larger than the 1548 maps, but also much improved, due, more than to any other single factor, to the rich information in the geographical chapter of the first "decade" of João de Barros's *Asia*, first published in 1552. Ramusio translated this chapter from the Portuguese and included it in this second edition of his volume one, but we know that Gastaldi had had immediate access to this text before it was published, because the many improvements in his depictions, which came directly from Barros, are truly striking. Striking also is the overall powerful attractiveness of the maps, and, in this writer's perception, the superb quality of their very sharp and clear woodcut engraving (though for some reason Biasutti [1920, 414] saw an engraver of little ability). Minella implies that they may have been engraved by Matteo Pagano (1993, 40), and this is the most likely conjecture, for there were few woodcutters working on maps in Venice at the time, and we know that Pagano had been engraving for Gastaldi since 1546, although Ramusio nowhere makes any mention of Pagano. On the other hand, since he never mentions any engraver for any of the maps or other illustrations in his *Navigazioni*, this fact does not detract much from Pagano's candidacy. We should note that all the woodcut maps in both this volume and in volume three (nos. 81-86) are replaced by less effective copperplates in all but the first editions, all the blocks probably having been destroyed by the printing-house fire which destroyed the blocks for volume two (Betz, 2007, 97). The maps are clearly the second prelude to the great maps of 1559-1564 (or the third prelude if we include the map of Near Asia for which Gastaldi obtained a privilege in 1550 (see no. 69), which may have been part of a larger initiative which aborted). We should mention that a shortcoming of the maps is their strange sparseness of detail and, especially, place names, although there is room for much more. This must have been Ramusio's decision, and I can offer no explanation for it.

The improvement over the 1548 maps, which we see here in the picture of Africa and southern Asia is entirely Gastaldi's. No other cartographer had stepped in with any improvements for extra-European areas between 1548 and the time these maps appeared. It is surprising that these maps have drawn so little attention. As to their sources, Ramusio himself tells us, both in the dedicatory letter to Fracastoro at the head of the volume, and in the volume's title itself, that the coasts are taken from Portuguese sea charts, and the interiors from the relations printed in the book, the most important of the latter being the accounts of Leo Africanus, Francisco Alvarez, and, added in the new edition, and most important of all for coastal Asia, João de Barros, although there are, of course, many others. We possess the *Navigazioni*, but what do we know of the Portuguese sea charts? Ramusio mentions Portuguese charts several times in the volume (1967-70, 1, 112v, 175v, 268v, 281r, on the second page of his dedication to Fracastoro, and on an unnumbered page entitled "Alli studiosi di Geographia" preceding the three maps; in Milanesi ed., 1978-88, respectively: 1, 554-55; 1, 904 and 905; 2, 435; 2, 501; 1, 5; and 1, [911]), but he says nothing in these places as to how he obtained his own maps. However, while we see in our discussion for maps 73-76 that Ramusio's main source for Spanish charts was Oviedo, his main source for Portuguese charts would most likely have been his friend Pietro Bembo, for it is clear from Andrea Corsali's letters of 1515 and 1517 (Ramusio, 1967-70, 1, 177r-188v: Milanesi ed., 1978-88, 2, 21-74; see also

Winsor, 1904, 31) that Portuguese charts were often sent to the Portuguese ambassador in Rome, a practice which no doubt continued after that time, and we know that Bembo, who was much interested in geography and in the collecting activities of his friend Ramusio, was a cardinal in Rome from 1539-1547, and had also been in Rome in 1513- 1521 as secretary to Pope Leo X. Undoubtedly among the main charts would have been an example of Ribero's famous marine-world maps, for, as we see in the entries for the American maps in the 1548 Ptolemy, Grande and Minella have shown that much of Ribero is reflected in those maps.

The three Ramusio maps are south-oriented, unusual for the time. Since the maps were made for Ramusio, this, too, was certainly his decision. This finds confirmation in the fact that the only other Gastaldi map in which we find this is the map of Asia and part of America in the Ducal Palace (no. 72), which almost certainly was made partly under the direction and supervision of Ramusio (while this map has almost certainly been much changed from Gastaldi's original depiction as a result of later repainting, its south orientation would not have changed.) This south-orientation in the Ramusio maps definitely does not come from recourse to Arab maps, which often (though not always) show south-orientation, as posited by Sezgin (see the second part of our chapter five), for Ramusio tells us the sources are Portuguese charts and his own relations in the *Navigazioni*. Rather it comes, I think, from elsewhere. Ramusio was a dedicated student of the classics (Parks, 1955), and Milanesi shows that in all of Ramusio's discourses there is a strong streak of Aristotle (Milanesi, 1994, "G. B. Ramusio", 97-101), whose works were enjoying their greatest heyday in history at the time, and that his friend Fracastoro, who much influenced Ramusio and the *Navigazioni*, was even more of an Aristotelian (Milanesi, cit., 95 and 98). In Aristotle's *De Caelo* (*On the Heavens*, available in a number of English translations), in Book two, Chapter two, Aristotle presents a case for south-orientation of the globe, as opposed to the north-orientation of the Pythagoreans, which, says Aristotle, is incorrect. The *De Caelo,* we should add, was one of Aristotle's most influential and widely read books. A simple search in online library catalogs revealed thirty-seven editions from 1540-1570, twenty-one of them published in Venice, and five by the Giunti, Ramusio's publishers and friends; also, we know that Simplicius wrote one of the most important commentaries on *De Caelo*, and that Bembo, in a letter to Ramusio, engages the latter's interest in "a proper text of an edition . . . of Simplicius on Aristotle" (Parks, 1955, 133). These sundry facts assuredly give us sufficient grounds to posit that it was Ramusio, influenced by Aristotle's conviction that south-orientaion for the globe was the correct orientation, who dictated the south-orientation of those Gastaldi maps in which he would have had a directing hand. The three present maps also appeared in the four later editions of Volume one, but as copperplates, the woodblocks no doubt having been consumed in the fire in the Giunti printing house in 1557. There was also a separate issuing of the maps in 1564/65 by Ferrando Bertelli, as see Karrow (1993, 228).

A NOTE ON THE DATES OF THE RAMUSIO MAPS

There has long been a much-repeated idea that all the maps in Ramusio probably date back to 1550 or earlier. I have traced down what I am pretty sure are the two original sources for this idea, which has no foundation. The first came from Johann Georg Kohl, who stated in 1869: "The discourse of Ramusio is dated, 'Venice, 20th June, 1553' at the time when he probably had collected all the materials for his third volume. As this would take him some time, we may put the date of the composition of these maps at about 1550, though they were not published by Ramusio until 1556, the date of the first edition of his third volume" (Kohl, 1869, 227). The statement, which seems at first to have a grain of truth in it, can perhaps be called a verbal illusion. A moment's reflection shows it to be devoid of any logic. Kohl's conclusion is a non sequitur. The second is just as meaningless. Nordenskiöld in 1889 says "The maps are considered to have been finished before 1550," upon which he refers to a note stating: "In a note at the end of Nomi de gli Autori in the first volume Ramusio says: 'To the year MDL, when the first volume of this work was laid under the press, answers Hegira's year of DCCCCLVII.'" What it was that Nordenskiöld saw in this phrase that made him take it as indicating that the maps would have been ready before 1550, we can't know, but it is as much a non sequitur as is Kohl's. No reason exists to date any of the maps in Ramusio other than by the date of their respective volumes (several scholars before us have contested the phantom 1550 date, at least as regards the Western Hemisphere map in Ramusio's volume three, including Caraci, 1936, 129 and 131; Gezelius, 1910, 133; Dahlgren, 1911, 16; and especially Cortesão, 1960, 5, 172). It has been largely due to the combination of this pernicious error and limited and incorrect interpretations of the passage quoted earlier that tremendous confusion surrounding these maps first arose and has persisted.

Location of copies (of the book):
New York PL(*KB + 1554)/ Cambridge Harv(Widener Ital 590.271.10 F)/ Oxford Bodl(Mason GG 179) and (Vet. F1 c.15)/ Edinburgh NLS(E.185.a, v. 1)/ London BL(566.k.1-3, v. 1)/ Edinburgh UL(JY 1094-6, v. 1)/ London WellcInst(5328/D)/ Basel UB(ET I 23a)/ Leiden UB(368 A 13)/ Wien ÖNB(393394-C.Kar, v. 1)/ Chicago Newb(Ayer 110 .R2 1554)/ New Haven Yale(Taylor 115 1) and (Eca +550Rb 1-2)/ Salamanca BU(BG/32217)/ Ithaca CU(G 159 .R18++, v. 1)/ Washington LC(G159 .R2 vol. 1 1554) and (Thacher A846 Vol. 1 Thacher Coll)/ Providence JCB(1-SIZE H554 .R184n, v. 1)/ San Diego UCSD(G159 .R22 1554)/ Amherst AC(G159 .R2 v. 1, 1554 +)/ Williamstown WC(Am1554 .R3 vol. 1 folio)/ Chicago UCL(fG159.R2 1554)

77. Africa
-Venice, 1554
-Woodcut, 37.5 x 38.0 cm., on two sheets
-No scale bar

Along the top border of the map:
PRIMA TAVOLA (FIRST MAP)

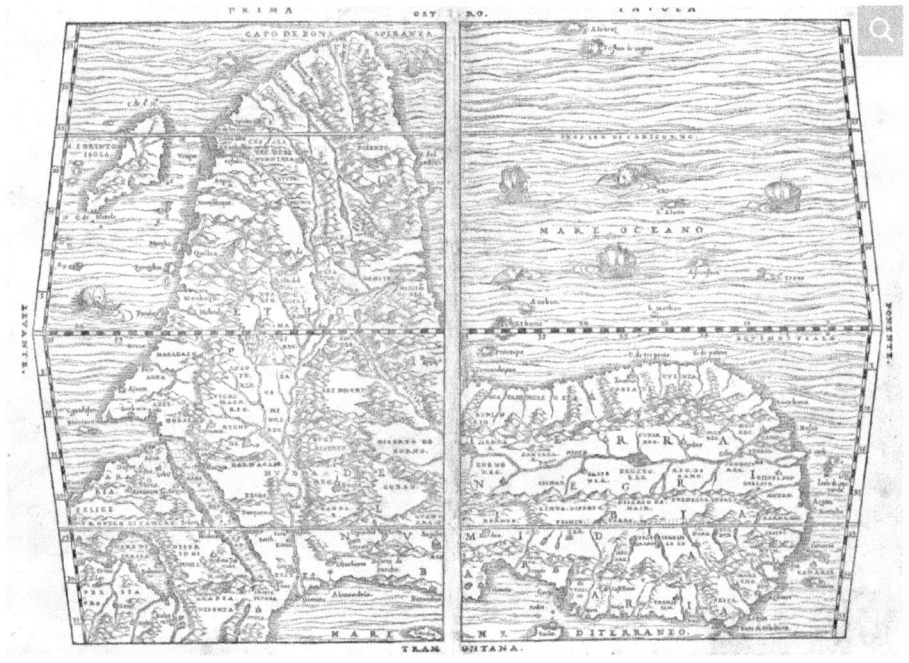

77 Africa 1554 Sanderus

Comments:
Graduated in whole degrees, in latitude at the sides, and in longitude on the
equator only, with each fifth degree numbered, from 37°00' S to 37°00' N,
and from 5°00' W to 94°20' E. Since the map is graduated in longitude only
on the equator, the projection is indeterminate, but from the form of the map
it is presumably to be taken as trapezoidal. The map has no formal title.
Though the map is clearly intended as illustrative material for the book, it is
sorely insufficient for that purpose because of the sparsity of detail and
names, mentioned in the comments above in entry (77-79), and Ramusio

himself admits in a short "Alli studiosi" just proceeding the maps that, if it had been attempted to include on the map all the information in the volume as regards Africa, even ten maps might not have sufficed. Nevertheless, that qualification aside, it is beyond doubt the best representation of Africa to date, as is stunningly apparent from a glance at the maps preceding it in Betz (2007). The sources, as Ramusio says, and as we have mentioned in the preceding comments, are Portuguese charts, and the accounts in the book. Biasutti seems to imply it's taken from the large Africa Gastaldi was compiling at the time he was working on the Ptolemy (1920, 913-14), and presumably still compiling in 1554, which is logical enough, and I think true, but the individual sources would ultimately be the same. The most important accounts would be that of Leo Africanus, for the Maghreb; Francisco Alvarez, for eastern Africa below Egypt; and Barros, which supplies much new information on southeast Africa (Betz, 2007, 96), but no true study of the source accounts has been made, and no doubt the map includes materials from a number of the many Africa accounts in volume one, as itemized in Parks (1970, 2-16). Several other copies and editions exist, and all are fully documented, including minor variants, in Betz (2007, nos. 5, 7, and 10).

References:
Biasutti, 1920, 411-14 and 433; Karrow, 1993, 227 (no. 30/73); Rizzo, 2006, 84: Betz, 2007, 57 and 95-97, no. 4; Bifolco and Ronca, 2018, 1: 434.

Reproductions:
Betz, 2007, 95 (no. 4).
https://sanderusmaps.com/our-catalogue/antique-maps/africa/old-antique-map-of-africa-by-g-b-ramusio-26311

78. The western part of the South of Asia
-Venice, 1554
-Woodcut, 27.5 x 38.0 cm., on two sheets
-No scale bar

Along the top border of the map:
SECONDA TAVOLA (SECOND MAP)

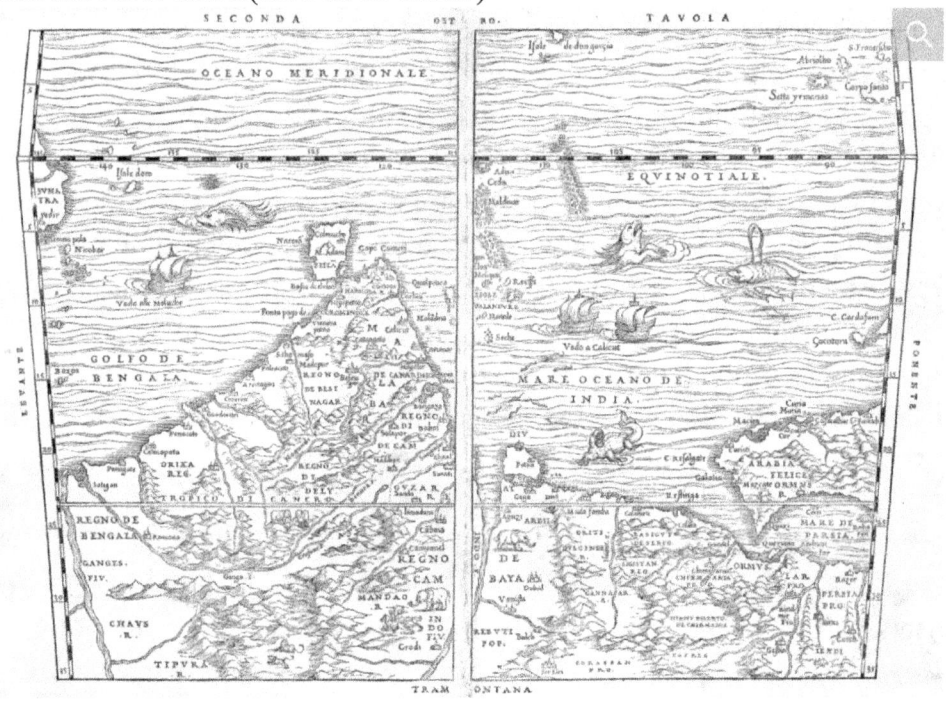

78 Western part of the south of Asia 1554 Sanderus

Comments:
Graduated in whole degrees, numbered at every fifth degree, in latitude and longitude, from 8°30' S to 35°10' N, and from 85°00' to 145°00' E. Since the map is graduated in longitude only on the equator, the projection is indeterminate, but from the form of the map it is presumably to be taken as trapezoidal. The map has no formal title. Just as with the Africa (no. 77), while intended as general illustrative material for the book, it is sadly inadequate for this, for the same reason, an unnecessarily sparse inclusion of detail and names. But also, just like the Africa, it is nonetheless

incomparably ahead of any previous depiction of the area, even more stunningly so than with the Africa. The general outline is essentially correct, and the improvement in the shape of India is truly superb. In the Indian Ocean there are vignettes of three ships, two west of India, and one east of it. Under the first two is the short inscription "Vado a Calicut" ("I am going to Calecut"), and under the other "Vado alle Maluche" ("I am going to the Moluccas"). This charming little touch consisting of the cartographer's writing under the vignette of a ship the words "I am going to such or other place" is borrowed from Ribero. But Gastaldi's tremendously improved India is not taken from Ribero, for, as good as Ribero's maps undeniably are, he still shows the misshapen narrow India we see on Gastaldi's 1548 "Calecut" (no. 54). In fact, in all the Portuguese charts showing India up to 1554 in Cortesão (1960), India is always depicted as too narrow, either far too narrow, or only slightly too narrow, but in Gastaldi's map, instead of approaching to the correct width of India, he rather exceeds it, though the general effect is better than on any other known map of the time. This is not seen on any of the Portuguese sea charts which have survived (see also our comments at no. 54). We would posit that this new India may not come from Portuguese charts at all, but from the excellent verbal description that Barros, in the geographical chapter of his 1552 first "decade", and included for the first time in this second edition of volume one, gives us, and which we have spoken of in chapter eight. All in all, the map definitely represents a fairly small but significant hallmark in the cartography of the area, and it deserves a study isolating its no doubt mainly Ramusian sources. But, for some reason, the map has received almost no attention in the literature so far. The shot-in-the-dark guess by Gole that the India was taken from Gastaldi's world map is completely wrong, as is her date for the map, although she does correctly mention Barros, even if not about the shape of the country, but its hydrography. The first stop in a full study would be, of course, Parks detailed run-down of the contents of this volume (Parks, 1970, 2-16). At least one separate edition of the map was later published, as see Karrow (1993, 228).

References:
Biasutti, 1920, 413 and 433; Gole, 1976, 34; Karrow, 1993, 228; Bifolco and Ronca, 2018, 1: 414.

Reproductions:
Ramusio, 1978-88, vol. 1, 914-15.
https://sanderusmaps.com/our-catalogue/antique-maps/asia/india-ceylon/old-antique-map-of-india-by-g-b-ramusio-26315

79. Further India and Archipelago Asia
-Venice, 1554
-Woodcut, 27.0 x 39.0 cm., on two sheets
-No scale bar

Along the top border of the map:
TERZA TAVOLA (THIRD MAP)

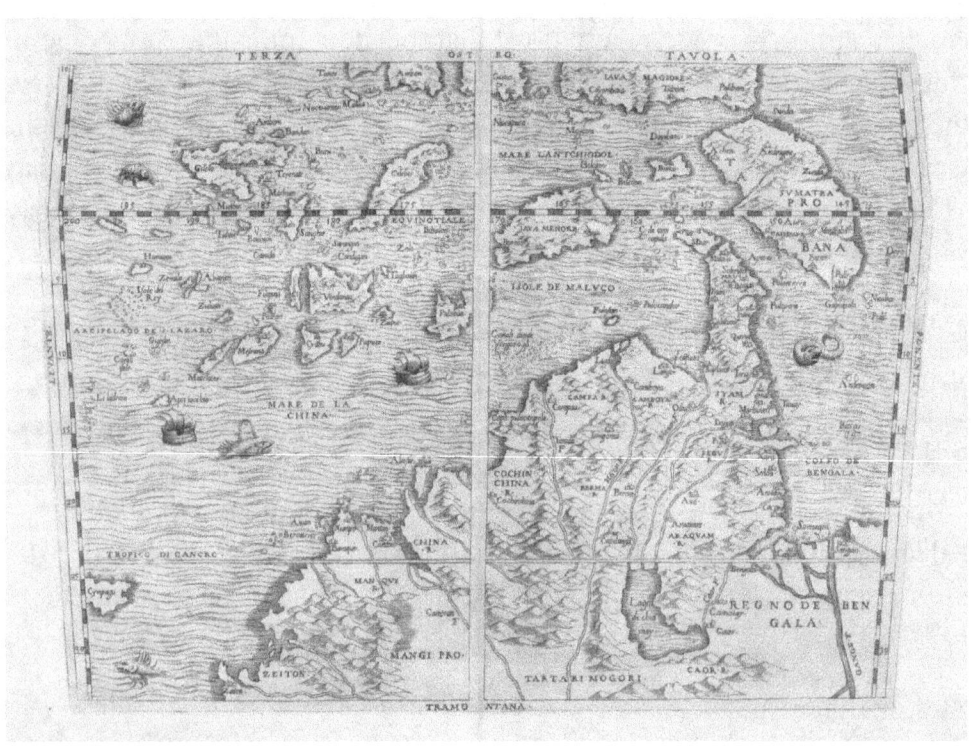

79 Further India and archipelago Asia 1554 Ruderman

Comments:

Graduated in whole degrees, numbered every fifth degree, in latitude and longitude, from 10°00' S to 33°00' N, and 140°30' to 200°00' E. Since the map is graduated in longitude only on the equator, the projection is indeterminate, but from the form of the map it is presumably to be taken as trapezoidal. The map has no formal title. Overall, there is considerable improvement over Gastaldi's 1548 map of the area (no. 56), but not at all as striking an improvement as in the previous map (no. 78), and Suarez says that it has no relation at all to the 1548 map (no. 78). Still, as with the other two maps, it is probably the best depiction of the area to date. The archipelago is significantly better, although considerable chaos remains, and the Gulf of Tonkin is actually better on the 1548 map. But it is the first map to include Celebes by name (Abendanon, 1918, 1783). Suarez principally surveys the archipelago, as opposed to the mainland parts, and not surprisingly finds that the main source is the Magellan voyage, as related by Pigafetta and Maximillian of Transylvania, both in Ramusio, and presumably Gastaldi used his versions, though Suarez does not specifically say so (Suarez, 1999, 130-47, passim, but very discursive, and including a lot of history which is not really related to this map and the others he is discussing). But, unfortunately, while to be sure, more attention has been given to this map than to the previous and better one, our fondness for imaginary geography takes center stage in most of what has been written, so that what is right about the map has received less treatment than what is wrong. The imaginary geography here is the "great" Lake Chiamay, utterly nonexistent, and introduced into the literature by Barros, usually a dependable source (Hedin, 231-32; Unno, 1985: Suarez, 152-56). The lake occupies a large area roughly corresponding to upper Burma, and perhaps a little of southwestern China. Gastaldi duly includes it, though for some reason he depicts only four great rivers flowing from it into the sea, instead of six, as given by Barros. Unno explores the question of whence Barros obtained this fictional feature (Unno, 1985). All in all, to repeat, except for Chiamay, the map introduces moderate improvement, but much still needs serious correcting. As usual, for one who might wish to explore all the map's sources, the first stop will be Parks (1970, 2-16). As with the other two maps, at least one separate edition was published, for which see Karrow (1993, 228).

References:
Hedin, 1917, 231-32; Abendanon, 1915-18, IV, 1783-85; Biasutti, 1920, 413 and 433; Unno, 1985; Suarez, 1999, 130-56, passim; Bifolco and Ronca, 2018, 1: 416.

Reproductions:
Ramusio, 1978-88, vol. 1, 916-17; Bifolco and Ronca, 2018, 1: 416-17.
https://www.raremaps.com/gallery/detail/49316/china-southeast-asia-philippines-etc-terza-tavola-ramusio

80. Piedmont
-Venice, 1555
-Woodcut, 52.5 x 76.0 cm., on two sheets
-100 Italian miles = 5.5 cm.

In a decorative cartouche, abutting the left border just below center:
IL PIAMONTE. | Opera de Iacomo gastaldo Piamontese | consmographo [sic] *in Venetia nella quale | e descritto la ragione dil Piamonte, e quella | di Monferra, con la maggior parte della ri | uiera di Genoa, & il teritorio Astesano, Ale | xandrino, Tortonese, Nouarese, & la piu | parte del Pauese, & parte del Milanese, | con le Separationi, Loro fatte da pontesini | picoli per maggiore cognitione loro. Et qui | sotto e la scala di miglia per sapere la di- | stantia ch'e da un luoco a l'altro; Hora se | per alcun tempo si trouasse qualche errore | da huomini piu periti di me in tal sientia mi | rimetaro al parer loro. | M. D. LV. (PIEDMONT. A work of Iacomo gastaldo Piamontese cosmographer in Venice in which is depicted the region of Piedmont, and that of Montferrat, with the greater part of the region of Genoa, and the territory Asti, Alexandria, Tortona, Novara, and the greater part of Pavia, and part of Milano, with Their Separations made by small dotted lines for better cognition of them. And here below is the scale in miles in order to know the distance which there is from one place to another: Now if in some*

time is found some error by men more expert than I in this science I defer to their opinion. 1555.)

Atop this cartouche is found:
In Vene | tia per Mathio | Pagan In Frezaria al segno de la Fede (At Venice by Matteo Pagano in Frezaria [Street] at the sign of Faith)

And below the cartouche the single word:
FEDE (FAITH)

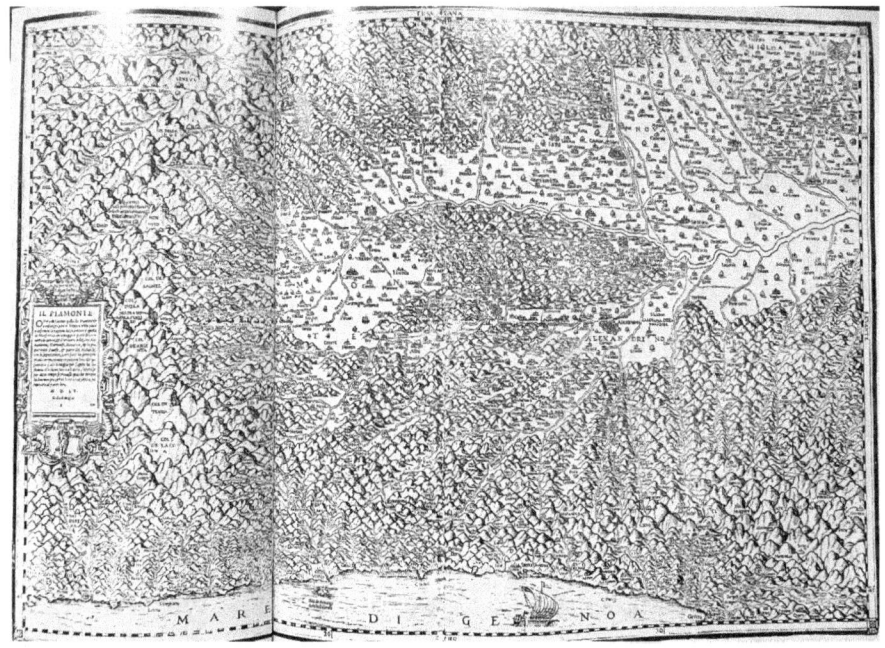

80 Piedmont 1555 Archivio di Stato, Firenze (from Bifolco and Ronca, 2018, 3:1886-87)

Comments:

Graduated in single minutes, with each whole degree numbered, from 42°56' to 44°13' N, and from ca. 28°02' to ca. 30°39' E on the top border, and from ca. 28°04' to ca. 30°37' E on the lower border, and thus on a trapezoidal projection with only a very slight convergence of meridians (and not rectangular, as some mistakenly state, as Biasutti, 1908, 37), the difference from top to bottom being only ca. six minutes. A considerable amount has been written about this map, but the judgements have differed sharply.

Almagià in 1915 spoke of all its individual aspects, its hydrography, orography, settlements and their relative positions, and the placement of coastline features at the bottom of the map in extremely glowing terms, though pointing up a few exceptions, notably the greatly insufficient inward curvature of the south coast. He also noted the exceptional richness and precision of detail, which no one could possibly disagree with, and he said that it had no connection at all with the very poor 1548 Piedmont (1915, 12-15); he elsewhere spoke of its magnificent engraving, another point on which no one could disagree (Almagià, 1925, 989). He also generally spoke of it in superlatives several times, of which we will quote but one: "It is by far the most important map of the Piedmont region to appear in the sixteenth century" (1915, 12), and elsewhere similarly (1915; 15; 1925, 989), and, perhaps surprisingly, usually the harshest critic of all, Lavis-Trafford, of whom we shall speak more in a moment, also said it was the best in the sixteenth century, and that nothing better would appear for sixty-five years (1950, 57; see also his always positive comparisons of it with many maps of the area, mostly maps later than Gastaldi's, at 61, 64, 75, 94, 95, 98, 104 and 120). Almagià repeats his high opinion later, and is followed by several others (Almagià, 1929, 27; Almagià, 1948, 25; Lago, 1992, 244; Perini, 1996, 43; and Mollo, in Lago, 2002, 1, 29). Lavis-Trafford, however, regardless of his high opinion of the map by comparison with others, noted a good many gross errors (1950, 53, 54-57), although it's true that he was studying only a small area of the map, and perhaps was applying an overly critical eye to a sixteenth century map, the progress and worth of which we believe cannot be judged on the basis of comparisons with reality, that is, the cartography of our own times, but on the basis of comparisons with maps of its own time and before. In any event, two scholars in 2002, in different works, strongly contest Almagià's stance, especially Milanesi. While she agrees that it is better than the 1548 map, she simply says that the "1548 errors are less accentuated" on the 1555 Map (2002, 1, 13), and implies that it is not after all so distant from the 1548 map. She accepts that the hydrography, slightly deformed, is good, as is the orography, and lauds the richness and precision of detail (2002, 2, 18). But as to relative positions of places, she considers it far inferior to the manuscript maps of Battista Agnese, and even of Nicolas Germanus (2002, 2, 18). Pressenda, too, says the map has much more in common with the 1548 map than commonly said, and regards Almagià's assertions as "excessive and disputable" (2002, 321), and Umek (2002, 525) says the 1548 and 1555 are definitely cognate. The truth must lie somewhere between. But though we have made no study of most of the facets of the map, we can say that the hydrography is greatly improved, especially as to the many important affluents of the Po, which are so glaringly incorrect on the 1548 map.

As to sources, except for the adoption of several Ptolemaic anchor points upon which to base his coordinate net (Almagià, 1915, 12-13; Almagià, 1929, 27; Milanesi, 2002, 2, 18), and the presumption that nautical charts were used for the coastline at the bottom of the map, in particular as to the placement of towns along that coastline, I find nothing written, and, oddly, the subject has not been gone into, a point noted by Almagià in 1952 (in the *Atti* of the fifteenth Italian Geographical Congress of 1950 at Torino, in vol. 2 (Torino, 1952), 761). Only the negative determination that neither the road guidebooks of Charles Estienne nor the historical works of Leandro Alberti were used has been made, by Lavis-Trafford (1950, 52 and 55-56). Umek says that the Vescovile atlas (see earlier in our Cartobibliography, in no. 4) *may* possibly have been used (2002, 512 and 524-25), but says the present map is much better in that area (cit., 536).

While we do not usually discuss derivatives in our Cartobibliography, other than to give references to works containing information on them when such exist, in this case, we must make a short exception. The first re-issue of the Piedmont was in the next year, 1556 (Karrow, 1993, 228, no. 76.1), and is a copperplate engraved by Fabio Licinio. This is the earliest known dated collaboration between Gastaldi and Licinio. It was probably about this time that Gastaldi, probably impressed with the fine engraving of the 1556 map, decided upon Licinio as his partner for the great maps of 1559-1564. One wonders if Giolito, the publisher of the 1552 copperplate Gastaldi Germany, and the 1556 Piedmont, had a hand in acquainting them with each other. The Piedmont was to have a notable future. For the later editions and derivatives besides the just mentioned 1556 edition, the reader is refered to Almagià (1915, 15-19); Almagià (1929, 27); Almagià (1948, 25-26); and Karrow (1993, 228-29).

Location of copies:
Simancas AGS(IV,45) (I am very grateful to Peter Meurer for apprising me of the existence of this copy, and to Pilar Chías Navarro for obtaining a reproduction of it for me.) There was a copy in the composite atlas at the Biblioteca dei Bardi at Firenze, but the holdings of this library were subsumed by the library of the Università degli Studi di Firenze, and a search in 1977-78 revealed no composite atlas present there. This is probably the copy now in the Archivio di Stato, reproduced in Bifolco and Ronca, and above. There is a 1940 photograph of the Bardi copy at the British Library, with call number (Maps 20865.(24.)), and there is a reproduction of it in Almagià, 1929, pl. 29. According to Meurer (1991, 53), there is an copy at the Leiden University Library. There exist no other copies to the best of my knowledge.

References:
Biasutti, 1908, 25 nt 1, 36-37, 41 and 44; Almagià, 1915, 10, 17-18, 22 and 26; Almagià, 1925, 989; Almagià, 1929, 27; Almagià, 1948, 25; Lavis-Trafford, 1950, 51-57, 61, 64, 74-75, 94, 95, 98, 99, 104, 107-08, 117 and 123; Meurer, 1991, 153; Lago, 1992, 243-45; Perini, 1996, 42-44; Milanesi, 2002, 1, 13-14 and II, 18-19; Mollo, 2002, 29; Pressenda, 2002; Umek, 2002, 9, 10, 11, 13 and 14; Bifolco and Ronca, 2018, 3:1886.

Reproductions:
Almagià, 1929, pl. 29; Bifolco and Ronca, 2018, 3: 1886-87. http://bibliografia-valdese.com/detail.php?id'7663&lang'fr (the Bardi copy, but very small)

(81.-86.) Six maps which appear in Volume Three of Ramusio's *Navigazioni*

We have already spoken, at our compound entry (73.-76.), of the most important maps for this volume, those four maps which were completed, at least preliminarily, in 1553, but which for some reason, were not published in the volume. They would presumably have been at the front of the volume, like those in the 1554 volume one (nos. 77-79), and would have had the useful purpose of serving (if not overly well) as general cartographic orientation and guide to the volume. In the event, we have a rather unsatisfactory hodge-podge of six maps at different places in the volume, a single-page map of Hispaniola, following the account by Peter Martire (in the 1967-70 reprint at 3, 36v), which is copied from the Hispaniola in the 1534 Venice edition of Martire and Oviedo, a rather good Western Hemisphere map of which more below, and four picturesque (*overly* picturesque) but geographically poor maps sent at an unknown time before 1553 by some unidentified Frenchmen to Ramusio or Fracastoro (see in entry (73.-76.). These four were accompanied by a six-page disjointed discourse purportedly by some unidentified sea captain of Dieppe near the end of volume 3 (see Parks, 1970, 35 for its location in other editions of volume three). This discourse briefly describes four unconnected parts of the world, New France, in North America, Brazil in South America, Guinea in Africa, and Sumatra in Archipelago Asia, with one map for each of these places. It also discusses one more place, Madagascar, but for some reason, includes no map in this case. Ramusio evidently included it in the volume on America simply because it deals with areas which fall within the areas covered by all three Volumes, and thus doesn't properly correspond to any of them. What could be the rationale for bringing together this sundry disconnected information in a would-be discourse one may wonder. The possibility that some unknown French voyage would have sailed to New France, from there to Brazil, from Brazil to Guinea, and from there to Sumatra, and then back to France, seems unlikely to me. Nor, in fact, does the account openly state that this was the case, for there are no transitional words between the sections. So why was it put together? What purpose was it supposed to serve? I cannot answer these questions. But for some reason, this disjointed discourse of little worth has attracted considerable attention (see Parks, 1970, 35-36), with some thinking that it is somehow connected with a voyage by the Parmentier brothers to Sumatra (which notion ignores the other four places), and some think that it was compiled by the French cosmographer Pierre Crignon. This last notion no doubt comes from the fact that the first full page of the discourse consists of a gratuitous and incongruous sort of preface, a pretentious and mock-erudite description of the terrestrial and celestial spheres, which basically consists of nothing but poorly presented rudimentary information, all of which can be found better expressed in Sacrobosco's *Sphera*, plus a fair dose of pure jabberwocky.

We much suspect that the whole discourse is apocryphal in nature, and was simply thrown together in disorderly fashion by some unknown person (though probably indeed of Dieppe) who happened to have gleaned from sundry sources various information on the thoroughly unrelated places of which he speaks. The four maps themselves do not just contain, but are stuffed with, vignettes of ships, boats, fish, sea monsters, animals, individual trees and plants, endless pictures of persons engaged in various activities, and more, giving them a somewhat childish appearance, although the vignettes are well done and well engraved, and thus in fact are attractive, and have ornamental value. But in terms of geographical value, the maps have little. None of them are graduated, which would tell us immediately that they are unlikely to be true Gastaldi maps, even if we did not know this otherwise. The map of New France alone, has a certain limited worth of which we shall speak in its individual entry. Biasutti was of the opinion, which we tend to agree with, that these four maps should not have been printed in the *Navigazioni* at all (1920, 409). In including these four maps among Gastaldi's, I have simply followed precedent (Grande, Bagrow, Karrow), though some might say a bit slavishly, for the originals of the maps were sent from Paris to Ramusio or Fracastoro, and Gastaldi's only hand in them would have been in working them up so that they were suitable for engraving and for inclusion in the *Navigazioni*, and this working-up could have consisted of nothing more than re-drawing them to size, so that they would fit the pages of Ramusio's book, italianization of the language, and perhaps some touching up here and there. The last map in the book, the Western Hemisphere mentioned above, appearing at the end of volume three, is truly from Gastaldi, and is of much greater value and interest; we shall speak of it in its individual entry. All of the maps also appeared in the two later editions of volume three (1565, 1606), but as copper engravings, all of the woodblocks probably having been destroyed in the printing house fire of 1557.

Location of copies (of the book):
New York PL(*KB + 1556)/ Cambridge Harv((SPEC. COLL. AM. DIS. R 149 + Portfolio)/ Oxford Bodl(H 88 Art.)/ Edinburgh NLS(E.185a, v. 3)/ London BL(566.k.1-3, v. 3)/ Edinburgh UL(JY 1094-6, v. 3)/ Cambridge UL(CCA.47.213) and (RCS.Case.a.99)/ Paris BN(G-1453)/ London WellcInst(5329/D)/ Basel UB(ET I 23a)/ Leiden UB((369 A 1-3, v. 3)/ Chicago Newb(Ayer 110 .R2 1556)/ New Haven Yale(Eca +550Rb 3) and (Eca +550Rc 3) and (Eca +563 3)/ Ithaca CU(G159.R18++)/ Washington LC(G159.R2 vol. 3 1556)(2 copies) and (Thacher A846 vol. 3 Thacher Coll.)/ Claremont CC(910..4 R15, v. 3)/ Hartford TC(QUARTO G159 .R2 v. 3 1556)/ Amherst AC(G159 .R2 v. 2-3 1559, 1556+, v. 3)/ Providence JCB(1-SIZE H550 .R184n, v. 3)(2 copies) and (1-SIZE G159 .D4x vol. 3 1556)/ Minneapolis Bell(R35, v. 3)

81. Hispaniola
-Venice, 1556
-Woodcut, 17.5 x 27.0, on one sheet
-No scale bar

At the top of the map, within the neat-line:
ISOLA SPAGNVOLA (ISLAND OF HISPANIOLA)

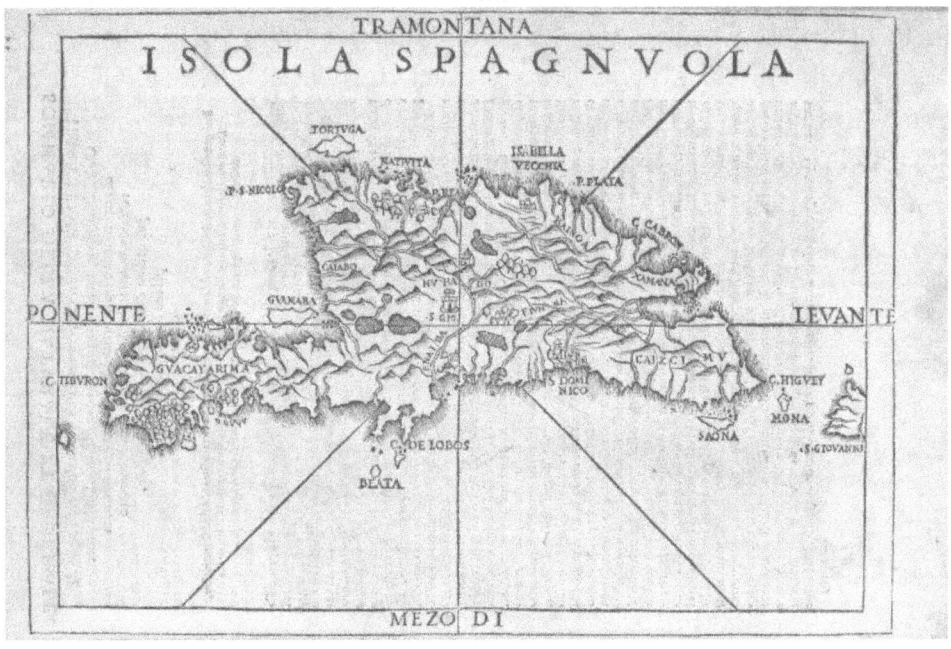

81 Hispaniola 1556 New York PL

Comments:
The map carries no graduation. Unlike the French maps, it is quite without décor. But, as with those maps (see the comments in the preceding compound entry, and nos. 82-85 following), Gastaldi's only part in this map would have been working it up to size for the *Navigazioni*, italianization of some forms, and perhaps adjustment of some details, for it is taken directly from the map of Hispaniola in the Venice edition of Martire and Oviedo, of 1534. This map, though it carries fewer names, is considerably closer to reality, especially as to its elongated form, than the map of Hispaniola in Gastaldi's 1548 Ptolemy (no. 62). One might ask why Gastaldi didn't use the

651

1534 map for his outline in the 1548 map, but perhaps Gastaldi had more faith in the sources he used for the map in the Ptolemy edition. That is, while the form is better in the 1534 original, than in the 1548 map, this doesn't necessarily mean that Gastaldi was aware of this fact. The map, along with no. 86, may well have been included by Ramusio by way of compensation for the fact that the intended four New World maps for some reason did not appear in the book, but if so, it is poor compensation.

References:
Winsor, 1884-89, II, 185 nt 1; Harrisse, 1892, 598: Nordenskiöld, 1897, 183, no. 164; Grande, 1905, *carte*, 88; Biasutti, 1920, 409.

Reproductions:
Ramusio, 1978-88, vol. 5, 217.
https://digitalcollections.nypl.org/items/7b7e9236-7661-da23-e040-e00a180652df

82. New France (Newfoundland area)
-Venice, 1556
-Woodcut, 27.0 x 37.0 cm., on one sheet
-No scale bar

On the face of the map itself, lower left:
LA NVOVA FRANCIA (NEW FRANCE)

Comments:
The map carries no graduation. It is filled with vignettes, like all the French maps, but perhaps its cartography should be taken more seriously than that of the other French maps, for reasons that shall soon be clear, regardless of the overall impression of a puerile work. At the lower right there is a ship with, below it, the words "Vado a la terra nuoua" ("I am going to New France"); cf. no. 78). The map is obviously cognate with our map no. 60, both of which give a good depiction of the Verrazzanian concepts of the cartography of northeastern North America, as opposed to the Gomez concepts (for more on this, see our comments at entry no. 60.). Consequently, the map has drawn

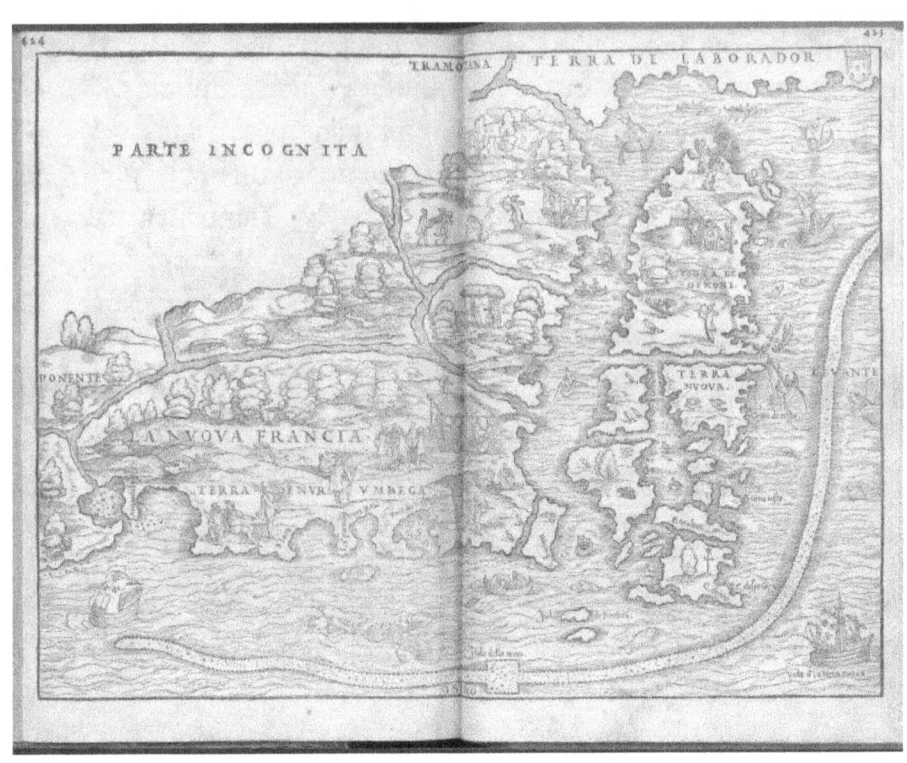

82 New France (Newfoundland area) 1556 New York PL

the interests of many scholars, as our list of references shows, and there have been various opinions as to its ultimate cartographic source. Stokes and Wieder say that it is from lost maps derived from Verrazzano (Stokes, 1915-28, 2, 162, in a section written by F. C. Wieder). Prowse (1933, 27) believes it to be based on the Harleian map (on this map, see Abendanon, 1921), while Anthiaume says it is from a Dieppe map of the Harleian type (1916, 2, 499-50), and, according to Winsor, Kohl believed that it was taken from a lost map by Jehan Denys (Winsor, 1904, 79, no. 159, without giving the Kohl reference). We shall not enter into the fray here further, letting the reader who might wish to do so pursue our many references, but we would like to make it clear that our own opinion differs from most in one important regard. It is best, I think, to usually accept the dates as given on maps as they are, and not play dating games when we have two or more cognate maps but leave the chronology as it is unless we have truly good reason to do otherwise. But here I think we have a case where we have such good reason. Gastaldi's map no. 60, from his Ptolemy, strongly resembles this one in its

653

northeast part (and a glance at map no. 60 will show that, in fact, other than in its northeast part, the map is almost without features). Map no. 60 of course was published in 1548, although it was very possibly made a few years earlier than this. The present map was published in 1556, perhaps as much as ten years, if not more, later. But any notion that the 1548 map might have influenced the 1556 map is, I think we may say without fear of error, certainly wrong. We know that Ramusio, in his 1553 prefatory dedication to Fracastoro at the head of his Volume three, where he has been speaking of Spanish maps received by him over a good number of years, suddenly interjects the observation: "Similarly have several excellent Frenchmen done, who have sent you [i.e. Fracastoro] from Paris the relations of New France, together with four maps, which shall be placed in this volume in their places" (cf. entry no. (73.-76.)). While it is unclear whether the phrase "the relations of New France" is in reference to the discourse which is accompanied by the four French maps, or perhaps the accounts in Ramusio of Cartier's first two voyages, of 1534 and 1535-36 (see Parks, 1970, 36), it *is* clear from another Ramusio discourse (Ramusio, 1967-70, 3, 348r [misnumbered 438]; Milanesi ed., 1978-88, 6, 879) that the anonymous French captain's discourse (see entry (81.-86.) was written in 1539, and so Fracastoro (and then through him Ramusio) could have received it at any time after 1539.

Now, while we know that Ramusio obtained Spanish maps, and we have strong foundation to believe he obtained Portuguese ones also, we have no indication of his having obtained major maps from the Dieppe school, or other French maps, other than the four small maps we are dealing with here. The present one of these four maps was compiled, as the above scholars have all perceived, from Dieppe-type maps, but this would have occurred in France, not in Italy. The scenario we are suggesting is that Fracastoro received the manuscript original of this New France (no. 82, the present map), and the other three French maps, sometime between 1539 and the time that Gastaldi began working on his Tierra nveva (no. 60), which would be some time between ca. 1542-1547, and that, in making that map (no. 60) Gastaldi was served by the manuscript original of the present map, and not directly by some Dieppe maps or lost Verrazzanian maps. Summarizing an argument which is admittedly a little involved, we think the following chronology the correct one: An unknown Frenchman made the manuscript original of our present map no. 82 at some time before Gastaldi began work on his "Tierra nveva" (no. 60), indeed very possibly before Gastaldi began work at all on his Ptolemy, and some time not long afterwards sent it (or a copy of it) to Fracastoro, who forwarded it to Ramusio, who then made it accessible to Gastaldi, who drew his "Tierra nveva" from it. Then, several years later, in 1556, Ramusio included a printed version of that manuscript original in the *Navigazioni*. In further support of this, we note that the area covered in the present map is larger in scale by a good many whole factors than the same area depicted by Gastaldi on the "Tierra nveva", implying that the latter was most likely generalized from the former. Thus the immediate source for both no. 60 and no. 82 is the same, the anonymous manuscript map sent from France, and for our purposes, this is all we need to know. The sources of the anonymous Frenchman who made the original manuscript of our no. 82, while no doubt of the greatest interest to historians of the discovery and exploration of the region, falls outside the story of Giacomo Gastaldi proper. It should be noted that some of the writers in the references which follow treat both nos. 60 and 82 as though they were maps derived by Gastaldi himself directly from Dieppe or Verrazzanian maps, which is surely incorrect. A point worth appending at the end here: All of this geography which has engendered so much discussion is dreadfully wrong in any event!

References:
Kohl, 1869, 226-32; Winsor, 1884-87, IV, 28, 77, 86-87 and 90; Harrisse, 1900, 251-54; Winsor, 1904, 79, no. 159; Grande, 1902, 73; Grande, 1905, *carte*, 74-83; Stokes, 1915-28, II, 162; Anthiaume, 1916, 1, 499-500; Prowse, 1933, 27; Wroth, 1970, 203, 205, 208-09 and 304; Verner, et al, 1979, 12-14.

Reproductions:
Ramusio, 1978-88, vol. 6, 904-05.
https://digitalcollections.nypl.org/items/7b7e9236-7662-da23-e040-e00a180652df

83. Brazil
-Venice, 1556
-Woodcut, 27.0 x 38.0 cm., on one sheet
-No scale bar

In the body of the map, in the center:
BRASIL (BRAZIL)

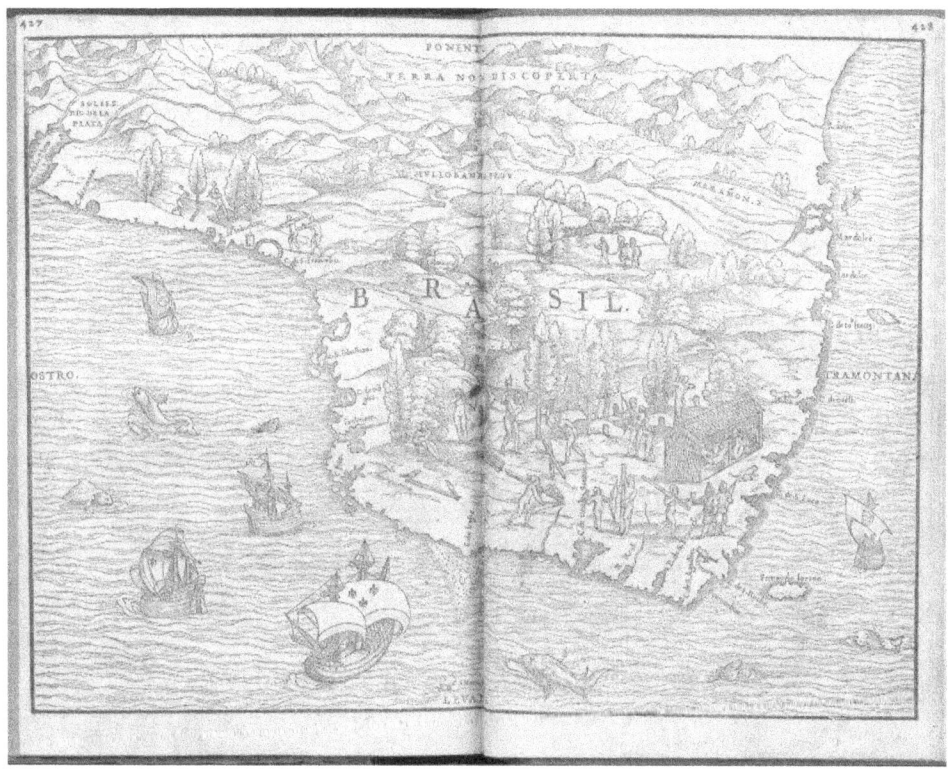

83 Brazil 1556 New York PL

Comments:
The map contains no graduation. It is oriented to the east. As with the other
French maps (nos. 82, 84, and 85), the original author was an unknown
Frenchman, and Gastaldi's part in the map would have been limited to
working it up to size for the *Navigazioni*, italianization of forms, and perhaps
some stylistic or other minor changes. Grande notes, interestingly, that the
coastal names follow exactly those of the accompanying account,

purportedly by a French sea captain (1905, *carte*, 87). As there is no point of controversy connected with it, and while strictly speaking it did not in the main emerge from the mind of Gastaldi, we need spend no more time on it.

References:
Ruge, 1892, 74 [wrongly dated as 1553]; Grande, 1905, *carte*, 84-87: Tooley, Bricker and Crone, 1989, 214; Minella, 1993, 41-43.

Reproductions:
Ramusio, 1978-88, vol. 6, 924-25.
https://digitalcollections.nypl.org/items/7b7e9236-7663-da23-e040-e00a180652df

84. West Africa below the Tropic of Cancer
-Venice, 1556
-Woodcut, 27.0 x 37.0 cm., on one sheet
-No scale bar

In the body of the map, above center:
PARTE DE LA FRICA [sic] (PART OF AFRICA)

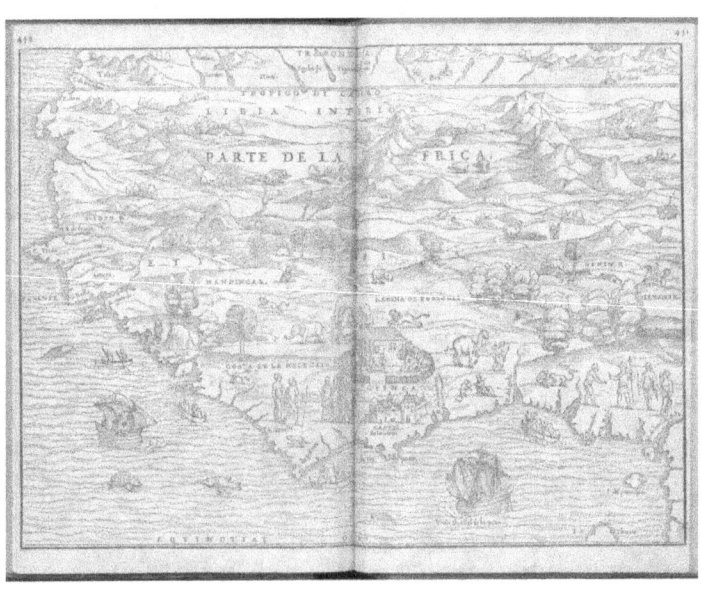

84 West Africa below the Tropic of Cancer 1556 New York PL

657

Comments:
The map contains no graduation. It is the third of the French maps (see nos. 82, 83, and 85). As usual with these French maps, stuffed with attractive vignettes, but of little geographical value. A ship near the lower right has below it the words "Vado al castol de la mina" ("I am going to Mina Castle") (cf. nos. 78 and 82). As with all the French maps, Gastaldi's role was simply to work up the map for inclusion in Ramusio's *Navigazioni*. The basic cartography is from an anonymous Frenchman, probably basing himself upon some Dieppe school maps. Biasutti's assertion that he detects some rapport between this map and the same area on the Gastaldi 1564 Africa should perhaps be taken with a grain of salt until a closer study has been made. Biasutti also does not seem to be aware of the origin of these maps.

References:
Biasutti, 1920, 409 and 411; Tooley, 1967?, 71, no. W12; Tooley, Bricker and Crone, 1989, 159; Norwich, 1997, 358.

Reproductions:
Ramusio, 1978-88, vol. 6, 1010-11.
https://digitalcollections.nypl.org/items/7b7e9236-7664-da23-e040-e00a180652df

85. Sumatra
-Venice, 1556
-Woodcut, 27.0 x 37.5 cm., on one sheet
-No scale bar

In the sea, just above the island:
SVMATRA (SUMATRA)

Comments:
The map carries no graduation. It is the last of the French maps (see nos. 82, 83, and 84), filled with appealing vignettes, but of little geographical value. Originally drawn by an anonymous French cartographer, Gastaldi's only contribution would have been to work it up for inclusion in the *Navigazioni*.

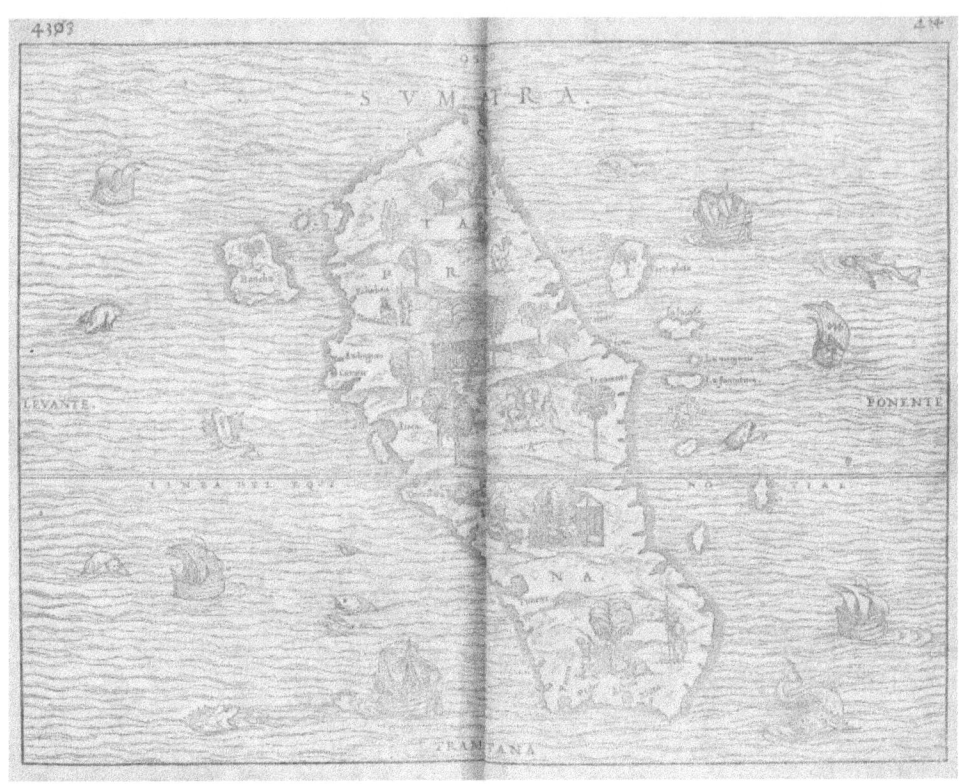

85 Sumatra 1556 New York PL

Suarez accepts the theory of the discourse accompanying the French maps as being connected with the voyage of the Parmentier brothers, which as we have seen is very questionable, since it ignores the other areas covered by the account and the maps. However, while that voyage cannot account for the whole of the discourse in Ramusio, nor the other maps, it certainly is quite possible that, as regards this map, the original information was based upon that venture, for, though both Parmentier brothers died in Sumatra, one ship of their company did return, and, as Suarez points out, the cartography is rather good for the time. Suarez also states that it "was the first separate map of any Southeast Asian island based upon actual observation." Again, however, this would be an accomplishment not of Gastaldi, but of the anonymous French cartographer, and is not really part of Gastaldi's story proper.

References:
Suarez:, 1999, 157.

Reproductions:
Nordenskiöld, 1997, 157.
https://digitalcollections.nypl.org/items/7e2af6f5-2c3e-b3db-e040-e00a18062ca5

86. Western Hemisphere
-Venice, 1556
-Woodcut, 27.0 cm. in diameter, on one sheet
-No scale bar

In the margin, outside the hemisphere, at upper left:
*VNIVERSALE DELLA PARTE DEL MONDO NVOVAMENTE RITROVATA
(GENERAL MAP OF THE PART OF THE WORLD NEWLY DISCOVERED)*

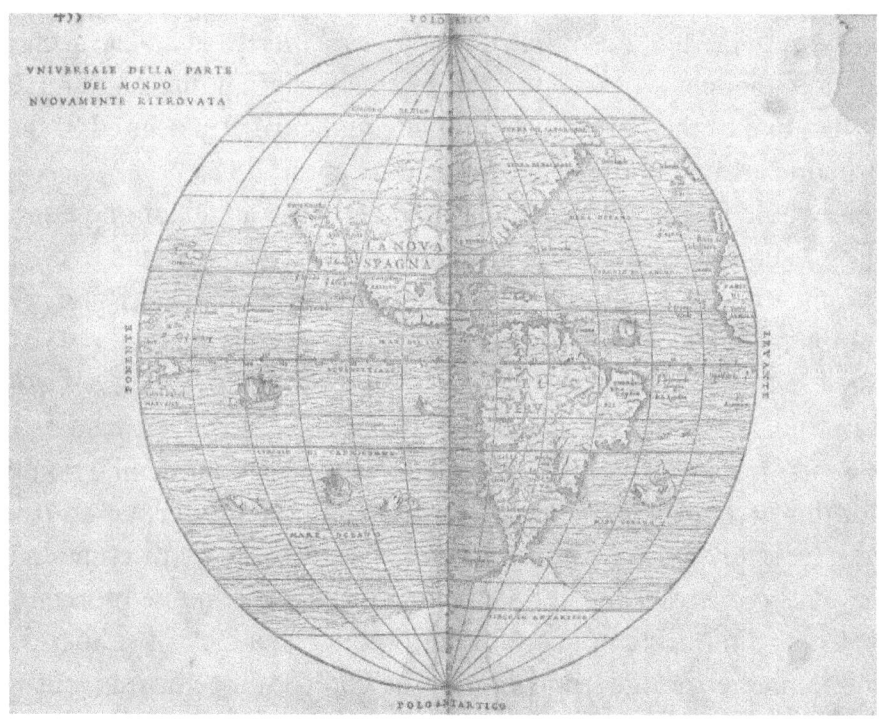

86 Western Hemisphere 1556 New York

Comments:

Graduated in numbered five-degree increments in latitude and longitude, in latitude along the central meridian from 90° S to 90° N, and in longitude along the equator, from 10°00' E to 170°00' W. The parallels and meridians are drawn in, at fifteen-degree intervals, the prime meridian running through the eastmost of the Azores, but also through the Cape Verde Islands, though in the midst and not touching any single island in the group, so the prime meridian is most likely to be taken as running through the Azorean island. The projection is hemispherical, which was not an innovation by Gastaldi, for he was preceded by Monachus in 1527 (Shirley, 1987, no. 57) and Tramezzini in 1554 (Shirley, cit., no. 97), and also by Agnese, and in fact the projection probably goes back to Roger Bacon (ca. 1220-1292)(See Fiorini, 1895, 172-73; Grande, 1905, *carte*, 115-16; Minella, 1993, 48-49). The projection, we might note, was better chosen for the area covered, than that chosen by him for his great map of America of ca. 1560 (no. 94). The first I know of to write about this map was Kohl, who came to the following conclusion: "The general [universal] map of America is a very accurate production, the result of the study of Spanish original maps and reports of the time. It is one of the best, most complete and correctly printed of the maps published near the middle of the sixteenth century" (1869, 227). And this keynote would then find agreement time and time again among later scholars, usually specifically with reference to improvements over previous depictions, improvements stemming from Spanish sources (Ruge, 1992, 72 [with map misdated 1550]; Grande, 1905, *carte*, 111; Wagner, 1937, 1, 46; Wheat, 1954, 30-31; Wheat, 1957, 21; Milanesi, 1984, 215). All is not perfect, true. The North American east coast is in general not so bad, but it has a generalized look, and, says Grande, is unique in this, like no other map. But for this area, Gastaldi could have gained no new information from Oviedo; he knew the only information extant was the conflicting data from the voyages of Verrazzano and Gomez in the 1520s, and he probably gave that coast its simplified noncommittal look out of a lack of solid information. Still odder is the strange truncation of the California peninsula, but wherever this feature comes from, the area was on the very remotest edge of Spanish activities, and no doubt little accurate information was available, even to the Spanish themselves. Note, incidentally, the exact same truncated depiction in the double hemispherical world map serving as insets at the bottom left and right of Gastaldi's great 1561 world map (no. 104).

Nevertheless, in all main areas, it corresponds very well with the best and most recent Spanish information. Now, we know (see compound entry no. (73.-76.)) that from a large assortment of recent maps provided to Ramusio by Oviedo, Gastaldi compiled a general map of the Western Hemisphere, which he then broke down into four regional maps covering the New World, but for some reason these four maps were not published, and we don't have them. Nor of course do we have the manuscript original which Gastaldi compiled covering the new world, which must have been a large and detailed map. Surely, then, our current map cannot but be a reduction, a generalization, of that original large and detailed manuscript compilation. In fact, several writers have essentially suggested the same thing, though making the observation in different ways (Biasutti, 1920, 409; Caraci, 1936, 129-30; Wagner, 1937, 1, 46; Minella, 1993, 481). This scenario surely gives us the origin of this map, and its purpose would have been (perhaps together with the Hispaniola map, no. 81, as another minor contribution to this end) to serve as compensation for the lack of the four intended maps. Still, as accurate as it is for its time, it is, like the three maps illustrating volume one (nos. 77, 78, and 79), sparse on interior detail and names; indeed, it is more so than even those maps, for the sparseness is extreme, and extends to coastal names as well. Caraci said that it has all the look of an expedient, an unfinished sketch of a map (1936, 130), and correctly noted, having in mind size and detail, that it definitely does not reflect the original manuscript map (cit., 130, n. 3). Still, it is certainly a greatly generalized reduction of that map, and its inclusion at the very end of the book, instead of at the start, suggests an apologetic attitude toward it on the part of Ramusio. On a final note, we recall that Gastaldi was seriously ailing from some unknown affliction in 1555, and that possibly, as we suggest in our compound entry no (73.-76.), while the four maps were ready, as Ramusio tells us in 1553, they may have been ready only in a preliminary way, and Gastaldi postponed the final working up of them until near the time the book was to be published, but found himself unable to do so because of his affliction. Perhaps the notably correct but very simplified and sketchy map we have represents a last-minute effort, the best that a recuperating Gastaldi could come up with before the volume went to press. While the original manuscript would necessarily have preceded the four maps which we can only date as 1553, since they did not reach the press, then that manuscript would also have been from 1553 or earlier. But the present reduction can only be dated as 1556, the date it was published, and just possibly also the date it was compiled.

References:
Kohl, 1869, 227; Ruge, 1892, 73 [misdating the map as 1550]; Fiorini, 1895, 174-75; Grande, 1905, *carte*, 110-16; Dahlgren, 1911, 16-18; Biasutti, 1920, 409; Caraci, 1936, 123-25, 127, 129-31, 133; Wagner, 1937, 1, 46-47; Wheat, 1954, 30-31; Wheat, 1957, 21; Milanesi, 1984, 215-16; Minella, 1993, 47-51.

Reproductions:
Nordenskiöld, 1897, 163.
https://digitalcollections.nypl.org/items/7ecd4264-713d-823d-e040-e00a18065730

87. Malta
-[Venice], ca. 1556 (?)
-Copper engraving, 21.0 x 31.0 cm., on one sheet
-5 Italian miles = 4.5 cm.

In text box in the lower right corner of the map:
La detta isola e discosta dall'isola | *de sicilia sesanta miglia uerso ostro* | *Giacomo di castaldi piamõtese F[ecit]* | *fabius licinius ex[cidit] (The said island is sixty miles distant from the island of sicily towards the south* | *Giacomo di castaldi piedmontese compiler* | *Fabio Licinio engraver)* **Note:** While the abbreviation "F" after a name usually denotes the engraver, it can, in rare cases, designate the author or compiler, as see Ganado (1994-95, 1, 3). See more in the comments below. Interestingly, this is the only map in which one of these standard forms, indicating function of the named person, abbreviated or full, appears after Gastaldi's name.

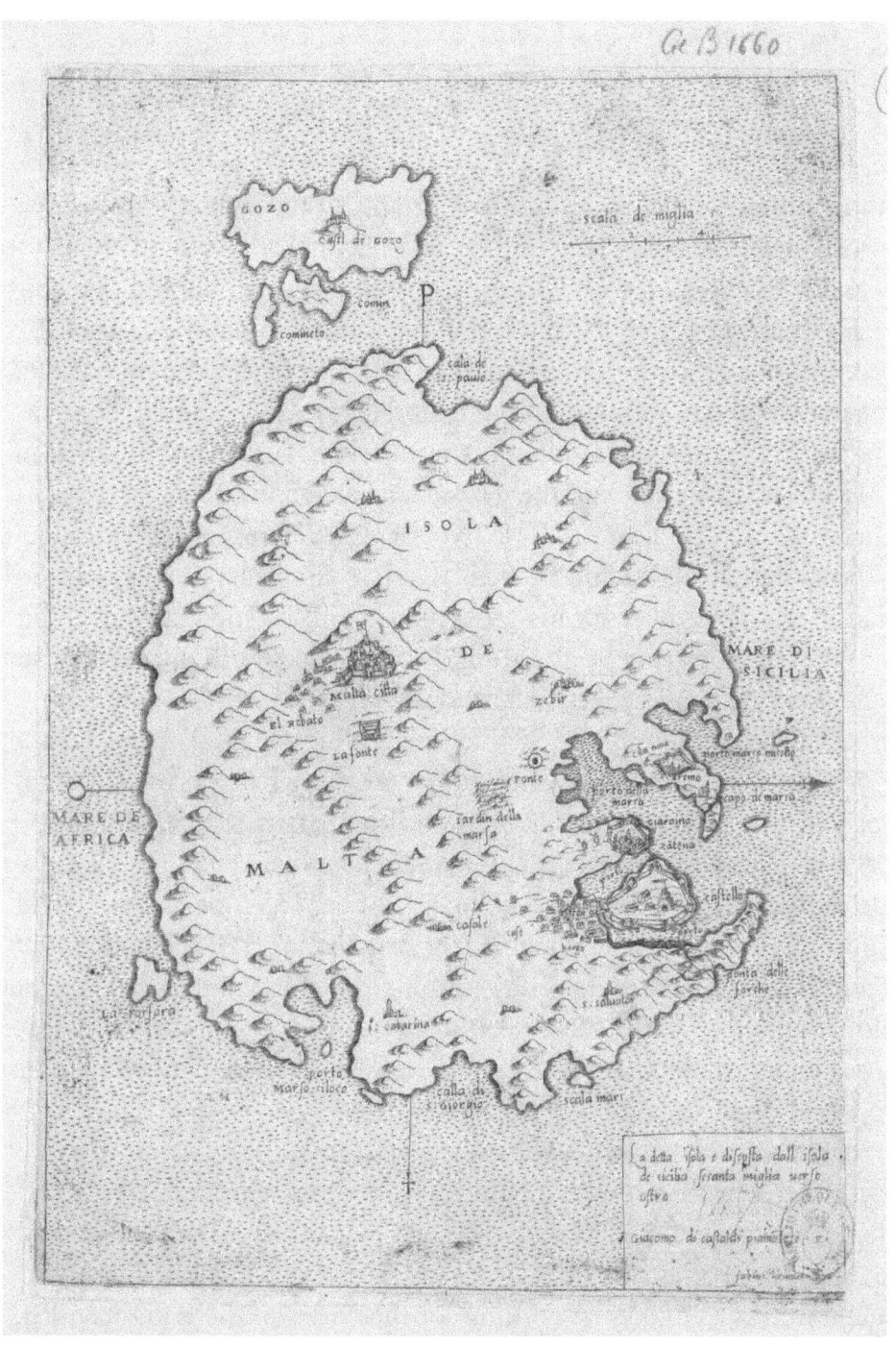

87 Malta 1556 Paris BN

664

On the island itself:
ISOLA DE MALTA (ISLAND OF MALTA)

Comments:
We should note first that there are two variants of the first edition, which differ only in the inclusion of two forts on one variant. We shall speak more below about this version with two forts, which is known only in one copy.

The map carries no graduation; it is oriented to the west. It is also undated, like our following map, Corsica, and a wide assortment of dates have been assigned to it, many of them simple guesses, ranging from ca. 1550 to ca. 1570, although the latter is impossible, since Gastaldi died in 1566. I have estimated it, and the Corsica, as ca. 1556 because all other Gastaldi-Licinio maps besides these two are dated maps, and they range from 1556-1564. Perhaps Gastaldi, in these two less significant maps, was trying out Licinio as an engraver for his great maps of 1559-1564, a project that he was very possibly gearing up for around 1556. Also, both maps carry scale bars, and with the single exception of the 1545 Sicily, no Gastaldi map carries a scale bar before his 1555 Piedmont, after which all carry scale bars. (The 1555 Antwerp edition by Cock of no. 69, showing west Asia, has a scale bar, but the original Gastaldi edition from between 1550 and 1555 has not survived, and it is possible that this scale bar was added by Cock.) Ganado, however, considers that the map is of ca. 1551, because it fails to show Forts St. Elmo and St. Michael, constructed in 1552 (Ganado, 1986, no. 5; and 2005, 52), but it does not seem to me quite valid to assume that Gastaldi would necessarily have been informed concerning two new structures on an island so remote to him. However, there is no way to be certain, and Ganado's point is a well-taken one.

The map is not, in any event, a remarkable production, and, by either date estimate, it was born without a destiny, for it is much inferior to an excellent anonymous 1551 Malta published by Lafreri (his earliest dated publication) which was no doubt the result of surveys made by highly competent military engineers working for the Order of the Knights of St. John, who effectively governed the island. This map took center stage for many years, and was reissued often by others (Ganado, 1985, 223; 1986, no. 2; 1994-95,1, 5; and 2003, 356-57).

There has been no discussion of the source of Gastaldi's map, though Ganado implies that a 1536 map by Johannes Quintinus, the earliest printed map of the island, might have served as a model (2003, 56). The island is actually somewhat oval-shaped, while the Gastaldi map and the Quintinus map have a rounded appearance, as does another map, an anonymous undated production which some have attributed to Giovanni Andreas Vavassore, and which Ganado has tentatively dated as 1551(?) (Ganado, 1986, no. 4; 1994-95, 1, 209 nt. 6; and 2003, 18), although the latter map is east-oriented, while the Quintinus and Gastaldi are west oriented.

A final interesting note. In 2004 Peter Meurer published a very full description of a large Veneto-Roman (VR, or Lafrerian) atlas, referred to by its owners as the "Strabo Illustratus Atlas", in which he included a reproduction of each map, and the atlas contains the Gastaldi Malta (Meurer, 2004, 57, no. 43). Since 2014 this atlas has been in the Bavarian State Library where it is known as the "Lafreri-Atlas" and has been completely digitized. Ganado noticed that, while on all other known copies of the map, there stands atop Mt. Sceberras a fortress oddly designated "cita nova", this fortress is not present on the map in the atlas described by Meurer. Since a fortress was indeed built there in 1552, the copy of the map now in the Bavarian State Library is clearly the unique copy of the map's first state, while all other known copies are of the second state (Ganado, 2005, 52-53). However, because there is uncertainty as to when Gastaldi would have first become aware of this new structure, the question of date as to either version is a somewhat shaky one, beyond the fact that we know that the variant with the forts came after the other.

Location of copies:
With the fort: München SB(2 Mapp. 464); without the fort: (Cambridge Harv(51-2498/ Paris BN(GE AF PF- 187(4451))/ Paris BN(GE B-1660)/ London BL(Maps C.7.e.1, no. 118)[2003]/ Roma BCas(Rari 1131, no. 43) [1982]

References:
Almagià, 1929, 23b; Almagià, 1939, *carta*, 9 with nt 4; Ganado, 1985, 223-24; Ganado, 1986, no. 5; Karrow, 1993, 224, no. 30/67; Ganado,

1994-95, 1, 3, 5 and 209; Ganado, 2003, 13 nt 16, 18, 53-54, 68, 356, 358-59 and 471; Meurer, 2004, 57, no. 43; Ganado, 2005, 52-53; Bifolco and Ronca, 2018, 3: 1706.

Reproductions:
First state, without fort: Meurer, 2004, no. 43; Bifolco and Ronca, 2018, 3: 1706-07.
https://www.digitale-sammlungen.de/en/view/bsb00107640?page'47; Second state, with fort: Almagià, 1929, pl. 25 (3); Bifolco and Ronca, 2018, 3: 1706.
https://gallica.bnf.fr/ark:/12148/btv1b532236355

88. Corsica
-[Venice], ca. 1556 (?)
-Copper engraving, 20.5 x 31.0 cm., on one sheet
-50 Italian miles = 9.0 cm.

In text box in the lower left corner of the map:
L'isola di Corsica, con i territori, citta, et castelle | forti et aperti, imonti, laghi, fiumi, golfi, porti | et isolette, la citta di genoa gli sta per tra- | mõtana miglia 125 in circa, la grandezza | della detta isola la ritrouarette con la sca- | la di miglia | giacomo di castaldi piamontese | fabius licinius | Ex (The island of Corsica, with territories, cities, and castles forts and plains, the mountains, lakes, rivers, gulfs, ports and islets, the city of genoa stands about 125 miles to the north of it, the size of the said island will be found with the scale of miles Giacomo di castaldi piedmontese fabius licinius engraver)

In the waters adjacent to the island:
ISOLA DI CORSICA (ISLAND OF CORSICA)

Comments:
The map carries no graduation. It is the largest map of Corsica printed before the time of Magini (Marinelli, 1906, 129 nt 2), and it is a rather good one, although it had only modest success (Ascari and Caraci, 1942-43, 211 [Caraci]). On this map too the abbreviation "Ex" follows the name of the engraver Licinio (cf. previous map, no. 87). The map, undated, has been

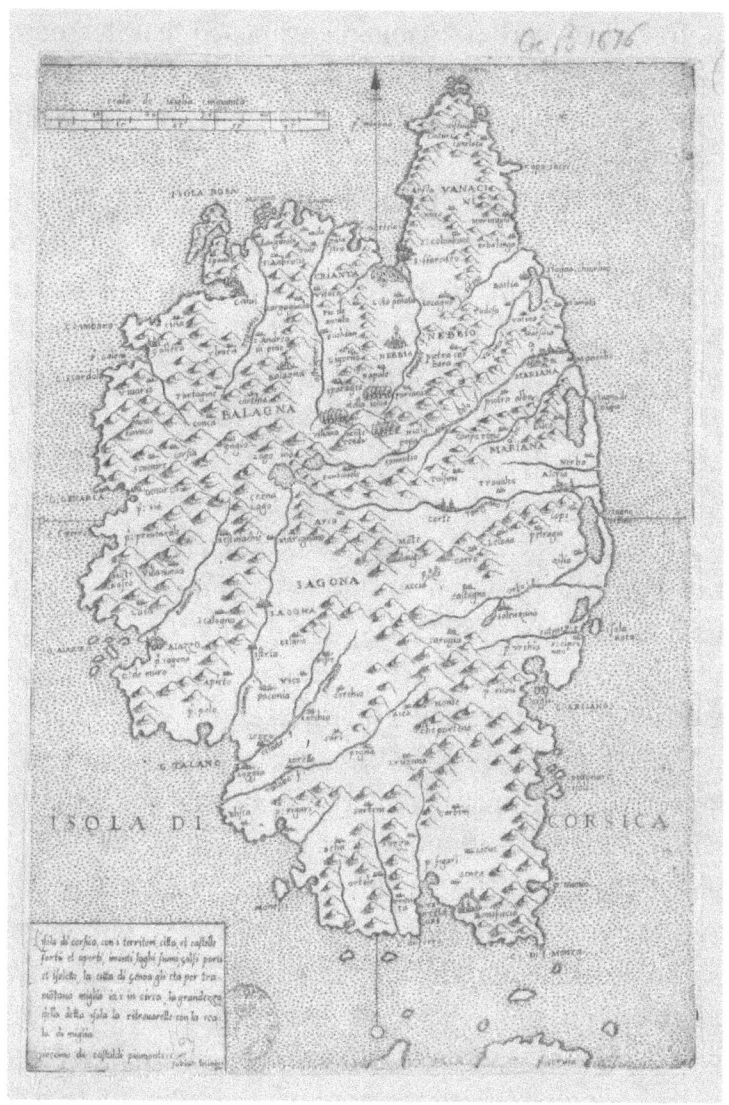

88 Corsica 1556 Paris BN

assigned various dates. Marinelli said 1560 (1906, 129 nt. 3); Caraci opined pre-1561 (1936, 490), and Ascari ca. 1550-61 (Ascari and Caraci, 1942-43, 181 [Ascari]). I have tentatively dated it ca. 1556(?) for the same reasons given for assigning the same date to the previous entry, no. 87, on Gastaldi's Malta (our no. 87). However, it was probable, on the basis of general similarity in size, subject, and depiction, that it was made at about the same time as the Malta, and, as we see at that entry, it is possible that that map dates from ca. five years earlier. Almagià proposed that the map was taken from a manuscript map of Corsica and its accompanying text, both by the well-known Genoese humanist, historian and churchman Agostino Giustiniani (Almagià, 1929, 32), and was followed in this by others (Caraci and Ascari, 1942-43, 182 [Ascari]; Karrow, 1993, 277-78, who, however, seems hesitant to fully accept the idea), or from some rendition of that map. Giustiniani, who had been made the bishop of Nebbio in Corsica traveled for nine years through the island, from 1522 to 1531 before returning to Genoa in 1531 (Almagià, 1929, 21 and 22; Karrow, 1993, 277), and wrote in 1531 a description of Corsica which remained in manuscript until 1882 (Karrow, 1993, 277), and supposedly, either at the same time, or in any event no later than July, 1535, he also made the mentioned manuscript map of Corsica (Almagià, 1929, 32; Karrow, 1993, 236 and 277). The Dominican geographer Leandro Alberti was also said to have made a map of Corsica which appears in his Venice, 1567 *Isole appartenenti alla Italia*, and it was presumed that this map was also taken from Giustiniani (Almagià, 1929, 21), but it is quite different in appearance than Gastaldi's, and the presumption was that it had been taken from a different recension of Giustiniani's map; but Caraci showed that the map in Alberti's book was in fact not made by him, but by some unknown author (Ascari and Caraci, 1942-43, 21-22 [1943, Caraci]). Several copies of Giustiniani's manuscript text exist, differing somewhat from each other (Almagià, 1929, 21), but no one seems to know what happened to the map, and there even seems to be uncertainty as to how generally available it might have been at the time, the presumption seeming to be that it was being held, perhaps jealously, by the Bank of Saint George in Genoa, clearly enough imparting a note of contradiction to the whole scenario, especially since, as Ascari brings out, Giustiniani's text contains almost no information on distances, and one could hardly use it alone for making a map (Ascari and Caraci, 1942-43, 185 [Ascari]). In fact, Caraci showed convincingly that it is not necessary to assume that Gastaldi had access to the supposed map to make his Corsica, and perhaps not to the text, either (Ascari and Caraci, 1942-43, 21-33 [1943, Caraci]), for all the information in the map was available from other sources at the time, including sea charts, the modern maps in the Strassburg and Lyon Ptolemy editions, and other sources (Ascari and Caraci, 1942-43, 211-13 [Caraci]).

He says basically the same as regards the map in Alberti's book (Ascari and Caraci, 1942-43, 18-23 [1943, Caraci]). This certainly more reflects the way Gastaldi customarily worked, and in our opinion, it is probably the way the map was actually made.

Furthermore, we have our doubts that the Giustiniani map in fact ever existed. It is attested only in one short passage which occurs in Giustiniani's 1537 annals of Genoa, where he states: "I minutely described the island of Corsica for the utility of my homeland, dedicated it to Prince Andrea Doria, and putting it in the form of a clear picture, presented it to the magnificent office of Saint George" (quoted from Karrow, 1993, 277). This is broadly interpretable language indeed, and without some such word as "also" or "furthermore" before the word "putting," the first and second clauses can be interpreted as referring to one and the same thing, the text, and the phrase "clear picture" is commonly used in a figurative sense in referring to text, probably in any language. In our opinion, Almagià was misled into thinking that still another source existed which attested to the map's existence. In one place, Almagià says that the map was of considerable size (1929, 21), though Giustiniani in the passage quoted says nothing of its size. But Lodovico degli Avanzi, the publisher of Alberti's 1567 *Isole appartenenti alla Italia,* tells us in a note to the reader that Alberti wished to show every detail, and that to do this, even thirty pages of maps would not have sufficed, and so it was decided to include but one map, showing the main places. But neither Alberti on his map nor Avanzi make any mention at all of Giustiniani, and Caraci makes it clear that the thirty-map depiction is not to be interpreted as having any reference to any supposed Giustiniani map, but has only to do with Alberti's ideas, and furthermore the reference is not to thirty or so maps already made by Alberti, but only to maps that he was contemplating making (Ascari and Caraci, 1942-43, 21-22 [1943, Caraci]). They could as well be daydreams, wishes, and the short mention cannot be taken as evidence that sources even existed for such a series of maps. And, although Ortelius, who used Alberti's map beginning from 1573, states on the map that Alberti made the map after Giustiniani, he makes no mention of Alberti following any map by Giustiniani, but only his text, telling us that the map "was drawn by Leandro Alberti from the commentary of Agostino Giustiniani" ("ex Augustini Iustiniani commentaries describit Leander Albertus") (quoted from

Almagià, 1923, 22; for a fuller English translation of the relevant passage, see Karrow, 1993, 278)). Giustiniani, incidentally, was also missing from Ortelius's list of cartographers in the first printing of the *Theatrum* in 1570, although he was added in a second printing in the same year (Karrow, 1993, xii), and remained in subsequent editions. But it is clear from his entry, reproduced in facsimile by Meurer (1991, 63), that Ortelius's source for his statement that Giustiniani made a map of Corsica is precisely the variably interpretable passage from Giustiniani's annals of Genoa from which we have quoted above. In our opinion, Giustiniani's map of Corsica is probably a mirage. Alberti apparently did make much use of Giustiniani's verbal description, although, as noted above, that description could hardly have sufficed alone. Gastaldi no doubt made his map as he usually did, using nautical charts for the coasts, for an island the most important feature in any event, and laying out the interior on the basis of various sources, which may or may not have included Giustiniani's verbal description, but if so, that description would not have played a role of great importance (see Caraci's comments in Ascari and Caraci, 1942-43, 213). Thus, the incongruity between the two depictions, Alberti's and Gastaldi's, is more naturally explained than by the presumption that, while both Gastaldi and Alberti used Giustiniani's supposed map, they used different recensions of it, as posited by Almagià (1929, 32). What, in fact, could these "recensions" be, and by whom would they have been made?

Location of copies:
Chicago Newb(Novacco 2F 78)/ Cambridge Harv(51-2496)/ Paris BN(GE B- 1676)/ Paris BN(GE AF PF- 187(4443))/ Budapest OSzK(TA 276, no. 38) [2005]/ London BL(Maps C.7.e.1., no. 103)[2003]/ Roma BCas(Rari 1131, no. 43)[1982]/ Vienna ÖNB (K I 109.514)[1970]/ Rostock UB(Q k 3, no. 42) [1904]

References:
Marinelli, 1906, 129 nt. 3; Biasutti, 1908, 50; Almagià, 1929, 21-22 and 32; Caraci, 1936, 490-93; Berthelot, 1939, 98-102; Ascari and Caraci, 1942-43, 181 and 183 (Ascari), and 210-13, 20-21 and 23-25 [1943] (Caraci); Karrow, 1993, 236 and 277-78; Bifolco and Ronca, 2018, 2: 996.

(89.-91.) Three(?) maps of sections of Interior Asia intended for volume two of Ramusio's *Navigazioni*, ca. 1556/57, but not published [not extant]

We see that there apparently existed a set of four regional maps of the New World which were to be included in volume three (1556) of the Navigazioni, which would have corresponded to the three known Gastaldi maps which appeared in volume one, beginning with the second edition (1554). From a much shorter passage in the Navigazioni, we learn that there were also maps for volume two, which volume covers interior or northern Asia, from its western boundaries to the Pacific. Tommaso Giunti, the publisher of the Navigazioni, tells us in his address to the reader in volume two (1559) that a few months before his death in July, 1557 Ramusio had given him several ready texts along with several maps of the areas covered by the volume. As with the maps made for America, we know that these maps existed in fully completed form, for Giunti's words are specific. Having spoken of "l'Incendio della mia Stamperia" ("the fire in my printing house"), which he says occurred on November 4, 1557, Giunti tells us that due to this fire, there was a great loss to geography, "essendo arsi alcuni essemplari, che'l Ramusio pochi mesi avãnti ch'egli passasse di questa vita, haueua apparecchiati, & daticigli per istãpare insieme con alcune tauole de I disegni de paesi, de quali nel libro uien fatto mentione" ("having been burned several items, which Ramusio, a few months before he passed from this life, had readied and given to us for printing together with several maps of lands, of which mention is made in this book") (Ramusio, 1967-70, 2, first and second pages of Giunti's notice to the reader; Milanesi ed., 1978-88, 3, 3 and 4). He tells us no more, but we are not without bases for some limited deduction as to the appearance of these maps. The 1555 Gastaldi-Membré map spoken of elsewhere here is of the western third of interior Asia, and would correspond pretty much exactly with the western portion of the area covered by the

Ramusio maps, and we can assume that the depiction on that map approximately reflects the western part of the maps which perished, though they would have been on a scale about a quarter to a third smaller, and probably would have had considerably less detail. Giunti's comments also accord well with Ramusio's statement that the volume one maps were included as a guide to the places in that volume, and they and the volume three maps were presumably intended to be placed at the front of their volumes, as those of volume one. How many there were, we don't know, for Giunti just says "several," but by comparison with the other two sets, there were probably three or four, the former perhaps more likely, considering the area covered, and that is the tentative assumption that we have made to enable us to include these lost Gastaldi maps in our Cartobibliography. We know no more of the maps, except that they must have been based on the relations in the volume, and that they must have been by Gastaldi, like the others.

89. (Western?) part of Interior Asia
Map not extant, and no details known other than those in the discussion in compound entry (89.-91.) above.

90. (Central?) part of Interior Asia
Map not extant, and no details known other than those in the discussion in compound entry (89.-91.) above.

91. (Eastern?) part of Interior Asia
Map not extant, and no details known other than those in the discussion in compound entry (89.-91.) above.

92. Western Inland Asia
-Venice, 1559
-Copper engraving, 43.0 x 73.0 cm., on two sheets
-100 Italian miles = 2.1 cm.

At the top of the map, right of center:

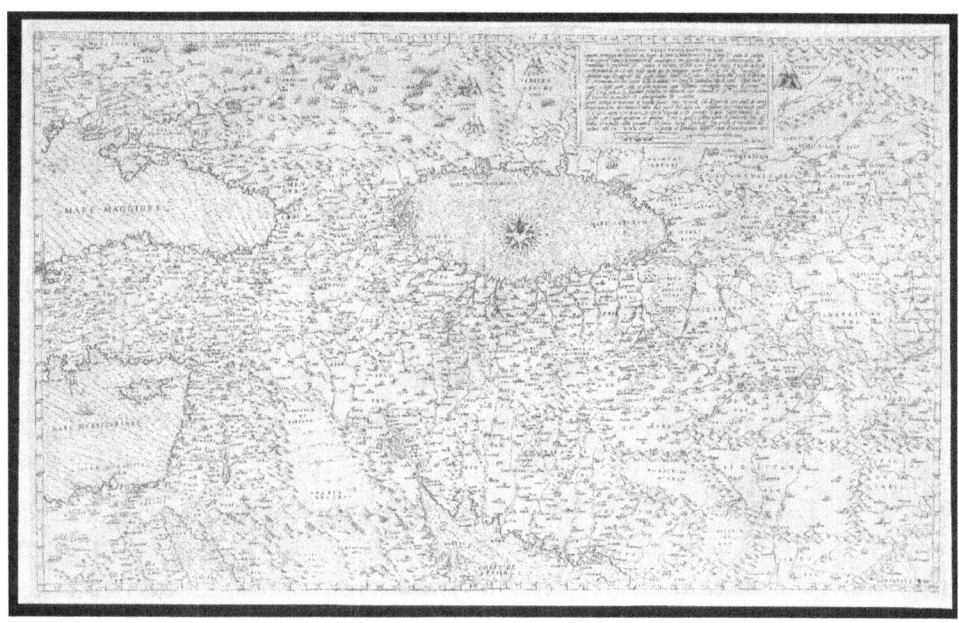

92 Western Inland Asia 1559 Chicago Newb

IL DISEGNO DELLA PRIMA PARTE DELASIA [sic] | Laquale principia da Leuante al Regno di Tarse, et alla prouincia di Charasã e quella di sablestã | et al Regno di Cabul, e la prouincia di Guzarate, et da ponente il stretto di Constantinopoli, da | Tramõtana la prouincia di Seuera, e Sibiera, et dal Ostro il mare Rosso, et il colfo di Persia | con la prouincia di Circam; Nella quale uie la maggior parte dil paese del sig[no]r. Turco, et similm te tutto il paese del sig[no]r Sophi. Diuisi luna dal' altro Con pontesini picoli, et altri pa | esi circonuicini a i due sopra detti: Graduato in Long[itudi]ne et Latitudinc tutte le citta, castelli mõti | Fiumi, colphi, porti, capi, et isole Misurato ogni distãtia con miglia italiani Al sereniss[i]mo | sig[no]r il sig[no]r Duca di sauoia Principe di piamõte suo naturale, et oss[equentissi]mo signiore Giacomo di Gastaldi piamõtese et cosmographo in Venetia | I nomi antiqui et moderni di questa parte sono separati del disegno in uno foglio di carta B Presto mandero alla stampa l'altre due parti del Asia, che sequitano la prima uerso ori | te, et uerso Austro con la Grecia che la sequita uerso Ponente le qual' parte sarãno de | scritte con i nomi moderni et antiqui come e questa prima parte, et similment faro all' | Italia, et a molte altre prouincie che saria lungo scriuerle, ma presto le mandaro all' | vostra Altezza MDLIX Con gratia et priuilegio dell'ill[ustrissi]mo senato di uenetia p[er] anni XV (MAP OF

674

THE FIRST PART OF ASIA Which begins in the East at the Realm of the Tartars, and at the province of Khorezm and that of Sablestan and at the Realm of Kabul, and the province of Guzerat, and at the west the strait of Constantinople, at the North the province of the North, and Siberia, and at the South the Red Sea, and the gulf of Persia with the province of Circam [Circassia?]; In which are the major part of the lands of the Turkish sovereign, and similarly all the countries of the Persian sovereign divided [on the map] the one from the other with small dotted lines, and other lands environing to the two above said: graduated in Longitude and Latitude all the cities, castles mountains Rivers, gulfs, ports, capes, and islands, every distance measured with Italian miles. To the most serene signor the signor Duke of Savoy, Prince of Piedmont [from] his compatriot and most respectful Signor Giacomo di Gastaldi piedmontese and cosmographer in Venice. The ancient and modern names of this part are separate from the map on a folio of paper. Soon I shall put into print the other two parts of Asia, which continue the first toward the east, and toward South with Greece which continues it toward the West which parts will be described with modern and ancient names as is this first part and I will do similarly for Italy, and for many other provinces, which it will be [too] long to write out, but soon I shall transmit them to your highness. 1559. With grace and privilege of the most illustrious senate of Venice for 15 years).

A scale bar follows, and below it and to the right is: *Fabio licinio f[ecit]* (*Fabio Licino engraver*)

Comments:
Graduated in whole degrees, with each degree numbered, in latitude and longitude, from 26°00' to 55°35' N, and, on the top border from 52°00' to 126°40' E, and on the bottom border from 60°00' to 118°00' E, on a trapezoidal projection. The map is sometimes found together with a list of ancient and modern name equivalents, which was intended to accompany the map (Karrow, 1993, 232).

Here we are in the presence of the first of those six Gastaldi maps which surpass his other maps by such leaps and bounds that it is difficult to adequately convey their supremacy in words. The maps are, besides the present one, the Second and Third Parts of Asia of 1561 (nos. 102 and 109), the wall maps of America (ca. 1560?) and Africa (1564) (nos. 94 and 118), and Gastaldi's giant *Cosmographia vniversalis* world map of 1561 (no. 109). If we take the three Parts of Asia as making up one continental depiction, the number of these maps is only four. In fact, in the 1570s, Gioan Francesco Camocio did in fact combine Gastaldi's three Parts of Asia into a single wall-map, and he did an excellent job of it, as see chapter eleven, and map no. III. Numerically, four is a tiny proportion of Gastaldi's output, but it is the story of these few maps which make up the heart and core of the present work. For in these four maps, largely by drawing on vast materials provided by his friend Ramusio, materials consisting not only of Ramusio's extensive accumulation of texts, but also of an indeterminate number of nautical charts brought together by him as well, Gastaldi succeeds in depicting all the extra-European continents in their generally correct lineations for the first time in history, as we show in our main text in chapters three and four. Gastaldi furthermore fills in the interior of these continents. Here, of course, there is more in the way of error, but an astonishing amount is basically correct, even if the relative placement of features often deviates from the true. The improvement brought by these maps to the picture of the world was in no sense incremental, but sweeping and revelatory. The world to be sure had been there before, but it was seriously out of kelter with reality in several broad ways, and interior features beyond Europe were in most places quite sparse. Then, suddenly, it had all become wrenched into generally proper form, and filled in as well, for the most part. Taken as a whole, no single improvement of such proportions would or could ever occur again in geography.

It will be clear from the preceding paragraph that, as regards these six crucial maps, we cannot hope to do more within the limits of our cartobibliographical entries than provide the skeletal overview which we have just presented, and for a fuller story of them, the reader must turn to the main text. It is for this reason that, except for the current entry, the entries for the remaining five of these most crucial maps may appear to the reader incommensurately short considering the level of importance of the maps covered by them, for, while we discuss them individually, central to each will be referrals back to the current entry, and to our main text.

A few words of caution are in order before proceeding in the present entry, in order to be certain that we maintain the correct perspective on things. We have said that Gastaldi's sources for his Asia, and his other continental maps, are the extensive materials gathered by Ramusio, both his texts and his copies of nautical charts. We know that this is true for several reasons. As shown in chapter four, all discussions which have broached the topic of Gastaldi's sources for the sundry parts of the extra-European continents have found that the principal, and usually the only source, was Ramusio and the sea charts. We also know, from chapter three, that no cartographical sources of note, that is, sources which could have provided anything close to the vast detail of Gastaldi's maps existed at all. From these facts, and from the further facts that no store of geographical knowledge on the far continents remotely comparable to Ramusio's existed, that Ramusio's stated purpose in gathering his texts was to provide the materials for making viable modern maps of the far continents, and that it is documented that Ramusio and Gastaldi were on close terms from at least 1546, but probably considerably earlier, it is valid to assume that the main source for the areas not yet studied will be Ramusio as well. Making a very rough estimate, I would say that at least 80% to 90%, probably closer to the latter, is from Ramusio's texts and charts.

Nevertheless, no one has made a comprehensive study comparing all names and features for all areas in the three Ramusio volumes and the maps of the three continents, and we know that other sources had to exist. For Africa, although Biasutti states without reservation at one point that all was from Ramusio (1920, 433), he earlier tells us that there were other sources (cit., 404). For America, it is well documented that Gastaldi made considerable usage of Gomara's 1552-53 *historia*. And the same cannot but be true for Asia. The known facts suggest that such other sources would surely have existed. For Gastaldi's great continental maps were made in 1559-1564, and not only did Ramusio die in 1557, but the indications are that he probably did no more collecting after about mid-1553, since it was then that he was promoted to the position of Secretary to the Council of Ten, and the closing portions of the mid-1553 discourses at the head of volumes two and three both seem to have been compiled in great haste, as if Ramusio were closing out his activities connected with the *Navigazioni* in order to concentrate fully on his new obligations. So, there are six years between this time and 1559, when the first of the continental maps appeared (the present one, no. 92), and eleven years between 1553 and 1564, when the Africa, the last of the continental maps, appeared. Certainly, it is natural to assume that Gastaldi himself in this period actively continued to pursue new information, no doubt partly based on connections which had been established for him by Ramusio, as well as sources sought out independently. For instance, as we have shown in chapter nine, he was almost certainly waiting in the early 1560s for expected information from Spanish sources on the results of the Legazpi expedition for which preparations were under way on the west coast of New Spain (Mexico).

In fact, the supposition that Gastaldi would have obtained new information on his own is perhaps truest of all for the present map no. 92, the First Part of Asia. It is, of all areas covered by these maps, that which is closest to Venice, and we know that Venice's principal maritime trade routes were to the eastern end of the Mediterranean, and that a good number of permanent Venetian trading colonies or outposts existed in the countries of the Near East. Also, Gastaldi personally knew Michel Membré, who had been to the area, and very possibly knew Guillaume Postel, who had also been there, and he probably knew others who had been there as well. Also, it was not unusual at the time for Venetian, and other European tourists, to make trips to the area, sometimes on pilgrimages to the Holy Land. Biasutti singles out the area covered by the First Part of Asia as the most impressive of all on Gastaldi's maps of Asia (1923, 310), and certainly it is the area for which his access to extra-Ramusian sources would be the best. In any event, not only a complete comparison between Ramusio and Gastaldi's maps, but also a search for other possible sources for the maps offers a ripe field for further study by future scholars.

One further note is necessary, to correct, and hopefully eradicate, an egregiously false notion that has arisen. One of the most important treatments of the question of Gastaldi's sources for Asia was that of Nordenskiöld (1899). Nordenskiöld found that almost all the place names in Ramusio's famous rendition of Marco Polo (the most frequently used version out of many in modern editions of Marco Polo), in Ramusio's volume two, are to be found on Gastaldi's Asia. But somewhere along the way since

1899, Nordenskiöld's finding became distorted in the literature. Saying that almost all the names in Ramusio's Marco Polo occur on Gastaldi's three Parts of Asia is of course not at all the same thing as saying that almost all Gastaldi's Asian names are from Polo's text. Nevertheless, we sometimes encounter the very misleading blanket statement that Gastaldi's Asia was based upon Marco Polo! An example is Tibbets (1978, 21). In no way does there exist such a comprehensive relationship between the Polian text and Gastaldi's Asia. Apart from the various Ramusian sources brought out in chapter four, we can be sure that Gastaldi made use of many other Ramusian texts. Mentioning only the most extensive accounts, there are the texts of Barbosa, Varthema, Barbaro, the two accounts on Magellan, Pires, Contarini, Lopez, Corsali, Angiolello, Hayton Armenio, Conti and Cabral, and there are many other shorter accounts. Gastaldi's Asia is a compilation from very many sources, of which Polo is only one.

As with all Gastaldi's maps, we give references at the end of this entry. But, for the present map, and indeed for all of the six crucial maps, the main reference will be the relevant chapters of the present work. For later editions of no. 92, the reader is referred to Karrow (1993, 231-33) and Meurer (2004, 118-21 (nos. 104-107)).

Location of copies:
Chicago Newb(Novacco 4F 373)/ Wien ÖNB(K I 109525 Kar)/ Cambridge Harv(51-2494[in 1st mat])/ Paris BN(GE DD- 655(77 RES))/ Paris BN(GE DD- 1140(69-70 RES))/ Kobenhavn KB(KBK 1-51(46))/ Basel UB(Kartenslg AA94)/ Kraków BCz(BCzK 1238 V)[1992]/ Firenze BN(12.-.44, v. 2, no. 12)[1980]/ Venezia BNM(138 c.4, no. 70)[1954]/ London RGS(Map Room, 264.G.2, no. 5)[1915]/ Washington LC(G1015 .L25 1575 Vault, no. 58)[1914]/ Dillingen SB(X,122, no. 71) [1911]/ Roma BN(711.6.G.2, no. 66)[1876]

*   *   *

Note: There is a letterpress broadside list of ancient and modern place name equivalents which accompanies some copies of this map: *Nomi antiqui e moderni della prima parte dell'Asia . . . per me Giacomo di castaldi piamontese cosmographo in Venetia. | Serenissimo. Signor mio Signore e principe Osseruandissimo. Il Signor Duca di Sauoia . . . M.D.LIX.*

Exemplars: Basel UB(Kartenslg AA94a)/ Firenze BN(12.-.44, v. 2, no. 11) [1980]/ Dillingen SB(X,123, no. 122)[1911]/ München SB(fol. Hist., no. 106)[1911]. Reproduction: Bifolco and Ronca, 1: 378.

References:
Nordenskiöld, 1897, 160, no. 118, and 161b; Nordenskiöld, 1899; Biasutti, 1923, 310; Bagrow, 1928-30, 1, 96; Tooley, 1939, 19, nos. 46-47; Luzio, 1947, 26-27; Almagià, 1948, 35-37 and 63-66; Gallo, 1954, 26-27, no. 68; Destombes, 1970, 87; Schilder, 1981, 7; Bella, 1986, 17, no. 9; Schilder, 1987, 63-79; Meurer, 1991, 150-51; Karrow, 1993, 231-33; Schilder, 1998, 109-11 and 114; Milanesi, in Dentoni Litta, et al, 2003, 48-52; Alai, 2005, 56-58, 135 and 136; Bifolco and Ronca, 2018, 1: 374-75.

Reproductions:
Bifolco and Ronca, 2018, 1: 374-75.
https://collections.Newberry.org/asset-management/2KXJ8ZSK4LRAX? &WS

93. Danube Basin
-Venice, 1559
-Copper engraving, 35.5 x 103.0 (102.0), on two sheets
-50 Italian miles = 4.5 cm.

In text box right of center of the right sheet:
M D L IX | Il disegno particolare delle Regioni che sono | da Constantinopoli á Venetia, da Venetia, | a viena, et da viena, a constantinopoli cõ | di molti altri paesi li quali sono fuori di | questi uiaggi cioe parte de ongària, Transil | uania valachia, et nelli detti viaggi Bulgaria, | Seruia, Dalmatia, Bossina, schiauonia, Austria, | Stiria, Carintia, Crouatia, Friuli, et Istria, | misurato et graduato con miglia italiani: | Opera noua di iacomo gastaldi piamõtese | alla magnifica Compagnia da ca Pisani (1559 Detailed map of the regions which are from Constantinople, to Venice, from Venice to Vienna, and from Vienna to Constantinople with many other lands which are outside of these areas Bulgaria, Serbia, Dalmatia, Bosnia, sclavonia, Austria, Styria, Carinthia, Croatia, Friuli, and Istria, measured

and graduated with Italian miles: [a] new Work by iacomo gastaldi piedmontese; to the magnificent Members of the house of the pisani)

Approximately two centimeters below this:
Con gratia et priuilegio del illustrissi | mo senato di uenetia per Anni XV
(With grace and privilege of the most illustrious senate of Venice for 15
Years)

Below and to the right of a scale bar approximately three centimeters still
further down:
Fabius licinius fecit (engraved by Fabio licinio)

Comments:
First we must note that in 1560, one year after this map was published, it was
combined with map 95, showing Greece, and with still another sheet, to
make up no. 96, Gastaldi's map of southeast Europe. The placement of these
sheets and their composition will be clarified by a diagram showing the full
map 96.

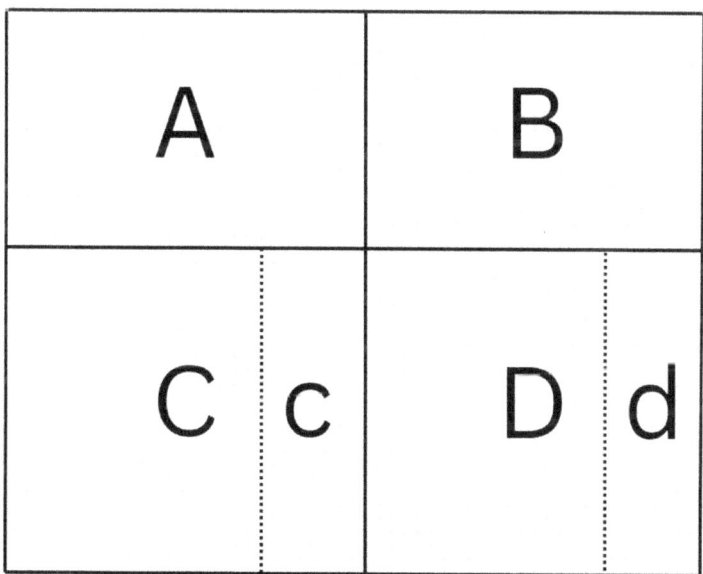

The two sheets of the present map showing the Danube basin (no. 93) are A
+ B. In 1560, one year after this map was published, there appeared a map
of Greece (no. 95) which was made up of c + D + d. And also in 1560, there
appeared a map of southeast Europe (no. 96) made up all the sheets in the
diagram: A + B + C + c + D + d. Note that sheets c and d are narrow, perhaps

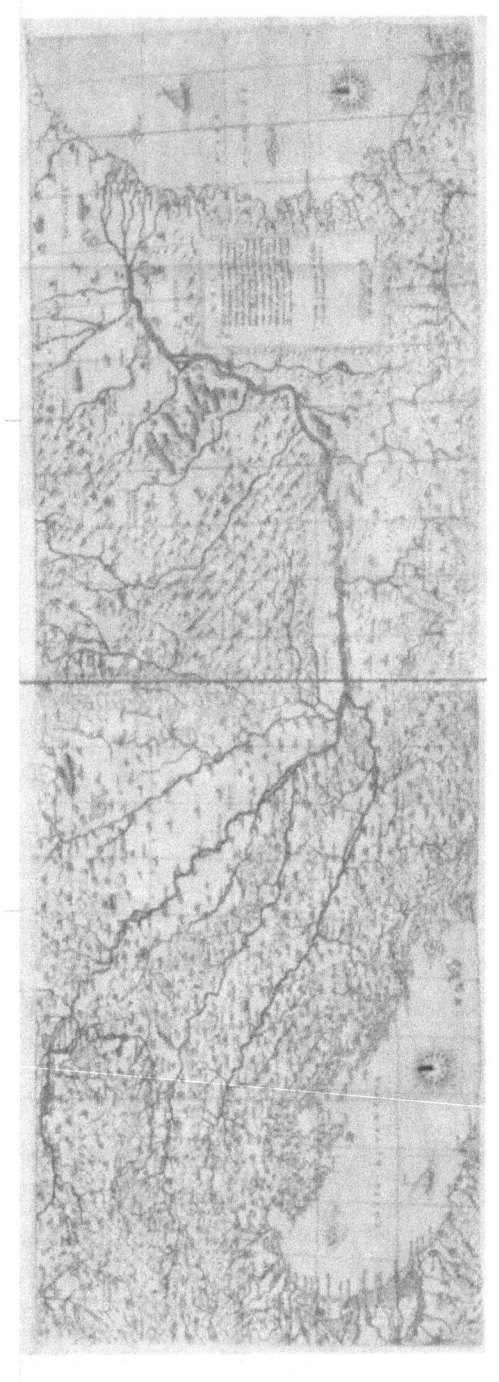

93 Danube Basin 1559 Dillingen SB

683

a third the width of the composite sheets C and D (their left edges are indicated by dotted lines). Now it would seem that the most logical process resulting in three separate maps would have been to first produce the large map of southeast Europe, comprising all six sheets. Then one could imagine printing the top two sheets together to form a map of the Danube basin, and then printing c, D, and d together to make a map of Greece. But in fact it can be demonstrated that the Danube basin map (no. 93) appeared first, that the map of Greece (sheets c, D, and d) appeared next, and that the full map of southeast Europe was the last to be printed. These changes in composition required a good many alterations to the plates, erasures and re-engravings, which we shall attempt to describe.

The present map is graduated in twelve-minute increments, with each whole degree numbered, from 43°00' to 48°28' N, and, along the top, from 33°09' to 56°50' E, and along the bottom from 33°35' to 56°28' E, on a trapezoidal projection, with parallels and meridians drawn in. This map is identical to the top two sheets of no. 96, Gastaldi's 1560 map of Southeast Europe, and is struck from the same plates, except that, as noted, for the 1560 map, the top half of the text box, here containing the main text quoted above ("M D L IX Il disegno particolare . . . da ca pisani"), has been burnished out and replaced with geography, and the privilege notice is expanded. Traces of the rim of the burnished out top half of the original text box are still quite visible, especially at its upper left.

It needs to be stated that, properly speaking, at least in this writer's opinion, there were no later editions of this map, although one finds references to a supposed Rome edition published by Lafreri. There is a definite and clear, if somewhat intricate, explanation for this misunderstanding. When Gastaldi extended the map to the south in 1560 to create our no. 96, he did so, of course, in Venice. The plates for the two added sheets were engraved in Venice, and the new map was sold in Venice, and it was a Venetian edition, as with all Gastaldi first editions without exception. That is, the first edition of no. 95, the four-sheet map of Southeast Europe, was published in Venice, to be followed later by a Rome edition. That the Venetian edition preceded the Roman edition, of which we shall speak more in a moment, and not vice versa as was once thought by some to be the case, has in fact come to be recognized by a number of scholars

(Almagià, 1948, 28; Zacharakis, 1982, 46-47; Szántai, 1996, 192 [wrongly dating the Rome edition as "1565(?)"]; Ganado, 1982, 29; Borroni-Salvadori, 1980, at nos. 255 and 279). In this extended new map, the lower half of the text box of the current map was given a new privilege notice, but the scale bar and the Licinio signature were not touched, and between the new privilege notice and this scale bar a blank space of about 2.5 cm. width remained, a new title text box was added in the southwest sheet, including a new date 1560, and at the lower edge of the southeast sheet was engraved: "fabius licinius fecit-- | venetiis" (engraved by Fabio licinio -- Venice). This is engraved very low on the sheet. The signature proper falls outside the neat line, and "venetiis", below it, falls outside even the outer graduation line, and sometimes, if the map has been trimmed too closely, the "venetiis" will be trimmed off, and occasionally the signature above it will be trimmed off as well.) Then, at an indeterminate time, as so regularly occurred in the Veneto-Roman map market, the plates were shipped to Lafreri in Rome, having presumably been purchased or leased by him. In the mentioned ample space of 2.5 cm. between the new privilege notice and the scale bar Lafreri added the short phrase "In Roma per Ant. Lafrerj" (In Rome by Antoine Lafreri). Nothing else was added or removed anywhere. Both of the Licinio signatures remain, as does the word "venetiis" in the lower right-hand corner of the southeast sheet. Thus, the rather complicated genesis of the 1560 Lafreri Rome edition of this map. In a number of cases it is clear that clients who were selecting maps to be bound for them into a Veneto-Roman (Lafrerian) atlas simply ordered the two top sheets of the Rome edition, but not the bottom two. In my opinion, these two-sheet artifacts cannot be considered as a 1560 edition of the 1559 map, our no. 93. They are simply incomplete copies of the Rome 1560 edition of the map of southeast Europe.

Without going into great detail, we should note, before giving our list of locations of exemplars of the map, that there is serious confusion concerning these interrelated maps in Tooley's well-known 1939 catalog of Veneto-Roman atlas maps, at Tooley's nos. 25-28 (Tooley, 1939, pp. 17-18). Tooley's no. 25 is our present map, no. 93. But his no. 26 is a giant red herring, probably the result of some organizational slip-up made during compilation of the catalog. The entry has the appearance of referring to a 1560 Rome Lafreri edition of our no. 93, and Tooley gives in the entry no less than twenty-one library locations for it. We have succeeded in looking into almost all of them, and all but a few are simply full four-sheet examples of a 1560 Lafreri Rome edition of our no. 96. Two more of the twenty-one are the same but lacking one sheet. One, his third entry in the list of twenty-one entries, is an example of the two north sheets of the Rome edition. In short, this entry in Tooley, as it is given in his catalog, *does not exist.* Moving on, his no. 27 also does not exist. It consists of two examples of the northeast sheet alone of the 1560 Venice edition and is nothing but an incomplete copy of that edition. Finally, Tooley's no. 28 could perhaps be taken as referring to the Venice four-sheet (i.e., complete) edition, but there is serious confusion here as well, for several of the eighteen examples listed are actually the Rome 1560 edition, and probably more than just several (though I have not attempted to check all), for, in fact, the 1560 Venice edition (our map 96) is much rarer than the Rome edition. Only Tooley's entry no. 25, out of entries 25-28, is correct (although he gives but one location, while there are at least four and probably more). All in all, Tooley's four entries on these maps amount to a total debacle.

Location of copies::
Cambridge Harv(51-2495)/ Leiden UB(COLLBN 002-01-023)/ Washington LC(G1015 .L25 1575b Vault Fol., no. 4)[1958]/ Dillingen SB(X,123, no. 71) [1911]

References:
Bagrow, 1928-30, 1, 86-87; Banfi, 1947, 36 and 37-38; Almagià, 1948, 28; Banfi, 1956, 89; Cucagna, 1964, 13; Dörflinger, et al, 1977, 56; Kret, 1978, 106; Lago and Rossit, 1981, 48; Meurer, 1991, 152; Karrow, 1993, 233; Szántai, 1996, 1, 191; Bifolco and Ronca, 2018, 1: 688-89.

Reproductions:
Karrow, 1993, pp. 636-37 (pl. 30/86); Bifolco and Ronca, 2018, 1:688-89. https://www.digitale-sammlungen.de/en/view/bsb00106663 (the Dillingen copy)

94. America (not extant in original form) (But see maps VIII and XII for mid-seventeenth century printings from the ca. 1596 plates)
-Venice, ca. 1560(?)(ca. 1575)(ca. 1596)
-Manuscript map, probably originally in eight sheets, intended for publication, but not properly published until ca. 1596
-unknown if original manuscript included a scale bar

This is the second of Gastaldi's six key maps, those which make up the core of our book, and of Gastaldi's work and career. As with the rest of these maps, in order to obtain a full and solid grasp of the story of this map one must read the chapters in which it is treated, that is, mainly, chapters three, nine and ten, although, as with Gastaldi's Asia, for a truly complete understanding of the fascinating thought processes which led Gastaldi to make this map, one also needs to consult chapters six to eight as well. Its story is a complex one, even more so than with the Asia, and we shall not attempt to do full justice to it in the present entry but shall only present a skeletal synopsis of our findings.

Unlike the other five key maps, this one was not published within Gastaldi's lifetime. We know that Gastaldi sometimes held back maps from publication if he was for whatever reason not yet satisfied with them. Without doubt the most prominent example of this was his Africa, for we know that he was working on a large Africa in the 1540s, which would eventually emerge as his great wall map of that continent in 1564 (no. 118), for as long as twenty years, although in his 1548 Ptolemy he speaks of it as a product which was near completion. The present map, like the Africa, was a very large one, and we can probably assume that it was in eight sheets, like the Africa. As we have shown, while this map was assuredly made before his giant 1561 world map (no. 104), he did not at the time prepare it for publication, and the reason, or at least the main reason, was almost certainly that he was waiting for the results of the pending expedition of Miguel López de Legazpi and Andrés de Urdaneta from the west coast of New Spain, in the hopes that it might provide a final resolution to the question of whether Asia and America were separated or joined. But this slow-starting expedition, the preparations for which had begun in the late 1550s, did not finally depart until 1564, and the first ship returned only in October 1565, so it is questionable if Gastaldi, who died in 1566, ever obtained word of its findings. It did not, in any event, provide an answer to the question of the relationship of the continents, nor would any expedition do so for well over another century and a half. In any event, very probably it was the wait for the expedition's outcome that was the main reason that the America remained in manuscript at the time of Gastaldi's death in 1566.

In the 1570s, this manuscript came into the hands of the well-known Venetian map publisher Giovanni Francesco Camocio. In the text, we broach the question of how this may have come about, but, for the moment, suffice it to say that, by no later than 1575, Camocio had obtained it, and with the purpose of using it to complement a series of three continental wall maps which he had already made, for Africa, Asia, and Europe, in order to create what would thus be the first set of wall maps of the four continents. The Africa and the Asia, incidentally, had also been taken from Gastaldi's maps, and much of the Europe also ultimately derives from Gastaldi's cartography, though in all cases, the models were maps which had been printed earlier. Camocio accordingly began to have the map engraved, but not following Gastaldi's original segmentation of eight sheets, but a segmentation into twelve sheets, precisely as he had done with Gastaldi's Africa. He used this segmentation on all four maps. This introduced complications, as it had with the other three maps. But the indications are that, after having already engraved several sheets, he introduced a further complication by deciding to actually correct one major feature in Gastaldi's cartography itself, that is, Gastaldi's unnatural overextension eastwards of the north part of the continent, a good and rational decision, for Gastaldi's error is indeed a disconcerting one. As noted, this of course introduced still further problems, as described in the text, and they were knotty ones.

Undaunted, Camocio proceeded with a plan to improve the depiction. But whether he would have succeeded in the end, or would have shied from the difficulties involved and reverted to Gastaldi's original depiction, we cannot know (nor would he in all likelihood have known yet himself), because the evidence we have indicates that he was suddenly taken by the great Venetian plague of 1575-77, leaving his work unfinished, and unfinished at a moment when Camocio was at a complicated and difficult pass in his tinkerings with the map. Those around him were left with a map much of which had already been engraved, but considerable parts of which had not. Nor, in all likelihood, did there yet exist, after Camocio's manipulations, completed *modeli* from which the rest of the map could be engraved. No doubt unable to follow, in the remnants, what Camocio's plan had been, it was unwisely, as well as unethically, decided to simply proceed with what had already been engraved, and, by making a few hopelessly ineffective adjustments in the existing plates, produce something which vaguely looked like a whole map, but certainly not a map which reflected geographical reality. It also was not the same size as the other three maps. To cover up the hopelessly misfit appearance of the would-be map of America, which clearly could not be sold as a bona fide wall map of the continent, it was decided to bind its sheets, together with those of all the other three maps, into atlas form, and sell the set in that form. How many of these bogus atlases were made is unknown, but I imagine not many. One copy of the would-be atlas has survived, as well as one copy of the incomplete America in loose sheets, along with loose sheets of the other maps, though with some sheets missing. We should mention that, since Camocio never succeeded in completing the map, the cartouche which would have contained the map's title text and its author remained empty, and so Gastaldi's name did not appear on the map.

Eventually, it is not clear how, the set of maps came into the hands of the famous San Marco establishment of the Bertelli's, and it can only have been Donato Bertelli who, about 1596, probably using as a model the depiction of America on a copy of Gastaldi's *Cosmographia vniversalis* world map, created *modeli* from which sheets were engraved producing a viable whole map, not attempting to incorporate Camocio's contemplated improvements (of which Donato was probably quite unaware) but simply producing a map of the continent as Gastaldi had originally conceived it. Three copies of Bertelli's restoration of the Gastaldi America survive, although in seventeenth century printings made by the Scolari's, into whose hands Donato's plates passed at some point. In most of the sheets, those which Camocio had had engraved, we have a faithful copy of Gastaldi's original depiction. In two sheets, we have Donato's restoration, but since the depiction in these two sheets is surely, as said, taken from the America on the giant Gastaldi world map from about the same time, they cannot but reflect very closely the depiction in the lost parts of Gastaldi's original, and so we may validly consider that we essentially have in the map Gastaldi's original depiction of America.

A final observation. As luck would have it, all three of the completed copies came to the attention of scholars only very late in the day, and for many years the only known copies were the two bizarrely butchered and distorted copies. Almagià (1923, 300-02) and after him Caraci (1927-32, 2, 37-48), who failed to perceive that the map's forlorn and repugnant appearance was due to unusual shop circumstances, mistakenly and, if I dare say so, rather irrationally attributed the map's condition to the original cartographer himself. Consequently, although everything in the surviving individual sheets was superb and beautiful cartography, which simply shouts the name Gastaldi, they balked unequivocally at attributing the map to Gastaldi, and Almagià contrived a scenario, which we show conclusively in chapter nine would have been impossible, by which the misbegotten map had attained its deplorable state due to some ill-defined but invalid procedure supposedly followed by some inept and incompetent cartographer, with the result that the map fell into a sort of limbo in the eyes of some scholars, an authorless curiosity, and by some later authors it came to be treated as such (Burden, 1996, 45-47, and Woodward, 1997, 9 and 22-23). This was, however, not the view taken by the majority of scholars, who correctly gave the map to Gastaldi with no reservations (Stokes, 1915-28, 4, 941, who notes besides that this was also the opinion of Charles Chadenat; Vignaud, 1921; Wagner, 1928, 358-59, and 1937, 1, 57 and 2, 283 (no. 83); Parker, 1956, 136; Layng, 1956, 136, and 1964, 486; and Tooley, 1979, 237). We have, I think it safe to say, justified the opinion of these latter scholars, and removed with finality any air of dissaprobation which has previously hung over the map, which is unquestionably one of Gastaldi's greatest achievements, fully the equal of our other five key maps. When Gastaldi first drew this map in ca. 1560, it was the first ever map of America which gave the whole of northwestern North America its generally proper form, and also the first map ever to show correctly the relationship between Asia and America. The sources for the map, discussed further in the main text, were, of course, Ramusio, with notable contributions from Gomara, and probably some lesser sources still unidentified.

Location of copies:

The original manuscript does not exist, but two copies of an abortive printing of ca. 1575(?), and three seventeenth century copies of a proper edition of ca. 1596, exist. For their locations, see entry nos. IV, VIII and XII below.

References:

Stokes, 1915-28, 4, 941; Vignaud, 1921; Almagià, 1923, 300-02; Caraci, 1926,-32, 2, 37-48; Wagner, 1929, 358-59; Wagner, 1937, 1, 57 and 2, 283 (no. 83); Kraus, 1949, 11; Parker, 1956, 5-8; Layng, 1956, 136; Layng, 1964, 486; Tooley, 1939, no. 83; Gallo, 1954, 52 (no. 70*); Kraus, 1969, 22, 24 and 26; Tooley, 1979, 237; Burden, 1996, 45-47; Woodward, 1997, 9 and 22-23. (The reader should be cautioned that the works of Almagià, Caraci, Burden and Woodward, written under the influence of powerful misconceptions introduced by Almagià, are distorting and misleading in the extreme.)

95. Greece

-Venice, 1560

-Copper engraving, 49.0 x 69.0 (66.0) cm., in 2(3) sheets (see elucidation below)

-50 Italian miles = 4.5 cm.

In a text box on the lower border, centered in the left half of the map:
TOTIVS GRAETIAE DESCRIPTIO | D[omi]ni iacobi de gastaldis cosmographi | Generoso ac Magnifico D[omi]no, D[omi]no | joanni jacobo fuggaro, Kirch | bergae et Weissenhorni comiti | &c. sacrae caes[aris], Maiestatis | consiliario | 1560 (MAP OF ALL OF GREECE by Master iacobo de gastaldi cosmographer [dedicated] to the Noble and Magnificent Lord, Sir johann Jacob fugger, count of Kirchberg and Weissenhorn etc. and counselor of the holy Sovereign emperor 1560)

In the margin, below the text box:

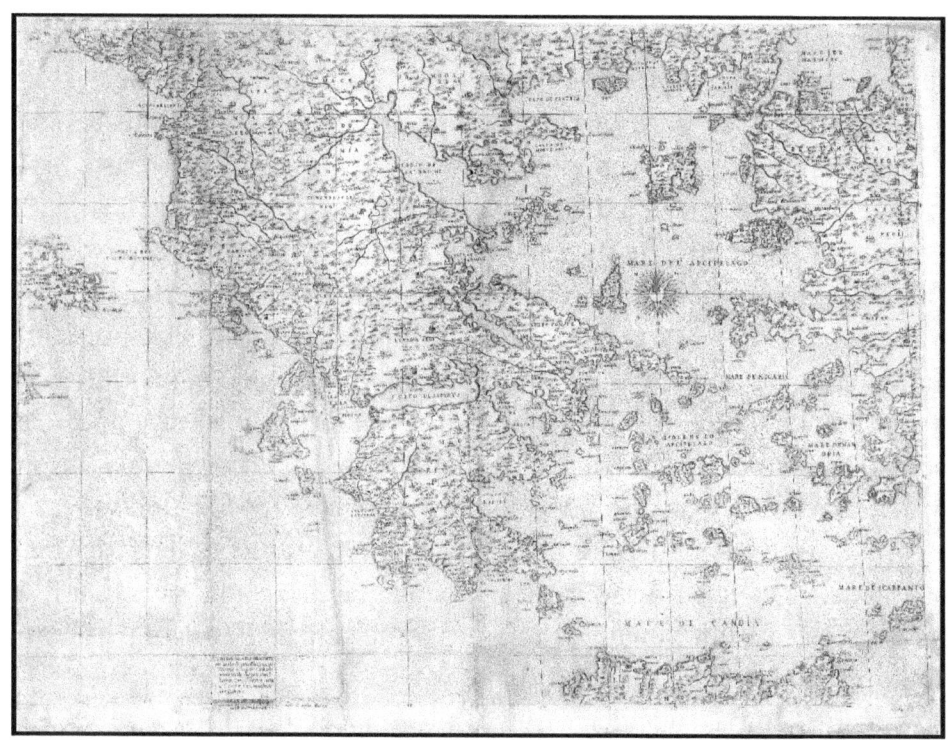

95 Greece 1560 Ruderman

Con gratia et priuilegio del jllustrissimo | senato di uenetia per anni XV
(With grace and privilege of the most illustrious senate of Venice for 15
years.)

In the lower right corner of the map, below the neat line:
Fabius licinius fecit (Fabio licinio engraver)

Comments:
Graduated in whole degrees, each numbered, in latitude and longitude (left
border not graduated), from 35°37' to 43°04' N, and, at the top, from 42°00' to
56°23' E, and at the bottom from 42°00' to 55°50' E, with parallels and
meridians drawn in. Technically, the map consists not of two sheets, a small
one to the left and a full one to the right, for, as the diagram above shows,
this right sheet itself is actually made up of two sheets, the large one to the
left, and the small one to the right, so actually the Greece consists of a
narrow sheet to the left, then a full-sized sheet to the right of that, and finally,

692

another narrow sheet to the right of the full sheet (c + D + d, in the diagram. In the case of the two right sheets they were firmly sealed together *before* printing, while the left narrow sheet was pasted to the compound sheet to the right *after* printing. It is a superb piece of work. It is true that it is simply a part of Gastaldi's map of southeast Europe (no. 96), but it is the best part of that map, and its superiority over the best previous map of Greece, the primitive Sophianus map (reproduced in a 1558 edition in Bella, 1986, 70, no. 62 and in a 1564 edition by F. Bertelli in Meurer, 2004, 114, no. 100), is so immediately obvious that the point does not need to be argued. A glance at the Sophianus map, Gastaldi's map, and a modern map shows progress which is quite startling, although the positioning of interior towns, the source for which is unknown, is often erratic (Almagià, 1914, 617), and the orography is arbitrary, although the hydrography is quite good (Almagià, cit., 616-17). While no specific sources can be named, Almagià says that it shows excellent fusion of nautical charts, some selected Ptolemaic points, and unknown information (cit., 636).

The reader may wonder why we have placed this 1560 Greece chronologically ahead of the map of southeast Europe (no. 96), when it seems that the logical chronology would be the opposite, and the Greece would have been derived from the southeast Europe when that map was already complete. But surprisingly, the facts indicate without doubt that the Greece was published first. There is no question that the whole of the area depicted on 95, and the same area on 96, the full map of southeast Europe, are from the same plates, the same engraving, and this applies both to the whole sheet and the small sheet of ca. 15 cm. width from the southwest sheet of 96. Yet, in this 15-cm. wide area on the southwest sheet of 96, we find, in large capital letters "TARANTO" (the end of "GOLFO DE TARANTO") below the Apulian peninsula, and near the bottom of this 15-cm. strip we find, in still larger capital letters "EDITERRANEO" (the end of "MARE MEDITERRANEO"), but neither is found on no. 95(!), and, unless someone performed a burnishing miracle, they most certainly were never there. Furthermore, in the southeast corner of the southeast sheet of no. 96, there always occurs (unless it has been trimmed off): "fabius licinius fecit," and just below it "venetiis". But, again, on 95, although there is an abundance of paper space remaining beneath "fabius licinius fecit", there is no "venetiis", and again, it is clear that it was not burnished out but was never present. I have not made a systematic investigation, but very possibly there are still other words or details on 96 which are not on 95. Yet, we repeat, there can be no doubt that the engravings are the same. The implication seems to be that 95 was printed from the full southeast sheet and the 15-cm. partial sheet and that only after that the partial sheet was completed, the words "GOLFO DI TARANTO", "MARE MEDITERRANEO", and "venetiis" were added in, all after what was considered a sufficiently large print run had been struck off to satisfy customer needs for the Latin Greece, our 95 (and, by this scenario, the reengraved small left sheet of 95 would probably indicate that the press run had been insufficient).

There is still one more problem we must deal with as regards this map of Greece. There has not been full agreement that the present map, no. 95 is truly the first edition, although it is carried as such both by Bagrow (1928-30, 87-88, no. 90) and by Karrow (1993, 235, no. 30/88). But Almagià (1948, 28) strongly implies that an Italian language edition could be the first edition. Almagià's map is undated, but it carries an Italian language text box (the text box of our no. 95 is in Latin) which could conceivably be the first edition (Almagià, 1948, 28). As with our no. 95, only one copy is known of Almagià's map. It is in the Biblioteca Marciana in Venice with call number 138.c.4, no. 56. It is undated, but printed in Venice, and its size, 50.0 x 68.0 (67.5) cm., is similar to the size of our no. 95. Its text box reads as follows:

DESCRITTIONE DELA GEOGRAFIA MODERNA DETVTTA | LA GRETIA | I confini della quale uerso oriente, il stretto di Constantinopoli | et quello di Galipoli, e ilmare dell'Arcipelago, da occidente il | golfo di Venetia et il mare Mediterraneo, da settentrione i mõti | de Romania, et ilmonte Argentato, dall Austro il Mare me- | ditterraneo. Graduata in longhezza e larghezza con la | misura de miglia italiane | Opera de Giac[om]o di castaldi cosmografo in Venetia | Al mag[nifi]co et generoso s[igno]r il sig[no]r Gio[vanni] Giac[om]o fuccaro dig[nissi]mo | conte de Kirchberga edi Weissenhorn, consigliero della | sacra ces[are]a Maesta suo grat[issi]mo si[gno]r | Con gratia et priuilegio (MAP OF THE MODERN GEOGRAPHY OF ALL OF GREECE, the confines of which toward the east, [are] the strait of Constantinople and that of Galipoli, and the sea of the Archipelago, at the west the gulf of Venice and the Mediterranean sea, at the north the mountains of Romania, and the mountain Argentato, at the South the Mediterranean Sea, graduated in longitude and latitude with the measure of Italian miles. Work of Giacomo di Castaldi cosmographer in Venice. To the magnificent and noble signor Johann Jacob fugger most dignified count of Kirchberg and of Weissenhorn, counselor of his most gracious holy and imperial Majesty. With grace and privilege.)

In the southeast corner of the map is: fabius licinius fecit-- | venetiis (Fabio licinio engraver-- venice)

Almagià's Marciana map is, as we have said, undated but it is accompanied by an Italian language sheet of ancient and modern place names, *I nomi latini tratti del greco et i uolgare, etc.*, which is securely dated 1560, and Almagià states that "This is also certainly the date of the map" (cit., 28). This is not very convincing, but the fact that this list of ancient and modern names exists gives some support for the notion that this Marciana map could be the first edition, for the first editions of most Gastaldi maps from the period when Gastaldi's maps were engraved by Licinio, are usually accompanied by such lists; further support is given by the fact that the main text box is in Italian, not Latin (as in no. 95), and this too is true of Gastaldi first editions cut by Licinio.

However, I am still inclined to give preference to no. 95 as the first edition of the Greece, based on the following: Both our no. 95 and the Marciana map have the parallels and meridians drawn in, but the Marciana map is very definitely a different engraving in its narrow left sheet, although the large sheet to the right is the same engraving in both maps, and also the same engraving as in the southwest sheet of no. 96. The present map, no. 95, is, in the small left sheet, *also* the same engraving as in the southwest sheet of no. 96. For this reason, I am inclined to consider no. 95 as the original, and the Marciana map as a later edition.

For information on the later editions and derivatives of the Greece, see Biasutti (1908, 27-28 nt. 3); Bagrow (1928-30, 1, 88); Almagià (1948, 28-30); Woodward (1990, 33, no. 54 (?)); and Karrow (1993, 235-36). These references, taken all together, will not provide a complete listing of the many derivatives of the Gastaldi map of Greece.

Location of copies:
Wolfegg SW (KuKa 154, no. 32 [former call number Histor. Geogr. 169, no. 32])/ Stanford SC(Barry Lawrence Ruderman Collection)

References:
This list contains references to both the Latin edition of the Greece, and the Italian edition of Almagià, as well as a couple of references to the 1566 edition, which is not changed: Ruge, 1904-16, Pt. 4, p. 124, no. 32 [Latin ed.]; Bonacci, 1905, 825-26 [any editions]; Biasutti, 1908 nt. 3 [Italian ed.]; Almagià, 1914, 614-20 and 636 [any editions]; Bagrow, 1928-30, 1, 87-88 [Latin ed.]; Tooley, 1939, 32, no. 281 [Latin ed.]; Almagià, 1948, 28-29 [Italian ed.]; Gallo, 1954, 23, no. 59 [Italian ed.]; Cucagna, 1964, 14 [Italian and Latin eds.]; Meurer, 1991, 151-52 [Latin ed.]; Karrow, 1993, 235, no. 30/88 [Latin ed.]; Meurer, 2004, 113, no. 99 [1566 ed., et al]; Bifolco and Ronca, 2018, 2: 1414-15 [Latin and Italian eds.]

Reproduction:
Bifolco and Ronca, 2018, 2: 1414-15.
https://exhibits.stanford.edu/ruderman/catalog/dp892wd0803 [reproduced here]

*   *   *

Note: There is a broadside list of ancient and modern place name equivalents which was made to accompany this map, of which more copies are known than of the map itself: *I nomi Latini tratti dall'antico Greco, & i uolgari hora nominati, di tutta la Prouincia della Grecia, & parte della Natolia di tutte le regioni, Città, Castelli, Monti, Laghi, Fiumi, Mari, Golfi, Porti, & Isole; graduato ogni luoco in longhezza e larghezza. Opera nuoua di Giacomo di Gastaldi Piamontese Cosmographo . . . MDLX Con Gratia & Priuilegio dell'Illustriss. Senato Veneziano, per anni, XV.* The following locations list is just a sampling. For those seven Gastaldi maps for which there exists an accompanying list of names, I have been less assiduous as to locating copies of the name lists than as to locating copies of the maps proper: Chicago Newb(Novacco 2F 175)/ Kobenhavn KB (KBK, 1-51, no.

282)/ London, BL (Maps C.&e.1, no. 131)/ Paris BN(Rés. Ge CC. 1380(64))/ Wolfegg SW (KuKa 154, no. 33)/ Firenze BN(12.-.44, v. 3, no. 55(54 written)[1980]/ Venezia BNM(138 c.4, no. 60)[1954]. Reference and reproduction: Bifolco and Ronca 2018, 2: 1416-17.

96. Southeast Europe
-Venice, 1560
- Copper engraving, 83.5 x 105.0 (102.0) cm., on four (six) sheets (see elucidation below)
- 50 Italian miles = 4.5 cm.

In text box at lower left of southwest sheet:
Geographia particolare d'una gran parte dell' | *Europa, nuouam te descritta co i confini suoi, e* | *prima uerso leuãte e il meridiano di constãtino* | *poli, e da pon te il meridiano della mag[nifi]ca cita di* | *Venetia, et da tramõtana il parallelo di vien* | *na in Austria, e uerso Ostro il parallelo che* | *passa per il mezzo dell'isola di Candia, et in* | *torno ui sono i gradi e minuti delle longhe* | *zze et larghezze, con lamisur a [!] de le miglia* | *italiani: Opera nuoua / di Giacopo di Castaldi piamontese.* (Detailed geography of a large part of Europe, newly drawn with its confines, and first toward the east is the meridian of Constantinople, and on the west the meridian of the magnificent city of Venice, and on the north the parallel of Vienna in Austria, and toward the South the parallel which passes through the midst of the island of Candia [Crete], and around [it] there are the degrees and minutes of longitude and latitude, with scale of Italian miles, a New work by Giacomo Gastaldi Piedmontese.) Immediately following: *All' Ill[ustrissi]mo Sig[no]r il S[igno]r Gio[vanni] Giacopo Fuccari* | *dig[nissi]mo Conte di Kirchberg e di Weisenhom [!],* | *conseglier della sa[cra] e ces[are]a M[aest]ia Suo gratissimo* | *signor.* (To the most Illustrious Lord Sir Johann Jacob Fugger most worthy Count of Kirchberg and of Weissenhorn, counsellor of His most gracious Lord the Holy and Imperial Majesty.)

In text box at lower middle right of northeast sheet:
MDLX | *Congratia et priuilegio del Nostro sig[no]r* | *papa pio iiii. per anni. x.* | *Et similmente della Serenissima sig[no]ria* | *di venetia per anni xv (1560*

*With grace and privilege of Our lord pope pius IV for 10 years. And likewise
of the most serene seignory of Venice for 15 years).*

Directly below the scale bar which follows the above, and in lower right
corner of same text box: *fabius licinius fecit (engraved by Fabio licinio)*

At far lower right of southeast sheet: *fabius licinius fecit | venetiis (engraved
by fabio licinio Venice)*

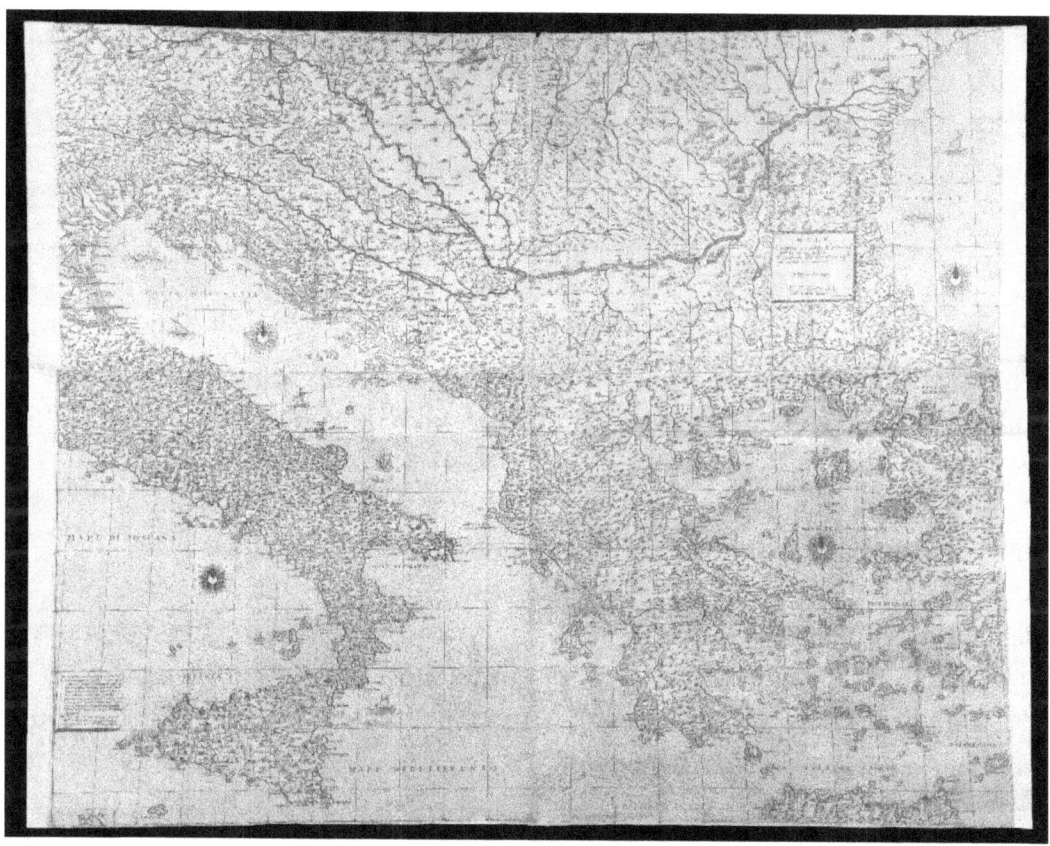

96 Southeast Europe 1560 Chicago Newb

Comments:

Graduated in twelve-minute increments, each full degree numbered, in
latitude and longitude, from 35°28' to 48°28' N, and at the top from 33°09' to
56°50' E, and at the bottom from 34°11' to 55°52' E, on a trapezoidal

698

projection, with parallels and meridians drawn in at every whole degree of longitude and latitude. The map itself is slightly trapezoidal in shape, as cf. dimensions above, and the top sheets are considerably different in size from the bottom ones (top ca. 35.0 x 51.5 [51.0], bottom sheets ca. 48.5 x 52.5 [51.5]). The bottom sheets are quite large, and in all exemplars I have seen, or have full descriptions of, each of the lower sheets "was made up from two pieces of paper, one of which was only 150-175 mm wide. It is clear from the printed surface that the sheets were first made up to size and then printed. The relatively large plates (ca. 490 x 540 mm) needed to print these quadrants apparently exceeded the size of paper available in the print shop." (Karrow, 1993, 234) The narrower of these two "welded" sheets is the eastern one, in both of the southern compound sheets, as we gather from Ruge (1911-14, IV, nos. 85(45) and 85(55)). It is difficult to even find the break line, so expertly were the two sheets pasted together, and one must inspect the back of the map to find it at all. Probably all copies are thus, and the map could be considered as a six sheet map in this sense. (This double sheeting does not occur in any copies of the smaller top two sheets.) The map was issued accompanied by a booklet of the same year giving ancient and modern names of the places on the map (see our "Note" below, after the listing of locations of copies). The top part of the map is the same as the Danube Basin map of 1559 (no. 93), and from the same plates, but in the east sheet the top half of the title text box has been removed and replaced by geography, while in the bottom half the old notice of privilege from the Venetian government has been removed to be replaced by indication of date in large numerals and a completely reworded notice of privilege from both the Venetian Senate and the Vatican. The scale bar and signature of Licinio at the lower part of the new reduced text box are unchanged, and not reengraved.

This map consists of a fusing together of two previous maps, our nos. 93 and 95, and the story of how this was done is lengthy, complex, and filled with uncertainties. For a basic discussion, see the beginning of our "Comments" to map no. 93, and further discussion of it can be found in chapter ten. There is good reason to think that Gastaldi had in mind the present map before he made map no. 93 in 1559, and map no. 95 in 1560, but a full investigation of this cannot be done in the present work. This very large map covers all of southeastern Europe. This fact provides the only real point of unity to the map, for there is very little in common culturally, historically or geographically between the sundry regions covered (we shall speak more of this lack of unity below). This map and Gastaldi's 1562 northeast Europe (no. 106) overlap slightly, and together provide coverage for all eastern Europe. But one must not presume from this that Gastaldi necessarily intended to provide corresponding coverage for western Europe, and in fact this is not too likely (see our chapter ten, for an in-depth discussion of this point).

As to sources, for the large part of continental Italy which is in the map, the known sources are, of course, the same as for the 1561 Italy (no. 101), that is, Gastaldi's own regional maps, where they apply (Apulia and Lombardy), and Bellarmato's 1536 Tuscany. For Sicily, too, the source is Gastaldi's Sicily. No source has been isolated for Greece, but, although Almagià says the style of drawing for the coasts is not the style of portolan charts, the outline must have come from them, directly or indirectly. Strangely, no one has mentioned as among Gastaldi's possible sources manuscript sources and other information obtained by the government of the Venetian Republic by diplomatic means, especially as regards the southern half of the map. The Republic actively pursued this accumulating of information, possibly including manuscript maps, probably more than any other nation, especially for areas of commercial or political significance (Biasutti, 1908, 53-54; and Colamonico, 1939, 170-71, and the works referred to by them). Almost all areas on this map's southern half (and part on the northern) are among those which were the most important of all to the Republic, and Gastaldi could no doubt easily have gained access to such material via Ramusio's influence. As usual with Gastaldi's European maps, investigators have concentrated too much on previously published maps, which in general seem not to have been Gastaldi's principal means of constructing his maps. Very few such maps in fact have been identified, and even in those cases, the identifications have not been made critically, and much disagreement exists, implying these few cartographical sources may be wrong altogether. For the northern half of the map, struck from the same plates as the 1559 map (no. 93), the known sources are Lazius's 1556 Hungary for Hungary, Yugoslavia, western Romania, and Bulgaria, with remaining sources mostly unidentified. This northern half of the map shows much the same area as that on the southern half of Gastaldi's 1546 map of the Danube countries (no. 4), but, although many toponyms are the same, there are between the two maps very considerable differences across the whole area, and it is clear that Gastaldi came into many new sources in the fourteen years between 1546 and 1560.

The fully assembled map, as said, is very large, much larger even than Gastaldi's third part of Asia, the largest of that set. It is an impressive accomplishment, and presents a grand panoramic picture, a feast for the eyes. But, as noted, it is not held together by any cultural, historical, or national theme, nor really even a geographical theme properly speaking. It crosses bounds in all these senses. It hits on Hungarian, Slavic, Italian, and Greek cultures and regions, and its top half is inland cartography, while the bottom is maritime lands. This duality is unappealing esthetically, as is the image of Italy wandering incompletely onto the map from the left, and there is a sense of a lack of a geographical center. It was no doubt as a consequence of this lack of unity that the map in completely assembled form was not well received by the public, and no derivatives of the full map were ever produced. When it occurs in atlases, the sheets of the map are usually found scattered in different places. Most commonly, the top two sheets occur as a map of the Danube Basin, the southwest sheet elsewhere as a map of Italy, and the southeast sheet somewhere else still as a separate map of Greece. In some atlases, only the top section appears, and the bottom sheets are replaced altogether by separate maps of Italy and Greece.

As to the general accuracy of the map, we can at present only make quite limited observations. The Italian parts are excellent, for they are almost exactly as on the generally accurate 1561 Italy. No scholars have commented on the other parts of the map in this regard, and this needs to be explored, although it is clear at a glance that the depiction of Greece is far better than any preceding one.

For an in depth discussion of the genesis of the present map from map no. 93, and of several points of confusion arising from that, see our comments at entry 93, and for still more points of confusion concerning this map, see our comments at no. 95. There were no other derivatives of this map other than the Rome Lafreri printing.

701

Location of copies:

Wien ÖNB(K I 109.404)/ Copenhagen KB(KBK 1-51 (26,27)(2 northern sheets only)/ London BL(Maps K.Top.113.24)(2 northern sheets only)/ Paris BN(GE B- 2408)(2 northern sheets only)/ Firenze BN(12.-.44, v. 3, nos. 34(33 written)(2 sheets together), 43, 56(55 written))[1980]/ Greenwich NMM(C3995, nos. 36, 37, 42, 61)[1971]/ London RGS(Map Room, 264.G.1, nos. 29, 30, 33, 54)[1929]/ Rostock UB(Q k 3, no. 28)(one sheet only)[1904]. The preceding six are all the original Venice printing. There is also a Rome edition of Lafreri. It is also dated 1560, but one must beware of any notion that the plates were transmitted to Lafreri in the year 1560. There were many instances where plates shipped to Rome from Venice contained dates earlier than the date of shipment, and yet maps were printed from these plates without changing the earlier date. I suspect this to be the case here. We do not usually, in our Cartobibliography, deal with derivatives. But because there is much confusion between the two editions, and the various sheets, we have decided to include the Rome editions, whole or partial, which we are aware of. The Rome edition, identical except for the words "*In Roma per Ant. Lafreri*" added between the privilege notice and the scale bar in the text box in the northeast sheet, is much more common. Examples are: Chicago Newb(Novacco 6F 35)/ Chicago Newb(Novacco 4F 118)(2 northern sheets only)/ London BL(M.T.11.g..(4).)/ New York PL(*KB+++1572, nos. 36, 35, 50, 40)/ Paris BN(GE DD- 1140(34,35,37,57 RES))/ Paris BN(GE DD- 655(53,62,63,70)/ Paris BN(GE AF PF- 103(33))(2 northern sheets only)/ Paris BN(B 464[83]0(northeast sheet only)/ Princeton UL(HMC01.2923 and HMC01.2096)(only ne and se sheets)/ London BL(C.7.e.2, nos. 20,21)(top 2 sheets only)[2003]/ Roma BCas(Rari 1131, no. 29 (top 2 sheets only))[1982]/ Helsinki AEN(HN[Mickwitz 130], nos. 30, 31, 42, 51)[1981]/ Firenze BN(12.-.44, v. 4, nos. 40(39 written), 41, 59(58 written), 63(62 written))[1980]/ Madrid PR(MAP/464, nos. 46(2 sheets), 70, 87)[1915]/ Washington LC(G1015 .L25 1575 Vault, nos. 29, 30, 44(southeast sheet missing)[1914]/ Roma BN(711.6.G.1, nos. 36, 37, 55, 68)[1876]

Note: The following also contain the map, but I do not know whether they are Venice or Rome editions: Leiden UB, Paris BN(4 other copies besides the 5 given above), London RGS (another copy), Madrid PR (2 other copies), Kraków BCz, Dillingen SB. The Leiden UB copy and one of the Madrid PR copies are probably Venice. Fully assembled copies of this map are extremely rare. I know of only three of the Rome edition, one in the Newberry Library, one in the British Library, and one privately owned by Graham Arader of New York; the only assembled copy of the Venice edition that I know of was until recently in the private collection of Margarita Savourkas of Greece, but is now in the possession of another Greek collector whose identity is unknown to me.

References:
Biasutti, 1908, 7, 50-51, 62-63; Almagià, 1939, carta, 15; Almagià, 1961 (1913-14), 265, 266-71; Bagrow, 1928-30, 1, 86-88; Almagià, 1929, 26 and 32; Colamonico, 1939, 167-68; Banfi, 1947, 36-42, 45, 49; Almagià, 1948, 27-31; Banfi, 1955, 102; Cucagna, 1964, 12-17, 18, 19, 160; Dörflinger, 1977, 56-57; Kret, 1978, 107; Lago and Rossit, 1981, 48-50; Bella, 1986, nos. 16, 61 and 68; Meurer, 1991, 152-53; Lago, 1992, 165, 328; Karrow, 1993, 234-35; Bifolco and Ronca, 2018, 1: 697. (Important Note: As discussed in entry 93, this map has been particularly subject to confusion in the literature, and many of these references contain inaccuracies, including false statements that the Rome edition was the first edition.)

Reproduction of the Paris BN(GE DD- 1140(34,35,37,57 RES)) copy: https://gallica.bnf.fr/ark:/12148/btv1b7200298s; of the Newberry Copy: Bifolco and Ronca, 2018, 1: 698-99; https://collections.Newberry.org/asset-management/2KXJ8ZSKAVUPT? &WS

*   *   *

Note: There is a list of ancient and modern place name equivalents which was made to accompany this map, in the form of a small (22 cm) booklet of eighteen leaves: *I nomi Latini tratti dall'antico Greco & ivolgari hora nominati, d'una gran parte dell'Europa nuouamente descritti. Opera nuova di Giacopo de'Castaldi Piamontese Cosmographo in Venetia . . . Con gratia*

& priuilegio del nostro Signor Papa pio IIII per anni 10. Et similmente della Serenissima Signoria di Venetia per anni 15.

Location of copies: I know of only three copies: Venezia BNM (in a volume of miscellaneous material together with a copy of Gastaldi's 1561 *La Vniversale descrittione del mondo*, at call number (6. D. 201)), according to Caraci (1936, 224)/ Roma BN(A-B8), to judge from the notice in the online OPAC Servizio Bibliotecario Nazionale; the SBN "Codice identificativo" given there is: IT\ICCU\BVEE\063163/ Firenze BN(1084. 16).

Reproduction: https://archive.org/details/bub_gb_PdwjGSwgxZ8C

(97.-100.) An uncompleted series of four maps intended for an edition of Ptolemy, ca. 1561(?)

In November 1999 Trajan auctioneers in Paris put up for sale a large Lafrerian type atlas with 164 plates including in all 191 prints, all of them Venetian imprints, the only instance I know of this, for usually such atlases contain an assortment of Venetian and Roman imprints. It was bought jointly by French and German antiquariats, and in 2004 Peter Meurer published a description of the atlas, as a book, and it is the fullest description of such an atlas ever made to date, with one full large page devoted to a description and a reproduction of each map, or other print (Meurer, 2004; a general description of the atlas is at pp. 5-7). The atlas is of particular interest to us, because it includes two sets of Gastaldi maps unknown before, one set an incomplete series of four maps intended for some edition of Ptolemy, and the other set an also incomplete series, in this case, of eleven maps, depicting the geographical ideas of Strabo, and intended for an edition of that writer's *Geography*. We spoke of them briefly at the end of chapter one. Meirere (cit., 6a) says the maps are "kinds of proof prints". On the basis of this rather extraordinary find, the atlas's joint purchasers gave to their atlas the appellation of the "Strabo Illustratus Atlas." In 2014 the atlas was acquired by the Bavarian State Library (where it is known as the Lafreri-Atlas) and the entire contents is digitally available https://www.digitale-sammlungen.de/en/view/bsb00107640?page'. Unfortunately, all the maps in both of the two Gastaldi series are undated. Most are also unsigned, but the two modern maps in the Ptolemy series are signed by Gastaldi, and a variant of one of the Strabonian maps, of Italy, has been known since 1881 (and another has recently surfaced, as see our compound entry (107.-117.)), and this Italy variant is signed "p[er] Iacomo Gastaldo", and on the basis of these signatures and the style of the maps, we can safely assign both sets to Gastaldi. But the question of the date presents a bigger problem, as we shall see.

The present entry is nominally devoted to the Ptolemy set. However, it will be useful for the moment to devote some discussion to both sets simultaneously. Meurer hypothesized that the Ptolemaic maps were being produced for the Ruscelli-Valgrisi Ptolemy published in Venice in 1561, but that the map series was halted, and was replaced by the set of maps which actually appeared in that edition, with the assumption evidently being that the Gastaldi maps were more expensive than the other maps. On the basis of the single map in the Strabonian series which was known before the Strabo Illustratus Atlas surfaced, the Italy, Almagià proposed a theory similar to Meurer's (Almagià, 1948c). He assumed that the Italy had been intended for a celebrated 1562-65 edition of Strabo, translated by Alfonso Buonacciuoli, and published in Venice and Ferrara by Francesco di Franceschi (Francesco Senese), but for some reason the map was not included in the work; consequently, the year 1562 has come to be often taken as a tentative date for the map. Logically enough, Meurer has extended Almagià's theory to the rest of the newly found Strabonian maps. These theories are certainly possible, but the following shows a much more probable origin for the maps.

We spoke earlier, in chapter one, about Gastaldi's membership in an elite scholarly academy, the Academia Venetiana, which, although prestigious, was closed after only four years of existence, by government intervention in August 1561. The academy published a prospectus, in 1558 in Italian, and in 1559 in Latin (see in our bibliography at "Accademia Venetiana" for all details). The prospectus presented an annotated listing of the academy's projected works, which amount to about 300 books, although only a small number were actually published (they are listed in Renouard, 1834, 266-81). The projected works are given in the prospectus under a series of headings corresponding to the various divisions and subdivisions of the various subjects dealt with by the academy (theology, metaphysics, physics, rhetoric, etc., etc.). As brought out in chapter one, Gastaldi and Livio Sanuto, represented the geographical (or cosmographical; the terms used interchangeably in the prospectuses, and other documents relating to the academy) faculty, which fell under the mathematical section, itself part of the Consiglio delle scientie. In the prospectus there are fifteen works listed under the heading "GEOGRAPHIA" (I cannot give a better citation, for the Italian edition of the prospectus has neither page numbers, folio numbers, nor signature numbers; in the Latin edition, the list is at f. 14v-15r, and in the 1808 Pellegrini Latin reprint mentioned in our bibliography, the section is at pp. 116-17.) Some of the works could be either maps or books. It is often impossible to be sure from the wording. But the eleventh and twelfth works are very definitely books with maps, one an edition of Ptolemy, and the other an edition of Strabo. Their titles are given thus in the Italian edition:

[no. 11] TOLOMEO con le tavole, molto piu fedeli, e molto piu copiose che non son quellé, le quali hoggidi si ueggono (Ptolemy with the maps, much more faithful [to the original], and much more copious than are those [editions] which are seen nowadays)

[no. 12] STRABONE con le sue tauole, a guisa di Tolomeo, di tutte tre le parti, Europa, Asia, and Africa, con le prouincie, regioni, città, monti, e fiumi, dichiarati co' nomi cosi antichi, come moderni, e con i climi, e paralleli, e con misure de gradi (Strabo with the maps, after the fashion of Ptolemy, in all three parts, Europe, Asia, and Africa, with the provinces, regions, cities, mountains, and rivers, given with names both ancient and modern, and with the *climata* , and parallels, and with the measure of degrees.)

The maps we have now must have been produced for these two works, which would have been in progress at the time when the government closed the academy in August 1561, which closure would explain the incompleteness of the sets we have. The Strabobian maps we have do not include *climata*, but, just as with the mentioned ancient and modern place names, these could have been in the text, similarly to the way in which Ptolemy gives a general locational description of the limits of the regions corresponding to his maps at the beginning of each of his sections. Possibly, too, since our maps have the feel of proofs (Meurer, 2004, 6a), they may not have been put in yet, for it is not unusual to find these *climata* indicated outside a neat line. Perhaps, too, they were simply omitted for some reason or other. Further evidence that the Strabo edition with maps which we find in the prospectus under the geography section corresponds to the maps in the Strabo Illustratus atlas is the fact that Meurer's comments on the sources of the Strabonian maps indicate that, in almost all cases, the coastlines and hydrography are taken from Gastaldi, while nomenclature is from Strabo.

This does not close the case, for the question of date remains. In fact, it is insolvable. The maps were made (drawn) sometime between 1557, when the academy opened, and 1561, when it closed. They were probably engraved then as well, although it is not impossible that they were engraved after the academy closed in 1561. In any event, we do not usually date maps by the time they were drawn or engraved, but by the date of publication, and in the case of maps in books, the date of publication of the maps is *ipso facto* the date of publication of the book. But in the present case, the book was never published. However, for the purpose of getting a date at which to place these maps, we can come up with some approximate dates by "compromise" so to speak. Firstly, for two of the maps, the modern "Ptolemaic" British Isles, and the Strabonian Italy, copies are known which are later states, so at least some of the plates continued in use after the academy closed in August 1561, so we know that their lives did not stop dead short at that time. Also, there is a possibility that the existence of the project and the maps had at least an inspirational effect on the starting of the 1561 Ptolemy and the 1562-65 Strabo of Meurer and Almagià. I therefore place the new Ptolemaic maps at ca. 1561 (?), and the Strabonian maps at ca. 1562 (?). While the grounds for these estimates are weak, we have nothing better, and the dates will probably not be very far from the truth.

97. Iberian Peninsula (Ptolemaic)
-[Venice?], n.d. [ca. 1561?]
-Copper engraving, 25.0 x 35.5 cm. (plate size), on one sheet
-No scale bar

At top right, outside the lateral border:
TAVOLA SECON | DA DELLA EV | ROPA, Secondo | la descritione del- | la Geografia di | Claudio Tolomeo | della parte della | Spagna. (SECOND MAP OF EUROPE, According to the description of the Geography of Claudius Ptolemy of the area of Spain)

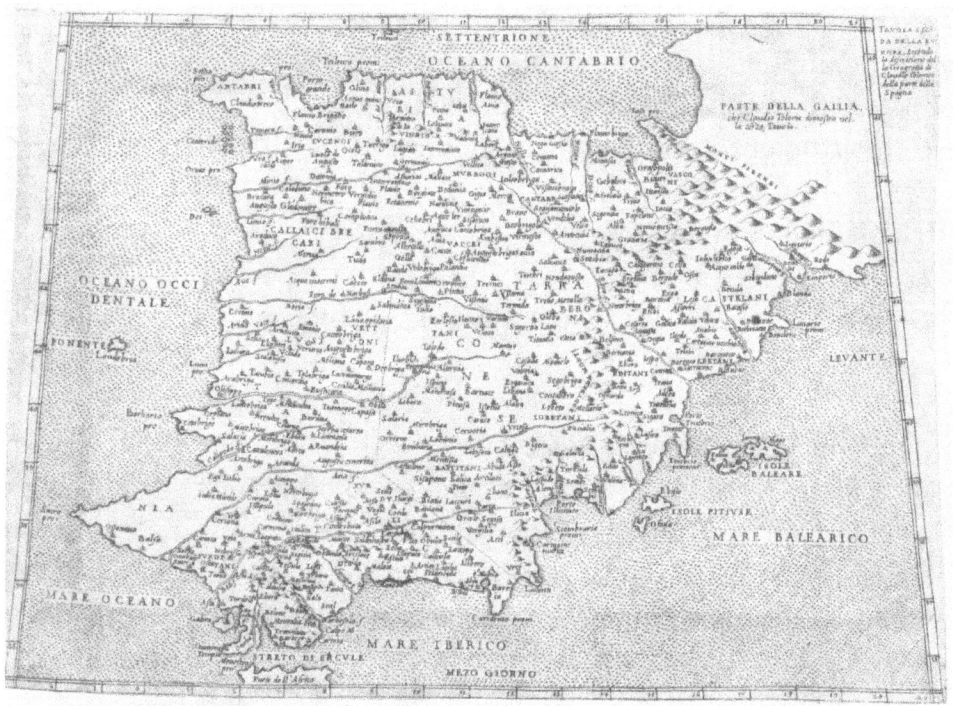

97 Iberian Peninsula (Ptolemaic) 1561? München SB

Comments:
Graduated in whole degrees, with each degree numbered, from ca. 35°30' to ca. 46°20' N, and from 1°00' to 21°00' E, on a trapezoidal projection. There is no difference between the longitudinal limits at the top and the bottom of the map, because the map itself is trapezoidal in shape, following the projection. The map is the second of Ptolemy's maps, according to his usual order. Like all four of the late Ptolemy series maps, it is far superior to Gastaldi's original Ptolemaic map of the Iberian Peninsula of 1548, partly of course because it is over four times as large, and can contain much more detail. But the technical execution is much better in general.

708

Location of copy:
München SB(2 Mapp. 464)

References:
Meurer, 2004, 34, no. 20; Bifolco and Ronca, 2018, 2: 1118.

Reproductions:
Meurer, 2004, no. 20; Bifolco and Ronca, 2018, 2: 1119.
https://www.digitale-sammlungen.de/en/view/bsb00107640?page'24"

98. British Isles (Ptolemaic)
-[Venice?], n.d. [ca. 1561?]
-Copper engraving, 25.5 x 33.0 cm. (plate size), on one sheet
-No scale bar

At top left, outside the lateral border:
TAVOLA PRIMA DE | L'EVROPA, secondo | la descrittione della Geografia di Clau | dio Tolomeo Ales- | sandrino del'Isol- | le de Bretagna, | ch'è una Prouincia. (FIRST MAP OF EUROPE, according to the description of the Geography of Claudius Ptolemy of Alexandria: of the Island of Britain, which is a Province.)

Comments:
Graduated in whole degrees, with each degree numbered, in latitude and longitude, from ca. 51°20' to ca. 63°30' N, and from 7°00' to 33°00' E, on a trapezoidal projection. There is no difference between the longitudinal limits at the top and the bottom of the map, because the map itself is trapezoidal in shape, following the projection. The first of the Ptolemaic maps, according to Ptolemy's usual order. Meurer notes that, while it generally follows the Ptolemaic geography, it seems to have taken some details from more modern sources, probably from a modern map of the British Isles of 1556 by a cartographer who signs himself simply as HIS (Meurer, 2004, 44). A peculiarity of the map is that the part of France which should be in the

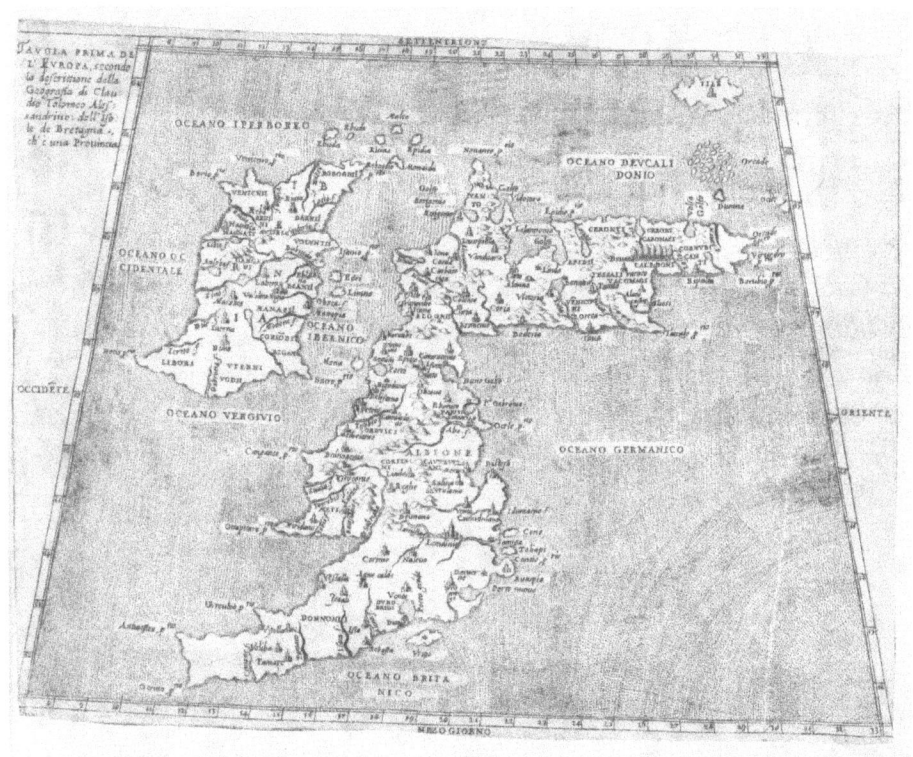

98 British Isles (Ptolemaic) 1561? München SB

southeast part of the map has been burnished out, and replaced by sea stippling (Shirley, 2000, "Updated," 13).

Location of copy:
München SB(2 Mapp. 464)

References:
Shirley, 2000, "Updated," 13; Meurer, 2004, 44, no. 30; Bifolco and Ronca, 2018, 1: 764.

Reproductions:
Meurer, 2004, no. 30; Bifolco and Ronca, 2018, 1: 764-65.
https://www.digitale-sammlungen.de/en/view/bsb00107640?page'34"

99. Iberian Peninsula (modern)
-[Venice?], n.d. [ca. 1561?]
-Copper engraving, 25.5 x 33.0 cm. (plate size), on one sheet
-100 Italian miles = 2.4 cm.

In a text box at the lower left corner:
*TAVOLA SECONDA | DELLA EVROPA SE- | CONDO La Geografia mo- |
derna della Prouincia della | Spagna, descritta per me Gia | como di
Gastaldi Piamontese. (SECOND MAP OF EUROPE ACCORDING TO The
modern Geography of the Province of Spain, drawn by me Giacomo di
Gastaldi Piedmontese)*

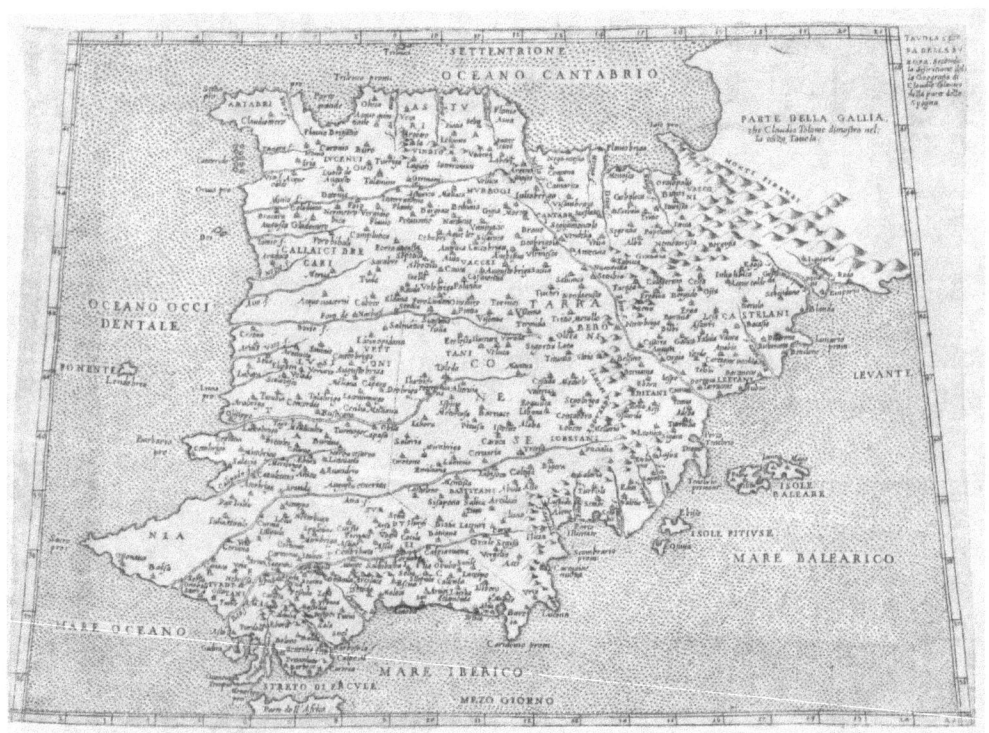

99 Iberian Peninsula (modern) 1561? München SB

Comments:
Graduated in thirty-minute increments, numbered at each whole degree, in
latitude and longitude, from 35°00' to 46°00' N; but, as to longitude, some

blunder has occurred, perhaps on the part of the engraver, for on the top border the graduation runs from 3°00' to 23°00' E, while on the lower border it runs from 1°00' to 21°00' E, so that, while there are exactly twenty degrees of longitude in both cases, if the meridians were drawn in, they would all run diagonally across the map. So we might say nominally on a trapezoidal projection, although actually the projection is lost in this longitude numbering error. Without actually mentioning Gastaldi's 1544 Spain, Meurer implies that the current map is more up to date, and this does seem to be the fact. He also notices some confusion and contradiction between the words of a little inscription in the northeast part of the map and an inscription on his map no. 33 (our following map, no. 100), ending with the observation that: "This general vagueness is evidence that the double Ptolemy series was probably never continued beyond the first two maps." (Meurer, 2004, 45).

Location of copy:
München SB(2 Mapp. 464)

References:
Meurer, 2004, 45, no. 31; Bifolco and Ronca, 2018, 2: 1120.

Reproductions:
Meurer, 2004, no. 31; Bifolco and Ronca, 2018, 2: 1120.
https://www.digitale-sammlungen.de/en/view/bsb00107640?page'35"

100. British Isles (modern)
-[Venice?], n.d. [ca. 1561?]
-Copper engraving, 23.5 x 23.0 cm. (plate size 24.5 x 39.0), on one sheet.
-No scale bar

At the top left outside the lateral border:
Tauola prima dell'Europa | secondo la Descrittione mo- | derna dela geografia de Gia- | como di Gastaldo piamontese (First Map of Europe according to the modern Description of the geography of Giacomo di Gastaldo piedmontese)

100 British Isles (modern) 1561? München SB

Comments:

Graduated in whole degrees, each numbered, in latitude and longitude, from
50°30' to ca. 62°20' N, and on the northern border, from ca. 3°30' to 29°00' E,
and on the southern border from 7°00' to 25°00' E, on a rectangular
projection. Shirley and Meurer believe that the source of the main island
may be Lily (Shirley, 1980 (1991 ed.), 32; Meurer, 2004, 47), and Meurer
considers that Ireland has affiliation with the Ireland on the 1548 modern
British Isles map in Gastaldi's Ptolemy (our no. 6), and to be sure there is
some resemblance, though the hydrography is much more developed on the
present map.

Location of copies:
The only known copy is in the Strabo Illustratus Atlas (München SB(2 Mapp. 464)). However, a variant copy evidently identical to this one, except for the addition of a second title in the broad left margin, "ISOLA DE IRLANDA ET SCOTIA INGHILTERRA", is in the Library of the Royal Geographical Society in London (call number RGS British Isles G.220), which is reproduced in Shirley (1980 (1991 ed.), 33).

References:
Shirley, 1980 (1991 ed.), 32-33; Shirley, 2000, 13-14; Meurer, 2004, 47, no. 33; Bifolco and Ronca, 2018, 1: 766-67.

Reproductions:
Meurer, 2004, no. 33; Bifolco and Ronca, 2018, 1: 766-67.
https://www.digitale-sammlungen.de/en/view/bsb00107640?page'37"

101. Italy (modern)
-Venice, 1561
- Copper engraving, 53.5 x 77.0 cm., on two sheets
- 50 Italian miles = 4.5 cm.

In text box at lower right of east sheet:
IL DISEGNO DELLA GEOGRAFIA | MODERNA DE TVTTA LA PRO | VINCIA DE LA ITALIA | Con sue regioni, citta, castella, Mõti, Laghi, Fiumi, | Mari, Colfi, Porti, capi et isole, ch' in quelli [!] si | ritrouano, et altre Regioni circonuicine ul golfo | Di Venetia, per maggiore lucida | tione dell' Italia. | All' Illustrissimo Et eccellentissimo sig[no]r il s[e]r Alfonso seconda da Este, duca di Ferrara quinto / Giacopo di Castaldi Piamõtese cosmografo In Venetia. / Con gratia et priuilegio del sémo põtifice | papa Pio iiij per anni X. E del serenissimo senato d' Venetia per anni · XV | M·D·LXI. (MAP OF THE MODERN GEOGRAPHY OF THE WHOLE COUNTRY OF ITALY With its regions, cities, castles, Mountains, Lakes, Rivers, Seas, Gulfs, Ports, capes and islands, which in those [!] are found, and other environing Regions to the gulf of Venice, for greater elucidation of Italy. To the Most Illustrious And excellent gentleman sir Alphonse the second of Este, fifth

714

duke of Ferrara / Giacomo Gastaldi Piedmontese cosmographer at Venice. With grace and privilege of the supreme pontiff pope Pius IV for 10 years. And from the most serene senate of Venice for 15 years.)

In lower right of same text box:
fabio licinio ex[cidebat](Fabio licinio engraver)

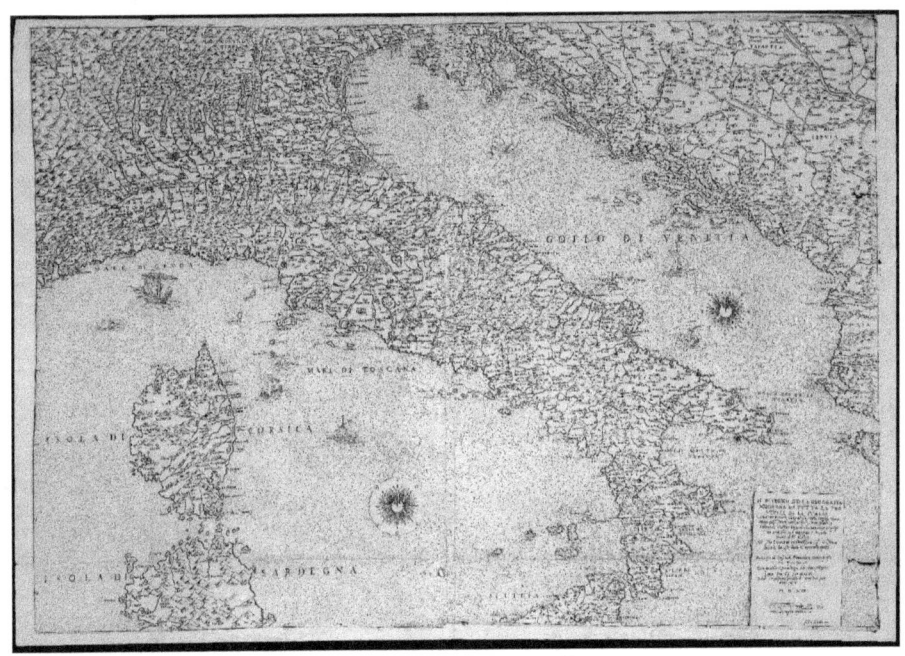

101 Italy 1561 Chicago Newb

Comments:
Graduated in full degrees, each numbered, in latitude and longitude, from ca. 37°30' to 45°35' N, and, at the top, from 27°40' to 44°50' E, and at the bottom, from 28°20' to 44°10' E, on a trapezoidal projection with very little meridional convergence. There is an accompanying list of ancient and modern name equivalents, though no copy of an edition before 1564 is known. It is often stated that the map was completed by 1559, since Gastaldi applied for and obtained a privilege for it in that year. But there is no validity to this. As we have seen in our first chapter, there was no standardized practice in this regard in applying for privileges. It was common for them to be applied for, and granted, before production of a work

had commenced, at any stage in production, or after production was completed.

The question of the occasion for this map is an interesting problem for which we cannot give a conclusive answer. As we saw in chapter ten, the indications are strong that from ca. 1559 most, though not all, of Gastaldi's energies were directed toward making a set of modern continental maps covering most of the world. For Africa, there was a giant single map, Asia was covered in three large blocks, and a map of America was completed in manuscript by ca. 1560. For Europe, Gastaldi succeeded only in making two large maps, one covering all of northeast Europe, and the other all of southeast Europe. The latter map (our no. 96), one of Gastaldi's largest, was published in four sheets in 1560, one year before the Italy. The southwest sheet of this large map covered the greater part, but not all, of Italy. The depiction of Italy here is nearly identical to that on the 1561 map as to the coasts (though not always as to the place names), and, most significantly to the present comments, the depictions are exactly the same size and scale. Several writers have referred to the 1561 Italy as being the southwest sheet of the larger map extended to the west to embrace the parts of Italy excluded in 1560, and, although there are certain differences (the 1560 map has parallels and meridians drawn in, while the 1561 Italy does not, and there are some toponymical differences), there is indeed the implication that the Italy is as much an outgrowth of the larger map, as it is an independent and discrete work unto itself. This interpretation receives some support from the fact that the Piedmontese Gastaldi had never before made a separate large map of his own homeland (here understood as Italy instead of the Venetian Republic), and his sights had always been mainly set on distant places, unlike most cartographers. On the other hand, in a 1559 application for and granting of privilege, and again in a legend on his 1559 First Part of Asia, he clearly refers to a forthcoming separate map of Italy (and also to one of Greece, which appeared in 1560 and is from the southeast part of the large map). Thus, some confusion remains as to the question of whether or not the Italy should be understood as a fully independently conceived production, and the question is perhaps unresolvable. As a further comment, on the large 1560 map, the density of names and detail is considerably lower for the areas adjacent to Italy than for Italy itself, and in the northeast parts of the map the density is several times lower, with the implication that Gastaldi did direct more attention to his own homeland than to others.

The principal source for the general shape of the country, the lay of its coastlines, and the axis of the peninsula, is portolan charts, and it is mostly these which account for the great general advances over Ptolemy in these respects. Gastaldi's usage of these was no novelty, for similar improvements in a number of previous maps (Syvanus, Waldseemüller, Münster, etc.) could only have come from the same source. Gastaldi, however, seems to have made more extensive use of them than any of his predecessors, and, since the coastal delineation is better in some places than in preserved general portolan charts, Gastaldi must have had at hand some now unknown more detailed local charts, or perhaps manuscript geographical maps which included parts of the coast. The sources for his enormous improvements, in quantity and quality, as to population centers and their placement, and, especially, as to hydrography, remain largely unknown, except in the area of Tuscany, where he used Bellarmato's great 1536 map, based on surveys. While Gastaldi used his own regional maps for some parts of Italy, this tells us nothing, since their sources are in turn unknown. The only other definite source of note was Lazius's 1556 Hungary, which gave the delineation for the northwest part of the Balkans on the map, but this is peripheral to Italy. We can assume with surety that Gastaldi did not trek through Italy, so he clearly had some sources unknown to us, perhaps military or diplomatic maps, as suggested by Almagià, but we know that throughout Europe at the time there had arisen among the scholarly-inclined a sort of fashion for local mapping, and I think sources of this type are more likely. The possibility cannot be excluded that Gastaldi actively canvassed for information from other parts of Italy, as his friend Ramusio did so successfully for the far parts of the world, and as Münster and Ortelius did in the north for many parts of Europe, also with success.

Once published, Gastaldi's Italy became the model which was followed by the great majority of cartographers for half a century, until it was superseded by Magini's 1608 Italy. Still, as with his other maps of European areas, we find in the Italy no stunning innovation of the kind seen in his maps of the other continents. Even the relatively notable improvements in axis and overall shape had already been made by others, as stated above.

Gastaldi, however, is first in one broader improvement, the reduction of the east-west extent of the country from Ptolemy's 13°00' to 11°23' (still ca. 2° overwide). What contributed to its resounding success was its size, wealth of detail, and (not irrelevant) its general esthetic appeal. Only one other map came up to it in size, Gormont's 1544 Italy (Borri, 1999, 41), but that is a drab production with nowhere near the amount of detail, and it has an unappealing horizontal orientation of the peninsula. It evidently had little success. But Gastaldi's Italy presents a grand panorama which arrests the viewer, as do most of his large later works. It contains approximately 2,000 place names, many not registered on any previous map, and a great wealth of hydrography, and, although there are exceptions in isolated areas, both the placement of population centers and the hydrography are far superior than on any previous maps, and in fact are largely correct, though in a general way, for it is clear that Gastaldi's placements were made by approximation. Certainly, nothing like it had been seen before. The map does have one bad flaw, serious enough that we cannot call the map a truly great one. The northern part of the peninsula is too broad, resulting in a Ligurian coast which is too flattened, and unlike previous modern maps, which show this coast much better. What led Gastaldi into this error I do not know. Nevertheless, on the basis of its great wealth of detail, its general correctness in all other areas, and its striking beauty, it is perhaps valid to call it the best printed map of Italy of the sixteenth century, although, with its Ligurian coast blunder, we may question if it was truly deserving of its astonishing longevity in reeditions. No doubt it was partly just Gastaldi's great renown that accounted for this. For listings of later editions and derivatives, see Bagrow, 1928-30, 1, 88-89; Almagià, 1929, 26-27; Almagià, 1948, 31-33; Karrow, 1993, 236-38; Perini, 1996, 31-32, and Borri, 1999.

Location of copies:
Chicago Newb(Novacco 4F 200)/ London BL(Maps K.Top.75.1)/ Leiden UB(COLLBN 002-06-016)/ Wilmington UNC(Drawer 9, Item 9-210)/ Paris BN(GE AF PF- 30(1 D)/ Paris BN(GE C- 5061 (RES))/ Paris BN(GE CC- 1380(31 RES))/ Paris BN(GE C- 9226))/ Paris BN(GE DD- 655(45 RES))/ Madrid PR(MAP/438, no. 31)/ Madrid PR(MAP/454, no. 36)/ Sint-Niklaas KOKW(Atlas 408 IATO(no. 31))[1994]/ Kraków BCz(BCzK 1208 V)

[1992]/ Helsinki AEN(HN[Mickwitz 130](no. 33))[1981]/ Firenze BN(12.-.44, v. 3, no. 36(35 written))[1980]/ Firenze BN(12.-.44, v. 1, no. 38) [1980]/ Firenze BN(12.-.44, v. 4, no. 45)[1980]/ Greenwich NMM(C3995, no. 40)[1971]/ Venezia Correr(Cartografia cartella, 32, no. 35)[1954]/ Venezia BNM(138 c.4, no. 34)[1954]/ London RGS(Map Room, 264.G.1, no. 31)[1929]/ London RGS(Map Room, 264.G.2, no. 66)[1915]/ Madrid PR(MAP/464, no. 54)[1915]/ Washington LC(G1015. L25 1575 Vault, no. 32)[1914]/ Dillingen SB(X,122, no. 43)[1911] /Wolfegg SW(Histor. Geogr., 169, no. 19)[1911] / Wolfenbüttel HAB(2.3 Geogr 20, no. 24)[1906]/ Roma BN(711.6.G.1, no. 36)[1876]

*   *   *

Note: There is a two-page list of ancient and modern place name equivalents which was made to accompany this map, although it appeared only in 1564: *I Nomi antichi et moderni della Italia delle: provincie, regioni, città, castelli, monti, laghi, fivmi, mari, golfi, porti, capi, & isole: grtaduati in lunghezza, & larghezza | Di Giacobo Gastaldi Piamontese, cosmografo. ; In Venetia MDLXIIII. Con privilegio.* Exemplars: Chicago Newb(Novacco 2F, nos. 109 and 110)/ Chicago Newb(Novacco 2F, nos. 107 and 108)/ Kobenhavn KB(KBK 1-51(331))/ Paris BN(GE DD- 655 (64,65)/ Kraków BCz((in atlas BCzK 1172-1278 V, between nos. 51 and 52)[1992]/ Firenze BN(12.-.44, v. 1, nos. 37 and 63)[1980]/ Firenze BN(12.-.44, v. 3, nos. 49, 50)[1980]/ Firenze BN(12.-.44, v. 4, nos. 60, 61)[1980]/ Venezia BNM(138 c.4, no. 35)[1954]/ London RGS(Map Room, 264.G.1, nos. 46, 47)[1929]/ London RGS(Map Room, 264.G.2, no. 36)[1915]/ Madrid PR(MAP/464, nos. 76,77)[1915]/ Washington LC(G1015 .L25 1575 Vault, between nos.45 and 46)[1914]. Reference and reproduction: Bifolco and Ronca, 2018, 3:1818-19.

References:
Biasutti, 1908; Almagià, 1961 (1912-13), 264, 266-71, 324; Bagrow, 1928-30, 1, 88; Almagià, 1929, 15, 26-27, 30, 31-33, 66; Colamonico, 1939, 163, 167; Almagià, 1948, 31-33, 102; Cucagna, 1964, 17-20; Lago and Rossit, 1981, 50: Lago, 1986, 84-85; Meurer, 1991, 153; Lago, 1992, 165-69,

244; Karrow, 1993, 236-38; Lago, 1996, 84-85; Perini, 1996, 16, 30-31; Schilder, 1996, 333-34; Borri, 1999, 46-47; Lago, 2002, 250-51, 326, 451; Umek, 2002, passim; Milanesi, 2004, 13; Mollo, 2002, 24-25; Bifolco and Ronca, 2018. 3: 1816.

Reproductions:
Almagià, 1929, pl. 28; Bella, 1986, no. 65; Meurer, 1991, pl. 30; Borri, 1999, no. 37; Bifolco and Ronca, 2018, 3: 1816-17.
https://gallica.bnf.fr/ark:/12148/btv1b55004648k/f1.vertical;
https://collections.Newberry.org/asset-management/2KXJ8ZSAPQ2_D?
&WS

102. Southwestern Asia
-Venice, 1561
-Copper engraving, 46.5 x 74.0 cm., on two sheets
-100 Italian miles = 2.1 cm.

In the text box at bottom middle of the right sheet:
IL DISEGNO DELLA SECONDA PARTE DELL'ASIA | Il quale principia da leuante al fiume indu gia detto indo, et alla prouintia | de malabar, e da Ponente il fiume Nilo, e parte luochi diserti, da setten | trione il Parallelo ch' è in 36 gradi di larghezza, et dall'Austro il mare d' | India, et il fiume di magadazo, et il Regno de Beleguanze: Nel detto di | segno si uedeno tutte le scale che fanno le naue, che vano e vengano con le | specciarie, dalla citta de calecut, et similmente tutti iluochi per terra | nominati al presente, ch' vanv e uengono le carouane dal Suachen. - | e Dalacca paese del prete giouãni, et similm te da Aden e ormus, | et dalla Balsara castello sopra il fiume frat: tutto graduato in | Longezza e Larghezza, et misurato con miglia italiane: | All' ill[ustrissi]mo sig[no]r il sig[no]r Marcho fucharo, Barone di Kirchberg e d' | Waissenhoren:-- | giacomo di castaldi Piamontese cosmographo in Venetia:-- 1561 | Con gratia et priuilegio del Sémo Pontifice Papa pio iiii p[er] anni x | E del serenissimo senato di Venetia per Anni XV (MAP OF THE SECOND PART OF ASIA which begins at the east at the Indus [indu] river formerly called the indo, and at the province of malabar, and at the West the Nile river, and the area of deserted places [and]

720

at the north the Parallel which is in 36 degrees of latitude, and at the south the Sea of India, and the river of Mogadishu [or magadoxo, or magadazo, or mecadesse, all the same]and the Realm of the Ganz people [or Gãnz people, the same]: In the said map are seen all the ports of call which are made by the ships, which go and come from the spice islands, from the city of Calcutta, and similarly all the places on land just named, [to] which go and come the caravans from Suakin, and Dahlak [the] country of Prester John, and similarly from Aden and Hormuz, and from Basra castle above the river Euphrates: all graduated in Longitude and Latitude, and measured with Italian miles: To the most illustrious signor the signor Marco fugger, Baron of Kirchberg and of Weissenhorn:--giacomo di Castaldi Piedmontese cosmographer in Venice:-- 1561 With grace and privilege of the Highest Pontiff Pope Pius IV for 10 years And of the most serene senate of Venice for 15 years)

Below the bottom right of the text box:
Fabio licinio f[ecit] (Fabio licinio engraver)

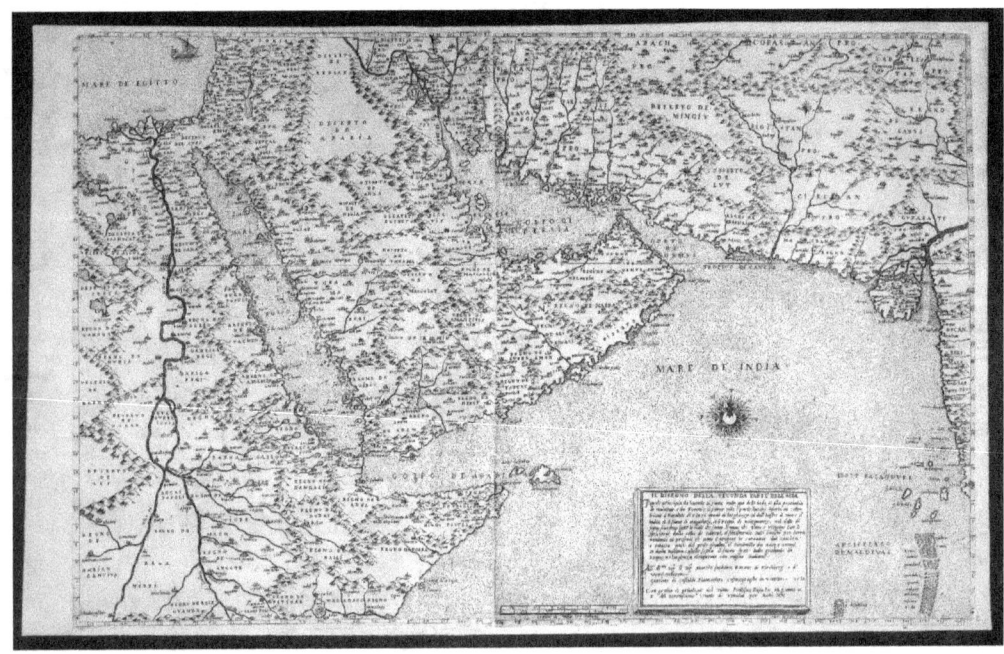

102 Southwestern Asia 1561 Chicago Newb

Comments:

Graduated in whole degrees, each numbered, in latitude and longitude, from 3°30' to 37°00' N, and, on the top border, from 57°40' to 121°30' E, and on the lower border from 64°20' to 114°20' E, on a trapezoidal projection. The map is often accompanied by a list of ancient and modern place name equivalents. This is the third of our six key or central Gastaldi maps, as defined and enumerated in entry no. 92, the first of these key maps. These maps are those in which Gastaldi breathed life into the extra-European continents for the first time in history, getting their geography on the whole correct, where before there had remained much confusion. For more perspective and greater depth on this, we refer the reader to entry no. 92, where one will also find references to the parts of the present book in which Gastaldi's tremendous achievement is discussed in detail. The present map is the second of his three Parts of Asia, the first and third parts being no. 92, and the entry following the present one, no. 103, and the three are sometimes referred to in a general way as "Gastaldi's Asia", a reasonable enough appellation, although the three parts cannot be combined into a single depiction, nor, clearly enough, did Gastaldi intend that they should be.

We wish to point out two aspects of this map which hold particular interest. Firstly, while it is principally a map of part of Asia, as its title states, and while, both in older and present day maps, it is normal, and indeed useful, for orientational purposes, to peripherally include on a map parts of adjacent lands, the amount of Africa which is shown in the map certainly exceeds the amount which would be necessary to depict in order to include the segment of Asia shown here. Perhaps this was for some reason unavoidable in order to achieve the correct meeting with the First and Second parts of Asia. But it is interesting that in Gastaldi's lengthy title box text, where he describes the coming and going of ships, at sea, and of caravans, on land, in the process of obtaining, transporting and distributing of spices (and other goods, though Gastaldi mentions only this most important one), he gives in general proportionately as much attention to this sizeable African segment as to the Asian segment, nominally making up the map. Out of sixteen geographical names in the text (including the name Asia), six are African place names: the Nile, the Realm of the Ganz people (one of a number of peoples in Ethiopia of whom almost nothing is known, and who disappeared at about Gastaldi's time, being assimilated into other peoples; the addition of Bell- or Bella- in some early European sources, as Gastaldi's map (Belleguanze), is not understood, but is generally considered as probably wrong, stemming from some unknown misunderstanding), the Mogadishu River, Suakin, Dahlak, and the Country of Prester John. Two of these, Suakin and Dahlak, on the Egyptian sea coast, were major ports of call in the movement of spices, and since this was to Gastaldi a major point of interest in this map, as we see from the legend, he wished to include them in his descriptive text. Another point of interest arising from the inclusion of a large chunk of Africa is the conspicuous inclusion at the west, of the Nile, all to the east of which is given in full detail, which could be taken as a reflection of the notion held anciently, and by some in the Middle Ages, and even a few in the Renaissance, that the Nile formed the western boundary of Asia. However, we know that Gastaldi did not adhere to this notion, for in his *La universale descrttione del mondo* of 1561 discussed in chapter two, when describing the boundaries of the continents, he espouses the modern notion that in this area the Red Sea is the boundary between Asia and Africa. In fact, it is hard to find a satisfactory explanation for Gastaldi's having pushed the western boundary of this map not only to the Nile, but considerably beyond. For later editions of this map, see Almagià, 1948, 36 and 63-66; and Karrow, 1993, 238-39.

Location of copies:
Chicago Newb(Novacco 4F 386)/ Leiden UB(COLLBN 002-07-019)/ Basel UB(Kartenslg AA95)/ Kobenhavn KB(KBK 1-51(54))/ Cambridge Harv(51-2495[in 2nd mat])/ Paris BN(GE C- 9228)/ Paris BN(GE CC-1380(67RES)/ Paris BN(GE CC- 2224(2))/ Paris BN(GE DD- 655(80 RES)/ Paris BN(GE DD- 1140(71,72))/ Roma BVat(Stampe Geogr.I.88-D)/ New York PL(*KB+++1572, no. 75)/ Madrid PR(MAP/454, no. 66)/ Madrid PR(MAP/438, no. 55)/ Firenze BMar(Stampe 423, 128-129)[2005]/ London BL(Maps C.7.e.1, no. 138)[2003]/ Sint-Niklaas KOKW(Atlas 408 IATO (no. 31))[1994]/ Kraków BCz(BCzK 1242 V)[1992]/ Roma BCas(Rari 1131, no. 57)[1982]/ Helsinki AEN(HN[Mickwitz 130](no. 613))[1981]/ Firenze BN(12.-.44, v. 4, no. 75)[1980]/ Firenze BN(12.-.44, v. 3, no. 66)(Licinio trimmed off)[1980]/ Firenze BN(12.-.44, v. 2, no. 16)(Licinio trimmed off)

[1980]/ Greenwich NMM(C3995, nos. 73,74)[1971]/ Venezia BNM(138 c.4, no. 74)[1954]/ London RGS(Map Room, 264.G.1, no. 65)[1929]/ London RGS(Map Room, 264.G.2, no. 60)[1915]/ Madrid PR(MAP/464, no. 106) [1915]/ Washington LC(G1015 .L25 1575 Vault, no. 61)[1914]/ Dillingen SB(X,122, no. 72)[1911]/ Dillingen SB(X,123, no. 125)[1911]/ Wolfenbüttel HAB(2.3 Geogr 20., no. 42)[1906]/ Roma BN(711.6.G.1, no. 71)[1876]

* * *

Note: There is a list of ancient and modern place name equivalents which was made to accompany this map: *I Nomi Antichi E Moderni Della Seconda Parte Dell'Asia . . . All'Illustrissimo Signor il Signor Marcho Fucharo dignissimo Barone di Kirchberg e di weissenhoren . . . Giacomo de Castaldi Piamontese, Cosmographo in Venetia 1561.* Exemplars: Basel UB(Kartenslg AA95a)/ Firenze BN(12.-.44, v. 2, no. 14)[1980]/ Firenze BN(12.-.44, v. 3, no. 68(67 written))[1980]/ Washington LC(G1015 .L25 1575 Vault, between nos. 61 and 62)[1914]/ Wolfenbüttel HAB(2.3 Geogr 20, no. 43)[1906]. Reproduction: Bifolco and Ronca, 1: 382.

References:

Nordenskiöld, 1897, 160 (no. 118) and 161b; Nordenskiöld, 1899; Pulle, 1901-32, III, 147 and 150; Magnaghi, 1910, 103, 164 nt 4, and 166; Biasutti, 1920, 405; Bagrow, 1928-30, 1, 89-90; Tooley, 1939, 19-20 (nos. 54-60); Lazio, 1947, 26-27; Almagià, 1948, 36 and 63-66; Kammerer, 26-28 with pl. cxliii; Gallo, 1954, 28 (no. 74); Destombes, 1970, 87; Tibbets, 1978, 21-24 and 46; Schilder, 1981, 7; Schilder, 1987, 63-79; Meurcr, 1991, 150-51; Karrow, 1993, 238-39; Schilder, 1998, 109-11 and 114; Milanesi, in Dentoni Litta, et al, 2003, 53-55; Bifolco and Ronca, 2018, 1: 380-81.

Reproductions:

Bifolco and Ronca, 2018, 1; 380-81. https://www.loc.gov/resource/ g3200m.gct00410/?sp'67&st'single" https://collections.Newberry.org/asset-management/2KXJ8ZSKAJT6M? &WS

103. Eastern Asia

-Venice, 1561 (but bottom two sheets evidently ca. 1565/66, as see below)
-Copper engraving, originally 48.5 x 72.5 cm. (two sheets), but after addition
of bottom two sheets in ca. 1565/66, 63.0 x 72.5 (four sheets)
-300 Italian miles = 4.2 cm.

In a small text box below the island of Sri Lanka (Zeilan):
IL DISEGNO DELLA TERZA PARTE | DELL' ASIA | All' ill[ustrissi]mo
Sig[no]r il s[igno]r March Fucharo Barone Di | Kirchberg e d'
Waissenhoren:-- | Giacomo di Castaldi Piamõtese Cosmographo in Venetia
(MAP OF THE THIRD PART OF ASIA To the most illustrious Signor the
Signor Marcus Fugger Baron of Kirchberg and of Weissenhorn:-- Giacomo
di Castaldi Piedmontese Cosmographer in Venice)

In a small text box flush with right border about 6°-8° above the equator:
Congratia et priuilegio del sumo pontifice | papa pio iiii per Anni X | E Del
serenissino senato di venetia p[er] An- | ni XV (With grace and privilege of
the highest pontiff pope pius IV for 10 years And of the most serene senate
of Venice for 15 years)

Below the right part of this same text box:
Fabius licinius Excudebat (Fabio licinio publisher)

In the lower left corner of the map:
Si uende alla libraria d'1 San Marco in Venetia (Sold at the San Marco
bookshop in Venice)

The date of the map, 1561, occurs isolated at the top of a tablet giving
ancient and modern place name equivalents, at the right side of the map, as
see under comments below.

Comments:
This is the fourth of our six key maps. Its original edition, of 1561, included
only the top two sheets. The latitude graduation, indicated in numbered five-
degree increments, on both sides of the map, with no markings for individual

725

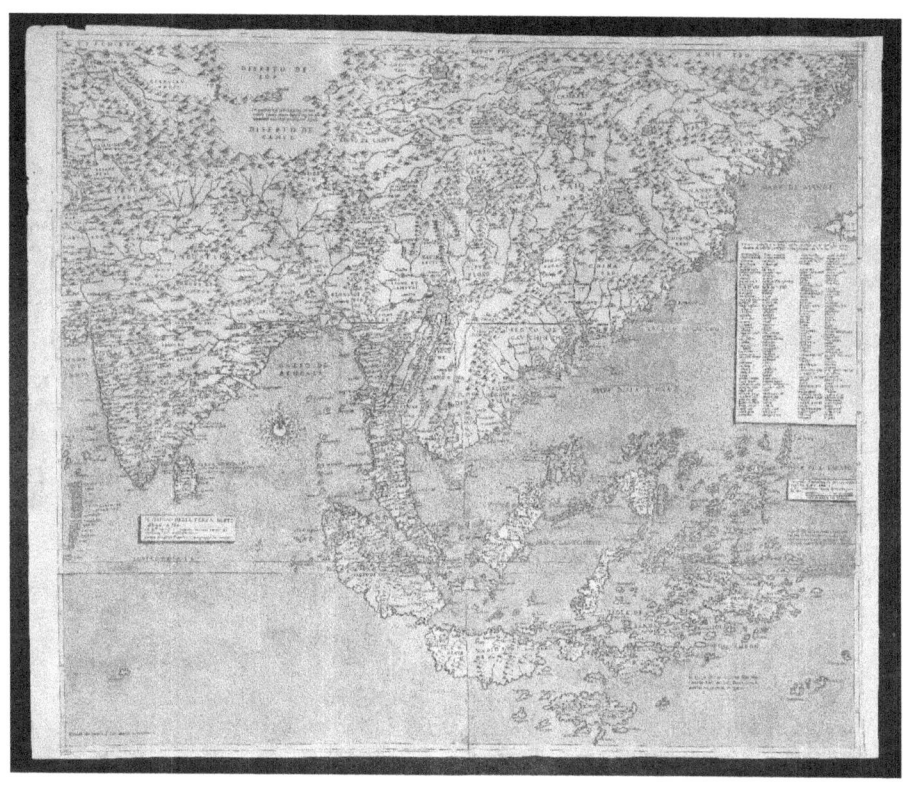

103 Eastern Asia 1565 or 66 Chicago Newb

degrees, runs from ca. 1°00' S to 50°10' N. The longitude graduation is shown only on the lower edge of the map, which is only about one degree south of the equator, and is shown, as with the latitude, only in numbered five-degree increments, with no markings for individual degrees, and runs from 110°00' to 190°00' E. Thus, one cannot say what projection is being used. Only after this original two-sheet edition had been on sale for a few years were the smaller two bottom sheets added (carrying the latitude down to ca. 17°30' S), as shown by Woodward (1990, 25 (no. 36), and, esp., 1992, 52). This, says Woodward, would have occurred ca. 1565/66, and the engraving was done by Paolo Forlani, although the cartography, certainly Gastaldi's, had probably been finished in manuscript by 1561. This four-sheet version is more common than the original two-sheet version of 1561, and in most cases, when this map was pasted together from its four sheets, the top edge of the lower sheets was, apparently intentionally, pasted high enough over the bottom edge of the upper sheets in order to obliterate the

726

approximately 4.5-millimeter-wide strip containing the longitude graduation. Perhaps, since the equator is drawn in, the presence, parallel to it and only about one degree south of it, of the two further horizontal lines making up the longitude strip, was found disconcerting. In any event, in almost all exemplars of the four-sheet version, the longitude graduation is thus obliterated, although examples exist where it was left showing, one being in the Ayer Collection at the Newberry Library, and another in the second Novacco Collection (assembled after Franco Novacco's first collection had been acquired by the Newberry), which is reproduced by Bella (1986, 18, no. 10).

An interesting and illuminating point concerned with the two added sheets of ca. 1565/66 is the presence of the little inscription quoted above telling us that the map was being sold at the famous San Marco shop of the Bertelli's. The only other Gastaldi map produced in his lifetime, besides these two 1565/66 sheets, which indicates publishing and vending by the San Marco shop is the 1564 Anatolia (no. 119), also engraved by Forlani, and certainly coming after the 1564 Africa, the last map engraved by Licinio. Concerning this fact and its significance to us, see our much lengthier discussion in chapter ten, in the section "Gastaldi and Licinio."

The present map differs in several ways from the first two Parts of Asia. For one thing, it is on considerably smaller scale. For another, while there exist separate lists of ancient and modern place name equivalents for the first two Parts of Asia, on the present map, this list occurs on a tablet in the map itself, at the right side of the map, a little above center. Oddly, at the head of this tablet is also found the map's date, 1561, not indicated elsewhere. Another point of difference is that this Third Part of Asia contains within the body of the map a good number of unboxed inscriptions, eighteen in all, describing some characteristic feature of a particular region, usually having to do with local customs, or with the presence in the area of some animal form (all of these inscriptions are quoted in full by Milanesi in Dentoni Litta, et al, 2003, 56-57). Finally, the map differs from the other two in its level of frequency in the Veneto-Roman atlases. Judging from the numbers, it was the most popular of all Gastaldi maps, evidently selling better not only than the other two Parts of Asia, but also better than the 1561 Italy, or any other map.

This popularity of our fourth key map is not surprising. It opens up, at a relatively large scale and in great detail (even if the detail is not always correct), a part of the earth which was extremely remote from Europe and was only very, very vaguely known before. It seems to take the map reader to the edge of the world, and certainly it did indeed take him to the extreme limits of European knowledge of the Old World at that time. And certainly too, it was this map, together with another of our key maps, the America (no. 94), which caused Gastaldi the greatest anguish, for, it was in creating these two maps that Gastaldi found himself willy-nilly in confrontation with the great question that so bewitched, but also perplexed and intractably foiled all geographers of the time, the relation between the Old World and the New World on the Pacific side. Gastaldi clearly spent much time pondering this question, and seeking an acceptable cartographic solution for it, and we have devoted much attention in our work to this great riddle of Gastaldi's time, and how he dealt with it. For references to the parts of our book where we deal with these intriguing topics, we refer the reader to our entry no. 92. For later editions of this map, see Almagià, 1948, 37 and 63-66; and Karrow, 1993, 239-40.

Location of copies:

The Third Part of Asia was originally published in two sheets, with a combined size of about 485 x 740 mm. In about 1565 or 1566 two smaller sheets (each about 155 x 370 mm), engraved by Forlani, were added at the bottom, extending the map southward to include archipelago Asia. Exemplars of the two-sheet version are: Leiden UB(COLLBN 002-07-021,022)/ Kobenhavn KB(KBK 1-51(61))/ Kobenhavn KB(KBK 2-2, v. 49, no. 17)/ Wien ÖNB(K I 109523 Kar)/ Paris BN(GE CC- 2224(3))/ Paris BN(GE CC- 1270(96))/ Paris BN(GE C- 9229)/ Paris BN(GE DD-5105(3))/ Roma BCas(Rari 1131, no. 58)[1982]/ Wolfenbüttel HAB(2.3 Geogr 20, no. 44)[1906]. Exemplars of the four-sheet version: Chicago Newb(VAULT Ayer 133.G25 1561/ Chicago Newb(Novacco 6F 40)/ Cambridge Harv(51-2494[in 3rd mat])/ Paris BN(GE DD- 655(82 RES))/ Paris BN(GE CC- 1380(68 RES))/ New York PL(*KB+++1572, no. 77)/ Basel UB(Kartenslg AA96-97)/ London BL(C.7.e.3, v. 1, nos. 12,13)[2003]/ PCK(BCzK 1243 V)[1992]/ Helsinki AEN(HN[Mickwitz 130](no. 62))

[1981]/ Firenze BN(12.-.44, v. 2, no. 17)[1980]/ Venezia BNM(138 c.4, no. 76)[1954]/ Washington LC(G1015 .L25 1575 Vault, no. 62)[1914]/ Dillingen SB(X,123, no. 126)[1911]. Exemplars unknown as to number of sheets: London BL(M.T.11.g.1.(6).)/ London BL(K.Top.115.21.)/ Madrid PR(MAP/454, no. 67)/ Madrid PR(MAP/438, no. 56)/ Sint-Niklaas KOKW(Atlas 408 IATO (no. 69)[1994]/ Firenze BN(12.-.44, v. 3, no. 69(68 written)[1980]/ Firenze BN(12.-.44, v. 4, no. 77(76 written)[1980]/ Greenwich NMM(C3995, no. 75)[1971]/ London RGS(Map Room, G.1, no. 67)[1929]/ London RGS(Map Room, 264.G.2, no. 62)[1915]/ Madrid PR(MAP/464, no. 108)[1915]

References:
Nordenskiöld, 1897, 160 (no. 118), and 161b; Nordenskiöld, 1899; Pulle, 1901-32, 3, 150 and 152-54; Dahlgren, 1916, *Hawaii*, 153; Hedin, 1917, xxv, xxvii, 179-86, 203, 232 and 243; Abendanon, 1915-18, 4, 1786; Herrmann, 1920, 211; Bagrow, 1928-30, 1, 90; Caraci, 1936, 123 and 124; Tooley, 1939, 20 (nos. 61-63); Almagià, 1948, 37 and 63-66; Gallo, 1954, 29 (no. 76); Wheatley, 1954, 67; Broek, 1962, 134-35; Quirino, 1963, 75-76; Destombes, 1970, 87; Roberts, 1973, 50-51; Schilder, 1981, 7; Gole, 1982, 18-20; Bella, 1986, 18 (no. 10); Schilder, 1987, 63-79; Woodward, 1990, 25 (no. 36); Meurer, 1991, 150-51; Woodward, 1992, 52 and 63 (no. 46); Karrow, 1993, 239-40; Schilder, 1998, 109-11 and 114; Suarez, 1999, 130-56, passim; Bury, 2001, 100-01; Milanesi, in Dentoni Litta, et al, 2003, 56-58; Bifolco and Ronca, 2018, 1; 384-87.

Reproductions:
Bifolco and Ronca, 2018, 1: 386-87.
https://www.loc.gov/resource/g3200m.gct00410/?sp'69&st'single"
https://collections.Newberry.org/asset-management/2KXJ8ZSAPADMO?&WS

104. World

-Venice, 1561 (original issue)

-Woodcut, ca. 90.0 x 182.0 cm., on ten sheets (eight full sheets and two half sheets)

-No scale bar

At the top border of the map:

COSMOGRAPHIA VNIVERSALIS ET EXACTISSIMA IUXTA POSTREMUM NEOTERICORVM TRADITIONEM (UNIVERSAL AND EXACT COSMOGRAPHY AFTER THE MOST RECENT SCHOLARSHIP)

And on the bottom border, continuing the above:

A IACOBO CASTALDIO NONNVLLISQUE ALIIS HVIVS DISCIPLINAE PERITISSIMIS NVNC P[RI]MVM REVISA AC INFINITIS FERE IN LOCIS CORRECTA ET LOCVPLETATA (BY IACOBUS CASTALDIUS AND [BY] SOME OTHERS MOST EXPERT IN THIS DISCIPLINE NOW FOR THE FIRST TIME REVIEWED AND IN NUMEROUS PLACES CORRECTED AND AUGMENTED)

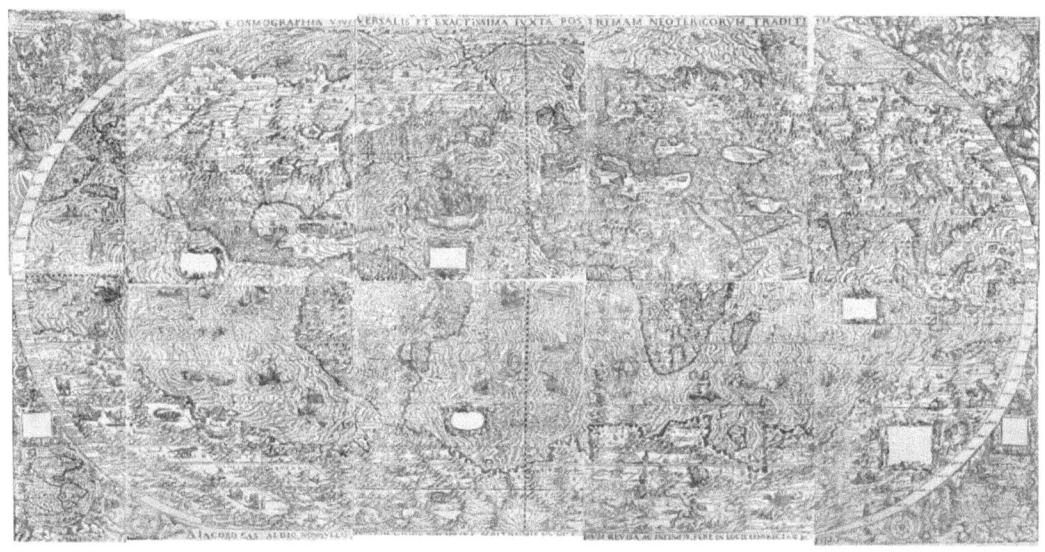

104 World 1561 London BL

Comments:

Graduated in whole degrees of latitude and longitude, along the prime meridian, which runs through both Madeira and Tenerife (just west of the middle of the Canaries), and the equator, numbered at every fifth degree, with parallels and meridians drawn in at every fifteen degrees, on an oval projection. This is the fifth of our six key maps (see entry 92 for the key maps), but it is very different from all the others, for it is a world map instead of a continental one, it is not engraved by Licinio, and it is a woodcut instead of a copperplate engraving. It was to be accompanied, at least in its earlier printings, by the booklet *La universale descrittione del mondo*, published, as the original edition of this map, by Matteo Pagano, and of which five editions are known, three in Italian (1561, 1562 and 1565) and three in Latin (1562, 1568, and 1571), on which see further in chapter two. It would seem that printings of the map occurred in all of these years. As with other key maps, for a full treatment we refer the reader to our main text, in the present case, chapter two.

Gastaldi had created a lasting world map model in 1546, with his "Vniversale" (no. 3), which was copied many times. In that model, he had shown Asia and America as connected by a broad land bridge, making them essentially one gigantic continent. Here he creates a new model, with a narrow strait separating Asia and America, making them definitely two separate and distinct continents. The model recurs through the 1560s in Italy, just as on this map, especially in the manuscript atlases of Joan Martines of Messina, and in the painted map series in the Vatican Terza Loggia, and in the painted series in the Guardaroba of the Palazzo Vecchio of the Medici family in Florence (see the last section of chapter six), and also in a somewhat hybrid form, in maps such as the "Totius Orbis Descriptio", touched on in chapter two, and the 1567 world map by Camocio (which also copies the main title of the present map), which combine much of the old model of 1546 with the new separation of the continents. At the end of the decade, the model began to be adopted outside Italy, in a slightly variant form giving greater bulk to North America, first with Mercator's 1569 world map, then with the world map in Ortelius's *Theatrum Orbis Terrarum* in 1570, after which it became the standard model for almost all cartographers' world maps.

This new model was basically the correct one. As we have stressed repeatedly, it was, in fact, the first world map to show all the world's major continents correctly in their main lineations, as a glance at the maps preceding it in Shirley instantly reveals to us. (One must bear in mind that, in the 1560 world map which is Shirley's no. 106, immediately preceding the present map, no. 107 there, the reproduction given for that map is a 1651 state, and reflects the continental separation between Asia and America established in 1561 in our map; the actual first state of his 106 is of the type of Gastaldi's 1546 world, with the continents solidly connected). It was, in short, no less than mankind's first generally correct map of the world. There could hardly be a better justification for having made the map than this, but we suspect that there was more to it. We recall that, when Gastaldi made this map, he was in the midst of his great project of creating copperplate maps of the continents and parts of Europe, in unison with his partner Licinio. But, as we have shown in chapter nine, he evidently felt constrained, until he had received more information, in particular information connected with the relation of America with Asia to the west, from committing himself to a depiction of America in a continental map, and he was especially undecided as to whether to show the two continents as connected or separated. But, as we saw in chapter eight, there were very good reasons to prefer the latter, reasons practical, esthetic, and perhaps psychological as well. The producing of this world map in woodcut was a far faster and less expensive proposition than producing it in copper, and how much less expensive, a major factor in our argument here, is probably not suspected by most. Woodward states, speaking of woodcuts: "Size for size, they cost about a tenth or a twelfth of the price of their copperplate equivalents" (1996, 33)! So here was a way to cheaply produce a world map which would act as a sort of self-affirmation, a statement by Gastaldi to himself that the depiction he chose was the correct depiction. Indeed, it was, although there was no way that Gastaldi or anyone could have been certain of this at the time. Thus, the woodcut world map allowed him to present his new idea to the world, even if he did not feel prepared to do this in a regional map, depicting but one continent. We may be going out on a limb somewhat here, for to be sure we can't read Gastaldi's mind, but we much suspect that the case was as stated.

A few comments on the fact that the map we reproduce is the only known copy of Gastaldi's famous map. As is shown irrefutably by several factors, presented in chapter two, there can be no question that the present copy gives us the depiction as produced by Gastaldi in 1561, and engraved for him by Matteo Pagano. But we know for several reasons that it is definitely not an exemplar of the original 1561 issue. The paper upon which the map is printed is apparently of the early seventeenth century, although, if the blocks from which our copy was printed are not the original blocks, they must have been cut by 1598 at the latest, since this is the death date of Philip II, who is depicted on the map in a way which clearly shows him as the current ruler. Also, the name of Pagano is missing, and the map's cartouches have been left empty. Furthermore, according to the text at the bottom of the map, quoted above, the map has been updated, though this can be taken with a grain of salt, since such claims were regularly made on maps to make the map seem more up to date, even if the changes were very small and insignificant, which is probably the case here. This surviving copy is not assembled, but on loose sheets, and on the excess paper below the bottom of the printing on the northeast sheet, we find a note, evidently written in pencil, which Pullè in 1932 (1901-32, III, 165) considered a recent jotting: "Riporodotta dal Jacobus de Judais Atlante del 1593." Clearly, whoever wrote this note was not well informed. The 1593 atlas referred to was the second edition of the *Speculum Orbis Terrarum* by Gerard (not Jacob!) de Jode (de Judaeis), and certainly this large map could not have been taken from anything in that atlas. Nevertheless, Pullè, evidently based on this little note, attributed the map to De Jode (cit., 165-67, and 182, at no. 8 in the list of plates, one of which is a reproduction of the northeast sheet). While Pullè's attribution is not justified, Gerard de Jode would in fact be a likely candidate for a later copying of Gastaldi's world map, for he created full-size new editions of Gastaldi's eight-sheet 1564 wall map of Africa, and of his 1561 Italy, as well as smaller editions of both of these maps, and also, for his *Speculum*, Gastaldi's three Parts of Asia (Karrow, 1993, respectively nos. 30/98.6, 30/90.2, 30/98.7 30/90.6, 30/85.3, 30/91.2 and 30/92.2); and the Officina Plantiniana account books seem to contain references to large Gastaldi world maps obtained from De Jode (Denucé, 1912-13, 1, 180). The problem here is that, to the best of my knowledge, neither De Jode nor his son Cornelis ever produced any woodcut maps. In any event, while perhaps not by De Jode, it seems likely that the present copy was printed from new blocks, and released by a new publisher, at a considerably later time than the original edition, perhaps in Italy, and perhaps somewhere else.

Location of copy:
London BL(Maps C.18.n.1) (only copy known). The British Library also has a photocopy at (Maps R.17.a.9), and the Newberry Library has a full 1979 photostat copy (Map 4F G3200 1561 .G3 1979).

References:
Pullè, 1901-32, 3, 160 and 165-67, with pl. 8; Almagià, 1939, "Intorno" ; Elte and Israel, 1978, 39 and 42-44; Shirley, 1987, no. 107; Astengo, 1990; Meurer, 1991, 149-50; Karrow, 1993, 240-41 (no. 30/93); Minella, 1993, 79-82; Bifolco and Ronca, 2018, 1: 246-49.

Reproductions:
Shirley, 1987, no. 107; Bifolco and Ronca, 2018, 1: 247-49; above.

105. World
-Venice, 1562
-Copperplate engraving, 39.5 x 67.5, on two sheets
-No scale bar

Along the top border of the map:
VNIVERSALE DESCRITTIONE DI TVTTA LA TERRA CONOSCIUTA FIN QVI (UNIVERSAL MAP OF ALL THE WORLD KNOWN TO NOW)

Along the bottom border:
IN VENETIA AL SEGNO DEL POZZO (IN VENICE AT THE SIGN OF THE WELL)

In the space outside the oval in the upper left corner, then continuing in the space outside the oval in the upper right corner, as indicated in the transcription:

AL MOLTO ILL[ustrissim]e SIG[no]or CÕTE GIER[oni]mo CANOSSA
SIG[no]r MIO SEMPRE OSS[ervantissi]mo | Molto tempo è ill[ustrissim]e
sig[n]or mio ch' ho un interno desiderio di dare al mondo | una Vniuersale
descrittione di tutta la terra conosciuta fin qui, al | qual desiderio ha dato
compimento l' ecc[elen]te m[esser] Giacomo gastaldo | cosmographo raro;
percioche egli questi mesi addietro me | ha dato un disegno, ó descrittione
uniuersale di tutta la | terra, per la piu piena et copiosa di quanti fin qui |
sene sono uedute; la quale hauendo io inta- | gliata inrame m' ha parso per
molti ri- | spetti farla uscir fuori sotto l'honor- | ato nome di V[ost]ra
Signoria ILL[ustrissim]e, | Impero che essendo ella di cosi nobile et
honorata famiglia | come è , son certo, che acce | ttata la protettione dell' |
opera, contra i mal | dicenti, iquali altro | non sa[nno] fare, che bia | simare
le altr- | ui operation- | ne mosse da buo | na et [From this point, the
dedication continues in the space outside the oval in the upper right corner of
the map] *na et* [repeated, perhaps intentionally] *utile intentione, spero poi*
oltre á cio, che l'opera da se le debba esser | cara, perche essendo V[ost]ra
Sig[no]ria ápar d'ogn'altra uirtuosá, et delattando si | sommamente delle
historie, con la qual lettione contempla i fatti d'suoi | progenitori, dalla uirtu
de quali uien stimulata sempre; et essendo | la geographia la chiaue per dir
cosi delle historie, et inquesto | Mappamondo uedendosi quasi tutta laterra
minutám te | descritta, et fidelmente, non dubbito punto, che | per
aleuiamento di pensieri et faticha ella | non lo debba hauer caro; et quando |
ella non l'hauesse grato per il suo | ualore, so che li sara gratissimo | per
non manchare alla sua | innata gentilezza et bonta, | alla quale di continuo |
mi raccomando, | D[i] V[ostro] S[ignor] ILLustre | protissimo ser[vo],
Paulo di for- | lani da | Verona (TO THE VERY ILLUSTRIOUS SIGNOR
COUNT GERONIMO CANOSSA MY ALWAYS REVERENT SIGNOR It is a
very long time my illustrious signor that I have had an internal desire to give
to the world a Universal map of all the world known to now, to which desire
the excellent master Giacomo gastaldo, exceptional cosmographer has given
fulfillment; for he gave me just a few months ago a drawing or universal map
of all the world, the most full and copious of any such seen up to now; [and]
having engraved it in copper, I judged for many reasons to have it brought
out under the honorable name of Your Illustrious Lordship, whose estate

being of such a noble and honored family as it is, I am certain, that you will accept the protection of the work, against the malcontents, who do nothing except fault others' operations advanced for good | [From this point, the dedication continues in the space outside of the oval in the upper right corner.] *and useful intentions: I hope then other than that, that the work in itself should be a thing of value, because Your Lordship being most of all a virtuous person, and delighting exceedingly in history, with the reading of which you contemplate the deeds of your progenitors, by the valor of which one is always stimulated; and geography being the key of history, and seeing in this Mappamondo almost all the lands minutely depicted, and faithfully, I do not doubt at all, that you surely will not find compensation of efforts and labors too expensive, and if you might not judge it a worthy thing, I know there will be much gratitude for [your] not failing in your innate kindness and goodness, to which I continuously turn in entreaty. Paulo di forlani of Verona most willing servant of Your Illustrious Lord)* [**Note:** The last few lines of this endless dedication are translated very freely indeed here, for Forlani's stilted syntax near the end becomes so impenetrable that a more literal translation is impossible, at least for the present writer.]

In the space outside the oval in the lower left corner:
À BENIGNI | LETTORI | Paulo di forlani | da Verona | Eccoui benigni Letto- | ri una nuoua descritti- | one di tutto il mondo, la | quale è la piu particolare, fidele, | giusta, et conformi alle nauigati- | oni et historie di quanti fin qui sene | sono uedute da noi: resta hora, che si co- | me da me è uolontiere per utilita commune | data al mondo, cosi parimente sia da uoi | accettata; percioche mentre, che jo uedrò poi, | che ui sara cara, mi sforzero appresso darui cose, | che non solamente non ui saranno discare, ma ui saran | de utile, et giouamento grandissimo, In Venetia l'anno | M D LXII. (TO THE GOOD READERS Paulo di forlani of Verona Here for you good Readers [is] a new map of all the world, which is the most detailed, true, correct, and in conformity with the voyages and histories of any which have been seen by you up until now; now it remains, that just as it is given by me to the world for the utility of all, that it thus be likewise accepted by you; for whereas if I later see, that it will be a useful thing to you, I will strive later on to give you

things, which not only will not be refused by you, but will be of the greatest usefulness and benefit to you. In Venice, the year 1562.

In the space outside the oval in the lower right corner:
IL modo | di trouare | la distanza | delle miglia tra | due luoghi per que | sta descrettione del | mondo. | Volendo trouare la dista- | nza tra due luoghi che sia- | no posti in questa descrittione | uniuersale, metterai un de' piedi | del compasso nell'uno de luoghi, et di- | stenderai l'altro piedi nell'altro luogo, | et senza piu stringere, ò slargare il comp- | asso et il metterai cosi aperto nell'equinotiale | della carta, conterai poi quanti gradi di quell- | lo, sono tra l'uno et l'altro piede del compasso, et qu- | el numero di gradi multiplicherai per, 60, et quel che ne | uerra saraño i miglia italiani tra quei due luoghi, auertendo, che | quella distanza si piglia per drittissima linea et non si considera obliquita | di uiaggio qui non accade essempio se si è inteso quel che s'è detto. (The method of finding the distance in miles between two places on this map of the world. [A short blank space follows these words, which thus are to be taken as a title to what follows.] *Wishing to find the distance between two places which are put on this universal map, place one of the legs of a compass on one of the places, and extend the other leg to the other place, and without further lessening or increasing the compass place it thus opened on the equator of the map, then count how many degrees of it* [the equator] *there are between the one and the other leg of the compass, and multiply this number of degrees by 60 and that which will be the result of this will be the Italian miles between these two places, bearing in mind, that this distance is gotten by a completely straight line and the obliquity of the traveling is not considered [but] it does not affect the example if that which has been said is heeded.)*

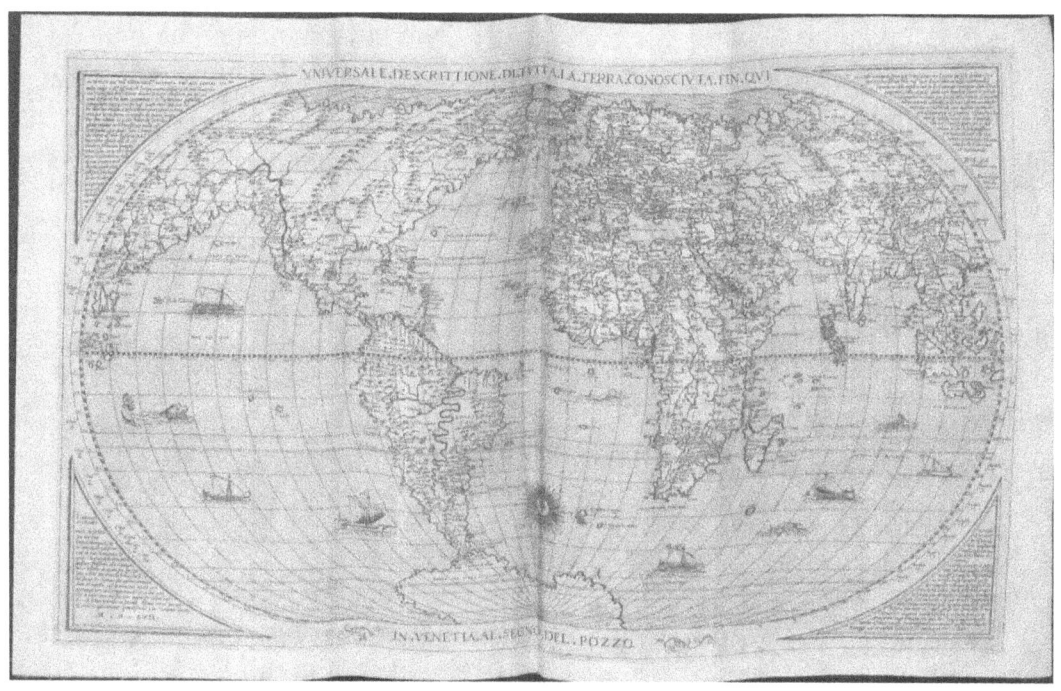

105 World 1562 LondonBL

Comments:
Graduated in whole degrees, in latitude and longitude, for latitude on the two sides of the oval, and in longitude on the equator, with each fifth degree numbered, and with the parallels and meridians drawn in at ten-degree intervals, on an oval projection. The prime meridian runs through the eastmost of the Canaries, unnamed on the map (Lanzarote?). There is some question as to how valid it is to consider this as a separate and new map, instead of just a derivative of Gastaldi's 1546 world map (no. 3). Bagrow treated it as a distinct map (1928-30, 1, 91, no. 97), but Karrow treats it as a derivative of the 1546 map (1993, 219, no. 30/3.3). Grande strongly considers it a new product (1902, 50, and, esp., 1905, *carte*, 119-22), but Grande regularly strains to paint the rosiest possible picture of Gastaldi, and wished to maximize the number of maps that Gastaldi made. Tooley seems to take a middle of the road stance, and his words sum up the situation well: "A new edition of Gastaldi's map, fundamentally the same as the edition of 1546, but engraved on a larger scale with new lettering, symbols and decorations, some new names, viz. Nueva Franza, Larcadia, etc., and a notable alteration in the river sytem of America" (1939, 16, no. 9). All in all,

while we tend a bit towards Karrow's stance, we have included the map as a separate entity, partly due to the changes enumerated by us in chapter eight, but partly due to the indirect consideration that the map plays a fundamentally crucial role in our demonstration in chapter eight that Gastaldi never really resolved completely the question of whether the continents of Asia and America were connected or separated. Forlani's exhaustingly lengthy, obsequious, and sometimes all but syntactically inscrutable dedication makes for tiresome reading, but it unquestionably provides us with some meat to chew on as regards the as yet never satisfactorily answered question of what these old map dedications are all about. See Woodward (1990, 5-8) for later issues of this map or variant.

Location of copies:
London BL(Maps K.Top.IV.4)/ ÖNB (K I 109.527). Before the present Cartobibliography, the British Library edition was the only one known in the English language literature. There is still a third copy in the Archivio di Stato di Torino, but I have not been able to succeed in getting its call number. It is cited by Fiorini, 1895, 193 nt 2; Grande, 1905, *carte*, 120; and Minella, 1993, 83.

References:
Fiorini, 1895, 193 with nt. 2; Grande, 1902, 50; Grande, 1905, *carte*, 119-20; Bagrow, 1928-30, 1, 91, no. 97; Tooley, 1939, 16, no. 9; Shirley, 1987, no. 112; Woodward, 1990, 5-8; Karrow, 1993, 219, no. 30/3.3; Minella, 1993, 83-85; Bifolco and Ronca, 2018, 1: 250.

Reproductions:
Shirley, 1986, no. 112; Bifolco and Ronca, 2018, 1:251; here.

106. Northeast Europe
-Venice, 1562
-Copper engraving, 53.0 x 75.5 cm., on two sheets
-100 Italian miles = 4.6 cm.

In text box at far right of lower sheet, about 5 cm. below the top of the sheet:

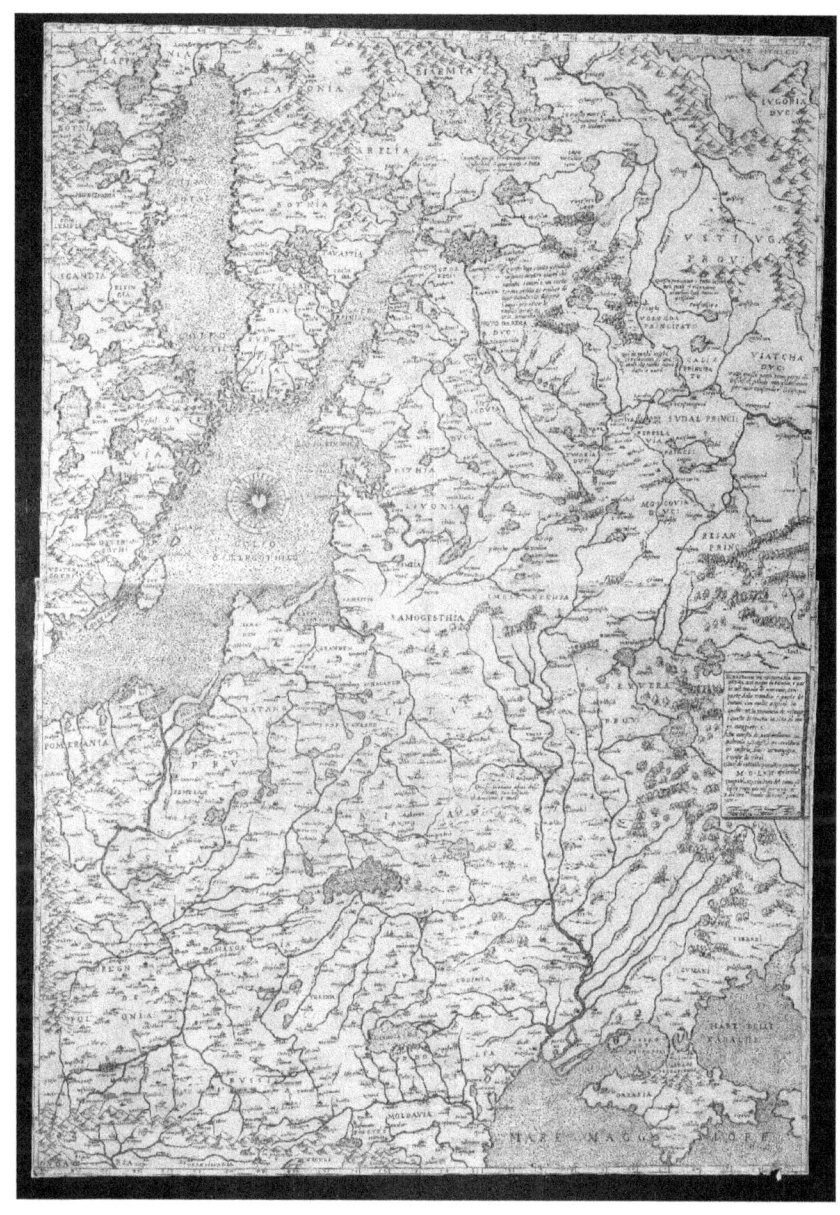

106 Northeast Europe 1562 Chicago Newb

*IL DISEGNO DE GEOGRAFIA MO |DERNA Del Regno di Polonia, e par |
te Del Ducado di Moscouia, con: | parte della Scandia, e parte de Sueuia,
con molte Regioni, in | quelli. Et la prouincia di Vstiuga, e quella di seuera
in sino al | re maggiore. | Alla maesta de Massimiliano Di | Bohemia ecc.
ecc. Re Arciduca | De Austria, Duc:De Borgogna, | e Conte de Tirol |*

Giac[om]o di castaldi, piamõtese cosmogr | afo | in vene[ti]a, | M.D.LXII. | Congratia et priuilegio del sumo põtifice papa pio iiij per Anni BX- | e del sere[nissi]mo senato di vene[ti]a, p[er] anni | XV. (MAP OF THE MODERN GEOGRAPHY of the Kingdom of Poland, and part of the Duchy of Moscovia, with part of Scandinavia, and part of Sweden, with many regions in the latter. And the province of ustiuga, and that of severa as far as the great sea. To his majesty, Maximilian of Bohemia etc. etc. Royal Archduke Of Austria, Duke Borgogno, and Count of Tirol. Giacomo Gastaldi Piedmontese cosmographer in Venice, 1562. | With grace and privilege of the supreme pontiff pope pius IV for 10 years and from the most serene senate of Venice for 15 years.)
The scale bar follows, beneath which is:
fabio li[cini]o f[ecit]. (engraved by fabio licinio)

Comments:
Graduated in full degrees, with each degree numbered, in latitude and longitude, from 48°00' to ca. 70°25' N, at the top from ca. 31°20' to 75°00' E, and, at the bottom, from ca. 40°50' to 65°15' E, on a trapezoidal projection. The map, to which so far no major study or discussion has been devoted, has drawn much less attention than the map of southeastern Europe (our no. 96). It covers all but a small westernmost sliver of modern Poland, the north half of the Ukraine, all of Belarus and all of the Baltic countries, most of Finland, part of western European Russia, and about the eastern half of Sweden. Although on a considerably smaller scale, it was, says Almagià, made as accompaniment to the map of southeastern Europe, and the present author completely agrees with this (although there are only twenty-four minutes of overlap between the two maps), and thus the two maps together cover eastern Europe. But the conclusion must not be drawn from this fact, as one could easily do, that the implication is that Gastaldi necessarily intended to make corresponding maps to cover western Europe as well. While such an idea is possible, it is unlikely (see chapter ten for a thorough discussion).

As to sources, Almagià considered that it preserved some of the elements of Gastaldi's own 1546 Danube countries map (no. 4), and for the area of the Black Sea followed closely the 1550 Moscovia, also of Gastaldi himself (no. 67), but that for the principal parts of Poland it used Grodecki's map of 1557 (mistakenly said by Almagià to be of 1558), and he stated that "it represents a sagacious elaboration of various sources" (Almagià, 1948, 40). Buczek, and after him Bagrow, considered that the map was taken from Mercator's 1558 Europe, but both essentially state that Gastaldi changed so many things that the original source seems lost, which to this writer suggests simply that the source suggested was the wrong one altogether. Finally, Kret, a Polish scholar, comes to Gastaldi's defense: "Buczek asserts, that Gastaldi's map is a clumsy and deformed adaptation from Mercator's map of Europe, published in 1544 . . . But one must point out, that the Gastaldi map, at least in its composition and territorial scope, corresponds to the lost map of Poland of Bernard Wapowski of 1526; and corresponds as well to the earlier work of Gastaldi from 1546. It is in any event the most magnificent map that Jagiellonian Poland obtained in the sixteenth century." (Kret, 1978, 37-38). The 1546 map Kret refers to is Gastaldi's 1546 map of eastern Central Europe (no. 4), mentioned above by Almagià as a source.

I much incline to the views of Almagià and Kret, which in fact are similar, for Grodecki's map itself was based on Wapowski's, so this is actually the same line of derivation. But we can add some important observations. This is Gastaldi, who regularly made use of textual sources, and who, the record seems to show (see chapter ten, note 45), was averse to simply copying other cartographers' maps without making some original additions of his own, and Kret's observations that the map corresponds to Wapowski's 1526 Poland, but that it is the most magnificent map of Poland of the sixteenth century implies that it has more to it than Wapowski's map alone. In fact, I think we may consider it as virtually certain that Gastaldi made use of the Italian edition of Maciej z Miechowa's history of the two Sarmatias, *Historia delle dve Sarmatie*, edited by the Venetian cartographer and translator of Bembo's poetry Tommaso Porcacchi, and published in Venice in 1561 by Gabriel Giolito. Giolito had published Gastaldi's map of Germany (no. 70), and I think it likely that it was precisely the publication of this translation that instigated Gastaldi to make this map the year after the book was published. The map, however, still awaits an in-depth study. Toward that end I note that in her preface to Kret's work, Maria Kielczewska-Zaleska observes that the main deficiencies in the map are west of the Vistula (in her preface to Kret's work, p. 11). On the single later edition of this map, see Almagià (1934, 147), Kret (1978, 39-40), and Karrow (1993, 242-43).

Location of copies:
Chicago Newb(Novacco 2F 96)/ Leiden UB(COLLBN 002-06-011,012)/ Paris BN((GE DD- 628 (59 69 RES)/ Paris BN(GE D- 13713)/ Paris BN(GE DD- 655(39,1-2 RES))/ Paris BN(GE DD- 1140 (28,1-2 RES))/ Copenhagen KB(KBK 1-51(453))/ Madrid PR(MAP/454, nos. 27,28)/ Madrid PR(MAP/ 438, nos. 22,23)/ London BL(Maps C.7.e.1, nos. 47,48)[2003]/ Roma BCas(Rari 1131, nos. 20,21)[1982]/ Firenze BN(12.-.44, v. 1, no. 88)[1980]/ Firenze BN(12.-.44, v. 3, nos. 26,27(25,26 written)[1980]/ Firenze BN(12.-.44, v. 4, nos. 32,33 (31,32 written))[1980]/ Greenwich NMM(C3995, nos. 32,33)[1971]/ Venezia BNM(138 c.4, nos. 23,24)[1954]/ London RGS(Map Room, 264.G.1, nos. 24,25)[1929]/ Madrid PR(MAP/464, nos. 35,36)[1915]/ Dillingen SB(X,122, nos. 31,32)[1911]/ Dillingen SB(X,123, nos. 56,57)[1911]/ Wolfegg SW(Histor. Geogr. 169, nos. 14,16) [1911]/ Roma BN(711.6.G.1, nos. 20,21)[1876]

References:
Almagià, 1934, 146-47; Almagià, 1948, 39-40; Buczek, 1966, 44; Bagrow, 1975, 88-90; Kret, 1978, 11 (in Maria Kielczewska-Zaleska's preface) and 37-38; Karrow, 1993, 242-43; Bifolco and Ronca, 2018, 2: 1198.

Reproductions:
Kret, 1978, atlas/portfolio, pl. 10 a,b; Bifolco and Ronca, 2018, 2: 1199. These are the only reproductions I know of showing both of the two sheets, top (north),. and bottom (south) together. However, separate reproductions of the two sheets exist: bottom (south) sheet in Kordt, 1st Ser., Part 1 (1899), pl. 22; and top (north) sheet in Bagrow, 1975, p. 94, fig. 44.
https://collections.Newberry.org/asset-management/2KXJ8ZSA2XX55? &WS (both sheets)
https://gallica.bnf.fr/ark:/12148/btv1b8491878k/f1.item.zoom (lower sheet)

(107.-117.) An incomplete series of eleven maps intended for an edition of Strabo, ca. 1562(?)

This set of maps first came to light in a large previously unknown Lafrerian type atlas which came up for sale at auction in 1999, and which was acquired by the Bavarian State Library in 2014. This atlas also contains an incomplete series of maps for an unrealized edition of Ptolemy. For the general background on this see our composite entry (97.-100.) above, where the Strabonian maps are dealt with as well, and the reader who is principally interested in the Strabobian maps is referred there also, where, among other things will be found my rationale for dating the Strabonian maps as ca. 1562 (?). As with the Ptolemaic maps, the copies of these Strabonian maps which occur in the atlas are unique with one exception, the map of Italy, which has been known in a slightly different variant since 1881, when it was first brought to light by Giovanni Marinelli (1881, 133, no. 634). Like the Ptolemaic maps, all the Strabonian maps are unsigned and undated.

These Strabonian maps hold a stronger element of interest than the incomplete Ptolemaic series, not just because the Strabo set is larger, but because there had, I believe, never before been an edition of Strabo which included maps. Strabo himself, as far as we know, never made any maps, although in his *Geography* he describes how to make maps (see Harley and Woodward, 1987, 173-75). It was because of the special interest of these maps that the original purchasers of the atlas in which they occur decided to give to the whole series the appellation "Strabo Illustratus Atlas" (the Bavarian State Library does not employ this term but calls it the "Lafreri-Atlas"). For further information on this atlas, and the Strabonian maps, see Meurer (2004, esp. pp. 5-7, and the individual entries there at pp. 35-43, 46 and 74).

107. Southern Germany and Illyria (Strabonian)
-[Venice?], n.d. [ca. 1562?]
-Copper engraving, 23.5 x 38.5 (plate size), on one sheet
-100 Italian miles = 4.8 cm.

The map has no title, but within the map at left center is a note:

Questa parte qui dispora della Sueuia | et Retia, Vindelicia, et Norica, Strabone | la descriue nel fine del quarto libro con | la Gallia, ame pare chestia bene in | questa tauola (This part here consists of Swabia and Rhaetia, Vindelicia, and Noricum, Strabo describes it at the end of the fourth book, with Gallia, to me it seems that it fits well in this map)

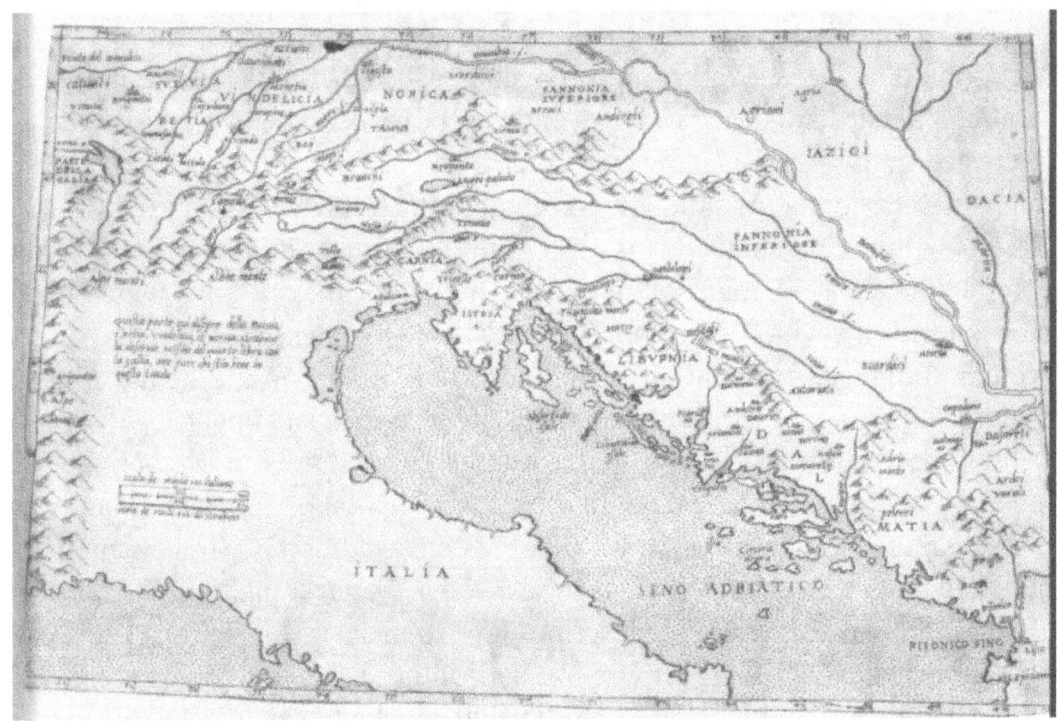

107 Southern Germany and Illyria (Strabonian) 1562? München SB

Comments:
Graduated in whole degrees, each numbered, in latitude and longitude, from 41°40' to 48°30' N, and from ca. 29°20' to 45°00' E, on a trapezoidal projection. The first of the Strabonian maps (according to the order in which they occur in the atlas). The coasts and hydrography are copied from Gastaldi's large map of Southeast Europe (our no. 95), while the nomenclature is taken from Strabo's *Geography* (Meurer, 2004, 35).

Location of copy:
The only known copy is in the Lafreri-Atlas (München SB(2 Mapp. 464))

References:
Meurer, 2004, 35, no. 21; Bifolco and Ronca, 2018, 2: 1322.
.

Reproductions:
Meurer, 2004, no. 21; Bifolco and Ronca, 2018, 2: 1322-23.
https://www.digitale-sammlungen.de/en/view/bsb00107640?page'25"

108. Iberian Peninsula (Strabonian)
-[Venice?], n.d. [ca. 1562?]
-Copper engraving, 26.0 x 35.5 cm. (plate size), on one sheet
-10 Italian miles = 3.4 miles

Above the top border:
Disegno della spagna, secondo la descritione della Geografia di strabone, nel libro Terzo Tavola I (Map of Spain, according to the description in the Geography of strabo, in the Third book First Map)

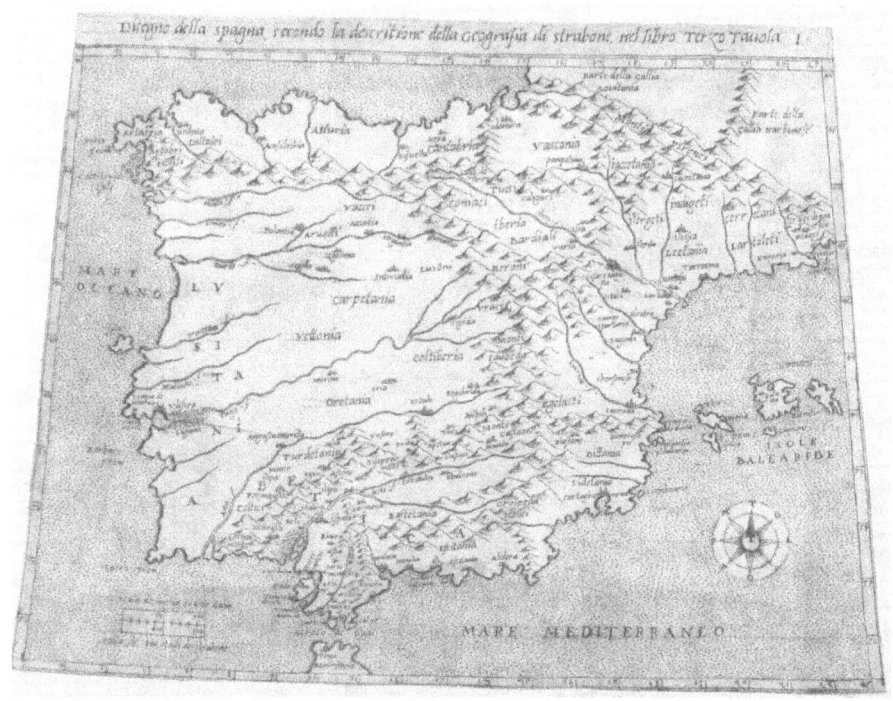

108 Iberian Peninsula (Strabonian) 1562? München SB

Comments:
Graduated in whole degrees, each numbered, in latitude and longitude, from 35°25' to 46°00' N, and from 3°00' to 23°00' E, on a trapezoidal projection. Meurer had considerable difficulty trying to discover the sources of this map, noting that it resembles the Gastaldi modern Spain from the new Ptolemy series (our no. 99), but differs much from other contemporary maps of the area, including Gastaldi's own 1544 Spain (no. 1), and he suggests that we have here the traces of a late work by Gastaldi which was not published elsewhere, an interesting proposition which we shall not attempt to follow up at the moment. The place names are taken from book 3 of Strabo (Meurer, 2004, 36, no. 22).

Location of copy:
The only known copy is in the Lafreri-Atlas (München SB(2 Mapp. 464))

References:
Meurer, 2004, 36, no. 22; Bifolco and Ronca, 2018, 2: 1121.

Reproductions:
Meurer, 2004, no. 22; Bifolco and Ronca, 2018, 2: 1121.
https://www.digitale-sammlungen.de/en/view/bsb00107640?page'26"

109. Western Greece (Strabonian)
-[Venice?], n.d. [ca. 1562?]
-Copper engraving, 26.0 x 34.0 cm. (plate size), on one sheet
-100 Italian miles = 6.7 cm.

Above the upper border:
Disegno della Macedonia. Et epiro. Secondo la descrittione della Geografia di Strabone nel libro settimo et nel principio dil X uisione gli Acornani et i Locri. Tauola VIII. (Map of Macedonia. And Epirus. According to the description in the Geography of strabo in book seven and at the beginning of the 10th [unclear phrase]. Eighth Map.)

109 Western Greece (Strabonian) 1562? München SB

Comments:
Graduated in whole degrees, each numbered, in latitude and longitude, from ca. 37°25' to 42°40' N, and from 42°30' to 51°35' E, on a rectangular projection. The third Strabonian map. Coastlines and hydrography are taken from Gastaldi's map of Greece (no. 95), while the toponyms are from books 7 and 8 of Strabo's *Geography* (Meurer, 2004, 37, no. 23).

Location of copy:
The only known copy is in the Lafreri-Atlas (München SB(2 Mapp. 464))

References:
Meurer, 2004, 37, no. 23; Bifolco and Ronca, 2018, 2: 1434.

748

Reproductions:
Meurer, 2004, no. 23; Bifolco and Ronca, 2018, 2: 1435.
https://www.digitale-sammlungen.de/en/view/bsb00107640?page'27

110. The Peloponnesus (Strabonian)
-[Venice?], n.d. [ca. 1562?]
-Copper engraving, 26.0 x 35.5 (plate size), on one sheet
-60 Italian miles = 6.2 cm.

Above the top border:
Disegno del Peloponeso secondo la descrittione della Geografia di Strabone
nel libro ottauo Tauola VIIII. (Map of the Peloponnesus according to the
description in the Geography of Strabo in the eighth book Ninth Map)

110 The Peloponnesus (Strabonian) 1562? München SB

Comments:
Graduated in whole degrees, each numbered, in latitude and longitude, from 35°25' to 38°30' N, and from 46°45' to 51°50' E, on a trapezoidal projection. Meurer found the topographical basis of this map to be not clear, although the basic outline again follows Gastaldi's Greece (no. 95), but with much more hydrography. As in all of the Strabonian maps, the nomenclature is from Strabo (Meurer, 2004, 38, no. 24).

Location of copy:
The only known copy is in the Lafreri-Atlas (München SB(2 Mapp. 464))

References:
Meurer, 2004, 38, no. 24; Bifolco and Ronca, 2018, 2: 1437.

Reproductions:
Meurer, 2004, no. 24; Bifolco and Ronca, 2018, 2: 1437.
https://www.digitale-sammlungen.de/en/view/bsb00107640?page'28

111. Central Italy (Strabonian)
-[Venice?], n.d. [ca. 1562?]
-Copper engraving, 26.5 x 37.0 cm. (plate size), on one sheet
-50 Italian miles = 8.5 cm.

Above the upper border:
Disegno particolare de parte d'Italia, secondo la descritionc della geografia di strabone la quale non s'a potesto descriuerla nel disegno dell'italia ch' e nel fine del sesto libro | ma per magior lucidatione di quelle ch' a descritto strabone nel quinto libro suo s'a fatto questa tauola iiii. (Detailed map of part of Italy, according to the description in the Geography of Strabo which it was not possible to include in the map of italy, which is at the end of the sixth book, but for greater elucidation of that which strabo described in his fifth book this fourth map has been made).

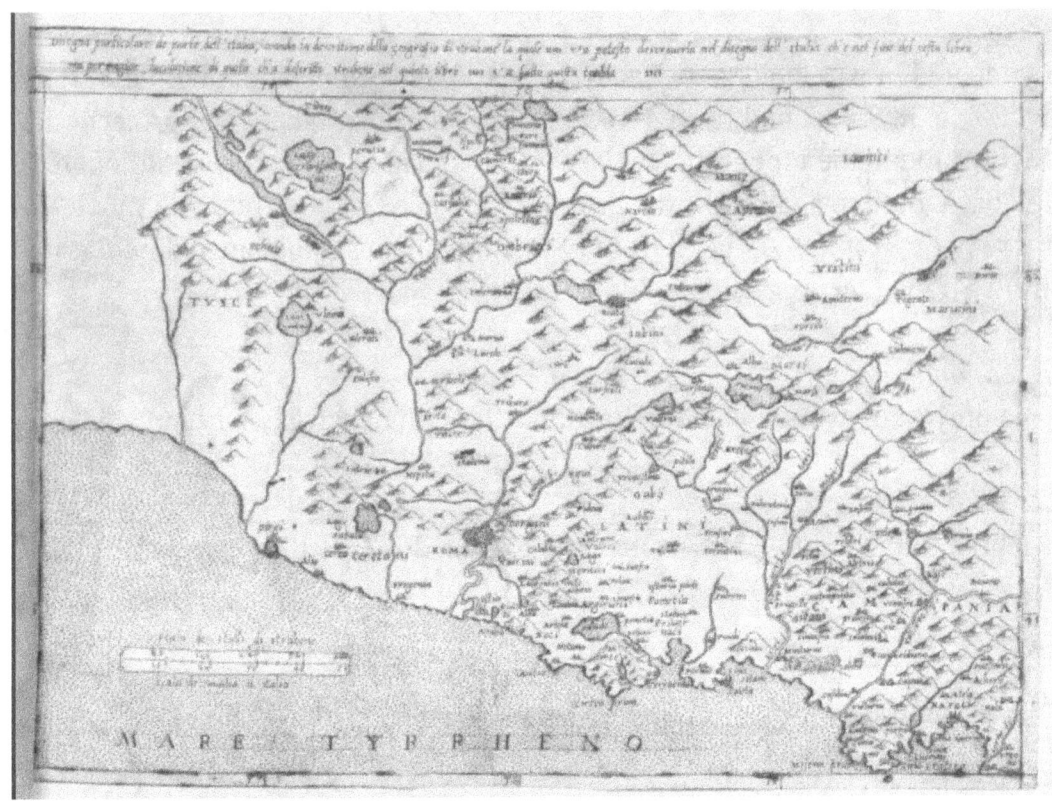

111 Central Italy (Strabonian) 1562? München SB

Comments:
Graduated in whole degrees, each numbered, in latitude and longitude, from
40°35' to 42°35' N, and from 34°50' to 38°00' E, on a trapezoidal projection
with barely discernible convergence of meridians due to the small area
covered. Interestingly, Meurer found that this fourth Strabo map is mainly
based on Gastaldi's 1561 Italy (no. 101) but supplemented by regional maps.
We shall not attempt to pursue this determination further. As usual, the place
names are from Strabo.

Location of copy:
The only known copy is in the Lafreri-Atlas (München SB(2 Mapp. 464))

References:
Meurer, 2004, 39, no. 25; Bifolco and Ronca, 2018, 3:2028.

Reproductions:
Meurer, 2004, no. 25; Bifolco and Ronca, 2018, 3: 2029.
https://www.digitale-sammlungen.de/en/view/bsb00107640?page'29

112. Thrace and the Crimea (Strabonian)
-[Venice?], n.d. [ca. 1562?]
-Copper engraving, 25.0 x 34.0 (plate size), on one sheet
-100 Italian miles = 3.0 cm.

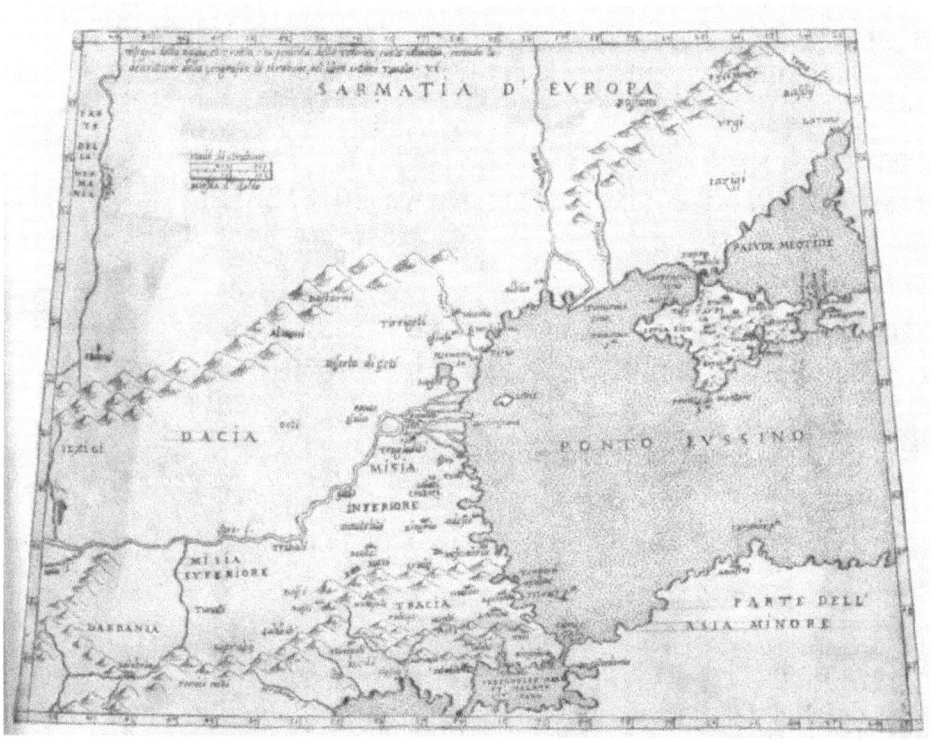

112 Thrace and the Crimea (Strabonian) 1562? München SB

At the upper left, within the border:
Disegno della Dacia, et tratia, e la penisola della Taurica, con la salmatia, secondo la | descrittione della geografia di strabone, nel libro settimo. Tauola VI. (Map of Dacia, and thrace, and the Peninsula Taurica [Crimean Peninsula]*, with sarmatia, according to the description in the geography of strabo, in the seventh book. Sixth Map.)*

Comments:
Graduated in whole degrees, each numbered, in latitude and longitude, from 42°00' to 54°00' N, and from 43°00' to 65°00' E, on a trapezoidal projection. Meurer found that the map is a combination of elements from Gastaldi's map of Southeast Europe (no. 96), and his First Part of Asia (no. 92), along with the description in book 7 of Strabo's *Geography.*

Location of copy:
The only known copy is in the Lafreri-Atlas (München SB(2 Mapp. 464))

References:
Meurer, 2004, 40, no. 26; Bifolco and Ronca, 2018, 2: 1212.

Reproductions:
Meurer, 2004, no. 26; Bifolco and Ronca, 2018, 2: 1213.
https://www.digitale-sammlungen.de/en/view/bsb00107640?page'30

113. Northern Germany (Strabonian)
-[Venice?], n.d. [ca. 1562?]
-Copper engraving, 26.0 x 36.5 (plate size), on one sheet
-No scale bar

Above the top border:
Disegno dela germania, secondo la descrittione della geografia di strabone nel Libro settimo. Tavola V. (Map of germany, according to the description of the geography of strabo in the seventh book. Fifth Map.)

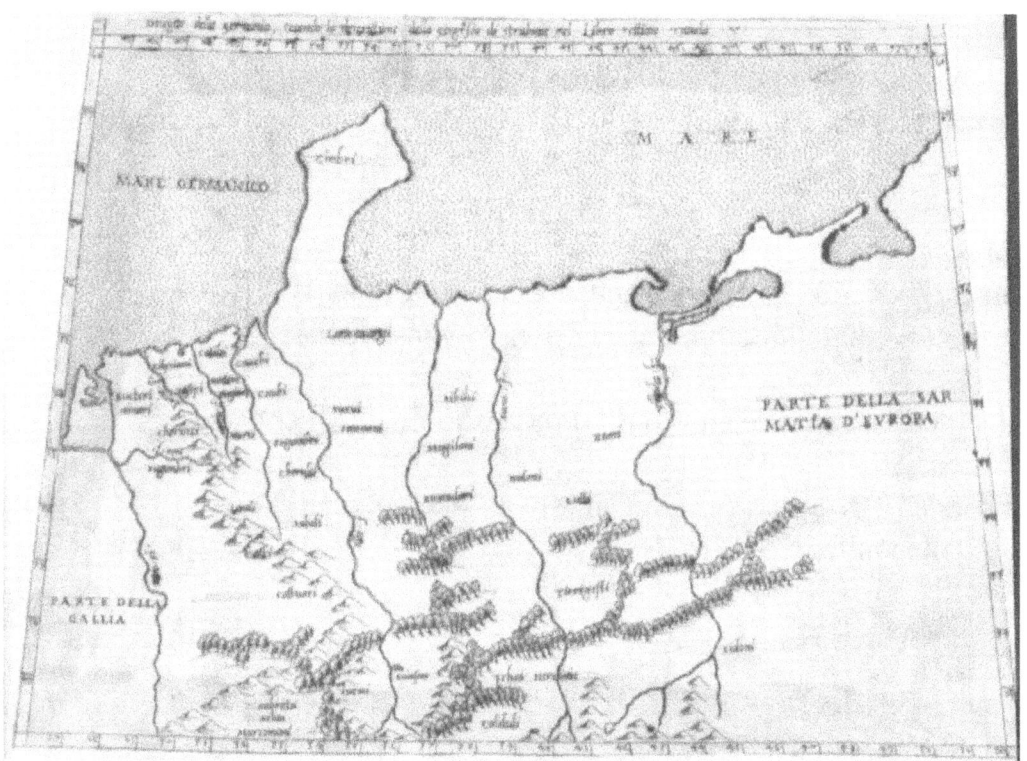

113 Northern Germany (Strabonioan) 1562? München SB'

Comments:

Graduated in whole degrees, each numbered, in latitude and longitude, from 48°00' to 60°00' N, in latitude. In longitude, there has been some blunder (perhaps an engraver's?), for the upper graduation runs from 25°00' to 54°00', while the lower border runs from 26°00' to 52°00'. The projection was intended to be trapezoidal. For this map, Meurer has made some quite interesting determinations, which we cannot at present follow up. The principal source would seem to be Anthoniszoon's map of the area around the North Sea and the Baltic Sea (of which a later edition is reproduced in Meurer, no. 8), while the coasts east of the Vistula River reflect Heinrich Zell's map of Prussia of 1542 in its first edition. As always with this map series, the nomenclature stays strictly with Strabo's *Geography.*

Location of copy:

The only known copy is in the Lafreri-Atlas (München SB(2 Mapp. 464))

754

References:
Meurer, 2001, p. 46; .Meurer, 2004, 41, no. 27; Bifolco and Ronca, 2018, 2: 898.

Reproductions:
Meurer, 2004, no. 27; Bifolco and Ronca, 2018, 2: 899.
https://www.digitale-sammlungen.de/en/view/bsb00107640?page'31

114. Northern Asia Minor and lands to the East (Strabonian)
-[Venice?], n.d. [ca. 1562?]
-Copper engraving, 24.5 x 38.5 cm. (plate size), on one sheet
-200 Italian miles = 3.4 cm.

114 Northern Asia Minor and lands to the East (Strabonian) 1562? München SB

Along the top border:
Disegno della Sogdiana, Battriana, Hircania, Parthia, et Media, Secondo la Geografia di Strabone, nel libro Vndecimo. Tauola [number missing]. (*Map of Sogdania* [Transoxiana], *Bactria, Hircania, Parthia* [Khurasan], *and Media, According to the Geography of Strabo, in the Eleventh book. Map number* [number missing].*)*

Comments:
Graduated in whole degrees, each numbered, in latitude and longitude, from 34°00' to 54°00' N, and from 84°00' to 122°00' E, on a trapezoidal projection. Meurer found that the map combines the depiction in the First Part of Asia by Gastaldi with toponyms from Strabo's *Geography.*

Location of copy:
The only known copy is in the Lafreri-Atlas (München SB(2 Mapp. 464))

References:
Meurer, 2004, 42, no. 28.

Reproductions:
Meurer, 2004, no. 28.
https://www.digitale-sammlungen.de/en/view/bsb00107640?page'32

115. France (Strabonian)
-[Venice?], n.d. [ca. 1562?]
-Copper engraving, 26.0 x 34.0 cm. (plate size), on one sheet
-100 Italian miles = 3.4 cm.

Above the top border:
Disegno della Gallia secondo la descrittione della Geografia di Strabone, nel libro Quarto Tauola II. (Map of France [Gaul] *according to the description in the Geography of Strabo, in the Fourth book Second Map.)*

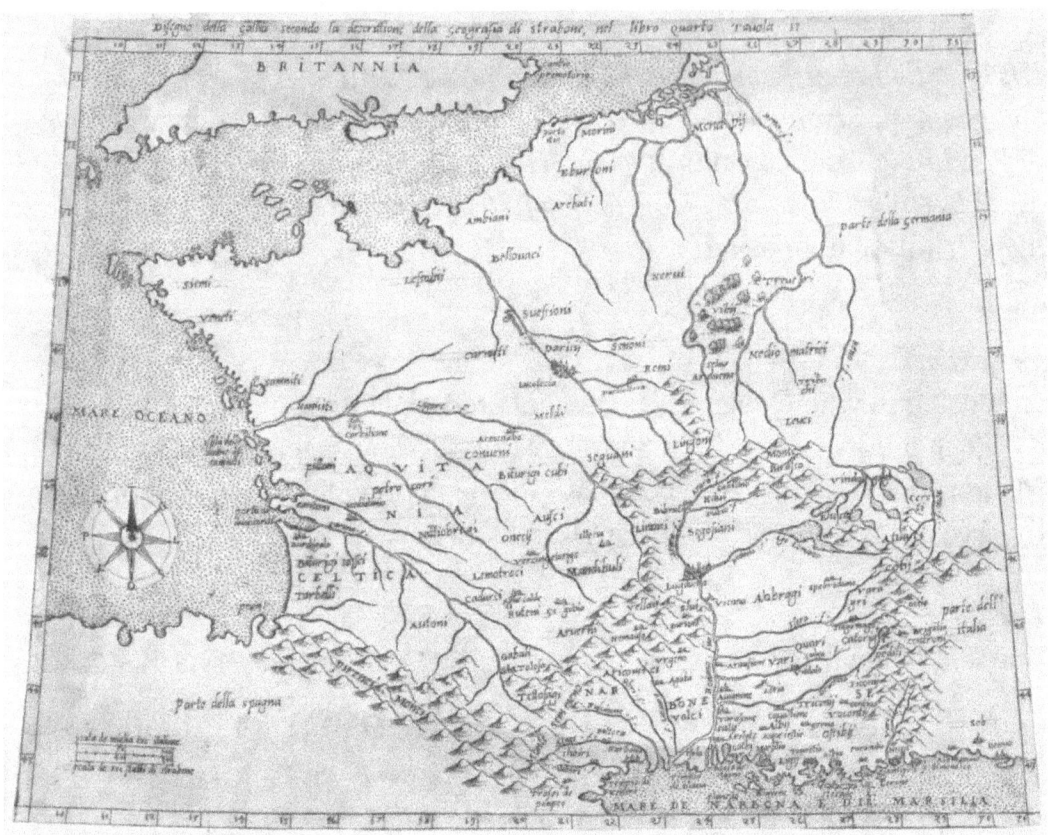

115 France (Strabonian) 1562? München SB

Comments:
Graduated in whole degrees, each numbered, in latitude and longitude, from
42°20' to 53°20' N, and from 9°00' to 31°00' E, on a trapezoidal projection.
The main outlines of the map are taken from a simplified adaptation of a map
of France by Fine, first published in 1538 in Paris, but the nomenclature as
always is from Strabo (Meurer, 2004, 43).

Location of copy:
The only known copy is in the Lafreri-Atlas (München SB(2 Mapp. 464))

References:
Meurer, 2004, 43, no. 29; Bifolco and Ronca, 2018, 2: 972.

Reproductions:
Meurer, 2004, no. 29; Bifolco and Ronca, 2018, 2: 972-73.
https://www.digitale-sammlungen.de/en/view/bsb00107640?page'33

116. Attica (East Central Greece) (Strabonian)
-[Venice?], n.d. [ca. 156
2?]
-Copper engraving, 25.5 x 33.5 cm. (plate size), on one sheet
-40 Italian miles = 5.4 cm.

There is no title. Meurer believes it may have been cut off in this copy, the
only copy known.

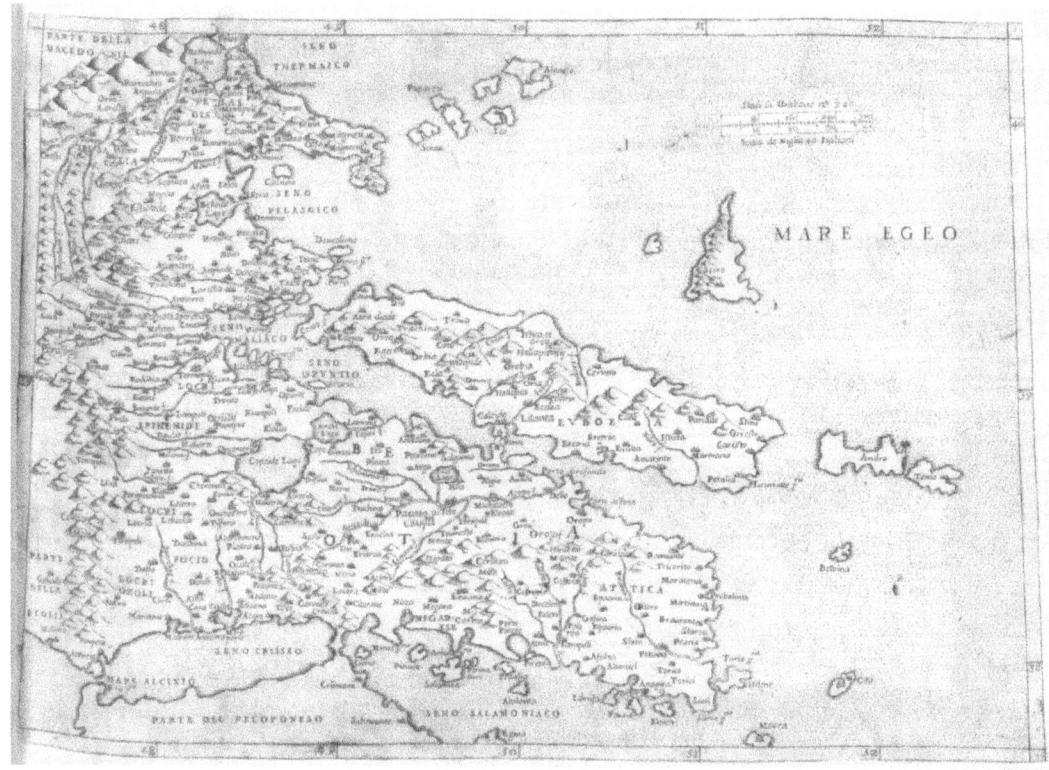

116 Attica (East Central Greece) (Strabonian) 1562? München SB

758

Comments:
Graduated in whole degrees, each numbered, in latitude and longitude, from 37°40 to 40°20' N, and from 47°00' to 53°00' E, on a trapezoidal projection in which the convergence of meridians is barely discernible, due to the small area covered. Meurer finds that this map follows Gastaldi's Greece (no. 95), with, as always in this series, the toponyms taken from Strabo's *Geography*, and he notes that the presence of a clear circular spot in the stippled sea is evidence that a wind rose was intended for this place, showing that the entire series as we have it was not yet ready for publication.

Location of copy:
The only known copy is in the Lafreri-Atlas (München SB(2 Mapp. 464))

References:
Meurer, 2004, 46, no. 32; Bifolco and Ronca, 2018, 2: 1436.

Reproductions:
Meurer, 2004, no. 32; Bifolco and Ronca, 2018, 2: 1436.
https://www.digitale-sammlungen.de/en/view/bsb00107640?page'36

117. Italy (Strabonian)
-[Venice?], n.d. [ca. 1562?]
-Copper engraving, 38.5 x 41.5 cm. (plate size), on one sheet
-100 Italian miles = 4.9 cm.

In the upper right corner:
Disegno dell'italia secondo la descrittione della Geografia di strabone, nel fine del | quarto libro, e sequita il quinto, et il sesto, Tavola iiii. [a short blank space follows] | *E per la particular sua descrittione di Latini, ombri et campagna, nel quinto libro, s'à fatta un | disegno particular de tutti i detti popoli che lui descrive per non poterli descriuerli | nella presente Italia.*
(Map of Italy according to the description in the Geography of strabo, at the end of the fourth book, and, following, the fifth, and the sixth. Fourth Map. [a short blank space follows] *And for his detailed description of Latium, umbria*

*and campania, in the fifth book, a detailed map has been made of all the said
areas* [peoples] *which were not able to be described in the present Italy.)*

117 Italy (Strabonian) 1562? München SB

Comments:
Graduated in whole degrees, each numbered, in latitude and longitude, from
35°00' to 46°00' N, and from 28°45' to 43°10' E, on a rectangular projection.
The most immediately striking fact about this map of Italy is that it is

considerably larger than the other maps in the series, and it apparently enjoyed some circulation, for it is the only map in the series which was already known to scholars, in a slightly different variation, before the emergence of the Strabo Illustratus Atlas. In its original state, known only through the 2004 Meurer reference found below, it does not contain Gastaldi's name. But a variant exists which gives below the title here: "p[er] Iacomo Gastaldo". This variant has been known since 1881, and in our list of locations of copies, all, except Meurer, 2004, refer to this latter variant, which is in the Correr Museum Library in Venice. Almagià seems to imply that the name might be a manuscript edition. But I have found a second copy of this variant with Gastaldi's name just as in the Correr copy, in the Newberry Library, so the addition of Gastaldi's name is a printed addition. Meurer found that the map's coastlines and hydrography follow Gastaldi's 1561 Italy (no. 101), while the toponymic content is from books 5 and 6 of Strabo's *Geography* (Meurer, 2004, 74). He also points out that the plate number given to this map in its title, no. 4, is the same as the number on the Strabonian map of Central Italy (no. 111), which provides further evidence of the unfinished state of the series as a whole.

Location of copies:
München SB(2 Mapp. 464); variants with Gastaldi's name Chicago Newb(Novacco 2F 104)/ Venezia Correr(Cartografia cartella 32/33).

References:
Marinelli, 1881, 133, no. 634; Grande, 1902, 67; Biasutti, 1908, 13 with nt. 2; Bagrow, 1928-30, 1, 96, no. 108; Almagià, 1939, *carta*, 9; Almagià, 1948, "Historical Map"; Gallo, 1954, 43, no. 33*; Karrow, 1993, 243, no. 30/97; Lago, 2002, 284; Meurer, 2004, 74, no. 60; Bifolco and Ronca, 2018, 3: 1820.

Reproductions:
Meurer, 2004, no. 60 (the original variant); Bifolco and Ronca, 2018, 3: 1820-21.
https://www.digitale-sammlungen.de/en/view/bsb00107640?page'36;
Almagià, 1948, op. p. 15 (variant with Gastadi's name printed): Karrow,

1993, p. 640 (pl. 30/37) (variant with Gastaldi's name printed); https://collections.Newberry.org/asset-management/2KXJ8ZSA2Z4L2?&WS

118. Africa
-Venice, 1564
-Copper engraving, 104.5 x 141.0 cm., on eight sheets
-300 Italian miles = 5.8 cm.

In plain text box near upper right corner:
Il disegno della geografia moderna de tutta la parte dell'Africa i confini | della quale stanno in questo modo, da ponente il mar' oceano computate l'isole | di capo verde, et le Canarie, da Tramontana il stretto de gibelterra, et il | mare mediterraneo, da siroco una linea che principia a feramida in sino al sues, | et dal sues per il mare Rosso, da leuante il mare oceano includendo l'isola | di s[an]to Lorenzo, insino al capo di Bona speranza; dall'ostro il mar' oc- | eano, graduata in longhezza, et in larghezza.-- | Composta per l'eccelente m[esser] giacomo di | Castaldi piamontese in uenetia [one full blank line follows here] *| Serenissimo et potentissimo Romanorum regi Boemie et ongarie | Maximiliano Inperatori Designato etc. D[omino] D[omino] Clem[mentissi]mo. (Map of the modern geography of all the contiment of Africa, the confines of which are thus, at the west the ocean sea counted [from] the islands of cape verde, and the Canaries, at the North the strait of Gibralter, and the meditteranean sea, at the southeast a line which begins at feramida as far as suez, and from suez by the Red sea, to the east the ocean sea including the island of St. Lorenzo* [Madagascar], *as far as the cape of good hope; at the south the ocean sea, graduated in longitude, and in latitude.* [a half-line blank space follows] *| Created by the excellent master Giacomo di Castaldi piedmontese in Venice* [Then, after skipping one full line:] *To the most Serene and powerful king of the Romans Bohemia and hungary Maximilian Imperor appointed etc. by the most merciful Lord God.)*

Below in the same text box, to the right:
fabius licinius ex[cidit] (fabio licinio engraver)

And just below the text box:

Con gratia et priuilegio dell''ill[ustrissi]mo senato di uenetia p[er] anni x.-- | 1564 (With grace and privilege of the most illustrious senate of Venice for 10 years.C1564)

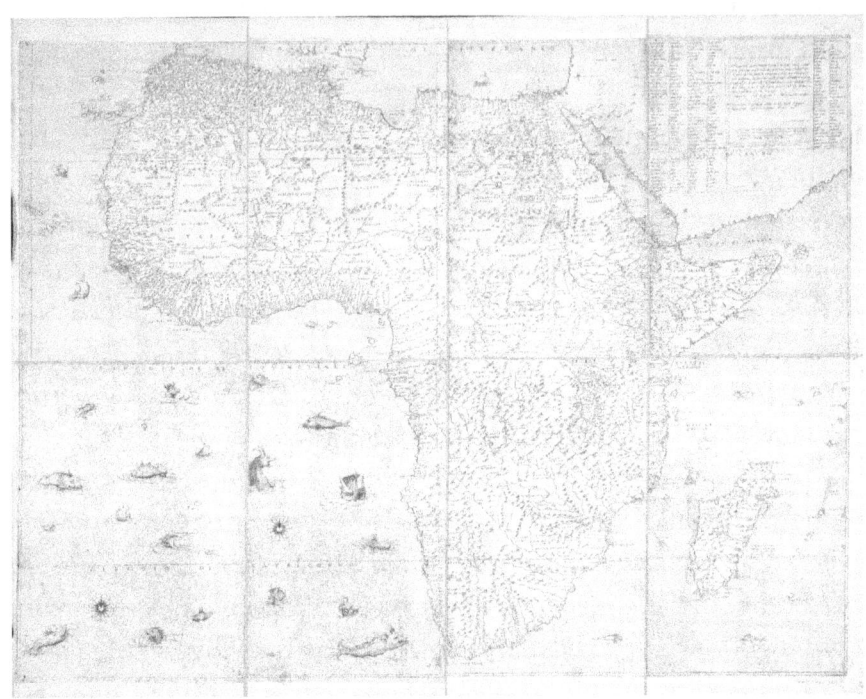

118 Africa 1564 Paris BN

Comments:

Graduated in whole degrees, with each degree numbered, in latitude and longitude, from ca. 38°00' S to 37°30' N, and from ca. 1°15' W to 98°20' E. The graduation on this map is applied irregularly. Latitude graduation occurs only in the following three places: (1) on the prime meridian, which runs through the island of Santa Lucia in the Cape Verde Islands (but is drawn in only in the upper left sheet, and not in the lower left sheet), about one degree and fifteen minutes in from the left border of the map, (2) along the 49th meridian, which is drawn in clear through the map, about one degree and twenty minutes left of the right border of the second sheet from the left in both the top and bottom rows, and (3) along the right border of the third

763

sheet in the top row; this last string of graduation is in some copies trimmed off, or pasted over by the sheet to the right); while the longitude graduation runs only along the equator (actually along the lower border of the top sheets, and the upper border of the bottom sheets, ca. 35 minutes south of the equator), all of which provides us with just enough to determine that the map is on a rectangular projection, as noted by Biasutti (1920, 330). We recall that this is the last map engraved by Licinio, who died the following year, and that there is the implication that he was, already beginning at some time in 1564, probably ailing in some way which prevented him from continuing with his engraving work. Both these awkward irregularities in the graduation, and the rather tentative, unassertive, and somewhat careless look of the lines outlining the text box containing both the dedicatory text and the list of ancient and modern names in the northeast corner imply that his expertise had already begun weakening before he had finished this map, although the map is on the whole a masterpiece, the last such to appear from the Gastaldi-Licinio coalition. There exists for the map no separate list of ancient and modern name equivalents as for the majority of these maps, but simply the rather short list just mentioned in the northeast corner of the map.

This is the sixth and last of our key maps, the few astonishing maps the study of which makes up the core of our work (see the comments at entry no. 92). Of the present map, Betz writes: "Without much dispute, it is probably the single most important and influential map of Africa of the sixteenth century. It represents a quantum leap from Sebastian Münster's significant Africa map of 1540" (Betz, 2007, 111). The map is as much an impressive accomplishment as the maps of Asia and America, as documented in our chapters three and four, although there is a lesser abundance of material in our book which is relevant to it than to the Asia and America, for our chapters seven and eight are mostly devoted to the great question of the relationship of Asia to America which looms so large in Gastaldi's work involving those two continents, a question which of course is irrelevant to Africa.

Biasutti states that the map was developed virtually entirely from the relations in Ramusio (Biasutti, 1920, 433), as does Skelton (1961, 562-67), although, of course, for the coasts, substantial information came from sea charts. The most important Ramusian accounts used were those of Leo

Africanus for the Maghreb and the whole of northern Africa, Alvarez for and east central Africa, with important material also from Barros, Cadamosto, Lopez, Cabral, Da Gama, and others. However, out of about 1,200 names total, Biasutti isolated some eighty-five names which are from elsewhere, and he lists them and suggests possible sources for some of them (cit., 398-403). As we have brought out elsewhere, Gastaldi tells us in the text accompanying two of his modern regional maps of parts of Africa in his 1548 Ptolemy, the "Marmarica" and the "Africa Nova" (nos. 35 and 38), that he is working at that time on a giant Africa like none seen before, and speaks of it as being almost ready to come out. Biasutti develops the theory that Gastaldi held this map back, improving it over time as more information became available, such as Barros in ca. 1553, and that it eventually developed into the present map, an idea which is surely basically correct. (Skelton, 1961, 563, nt. 1 misunderstands Biasutti here.) I have not yet explored the possible correspondence between the 1548 Ptolemy modern maps and this map, and so there is still more work to occupy other scholars. The same needs to be done regarding Asia and America as well.

The map's only real fault is its poor choice of projection. The rectangular projection is not well suited to a map covering such a large area, especially when the projection is developed such that the length of a degree of longitude is greater than the length of a degree of latitude, an unnatural ratio which Gastaldi evidently found it necessary to use in order to fit the continent into what we would call landscape format today. As Biasutti notes, this unnatural ratio distorts the map some, especially far from the equator (cit., 330). A better choice would have been the trapezoidal projection which Gastaldi uses on most of his later maps, including the First and Second Parts of Asia, but Gastaldi apparently disliked the effect produced when using this projection on an area which crosses the equator, although it was used by several later cartographers of Africa (see, for example, the list of examples in Betz given in our entry no. 37). Gastaldi used the same inappropriate projection for his America, but here the ratio of a degree of latitude to a degree of longitude is still worse, resulting in still greater distortion. Curvilinear projections would have been best, but Gastaldi seems to have not felt confident using them on regional maps. Consternation over the problem of an appropriate projection which crosses the equator probably also explains

Gastaldi's hesitance in bringing out the lower parts of the Third Part of Asia until ca. 1565/66.

There is a little mystery connected with this map. Forlani published in 1562, two years before this map came out, a smaller 2-sheet Africa (Betz, 2007, 101-02, no. 6; Biasutti, 1920, 414-15) which clearly seems to be a reduction of this map. Karrow suggests that perhaps Forlani used as a model the Gastaldi map which was painted on a wall of the Ducal Palace in 1549 (no. 65), and I tend to agree with this. However, prominent in the 1564 map is the influence of Barros, which was not available until ca. 1553, so if the 1562 Forlani includes the Barros features of the 1564 map, then that cannot be the whole answer, but no one has yet taken on the task of making the necessary comparisons. For other editions and derivatives of this map, including the 1562 Forlani and derivatives of that, see Biasutti, 1920, 414-15, 423-25 and 428-29; Karrow, 1993, 243-45; Meurer, 2004, 130, no. 116; and esp. Betz, 2007, nos. 6, 8, 11, 13, 19 and 33.

Location of copies:
This is an 8-sheet map. But in many copies, the southwestmost of 8 sheets, which shows only ocean, is missing, producing a 7-sheet map, as indicated in the following list: Chicago Newb(Novacco 6F 39)(7 sheets)/ Basel UB(Kartenslg AA110-113)/ Modena Estense(A.49.Q.7, nos. 93,94)(7 sheets)/ Stanford SC(Norwich no. 0008)/ Milwaukee AGS(OV / 300 / A-1564)(7 sheets)/ Paris BN(GE DD- 5077(RES)/ London BL(Maps 189.c.1)(7 sheets)/ Helsinki AEN(HN)(in Nordenskiöld Collection)/ Greenwich NMM(G290: 1/8 A-H)/ Greenwich NMM(BP C 5309, no. 144)/ Firenze BMar(in atlas Stampe 423)(7 sheets)[2005]

References:
Schilling, 1892, 6-7, 25, 30, 32, 39, 51; Nordenskiöld, 1897, 132; Ruge, 1904-16, Pt. IV, 116-17, no. 86 (110-113); Biasutti, 1920; Tooley, 1939, 20-21; Gallo, 1954, 24-26; Randles, 1956, 77-84, 85, 87; Randles, 1958, 131-55; Skelton, 1961; Skelton, 1962; Teixeira da Mota, 1964, 28-30; Tooley, 1966, 20-21, no. 56; Tooley, Bricker and Crone, 1989, 160-61; Skelton, 1970, p. xiii; Eversole, 1983, 2-3; Mano, 1987, 6; Meurer, 1991, 151; Karrow, 1993, 243-44; Relaño, 1995, 54-55, 56, 58, 59, 60, 61, 62;

Schilder, 1996, 46; Norwich, 1997, 11-12; Meurer, 2004, nos. 117-119; Rizzo, 2006; Betz, 2007, 55, 58-59, 60, 84, 101-02, 105-13, 116-17, 122, 123; Bifolco and Ronca, 2018, 1: 430-33.

Reproductions:
Bifolco and Ronca, 2018, 1: 430-33.
https://collections.Newberry.org/asset-management/2KXJ8ZSKAJ9WN";
https://www.loc.gov/resource/gdcwdl.wdl_06764" (seven sheets); https://gallica.bnf.fr/ark:/12148/btv1b72003094/f9.item" (eight sheets)

119. Anatolia
-Venice, 1564
-Copper engraving, 38.5 x 52.0 cm., on two sheets
-100 Italian miles = 4.8 cm.

In the southeast corner of the map, in a decorative cartouche:
IL DISEGNO D'GEOGRAFIA | MODERNA | Della prouincia di Natolia, et Caramania, patria | de gli Sin[no]ri Turchi della casa Ottomana, i con- | fini suoi da Leuãte il Fiume Eufrates, da Po- | n te il stretto di cõstãtinopoli, et quello di Ga- | lipoli, et il Mare dell'Arcipelago, comp[re]so nella | detta prouincia molte Isole, da Tramõtana | il Mare Maggiore, dal Ostro il Mare Medi- | terraneo, nel qual'u'e l'Isola di Candia, et | quella di Cipro, di Mag[nifi]ci Venetiani, Gradua- | ta et una Scala de Miglia Italiani. | Al Sig[no]r Cosimo Bartoli Gentil'Huomo, et | Accademico Fiorentino | Giac[om]o di Castaldi Cosmografo in Venetia | L'Anno M D LXIIII. | Alla libraria d'la insegna di S[an] Marco. (MAP OF THE MODERN GEOGRAPHY Of the province of Anatolia, and Karamania, land of the Turkish Lords of the house Ottoman, its confines on the East, the Euphrates River, on the west the strait of Constantinople, and that of Gallipoli, and the Sea of the Archipelago [Aegean Sea], comprehended in the said province [are] many Islands, at the North the Black Sea, at the South the Mediterranean Sea, in which there is the Island of Candia, and that of Cyprus, of the Magnificent Venetians, Graduated and [with] a Scale of Italian Miles. To the Signor Cosimo Bartoli Gentleman, and Florentine

Academician. Giacomo di Castaldi Cosmographer in Venice The Year 1564. At the bookstore of St. Marks.

Follows a scale bar, beneath which is:
Cum priuilegio (With privilege)

Below the decorative cartouche:
Paulo Forlani Veronese intagliatore (Paolo Forlani of Verona engraver)

119 Anatolia 1564 Paris BN

Comments:
Graduated in whole degrees, each numbered, in latitude and longitude, from 34°40' to 45°35', and, on the top border, from 51°45' to 72°40' E, and on the lower border from 52°50' to to 71°00' E, on a trapezoidal projection. We can assume that the inclusion of the dedicatory inscription in a decorative cartouche was Forlani's idea. Gastaldi and Licinio always used very unpretentious and plain text boxes or tablets for their inscriptions. What was

the occasion for this map? The same area, though in smaller scale is shown on Gastaldi's First Part of Asia, although possibly due to bad planning, the westernmost sliver of the peninsula falls off that map. Perhaps it was a combination of wishing to rectify this deficiency and the fact that the area was of much importance to the commerce of the Venetian Republic, that induced Gastaldi to make this map. It has been very little studied. The only treatment of it worthy of being called a discussion is that of Almagià (1948, 34). The question of sources is puzzling, both for the area on this map and the same area on the First Part of Asia, for, this is an area with a large interior, and Ramusio has little to offer on it. Barbaro's travels would contain something on the east part of Turkey (see Parks, 1970, 21 for background on that account in Ramusio.); and perhaps something in the accounts of Hayton Armenio, Angiolello, Contarini, Interiano, and Ramusio's lost edition of Caterino Zeno's embassy would have something (respectively in Parks, pp. 21, 20, 21, 22, and 23-24), though none of them seem to deal with the principal part of the peninsula. Another possibility would be Giovio's history of the Turks of 1530, which went into several editions in various languages (Karrow, 1993, 269). Almagià mentions one previous map of the area by Henricus Martellus Germanus (cit., 34) but admits that this map has nothing to do with the Gastaldi map. Another possibility is information obtained by Michel Membré during his journey to the Persian Court (see Cartobibliography entry no. 69), but I can offer no more than these vague clues. Of course nautical charts were used for the coastlines, and a few Ptolemaic points were apparently picked out to help make a coordinate frame (Almagià, 1948, 34), but beyond that, nothing more can yet be said with certainty. The map has considerable importance for us in that it was engraved by Forlani, not Licinio, and was marketed through the San Marco shop of the Bertelli's, and, as we have already shown in entry no. 103, this and some other facts lend confirmation to our interpretation of the independent nature of the Gastaldi-Licinio business before Licinio apparently became incapacitated. For later editions, derivatives, etc., see Tooley, 1939, 20; Almagià, 1948, 34-35; Woodward, 1990, 16-17; Meurer, 1991; and Karrow, 1993, 246.

Location of copies:

Paris BN(GE DD- 2987(6504))/ Paris BN(GE D- 17044)/ Paris BN(GE AF PF- 192(4765)) /Madrid PR(MAP/454, no. 64)/ Roma BCas(Rari 1131, no. 54)[1982]/ Greenwich NMM(C3995, no. 70)[1971]/ Venezia BNM(138 c.4, no. 68)[1954]/ Madrid PR(MAP/464, no. 97)[1915]/ Wolfegg SW(Histor. Geogr., no. 34)[1911]/ Rostock UB(Q k 3, no. 60)[1904]

Refererences:
Ruge, 1904-16, 1, no. 67(60); Bagrow, 1928-30, 1, 34, no. 101; Tooley, 1939, no. 64; Almagià, 1948, 34; Gallo, 1954, no. 68; Woodward, 1990, 16-17; Meurer, 1991, 151; Karrow, 1993, 246, no. 30/103; Bifolco and Ronca, 2018, 1: 556.

Reproductions:
Schilder, 2007, 98-99; Bifolco and Ronca, 2018, 1: 557-59.
https://gallica.bnf.fr/ark:/12148/btv1b8494691p/f1.item" (GE D-17044)

(120.-124.) Gastaldi maps published posthumously

We have included in our Cartobibliography several composite entries, to give a general overview of several sets of maps, sets which make distinct entities within themselves, as with the 1548 Ptolemy Gastaldi maps, the three sets of Ramusian maps, and the incomplete Ptolemaic and Strabonian series of maps now in the Bavarian State Library. It might at first seem superfluous to follow that precedent for the present five maps, but in fact such is not the case, for in considering these maps as a distinct set, we find that we are able to bring into view still one other aspect of our cartographer, perhaps of very considerable importance. The maps produced before Gastaldi's death were almost all produced in unison with parties with whom Gastaldi was personally associated, and here we have in mind in particular the Gastaldi-Licinio partnership. But on these posthumous maps, we find names which do not occur at all on any of Gastaldi's first editions, names of persons who were not involved with Gastaldi in producing the originals of his maps, Ferrando Bertelli, Girolamo Olgiati, Giorgio Tilman, Antoine Lafreri, and Paolo Forlani. Forlani alone does occur twice on maps produced in Gastaldi's lifetime, the 1564 Anatolia (no. 119) and the 1562 Canossa edition of Gastaldi's world map (no. 105), and what we have to say here regarding the posthumous maps applies as well to this latter map, for which Forlani wrote the dedication (while Gastaldi himself wrote the dedication for the 1564 Anatolia). As we have done in all the maps in our Cartobibliography, we have given all dedicatory texts and all other peripheral verbal matter in full, with no ellipses anywhere, and have also given an English translation of each, also in full and with no ellipses.

In the case of the present maps, taken by comparison with all the other maps, this policy has unexpectedly revealed something of much interest, and it is revealed precisely in the dedicatory notices. These non-Gastaldian dedicatory notices are, in most cases (the Padua, the Gulf of Venice, the Lombardy, and the 1562 Forlani world), exhaustingly long-winded and obscure, with syntax and diction which often approaches unintelligibility, though we have striven to render them as well as we can, sometimes alas with limited success. But it is not this fact, but another one, which makes these dedications so revealing. They are filled not just with expressions of respect for their dedicatees, but with volley after volley of phrases and expressions which are so excruciatingly obsequious that it is almost painful and unpleasant to read them. They make one wince. We shall not enter here into the question of the motives behind these verbal avalanches of self-demeaning outbursts. The question in general of the significance of map dedications has been little discussed and is far from being resolved. What we wish to point out here is that other than including the usual standard courteous forms of address to dedicatees, the dedicatory epistles on the maps produced by Gastaldi and Licinio are absolutely lacking in language couched in this obsequious tone. There is not the slightest hint of it on any map. Gastaldi is quite restrained and clearly unconcerned with making special efforts to impress his dedicatees or with convincing them of his affection for them. The Gastaldi-Licinio business enterprise thus seems to have had a quite different air about it than that about the businesses of the Bertelli's, Forlani, Camocio and many others, since there is no sign of any impulse in Gastaldi to indicate that he felt that his status in society was so greatly lower than the persons whom he addressed. He was after all affiliated with such persons as Ramusio and ambassador Mendoza, and was obviously in the good graces of the Venetian Senate and Council of Ten. But perhaps more important was the fact that he was the map *maker*, the *creator* of something, instead of being involved in the technical aspects of the final production of the works. And, just possibly, could his aloofness from, or at least indifference to the obsequious perhaps stem in part from possible connections with persons of importance in his original environment in Piedmont, of which hints exist, as we saw in our first chapter? However that may be, it is clear that the Gastaldi-Licinio enterprise was a thing apart from the rest of the map producing establishment.

120. Apulia
-Venice, 1567
-Copper engraving
-No scale bar

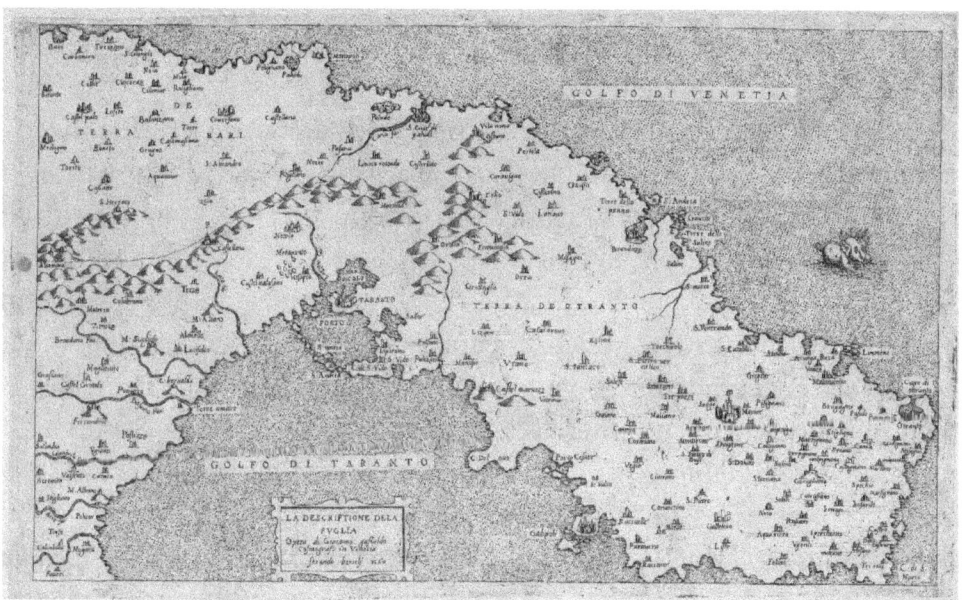

120 Apulia 1567 Chicago Newb

772

In text box just left of middle bottom of the sheet:
LA DESCRIPTIONE DELA | PVGLIA | Opera di Giacomo gastaldo | Cosmografo in Venetia | ferando bertelj 1567 (THE DESCRIPTION OF APULIA Work of Giacomo Gastaldi in Venice Ferando Bertelli 1567)

Comments:
The map contains no graduation. This posthumous map, one of Gastaldi's five Italian provincial maps, is the first known map, printed or manuscript, of the province of Apulia alone (There is a 1558 Ligorio map of the Neapolitan Kingdom which includes Apulia, but it is not a separate map of that area (Biasutti, 1908, 49, nt. 1)). As noted in our chapter ten, these province maps cannot be taken as representing an attempt to provide maps of all the Italian provinces, but probably are simply areas for which Gastaldi either came into, or intentionally sought, sufficient information to justify making a large-scale map of the area. The question of the map's sources, as is usual with Gastaldi's maps of European areas, is foggy. The following is perhaps the most likely scenario, though it is conjectural.

As Colamonico (1939, 163-67) has shown convincingly, the map probably precedes its publication date by at least ten years, and probably goes back to something like 1555 or 1556, as opposed to Almagià's earlier suggestion that the map probably came after the 1561 Italy. As Colamonico also points out (1939, 171), on the basis of an important study by Giovanni Marinelli, the Venetian Republic, probably more than any other state at the time, actively concerned itself with the obtaining, via diplomatic means, of cartographic documents of other areas, but especially those with which it had important commercial or political ties, of which the area of the central southern Apulian coastal towns was among the more important, with major ports of call before Venetian trading ships left Italian territory for the Levant. He suggests plausibly enough that Gastaldi could have obtained a manuscript map of Apulia around the time stated through such channels (1939, 170-71), which would have served as the basis of Gastaldi's map. We might add that Ramusio's influence lends further credibility to such an idea.

But we know that Gastaldi did not publish such a map at the time, and the map then becomes one of a number of maps which we know that Gastaldi held in manuscript, out of dissatisfaction with them and a wish to improve them on the basis of other sources. Colamonico mentions as definitely being among such sources portolan charts, which is usual with Gastaldi, and Leandro Alberti's famous description of Italy (Alberti, 1550), which Colamonico shows was unquestionably used (1939, 173-74), and finally, Colamonico discusses the Vescovile atlas as a possible source (cit., 179-84), as does also Umek (2002, 527 and 533). Colamonico also mentions the possible use of lists of towns and oral information.

Assessments of the map's worth vary somewhat. Biasutti said that the map was "one of the most beautiful and exact of Gastaldi's" and that "the peninsula is depicted in a way far more correct than in other terrestrial maps of the time" (1908, 49), and Colamonico states that "the great Piedmontese has accomplished in this a personal work of harmony and fusion, creating a work of original production" (1939, 168), both high praise considering that the map is the first known map of Apulia. But frequent mention is made by both Almagià and Colamonico of inexact locations of places, although this is common to almost all maps of the time, and to the fact that there are a good number of place-name duplications on the map, a common fault with Gastaldi. Perhaps the most realistic assessment, also by Colamonico, is that it is a fine sixteenth century map whose negative points are outweighed by its positive ones (Colamonico, 157). Colamonico is unquestionably mistaken in his unexpected observation (1939, 163) that an early edition in woodcut would have existed, an idea which has no basis at all, and probably is inspired by Almagià's questionable 1929 idea that Gastaldi's 1570 map of Lombardy first appeared in a 1559 woodcut edition. For the later editions of this map, see Almagià (1929, 32); Colamonico, 1939 (174-79); and Karrow (1993, 247).

Location of copies:
Chicago Newb(Novacco 2F 173)/ Cambridge Harv(51-2500)/ Paris BN(GE AF PF- 187(4391)/ Paris BN(GE B- 1657)/ Copenhagen KB(KBK 1-51(114))/ Roma BVat(Stampe.Geogr.I.65)/ Madrid PR(MAP/455, no. 40)/ Budapest OSzK(TA 276,no. 47)[2005]/ London BL(Maps C.7.e.1., no. 100) [2003]/ Sint-Niklaas KOKW(Atlas 408 IATO(no. 41))[1994]/ Firenze BMar(Stampe 473, 81-82)[1980]/ Firenze BN(12.-.44, v. 1, no. 60)[1980]/ Firenze BN(12.-.44, v. 4, no. 54(53 written)[1980]/ Madrid PR(MAP/464,

no. 69)[1915]/ Metten BBa(Mapp.XIV, 142c)[1911]/ Greifswald UB(Pb,883)
[1904]/ Roma BN(711.6.G.1, no. 46)[1876]

References:
Bonacci, 1905, 214-15; Biasutti, 1908, 38 and 47-49; Colamonico, 1921,
296; Almagià, 1929, 32a; Colamonico, 1939; Tooley, 1939, no. 114;
Almagià, 1948, 38-39; Almagià, 1951, 8; Almagià, 1961(1913-14), 278-79;
Borroni-Salvadori, 1980, no. 60; Bella, 1986, no. 107; Meurer, 1991, 154;
Lago, 1992, II, 282; Karrow, 1993, 247; Luisi, 2002, 456-67; Rossit, 2002,
454; Umek, 2002, 527, 533, 535; Meurer, 2004, 93, no. 79; Bifolco and
Ronca, 2018, 3: 2078.

Reproductions:
Almagià, 1929, pl. 36 (2); Meurer, 2004, no. 79; Bifolco and Ronca, 2018, 3:
2078.
https://collections.Newberry.org/asset-management/2KXJ8ZSAPDYLX?
&WS

121. Madagascar
-[Venice], 1567
-Copper engraving, 19.0 x 25.5 cm., on one sheet
-No scale bar

In the body of the map itself:
ISO | LA | DE | SAN | LO | REN | ZO (ISLAND OF MADAGASCAR [SAN
LORENZO]*)*

In text box in the upper left corner:
In questa isola vi sono Elefanti é boschi d'legni | setin che hora si
adimandano sandari iquali | sono Rosi D   M567 | Op[er]a di gac[om]o
gastaldo p[iamontese] | Ferando berteli exc[udebat] (In this island there are
Elephants and forests of [satin-like?] woods which nowadays are called
sandalwoods which are red [I am uncertain of the translation in this strange
and difficult little passage] 1567 Work of gacomo gastaldo piedmontese

Ferando Berteli publisher) (For reference to an explanation of the peculiar form of the date expression on this map, see in the comments below.)

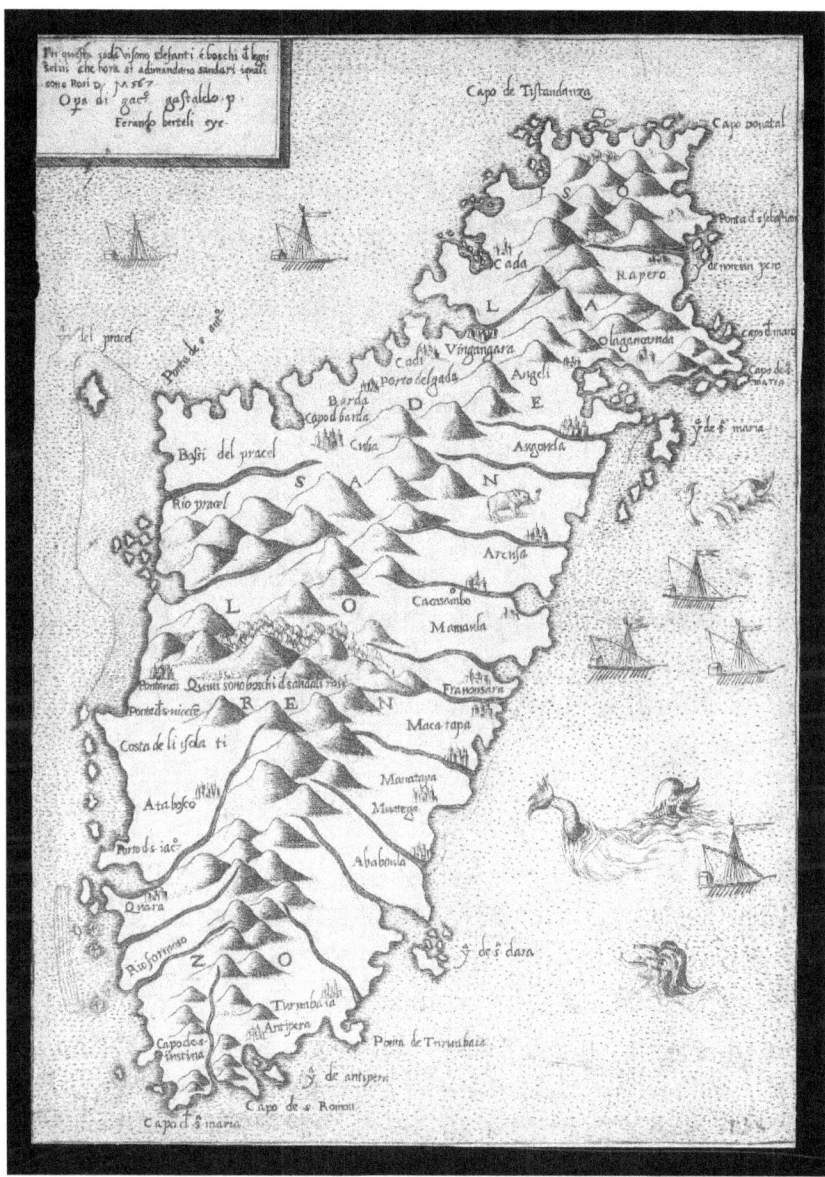

121 Madagascar 1567 Chicago Newb

Comments:
The map is not graduated. It is nothing but a copy, in a different style of engraving, of the Madagascar on Gastaldi's 1564 Africa (no. 118), as recognized by Almagià (1939, carta, 9) and Meurer (2004, 126, no. 112), and the few comments that have been made about it apply equally to the Africa, as Gravier's observation that the west coast is of remarkable exactitude for its era (1896, 91), and Biasutti's comment that Gastaldi seems to have used sources in advance of the world-map type nautical charts of the first half of the sixteenth century (1920, 336). There is no 1556 edition of this map, as mistakenly stated by Biasutti (1920, 336). This notion is based on an error that stems from Grande (1902, 44), as shown by Karrow (1993, 247), who also offers an explanation for the peculiar rendering of the date on the map. There may be a single derivative, though this is unclear (see Gravier, 1896, 93 and Biasutti, 1920, 337, in nt. 2 from preceding page).

Location of copies:
Chicago Newb(Novacco 2F 245.5)/ Paris BN(GE B- 1693)/ London BL(Maps C.7.e.1, no. 146)[2003]/ Roma BCas(Rari 1131, no. 59)[1982]/ Roma BA(in Bancs. a, 43[Is this call number now Rari 272?])[1918]/ Nürnberg GNM(Kartensamml. Afrika)[1911]/ Rostock UB(Q 7 3, no. 82) [1904]

References:
Nordenskiöld, 1889, 120, no. 90; Mallat de Bassilan, 1890(?), 7; Gravier, 1896, 89-91 and 93; Grande, 1902, 44; Ruge, 1904-16, Pt. 1, no. 67(82); Biasutti, 1920, 336-37 and 405; Almagià, 1939, *carta*, 9; Tooley, 1939, nos. 504 and 505 [These two entries probably describe the same map, as noted by Ganado and Karrow in the following references]; Ganado, 1982, 37, no. 59; Karrow, 1993, 247; Meurer, 2004, no. 112; Bifolco and Ronca, 2018, 1: 463.

Reproductions:
Meurer, 2004, no. 112; Bifolco and Ronca, 2018, 1:463.
https://collections.Newberry.org/asset-management/2KXJ8ZSA2MCWX? &WS

122. Padua region

-Venice, 1568
-Copper engraving, 44.0 x 55.0, on two sheets (right sheet only ca. 18 centimeters wide)
-5 Italian miles = 5.3 cm.

In the lower left corner, in an ornate cartouche:

AL R[EVERENDISSI]MO MONS[IGNORE] GIO[VANNI] DELFINO, | meritissimo Vescouo di Torcello. | Il gran ualore di V[ostra] S[ignoria] R[everendissi]ma fa, che io hora ardisca di appre- | sentarle questo nouo Disegno del Territorio Padoano, non ancora | da altri dato in luce, di mano di M[esser] Giacomo gastaldo, Piamontese, | Cosmografo eccellentissimo: Il qual Disegno, come che per se sij di pic- | ciolo momento, et non uguale a' meriti di V[ostra] S[ignoria] Reuer[endissi]ma accompagna- | to però con la deuotione, con che io glie lo presento, douerà perauu - | tura esserle caro. Stimi adunque V[ostra] S[ignoria] R[euerandissi]ma l'animo mio tale, che non | sij per mai stancar si, doue a' Seruigi suoi si possa adoperare. Et ac- | cetti questo mio debel dono, insieme col desiderio di seruirla, douun- | que, lei giudichera, che io sia buono. Che N[ostro] S[ignore] Dio presti a' suoi giu- | sti desiderij prospero fine. Di Venetia a di 3 di Zugno.M.D.LXVIII | Di V[ostra] S[ignoria] R[euerendissi]ma | Ser[uito]re diuotissimo | Ferrando Bertelli. (TO THE MOST REVEREND MONSIGNOR GIOVANNI DELFINO, most meritorious Bishop of Torcello. The great valor of Your Most Reverend Lordship has now made me [so] bold as to present to you this new Map of the Paduan Territory, not yet published by others, from the hand of Master Giacomo gastaldo, Piedmontese, most excellent Cosmographer: Which Map, although in itself be as a little trifle, and not equal to the merits of Your Most Reverend Lordship, but accompanied with the devotion, with which I present it to you, it will perhaps be to you a thing of worth. Regard then Your Most Reverend Lordship my spirit such, that will not ever fade, where I might be able to exert myself to your services. And accept this poor donation of mine, together with the desire to serve you, wherever you will find, that I might be fit. May Our Lord God give to your righteous desires successful conclusion. In Venice the 3rd day of June 1568 most devoted Servant of Your Most Reverend Lordship Ferrando Bertelli.)

In the scrollwork at the bottom of the cartouche:
Girolamo Olgiato fec[it] (Girolamo Olgiato engraver)

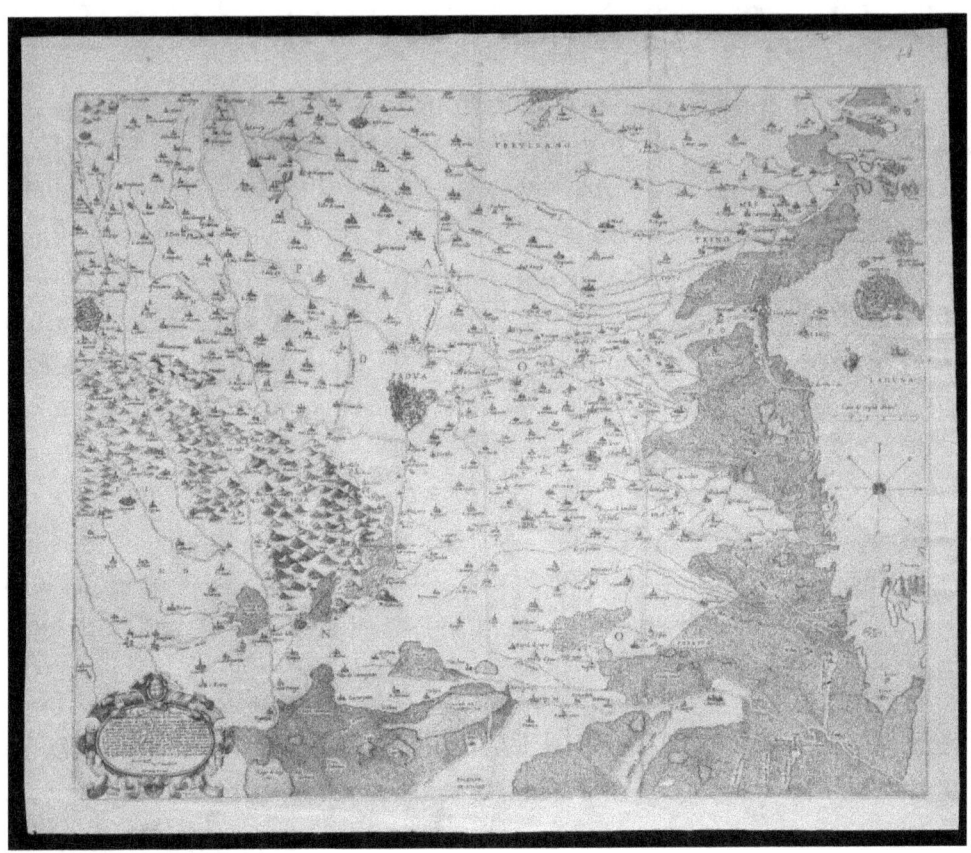

122 Padua region 1568 Chicago Newb

Comments:
The map carries no graduation. Almagià calls it a map of notable worth
(1948, 39), and Biasutti and Perini say that the hydrography is clear,
accurate, and easily recognizable (Biasutti, 1908, 45; and Perini, 1996, 76),
which is perhaps not surprising considering its sources as determined by
Almagià. The source for the map's prominent hydrographical net stems from
a map by Cristoforo Sabbadino (Almagià, 1929, 30a, with a reproduction of
the Sabbadino map at pl. 20(2); and 1948, 39), with whom Gastaldi
collaborated in his work as a hydrographical engineer for the State, but

779

Gastaldi has added to the landscape a large number of settlements, either from other maps or from written descriptions, says Almagià. Umek notes briefly that he sees some similarity with the Vescovile atlas (2002, 523c). It is worth pointing out that this, the only Gastaldi printed map which derived benefit from maps produced from the government body for which Gastaldi worked (whether occasionally or as a regular employee is still not clear) derived that benefit not from a work by Gastaldi, but a work by Sabbadino, who in fact generally outshone Gastaldi in this technical work. For later editions and derivatives of this map, see Almagià (1929, 29-30; and 1948, 39), Karrow (1993, 247-48), Perini (1996, 76-77), and Meurer (2004, 73).

Location of copies:
Chicago Newb(Novacco 4F 311)/ London BL(C.7.e.1., no. 89))/ London BL(*22910.(4.))/ London BL(Maps K.Top.79.15)/ Wien ÖNB(K I 109485 Kar)/ Paris BN(GE D- 13999)/ Paris BN(GE DD- 626(8 RES))/ Basel UB(Kartenslg AA69)

References:
Marinelli, 1881, 109, no. 544: Grande, 1902, 64; Biasutti, 1908, 38, 44-45, 63: Almagià, 1929, 29b-30a and 30b; Almagià, 1948, 39a-b; Meurer, 1991, 153-54; Karrow, 1993, 247-48; Gambi, 1994, text volume, 292; Perini, 1996, 76-77; Umek, 2002, 523c; Meurer, 2004, 59; Bifolco and Ronca, 2018, 3: 1928.

Reproductions:
Perini, 1996, 76; Bifolco and Ronca, 2018, 3: 1929.
https://collections.Newberry.org/asset-management/2KXJ8ZSKA83W0

123. Gulf of Venice (Adriatic Sea)
-[Venice], 1568
-Copper engraving, 23.5 x 42.5 cm., on one sheet
-80 Italian miles = 4.9 cm.

In triangular space at the upper left, outside the map proper:

*Ai Mag[nifi]ci Sig[no]ri miei oser[uantissi]mi il Sig[n]or PIERO
BADOERO, et il sig[n]or ANTONIO DIEDO, | Paolo Forlani | IL GOLFO
DI VENETIA si come è il piu famoso et illustre di | quanti sono dal Mare
circondati, cosi douendo uscire al mondo | nelle mie stampe piu copioso di
quanti fin hora sono, stati ue- | duti opera del dotto Gastaldo, et desiderando
io di darlo in | luce sotto il nome dell'una di V[ostre] S[ignorie]; ne
sappendo deliberare, | finalmente mi sono risoluto di indrizzarlo all'uno et
all'| altro, et non senza ragione essendo che ambedue uoi | siate pari di
ualore, cortesia simili di costumi et | di professione, compagni nelli studii et
amici in- | comparabili, dal che ne seguita che porgendo io | all'uno questo
mio picciol Dono seria stato | giudicato poco accorto quasi che uolessi | tra
il latte et latte far giudicio di maggior | bianchezza, Bene ho fatto adunq[ue]
ad inui- | arlo a V[ostre] S[ignorie] le quali essendo conosciuti | colmi di
ogni Virtu et Gentilezza lo accettarono con quell largo | animo con loquale
io loro | l'appresento et me ri- | poranno nel numero | de suoi affetio- | nati
seruitori. (To my Most Magnificent Signors Most Devout Signor PIERO
BADOERO, and Signor ANTONIO DIEDO. THE GULF OF VENICE since
it is the most famous and celebrated of all the circumenvironing Seas, thus
should be published to the world in my print, more copious than all of the
works of the learned Gastaldi seen up to now, and desiring to publish it
under the name of one of Your Lordships; not knowing how to decide I have
finally resolved to address it to the one and to the other, and not without
[the] reason being that you are both equal in valor, similar courtliness of
manners and of professions, companions in study and incomparable friends,
from which it followed that offering to one this small donation of mine I
would have been judged as of little wisdom as if I had wished to make a
judgement of greater whiteness between milk and milk. Properly then I have
had it sent to Your Lordships who as is well known are overflowing with*

every virtue and kindness [and] will accept it with that liberal affection with which I present it to you and you will count me in the number of your devoted servants.

At upper left of triangular space in upper right corner:
ALLA LIBRARIA DELLA COLONNA IN MERZARIA (AT THE BOOKSHOP OF THE COLUMN IN MERZARIA)

In the lower right of the same triangle, below the scale bar:
Intagliato da Paolo Forlani con ogni diligenza l'anno M.D. LXVIII.
(Engraved by Paolo Forlani with all care and diligence the year 1568.)

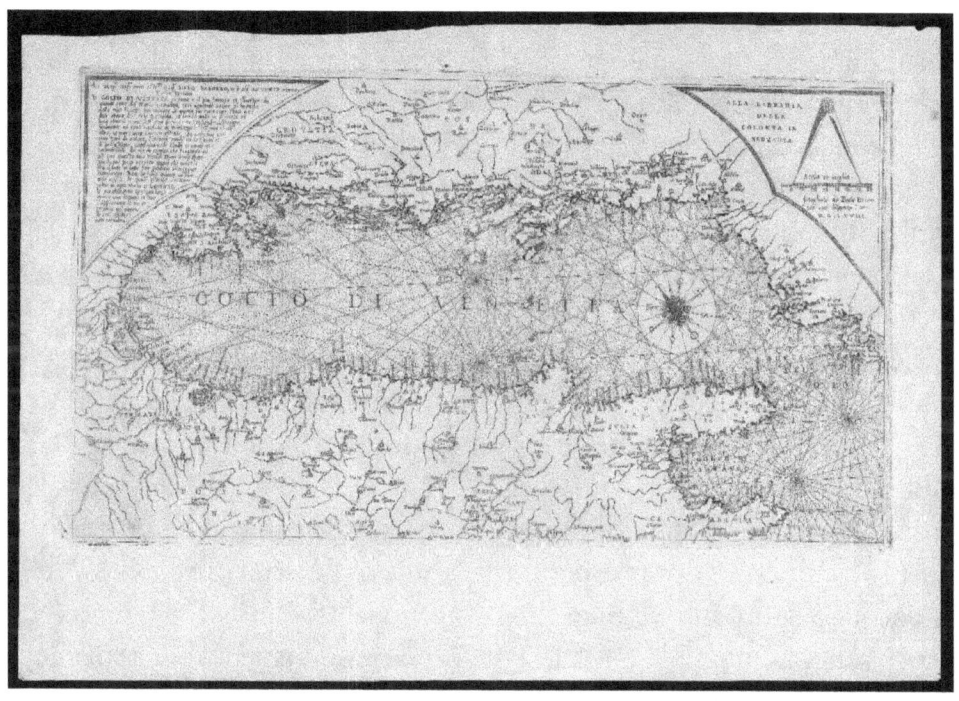

123 Gulf of Venice (Adriatic Sea) 1568 Chicago Newb

Comments:
The map has no graduation and is oriented to the northeast. It much reflects the same areas covered on Gastaldi's 1561 Italy (no. 101), and two scholars, Almagià (1929, 30a; and 1948, 33) and Cucagna (1964, 24), are of the

opinion that it should not be considered a Gastaldi map, but was drawn by someone else, probably from the second edition of the Italy, published in 1567 by Domenico Zenoi (for this map, see Almagià, 1929, 27(A) and Karrow, 1993, 237, no. 30/90.1). However, we are uncertain, and since my predecessors Bagrow and Karrow both include it among Gastaldi's maps, and all the authorities listed under our "references" below besides Almagià and Cucagna give the map to Gastaldi with no reservation, we have again opted not to break their precedence. At least two scholars have expressed their opinion that the 1568 edition may not be the first edition, but that a 1567 issue preceded it. Their opinion is based upon the fact that, the last of the three Roman numerals "I" in the date is higher than the other two, implying to them that this last "I" was, evidently carelessly, added later. I am quite convinced that this is incorrect. At the time, increasing of the height of the last of a series of Roman numeral I's was a common affectation. Other clear examples of it can be seen on Gastaldi's 1564 map of Anatolia (no. 119), reproduced here, and in a 1562 Bertelli-Forlani map of the British Isles, reproduced by Meurer (2004, 20, no. 6), and I have seen several other examples, into the seventeenth century. Exactly when and why this affectation arose, I cannot say. There is still one other factor which I suspect adds some fuel to this notion that there was a 1567 edition of this map. For some peculiar reason, the 1567 Zenoi derivative of Gastaldi's 1561 Italy, although it is quite clearly a map of Italy (reproduced in *Remarkable Maps*, 1894-99, 5/6, pl. 22), is not titled as a map of Italy, but rather carries the title: "Il Golfo di Venetia . . . ." (Almagià, 1929, 261). Obviously, anyone seeing the title of this 1567 map with no reproduction of it at hand could easily take it as a 1567 edition of our present map. Tooley, it is true (Tooley, 1939, no. 591), carries a short entry which reads: "Venetia 1567. BM. (Mar. 5(68)). Il Golfo di Venetia Intagliata da P. Forlani", but, as indispensable as Tooley's work may be, it is peppered with errors and inaccuracies, and I feel certain this entry results from some confusion concerning the 1567 mistitled Zenoi Italy and the present 1568 Forlani map. The question of derivatives and variants of our 1568 Gulf of Venice is complex, confused, and by no means settled. He who might wish to get a start on it should consult all the various works given in our references below.

Chicago Newb(Novacco 2F 150)/ Chicago Newb(Novacco 2F 151)/ London BL(Maps K.MAR.5.(63.))/ Kobenhavn KB(KBK 1-51(588))/ Paris BN(GE DD- 655(57 RES))/ Paris BN(GE DD- 2987 (5848)/ Paris Bn GE B- 1651)/ Roma BVat Stampe.Geogr.I.24/ Roma BVat Stampe.Geogr.I.25/ London BL(Maps C.7.e.1., no. 105)[2003]/ Venezia Correr(Cartografia cartella 32, no. 45)[1954]/ Madrid PR(MAP/464, no. 52)[1915]/ Madrid BN(MAPAS VÁRIOS(BAG 1861), no. 41)[1915]/ Nürnberg GNM(Kartensamml. Italien 3)[1911]

References:
Marinelli, 1881, 108-09, no. 543; Grande, 1902, 65; Ruge, 1904-16, Pt. IV, 153-54 (no. 8); Biasutti, 1908, 38; Bagrow, 1928-30, 1, 96, no. 106; Almagià, 1929, 27a (in A) and 30a; Tooley, 1939, nos. 587-593; Almagià, 1948, 33-34; Gallo, 1954, 46, no. 45*; Cucagna, 1964, 22-24; Borroni-Salvadori, 1980, 19 (no. 48); Bella, 1986, 9 (no. 1); Woodward, 1990, 42-44, nos. 73.01-74.02, and pl. 74.01; Lago, 1992, II, 344, in caption; Woodward, 1992, 53, 55, 63 (no. 56) and 64 (no. 60); Karrow, 1993, 248; Meurer, 2004, 77, no. 63; Bifolco and Ronca, 2018, 3: 1878.

Reproductions:
Woodward, 1990. pl. 74.01; Bifolco and Ronca, 2018, 3: 1879. https://collections.Newberry.org/asset-management/2KXJ8ZSAP73F7?&WS

124. Lombardy
-Rome, 1570
-Copper engraving, 48.5 x 73.0 cm., on two sheets
-50 Italian miles = 11.6 cm.

In text box in the upper left corner:

LA NOVA DESCRITTION DELLA LOMBARDIA. | All' Ill[ustrissi]mo et R[erendissi]mo Mons[ignore]:mio Col[tissi]mo Christoforo Madrutio Car[dina]le di Trento Dignissimo. | Non ho potuto Ill[ustrissi]mo et R[everendissi]mo Sig[no]r mio, con altro che con l'istesse fatighe dimostrarli l'animo mio à | benche indegno di tanta bonta et clemenza, al suo seruitio; però che industriatomi à fare la descrittione | de la Lombardia con tutti suoi confini, nella quale ci sono non poche considerationi, ne potendo darli mag- | gior reputatione che drizzarla à tal Prencipe, essendo cosa uirtuosa curiosa & degna di esser ligata con tal | modello, et patroneggiata da tal Marinaro, l'ho uoluta dedicare à V[ostra] S[ignoria] Ill[ustrissi]ma et R[everendissi]ma Prego adunque sua | bontà e clemenza si degni accettarla, et me nel numero di suoi minimi & affetionati seruitori. Detta | opera è descritta da Jacobo Gastaldi Cosmografo in Venetia, la quale, anchora che da Diuersi sia stata | più uolte fatta e descritta, dimostrerà più apertamente i suoi confini, Le fonti del Pò il suo corso con le Fiu- | mare che ui entrano, e doue sbocca nella Marina, il quale causa la fertilità del Paese. Dimostra anco le | Città principali nelle quali fioriscono tutte le scientie & arti; la regione temperate abondante, e popu- | lata come qual si uoglia altra del Mondo, et signoreggiata da diuersi Prencipi, Li confini di questa | uerso Tramontana sono le Alpi, doue sono li Suizzeri, li Grissoni, il Contado di Tirolo et il Friuli. Verso Mezzogiorno il Mare Mediterraneo di Genoua et la Toscana. Verso Leuante il Frioli il Mare | Adriatico di Venetia & la Romagna. Verso Ponente la Prouenza il Delfinato & la Sauoia fatta con la | graduatione & con la scala delle miglia.---- Stampata « Roma Appresso Antonio Laffreri.L'A[nno]: 1570. | Di V[ostra] S[ignoria] Ill[ustrissi]ma et R[everendissi]ma aff[ettuosissi]mo s[eruitor]e | Giogio Tilman. Fecit. (MODERN MAP OF LOMBARDY. To The Most Illustrious and Reverend Monsignor Christoforo Madrutio Most Dignified Cardinal of Trent. I have not been able my Most Illustrious and Reverend Signor to demonstrate my devotion, although unworthy of such exaltedness and delicacy, other than with these very efforts; however I have done my best to make a map of Lombardy with all the confines, in which there are not a few things, [and] being able to give them greater renown so as to address it to such a prince. [and] being a thing thus virtuous, interesting and worthy of being connected with such an exemplary person, and patronized by such an [excellent man??C"Marinaro"---unclear in present context], I have desired to dedicate [it] to Your Most Illustrious and Most Reverend Lordship. Thus I implore that your kindness and mercifulness deign to accept it, and me into the number of your most insignificant and adoring servants. The said work is drawn by Jacobo Gastaldi Cosmographer in Venice, [and] it, even though it has been made and drawn several times, will demonstrate more clearly its confines, The sources of the Po, its course, with the tributaries which enter into it, which results in the fertility of the country, and where it discharges at the coast. It shows also the principal cities in which all the sciences and arts flower; the bountiful temperate region, and populated such as the rest of the world might wish, and ruled by diverse Princes. The confines of this toward the North are the Alps, where are the Swiss, the Grisonians, the Country of Tyrol and Friuli, Toward the South the Mediterranean Sea of Genoa and Tuscany. Toward the East Friuli the Adriatic Sea of Venice and Romania. Toward the West Provence, Dauphiné and Savoy made with graduation & with the scale of miles.----Printed in Rome by Antonio Lafreri The Year 1570.----engraved by Giorgio Tilman most affectionate servant of Your Most Illustrious and Most Reverend Lordship) [I cannot in all places fully vouch for the accuracy of the necessarily very free translation, admittedly barely comprehensible at times, for the impenetrably troubled syntax and diction of Tilman rather often approaches to complete unintelligibility.])

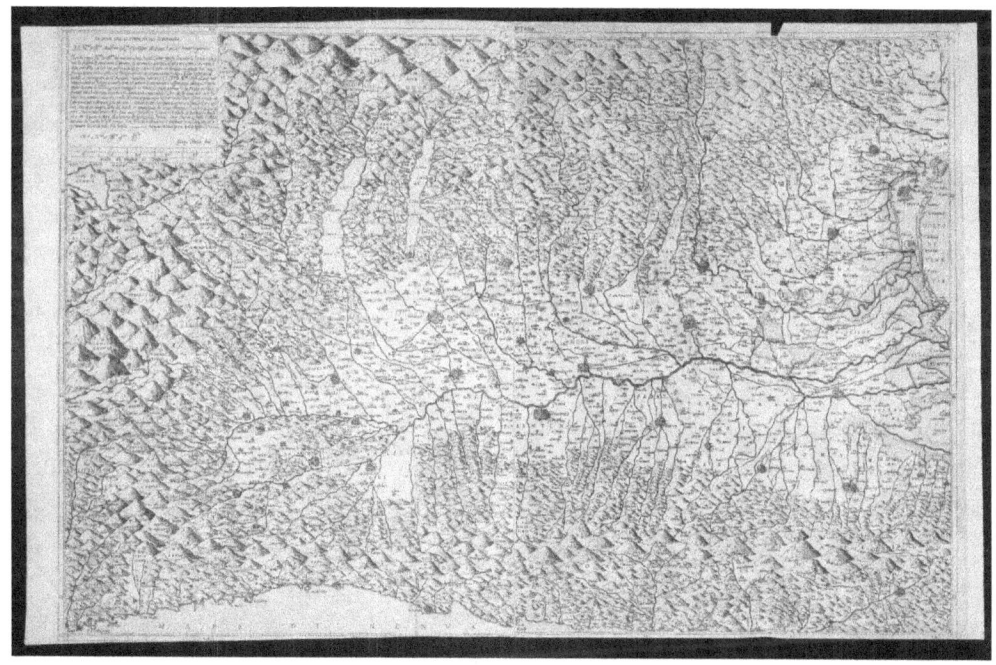

124 Lombardy 1570 Chicago Newb

Comments:

Graduated in whole degrees, each numbered, in latitude and longitude, from 42°52' to 45°45' N, and from 27°58' to 34°07' E, on a rectangular projection. The map includes much more than just Lombardy, embracing virtually all of northern Italy, and the areas covered by Gastaldi's Piedmont and Padua are entirely included within it, though of course on a smaller scale. The map is one of Gastaldi's finer works, and Almagià even went so far as to suggest that it was perhaps his most valuable work (1929, 28b), but the statement reflects the usual tendency of Italian scholars to focus on Italy at the expense of his other maps, for, regardless of its outstanding qualities, the map cannot touch in historical importance Gastaldi's maps of the far continents. But, as Almagià notes, the richness of the hydrography, and the accurate representation of the lagoons, valleys and marshy areas is truly impressive, as is the abundance of towns, although here there are some singular omissions (Almagià, cit., 28b). The sources are unclear. For Piedmont, it is essentially identical to Gastaldi's Piedmont of 1555, but the rest is completely different from any known previous maps, and Almagià simply states that it is an elaboration of original material selected with great care (Almagià, cit., 28b). Umek observes that there is much similarity between it and the same area in the Vescovile atlas (Umek, 2002, 520, 521, 523 and 525), but he concedes that the Lombardy gives a more advanced depiction than the Vescovile atlas (521 and 525), so its usage as a source must be considered as debatable.

Regardless of the fact that the earliest printing known is the current 1570 edition, Almagià did not consider that this map was among those which Gastaldi held back for whatever reasons and were therefore only published after his death. He developed a theory that, although no copy is known or attested, the map was first published in 1559 as a woodcut which would have been larger, and covered a somewhat larger area, and his theory has been accepted by several scholars (Lavis-Trafford, 1950, 53 nt. 5; Karrow, 1993, 230; Perini, 1996, 55-56; and Lago, 2002, 339). He bases his argument on the facts that there exists a July 29, 1559 request and granting of a privilege for a Lombardy (as well as a September 11, 1564 privilege also for a Lombardy), the fact that there exists an undated but probably early seventeenth century issue of the Lombardy by F. Valeggio which is much larger and also extends the area coverage seen in the 1570 map, and the supposition that there exists a pattern by which Gastaldi would publish a map first in a woodcut edition, and then only later in an edition in copperplate. Basically, his scenario is that the first privilege, of 1559, was for a woodcut, which was duly published at that time, and the 1564 privilege was for the copperplate edition, but it was not realized because of Gastaldi's death (which at the time Almagià wrote this was still considered to have occurred in ca. 1565, his real death date of 1566 not being established until 1939), due to which it did not make it to the press, and first appeared only in the known 1570 printing. Later, in the early seventeenth century, Valeggio used a copy of the presumed original woodcut edition to make his issue of the Lombardy (discussed and reproduced in Bifolco and Ronca, 2018, 3: 1858-60).

But this scenario does not stand up well for several reasons. In the first place, there exists no pattern of Gastaldi maps being first published in woodcut, and then in copperplate. This occurs only once, with the 1555 Piedmont, which was then reissued in the next year 1556 as a copperplate engraved by Licinio. A single instance does not make a pattern, and reason exists to surmise that the case with the Piedmont was a special case, and Gastaldi may simply have been trying out Licinio as an engraver to use in his projected great series of maps which began to be published in 1559 (see our no. 80). Then there are problems with the privilege notices. As we have seen, privilege dates are never a reliable basis for determining dates of publication in general, and in the present case there are two more problems. One, the July 29, 1559, privilege was a blanket sort of privilege, which was for six maps, the First, Second, and Third Parts of Asia, the Greece, the Italy, and the Lombardy. All but the Lombardy are known, and they were published, all in copperplate, respectively in 1559, 1561, 1561, 1560, and 1561. (Note, incidentally, that we have here a perfect example of the unwiseness of taking a privilege date as being the date of publication.) It seems likely, since the five that were published were copperplates, that all were intended as copperplates.

While the point just made is perhaps not waterproof, there is still another problematic point with the privileges. By Almagià's scenario, the explanation for the September 11, 1564, second privilege for a Lombardy was that this time the privilege was for a copperplate edition of the supposed woodcut covered by the 1559 privilege. But there is a different possible explanation for the double privilege notice which I think is more likely. By the year 1517, a problem had developed in the Venetian system of privileges. More and more publishers had taken to the practice of obtaining privileges for works which promised to sell well, mostly the classics, which were quite popular at the time, even though these publishers had not yet actually prepared, or even begun preparing, these works for the press and might not even start preparing them for an indeterminate amount of time. In the meantime, since these publishers held the privileges, other publishers could not print these works, and, as the practice became widespread, the entire Venetian publishing business came to be in a sort of stranglehold (Brown, 1891, 54, 74, 75). The government acted, passing a law in 1517 to deal with the problem (Brown, cit., 54, 74), but the new law was poorly worded, and the abuse continued. Then, in 1533, a law was passed which dealt adequately with the problem. The new law stated that when one acquired a privilege for a work, he must produce the work within a year if possible, and if not possible, as could be the case with more extensive and extravagant works, he must be able to show that he was making regular and significant progress on it. Otherwise, the privilege would become invalid (Brown, 1891, 57, 75, 76, and, printing the text of the original law in full, 208-09). The law is worded as if books were had in mind, but we can be sure that it came to be applied as well to maps and other prints as those industries developed. Thus, a likely explanation for the privilege of 1564 is simply that Gastaldi had not managed to produce the Lombardy fast enough, the 1559 privilege became void for that map, and he had to re-apply. We see this also, incidentally, with another Gastaldi map, his Anatolia. A privilege for it, along with another map (our no. 93), was taken out on April 29, 1559. While the other map came out, the Anatolia did not, and Gastaldi reapplied for a second privilege for it in 1564 (in the same second privilege request of September 11 for the Lombardy), and it appeared that year, though there was still no sign of the Lombardy.

In my opinion, Gastaldi was having some sort of difficulties with the Lombardy, failed to resolve them before he died in 1566, and thus the map did not appear until 1570 with the Lafreri-Tilman edition. As to the moderate extensions given to the Gastaldi Lombardy by F. Valeggio in the early seventeenth century, the data for this could no doubt easily have been obtained from other maps that had been made in the interim, for instance the many excellent maps of Italian and other areas made by Magini, or some other maps. In conclusion, until a copy of Almagià's hypothesized 1559 woodcut Gastaldi Lombardy should surface, an eventuality we do not expect since we doubt that such a map ever existed, we find Almagià's scenario quite unconvincing, and we consider that the 1570 Lafreri-Tilman map was the first printing ever made of Gastaldi's Lombardy, and, accordingly we enter the map in our Cartobibliography at 1570, instead of at 1559. For data on later editions of the 1570 map, see Almagià (1929, 28-29), Almagià (1948, 40-41), and Karrow (1993, 230-31).

Location of copies:
Chicago Newb(Novacco 4F 309)/ ULC (G1015.L25 1575 Vault, no. 38)/ London BL(Maps C.7.e.2, no. 40)/ London RGS (Map Room, 264.G.", no. 31)/ Valletta NLM (progressive number 15963, v. 6, no. 112 [s. Ganado, 1984, 207 with 142, nt. 15])/ Firenze BN (12.-44., v. I, no. 44)/ Roma BN (711.6.G.1, no. 40)/ Madrid PR (MAP/464, no. 59)/ Madrid PR (ARCH1/ CART/29 (35)

References:
Marinelli, 1881, 119, no. 578; Grande, 1902, 68-69; Biasutti, 1908, 37-38, 55 and 65; Almagià, 1914-15, 18-19; Bagrow, 1928-30, 1, 96; Almagià, 1929, 27b, 28b-29a, 30a and 31a; Almagià, 1948, 40-41; Lavis-Trafford, 1950, 52-53; Aliprandi, 1974, 42-43, 110, 191, 222; Karrow, 1993, 230-31; Gambi, 1994, text, 279; Perini, 1996, 54-57; Umek, 202, 520, 521, 523, 525; Bifolco and Ronca, 2018, 3: 1868.

Reproductions:
Almagià, 1929, pl. 31; Bifolco and Ronca, 2018, 3: 1869.
https://collections.Newberry.org/asset-management/2KXJ8ZSKA8G2M

The above entry, no. 124, concludes our Cartobibliography of Gastaldi maps proper. The twelve entries remaining, numbered in Roman numerals from I to XII, while they were not produced directly by Gastaldi, are of much importance to our Cartobibliography and our book. They represent three sets of wall maps of the four continents which were made by other hands, G. F. Camocio, then D. Bertelli, using almost entirely Gastaldi's cartography. They can be considered, in a very real sense, the final culmination of the main part of his work, and the first of the three sets, by Camocio, which aborted, was the first attempt ever at such a four-continent set, while the last sets are two variants of essentially the same set, completed by Donato Bertelli, all of which is explained in detail in the compound entry (I.-XII.) which precedes them.

(I.-XII.) The Gastaldian Four-Continent Sets of Wall Maps of G. F. Camocio and D. Bertelli

With entry no. 124, we concluded our chronological cartobibliography of Gastaldi maps proper, that is, maps which were produced by Gastaldi personally, including five posthumous works which were made by him at unknown points in his life. As we have, with intentional repetition, pointed out, among this large number of maps, there are six which incomparably surpass all the rest in historical importance, the maps of the far continents and the great 1561 *Cosmographia vniversalis* world map, since they alone show a true geographical quantum leap, like none other, resulting suddenly as it were in a modern and generally correct picture of the world. In a word, they *do*, for the first time since people first began to show interest and curiosity in the world around them, depict that world essentially as it truly is. Nobody had ever seen a picture of the planet he or she lived on which showed it in the main correctly everywhere, or nearly everywhere. In general terms, in the story of the growth of human knowledge, here, beyond any doubt, is an advance which cannot but be numbered among the major steps forward.

      He did this, and this is his main legacy. But he did not, and apparently never formulated an intention to, present them in the form of a unified whole. They were simply six extraordinarily impressive maps among the total of 124. While printed atlases existed, they were all the ancient atlas of Ptolemy. In some, modern maps were added (more in Gastaldi's Ptolemy than in any other), but the books still basically remained the atlas of Ptolemy, and the modern additions were more adjuncts than anything else. Even the titles alone of these books were enough to show this, for they are without exception called Ptolemy's *Geography*, even if in smaller print the titles sometimes noted the fact that some modern maps had been subjoined. No atlas which roundly and conclusively broke away from the ancient model existed, and even if the modern maps had been removed as a body and bound together (I know of no such case), the coverage of the world beyond Europe would not have been sufficient. It is true that one of the six great maps, Gastaldi's 1561 world map answered in a limited way to this need, but the scale was not at all up to what was available in his separate continental maps.

Very shortly after Gastaldi's death, in the 1570s, first with Ortelius's *Theatrum Orbis Terrarum* of 1570, and shortly after that in the form of a series of four large maps of all the then recognized four continents, the two great forms which answered to the need for a unified modern presentation of the world, and lasted for centuries, indeed until today, began to appear. These new forms broke with finality the old bond to the revered but no longer valid ancient geography, a fact not diminished in importance significantly by the other fact that, here and there, in interiors, traces of Ptolemy remained, and would not disappear completely until the eighteenth century, if not perhaps the nineteenth. No, the break was a virtually complete one, and in spirit literally 100% complete. As to the far continents, Africa, Asia, and America, it was virtually entirely the continental depictions of Gastaldi which made the appearance of both of these forms possible, for it was mainly his geography which filled in these pictures of the extra-European world, which, in terms of physical land coverage, accounts for as much if not more than 90% of the world's land surface. The story of the advent of the modern atlas in Ortelius's *Theatrum* has been well covered elsewhere. But the story of the inception of the sets of maps of the four continents has languished. It is the story of the metamorphosis of Gastaldi's greatest works into a unified whole, first in the hands of Giovanni Francesco Camocio in the 1570s, an enterprise which unfortunately did not quite make it to the finish due to Camocio's death, evidently from the plague at the middle or shortly after the middle of the decade, followed in the mid-1590s by the final culmination of the project by Donato Bertelli.

The story of the genesis, filled with birth pains, of this four-continent form has been, we trust, well and concisely covered in our last chapters, eleven and twelve. But we felt it appropriate and necessary to individually present the maps of those sets at the end of our Cartobibliography, for, although not compiled directly by Gastaldi, they are, as we have said, the rightful culmination of his most important work. And it is only in these sets, intended to be proudly displayed on wall space, such that Gastaldi's grand achievement, the capturing of the world on paper, can be seen and perused as a whole, the virtual entirety of the world at a glance as it were.

Even if the question of how much of the picture of one of the continents, Europe, comes from Gastaldi is still not perfectly ascertained, it is valid, we feel, to refer to the four-continent set as Gastaldi's, and it was in fact so referred to in the account books of the Officina Plantiniana, as we have seen. Since the original maps from which these depictions were taken have already been dealt with earlier in our Cartobibliography, and since the technical execution of this cartography in four-continent form took place at the hands of others and is covered in chapters eleven and twelve, we restrict these entries principally to the usual cartobibliographical technical details of size, scale, date, publishing data and partial dedicatory information, etc., and provide only limited further comments, since the human story, covered thoroughly in the two mentioned chapters is rather complicated and intricate, and does not lend itself well to an abbreviated presentation. But we will include a few facts of secondary importance which were left out in the presentations in chapters eleven and twelve.

We present twelve maps, numbered I to XII, in three sets, first those four created in the 1570s by Camocio (nos. I-IV), and then the maps of the set completed by Bertelli in the 1590s, but in printings made from Bertelli's plates in the mid-seventeenth century, for regrettably no copies of the original Bertelli printings have survived, or if they have, they have not yet surfaced. We present these in two sets of four maps each (nos. V-VIII and IX-XII), for two reasons. In the first place, the first set, tentatively dated as 1655 on the basis of the Asia, the only dated map, differs in some respects from the second set, tentatively dated as 1662, also on the basis of the Asia, again the only dated map. In the second place, it seemed advisable to include both sets, for there remain some mysteries regarding the make-up of these two sets by relation to each other which we have not been able to fully resolve, and so the best policy, in the interests of future scholars who may wade into the question of these unresolved points, seemed to be to reproduce and document both sets. Lending further fuel to the advisability of reproducing both sets is the fact that the final set (nos. IX-XII) is the fullest and best preserved of the sets, and, since the set is at present in private hands, a real possibility exists that the set will become inaccessible to scholars for an indefinite period of time, with its whereabouts becoming perhaps altogether unknown, so that the present reproductions and documentation may well be the only such which will be available to the scholarly world for study. We begin with the set, unique, which was produced by Camocio in the 1570s, in which set one map, the America, remained incomplete at the time of Camocio's death, as seen in our reproduction of that map. We note that in the map listings for all three sets, even though in Camocio's original attempt he produced the Aftrica first, we have listed the Europe first, both in order to adhere to the most usual practice, and also because, by doing so, the listing of the far-continent maps, our main interest, are not broken up by the Europe. The actual chronology of production is clear from the dates given here (see also the discussion on probable chronology of the original set in section 11.3.3 of chapter eleven).

(I.-IV.) The Camocio Gastaldian Four-Continent set, ca. 1570-1575 (?) (uncompleted)

It is not known exactly when Camocio produced each of these maps, nor is it certain in which order he produced them, but we present what we believe to be the most reasonable hypothesis in the section "ASIA" in chapter eleven.

I. Gastaldi (partially)-Camocio Europe
-Venice, ca. ca. 1572-73 (?) (original date; date of the Bell Library copy described changed to 1579 [MDLXXIX].)
-Copper engraving, 103.5 x 145.5, in twelve sheets (nine full and three half sheets)
-100 Italian miles = 3.4 cm.
This map bears no title.

In an ornate cartouche in the upper left sheet of the map:
A dedicatory epistle to Count Antonio Valmarana (on whom see Gallo, 1950, 101-02 and Woodward, 1997, 8), signed by Camocio. See Gallo (1954, 36, no. 4*) for a full transcription in Italian, our fig. 11.5 for an enlarged reproduction of the dedication, and Gallo (1950, 101) for a full English translation.

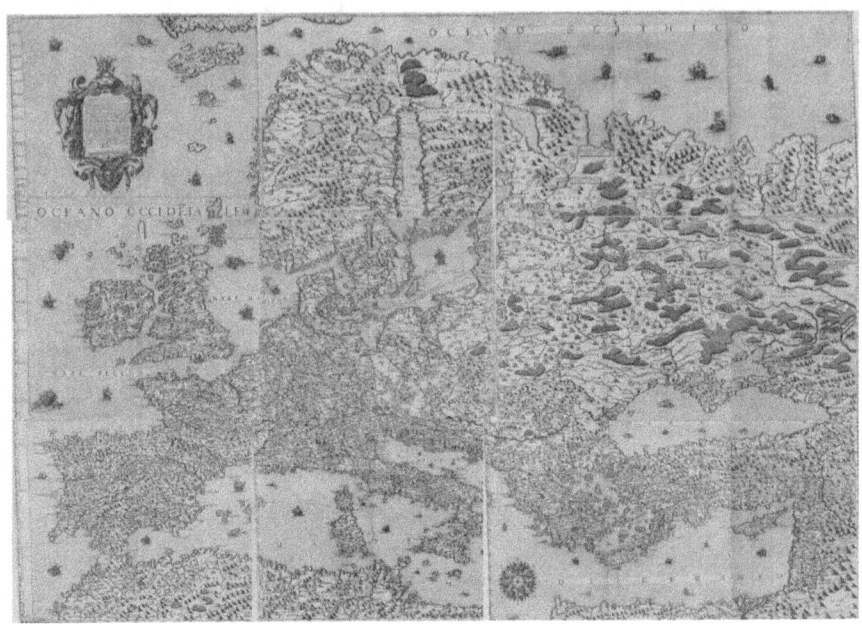

I. Gastaldi (partially)-Camocio Europe 1572-73? Minneapolis Bell

At the bottom of the cartouche, under the scale bar:
Alla libraria della Piramide (At the bookshop of the Pyramid)

Comments:
Graduated in latitude in twelve-minute increments, each whole degree marked, with each fifth degree numbered, from 30°17' to 80°00' N; graduated in longitude at the top in fifteen-minute increments, each degree marked, with each fifth degree numbered, from 320°00' to 103°00' E, and at the bottom graduated in ten-minute increments, with each degree numbered, from 9°20' to 70°00' E, on a trapezoidal projection with very sharp convergence of the meridians. As we have brought out in the text and

mentioned above here, while much in the Contarini map, from which Camocio directly copied the present map, is from Gastaldi, the amount that Contarini took from Gastaldi has not been determined.

Location of copies:
The copy in the four-continent set under discussion, bound as individual sheets in atlas form, is in the James Ford Bell Library of the University of Minnesota, under call no. B1560 fCa. A copy missing seven of the twelve sheets is in the incomplete four-continent set in the Library of the Correr Museum in Venice discussed in the text, call no. Cartografia cartella 32, no. 4 (reproduced in Heijden, 1992, 94-95); and a superb separate copy, dated July 26, 1573 (which I suspect is the original date of completion of the map) is in the Prins Hendrik Maritiem Museum in Rotterdam, with call no. K263 (reproduced in Koeman, 1978, p.8); according to Heijden (1992, 93) there is a seventeenth century copy in the Yale University Library, in very bad condition, with extensive added illustrative framework pasted around the edges, showing city views, persons in traditional dress, etc., but I could find no such copy there. To the best of my knowledge, there are no other copies, except those two given in entries V and IX below.

References:
See our text in chapters eleven and twelve, and Bifolco and Ronca, 2018, 1:670.

Reproductions:
Bifolco and Ronca, 2018, 1:671-73, above.

II. Gastaldi-Camocio Africa
-Venice, ca. 1571-72 (?)
-Copper engraving, 106.0 x 146.0 cm., in twelve sheets (nine full and three half sheets)
-100 Italian miles = 1.9 cm.

The map bears no title, and the only text is at the head of a large cartouche in the upper right corner containing ancient and modern place name equivalents:
Tavola de nomi antichi et moderni dela presente carta (Table of the ancient and modern names of the present map)

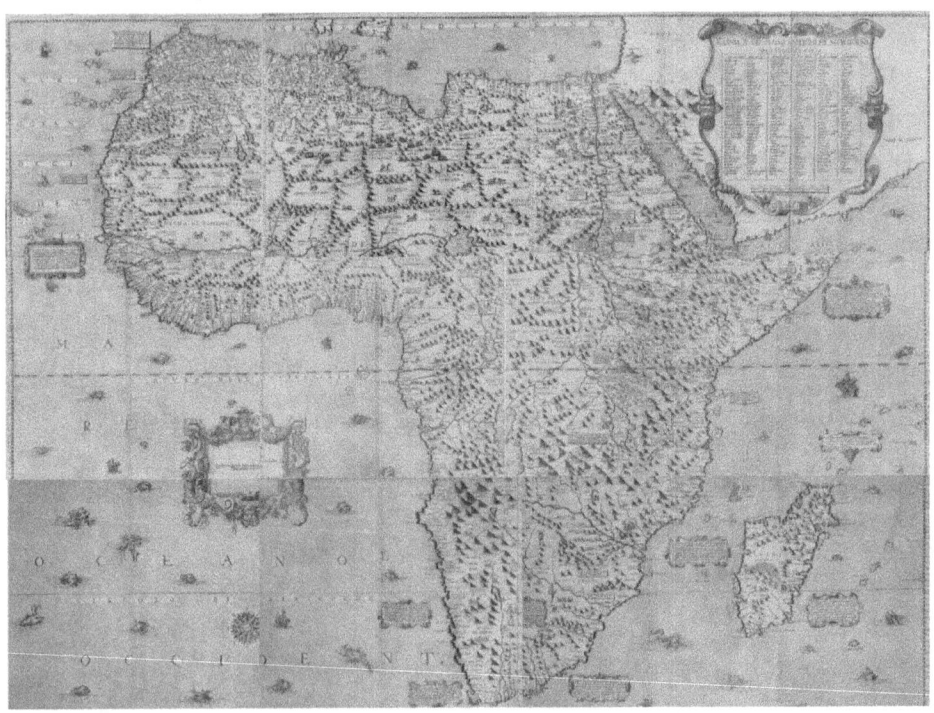

II. Gastaldi-Camocio Africa 1571-72? Minneapolis Bell

Comments:
Graduated in latitude in ten-minute increments, with each whole degree numbered, from ca. 31°25' S to ca. 31°20' N. Graduated in longitude only on the equator in whole degrees, each fifth degree numbered, from 7°00' W to

99°00' E, although there is confusion in the numbering towards the left end of the map, so that the actual longitude at the west edge of the map should probably be considered as at 2°00 W, putting the prime meridian, not drawn in, somewhere in the western Cape Verde Islands. The projection is indeterminate. The map is a clear-cut copy of Gastaldi's 1564 Africa except for a few small and insignificant changes, probably arbitrary, and the addition of characteristically ornate Camocian decorative touches, such as the elaborate cartouche around Gastaldi's list of ancient and modern place names, or around the sundry informational inscriptions, and is thus simply an edition of the 1564 Africa. Camocio's name does not appear on the map, but there is a large blank dedicatory cartouche in the Bight of Benin, oddly containing only the words: *Qui dentro va posta la epistola dedicatoria et espositoria della presente carta (Here inside is to be placed the dedicatory epistle and explanatory note of the present map)*, which no doubt would have included his name, and, in any event, on the basis of style by comparison with the other maps there is no question that it is Camocio's work.

Location of copies:
The only known full copy, bound as individual sheets in atlas form, is in the James Ford Bell Library of the University of Minnesota, under call no. B1560 fCa. An incomplete copy is known, which is in private possession (Betz, 2007, 117).

References:
See our text in chapters eleven and twelve, and Bifolco and Ronca, 2018, 1:440.

Reproductions:
Bifolco and Ronca, 2018, 1:441-43; above.

III. Gastaldi-Camocio Asia

-Venice, ca. 1573-74 (?) (original date; changed to 1579 [written MDLXXV4] in the present copy)
-Copper engraving, 97.0 x 145.0 cm., on twelve sheets (nine full sheets and three half sheets)
-100 Italian miles = 1.4 cm.

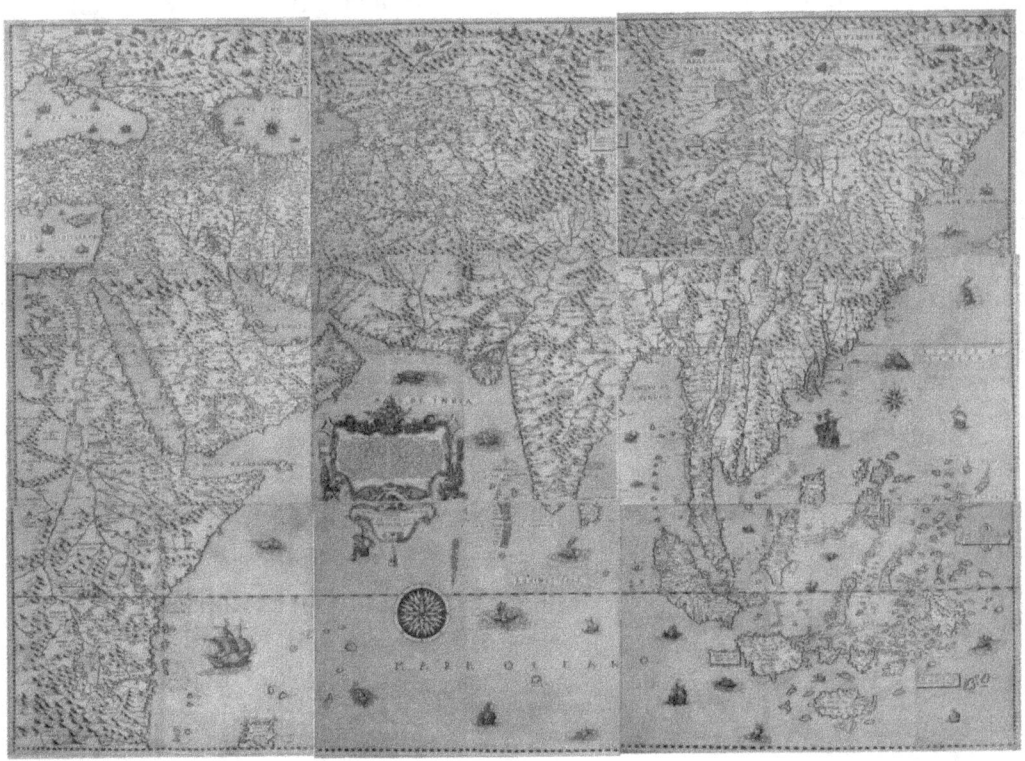

III. Gastaldi-Camocio Asia 1573-74? Minneapolis Bell

The map has no formal title, but contains in an ornate cartouche in the sea west of India, a lengthy dedicatory text from Camocio to Gottardo Murari, in the essential parts of which text Camocio identifies the cartography of the map as being from Gastaldi's Three Parts of Asia, tells us that according to the ancient and modern writers, there are four continents, Asia, Africa, Europe and the New World, notes that he has already produced a Europe and an Africa, and states that he now hopes to produce the fourth continent, "so that the whole said universe might be enjoyed," the earliest known declaration of an intent to complete a four-continent set of wall maps. We have transcribed and translated this section elsewhere here (see chapter eleven at the section "ASIA"). Camocio then proceeds to note that the contents of the map has come from only those writers which are so ample that they exceed description of only Europe and Africa, then gives the confines of the map in each direction, noting that the area covered contains forty-eight provinces or kingdoms, each of which he then proceeds to name, and ends by saying that the map cost him much labor and expense, and that it is perhaps a thing worthy of adorning the home of a dignified and honorable person, and that the fine, virtuous, noble, honorable, etc. Murari House came to his mind and he has thus dedicated it to Gottardo Murari and prays God to give perpetual felicity to Murari.

Below the cartouche, in a sort of secondary cartouche, dangling as it were from the main one, is the inscription: *In Venetia Appresso Giovan Francesco Camoscio alla libraria di la Piramide (In Venice by Giovan Francesco Camoscio at the bookshop of the Pyramid).*

Comments:
Graduated in twelve-minute increments, with each full degree numbered, in latitude from 15°00' S to 56°00' N. Graduated in longitude only on the equator in whole degrees, each fifth degree numbered, from 55°00' to 195°00' E, with projection indeterminate. Oddly, the map contains three compass roses. The map, of which only one copy exists, is of inestimable value, although this fact seems to have gone unnoticed by the few writers who have devoted any attention to it. Gastaldi, as we know, made a magnificent map of Asia, the first viable map of the continent ever, but in three parts which could not be put together to make up a single map, a fact for which he was criticized. Here, Camocio has done a superb job of combining these three parts into a single map, preserving all of Gastaldi's original detail as it was. It is the only extant copy of the only existing single image which brings together, and with great fidelity to the original, the whole of Gastaldi's image of Asia. This was a truly remarkable achievement by Camocio, and, in our opinion, the present map stands among the most important of the sixteenth century.

References:
See our text in chapters eleven and twelve and Bifolco and Ronca, 2018, 1:396.

Reproductions:
Bifolco and Ronca, 2018, 1:397-99; above.

IV. Gastaldi-Camocio America

-Venice, ca. 1574-75 (?), but uncompleted, although printed, evidently in proof form.
-Copper engraving; if the extant sheets were laid out in the positions and arrangement which was intended, the full height would be 98.5 cm., and the full width 140.5 cm., but there would remain two large gaps in the map (as see our reproduction here); in nine sheets (six full sheets and three half sheets)
-No scale bar

The map bears no title, and there are no legends or inscriptions giving any publishing or dedicatory data, although there is a large blank cartouche west of South America which no doubt was intended to carry such information, but the map is unquestionably Camocio's work.

Comments:
Graduated in twelve-minute increments in latitude, with each whole degree numbered, from 81°00' S to 78°20' N. Graduated in longitude in whole degrees, every fifth degree numbered, on the top and bottom borders, and on the equator. But none of the three series of numberings is complete, because of the missing parts of the map. The equatorial series runs from 12°00' at the right side westward to 109°00' W at the left, which is as far as the uncompleted map extends at that point. The bottom series runs from 13°02' E at the right side westward to 107°00' W, again, as far as the unfinished map

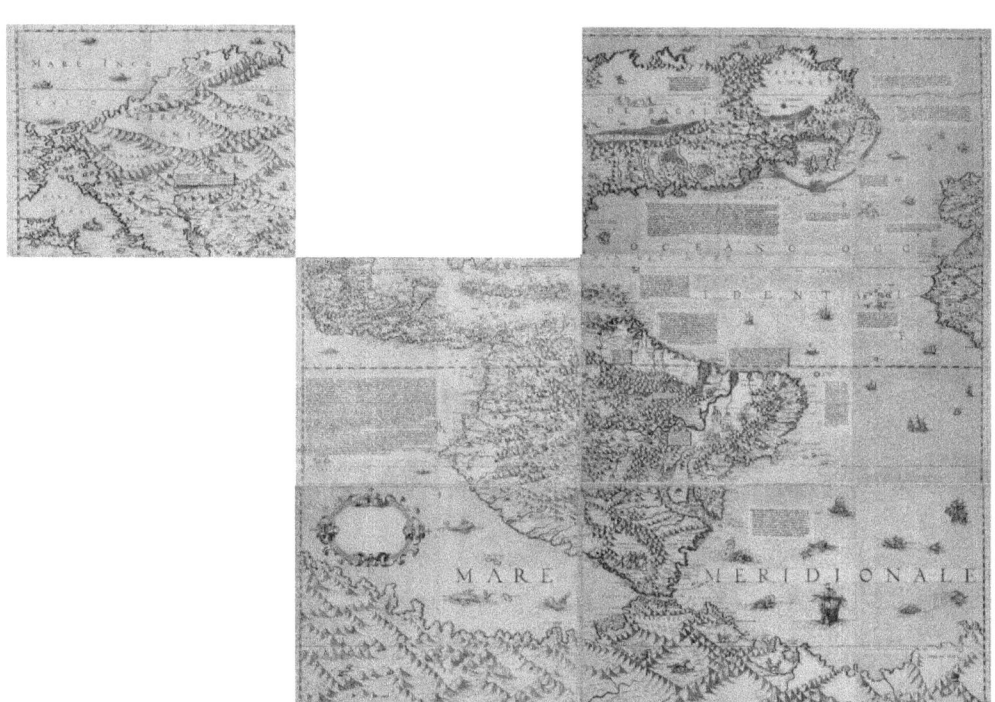

IV. Gastaldi-Camocio America 1574-75? Minneapolis Bell

extends in that direction. The top series runs from 13°10' E at the right side westward to 58°10' W, where starts a large gap in the top part of the map. The cartography then continues after this gap, in what amounts to the upper left sheet, and this graduation nominally runs from 58°10' W to 106°05' W, but this stretch of numbering is bogus, as we have demonstrated in chapters nine and eleven. The incomplete condition of the map in its present state, the peculiar placement of the sheets which are present that is necessary in order to achieve an incomplete but fair image, or visual impression, of the continent of North America, the bogus longitude graduation in the northwest sheet, and still other oddities are the result of Camocio's death having occurred in the midst of making some unusual and complex adjustments to the map, and ensuing unethical actions of unidentified shop personnel. We cannot present a more complete explanation within the confines of the present entry, but we do so fully in our main text, in chapters nine and eleven.

References:
See our text in chapters nine and eleven and Bifolco and Ronca, 2018, 1:342

Reproductions:
Bifolco and Ronca, 2018, 1: 343-47; above.

(V.-XII.) The Camocio-D. Bertelli (-Scolari) Gastaldian Four-Continent set, i.e., the finally culminated set, ca. 1596 (?)

What befell the near complete remnants of the abortive attempt at the basically Gastaldian four-continent set after Camocio's death, and up to the time it was eventually brought to fruition ca. 1596(?) by Donato Bertelli remains obscure. What party or parties possessed the plates, what use (and how much use) was made of them, and by what means they came to rest in the hands of Donato Bertelli probably in the first lustrum of the 1590s, but possibly earlier, is not known; we speculatively discuss the question a little in our text, though we are unable to come up with anything like solid results. We *can* note one perhaps significant fact in the case of that set which was bound as an atlas and rests in the Bell Library. Other than dedicatees, in two cases, and Gastaldi himself, on the Asia, there are no names on the maps except that of Camocio, the publisher, and the original brains behind the project. Now, usually, when plates change hands, we find that a new publisher's name and often address as well, has been added to the plate. Occasionally, especially later in the period, we find the old publisher still left on the plate, but the new publisher is added as well. This was the case with De Nobilibus in Rome, from about the 1580s, and in the maps of F. Valeggio and the Scolaris. But here we find no new publisher's name, or any other name (engraver, printer, etc.). Most important here is the lack of a publisher's name other than, of course the name of Camocio himself, the original publisher, whose name is on the Europe and the Asia. Adding to this the facts, one, that Camocio evidently died from the plague, probably in 1575, and two, that two of the maps in the set carry dates, in both cases 1579, though in both cases the date has very definitely been changed, and clumsily, we see that there are only two to four years between the time Camocio died and this defective set, which we can probably assume was from 1579.

All these facts together do not actually *prove* anything, but they do rather strongly suggest that the bogus atlas, a subterfuge, was unethically put together by the hands around Camocio who were involved in the project with him, sundry shop personnel, from the engraver, to the printer (Camocio, also a publisher of books, probably had a type printing press on his premises, so it is quite possible he had a rolling press as well), to, possibly, personnel who worked up the *modelli* for the engraver, and possibly others of significance, as well as some menial hands, and even these would not be incapable of contributing occasionally new ideas. All of these, when Camocio died, and business at the sign of the Pyramid died, would presumably have been out of work. The suggestion is that it was they who contrived the bogus atlas, sometime between 1575, when Camocio died, and 1579, when the atlas appeared. However, Woodward (1997) tentatively suggests De' Nobili, of Rome, as the atlases' compiler. It is not clear why he chose De' Nobili, but it is clear why he chose Rome. The watermarks in the paper suggested that the atlas was printed in Rome, but for a number of reasons, I have never found watermark evidence overly convincing, and, as we have shown at the end of our chapter eleven, the suggestion is not a logical one in this case.

In any event, either from the survivors of Camocio's establishment, or from some other party, the set's plates came into the possession of Donato Bertelli, and it was he who brought the set to life at last, and as we show clearly in our text. The indications are that this most likely would have occurred sometime between 1594 and 1596. To complete the missing parts of America, which in both cases were areas with very little detail compared to other parts of the map, he probably used the America on a copy of Gastaldi's *Cosmographia vniversalis* world map, which shows essentially the same depiction of America throughout as on the America of the four-continent set. Donato replaced in his set two of Camocio's maps, the Africa and the Asia, with wall maps of these two continents which were approximately of the same size as the Camocio maps, and were of his own making, although they are in both cases simply slavish copies of earlier maps. The Africa is, as with Camocio's, simply a copy of the 1564 Gastaldi Africa, although done in Bertelli's own style instead of Camocio's. It cannot be said that Bertelli's Africa is an improvement over Camocio's, indeed, in our opinion, the Camocio variant is rather better, including its engraving. Regardless of its stylistic differences from Camocio's map, it is, like the latter, simply an edition of the original 1564 Gastaldi Africa of 1564.

The case is quite different, and much more interesting, with the Asia map. Here Bertelli has exactly copied Ortelius's 1567 wall map of Asia, but that map itself is basically Gastaldi, even to each of its coordinates. But Ortelius introduced four changes, enough that we probably can't really consider it an edition of Gastaldi's Asia, but we can consider it a derivative of Gastaldi's Asia. Classifying the map in this sense is in fact problematical, irresolvable, and is perhaps best considered a matter of opinion. Ortelius's four changes are as follows. He has combined the Gastaldi three Parts of Asia into a single map (as did Camocio a little later, though in a different way); he has considerably improved the depiction of Archipelago Asia, probably on the basis of information brought back by Andres Urdaneta or others in the Legazpi expedition; he has added the northern coast of Asia, this an imaginary addition, but nevertheless well within the spirit of the times; and, last but not least, he has replaced Gastaldi's projection with a different one, a truly striking and stunningly effective curvilinear projection, with all parallels and meridians drawn in at ten-degree intervals, and having all the appearance of a modern projection. I know of no other regional map of the time which contains such a marvelous projection. The engraving also seems almost impossibly well done, though the engraver's identity is not known, so that both in conceptualization as well as execution, this 1567 Asia must also be numbered among the greatest maps of the century. As fine a job as Camocio's Asia is, it must be admitted, unlike the case with the Africa, that Bertelli did well in replacing the original Asia with this masterpiece of Ortelius. However, the engraver (also unknown) of the Bertelli copy, though he did a quite acceptable job, was far behind Ortelius's near miraculous engraver in expertise (cf. our reproductions of maps nos. VII and XI with the reproduction of Ortelius's 1567 original in Schilder (1987, in portfolio, pls. 31.-38.)).

Bertelli's two maps are also known in a couple of separate copies, and they are both undated. Exactly when Bertelli made these two maps, and why, is not clear. The Africa stems directly from Gastaldi's 1564 Africa, and the Asia stems from Ortelius's 1567 Asia, and both were used in ca. 1596 to complete Bertelli's four-continent wall map set. We can narrow down the *terminus a quo* considerably, for both maps are dedicated to Paolo Nani in the capacity of Procurator of St. Mark's, to which office he was elected only on November 22, 1573, and held until 1608 (Caraci, 1926-32, II, 37 nt. 3). However, though I have, for well over 20 years, sought some basis to narrow these spans down further, I have so far not found a single shred of information which throws any helpful light. The only conjecture which I can come up with is that, since it probably would have been shortly after Nani's election, say about 1574, that Bertelli caught wind of Camocio's four-continent attempt being under way, he decided, in competition, to create his own, but he stopped when the plague hit Venice, having succeeded in making only two of the continents, and perhaps temporarily retiring to Padua, where much of his family lived, and when he returned, either had no time to pursue the project, or had for some reason lost interest in it. Certainly, the two maps are stylistically very similar in several ways to each other, and the implication that they might have been originally conceived as part of a four-continent set is inescapable. But we have no definite evidence of this, and so far, we can say with assurance only that the maps were made at some time between late 1573 and ca. 1596, a 23 year span!

As to Europe, Bertelli used Camocio's original, although he removed Camocio's name and address, so there is nothing on any of the maps of the Bertelli set to indicate that Camocio had ever had any connection with the set at all, although in fact he is the original father of it. The America, as we have seen, was also the Camocio-Gastaldi America, but brought to completion. This new set evidently sold well. We have, as mentioned elsewhere, a 1604 record of ten full sets being sold by the Officina Plantiniana to Baptiste Vrients (see chapter twelve, at the section, "A terminus a quo and a terminus ad quem"). Nevertheless, no copies printed and sold by Bertelli's famous San Marco shop are known. The plates passed later, perhaps ca. 1640, into the hands of the Scolari family, who began issuing the set. We possess three such sets. In all three sets, the only map carrying a date is the Asia. We have one set in which the Asia is dated 1655, at the Ransom Center of the University of Texas at Austin (our nos. V-VIII), and two sets (one of them lacking the Europe) in which the Asia is dated 1662, both in the possession of Graham Arader of New York (see.nos. IX-XII). The maps in these Scolari sets all contain, at the top, added titles, pasted on from separately printed strips, which added titles are discussed in our text in chapter eleven.

(V.-VIII.) The ca. 1655 Printing of the Four-Continent set

This set presents something of a mystery. We know the Asia is earlier than the other set (nos. IX-XII), because it is dated seven years earlier. We also know that the Africa is earlier, for while this Africa carries a Scolari signature in two places, in the other set, one of the two Scolari addresses has clearly been clumsily rubbed out. And we know that the America is earlier, for in the 1662 set Drake's Passage has been cut through, and the name "STRETO D'ANIAN" has been added above the strait separating Asia and America, and on land next to it, on the American side, a little kingdom "regno d'Anian" appears, none of which changes have yet been made in the America of the 1655 set. But with the Europe we encounter a strange problem. In the 1655 set, the Europe is a completely new engraving, with a completely different ornate cartouche in the upper left sheet, and with different, and differently placed, ships, fish, sea monsters, and other maritime décor, while in the 1662 set, the Europe is still very clearly that produced by Camocio, but with Camocio's dedicatory epistle replaced simply with the title EVROPA in very large capital letters, although shadowy traces of the former presence of the dedication are still detectable behind the lettering.

What accounts for this, I do not know for certain. One possible explanation is that the sets sold so well that a good number of framed or unframed copies were regularly made up and stored aside somewhere. We recall that in 1604 Vrients had ordered ten sets from the Officina Plantiniana, and since the Officina itself must have obtained the sets from the Bertellis in Venice there could be the implication that they already had more than ten sets in stock, and, accordingly, if sales were that good the Bertellis

807

themselves may have kept quite a large stock always on hand. The same could have been true of the Scolaris. They could have had stock that had accumulated over years, and so it is not impossible that on some occasions, when a customer ordered such a set, it could easily occur that a combination of older and more recent printings of the four maps were pulled from the stockroom. Considering that, in all likelihood, sometimes orders for single continents, or perhaps two, were surely made, disorder in the stockroom between older and newer printings of things would be likely, and there is no reason why seller or buyer should much concern himself with the matter. Another possible scenario could be as follows. The original Europe became too worn for continued use. This would not be surprising, for it was probably the oldest of the plates, and individual orders for the Europe probably much exceeded individual orders for the other continents, so the Scolaris had it reengraved. But the reengraved Europe which occurs in the 1655 set is not a good engraving. In fact, it is an extremely poor one. Several writers have mentioned that there was a shortage of good engravers in seventeenth century Italy, and certainly in this case, if this scenario be correct, the Scolaris hired a very poor one indeed. Now we know that throughout the history of engraving there were cases where old but very successful plates were restored, and there were even persons who specialized in this, sometimes adding to their signatures the word "restituit" or "reddidit" (Woodward, 1992, 46). There is no such word on the 1662 set's Europe, but it is unlikely that this designation was always added. In short, the Scolaris may have been so dissatisfied with the new Europe as in the 1655 set, that they hired someone, this time an artisan of more expertise, to restore the plates for the old Europe, and began using the refurbished old plate again, instead of the undesirable new engraving, and the Europe in the 1662 set is from this restored plate.

V. Europe
-Venice, ca. 1655(?)
-Copper engraving, 101.5 x 142.0 (with added title strip ca. 107.0 x 142.0) cm., on 12 sheets (9 full and 3 half sheets)
-100 Italian miles = ca. 3.4 cm.

V. Camocio-Scolari-Gastaldi Europe 1655? Austin UT

On the title strip added at the top:
NOVA ET ACVRATA TOTIVS EVROPAE TABVLA, auct. G. I: (ACCURATE MAP OF ALL OF EUROPE [For the translation of the notation at the ending "auct: G. I:", see chapter eleven])

In an ornate cartouche at the upper left:
EV | RO | PA (EUROPE)

In the scrollwork at the bottom of the cartouche:
Stefano Scolari forma (Stefano Scolari plate owner/publisher)

Comments:
Graduated in latitude in ten-minute increments, with each whole degree numbered (though there are some discrepancies), from 27°15' to 80°10' N; in longitude graduated at the top in fifteen-minute increments, each whole degree numbered, from 317°40' to 103°00' E; and at the bottom in ten-minute

809

increments, with each whole degree numbered, from 9°55' to ca. 71°00' E, on a trapezoidal projection, with sharp convergence of the meridians. In some places, there are spacing errors. This map is a reengraving, and a very poor one, as note for example in the southeast part of the map the very different type of mountains, and the badly written large words "ARABIA PETRIA" by comparison with the Europe map in the other sets, and similar signs of very poor engraving can be found throughout the map with no difficulty.

Location of copy:
The only copy known is in the Harry Ransom Humanities Research Center at the University of Texas at Austin. It has not been formally catalogued as of this writing, but is identified by the interim call no.: Kraus 12/IV.

References:
Bifolco and Ronca, 2018, 1: 646; see also our text in chapters eleven and twelve.

Reproductions:
Kraus, 1949, pl. XIV; Kraus, 1969?, 25; Bifolco and Ronca, 2018, 1: 647-49.

VI. AFRICA
-Venice, ca. 1655 (?)
- Copper engraving, 91.5 x 125.0 (with added title strip ca. 97.0 x 125.0) cm., on 8 sheets, 4 up and 4 down.
-   -200 Italian miles = 3.4 cm.

On the title strip added at the top of the map:
NOVA ET ACVRATA TOTIVS AFRICAE TABVLA, auct: G. I: (NEW AND ACCURATE MAP OF ALL OF AFRICA [For the translation of the notation at the ending "auct: G. I:", see chapter eleven]*)*

On the body of the map proper, in large capital letters, in the Gulf of Guinea, the original title:
NOVA TOTIVS AFRICAE DESCRIPTIO (NEW MAP OF ALL OF AFRICA)

At lower left, at the head of a cartouche containing ancient and modern place name equivalents for African localities, a dedication from Bertelli to Paolo Nani:

Clarissimo | Domino Paulo Nani digni | ssimo Procuratori Sancti | Marci
Domino et Patron | suo semper obseruandissimo | D. B. (To the Most
Renowned Lord Paulo Nani most dignified Procurator of Saint Mark's
Master and Patron [from] your ever respectful D[onato] B[ertelli]) (There
follow four more short lines the smaller lettering of which has become badly
worn and which unfortunately I am unable to make out)

At the bottom of the list of names in the border of the cartouche:
Ad signum bibliothecae Diui Marci (At the bookshop of Saint Marks)

And still lower, in the scrollwork:
Stefanus Scolarus(?) formis (Stefano Scolari plate owner/publisher)[I am
unable to make out with certainty the last two (three?) letters in the word
"Scolarus", and cannot vouch securely for the word's ending.]

VI. Camocio-Scolari-Gastaldi Africa 1655? Austin UT

Finally, we find, peculiarly, a second signature of Scolari in Italian instead of Latin at the end of a small informational text box located next to the Canary Islands and giving the map-reader information about the islands:
Stefano Scolari forma (Stefano Scolari plate owner/publisher)

There is nothing more in the way of publishing or dedicatory information on the map, but in the upper right in a cartouche is a sort of general informational text about Africa, a considerable portion of which has worn away and can't be read. It tells us that the ancients called Africa the Third Part (continent) of the world, and that Giacomo Gastaldi has made this full map of it, after which the major portion of the text follows, giving some description of African geography.

Comments:
Latitude is not indicated on the borders, but only very cursorily along the central meridian, where we find latitude numbering at every five degrees (though there are no actual graduation markings), approximately from 34°00' S to 36°30' N. Longitude is given only on the equator in whole degrees, with each fifth degree numbered. For some reason, Bertelli leaves about the first four degrees west of the zero point (the prime meridian is not indicated) unmarked, but the whole longitude coverage is from ca. 4°00' W to ca. 93°30' E. The projection is indeterminate.

Location of copies:
Besides the present copy, at the Harry Ransom Humanities Center of the University of Texas at Austin, with provisional call no. of Kraus 12/III, and two copies in the private possession of Graham Arader of New York (see entry no. X), there is an excellent copy, not bearing the title strip, in the Library of the Correr Museum, under the call number Cartografia cartella 32, no. 68. It makes up part of the sort of hybrid set of these four-continent maps discussed in the text at chapter nine, in the section, "The Correr Museum Library set", and at the end of chapter eleven. Caraci spoke in 1927 of a copy in the private collection of one W. Ashburner of Florence (1926-32, 2, 37 nt. 3; and 1927, 190-92, with two small reproductions from it), but I

have not been able to discover more about it and have no notion of its present whereabouts.

References:
See our text in chapters eleven and twelve and Bifolco and Ronca, 2018, 1: 436.

Reproduction:
Kraus, 1949, pl. XIII; Bifolco and Ronca, 2018, 1: 436-37.

VII. Asia
-Venice, ca. 1655 (?)
-Copper engraving, 98.0 x 143.0 (with added title strip ca. 103.5 x 143.0) cm., on 8 sheets, 4 up and 4 down.
-250 leagues = 10.5 cm.

VII. Camocio-Scolari-Gastaldi Asia 1655? Austin UT

On the title strip added at the top of the map:
NOVA ET ACVRATA TOTIVS ASIAE TABVLA, auct.: G. I: (NEW AND ACCURATE MAP OF ALL OF ASIA [For the translation of the notation at the ending, "auct: G. I:", see chapter eleven*)*

Centered along the top border of the map, the original title:
ASIAE ORBIS PARTIVM MAXI | MAE NOVA DESCRIPTIO (NEW MAP OF ASIA THE LARGEST PART OF THE EARTH)

In the left half of the lower decorative border, the exact same dedication to Paolo Nani which occurs on no. VI, except written all in capital letters (see in no. VI for transcription and translation)

In the right half of the lower decorative border, Bertelli's signature:
DONATVS BERTELLI BIBLIOTHECAE VENETVS | AD SIGNVM SANCTI MARCI (BY DONATO BERTELLI OF THE VENICE BOOKSHOP AT THE SIGN OF SAINT MARK'S)

Immediately following the word "MARCI" in a smaller script, added later and rather awkwardly squeezed into the frame around Bertelli's signature:
Stefano Scolari Forma 1655 (Stefano Scolari plate owner/publisher 1655)
Oddly, as noted elsewhere, both in the Ransom Center set and in the Arader sets, it is only the Asia which is dated. The digits of the date are much abraded, but the "55" is clear and one can make out the ascender of the "6" so the date can be confidently read as 1655.

There is nothing more in the way of publishing or dedicatory information on the map, but a special notice to the map-reader from Ortelius (from whose 1567 Asia after Gastaldi Bertelli had copied this map exactly, including this notice) is in the southeast corner, where Ortelius credits the geography of the map to Giacomo Gastaldi, though he also posits that Gastaldi obtained his information for the map from the Arab geographer

Abulfeda, which we show to be mistaken in our chapter five, in the section "Gastaldi and Abulfeda" where there is also a partial translation of Ortelius's text, and for a full transcription and translation into English and Dutch, see Schilder (1987, 63-64).

Comments:
As noted in composite entry (V.-XII.) above, Ortelius applied a superb curvilinear projection to the map, very unusual for the time in a regional map, however large. The result is so stunningly successful that one may wonder if his friend Mercator did not assist him with it, for Mercator had used the same sort of projection in his 1554 map of Europe some years earlier, although, since that continent is much smaller, the projection did not produce the breathtaking effect produced by its use on the Asia map, where one almost has the impression of looking down upon the continent from space. It is unquestionably a much more appropriate projection than that originally used by Gastaldi. The parallels and meridians are drawn in at ten degree intervals, with the former numbered at their eastern ends, while the meridians are numbered along the equator, from 57° E to 194°E, although of course the longitudinal span covered will vary from parallel to parallel in this projection.

Location of copies:
Besides the present copy, at the Ransom Center of the University of Texas at Austin, with provisional call number of Kraus 12/II, and two copies in the private possession of Graham Arader of New York (see entry no. XI) there is an excellent copy, not bearing the title strip in the Library of the Correr Museum in Venice, under call no. Cartografia cartella 32, no. 67, which makes up part of the hybrid set of these four-continent maps discussed in the text at chapter nine, in the section, "The Correr Museum Library set" and at the end of chapter eleven. Finally, there is a copy in the Vatican Library, with call no. Stampe.Geogr. I.9, contributed to the library by Thomas Ashby.

References:
See our text in chapters eleven and twelve and Bifolco and Ronca, 2018, 1: 400-401

VIII. Camocio-Scolari-Gastaldi America 1655? Austin UT

Reproductions:
Kraus, 1949, pl. XVI; Bifolco and Ronca, 2018, 1: 401.

VIII. America
-[Venice], ca. 1655 (?)
-copper engraving, 98.5 x 140.5 cm. (with added title strip ca. 104.0 x 140.5) cm. on 12 sheets, some of irregular size (cf. figs. 9.12 and 9.3), the explanation for which is given in chapters nine and twelve.
-No scale bar

On the title strip added at the top of the map:
NOVA ET ACVRATA TOTIVS AMERICAE TABVLA, auct.: G. [There was presumably an "I" following this, as see at the previous three entries, but the paper has torn away] *(NEW AND ACCURATE MAP OF ALL OF AMERICA*

[For the translation of the notation at the ending, "auct. G. [I:]", see chapter eleven]*)*

To the left of South America, in a cartouche which was no doubt originally intended for publication information and a dedication, the word:
AMERI | CA (AMERICA)

There are no publication statements on the map, nor is there any dedicatory statement or epistle. There is in the low left a lengthy letterpress descriptive text intended as accompaniment to the entire set of four maps, with the title *DICHIARATIONE DELLE QVATRO PARTI DEL MONDO DI GIACOBO GASTALDO RACCOLTA DA PIV FAMOSI COSMOGRAFI ET HISTORICI (DESCRIPTION OF THE FOUR PARTS OF THE WORLD BY GIACOBO GASTALDO GATHERED FROM THE MOST FAMOUS COSMOGRAPHERS AND HISTORIANS),* which text we discuss, at the beginning of chapter twelve.

Comments:

Graduated in whole degrees, every fifth degree numbered, in latitude and longitude, in latitude from ca. 81°00' S to 78°20' N; in longitude, it is graduated on both upper and lower borders as well as on the equator. On the top border, the graduation runs from 148°00' W to 13°10' E, on the bottom border from ca. 147°30' W to 13°00' E, and on the equator, from 109°00' W (starting not at the left edge of the map, but at the right border of the large text box mentioned above) to 12°00' E. The projection is essentially a rectangular one, and we treat it as such in the text. But the reader will note that, on the right side, where the equator runs all the way to the border, the eastern end of the longitude graduation is about one degree greater at the top and bottom than at the equator. This may simply represent some carelessness in the spacing of the degrees, but if not, we have a projection which contains just a hint of a trapezoidal projection. This makes no sense at all on a map covering such a vast area in both longitude and, especially, latitude. In a proper trapezoidal projection on such a map, the longitude difference at the far right between the top or the bottom of the map and the equator should be many degrees. We don't know what to make of this little peculiarity, but we recall that it is not impossible that Gastaldi added the graduations in his maps after they were finished. Since he was still holding this map in manuscript at the time of his death, it is possible that he had not yet applied a graduation to it, and it was applied first by Camocio. In any event, even without looking at the numbers, it is clear from the great elongations east to west of all bodies of land on the map that the projection is one in which there is an unusually high ratio between the length of degrees of longitude and the length of degrees of latitude, with the former notably longer than the latter, and the ratio does not vary noticeably anywhere in the depicted graduations, and so we can rest easy in referring to the projection as a rectangular one.

Location of copies:
Besides the present copy, at the Ransom Center of the University of Texas at Austin, with provisional call no. Kraus 12/I, there are two copies in the private possession of Graham Arader of New York (see entry no. XII), which are slightly different variants, as mentioned in compound entry (V.-VIII).
References:
For references, see our text, in chapters nine, eleven, and twelve, Bifolco and Ronca, 2018, 1: 342-43.

Reproductions:
Kraus, 1949, pl. XI; Kraus, 1969?, 24; Bifolco and Ronca, 2018, 1: 346-47.

(IX.-XII.) The ca. 1662 Scolarian printing of the Four-Continent set

Two copies are known of this set, both in the private possession of Graham Arader of New York. The contents of the two sets are the same, except that one set is lacking the Europe. There are some differences between all the maps in this set and those in the set V-VIII, though at first glance they appear the same. The Europe is quite different all over, for it is printed from the much superior original plate, very possibly after a restoral of that plate, while the Europe in the set V-VIII was printed from the much inferior reengraving discussed in composite entry no. (V.-VIII.). The America differs in that Drake Passage has been cut through and the famous Strait of Anian has been named. There are quite possibly other changes, for I have not attempted an in-depth search. The Africa differs because Scolari's Latin language signature has been burnished out (cf. entry no. VI), and the Asia differs because the signature and date line has been much lengthened, the date has been changed from 1655 to 1662, and the entire line has been differently located, with the old line burnished out. As with the America, there may be other differences in the Africa and Asia, for I have not scrutinized those maps minutely. But the greatest difference between the surviving complete 1662 set and the 1655 set is of a different nature, and will be obvious to the reader upon comparing the reproductions here of maps V-VIII with those of maps IX-XII. That is, the set IX-XII is the only set extant which can be said to be in optimum condition, having undergone a single minor restoration. The Ransom Center set is unfortunately in a deplorable state of preservation, while the other three extant sets, viz. our set I-IV in the Bell Library, the set in the Correr Museum, and the second set owned by Graham Arader are all incomplete, missing sundry parts, either of the America, or the Europe, or, in the case of the Correr set, both. Thus, we must make no mistake as regards the significance of this set of maps, not just in the history of cartography, but in terms of humankind's heritage in general. We invite the reader to survey our reproductions of these maps. Here before our eyes in this set is the only known artifact which gives a clear and complete picture of Gastaldi's conception of the world at the height of his career, and that conception was the first generally correct conception of the world which had ever existed, a point worthy of note indeed. It is truly astonishing that, due to nothing but the caprices of fate, this set of maps, arguably representing the greatest milestone ever in our cognizance of the world we inhabit, has remained virtually unknown to historians of cartography, and indeed to historians in general, and it is with no small satisfaction and pride that we reproduce and adequately discuss them here for the first time.

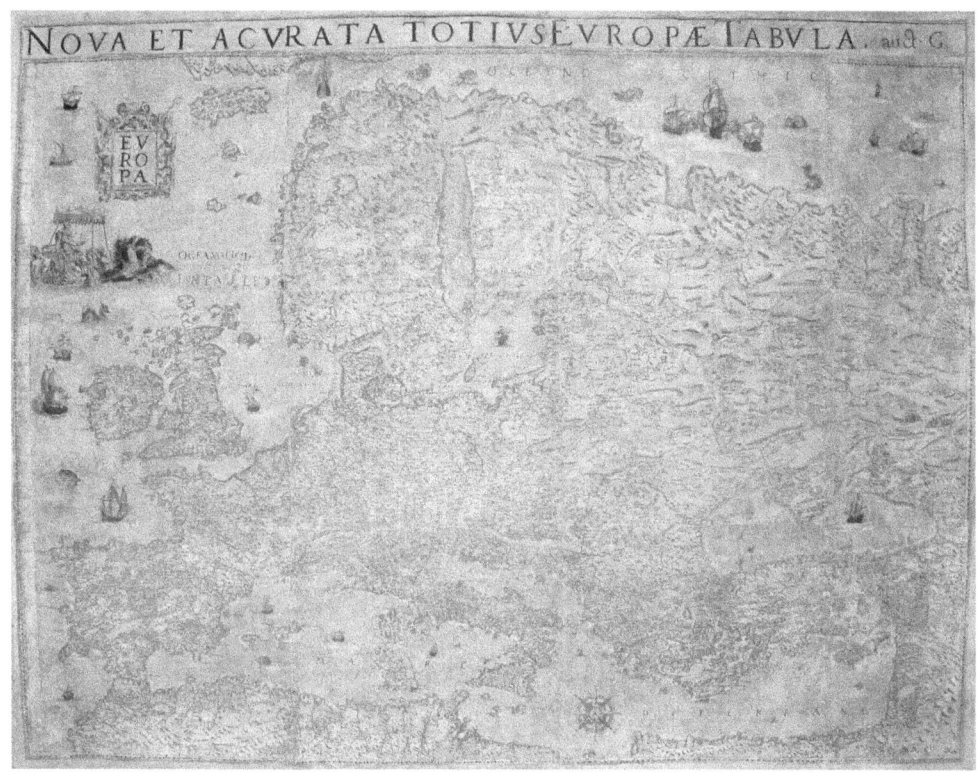

IX Europe 1662 Arader

IX. Europe

-Venice, ca. 1662 (?)

-Copper engraving, 103.5 x 145.5 (with the added title strip ca. 109.0 x 145.5) cm., in twelve sheets (nine full and three half sheets)

-100 Italian miles = ca. 3.4 cm.

On the title strip added at the top:

NOVA ET ACVRATA TOTIVS EVROPAE TABVLA, auct. G. I: (ACCURATE MAP OF ALL OF EUROPE [For the translation of the notation at the ending "auct: G. I:", see chapter eleven]*)*

In an ornate cartouche at the upper left:

EVRO | PA (EUROPE)

Below the scale bar at the bottom of the cartouche:

Alla libraria della S[an] Marcho (At the bookshop of Saint Mark's)

Comments:
The graduation on the map is as in entry no. V. Some of the longitude graduation at the top has been partially obscured by the lower edge of the added title strip. As noted in composite entry no. (IX.-XII.), this variant is from the original Camocian plate, very possibly after a plate restoral, which is much superior to the very poorly engraved plate of entry no. 5.

Location of copy:
The only copy known is in the private possession of Graham Arader of New York.

References:
See our text in chapters eleven and twelve.

Reproduction:
Reproduced above.

X. Africa
-Venice, ca. 1662 (?)
-Copper engraving, 91.5 x 125.0 (with added title strip ca. 97.0 x 125.0) cm., on eight sheets, four up and four down.
-200 Italian miles = 3.4 cm.

On the title strip added at the top of the map:
NOVA ET ACVRATA TOTIVS AFRICAE TABVLA, auct: G. I: (NEW AND ACCURATE MAP OF ALL OF AFRICA [For the translation of the notation at the ending "auct: G. I:", see chapter eleven]*)*

X. Africa 1662 Arader

On the body of the map proper, in large capital letters, in the Gulf of Guinea, the original title:
NOVA TOTIVS AFRICAE DESCRIPTIO (NEW MAP OF ALL OF AFRICA)

At lower left, at the head of a cartouche containing ancient and modern place name equivalents for African localities, a dedication from Bertelli to Paolo Nani (same as on no. VI, q.v.)

At the bottom of the list of names in the border of the cartouche:
Ad signum bibliothecae Diui Marci (At the bookshop of Saint Marks)

At the end of a small informational text box located next to the Canary Islands and giving the map-reader information about the islands:
Stefano Scolari forma (Stefano Scolari plate owner/publisher)

The cartouche at the upper right mentioning Gastaldi as the map's author, and giving information about African geography is the same as in no. VI, q.v.

Comments:
Latitude is not indicated on the borders, but only very cursorily along the central meridian, where we find latitude numbering at every five degrees (though there are no actual graduation markings), approximately from 34°00' S to 36°30' N. Longitude is given only on the equator in whole degrees, with each fifth degree numbered. For some reason, Bertelli leaves about the first four degrees west of the zero point (the prime meridian is not indicated) unmarked, but the whole longitude coverage is approximately from 4°00' W to ca. 93°30' E. The projection is indeterminate. As has been noted in composite entry no. (V.-VIII.), the Latin Scolari signature which occurs in no. VI in the scrollwork at the bottom of the cartouche containing the list of ancient and modern name equivalents has been rubbed out in this issue of the map, although it was done, as often, clumsily, and traces of the old signature are still clearly discernible.

Location of copies:
The only two copies known are in the possession of Graham Arader of New York.

References:
See our text in chapters eleven and twelve.

Reproduction:
Reproduced above.

XI. Asia
-Venice, ca. 1662 (?)
-Copper engraving, 98.0 x 143.0 (with added title strip ca. 103.5 x 143.0) cm., on eight sheets, four up and four down.
-250 leagues = 10.5 cm.

On the title strip added at the top of the map:
NOVA ET ACVRATA TOTIVS ASIAE TABVLA, auct.: G. I: (NEW AND ACCURATE MAP OF ALL OF ASIA [For the translation of the notation at the ending, "auct: G. I:", see chapter eleven]*)*

Centered along the top border of the map, the original title:
ASIAE ORBIS PARTIVM MAXI | MAE NOVA DESCRIPTIO (NEW MAP OF ASIA THE LARGEST PART OF THE EARTH)

In the left half of the lower decorative border, the exact same dedication to Paolo Nani which occurs on no. VI, except written all in capital letters (see in no. VI for transcription and translation)

In the right half of the lower decorative border, Bertelli's signature:
DONATVS BERTELLI BIBLIOTHECAE VENETVS | AD SIGNVM SANCTI MARCI (BY DONATO BERTELLI OF THE VENICE BOOKSHOP AT THE SIGN OF SAINT MARK'S)

Just above the right half of the lower decorative border, within the body of the map:
Stefano Scolari Forma 1662 Venetia al signa delle tre Virtu (Stefano Scolari plate holder/publisher 1662 Venice at the sign of the three Virtues) [This entire line, incuding the new date 1662, is added to the plate in the present map, and does not occur in no. VII, the Ranson Center Texas variant; the shorter and differently located Scolari signature with the date 1655 as in no.

VII, is rubbed out, although, as usual, traces of the old line are still slightly visible.]

The special (and erroneous) notice from Ortelius concerning Gastaldi's purported souce for the map, copied by Bertelli from the 1567 Ortelius original of the map and located in the southeast corner of the map is unchanged from the 1655 edition no. VII, q.v.

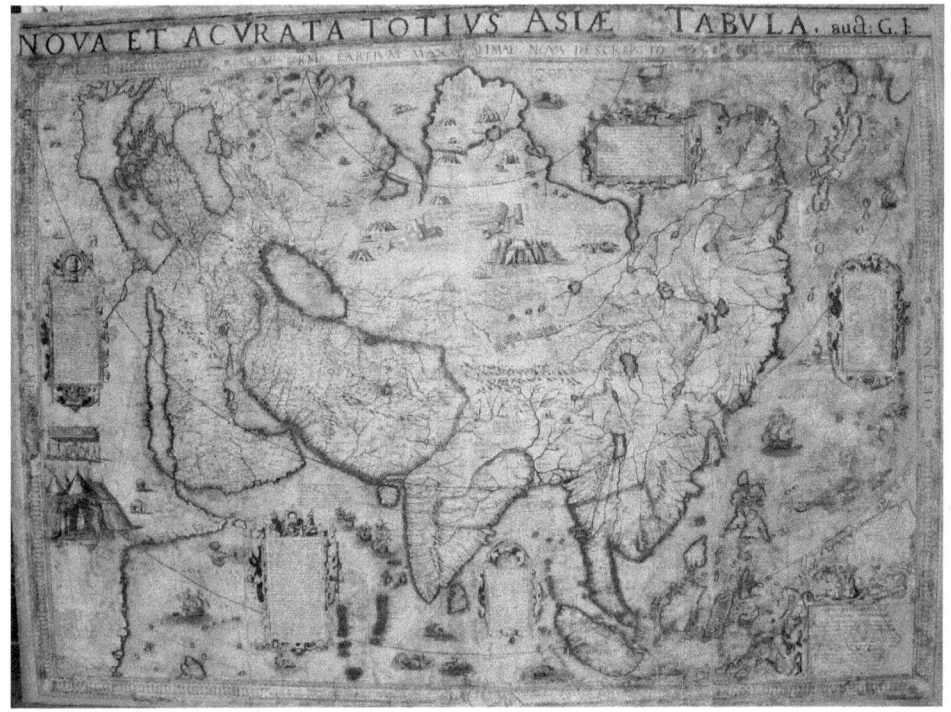

XI Asia 1662 Arader

Comments:
Information on the structure of the coordinate net of the map, and its remarkable projection, is exactly the same as in entry no. VII, for the 1655 Asia, q.v.

Location of copies:
The only two copies known are in the possession of Graham Arader of New York.

References:
For references, see our text, in chapters eleven and twelve.

Reproduction:
Reproduced above.

XII. America
-Venice, ca. 1662 (?)
-Copper engraving, 98.5 x 140.5 (with added title strip ca. 104.0 x 140.5) cm., on twelve sheets, some of irregular size (cf. figs. 9.12 and 9.3), the explanation for which is given in chapters nine and twelve.
-No scale bar

On the title strip added at the top of the map:
NOVA ET ACVRATA TOTIVS AMERICAE TABVLA, auct.: G. I: (NEW AND ACCURATE MAP OF ALL OF AMERICA [For the translation of the notation at the ending, "auct. G. I:", see chapter eleven])

To the left of South America, in a cartouche which was no doubt originally intended for publication information and a dedication, the word:
AMERI | CA (AMERICA)

There are no publication statements on the map, nor is there any dedicatory statement or epistle. There is in the low left a lengthy letterpress descriptive text intended as accompaniment to the entire set of four maps, with the title *DICHIARATIONE DELLE QVATRO PARTI DEL MONDO DI GIACOBO GASTALDO RACCOLTA DA PIV FAMOSI COSMOGRAFI ET HISTORICI (DESCRIPTION OF THE FOUR PARTS OF THE WORLD BY GIACOBO GASTALDO GATHERED FROM THE MOST FAMOUS COSMOGRAPHERS AND HISTORIANS),* which text we discuss, at the beginning of chapter twelve.

XII America 1662 Arader

Comments:
The information on longitudinal and latitudinal limits of the map, and on its
projection, is exactly the same as for no. VIII, q.v. As noted elsewhere, this
1662 variant has Drake Passage cut through, and has the name "STRETO
D'ANIAN" added above the strait between Asia and America, unlike other
copies of the America. It also has, unique on any map of America to the best
of my knowledge, a small "regno di Anian" on the Arctic shores above and
just east of the strait, and there may be other differences.

Location of copies:
The only two copies known are in the possession of Graham Arader of New
York.

References:
For references, see our text, in chapters nine, eleven, and twelve.

Reproduction:
Reproduced above.

An Endnote to the Cartobibliography: Gastaldi's Manuscript Hydrographical Drawings, Diagrams and Field Plans Made for the Venetian State

The following comments are made by way of an expansion and complement to the observations in this area made in our first chapter. The Venetian Republic was compelled from time to time in its history to take action of one kind or another to ensure against what we today might call environmental or ecological instabilities arising as a result of its watery surroundings. For various reasons arising no doubt from the growth of the city and its environs, this situation had become of a more urgent and crucial nature by the end of the 15th century, and in 1501 the government established a permanent separate department to deal with it, the Savi alle Acque, which was expanded in 1531 to the Savi ed Esecutori alle Acque. The phrases are clumsy to translate, and I shall refer to the department here as the Ministry for Water, a phrase Denis Cosgrove sometimes used to refer to the office (1993, 44, for example). In 1556, another, related, ministry was added, the Magistratura per i Beni Inculti (The Ministry for Uncultivated Lands), whose responsibility was to create from uncultivated lands tillable soil in which wheat could be grown so that Venice would not have to depend on foreign sources to keep itself fed. These bodies, still extant under different names, were headed by provveditori, executive officers chosen by the Senate from the patrician class. Below them and advising them was a body of technical experts called proti, and below the proti, but often working together with them, were the periti, the basic survey engineers who worked in the field. These periti were entrusted with sundry tasks in the field, after the completion of which they submitted reports, often accompanied by various descriptive materials, as drawings, diagrams, or maps, based on surveys. It should be pointed out, however, that, while at a later time, the periti would base their surveys on triangulation and other sophisticated techniques, in the sixteenth century their methods, described by Cosgrove, were much more primitive (1993, 175 and 181).

In 1914, Mario Baratta discovered in the Venetian archives six such diagrams and maps which had been made by Gastaldi between 1551 and 1565 (Baratta, 1914), and Bagrow duly included them in his list of 109 maps by Gastaldi (Bagrow, 1928-30, 1, 74-96). Then Almagià discovered in the archives 14 more such items by Gastaldi (Almagià, 1947), though he described only two of them, and he noted that, "it is not to be excluded that still some others may exist" (1947, 199). Karrow includes in his list of 108 Gastaldi maps the six maps found by Baratta and also those two further maps which Almagià described. Sometime later a massive project was begun by archives personnel to systematically unearth such drawings and maps in the archives, concentrating mainly but evidently not entirely on the archives of the two ministries named above, apparently under the direction of Ferruccio Zago (Zago, 1984). Zago, already retired as head of the archives when he wrote his article, does not say when the project began, but it must have been quite some years before he wrote. Some 2,000 items were unearthed, and they were catalogued, photographed, and filed according to a particular procedure (Zago, cit., 629-30). The procedure, however, was found to be wanting, and another was developed, and another 15,000 maps and drawings were ferreted out and catalogued, photographed and filed, according to this new procedure. Zago of course does not in his article name all the engineers involved, nor how many items were produced by this or that engineer, but he names some of the older periti, among them Gastaldi (Zago, cit., 622 and 636).

How close this project came to completion, Zago does not say, and whether or not it was continued after Zago's time I have not been able to discover. But a later head of the archives, now also retired, Maria Francesca Tiepolo published in 1994 a 291-page basic description of the contents of the archives, and the only mention evidently corresponding to the information given by Zago, whose name she does not mention, is a single paragraph entitled "Miscellanea mappe, pezzi 2.000 ca. (secc. XV-XX). Schedatura e fotoriproduzione" (Tiepolo, 1994, 1130), which is the last bit of information I have been able to find concerning Zago's maps. Clearly, Tiepolo's entry can only refer to the 2,000 items mentioned earlier as catalogued according to a procedure which was then abandoned for a new one. Where, then, are the 15,000 maps and drawings catalogued and photographed according to the later procedure? I have made no personal inquiries, for, even if they were met with success, the expenditure in terms of time and financial resources which would be necessary in order to pursue the matter would far exceed the capacities of the present researcher, not to mention the fact that it is unknown, as mentioned above, to what extent Zago exhausted these massive archives before his retirement. Tiepolo's apparent lack of knowledge of the 15,000 maps and drawings suggests that the project was very possibly abandoned before completion, and if so, continuing the hunt would be quite beyond the powers of an individual outsider to the archives, who probably could not obtain the permission to do so in any event.

In light of the above facts, along with the further fact that the present work is for all practical purposes concerned exclusively with Gastaldi's printed maps, the maps which were made for public eyes and which so strongly influenced world geography, we have opted not to include in our cartobibliography maps those few manuscript periti maps for which information is available. We feel that the appropriateness of our decision, which is firstly based upon this fact that these manuscript maps are essentially extraneous to the spirit of the present work, is reinforced both by the fact that the eight such maps for which information is available represent only a smattering of the total number of these maps and drawings, making their inclusion problematical, and also by further factors brought out in our discussion in this area in chapter one. The reader who wishes information on these maps may consult the cited works of Baratta, Almagià, and Karrow (1993, at pp. 225, 230, 242, 245-46, 247 and 249). In the meantime, the present notice should provide a helpful starting point for the scholar who might have a particular interest in this area.

KEY TO LIBRARY ABBREVIATIONS GIVEN IN THE CARTOBIBLIOGRAPHY

The abbreviations given in the Cartobibliography all begin with the full name, in the local language, of the city or town in which the library is located, followed by an abbreviation for the library's name. Accordingly, the following list is alphabetized by cities, followed by the abbreviation given in the entries, after which the library's name is given in full; at the end of each entry, the international country code is given in parentheses.

Amherst AC = Amherst College, Amherst, Massachusetts (USA)
Ann Arbor UML = University of Michigan Libraries (USA)
Athens UGL = University of Georgia Libraries (USA)
Austin UTL = University of Texas Libraries (USA)
Basel UB = Universitätsbibliothek (CH)
Boston BA = Boston Athenaeum (USA)
Budapest OSzK = Országos Széchényi Könyvtár (H)
Cambridge Harv = Harvard University (USA)
Cambridge UL = Cambridge University Library (GB)
Chicago Newb = The Newberry Library (USA)
Chicago UCL = University of Chicago Libraries (USA)
Claremont CC = Claremont Colleges Libraries (USA)
Dillingen SB = Studienbibliothek, Dillingen an der Donau (D)
Edinburgh NLS = National Library of Scotland (GB)
Edinburgh UL = University Library (GB)
Firenze BMar = Biblioteca Marucelliana (I)
Firenze BN = Biblioteca Nazionale Centrale (I)
Greenwich NMM = National Maritime Museum (GB)
Greifswald UB = Universitätsbibliothek (D)
Hartford TC = Trinity College Library (USA)
Helsinki AEN = University Library, A. E. Nordenskiöld Collection (FIN)
Ithaca CU = Cornell University Library (USA)
København KB = Det Kongelige Bibliotek (DK)
Kraków BCz = Biblioteka Czartoryskich (PL)
Leiden UB = Universiteitsbibliotheek (NL)

London BL = The British Library (GB)
London RGS = Royal Geographical Society (GB)
London WellcInst = Welcome Institute for the History of Medicine Libr (GB)
Los Angeles UCLA = University of California at Los Angeles Libraries (USA)
Louisville UL = University of Louisville Libraries (USA)
Madrid BN = Biblioteca Nacional (E)
Madrid PR = Biblioteca del Palacio Real (E)
Madrid UB = Universidad Complutense de Madrid (E)
Metten BB = Bibliothek des Benedictinerstiftes (D)
Middletown WU = Wesleyan University Libraries (USA)
Milwaukee AGS = American Geographical Society Collection (USA)
Milwaukee UW = University of Wisconsin at Milwaukee Libraries (USA)
Minneapolis Bell = James Ford Bell Library, University of Minnesota (USA)
Modena Estense = Biblioteca Estense Universitaria (I)
München SB = Bayerische Staatsbibliothek (D)
New Haven Yale = Beinecke Rare Book & Manuscript Library (USA)
New York PL = New York Public Library (USA)
Northridge CS = California State University at Northridge Libraries (USA)
Nürnberg GNM = Bibliothek des Germanischen Nationalmuseum (D)
Oxford Bodl = Bodleian Library (GB)
Paris BN = Bibliothèque Nationale de France (F)
Paris Med = Bibliothèque Médiothèque MQB (F)
Princeton UL = Princeton University Library (USA)
Providence JCB = John Carter Brown Library (USA)
Provo BY = Brigham Young University (USA)
Rochester UR = University of Rochester (USA)
Roma BA = Biblioteca Alessandrina (I)
Roma BCas = Biblioteca Casanatense (I)
Roma BN = Biblioteca Nazionale Centrale Vittorio Emanuele II (I)
Roma BVat = Biblioteca Apostolica Vaticana (I)
Rostock UB = Universitätsbibliothek (D)
Rotterdam MMPH = Maritiem Museum "Prins Hendrik' (NL)
Salamanca BU = Universidad de Salamanca, Biblioteca Universitari (E)
San Diego UCSD = University of California at San Diego Libraries (USA)

Simancas AGS = Archivio General de Simancas (E)

Sint-Niklaas KOKW = Koninklijke Oudheidkundige Kring van het Land van Waas (B)

Stanford SC = Stanford University Libraries Special Collection (USA)

Stuttgart SC = Württembergische Landesbibliothek (D)

Syracuse SU = University of Syracuse Libraries (USA)

Torino AST = Archivio di Stato di Torino (I)

Trondheim UB = Universitetsbiblioteket (N)

Urbana UIL = University of Illinois (USA)

Valletta NLM = National Library of Malta (MT)

Venezia BNM = Biblioteca Nazionale Marciana (I)

Venezia Correr = Biblioteca del Museo Correr (I)

Venezia QS = Biblioteca Querini Stampalia (I)

Vilnius UVL = University of Vilnius Library (LT)

Washington GU = Georgetown University (USA)

Washington LC = Library of Congress (USA)

Wien ÖNB = Kartensammlung und Globenmuseum (A)

Wien UB = Universitätsbibliothek (A)

Williamstown WC = Williams College (USA)

Wilmington UNC = University of North Carolina Libraries (USA)

Wolfegg SW = Schloss Wolfegg, Kupferstichkabinet (D)

Wolfenbüttel HAB = Herzog August Bibliothek (D)

BIBLIOGRAPHY

Abendanon, Eduard Cornelius. 1915-18. *Midden-Celebies-expeditie: geologische en geographische doorkruisingen van Midden-Celebes.* 4 vols. and atlas. Leiden.

Abendanon, Eduard Cornelius. 1921. An Important Map in the British Museum. *Geographical Journal*, 57: 284-89.

Abulfeda. See Holt, Greaves, and Reinaud and Guyard.

Accademia Venetiana. 1559. *Somma delle Opere che in tvtte le scienze et arti piv nobili, et in varie lingve, ha da mandare in lvce l'Academia Venetiana, parte nvove, et non piv stampate, parte con fedelissime tradottioni, giudiciose correttioni, & utilissime annotationi riformate* [*Summary of the works which in all the most noble sciences and arts which the Venetian Academy is to publish, some new, and not printed before, some in most faithful translations, judiciously corrected, and amended with most useful annotations.*]. Venice, 1558. (Latin edition: *Svmma librorum, qvos in omnibvs scientiis, ac nobilioribvs artibvs, variis lingvis conscriptos, vel antea nvmqvam divvlgatos, vel vtilissimis, et pvlcherrimis scholiis, correctionibvs qve illvstratos, in lvcem emittet ACADEMIA VENETA.* Venice, 1559, which is reprinted in Pellegrini, 1808). The work, very rare, is a prospectus of proposed projects of the academy.

Acosta, Jose de. 1588. *De Natvra Novi Orbis Libri Dvo*, etc. Salamanca.

Acosta, Jose de. 1590. *Historia natvral y moral de las Indias, en qve se tratan de las cosas notables del cielo, y elementos, metales, plantas, y animales dellas*, etc. Seville.

Acosta, Jose de. 1604. *The natvrall and morall historie of the East and West Indies. Intreating of the remarkeable things of heaven, of the elements, mettalls, plants and beasts which are proper to that country: together with the manners, ceremonies, lawes, governements, and warres of the Indians.* London. (English trans. of above; this was reprinted by the Hakluyt Society in 2 volumes in 1880 as volumes 60-61 of the first series.)

Ahmad, S. Maqbul. 1992. Cartography of al-Sharif al-Idrisi. In *The History of Cartography*, vol. II, Book 1. *Cartography in the Traditional Islamic and South Asian Societies*, ed. John Brian Harley and David Woodward, 156-74. Chicago.

Aiton, Arthur Scott. 1927. *Antonio de Mendoza, first viceroy of New Spain.* Durham, N.C.

Alai, Cyrus. 2005. *General Maps of Persia, 1477-1925.* Leiden.

Alberti, Leandro. 1550. *Descrittione di tvtta Italia*, etc. Bologna, 1550 (and other editions).

Alexo de Orrio, Francisco Xavier. 1763. *Solucion del gran Problema acerca de la Poblacion de las Americas, en que sobre el fundamento de los Libros Santos se descubre facil camino a´ la transmigracion ... del uno al otro Continente ... Sacala a` luz Don F. Carmona, Godoy y Bucareli, etc.* Mexico. (Reprinted in León, 1902-08 [q.v.], 379-409).

Aliprandi, Laura. 1974. *Le Grandi Alpi nella cartografia dei secoli passati, 1482-1865: con gli itinerari dei valichi tra la Val d'Aosta e la Savoia e il Vallese e considerazioni sul lazona del Gran Paradiso 'The cartography of the Great Alps over passed [sic] centuries (1482-1865), with the routes of passes between the Aosta Valley, Savoy and the Valais, and some considerations on the Gran Paradiso area.* Ivrea.

Allen, Don Cameron. 1949. *The Legend of Noah: Renaissance Rationalism in Art, Science, and Letters.* (Illinois Studies in Language and Literature, vol. 33, no. 3-4). Urbana.

Allen, John Logan, ed. 1997. *North American Exploration.* 3 vols. Lincoln, Neb.

Almagià, Roberto. 1914. Le più antiche rappresentazioni cartografiche della regione albanese. *Bollettino della Società Geografica Italiana*, 51: 601-37.

Almagià, Roberto. 1914-15. La cartografia dell'Italia nel conquecento con un saggio sulla cartografia del Piemonte. *Rivista Geografica Italiana*, 21: 640-56 and 22: 1-26. (Reprinted in *Acta Cartographica*, 18 (1974), 1-43).

Almagià, Roberto. 1922. L'Italia *di G. A. Magini e la cartografia dell'Italia nei secoli XVI e XVII.* (Comitato geografico nazionale italiano. *Pubblicazione*, 1). Napoli.

Almagià, Roberto. 1923. Su alcuni importanti cimelî cartografici conservati a Venezia. *Atti dello VIII Congresso Geografico Italiano tenuto in Firenze dal 29 marzo al 6 aprile 1921*, 2: 295-302. Firenze.

Almagià, Roberto. 1925. La più antica carta stampata del Piemonte. *L'Universo*, 6: 985-89.

Almagià, Roberto. 1929. *Monumenta Italiae Cartographica*. Florence.

Almagià, Roberto. 1934. Sulle carte della Polonia di Giacomo Gastaldi. In *Zbiór Prac poswiecony przez towarzystwo geograficzne we Lwowie Eugenjuszowi Romerowi w 40-lecie jego tworczosci naukowej*, ed. H. Arctowski, 143-48. Lvov.

Almagià, Roberto. 1937. *L'opera del genio italiano all'estero: Gli Italiani primi esploratori dell'America.* Rome.

Almagià, Roberto. 1939. *La carta dei paesi danubiani e delle regioni contermini di Giacomo Gastaldi (1546)*. Roma.

Almagià, Roberto. 1939. Intorno ad un grande mappamondo perduto di Giacomo Gastaldi (1561). *La Bibliofilia*, 41: 259-66.

Almagià, Roberto. 1941. Un prezioso cimelio della cartografia italiana: Il planisfero di Urbano Monti. *La Bibliofilia*, 43: 156-93.

Almagià, Roberto. 1944. *Planisferi, carte nautiche e affini dal secolo XIV al XVII esistenti nella Biblioteca Apostolica Vaticana*. (Monumenta Cartographica Vaticana, vol. 1). Vatican City.

Almagià, Roberto. 1947. Nuove notizie intorno a Giacomo Gastaldi. *Bollettino della Società Geografica Italiana*, 84: 187-89.

Almagià, Roberto. 1948. *Carte geografiche a stampa di particolare pregio o rarità dei secoli XVI e XVII esistenti nella Biblioteca Apostolica Vaticana*. (Monumenta Cartographica Vaticana, vol. 2). Vatican City.

Almagià, Roberto. 1948. The First 'Modern' Map of Spain. *Imago Mundi*, 4: 27-31.

Almagià, Roberto. 1948. An Historical Map by Giacomo Gastaldi. *Imago Mundi*, 5: 14-15, with map opp. p. 15.

Almagià, Roberto. 1951. Note sulla cartografia dell'Italia nei secoli XV e XVI. *Atti della Accademia Nazionale dei Lincei. Classe di scienze morali, storiche e filologiche. Rendiconti*, Ser. 8, vol. 6: 3-8.

Almagià, Roberto. 1952. *Le pitture murali della Galleria delle Carte Geografiche*. (Monumenta Cartographica Vaticana, vol. 3). Vatican City.

Almagià, Roberto. 1955. *Le pitture geografiche murali della Terza Loggia e di altre sale vaticane*. (Monumenta Cartographica Vaticana, 4). Vatican City.

Almagià, Roberto. 1960. A proposito del mappamondo in lingua turca della Biblioteca Marciana. Istituto Veneto di scienze, lettere ed arti, Classe di scienze morali e lettere. *Atti*, 118: 53-59.

Almagià, Roberto. 1960. *Documenti cartografici dello stato pontificio*. Vatican City.

Almagià, Roberto. 1961. Studi storici di cartografia napoletana. In *Scritti geografici (1905-1957)*, by Roberto Almagià, 231-324. Roma. (Originally published in *Archivio storico per le provincie napoletane*, 37 [1913] and 38 [1914]).

Almagià, Roberto. 1962. A proposito di una presunta carta dell'Asia anteriore di Giacomo Gastaldi. *Rivista Geografica Italiana*, 69: 2-9.

Alves Gaspar, Joaquim. 2007. The Myth of the Square Chart. e-*Perimetron*, 2, no. 2: 66-79.

Ambrosini, Federica. 1980. Rappresentazioni allegoriche dell'America nel Veneto del Cinque e Seicento. *Artibus et Historiae*, 2: 63-78.

Ambrosini, Federica. 1981. Descrittioni del mondo' nelle case venete dei secoli XVI e XVII. *Archivio Veneto*, 117: 67-79.

Amoretti, Carlo. 1811. *Viaggio dal mare Atlantico al Pacifico per la via del Nord-Ovest, fatto dal capitano Lorenzo Ferrer Maldonado l'anno MDLXXXVIII. Tr. da un manoscritto spagnuolo inedito*. Milan. (Also a French edition, 1812).

Anania, Giovanni Lorenzo d'. 1576. *L'Vniversale Fabrica Del Mondo, Overo Cosmografia Di M. Gio. Lorenzo D'Anania, Diuisa in quattro Trattati, Ne i quali ... si misura il Cielo, e la Terra, & si discriuono ... le Prouincie, Città ... Fiumi, & Fonti, Et si tratta delle Leggi, & Costumi di molti Popoli ... Di nuouo posta in luce*, etc. Venice. (First edition, 1573).

Anthiaume, Albert. 1916. *Cartes marines, constructions navales, voyages de Cartes marines, constructions navales, voyages de découverte chez les Normands, 1550-1650*. 2 vols. Paris.

Apian, Peter. 1524. *Cosmographicus liber Petri Apiani mathematici studiose collectus*. Landshut.

Apian, Peter. 1544. *La Cosmographie de Pierre Apian, libure tresutile, traictant de toutes les regions & pays du monde par artifice Astronomicque, nouuelleme[n]t traduict de Latin en François. Et par Gemma Frison ... corrige. Auecq aultres libures du mesme Gemma Fr. appartenantz audict artifice*, etc. Antwerp.

Arbel, Benjamin. 2002. Maps of the World for Ottoman Princes? Further Evidence and Questions Concerning `The Mappamondo of Hajji Ahmed.' *Imago Mundi*, 54: 19-29.

Archivio biografico italiano. 1988. *[microform]* = *Italian biographical archive*. München (and later additions in microfiche).

Arias Montanus, Benito. 1572. Phaleg, Sive, De Gentium Sedibvs Orbisqve Terrae Sitv. In *Biblia Sacra Hebraice, Chaldaice, Græce, & Latine*, ed. Benito Arias Montanus. vol. 8, 4th individually paginated treatise. (16pp). Antwerp. (The numbering sequence of treatises in volume 8, 18 in all, can vary in copies of this polyglot bible.)

Armao, Ermanno. 1957. *Il 'Catalogo degli autori di Vincenzo Coronelli'; una biobibliografia geografica del '600 [di] Ermanno Armao*. Florence, 1957.

Ascari, Mario Celsi, and Cagaci, Giuseppe. 1942-43. La cartografia terrestre della Corsica. *Archivio Storico di Corsica*, 18: 1-36 and 179-213; and 19: 1-34.

Astengo, Corradino. 1990. I mappamondi di Giacomo Gastaldi e lo Stretto di Anian. *Annali di ricerche e studi di geografia*, 46: 1-18.

Astengo, Corradino. 1991. Il globo terrestre di Franciscus Bassus. In: *La lettura geografica, il linguaggio geografico, i contenuti geografici a servizio dell'uomo: studi in onore di Osvaldo Baldacci*, ed. Cosimo Palagiano, et al., 115-22. Bologna.

Astengo, Corradino. 1993. La produzione cartografica di Francesco Ghisolfi. *Annali di richerche e studi di geografia*, 49: 1-16.

Astengo, Corradino. 1996. *Elenco preliminare di carte ed atlanti nautici manoscritti eseguiti nell'area mediterranea nel periodo 1500-1700 e conservati presso enti pubblici*. Genova.

Atanagi, Dionigi, ed. 1582. *Lettere di XIII. Huomini illlustri*, etc. Venice.

Avalos Guzmán, Gustavo. 1991. *Don Antonio de Mendoza: semblanza*. 2nd ed. Morelia.

Avezac-Macaya, Armand d'. 1865. Note sur une mappemonde turque du XVIe siècle, conservée à la Bibliothèque de Saint-Marc à Venise. *Bulletin de la Société de Géographie de Paris*, Ser. 5, 10: 675-757.

Badoer, Federico (Accademkia Venetiana). 1560. *Instrumento de Deputazione, & c. di Federico Badoero, in data 1560, 30 decembre: o sia Fondatione ed ordine dell'Academia Venetiana*. Venice, Aldine Press. (12 unnumbered leaves). This is the title as given by Renouard, 1834 (see in this bibliography), in his catalog of Aldine Press works, p. 280, no. 52, and the title most often given elsewhere. Actually, the booklet has no formal title. The Pierpont Morgan Library in New York gives the title as *Il testomento in data 30 Decembre. 1560. Osia fondatione ed ordine dell'Academia Venetiana*. The notes in the OCLC entry for the copy formerly in the John Rylands Library, which library merged with the University of Manchester Library in 1972, give the incipit as "1560. 30. Decembre. In Venetia in contrada di San Cantian nella casa dell'habitatione del clarissimo M. Federigo Badoer." The Morgan and Ryland copies (call numbers respectively 001177 and Aldine Collection [20989]) are the only copies known; I have seen neither. Fortunately, it was reprinted in full, though carelessly and with many orthographical and other irregularities, by Pellegrini (q.v.), in vol. 23, at pp. 49-68. Renouard (1834, 280, no. 52) says this is the most important of the fifty-seven works published for the Academia Venetiana by the prestigious Aldine Press, under Paolo Manucio.

Bagrow, Leo. 1927. Der Deutsch Kartograph Heinrich Zell. *Petermanns Mitteilungen*, 73: 63-66.

Bagrow, Leo. 1928-30. *A. Ortelii Catalogus Cartographorum*. 2 vols. (Petermanns Mitteilungen, Ergänzungshefte, 199 and 210). Gotha.

Bagrow, Leo. 1939. *Giovanni Andreas di Vavassore, a Venetian Cartographer of the 16th Century, a Descriptive List of His Maps*. Jenkintown, Pa.

Bagrow, Leo. 1940. *Matheo Pagano, a Venetian Cartographer of the 16th Century: A Descriptive List of His Maps*. Jenkintown, Pa.

Bagrow, Leo. 1945. The Origin of Ptolemy's Geographia. *Geografiska Annaler*, 27: 318-87.

Bagrow, Leo. 1948. A Page from the History of the Distribution of Maps. *Imago Mundi*, 5: 53-62.

Bagrow, Leo. 1956. Italians on the Caspian. *Imago Mundi*, 13: 2-10.

Bagrow, Leo. 1962. At the Sources of the Cartography of Russia. *Imago Mundi*, 16: 33-48.

Bagrow, Leo. 1975. *A History of Russian Cartography up to 1600*. Wolfe Island, Ont. (vol. I of his *A History of the Cartography of Russia up to 1800*.)

Bagrow, Leo, revised and enlarged by Raleigh Ashlin Skelton. 1985. *History of Cartography*. Chicago.

Baião, António. 1932. Dois inéditos de João de Barros a sua Geografia. In *Ásia; dos feitos que os Portugueses fizeram no descobrimento e conquista dos mares e terras do Oriente. 1. decada.*, by João de Barros. 4th ed. Rev., li-lxxxii. Coimbra. (With material not in 1945-46 edition).

Baião, António. 1945-46. Dois inéditos de João de Barros a sua Geografia. In *Décadas*, by João de Barros. 4 Vols. vol. 1, xlix-lxxv. Lisbon. (A revised edition of above).

Baldi, Bernardino. 1590. La nautica. In his *Versi e prose, di Monsignor Bernardino Baldi da Vrbino, abbate di Guastalla*. Venice. (First edition 1576).

Balteau, J., et al, eds. 1933-. *Dictionnaire de biographie française*. Paris.

Bancroft, Hubert Howe. 1886. *The Native Races: Primitive History*. (Works of Hubert Howe Bancroft, vol. 5). San Francisco.

Banfi, Florio. 1947. *Imago Hungariae nella cartografia italiana del rinascimento*. (Biblioteca dell'Accademia d'Ungheria in Roma diretta da Tiberio Kardos, N.S., XI). Rome.

Banfi, Florio. 1955. The Cartographer Stephanus Florentinus. *Imago Mundi*, 12: 92-102.

Banfi, Florio. 1956. Sole Surviving Specimens of Early Hungarian Cartography. *Imago Mundi*, 13: 89-10.

Baratta, Mario. 1914. Ricerche intorno a Giacomo Gastaldi. *Rivista Geografica Italiana*, 21: 117-36 and 373-79.

Barbat, P. 1997. Charles Chadenat. *Bulletin du bibliophile*. 1: 154-62.

Barcía Carballido y Zúñiga, Andrés González de, ed. 1737-38. *Epitome de la bibliotheca oriental, y occidental, nautica, y geografica de Don Antonio de Leon Pinelo ... añadido, y enmendado nuevamente, en que se contienen los escritores de las Indias orientales, y occidentales, y reinos convecinos, China, Tartaria, Japon, Persia, Armenia, Etiopia, y otras partes ... 3 vols. Madrid.

Barlow, Roger. 1932. *A Brief Summe of Geographie*, ed. Eva Germaine Rimington Taylor. (Works issued by the Hakluyt Society, Ser 2, No. 69). London. (Written 1540-41).

Barozzi, Francesco. 1588. *Cosmographia In Qvatvor Libros*, etc. Venice.

Barros, João de. 1552. *A[s]ia de Joam de Barros/dos fectos que os Po[r]tugue[s]es fizeram no de[s]cob[r]imento et conqui[s]ta dos mares et terras do O[r]iente*. Lisbon. (First of four *decadas* of Barros; first editions of other three were 1553, 1563 and 1615.)

Bartold, Vasilii Vladimirovich. 1947. *La découverte de l'Asie; histoire de l'orientalisme en Europe et en Russie.* Paris.

Bayle, Pierre. 1697. *Dictionaire historique et critique*, etc. 2 vols. Rotterdam.

Beans, George Harry. 1933. *A Large World Map Dated 1569 Sold at the Sign of the Pyramid in Venice by Joan Franciscus Camotius, now in the George H. Beans Library.* Philadelphia.

Beans, George Harry. 1943. *A Collection of Maps Compiled by Luis Hurtado de Toledo, Spanish Ambassador in Venice 1568.* Jenkintown, Pa.

Beckingham, Charles Fraser. 1983. Arabic Texts and the Hakluyt Society. In his *Between Islam and Christendom: Travellers, Facts and Legends in the Middle Ages and the Renaissance*, essay no IV (13pp). London.

Bella, Valeria and Piero. 1986. *Cartografia Rara: Antiche carte geografiche, topografiche e storiche dalla collezione Franco Novacco.* Milan.

Bellinato, Francesco. 1573. *Discorso Di Cosmografia, In Dialogo. Doue si ha *piena notitia Di Prouincie, Città, Castella, Popoli, & Monti, Mari, Fiumi, Laghi, di tutto'l Mondo. Nuouamente stampato.* Venice.

Bembo, Pietro. 1556. *L'histoire du noveau monde descouvert par les Portugalois, escrite par le Seigneur Pierre Bembo.* Paris.

Bembo, Pietro. 1809. *Lettere di M. Pietro Bembo Cardinale.* Milano. (Opere del cardinale Pietro Bembo, v. 6). Milano.

Berg, Lev Semenovich. 1919. Izvestiia o Beringovom prolive i ego beregakh do Beringa i Kuka. *Zapiski po gidrografii,* N.S., 43, no. 2: 77-141.

Berg, Lev Semenovich. 1935. Anianskii proliv. In his *Otkrytie Kamchatki i ekspeditsii Beringa.* 2nd ed., 7-25. Leningrad.

Berg, Lev Semenovich. 1935. Kartograficheskii mif Anianskii proliv. Geograficheskoe obshchestvo SSSR. *Izvestiia,* 68: 806-10.

Berggren, J. L., and Jones, Alexander. 2000. *Ptolemy's Geography: An Annotated Translation of the Theoretical Chapters.* Princeton.

Bernard, Edward. 1704. Veterum Mathematicorum, Graecorum, Latinorum, & Arabum, Synopsis. In *Admodum Reverendi & Doctissimi Viri D. Roberti Huntingtoni, Episcopi Rapetensis Epistolae: Et Praemittuntur*

D. Huntingtoni & D. Bernardi Vitae, by Robert Huntington, et al., pp. 1-44 (third Arabic numeral pagination in book). London.

Berthelot, André. 1939. *Les cartes de la Corse de Ptolémé au XIXe siècle.* Paris.

Bertolini, Gian Lodovico (Zanetti, Girolamo). 1925. Relazione sul restauro delle carte geografiche del Palazzo Ducale di Venezia (1762) di Girolamo Zanetti. *Bollettino della Società Geografica Italiana,* 62: 309-40.

Bertolini, Gian Lodovico. 1929. Dell'espressione 'Le Quattro parti del mondo e la Quarta parte del Mondo' nei documenti medievali. *Rivista Geografica Italiana,* 36: 136-38.

Best, George. 1867. *The Three Voyages of Martin Frobisher in Search of a Passage to Cathaia and India by the North-West, A.D. 1576-8,* etc. (Works issued by the Hakluyt Society, 38). London. (First published 1578).

Betz, Richard. 2007. *The Mapping of Africa: A Cartobibliography of Printed Maps of the African Continent to 1700.* 't Goy-Houten.

Biagiotti, Marco. 1990. L'America in un atlante anonimo del XVI secolo attribuite a Joan Martines. *Bollettino della Società Geografica Italiana,* Ser. XI, 7: 347-67.

Biasutti, Renato. 1908. *Il 'Disegno della geografia moderna' dell'Italia di*

Giacomo Gastaldi (1561). (Memorie geografiche pubblicate come supplemento alla Rivista Geografica Italiana, vol. 2, No. 4). Florence.

Biasutti, Renato. 1920. La carta dell'Africa di G. Gastaldi (1545-1564) e lo sviluppo della cartografia Africana nei sec. XVI e XVII. *Bollettino della Società Geografica Italiana*, Ser. 5, 9: 327-46 and 387-436.

Biasutti, Renato. 1923. La carta dell'Africa del De Jode (1593) e l'influsso del Gastaldi sulla cartografia olandese. Congresso Geografico Italiano, 8th, Florence, 1921. *Atti*, vol. 2, 307-10. Florence.

Biasutti, Renato. 1930. Lo sviluppo della cartografia dell'Italia nel secoli XIV-XVII. *L'Universo*, 11: 549-57.

Bifolco, Stefano and Fabrizio Ronca. 2018. *Cartografia e topografia italiana del XVI secolo: catalogo ragionato delle opere a stampa.* 3 vols. Roma.

Biondo, Flavio. 1474. *Italiae illustratae libri viii.* Rome (and many later editions).

Björnbo, Axel Anthon, and Petersen, Carl S. 1909. *Der Däne Claudius Claussøn Swart (Claudius Clavus) & der älteste Kartograph des Nordens, der erste Ptolemäus-Epigon der Renaissance:ein Monographie.* Innsbruck.

Bjørnbo, Axel Anthon. 1912. *Cartografia Groenlandica* (Meddelelser om Grønland, 48). Copenhagen.

Bochart, Samuel. 1646. *Phaleg, Sev De Dispersione Gentivm Et Terrarvm Divisione Facta In Aedificatione Turris Babel.* Part 1 of his *Geographiae Sacrae Pars Prior [-Altera]*, etc. Cadomi [Caen].

Bochart, Samuel. 1663. *Hierozoicon, Sive, Bipertitum Opus De Animalibus Sacrae Scripturae*, etc. London.

Bodenstein, Wulf. 1998. Ortelius' Maps of Africa. In *Abraham Ortelius and the First Atlas: Essays Commemorating the Quadricentennial of His Death 1598-1998*, ed., Marcel van den Broecke, Peter van der Krogt, and Peter Meurer, 185-207. Utrecht.

Boileau de Bouillon, Gilles. 1555. *La sphere des deux mondes, composée en françois, par Darinel pasteur des Amadis* [pseud], etc. Antwerp.

Bonacci, Giovani. 1905. Note intorno a Pirro Ligorio e alla cartografia napoletana della seconda metà del secolo XVI. *Atti del V. Congresso Geografico Italiano tenuto in Napoli dal 6 a 11 Aprile 1904.* vol. 2, 812-27. Napoli.

Boorsch, Suzanne. 1976. America in Festival Presentations. In *First Images of the New World*, ed. Fredi Chiapelli. vol. 1, 503-15. Berkeley.

Bordini, Francesco. 1573. . . . *Qvaesitorvm, Et Responsorvm Mathematicæ disciplinæ ad totius Vniuersi Cognitionem spectantium Chilias. Ex quibus, quæ ad sphere, Cosmographiæ, Geographiæ*, etc. Bononiae.

Borrhaus, Martin. 1555. *Martini Borrhai In Cosmographiae Elementa Commentatio. Astronomica. Geographica. Libellus, ut mole exiguous*, etc. Basle.

Borri, Roberto. 1999. *L'Italia nell'antica cartografia 1477-1799*. Torino.

Borroni, Fabia. 1967. Bertelli, Donato. *Dizionario Biografico degli Italiani*, 9: 490-91.

Borroni, Fabia. 1967. Bertelli, Ferdinando. *Dizionario Biografico degli Italiani*, 9: 491-92.

Borroni, Fabia. 1967. Bertelli, Luca. *Dizionario Biografico degli Italiani*, 9: 492-93.

Borroni, Fabia. 1967. Bertelli, Pietro. *Dizionario Biografico degli Italiani*, 9: 499-500.

Borroni Salvadori, Fabia. 1980. *Carte piante e stampe storiche delle raccolte lafreriane della Biblioteca Nazionale di Firenze*. Rome.

Botero, Giovanni. 1591-92. *Relationi vniversale*, etc. Rome (and many later editions).

Bourne, Molly. 1999. Francesco II Gonzaga and Maps as Palace Decoration in Renaissance Mantua. *Imago Mundi*, 51: 51-82.

Bouwsma, William J. 1957. *Concordia Mundi: The Career and Thought of Guillaume Postel (1510-1581)*. Cambridge, Mass.

Boxer, Charles Ralph. 1981. *João de Barros, Portuguese Humanist and Historian of Asia*. New Delhi.

Bragantini, Renzo. 1987. L'enigma di una raccolta di enigmi. In his *Il riso sotto il velame: la novella cinquecentesca tra l'avventura e la norma*, 127-50. Florence.

Brand, Donald D. 1967. Geographical Exploration by the Spaniards. In *The Pacific Basin: A History of Its Geographical Exploration*, ed. Herman R. Friis, 109-44. (American Geographical Society, Special Publication, 38). New York.

Braudel, Fernand. 1972-73. *The Mediterranean and the Mediterranean World in the Age of Philip II*. 2 vols. New York.

Brockelmann, Carl. 1938. *Geschichte der arabischen Litteratur*. 2nd supplement. Leiden.

Broek, Jan O. M. 1962. Place Names in 16th and 17th Century Borneo. *Imago Mundi*, 16: 129-48.

Brogan, Howard O., et al, comp. 1952. *The Leopold von Ranke Manuscripts of Syracuse University: The First One Hundred Titles, Dealing Primarily with the Republic of Venice in the 16th, 17th and 18th Centuries*. Syracuse, N.Y.

Brown, Horatio F. 1891. *The Venetian Printing Press. An Historical Study Based upon Documents for the Most Part hitherto Unpublished*. New York.

Brown, Lloyd A. 1949. *The Story of Maps*. Boston.

Brown, Lloyd A. 1951. *Jean Dominique Cassini and His World Map of 1696*. Ann Arbor.

Brown, Lloyd, introd. 1952. *The World Encompassed: An Exhibition of the History of Maps Held at the Baltimore Museum of Art October 7 to November 23, 1952*. Baltimore.

Brown, Rawdon. 1864. Preface to *Calendar of State Papers and Manuscripts, relating to English Affairs, Existing in the Archives and Collections of Venice, and in Other Libraries of Northern Italy*. vol. 1. London.

Browne, Janet. 1983. *The Secular Ark: Studies in the History of Biogeography*. New Haven.

Buache, Philippe. 1753. *Considerations geographiques et physiques sur les nouvelles decouvertes au nord de la grande mer, appellée vulgairement la mer du Sud; avec des cartes qui y sont relatives*. Paris.

Buczek, Karol. 1966. *The history of Polish cartography from the 15th to the 18th century*. Wroclaw.

Buisseret, David, ed. 1992. *Monarchs, Ministers and Maps: The Emergence of Cartography as a Tool of Government in Early Modern Europe*. Chicago.

Burden, Philip D. 1996. *The Mapping of North America: A List of Printed Maps 1511-1670*. Stamford, Conn.

Burgaleta, Claudio M. 1999. José *de Acosta, S.J. (1540-1600): His Life and Thought*. Chicago.

Bury, Michael. 1990. *Giulio Sanuto, a Venetian Engraver of the Sixteenth Century*. Edinburgh.

Bury, Michael. 2001. *The Print in Italy, 1550-1620*. London.

Busolini, D. 1999. Giacomo Gastaldi. *Dizionario Biografico degli Italiani*, 52: 529-32.

Calancha, Antonio de la. 1638. *Corónica moralizada del Orden de San Avgvstin en el Perv, con svcesos egenplares vistos en esta monarqvia*, etc. Barcelona, 1638.

Camden, William. 1691. *V. Cl. Gulielmi Camdeni, et Illustrium Virorum ad G. Camdenum Epistolae*, etc. London.

Capello, Carlo F. 1952. *Studi sulle cartografia piamontese. I. Il Piemonte nella cartografia moderna*. Torino.

Caraci, Giuseppe. 1926-32. *Tabulae Geographicae Vetustiores in Italia Adservatae: Reproductions of Manuscript and Rare Printed Maps, Edited and Explained, as a Contribution to the History of Geographical Knowledge in the Period of the Great Discoveries*. 3 Vols. Florence.

Caraci, Giuseppe. 1927. Avanzi di una preziosa raccolta di carte geografiche a stampa dei secolo XVI e XVII. *La Bibliofilia*, 29: 178-92.

Caraci, Giuseppe. 1927. A Large printed anonymous map of the New World (second half of the 16th century). In Caraci, 1926-32 (q.v.), vol. 2 (1927), pp. 37-48 and plates XXXI-XL.

Caraci, Giuseppe. 1927. Giacomo Gastaldi, Enrico Zell e la cartografia più antica a stampa della Germania. *Archeion; Archivio di storia della scienza*, 8: 377-400. (Also in German in *Petermanns Mitteilungen*, 73 (1927), 200-05.)

Caraci, Giuseppe. 1935. Il cartografo messinese Joan Martines e l'opera sua. In *Atti della Accademia Peloritana*, 619-67.

Caraci, Giuseppe. 1936. La carta della Corsica attribuita ad Agostino Giustiniani. *Archivio Storico di Corsica*, 12: 129-72, 268-315 and 461-95.

Caraci, Giuseppe. 1936. Note critiche sui mappamondi gastaldini. *Rivista Geografica Italiana*, 43: 120-37 and 202-37.

Caraci, Giuseppe. 1937. Di un atlante poco noto di Vesconte Maggiolo. *La Bibliofilia*, 39: 1-29. (Reprinted in English in *Imago Mundi*, 2 (1937), 37-54).

Caraci, Giuseppe. 1942-43. Note e aggiunte alla cartografia terrestre della Corsica di M. Ascari. *Archivio storico di Corsica*, 1942, 28-36 and 206-13; and 1943, 18-34.

Caraci, Giuseppe. 1958. La produzione cartografica di Vesconte Maggiolo (1511-1549) ed il Nuovo Mondo. Roma. Università. Facoltà di magistero. Istituto di scienze geografiche e cartografiche. *Memorie geografiche*, 4: 221-89.

Caraci, Giuseppe. 1962. La prima raccolta moderna di grandi carte murali rappresentati i quattro continenti. *Atti del XVIII Congresso Geografico Italiano, Trieste, 1961*. vol. 2, 49-60. Trieste.

Chapin, Seymour L. 1957. The Astronomical Activities of Nicolas-Claude Fabri de Peiresc. *Isis*, 48: 13-29.

Chaufepié, Jaques George de. 1750-59. *Nouveau dictionnaire historique et critique: pour servir de supplement ou de continuation au Dictionnaire historique et critique de Pierre Bayle*. 4 vols. Amsterdam.

Chesneau, Jean. 1887. *Le voyage de Monsieur d'Aramon, ambassadeur pour le roy en Levant, escript par noble homme Jean Chesneau; publié et annoté par Ch. Schefer. (Recueil de voyages et de documents pour servir à l'histoire de la géographie depuis le XIIIe jusqu'à la fin du XVIe siècle*, 8). Paris. (Often spelled Chesneaux in catalogs).

Cicogna, Emmanuele Antonio. 1824-53. *Delle Inscrizioni veneziane*. 6 vols. in 7. Venice.

Cirillo Sirri, Teresa. 1994. L'*Imago Mundi* nella poesia epica del Rinascimento. In *Esplorazioni geografiche e imagine del mondo nei secoli XV e XVI*, ed. Simonetta Ballo Alagna, 269-85. Messina.

Citolini, Alessandro. 1561. *La tipocosmia*. Venice.

Civici musei veneziani d'arte e di storia. 1986. Una città e il suo museo. *Bollettino*, N.S., 30, nos. 1-4.

Clagett, Marshall. 1974. The Works of Francesco Maurolico. *Physis*, 16: 149-98.

Clarke, James Stanier. 1803. *The Progress of Maritime Discovery, from the Earliest Period to the Close of the Eighteenth Century, Forming an Extensive System of Hydrography*. London.

Cline, Howard F. 1962. The Ortelius Maps of New Spain, 1579, and Related Contemporary Materials, 1560-1610. *Imago Mundi*, 16: 98-115.

Coccio, Paola. 1991. Le illustrazioni dell'*Orlando Furioso* (Valgrisi, 1556) già attribuite a Dosso Dossi. *La Bibliofilia*, 93: 279-309.

Cochrane, Eric W. 1981. *Historians and Historiography in the Italian Renaissance*. Chicago.

Codazzi, Angela. 1953. Una Descrizione' del Cairo di Guglielmo Postel. In *Studi di paleografia, diplomatica, storia e araldica in onore di Cesare Manaresi*, 169-206. Milan.

Codazzi, Angiolina. 1922. Di un atlante nautico di Giovanni Martines. *L'Universo*, 3: 905-25.

Colamonico, Carmelo. 1921. Appunti storici sulla cartografia della Puglia. *Bollettino della Società Geografica Italiana*, 58: 295-326.

Colamonico, Carmelo. 1939. La più antica carta regionale della Puglia. *Iapigia*, 10: 145-85.

Colección de documentos (1886) ineditos relativos al descubrimiento, conquista y organización de las antiguas posesiones españolas de ultramar. Segunda serie publicada por la Real Academia de la Historia. vol. 2. Madrid.

Colón, Fernando. 1988. *Descripción y Cosmografía de España*. 3 vols. Sevilla. (First published 1908-1915).

Comba, Rinaldo, and Sereno, Paola, eds. 2002. *Rappresentare uno Stato: Carti e cartografi degli Stati Sabaudi del XVI al XVIII secolo*. 2 vols. Torino.

Coronelli, Vincenzo. 1695. Catalogo degli avtori antichi, et moderni, che hanno scritto, e trattato di Geografia. In his *Atlante veneto*. Venice. (Reprinted in Armao, 1957, q.v. in this bibliography).

Cortes, Hernan. 1986. *Letters from Mexico*, trans. and ed. Anthony Pagden. New Haven.

Cortés, Martín. 1551. *Breue compendio de la sphera y de la arte de nauegar con nueuos instrumentos y reglas exemplificado con muy subtiles demonstraciones*. Seville.

Cortesão, Armando. 1960. *Portugaliae monumenta cartographica*. 5 vols. Lisbon. (Also has small index volume dated 1962).

Cosgrove, Denis. 1988. The Geometry of Landscape: Practical and Speculative Arts in Sixteenth-Century Venetian Land Territories. In *The Iconography of Landscape: Essays on the Symbolic Representation, Design and Use of Past Environments,* 254-76. (Cambridge Studies in Historical Geography, 9). Cambridge.

Cosgrove, Denis. 1992. Mapping New Worlds: Culture and Cartography in Sixteenth-Century Venice. *Imago Mundi,* 44: 65-89.

Cosgrove, Denis. 1993. *The Palladian Landscape: Geographical Change and Its Cultural Representations in Sixteenth-Century Italy*. University Park, Pa.

Crane, Nicholas. 2002. *Mercator: The Man Who Mapped the Planet*. New York.

Cucagna, Alessandro. 1964. Il Friuli e la Venezia Giulia nelle principali carte geografiche regionali dei secoli XVI, XVII e XVIII: Catalogo ragionato della mostra storica di cartografia. *Atti del XVIII Congresso Geografico Italiano Trieste 4-9 aprile 1961, volume terzo, mostre,* pp. xvii-xxviii and 1-372. Trieste.

Cuesto Domingo, Mariano. 1983-84. *Alonso de Santa Cruz y su obra cosmográfica*. 2 vols. Madrid. (There is an English translation of the Santa Cruz work which is of interest to the present book [*Libro de las Longitudines*] in *The Book of Longitudes*, trans. J. Bankston. Bisbee, Arizona, 1992.)

848

Dahlgren, Erik Wilhelm. 1892. [Santa Cruz, Alonso de]. *Map of the World, 1542*. Stockholm.

Dahlgren, Erik Wilhelm. 1911. *Les débuts de la cartographie du Japon*. (Archives d'études orientales, 4). Uppsala.

Dahlgren, Erik Wilhelm. 1916. *Were the Hawaiian Islands Visited by the Spaniards before their Discovery by Captain Cook in 1778?: A Contribution to the Geographical History of the North Pacific Ocean Especially of the Relations between America and Asia in the Spanish Period*. (Svenska vetenskapsakademien Handlingar, vol. 57, No. 4). Stockholm.

Da Mosto, Andrea. 1937-40. *L'Archivio di Stato di Venezia: indice generale, storico, descrittivo ed analitico*. 2 vols. Roma.

Dannenfeldt, Karl H. 1955. The Renaissance Humanists and the Knowledge of Arabic. *Studies in the Renaissance*, 2: 96-117.

Deane, Charles. 1885. [untitled comments on Johann Schöner's 1533 *Opusculum Geographicum*]. Amarican Antiquarian Society. *Proceedings*, N.S., 3: 26-34.

De Ghein, Rik. 1994. De oudste kaarten van het graafschap Vlaanderen 1538-1656. Cercle archéologique du pays de Waes, *Annalen*, 97: 233-456.

De Jode, Gerard. 1578. *Speculum Orbis Terrarum*. Antwerp.

Delano-Smith, Catherine. 1991. *Maps in Bibles, 1500-1600: An Illustrated Catalogue*. Genève.

Del Piero, Antonio. 1902. Della vita e degli studi di Gio. Battista Ramusio. *Nuovo Archivio Veneto*, N.S., 4: 5-112.

Della Giustina, Lisa. 1999. La *Tipocosmia* di Alessandro Citolini (1561): Nuove forme di enciclopedismo nel XVI secolo. *Archivio Storico Italiano*, 157: 63-87.

Dentoni Litta, Antonio, and Massabò Ricci, Isabella, eds. 2003. *Architettura militare: Luoghi, città, fortezze, territori in età moderna*. vol. 1. Roma.

Denuce, Jean. 1912-13. *Oud-nederlandsche kaartmakers in betrekking met Plantin*. 2 vols. Antwerp.

De Stefano, Francesco. 1920. Intorno alla carta gastaldina della Sicilia (1545). *Rivista Geografica Italiana*, 27: 196-99.

Destombes, Marcel. 1970. An Antwerp *Unicum:* an Unpublished Terrestrial Globe of the 16th Century in the Bibliothèque Nationale, Paris. *Imago Mundi*, 24: 85-94.

Destombes, Marcel. 1973. La grande carte d'Europe de Zuan Domenico Zorzi (1545) et l'activité cartographique de Matteo Pagano à Venise de 1538 à 1565. In Jòzef Babicz, ed. *Studia z dziejów geografii i kartografii,* 115-29. Wroclaw.

Destombes, Marcel. 1985. Guillaume Postel cartographe. In *Guillaume Postel, 1581-1981: actes du colloque international d'Avranches, 5-9 septembre 1981,* 361-71. Paris.

Dilke, O. A. W. 1985. *Greek and Roman Maps.* London.

Dilke. O. A. W. 1987. Cartography in the Byzantine Empire. In *The History of Cartography.* vol. 1. *Cartography in Prehistoric, Ancient, and Medieval Europe and the Mediterranean,* ed. John Brian Harley and David Woodward, 258-75. Chicago.

Di Palma, Maria Teresa. 1991. Le Quattro carte murali dei continenti della Società Geografica Italiana. *Bollettino della Società Geografica Italiana,* Ser. XI, 8: 525-30.

Di Vita, Giuseppe. 1905. Lo schema triangolare e la posizione geografica della Sicilia secondo i geografi e i cartografi antichi da Strabone sino a Giacomo Gastaldo. *Atti del V. Congresso Geografico Italiano tenuto in Napoli dal 6 a 11 Aprile 1904.* vol. 2, 751-61. Napoli.

Dodoens, Rembert. 1548. *Cosmographica In Astronomiam Et Geographiam Isagoge.* Antwerp.

Doglioni, Giovanni Nicolo. 1594. *Compendio historico vniversale,* etc. Venice. (Also 1605 edition, and others).

Donattini, Massimo. 1992. Orizzonti geografici dell'editoria italiana (1493-1560). In *Il Nuovo Mondo nella coscienza italiana e tedesca del Cinquecento,* ed. Adriano Prosperi and Wolfgang Reinhard, 79-154. (Annali dell'Istituto storico italo-germanico, Quaderno, 33). Bologna.

Donazzolo, Pietro. 1929. *I viaggiatori veneti minori: Studio bio-bibliografico.* (Memorie della Società Geografica Italiana, 16). Rome.

Dörflinger, Johannes, et al. 1977. *Descriptio Austriae: Österreich u. seine Nachbarn im Kartenbild v. d. Spätantike bis ins 19. Jh.* Wien.

Dryander, Joannes (Apian, Peter). 1544. *Cosmographiae Introdvctio, Cvm Quibusdam Geometriae Ac Astronomiae Principijs, Ad Eam Rem Necessarijs.* Coloniae. (An edition of Apian's cosmography by Dryander, also known as Joannes Eichmann).

Durand, Dana Bennett. 1952. *The Vienna-Klosterneuburg Map Corpus of the Fifteenth Century; a Study in the Transition from Medieval to Modern Science.* Leiden.

Dürst, Arthur. 1998. The Map of Europe. In *The Mercator Atlas of Europe,* ed. Marcel Watelet, 31-41. Pleasant Hill, OR.

[Eames, Wilberforce]. 1886. *A List of Editions of Ptolemy's Geography 1475-1730*. New York. (Extracted from Sabin, 1868-1939, ad nomen Ptolemy).

Eichmann, Joannes. See Dryander, Joannes.

Elte, Meijer, firm, The Hague, and Nico Israel, firm, Amsterdam, booksellers. 1978. *Important Old Books on Various Subjects offered for sale jointly by Nico IsraelCRare Books, Amsterdam [and] Antiquariaat Meijer Elte, The Hague*. (Catalog 20 Fall, 1978). Amsterdam.

Enciso, Martin Fernandez de. 1519. *Suma de geographia q[ue] trata de todas las partidas & prouincias del mundo: en especial delas indias. & trata largam te del arte del marear: juntam te con la espera en romãce: con el regimi to del sol & del norte*. Seville.

Enckell, Carl. 1951. The Representation of the North of Europe in the Worldmap of Petrus Plancius of 1592. *Imago Mundi*, 8: 55-69.

Engel, Samuel. 1765. *Mémoires et observations géographique et critiques sur la situation des pays septentrionaux de l'Asie et l'Amérique : d'après les relations les plus récentes : aux quelles on a joint un Essai sur la route aux Indes par le nord & sur un commerce très vaste & très riche à établir dans la mer du Sud*, etc. Lausanne.

Engel, Samuel. 1767. *Essai sur cette question: quand et comment l'Amérique a-t-elle été peuplée d'hommes et d'animaux?* 5 vols. Amsterdam.

Enrile, Antonino. 1905. Intorno alle ricerche fatte per la compilazione di un Saggio di Cartografia della Regione Siciliana da Giacomo Gastaldo ai nostri giorni. In *Atti del V. Congresso Geografico Italiano tenuto in Napoli dal 6 a 11 Aprile 1904*. vol. 2, 762-79. Napoli.

Enrile, Antonino. 1908. *Primo saggio di cartografia della regione siciliana*. Palermo.

Eversole, Richard. 1983. An Ethiopean Mountain in Maps and Literature. *Mapline*, no. 29 (March): [1]-[5].

Fabris, Antonio. 1989. Note sul mappamondo cordiforme de Haci Ahmed di Tunisi. *Quaderni di studi araba*, 7: 3-17.

Fahy, Conor. 1993. The Venetian Ptolemy of 1548. In *The Italian Book 1465-1800: Studies Presented to Dennis E. Rhodes on his 70th Birthday*, ed. Denis V. Reidy, 89-115. London.

Faldi, Italo. 1981. *Il Palazzo Farnese di Caprarola*. Torino.

Feuerstein, Arnold. 1912. Die Entwicklung des Kartenbildes von Tirol bis um die Mitte des 16. Jahrhunderts. *Mitteilungen der Geographischen Gesellschaft in Wien*, 55: 328-85.

Fine, Oronce. 1551. *Sphaera Mundi, Siue Cosmographia Quinque Libris*, etc. Paris.

Fiorani, Francesca. 1996. Post-Tridentine 'Geographia Sacra.' The Galleria delle Carte Geografiche in the Vatican Palace. *Imago Mundi*, 48: 124-48.

Fiorini, Matteo. 1881. *Le projezioni delle carte geografiche*. 2 vols (text + atlas). Bologna.

Fiorini, Matteo. 1895. Sopra tre speciali projezioni meridiane e i mappamondi ovali de secolo XVI. *Memorie della Società Geografica Italiana*, 5: 165-201.

Fracanzano da Montalboddo. 1507. *Paesi Nouamente retrouati. Et Nouo Mondo da Alberico Vesputio Florentino intitulato*. Vicenza.

Fracastoro, Girolamo. 1538. . . . *Homocentrica. Eivsdem De cavsisb criticorvm diervm per ea qvae in nobis svnt* . . . . Venetiis.

Franzoi, Umberto and Dina di Stefano. 1976. *Le chiese di Venezia*. Venice.

Franck, Sebastian. 1534. *Weltbuch: Spiegel vñ Bildtnisz des gantzen Erdbodens von Sebastiano Franco Wördensi in vier Bücher nemlich in Asiam Aphricam Europam vnd Americam gestelt vnd abteilt ... Auch etwas võ new gefundenen Welten vnd Inseln*, etc. Tübingen.

Fueck, Johann. 1955. *Die arabischen Studien in Europa bis in den Anfang des 20. Jahrhunderts*. Leipzig.

Gallo, Rodolfo. 1943. Le mappe geografiche del Palazzo Ducale di Venezia. *Archivio veneto*, Ser. 5, 32-33: 47-113.

Gallo, Rodolfo. 1949. Antonio Florian and his Mappemonde. *Imago Mundi*, 6: 34-38.

Gallo, Rodolfo. 1950. Gioan Francesco Camocio and his Large Map of Europe. *Imago Mundi*, 7: 93-102.

Gallo, Rodolfo. 1954. *Carte geografiche cinquecentesche a stampa della Biblioteca Marciana e della Biblioteca del Museo Correr di Venezia*. Venice.

Gallo, Rodolfo. 1955. La mappa dell'Asia della Sala dello Scudo in Palazzo Ducale e il Milione di Marco Polo. In *Nel VII centenario della nascita di Marco Polo,* 195-232. Venice.

Gallois, Lucien Louis Joseph. 1890. *Les Geographes Allemands de la Renaissance*. Paris. Reprinted in facs., Amsterdam, 1963.

Gallucci, Giovanni Paolo. 1588. *Theatrvm mvndi, et temporis, in quo non solvm precipvæ horvm partes describuntur*, etc. Venice.

Gambi, Lucio, and Antonio Pinelli, ed. 1994. *La Galleria delle carte geografiche in Vaticano ' The Gallery of maps in the Vatican.* 3 vols. Modena.

Ganado, Albert. 1982. Description of an Early Venetian Sixteenth Century Collection of Maps at the Casanatense Library in Rome. *Imago Mundi*, 34: 26-47.

Ganado, Albert. 1985. Italy's 16th Century Contribution to the Cartography of Malta. In *Imago et Mensura Mundi: Atti del IX Congresso Internazionale di Storia della Cartografia*, ed. Carlo Clivio Marzoli, vol. 1, 221-33. Roma.

Ganado, Albert, et al. 1986. The Pre-Siege Maps of Malta, 1536-1563. In *Annual Report and Accounts 30th September 1986, Investment Finance Bank Ltd., Malta*. Malta. (17 unnumbered pages).

Ganado, Albert. 1994-95. *A Study in Depth of 143 Maps Representing the Great Siege of Malta of 1565.* 2 vols. Valletta.

Ganado, Albert. 2003. *Velletta Città Nuova: A Map History (1566-1600)*. Valletta.

Ganado, Albert. 2005-6. A New State of a Rare Pre-Siege Malta Map. *Treasures of Malta*, 12, no. 2: 52-53.

Ganong, William Francis. 1964. *Crucial Maps in the Early Cartography and Place-Nomenclature of the Atlantic Coast of Canada*. Toronto.

Garcia, Gregorio. 1981. *Origen de los indios del Nuevo Mundo*. Mexico. (First edition 1607).

García Mercadal, José, ed. 1952-62. *Viajes de extranjeros por España y Portugal*. 3 vols. Madrid.

Garzoni, Tomaso. 1996. *La piazza universale di tutte le professioni del mondo*. 2 vols. Florence. (Original edition 1585).

Gasparrini Leporace, Tullia. 1954. *Mostra L'Asia nella cartografia degli occidentali*. Venice.

Gastaldi, Giacomo (Ptolemy). 1548. *La Geografia di Claudo Ptolemeo Alessandrino . . . con le tauole non solamente antiche & moderne solite di stamparsi, ma altre nuoue aggiunteui*, etc. Venice.

Gastaldi, Giacomo. 1561. *La Vniversale descrittione del mondo*. Venice. (Also editions 1562, 1565 and in Latin, 1562 and 1568. We use the pagination scheme initiated by Caraci in 1936, as explained in chapter 2, at note 68).

Gatti, Isidoro. 1976. *Il P. Vincenzo Coronelli dei Frati Minori Conventuali negli anni del generalato (1701-1707)*. (Miscellanea Historiae Pontificae, 41-42). Rome.

Gemma, Frisius. 1530. *De Principiis Astronomiæ & Cosmographiæ, Deq[ue] vse Globi ad eodem editi. Item de Orbis diuisione, & Insulis, rebusq[ue] nuper inuentis.* Antwerp.

Gerbi, Antonello. 1973. *The Dispute of the New World; the History of a Polemic, 1750-1900.* Rev. and enl. ed. Pittsburgh.

Gerbi, Antonello. 1985. *Nature in the New World: from Christopher Columbus to Gonzalo Fernández de Oviedo.* Pittsburgh.

Gezelius, Birger. 1910. *Japan i västerländsk framställning till omkring år 1700; ett geografiskt-kartografiskt forsook.* Linköping.

Giachery, Alessio. 1998. Un' Università di stampatori e librai: la mariegola dell'Arte veneziano. *Charta*, 7, no. 37: 36-38.

Giglio, Geronimo. 1560. Gli costvmi, et l'vsanze dell'Indie, overo Mondo Nvovo. In *Gli Costvmi, Le Leggi, Et Lvsanze Di Tvtte Le Genti; Raccolte, Qvi Insieme Da molti illustri Scrittori per Giouanni Boemo ... E tradotti Lucio Fauno in questa nostra lingua volgare. Aggiontovvi Di Nvovo Gli costumi, & l' usanze dell' Indie occidentali, ouero Mondo Nuouo, da P. Gieronimo Giglio*, by Joannes Boemus, 189r-236r. Venice. (First ed. with Giglio 1558)

Giovio, Paolo. 1550-52. *Historiarvm svi temporis; tomus primus [secundus].* 2 vols. in 1. Florence (and many later editions).

Girava, Gerónimo. 1556. *Dos Libros De Cosmographia Compuestos nueuamente.* Milan.

Giustiniani, Bernardo. 1608. *Historia di Bernardo Giustiniano caualiere, et procuratore di S. Marco. Dell'origine di Venetia*, etc. Venice.

Glareanus, Henricus. 1527. ...*De Geographia Liber Vnvs.* Basle.

Glaser, Lynn. 1973. *Indians or Jews? An Introduction to a Reprint of Manasseh ben Israel's The Hope of Israel.* Gilroy, CA.

Gliozzi, Giuliano. 1977. *Adamo e il Nuovo Mondo: La nascita dell'antropologia coloniale: dalle genealogie bibliche alle teorie razziali (1500-1700).* Firenze.

Globus mundi (1509)*Declaratio siue descriptio mundi et totius orbis terrarum. globulo rotundo comparati vt spera solida*, etc. Strassburg.

Goldson, William. 1793. *Observations on the Passage between the Atlantic and Pacific Oceans, in Two Memoirs on the Straits of Anian, and the Discoveries of De Fonte*, etc. Portsmouth.

Gole, Susan. 1976. *Early Maps of India.* New Delhi.

Gole, Susan. 1982. India Proper. *Map Collector*, 20: 16-20.

Gómara, Francisco López de. See López de Gómara, Francisco.

Gordeev, Anton Yu. 2006. *Kartografiia Chernego i Azovskogo morei: Retrospektiva do 1500 g., period 1500-1600 gg., period 1600-1700.* (work on 2 CD-ROMs). Kiev.

Goss, J. J. S. 1981. An Unusual Manuscript Wall Map by Urbano Monti 1544-1613. *Map Collector*, 15: 18-22.

Gould, Rupert Thomas. 1929. The Strait of Anian. In his *Enigmas: Another Book of Strange Facts*, 143-77. London.

Grande, Stefano. 1902. *Notizie sulla vita e sulle opere di Giacomo Gastaldi cosmografo piemontese del secolo XVI.* Torino.

Grande, Stefano. 1905. *Le carte d'America di Giacomo Gastaldi: contributo alla storia della cartografia del secolo XVI.* Torino.

Grande, Stefano. 1905. Le relazioni geografiche fra P. Bembo, G. Fracastoro, G. B. Ramusio, G. Gastaldi. Società Geografica Italiana, *Memorie*, 12: 93-197.

Grande, Stefano. 1953. *Gli 800 anni di storia di Villafranca Piemonte.* Moretta, 1953. Reprinted as *La storia di Villafranca Piemonte: la storia di Villafranca Piemonte comprende gli 800 anni di storia.* Cavour.

Gravier, Gabriel. 1896. *La cartographie de Madagascar.* Paris.

Greaves, John, trans. and ed (Abulfeda). 1650. *Chorasmiae et Mawaralhahrae: Hoc Est Regionum Extra Fluvium Oxum Descriptio Ex Tabulis Abulfedae.* London.

Gregorii, Johann Gottfried. 1713. *Curieuse Gedancken von den vornehmsten und accuratesten alt- und neuen Landcharten*, etc. Leipzig.

Gróf, László. 1988. *Carta Hungarica: térképgyüjtemény (1540-1841).* Budapest.

Grotius, Hugo. 1884. *On the Origin of the Native Races of America*, etc. Edinburgh. (Original edition in Latin, 1642: *Dissertatio de origine gentivm Americanarvm*).

Grynaeus, Simon, ed. 1532. *Novvs Orbis Regionvm Ac Insvlarvm Veteribvs Incognitarum, unà cum tabula cosmographica.* Paris. (Edited by Simon Grynaeus from material collected by Johann Huttich).

Hakluyt, Richard. 1903-05. *The Principal Navigations Voyages Traffiques & Discoveries of the English Nation : Made by Sea or Over-Land to the Remote and Farthest Distant Quarters of the Earth at Any Time within the Compasse of These 1600 Yeeres.* 12 vols. Glasgow.

Hanke, Lewis. 1935. *The First Social Experiments in America: A Study in the Development of Spanish Indian Policy in the Sixteenth Century.* Cambridge, Mass.

Hanke, Lewis. 1937. Pope Paul III and the American Indians. *The Harvard Theological Review*, 30: 65-102.

Harald Sigurpsson. 1971. *Kortesaga Islands.* Reykjavik.

Harley, John Brian. 1987. The Map and the Development of the History of Cartography. In *The History of Cartography.* vol. I. *Cartography in Prehistoric, Ancient, and Medieval Europe and the Mediterranean,* ed. John Brian Harley and David Woodward, 1-42. Chicago.

Harley, John Brian, and David Woodward, eds. 1987. *The History of Cartography.* vol. I. *Cartography in Prehistoric, Ancient, and Medieval Europe and the Mediterranean.* Chicago.

Harley, John Brian, and David Woodward, eds. 1992. *The History of Cartography.* vol. 2, Book 1. *Cartography in the Traditional Islamic and South Asian Societies.* Chicago.

Harley, John Brian, and David Woodward, eds. 1994. *The History of Cartography.* vol. 2, Book 2. *Cartography in the Traditional East and Southeast Asian Societies.* Chicago.

Harrison, J. B. 1961. Five Portuguese Historians. In *Historians of India, Pakistan and Ceylon,* ed. C. H. Philips, 155-196. London.

Harrisse, Henry. 1966. *Bibliotheca Americana Vetustissima : A Description of Works Relating to America, Published between the Years 1492 and 1551.* New York.

Harrisse, Henry. 1892. *The Discovery of North America; a Critical, Documentary, and Historic Investigation ... .* London.

Harrisse, Henry. 1900. *Découverte et evolution cartographique de Terre-Neuve et des pays circonvoisins 1497-1501-1769.* Paris.

Hébert, John, and Richard Pflederer. 2000. Like No Other: The 1562 Gutiérrez Map of America. *Mercator's World*, 5, no. 6: 47-51.

Hedin, Sven Anders. 1917. *Lake Manasarovar and the Sources of the Great Indian RiversCFrom the Remotest Antiquity to the End of the Eighteenth Century.* Stockholm. (Vol. 1 of his *Southern Tibet*, 1917-22).

Hedin, Sven Anders. 1919. Early European Knowledge of Tibet. *Geografiska annaler*, 1: 290-339.

Heijden, H. A. M. van der. 1987. *The Oldest Maps of the Netherlands: An Illustrated and Annotated Cartobibliography of the 16th Century Maps of the XVII Provinces*. Utrecht.

Heijden, H. A. M. van der. 1992. *De Oudste gedrukte kaarten van Europa*. Alphen aan den Rijn.

Hellwig, Fritz. 1994. On Giov. Lorenzo Anania and his *Fabrica del Mondo*: The Hitherto Unknown Maps of the First Edition (Naples, 1573). In *Liber Amicorum: Essays on Art, History, Cartography and Bibliography in Honour of Dr. Albert Ganado*, ed. Joseph Schirò, et al., 105-120. Msida, Malta.

Hennig, Richard. 1935. Eine Kenntnis der Bering-Strasse im 16. Jahrhundert? *Petermanns Mitteilungen*, 81: 122-25.

Herberstein, Sigmund von. 1550. *Comentari Della Moscovia Et parimente della Russia, & delle altre cose belle & notabili, composti gia latinamente per il signor Sigismondo libero Barone in herberstain*, etc. Venice. (First edition, Latin, Vienna, 1549).

Hernando Rica, Agustín. 1995. *El mapa de España: siglos XV-XVIII*. [Madrid?].

Herrera y Tordesillas, Antonio de. 1601-13. *Historia general de los hechos de los castellanos en las islas i tierra firme del mar oceano*. 9 parts in 4 vols. Madrid.

Herrmann, Albert. 1920. Der Manasarover und die Quellen der Indischen Ströme. *Zeitschrift der Gesellschaft für Erdkunde zu Berlin*, 193-215.

Hessels, Jan H. 1887. *Abrahami Ortelii (geographi antverpiensis) et vivorum eruditorum ad eundem et ad Jacobum Colium Ortelianum . . . epistulae.* (*Ecclesiae londino-batavae archivum*, 1). Cambridge.

Hettner, Alfred. 1927. *Die Geographie; ihre Geschichte, ihr Wesen und ihre Methoden*. Breslau.

Hieronymus, Frank. 1985. Sebastian Münster, Conrad Schnitt und ihre Basel-Karte von 1538. *Speculum orbis*, 1, no. 2: 2-38.

Hobson, Anthony. 1999. *Renaissance Book Collecting: Jean Grolier and Diego Hurtado de Mendoza, Their Books and Bindings*. New York.

Hoff, Bert van 't. 1953. *Jacob van Deventer, keizerlijk-koninklijk geograaf*. The Hague.

Holt, Peter Malcolm, trans. and introd. 1983. [Abulfeda] *The Memoirs of a Syrian Prince: Abu'l-Fida, Sultan of Hamah (672-732/1273-1331)*. Wiesbaden.

Holzheimer, Arthur, and David Buisseret. 1992. *The Ramusio Map of 1534: A Facsimile Edition*. (The Hermon Dunlap Smith Center for the

History of Cartography. Occasional Publication, 6). Chicago.

Honter, Johannes. 1542. *Rvdimenta Cosmographica*. Brasov.

Horn, Georg. 1652. . . . *De originibvs americanis libri qvatvor*. The Hague.

Horn, Georg. 1666. . . . *Arca Noæ: Sive, Historia imperiorum et regnorum à condito orbe ad nostra tempora*. Leiden.

Hrenko, Pal. 1975. Magyarország Gastaldi térképén. *Geodezia es Kartográfia*, 27: 110-21.

Hübner, Christian E. 1710. *Dissertatio Philosophica de Studio Geographico in Genere*. Halle.

Huddleston, Lee. 1967. *Origins of the American Indians; European concepts, 1492-1729*. Austin.

Humphreys, Arthur Lee. 1926. *Old Decorative Maps and Charts*. London.

Hyde, J. 1924. L'Iconographie des quatre parties du monde dans les tapisseries. *Gazette des Beaux-Arts*, Ser. 5, 10: 253-72.

Hyde, J. 1926-27. Four Parts of the World in Old-Time Pageants and Ballets. *Apollo*, 4: 232-38, and 5: 19-27.

Ivins, William Mills. 1969. *Prints and Visual Communication*. New York.

Jourdain, Amable Louis. 1811. Notice historique sur Aboul-Féda et ses ouvrages. *Annales des voyages de la géographie de l'histoire*, 14: 180-230.

Juynboll, Wilhelmina. 1931. *Zeventiende-eeuwsche beoefenaars van het Arabisch in Nederland*. Utrecht.

Kagan, Richard L. 1989. *Spanish Cities of the Golden Age: The Views of Anton van den Wyngaerde*. Berkeley.

Kammerer, Albert. 1952. *La Mer Rouge, l'Abyssinie et l'Arabie aux XVIe et XVII siècles*. vol. 3, parte 3. Cairo.

Karamustafa, Ahmet T. 1992. Introduction to Islamic Maps. In *The History of Cartography*, vol. II, Book 1. *Cartography in the Traditional Islamic and South Asian Societies*, ed. John Brian Harley and David Woodward, 3-11. Chicago.

Karrow, Robert W., Jr. 1993. *Mapmakers of the Sixteenth Century and Their Maps: Bio-Bibliographies of the Cartographers of Abraham Ortelius, 1570*. Chicago.

Kelsey, Harry. 1986. Finding the Way Home: Spanish Exploration of the Round-Trip Route across the Pacific Ocean. *Western Historical Quarterly*, 17: 145-64.

Kelsey, Harry. 1986. *Juan Rodrìguez Cabrillo*. San Marino, CA.

Kennedy, Edward S. 1983. *Studies in the Islamic Exact Sciences*. Beirut.

Kish, George. 1951. The Japan on the 'Mural Atlas' of the Palazzo Vecchio, Florence. *Imago Mundi*, 8: 52-54.

Kish, George. 1953. The 'Mural Atlas' of Caprarola. *Imago Mundi*, 10: 51-56.

Kish, George. 1976. Early Thematic Mapping: The Work of Philippe Buache. *Imago Mundi*, 28: 129-36.

Klemp, Egon. 1989. *Asien auf Karten: von der Antike bis zur Mitte des 19. Jahrhunderts*. Weinheim.

Knauer, Elfriede Regina. 1981. *Die Carta Marina des Olaus Magnus von 1539: Ein Kartographisches Meisterwerk und seine Wirkung*. Göttingen.

Koeman, Cornelis. 1978. Oude wandkaarten. *Mededelingen van de nederlandse vereniging voor zeegeschiedenis*, 36: 5-10.

Koeman, Cornelis, et al. 2007. Surveying and Official Mapping in the Low Countries, 1500-ca. 1670. In *The History of Cartography: Cartography in the European Renaissance.*, ed. David Woodward, vol. 3, part 1, 1246-95. Chicago.

Kohl, Johann Georg. 1869. *History of the Discovery of Maine*. (Documentary History of the State of Maine, ed. William Willis, vol. 1). Portland.

Kohl, Johann Georg. 1911. Asia and America : An Historical Disquisition concerning the Ideas Which Former Geographers Had about the Geographical Relation and Connection of the Old and New World. American Antiquarian Society, *Proceedings*, N.S., 21: 284-338. (Written in the 1850s).

Köllmann, Erich, et al. 1967. Erdteile. In *Reallexikon zur deutschen Kunstgeschichte*. Vol 5, cols. 1107-1202. Stuttgart. (This article is in no way restricted to German art, regardless of the title of the work in which it appears).

Kordt, Veniamin A. 1899. *Materialy po istrii russkoi kartografii*. First series, Part 1. Kiev.

Krachkovskii, Ignatii Iulianovich. 1957. *Arabskaia geograficheskaia literature*. (Izbrannye sochineniia, vol. 4). Moscow.

Kraus, H. P., firm, booksellers, New York. 1949. *Early Geography and Cartography: A Catalogue of a Fine Collection of Atlases, Books on Navigation, Maps and Choice Geographical Works Relating to America* (Catalogue 51). New York.

Kraus, H. P., firm, booksellers, New York. 1969? *Monumenta Cartographica* (Catalogue 124). New York.

Kret, Wojciech, comp. 1978. *Katalog dawnych map Rzeczypospolitej Polskiej w Kolekcji Emeryka Hutten Czapskiego i w innych zbiorach. vol. 1. Mapy XV-XVI wieku.* Text and 28 maps on 37 sheets in a portfolio. Wroclaw.

Kretschmer, Ingrid, Johannes Dörflinger, and Franz Wawrik, eds. 1986. *Lexikon zur Geschichte der Kartographie : von den Anfängen bis zum Ersten Weltkrieg.* 2 vols. Vienna.

Kretschmer, Konrad. 1892. *Die Entdeckung Amerika's in ihrer Bedeutung für die Geschichte des Weltbildes.* Text and atlas. Berlin.

Lach, Donald F. 1965-93. *Asia in the Making of Europe.* 3 vols. in 9. Chicago.

Lagarde, Lucie. Philippe Buache. In *Lexikon zur Geschichte der Kartographie,* ed. Ingrid Kretschmer, et al., vol. 1, 119-21. Vienna.

Lagarde, Lucie. 1989. Le Passage du Nord-ouest et la Mer de l'Ouest dans la Cartographie française du 18e Siècle, Contribution à l'Etude de l'Oeuvre des Delisle et Buache. *Imago Mundi,* 41: 19-43.

Lago, Luciano, ed. 1992. *Imago mundi et Italiae : la versione del mondo e la scoperta dell'Italia nella cartografia antica (secoli X-XVI) / [a cura di] Luciano Lago: contributi di L. Gambi, M. Milanesi, L. Rombai.* 2 vols. Trieste.

Lago, Luciano. 1996. *Imago Adriae: La patria del Friuli, L'Istriae e la Dalmazia nella cartografia antica.* Trieste.

Lago, Luciano, ed. 2002. *Imago Italiae: la fabbrica del'Italia nella storia dells cartografia tra Medioevo et età moderna: realtà, imagine ed immaginazione dai codici di Claudio Tolomeo alatlante di Giovanni Antonio Magini.* Trieste.

Lago, Luciano, and Rossit, Claudio. 1981. *Descriptio Histriae: La penisola istriana in alcuni monumenti significativi . . . sino a totto il secolo XVIII.* Trieste.

Lago, Luciano, and Claudio Rossit. 1986. *Pietro Coppo: Le 'Tabulae', 1524-1526: una preziosa raccolta cartografica custodita a Pirano.* 2 vols. Trieste.

Landín Carrasco, Amancio. 1992. *Descubrimientos españoles en el Mar del Sur.* 3 vols. Madrid.

Laor, Eran. 1986. *Maps of the Holy Land: Cartobibliography of Printed Maps, 1475-1900.* New York.

Lavis-Trafford, Marc Antoine de. 1950. *L'évolution de cartographie de la région du Mont-Cenis et de ses abords aux XVe et XVIe siècles; étude critique des méthodes de travail des grands cartographes du XVIe siècle: Fine, Gastaldi, Ortelius, Mercator, La Guillotière et Magini, ainsi que de Jacques Signot et de Boileau de Bouillon.* Chambéry.

860

Layng, Theodore E. 1956. *Sixteenth-Century Maps Relating to Canada: A Check List and Bibliography*. Ottawa.

Layng, Theodore E. Commentaries and Map Notes. In *Crucial Maps in the Early Cartography and Place-Nomenclature of the Atlantic Coast of Canada*, by William Francis Ganong, 469-98. Toronto.

Le Corbeiller, Clare. 1961. Miss America and Her Sisters: Personifications of the Four Parts of the World. Metropolitan Museum of Art, *Bulletin*, N.S., 19, no. 8: 209-23.

Ledyard, Gari. 1994. Cartography in Korea. In *The History of Cartography*. vol. 2, Book 2. *Cartography in the Traditional East and Southeast Asian Societies*, ed. John Brian Harley and David Woodward, 235-345. Chicago.

Lefevre, Renato. 1942. L'Africa di Livio Sanuto geografo veneto del '500. *Rivista delle colonie*, 16: 842-52.

Lelewel, Joachim. 1852-57. *Géographie du moyen âge*. 4 vols. and epilogue. Brussels. (Accompanying atlas in two editions, 1845 and 1850).

Lentz, Lamar, ed. 1994. *A Portable World: Abraham Ortelius & Art, Cartography & Printing in 16th Century Antwerp* [exhibition catalog]. Austin, Tex.

León, Nicolás. 1902-08. *Bibliografía mexicana del siglo XVIII, por el dr.*

Nicolás de León ... Sección primera, 1.-5. pte. 5 vols. in 6. (Boletín de Instituto bibliográfico mexicano, nos. 1,4,5,7,8,10). México.

Lévesque, Rodrigue, comp. and ed. 1992. *History of Micronesia: A Collection of Source Documents*. vol. 1, *European Discovery 1521-1560*, and vol. 2. Québec.

Levi della Vida, Giorgio. 1935. *Elenco dei manoscritti arabi islamici della Biblioteca Vaticana*. Vaticn City.

Levi della Vida, Giorgio. 1939. *Ricerche sulla formazione del più antico fondo dei manoscritti orientali della Biblioteca Vaticana*. Vaticn City.

Levi-Donati, Gemmarosa. 1995. *The Geographical Panels in the Medici Guardaroba of Palazzo Vecchio in Florence*. Perugia.

Levin, Michael Jacob. 2005. *Agents of Empire: Spanish Ambassadors in Sixteenth-Century Italy*. Ithaca, New York.

Lewis, Martin W. and Kären Wigen. 1997. *The Myth of Continents: a Critique of Metageography*. Berkeley.

Licini, Patrizia. 1988. *La Moscovia rappresentata: l'immagine Acapavolta della Russia nella cartografia rinascimentale europea*. Milan.

861

Linderski, Jerzy. 1964. Alfred the Great and the Tradition of Ancient Geography. *Speculum*, 39: 434-39.

Lipsius, Justus. 1604. ... *Physiologiae Stoicorum Libri Tres L. Annaeo Senecae, Aliísque Scriptoribus Illustrandis*. Paris.

Lister, Raymond. 1970. *Antique Maps and Their Cartographers*. London.

López de Gómara, Francisco. 1552-53. *Primera y segunda parte dela historia general de las Indias*, Saragossa. (References are to the 1852 edition of Enrique de Vedia).

Lorenzi, Giambattista. 1868. *Monumenti per servire alla storia del Palazzo Ducale di Venezia*. Venice.

Lossen, Max, ed. 1886. *Briefe von Andreas Masius und seinen Freunden 1538 bis 1573*. (Gesellschaft für Rheinische Geschichtskunde, *Publikationen*, 2). Leipzig.

Ludwig, Gustav. 1903. *Archivälische Beiträge zur Geschichte der venezianischen Malerei*. (*Jahrbuch der Königlich preussischen Kunstsammlungen. Beiheft zum XXIV Band*). Berlin.

Luisetto, Giovanni, ed. 1988. *Archivio Sartori: documenti di storia e arte francescana. III/2: Evoluzione del francescanesimo nelle tre Venezie: monasteri, contrade, localita abitanti di padova medioevale*. Padova.

Luisi, Guido. 2002. La corologia del Territorio pugliese. In Luciano Lago, ed. *Imago Italiae: la fabbrica del'Italia nella storia dells cartografia tra Medioevo et età moderna*, 456-67. Trieste.

Luzio, Leopoldina. 1947. Alcune notizie intorno al viaggiatore fiorentino Andrea Corsali. *Bollettino della Società Geografica Italiana*, 84: 24-28.

Lynam, Edward. 1938. Gifts from the Friends of the National Libraries [on 1564 Contarini map of Europe]. *British Museum Quarterly*, 12: 21-24.

Maciej z Miechowa. 1561. *Historia delle due Sarmatie . . . Con la tauola delle cose notabili*. Venice, Gabriel Giolito.

Macrì, Giacomo. 1896. Francesco Maurolico nella vita e negli scritti. In *Commemorazione del IV centenario di Francesco Maurolico MDCCCXCIV*, ed. Accademia R[eale] Peloritana dei Pericolanti di Messina, 1-198. Messina. (Second edition, enlarged with manuscript documents, printed separately with same title in Messina, 1901).

Magnaghi, Alberto. 1910. Il Golfo di Suez e il Mar Rosso in una Relazione inedita di Filippo Pigafetta (1576-77). *Bollettino della Società Geografica Italiana*, 47: 145-77 and 284-312.

Mallat de Bassilan, Marcel Jacques Saint-Ange. 1890? *Essai sur la cartographie de Madagascar*. Paris, 1890? Reprinted in *Acta Cartografica*, 21: 1-27.

Mallet, Alain Manesson. 1683. *Description de l'univers, contenant les differents systêmes di monde, les cartes generales & particulieres de la geographie ancienne & moderne*, etc. 5 vols. Paris.

Malombra, Giuseppe (Ptolemy). 1574. *La Geografia di Clavdio Tolomeo . . .* Venetia.

Manasek, Francis J. 1998. *Collecting Old Maps*. Norwich, Vt.

Mangani, Giorgio. 1992. *Carte e cartografici delle Marche: Guida alla cartografia storica regionale (sec. XVI-XIX)*. Ancona.

Manno, Antonio, and Vincenzo Promis. 1880-81. Notizie di Jacopo Gastaldi cartografo piemontese del secolo XVI. Accademià delle Scienze di Torino. *Atti*, 16: 847-69.

Mano, Jo Margaret. 1987. Symbol as Signature: Gastaldi and His Engravers. *Mapline*, 47: 5-7.

Marcel, Gabriel. 1899. Les Origines de la carte d'Espagne. *Revue hispanique*, 6: 163-93.

Marinelli, Giovanni. 1881. *Saggio di cartografia della regione veneta*. Venice.

Marinelli, Olinto. 1902. Materiali per la storia della cartografia marchigiana. *Le Marche illustrate nella storia, nelle lettere e nelle arti*, 2: 130-79. (Expanded version of work originally in *Rivista Geografica Italiana*, 7 (1900), 353-70, which is lacking much which is in the 1902 edition, including a discussion of a Gastaldi map).

Marinelli, Olinto. 1906. Notizia di una grande carta manoscritta della Corsica. *Rivista Geografica Italiana*, 13: 126-32.

Marinelli, Olinto. 1917. Lo Stretto di Anian e Giacomo Gastaldi. *Rivista Geografica Italiana*, 24: 39-49.

Martinez del Rio, Pablo. 1952. *Los Origenes Americanos*. 3rd ed. Mexico.

Martín Merás, María Luisa. 1986. Santa Cruz, Alonso de. In Kretschmer, Ingrid, et al., *Lexikon zur Geschichte der Kartographie*, vol 2, 701-02. Vienna.

Maruli, Francesco, Baron della Foresta. 1613. *Vita dell'Abbate del Parto D. Francesci Mavrolyco . . . .* Messina.

Mathes, W. Michael. 1997. The Early Exploration of the Pacific Coast. In *North American Exploration*, ed. John Logan Allen, vol. 1, 400-51. Lincoln, Neb.

Maurolico, Francesco. 1543. *Cosmographia Francisci Mavrolyci ... in tres dialogos distincta*. Venice.

Maurolico, Francesco. 1546. *Descrittione dell'isola di Sicilia.* Venice.

Mazzarella, Salvatore, and Zanca, Renato. 1985. *Il libri delle torri: le torri costiere di Sicilia nel secoli XVI-XX.* Palermo.

Mazzatinti, Giuseppe. 1979. *Inventari dei manoscritti delle biblioteche d'Italia. vol. 91. Venezia. Biblioteca Marciana.* Firenze.

McClymont, James Roxburgh. 1921. Terra Australis and Java La Grande. In his *Essays in Historical Geography and on Kindred Subjects,* 9-18 and 41-42. London.

McMin, Stuart. 1986. Mapping of Arabia, Real or Imagined. *Map Collector*, 37: 36-40.

Medina, Pedro de. 1545. *Arte de nauegar en que se contienen todas las Reglas, Declaraciones, Secretos, y Auisos, ~q a la buena nauegaciõ son necessarios, y se deu saber.* Valladolid.

Ménage, V. L. 1958. The Map of Hajji Ahmed and its Makers. University of London, School of Oriental and African Studies, *Bulletin*, 21: 291-314.

Menato, Marco, et al, eds. 1997. *Dizionario dei tipografi e degli editori Italiani. Il Cinquecento.* vol. 1 (A-F). Milano.

Mendes Pinto, Fernão. 1627. *Historia oriental de las peregrinaciones de Fernan Mendez Pinto portvgves*, etc. Madrid.

Mercier, Raymond P. 1992. Geodesy. In *The History of Cartography*, vol. II, Book 1. *Cartography in the Traditional Islamic and South Asian Societies*, ed. John Brian Harley and David Woodward, 175-88. Chicago.

Meurer, Peter. 1986. Die Karten der Kronstädter Ausgabe 1542 von Johannes Honters 'Rudimenta Cosmographica.' *Speculum orbis*, 2, no. 1: 34-39.

Meurer, Peter H. 1991. *Fontes cartographici Orteliani : das 'Theatrum orbis terrarum' von Abraham Ortelius und seine Kartenquellen.* Weinheim.

Meurer, Peter H. 2001. *Corpus der älteren Germania-Karten: ein annotierter Katalog der gedruckten Gesamtkarten des deutschen Raumes von den Anfängen bis um 1650.* 2 Vols (1 vol. Text, and one portfolio of maps). Aalphen an der Rijn.

Meurer, Peter H. 2002. Op het spoor van de kaart der Nederlanden van Jan van Hoirne *Caert-Thresoor*, 21: 33-40.

Meurer, Peter H. 2004. *The Strabo Illustratus Atlas: A Unique Sixteenth Century Composite Atlas from the House of Bertelli.* Bedburg-Hau.

Michieli, Adriano. 1919. Il fiume Sile. *Bollettino della Società Geografica Italiana*, 56: 27-41.

Michow, Heinrich. 1884. *Die ältesten Karten von Russland, ein Beitrag zur historischen Geographie.* Hamburg.

Michow, Heinrich. 1906. Das erste Jahrhundert russischer Kartographie, 1525-1631, und die Originalkarte des Anton Wied von 1542. *Mitteilungen der geographischen Gesellschaft in Hamburg*, 21: 1-61. Reprinted in *Acta Cartographica*, 12 (1971), 288-351.

Michow, Heinrich. 1907. Weitere Beiträge zur älteren Kartographie Russlands. *Mitteilungen der geographischen Gesellschaft in Hamburg*, 22:125-72. Reprinted in *Acta Cartographica*, 11 (1971), 311-58.

Mickwitz, Ann-Mari and Leena Miekkavaara. 1979-95. *The A.E. Nordenskiöld collection in the Helsinki University Library: annotated catalogue of maps made up to 1800.* Helsinki.

Milanesi, Marica. 1983. Nuovo Mondo e Terra Incognita in margine alla mostra 'The Italians and the Creation of America.' *Rivista Geografica Italiana*, 90: 81-92.

Milanesi, Marica. 1984. *Tolomeo sostituito: Studi di storia delle conoscenze geografiche nel XVI secolo.* Milano.

Milanesi, Marica. 1988. Guillaume Postel. In: *L'Italia che cambia. Il contributo della geografia*, ed. Alberto di Blasi, vol. 1, 24-30. (Atti del XXIV Congresso Geografico Italiano [Taormina, 1988]). Catania.

Milanesi, Marica. 1990. *Atlante nautico di Battista Agnese, 1553.* Venezia.

Milanesi, Marica. 1992. Arsarot o Anian? Identità e separazione tra Asia e Nuovo Mondo nella cartografia del Cinquecento (1500-1570). In *Il Nuovo Mondo nella coscienza italiana e tedesca del Cinquecento*, ed. Adriano Prosperi and Wolfgang Reinhard, 19-78. (Annali dell'Istituto storico italo-germanico, Quaderno, 33). Bologna.

Milanesi, Marica. 1993. La cartografia italiana nel Medio Evo e nel Rinascimento. In *La cartografia italiana*, 13-78. (Cicle de conferències sobre Història de la Cartografia, 3er curs). Barcelona.

Milanesi, Marica. 1994. G. B. Ramusio e le 'Navigazioni e viaggi' (1550-59). In *L'epopea della scoperte*, ed. Renzo Zorzi, 75-101. Firenze.

Milanesi, Marica. 1994. Geography and Cosmography in Italy from XV to XVII Century. *Memorie della Società Astronomica Italiana*, 65: 443-68.

Milanesi, Marica. 2002. Il Piemonte sud-occidentale nelle carte del Rinascimento. In *Rappresentare uno Stato: Carte e cartografici degli Stati*

Sabaudi dal XVI al XVIII secolo, ed. Rinaldo Comba, and Paolo Sereno, vol. 1, 11-17; vol. 2, 12-19 and plate 6. Torino.

Milanesi, Marica. 2002. Le ragioni del ciclo delle carte geografiche/The Historical Background to the Cycle in the Gallery of Maps. In *La Galleria delle carte geografiche in Vaticano/The Gallery of maps in the Vatican*, eds. Lucio Gambi, and Antonio Pinelli, text volume, 97-123. 3 vols. Trieste.

Milanesi, Marica. 2016. *Vincenzo Coronelli cosmographer (1650-1718)*. (*Theatrum Orbis, 13*). Turnhout, Belgium.

Milanesi, Marica. See also Ramusio, 1978-88.

Miller, Konrad. 1926-31. *Mappae Arabicae, arabische Welt- und Länderkarten des 9.-13. Jahrhunderts in arabischer Urschrift, lateinischer Transkription und Übertragung in neuzeitliche Kartenskizzen. Mit einleitenden Texten*. 6 vols. In 3 portfolios. Stuttgart.

Miller, Konrad. 1931. *Die ältesten Separatkarten der 3 Erdteile wahrscheinlich von Nikophoros Gregoras in 1350 in Konstantinopel entworfen*. Stuttgart, 1930; and *Die ältesten Separatkarten der drei Erdteile. Ergänzungsblatt*. Stuttgart.

Minella, Massimo. 1993. *Il mondo ritrovato: Le tavole sudamericane di Giacomo Gastaldi. Con la riproduzione anastatica del libro La universale descrittione del mondo (1561)*. Genova.

Minow, Helmut. 2001. Review of: *Mathematische Geographie und Kartographie im Islam und ihr Fortleben im Abendland*, by Fuat Sezgin. 2 vols. Text, and atlas. (Geschichte des arabischen Schrifttums, vols. 10-12). Frankfurt, 2000. In *Cartographica Helvetica*, 24: 48-49.

Mitchell, Mairin. 1964. *Friar Andrés de Urdaneta, O.S.A.* London.

Mollo, Emanuela. 2002. L'attività di un cartografo piemontese fuori dello stato: Giacomo Gastaldi. In *Rappresentare uno Stato: Carte e cartografici degli Stati Sabaudi dal XVI al XVIII secolo*, ed. Rinaldo Comba, and Paolo Sereno, vol. 1, 27-31; vol. 2, 24-25. Torino.

Monachus, Franciscus. 1529 ca. *De Orbis Sitv*, etc. Antwerp.

Monga, Luigi. 1999. El Nuevo Mundo y los diarios de las viajeros italianos en España. In *Literatura de viajes: el Viejo mundo y el Nuevo* (Actas del congreso 'El Viejo Mundo y el Nuevo'), 39-49. Madrid.

Monga, Luigi, ed. 2000. *Due ambasciatori veneziani nella Spagna di fine Cinquecento : i diari dei viaggi di Antonio Tiepolo (1571-1572) e Francesco Vendramin (1592-1593)*. Torino.

Monte, Urbano. 1994. *Descrizione del mondo sin qui consciuto*, ed. Maurizio Ampollini. (Le chimere, 2). Lecco (Como).

Morison, Samuel Eliot. 1971. *The Northern Voyages, A. D. 500-1600.* (The European Discovery of America, vol. 1. New York.

Morison, Samuel Eliot. 1974. The *Southern Voyages, 1492-1616.* (The European Discovery of America. vol. 2). New York.

Moscheo, Rosario. 1988. *Francesco Maurolico tra Rinascimento e scienza galileiana: Materiali e ricerche.* Messina.

Münster, Sebastian. 1540. *Geographia vniversalis, vetvs et nova, complectens Clavdii Ptolemæi Alexandrini enarrationis libros VIII*, etc. Basle.

Münster, Sebastian. 1550. *Cosmographiæ uniuersalis Lib. VI. in quibus, iuxta certioris fidei scriptorum traditionem describuntur, Omnêi habitabilis orbis partié situs, ppriæq[ue] dotes*, etc. Basle.

Myritius, Joannes. 1590. *Opvscvlvm Geographicvm Rarvm, Totivs Eivs Negotii Rationem, Mira Indvstria Et Brevitate Complectens, Iam Recens Ex Diversorvm Libris ac chartis*, etc. Ingolstadt.

Needham, Joseph. 1959. *Science and Civilization in China.* vol. 3. Cambridge.

Nicolay, Nicolas de. 1577. *Les navigations, peregrinations et voyages, faicts en la Tvrqvie, par Nicolas de Nicolay Daulphinoys, seigneur d'Arfeville ... contenants plusieurs singularitz que l'autheur y a veu & obserue*, etc. Anvers. (This is the earliest edition I have seen, but according to Chesneau, 1887, q.v. in this bibliography, at p. lvi, the first edition is 1567).

Nordenskiöld, Adolf Erik. 1883. *Om bröderna Zenos resor och de äldsta kartor öfver Norden* (Bihang til K. Svenska Vetenskaps-Akademiens Handlingar, VIII, No. 2). Stockholm. Reprinted in *Acta Cartographica,* 13 (1972).

Nordenskiöld, Adolf Erik. 1889. *Facsimile-Atlas to the Early History of Cartography with Reproductions of the Most Important Maps Printed in the XV and XVI Centuries.* Stockholm.

Nordenskiöld, Adolf Erik. 1897. *Periplus: An Essay on the Early History of Charts and Sailing-Directions.* Stockholm.

Nordenskiöld, Adolf Erik. 1899. The Influence of the Travels of Marco Polo on Jacobo Gastaldi's Maps of Asia. *Geographical Journal,* 13: 396-406.

Nores, Giasone de. 1571. *Breve trattato del mondo, et delle sue parti*. Venice.

Nores, Giasone de. 1589. *Discorso di Iason De Nores intorno alla geographia*. Padua.

Norwich, Oscar. 1997. *Norwich's Maps of Africa : an Illustrated and Annotated Carto-Bibliography*. Norwich, Vt.

Nunes, Pedro. 1940- .*Obras*. Lisbon. (Projected in 6 volumes; volumes 1-3 and 6 have so far been published).

Nunes, Pedro. 1940. Tratado . . . em defensam da carta de marear . . .In his *Obras*, ed. Academìa das Ciéncias de Lisboa. vol. 1, 175-242. Lisbon. (This is the last part of his Tratado da sphera (orig. 1537), all of which is 1-242 in the present volume).

Núñez de las Cuevas, Rodolfo. 1991. Historia de la cartografía española. In: *La cartografia de la Península Ibèrica i la seva Extensió al Continent Americà* (Cicle de conferècies sobre Història de la Cartografia, 2), 153-223. Barcelona.

Nunn, George Emra. 1929. *Origin of the Strait of Anian Concept*. Philadelphia.

Nunn, George Emra. 1992. *The Geographical Conceptions of Columbus: A Critical Consideration of Four Problems*, etc. New York.

Oehme, Ruthardt. 1978. Das Geograph und Kartograph. In *Wilhelm Schickard,*

1592-1635 : Astronom, Geograph, Orientalist, Erfinder d. Rechenmaschine, ed. Friedrich Seck, 310-75. Tübingen.

O'Gorman, Edmundo. 1972. *Cuatro historiadores de Indias, siglo XVI: Pedro Martír de Anglería, Gonzalo Fernández de Oviedo y Valdés, Bartolomé de las Casas, Joseph de Acosta*. Mexico.

Ortelius, Abraham. 1570. *Theatrum Orbis Terrarum*. Antwerp.

Ortelius, Abraham. 1596. . . . *Thesavrvs geographicvs recognitvs et avctvs in qvo omnivm totivs terræ* etc. Antwerp.

Oviedo y Valdés, Gonzalo Fernández de. 1535. *La historia general delas* [sic] *Indias*. Seville.

Oviedo y Valdés, Gonzalo Fernández de. 1959. *Natural history of the West Indies*, trans. and ed. Sterling A. Stoudemire. Chapel Hill, NC.

Palagiano, C. 1974. Camocio, Giovan Francesco. *Dizionario Biografico degli Italiani*. 17: 288-91.

Parker, Geoffrey. 1992. Maps and Ministers: The Spanish Hapsburgs. In *Monarchs, Ministers and Maps: The Emergence of Cartography as a Tool of Government in Early Modern Europe*, David Buisseret, ed., 124-52. Chicago.

Parker, John. 1956. *The Strait of Anian*. Minneapolis.

Parker, John, commentary and notes. 1957. *Tidings out of Brazil*. London.

Parker, John, et al (ed. Carol Urness). 1991. *A Book for Jack: Words To, By and About John Parker, Curator of the James Ford Bell Library, University of Minnesota*. Minneapolis.

Parks, George Bruner. 1955. Ramusio's Literary History. *Studies in Philology*, 52: 127-48.

Parks, George Bruner. 1970. The Contents and Sources of Ramusio's *Navigationi*. In Ramusio, 1967-70, q.v. here, vol. 1 (1970), 1-39. (Originally in *Bulletin of the New York Public Library*, 1955, 279-313, but lacking the useful index of the 1970 edition).

Parry, James V. 2004. Mapping Arabia. *Saudi Aramco World*, Jan.-Feb.: 20-37.

Parry, John Horace. 1981. *The Age of Reconnaissance*. Berkeley.

Partridge, Loren. 1975. The Room of Maps at Caprarola, 1573-75. *Art Bulletin*, 77: 413-44.

Passi, Carlo. 1564. *La selva di varia istoria di Carlo Passi. Laquale auanti andaua attorno stampata sotto nome fittitio di annotationi dell'infortvnio nella prima, e seconda parte delle Istorie di Monsig. Giouio*, etc. Venice (and other editions).
[Passi, Carlo], attrib. 1564. *Tavole delle provincie, citta, castella, popoli, monti,* *mari, fivmi, et laghi. De' qvali il Giovio ha fatto nelle sve istorie mentione. Con i lor nomi moderni, & antichi, raccolti in vno a beneficio di chi si diletta della Geografia, & della Istoria*. Venice.

Pastor Bodmer, Beatriz. 1992. *The Armature of Conquest: Spanish Accounts of the Discovery of America, 1492-1589*. Stanford, CA.

Pellegrini, Domenico Maria. 1808. Breve dissertazione previa al sommario dell'accademia veneta della Fama. *Giornale dell'italiana letteratura*, 22: 3-32, 113-28, 193-212, and 23: 49-68. (Most of this is a reprint of the Latin edition (1559) of the prospectus of the Accademia Venetiana, q.v. above in this bibliography; see also chapter 1, note 112 for important information on this reprint).

Pereira, Duarte Pacheco. 1937. *Esmeraldo de situ orbis*. (Works issued by the Hakluyt Society, Ser. 2, No. 79). London.

Perini, Carlo. 1996. *L'Italia e le sue regioni nelle antiche carte geografiche*. Verona.

Perocco, Daria. 1994. Giacomo Gastaldi e la *Universale descrittione del mondo*. In *Esplorazioni geografiche e imagine del mondo nei secoli XV e XVI*, ed. Simonetta Ballo Alagna, 211-22. Messina.

Peschel, Oscar. 1877. *O. Peschel's Geschichte der Erdkunde bis auf*

Alexander von Humboldt und Carl Ritter. München.

Phipps, Michel, and Ahmed Sdiri. 1994. Al-Hasan ibn Muhammad al-Wazzân az-Zayyâtî *alias* Leo Africanus. *Geographers: Biobibliographical Studies*, 15: 1-9.

Pigler, Andor. 1974. Die vier Weltteile. In his *Barockthemen; eine Auswahl von Verzeichnissen zur Ikonographie des 17. und 18. Jahrhunderts*, v. 2, 521-23. 2nd ed., enlarged. Budapest.

Piloni, Luigi. 1974. *Carte geografiche di Sardegna*. Cagliari.

Plihál, Katalin. 1998. Ungarn auf der Landkarte La vera descrittione di tutta la Ungheria: . . . von Giacomo Gastaldi. *Cartographica Hungarica*, 6: 2-8. (Article is in Hungarian, with German résumé, title of which is given here).

Plumb, John H. 1964. *The Penguin Book of the Renaissance*. Harmandsworth, England.

Polo, Marco. 1533. *Opera stampata nouam te delle marauigliose cose del mondo: cominciãdo da Leuante a ponente fin al mezo di. El mondo nouo & isole & lochi incogniti & siluestri ... doue abõda loro & largento*, etc. Venice

Polo, Marco. 1555? *Marco Polo Venetiano. In Cvi Si Tratta Le Meravigliose cose del mondo per lui uedute, del costume di uarij paesi, dello stranio uiuere di quelli; della descrittione de diuersi animali, e del trouar dell'oro, dell'argento, e delle pietre preciose, cosa non men utile, che bella*. Venice, Mathio Pagan.

Porcacchi, Thomaso. 1572. *L'isole piv famose del mondo descritte da Thomaso Porcacchi da Castiglione Arretino e intagliate da Girolamo Porro Padovano*. Venice.

Porena, Filippo. 1888. La geografia in Roma e il Mappamondo Vaticano. *Bollettino della Società Geografica Italiana*, 25: 221-38, 311-39 and 427-53.

Porena, Filippo. 1895-96. La rapprezentazione della Sicilia nelle varie fasi della cartografia. *Atti della R[eale] accademia Peloritana*, 10: 200-07.

Porena, Filippo. 1905. Schiarimenti intorno al passaggio del primato cartografico dall'Italia ai Paesi Bassi nel secolo XVI. *Atti del V. Congresso Geografico Italiano tenuto in Napoli dal 6 a 11 Aprile 1904*, vol. 2, 790-804. Napoli.

Portinaro, Pierluigi, and Knirsch, Franco. 1987. *The Cartography of North America 1500-1800*. New York.

Portoghesi, Paolo. 1996. *Caprarola*. Rome.

Postel, Guillaume. 1538? *Grammatica Arabica*. Paris.

Postel, Guillaume. 1561. *Cosmographicæ disciplinæ compendium, in suum finem, hoc est ad Diuinae Prouidentiae certissimam demonstrationem conductum*, etc. Basle.

Potter, Jonathan. 1988. *Country Life Book of Antique Maps: An Introduction to the History of Maps and How to Appreciate Them*. London.

Pressenda, Paolo. 2002. Le carte del Piemonte di Giacomo Gastaldi. In Lago, 2002 (q.v.), 321-26.

Prowse, George Robert Farrar. 1933. *Exploration of the Saint Lawrence, 1499-1525*. Winnipeg.

Pullè, Francesco. 1901-32. *La cartografia antica dell'India*. 3 vols. (Studi italiani di filologia indo-iranica, vols. 4 [1901], 5 [1905], and 10 [1932]). Florence.

Puppi, Lionello, ed. 1968. *Giornale (1573-1606)*, by Paolo Farinati. (Civilta veneziana, 8). Florence.

Pythius, Joannes. 1656. *Responsio exetastica ad tractatum, incerto autore, nuper editum, cui titulus Præadamitæ. Libro duo*. 2 vols. in 1. Leiden.

Quinn, David B., ed. 1979. *New American World : a Documentary History of North America to 1612*. 5 vols. New York.

Quirino, Carlos. 1963. *Philippine Cartography, 1320-1899*. Amsterdam.

Rainero, Romain. 1982. Attualità ed importanza dell'attività di Giacomo Gastaldi 'cosmografo piemontese.' *Bollettino della Società per gli studi storici, archeologici ed artistici della provincia di Cuneo*, no. 86: 5-13.

Ramusio, Giovanni Battista, (1534) trans. and ed., attrib. (Pietro Martire, and Gonzalo Hernandez de Oviedo). *Libro Primo [-Vltimo] Della Historia De L'Indie Occidentali*. 3 vols. in 1. Venice. (The book is often cited under the title of first of the three works included in it: *Summario de la generale historia de l'Indie Occidentali*, etc.).

Ramusio, Giovanni, (1536) trans. and ed., attrib. (Maximilianus Transylvanus, and Antonio Pigafetta). *Il Viaggio Fatto Da Gli Spagnivoli Atorno A'l Mondo*. Venice.

Ramusio, Giovanni Battista. 1550-59. *Navigationi et Viaggi*. 3 vols. Venice (and later editions, see chapter 4, note 1 for details).

Ramusio, Giovanni Battista. 1837. *Il viaggio di Giovan Leone e le navigazioni di Alvise da Ca da Mosto, di Pietro di Cintra, di Annone, di un piloto portoghese e di Vasco di Gama; quali si leggono nella raccolta di Giovambattista Ramusio*. Venice.
Ramusio, Giovanni Battista. 1967-70. *Navigationi et Viaggi*. 3 vols. Amsterdam. (Facsimile reprint of

1563-1606 edition of the above, ed. R. A. Skelton)

Ramusio, Giovanni Battista. 1978-88, Marica Milanesi. *Navigazioni et Viaggi.* 6 vols. Torino. (Scholarly edition of the above).

Randles, W. G. L. 1956. South-East Africa as Shown on Selected Printed Maps of the Sixteenth Century. *Imago Mundi*, 13: 69-88.

Randles, W. G. L. 1958. *South-East Africa and the Empire of Monomotapa as Shown on Selected Printed Maps of the 16th Century.* (Centro de estudos historicos ultramarines. *Studia*, 2, 103-63). Lisbon.

Raynaud-Nguyen, Isabelle. 1985. L'hydrographie et l'évènement historique: deux examples. *Revista da Universidade de Coimbra*, 32: 199-210.

Regier, Mary H. 1987. Kennedy's Geographical Tables of Medieval Islam: An Exploratory Statistical Analysis. *Annals of the New York Academy of Sciences*, 500: 357-72.

Reinaud, Joseph Toussaint, (1840) transcription and introduction (Abulfeda). *Géographie d'Aboulféda. Texte arabe publié d'après les manuscripts de Paris et de Leyde*, etc. Paris.

Reinaud, Joseph Toussaint, and Stanislas Guyard, trans. 1848-83. (Abulfeda). *Géographie d'Aboulféda;* *traduite de l'arabe en français et accompagnée de notes et d'éclaircissements*, etc. 2 vols. in 3. Paris.

Reinhartz, and Oakah L. Jones. 1997. H*acia el Norte!* The Spanish *Entrada* into North America, 1513-1549. In *North American Exploration*, ed. John Logan Allen, v. 1, 241-91. Lincoln, Neb.

Relaño, Francesc. 1995. Against Ptolemy: The Significance of the Lopes-Pigafetta Map of Africa. *Imago Mundi*, 47: 49-66.

Remarkable Maps (1894-99) of the XVth, XVIth, XVIIth Centuries Reproduced in Their Original Size (introd. C. H. Coote). Amsterdam.

Renaudot, Eusebe. 1733. *Ancient Accounts of India and China, by two Mohammedan Travellers, Who Went to Those Parts in the 9th Century; tr. from the Arabic, by the late learned Eusebius Renaudot. With notes, illustrations and inquiries by the same hand.* London.

Renieri, Anna Antonini. 1997. La Tipocosmia di Alessandro Citolini: un repertorio linguistico. In *Repertori di parole e immagini. Esperienze cinquecentesche e moderni data bases*, ed. P. Barocchi and L. Bolzoni, 159-231. Pisa.

Renouard, Antoine Augustin. 1834. *Annales de l'imprimerie des Alde ou histoire des trios Manuce et de leurs editions*. 3rd ed. Paris.

Richter, Herman. 1967. *Olaus Magnus Carta marina 1539*. Lund.

Rickard, Thomas Arthur. 1941. The Strait of Anian. *British Columbia Historical Quarterly*, 5: 161-83.

Rithaymer, Georg. 1538. . . . *De orbis terrarvm sitv compendium*, etc. Nuremberg.

Rizzo, Gerald J. 2006. The Patterns and Meaning of a Great Lake in Western Africa. *Imago Mundi*, 58, 1: 80-89.

Roberts, Gail. 1973. *Atlas of Discovery*. New York.

Rohr, Heinz. 1939. *Die Entwicklung des Kartenbildes Westeuropas zwischen Kanal und Mittelmeer von den ältesten Weltkarten bis Mercator*. Leipzig.

Roland, François. 1912. *Les cartes ancienes de la Franche-Comte: Etude historique et descriptive (Première Partie)*. Besançon. (Originally in: Société d'émulation du Doubs, Besançon. *Mémoires*, Ser. 8, 7: 187-299.)

Rosaccio, Giuseppe. 1598. Descrittione di tutta la terra, 127-pages, separately paginated, in *Geografia Di Clavdio Tolomeo ... Tradotta Di Greco nell' Idioma Volgare Italiano Da Girolamo Rvscelli, Et hora nuouamente ampliata Da Gioseffo Rosaccio, Con varie*

Annotationi, & Espositioni ... Et vna Geografia vniuersale del medesimo, etc. Venice.

Rose, Paul Lawrence. 1969. The Accademia Venetiana: Science and Culture in Renaissance Venice. *Studi veneziani*, 11: 191-242.

Rossit, Claudio. 2002. I primi documenti cartografici del Reame di Napoli. In Lago, 2002 (q,v.), pp. 448-55.

Ruge, Sophus. 1888. *Fretum Anian (Die Geschichte der Beringstrasse vor ihrer Entdeckung)*. (Programm . . . der Annen-Realschule . . . .). Dresden. Reprinted, considerably revised, and with some new material added, in Ruge's *Abhandlungen und Vorträge zur Geschichte der Erdkunde*, 53-70. Dresden, 1888.

Ruge, Sophus. 1892. *Die Entwicklung der Kartographie von Amerika bis 1570*. Gotha.

Ruge, Sophus. 1975. Marco Polo und die Anianstrasse. *Globus*, 69 (1896), 133-37. Reprinted in *Acta Cartographica*, 21: 460-64.

Ruge, Walter. 1904-16. Alteres kartographisches Material in deutschen Bibliotheken. Gesellschaft der Wissenschaften zu Göttingen, Philologisch-historische Klasse, *Nachrichten* (1904), 1-69; (1906), 1-39; (1911), 35-166; (1916, Beiheft), 1-128.

(all reprinted *Acta Cartographica*, 17 (1973), 105-472).

Ruitinga, Lida, and Jan Werner. 1994. Nico Israel: 'Ik heb altijd gedaan waar ik zelf plezier in had': Een interview met antiquaar Nico Israel ter gelegenheid van zijn 75ste verjaardag. *Caert-Thresoor*, 13: 93-101.

Ruscelli, Girolamo (Ptolemy). 1561. *La Geografia di Claudio Tolomeo Alessandrino, nuouamente tradotta di Greco in Italiano*, etc. Venice.

Ruscelli, Girolamo, comp. 1562. *Lettere di principi, le qvali o si scrivono da principi, ò à principi, ò ragionan di principi. Libro primo*, etc. Venice (also edition of 1564, same title).

Sabin, Joseph, et al, comp. 1868-1936. *Biblioteca Americana. A Dictionary of Books Relating to America, from its Discovery to the Present Time*, etc. 29 vols. New York.

[Sale, George]. 1734-35. Abu'lfeda. In *A General Dictionary, Historical and Critical; in which a new and accurate translation of that of the celebrated Mr. Bayle, with the corrections and observations printed in the late edition at Paris, is included and interspersed with several thousand lives never before published*, etc. vol. 1, 114-16. London.

[Sale, George]. 1737. Greaves (John). In *A General Dictionary, Historical and Critical; in which a new and accurate translation of that of the celebrated Mr. Bayle, with the corrections and observations printed in the late edition at Paris, is included and interspersed with several thousand lives never before published*, etc. vol. 5, 521-30. London. (The valuable Sale articles appear *only* in the 1734/35-41 editions of Bayle).

San Pío, María Pilar de. 1992. *Expediciones españolas del siglo XVIII: el paso del noroeste. (Coleccion Mar y America*, 12). Madrid.

Sandler, Christian. 1894. Die Anian-Strasse und Marco Polo. *Zeitschrift der Gesellschaft für Erdkunde zu Berlin*, Ser. 3, 29: 401-08.

Sanuto, Livio. 1987. [Facsimile of gores for a terrestrial globe of 69 cm. diameter, engraved after ca. 1564]. Accompanied by descriptive text by David Woodward, *The Holzheimer Venetian globe gores of the sixteenth century*. Madison, WI.

Sanuto, Livio. 1588. *Geografia di M. Livio Sanvto distinta in XII libri. Ne' quail, oltra l'esplicatone de molti luoghi di Tolemeo, e della Bussola, e dell'Aguglia, si dichiarono le provincie, popoli, regni, città dell'Africa*, etc. Venice.

Sarton, George. 1947. *Introduction to the History of Science*. vol. III. Baltimore.

Sauer, Carl Ortwin. 1971. *Sixteenth Century North America: The Land and the People as Seen by the Europeans*. Berkeley.

Schiavo Musi, Adriana. 1952. Intorno alla raccolta italiana di relazioni di viaggi edita a Vicenza nel 1507 con la designazione: 'Paesi nouamente retrovati et Nouo Mondo da Alberico Vesputio intitulata.' *Studi colombiani*, 2: 419-41.

Schilder, Günter. 1981. The cartographical Relationships between Italy and the Low Countries in the Sixteenth Century. *Map Collector*, 17: 2-8.

Schilder, Günter. 1987. *Monumenta Cartographica Neerlandica, II.* (one text volume and accompanying portfolio of maps). Alphen aan den Rijn.

Schilder, Günter. 1996. *Ten Wall Maps by Blaeu and Visscher*. (*Monumenta Cartographica Neerlandica*, V)(text volume and accompanying portfolio of maps). Alphen aan den Rijn.

Schilder, Günter. 1998. The Wall Maps by Abraham Ortelius. In *Abraham Ortelius and the First Atlas: Essays Commemorating the Quadricentennial of His Death 1598-1998*, ed. Marcel van den Broecke, Peter van der Krogt and Peter Meurer, 93-123. Utrecht.

Schilder, Günter. 2000. *Dutch Folio-Sized Single Sheet Maps with Decorative Borders, 1604-60.* (*Monumenta Cartographica

Neerlandica*, VI). Alphen aan den Rijn. (Text volume and accompanying portfolio of maps).

Schilder, Günter. 2007. *Jodocus Hondius (1563-1612 and Petrus Kaerius (1571-after 1646)* (Monumenta Cartographica Neerlandica, VIII). Alphen aan den Rijn.

Schilling, Oskar. 1892. *Das Reich Monomotapa, sein erstes Bekanntwerden, sein Name und seine Darstellung auf den Karten des 16. bis 19. Jahrhunderts. (Programm der Realschule zu Dresden-Friedrichstadt, 1892)*. Dresden. Reprinted in *Acta Cartographica*, 2 (1968), 449-510.

Schmidt, Francis. 1988. Arzareth en Amérique: l'autorité du quatrième livre d'Esdras dans la discussion sur la parenté des Juifs et des Indiens d'Amérique (1530-1729). In *Moïse géographe: recherches sur les représentations juives et chrétiennes de l'espace*, ed. Alain Desreumaux et Francis Schmidt, 155-201. Paris.

Schnayder, Eduard. 1972. Bernhard Wapowski's Lost Maps of Poland, Sarmatias and Scandinavia. Imago mundi 26: 76-77.

Schöner, Johann. 1515. *Luculenti[ss]ima quaedã terrae totius de[s]criptio: cé multis vtili[ss]imis Co[s]mographiæ iniciis. Nouaq[ue] & ˜[?q] ante fuit verior Europæ no[s]træ formatio*, etc. Nuremberg.

Schöner, Johann 1533. . . . *Opvscvlvm Geographicvm Ex Diversorvm Libris ac cartis ... collectum, accomodatum ad recenter elaboratum ab eodem globum descriptionis terrenæ*, etc. Nuremberg.

Schulz, Juergen. 1987. Maps as Metaphors: Mural Map Cycles of the Italian Renaissance. In *Art and Cartography: Six Historical Essays*, ed. David Woodward, 97-122. Chicago.

Schwartz, Seymour I., and Ehrenberg, Ralph E. 1980. *The Mapping of America*. New York.

Seaver, Kirsten A. 1998. Norumbega and *Harmonia Mundi* in Sixteenth-Century Cartography. *Imago Mundi*, 50: 34-58.

Seck, Friedrich. 1978. Leben und Werk im Überblick. In *Wilhelm Schickard, 1592-1635 : Astronom, Geograph, Orientalist, Erfinder d. Rechenmaschine*, ed. Friedrich Seck, 13-40. Tübingen.

Secret, François. 1959. Notes sur G. Postel. *Bibliothèque d'Humanisme et Renaissance*, 21: 453-67.

Secret, François. 1962. Guillaume Postel et les etudes arabes à la Renaissance. *Arabica*, 9: 21-36.

Secret, François. 1998. *Postel revisité: nouvelles recherches sur Guillaume Postel et son milieu*. Paris.

Secret, François. *See also* Weill, Georges.

Sereno, Paolo. 2002. Dalle rappresentazioni tolomaiche del Piemonte alla prime imagini moderne. In Lago, 2002 (q.v.), 315-20.

Severt, Jacques. 1598. *De orbis catoptrici, seu, Mapparum mundi principiis*. Paris.

Sezgin, Fuat. 2000. *Mathematische Geographie und Kartographie im Islam und ihr Fortleben im Abendland*. 2 vols. text, and atlas. (*Geschichte des arabischen Schrifttums*, vols. 10-12) Frankfurt.

Sezgin, Fuat. 2001. Arabischer Ursprung europäischer Karten. *Cartographica Helvetica*, no. 24: 21-28.

Shirley, Rodney. 1991. *Early Printed Maps of the British Isles, 1477-1650: A Bibliography*. King of Prussia, Pa. (Second edition, revised and updated. East Grimstead, 1991).

Shirley, Rodney. 1987. *The Mapping of the World: Early Printed World Maps 1472-1700*. London.

Shirley, Rodney. 2000. Updated News about Sixteenth-Century Italian Atlases. *IMCoS Journal*, 80: 11-14.

Sicco, Maria, ed. 1985- *Le edizioni italiane del XVI secolo: censimento nazionale*. Roma.

Sider, Sandra. 1992. *Maps, Charts, Globes : Five Centuries of Exploration : a New Edition of E.L. Stevenson's Portolan Charts and Catalogue of the 1992 Exhibition.* New York.

Signot, Jacques. 1539. *La division du monde, contenant la declaration des provinces et regions d'Asie, Europe, et Affrique,* etc. Lyons (and later editions).

Simar, Théophile. *Le Congo au XVIe siècle: d'après la relation de Lopez-Pigafetta.* Brussels.

Simler, Josias (Konrad Gesner). 1555. *Epitome Bibliothecae Conradi Gesneri.* Zurich.

Skelton, Raleigh Ashlin. 1961. Gastaldi's Map of 1564. In *The Prester John of the Indies: A True Relation of the Lands of the Prester John Being the Narrative of the Portuguese Embassy to Ethiopia in 1520 Written by Father Francisco Alvares,* vol. 2, 562-67. (Hakluyt Society publications, Ser. 2, vol. 115). Cambridge.

Skelton, Raleigh Ashlin. 1962. Appendix XX [Note on Gastaldi's 1564 Map of Africa.] In Somali Republic, *The Somali Peninsula: A New Light on Imperial Matters,* 82-83. Rev. ed. Mogadishu.

Skelton, Raleigh Ashlin. 1965. Bibliographical Note. In *Geografia dell'Africa, Venice 1588,* etc., by Livio Sanuto, v-ix. (Theatrum orbis terrarum, 1) Amsterdam.

Skelton, Raleigh Ashlin. 1966. Bibliographical Note. In Münster, Sebastian. *Geographia: Basle, 1540,* v-xxiii. (Theatrum orbis terrarum, 3d ser., v. 5) Amsterdam.

Skelton, Raleigh Ashlin., trans. and ed. 1969a. *Magellan's Voyage: A Narrative Account of the First Circumnavigation,* by Antonio Pigafetta. New York.

Skelton, Raleigh Ashlin. 1969b. *A Venetian Terrestrial Globe, Represented by the Largest Surviving Printed Gores of the 16th Century.* Bologna.

Skelton, Raleigh Ashlin. 1970. Introduction. In *Navigationi et Viaggi,* by Giovanni Battista Ramusio. vol. 1, v-xvi. Amsterdam.

Skelton, Raleigh Ashlin. 1974. *Saxton's Survey of England and Wales, with a Facsimile of Saxton's Wall Map of 1583.* Amsterdam.

Smith, Thomas. 1707. *Vitae Quorundam Eruditissimorum.* London. (See Greaves [Gravius] in this bibliography).

Solórzano Pereira, Juan de. 1629-39. *...Dispvatationem de Indiarvm ivre, sive De iusta Indiarum Occidentalium inquisitione, acquisitione, et retentione tribvs libris comprehensam, d. e. c.* Matriti [Madrid].

Spagni, Emilio. 1900. Una sultana veneziana. *Nuovo Archivio Veneto*, 19: 241-348.

Spekke, Arnolds. 1948. A Brief Cartographic-Iconographic View of the Eastern Baltic Coast up to the 16th Century. *Imago Mundi*, 5: 39-51.

Spivakovsky, Erika. 1970. *Son of the Alhambra; Don Diego Hurtado de Mendoza, 1504-1575*. Austin.

Stams, Werner. 1986. Wandkarte. In *Lexikon zur Geschichte der Kartographie von den Anfängen bis zum ersten Weltkrieg*, ed. Ingrid Kretschmer, et al. vol. 2, 872-77. Vienna.

Stevenson, Edward Luther. 1911. *Portolan Charts; Their Origin and Characteristics, with a Descriptive List of Those Belonging to the Hispanic Society of America*. New York.

Stevenson, Edward Luther. 1921 *Terrestrial and Celestial Globes; Their History and Construction, including a Consideration of Their Value as Aids in the Study of Geography and Astronomy*. 2 vols. New Haven.

Stevenson, Edward Luther, trans. and ed. (Ptolemy). 1932. *Claudius Ptolemy: The Geography*. New York. Reprinted, New York, 1991.

Stobnicza, Jan ze. 1512. *Introductio in Ptholomei Cosmographia cu longitudinibus et latitudinibus regionum et ciuitatum celebriorum*. Cracow.

Stöffler, Johann. 1537. *Cosmographicae Aliqvot descriptiones Ioannis Stofleri ... De Sphaera Cosmographica, hoc est, de Globi terrestris, artificiosa structura*, etc. Marburg.

Stokes, Isaac Newton Phelps. 1915-28. *The iconography of Manhattan Island Compiled from Original Sources and Illustrated by Photo-Intaglio Reproductions of Important Maps, Plans, Views and Documents in Public and Private Collections*. 6 vols. New York.

Suárez, Thomas. 1999. *Early Mapping of Southeast Asia*. [Singapore?].

Sykes, Godfrey Glenton. 1915. The Mythical Straits of Anian. American Geographical Society. *Bulletin*, 47: 161-72.

Szántai, Lajos. 1996. *Atlas Hungaricus: Magyarország nyomtatott térképei, 1528-1850*. 2 vols. Budapest.

Tafuri, Manfredo. 1989. *Venice and the Renaissance*. Cambridge, MA.

Tasso, Bernardo. 1560. *L'amadigi del S. Bernardo Tasso*. Venice.

Tadini, Guido. 1977. *Ferramolino da Bergamo: l'ingegnere militare che nel '500 fortificò la Sicilia*. Bergamo.

Taylor, Eva Germaine Rimington. 1930. *Tudor Geography 1485-1583*. London.

Taylor, Eva Germaine Rimington, introd.and notes. 1935. *The Original Writings & Correspondence of the Two Richard Hakluyts*. (Works issued by the Hakluyt Society, Ser. 2, Nos. 76-77). London.

Teixeira da Mota, Avelino. 1964. *A cartografia antiga da África central e a travessia entre Angola e Moçambique 1500-1860*. Lourenço Marques.

Tenenti, Alberto. 1973. The Sense of Space and Time in the Venetian World of the Fifteenth and Sixteenth Centuries. In *Renaissance Venice*, ed. John Hale, 17-46. London.

Thévenot, Melchisédec. 1663-72? *Relations de divers voyages cvrievx*, etc. 5 parts in 2 vols. Paris.

Thevet, André. 1558. *Les singvlaritez de la France Antarctiqve, avtrement nommée Amerique: & de plusieurs terre & isles decouuertes de nostre temps*. Paris.

Thevet, André. 1575. *La Cosmographie Vniverselle*, etc. Paris.

Tibbetts, Gerald Randall. 1978. *Arabia in Early Maps*. Naples.

Tibbetts, Gerald Randall. 1992. The Beginnings of a Cartographic Tradition. In *The History of Cartography*, vol. II, Book 1. *Cartography in the Traditional Islamic and South Asian Societies*, ed. John Brian Harley and David Woodward. 90-107. Chicago.

Tiepolo, Maria Francesca. 1994. Archivio di Stato di Venezia. In *Guida Generale degli Archivi di Stato Italiani*, ed. Paolo Carucci, et al. vol. 4 (S-Z), 8571148. Roma.

Tooley, Ronald V. 1939. Maps in Italian Atlases of the Sixteenth Century. *Imago Mundi*, 3: 12-47.

Tooley, Ronald Vere. 1966. *Printed Maps of the Continent of Africa and Regional Maps South of the Tropic of Cancer*. (Map Collectors' Series, no. 29). London.

Tooley, Ronald Vere. 1967? *Printed Maps of the Continent of Africa. Part II. 1500-1600, Regional Maps South of the Tropic of Cancer*. (Map Collector's Series, no. 30). London.

Tooley, Ronald Vere. 1979. *Tooley's Dictionary of Mapmakers*. New York.

Tooley, Ronald Vere. 1985. *Tooley's Handbook for Map Collectors: A Subject Index Record*. Chicago.

Tooley, Ronald Vere; Bricker, Charles; and Crone, Gerald Roe. 1989. *Landmarks of Mapmaking: An Illustrated Survey of Maps and Mapmaking*. New York.

Torquemada, Juan de. 1615. *Los veynte y un libros rituals y monarchia yndiana con el origin y guerras de los Yndios Occidentales de sus poblaçones, descubrimiento conquista, conuersion y otras cosas marauillosas de la mesma tierra*, etc. Seville.

Toscanella, Orazio. 1567. *I Nomi Antichi E Moderni Delle Provincie, Regioni, Città, Castella, Monti, Laghi, Fiumi, Mari, Golfi, Porti, & Isole dell'Evropa, dell'Africa & dell'Asia; Con le graduationi loro in lumghezza, e larghezza & una breue descrittione delle suddette partide mondo.* Venice.

Trimingham, J. Spencer. 1975. The Arab Geographers and the East African Coast. In *East Africa and the Orient: Cultural Syntheses in Pre-Colonial Times*, ed. H. Neville Chittick and Robert I. Rotberg, 115-46. New York.

Tudeer, Lauri Oskar Theodor. 1917. On the Origin of the Maps Attached to Ptolemy's Geography. *Journal of Hellenic Studies*, 37: 62-76.

Tyard, Pontus de. 1557. *The Universe of Pontus de Tyard; a Critical Edition of L'univers, with introd. and notes by John C. Lapp.* Ithaca. (Original edition in French, 1557).

Ullmann, Manfred. 1978. Arabische, türkische und persische Studien. In *Wilhelm Schickard, 1592-1635 : Astronom, Geograph, Orientalist, Erfinder d. Rechenmaschine*, ed. Friedrich Seck, 109-28. Tübingen.

Umek, Dragan. 2002. L'Atlante d'Italia manoscritto, anonimo e senza data, del Seminario Vescovile di Padova. In Lago, 2002 (q.v.), pp. 509-36.

Unno, Kazutaka. 1985. The Asian Lake Chiamay in the Early European Cartography. In *Imago et mensura mundi : atti del IX Congresso internazionale di storia della cartografia*, ed. Carla Clivio Marzoli, vol. 1, 287-96. Rome.

Uzielli, Gustavo. 1893. Le quatrième continent avant la découverte de l'Amérique. *Toscanelli*, 1: 26-27.

Vadianus, Joachim. 1534. *Epitome Trivm Terræ Partivm, Asiæ, Africæ Et Evropæ compendiariam locorum de[s]criptionem continens*, etc. Zurich.

Valerio, Vladimiro, and Spagnolo, Santo. 2013. *Sicilia 1477-1861: La collezione Spagnolo-Palermo in quattro secoli di cartografia.* 2 vols. Palermo.

Van der Heijden, H. A. M. See Heijden, H. A. M. van der.

Van der Krogt, Peter. 1995. Commercial Cartography in the Netherlands with Particular Reference to Atlas Production (16th-18th Centuries). In *La Cartografia dels Països Baixos,* 71-140. (Cicle de conferències sobre Història de la Cartografia, 4). Barcelona.

Vasari, Giorgio. 1906. *Le vite de' più eccellenti pittori, scultori ed architettori scritte da Giorgio Vasari, pittore aretino, con nuovo annotazioni e commenti di Gaetano Milanesi.* 9 vols. Florence.

Vázquez, Germán. 1987. *Antonio de Mendoza*. Madrid.

Verner, Coolie. 1975. Copperplate Printing. In *Five Centuries of Map Printing*, ed. David Woodward, 51-75. Chicago.

Verner, Coolie; and Basil Stuart-Stubbs. 1979. *The Northpart of America*. Toronto.

Vernet, J. 1970. Abu'l-fida' Isma'il ibn 'Ali ibn Mahmud ibn . . . Ayyub, 'Imad al-Din. In *Dictionary of Scientific Biography*. vol. 1, 28-29. New York.

Vespucci, Amérigo. 1951. *El nuevo mundo; cartas relativas a sus viajes y descubrimientos*. Buenos Aires.

Vignaud, Henri. 1921. Une ancienne carte inconnue de l'Amérique, la première où figure le future détroit de Behring. *Journal de la Société des Américanistes de Paris*, N.S., vol. 13: 1-5. (English translation in *Washington Historical Quarterly*, 22 (1931), 112-16.)

Vigneras, L. A. 1962. The Cartographer Diogo Ribero. *Imago Mundi*, 16: 76-83.

Vogel, E. G. 1853. Über Wilh. Postel's Reisen in den Orient. *Serapeum: Zeitschrift für Bibliothekswissenschaft, Handschriftenkunde und ältere Litteratur*, 14: 49-58

Wagner, Henry Raup. 1926. Some Imaginary California Geography.

American Antiquarian Society, *Proceedings*, N.S., 36: 83-129.

Wagner, Henry Raup. 1929. *Spanish Voyages to the Northwest Coast of America of America in the Sixteenth Century*. San Francisco.

Wagner, Henry Raup. 1937. *The Cartography of the Northwest Coast of America to the year 1800*. 2 vols. Berkeley.

Wagner, Henry Raup. 1941. *Juan Rodríguez Cabrillo, Discoverer of the Coast of California*. San Francisco.

Wagner, Henry Raup (Grijalva, Juan de). 1942. *The Discovery of New Spain in 1518*. Berkeley.

Wagner, Henry Raup. 1947. The Manuscript Atlases of Battista Agnese. *Papers of the Bibliographical Society of America*, 25: 1-110 (Plus additions in *Imago Mundi*, 4 (1947), 28-30).

Wagner, Henry Raup. 1948. Francisco Lopez de Gomara and His Works. *Proceedings of the American Antiquarian Society*, 58: 262-82.

Wagner, Henry Raup. 1967. *The Spanish Southwest, 1542-1794; an Annotated Bibliography*. New York.

Waldseemüller, Martin. 1507. *Cosmographiae Introdvctio Cvm Qvibvs dam Geometriae Ac Astronomiae Principiis Ad Eam Rem Necessariis*

Insuper quattuor Americi Vespucij nauigationes, etc. St. Dié.

Waldseemüller, Martin. 1513. *In Claudii Ptolemei Supplementum*, etc. Strassburg. (This amounts to the modern maps section of his 1513 Ptolemy; see Karrow, no. 80/Eb).

Watelet, Marcel, ed. 1998. *The Mercator Atlas of Europe*. Pleasant Hill, OR.

Weill, Georges, and François Secret. 1987. *Vie et caractère de Guillaume Postel*. Milan. (This is a translation by Secret of a Weill 1892 work in Latin, to which Secret has made extensive additions, in smaller type and set off by brackets.)

Werner, Johannes. 1514. *Geographia*. Nuremberg, 1514. (On fol. [a1] recto: *In hoc opere haec cõtinentur: Noua translatio primi libri geographiae Cl' Ptolomaei*, sometimes given as a title.)

Westrupp, Thomas Johnson. 1912-13. Early Italian Maps of Ireland from 1300 to 1600, with Notes on Foreign Settlers and Trade. *Proceedings of the Royal Irish Academy*, vol. 30, Sec. C: 361-428.

Wheat, Carl I. 1954. Mapping the American West 1540-1857: A Preliminary Study. *Proceedings of the American Antiquarian Society*, 64: 19-194.

Wheat, Carl Irving. 1957. *Mapping the Trans-Mississippi West 1540-1861. vol. I. The Spanish Entrada to the Lousiana Purchase 1540-1804*. San Francisco.

Wheatley, Paul. 1954. A Curious Feature on Early Maps of Malaysia. *Imago Mundi*, 11: 67-72.

Wieder, Frederik Caspar. 1914-15. Nederlandsche historisch-geographische Documenten in Spanje. Uitkomsten van twee maanden Onderzoek. (Koninklijk) Nederlandsch Aardrijkskundig Genootschap. *Tijdschrift*, Ser. 2, vol. 31: 693-724; 32: 1-34, 145-87, 285-318 and 775-824; and also a 158-page special issue to accompany volume 32 (1915). Reprinted in *Acta Cartographica*, 23 (1976), 115-464.

Wieder, Frederik Caspar. 1925-32. *Monumenta Cartographica; Reproductions of Unique and Rare Maps, Plans and Views in the Actual Size of the Originals*. 5 vols. The Hague.

Wilford, John Noble. 1981. *The Mapmakers*. New York.

Wilkins, Ernest N. 1957. Arcadia in America. *Proceedings of the American Philosophical Society*, 101: 4-30.

Williams, S. 1960. Les Ommegangs d'Anvers et les Cortèges du Lord-Maire de Londres. In *Les Fêtes de la Renaissance*, ed. J. Jacquet, vol. 2, 349-57. Paris.

Winsor, Justin. 1883-84. A Bibliography of Ptolemy's Geography. *Bulletin of Harvard University*, Nos. 24-29. (Also published separately Cambridge, Mass., 1884.)

Winsor, Justin. 1884-89. *Narrative and Critical History of America*. 8 vols. Boston.

Winsor, Justin. 1904. *The Kohl Collection (Now in the Library of Congress) of Maps Relating to America*. Washington.

Witcombe, Christopher L. C. E. 2004. *Copyright in the Renaissance: Prints and the Privilegio in Sixteenth-Century Venice and Rome*. Leiden.

Woodward, David. 1975. The Woodcut Technique. In *Five Centuries of Map Printing*, ed. David Woodward, 25-50. Chicago.

Woodward, David. 1979. *La Geografia Moderna: The Work of the Sixteenth-Century Italian Cartographers. An Exhibition Held at the Newberry Library, Chicago 30 April 1979 to 16 June 1979*. (Mapline, Special Number, 4). Chicago.

Woodward, David. 1980. The Study of the Italian Map Trade in the Sixteenth Century: Needs and Opportunities. *Wolfenbütteler Forschungen*, 8: 137-46.

Woodward, David, ed. 1987. *Art and Cartography: Six Historical Essays*. Chicago.

Woodward, David. 1987. [Livio Sanuto. *Venetian globe gores*]. Madison, WI. (Title of accompanying text: *The Holzheimer Venetian globe gores of the sixteenth century*.)

Woodward, David. 1990. *The Maps and Prints of Paolo Forlani: A Descriptive Bibliography* (Hermon Dunlap Smith Center for the History of Cartography. Occasional Publication, 4). Chicago.

Woodward, David. 1992. Paolo Forlani: Compiler, Engraver, Printer, or Publisher? *Imago Mundi*, 44: 45-64.

Woodward, David. 1994. The Forlani Map of North America. *Imago Mundi*, 46: 29-40.

Woodward, David. 1996. Italian Composite Atlases of the Sixteenth Century. In *Images of the World: The Atlas through History*, ed. John A. Wolter, and Ronald E. Grim, 51-70. New York.

Woodward, David. *Maps as Prints in the Italian Renaissance: Makers, Distributors & Consumers*. (The 1995 Panizzi Lectures). London.

Woodward, David. 1997. *The Four Parts of the World: Giovanni Francesco Camocio's Wall Maps*. (James Ford Bell Lectures, 34). [Minneapolis].

Woodward, David. 2007. The Italian Map Trade, 1480-1650. In *The History of Cartography*. vol. III: *Cartography in the European Renaissance*, ed. David Woodward, part 1, 773-803. Chicago.

Wright, Ione Stuessy. 1945. Early Spanish Voyages from America to the Far East, 1527-1565. In *Greater America: Essays in Honor of Herbert Eugene Bolton,* 59-78. Berkeley.

Wright, John Kirtland. 1923. Notes on the Knowledge of Latitudes and Longitudes in the Middle Ages. *Isis,* 5: 75-98.

Wroth, Lawrence C. 1970. *The Voyages of Giovanni da Verrazzano, 1524-1528.* New Haven.

Wytfliet, Corneille. 1598. *Descriptionis Ptolemaicæ Avgmentvm. siue Occidentis Notitia Breui commentario illustrata,* etc. Louvain. (First edition 1597)

Yee, Cordell D. K. 1994a. Reinterpreting Traditional Chinese Geographical Maps. In *The History of Cartography.* vol. 2, Book 2. *Cartography in the Traditional East and Southeast Asian Societies*, ed. John Brian Harley and David Woodward, 35-70. Chicago.

Yee, Cordell D. K. 1994b. Taking the World's Measure: Chinese Maps between Observation and Text. In *The History of Cartography*, vol. II, Book 2: *Cartography in the Traditional East and Southeast Asian Societies*, ed. John Brian Harley and David Woodward, 96-127. Chicago.

Zacharakis, Christos G. 1982. *A Catalogue of Printed Maps of Greece, 1477-1800.* Nicosia.

Zago, Ferruccio. 1984. 'Corpus' cartografico veneziano. *Bollettino della Società Geografica Italiana,* 121: 621-38.

Zanetti, Girolamo. 1925. Descrizione Delle antiche Tavole Geografiche collocate già nella Sala detta dello Scudo del Ducal Palagio di Venezia e rinnovate per decreto dell' Ecc.mo Senato nel presente Ano MDCCLXII. In Bertolini, 1925, 326-40 (q.v.) (Originally written in 1762).

Zerubavel, Eviatar. 1992. *Terra Cognita: The Mental Discovery of America.* New Brunswick.

Zurla, Placido. 1918. *Sulle antiche mappe idro-grafiche lavorate in Venezia.* Venice.

SOURCES OF PHOTOGRAPHS

Arader Galleries: 820, 822, 825, 827.

Austin UTL: 809, 811, 813, 817.

Chicago Newb: 461-62, 465, 476, 617, 674, 698, 715, 721, 726, 740, 772, 776, 779, 782, 786.

Dillingen SB: 683.

London BL: 602, 730, 738.

Minneapolis Bell: 795, 797, 799, 802.

München SB: 708, 710-11, 713, 745-46, 748-49, 751-52, 754-55, 757-58, 760.

National Galleries of Scotland: 133.

New York PL: 651, 653, 656-57, 659-60.

Paris BN: 664, 668, 763, 768.

Ruderman Antique Maps: 641, 692.

Rumsey Collection (Stanford University): 489-90, 492, 494-96, 498, 501-2, 504, 506, 508, 510, 513, 516, 518, 520, 522, 524, 526-27, 529, 531, 533, 536-37, 539, 540, 542-43, 545-46, 549, 551-52, 554, 556, 558, 560, 561, 563-64, 567-68, 570, 572-75, 578, 579, 581, 584, 589-90, 592, 594, 596.

Sanderus Antique Maps and Books: 637, 639.

Wolfenbüttel HAB: 610.

INDEX

In all sub-headings, "Gastaldi" is abbreviated with the letter G. Page numbers in bold include an illustration of the map referenced.

886

888

891

904

www.ingramcontent.com/pod-product-compliance
Lightning Source LLC
Chambersburg PA
CBHW081526120626
46550CB00009B/2630